BIG WONDERFUL THING

**THE PUBLICATION OF THIS BOOK WAS MADE POSSIBLE
BY THE GENEROUS SUPPORT OF THE FOLLOWING:**

Christine and Charles Aubrey
Roger W. Fullington
Jeanne and Mickey Klein
Marsha and John Kleinheinz
Lowell H. Lebermann, Jr.
Joyce and Harvey Mitchell
Office of UT President William Powers, Jr.
Ellen and Ed Randall
Jean and Dan Rather
Tocker Foundation
Judith Willcott and Laurence Miller
Suzanne and Marc Winkelman

big
wond
thing

A HISTORY OF TEXAS

Stephen Harrigan

erful

UNIVERSITY
OF TEXAS PRESS
AUSTIN

THE TEXAS BOOKSHELF

The theme song from *The Adventures of Jim Bowie* is quoted on page 132. © 1956
(Renewed 2002) Flea Market Music, Inc. Reprinted by permission of Flea
Market Music, Inc.
A stanza from "The End of the Line" by Bonnie Parker appears on page 547.
Dallas Police Department Historial Reports, Records, and Newsletters,
1930–Current (Box 13, Folder 14), Dallas Municipal Archives,
City Secretary's Office, City of Dallas.
Lines from "Negro Hero" by Gwendolyn Brooks, on page 596, are reprinted
by consent of Brooks Permissions.
"What are you looking at me for?," on page 820, is from *The Facts of Life:
And Other Dirty Jokes* by Willie Nelson, copyright © 2002 by Willie Nelson.
Used by permission of Random House, an imprint and division
of Penguin Random House LLC. All rights reserved.

Requests for permission to reproduce material from this work should be sent to:
Permissions
University of Texas Press
P.O. Box 7819
Austin, TX 78713-7819
utpress.utexas.edu/rp-form

♾ The paper used in this book meets the minimum requirements of ANSI/NISO
Z39.48-1992 (R1997) (Permanence of Paper).

Library of Congress Cataloging-in-Publication Data

Names: Harrigan, Stephen, 1948–, author.
Title: Big wonderful thing : a history of Texas / Stephen Harrigan.
Description: First edition. | Austin : University of Texas Press, 2019. | Series:
The Texas bookshelf | Includes bibliographical references and index.
Identifiers: LCCN 2018060912
ISBN 978-0-292-75951-0 (cloth : alk. paper)
ISBN 978-1-4773-2003-7 (library e-book)
ISBN 978-1-4773-2004-4 (nonlibrary e-book)
Subjects: LCSH: Texas—History.
Classification: LCC F386 .H267 2019 | DDC 976.4—dc23
LC record available at https://lccn.loc.gov/2018060912

doi:10.7560/759510

For Sonny and Gladys

───── ★ ─────

*I hope that a dead calm will reign all over Texas
for many years to come—and that there will be no more
excitements of any kind whatever.*

—STEPHEN F. AUSTIN, FEBRUARY 6, 1835

———— ★ ————

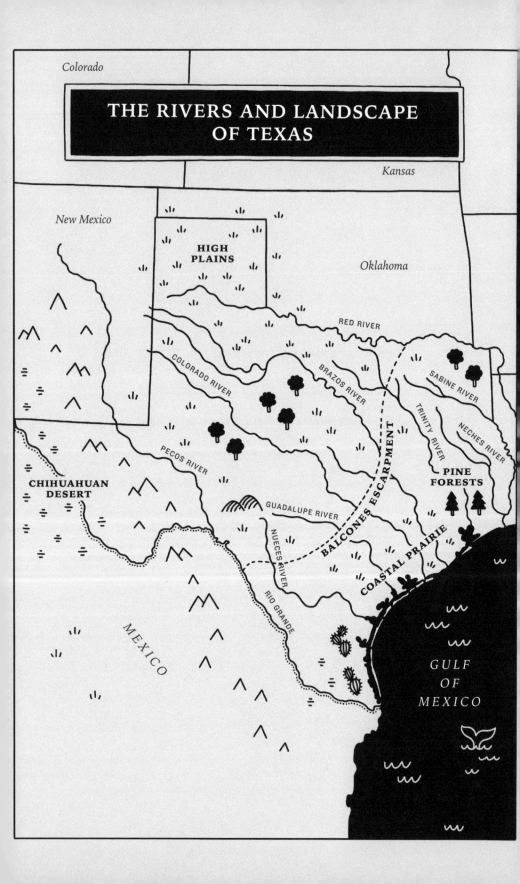

CONTENTS

———— ★ ————

"I couldn't be
was real. . .
big wonde
that oceans
highest mou

lieve Texas
the same
rful thing
and the
ntains are."

—GEORGIA O'KEEFFE

—— Prologue ——

BIG TEX

THE FIRE STARTED IN BIG TEX'S RIGHT BOOT. IT WAS
October 2012. Big Tex was fifty-two feet high and sixty years
old. He had come into being when the chamber of commerce
of Kerens, Texas, decided to build the world's largest Santa
Claus as a lure to draw Christmas shoppers to their little
East Texas town. Beneath his Santa suit of painted oilcloth
was a sturdy armature made of drill pipe and structural steel scavenged
from nearby oil fields. The giant Santa generated considerable attention at
first, but after a windstorm blew away his clothes and the initial excitement
of his presence wore off, the figure was sold to the State Fair of Texas in 1951
for $750. He was retrofitted as a cowboy and placed in front of the Cotton
Bowl in Dallas, where he greeted fair visitors for the next six decades.

Big Tex had a massive hinged jaw that opened and closed to an approxi-
mation of the welcoming words "Howdy, folks!" broadcast over loudspeakers by an announcer with an impeccably unhurried Texas accent. His outfits changed somewhat over the years, but he always wore a cowboy hat and
jeans and a belt buckle as big as a turkey platter. His right arm, bent at the
elbow, waved stiffly at fairgoers. His left arm, flung out awkwardly against
the blue sky in a gesture meant to seem expansive, looked painfully broken.

For all his creepiness, Big Tex was beloved, a nostalgic reminder of a
midcentury time when Texas had agreed to embrace a gentle caricature of
itself as a cowboy state, outsized and outlandish, proudly unconcerned with
taste. Big Tex was a homely, homegrown icon, the sort of thing that was fea-

tured along with the Alamo and the Astrodome on souvenir dinner plates and illustrated tourist maps.

The cause of the fire was an electrical short at the base of the figure, but the first indication that something was wrong with Big Tex appeared much higher up when greasy black smoke began to seep from beneath his shirt collar. Soon, bright flames crept up to consume his face and cowboy hat, and then they appeared along the crotch and seams of his jeans. Within a few minutes the conflagration was complete, nothing left but his blackened steel frame, his right hand, and the outlines of his charred face.

In less than a year, in time for the next state fair, a new Big Tex was erected in the same spot. The updated version cost half a million dollars, was three feet taller and nineteen thousand pounds heavier. But the sight of the new Big Tex being unveiled could not eclipse the weirdly horrifying image of the old one in flames. It's too much to say that the original Big Tex was a symbol of a simpler time—there have been no simple times in Texas history—but it belonged to a different Texas, a Texas that had not yet entered an age of ironic reflection. The new Big Tex was sort of a joke in the way the old one never had been. Everyone understood that it had been reconstructed simply for nostalgia's sake, to fill an empty place in the Lone Star psyche. But it was no longer possible for a single image—that of a waving, welcoming cowboy—to truly evoke the heaving twenty-first-century mix of cultural allegiances and colliding identities that Texas had become.

Both the original Big Tex and the new one stood dead center in the very place where that old half-mythical cohesive identity had been codified and triumphantly proclaimed to the world. Fair Park, which is a few miles east of downtown Dallas, is not just the location of the annual state fair and the Cotton Bowl football stadium. It was also the site of the 1936 Texas Centennial Exposition, the gigantic birthday party that Texas staged for itself on the occasion of the 100th anniversary of its independence from Mexico. One of the core goals of the exposition was to "Texanize Texans," to acquaint the citizens of the state with the marvels of its industrial might and its unparalleled history. It was also an announcement to the rest of the world of the state's poignantly unguarded self-love, a way to "mirror the accomplishments of Texas to all the sons and daughters of earth."

Most of the art moderne buildings of the great exposition are still there in Fair Park, hauntingly so. When there is no football game in the Cotton Bowl, no state fair in session, the grounds are often empty. The vast exhibition edifices, with their gilded sculptures and heroic friezes, still flank the grand esplanade, where fountains lining a seven-hundred-foot reflecting pool are programmed to erupt in rhythm with "The Yellow Rose of Texas."

But the place looks like an abandoned movie set from some futuristic epic of long ago. The exposition had been created on the scale of a World's Fair. It was rushed into being with remarkable speed, more than fifty new buildings thrown up in the hinterlands of Dallas in less than ten months. There were life-size robotic dinosaurs, a reproduction of the Globe Theatre, a colossal cash register on top of the National Cash Register Building that tallied up the number of each day's visitors—an average of about 36,000. The exhibition halls displayed new advances in electricity, transportation, and domestic life. There was a meant-to-be-progressive Hall of Negro Life, where visitors could learn about black Americans' "patient, loyal, patriotic attitude toward their country and . . . their gifts of soul and song." And somehow, there in the middle of Dallas, which would become famous as one of the most morally repressive cities in the country, there was a sanctioned "Streets of Paris" section, whose artistic focal point was live naked women. The best glimpse of them was via an attraction that passed itself off as an artist's studio, where patrons were handed a pad and pencil and shuffled quickly along so that they could "sketch" a nude model.

This glimpse of what passed for European sophistication was predictably popular, but the biggest crowd pleaser at the Centennial Exposition was *Cavalcade of Texas*, an extravagantly ambitious outdoor pageant chronicling the history of Texas from the arrival of the first European explorers to the great cattle drives in the waning years of the nineteenth century. It took place on what was billed as the world's largest stage, a performance space 300 feet wide and 170 feet deep. The stage was commodious enough to accommodate an artificial lagoon representing the Gulf of Mexico, in which a full-scale Spanish caravel sailed onto the Texas shore in the opening minutes of the production. Eighty-foot-high mountain peaks formed the back of the stage, and there were rocky cliffs and broad plains across which thundered mounted Indians and stagecoaches and herds of longhorn cattle.

Film footage of *Cavalcade of Texas* is scarce, though there is a glimpse of the great stage in an old Gene Autry movie, *The Big Show,* that was filmed at the exposition. And you can still find copies of the souvenir program in libraries and for sale online. When you page through this booklet, it's immediately apparent how earnest and comprehensive the intentions were for this extravaganza. It began with Indians holding aloft torches and chanting to the sun god and ended with Judge Roy Bean, the frontier magistrate who idiosyncratically represented "the law west of the Pecos." In between were Spanish castaways and conquistadors, French interlopers, American colonists, the Alamo and the Texas Revolution, Comanche raids, the rise and eventual dissolution of the independent Republic of Texas, secession, and the Civil War.

The Indians were played by white men in wigs and breechcloths whose bodies were sprayed with swarthy makeup. The "Pantomime Cast"—so named because the performers mouthed their lines while actors in a backstage sound room spoke them over a powerful public-address system—numbered 300 people. They are all listed in the program, and though the show prominently featured Spanish friars and explorers and the Mexican army, only 2 or 3 of the actors out of 300 have Hispanic surnames. Texans in 1936 would not have expected otherwise. The state's history was seen through an unbothered Anglo perspective. Other races or cultures had participated in that history, but were not considered part of its triumphant conclusion. And conclusion feels like the right word. Even though the souvenir program declared, "The Cavalcade of Texas will march on forever!" and even though the Centennial Exposition set a swaggering course for the future, there was a detectable sense that the history of Texas was essentially a settled issue. The question of whom Texas belonged to was presented at the exposition as the immutable result of four centuries of conflict. The future would bring wonders and hazards of all sorts, but Texas would never again be a fragmented, fought-over place. It had cohered into a singular nation-state whose people were pridefully united in their narrative of the past.

But just as the great panoramic stage could only hint at the breadth of the real Texas landscape—an immensity of plains and prairies and broken escarpments, deserts, fertile river valleys, spectral forests, wild coastal marshes merging into the stormy waters of the Gulf of Mexico—the moment in time when the Centennial Exposition took place enforced its own limitations on how Texas history could be understood. Every moment in time does that, of course. Every writer who attempts to portray history, including me every bit as much as Jan Isbelle Fortune and Clinton Boltons, the authors of the script of *Cavalcade of Texas*, is a hostage to contemporary values and unexposed biases.

There's a stopped-clock feel to the grounds of the exposition that reinforces the idea that this place, and this moment in Dallas, was meant to function as a bulwark against the erosive identity waves of the future. When you walk into the Hall of State, one of the few buildings left from the great fair that still aspires to serve its original purpose, you sense the ghostly emptiness even more. The Hall of State was originally called the State of Texas Building. It still sits at the head of the reflecting pool, the focal centerpiece of the grand esplanade. It was built to impress and to last—"the Westminster Abbey of the Western World," as a former Texas governor described it. It is partly a museum, with historical exhibits scattered here and there (including one honoring the inventor of the frozen margarita machine), but mostly it is a maximum-impact visual statement, its great central room dominated by a blindingly gold lone star emitting sun rays of Texas optimism. In front of the great room is the Hall of Heroes, with bronze statues by the San Antonio sculptor Pompeo Coppini of Sam Houston, William Travis, Stephen F. Austin, and other prominent figures from the revised standard version of Texas history, all standing guard in an empty marble corridor.

Almost another century has rolled past since this building was erected in 1936, and it's probably no longer possible to think about Texas in the way this consecrated place intended us to, as the culmination of an imperial dream. Locked in our own time, we are more likely to look back on the history trumpeted at the exposition with the accumulated detachment of the generations. That particular vision of Texas belongs to another age.

But when you leave the Hall of State, with its heroic statues and its sprawling, muscular murals, when you exit its mighty bronze doors and walk past limestone buttresses engraved with the dreamily thematic words "Romance," "Fortune," "Adventure," and "Honour"; when you drift toward the Cotton Bowl and find yourself staring up at the rebuilt Big Tex, his new white shirt brilliantly billowing against the searing blue sky of a Texas summer, you can't help but feel just a little bit Texanized. The state has nation-sized measurements: 268,000 square miles in all, 827 road miles from its westernmost city, El Paso, to Beaumont, near the Louisiana border. But its insistent and imposing sense of itself has created a vast mythical mindscape as well. Because it looms large in the world's imagination, and in fact is large, Texas has a history that is of consequence not just to itself, and not just to the nations it was once part of or the nation it briefly became. It sits at the core of the American experience, and its wars, its industries, its presidents, its catastrophes, its scientific discoveries have never stopped shaping the world.

"I salute the Empire of Texas!" President Franklin Roosevelt grandly declared when he visited the Centennial Exposition the week after it opened. His tongue may have been slightly in his cheek, and he may have been playing to the besotted native pride of his audience. But it was not much of a stretch to call the state an empire, and still isn't. The scale of Texas has always been, to borrow a word invented to describe the exposition's architecture, Texanic. In every dimension that matters, it is a very big place.

"I couldn't believe Texas was real," remembered Georgia O'Keeffe, who arrived in the Panhandle as a young artist and teacher in 1912. Her first impression was grander than even Roosevelt's. Her new home was not a state, not an empire, but a world. Texas, she thought, was "the same big wonderful thing that oceans and the highest mountains are."

★

PART ONE

They
CAME
— *from the* —
SKY

★

—1—

CASTAWAYS

THE LANDSCAPE OF THE TEXAS PANHANDLE IS CALLED the High Plains for a reason. Even though the elevation in this part of Texas is less than five thousand feet, when you drive north from Amarillo on State Highway 136, the overwhelming flatness of the land creates a top-of-the-world sensation, a feeling that you are rising upon the surface of a brimming, borderless sea. About twenty miles out of town, however, the land takes on texture. Shallow gullies and grassy declivities begin to appear, like ocean swells building under the stir of a gentle wind. Farther on, the change is dramatic. The flat land suddenly disappears entirely, replaced by a beautiful broken country where the Canadian River and its tributaries have sluiced deep below the limestone caprock into red Permian clay.

This is the site of the Alibates Flint Quarries. It is an important place, one of only three locations in Texas to be designated a national monument by the federal government. But a safe guess is that most of the people who find their way to the modest little visitor center at the bottom of a winding canyon road are drawn there less by the site's beckoning fame than by spur-of-the-moment curiosity. In truth, there isn't all that much to see, though what you do see you could spend a lifetime thinking about. Scattered over a series of windswept mesas above the Canadian River valley are seven hundred or so pits that were dug into the ground by ancient toolmakers in search of high-quality flint for knives, spear points, and arrow points. The pits were only a few feet deep, and over the millennia most of them have filled up with soil and plant life, so they register only as shallow depressions under a carpet of native prairie grasses and yellow broomweed flowers.

But pieces of the flint that was once quarried from these pits lie all around, flakes of agatized dolomite with intriguing striations and swirling colors, most characteristically a milky, muted shade of oxblood. There are natural outcroppings of this rock as well, big colorful boulders, but the paleo and archaic peoples who lived here appear to have mostly ignored the surface rock and dug with bone axes and hammerstones to get to the unweathered flint beneath the soil. They shaped it into what archaeologists call bifaces or trade blanks, hand-sized blocks of stone that they would carry back to their slab-housed villages or nomadic camps to be chipped and flaked into working implements. These unfinished pieces of flint also served as currency in a trade network that flourished throughout North America for many thousands of years. In Texas, a state whose identity would become fused with the practice and ethos of business, with cotton, cattle, oil, real estate, shipping, aerospace, banking, and high tech, the production and distribution of flint was the first thriving enterprise.

Alibates flint went everywhere, carried along by ancient peddlers through draws and along riverbeds and game trails, traded as far away as Minnesota and the Pacific coast. These quarries along the Canadian date back to the twilight of the last great Ice Age. The people of that time and place shared the grasslands and forested savannas of early Texas with vanished megafauna like bear-sized sloths and camels and saber-toothed cats and gigantic proto-armadillos. The earliest inhabitants shaped Alibates flint into the distinctively styled spear and projectile points that are classified today as Clovis, named for the town in New Mexico near which they were first discovered. Clovis points were long, often three or four inches, and painstakingly flaked to create a groove on either side for fastening the point to a split shaft. Clovis-era hunters used these weapons to kill the great Columbian mammoths—less shaggy than their northern cousins but, at fourteen feet high, even taller—that flourished in the warming landscape below the retreating ice sheets.

The long-held archaeological conviction that Clovis artifacts represent the earliest inhabitants of North America—people who had threaded their way onto the continent when it was joined to Asia by an Ice Age landmass—has been challenged in recent years, the attacks originating from excavations at places like the Gault Site, fifty miles north of Austin, in a rich transition zone between the rocky highlands of the Edwards Plateau and the deep black soil of the coastal prairie. Some of the tools found there—made out of local chert—lie deeper than the Clovis material. And they suggest an older technology that belonged to an earlier people, a people who had not yet developed Clovis innovations like fluted spear points, and who had taken up residence in the Americas several thousand years earlier than archaeologists' previous estimates of when humans first lived here.

Between this earliest-known period of human habitation in Texas and the first encounters with Europeans in the early sixteenth century lies an unimaginable stretch of deep time: fifteen thousand years, five hundred generations of people for whom we have no tangible history, not the name of a single person or even of a tribe. We know them only by buried artifacts in the strata of flood deposits and trash pits, by mementoes or offerings left behind in their graves, by the puzzling imagery they carved or painted on rock walls, and by the traces of illness, old wounds, and lifelong wear visible in their bones and teeth.

Four hundred and fifty miles due south of the Alibates Flint Quarries, in the desert canyon lands where the Pecos River meets the Rio Grande, are hundreds of rock shelters that were carved out of the limestone by Pleistocene rivers. The shelters are sweeping and commodious, natural gathering places for people seeking refuge from harsh weather or perhaps in search of panoramic vistas from which to contemplate their place in creation. Excavations in the soil of the shelter floors have revealed a great deal of information about how these early inhabitants lived. There are sandals and bedding woven from lechuguilla fibers, weapons and implements demonstrating the advances of Stone Age technology, the remains of earth ovens where the fibrous bulbs of sotol plants were baked for days to make them edible. But when you look up at the colorful, faded rock art on the ceilings and walls of the shelters, all you see is something our modern minds must struggle to grasp, the consciousness and cosmology of a people who long ago moved on from these painted canyons.

The pictographs feature strange, provocative forms: elongated, vaguely human shapes with antlers or rabbit ears sprouting from their featureless heads, sometimes rising with outstretched arms in a posture that suggests flight or resurrection from some dark underworld. There are bat-like creatures and headless entities in the shapes of rectangles or gourds, and scattered renderings of dead animals impaled by arrows or atlatl darts. There are waving, serpentine lines and spiky paramecium-shaped blobs that some scholars believe represent the peyote cactus buttons that might have been the means of accessing an archaic mythical or spiritual realm. These tableaux

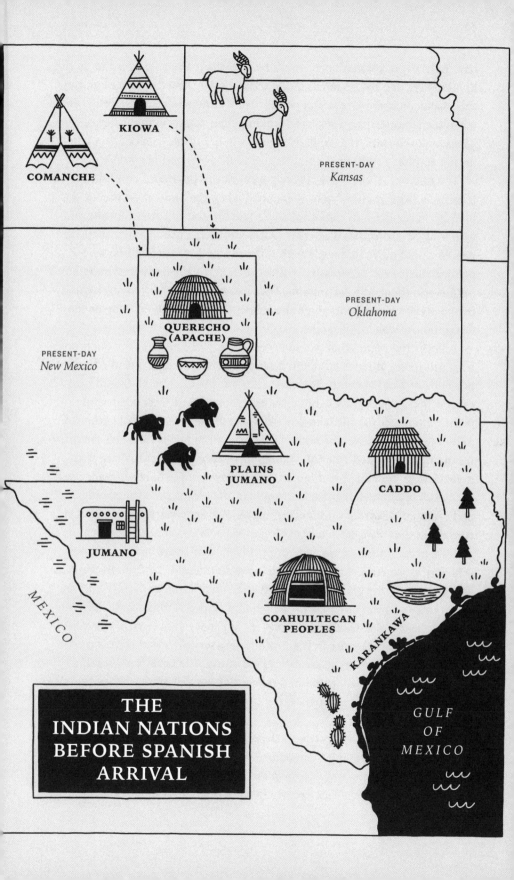

KIOWA

COMANCHE

PRESENT-DAY
Kansas

PRESENT-DAY
Oklahoma

QUERECHO
(APACHE)

PRESENT-DAY
New Mexico

PLAINS
JUMANO

CADDO

JUMANO

COAHUILTECAN
PEOPLES

KARANKAWA

MEXICO

GULF
OF
MEXICO

THE
INDIAN NATIONS
BEFORE SPANISH
ARRIVAL

have been degraded in modern times by vandalism and pollution and by the humidity created by the construction of the nearby Amistad Reservoir, but their hallucinogenic vibe is still potent. They were painted around the time when the Egyptian pharaohs were building their tombs in the Valley of the Kings, and they hint at a similarly complex belief system, one of soul journeying and form shifting and travels to and from mysterious otherworlds.

The canyons of the Lower Pecos appear not to have been continuously inhabited. Rock shelters were abandoned when the population moved on, perhaps in response to climate changes and the rise of better hunting and gathering opportunities elsewhere. After stretches of time, other sorts of people would move in, people with different tools and aesthetics, who painted the rock in accordance with a different understanding of humanity's origins and the soul's destination. The already ancient designs left behind by the previous occupants might have been as inscrutable to them as the Great Sphinx was to Alexander the Great.

All over the region that would become Texas, throughout the unchronicled centuries, populations shifted as resources surged or dwindled, or as one tribe or band violently displaced another. (At the Harrell Site in north-central Texas, mass graves contain human bones with embedded arrow points, along with skulls whose missing mandibles were probably carried away as war trophies.) The nomadic people of the plains followed the mammoth migrations, and when the mammoths were gone—casualties of climate change, human predation, or both—these people hunted an ancestral species of big-boned, big-horned ruminant that dominated the grasslands and eventually evolved into modern bison. The expressions of human culture evolved as well, from simple thrusting spears to atlatls to bows and arrows, from designs scratched onto pebbles to intricate ornamental pottery. In the forests and deep-soiled prairies to the east, far from the deserts and drought-prone plains that lie above the great rampart of uplifted limestone known as the Balcones Escarpment, a settled farming and village life began to take hold. This part of Texas lay at the western edge of the Mississippian culture that arose in the southeastern woodlands of the continent in the centuries before the arrival of Europeans. The Caddoan-speaking people here built great ceremonial centers whose elaborate earthen temples and burial mounds can still be traced in the hummocky contours of the East Texas landscape.

By the beginning of the sixteenth century, Texas was well populated with indigenous peoples living in nomadic family groups or in settled villages that, according to one early Spanish estimate, might have had populations of up to ten thousand. They spoke a bewildering spectrum of languages, and were splintered into so many tribes and bands that Juan Domínguez de Mendoza, exploring Texas in 1684, counted sixty-four "nations" in attendance at some sort of rendezvous or trading fair on the Colorado River near present-day Ballinger.

———————— ★ ————————

ON THE GULF OF MEXICO LIVED A PEOPLE THAT CAME TO BE known as the Karankawas. They were divided into bands spread out along the margins of the Texas coast. Karankawas moved with the seasons. They spent the summers hunting and harvesting on the mainland prairies, and in the fall and winter they set up camp along the bay shores or paddled their dugout canoes across the lagoons to the string of low-lying barrier islands that protected the inland waters from the open Gulf. They moved seaward to take advantage of the spawning seasons of drum and redfish and speckled trout, catching the fish in weirs and nets or through the deadly accurate use of their distinctively long bows. Karankawas were famously tall; everyone who encountered them remarked on it. They were tattooed and mostly naked, their lower lips sometimes pierced with short lengths of cane, their skin glistening with the alligator grease they employed to ward off mosquitoes. They made pottery and painted designs on it with black beach tar. They lived in willow-framed huts that could be gathered up and moved quickly as they followed the food sources from season to season.

On a freezing November day in 1528, on some narrow windswept stretch of the Texas coast (most likely Galveston Island or nearby Follett's Island), a hunting party of three Karankawa men encountered a shocking apparition. It was a man, or at least something like a man, carrying a pot he had stolen from their camp while all the people were away. He had taken some fish as well, and was either carrying or being followed by one of the village dogs. The stranger was starving and haggard. His skin was oddly pale, his hair and beard matted. His emaciated body shivered beneath the few loose rags that covered it. He looked back at the Karankawas but ignored their attempts to communicate with him and kept walking toward the desolate ocean beach. When he reached it, the Karankawas held back a little, staring in amazement. There were forty other men there, sprawled in the sand around a driftwood fire. Near them, half buried in the sand where it had been violently driven in by the waves, was some sort of crude vessel, a thirty-foot-long raft of lashed pine logs, with a rough-hewn mast and spars and a disintegrating sail made out of sewn-together shirts.

Within a half hour, another hundred or so Karankawa warriors had arrived to gawk at the castaways. The newcomers did not seem to be a threat,

The Karankawas, who lived along the coast, were the first inhabitants of Texas to encounter Europeans. The meeting did not go well.

since they had no weapons and most of them were too weak to stand. Finally two of the men rose from the sand and staggered over to the Indians. The one who seemed to be the leader did his best to communicate by signs that they meant no harm, and he presented them with trading goods, some beads and bells that had somehow survived as cargo during whatever disastrous voyage had just taken place.

The Karankawas made signs that they intended to return the next morning with food. They made good on their promise, bringing fish and cattail roots, and kept coming back to feed the men for several days. One evening they returned to find the strange visitors in even more desperate shape. During the day, they had tried to resume their ocean journey, digging their raft out of the sand, stowing their clothes on board, and paddling out toward the open Gulf. Not far from shore, they had been hit by a wave, and the raft had capsized and been pounded apart against the sandbars that run parallel to the Texas shoreline. Three men had drowned, and the survivors were all now naked and so close to death from exposure that the Karankawas broke out into loud ritualistic lamentations. Then, realizing that the men would not survive the night, they got to work, some of them running off to build a series of bonfires to warm the castaways en route to their camps, others bodily picking up the starving, freezing men and carrying them to shelter.

———————— ★ ————————

THE KARANKAWAS WERE NOT A SEAFARING PEOPLE. THEY probed the bays and lagoons and paddled back and forth from the mainland to the barrier islands, but the open Gulf of Mexico remained a mysterious immensity beyond the reach of their dugout canoes. And far to the east, beyond the Straits of Florida, there was a much greater sea of whose existence they might only have heard through stories passed along by other native peoples. It was from the far side of this unknown ocean that the ghostlike men trying to revive themselves around the fires in the natives' willow-framed lodges had come. They were adventurers from Spain, part of a great wave of expansion and exploration generated by the completion of a struggle that had lasted almost eight centuries, the Christian reconquest of the Muslim-dominated Iberian Peninsula. By 1492, King Ferdinand II and Queen Isabella, whose marriage had allied the Catholic kingdoms of Aragon and Castile, had conquered Granada, the last stronghold of al-Andalus, the name by which Muslim Iberia had long been known. That same year, Isabella financed Columbus's first voyage of discovery, and his landfall in the West Indies gave Spain a new horizon toward which to direct its surging national confidence, and a new world to exploit.

The men who had washed up naked on this forsaken Gulf beach were, in all likelihood, the first Europeans to set foot in Texas. (A Spanish expedition led by Alonso Álvarez de Pineda had sailed along this coast in 1519 and produced a map of it, but there is no record of them going ashore.) They came thirty-six years after Columbus, when the Spanish colonization and conquest of the Caribbean basin and Mexico were well under way, and when the invasion of the Inca Empire in Peru was about to begin. The doorway to two great continents had been breached, and it was crowded with men of rampant ambition trying to beat each other through it. Some of these men were adelantados, licensed by the Crown to risk their own fortunes in order to find and subjugate new lands. If their ships didn't go down in a hurricane or run aground on uncharted shoals, if they didn't starve or die of disease or get killed by the native inhabitants they had come to conquer, they would be granted titles and far-reaching administrative powers and inexhaustible wealth.

Others, like Hernán Cortés, lacked that official sanction, but they made up for it in bravado. In 1518, Cortés was commissioned by Diego Velázquez de Cuéllar, the governor of Cuba, to explore the newly discovered coast of the Yucatán, from which two previous expeditions had returned with reports of sophisticated cities with towering stone temples and a casual abundance of gold. Velázquez had never really trusted Cortés, and as he began to suspect his commander of being a competitor and not a subordinate partner, he withdrew the commission and even ordered his arrest. But Cortés was too fast and too crafty, and the order came too late. By late February 1519 his fleet of eleven ships had sailed, heading westward across the Yucatán channel toward the Mexican Gulf Coast. There Cortés and his men encountered the unimaginable and proceeded to accomplish the unthinkable. Tenochtitlán, the capital of the Aztec Empire, was as proud and populous as any city in Europe. To the Spaniards who beheld it after fighting their way inland from the coast, it was a sprawling, glittering, dreamlike metropolis, a place whose temple pyramids and strange sculptures and frescoes were startling in their alien beauty, and whose culture of human sacrifice—of ripped-out hearts and priests with blood-caked hair—struck their fervently Catholic minds as a devil's pageant of horror. In only a little over two years, with a fighting force that began with fewer than six hundred men and sixteen horses but was exponentially increased by Cortés's dynamic diplomacy among subjugated tribes primed to rebel against Aztec domination, the Spaniards had conquered Tenochtitlán and begun the work of tearing down its temples, determined to erase this wondrous abomination of a city from human memory.

There was no Aztec grandeur on the Texas coast, over seven hundred miles north of Tenochtitlán, where the Karankawa bands pieced together a subsistence existence by following the cycles of spawning fish and ripening fruits and nuts. And they could hardly have considered the desperate wraiths they had taken into their village to be conquerors. Unlike Cortés, these Spaniards had no ships, no armor, no weapons, no intimidating beasts like the never-before-seen horses. But a year and a half earlier, these men had sailed pridefully out of the harbor in Seville and down the Guadalquivir River into the open Atlantic, part of an expedition made up of five ships and six hundred people. The expedition had a grant from King Ferdinand's grandson Charles, now king of Spain and Holy Roman emperor, to conquer and populate all the land from the northern border of Cortés's Mexican possessions to the Florida Peninsula.

The voyage was led by a ruthless soldier and tireless schemer named Pánfilo de Narváez. Narváez had been Diego Velázquez's sword arm in the conquest of Cuba, where he watched impassively from horseback as his men butchered the inhabitants of a village on the Caonao River. In 1520, Velázquez, still fuming over Cortés's usurpation of the Yucatán mission, put together a powerful fleet of nineteen ships to intercept Cortés, throw him in irons, and neutralize any claim he tried to make on the plundered wealth of Mexico. Narváez, who had served Velázquez cruelly well in Cuba, commanded the expedition. When Narváez's armada landed, Cortés had already entered Tenochtitlán, where, in an unnervingly brazen stroke, he had taken the Aztec leader Moctezuma hostage in his own palace. Even though his position was exquisitely vulnerable, he left a couple hundred men behind in the city and marched the rest of his army to the coast. Cortés swiftly outwitted and outfought Narváez, peeling away some of his officers with bribes and overpowering his force in a surprise nighttime attack. Narváez lost an eye in the fight and spent two and a half years in a fetid dungeon while Cortés finished conquering Mexico with the help of the soldiers Narváez had brought to arrest him.

But his career still held an even more disastrous third act. Once he was released from prison, Narváez sailed to Spain, where he spent five years lobbying Charles V and the Council of the Indies for permission to "explore, conquer, populate and discover all there is to be found of Florida." The name "Florida" at that time meant the entire sweeping coastline of the Gulf of Mexico from Mexico's Río de las Palmas to the Florida Keys. In 1526, Narváez's petition to become an adelantado was finally granted, and the next year he set out across the Atlantic with five ships bearing six hundred men and women—soldiers, colonists, slaves, and priests—to claim and somehow try to possess an unknown part of the world that was four times as large as Spain itself.

The fleet stopped in Cuba, where a hurricane destroyed two of Narváez's ships and drowned sixty men, and where the surviving vessels ran aground onto shoals and encountered more storms once they were under sail again. But the hard luck had barely started. From Cuba, Narváez sailed due westward for the Río de las Palmas, on the northerly coast of Mexico, which was the western boundary of his vast territorial claim. He never reached it. After a month at sea, caught up in the fast-moving swirl of the Gulf Stream, which bore the ships in the opposite direction, and with food running low and horses dying in the holds, the fleet made landfall on the western coast of Florida, all the way across the Gulf of Mexico from its planned landing site.

Even though they were a thousand miles away from the Río de las Palmas, the thoroughly disoriented Spaniards thought they had nearly reached their destination. They encountered Indians who encouraged them to believe that there was a great kingdom, full of gold, not far to the north. Narváez decided to reconnoiter on land, taking 300 men and sending the rest of the expedition ahead on the ships to wait for them farther up the coast. The two parts of the expedition never saw each other again. Narváez and his land party spent four months wandering lost and starving through nearly impassable swamps and forests, and blundering into sieges and skirmishes with the native inhabitants. Desperate and unable to find the ships with which they were supposed to rendezvous, they killed and ate their horses and then set about the almost impossible task of building five seaworthy vessels to carry them to the Río de las Palmas. They still believed that the river lay somewhere just along the coast, and that once they found it they could make their way to Pánuco, Mexico's northernmost Spanish settlement. The 242 men who were left—fifty had died of disease or drowning or starvation—constructed a crude forge and melted down their crossbows and stirrups in order to make axes and nails with which to build wooden rafts.

The men were at sea on their rafts for a month and a half. They sailed westward along the Florida Panhandle, then across the mouth of the Mississippi. They were nearly dead from dehydration when the rafts finally drifted apart, strung out along the length of the Texas coast. Most of the men made it to shore somewhere. But Pánfilo de Narváez, the adelantado whose claim to all the lands of Florida was now a pathetic presumption, was last seen drifting out into the Gulf on his raft.

AS THE MEN WHO HAD BEEN TAKEN INTO THE KARANKAWA camp began to revive somewhat around the fire pits, watching the Karankawas dance all night in a frighteningly ambiguous celebration, they grew alarmed. In the months since leaving Cuba, they had encountered numerous native peoples whose reaction to their presence had been mercurial, unreadable, and often violent. And they had heard the stories of what had befallen other Spaniards in Mexico, men who had been captured and sacrificed to alien gods, then flayed so thoroughly and expertly that their comrades, finding their skins strung up on temple walls, were still able to recognize their boneless, bearded faces. They were convinced that something similar was in store for them. But as the days passed, the Karankawas continued to treat them as unfortunate refugees and not as captives to be sacrificed.

The leader of the Spaniards, the man who had approached the Karankawas on the beach, asking for help and offering trade goods, was Álvar Núñez Cabeza de Vaca. He was probably in his late thirties, from a distinguished family with ties to the royal court. A functionary in the houses of Andalusian dukes when younger, he had spent most of his career as a soldier, fighting the French at the Battle of Ravenna in 1512 and insurrectionists in Castile. On Narváez's expedition, he was the royal treasurer, whose mission was to ensure that the Crown received its share of any New World wealth.

But there was no longer any need for wealth to be accounted for, and only a very slim possibility of surviving. Three of the five rafts had drifted south of the island that Cabeza de Vaca and his companions came to call Malhado—"ill fortune"—and the men on those rafts were either killed outright by Indians or eventually died of starvation and exposure. Another raft had landed with Cabeza de Vaca's on Malhado, bringing the total number of survivors on the island to eighty or so. But most of the men were too sick or malnourished to survive, and within weeks only sixteen were left. Five of the Spaniards from Cabeza de Vaca's raft had stayed behind on the beach rather than face the horrors they imagined waiting for them in the camp. Starving there, they turned to cannibalism. When the Indians discovered this, the relationship between the castaways and their hosts quickly began to deteriorate. The Karankawas appear to have practiced ritualistic cannibalism against their enemies, but they could not abide the idea of human beings actually eating one another for food. This is a resonant historical irony, since they have long been saddled with the reputation of being rapacious man-eaters themselves. ("Cannibal Indians," intones the narrator of a 1960 Texas Department of Public Safety travelogue, "used to waylay shipwrecked sailors and then chase them up and down the island one at a time as the menu indicated.")

The Karankawas watched the Spaniards die, and then they began to die themselves. During the course of that terrible winter, over half the natives on the island perished. So many died so suddenly that the Indians' mourning customs—elaborate burials and cremations, the drinking of water mixed with the pulverized bones of the deceased, a year of ritual weeping at every sunrise—became impossible to carry out. Undone with grief and bewilderment, they assumed the Spaniards were murdering them through some sort of dark magic. And there was indeed an invisible lethal force at work, one that had already ravaged the indigenous people of the Indies and in years to come would bring unimaginable catastrophe to native populations throughout the Americas: Old World pathogens like smallpox and measles, for which the Karankawas had no immunity.

The traumatized Indians who survived this initial epidemic spared the Spaniards' lives, but grudgingly. Having first taken in their visitors out of charity, they now cast them into a kind of slavery. Continually beaten and threatened, the castaways were forced to dig up roots from the freezing saltwater marshes with their bleeding fingers. In the spring of 1529, thirteen of the Spaniards managed to escape from Malhado and make their way south along the coast, determined to somehow still reach the Spanish settlement at Pánuco. Cabeza de Vaca was too ill to join the trek, but when he recovered he too fled the island for the mainland, where he fell in with a tribe called the Charrucos, who treated him better and put him to work as a long-distance peddler. They sent him off on long solitary trading missions deep into the heart of the country, where he bartered for hides and flint, offering seashells and pearls from the coast in exchange. Traveling alone in an alien land, in constant peril from hunger and thirst and hostile weather, he was nevertheless exhilarated by his liberation from enslavement on Malhado and by a newfound sense of purpose and confidence: "This occupation served me very well, because practicing it, I had the freedom to go where I wanted, and I was not constrained in any way nor enslaved."

Those words are from a book Cabeza de Vaca wrote that has come to be known as *La relación* (The account). Acknowledging in a preface that its contents would be "very difficult for some to believe," he published the book in Spain in 1542, with a second edition thirteen years later. It is an extremely rare book, but there are places, such as the Wittliff Collections at Texas State University in San Marcos, where you can ask for it and hold it in your hands. The double-headed eagle of Charles V is on the frontispiece, the ancient rag paper is pleasingly supple and tactile, the pages so dense with sixteenth-century typography there are hardly any margins. *La relación* is the first book ever written about Texas. It's a work of survival literature, of natural history, of anthropology, and of what must have seemed to readers of the time to be extraterrestrial travel.

The book recounts the doomed voyage from Cuba to Florida and the desperate attempt to sail on to Pánuco on rafts, as well as the almost six years that Cabeza de Vaca spent wandering with his trade goods through the interior of Texas and up and down its desolate coast. He wrote about the strange and frightening customs he witnessed among the people he encountered—their theatrical weeping and fluid gender roles, the way that unwanted female babies were sometimes buried alive or fed to dogs, the contrasting tenderness toward children and the unstoppable grief when they died. He wrote about "vipers that kill men when they strike" and about great herds of "cows" that ranged down from the north, creatures with long fur and curved horns like Moorish cattle—the first-ever written reference to bison.

FOR MOST OF THOSE YEARS, HE WAS SEPARATED FROM HIS fellow Spaniards. But in 1533, in the pecan forests near the mouth of San Antonio Bay, where all the bands of the region migrated in the spring to gather nuts, Cabeza de Vaca encountered what was left of the group that had set out years earlier for Pánuco when he was too sick to join them. Of those thirteen men, only three were still alive, and their long odyssey to the Spanish settlement had been interrupted by years of captivity and servitude among tribes that inhabited the coastal prairies of South Texas. Two of the men, Andrés Dorantes and Alonso del Castillo, were, like Cabeza de Vaca, soldiers of noble rank. The third is referred to in *La relación* by the diminutive version of the Christian name—Esteban—that had been assigned to him after he was captured by slavers somewhere in Africa and then sold in the markets of Morocco or Spain. He had come to the New World as the human property of Dorantes, probably the first African and the first Muslim to find himself in the American Southwest. Now, along with his master, Estebanico was a new sort of slave, in bondage not just to the inscrutable mores of the alien peoples he had encountered but also to the imprisoning wilderness all around him.

It had been five years since their rafts went ashore on Malhado, but the four men still dreamed of reaching the Spanish settlement at Pánuco. It would be two more frustrating years before they could coordinate their escape. They finally slipped away in the summer of 1535, during the time of year when the native groups throughout the region moved south toward the Nueces River for the annual harvest of the prickly pear fruits, which grew there in staggering abundance.

The four escapees trekked through an inhospitable landscape of cactus, thorny brush, and shadeless, spindly trees. Though the Spanish outpost of Pánuco lay on the coast three hundred miles south, they kept well inland, where they had learned from experience that the people tended to be more welcoming to strangers. They came to the Rio Grande, shallow enough to

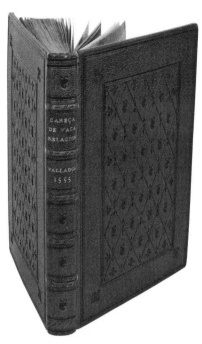

La relación, *Álvar Núñez Cabeza de Vaca's account of his eight-year odyssey after washing ashore on a Texas island, gave sixteenth-century European readers their first glimpse of the American Southwest.*

wade across but, as Cabeza de Vaca wrote, wider than the Guadalquivir, down which Narváez's impressive fleet had first sailed.

The country was harsh, but the four castaways were no longer wretched. They had learned the languages and the customs of the people among whom they had passed, and they were conditioned to hardship and unsurprised by it. Also, they were beginning to emerge from servitude into celebrity.

Back on Malhado, the castaways had been pressed into service as healers. Cabeza de Vaca and the others were nervous about practicing an art about which they knew nothing, one with high stakes and unpredictable results. But the Karankawas threatened to let them starve if they didn't comply. So the Spaniards cautiously began, adding Christian flourishes—the sign of the cross, the Lord's Prayer—to the native repertoire of ritual healing. The two forms of magic turned out to be compatible enough for at least some healing to take place, and the castaways, even though they were still slaves, began to take on the power of shamans.

By the time they crossed the Rio Grande, they had developed a surging reputation. Each tribe they encountered had heard of their cures, and as they ventured deeper into Mexico they accumulated a constant following of people eager to see the foreigners and witness their miracles. Often Estebanico went ahead as a kind of mysterious herald, the inhabitants startled and mesmerized by his black skin.

The route of Cabeza de Vaca, Estebanico, and the others has been the subject of debate for many decades, and it's still impossible to know at this point precisely where the journey took them. They were possibly only about two hundred miles from Pánuco, the Spanish province that had been the focus of all their dreams of salvation, when they turned west, moving far away from the coast and toward the peaks of the Sierra Madre. No longer starving, no longer enslaved, they now enjoyed superhuman status among the people they met, who followed them from one village to the next in processions that grew to number in the thousands. If they had felt forsaken by God in the previous years, perhaps now they sensed his guiding hand as they blew their healing breath over the bodies of the afflicted or even performed surgery on them with flint knives and sutured the incisions with deer-bone needles. Cabeza de Vaca recounted one of these operations in *La relación*, which many years later inspired the Texas Surgical Society to choose a cow skull—in homage to the English translation of the explorer's name—for its logo.

It seems plausible that the four survivors of Narváez's expedition turned away from the coast and moved deeper into the interior out of a reawakened sense of discovery. Along the way they encountered things that encouraged them: an intricately worked copper bell with a human face, cotton blankets, baskets of maize. All this indicated that if they kept going they might still fulfill one of the original purposes of the Narváez expedition—to discover cities of vast wealth like the one Cortés had found in the Valley of Mexico.

They found further hints of what might lie ahead when they turned north again and recrossed the Rio Grande back into what is now Texas, many miles upstream from where they had first crossed it. Beyond, where the Rio Grande met the Conchos in the Junta de los Ríos, near where the town of Presidio is today, they entered the fertile country of the Jumanos, an agricultural people who lived in flat-roofed stone apartments—"the first dwellings we saw that had the semblance and appearance of houses."

They lingered with the Jumanos and then kept on, believing that by "going the route of the setting sun we would find what we desired." They were constantly followed by a great crowd of native disciples. "They always accompanied us," Cabeza de Vaca wrote, "until they left us handed over to others. And among all these peoples, it was taken for certain that we came from the sky." And it was in the sky, the Spaniards preached to the Indians, that their God lived. If they too believed in him, if they obeyed his teachings, things "would go very well for them."

But things did not go well for the people who accompanied Cabeza de Vaca. After following the Rio Grande north for several weeks, the party turned southwest, still moving in the direction of the setting sun, searching for the cities of great wealth and sophistication they had come to believe lay beyond the horizon. They made their way through the Chihuahuan Desert, through the mountain passes of the western Sierra Madre, down to the coastal plateaus of the Gulf of California. In something like six months, they had walked across the continent of North America. And now they were among people who were not naked hunter-gatherers, but who lived in stable houses and grew crops and wore shirts and robes of finely woven cotton. By this time, the desperate men from Malhado had reached their highest level of spiritual influence. In one village, they were given a gift of six hundred deer hearts. Mothers who had just given birth presented their infants to the healers so that they could be blessed with the sign of the cross.

They met an Indian wearing a necklace fashioned from the buckle of a Spanish sword belt. This could only mean that the countrymen they had been seeking in the wilderness for almost eight years were at last somewhere nearby. Cabeza de Vaca and the others pressed anxiously on, reassuring their Indian followers, telling them they would intercede with any Christians so that "they should not kill them or take them as slaves."

But they now moved through a country that had been devastated—villages burned and almost deserted, the few remaining people sick and starving, the rest having fled to the mountains or been taken captive. Finally, at the end of Cabeza de Vaca's unthinkably long road, he encountered the cause of this havoc. One day he found himself staring up at four Spaniards mounted on horseback. "[They] experienced great shock upon seeing me so strangely dressed," he wrote, "and in the company of Indians. They remained looking at me a long time, so astonished that they neither spoke nor managed to ask me anything." The bearded, helmeted men looking down in stupefaction from their horses were part of a slave-hunting expedition in the service of Nuño de Guzmán, the rapacious governor of the Mexican province of Nueva Galicia.

It was 1536, a time when a fervent argument was raging over the "capacity" of the people the Spanish had discovered inhabiting the New World. Were they some low, half-bestial variant of humanity, or had God given them souls that might be brought to salvation, and slumbering intellects that could be awakened and made to understand the Gospels and the mysteries of faith? Passionate, conscience-torn priests such as Antonio de Montesinos, who in 1511 shocked the conquistadors of Hispaniola by asking, "Are these Indians not men? Do they not have rational souls?," and Bartolomé de las Casas, who as a young man had witnessed Narváez's rampages in Cuba, had begun to win the argument, at least in the courts of philosophy. And a year later, in 1537, Pope Paul III issued the bull *Sublimis Deus*, which decreed that "Indians and all other people who may later be discovered by Christians, are by no means to be deprived of their liberty or the possession of their property . . . nor should they be in any way enslaved." But such distant moral declarations were only limp pieties on the ground in New Spain, where men like Guzmán needed slaves to work their extensive lands and their silver and gold mines, and to export to the Antilles in exchange for livestock and other commodities.

Cabeza de Vaca pleaded for the freedom of the Indians who were traveling with his party, but the Spanish captain, interested only in enslaving them, sent the castaways off under armed guard to the town of Culiacán, where they could not interfere. A few months later they arrived in Mexico City, where they astonished Viceroy Antonio de Mendoza and Hernán Cortés himself with their story of having survived the doomed Narváez expedition and managing to stay alive for eight long years in a vast wilderness realm no other European had ever seen. The wanderers had trouble readjusting to Spanish life, feeling weighed down by their borrowed clothes and unable to sleep comfortably anywhere except on the ground. And Cabeza de Vaca's conscience—expanded by the experience of being saved, enslaved, and finally venerated by an ever-changing cast of native peoples—was no longer a natural fit with the hubristic spirit of conquest.

— 2 —

GOLDEN CITIES

THE GHOSTLY REAPPEARANCE OF CABEZA DE VACA AND his companions startled the inhabitants of New Spain and set in motion a new wave of exploration. If there were civilizations far to the north capable of fabricating copper bells and weaving fine cotton, wasn't it logical to assume that somewhere in this "Tierra Nueva" there might be another golden city like Tenochtitlán? In fact, there might be seven such cities, a legend that had taken root in the Iberian imagination as far back as the eighth century, when it was believed that seven bishops had sailed away from Moorish-conquered Spain and founded Christian cities far from Europe in some unknown land beyond the Ocean Sea.

Viceroy Mendoza tried to recruit the three white survivors of the Narváez expedition to retrace their steps northward in search of the seven cities, but they turned him down. In the end there was only one man available who knew anything about the country and the people who lived north of Nueva Galicia. Though in the wilderness he had achieved a sort of freedom through the leveling hardships he shared with his fellow castaways, Estebanico was now a slave again, and he was ordered into service as the guide for a new entrada. He may very well have welcomed the mission, given the swagger he showed on the expedition, which was led by a Franciscan cleric named Fray Marcos de Niza.

Accompanied by two Castilian greyhounds and bearing a talismanic gourd decorated with feathers and rattlesnake rattles to present to the chieftains he would meet, Estebanico scouted far in advance of Fray Marcos's main party, following rumors that the "greatest thing in the world" lay ahead. Both Estebanico and Marcos became increasingly confident that they were soon to encounter a land called Cíbola, where there would indeed be seven cities, splendid cities where the people lived in towering houses made of stone and inlaid turquoise and slept on canopied beds.

When he arrived at Hawikuh, the first of these cities, Estebanico made a fatal miscalculation. The presentation of his ceremonial gourd was refused, and the inhabitants—probably alerted by stories of Spanish atrocities in Nueva Galicia—warned him and his large Indian entourage not to approach the city. But Estebanico had spent so many years as a celebrated guest among multitudes of native peoples—some friendly, others hostile, some inscrutably in-between—that he appears not to have taken the lack of welcome seriously. Perhaps he was feeling a bit indomitable. He had, after all, survived shipwreck, disease, starvation, thirst, and innumerable skirmishes and standoffs, and had made one of the greatest odysseys in human history. He may have still been a slave but he was also a celebrated shaman who now presented himself as a plenipotentiary from a distant culture. He refused to be refused by Hawikuh's leaders and insisted on approaching the city, but before he reached its walls archers sallied forth and killed him and many of his followers.

Fray Marcos reported that when he heard the news of Estebanico's death, he hurried forward but stopped short of trying to enter Hawikuh. He was "satiated with fear" and did no more than glimpse the terraced stone city from across the plains. His impression was that it was "bigger than the city of Mexico." It wasn't. From a distance, the seven cities of Cíbola might have looked like sprawling metropolises to a weary and traumatized friar, but they were only modest pueblos scattered along the Zuni River basin in what is today western New Mexico.

Nevertheless, the tantalizing prospect of more rich kingdoms to investigate and conquer led to a massive reconnaissance expedition that left from Compostela, on the Pacific coast of Mexico, the next year, 1540, under the command of Francisco Vázquez de Coronado. Coronado was thirty years old, the beneficiary of a noble birth and an even nobler marriage to a woman whose father was said to be the illegitimate son of King Ferdinand. He was also the protégé of Viceroy Mendoza and had recently replaced Nuño de Guzmán as governor of Nueva Galicia. His entrada was a swarming mass of humans and livestock: thousands of cattle, sheep, and hogs to feed an expeditionary force made up of between three hundred and four hundred Spanish soldiers, probably an equal number of slaves and servants, and an accompanying army of thousands of *indios amigos*, native allies from Mexican nations, who were armed with obsidian-edged swords and featherwork shields.

When Coronado reached Hawikuh, he ordered the *Requerimiento* read aloud to the Zuni-speaking warriors behind the city walls. The *Requerimiento* was a document created by pedantic legal minds in Castile to provide a veneer of justification for the seizing of native lands and people. It offered a summary of the creation of the world, including the story of the first man and woman, and told how God had bestowed ecclesiastical authority upon Saint Peter, and how Peter's successors as pontiff had granted the land upon which the Indians were living to Spain. "You can inspect the documents," the Zunis were told, "that recorded this grant." They were exhorted to "recognize the Church as owner and administrator of the entire world," and if they complied, they would receive a number of unspecified benefits. The alternative, Coronado made plain, was grim: "If you do not do what I ask . . . I assure you that, with the help of God, I will attack you mightily . . . I will take your wives and children, and I will make them slaves . . . I declare that the deaths and injuries that occur as a result of this would be your fault and not His Majesty's, nor ours, nor that of these gentlemen who have come with me."

After the Zunis heard this incomprehensible pronouncement and "refused to have peace," Coronado and his Spanish men-at-arms and Indian allies attacked, overrunning and capturing the city. They eventually moved on to another complex of pueblos called Tiguex, near present-day Albuquerque, and spent the winter fighting a brief, savage war with the Tiwa people who lived there. It was while he was near Tiguex that Coronado met the Turk, so named because his features reminded the Spaniards of their Old World Ottoman enemies. Nobody thought to record the Turk's real name, but he was the man who, thirteen years after the remnants of Narváez's expedition had washed ashore on Malhado, was responsible for bringing Europeans back onto Texas soil.

The Turk was a member of an unknown tribe far to the east. He had been captured and enslaved at some point before Coronado's entrada by the people of Cicúique, a populous pueblo eighty or ninety miles northeast of Tiguex, near present-day Santa Fe. What the Turk told the expeditionaries made them forget how lackluster the Seven Cities of Cíbola had turned out to be. There was another place, he said, called Quivira, where there was a great river seven miles across, with fish swimming in it that were the size of the Spaniards' horses, and where the rulers cruised along in ships with eagle figureheads

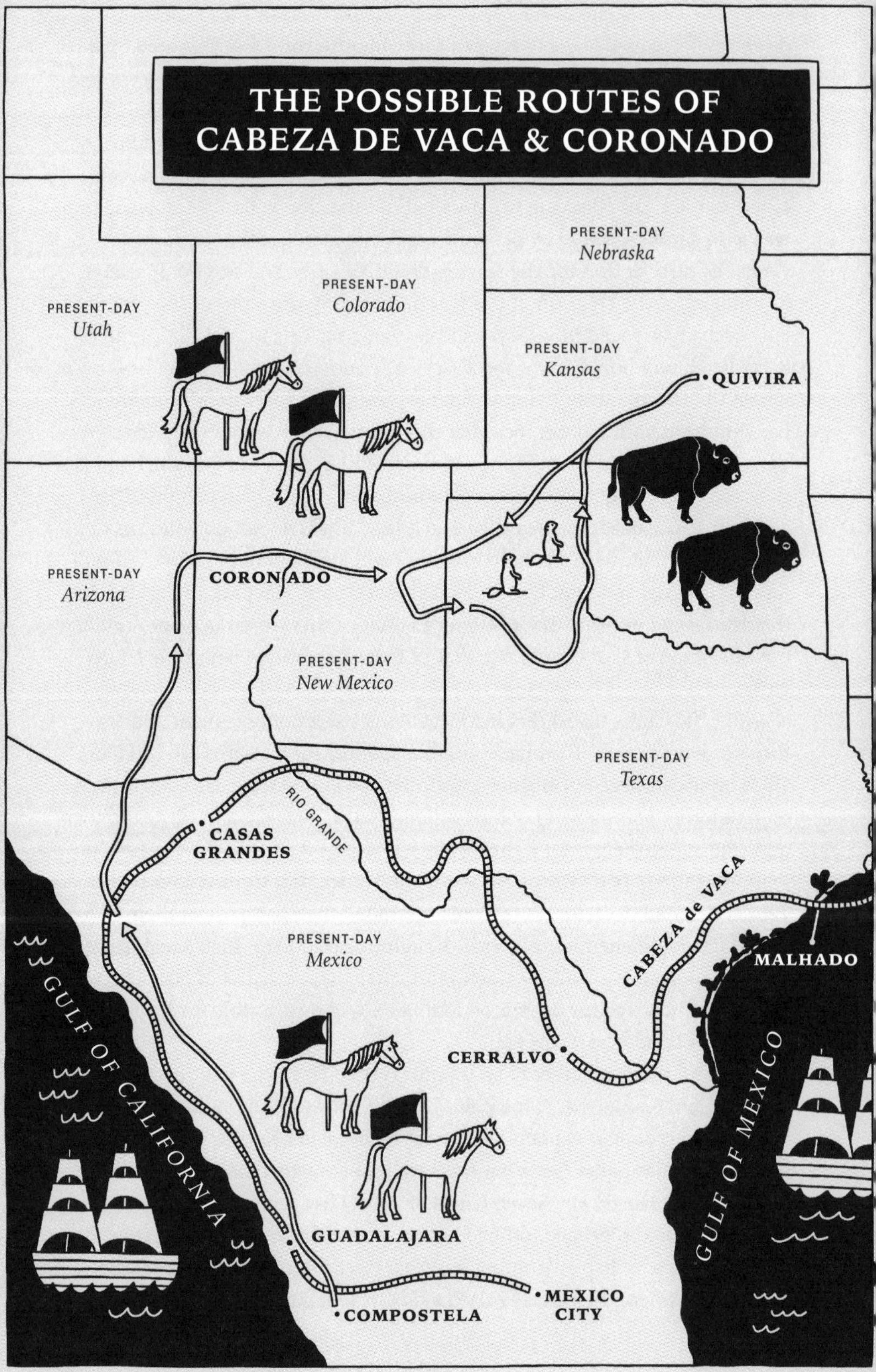

THE POSSIBLE ROUTES OF CABEZA DE VACA & CORONADO

PRESENT-DAY
Nebraska

PRESENT-DAY
Colorado

PRESENT-DAY
Utah

PRESENT-DAY
Kansas

•QUIVIRA

PRESENT-DAY
Arizona

CORONADO

PRESENT-DAY
New Mexico

PRESENT-DAY
Texas

RIO GRANDE

•CASAS
GRANDES

CABEZA de VACA

PRESENT-DAY
Mexico

MALHADO

GULF OF CALIFORNIA

CERRALVO

GULF OF MEXICO

GUADALAJARA

•MEXICO
CITY

•COMPOSTELA

fashioned out of gold and drifted to sleep beneath the forest canopy to the music of golden wind chimes. Coronado wasn't gullible, but he was intrigued enough to allow the Turk, when the spring came, to lead his expedition toward the hypnotic immensity of land that lay beyond the Pecos River.

Much of this region was what would become known as the Texas Panhandle or, more lyrically, the Llano Estacado. "Llano Estacado" is Spanish for "Staked Plains" or "Palisaded Plains." The term probably has to do with the stockade-like appearance of the eroded rock where the landscape east of Lubbock and Amarillo drops down suddenly from the tableland of the High Plains. A less likely explanation, but a more colorful and persistent one, refers to the wooden stakes that Coronado's men supposedly drove into the ground to create a trail they could follow across an utterly featureless grassland void. There is no mention of this particular breadcrumb trail in any of the expedition reports, but the vanguard of the army would sometimes leave piles of bones and cow dung to mark the way for those following behind.

The haunting monotony of the llano made a deep impression. There were, Coronado wrote, "no more landmarks than as if we had been swallowed up in the sea . . . There was not a stone, nor a bit of rising ground, nor a tree, nor a shrub, nor anything to go by." One of the soldiers on the expedition, Pedro de Castañeda, was an especially close and curious observer of this unsettling environment and the effect it had on human perception: "The country is like a bowl, so that when a man sits down, the horizon surrounds him all around at the distance of a musket shot. There are no groves of trees except at the rivers, which flow at the bottom of some ravines where the trees grow so thick that they were not noticed until one was right on the edge of them. They are of dead earth."

But this seemingly blank world teemed with life: vast prairie dog towns, pale, wraith-like wolves, and "foolish" rabbits that could not seem to evade the lances of the Spanish horsemen. The strangest and most unforgettable creatures they encountered were the buffalo, the same shaggy "cows" that Cabeza de Vaca had seen years earlier when he was a traveling salesman on the coastal prairies. Now, amazed Spanish eyes saw them again. The animals congregated in herds so great that in weeks of trekking the expedition never lost sight of them. "The country they traveled over," marveled Castañeda, "was so level and smooth that if one looked at them the sky could be seen between their legs, so that if some of them were at a distance they looked like smooth-trunked pines whose tops joined."

There were other humans on the plains as well, a nomadic tribe called the Querechos, who hunted the bison and "lived like Arabs" in temporary encampments, teams of dogs hauling their goods and hide tents on travois from one place on the llano to the next. The Querechos would become better known as a division of the Apaches, the Athabaskan-speaking people who for generations had been migrating southward on the Great Plains. Along with the Comanches, they would evolve into an iconic horse culture, but in 1541 the horses that accompanied the Coronado expedition were the first such animals they had ever seen.

The Querechos, who hunted buffalo for their own subsistence, were also traders who were at that point making their presence felt in a thriving exchange network that linked the terraced pueblos of New Mexico with the woodland cultures of East Texas and beyond. Specifically, they were muscling in on the hide trade of another plains people, the Teyas, whom the Spaniards encountered when they entered the venous network of canyon lands that occasionally provided a shock of scenery when glimpsed from the flat surface of the llano. The Teyas warned Coronado that they knew all about Quivira, and that it was not an imposing city at all but a place of "straw and skins."

The Spaniards, their *indios amigos,* and the animals they herded along with them suffered constantly from thirst; there was no water on the llano except for buffalo wallows and evaporating playa lakes that were sometimes covered with a thick rime of salt. A devastating hailstorm injured many of the expedition's horses, broke all the crockery, and left the camp in tatters. Nevertheless, Coronado was determined to get at least a glimpse of Quivira. Ordering the greater part of his army back to Tiguex, he pressed ahead with thirty horsemen and a half-dozen foot soldiers, accompanied by Teyas guides. The increasingly suspect Turk was now under armed guard. It took them six weeks to reach their goal. The province of Quivira was as unimpressive as the Teyas had warned it would be, just a scattering of villages of grass houses on the Kansas plains.

The Turk admitted, probably as he was being tortured, that he had misled the expedition on orders of the pueblo leaders back in Cicúique, who wanted to see Coronado and his invaders as far away as possible, hoping they would starve or die of thirst or become forever lost out on the inhospitable llano. The Spaniards also suspected him of trying to stir up the people of Quivira into an attack. Coronado ordered that justice be administered, and left it to his *maestre de campo* to arrange the details. A soldier named Pérez crept up on the Turk from behind, slipped a cord over his neck, and strangled him by tightening the cord with a stick.

After that, Coronado took his reconnaissance party back to Tiguex, where the rest of the army had withdrawn for the winter. There were plans to return to the plains in the spring, to keep pushing farther east despite the previous dispiriting results, but new crises intervened. A native insurrection in the South suddenly threatened the expedition's supply line to New Spain, and Coronado suffered a serious head trauma when the cinch strap of his saddle broke and sent him tumbling beneath the hooves of a comrade's galloping horse. After that, writes his biographer Herbert E. Bolton, "the real Coronado was no more." He was confused and cautious, and his passion for exploration and conquest had dimmed. He recalled the predictions of a "scientific friend" of his back in Salamanca who had said that he would one day become a powerful lord in distant lands, but that he would suffer a fall from which he would never recover. "This expectation of death," Castañeda writes, "made him desire to return and die where he had a wife and children."

Coronado lived for twelve more years after returning to Mexico as the leader of a failed and expensive expedition, one that for all its far-ranging investigations into Texas had found very little real material wealth. Beset in his last years by charges of bribery and corruption, he was forced to step down as the governor of Nueva Galicia. The year before he died, he became a target of reformers whose consciences were inflamed by the atrocities committed by the rulers of New Spain. He was tried on—but acquitted of—charges of inflicting cruelty and abuse on the inhabitants of Tierra Nueva, including burning thirty people at the stake during the Tiguex War, setting dogs on others, and murdering the Turk.

— 3 —

WOE TO US

AS CORONADO, IN HIS CONCUSSED AND FATALISTIC STATE,
was leading his men back to Mexico in 1542, another Spanish
expedition was in the process of unraveling a thousand miles
to the east. Hernando de Soto, an adventurer who had made
his enormous fortune and reputation in the conquest of the
Incas, and who had been awarded the imperial contract to

explore and conquer—where Narváez had failed—the vast territory from
Florida to Río de las Palmas, was dying in a brush house in the Indian
kingdom of Guachoya, somewhere in southeastern Arkansas. Guachoya was
one of many native principalities that de Soto had attacked, courted, or intimidated in his grueling three-year reconnaissance of the southeastern quadrant
of North America. He had fought many battles as he and his six hundred men
marched from one Indian capital to the next, searching for the new Tenochtitlán, which was sure to lie just beyond the next river. They had deployed
their horses to powerful strategic effect, running down and lancing the Indian
warriors who opposed them. They had routinely taken chieftains hostage,
enslaved their subjects, cut off the hands and noses of Indians they suspected
of duplicity. Others they had burned alive or fed to their voracious war dogs.

They had wandered from Florida swamps to Appalachian forests, through
a country vastly different and far more populated than the treeless empti-

ness that Coronado had encountered on the South Plains of Texas. Instead of pueblos and nomadic camps, there were consolidated metropolitan districts ruled by powerful chieftains, some of them female, and cities and ceremonial centers dominated by temple mounds and guarded by palisaded walls.

But there was no gold—only endless rumors of it, enticing the Spaniards ever deeper into the heart of the continent. They had done little to make themselves welcome, and after three years of constant warfare and hardship almost half of them were dead, along with most of their horses. De Soto's journey came to an end on the western side of the Mississippi. He "sank into a deep despondency" when he realized the extent of the impassable terrain that separated him from the Gulf Coast, where he had hoped to build ships to sail the survivors of his expedition to Mexico or Cuba. His health collapsed along with his spirits. As he lay dying of fever on his pallet, he committed his soul to God and appointed Luis de Moscoso to succeed him. Moscoso was thirty-seven. He had fought alongside de Soto in Peru and had served as his chief subordinate during the embattled and disastrous trek through La Florida.

Among Moscoso's first decisions as the new governor of this decidedly unconquered region was to exhume his predecessor's body almost as soon as it was buried. He needed to keep de Soto's death a secret from the people of Guachoya, with whom the Spaniards had only a tremulous alliance. In the will that de Soto had made in Havana before his fleet sailed, he stipulated that his body be buried in his homeland of Extremadura, in a chapel built especially to receive it, whose walls would bear his family's coat of arms and whose altar would be decorated with the cross of the order of the Knights of Santiago. But in the end, he was interred in a tomb of moving water. His remains were wrapped in a shawl, weighted with sand, and deposited in the Mississippi.

Moscoso's worn-out and disillusioned men were ready to go home, and so was he. "The Governor," one chronicler of the expedition recalled, "longed to be again where he could get his full measure of sleep." From the Mississippi, the remains of the entrada headed west, believing they would find their way to Mexico and Spanish civilization. The way forward led them into the rolling grasslands and woodlands of East Texas, the land of the Caddos. Like many of the other Indians whom de Soto and his men had encountered, the Caddos were a settled agricultural people with a complex political system of towns and villages confederated into chiefdoms. They built temple mounds, lived in tall conical houses amid extensive cornfields, and worshipped a deity they called "Leader Up Above." The Caddos, who had heard all about the depredations of the foreign intruders coming from the east, rose up against them, but Moscoso and his men continued to fight their way forward, winning pitched battles, burning villages, and seizing Indians to serve as guides and hostages. They reached a river named the Daycao—which could have been the Trinity or the Navasota, or possibly the Brazos—before realizing they had to turn back. Winter was coming, the country was growing more rugged and inhospitable, and the hope of finding a Spanish outpost in that direction was proving to be a dream.

So Moscoso ordered a retreat all the way to the Mississippi. The Spaniards backtracked through lands they had already despoiled, facing ambushes from people they had already fought, who were enraged by their reappearance. Some four hundred miles upriver from the Gulf of Mexico, they spent the winter of 1542–1543 doing what Narváez had done fifteen years earlier: building boats. Salvation lay seaward, down the Mississippi, around the westward curve of the Gulf to the Spanish outpost of Pánuco. The Spaniards built seven flat-bottomed, barge-like vessels that they spent over two weeks rowing down the river. They covered the sides of the boats with thick fiber mats for protection against enemy arrows, and towed lashed-together dugout canoes in which their few remaining horses teetered.

Moscoso and his men were attacked along the way by fleets of Indian canoes, leading to pitched naval battles in the middle of the Mississippi and to harrying attacks that continued almost all the way to the mouth of the river. They headed toward the open sea at first, but they were short on water and the boats were leaky, so they sailed shoreward and hugged the coast, rowing hard against contrary winds that threatened on some days to drive them back out to sea, on others to send them crashing onto the shore.

After a ten-day voyage westward from the mouth of the Mississippi, the Spaniards were introduced to the abundant discomforts of the Texas coast. One night they were blown toward shore, dragging their improvised anchors, along a desolate stretch of exposed beach. They were probably not far from where the remnants of Narváez's expedition had washed ashore, maybe even on the same island, Malhado. They had the advantage of not making landfall on a fierce winter day, as Cabeza de Vaca had done, but the summer wind, howling in from the south, was such a threat that half of the men had to jump into the shallow water and point the bows of the boats into the gale to keep them from being swamped. They did that all night long, and in the morning, when the wind finally died down, the mosquitoes were so dense that they covered the white sails of the boats and turned them black. The men were so tormented by mosquito bites, one of them later wrote, "they could but laugh."

But this otherwise inhospitable coast had at least one welcome feature. A dark viscous "scum" seeped up from the sea floor, which the voyagers used to seal the leaky gaps in the planking of their boats. It was the same substance that coastal Indians painted onto their pots for decorative effect. It would be another few centuries before a broader purpose was found for Texas oil.

Their boats patched, their water casks filled, Moscoso and his men embarked in a cloud of mosquitoes and sailed south along the Texas coast in high summer. They stayed generally seaward of the barrier islands and their treacherous rows of offshore sandbars, though they cautiously entered the bays and lagoons to set nets for fish and to dig in the sand for more fresh water. Fifty-four days after embarking from the mouth of the Mississippi, they finally made it to Pánuco, the Spanish settlement that the doomed Narváez expedition had been destined never to reach.

The surviving half of the de Soto expedition had managed to escape Texas without running aground or starving to death or being killed by its aggrieved inhabitants. But for many years to come, the low-lying coast, assaulted by storms in summer and winter, with no landmarks except shifting dune fields, remained a lethal barrier to any secure European foothold in Texas.

"WOE TO US WHO ARE GOING TO SPAIN," A PRIEST NAMED JUAN Ferrer supposedly prophesied before embarking from the Mexican port of Veracruz a decade after Moscoso's homemade ships came limping back to Spanish territory, "because neither we nor the fleet will arrive there. Most of us will perish, and those who are left will experience great torment, though all will die in the end except a very few."

Fray Ferrer and five other Dominican clerics were among the four hundred passengers who left the shores of Mexico for Spain in April 1554. They traveled in a fleet of four ships, bearing the wealth of New Spain back to its mother country and into the imperial treasury of Charles V. Most of this wealth was in the form of gold and silver from the mines of northern Mexico, the Crown's share stored in dozens of custom-designed trunks. There was a great deal of coinage as well, minted in Mexico City, that represented the private fortunes of merchants and individual passengers headed home to Spain, or the legacies and bequests of men who had died in the conquest. Included in the cargo were other New World products such as cowhides, resin, cochineal, silk thread, and sugar.

The ships were to stop in Havana before crossing the Atlantic, but before they made it to Cuba a powerful spring storm erupted in the Gulf. One of the ships managed to escape, but the other three were driven westward and broke apart on the shores of what is now called Padre Island. Padre, the longest of the barrier islands that shadow the Texas coast, is an even worse place to be shipwrecked than the Narváez expedition's fatal island of Malhado, which is farther north and east. Padre is a 113-mile-long stretch of tidal flats and wind-scoured dunes, separated from the mainland along its whole length by a forbidding saltwater lagoon.

The details of what exactly happened to the three hundred or so survivors of the shipwreck are hazy, but there is no doubt that the apocalyptic predictions of Fray Ferrer were largely borne out. Although it appears that several dozen castaways managed to salvage one of the ships' boats and sail it back to Veracruz with news of the disaster, the rest of the men, women, and children stranded on the forsaken beach decided that their best hope for survival was to walk south along the coast. Like the unfortunate members of the Narváez and de Soto expeditions before them, they would try to reach Pánuco. But after twenty days at sea in hostile weather, driven all over the western Gulf by uncertain winds, they were severely disoriented. They thought they were much farther south than they really were, and that a march of two or three days would deliver them from the wilderness. In fact, they were over three hundred miles from Pánuco: three hundred miles of barren sand, boggy marshlands, tangled mangrove swamps, and broad rivers they had no means of crossing.

They had been walking for a week when they encountered Indians. These people may have been Karankawas or perhaps one of the other tribes that Cabeza de Vaca had encountered on his march south from Malhado. According to an account set down forty years later by a priest who claimed to have interviewed one of the party's two survivors, the Indians brought food and made signs of peace. Something in their demeanor, though, must have made the Spaniards nervous. As they sat down to eat their first meal in a week, they gripped their sabers and readied the two crossbows they had managed to salvage from the wrecks. While they were eating, their hosts attacked. The castaways managed to drive them away without suffering any immediate casualties, but the skirmish was only a prelude to a hellish retreat.

The survivors of the shipwrecks continued marching down the coast as the Indians followed, killing stragglers with arrows while the main party stumbled blindly south. Harassed every step of the way, with nothing to eat and nothing to drink except the dew they were able to lick from the dune grasses, they managed to make it fifty miles, past the southern tip of Padre Island, where their way was barred by the mouth of the Rio Grande. After lashing driftwood rafts together with cord that they had carried from the wrecks, they crossed precariously to the other side. They lost their two crossbows in the middle of the river and came to shore virtually defenseless and still at the mercy of their pursuers, possibly the same Indians who had followed them along the length of Padre Island, but more likely another tribe that had taken up the relay mission of annihilating the intruders.

Because the Indians soon stripped the clothes off two captured Spaniards without killing them, the castaways allowed themselves to hope that if they threw off their own ragged garments, they would be left alone. Under the crushing burden of sixteenth-century Catholic shame, they made their way forward naked. The lone (and at least somewhat dubious) chronicler of the disaster wrote that several of the women died of embarrassment, "helpless to protect the decency that normally would be bought at the cost of one's life."

To preserve some scrap of modesty, the priests sent the women and children ahead in a kind of vanguard, where they could remain out of sight. But by the time the men caught up with them on the banks of Mexico's Río de las Palmas, they were all dead, killed by native arrows. That left something like two hundred survivors of the shipwreck, all of them men, five of them priests. Fifty were killed after they crossed the river, the rest one by one or in small groups as they staggered onward toward Pánuco. One of the two ultimate survivors was Francisco Vázquez, who somehow backtracked alone all the way to the shipwreck site, where he was rescued by a ship that had been sent to search for the lost fleet. The other was one of the priests, Fray Marcos de Mena, who, despite suffering from seven maggot-infested arrow wounds, managed to make his way at last to a village near Pánuco and astound the residents of a Spanish house when he knocked on their front door.

By that point or shortly after, a salvage fleet was on the way from Veracruz to recover the boxes of bullion and coinage that had been lost when the ships broke apart and sank in the Texas surf, money that the aging Charles V acutely needed to fight the latest of his chronic wars with France. A great deal of the treasure—perhaps half of it—was brought up by divers, but the rest was buried and scattered by months, and then years, and then centuries of ceaseless wind and waves. The silver *reales*—covered with tar, worn thin as communion wafers—still wash up on the Padre Island beach.

The Spanish presence in Texas had by now run aground as surely as had its treasure fleet. The Narváez expedition was a gruesome failure that gave rise to chimerical stories of golden cities, luring Coronado out onto the empty buffalo plains and sending him home a ruined man. Moscoso, in his sally into Texas after de Soto's death, found nothing to conquer but much to destroy. With the loss of the treasure fleet added to this list of disasters, it was no accident that Texas found its way to the bottom of New Spain's priority list of territorial ambition. The wave of conquest lapped briefly over the Rio Grande, then receded for decades. The urgency to explore a region that seemed to offer very little was gone, especially after silver was discovered in Zacatecas in 1546, sparking a mining boom and a fierce decades-long war with the Chichimeca peoples of north-central Mexico. But the vast Texas unknown was still there, and the European hunger for its domination had not gone away.

—4—

THE LADY IN BLUE

SOR MARÍA DE JESÚS DE ÁGREDA, THE ABBESS OF THE
Convent of the Immaculate Conception, was forty-seven
years old in the winter of 1650. She had lived her whole life
in Ágreda, a village in northeastern Spain at the base of the
mountain range known as the Sistema Ibérico. It had been a
life of spiritual wonder and turmoil, marked by ecstatic
visions but also by horrible doubts and temptations. As a child, she had
watched her mother meditate on mortality in front of a human skull. She
had woken at three in the morning to the sound of her devout father shuf-
fling along the floor under the weight of a hundred-pound iron cross. Suffering and mortification, she understood, were what led a soul into the
presence of God. When she entered the convent at eighteen, she slept two
hours a day on the hardest surface she could find, grudgingly ate a few
vegetables for the sake of staying alive, and petitioned her superior for a
habit made of coarser cloth.

But now there were lingering concerns about Sor María, concerns that
the Holy Office of the Inquisition felt the need to investigate. They wanted
to know more about her mystical revelations, the claims that she levitated
during prayer, and above all her mysterious *exterioridades*, in which she was
said to exist in two places at the same time.

It was a January day. Sor María, who was so weak with fever that she could not walk, had to be carried down from the infirmary to the library, where the interrogation was to take place. No allowances were made for her illness. To protect their isolation, the cloistered nuns at the convent usually spoke with visitors through a grillwork covered with projecting spikes. But Sor María was instructed to kneel at a communion rail and answer her examiner, a priest named Antonio Gonzalo del Moral, face to face.

In the presence of a notary, Moral began assaulting the abbess with questions as she struggled to remain conscious and upright on the communion rail. Most of the questions had to do with something that had begun happening three decades earlier, when the young Sor María claimed that—while her body remained in the convent in Ágreda—she had crossed the Atlantic and appeared "in the kingdoms of Quivira and the Jumanas," preaching the Gospel to the pagan inhabitants of New Spain.

It was Moral's objective to determine whether these "bilocations" were real, and if so, whether they were holy miracles or some sort of mischief stirred up by the devil. Sor María's spirit journeys could not be dismissed out of hand. There was evidence that something of the sort had taken place.

In the first third of the seventeenth century, Texas remained little more than an enticing blank when it came to serious Spanish initiatives. But two expeditions that had ventured north along the Rio Grande, into the Pueblo country of New Mexico, helped reignite the old dreams of finding golden or silver cities somewhere just over the horizon. In 1598, Juan de Oñate, married to a woman of noble Castilian and Aztec blood—a descendent of both Cortés and Moctezuma—followed up earlier scouting entradas with a much grander colonizing expedition, creating a line of Spanish settlements along the upper Rio Grande. There, beyond the western margins of Texas, among Pueblo peoples whose existence had already been destabilized by Coronado, Franciscan friars with a fervent determination to Christianize the Indians created a hardscrabble cluster of missions.

In 1629, a delegation of Jumano Indians appeared at one of these missions. They came from the east, from the Texas plains. The Jumanos were mostly a farming people, living in extensive villages of flat-roofed houses along the Rio Grande and in the fertile river juncture where the Rio Grande met the Conchos, known to the Spanish as La Junta de los Ríos. But this band lived much farther north. They hunted buffalo on the vast grasslands and played a vibrant role in the trading economy that had developed between the Spanish newcomers in the mission outposts in New Mexico and the multitudes of indigenous peoples that lived far to the east.

The Jumano delegation told the friars that they wanted missionaries to come with them to their home territory, to live with them and establish missions and baptize them as Christians. They said that for a number of years they had been receiving mysterious visitations from a woman who was young and beautiful and spoke their language. She was barefoot and wore a gray sackcloth habit and a heavy blue cloak. This "Lady in Blue," they said, had visited the Indians hundreds of times, preaching to them about Christ and the Trinity, imploring them to seek out the friars who could bring them into the light of salvation.

The Franciscans were excited by the spectacle of these tattooed visitors appearing from the wilderness after apparently having experienced a spontaneous conversion by what could only have been a blessed apparition. Two friars were assigned to accompany the Jumanos back to the buffalo plains to assess the feasibility of building a mission in the heart of the little-known country that lay north and east of the line of Spanish settlement.

The tough priests who trekked three hundred miles through the summer heat to visit the Jumanos in their homeland were greeted with jubilation, though the mission they hoped to build never got further than the planning stages. The Indians may indeed have had a cultural epiphany prompted by the appearance of a bilocating Spanish nun, but that didn't rule out a more pragmatic strategy. The Jumanos of the plains were in trouble. The Apaches, rising in power, were raiding from the north and threatening the Jumanos' control of the buffalo grounds and lucrative trading routes. A Spanish mission would have meant not just priests but soldiers, the beginning of an alliance against a powerful enemy. But the Jumanos lived far away from the Spanish outposts, and the country between was so vast and inhospitable that the alliance never happened.

It was twenty years later that Father Moral began to question María de Ágreda, and by then the Jumanos had surrendered the plains to the Apaches. They retreated to the farming pueblos along the rivers and began to melt into history. But the question of whether a lady in blue had actually appeared to them was still of acute interest to the Inquisition.

Moral questioned the abbess unrelentingly, three hours a day for eleven days as she knelt at the communion rail. When she returned from her first miraculous journey to the New World, had she told her confessor what had happened? Had she indeed flown to that region on the wings of St. Michael the Archangel? What places did she see as she was being transported across the world? When it rained in the kingdoms she visited, were her clothes wet when she returned? How did she carry physical objects like rosaries to the Indians? What was their language like? What sort of weapons did they have? What happened to her body in the convent while she was preaching to the Indians on the other side of the ocean? Did an angel inhabit it so that she could continue performing her duties as abbess?

Sor María never objected to any of these questions nor tried to evade them. Ill and uncomfortable as she was, she answered everything with striking patience and candor. She was now much older than she was when her mysterious travels began, and she testified honestly that she did not know exactly what had happened, whether she had actually been carried by angels to rescue the souls of people in faraway lands or whether, in her zeal and youthful confusion, she only thought that she had. All she knew for certain was that her *exterioridades* were not the work of the devil.

Moral agreed. He was moved by her obvious devotion, her "sublime holiness." "I say that she is a catholic and faithful Christian," he concluded in his report to the inquisitor-general, "well-founded in our holy faith. She embroidered no fiction into her accounts, nor was she deluded by the devil."

The abbess was judged to be authentic, but the land she claimed to have visited might still have seemed to her inquisitors as the projection of a mind inflamed. She mentioned numerous Indian nations besides the Jumanos to whom she had appeared, though she couldn't vouch for having their names right. Among these people were the Cambujos, the Chillescas, and the Titlas, who lived in the forested realms farther east. In Sor María's telling, they were reminiscent of the fantastical sophisticated Indian kingdoms, like Quivira, that had once lured Coronado—places of wealth and glorious indolence longing to be shown the path to God.

Texas at this time was hardly a void. It was peopled in its North and West by a swirling complex of nomadic buffalo-hunting tribes such as the Teyas and Apaches and plains Jumanos; by the settled agricultural branches of the Jumanos at the Junta de los Ríos; by the numerous Coahuiltecan peoples of the southern prairies; by the Karankawas along the Gulf Coast; and by the extensive Caddo tribes in the eastern forests, gathered into the Hasinai Confederacy. But the strangers who had come from across the sea to the New World over a hundred years before still knew very little about it. From a European perspective, it remained largely unseen and unsettled, a speculatively rendered immensity on a series of inaccurate maps. To the mind of a brilliant and confused young nun who had never left her village in Spain, it was more than that—it was a shining emptiness that had the power to lure her away and liberate her from her cloistered body.

At the time Sor María was being questioned by the Inquisition, Spain had been hovering at the edges of this Texas mirage for a hundred years. No mercenary reason or national rivalry was strong enough to warrant any serious further explorations beyond the Rio Grande. Coronado had proved only that the golden cities did not exist, and Moscoso had triggered unrelenting hostility but had found nothing worth fighting for. For the castaways of the Spanish treasure fleet of 1554, Texas was almost literally a hell. But it was also a place from which the Spanish mind could not release its material dreams, its mystical claims. No matter how blank Texas was, no matter how bleak, Spain was not going to give it up without a fight.

—5—

VOYAGEURS

SITTING ON A HIGH SHELF IN A BACK ROOM OF THE MUSEUM
of the Coastal Bend in Victoria, Texas, is an archival storage
container the size of a hatbox. Its contents are not among the
artifacts on exhibit in the museum, which holds a fascinating collection of seventeenth- and eighteenth-century objects
chronicling the culture of the local native peoples and the
struggle for European dominance along the middle stretch of the Texas coast.

Inside the box, protected by Styrofoam packing peanuts, is something
not immediately identifiable, a mashed oval of bone or, maybe, rock. It is so
weathered and misshapen that it is unrecognizable as a human skull, but
that's what it is. It very likely belonged to a French woman, a mother of six,
named Isabelle Talon. Its distorted shape is the result of a killing blow from
a Karankawa war club.

On an April morning in 1689, a Spanish expedition arrived at a modest bluff above Garcitas Creek, seven or eight miles upstream from a vast
sheet of shallow water known as Matagorda Bay. The expedition was led by
Alonso de León, the governor of New Spain's province of Coahuila. It had
set out a month earlier from northern Mexico, and its official roster listed
113 men: soldiers, priests, servants, and mule drivers. The entrada was
accompanied by an unrecorded number of *indios amigos*, along with multi-

tudes of horses, cattle, and pack mules. Provisions included five hundred pounds of chocolate. They had crossed the Rio Grande at a low-water ford that would soon be called Paso de Francia and then headed north and east through the deserts and grasslands of South Texas, marching behind a standard embroidered with the image of the Virgin of Guadalupe.

For three frantic years, through four punishing expeditions, de León had been pursuing the same goal: to find a rumored French fort—"this thorn which has been thrust into the heart of America" —that could mean the end of Spain's hard-won hegemony in the Gulf of Mexico. The possibility that the French had made a significant incursion into Spanish territory had galvanized the viceregal authorities of New Spain and turned the long-neglected expanse of Texas into decisive ground from which the French would have to be expelled and the mostly rhetorical Spanish claim secured. At the time the French alarm bell sounded, Spain was in retreat not just from Texas but also, catastrophically, from its possessions along the northern Rio Grande in New Mexico. The ranchos and missions established there had depended on the forced labor of the native Pueblos, and the Spanish priests had demanded the surrender of the Indians' souls to the Christian God. By 1680, after years of drought and famine, and after watching their medicine men being hanged and scourged by Spanish officials, the Pueblos had had enough. They rose up against the intruders and drove them south down the Rio Grande, where the Spaniards retrenched at the little village of El Paso del Norte. The loss of New Mexico meant that Texas was essentially abandoned as well. Yet Spain could not allow France to fill the resulting power vacuum.

Garcitas Creek, the watercourse that de León and his men followed that April day, is a wide brownish stream whose banks are either overgrown with tangled vegetation or slick with stinking mud. The site of the French colony above the creek that they were looking for is on private property today, and even if you have permission to visit, it is an uncomfortable place to approach. You travel by boat downstream from a highway overpass near the barely there hamlet of La Salle, Texas. No dock or man-made mooring of any sort marks the disembarkation spot. The boat simply noses up to the bank, and you hop off into clumps of needle-sharp cordgrass and throbbing clouds of mosquitoes. As the mosquitoes swarm up your pant legs and down your shirt collar, you bushwhack to the top of the bluff, where there is no breeze and little relief from the insects, and nothing much to see but a weedy meadow with a few scraggly trees and stands of prickly pear.

But this desolate place is saturated in history. It was the site of the French power base that had set Spain into such a frenzy of mobilization. When the de León expedition finally reached what has become known as

Fort St. Louis, though, it found not an unassailable imperial fortress but a cluster of ransacked mud huts and a rude two-story wooden building made from the timbers of a wrecked ship. There was no one there, just an ominous stillness, the ground strewn with the rotting pages of hundreds of ripped-apart books, the rickety houses sagging under the weight of their buffalo-hide roofs. There were untended cornfields and herb gardens, numerous dead pigs, harquebus parts and broken weapons scattered everywhere, and eight cannons lying useless on the ground. Juan Bautista Chapa, an Italian-born member of de León's expedition, over sixty years old and with literary aspirations, took careful notes of what he saw. He drew a rough map of the layout of the fort and sketched the carvings over the doorway of the main building. They included the outline of a heart with the puzzling, ominous words "Mal ecl" inside it, and a date of 1684.

That suggested that the French had been in Texas for five years, but the people who had lived at this settlement, who had been part of the great colonial enterprise to seize the New World from Spain, were gone. They had been wiped out by disease or misadventure, or by their Karankawa enemies, who had finally assaulted the fort. Inspecting the ground, the Spaniards found the moldering remains of three French bodies. One of them was a woman, probably Isabelle Talon. A torn dress was still draped over her bones.

De León ordered the bones gathered and buried, and a requiem mass sung. The scene at the devastated fort, and particularly the sight of the tattered dress clinging to the woman's skeleton, caused, Chapa wrote, "much pity among us." One of the expedition members—Chapa doesn't tell us who, but it was probably himself, since he was given to anonymous authorship—struggled to express himself in verse. As far as we know, it was the first poem written in Texas. Among its stanzas:

> Oh, beautiful French women
> Who once walked among these blooming prairie roses,
> and whose hands white as snow
> brushed against the white irises of the fields.

Chapa included the poem in a history he later wrote about Texas and northeastern Mexico, but in the following paragraphs of his account he remembered that France was an enemy, and his elegiac tone turned icy. He wrote that the dead French colonists had more or less gotten what they deserved for ignoring Pope Alexander VI's 1493 papal bull decreeing that all the lands west and south of the Azores or Cape Verde Islands—that is, almost all the New World—belonged to Spain.

The French had trespassed in the winter of 1685. They arrived in three ships, though four had sailed from the port of La Rochelle the previous summer. One ship was captured en route by Spanish privateers off Haiti, the first of many turns of bad luck. René-Robert Cavelier, the forty-one-year-old leader of the expedition, is better known to history as La Salle, the name of his wealthy family's estate near Rouen. In his youth, he studied with the Jesuits and took holy orders, but after a few miserable years he managed to be released from the religious life. If there was ever an unpriestly nature, it was his: restless, aggrandizing, obsessively driven, intolerantly proud. Within months of being absolved from his vows, he arrived on the harsh Canadian frontier, throwing himself into the fur trade and founding a colony and trading base on the St. Lawrence River. But he was too ambitious and too curious about the unknown country of New France to remain a mere seigneur. He had the heart of an explorer, and the obsessive focus of his explorations was a river that was said to lead all the way through the heart of the continent to the Gulf of Mexico. Control of that river, and the warm-water port that could be created at its mouth, would frustrate Spanish—and English and Dutch—ambitions, and provide France a powerful trading corridor through which to move its New World goods.

The explorers Louis Jolliet and Father Jacques Marquette made an epic canoe voyage down the Mississippi in 1673, but it was La Salle who, nine years later, managed to finally follow the river all the way to the Gulf. There he converted a tree trunk into a triumphal column bearing the crest of Louis XIV. He announced that in the king's name he took "possession of this country of Louisiana, the seas, harbors, ports, bays, adjacent straits, and all the nations, peoples, provinces, cities, towns, villages, mines, minerals, fisheries, streams and rivers." It was the French version of the Spanish *Requerimiento*: a formulaic declaration of ownership, claiming everything, announced to the wind.

Backing up these words would be a much harder proposition, but La Salle's ambition was as broad and implacable as the course of the river he had just followed to its mouth. He sailed to France, where he pitched his scheme directly to the king. He would return to the Gulf with a small fleet, sail westward along its shores until he returned by sea to the mouth of the Mississippi, and then establish a fort some distance upriver from which France could control the commerce of the continent. From this base La Salle could march west and seize for the king the Spanish silver mines of northern Mexico.

La Salle won his commission but ran afoul of the realities of geography. The mouth of the Mississippi—a wilderness of deltaic marshes—turned out not to be discernible from offshore. And faulty latitude readings from his earlier voyage, along with the sketchy maps he consulted, had convinced him that the river discharged into the Gulf far to the west, hundreds of miles beyond where he had placed his tree-trunk monument to Louis XIV.

In short, he ended up in Texas. He surmised that Matagorda Bay—a broad sheltered anchorage visible through a narrow pass between the barrier islands—was the river mouth he had been searching for, or at least one of the Mississippi's major tributaries. La Salle had set out from France with a colonizing contingent of three hundred, most of them soldiers, many of questionable conviction or worth—"a Noah's Ark," in the words of Henri Joutel, who wrote a memorable chronicle of the expedition, "where there were all sorts of animals." There was also a small contingent of women, including Isabelle Talon. Born in Paris, she had immigrated at a young age to French Canada, where she met and married her husband, Lucien, a carpenter. Their livelihood must have been tenuous enough, or their spirits adventurous enough, to make it seem worthwhile to join La Salle's great colonial enterprise. It was a bold decision that meant sailing from Canada to France with their five children and then boarding the ship that would take them back across the Atlantic to the Gulf. On the voyage, Isabelle gave birth to her sixth child, Robert, named after La Salle, who stood up as the boy's godfather during his open-sea baptism.

The expedition made landfall in Matagorda, but only after losing one of its ships, *L'Aimable*, when it foundered on a submerged sandbar in the treacherous pass leading into the bay. The next month, one of the two remaining ships sailed back to France, taking over a third of La Salle's colonists with it.

That left La Salle's remaining force in an increasingly perplexed and isolated condition. It was clear by this time that they were on the wrong river and that it would take extensive reconnaissance by land to find the Mississippi. The Karankawas living in the vicinity were warily friendly at first, but war erupted when the French, after accusing the Indians of scavenging cargo from the wreck of *L'Aimable*, stole some dugout canoes in retaliation. The newcomers began to perish at a frightening rate from Indian arrows, disease, fatigue, and all sorts of novel calamities. Isabelle Talon's husband became lost on a scouting expedition and was never seen again. One man died a lingering death after being bitten by a rattlesnake, and another was seized by an alligator while swimming across a river. Another ate prickly pear fruit, which had helped sustain Cabeza de Vaca, but didn't know to remove the thousands of almost invisible hairlike spines that covered it. He died from "a tremendous inflammation of the throat."

Searching for a reasonably hospitable site for a settlement, La Salle chose the bluff on Garcitas Creek four miles upstream from the bay. The colonists built their fort from salvaged timbers from the wreck of *L'Aimable* and hides from the buffalo they were slowly gaining expertise in killing. (Two of their priests, still learning, were trampled by wounded bulls.) They planted crops and watered them from a nearby spring, though the Indians discouraged their use of the spring by shooting arrows into the ground to mark a no-go zone. Aware that they were outnumbered by the seething Karankawas, the French held frequent target practice and made a point of teaching the women and girls how to shoot.

La Salle left the fort and his one remaining ship—*La Belle*—to go in search of the Mississippi. Evidence suggests that he—or perhaps another scouting party he sent out—headed west instead of east. That expedition went far up the Rio Grande—perhaps 350 miles—without finding either the Mississippi or the Spanish silver mines that they mistakenly assumed were nearby. We know for certain that La Salle led twenty men northeast in the spring of 1686 and made contact with the Caddos near the Neches River. The country in that part of Texas was more bounteous, the people more settled and welcoming. But the journey there and back was brutal. Along the way, four of his men deserted to live with the Indians, and eight more died or were lost to the wilderness and never seen again. Before he left, the experienced sailors who had until then manned *La Belle* were killed by Karankawas. They were replaced by a pieced-together crew of landsmen, of dubious skill and character, who lost control of the ship when a storm struck that May, driving it onto a sandbank on the lee side of Matagorda Island. When La Salle straggled back with his remaining men to the settlement on Garcitas Creek, *La Belle* was at the mud bottom of the bay, along with its store of precious provisions. Worse, he had lost his lifeline. The surviving colonists no longer had a vessel to transport them out of their miserable surroundings or to send for help. La Salle's only chance was to strike out overland again, find the Mississippi, make his way twelve hundred miles back to Canada, and come back to rescue those left behind at Garcitas Creek.

"It is better not to mope in such circumstances," Henri Joutel wrote later, but his spirits must have been heavy as he set off in January 1687 with La Salle and fifteen other men for the unimaginably distant destination of New France. Most of their clothes had long since worn out, with some notable exceptions, including La Salle's gold-laced scarlet coat. They wore shirts cut from the sails of *La Belle*, and their shoes were of buffalo hide, and they carried armor made from barrel staves. They left behind about twenty colonists, including seven girls and women.

The country they marched through was often open and beautiful, but it was a miserably wet winter, and the rivers that cut through the coastal plain were swollen and treacherous to cross. At every turn on their way to the Caddo lands, they encountered other native peoples. Some of them were suspicious, but most were willing to help the outlanders on their journey in exchange for some of the hatchets and knives from La Salle's dwindling stock of trade goods. Although the foreign diseases introduced by the de Soto expedition and other European arrivals had apparently dealt a shattering blow to the Indians of East Texas in the previous century, the country was still populous. Joutel mentions in his account the names of twenty-two tribes inhabiting the prairies north of the Colorado River, and of twenty more to the northwest.

La Salle had spent several decades on the frontiers of the New World and—his diplomatic failure with the Karankawas aside—he was generally skillful when it came to interacting and making deals with local tribes. But to his own men he was arrogant, autocratic, and so inscrutable that he was judged by some to be insane. "This is a man who has lost his mind," wrote one of his aggrieved subordinates, who also declared that La Salle regarded anyone who questioned his judgment as "lice on his gown." Even Henri Joutel, whose loyalty to La Salle was unflagging, had to admit that the explorer "was interested only in his own opinion."

A better disposition might have spared La Salle from being killed by his own men, which might in turn have altered the fate of the desperate colonists left behind on Garcitas Creek. But two months after setting out, the hungry expedition that he led dissolved into murderous factionalism after a dispute over the distribution of buffalo meat. As La Salle's nephew and two other men lay sleeping in camp, they were dispatched one after the next by an axe wielded by La Salle's embittered surgeon. La Salle himself was at that point camped some miles away. When his nephew didn't return, he went ahead alone to look for him. The conspirators knew he was coming and knew there was no way out for them except to kill him. They set up an ambush, and one of the men walked out of the trees and shot the Sieur de la Salle through the head with a musket. His body was left to the "discretion of wolves."

A month and a half later, the assassins turned on themselves. Their argument over who was to take possession of La Salle's belongings—including his scarlet coat—erupted in a gunfight before a crowd of astonished Caddos. When it was over, the man who had killed La Salle was dead, his shirt on fire from the close-range discharge. The surgeon who had murdered the others with an axe was shot three times. He lived long enough to be confessed by La Salle's brother, a Sulpician priest.

Joutel and a half-dozen others, including a repentant accomplice in the plot against La Salle, managed to make their way to a lonely French outpost on the Arkansas River, from there up the Mississippi, and finally to Montreal in the summer of 1688. By then, most of the people left behind in Texas were beyond rescue.

After La Salle and his party left to find their way to Canada, the remaining colonists at the settlement managed to establish a tense peace with their Karankawa enemies, even—the archeological evidence suggests—trading with them. But at some point the Indians decided to strike. One winter day, they approached the fort with gestures of friendship, and the settlers walked out of their houses to meet them. One of the few people who lived to describe what happened next was Jean-Baptiste Talon. Jean-Baptiste, nine years old, was one of Isabelle Talon's five surviving children. (One of her two daughters had perished from disease or hunger.) Of these five children, only four were in the fort. La Salle had taken Jean-Baptiste's older brother, Pierre, along with him on his last expedition, with the intention of leaving him behind with the Caddos so that he could learn their language and serve as an interpreter when the explorer returned from New France.

The colonists were off their guard and lightly armed. The fort had eight cannons, but the cannonballs had all gone down with the ships in Matagorda Bay. The Indians, Jean-Baptiste later testified, "had little trouble slaughtering them all." His mother was killed in front of him, but he and the rest of Isabelle's children were saved by a group of Karankawa women who grabbed them and carried them away from the site of the massacre. Jean-Baptiste and his siblings ended up being adopted into the tribe. Their French rags were thrown away, their faces and arms heavily and permanently tattooed when the Indians scratched their skin with thorns and rubbed charcoal into the wounds. The Karankawas mocked the children's forlorn attempts to console themselves with prayer, snatching a tattered prayer book from their hands and pretending to read it with pious expressions before breaking out in raucous laughter. But for the most part, they treated the Talons not as captives but as family members, and when the children were ransomed by the Spanish two years later, they wailed in grief when it was time to give them up.

———————— ★ ————————

WALKING THROUGH THE KNEE-HIGH BRUSH THAT NOW COVERS the site of the French fort, it's easy to imagine the terror and isolation that La Salle's colonists must have felt while stranded in this spot. Almost three and a half centuries later, it still stands at a distance from any palpable human mark, any road or habitation. The view from the bluff above Garcitas Creek is of a sumptuous coastal plain receding far into the distance, finally melding into the mirage-like shimmer of Matagorda Bay and the limitless Gulf beyond. What would it have been like to be trapped in this strange, beyond-the-world place and learn, on a spring day in 1686, the worst possible news—that *La Belle*, the last ship, the only way out, had sunk in the bay with all the expedition's remaining provisions?

In the summer of 1978, I spent a few weeks in Matagorda Bay, reporting a magazine article about the Texas Antiquities Commission's search for La Salle's ships. We traveled back and forth across the greenish surface of the bay in a boat called the *Anomaly*. When the boat's magnetometer registered the presence of a metal object in the water below, we would put on our diving gear and slip overboard. The visibility, low to begin with, became nearly zero once the prop deflector was attached. This was a big elbow-shaped device that was bolted over one of the boat's twin props. When the motor was turned on, the power was directed downward, blasting a hole through the mud and shell bottom of the bay. Searching for the ships was an eerily hands-on proposition. It meant groping blindly with one hand through the riled-up muck for any sort of metal object while holding on to a guide rope with the other, trying not to be blown away by the underwater hurricane generated by the prop deflector.

The archeologists located a number of sunken vessels that summer. Pass Cavallo, the entrance to Matagorda Bay, has historically been a notorious ship trap. But none of them was *L'Aimable* or *La Belle*. It would be another seventeen years before one of the ships, *La Belle*, was finally found, its worm-eaten wooden hull buried beneath the mud in twelve feet of water off the lee side of Matagorda Peninsula. In the wreck was the skeleton of one of the luckless sailors who had gone down with the ship. He was lying over a coil of anchor rope. His name might have been C. Barange, since that was the name inscribed on a pewter cup lying next to him. He had a battered workman's body: missing teeth, a badly sprained ankle, a broken nose, a damaged back that would have given him an awkward gait. His bones were extracted from La Salle's doomed ship and interred at the Texas State Cemetery in Austin, with the French ambassador to the United States in solemn attendance.

The next year, archeologists found the site of La Salle's settlement. It had been burned by de León, and a Spanish fort was later erected on the site as a blatant gesture of ownership. But there was still abundant evidence of the brief French occupation of Texas. Among the artifacts were the expedition's eight cannons, which had been ultimately useless in defending the settlement from attack. The archeologists also located the grave where the Spaniards of de León's expedition had given a Christian burial to the bones of Isabelle Talon and her fellow colonists. That she was a "beautiful" Frenchwoman was only a supposition of Juan Bautista Chapa, the author of Texas's first poem. Her children, who would eventually return with tattooed faces to Europe or to European outposts in the New World, left no description of the mother who took them from France to what she and her husband thought would be a bright new beginning in an unknown land.

— 6 —

GOD'S WORK

A CENTURY OR SO OF COWBOY MOVIES HAS CREATED A
persistent misperception that Texas is a desert land. It's not
true, but not entirely false, either, since the state's southwestern extremity—from El Paso eastward to the Big Bend
country—contains a sizable piece of the Chihuahuan Desert,
along with a series of 8,000-foot peaks that represent the

trailing edge of the Rocky Mountains. But the Texas landscape is stagger-
ingly varied, from abrupt mountain ranges to hypnotically featureless plains
to forests so tropically thick and humid that every breath feels like something that must be seized from the greedily respiring trees.

It is an emphatic landscape, if not always a beautiful one, a fathomless transition zone between the mountainous West of the continent and the wooded
East, between the sea of grass of the Great Plains and the actual sea of the
Gulf of Mexico. Fifteen major rivers thread directly or circuitously across Texas
toward the Gulf, most of them running roughly parallel on a southeasterly
course that leads down from elevated plains to sea-level blackland soil. One
of the most commanding and fateful elements of Texas geography is a great
upthrust salient of Cretaceous rock called the Edwards Plateau, which sweeps
across much of the state in a bold eastward arc. The buckled, jumbled, eroded
limestone pediments at the ragged fringe of the Edwards form the Balcones

Escarpment. The Balcones is the stark dividing line that separates west from east, that distinguishes the open range country of nomads and ranchers from the places where stay-at-home agricultural economies could take root.

The fractured limestone of the escarpment creates a venous network of underground streams. All across the Hill Country, as this part of Texas is known, the water that sinks into the cracked streambeds of creeks and rivers erupts from spring openings farther downstream, creating transparent pools bubbling with artesian force and river tributaries filled with clean, rock-scoured water bordered by towering pillars of cypress trees.

In May 1718, near one of these bucolic spring openings that fed into the San Antonio River, a priest named Fray Antonio de San Buenaventura y Olivares said Mass in a temporary chapel built by himself and three Jarame Indians who had made the long journey from their homes south of the Rio Grande. Fray Olivares was old, but tireless and impatient. He was one of the fervid Franciscan priests who had been trained at a missionary college in Querétaro, Mexico before being sent forth into Texas. The business of saving souls was an urgent one, and he had grown so tired of waiting on the Spanish expedition that was to accompany him that he had struck out with a few companions from the mission settlement of San Juan Bautista near the Rio Grande.

The chapel they built on the San Antonio River was a modest jacal of sticks and mud. But if Fray Olivares had hauled in his oxcarts the usual furnishings necessary to start a mission, the little church would have been outfitted with brass candlesticks and copper fonts for holy water, its communion wafers already baked in the altar-bread irons. From the Marqués de Valero, who had recently been installed as the viceroy of New Spain, Olivares had requested a six-foot-tall portrait of St. Anthony, the namesake and patron saint of this little seedling of an outpost. In attendance at the Mass, most likely, were three or four other Franciscan missionaries, wearing their habits of undyed gray wool in the heat of a late Texas spring. There would also have been the thirty-four soldiers and seven families that Martin de Alarcón, the new governor of the Spanish provinces of Coahuila and Tejas, had brought to settle on the banks of the gleaming river. Also likely present during the singing of the "Te Deum" and the royal salute fired after Mass were members of the Payaya tribe, whose souls Fray Olivares had come to save from the fires of hell. The Payayas were one of dozens of native groups who inhabited the scenic margins of the Edwards Plateau and the monotonous brush country to the south. Speaking many languages and governed by many customs, these peoples had been so fragmented by European diseases and so harried by more powerful tribes that over time their individual tribal names became absorbed into the homogenous term "Coahuiltecan."

The Mass that Fray Olivares celebrated in this rude chapel marked the founding of a mission that bore the names of the saint who would protect it and the viceroy who had funded it: San Antonio de Valero. The next year, the mission would be moved to a more favorable site on the east side of the river, and in five years moved again to its final location, less than a mile north. It kept the name San Antonio de Valero until it was secularized and became the headquarters of a company of presidial soldiers sent to Texas in 1803 from a Mexican village named Álamo de Parras. From them, it developed the most ineradicable name in Texas history: the Alamo.

A few days after the mission was established, Alarcón formally took possession of a site a short distance upstream and decreed into existence a town and a fort. The Payayas called this place Yanaguana. To Alarcón and his soldiers and settlers, it was San Antonio de Béxar.

---------- ★ ----------

THE PLANTING OF A SPANISH TOWN IN THIS PLACE, AT THIS time, was a crucial gambit in an ongoing multidimensional international chess game involving Spain, France, England, and an ever-wary spectrum of native peoples, each with its own strategic imperatives. It had been thirty years since the de León expedition found the ruins of La Salle's colony on Garcitas Creek, but the Spanish claim on Texas was still in danger of evaporating.

Less than a year after returning to Mexico, de León had once again been on the march to Texas, this time to establish a permanent presence that would back up the notion that Texas was Spanish territory and that would serve as an early-warning system against any further incursions.

The best bet for such an enterprise was in the land of the Caddos. The Caddos had impressed both La Salle and the Spanish with their friendliness and sophistication. They lived a settled way of life and gave the impression of having a centralized governmental system upon which a Spanish superstructure might be painlessly imposed. The French called the Caddos the Ceni. The Spanish soldiers and priests referred to them by a word they heard the Caddos use when discussing their friends and allies. The Indians did not have a written language; the word had no spelling. But it was pronounced something along the lines of "Tayshas" or "Techas" or "Texias" or any of a dozen other variations. The missionaries called these Caddo people "Tejas," their territory the kingdom of the Tejas. The slurry Spanish j eventually evolved into a hard English x, and the word "Texas" came into being.

De León and Fray Damian Massanet, the priest in charge of creating the missions, were very much taken with the architecture and order of the home of the village chief, the *caddi*, whom they called the governor. The gov-

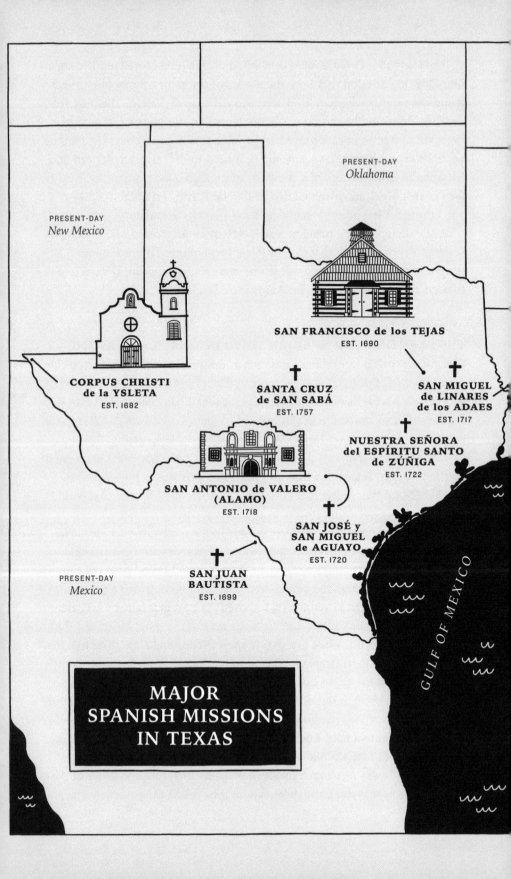

PRESENT-DAY
Oklahoma

PRESENT-DAY
New Mexico

SAN FRANCISCO de los TEJAS
EST. 1690

✝

✝

**CORPUS CHRISTI
de la YSLETA**
EST. 1682

**SANTA CRUZ
de SAN SABÁ**
EST. 1757

**SAN MIGUEL
de LINARES
de los ADAES**
EST. 1717

✝

**NUESTRA SEÑORA
del ESPÍRITU SANTO
de ZÚÑIGA**
EST. 1722

**SAN ANTONIO de VALERO
(ALAMO)**
EST. 1718

✝

**SAN JOSÉ y
SAN MIGUEL
de AGUAYO**
EST. 1720

✝

PRESENT-DAY
Mexico

**SAN JUAN
BAUTISTA**
EST. 1699

GULF OF MEXICO

MAJOR
SPANISH MISSIONS
IN TEXAS

ernor's house was round and commodious, framed by poles lashed together and covered with grass. There were reed mats on the floor, a fire that was never allowed to go out, and neatly arranged storage shelves holding reed baskets full of acorns and corn and beans. Ten people slept in the house, on beds raised off the floor and covered with buffalo hides. The beds were set end to end, separated at their heads and feet by a "very pretty alcove." Every morning at dawn, ten women would enter the house and begin cleaning and sweeping and grinding corn.

"I delivered to the governor a staff with a cross," de León wrote, "giving him the title of all his people, in order that he might rule and govern them, giving him to understand by means of an interpreter that which he should observe and do, and the respect and obedience which he and all his people ought to have for the priests, and that he should make all his families attend Christian teaching, in order that they might be instructed in the affairs of our holy Catholic faith so that later they might be baptized and become Christians. He accepted the staff with much pleasure, promising to do all that was desired of him, and the company fired three salutes."

The Caddo leader to whom de León addressed these remarks probably regarded them as the usual sort of rhetorical babble common to Indian diplomacy. It seems unlikely he could have really believed that the Spanish meant every word of it, that they considered themselves the new masters of this woodland empire, that he himself now ruled at their discretion, and that his people were expected not just to change their way of life but their entire cosmology.

The Caddos, unlike many of the Indian groups that had been struck by the European shock wave, still had a cohesive identity. Though the great earthen temples and burial mounds of their ancestors were by now mostly just unmarked grassy swales, and though the violent rampages of the de Soto and Moscoso expedition 150 years earlier, and the epidemics it had left behind, had shattered their world, by the 1680s the Caddos had begun to reorganize themselves into three powerful confederacies. The lush strip of land between the Trinity and Neches Rivers in East Central Texas, where Fray Massanet planned to build the first of many missions, was the heart of one of these confederacies, known as the Hasinai.

Things looked promising at first. The Hasinai Caddos were always eager for the manufactured goods of New Spain, and their supply line had recently been disrupted by the Apaches, who had moved down onto the Southern Plains and begun controlling the trade routes that led east from the New Mexico pueblos.

And the Caddos seemed receptive to the idea of Christianity, or at least mystically drawn to the trappings of it. Like every other priest on the frontiers of New Spain, Massanet was fervently aware of the miraculous appearances of the Lady in Blue earlier in the century, and he was very much in hopes that he would encounter native tribes who might have seen her and heard her message of conversion. Here in the kingdom of the Tejas, it appeared that that divine quest had been fulfilled. One evening the caddi asked Massanet for a length of blue cloth. His mother was elderly, and he wanted the material to set aside for her as a shroud when she died. He was puzzlingly insistent on the color. Blue was important to him. When Massanet asked why, the man said that many years before, his mother and some of the other village elders had seen a woman descending from the heavens. They had never forgotten her sky-blue cloak and her kindly radiant face. "From this," Massanet reported in wonder, "it is easily to be seen that they referred to the Madre María de Jesus de Ágreda."

But the sense of miraculous destiny quickly soured. Within a few years, the two missions that the Spanish built in the heart of the Tejas country turned out to be dismal misfires. Five hundred miles from the nearest Spanish outpost, they were undersupplied and—in Fray Massanet's opinion—overstaffed with bored, troublesome soldiers. The priests, deceived into thinking the Caddos were as interested in a religious overhaul as they were in a trade alliance, overplayed their hand, growing more and more intolerant of the "witchcraft, superstitions, and deceits of the devil" that, to their minds, infected native worship. At one point a frustrated priest infuriated a *caddi* by trying, and almost succeeding, in throwing sacred Caddo icons into a fire. Worse than the spiritual abuses of the priests was the sexual rampaging of some of the soldiers, one of whom tried to rape the wife of the *caddi*'s brother. And then there was the by-now inexorable introduction of smallpox, which flared through the villages of the Hasinai confederacy, killing hundreds, or more likely thousands, of Indians, who now regarded the sacraments and the baptismal waters of the Franciscans as the source of a deadly incubus. One of the two missions was swept away by a flood. The other was burned down by the priests themselves, who were evicted from the Tejas country under threat of death and barely survived a four-month wilderness trek back to Coahuila.

Twenty years passed before Spain made another serious attempt to occupy East Texas. Around that time, France finally made good on La Salle's dream of establishing a colony at the mouth of the Mississippi. The long and complex European war in which France and Spain had been fighting each other had been temporarily resolved, and Louis XIV's grandson Philip V now sat on the Spanish throne. In the New World, though, the two nations were still edgy competitors, with the French steadily encroaching toward the Red River from their Louisiana base and winning the goodwill of the Caddos by treating them more as business partners and not, as the Spanish tended to do, as pagans in need of salvation from their unholy beliefs. They were also more than willing to sell them firearms, something that official Spanish policy forbade.

Relations between Spain and France were murky enough at this point that a Spanish Franciscan priest wrote a letter to the French governor in Louisiana. The priest, Francisco Hidalgo, had endured the humiliating abandonment of the East Texas missions and Spain's intolerable lack of interest in making another try at settling the region. If Spain would not reestablish the Tejas missions, he proposed, maybe France would be interested in doing so. It was a desperate, maybe treasonous gambit, one that shines a light on the unstoppable missionary spirit that worked in conflict as much as in concert with the Spanish drive for worldly power. It was also consequential. It led to the arrival on the Texas stage of a French-Canadian entrepreneur named Louis Juchereau de St. Denis, who showed up in San Juan Bautista, south of the Rio Grande near present-day Eagle Pass, in 1714, ready to take up Father Hidalgo on his invitation, even though foreigners—especially the French— were still barred from Spanish territory. Serving as guides for St. Denis were two of the formerly captive Talon brothers, marked with tattoos and fluent in multiple Indian languages. The commandant at the San Juan Bautista presidio, Diego Ramón, assumed St. Denis was some kind of spy, politely arrested him, and sent him on to Mexico City—though not in time to prevent the ingratiating Frenchman from becoming engaged to his step granddaughter. In Mexico City, St. Denis not only talked the authorities out of sending him to prison, but also inspired them to outfit an expedition back to East Texas to establish six new missions between the Trinity and Red Rivers. One of these mission settlements, Los Adaes, represented the easternmost reach of Spanish Texas—so far east, in fact, that it was in present-day Louisiana, only a few miles from the French trading center of Natchitoches.

Ramón and St. Denis embarked on this expedition in 1716. When Mission Valero was created near the San Antonio River, two years later, the idea was that it and the nearby settlement and presidio would serve as a crucial halfway point on the long stretch of empty country between San Juan Bautista and the new East Texas missions. But those faraway new missions were still so hard to supply that the priests reported being forced to eat the "despicable meat of crows." War flared up again between France and Spain and spilled over into Texas and Louisiana, ruining the atmosphere of amicable trade that St. Denis had represented and setting off an opéra bouffe skirmish known as the "Chicken War," in which a French commander attacked

Spain's Los Adaes settlement, capturing its two remaining human occupants along with a dozen or so chickens. The "monsieur commandant," wrote a Spanish historian in a mocking account, "did not spare, according to civilized rules, the lives of the chickens."

The Chicken War might have been risible in hindsight, but the threat of a real war with France led to the abandonment, for the second time, of the East Texas missions. Texas, now practically defenseless against French incursions, might have remained that way had it not been for the newly appointed governor of the province of Coahuila y Texas, a Spanish aristocrat named Don José de Azlor y Virto de Vera, better—if not more briefly—known as the Marqués de San Miguel de Aguayo. Aguayo took it upon himself to preserve the "far flung heathen land" of Texas for Spain. He organized and paid for a force of over six hundred men and led them from below the Rio Grande deep into the East Texas forests. It ended up being a punishing wilderness journey, the rivers so swollen that the expedition had to build bridges—the first in Texas—to cross them. The weather was so brutal that only fifty of the expedition's four thousand horses survived the return journey. But Aguayo rebuilt the six abandoned missions in East Texas and established four new ones, including two in San Antonio.

Thanks to him, the Spanish presence in Texas turned out to be tenacious and enduring, in no place more so than San Antonio de Béxar. By 1731 there were five missions situated along the San Antonio River. They were administered by Franciscan priests and populated and maintained by hundreds of "neophytes." This was the term for the Indians from the harassed and destabilized tribes who had decided it was to their advantage to seek out a new life under the protection of an ordered Spanish world. The goal of the missions was to Catholicize and Hispanicize native people, to draw them into the embrace of the Church, to appoint them as governors and magistrates and town councilmen in a harmonious simulacrum of Spanish civil culture. They were to become farmers in the mission fields, weavers, stonemasons, vaqueros who tended the cattle on the mission ranchos. It worked and it didn't. For the Indians—Payayas, Pamayas, Pampopas, Pastias, Sulujams, and Jarames, among many other tribes and bands—the missions could be a refuge in an acceleratingly chaotic world. But many of them tended to view a mission as a supply base more than a home, a place to congregate in times of threat or want, and to move on from when it came time for traditional hunts and migrations.

In addition to this fluctuating population of Indians, San Antonio was inhabited by priests and brothers, by the soldiers of the nearby presidio, by the original settler families who had come with Alarcón from Mexico, and by a cluster of families from the Canary Islands who had responded to an official appeal for colonists to help make tangible the Spanish presence in Texas.

Life in the frontier village wasn't serene. The Canary Islanders—from an archipelago off the coast of Morocco that had been conquered by Castile in the fifteenth century—arrived in Texas with a long-fixed sense of identity that helped lead to clashes with the original settlers and disputes about land and water rights. And other racial and class frictions drove divisions between citizens who regarded themselves as pure-blood *españoles* and the mixed-blood mestizos, who made up the bulk of the Spanish population in Texas. Every three or four years came a new wave of epidemic disease, striking hardest, as always, at the vulnerable Indians clustered in the missions.

And then there were the Apaches, for whom San Antonio was a persistent target of opportunity. Like the Spanish, the Apaches were relative newcomers to Texas. When Coronado encountered them on the llano in the 1540s, they had been on the Southern Plains for perhaps only a hundred years. Also like the Spanish, they were an ambitious and aggressive-minded people, the same drive for wealth and opportunity pushing them on into unknown country. They were a powerful presence even before they began adapting themselves to the revolutionary horse culture made possible by the herds that the Spanish entradas introduced into New Mexico and Texas. Mounted Apaches soon were a dominant force on the Texas plains, driving other buffalo-hunting tribes such as the Jumanos and Wichitas to the south, and installing themselves as the premier suppliers of the hides that were one of the cornerstone commodities of the Indian trading networks.

Some Apaches had branched westward into New Mexico and Arizona, but those in the eastern division—who became the ancestral enemies of the Spanish—were known as the Lipans. Lipans had a mobile culture and a martial attitude—their word for the sun, for instance, was Killer-of-Enemies. They fought with tactical complexity—feints, encirclements, ambushes—that to the Spanish way of thinking amounted to mere deviousness. To the Franciscan clerics, the Lipans were a supreme and urgent challenge. Without the light of Christ, they would remain "eternal dwellers in the infernal caverns."

Lipans thought Spaniards dwelt in some pretty dark places themselves, especially since their repeated attempts to secure a foothold in East Texas meant they were friends—or at least trying to be friends—with the Caddos, who were bitter enemies of the Apaches. Over the early decades of the eighteenth century, the Lipans began to find themselves increasingly boxed in. There was a new threat to their north in the form of the Comanches, an even more mobile and warlike people, who were gaining control of the llano and allying themselves with the Wichitas and other tribes along the Red River who made up an anti-Apache coalition known as the Norteños. To the south were the encroaching Spanish, and to the east—blocking trade with the French and the procurement of French firearms and ammunition—were the Caddos.

All this naturally set the Lipans in conflict with the Spanish in Texas, and especially in San Antonio de Béxar. Almost from the founding of the town there developed a pattern of escalating raids and reprisals that spanned generations and created a lasting blood enmity between the Apaches and the Spanish settlers. Only a few conflicts could be described as battles. In November 1732, a Spanish expeditionary force attacked a Lipan stronghold on the San Saba River, killing a reported two hundred warriors and capturing thirty women and children to take back to San Antonio as hostages or as involuntary converts to mission society. Thirteen years later, Apaches mounted a major attack on the San Antonio presidio, the first of perhaps a half-dozen attempts over the next century by one hostile party or another to seize control of the most fought-over city in Texas. The assailants would have succeeded if not for a force of armed mission Indians who sallied out of Mission Valero to reinforce the presidial soldiers.

For the most part, the warfare was vicious and small scale: horse stealing; brief, bloody skirmishes that left behind mutilated Spanish bodies, their flesh stripped from their limbs; attacks on supply trains; punitive expeditions of a few dozen soldiers riding out into the vast Indian territory known as Apachería; captives taken into slavery or held as hostages for peace negotiations that as often as not only engendered more hostilities. The fighting was chronic but inconclusive. The Spanish presence in Texas was not substantial enough to conquer the Apaches outright, and the Apaches—at war on all sides, and effectively blockaded from acquiring modern weaponry from the French— could not realistically drive the Spanish from Texas.

For the Lipans, the line of Spanish settlement was an anvil upon which they were being pounded by multiple hammers, the most relentless of which was the Comanches. "Each year at a certain time," wrote a Spanish brigadier from New Mexico in 1726, "there comes to this province a nation of Indians very barbarous and warlike. Their name is Comanche. They never number less than 1,500. Their origin is unknown, because they are always wandering in battle formation, for they make war on all the Nations."

"Their name is Comanche." It's a simple enough statement, but one that, when considered against the next few hundred years of Texas history, takes on an ominous, oracular force. Long before the Comanches began to clash with the Spanish in Texas, they were well known to the soldiers and settlers and priests of New Mexico, and to the Pueblo Indians there, who were restively under Spanish control. The Comanches were a Shoshone-speaking

The Lipan Apaches
were mounted and
mobilized in Texas
against the Spanish
threat. To Fran-
ciscan clerics, the
Lipans were "eternal
dwellers in the infer-
nal caverns."

people who had filtered down—or been driven down—onto the plains from the heights of the Rockies. They arrived as pedestrians who lived a hunter-gatherer way of life; when traveling and changing camps, they stashed their belongings on travois pulled by dogs. But that began to change after the first Spanish explorers arrived and brought horses to a world in which such animals had been extinct for as long as ten thousand years. The tough Iberian mustangs were as at home on the plains of Texas as they had been on the exposed grasslands of Spain, and of all the native peoples on the North American continent, the Comanches were the ones who most fully grasped and exploited the transformative potential of the horse. Apaches and other tribes began acquiring horses—through theft or barter—from the New Mexico pueblos in the years after Don Juan de Oñate founded the Spanish colony there in 1598. The Pueblo revolt of 1680 not only drove the Spanish out of New Mexico for a decade, but also unleashed hundreds of horses onto the plains, where they were captured and trained and bred by enterprising tribes like the Comanches.

Apaches used horses to great effect to raid the New Mexico pueblos and extend their own hunting and trading ranges. But since the Apaches came from a partly agricultural tradition, for them the horse represented a powerful new tool but not necessarily an identity makeover. For the Comanches, horses became their culture. Horses were the most important form of property, a key measure of wealth and prestige. Every warrior had his own remuda, often several hundred animals, and chiefs were known to amass as many as fifteen hundred. Comanche children, strapped to the saddle of their mothers' mares as infants, grew up on horseback to the rhythm of hooves striking the grassy sod of the llano. Boys spent much of their days not just learning to ride but also training to transform extraordinary feats of horsemanship into instinctive movements. A Comanche rider, marveled an observer named Homer S. Thrall, was "the model of the fabled Thessalian 'Centaur', half horse, half man, so closely joined and so dexterously managed that it appears but one animal, fleet and furious."

Apaches tended to fight like dragoons, using horses for transportation but dismounting for combat. Comanches, on the other hand, gave new meaning to the idea of mounted warfare. They were a highly mobilized strike force in which rider and horse were melded into an almost indissoluble fighting unit. When the Spanish managed to reestablish their foothold in New Mexico after the Pueblo revolt, they came face to face with the new Comanche war machine, which presented itself in a series of brutal lightning raids on pueblos and presidios.

The Comanches helped create a militarized barrier to Spanish expansion

—a barrier that would become more and more formidable over the decades —and drove their other enemies, the Apaches, to the edge of the map. Apachería was inexorably turning into Comanchería, and by the middle of the eighteenth century the Lipans had been pressured for so long and so hard by the Comanches and their Norteño allies that they had few options left. It was time to cut a deal with the Spanish.

On an August day in 1749, Lipans appeared once again in San Antonio, this time not to attack the village but to negotiate a peace treaty. They were received with elaborate diplomatic courtesy. The presidial commander, Captain Toribio de Urrutia, was an incorrigible Apache hunter, but he had ordered a special reception hall built, and even invited several members of the Indian delegation to stay in his own home. The negotiations went smoothly, and soon the entire community gathered in the plaza in front of the presidio, where a great pit was dug to symbolically bury the implements of war. These items included six arrows, a hatchet, a lance and—we are told—a live horse, who was entombed along with the inanimate weapons after Urrutia and the Apache chiefs held hands and danced around the pit.

The peace conference eventually led, in 1757, to the establishment of a new mission—with a presidio to protect it—along the San Saba River a hundred and fifty miles northwest of San Antonio. The mission, built for the Apaches, was situated in the very heart of shrinking Apachería. This was a remarkable change of policy for both the Spanish and the Lipans. In 1749, Spain had built three missions along the San Gabriel River. They were about as far northeast of San Antonio as the new San Saba mission was to the northwest. Those missions, designed for refugee tribes throughout Texas, had failed because of spectacularly corrupt mismanagement and relentless Apache attacks. Now the Apaches, desperate for peace and security, were ready—or at least gave the appearance of being ready—to welcome a mission of their own. For the Franciscan friars, the chance to plant the cross in Apache territory and convert their most determined enemies was a glorious challenge. It also made secular sense to the government in Mexico City, since hidden somewhere in the mineral-rich San Saba country was supposedly a mountain of pure silver. A viable presence north of San Antonio could mean discovery at last of the mineral wealth that had been eluding Spain in Texas since the days of Coronado and the Seven Cities of Cíbola. It would also cement peace with the Lipans, extend the range of Spanish influence in Texas, and help hold the line against the encroaching French.

For the Lipans, the mission and the presidio represented a buffer as well, a way to draw their new Spanish allies into the fight against the Comanches and the Norteños. The ever-optimistic priests believed the Apaches would

A mounted Comanche, according to one bewitched observer, was "half horse, half man, so closely joined and so dexterously managed that it appears but one animal, fleet and furious."

seize the opportunity to transform their traditional way of life. But it is just as likely the Indians had calculated that welcoming the mission was the only means left of sustaining that life. In any case, they paid scant attention to the mission once it was built. The priest in charge was fifty-eight-year-old Fray Alonso Giraldo de Terreros. He had devoted his career to "persuading and catechizing [the] confused and irresolute wills" of Indians in Texas and Mexico. His own will was focused and resolute, but his success had been mixed at best. His previous mission, in Coahuila, Mexico, had been burned down by its own neophytes. And at the newly built Mission Santa Cruz de San Sabá, he and his fellow missionaries waited forlornly for the Apaches to show up. They did arrive, several thousand of them, but only briefly, and only to use the mission to stock up on supplies. In a few days they were all gone, some of them to hunt buffalo, others to hunt Comanches.

"All Hell is joined to impede this enterprise," Terreros wrote, and he was right. Almost a year passed with no Lipan converts, and within the stockade walls of the mission there were only three priests, a few soldiers, and a handful of Christianized Tlaxcalan Indians from Central Mexico, descendants of the nation that had fought with Cortés against Moctezuma. The Tlaxcalans were there to help instruct the Apaches in the ways of mission life, but no Apaches were willing to be instructed. Four or five miles away, on the opposite bank of the San Saba River, stood the presidio that had been built to protect the mission enterprise. It was commanded by Colonel Diego Ortiz Parrilla and inhabited by over three hundred people, most of them the wives and children of the presidial soldiers. Parrilla was a man of noble birth and grizzled experience, having fought in campaigns against Indians throughout Mexico and even against the English in Cuba. He did not believe the Apaches were serious in wanting a mission, he had little patience for priests and their martyrs' zeal, and he had already written to the viceroy, recommending that the whole enterprise be abandoned.

What neither he nor anyone else seemed to grasp until it was too late was that the decision to build a mission and presidio on the San Saba, to make such an emphatic gesture of common cause with the Apaches, was a provocation that the Comanches couldn't ignore. But perhaps that had been the Lipan strategy all along: to engineer a war between their two most obstinate enemies.

One March morning in 1758, one of the three mission priests, Fray Santiesteban, was just starting to say Mass when the stockade walls of Mission San Sabá were suddenly surrounded by a huge combined force—perhaps several thousand in all—of Comanches and Norteños. The only surviving priest, Fray Miguel Molina, recorded the scene: "[I was] filled with amazement and fear when I saw nothing but Indians on every hand, armed with guns and arrayed in the most horrible attire. Besides the paint on their faces, red and black, they were adorned with the pelts and tails of wild beasts, wrapped around them or hanging down from their heads, as well as deer horns. Some were disguised as various kinds of animals, and some wore headdresses. All were armed with muskets, swords and lances."

For the several dozen people in the mission, it was a blood-freezing display, but the Indians didn't attack at once. Instead, they pretended that they had come in peace and managed to gain entrance to the interior of the mission. The Comanche leader, wearing a red French military jacket, remained mounted imperiously as his warriors looted the mission and the priests desperately tried to placate him with gifts of tobacco, though "his face was hideous and extremely grave."

A few days earlier, Colonel Parrilla had become aware of hostile activity in the area, and had ridden to see Father Terreros to try to convince him to leave the mission for the relative safety of the presidio. Terreros, true to his stubborn missionary ethos, refused to move. Parrilla had left eight soldiers behind, but there was not much they could do once the uneasy stasis erupted into outright carnage. Terreros was killed first—by a musket ball through his head. One of the soldiers next to him fell dead an instant later, and two more were killed and hacked to pieces in the mission courtyard. Father Santiesteban, whose Mass had been interrupted by the assault, remained in the church during the assault, and presumably died there. His body was never found, though his head was later discovered in the ashes of a mission storehouse.

Father Molina and a handful of survivors managed to hide themselves, moving from building to building as the Indians plundered the mission and set fire to it. At some point they were joined by a soldier named Joseph Vásquez, who was part of a relief mission sent by Parrilla from the presidio. But an Indian attack drove them back and left Vásquez, wounded by a lance thrust, lying midway between the mission and the presidio. Thinking he was dying, he decided the better course of action was not to try to reach the safety of the presidio but the sanctity of the burning mission, where, if he could find a living priest, he could at least confess his sins. He managed to drag himself there, was promptly discovered by the Indians, and heaved into a fire. But while the Comanches' attention was elsewhere, the unkillable Vásquez rolled out of the flames and crawled toward Father Terreros's headquarters room, where Father Molina and the other survivors had gathered. It is not known whether the priest, who was wounded by a musket ball, was able to hear Vásquez's confession, but both men managed to survive by sneaking out the mission that night and making their way to the presidio.

With only about sixty men under arms in the presidio, Parrilla could do little but shore up his defenses and get ready for an attack. But the attack didn't come. The enemy withdrew, apparently satisfied to have made the point that a Spanish presence in their country was not just unwelcome but untenable. A year later they were back, killing and mutilating nineteen soldiers and riding off with a sizable portion of the San Saba presidio's horse herd. Parrilla and his men were staggered not just by the hostility and coordination of the northern tribes but also by the realization that they were fighting a new kind of enemy. For centuries, guns and horses and steel had given Spain a determining advantage in its wars against native peoples. But now the tribes had horses and, especially in the case of the Comanches, a revolutionary way of using them. And courtesy of their French trading partners, almost all of them carried firearms, which replaced or augmented their Stone Age weapons.

It took until August 1759, a year and a half after the massacre at the mission, for Parrilla to manage to put together a punitive expedition. He had almost six hundred men, but it was far from a cohesive force, made up of presidial soldiers, militiamen from all over Texas and New Spain, mission Indians, Apache auxiliaries, and an assortment of armed tailors, cigar sellers, and shoemakers. His army, Parrilla later felt it necessary to confess, was largely made up of undisciplined civilian soldiers distinguished by "personal defects and a complete ignorance of the use of arms."

They marched northeast some three hundred miles and found the enemy in a Taovaya village on the bank of the Red River. But it was more than a village. It was a fort, with a strong stockade and even a moat, defended by a well-prepared force of Norteños and Comanches, who immediately sortied out under covering fire from the stockade to drive Parrilla's forces off the road into a deep sandbank, where they couldn't maneuver and were quickly overwhelmed.

His thrown-together army demoralized and disoriented, Parrilla ordered a retreat all the way back to the San Saba presidio. Just as the attack on the mission had been a minor massacre (only eight people dead), the attempted assault on the Red River fort was a minor military defeat, with the Spanish losses amounting to fifty-two dead, wounded, and missing. But the long-range impact shattered Spain's ambition to thrust beyond its beleaguered settlement line in Texas and extend its claim into the middle of the continent. By moving into the San Saba country to cement its peace with the Apaches, Spain had ended up with new enemies, most formidably the Comanches. For generations to come, it would be the Comanches who would frustrate the reach of Spain's frontier, and the Mexican and American frontiers that followed, and shape the destiny of Texas.

The destruction of the San Saba mission is the subject of one of Texas's earliest paintings, commissioned by a wealthy mine owner in Mexico who was a cousin of the slain Father Terreros and the man who had bankrolled the construction of the mission. It's a gloomy, haunted canvas, dominated by the two martyred friars standing on either side in saintly placidity, displaying their wounds as blood streams down the front of their robes. The center of the painting is all boiling, firelit chaos, a crushing mob of demonic warriors pressing in on the frail mission walls. From the perspective of those warriors, however, the attack was not a heathen massacre but a triumph of intertribal diplomacy and coordinated military planning against common invaders.

The wooden mission was completely burned, and its location wasn't pinpointed until the 1990s, when archaeologists excavated an alfalfa field a mile and a half outside the town of Menard and found a scattering of artifacts and charcoal stains that marked the location of the mission's stockade logs. But the presidio, downstream along the clear, shallow San Saba River, was never lost to history. Two years after the attack, the wooden fort was rebuilt in stone, and those walls, or at least their foundations, remained prominently visible. They were partially rebuilt in the 1930s, though not with scrupulous authenticity. It doesn't much matter. The presidio's entrance gate and its blockhouse, directly adjacent to a nine-hole golf course, manage to cast a brooding spell. When you stand there, you are at the high-water mark of the great Spanish adventure in Texas.

In 1767, a field marshal in the royal army of Spain with the resounding name of Cayetano María Pignatelli Rubí Corbera y San Climent, shorthanded by history to one of his many titles, the Marqués de Rubí, stood on this spot and registered his firm disapproval of the San Sabá presidio. It was still in existence almost a decade after the attacks of 1758, but by that time it was a feeble and forlorn place. "It affords as much protection to the interests of His Majesty in New Spain," Rubí observed, "as a ship anchored in mid-Atlantic would afford in preventing foreign trade with America."

Rubí was in the middle of a twenty-three-month inspection tour of New Spain's frontier defenses, a vast journey of 7,600 miles that took him and his extensive party from the Gulf of California throughout New Mexico and Texas to the Gulf of Mexico. It was a crucial time for the Spanish king, Charles III, to reassess exactly what sort of business Spain had in Texas and how well it was going about it. In the last few years, everything had changed. France was no longer a threat to Spain's dominion in the New World. The two Bourbon empires had become allies against England in the Seven Years' War, a kaleidoscopic European struggle that manifested itself in North America as the French and Indian War. When the pieces of the world were reshuffled at the Treaty of Paris in 1763, England and its colonies had control of, among other French possessions, Canada and the southeastern part of North America. Louisiana, or at least that part of it west of the Mississippi, was ceded to Spain by France.

Spain had been obsessively fortifying its borders against potential French invasions ever since it had heard the first rumors of La Salle's colony almost eighty years before. Now, suddenly, there was no longer a French threat. The French inhabitants of Louisiana were no longer seen as a destabilizing presence on the Spanish border, since they were now officially Spaniards themselves. Among the Frenchmen whom the Treaty of Paris decreed to be Spanish subjects was a man named Athanase de Mézières, an upper-class soldier, born in Paris, who had lived in Louisiana since 1733. When Mézières entered Spanish service after the Treaty of Paris, his administrative verve and deep knowledge of the murky borderland region turned out to be critical, particularly when it came to making treaties with the numerous Indian nations along the Red River. The former Frenchman, a Spanish official testified, had "such a knowledge of these provinces of Texas and Louisiana as is possessed by no one else, and, likewise, of the tribes which surround them."

Among the things Mézières learned about during an expedition he made into the Texas interior in 1772 was "a mass of metal which the Indians say is hard, thick, heavy, and composed of iron." Local tribes treated it as an object of worship: "They venerate it as an extraordinary manifestation of nature. . . . There is not a person in the village who does not tell of it." It was probably the Tawakonis who told Mézières about this 1,635-pound chunk of alien rock, the largest meteorite ever found in Texas, but they were not the only Indian people who thought it sacred and claimed it as their own. The Comanches called it Po-a-cat-le-pi-le-car-re, a name that translates as "Medicine Rock." A George Catlin painting, *Comanches Giving Arrows to the Medicine Rock*, depicts a Comanche war party appeasing the gods by shooting arrows at what may have been the Texas Iron, the meteorite that Mézières heard about. In the end, though, neither the Tawakonis nor the Comanches nor any other native group could keep possession of the rock, any more than they could keep possession of the earth it had struck. It was dug up and is on display today at Yale's Peabody Museum of Natural History.

Now that the French invasion of Texas had disappeared as a live menace, the Spanish no longer needed to support isolated missions and presidios filled with disappointed friars and demoralized troops. Outposts like San Saba, Rubí concluded in his report to the king, guarded only an "imaginary frontier." The solution was for Spain to pull back to its "true dominions" and shrink the boundaries of Spanish Texas. San Saba was abandoned, as was the capital of Texas, the mission and settlement of Los Adaes, which had been pointedly established across the Sabine in French Louisiana.

Though a cluster of Spanish settlers defiantly remained in East Texas and formed the town of Nacogdoches, San Antonio de Béxar, deep in the interior, became the new provincial capital.

Texas during this time remained, in the Spanish view of things, unsettled, remote, and largely inhospitable, with maybe twenty-five thousand people, including Indians, Spaniards, and a handful of African slaves. Below the Rio Grande, in the more populated precincts of Mexico, a teeming human presence numbered in the millions. This part of New Spain had become a thickly peopled, conquered land of pueblos and villas and great cities, its inhabitants living in everything from brush shacks to viceroy palaces. There was sprawling (and ominous) growth as well in the English colonies, where the restless Americans—"distinguished," in the words of a wary Spanish governor, "only in their color, language, and the superiority of their depraved cunning and untrustworthiness"—were headed unstoppably westward. Revolution was coming to both places, to colonial England and colonial Spain, and as a consequence, it would come to Texas as well, turning an imaginary frontier into a realm of fiery reality.

★

PART TWO

The

RIPE
PEACH

★

—7—

FILIBUSTERS

IN THE HALF CENTURY FOLLOWING THE MARQUÉS DE
Rubí's recommendation that Spain scale back its Texas ambitions, one intrigue after another blew through the province, reinforcing the old idea that Texas was more than anything a critical buffer zone, a listening post that would detect the first stirrings of a foreign invasion and a wilderness that would dissipate the impact of such an invasion like a tidal marshland absorbing a crashing wave.

There was no wave yet, just a probing rivulet in the form of a young Irish-born Kentuckian named Philip Nolan. Nolan was a shipping clerk and bookkeeper in the office of his supremely slippery mentor, James Wilkinson. Wilkinson was known to the Spanish—to whom he was in the habit of cheerfully selling U.S. government secrets—as Agent 13. He had been a brigadier general in the American Revolution as well as a participant in a secret campaign to remove George Washington from command of the Continental Army. Wilkinson was predisposed to scheming and aggrandizing of every sort, a trait that ultimately led him into a notorious conspiracy with Aaron Burr to allegedly break up the United States and form their own continental empire.

In 1791, Philip Nolan began traveling into Texas through Spanish Louisiana for the stated purpose of capturing and selling mustangs. On his first few expeditions, he traveled with a passport and managed to cultivate friendly relations with crucial officials, including the governor of Texas and the commandant general of the Interior Provinces, the vast administrative area of which Texas was a part. But by the turn of the century he was being regarded with deep suspicion, and his passport was not renewed. New Spain was very nervous about foreign interlopers coming into Texas, particularly Americans, and most particularly an American who might reasonably be suspected of being the agent of a habitual nation wrecker like James Wilkinson.

Lack of a passport notwithstanding, Nolan persisted in his Texas enterprise, riding west from Mississippi in 1800 at the head of an expedition of a couple dozen heavily armed men. They built corrals and a log fort near the Brazos River somewhere on the Central Texas prairie. No one knows exactly what they were up to, if anything, besides catching mustangs, but the Spanish authorities clearly regarded Nolan and his men as a threat. Perhaps the threat was immediate—a direct filibustering expedition that would rely on stirring up anti-Spanish feeling among the Indians. Or perhaps it was some sort of scouting or spying party that would prepare the ground for a U.S. invasion of Spanish America. Either way it had to be stopped. The commandant of the presidio at Nacogdoches rode out with 120 men to confront the intruders. Nolan's men were hungry and haggard after five months of surviving in the field on a diet of horsemeat. (Mustanging in Texas, Nolan had written to Wilkinson, was "less pleasing in practice than in speculation.") Nolan, though, was ready for a fight and did his best to rally his dispirited men, warning them that if they were captured they would spend the rest of their lives as Spanish slaves. But the mustangers were outnumbered, and only their leader seemed to be truly filled with the spirit of resistance. Nolan was killed in action, struck in the head by a musket ball. After being bombarded with grapeshot fired from a swivel gun attached to the back of a mule, the rest of his men promptly surrendered. Nolan was buried on the battlefield, though not before his ears were cut off and sent to the provincial governor.

His men were taken to San Antonio and then to prisons in Chihuahua and San Carlos. They were eventually tried and found guilty of taking up arms against Spain. They were sentenced to ten years of hard labor, though one day a colonel came to read them a decree from the king, informing them that one of their number must hang. To decide who would die, they threw dice out of a glass tumbler onto the head of a drum. The man with the lowest score, and hence the one to be executed, turned out to be the oldest of the filibusters, fifty-three-year old Ephraim Blackburn. He was led off the next day to the gallows, after being baptized as a Catholic and confessing his sins. The rest were dispersed into solitary confinement in different prisons. One of them, a restless young man from Tennessee named Peter Ellis Bean—who would survive to live a colorful life that included fighting under Andrew Jackson at the Battle of New Orleans, serving as an officer in the Mexican Army, becoming a wealthy landowner in Texas, and marrying two women at once—reflected on his imprisonment in his memoir. The most affecting passage was an account of his relationship with a small lizard he discovered in his cell. He tamed the lizard and called him Bill. "I found," the lonely prisoner wrote, "that he was sincerely my friend."

★

BY THE TIME THE EARLESS BODY OF PHILIP NOLAN WAS GIVEN a trespasser's burial on the Texas prairie, the balance of power in the New World had shifted again. In the flurry of international horse-trading following the chaos and global upheavals of the French Revolution, Spain lost possession of Louisiana, ceding the territory back to France in 1800. Thus, its old international enemy was once more adjacent to Texas, not a good thing, though all in all a better prospect for New Spain than being neighbors with the alarming new United States, which was throbbing with expansionist designs.

But that relatively tolerable situation abruptly changed three years later when Napoleon decided to sell Louisiana to the new American republic. Now New Spain and the United States faced each other directly across a fuzzy boundary. Nobody knew, or at least nobody cared to agree on, the exact extent of the Louisiana Purchase. In President Jefferson's opinion, Louisiana stretched west to the Rio Grande, engulfing all of what had historically been understood as Texas. To Spain, this was absurd. It maintained that Louisiana ended far to the east, near Texas's abandoned provincial capital of Los Adaes, across the Arroyo Hondo from Natchitoches. The lack of any agreed-upon border between New Spain and the United States enhanced the possibility of war and guaranteed the existence of smuggling, spying, and wild adventurism. "God keep us from their hands," a Spanish official wrote about the U.S. government soon after the Louisiana Purchase, calling it "the most ambitious, restless, unsteady, caviling and meddlesome government on earth."

During a rare spell of productive diplomacy, Wilkinson, who was now the commander of U.S. troops in Louisiana, brokered an unofficial truce with the Spanish governor of Nuevo León, Simón de Herrera, and brought into being something called the Neutral Ground, a strip of land roughly between the Sabine and the Arroyo Hondo. It was a zone where American Louisiana and Spanish Texas could abut each other for the time being without the necessity of either nation having to draw a clear line in the dirt. The Neutral Ground was created just in time, because ever since the Philip Nolan adventure, Spain had been preparing for war with the United States, strengthening its habitually neglected East Texas presidios against an invasion it considered almost inevitable.

The threats from the United States were just ambiguous enough to create alarm without quite provoking war. In 1806, Spanish forces turned back an expedition that Jefferson had sent to explore the headwaters of the Red River, which, according to America's understanding of reality, were contained within its new Louisiana possessions. That same year, members of an expedition led by Zebulon Pike were arrested in Colorado, imprisoned briefly in Chihuahua, and then escorted across Texas back to Natchitoches on the U.S. side of the Neutral Ground. American officials could properly claim that these were scientific and geographic expeditions, but Spain had no interest in parsing the distinction between drawing maps to enhance knowledge and drawing them to facilitate conquest. Spain knew filibusters when it saw them. What it faced now were only recent iterations of the semi-sanctioned adventurers like Hernán Cortés who had made possible their country's imprint on the continent in the first place. This time it was Spain's turn to absorb the shock.

NOW IT WAS 1813, AND A YOUNG LIEUTENANT IN THE SPANISH royalist army had just set foot in Texas for the first time. Antonio López de Santa Anna was only nineteen but had already fought in a number of battles and skirmishes against defiant Indian tribes—and been shot through the left hand by a Chichimec arrow. He had also helped put down rebellious Mexicans inflamed by the desire to free themselves from imperial Spanish rule, and been commended for his courage and initiative. Santa Anna was lean, dark haired, and light skinned—a criollo, born in Mexico from unalloyed Spanish blood. He was the son of middle-class parents in Xalapa, a town of flowery splendor in the tropical highlands above the miasmic port city of Veracruz. His character would grow more variegated with age, but even in his youth he was both disciplined and insubordinate, strategic and heedless, decadent and devoted.

He was in Texas with the army of General Joaquín de Arredondo, a headstrong and ruthlessly efficient commanding officer whose tactics Santa Anna would remember and adopt two decades later when he was president of Mexico and his country was under another threat from its troublesome northern province. The insurrection facing Arredondo had begun several years earlier, on September 16, 1810, when a rural priest named Father Miguel Hidalgo y Costilla, inspired by the success of the American and French Revolutions, aggrieved by New Spain's racial and class oppression against its Indian and mestizo populations, and driven by his own boiling temperament, had stirred up a bloody insurrectionist whirlwind.

The whirlwind began in the Bajío region of north-central Mexico and eventually swept north. The revolutionaries were an uneasy mixture of desperate campesinos eager to pull down the scaffolding of Mexican society and highborn criollos protecting their interests from a distant Spain that was itself in mortal confusion, at war with the French yet again and its new king, Fernando VII, a prisoner of Napoleon. Texas was far from the center of the conflagration, but it was, inevitably, decisive ground. Its position on the border with the United States meant that if it did not hold firm against the revolutionaries from the south, it would provide an irresistible climate of destabilization for its meddlesome neighbor on the other side of the Neutral Ground.

At the time of Hidalgo's revolution, the governor of Texas was Manuel María de Salcedo. Salcedo was Spanish born, in his early thirties, the son of the last Spanish governor of Louisiana and the nephew of the commandant general of the Interior Provinces. He was an energetic administrator whose main priority was to make sure the Texas frontier would not be overwhelmed by the United States. He was also—no surprise, given his pedigree—a stalwart royalist. He acted vigorously when word came of Hidalgo's revolt, tightening defenses, prohibiting travel and private mail, declaring martial law. But the revolutionary fever had come on too fast. A rebellious junta, led by a captain named Juan Bautista de las Casas, rose up in San Antonio de Béxar, arrested Salcedo and his fellow governor Herrera, and sent them south of the Rio Grande in chains. That was in January 1811. But less than a year later, Salcedo was back in San Antonio and restored to office. The junta that had expelled him had been deposed by royalist sympathizers. Casas and the other main leaders of the revolt had been captured and killed, and Hidalgo's head was hanging on display in an iron cage in Guanajuato.

But even with Hidalgo dead, the revolution still simmered, and there was a jittery expectation that the United States would meddle in it one way or another. José Bernardo Gutiérrez de Lara was one of the people who took it upon himself to ensure that outcome. A wealthy merchant from the small town of Revila below the Rio Grande, he led a party that made its stealthy way across the breadth of Texas in the summer and fall of 1811, narrowly missing being captured by Salcedo's royalist troops. When he emerged on the American side of the Neutral Ground, Gutiérrez's well-spoken, businesslike manner appealed to the American officials he encountered, who were chummily concerned about the out-of-control Mexican Revolution "assuming a proper direction."

He was sent on to Tennessee and then to Washington, where he conferred with various high-ranking officials, including Secretary of State James Monroe, about what kind of role it would be seemly for the United States to play in Gutiérrez's proposed liberation of Texas from the tyranny of royalist Spain. He was unwilling to go along with a U.S. proposal to send an army into Texas to enforce its claim that the Louisiana Purchase extended to the Rio Grande, but by the summer of 1812 he was back in Louisiana, industriously recruiting a filibustering force made up of shades-of-gray characters from the Neutral Ground and high-minded American idealists. ("Behold the empire of Mexico," declared a Nashville newspaper, "a celestial region whose valiant sons are now struggling for their independence as we struggled for ours thirty years ago.")

The degree to which Gutiérrez's enterprise was smiled on by the U.S. government can be gauged by a letter sent by William Shaler, an American special agent stationed in Louisiana, to Monroe: "The volunteer expedition from the most insignificant beginning is growing into an irresistible torrent that will sweep the crazy remains of Spanish Government from the Interior Provinces and open Mexico to the political influence of the United States and to the talents and enterprise of our citizens."

Joining Gutiérrez at the head of the expedition was Augustus Magee, an ambitious West Point graduate who resigned his commission in the army for the opportunity to invade Texas. He recruited sixty men to join him, some of them border ruffians from the Neutral Ground. Magee led the self-proclaimed Republican Army of the North across the Sabine River in Texas. The key town of Nacogdoches surrendered to them without a shot being fired, and the emboldened filibusters—joined now by Gutiérrez—marched on to La Bahía. That settlement was located in South Texas on the banks of the San Antonio River about forty miles upstream from the Gulf. A mission and an imposing stone presidio there were legacies of the Spanish imperative to protect Texas from the French threat. It was a crucial location, since it guarded the main north-south road in Texas and—being near the coast—had the potential to check any invasion coming from the sea.

The strategic importance of La Bahía was not lost on Salcedo and Herrera, who rode out from San Antonio and promptly besieged the invaders in the presidio with a force of over a thousand men. The siege lasted almost four months. At some point in its waning weeks, Augustus Magee got sick and died. It is unknown whether he lived to take part in the fight against an all-out Spanish assault, which failed to carry the fort and ended up sending Salcedo and Herrera and their depleted forces back to San Antonio de Béxar.

The filibusters, emboldened by their victory at La Bahía, set off in pursuit. They were determined to take the capital. Salcedo's army met them a few miles southeast of San Antonio on Rosillo Creek, but they were overwhelmed in a brief, brutal battle by the invading forces. The Republican Army of the North by now numbered six hundred to nine hundred men. It represented an inevitably volatile mix of interests: American dreamers, schemers, and adventurers; native Mexicans determined to overthrow Spanish rule in Texas without, in the process, accidentally turning over the province to the United States; deserters from Salcedo's royalist army; and perhaps a hundred Indian allies from a half-dozen tribes, each continually factoring where its interests lay.

Gutiérrez and Samuel Kemper, who had taken over American leadership from the dead Augustus Magee, led the army into San Antonio and forced the defeated Salcedo to unconditionally surrender the capital of Texas. Gutiérrez had promised Shaler that the "cheering beams of the sun of Liberty," which his army would bring to Texas, would dispel "the dark myst of ignorance, slavery and corruption." But dark mists have a way of lingering, especially in the middle of a bitter partisan war like the one that Gutiérrez and his confederates had orchestrated. He put Salcedo and Herrera and a dozen other royalist officers on trial for treason and, when they were convicted, sent them under guard on the road to La Bahía. In the agreement he had worked out with Kemper and the other Americans, the royalists' lives were to be spared and they would be banished from New Spain. But he entrusted the safety of the prisoners to a man named Delgado, who claimed that Salcedo had ordered the death of his father and brother and then dragged their heads through the streets. The prisoners never made it to La Bahía. They were murdered en route, their throats cut, Salcedo's tongue cut out, their bodies left unburied.

The brutal executions deepened the growing divide between the American contingent, which saw itself as generously sweeping into Texas to liberate it from Spain, and their Mexican comrades—many of whom, like Delgado, had deep, complex roots in the province and ancient scores to settle. Almost as soon as the Republican Army of the North's green banner was raised over San Antonio and independence declared for the new Republic of Texas, the coalition was in jeopardy. Gutiérrez did not trust the Americans to be a part of his new government, and many of them rode home just as many others—having read of a fabulous conquest that would "rank among the most extraordinary expeditions ever undertaken, that of Cortez not excepted"—surged west from the Neutral Ground into Texas. In June, the filibusters held their army together long enough to repel a royalist force at a brief battle near Alazán Creek, near the western edge of San Antonio. But the brand-new Republic of Texas soon deteriorated into a fractious government at cross-purposes with itself, with the Mexicans and Americans distrusting each other's revolutionary motives and everyone losing confidence in Gutiérrez. Feeling betrayed by his former U.S. sponsors and withdrawing into moody isolation—his "whole time," according to one American correspondent, was "employed in lolling on his sofa and catching flies"—he was soon forced to resign and endure a friendless retreat back across the Sabine to the United States.

SUCH WAS THE SITUATION IN TEXAS WHEN THE YOUNG SANTA
Anna arrived as a member of Arredondo's avenging army. History has forever entwined Santa Anna's name with that of the Battle of the Alamo, an event that in 1813 was still almost a quarter century in the future. The Alamo has loomed so enormously large in the imagination of Texans that it has crowded out the memory of other, bloodier conflicts that for one reason or another do not rise to nearly its level of mythic resonance. Still, the Alamo was a smaller battle than those that took place during the Green Flag invasion of Gutiérrez and Magee—smaller than Salcedo's assault of La Bahía and the clashes that took place on Rosillo and Alazán Creeks. And then, on an unbearably hot August day in 1813, there was the Battle of Medina, where the forces of the presumptive Republic of Texas—minus now both Gutiérrez and Magee—were destroyed by Arredondo's army.

Years after the battle, travelers along the road from Béxar to Laredo were still encountering the unburied bones, scattered for miles throughout the thick oak forest where the fighting took place, of the American and Mexican and Indian republicans who died that day. In our own time, those bones have long since moldered away, and the precise site of the battlefield has been lost. But it was somewhere between the Medina and Atascosa Rivers about twenty miles south of San Antonio.

Leading the filibusters that day instead of Gutiérrez was a Cuban-born revolutionary named José de Álvarez de Toledo. He was the new favorite of the American spymasters but warily regarded by the insurgent troops under his command, especially by the Tejanos, native Texans of Mexican descent, who considered him a foreigner with suspect motives.

On hearing that Arredondo's forces were marching toward San Antonio, Toledo led his army of 1,400 men south of the town to meet them. Toledo's plan was to ambush the royalists, but it ended up working out the opposite way. Arredondo's cavalry lured the rebels out of their fortified positions and toward the entrenched royalist army. Toledo's men were exhausted even before the enemy opened fire. They advanced through the heat and humidity of an August day in South Texas across boggy sand flats, hauling their cannons over the soft ground themselves because their depleted draft animals were no longer of use. The men too were at the edge of dehydration. Before the battle began, they had already abandoned most of their artillery.

The tired and thirst-crazed, fractious and undisciplined army that faced Arredondo's artillery fought well enough that for four hours or so it seemed as if the would-be liberators of Texas would have a chance of carrying the field. But then their luck turned, their lines broke, and the royalist cavalry rode them down as they fled in desperation back in the direction of San Antonio. Most of them never made it. Those who were not cut down by cannon fire were shot or lanced. Their bodies were left to rot on the prairie or cut apart and hung from tree limbs.

Arredondo's reprisal against the citizens who had harbored the rebels was equally brutal. Though it is not true that Dolorosa Street, which still runs through downtown San Antonio, got its sorrowful-sounding Spanish name in the aftermath of the Medina battle (it was a street name as early as 1778), there is a poetic tradition that insists upon it. And it was certainly true that the suppression of the upstart republic cast a dolorous shadow over the town and over its history. Hundreds of suspected republicans or collaborators were executed, some of their heads cut off and displayed in the plazas. Women who had not joined the refugees streaming east out of Béxar toward the Sabine were separated from their terrified and hungry children and forced to cook for Arredondo's occupying troops.

Santa Anna saw and no doubt participated in this decisive and merciless extirpation of a rebellion. In the future, he would prove to have no qualms about summarily executing men he considered traitors or lawless adventurers acting as land pirates. And he had fought well in the Battle of Medina, being cited, along with other officers, in Arredondo's report for "great bravery." He stayed on in Texas with the army for almost a year, time enough for the slippery side of his nature to make an early appearance. To cover a heavy gambling debt, he audaciously forged General Arredondo's name in order to withdraw money from the army payroll. The crime was quickly discovered, but Santa Anna apparently deployed enough charm to avoid being stripped of his rank or sent to jail. He did have to sell almost everything he owned to repay the debt, including his sword, but the resilient Antonio López de Santa Anna would find another sword soon enough.

— 8 —

GOD SPEED YE

THE DESTRUCTION OF THE REPUBLICAN REBELS AT THE
Medina turned out to be only a passing triumph. Arredondo's
terrorizing tactics drove almost half the Spanish-speaking
population out of Texas, and when he and his army left after
only a few weeks, the province reverted to its usual vulnerable
and neglected condition. Governor Antonio María Martínez,
who took office in Béxar a few years later and would turn out to be the last
governor of Spanish Texas, watched in alarm as the region "advanced at an
amazing rate toward ruin and destruction."

Meanwhile, across the Sabine in the tempestuous U.S. borderlands,
the enthusiasm for vainglorious expeditions to seize Texas was still stirring, kept alive in part by the patriotic frenzy brought on by the War of 1812
against Great Britain. Despite being rejected by his Green Flag comrades,
Gutiérrez was considering a return engagement. Toledo, who had fled on
horseback from the Medina battlefield and managed to reach the safety of
Natchitoches without being captured by Arredondo's cavalry, briefly embroiled himself in an abortive plot to retake Nacogdoches, and Samuel
Kemper—who also survived Medina—might have joined him if he hadn't
died of measles. Over the next few years, one grand filibustering initiative
after another failed to catch fire. They had names like the Committee to

Free Mexico, the New Orleans Association, the Mexican Patriotic Army, the Friends of Mexican Emancipation, the Provisional Government of the Free Men of the Interior Provinces of Mexico, and, most winningly, the Society for the Cultivation of the Vine and Olive.

This last organization referred not to an American scheme but to a French one, a colony planted on the Trinity River in 1818. During its brief existence and in its romantic afterlife in Gallic memory, the colony was called Champ d'Asile (Field of Asylum). It purported to be a bucolic agricultural community, but it was more likely a French version of the American incursions that had been prompted by the ongoing Mexican struggle for independence unleashed by Hidalgo. Many of the soi-disant olive and vine cultivators just happened, suspiciously enough, to be tough veterans of Napoleon's Peninsular War, and their focus seemed to be less on planting crops than on building a fortress, manufacturing uniforms, and capturing wild horses to use as cavalry mounts. But a French colony in Texas brought back bad memories for the Spanish, and the United States likewise had no patience for a meddling foreign power in its disputed territory with Spain.

Nevertheless, remembered two of the settlers who wrote a history of the colony published in 1819, "We enjoyed the greatest tranquility. Deep peace surrounded us, calm and satisfaction reigned in all hearts. Our camp was sacred ground, where the golden age was to be born again. . . . The echoes of Texas resounded also with our songs; love and glory were celebrated. And the God of Wine—that conqueror of the Indies—was not forgotten."

In the end, the colonists packed up their wine, left Champ d'Asile, and sailed away from Texas before their deep peace could be shattered by the hard reality of a Spanish attack. But nostalgia for this imagined paradise on the Trinity lingered on in the French imagination and would be remembered decades later when France became the first European nation to recognize the Republic of Texas. It also produced what was likely the first novel ever set in Texas, a wistful love story called *L'Heroine du Texas*, published in Paris in 1819.

The next would-be Texas liberator of note was an ambitious debt-ridden Tennessean named James Long. In 1819, when he decided to try to accomplish what the Gutiérrez-Magee expedition had failed to do, he was twenty-six. He was a physician, an emblematic specimen of a certain kind of blustery nineteenth-century doctor equally at home with war and agitation as with healing. He served in Andrew Jackson's army during the War of 1812 and may have been present at the Battle of New Orleans. Afterward, he met his wife, Jane, over a game of backgammon at a plantation near Natchez, Mississippi. Jane was the niece of none other than James Wilkinson, which might explain why she found her new husband and his empire-shattering schemes such a perfect fit for her own adventurous temperament.

"Our intention," wrote one of the hundred or so men Long recruited for his expedition, "is to take the country, make an offer of it to the United States, and to be formed into a state or states." Such plainspoken declarations were rare. The rationale for Long's venture was more likely to be wrapped in the noble rhetoric that Americans had deployed to give an impression of common cause with the Mexican fight for liberation from Spain. A typical example was the send-off Long received from a Mississippi newspaper: "God speed ye, [and] may no difficulties or obstacles oppose you—until the flag of liberty waves triumphant over the prostituted insignia of time-serving priests and the broken truncheons of substitute kings."

Long's enterprise was lent momentum by the Adams-Onís Treaty of 1819, the result of negotiations between U.S. Secretary of State John Quincy Adams and Luis de Onís y Gonzales, the Spanish minister to the United States. The treaty ended, at least on paper, the lingering border dispute between the United States and Spain. The old Neutral Ground, which had operated as a demilitarized zone between the two countries, was gone from the map, replaced by a fixed border. The western boundary of the United States was now the Sabine River. The land across the river was officially recognized as Spanish Texas.

But to certain sorts of Americans with westward dreams, the idea of agreeing to place the border at the Sabine rather than much farther west at the Rio Grande meant surrender. It meant giving up Texas to Spain, a declining European power that was fast losing its grasp on a Mexican population that had risen up against it. Arredondo had managed to stop Gutiérrez and Magee and keep Texas in Spanish control, but the province was still vulnerable, and still rich (it was thought) in mineral wealth, and still, in the opinion of Long, a country "beyond description, beautiful, fertile, well watered and healthy."

Such a dreamy characterization might not have applied to the arid western regions of the province, but for people like Long, Texas meant mostly East Texas, the fertile crescent of arable deep-soiled land, rich river bottoms, and coastal prairies extending roughly from San Antonio de Béxar to Nacogdoches, from the Colorado River to the Sabine. The fact that Spain had neglected this paradise, had failed to people it and protect it, to cultivate it and mine it, was an affront almost against nature itself. And the fact that the United States was already locked in a struggle over the expansion of slavery, with eleven free states tipping the balance against ten slave states at the time of Long's invasion, meant that Texas offered a potentially ripe opportunity to extend the dominion of human bondage.

Long and his men left Natchez for Texas in June 1819. Riding with him, eager to recapture the republic that had slipped through his hands six years earlier, was Gutiérrez. Jane Long, though determined to be an active participant in the enterprise, was pregnant with her second child and so for now had to stay home and settle for designing a flag for her husband to carry. It featured red and white stripes and one big white star, an icon that would reappear decades later in the Lone Star flag of Texas. Long unfurled his wife's flag after he reached Nacogdoches and occupied the easternmost Texas settlement without hostilities. Nacogdoches was hardly in a condition to offer much resistance. It had been almost abandoned after Arredondo's purge of suspected rebels in the wake of the Green Flag uprising. Now there were only a few scattered families, a church, and a substantial two-story stone building that had been built as a trading warehouse forty years before and had fallen into use as a jail and de facto government headquarters.

From this nearly empty place, four hundred miles from Béxar and two hundred and fifty miles from La Bahía, the only two Spanish settlements in Texas that could still be thought of as population centers, Long declared yet another new republic, with himself as president of its Supreme Council and Gutiérrez as vice president. On a printing press they had hauled along, they published a short-lived newspaper called the Texas Republican, which reported all the aspirational plans of the new country: industry in the form of sawmills and grist mills, and a national school and a board of trustees to run it.

There was only one problem: the rest of Texas. Though Long's overconfidence led him to expect, as one of his officers expressed it, "nothing . . . [but] tame submission" as he and his men marched through the province, Spain intended a fight. Texas was, as usual, chronically underpopulated and undergarrisoned, still a wilderness outpost of New Spain whose survival was constantly threatened by attacks from Comanches and other Indians. But Governor Martínez managed to scrape together an army of six hundred to seven hundred men under the command of Colonel Juan Ignacio Pérez and send it off to meet the invading forces, which Long—as the inexperienced commander in chief of his new republic—had dispersed at river crossings throughout East Texas.

Long, meanwhile, sent himself off on a diplomatic mission to Galveston, possibly the same narrow, weather-beaten island facing the Gulf of Mexico that Cabeza de Vaca and his companions had called Malhado when they washed up there in 1528. Galveston had not changed much since then, but it now had a few year-round residents in addition to the Karankawas who paddled across from the mainland in their canoes during the winter fishing season. It had become the base of Jean Lafitte, who, together with his older brother Pierre, had long been involved in every sort of profiteering scheme imaginable along the Gulf coast. The brothers ran a shakily sanctioned privateering business that merged easily enough into piracy, and they were also robustly enterprising smugglers, especially of slaves. A U.S. law that went into effect in 1808 banned the importation of slaves, but if Africans just happened to be found already in the country, they could be seized and turned over to the authorities, who would sell them at a sheriff's auction, with half the profits going to the person who had "discovered" them. In effect, the Lafittes ran a slave-laundering business out of Galveston, receiving their human cargo at the island and selling them in Spanish Texas to buyers who would then smuggle them to American Louisiana, where they would be sold again, with the Lafittes getting a second payday in the form of a kickback.

Aware that Lafitte was in strategic maritime control of Texas through his Galveston base, Long offered him a governorship in his brand-new Texas Republic, with the power to commission privateers of his own. Lafitte for his part was happy to receive any honorifics Long sent his way and equally happy to report on Long's activities to the Spanish authorities, who were determined to drive him out of Texas. In the end, Lafitte's double-crossing wasn't crucial, because Pérez's army quickly routed the spread-out forces of the filibusters. It's unclear whether Long made it to Galveston before having to turn around and head back to Nacogdoches to try to take command of his men. By the time he got there, almost all of them had fled across the Sabine back to Louisiana.

Long barely made it out of Texas without being captured by Pérez. The latest great war of conquest, characterized by one skeptic as a "trifling expedition," had reached its trifling end. But James Long didn't accept that conclusion. Even though his invasion had been a fiasco, even though he was now under intense scrutiny from U.S. officials concerned about a reprise of his unlawful invasion of a nation with which it was supposed to be at peace, and even though he was so broke that he had to sell his horse, bridle, and saddle to make a payment on his debts, Long had the resiliency—and somehow still the credibility—to make another attempt.

In the spring of 1820 he and Jane—who had just lost her second daughter, Rebecca, in infancy—arrived at Bolivar, a narrow peninsula that faced the eastern point of Galveston Island across the ocean pass that led into Galveston Bay. Long had come to seek Jean Lafitte's assistance in the second phase of his attempt to seize Texas. But Lafitte's mind was elsewhere. Accused by the United States of piracy—a capital offense—he and his brother had cut a deal to vacate their Galveston headquarters and relocate beyond American jurisdiction. By the time the Longs arrived, Lafitte had already dismantled the rough but commodious two-story house he had built for himself—known as the Maison Rouge—and his men were busy tearing down or burning their plank shanties and getting ready to embark for friendlier waters. Nevertheless, the distracted pirate invited the Longs to dinner on one of his ships. Many years later, Mrs. Long gave an account of the evening to a friend, who colorfully recalled that Jane found Lafitte not to be, as her imagination had foreseen, "an uncouth giant, ferocious in temper, and in manners as rough and boisterous as the winds and waves he dealt with." Though Jane was struck by his physical presence, in particular his fierce black eyes, she thought him to be a rather boring pirate, politely uncommunicative and "altogether unjocular."

Before Lafitte sailed away in early May, the Longs traveled to New Orleans, where James managed to raise fifty recruits for his second attempt to seize Texas. In June he returned to Bolivar Point, where he and his men, using lumber left behind by Lafitte, built a fort guarding the pass to Galveston Bay. In Long's mind, the Texas republic he had declared when he conquered Nacogdoches was still very much a live entity, and he was still the president of its Supreme Council and its chief policy maker. Under his leadership, the government passed an ad valorem tariff, created a court of admiralty, named a collector of revenues, and established a code of military law that, among other things, outlawed profanity. The presumptive nation also went to war, with Long leading a raid across Galveston Bay to attack a Karankawa village on the mainland, which resulted in thirty or forty dead Indians, among them women and children. True to form, the grandiose president of his republic of fifty people passed out citations and acted as if the grubby fight had been the Battle of Agincourt, an action "unexampled in the annals of war."

Jane arrived back at Bolivar several months later, along with her four-year-old daughter and a young female slave named Kian. In September of the next year, 1821, Jane and her husband were parted again, this time forever, when Long sailed off with his little army to seize La Bahía, which he believed, or perhaps hoped, was still in royalist hands. While he was organizing his government on Bolivar, the geopolitical ground had shifted beneath him. Seven months earlier, Agustín de Iturbide, the royalist military commander, had signed an agreement with Vicente Guerrero, who commanded the largest rebel army fighting against Spain. The agreement, called the Plan of Iguala, created a workable alliance between the insurrectionists, who had been fighting to free Mexico from Spanish rule, and the loyalist forces, who had grown disenchanted when King Ferdinand, restored to the throne in 1814 after six years of French imprisonment, rejected the liberal constitution that

JANE LONG

shared the filibustering temperament of her doomed husband, James. As a young widow, her "masculine vigor," combined with her "wholly feminine" demeanor, strongly appealed to imperial-minded admirers like Mirabeau Lamar and Sam Houston.

had been created in his absence. When the Treaty of Córdoba was signed in August, it was official: Mexico—with its Texas province—was an independent country. Three centuries of Spanish rule, from the conquest of Tenochtitlan to the last attempts to put out the fires of Hidalgo's revolution, were over.

James Long was aware of the Plan of Iguala when he set out for La Bahía, and no doubt his plans for maintaining his independent nation were complicated by it. He and his men promptly seized the presidio without much of a fight. He later declared to Governor Martínez—who, along with almost everybody else in Texas, had pledged himself by that time to the new Mexican nation—that false information "gave me the unfortunate idea to take the place by force, which I did."

But Martínez appears to have taken a once-a-filibuster, always-a-filibuster attitude toward James Long. After Pérez's troops attacked La Bahía and forced Long's surrender, Long and his men were arrested and sent to prison in Monterrey. They were released after eight months, and Long was granted a much-sought-after audience with Iturbide, but before it could come to pass, he was accidentally—or maybe on purpose—shot dead by a sentry in Mexico City in April 1822.

It was a long lonely time—almost a year—before Jane learned of her husband's death. After he set off to conquer La Bahía, she and their surviving daughter, Ann, remained at Bolivar with Kian and the several dozen men who had been left behind to garrison the fort. After no news from Long for a month or so, his followers began to drift away. Jane refused to go—"My husband left me here and I shall stay until he returns," she reportedly declared—and spent the bitter winter of 1821–1822 shivering with Kian and Ann inside the fort, staring nervously at the Karankawa campfires across the bay.

She gave birth to a daughter named Mary James one freezing December night while Kian was delirious and half dead with fever. In Texas lore, Jane

Long ended up transformed into as much a shining Texas emblem as the Lone Star flag that she sort of invented: the steadfast twenty-four-year-old woman who still believed that her husband would return and that together they would yet conquer Texas; who ran a red flannel petticoat up the flagpole and fired off a cannon to scare off the Karankawas and then delivered a baby by herself when the enslaved Kian was out of commission. When I was growing up, she was still called the "Mother of Texas," though the title rested on the dual misconception that her daughter was the first Anglo baby born in Texas (now thought not to be the case), and that the sole fact of her being a white woman entitled her to seize a title denied to the other mothers who had been on the scene in Texas for perhaps fifteen thousand years before her. But by any measure, the niece of James Wilkinson was a resolute and remarkable woman who deserves her place in not just Texas lore but also Texas history. Although Mary James died at the age of two, Jane lived to be eighty-two, having paid off her husband's considerable debts and become a wealthy pipe-smoking plantation owner in Fort Bend County. When she was thirty, she made quite an impression on J. C. Clopper, a besotted visitor from Cincinnati, who observed that she had "the energies of masculine vigor yet moving with a grace that is truly and wholly feminine . . . her features are regular—her aspect smiling—her eyes sparking her tongue not too pliant for a female being."

She was drawn to bold men with big strategic dreams, and they to her. Among her clients and admirers, after she opened a boardinghouse in the coastal town of Brazoria in 1832, were Sam Houston and Mirabeau Buonaparte Lamar. Both men were to become presidents of the Republic of Texas, though a different and more consequential republic than the one her late husband had proclaimed. Of the two, Lamar, who had serious poetic ambitions, appears to have been the more deeply smitten. "Oh, brighter than that planet, love," he wrote in a poem titled "Bonnie Jane," "Thy face appears to me; / But when shall I behold its light, / Through bridal drapery?"

Lamar might have been as much in love with Jane Long's legend as with her face, but if so he would have been merely in step with the unbridled mythmaking that was already forming the core of the Texas identity.

9

THE TEXAS DREAM

JUST WHEN IT SEEMED THAT MOSES AUSTIN'S LONG RUN of bad luck was about to turn, a panther leapt out of a tree and grabbed him in its claws. Austin and an enslaved man named Richmond, who had traveled with him to Texas, were camped somewhere along the Trinity River on their way back home to U.S. territory. They had just been robbed along the Camino Real—the road that ran eastward from San Antonio to Natchitoches—by a man who had ingratiated himself into their company and then made off with their horses and all their food and supplies. The panther attacked on a cold January night in 1821 while Austin shivered on the ground beneath a buffalo robe. The startled man sprang to his feet, threw off the robe, and shouted and gesticulated enough to drive the panther away. Austin didn't record whether he was hurt, or how badly, but by the time he and Richmond reached a settler's cabin on the Louisiana side of the Sabine a week or so later, they were both half dead. They had had nothing to eat except what they could scavenge by hand, been forced to cross one rain-swollen river after another on improvised rafts, and fallen ill with pneumonia. Richmond, who was the property of Moses Austin's son Stephen, was left in Louisiana until he could regain his health, after which time his labor was to be leased out at twelve dollars a month to a local resident.

Moses Austin was not young. He was almost sixty when he made his painful way home to Missouri and arrived, in the words of his distressed wife, Maria, "but a shadow of his former self." But he had accomplished something significant in Texas, and even in his weakened state he was filled with hope and determined not to fall behind in his plans or deeper into debt than he already was. A man of keen self-regard and colossal ambitions, in 1798 he had moved his family in a hazardous journey from the settled precincts of Virginia to eastern Missouri, which was then part of Spanish Louisiana. "Can any thing be more Absurd than the Conduct of man," he wrote of himself and the throngs of fellow pilgrims who were venturing west, "here is hundreds Travelling hundreds of Miles, they Know not for what Nor Whither."

But Austin knew both what and whither. Just as he would later do in Texas, he applied to the Spanish government for a grant of land, took an oath of allegiance as a Spanish subject, and went to work developing a prosperous lead mine. In a little over ten years, he had assets of $190,000, lived in a mansion that he called Durham Hall, and was sufficiently confident of his own grand legacy that he could lecture his son Stephen, then only eleven years old, about the necessity to "lay the foundation for your future greatness in life."

But his own foundation began to break apart. A decline in lead prices, failed investments, mounting liabilities, and the financial panic of 1819 reduced the once-baronial Austin to a bankrupt debtor. The low point came when the sheriff arrived to serve a writ and Austin wouldn't let him inside, even when, in Austin's words, the sheriff "swore he would force his way into my house by Brakeing Down my door with an ax."

Moses Austin had a tempestuous personality but a resilient spirit, and it wasn't long before he was making inventive plans to get himself out of debt and to once again occupy a big place in the world. Like many others before him, from Coronado to James Long, he imagined that Texas was the place where his destiny slumbered. As his debts deepened, he avidly followed the news of Long's adventures. But there was a crucial difference between Moses Austin and James Long. For all the bravado in his character, Austin was at heart a businessman, not a filibuster. Unlike Long, he did not regard the Adams-Onís Treaty as an evil bargain, one that demanded an American invasion to take by force the land that the United States had surrendered at the negotiating table. The treaty might just as well offer a different opportunity. With the contentious border issues that had bedeviled the relationship between the United States and Spain at an end, Spain had clear title to Texas. A grant of land, if he could somehow acquire one from the Spanish authorities, would be secure by law.

Austin arrived in San Antonio de Béxar in November 1820, after Pérez's army had driven Long's first expedition back to Louisiana. He represented himself to Governor Martínez as a colonizer, not a conqueror. He displayed the old Spanish passport that had been issued to him when he moved to Missouri to begin his lead-mining business, and he brought with him a history of working uncomplainingly under Spanish jurisdiction. Martínez was not impressed. He dismissed Austin's idea of settling American families in Spanish Texas, and he dismissed Austin himself, ordering him out of San Antonio. But startlingly good fortune intervened in the form of an old acquaintance, the Baron de Bastrop, a roving Dutch aristocrat (or at least he styled himself as one) whom Austin had met years before in New Orleans and who was now, improbably, an influential citizen of San Antonio. With Bastrop's support, Austin was able to pitch his idea to the governor again, and this time Martínez was sympathetic. Although he was under orders from his superiors in Mexico not to admit any Americans into Texas, Martínez knew that Long's incursion and the others that had preceded it were the direct result of the impression that Texas was an unsettled, empty land, always at the risk of being seized away. Since Spain had failed to populate Texas itself, maybe it wasn't such a bad idea to invite in the sort of Americans that Moses Austin promised to bring—stable families who would pledge loyalty to the beleaguered Spanish Crown, and who would not be invaders but willing citizens of an adopted country.

With the promise of a contract and a new start in life, Austin left San Antonio at once to begin recruiting his three hundred families and to round up thirty men who could immediately begin building his settlement on land he had chosen near the mouth of the Colorado River, a town that would be called Austina and that he confidently predicted would, in only a few short years, be the rival of New Orleans.

But the thriving city of Austina never happened. The perilous trip back to Missouri from Texas—in which the panther attack on the banks of the Trinity was only the start of his troubles—had broken Moses Austin's health, and his frantic efforts to settle his crushing debts and restore some liquidity to his finances ("I am . . . with out a Dollar to get a shirt washed") landed him on his deathbed in the summer of 1821.

"His fever has returned this day with great violence," Maria Austin wrote her son Stephen during the patriarch's last hours. "He breathes with much difficulty and seems in great distress boath in body and mind."

Much of what distressed Moses Austin's mind was the fate of his great Texas project, which held the promise of not only saving his family from immediate ruin but also seizing back the proud Austin name from the financial ignominy into which it had fallen. "He called me to his bed side," Maria went on in the same letter to tell Stephen, "and with much distress an difficulty of speech, beged me to tell you to take his place and if god in his wisdom thought best to disappoint him in the accomplishment of his wishes and plans formed for the benefit of his family, he prayed him to extend his goodness to you and eneable you to go on with the business in the same way he would have done had not sickness and oh dreadful to think of perhaps death, prevented him from accomplishing—"

So there it was, the dying request from imperious father to faithful son that changed the course of Texas history.

Stephen Fuller Austin at this time was twenty-seven. He had a slender frame and a quiet, temperate, studious manner—"a small, quite handsome gentleman," in the words of one acquaintance. He was susceptible to depression and privately believed he was as impetuous as his father. But it was the deliberate side of his nature that he showed to the world. His ambition, though less visible than Moses Austin's, was every bit as capacious, and his professional risk taking—as a mine operator himself and as a land speculator in Arkansas, among other pursuits—had left him broke and marooned in Louisiana. At the time Moses was blazing his trail to Texas, Stephen was walking a more cautious path. In New Orleans, he had found a newspaper job and begun studying law, hoping to gain enough financial security to begin paying off the family debts, both the extravagant ones his father was responsible for and those he had acquired on his own.

Much has been written about Stephen's reluctance to accept the burden of destiny his father placed on him, but perhaps too much. It's hard to imagine his entrepreneurial spirit remaining unstirred for long by the live prospect of creating a colonial empire and carving out a fortune. "I hope and pray you will Discharge your Doubts, as to the Enterprise," Moses urged in his last letter to his son, a month or so before he died, and "raise your Spirits times are changing a new chance presents itself nothing is now wanting but Concert and firmness."

In any case, Stephen must have discharged his doubts to some degree, because by the time he learned that Moses Austin was dead he was already on the way to Texas and already promoting his colonization plans in the newspapers. "I started on with a heavy heart," he wrote in his journal after hearing the news. A few days later, he forded the Sabine and entered Texas. He was accompanied by a small party of American citizens and by a Spanish delegation led by Erasmo Seguín, who was the alcalde of San Antonio, a position more or less equivalent to that of an American mayor. Seguín and his men had been sent to meet Moses Austin and accompany him to San

Antonio, where his grant could be confirmed. But when they realized he was dead, they escorted his son in his place.

The journal that Stephen Austin kept on this trip is alert and precise, full of the observations of a man who understands that his success hangs on reliable knowledge of the territory he is passing through. "The general face of the country," reads one representative passage, "from within 5 miles of the Sabine to Nacogdoches is gently rolling and very much resembles the Barrens of Kentucky, except that the growth of timber is larger and not so bushy—Black Jack and Black Hickory, Mulbery, is the principal timber, but it [is] all too low and scruby for Rails, or building except on the Creeks where the timber is very good and lofty—"

His party traveled southwest three hundred miles from the once thriving but now almost deserted hamlet of Nacogdoches to San Antonio. Sickness and misery and the fear of Indian attack were with them most of the way, and it was easy for members of the entourage to get lost on the grandly named but poorly defined Camino Real. Austin later described his first impressions of Texas: "It was a wild, howling, interminable solitude." But the more of it he saw, the more acclimated to it he became, and the more it spoke to him. He was heartened by the rolling prairies populated with buffalo, by rich soil and substantial rivers with clear, good-tasting water, by thick timber, and intricate tangles of low-growing vines studded with grapes that his future colonists could put to use making red wine.

On August 12, 1821, three men that Seguín had sent ahead to San Antonio came riding back at dawn to announce "the glorious news of the Independence of Mexico." Austin reported that the Spaniards—now officially Mexicans—who were traveling with him were overcome with joy, and the men who had ridden back from San Antonio brought with them a celebratory breakfast packed by their wives—"various Spanish dishes" that apparently represented Stephen Austin's first real encounter with Mexican food.

Later that morning, they entered San Antonio, the first settlement they had encountered in this strangely empty country since leaving Nacogdoches. Austin must have been anxious about the fate of his father's land concession, now that he was suddenly dealing with a Mexican government instead of a Spanish one, but Governor Martínez showed no hesitation in honoring the agreement, and he and Austin went to work addressing the specifics of the colony, such as where its boundaries would lie, and how much land each family who came to live there would receive.

After a week and a half in San Antonio, Austin and his party set out to explore the country his father had envisioned for his colony. They first rode southeast to La Bahía. A lonely garrison town in the best of times, it was in a state of ruin after the revolutionary battles that had taken place there between royalist armies and bellicose liberators like Gutiérrez and Long. The inhabitants were poor, had little in the way of furniture or possessions, and lived in peril of Indian attacks.

From La Bahía—or Labaddie, as Austin and the Anglo settlers who followed him would refer to it—the company wandered across the coastal prairies, encountering plentiful deer and wild mustangs and brackish waters teeming with alligators. They moved inland and eastward, following the Atascocito Road, the main Spanish trail leading out of La Bahía. Along the way, Austin never ceased to grade the quality of the soil, the abundance of the timber, the purity of the water. He found the land along the Colorado River to be "first rate," and when he came to the Brazos, another few days' travel farther east, he liked it even better. The soil was thick and black, the prairies crossed by clear-running streams that drained into the wide and seemingly navigable river that was a highway to the sea. On a high bluff above the Brazos, Austin envisioned "a most beautifull situation for a Town or settlement."

The site was in the very center of Austin's colony, and within a decade or so it would grow into a promising, thriving town of fifty or sixty buildings, with a ferry landing, a post office, a hotel, stores and taverns, and public squares with stalwart names like Commerce and Constitution. But today the aspiring capital city known as San Felipe de Austin is nothing much more than a lonesome state historic site, a detour off Interstate 10 between Houston and San Antonio. Burned to the ground in the panic that seized Texas after the fall of the Alamo in 1836, the town never recovered, leaving only a fading footprint on the bluff above the Brazos: a visitor's center, a replica log cabin, a well. Its most imposing current feature is a statue of Stephen Austin sitting on a massive granite block with his legs leisurely crossed, dressed in a frock coat and cravat and gazing firmly off into the distance.

It was not this impeccably dressed sage who made his way back to Natchitoches in the fall of 1821, but a young man still in his twenties, weary and bedraggled after months of reconnoitering in strange country, swimming across rivers, losing his way whenever a barely detectable trace disappeared entirely, or leading the party into towering canebrakes that squeezed out the light of the sun. And he had a colossal job ahead of him once he emerged. He had determined the future boundaries of his colony. It was a huge swath of Southeast Texas that ran all the way to the coast and encompassed the region's two greatest rivers—the Brazos and the Colorado—and all the prime farmland nurtured by them.

Austin had his colony, at least in theory, and there were plenty of cash-poor families from the United States eager to take advantage of an opportu-

STEPHEN AUSTIN
commissioned this painting of himself by British artist
William Howard in 1833. It depicts a frontiersman very much at home in the
"wild, howling, interminable solitude" of Texas.

nity to own land, even if it meant becoming a citizen in a foreign land. But he was still trapped in personal debt and had to scramble to find investors who could front him the money to buy a ship and supplies so that the first of his colonists could sail to Texas to begin building houses and planting crops. Austin headed quickly back to San Antonio, crossing the Sabine once more and leaving behind the United States for fifteen years.

Only a year after Moses Austin's death, Stephen was the empresario his father had dreamed of becoming. But it was a wildly uncertain role. Austin was overwhelmed by families clamoring to be part of the new enterprise ("it appears to be the General rage in every quarter to Move to Texas," wrote his brother-in-law and business partner James Bryan), and the first wave of colonists got lost and wandered up the Brazos while Austin anxiously searched for them on the Colorado. Far worse was the news that the bureaucracy in Mexico City had examined Austin's agreement with Governor Martínez and emerged with second thoughts. Without the supreme government's specific approval, the whole project would be invalid.

With his settlers already building homes and planting crops, Austin was desperate to secure a firm title to his colony. In the spring of 1822, he began a long journey on horseback to Mexico City. He was robbed along the way by Comanches, who left him his scalp but helped themselves to one of the most crucial possessions for a man about to lobby the Mexican government: his Spanish grammar book.

Austin hoped his time in the Mexican capital would be brief, but in the end he spent a year there. He found he was not alone in his ambitions. The city was buzzing with Americans who, like Austin, had come to petition the government for colonial grants for themselves or the consortiums they represented. Among them—always to be found stirring any potential cauldron of intrigue—was James Wilkinson.

During the first few weeks Austin was in Mexico City, the government was far too preoccupied to hear his cause, since it was in the process of remaking itself and proclaiming Iturbide, the head of the provisional junta that ruled the country, Emperor Augustín I. The Treaty of Córdoba decreed that an independent Mexico would be a constitutional monarchy, not a republic. Neither Ferdinand nor any of the other European nobles to whom the crown was offered would accept it, and so Iturbide, with a seemly show of reluctance, had allowed himself to be seated upon the golden throne of Mexico. Stephen Austin was in the cathedral for the coronation, and he wasted no time pledging his allegiance to the new empire. "This solemn act," he wrote to the emperor, "cuts me off from all protection or dependence on my former government—my property, my prospects, my future hopes of happiness, for myself and family, and for the families I have brought with me, are centered here. This is our adopted Nation."

Austin was still in the throes of culture shock when he wrote this. He was appalled by the stupefying poverty visible behind the face of what he sardonically called the "City Magnificent," and he was contemptuous of the Catholic clergy and the superstitious thralldom in which he believed it held the people. But his claim of loyalty to his new country was not just opportunistic rhetoric. He was sincere. As soon as he found a replacement for the grammar book the Comanches had stolen, he applied himself to the study of the Spanish language with furious concentration, and he made sure to befriend, and bribe when necessary, the powerful men in Mexico City who could help him confirm his Texas grant. In his spare time, aware that Mexico did not yet have a constitution for its constitutional monarchy, he took it upon himself to write one. I asked to see this document recently at the Briscoe Center for American History at the University of Texas. It was brought to my reading table, modestly filed away in one of the archival boxes containing Austin's papers. Staring at Austin's handwriting, I could almost feel the industrious beating of his heart, the ambition and presumption that lay beneath his patient demeanor. "We the people of the Mexican nation," it read, in bold language lifted from the founding document of the country he had just sworn to forsake, "having assumed those natural and imprescriptable rights which appertain to us as members of the great human family."

Before Austin's case for his land grant could be taken up, the Mexican government had to pass a bill defining its overall colonization policy—which it was slow in doing, mainly because the government was falling apart. Iturbide had nineteen members of congress arrested for treason, and later dissolved congress altogether and replaced it with a governing junta, and then with stunning rapidity the emperor himself was gone, on his way to a brief exile in Italy and then a firing squad upon his return to Mexico.

The man most responsible for his ouster was Santa Anna. In the years since serving with Arredondo in Texas, he had gone on to carve out a spectacular career for himself, first as a royalist hero hunting down Mexican rebels and then abruptly changing sides and becoming a revolutionary leader under Iturbide. He was also prominently present at the signing of the Treaty of Córdoba. Santa Anna, at twenty-nine, was barely a year younger than Stephen Austin, but more or less his opposite in temperament, all passion and impatience and undisguised ambition. Iturbide made him a brigadier general, but it wasn't long before Santa Anna developed a grievance against the emperor and a supposed distaste for autocratic rule, and engineered a revolt from his power base in Veracruz.

Austin looks more robust in this portrait, painted in New Orleans in 1836,
than he probably did in real life, at a time when he was beset with illness and with worry
about the precarious future of Texas.

Santa Anna spoiled Austin's plans, too, and not for the last time. With Iturbide out of power, the colonization law, which had finally been passed, was repealed, and Austin's land grant along with it. But after a month of creative lobbying, the empresario received the blessing of the new, interim government to establish his colony.

When he returned to Texas after a year away, the first of the families he had recruited—they would become known as the Old Three Hundred—were hard at work establishing themselves in the fertile lands between the Colorado and Brazos that were now, Austin promised, securely theirs. They were

Mexican citizens and had pledged to become Catholic, though no one in the colony could perform baptisms until the arrival several years later of a worldly Irish priest named Michael Muldoon, who wrote jaunty verse and hung out in grog shops and whose application of the sacrament was light-handed enough for the colonists to consider themselves "Muldoon Catholics." Following the example of their priest, they exempted themselves from any tortured application of their new faith.

Mexican law applied to the colonists, though Austin had to improvise some of the law himself, since he was operating far from the Mexican government, which still had no constitution. He organized his colony into districts, appointed alcaldes and other Spanish-sounding offices, and wrote civil and criminal codes that had echoes of both Mexican and American legal traditions.

When Mexico finally had a new constitution, in 1824, it was an aspirational document true to the liberal spirit of the age. The country was a federal republic called the United Mexican States, made up of nineteen semiautonomous units. Texas, though large in territory, was still thinly populated, so it remained attached to Coahuila. This was not necessarily the best of news, since the capital of the new state of Coahuila y Tejas was Saltillo, five hundred miles from San Felipe. Coahuila also had ten times the number of inhabitants as Texas. Underrepresentation in the new state government—for Austin and his colonists, and for the Tejanos in the frontier outposts of San Antonio, La Bahía, and elsewhere—was inevitable, and would be the cause of much turmoil to come.

But the formation of the state of Coahuila y Tejas also greatly benefited Austin and the other empresarios eager to bring Americans into Texas and to enrich themselves through the fees they charged to the colonists. (In Austin's case, that was twelve and a half cents an acre, and most families were granted a league of land, which was 4,428 acres.) In 1825 the new state passed a generous colonization law that opened the door to foreign immigration, providing that the new settlers arrived under a sanctioned agent of the Mexican government. In the land rush that followed, Austin applied for and ultimately received four more contracts, and other empresarios were clamoring to claim their places on a Texas map that was rapidly filling up.

Before it all fell apart in 1835, more than thirty empresarios attempted to bring settlers to Texas, though almost half of them failed to fulfill the terms of their contracts. Among those who succeeded was Martín De León. De León, who was just approaching his sixties, was one of the most renowned figures north of the Rio Grande when he filed for empresario status. The son of aristocratic *peninsulares*, he and his equally industrious wife, Patricia, had staked out a future in Texas, combining their fortunes to create a vast rancho along the same coastal plains that La Salle had once tried to claim for France. They founded the town of Victoria (named for Guadalupe Victoria, the newly elected president of the Mexican Republic), captured and tamed mustangs, and drove cattle all the way to New Orleans. De León's herds were so numerous that he was known as Capitán Vacas Muchas—"Captain of Many Cows."

Empresarios such as De León and Lorenzo de Zavala, a Mexican statesman, historian, linguist, newspaper owner, and political prisoner who would eventually become the vice president of the Republic of Texas, were on their way to becoming minority citizens in a land they had grown used to thinking of as Hispanic.

The balance of population, if not yet of power, was beginning to shift as more and more Anglo American settlers, under American empresarios who did not always share Austin's rigorous fealty to the Mexican government, began to stream into Texas. They built farms and plantations and towns and forts. Their habitations were architecturally distinct from the low-lying, flat-roofed, thick-walled buildings that lined the streets of old Spanish villages like San Antonio. They also, in the worried opinion of one Mexican official, "go about with their constitution in their pocket," never quite accepting that they had become foreign citizens in a foreign land.

Austin confided as much in his private correspondence. "Strangers to each other," he wrote, "to me, and to the laws and languages of the country, they come here with all the ideas of americans and expect to see and understand the laws they are governed by, and many very many of them have all the licentiousness and wild turbulence of frontiersmen."

Wild turbulence was what soon came to pass. It occurred in a colony founded by Haden Edwards, a Kentucky senator's son whose grant in Northeast Texas included the historically contentious community of Nacogdoches. Haden promptly got into a dispute with settlers who were already in the area. These included long-resident Tejanos, displaced Cherokee Indians, squatters from the Neutral Ground, and veterans of one stripe or another who had taken part in the filibustering conflicts of the previous decades and had lingered on in Texas. Edwards wanted them all to provide valid titles to the lands they were living on, documentation that wasn't easy to produce on the lawless fringes of one of Mexico's most neglected possessions. The empresario had a talent for ratcheting up tensions. He was hot tempered and grievance minded to begin with (traits he shared with his brother Benjamin), and with a huge, $50,000 investment riding on the success of his colony, he was inclined to precipitous action. The result was a bitter power struggle among the settlers that led José Antonio Saucedo, the political chief of San Antonio, to begin an investigation into Edwards's conduct, which resulted in him losing his grant and being formally expelled from Texas. Among the reasons cited by the alarmed Mexican authorities was that the empresario believed himself to be an "absolute Lord and Master."

He certainly believed himself, as his brother Benjamin wrote, to be the victim of the "corrupt and despotick" Mexican government. The Edwards brothers, and Martin Parmer, another outraged colonist who called himself the Ringtailed Panther, launched a rebellion, wrote yet another declaration of independence, designed yet another flag, and established yet another evanescent republic. This one was called the Republic of Fredonia, a brandnew country that in the Edwardses' mind included not just the territory of his former colony but the greater part of Texas itself. Though it was at heart an Anglo rebellion, Haden Edwards managed to enlist a smattering of Cherokee allies, under the leadership of Richard Fields, who was a tireless advocate of the tribe despite his run-of-the-mill Anglo American name and his one-eighth measure of Cherokee blood. "The flag of liberty," Edwards exulted, "now waves in majestic triumph on the heights of Nacogdoches and despotism stands appalled at the sight."

But it was Stephen Austin who stood appalled. "A small party of infatuated madmen" was the way he characterized the Fredonian rebels. He swiftly went about doing everything he could to help suppress what he regarded as an absurd eruption, one that threatened to destroy the delicate coexistence he had worked so hard to achieve with the Mexican authorities. He embarked on a propaganda campaign to keep his own colonists in line and negotiated with the Cherokee chiefs who had resisted Edwards's airy promises of a vast homeland within Fredonia. (He was aided in this by Peter Ellis Bean, the young adventurer from the Philip Nolan expedition whom we last encountered in a Mexican jail, confiding to a lizard. He was now Pedro Elias Bean, an Indian agent in the employ of the Mexican government.) And in a crucial display of national loyalty, Austin assembled his own militia to march along with Mexican forces to take back Nacogdoches. By the time they got there, though, the rebellion had fallen apart and the Fredonians had fled. The Ringtailed Panther and the Edwards brothers escaped to the United States, though Richard Fields was not so fortunate. He was captured, tried by the Cherokee council, and executed.

<hr>

★

<hr>

THE FREDONIAN REBELLION WAS ONLY ONE WRONG TURN IN the "Labyrinth of trouble and Vexation and responsibility" in which Austin increasingly found himself trapped. In addition to the constant political

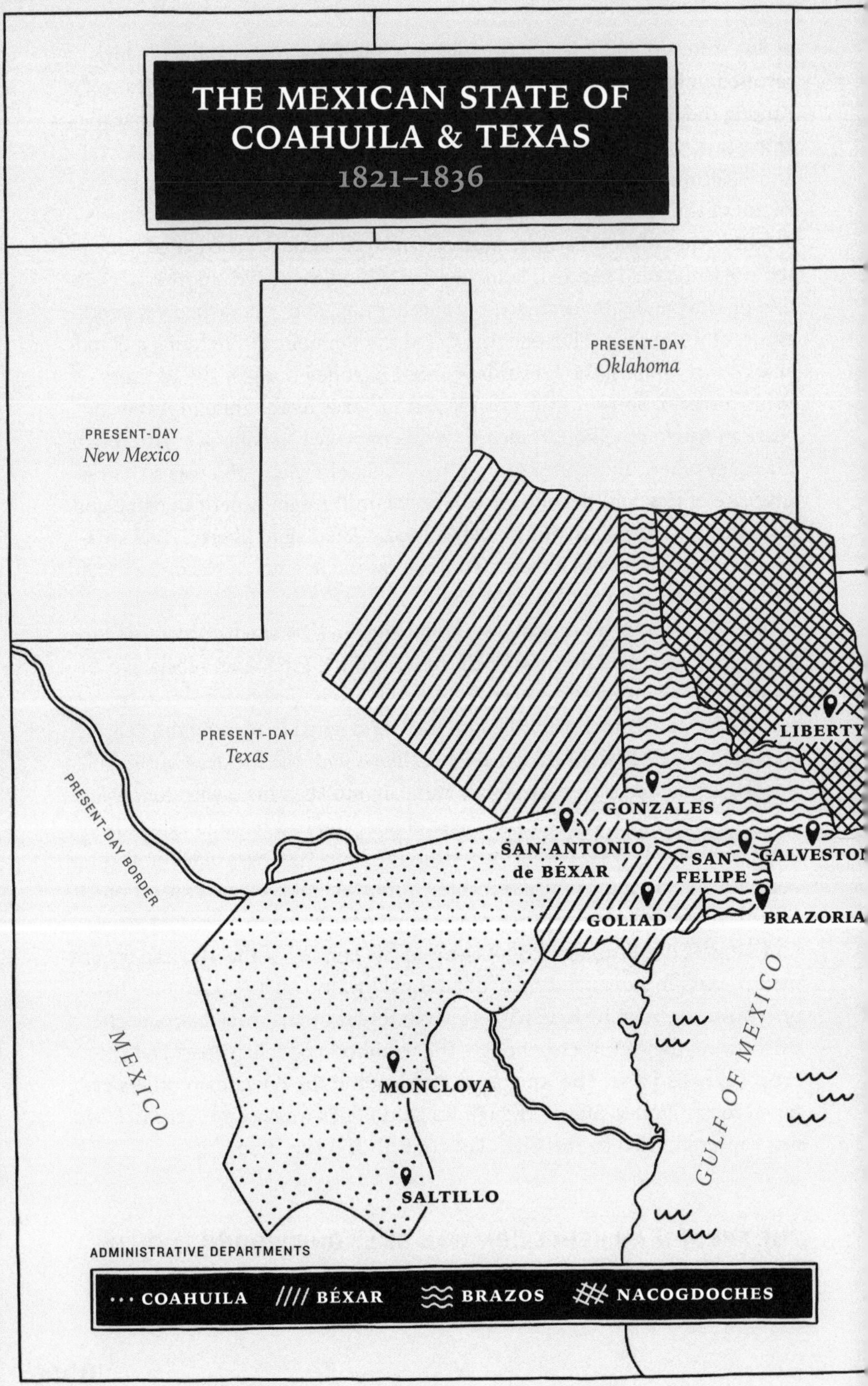

THE MEXICAN STATE OF COAHUILA & TEXAS

1821–1836

PRESENT-DAY
Oklahoma

PRESENT-DAY
New Mexico

PRESENT-DAY
Texas

PRESENT-DAY BORDER

LIBERTY

GONZALES

SAN ANTONIO
de BÉXAR

SAN
FELIPE

GALVESTON

GOLIAD

BRAZORIA

MEXICO

GULF OF MEXICO

MONCLOVA

SALTILLO

ADMINISTRATIVE DEPARTMENTS

··· COAHUILA   //// BÉXAR   ≋ BRAZOS   ⧰ NACOGDOCHES

troubles he had to confront both within and without his colony, he still had overhanging debts and a creeping weariness of soul. In a letter to his brother-in-law in 1830, he diagnosed himself with "something like disgust towards the world and human affairs." This was after his younger brother Brown, his closest confidant and the only family member who had joined him in Texas, died of yellow fever. It was a crushing emotional blow that weakened his spirit and drove his health into a downward spiral from which it never really recovered.

One of Austin's primary vexations was the "difficult and dark question" of how the plantation economy he foresaw for Texas could be put in place. There was the problem of slavery—or in the thinking of Austin and the other empresarios, the problem of no slavery. The Mexican Constitution of 1824 had little to say on the subject. True to its federalist philosophy, it left the states to decide whether human bondage would be tolerated. This was a crucial question for Texas. Without slavery, Austin was convinced, "we will have nothing but poverty for a long time, perhaps the rest of our lives." He was thus alarmed when he learned about a new draft of the Coahuila y Tejas state constitution, which included an article that read: "The state prohibits absolutely and for all time slavery in all its territory, and slaves that already reside in the state will be free from the day of the publication of the constitution in this capital."

To the empresarios, the wording was intolerably clear. Many of the colonists had already brought enslaved people into Texas. In Austin's colony alone, which had 1,800 residents in 1826, 443 of them were in bondage. Austin allowed himself a certain philosophical ambivalence when it came to the idea of slavery—that "curse of curses," he called it, "that unanswered, and unanswerable, inconsistency of free and liberal republicans"—but such enlightened feelings stood beside the point when it came to the success or failure of his Texas dream. It was not just Austin and his fellow Anglo empire builders who felt that way. Tejanos who had risen to local power in San Antonio—men such as Erasmo Seguín, José Antonio Navarro, and Juan Martín de Veramendi—knew that their fortunes were linked with the imperative of transforming the undernoticed backwater that was Texas into a place with a live economy and a real voice in its own affairs. And there were other power players farther south, closer to the state capital of Saltillo, who felt the same. Their tireless lobbying paid off, at least in the short term, with the passage by the state legislature of a law that allowed the practice to exist as long as slaves were cosmetically referred to as servants or hirelings that were working under contracts. Austin drew up the sample contracts for his colonists to follow: one-sided agreements in which the price for a worker's buyout was so high, and his wages were so imaginary, that the debt would be impossible to retire and could reliably be passed on to the next enslaved generation.

So slavery as an institution kept creeping into Texas, ensuring that there would be more Estebanicos and Kians and Richmonds, men and women who were active agents in the unfolding story of Texas but who would leave behind no last names, no title greater than faithful servant, whose lives would be overwritten by the very history they were creating.

There were, inevitably, other shoved-aside peoples. When Austin first explored the future site of his colony in 1821, he "descried an Indian," who approached at the head of fourteen warriors. They belonged to the Cocos, a band of the Karankawas. They were friendly enough, but Austin kept a wary eye on the Indians as they traded and talked in Spanish. The Karankawas, he wrote in his journal, "may be called universal enemies to man—they killed of [sic] all nations that came in their power, and frequently feast on the bodies of their victims." Coexistence with such people was out of the question: "An American population will be the signal of their extermination for there will be no way of subduing them but extermination."

The Karankawas had a warrior culture without the resources of a war economy. Before the Spanish came, they had mastered life on the inhospitable seacoasts and on the open prairies and thorny brushlands of South Texas, but in the end they didn't have the horse mobility of the Comanches or Apaches or the control of established trading routes, as the Caddos did. They became a people on the edge, crowded out, hunted down, forced to choose between a constrained existence in the missions at La Bahía and Refugio or an increasingly hazardous raiding life. They clashed with the Lafitte brothers and their heavily armed pirate army on Galveston, and with James Long and his men, and were finally driven off the island they had once commanded. When the first wave of Austin's colonists arrived at the mouth of the Colorado River, a Karankawa band didn't hesitate to attack. They killed four men and made off with the supplies the settlers had brought with them by schooner. Austin led a militia to hunt down Karankawas in the sporadic war that followed, a conflict that flared for decades and in the long run did become the war of extermination that he had predicted. The surviving Karankawas who were not wiped out in Texas melted away across the Rio Grande in the 1850s to blend with other coastal tribes, losing their coherent identity as a people and leaving behind only a lingering legend of cannibal ferocity.

"My lot is cast in the wilderness," Austin wrote to his sister Emily in 1824. He meant to do everything in his power to hold on to his piece of Texas and to turn it from a wilderness into a pastoral paradise where he would spend his summers on a "mountain retreat" that he envisioned on a particularly scenic stretch of the upper Colorado, and where, in his words, he would found an academy to "amuse myself and do good to others." In the way of this dream were the Karankawas and the other tribes—Comanches, Tonkawas, Tawakonis—whose conviction that the land belonged to them was no less absolute. Also in the way was an increasingly nervous Mexican government. Even though the commandant general of the Interior Provinces had personally thanked Austin for his role in putting down the Fredonian Rebellion, the fact that it had occurred in the first place meant that that something like it was bound to happen again. There were too many restless Americans in Mexico with their Constitutions in their pockets, growing more and more independent in their expectations, and more and more detached from a distant state government in Saltillo, whose workings only a handful of them had ever witnessed.

J. C. CLOPPER, THE YOUNG MAN FROM CINCINNATI WHO HAD taken such an enthusiastic interest in the charms of Jane Long, kept a journal of his 1828 travels in Texas, a spectacularly rhapsodic account in which he took note of the wild horses on the prairie ("their lofty gambols and wild manoeuvres unconstrained and unshackled by the thraldom of Man"), a Tejana at a fandango in San Antonio ("the snowy brightness of her well turned forehead beautifully contrasting with the carnation tints of her cheeks") and the death from fever of his brother and traveling companion. ("Farewell! Edward, thou most dutiful and affectionate of sons; thou tenderest of brothers . . . short were the wanderings of thy pilgrimage.")

Clopper met Austin in San Felipe and seems not to have encountered the empresario on one of his best days. Though he was grudgingly impressed by Austin's common sense and statesmanship, he basically found him to be a "small spare little old batchelor."

Austin would have had much on his mind. At about the time Clopper met him, Mexico had entered a new state of turmoil as the centralist faction under Manuel Gómez Pedraza rose to power and then abruptly lost it in a bloody revolt, one orchestrated yet again by Santa Anna. The caudillo had spent the last few years in strategic retirement, growing his power base in Veracruz, marrying a fourteen-year-old girl with an enormous dowry, and breeding fighting cocks for famous gladiatorial fiestas. (He was, according to an observer who saw him in action at the cockfighting pit, "the soul of this emporium of chaos and licentiousness.")

He was also a self-proclaimed "friend of liberty" who at this time—until he developed a taste for centralized power himself—was a resolute federalist. His coup d'etat forced the resignation of Gómez Pedraza and installed Vicente Guerrero, a rebel hero in the war for independence, as the new president of Mexico.

But despite this momentary federalist triumph, centralist sentiment was on the rise. The United Mexican States was turning out to be a very unruly place to govern. Powerful and even liberal-minded people feared that this was especially true in Texas, where the colonization project, instead of stabilizing the frontier, seemed to be incubating a foreign presence to take over the region.

Clopper was driving thirty head of cattle west from San Felipe to San Antonio when he encountered an "indescribable machine" which, characteristically for this verbose diarist, he could not resist describing in abundantly florid detail. "Suffice it to say," he marveled, "that the long vista which discovers to the mind's eye the gradual advancement of civilization arts and sciences show'd me the unseemly vehicle standing in its proper place—a splendid specimen of the ingenuity and cunning workmanship of man when the last shades of the dark ages were vanishing from before the dawning of the intellectual world."

In other words, a fancy carriage. It was escorted by thirty-five soldiers, and its principal passenger was a Mexican general named Manuel de Mier y Terán. Terán was at the head of a commission whose official purpose was to mark the still somewhat nebulous boundary between Mexico and the United States and to record the natural features and resources of Texas. Its roster included a mineralogist, a cartographer, and a Swiss botanist internationally renowned as an authority on gooseberries.

Terán was thirty-eight. He was a man of broad learning and high purpose who had fought in the war against Spain, sat in Mexico's first congress, and later served as its minister of war. As a member of the national colonization committee, he had become concerned about the steady foreign migration from the United States into Texas. In addition to the nature studies of his boundary commission, he was deeply interested in observing with his own eyes the nature of these new inhabitants and calculating what they might portend for the future of his country.

He was alarmed. "There is no power like that to the north," he warned in a report to the War Department the year after his inspection, "which by silent means has made conquests of momentous importance. Such dexterity, such constancy in their designs, such uniformity of means of execution which always are completely successful, arouses admiration."

He had admiration for Americans, but he also had scorn for their querulous demands and their contempt for their host nation's authority. And his worry about what would happen if Mexico did nothing to stop Texas from being overtopped by foreigners bordered on the apocalyptic. "In the act of ceding Texas [Mexico] would have to renounce all pretensions of having its own industries with which to maintain and enrich its eight million inhabitants, who within a few years could not avoid seeing the bread and sugar, and even the corn and beans consumed in the federal district, furnished by the foreign harvest of Texas." Anyone who did not oppose the loss of Texas, Terán insisted, "is an execrable traitor who ought to be punished with every kind of death."

His diary is more temperate. He seems to have liked the place and at least some of the newcomers. He lovingly described the cotton gin that Jared Groce, who was the biggest landowner in Austin's colony, had built on his land along the Brazos, and was impressed by the fact that Groce's 105 slaves seemed well cared for and that they gathered at the master's house every Saturday night for a dance. (Though he didn't turn a blind eye to the barbarities he saw practiced by other slave owners: "They pull their teeth, they set dogs upon them to tear them apart, and the mildest of them will whip the slaves until they are flayed.") He paints a portrait of a primeval land rapidly being transformed: African slaves laboring in cultivated fields enclosed by wooden fences, trees cinched and left to rot to clear more land for crops, the skins of the ocelots that roamed the vanishing forests hanging on the walls in the settlers' cabins.

Terán and his entourage visited San Felipe and stayed there for two weeks or so, giving him time to get to know Austin. The two men were on opposite sides of the debate about how welcoming Mexico should be to foreign colonists, but intellectually and temperamentally they were kindred spirits. Judging by Terán's brief notes, they seem to have had robust discussions about the mineral content of Texas rivers and the bones found by a settler along the banks of the Brazos that Austin felt sure were those of a mammoth.

But the personal connection they made did not in the end translate to policy. "If the colonization contracts in Texas are not suspended," Terán concluded after his boundary survey, "and if the conditions of the establishments are not watched, it is necessary to say that the province is already definitely delivered to the foreigners."

At the end of 1829, in another coup in Mexico, the centralist vice president Anastasio Bustamante seized power from Vicente Guerrero. On April 6, 1830, a new law was passed, one that would ultimately arrange the conditions in Texas for outright insurgency. The law halted the issuance of any further empresario contracts and put a stop to the immigration of colonists from the United States. It also prohibited the introduction of slaves.

Austin, thanks to his demonstrated loyalty to Mexico and his careful cultivation of key governmental contacts, managed to get the immigration ban lifted from his own colonies, but he couldn't control the overall outrage of the American settlers in Texas, especially the newcomers who kept arriving on their own, forgoing the formalities of official land titles and Mexican citizenship and just carving out a place for themselves to live. They were quick to imagine both their prosperity and their propensity for self-government directly threatened by the new law. At the same time, a crucial benefit that the colonists had come to rely on—an exemption from Mexican customs laws—was being phased out. At one point, at the new village of Anahuac, situated at the mouth of the Trinity River and home to a fort and customshouse, ship captains headed down the Brazos into the open Gulf refused to make a detour up Galveston Bay to stop and show their papers and ended up exchanging fire with government troops. There was only one casualty, a wounded Mexican soldier, but those echoing shots were a modest foretaste of the war that would tear Texas away from Mexico.

FOR AUSTIN, THOUGH, THERE WAS AN UNCHARACTERISTIC
spell of personal peace. It came in the person of his cousin Mary Austin Holley. When she visited Texas in 1831, she was forty-seven, nine years older than Austin, but very much his peer when it came to swoony daydreams of what life might still have to offer. She was a widow. Her late husband had been the president of Transylvania University, in Kentucky. She was also a considerable writer. Almost from the moment she arrived at Brazoria, the brand-new river town near where her brother Henry had settled, she was at work on a Texas adventure novel for young boys, a Texas song ("The Brazos Boat Song"), and—most ambitiously and enduringly—a vivid travel narrative of Texas.

She and Austin spent ten days together in Henry's cabin on the lower Brazos while he told her all about Texas, joined in the singing as the family tested out her river song, and listened as she read aloud from the impressions of Texas that she was setting down during the day. "One's feelings in Texas are unique and original," she wrote toward the end of her musings, "and very like a dream or youthful vision realized."

Judging from the fervent correspondence that followed Mary's departure, the cousins had formed a soulmate bond in Texas. She had barely boarded her ship on Christmas Day when Austin managed to get a letter aboard so that he could say "farewell once more." He followed up with a soul-baring stream of letters. Sometimes he was throbbing with noble purpose. "My ambition," he confided, "was to redeem this fine country—our glorious Texas—and con-

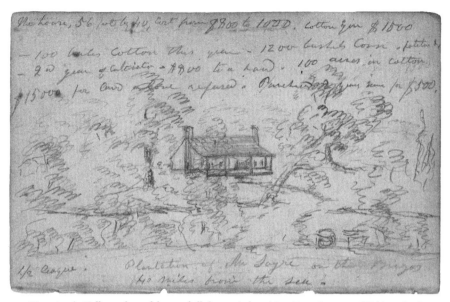

Mary Austin Holley took careful note of all she saw in her visit to Texas in 1831, publishing a book of her observations two years later. She was one of Texas's first travel writers and most ardent boosters. "We were all enchanted with Texas, and, with one accord, exclaimed, 'This is the spot.'"

vert it into a home for the unfortunate, a refuge from poverty, an asylum for the sufferers from selfish avarice." Sometimes he forgot his statesman's pose and gave her a glimpse of raw grandiloquence: "One word from me now," he boasted, "would annihilate every Mexican soldier in Texas."

But mostly he was wrenchingly wistful. "Gardens, and rosy bowers, and ever verdant groves, and music, books, and intellectual amusements can all be ours," he predicted in one letter. And in another, he cast his dreaming mind further than it had ever gone before, into some Elysium that he seemed to sense he could never truly behold: "On our ponies we will scamper over the flowery prairies to the sea beach, and along it with the wide waste of the ocean on one hand, the level green carpet of nature fringed by distant woods, on the other, and friendship and happiness in our hearts."

AUSTIN MADE THE LONG JOURNEY TO SALTILLO IN MARCH 1832 to try to persuade the state legislature to reverse the immigration ban, restore free trade, and rethink its ban on slavery. He traveled on horseback with a fourteen-year-old nephew named Moses, after his grandfather. On the way, they stopped outside San Antonio to wander across the site of the Battle of Medina, where General Arredondo—aided by the heroics of his junior officer Santa Anna—had destroyed the republican rebels of 1813. It must have been a sobering place to visit for a man who was already harboring dangerous revolutionary dreams if the Mexican government continued to defy his aspirations. "We shall go for Independence," he had already confided to Mary, "and put our trust in our selves, our riffles [*sic*], and—our God."

Mexico was in the midst of another convulsion when Austin arrived. Santa Anna, whose hero status had been dramatically boosted by his defeat of a Spanish invasion force in 1829, was leading his latest revolt, this one against the Bustamante regime. Terán, who had served with Santa Anna against the Spanish, was now his enemy, leading the outnumbered centralist forces against a man who—it was becoming apparent—drew his strength from instability and chaos. Here was the irony, though: Santa Anna's political philosophy, to the extent it could be disentangled at any particular moment from his Brobdingnagian personal ambition, was federalist. Austin had cause to hope that a victory by Santa Anna would mean a relaxation of the Mexican government's tightening grip on Texas.

Austin was still friendly with Terán, even though their conflicting interests kept drawing them apart. And he recognized that the general who had caused him so much trouble by setting into motion the law cutting off immigration to Texas was a principled man who was acting only out of a fervent longing to hold the Mexican nation together. After his trip to Saltillo, Austin visited Terán at his field headquarters. He found him in poor health and low spirits, distracted not just by the war he was fighting but also by some deeper personal struggle. "How horrid is civil war," Austin reflected in a letter home after he had seen the general. "God keep it away from Texas."

Two days later, at dawn, General Manuel de Mier y Terán, the man who had devoted so much of his thought and life's energy to keeping Texas from being pried away from the rest of Mexico, put on his dress uniform and walked to the wall in front of a crumbling church. Then he took out his sword and drove it through his heart. The day before, he had written a letter to Mexico's chief minister. It turned out to be his suicide note, and its core prediction was also its most heartbroken sentence: "Texas is lost."

— 10 —

THE CONSEQUENCE
OF FAILURE

"THE TIME HAS COME TO STRIKE A DECISIVE BLOW UPON
the enemy occupying the Fortress of the Alamo," declared
the general order passed down to the Mexican troops in San
Antonio on March 5, 1836. The Alamo had been under siege
since February 23, and the attack was to take place the next
day. The assault force of 2,000 men was ordered to turn in

as soon as it was dark. By midnight, they would be on the move, separated
into four columns and creeping silently beneath the rising moon to within a
musket shot of the entrenchments the rebel defenders had dug outside the
walls of the old mission. There they would lie, shivering on the ground for
hours, waiting for the bugle calls and Congreve rockets that would signal
the moment of attack.

The men were without blankets or overcoats. Such items would, in the
words of the general order, "impede the rapidity of their motions." They
wore blue woolen tunics and white cotton trousers, and on their heads the
tall billed caps known as shakos. The more fortunate soldados had shoes
to protect their feet against the cold; others wore only sandals. Most of
the men in the line companies carried surplus Brown Bess muskets, the

smoothbore firearm that had helped Britain win its empire. ("And if ever we
English had reason to bless / Any arm save our mothers'," wrote Rudyard
Kipling, "that arm is Brown Bess.")

But these weary and footsore Mexican soldiers—many of them con-
scripts—had no particular reason to be sentimental about a musket that
weighed almost ten pounds and, at close to five feet in length, almost
equaled some of them in height. They had carried these cumbersome
weapons on a brutal forced march from Saltillo for almost four hundred
miles. They had endured desert heat and a freakish blizzard, been attacked by
Indians and ravaged by dysentery. Now Santa Anna had ordered them to lie
on the ground in the freezing dark, far from their homes, in a desolate and
remote pocket of Mexico, waiting for his order to attack a fortified and long-
deconsecrated mission so that the battle for Texas could begin in earnest.

HOW HAD IT COME TO THIS? HOW HAD THE MEXICAN GOVERN-
ment's attempt to populate Texas with loyal Mexican citizens created instead
the opposite result: a breakaway republic that—three days before Santa Anna
ordered his troops into position to attack the Alamo—had declared its independence? The insurrection had taken a few years to cohere but had perhaps been inevitable from the moment Austin's first colonists arrived at the
mouth of the Brazos to try to make a foreign land their own. Austin himself later concluded that "the country was placed during the whole of that
eventful period upon a volcano." There was of course the magma chamber
of Mexican politics, continually churning and seething with revolutions and
counterrevolutions. But there were also the divergent priorities of the residents of Texas: Tejanos who found their interests allied with the empresarios' dream of a surging economy based on slave power; other Tejanos who
were disposed to side with a centralist Mexican authority over an alarming
influx of American pilgrims; colonists terrified of losing their expectation of
representative government, along with the lands they had cultivated and the
towns they had built; adventurers who sensed a brewing fight; political exiles
eager for a second chance; speculators from the United States and Mexico
looking for opportunity in chaos; and Indian peoples, displaced and watchful,
trying to decide whether to enter the coming fight, and on whose side.

Stephen Austin was still in Mexico when the volcano began to rumble in
the spring of 1832. At Anahuac, the village at the mouth of the Trinity that
was proving to be a serious hot spot, Texas settlers' growing outrage centered on a fellow Anglo named Juan Davis Bradburn. Known as "John Davis
Bradburn" when he had joined the Gutiérrez-Magee expedition, twenty

years earlier, he had since gone on to become a Mexican lieutenant colonel, fighting with Iturbide against the Spanish and marrying a prominent heiress in Mexico City. Now the commander of the Mexican garrison at Anahuac, Bradburn was charged with enforcing Mexican customs laws. His blunt, unyielding temperament was a poor match for a volatile place whose governance required the skills of a diplomat. Anahuac was a ragged little village of several dozen huts and log houses near the strategic shores of Galveston Bay. The barrack housing Bradburn and his Mexican soldados was the only structure resembling a real building. The town was populated by restive settlers and speculators who saw their horizons circumscribed by the anti-immigration law of 1830 and by a new zeal on the part of the Mexican government to put a stop to smuggling and collect tariffs.

The disenchantment on the part of the emigrants from the United States was not only political—it was also personal. They didn't like the inflexible Bradburn and they didn't like the Mexican troops he commanded. "The common soldiers at this post," wrote a man named Robert Gray in a book he compiled about his adventures in Texas, "were men of a most depraved character, while they were believed to be as cowardly as they were wicked and ignorant."

But it was not only the Mexicans whom Gray was wary about. "Among these strangers," he wrote of the American settlers, "I found a number of very intelligent men; but I learnt that a portion of them had fled from justice, or as they chose to call it, from law, in their own country. It is a well known fact, that a considerable portion of our countrymen who are found in Texas, are of this character. I saw at the breakfast table one morning, among those who were seated with me, four murderers who had sought safety in this country, and a gentleman assured me, that on one occasion, he had sat down with eleven."

William Barret Travis was not a murderer, but like a lot of people whom Gray had encountered in Texas he was on the run. He was twenty-one years old when he came to Texas in 1831 from Alabama. He left behind a disaffected wife, a son, another child on the way, a trail of false starts, and a shredded reputation. He had failed as a newspaper editor and as a lawyer. Desperate to find a way to dodge his creditors, he had tried to have his debts—incurred before he had reached the legal age of twenty-one—dismissed on the grounds of "infancy." He was promptly found liable and laughed out of court. Before he could be arrested, he was on his way to Texas.

Travis had only a few years to live. He would die spectacularly at twenty-six, leaving behind a name that is still powerfully resonant in Texas today. (I live in Travis County, just a few miles from Lake Travis and one of the many

Travis High Schools in the state, and one of my grandchildren is named Travis.) No doubt he would have wished for a longer life, but maybe not at the expense of making such an enduring mark. "He was very ambitious," remembered his friend J. H. Kuykendall. "He hungered and thirsted for fame—not the kind of fame which staisfies [sic] the ambition of the duelist and desperado, but the exalted fame which crowns the doer of great deeds in a good cause."

Anahuac, a contentious and grubby little coastal settlement on the edge of nowhere, might have seemed an unpromising spot for great deeds to begin, but as soon as Travis arrived and began rekindling his legal practice, he also joined in fanning the flames of outrage against Juan Bradburn. He probably helped organize a response—in the form of a riot—after some of the settlers claimed they had been assaulted by Bradburn's troops. He was instrumental in forming a civilian militia, which was proscribed by Mexican law and which Bradburn could not help but see as a direct threat to his authority. And he provoked the commander further by representing a Louisiana slave owner who appeared in Anahuac to reclaim two escaped slaves. Bradburn took seriously his government's official opposition to slavery and refused to give them up. He was soon confronted with a rumor that a full-scale uprising was in the works—-a hundred men were riding toward Anahuac to seize the slaves and send them back across the Sabine into bondage.

The uprising turned out to be a ruse. Bradburn, suspecting that Travis and his law partner, Patrick Jack, were behind it, had them arrested, which promptly provoked a real uprising. In the middle of it, Bradburn—believing an attack was immediate—had Travis and Jack dragged out of their cell and ordered them to be immediately shot if hostilities began. Lying on the ground, bound hand and foot, with muskets pointed at him, Travis called out to his friends to ignore his situation and "blaze away upon the fort."

They held their fire, Travis postponed his martyrdom, and after a few weeks of skirmishes and deliberations, Travis and Jack were released from jail and Bradburn was relieved of duty. It was only a small insurrection, but to Travis and his fellow war-minded Texians (the word "Texan" had not yet entered the language), it amounted to not just a strategic victory but also a triumphant assertion of identity. "Mexicans have learned a lesson," he declared. "Americans know their rights and will assert and protect them."

Travis would have known that Americans had no rights at all in Texas except for those that the Mexican colonization laws granted them, but rhetorical precision was not what he had in mind. He was speaking for people who were determined to have an American way of life in Mexico, one way or another. For a while, it was possible to imagine achieving that end without an outright war for independence. If Texas could be its own state within the Mexican federation and not a powerless appendage to the state of Coahuila, it might at last have the influence to set its own course and demand the exemptions—on tariffs, on slavery, on immigration—that it felt it needed in order to survive.

Those hopes rested, for now, on Santa Anna. Though Austin regarded him as a "sort of Mad Cap," Santa Anna was in the middle of leading a revolution to depose the Bustamante regime, a development that would very much favor Texas's aspirations to be free of the iron grip of centralized government. The Texas insurgents who had driven Bradburn out of Anahuac drank toasts to the Mexican general and even named one of their militias the Santa Anna Volunteer Company.

Stephen Austin returned to Texas from south of the Rio Grande in the summer of 1832. Despite his wariness about the madcap liberator, he began a campaign in support of Santa Anna, convinced that he offered the best chance of Texas being able to separate from Coahuila without having to take the drastic step of separating from Mexico.

By the end of 1832, Santa Anna had driven Bustamante from power. A few months later he was elected president. But he was a very strange president. He chose not to attend his own investiture and promptly left the governing of the nation to the discretion of his vice president, the staunchly liberal-minded doctor Valentín Gómez Farías. Santa Anna preferred to stay far from the capital of Mexico City in his beloved hideaway in Xalapa. For a man who would soon become infamous as a dictator and tyrant, he wielded political power from a puzzling remove. Perhaps this was a brilliant strategic gambit—the detached scrutiny of a cat waiting to pounce—or perhaps it was the natural indifference of a born soldier who took no real satisfaction in politics.

A few months before Santa Anna came to power, the Texian settlers of San Felipe issued a call for a convention to decide how to press their case for reforms. Under Mexican law, this was an illegal assembly, but the Anglo population of Texas had been emboldened by the showdown at Anahuac and by later armed conflicts in Nacogdoches and in the port town of Velasco. Tejano leaders, among them Juan Seguín—the son of Erasmo Seguín, who had ushered Stephen Austin into Texas in 1821—were cautious about merging their fortunes with those of the aggrieved Texians. The Tejanos were mostly clustered in San Antonio, which was 150 miles west of San Felipe, the center of Anglo influence. But in its identity, San Antonio de Béxar was a world away. It was a hundred years older, its landscape craggier and shadowier, its inhabitants—its Seguíns and Navarros and Veramendis—Mexicans not by choice and opportunity but by blood and destiny. They still had keen memories of Arredondo's punitive incursion of 1813, and a wariness about being forced to choose sides in yet another civil war. Austin was wary too. He was a man of careful measures caught in a growing climate of headlong action.

In April another meeting, the Convention of 1833, met in San Felipe. This time the delegates, encouraged by the rise of Santa Anna, decided to send a representative to Mexico City to present their petition for separate statehood, along with a proposed state constitution whose provisions were borrowed from the 1780 constitution for the Commonwealth of Massachusetts, a copy of which somebody managed to produce from one of the log cabins of San Felipe. They chose Austin for this mission, and Austin knew the stakes. He had to deliver some sort of meaningful autonomy for Texas. "The consequence of a failure," he wrote, "will no doubt be war."

He mounted his mule and set out on the long journey to the "City of Montezuma." He arrived there just as a catastrophic epidemic of cholera was sweeping through Mexico, and he almost perished. "Others have died in less than one hour," he reported, "whose simptoms were similar to mine." Afterward, his health was more fragile than ever, but his hopes were unexpectedly high. He met with Vice President Gómez Farías and then with Santa Anna on one of the president's rare appearances in the capital city. Santa Anna seemed to be very much the federalist hero of Texian fantasies. He was friendly and sympathetic to the idea of lifting the ban on Anglo immigration into Texas. Separate statehood was off the table, but when Austin left Mexico City in December 1833, he had reason to believe he had gained enough concessions to head off a war.

Then he got arrested. His crime was to have written a letter advising the people of Texas to form an independent state government despite the unwillingness of Santa Anna or Gómez Farías or any other Mexican official to separate Texas from Coahuila. It is unclear why he wrote such a provocative message. Maybe it was out of frustration, maybe out of world-weary despair (he had just lost his niece and three friends to cholera—"Good God what a blow"), maybe out of the need to assert his leadership back in Texas at a time when he was absent and worried that events were moving beyond his control. In any case, the letter was intercepted before he got home, and its seditious content shattered the trust he had spent so many years building with people in high office in Mexico. Considered a "state criminal of the greatest seriousness," he was confined to a dungeon in Mexico City left over from the Inquisition, with only a mouse for company and with only a smuggled French-language biography of Philip II to read.

He was in prison for almost a year before being released on bond at the end of 1834. His case was still pending, though his place of confinement broadened to include all of Mexico City, its opera palaces and ballrooms and the attentions, we are told, of a "very sprightly young lady." In Texas, meanwhile, as in the rest of Mexico, turmoil continued to grow. The ban on immigration into Texas had been lifted, but the resulting influx of new settlers from the United States only added to the alarm of the centralists, who warned that Texas was rapidly calving away from the Mexican iceberg. By now there was an openly declared War Party in Texas, whose most influential members were combative souls like Travis and William Wharton, and Wharton's younger brother John, who had barely arrived in Texas before he got into a duel that cost him the use of his right hand.

And it soon became evident that the Texians no longer had a friend in Santa Anna; in fact they now had a decisive enemy. Santa Anna had watched with neutral interest to see whether Mexico would absorb or reject the radical reformist agenda of his vice president and his even more radical congress. When discontent arose, he swept back into the capital, dismissed Gómez Farías, shut down congress, and allowed the new lawmakers to abolish the cherished 1824 Constitution. Santa Anna still flattered himself with the self-description of a moderate whose mission was to calm "excessive passion," but the truth was that his own ambitions were now better served by the policies of an iron-fisted centralist—and one who was ready to fight any restive province, like Texas, that got in his way.

—11—

COME AND TAKE IT

AUSTIN WAS RELEASED FROM HIS MEXICO CITY CONFINE-
ment in June 1835 and finally made his way back to Texas at
the end of the summer. By this time, uprisings against Santa
Anna, the sudden new enemy of federalist freedoms, had
broken out across Mexico, most notably in Zacatecas. The
president put down that revolt personally, leading his regular
army troops against a defiant militia and then allowing his men to plunder
the city while he helped himself to a caudillo-scale prize: the proceeds of a
local silver mine. And there had been yet another confrontation at Anahuac,
with Travis again taking a crucial, incendiary role. When the old dispute
about customs duties flared up once more, he raised a force of twenty men
and compelled the surrender of the Mexican commander who had taken
over the garrison from Bradburn.

Travis had decided that "all are for energetic resistance to the oppres-
sions of a govt. that seems determined to destroy, to smash & to ruin us."
He wasn't right. Most people in the Anglo colonies were far more cautious.
The "Tories" and "submission men"—as Travis termed them—saw no particular benefit in going to war against Santa Anna, and there was widespread resentment against Travis for stirring up trouble. "Listen not to men

who have no home," a member of the Peace Party warned, "who have no family, who have nothing to lose in case of civil war."

Stephen Austin still had plenty to lose, and he didn't have the War Party temperament of Travis. But his long imprisonment and his exasperation with the chaos of Mexican politics had led him to a fateful position. "A gentle breeze," he wrote to Mary Austin Holley, "shakes off a ripe peach. Can it be supposed that the violent political convulsions of Mexico will not shake off Texas so soon as it is ripe enough to fall? . . . The fact is, we must, and ought to become a part of the United States."

It would take more than a gentle breeze, though the carnage of the Texas Revolution started with the smallest of battles, fought over the possession of a single small cannon. It happened early in October, shortly after General Martín Perfecto de Cos, the commander of Mexico's Eastern Internal Provinces, landed at Copano, on the Texas coast, with three hundred men. It was a show of force brought on by the latest troubles in Anahuac. Cos planned to arrest Travis and the other agitators and "let those ungrateful strangers know that the Govno. has sufficient power to repress them."

But the arrival of Cos's army, which looked a little too much like an invasion, fused the various Texian and Tejano factions into a united sense of outrage against Santa Anna's centralist overreach. Seventy miles northeast of San Antonio, along the far bank of the Guadalupe River, sat the log buildings that made up the town of Gonzales, the center of the struggling colony of Green DeWitt. DeWitt was a militia captain who had served in the War of 1812 and had come to Texas to be an empresario. Thanks partially to the bankrolling of his wife, Sarah, who had sold her property in Missouri to finance the enterprise, he had been awarded a grant in 1825 adjacent to Austin's colony. DeWitt was a born promoter. He was, according to an acquaintance, "as enthusiastic in praise of the country as the most energetic real estate dealer of boom towns." But J. C. Clopper thought DeWitt had problems with "dissipation [and] neglectful indolence." In any case, he was dead—of cholera, probably, during a trip to Mexico—by the time Gonzales became the flashpoint for the Texas Revolution.

Before he died, DeWitt had convinced the political chief of San Antonio to lend the citizens of Gonzales a cannon for defense against Indians. It was only a small-caliber cannon that fired a six-pound ball, but with so much insurrection brewing in the colonies, Domingo de Ugartechea, the military commander at Béxar, now wanted it back. He sent a squad of the presidial soldiers stationed at the Alamo to retrieve it. When the citizens of Gonzales would not give it up, Ugartechea sent a hundred dragoons. The Guadalupe was high from recent rains, all the fords were under water, and the

Texians had made sure that the ferry and all other boats that might be used to cross the river were on their side. With the dragoons on one bank and the Texians on the other, there was an inconclusive flurry of diplomacy, during which the cannon was buried. It was dug up a few days later after more than a hundred volunteers swarmed in from the settlements with their rifles and shotguns and fowling pieces to reinforce the men who had decided to make a stand at Gonzales. The resistance this time was widespread, not confined to a few War Party firebrands.

In today's Texas, "Come and Take It" has evolved into an all-purpose cri de coeur of defiance that can be found on T-shirts and coffee cups in every gas station gift shop and cowboy boutique. The words come from a flag hastily sewn from her daughter's wedding dress by Sarah Seely DeWitt, the take-charge widow of Green DeWitt. (A few years before, she had successfully petitioned the Mexican government for a grant of land in her own name after, as she put it, her husband became "much embarrassed in his affairs.")

The Texians were flying the flag when they crossed the river downstream and charged the dragoons. The Mexican leader, Lieutenant Francisco Castañeda, seems to have been genuinely bewildered by the colonists' hostile reaction. He had come only to request the cannon, not to fight a war over it. Since he was outnumbered, he ordered his men to withdraw. It is unknown how many Mexicans were killed—the best guess has been one or two. The tally on the Texian side is more accurate: one casualty. As Noah Smithwick recorded it in his sometimes too-colorful memoir of the Texas Revolution, one of the insurgents "took a header from his horse, thereby bringing his nasal appendage into such intimate association with Mother Earth as to draw forth a copious stream of the sanguinary fluid."

The Battle of Gonzales was not a battle, but it was a salvo. In crossing the Guadalupe, the Texians had crossed the Rubicon. Texas, more or less, had risen up in arms, though the rebels' strategic objective had not quite been determined. "I can not remember," wrote Smithwick, "that there was any distinct understanding as to the position we were to assume toward Mexico. Some were for independence, some for the constitution of 1824; and some for anything, just so it was a row."

They lost no time in pressing the fight. Cos had taken his army to invest San Antonio, leaving behind a force of fifty or so men at the presidio in La Bahía, which had been rechristened in 1829 to honor the hero of the Mexican independence movement. The town was now known as Goliad, a scrambled reworking of the name Hidalgo. Texians assaulted the presidio and forced the surrender of its outnumbered defenders in less than half an hour. The capture of the fort at Goliad, which guarded the road leading from the crucial port of Copano, effectively put the rebels in command of the Texas coast and blocked the likelihood of Santa Anna sending more troops by sea.

Then it was on to confront Cos in San Antonio, which was strategically situated on the Camino Real leading up from Mexico. San Antonio was a community that had been fought over for so long and so savagely that it was on its way to becoming the Jerusalem of Texas. At the head of this army—an unstable assemblage of headstrong individualists ("We are all captains," one of them decided)—was Stephen Austin. By this point, Austin had given up any pretense of avoiding conflict. When word came that Cos had landed in Copano, Austin flatly stated, "War is our only recourse." He was perhaps an inevitable choice for commander in chief: a respected patriarch who stood the best chance of uniting the Texian factions, which had, before the arrival of Cos, been as likely to go to war with one another as to band together against the *centralistas*. But he was so physically weak when he left San Felipe to join the volunteers in Gonzales that he couldn't get onto his horse without help. And his gravitas was a better fit for the negotiating table than the battlefield.

NOAH SMITHWICK—AGED 66.

NOAH SMITHWICK,
a blacksmith, served in the Texas Revolution and, many years later, his eyesight failing, dictated his memoirs to his daughter. He left behind a vivid description of the conflicting aims of the insurgent Texians: "Some were for independence . . . and some for anything, just so it was a row."

Nevertheless, he led his "Army of the People" west. "It certainly bore little resemblance to the army of my childhood dreams," recalled Smithwick. "Buckskin breeches were the nearest approach to uniform, and there was wide diversity even there, some being new and soft and yellow, while others, from long familiarity with rain and grease and dirt, had become hard and black and shiny . . . some wore shoes and some moccasins. Here a broad-brimmed sombrero overshadowed the military cap at its side; there a tall 'beegum' rode familiarly beside a coonskin cap, with the tail hanging down behind."

When they arrived at Salado Creek, five miles east of San Antonio, it became clear they could not assault the town outright. Cos had blocked the streets with breastworks, turned the Alamo mission into a fortress, and put over twenty pieces of artillery in place. A siege was the only realistic option, and for it to be successful Austin would need the cooperation of local Tejanos who knew the roads and could serve as express riders and scouts for foraging parties.

Juan Nepomuceno Seguín was a natural fit for this crucial role. He was a few weeks from his twenty-ninth birthday, and his family had been connected with the Austins since his boyhood, ever since his father, Erasmo, had encouraged Moses in his colonization efforts and, after Moses's death, escorted Stephen across the Sabine to take up his father's work. The Seguíns had been in Texas since the 1740s. They were prosperous landholders who owned, among other properties, a nine-thousand-acre rancho a day's ride south of San Antonio, whose headquarters was a heavily fortified castle-like ranch house called Casa Blanca. They were also players in the unsteady, whipsawing political world of Mexican Texas. Erasmo had been the alcalde of San Antonio, and by the time the revolution broke out, his son had served in that office as well and been the *jefe político*, the highest-ranking administrator in the department of Béxar.

When the trouble began brewing in Gonzales, Seguín rode south along the San Antonio River to the rancho of another prominent landowner, Salvador Flores, where a meeting had been called. The participants were Flores's neighbors, Tejanos who were about to be thrust into the middle of yet another bloody and complicated conflict. Seguín wrote that he told them he was "well satisfied that the beginning of the revolution was close at hand." There is no record of what was otherwise said at the meeting, but one can imagine the deliberations about the wisdom of backing an insurrection that, if successful, would inevitably favor the interests of the Anglo settlers, most of whom now viewed Texas as an extension of the America they had left behind. For the Tejanos, Texas was and had to forever be Mexico. The question was which Mexico would prevail: one ruled by a distant and autocratic government or one that supported the freedoms of the 1824 Constitution.

For a public man like Seguín, the choice to be made was both wrenching and particularly dangerous. General Cos, learning of Seguín's federalist leanings the year before, had warned him, "This conduct, all the more scandalous when observed in an officer who would be better occupied in putting out the flames of revolution rather than fanning them, has caught my complete attention, as well as that of every Mexican who wonders what ideas move those who promote disturbances in Texas."

MAJOR BATTLES OF THE TEXAS REVOLUTION

1835–1836

SABINE RIVER

TRINITY RIVER

BRAZOS RIVER

COLORADO RIVER

PECOS RIVER

WASHINGTON-ON-THE-BRAZOS

SIEGE OF THE ALAMO
FEBRUARY 23–MARCH 6, 1836

SAN JACINTO
APRIL 21, 1836

SIEGE OF BÉXAR
OCTOBER 12–DECEMBER 9, 1835

SAN FELIPE

SAN ANTONIO

GONZALES

GALVESTON

PRESIDIO de RÍO GRANDE

COLETO CREEK
MARCH 19–20, 1836

MATAGORDA

GOLIAD MASSACRE
MARCH 27, 1836

REFUGIO
MARCH 12–15, 1836

MONCLOVA

RIO GRANDE

GULF OF MEXICO

LEGEND

✕ **BATTLE SITE**

— **MAIN MEXICAN ARMY LED BY SANTA ANNA**

—·— **MEXICAN FORCE UNDER URREA**

—· **HOUSTON**

MATAMOROS

Despite Cos's obvious threat, Seguín and the rancheros he met with that day decided that their best chance to hold on to their economic and political power, and to preserve their national identity, was to rise up with the Anglos against Santa Anna. Seguín raised a mounted company of thirty-seven men, including Flores, and reported to Austin, who named him a captain of what had been grandly termed the Federal Army of Texas. Seguín and his men, along with a Tejano company led by Placido Benavides, served as Austin's eyes and ears during the early days of the siege of Béxar, patrolling the roads and intercepting messages sent out by Cos.

Also playing a crucial role was James Bowie. Bowie is one of those historical Texas personages who has pretty much been absorbed by myth. I still remember (in fact, seem incapable of forgetting) the theme song from *The Adventures of Jim Bowie*, a television series from the 1950s: "He roamed the wilderness unafraid / From Natchez to Rio Grande / With all the might of his gleaming blade / He fought for the rights of man!"

The first part of the song is true enough. Bowie did indeed roam the wilderness unafraid. He was the son of a rootless, self-reliant Georgian, one of the men who followed Daniel Boone across the Mississippi to Spanish Missouri. Like his father, Jim Bowie practiced what Tocqueville called "democracy in its most extreme form." He came of age in the swamps and bayous of Louisiana, and like most people in that unsettled region, which was sometimes part of France, sometimes part of Spain, and sometimes part of the United States, he fought mostly to advance himself and his family. He was first and foremost a daring and supremely crooked businessman. His older brother Rezin may have been a participant in the Gutiérrez-Magee expedition, and Jim himself was introduced to Texas when he signed on with the filibustering adventure of James Long. He met Jean Lafitte on Galveston, and soon the Bowie brothers were in business with the pirate, buying slaves from him for a dollar a pound and then smuggling them into Louisiana, where they could be legally sold for a considerable profit. Jim Bowie then moved on to a much bigger scheme, forging Spanish land grants and trying to pass them off as real, on what a biographer, William C. Davis, calls an "almost industrial scale."

As for the "gleaming blade" mentioned in the song, there really was a Bowie knife, or at least the name "Bowie" and the word "knife" became fused to some degree during his lifetime and raised to a legendary level after his death. Bowie was a convivial and magnetic figure, and a natural leader, but he had a simmering, lethal temper. "When fired by anger," a friend remembered, "his face bore the semblance of an enraged tiger." In 1826 he got into a nasty fight in a Louisiana hotel with a political and business enemy

JUAN SEGUÍN
was a rising political figure in Texas and led a company that fought with Sam Houston at San Jacinto. But he soon found that it was not all that easy for a Tejano to be a Texas patriot in the infant republic.

named Norris Wright, who shot Bowie in the chest. The underpowered bullet, however, didn't penetrate. With one hand busy holding Wright to the floor, the maddened Bowie desperately tried to open a clasp knife with his teeth. His friends pulled him off before he could do so. Wright survived; so did Bowie, though he came away with a severe bruise from his assailant's bullet and a missing tooth. Well, not missing exactly—it was found in Wright's finger, which Bowie had tried a little too hard to bite off.

The lesson Bowie took away from the fight was that he needed something more efficient than a clasp knife. His brother Rezin made one for him. It wasn't the ornate swordlike weapon with the clip point on top of the blade that later became the prototype of the Bowie knife. It was just a straight-bladed no-nonsense implement suitable for sticking into an enemy.

Bowie and Wright had a spectacular rematch when they were both supporters—on opposite sides—at a duel held on a sandbar on the Mississippi near Natchez. The duel ended amicably. The quarreling principals exchanged shots, missed, shook hands, and decided they were friends after all. But their associates on the field all held seething grudges of one sort or another, and the gentlemanly duel soon erupted into a lethal brawl. Wright shot Bowie in the chest yet again, this time the ball penetrating and passing through his lung. Before it was over, Bowie was all but dead—with two gunshots and at least seven stab wounds—but Wright was dead indeed. The grievously wounded Bowie had managed to plunge his new knife into Wright's chest and "cut his heart strings."

The sandbar fight made Jim Bowie and his knife famous, and as suspicion tightened on his ever-escalating scheme to cash in on fraudulent land schemes, he was becoming notorious enough that a move to Texas seemed like a very good idea. All across the United States, scrawled on the doors of abandoned cabins, written in the dockets of debtors' trials in which the accused failed to appear in court, were the words "Gone to Texas" or simply the instantly recognized initials "GTT." Bowie became part of this exodus in 1830. He had been to Texas before, as part of the James Long expedition and on a kind of business scouting trip in 1829, during which he visited San Antonio and ingratiated himself with the head of one of its leading families, Juan Veramendi, a former two-term alcalde and rising star in the state government of Coahuila and Texas.

Bowie also traveled to the San Saba country to look for a "lost" silver mine

This portrait of James Bowie is believed to have been painted from life by the artist George Peter Alexander Healy in New Orleans about ten years before Bowie's death in the Alamo. The hilt of a sword or a big knife can be seen in the subject's right hand, but it's likely not the knife most associated with his name.

the Spanish had worked with negligible success nearly eighty years before and then abandoned after the Comanches and Norteños wiped out Father Terreros and his hopeful mission. Bowie and his companions found no silver on that trip, but the failure didn't deter him. He was still a restless con man and entrepreneur. When he returned to Texas the next year, a silver strike remained on his wish list of get-rich-quick possibilities, along with a cotton-milling enterprise and big-time land speculation. He was short on cash but always flush with charm. He was "very successful," remembered one of his brothers, "in securing a fair portion of the friendship of the better class of the people." And he made sure he married very well. His nineteen-year-old bride—sixteen years younger than himself—was Ursula Veramendi, the daughter of Juan Veramendi.

Bowie had every reason to face the future with optimism on that April day in 1831 when he and Ursula said their vows in San Fernando Church in the heart of San Antonio. But misfortune came crowding in. Another silver search near the San Saba, bankrolled by his father-in-law, was abandoned when Bowie and his party were attacked by a mixed force of Tawakonis, Wacos, and Caddos. Caught out in the open, they were besieged as the Indians sniped at them and repeatedly set fire to the prairie to burn them out. The attackers finally withdrew after losing several dozen warriors. All of Bowie's party except one man managed to stagger back to San Antonio. Then, in 1833, while he was in Natchez recovering from a near fatal bout of malaria, he learned that Ursula, along with her parents, had perished in the cholera epidemic.

Bowie has often been depicted in movies as shattered by grief and lost in dissipation after the death of his wife. He was sad, of course ("I know that she had a deep hold on Bowie's affections," Noah Smithwick recalled. "Strong man that he was, I have seen the tears course down his cheeks while lamenting her untimely death"), and he definitely drank. But in real life he sprang back. He did not pause long, if at all, in his drive to achieve vast wealth. In 1833, after the capital of Coahuila and Texas was moved north from Saltillo to Monclova, he became a major participant in an insider-trading scheme in which the federalist governor and legislature colluded with a small group of Anglo speculators in a bargain-basement sale of Texas lands. For a brief time, Bowie held title to close to a half million acres. But when Santa Anna reclaimed centralist control of the government, his fortune evaporated. He was arrested, but slipped out of custody and made his way back to Texas, where he was more than ready to fight the dictator who had cheated him out of the biggest score of his life.

The sandbar duel, the San Saba siege, and his commanding presence during a bloody fight in Nacogdoches after the latest Anahuac disturbance had firmed up Bowie's reputation as a rare combination of cool strategic thinker and hot-blooded fighter. It was natural for Austin to put him in command of a ninety-two-man reconnaissance force in search of a base of operations from which to conduct the siege of San Antonio. Late in the day, Bowie settled on the spot, downstream from the town, where the old mission La Purísima Concepción sat in a field above a shallow oxbow of the San Antonio River. The ground was favorable for defense, which was fortunate, because Bowie and his men soon had to defend it.

Upon learning of their presence, General Cos dispatched two hundred dragoons and seventy-five infantrymen out from behind their fortifications in San Antonio to confront the rebels dug in along the riverbank. The Mexicans opened with cannon fire, the grapeshot tearing through the pecan limbs overhead, showering the defenders with nuts, which some of the cool-under-fire Texians cracked open and ate. For Cos, the attack was a disaster. The Kentucky rifles that many of the rebels carried could hit a target at two hundred yards, and their cartridges and powder horns held excellent DuPont powder. Most of the soldados had only their short-shooting muskets with inferior powder—"little better than pounded charcoal," according to one Texian—and on the open ground they were dangerously exposed before they could come within range to do any killing. The Mexicans withdrew with close to fifty dead and wounded. The Texians under Bowie's leadership lost only one man.

Jim Bowie and a defiant band of Texas rebels defending an old Spanish mission against a greatly superior Mexican force: the same scenario would reoccur in only a few months, though the battle would be at the Alamo, not at Concepción, and the outcome would be resoundingly different. For the moment, though, the thrown-together Texas army was victorious and confident. The usually cautious Austin tried to rouse his men to go after the defeated Mexicans and make an immediate attack upon San Antonio, declaring, "The Army must follow them right into the town!" But that was too bold a gamble even for Bowie, who, together with some of the other officers, talked Austin out of it.

So the siege of San Antonio—the siege of Béxar—continued, and as it dragged on, the weaknesses in the rebel forces became apparent. It was a brand-new volunteer army made up of restive and independent-minded soldiers who had come for a quick fight and were mentally and physically unequipped for a static siege. They did not have warm clothing for the winter that was closing in, they worried about the welfare of their families back home in the colonies, they had varying degrees of confidence in the officers they had elected to lead them, and there was no consensus about tactics or even about what exactly they were fighting for. Widespread drunkenness was a problem ("In the name of almighty God," Austin wrote to what was then passing as a Texas government, "send no more ardent spirits to this camp"), and so was desertion. Austin knew he needed reinforcements, but was openly doubtful that he could hold the army together before they arrived.

He was also more than aware of his own limitations. His health was worse than ever, and his military portfolio—beyond some militia experience back in Missouri and his harassment of the Karankawas—was thin. The fact that he had been essentially overruled by Bowie and others when he wanted to attack Cos directly after the Concepción victory was a clear enough demonstration of a natural deficit in his command authority. "The taking of Bexar is very difficult," he admitted on November 5 in the same letter to the Texas government. He recorded his concerns about his health and the conditions of his army, which had "no law but moral principle and enthusiasm to keep them together." He pleaded for "the organization of a regular army, with a Genl. of well known military talents experience, integrity and moral influence. This is very important."

He sent this letter to San Felipe, where a crucial political assemblage was trying to make sense of what the war was all about and how to conduct it. The delegates to the Consultation, as it was known, made up a clanging

chorus of agendas and opinions about whether Texas should seize this moment to announce its outright independence or still strive to remain part
of the larger Mexican federalist movement fighting to defeat Santa Anna
and restore the beloved Constitution of 1824. They compromised on a declaration that was not all that declarative, full of revolutionary rhetoric but
essentially keeping all options open. They also created a provisional government that, in its structure and personalities, would soon prove to be all but
unworkable. At its head was Henry Smith, a pinch-faced War Party stalwart
not prone to diplomacy.

A few days after the deliberations of the Consultation began, a delegate
named Gail Borden wrote to Austin, still encamped with the army outside
San Antonio. The thirty-four-year-old Borden was the publisher of a newspaper called the *Telegraph and Texas Register*, which had debuted in San Felipe
only the month before. He was also a buzzing inventor who would later
try to market an amphibious conveyance called a "terraqueous machine"
and the repulsive-sounding "meat biscuit," which also went by the name of
"Portable Dessicated Soup Bread." The meat biscuit was life sustaining but
unappetizing, and it never quite found its market. Borden would have much
better success with his next product: condensed milk.

In his letter, Borden informed Austin that he had just listened to "the
best speech . . . I have ever heard." The orator was a delegate from Nacogdoches who had been in Texas since 1832. In the words of Washington Irving,
who had met Sam Houston briefly around that time, he was a "tall, large,
well formed, fascinating man—low crowned large brimmed white beaver
[hat]—boots with brass eagle spurs—given to grand eloquence. A large &
military mode of expressing himself."

It's no accident that Irving used the word "large" three times in his on-
the-fly description. Houston had a big, commanding face dominated by a
chin dimple and bushy side-whiskers. He had, remembered a future Texas
governor, Francis Lubbock, "a most remarkable foot, measuring more
around the instep than in length." His hairline was probably receding by
1835, but judging from later portraits his chestnut hair was still abundant
on the sides of his head, where it was brushed into swooping eagle's wings
over his ears. He was tall, six feet two, but his largeness was less a matter
of size than of measureless impact. He loomed over the Texas Consultation just as he looms over the Texas consciousness today. On Interstate
45 between Houston and Dallas, there is a startling, sixty-seven-foot-high
all-white concrete statue of Sam Houston by the sculptor David Adickes.
It pops suddenly into view around a bend of the highway and looks like a
cloud-striding giant. People sometimes complain that the statue is freak-

ishly overbearing, but I've never heard anybody say it's out of scale with its subject.

Part of what has always appealed to Texans about Houston is that he was the embodiment of the start-over saga: a drunken and disgraced former governor of Tennessee who found a second chance and a colossal destiny in Texas. Houston was thirty-nine when he threaded the quicksand beds of the Red River and entered the Mexican state. His mission appears to have been primarily entrepreneurial, since he was a celebrity partner in the Galveston Bay and Texas Land Company, a kind of brokerage firm that was trying to recruit new colonists for a failing empresario grant to the north of Austin's original colony. ("If we should live," Houston wrote to a friend whom he hoped to enlist in the journey, "our wealth must be boundless.") But his journey had a diplomatic component as well, since Houston's mentor, President Andrew Jackson, had appointed him envoy to the Comanches. Houston was a logical person to be entrusted with such an errand—his Indian bona fides were strong. As a teenager in Tennessee, he had run away from home and lived with the Cherokees, learned their language, and adopted their dress. Later, as a U.S. government subagent to that same tribe, he had performed the painful duty of helping convince them to bow to American pressure to give up their lands and move west across the Mississippi.

Houston's purpose in going to Texas, as it was told to his hand-chosen biographer and memoirist, C. Edwards Lester, was to become "a herdsman, and spend the rest of his life in the prairie solitudes." Houston did have a weakness for the idea of romantic exile, but he was too much a natural world shaker for that statement to be regarded as anything but laugh-out-loud self-delusion. We can be sure that whatever dreams drove Sam Houston to Texas, they were big.

One undying source of speculation is whether Houston's presidential mission to the Comanches was just a convenient pretext, that his real reason for going to Texas was to help the ripe peach fall and to make sure it fell into Andrew Jackson's basket. Jackson wanted Texas for the United States and had tried to buy it outright from Mexico. But if he was using Houston as some sort of agent provocateur, he must have been aware that there was no telling exactly what sorts of things his agent might provoke. Houston by then was, to say the least, unpredictable.

───────── ★ ─────────

"MY GOD, IS THE MAN MAD?" HAD BEEN JACKSON'S REACTION— along with the rest of the country's—when Houston abruptly resigned the governorship of Tennessee in 1829 after his marriage to nineteen-year-old

Eliza Allen inscrutably misfired on the couple's wedding night and ended eleven weeks later. Jackson had more reason than anyone to be shocked. Houston had started out as his protégé and had risen so fast and so reliably that he was considered almost his heir, Old Hickory's likely successor to the presidency of the United States. The two men had met in 1814, when Third Lieutenant Sam Houston had fought under General Andrew Jackson in his campaign against the Creek Indians, who had allied with the British in the War of 1812. Houston had played a highly visible part in an assault on the log fort the Creeks had built where the Tallapoosa River in Alabama formed a loop known as Horseshoe Bend. He was struck by an arrow in the groin during the desperate fighting to get over the breastworks. Though the wound was severe, and Jackson wanted him out of the fight, Houston volunteered to lead a charge later in the day against the Creeks, where they were making a last stand in a fortified ravine. Probably mad with pain, certainly throbbing with dreams of gallantry, Houston rushed out ahead of his men and found himself alone on the field, where he was hit by Creek musket balls in his shoulder and arm.

He should not have survived the Battle of Horseshoe Bend, but he did. Though his wounds never healed and troubled him the rest of his life, he went on to become a United States congressman and, at thirty-four, the governor of Tennessee. It was after he married Eliza Allen, the daughter of a wealthy family from Sumner County, that everything fell apart. Nobody has ever figured out what exactly went wrong in that marriage. "There is a thousand different tails a float," buzzed one correspondent. The theories alive at the time and still alive today include: Eliza, though in love with somebody else, was pressured by her family to marry the governor; Houston confronted her about his suspicion that she might not be "virtuous"; Eliza was afraid of Houston somehow, thought him controlling and downright weird; she was repulsed by his "running sore," the long-unhealed wound in his groin caused by a Creek arrow.

Whatever the cause, Eliza's disenchantment with her dazzling new husband was immediate. The second morning after the wedding, the Houstons were staying with friends on the way to Nashville. Eliza, seeing her new husband in a snowball fight with the family's young daughters, confided to their mother, "I wish they would kill him."

The disaster of his marriage caused Houston to collapse. After Eliza ran back to her family, he abruptly resigned the governorship, refused to explain anything, and moved to the Arkansas Territory to live with the Cherokees again. He looked, according to one supposedly firsthand description, "like some magnificent ruin." To the Cherokees, though, he was mostly just a ruin. He did manage to marry again, to a mixed-race Cherokee widow named Tiana Rogers, and was functional enough to operate a trading post for a while, but his theatrical temperament had driven him into such glorious dissipation that the Cherokees—who had previously bestowed upon him the mystical-sounding name the Raven—now just called him Oo-tse-tee Ar-dee-tah-skee, which translates as "Big Drunk."

But now Sam Houston was in Texas, not totally sobered up but definitely in a regenerative frame of mind. He had a fortune to make, a reputation to rebuild, and maybe—it couldn't have been far from his grandiose consciousness—a Texas-sized world to conquer.

By this time he seems to have left behind the Cherokee costuming, the colorful hunting shirts, beaded sashes, and turbans he had once worn to impress and annoy the citizens of Washington and Nashville. But he still wore the ring that his mother had given him when he first marched off to fight the Creeks, a slim gold band with the word "Honor" engraved on the inside. (It is on display at the San Jacinto Museum, along with his dictionary, in which he crossed out the word "temporize" and wrote "Out with it!" in the margin). In Texas he is described as wearing buckskins, "greasy" buckskins at that, and one of his many political enemies, a Massachusetts doctor named Anson Jones, decided that he looked like "a broken-down sot and debauchee." But enough delegates to the Consultation, like Gail Borden, felt otherwise and elected him to be the "Genl. of well known military talents experience, integrity and moral influence" that Austin had pined for.

Houston was named commander in chief of the regular army. One problem: there was no regular army. The men fighting with Stephen Austin outside San Antonio were all volunteers. Houston would have to create the official Texas army and somehow also assume command of the rowdy self-governing militias who made up the only fighting force the Texians had in the field. The Consultation presented Houston with a handsome proclamation that congratulated him and detailed his responsibilities but in certain subtle phrases—"be careful in executing the great trust reposed in you," "you are to regulate your conduct"—betrayed a wariness that he had once been, and could be still, a magnificent ruin.

───────── ★ ─────────

WHILE HOUSTON BUSIED HIMSELF IN SAN FELIPE AND THEN IN
Gonzales with the details of inventing an army, the siege of San Antonio continued. Houston had no control over the men there, who were growing distracted and disheartened as the siege dragged on. Houston thought the effort to dislodge Cos was a mistake, or at least would be until he could

build up an army capable of seizing San Antonio and holding on to it. He believed the Texians should retreat to the east and establish themselves along a line between Gonzales and Goliad, where they would fight a defensive war primarily aimed at keeping Mexican forces out of the Anglo colonies.

But the Consultation had not placed Houston in command in San Antonio. Austin still held that position, though barely. Houston had no great regard for Austin's military leadership. The "little Gentleman," he had written earlier in the year to John Wharton, "shewed the disposition of a viper without its fangs." By contrast, he was pleased to say about himself that he was "one of the most steady men in Texas!"

In late November, Austin once more tried to convince his army to make an attack on Cos's defenses, but the majority of his men wouldn't follow him. It was a crushing blow to his confidence. He was reported to be "greatly astonished & mortified," and he admitted in a letter to his brother-in-law the next day that he had done the best he could, but the army was basically unmanageable, and he really needed a break. Fortunately, the Consultation had already agreed with him that his talents were being misused. He was informed that he would be sent with William Wharton and another delegate, Branch T. Archer, to the United States to raise money and moral support for the Texian cause. The mission was a perfect fit. If there was one thing Austin was good at, it was selling people on the idea of Texas.

The United States was already ablaze with interest in the Texian cause. Embattled colonists fighting for their rights as free citizens under a tyrannical government from which they were no doubt about to declare their independence was almost a reprise of America's origin story. In New Orleans, only a week and a half after the revolt was sparked at Gonzales, there was a public meeting at a commodious coffeehouse on Magazine Street. Ten thousand dollars for the relief of Texas was raised, and many of the young men in the audience, pumped up by all the inspiring speeches and the patriotic banners, volunteered to cross over into Texas and join in the fight. One of the people caught up in the excitement was a young Prussian immigrant not yet out of his teens named Herman Ehrenberg. He enlisted with 120 other men in an organization called the New Orleans Greys. Unlike the militias and ranging companies that made up most of the rebel forces, with their mismatched Leatherstocking outfits and Dickensian frock coats and top hats, the Greys had actual uniforms—grey jackets and trousers with floppy sealskin forage caps. As soon as they crossed the Sabine at Gaines Ferry, they were greeted as saviors by the local Texians. "A pretty Texas girl," Ehrenberg remembered, "held out to us a beautiful banner of blue silk, bearing the following inscription: To the first company of volunteers sent by New Orleans to Texas." Before it was all over, this flag—which would fly over the Alamo and be taken as a battle prize to Mexico City, where it remains today, frayed and faded—would be almost all that was left of the New Orleans Greys.

By the time Ehrenberg and the Greys joined the Texian forces besieging San Antonio, Austin had left on his diplomatic mission to the States and Bowie had been dispatched to Goliad, to oversee the critical defenses of the presidio there—now called Fort Defiance. Edward Burleson was in charge in San Antonio. Burleson, who would one day be memorialized by the Texas Legislature as "the hero of thirty battles who was never known to retreat," was a tough thirty-seven-year-old veteran militia commander who had developed a reputation in Texas as a fearsome Indian fighter. The previous summer, an observer had deemed Burleson and his companions, as they rode out on a reprisal against a group of Indians, as much a "don't care a looking company of men as could be found on the top of the ground."

Ehrenberg found the Texian camp to be a colorful mess: tents pitched here and there without any regard for organization, volunteers ignoring the muster drum as they sat by their fires, slicing off roasting meat with their Bowie knives, buzzards and coyotes congregating to feed on the carcasses of butchered cattle. He took note of the enemy's fortifications, not just the breastworks and battlements that Cos had placed in the city itself, but also the solitary old mission, bristling with artillery, visible on the other side of a cornfield: "On the left, denuded shore of the river, rose the Alamo, the sombre fortress of the ancient province of Texas."

— 12 —

THE ALAMO IS OURS!

VISITORS TO THE ALAMO TODAY ARE IMPRESSED MOSTLY by how unimpressed they are. Instead of a commanding castle-like fort in the middle of a Texas prairie, they encounter a squat, brooding edifice tucked away into the bustling downtown of San Antonio. What most of them don't understand is that this iconic building, with its bedstead-shaped parapet, is not really the Alamo. It is a church, one of only two surviving buildings of the large mission compound that was the Alamo proper. At the time the Mexicans held San Antonio, the Alamo was a sprawling three-acre expanse whose church, convent, and quarters for priests and Indians had been turned into an imperfect fortress where Cos concentrated much of his defenses.

The rebel assault on San Antonio, which began at last on the morning of December 5, almost didn't happen. Burleson had the military experience and demeanor that Austin lacked, but when he proposed an attack he had the same problem of being overruled by his officers. Their caution might have been justified, since the army was falling apart. It was short on supplies, confused about its aims, and filled with soldiers who viewed insubordination as a birthright. The so-called Texas government, which was supposed to be setting policy and supplying its army, was of no help, since it turned out to be a wasp's nest of men whose interests and egos were at perpetual cross-purposes. And many of the volunteers were considering moving on to greener pastures by joining an ill-advised expedition to conquer Matamoros, the Mexican port city at the mouth of the Rio Grande. The Matamoros adventure wasn't entirely without military logic. Austin had strongly recommended that the city be captured—"It is all important," he had written to the Consultation on November 5. He thought that if Matamoros fell to the rebels, it would keep Santa Anna from sending more troops to Texas. But Austin had in mind a well-planned diversionary expedition originating from New Orleans, not an impromptu change of scene for the frustrated and disillusioned citizen-soldiers who had been trying without success for weeks to take San Antonio from the Mexican Army.

The Texians might have melted away and given up the attempt to take San Antonio if not for the appearance in camp of Jesús Cuellar, a Mexican lieutenant, former Comanche captive, and newly minted enemy of Santa Anna. Cuellar, who had been fighting with the Mexicans in San Antonio, decided to change sides. He told Burleson that Cos's defenses in the city were weaker than the Texians thought, and offered to guide them in an attack. On hearing the news, Burleson reconsidered the decision to abandon the siege and go into winter quarters, and the men were soon galvanized by a challenge thrown down by one of their officers, Ben Milam. Milam had tried to seize Texas once before as a player in James Long's 1819 expedition. He survived that disaster, and after being released from prison he flourished in the hopeful atmosphere following Mexican independence from Spain, eventually becoming a colonel in the Mexican Army. He wasn't in the mood to let another opportunity to liberate Texas pass.

"Who will go with Old Ben Milam into San Antonio?" he is reported to have said. It was just the rallying cry the men needed, and before dawn the next morning a strike force made up of two divisions set out to try to infiltrate the city as far as possible before they could be discovered. By this time, the rebel forces had acquired a few pieces of artillery, and at around five in the morning they opened fire on the Alamo to create a diversion and draw the Mexicans away from the city and toward the mission. The diversion worked well enough for the insurgents to stealthily make their way into almost the center of the town before being spotted. Then canister fire from the Mexican artillery blasted jagged metal fragments into the narrow streets, driving the rebels into residents' houses, where Bexareño families cowered in terror. For the next four days, the Texians advanced with their Kentucky rifles and crowbars, moving from house to house, prying open doors, digging through walls, taking the city inch by inch as the defenders fought furiously to stop them. But the Texians kept on, seizing control of key positions.

Among these was the house once owned by the Veramendi family and, since they were all dead of cholera, now belonged to their son-in-law Jim Bowie.

On the third day of the siege, a Mexican sniper named Felix de la Garza, armed with an excellent British-made weapon called a Baker rifle, climbed into a tree along the riverbank. He saw Ben Milam standing in front of the Veramendi house, took careful aim, and killed the inspirational Texian leader with a single shot to the head. But the powder flash from de la Garza's rifle betrayed his position, and in an instant enraged rebels shot him out of the tree.

During the nighttime lull in the fighting, Milam was buried in the Veramendi courtyard with full Masonic rites. The house-to-house fighting continued the next day and the next. Cos received reinforcements, though the initial jubilation at their arrival quickly wore away when it was discovered that many of them were convicts who had been hauled into the fight in manacles and didn't know how to load a musket. One of the officers of the relief column was a lieutenant colonel of engineers named José Juan Sánchez-Navarro. After taking part in the street fighting in the city, he made his way across the river to report to Cos in the Alamo. He found a scene of despair: frightened girls and women who had fled the town to seek refuge behind the walls of the fort, starving horses, demoralized troops muttering, "We are lost." Cos was of much the same opinion. He told Sánchez-Navarro to arrange surrender on the best terms he could: "Save the dignity of our Government, the honor of its arms . . . even though I myself perish."

Sánchez-Navarro rode out under a white flag to meet the Texians. He was alarmed and revolted by the enemy that had just vanquished the Mexican forces: "We were surrounded with crude bumpkins, proud and overbearing. (Whoever knows the character of North Americans may appreciate the position in which we found ourselves.)"

However bumpkinish they might have appeared, the Texians treated the Mexican forces with military respect and with a generosity that would not be reciprocated the next time the Alamo fell. Cos and his men were given food and medical care and, after pledging not to take up arms against the colonies, allowed to return to the interior of Mexico.

The rebels had driven the Mexican Army out of Texas, and out of San Antonio, with the loss of only four men. "We considered ourselves," Herman Ehrenberg wrote, "almost invincible."

IN JANUARY OF THE NEXT YEAR, 1836, A LITTLE MORE THAN A month after the rebels took San Antonio, a Nacogdoches resident named John Forbes stood before fifty-four Texas newcomers, most of them Tennesseans, who had crowded into the room that served as his office. Forbes himself had not been in Texas long, but he had risen quickly enough for the provisional government, which had begun creating its own local officials, in defiance of the old Mexican order, to appoint him judge. As judge, one of his duties was to administer the oath of allegiance to volunteers from the United States who had come to fight in the Texas cause.

Forbes had written the oath himself. It was something of a conditional statement, because Texas had not yet declared its independence from Mexico and nobody could yet be certain exactly what entity the men taking the oath were pledging their allegiance to: "I do solemnly swear that I will bear true allegiance to the provisional government of Texas, or any future government that may be hereafter declared, and that I will serve her honestly and faithfully against all her enemies and oppressors whatsoever, and observe and obey the orders of the governor of Texas, the orders and decrees of the present and future authorities, and the orders of the officers appointed over me according to the rules and articles for the government of Texas so help me God."

The men in the room stepped forward and signed willingly, but one of them hesitated, which must have caused a bit of commotion, because David Crockett was one of the most famous people in the United States, better known than Jim Bowie or maybe even Sam Houston. At forty-nine, he was considerably older than almost all the other volunteers. He had lank black hair that was parted in the middle and fell to his shoulders. His nose was sharp and straight. In every credible surviving portrait of him there is a striking warmth of expression, an unexpected mildness. ("He has rather an indolent appearance," wrote a woman who saw him at a ventriloquist's performance in New York, "and looks not like a 'go-ahead' man.") His health was good, for now, but malaria had almost killed him on several occasions and could recur at any time. He might have been a little paunchy before he left for Texas—he seems so in a full-length portrait painted in a Washington studio a few years before by John Gadsby Chapman—but he had probably lost weight on the lengthy overland journey. As for dress, he may or may not have had buckskins and a coonskin cap in his baggage, but he preferred to dress like a normal gentleman, just as he preferred to be known in formal circles as "David" and not "Davy."

The reason he hesitated before signing the oath was a concern about its wording, in particular its promise of loyalty to "the provisional government of Texas, or any future government." Since a future government might be despotic, he told Forbes, he insisted on altering the phrase so that it read "any future republican government." Forbes agreed, Crockett signed, and he became

Congressman Davy Crockett was an enthusiastic model when John G. Chapman painted this full-length portrait of him in 1834. It was Crockett's idea to appear as a bear hunter, though he had to look far and wide in Washington, DC, to locate the right backwoods gear and clothing.

a soldier in the Texas cause, eligible for a headright claim of 640 acres. The land was definitely an enticement for the always-strapped Crockett, but so was the opportunity to get involved in a big way in the future of a region that was most likely to become either its own country or a part of the United States.

"He could not live without being before the public," wrote someone who encountered Crockett in New York at the height of his renown, when it seemed entirely plausible that he might become president. Crockett had been an officeholder off and on for almost twenty years, ever since, as a young veteran of the same Creek War in which Sam Houston had received his unhealing wounds, he was named a justice of the peace in West Tennessee. He had risen to national prominence as a three-term congressman on the strength of his natural electioneering wits and as the manufactured embodiment of the common-man ideal that began to take hold during the age of Andrew Jackson. Crockett was not in any real sense a fraud. He *was* a common man, a restless, uneducated frontier denizen continually beset by hard times and hard luck, but with such a store of humor and rustic magnetism that he had been elected to the House of Representative and been the backwoods subject of humorous plays and books and almanacs, as well as the author of a best-selling and wonderfully idiosyncratic autobiography.

Why then was he in Texas? Like so many others, like Travis and Bowie and Houston, he had outlasted his prospects in the States. Though Crockett was an amusing and talented campaigner, as a politician he had proved to be principled but inflexible. The battles he waged—reforms to benefit the landless and luckless class from which he had sprung, and fair treatment of Indians—were waged without the savvy cynicism of his political enemies. And he had made a merciless enemy in Andrew Jackson. He had fought under Jackson during the Creek War, but the more Crockett saw of "King Andrew," the less he liked him. Though he began his political career as a member of Jackson's Democratic Party, he had allowed himself and his celebrity to be taken up by the Whigs, who had toyed with the idea of running him against Martin Van Buren in the 1836 presidential election.

In the end, he was defeated by a Jackson man for reelection to his congressional seat. He was also short on money, as usual, estranged from his wife, and a victim of the frontier caricature that had once been his ticket out of obscurity. Along with "Come and Take It," the most popular slogan to be found today on souvenir coffee mugs and baseball caps are the bitter words he reportedly spoke to the constituents who had voted him out of office: "You may all go to hell, and I will go to Texas."

Full of bright prospects ("I am rejoiced at my fate," he wrote home to his family), Crockett left Nacogdoches with an entourage that dubbed itself the

Tennessee Mounted Volunteers. Among them was Micajah Autry, a once-prosperous lawyer from Jackson, Tennessee, who had made the mistake of investing in a doomed mercantile business. Now Autry was determined to help Texas win its independence and make a new life for his family. He was optimistic but weary and homesick. In his last letter to his wife, less than two months before he would die at the Alamo, he wrote in a postscript: "We stand guard of nights and night before last was mine to stand two hours during which the moon rose in all her mildness and splendor and majesty. With what pleasure did I contemplate that lovely orb chiefly because I recollected how often you and I had taken pleasure in standing in the door and contemplating her together. Indeed I imagined that you might be looking at her at the same time. Farewell Dear Martha."

Crockett and the Tennesseans arrived in San Antonio in early February. A lot had happened there since the Texians seized the town, and very little of it was good. A Scottish-born doctor named James Grant, whose complex career included world-spanning voyages as a ship's surgeon, possible espionage for the British government, and Mexico representative for a London banking house, had—along with Frank Johnson, a hero of the battle for Béxar—reenergized the dream of taking the fight to Matamoros. The tactical reason for taking Matamoros was to open up a diversionary second front in the war, and it may have been defensible. But the initiative appealed more strongly to the simpler motives of greed and adventure. Added to that was the fact that the provisional Texas government, which had dissolved into toxic personal factionalism between Governor Smith and his Council, was such a complete failure that it could present no coherent policy on the war or anything else.

There were less than a hundred men left to defend San Antonio and the Alamo by the time the Matamoros expedition marched out of town. Among the men following Grant and Johnson were Herman Ehrenberg and half of the New Orleans Greys. They stripped the garrison of horses and cattle, clothing and military supplies. The enraged Alamo commander, James Neill, warned the provisional government, "We know not what day, or hour, an enemy of 1000 in number may be down upon us, and as we have no supplies of provisions within the fortress could be Starved out in 4 days by any thing like a close Seige."

Neill did not know it, but he was being optimistic. As he was writing his letter, a Mexican army of over six thousand men, led by Santa Anna, was being assembled in San Luis Potosí and was about to begin a brutal overland journey to retake San Antonio.

The depleted garrison must have been astonished to discover that none other than the legendary David Crockett, the "half horse, half snapping turtle" backwoods congressman, had chosen to join them at their forlorn outpost. They demanded a speech from him, and he mounted a box in the middle of San Antonio's bullet-scarred plaza, did his "you may all go to hell and I will go to Texas" routine, and concluded with, "I shall identify myself with your interests, and all the honor that I desire is that of defending, as a high private, in common with my fellow-citizens, the liberties of our common country."

The "high private" remark was in response to an offer of command, which Crockett refused, preferring his common-man credentials. And his offhand reference to "our common country" could very well have struck a disturbing chord for the Tejanos in his audience. What common country was he referring to? The country from which he and his fellow Anglo insurgents had risen, the country to which they now planned to deliver Texas?

In any case, Crockett took his place as a "high private" under the command of James Neill. Crockett's was not the only notable name on the muster roll. Jim Bowie was back in San Antonio, having been dispatched there by Sam Houston with the recommendation that the town be abandoned and the Alamo demolished. But when he got to San Antonio, Bowie came to a different conclusion. He and Neill had fought to take this place from Cos's army, its defenses had been considerably strengthened in the meantime, and it made no strategic sense to them to give it up. "The salvation of Texas," Bowie wrote to Henry Smith, "depends in great measure in keeping Bejar out of the hands of the enemy. It serves as the frontier picquet guard and if it were in the possession of Santa Anna there is no strong hold from which to repel him in his march towards the Sabine." Bowie was at this point certain that the Mexican Army was on its way to reclaim its Texas capital, and he declared, "Col. Neill & Myself have come to the solemn resolution that we will rather die in these ditches than give it up to the enemy."

Smith apparently agreed that the Alamo and San Antonio should be defended, not abandoned, because by the time he received Bowie's letter, he had already ordered William Travis to raise a hundred men and ride from San Felipe to reinforce the garrison. It is unclear whether the custom uniform that Travis had ordered for himself arrived before he left, but we know from the liberal clothing purchases recorded in his diary that he made it a priority to dress for the occasion. Travis "strained every nerve" to comply with Smith's request, but in the end he was able to recruit only about thirty men. By the time he had reached the Colorado, he was exhausted and fed up. "The people are cold & indifferent," he reported. "They are worn down & exhausted with the war, & in consequence of dissentions between contending & rival chieftains, they have lost all confidence in their own Govt. & officers." He asked to be relieved and threatened to resign if Smith could not find something more worthwhile for him to do than lead a group of underequipped volunteers to an outpost that Sam Houston believed ought to be abandoned.

But when Travis got to San Antonio, he too changed his mind and became invested in the idea of holding the town. "We are determined to sustain it," he wrote to Smith, "as long as there is a man left, because we consider death preferable to disgrace, which would be the result of giving up a Post which has been so dearly won, and thus opening the door for the Invaders to enter the Sacred Territory of the Colonies."

Two weeks after he arrived in San Antonio, Travis found himself in command when Neill left on what was supposed to be a brief furlough due to a family illness. Travis knew he had to make his leadership acceptable to both the regulars that he commanded and the volunteers, over whom he had no official authority. He ordered an election so that the volunteers could choose their leader to share command, an unruly solution that led to something like anarchy. The volunteers chose Bowie, and for some reason the cool-headed fighter who had held off Indians at San Saba and beat Cos's Mexican dragoons at the Battle of Concepcíon promptly lost all control of himself. He embarked on an epic bender during which he stopped terrified Tejano families from fleeing the city and arbitrarily ordered the release of duly convicted prisoners from the jail. But his drunken power grab seemed to subside with his hangover, and only a few days later he and Travis were peacefully cosigning a plea to Smith for reinforcements.

None arrived. By the third week of February, Travis and Bowie had only 150 men. Half of them were quartered in the Alamo, the other half in town. They held a raucous fandango on the night of February 22 to celebrate George Washington's birthday, and on the bleary morning after they noticed the Bexareños were almost in full flight, desperately evacuating the town on foot or on horseback, their carts loaded with furniture and valuables. Early that afternoon, a sentinel in the bell tower of San Fernando Church rang the bell and called out that he had seen Santa Anna's forces approaching, but several other men who came running and climbed the tower saw nothing. Whatever the sentinel had seen had vanished, mirage-like, in the mesquite-screened defiles of the shallow hills west of town. But two scouts that Travis sent out in that direction soon returned at a breathless gallop to confirm the news that the Mexican Army had just arrived.

The surprised garrison had known that Santa Anna was on his way, but they thought he would take his time, waiting until the spring so that his army's cavalry mounts and livestock could forage on fresh prairie grass. But he had thrown together his punitive expedition and led it north, in the middle of the winter, with merciless speed. "The great problem I had to solve," he later wrote, "was to reconquer Texas and to accomplish this in the shortest time possible, at whatever cost."

The rebels gathered what provisions they could at the last minute and raced across the river to barricade themselves behind the walls of the Alamo. Some of the Tejano women who had not left town stood in their doorways, weeping, as the defenders made their way to the footbridge spanning the river. "Poor fellows," they called out. "You will all be killed."

Travis sent out riders with pleas for help to Gonzales and to Goliad, where there were more than four hundred men under the command of James Fannin, who had been a key presence in the siege of Béxar. Meanwhile, the Mexican forces quickly invested San Antonio and raised a red banner from the bell tower of San Fernando Church. The flag was a signal that no quarter would be given to the pirates who had unlawfully seized Mexican soil. Travis ordered a response in the form of a defiant blast from the Alamo's largest piece of artillery, a cannon firing an eighteen-pound ball.

Travis apparently had not cleared this gesture with his co-commander Bowie, who wasted no time writing a letter and sending it out with a messenger under a white flag to ask whether a parley was still possible. The reply was as unequivocal as the red flag: "The Mexican army cannot come to terms under any conditions with rebellious foreigners."

Something was wrong with Bowie. You can see it in a facsimile of a letter he wrote that is on display today at the Alamo. The letter is in Spanish. Bowie appears to have dictated it, most likely to Juan Seguín, who had entered the Alamo with about fifteen other Tejanos from his company. The handwriting is smooth and precise, but Bowie's signature at the bottom is nothing more than a ragged scratch. The siege of the Alamo had only just begun, and he was already so sick that he could barely sign his name. He was probably suffering from typhoid, or at least that was what Juana Alsbury believed.

Juana Alsbury and her younger sister, Gertrudis, were the closest thing to family members Bowie had left in Texas. Juana was twenty-four. Her maiden name was Navarro. She and Gertrudis were members of two of the most powerful families in San Antonio, the Navarros and the Veramendis. Their father was José Ángel Navarro, who had been both the alcalde and *jefe político*. Their aunt, Josefa Navarro, had married Juan Martín Veramendi. After their mother's death, Juana and Gertrudis Navarro were sent to live in the Veramendi household with their cousin Ursula, who later married Jim Bowie.

Ursula Veramendi died with her parents in the cholera epidemic of 1833, but the Navarro sisters were still close to her husband, and they had gone into the Alamo either to be under Bowie's protection or to look after him during the illness that apparently struck him on the first day of the siege.

Until very recently, Juana had been a widow. Her husband, Alejo Pérez, had died in 1834, but only a month before Santa Anna's army arrived she remarried. Her new husband was a Texian doctor named Horace Alsbury, who had been with the rebels when they defeated Cos. But Alsbury was out of town, and Juana had retreated to the Alamo with her late husband's son, an infant who was named, like his father, Alejo Pérez.

Around 2008 or 2009, I was in a hotel conference room in San Antonio, at the annual meeting of the Alamo Society, an organization made up of historians and reenactors who share a close-to-obsessive interest in the famous battle. Somebody pointed out a man in his eighties who was sitting on one side of the room. He was the grandson of Alejo Pérez, the baby that Juana Alsbury had carried in her arms when she entered the Alamo on February 23, 1836. Pérez had had two children with his first wife and then had remarried and had another family late in life before he died in 1918. The old man in that conference room was born in 1914, in time to meet his grandfather. If I had thought to introduce myself, I would have been only a handshake away from someone who had known a participant in the siege and fall of the Alamo.

The Alamo has generated such mythic resonance—especially, though not exclusively, in the minds of Texans—that it is easy to forget that it was an actual historical event and not some sort of pageant that took place deep in the gauzy mists of time. The fact that a minor battle on the fringes of a minor war was elevated to a Homeric struggle is partly due to the letter that Travis wrote on the second day of the siege and sent out with a courier named Albert Martin.

> To the People of Texas & all Americans in the world—Fellow citizens and compatriots—
> I am besieged, by a thousand or more of the Mexicans under Santa Anna—I have sustained a continual Bombardment & cannonade for 24 hours & have not lost a man—The enemy has demanded a surrender at discretion, otherwise, the garrison will all be put to the sword, if the fort is taken—I have answered the demand with a cannon shot, & our flag still waves proudly from the walls—*I shall never surrender or retreat.* Then, I call on you in the name of Liberty, of patriotism & everything dear to the American character, to come to our aid, with all dispatch—The enemy is receiving reinforcements daily & will no doubt increase to three or four thousand in four or five days. If this call is neglected, I am determined to sustain myself as long as possible & die like a soldier who never forgets what is due to his own honor & that of his country—Victory or Death,

William Barret Travis
Lt. Col. Comdt.

P.S. The Lord is on our side—when the enemy appeared in sight
we had not three bushels of corn—we have since found in deserted
houses 80 or 90 bushels & got into the walls 20 or 30 head of
Beeves—
Travis

I have reproduced the letter in its entirety here because it is almost unthinkable not to. William Barret Travis, the washed-up Alabama lawyer,
the grievance-minded provocateur who "hungered and thirsted for fame,"
had unknowingly produced the sacred text of Texas history—a document
of epic, eloquent defiance that schoolchildren throughout the state are
instructed to memorize.

When he wrote his letter, in his headquarters room in one of the buildings
on the western side of the Alamo compound, Travis was obviously grasping
for resounding rhetoric, but so much was happening so fast that it is hard to
imagine him consciously writing for the ages. He just needed help, and soon.
He had something like 150 men to defend a shored-up old mission that was
not quite a proper fortress. Its walls were so low and so extended that to have
any realistic chance of holding off a direct attack from Santa Anna, he needed
a force at least three times as large as the one he had.

A few days after the siege began, Juan Seguín managed to slip out of the
fort with another message from Travis, an urgent plea for help from Goliad,
where James Fannin was in command of the only force in Texas sizable
enough to make up an effective reinforcement. Fannin promptly set out for
San Antonio with three hundred of his men, along with four pieces of artillery, but they had barely begun the march when one of the wagons broke
down, creating a delay that turned into a fatal opportunity for doubt. Fannin
was one of the heroes, along with Bowie, of the Battle of Concepción, and
the two years he had spent at West Point before withdrawing had given him
at least some basic understanding of traditional war craft. But he had the
wrong temperament for this kind of emergency, and he seemed to know it.
"I am a better judge of my military abilities than others," he wrote on February 22 to the lieutenant governor of the provisional government, "and if I
am qualified to command an Army, I have not found it out."

He was not the only one who had doubts about continuing on to the
Alamo. His officers were of the opinion that it would be a strategic mistake to abandon a crucial coastal stronghold in order to strengthen an out-

post that was likely to be overwhelmed in any case. And they were aware that another Mexican force under the command of a very capable general, José de Urrea, was in the vicinity, aided—just as the rebels were—by Tejano scouts who knew the country. At the moment, Urrea was busy killing and capturing the fifty or so men led by Frank Johnson and James Grant who had persisted in marching on to Matamoros after their expedition had more or less fallen apart.

So Fannin turned his men around and marched back to Goliad, to the security of the presidio. Herman Ehrenberg and his fellow New Orleans Greys were with Fannin on this aborted relief expedition. Ehrenberg recalled that they tried to talk their commander out of his "selfish resolution" to turn back: "We reminded him constantly of the probable fate of our brothers-in-arms if we turned a deaf ear to their appeal."

"Col. Fannin is said to be on the march to this place," Travis wrote forlornly from the Alamo on March 3, "but I fear it is not true." In this letter, as well as in another he managed to send out on the same day, he gives a vivid account of the conditions in the Alamo after ten days of being besieged and bombarded. "We have had a shower of bombs and cannon balls continually falling among us the whole time, yet none of us have fallen. We have been miraculously preserved." He makes a reference to the gathering that he knows has been called in a last attempt to try to forge the poisonously partisan and almost laughably inept Texas government into a functional body with a coherent purpose. In Travis's mind, that purpose had been obvious for a long time: "Let the Convention go on and make a declaration of independence; and we will then understand and the world will understand what we are fighting for. If independence is not declared, I shall lay down my arms and so will the men under my command. But under the flag of independence, we are ready to peril our lives a hundred times a day, and to dare the monster who is fighting us under a blood-red flag, threatening to murder all prisoners and to make Texas a waste desert."

TRAVIS DIDN'T KNOW IT, BUT INDEPENDENCE HAD BEEN DE-clared the day before. Fifty-nine delegates were convened in Washington, a hamlet of a hundred or so people fifty miles north of San Felipe at a strategic river crossing on the Brazos just below its confluence with the Navasota. William Fairfax Gray, a lawyer and land agent who happened to be visiting at the time, and whose dyspeptic judgment might have been informed by weeks of terrible food and even worse coffee, thought Washington a "disgusting" place. "It is laid out in the woods; about a dozen wretched cabins

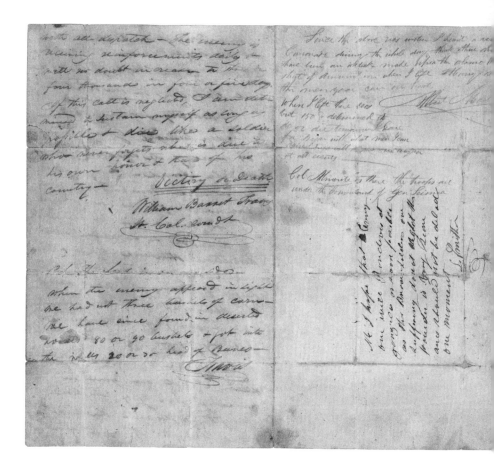

or shanties constitute the city; not one decent house in it, and only one well defined street, with stumps still standing. A rare place to hold a national convention in. They will have to leave it promptly to avoid starvation."

The delegates gathered in what passed for an assembly hall, a drafty and unfinished frame building, with cloth stretched across the open windows to provide some sort of barrier against the cold wind. In less than an hour, they approved a declaration of independence that had been largely written in advance by a Tennessee lawyer named George Childress. José Antonio Navarro was one of the men who signed the document. He was the uncle of Juana Alsbury and Gertrudis Navarro, who were at that moment under siege behind the walls of the Alamo. He and his own uncle, Francisco Ruiz, were Tejano delegates to the convention from Béxar. They had both been participants on the rebel side when Arredondo invested Texas in 1813 and had spent years in political exile afterward. Now it was time for them to put themselves on the line again, for yet another uprising engineered by Anglo

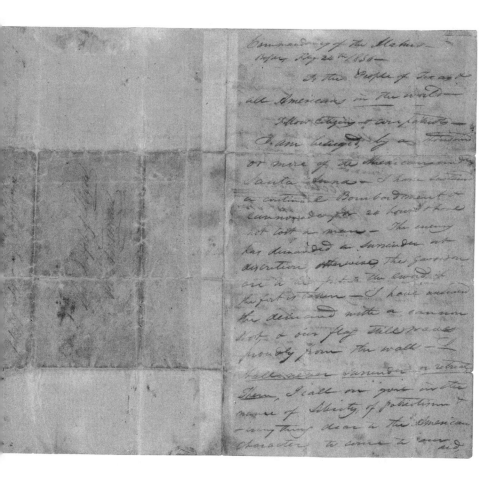

The sacred text of Texas history: William Travis's eloquent, defiant letter from the Alamo, calling upon the conscience of "the people of Texas, and all Americans in the world." When he closed his letter, Travis underlined "Victory or Death" three times.

outlanders that would place them at war with their native country. "The pang of severing national allegiance unnerved him for the act," wrote a contemporary, the historian Reuben M. Potter, of the moment, "till Ruiz took him by the arm and led him to the desk where the instrument awaited his signature. He signed it, and felt that the first plunge which puts an end to all shrinking was over." The document Navarro and Ruiz signed, along with the fifty-eight other men gathered in what amounted to Texas's Independence Hall, began with a Jeffersonian philosophical preamble about the purpose of government, continued with a summary of grievances and betrayals, and concluded that "the people of Texas do now constitute a free, Sovereign, and independent republic, and are fully invested with all the rights and attributes which properly belong to independent nations."

THE MEN AND WOMEN IN THE ALAMO KNEW THAT SANTA
Anna's noose was drawing tight. The Mexican entrenchments were creeping closer from all directions, and the defenders could hear cheering from
San Antonio de Béxar as the trailing brigades of Santa Anna's army arrived
in town, worsening the odds against those in the Alamo. But there was as
yet no reason to give up hope. A mounted company of thirty-two men from
Gonzales had made its way in the darkness past the screen of Mexican cavalry and into the fort. And on March 3, the day that Travis wrote his last
letters, James Bonham daringly rode in in broad daylight. Bonham, born in
South Carolina a couple of years before Travis, is thought to have been his
second cousin. He shared with Travis an activist temperament and had once
been expelled from South Carolina College for leading a student protest
against the quality of the food in the dining hall. He rode through the gates
of the Alamo with a letter in his saddlebag from another warrior-lawyer,
Robert Williamson. "You cannot know my anxiety, sir," Williamson wrote.
"Today makes four full days that we have not received the slightest report
regarding your dangerous situation." Hold firm, Williamson urged. Help
was on the way, not just Colonel Fannin (he had not yet heard of Fannin's
reversal) but also another sixty men from Gonzales and three hundred more
from other settlements.

Santa Anna was also aware that at least some reinforcements might still
arrive, and that may have been part of the reason he decided to make a final
assault on the Alamo after thirteen days of siege warfare and skirmishing
with the rebels. Not all his officers were in agreement. During a council of
war, several of them argued that it would be far better to wait for the siege
cannon they were expecting to arrive within the next few days. The artillery on hand—a few mortars that fired grenades and light field pieces that
hurled six- or eight-pound balls—had done significant damage to the Alamo's walls. But those walls—especially the crumbling north wall—could be
battered down in a matter of hours with proper siege weapons, and a rebel
surrender would most likely follow. But Santa Anna was determined not to
wait. A lieutenant colonel named José Enrique de la Peña—who, like many
other officers in Santa Anna's army, would later try to put as much distance as possible between himself and the man who lost Texas—thought he
knew the reason: "He wanted to cause a sensation and would have regretted
taking the Alamo without clamor and without bloodshed, for some believed
that without these there was no glory."

"Night came," de la Peña wrote in his memoir about the Texas war, "and

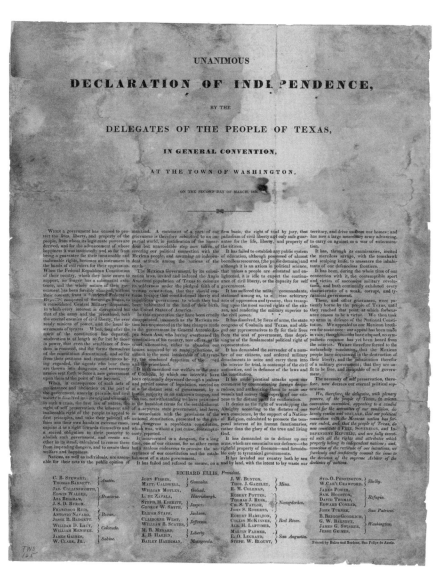

The defenders of the Alamo died without knowing that Texas had declared independence from Mexico on March 2, 1836, proclaiming a "free, Sovereign, and independent republic." But as long as Santa Anna's army was on the march, those were only words.

with it the most sober reflections. . . . Each one individually confronted and prepared his soul for the terrible moment, expressed his last wishes, and silently and coolly took those steps which preceded an encounter."

The assault began at 5:30 a.m. It proceeded in silence and darkness: a sneak attack, not the broad-daylight open-ground charge depicted in so many Alamo movies. The soldados who had been lying on the cold ground for half the night were finally ordered to stand and form into the four col-

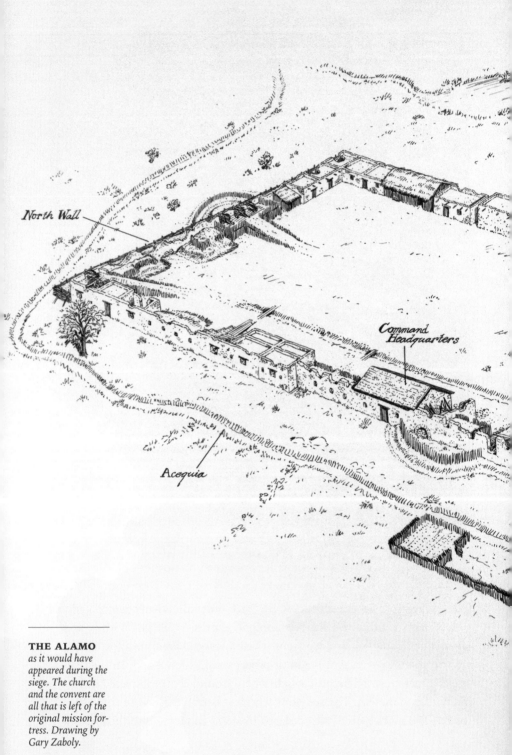

North Wall

Command Headquarters

Acequia

THE ALAMO *as it would have appeared during the siege. The church and the convent are all that is left of the original mission fortress. Drawing by Gary Zaboly.*

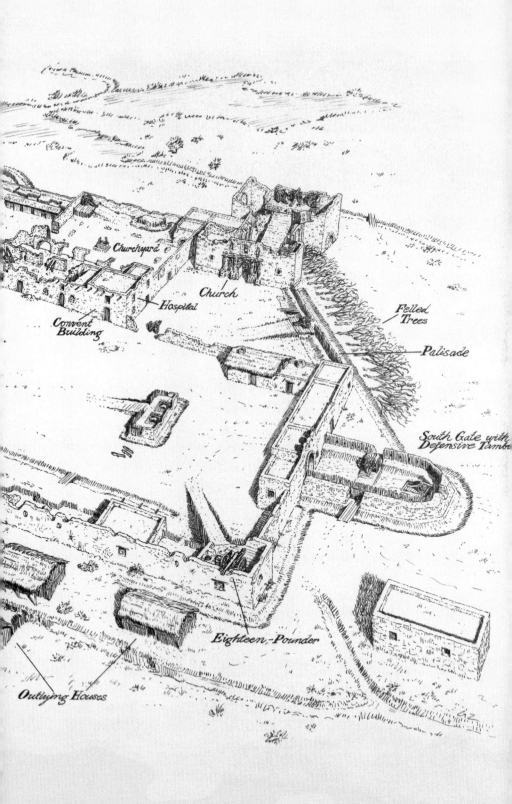

Churchyard

Church

Hospital

Convent
Building

Felled
Trees

Palisade

South Gate with
Defensive Tambo

Eighteen-Pounder

Outlying Houses

umns that would attack the fort from each point of the compass. Santa Anna had ordered a stop to the near-constant bombardment from his artillery positions, and inside the Alamo the defenders who had spent almost two weeks in a state of high-alert exhaustion were mostly asleep. For a while, the columns advanced unimpeded, armed with crowbars and axes and scaling ladders to make their way over the walls or through them. But the pressure for action that had been building all night broke through as the Mexican Army began to reach its target. Cries of "¡Viva Santa Anna!" and "¡Viva la República!" erupted through the ranks and alerted the sleeping men in the Alamo.

Travis was one of the first to react. He reached his station on the north wall just in time to be shot through the head by a Mexican sharpshooter. We know this because Joe, Travis's twenty-one-year-old slave, was an eyewitness to his master's death. The common understanding that none of the defenders survived the battle of the Alamo is false. Joe survived, and though he was presumably an unwilling defender, he was a defender nonetheless. He fought alongside Travis at the north wall in the fierce opening moments of the battle. Once Travis was dead and his position overrun, Joe fled with other survivors to one of the rooms in the convent building across the courtyard and continued firing from there until, near the end of the battle, he was saved by a Mexican captain who called out through the chaos, "Are there any Negroes here?" The captain was honoring a principle that the Mexican republic did not make war on slaves. Joe was later interrogated by Santa Anna before being sent on to the Texian lines. One of the men who interviewed him there about what had happened at the Alamo found that "he related the affair with much modesty, apparent candor, and remarkably distinctly for one of his class."

Mercy may have been shown to Joe, but Santa Anna was determined to make an example of people he regarded as pirates, invaders, and adventurers. Before the battle, according to de la Peña, he informed his officers that he intended to follow the "example of Arredondo," the general whose ruthless treatment of prisoners Santa Anna had observed as an impressionable young lieutenant in 1813. Several officers "voiced principles regarding the rights of men," but Santa Anna wouldn't listen to their arguments. Any rebels who didn't die in battle were to be executed. And once the fighting was over, his soldiers would be permitted, perhaps even encouraged, to loot.

It didn't take long for the battle of the Alamo to be over—less than an hour, according to most of the reliable accounts. When the Texians discovered the attack and opened fire, the Mexican forces were already lethally close to the walls of the fort. The damage to the attackers was terrible in those first few salvos. The Alamo artillery opened up with canister shot that sprayed jagged metal fragments through the columns, and with solid cannon balls that killed at first with direct force and then bounded and ricocheted deep into the ranks, tearing off arms and legs and heads. The neat order of the columns collapsed, and the attack stalled for a few minutes as the men huddled at the base of the north wall. Then there was nowhere to go but into the fort. The Mexicans clawed their way up the wall or battered their way through it, confronting the Texians at the parapets in hand-to-hand fighting with bayonets and hatchets and Bowie knives. "It seemed as if the furies had descended upon us," de la Peña recalled.

Once the defenders at the north wall were overwhelmed, the battle was effectively won. The Texians ran across the courtyard to the stone-walled convent, where they were blasted out by their own cannon. Others fled from the south end of the fort to try to make a stand out in the open, but they were run down by mounted Mexican lancers. As far as we know, Joe was the only combatant who survived. Bowie was probably bayonetted on his bed, if he was even alive. (One of the survivors, Susanna Dickinson, testified many years later that Bowie had been so sick he had "even been expected to die.")

By the time the winter sun had risen, most of the shooting was over. Santa Anna rode into the Alamo to inspect the results. "The bodies," de la Peña wrote, "with their blackened and bloody faces disfigured by a desperate death, their hair and uniforms burning at once, presented a dreadful and truly hellish sight." A half-dozen or more Texians had survived the initial assault and were captured and brought before Santa Anna. A general named Manuel Castrillón, one of the officers who had wanted to wait for the siege guns before attacking the Alamo, pleaded with Santa Anna to spare the men's lives, but the president general would not listen to his arguments and ordered the men executed on the spot.

The question whether Crockett was one of these captured and executed men has haunted and inflamed the historical discussion of the Alamo for many years. Whole books have been written about the issue, arguing the merits of this or that crucial passage in memoirs, letters, or testimonies. I don't have a strong opinion—it seems to me the most authoritative statement about Crockett's death is to be found in survivor Susannah Dickinson's 1876 interview with the Texas adjutant general's office, where it is simply recorded that "he was killed, she believes."

The intense curiosity about Crockett's demise is natural. He was one of the most famous men in America at the time, and his death and the national stir it caused are among the reasons why the phrase "Remember the Alamo" entered the American vocabulary. "Alas! poor Davie Crockett!" proclaimed the *New York Herald* upon hearing the flabbergasting news. "Where be thy sarcasms now! thy shrewd remarks! thy pointed absurdities! thy cunning stories whose very vanity made them a delightful study to the philosopher!—all gone—all chopfallen—all lost but in the recollection of those who knew thee!"

Crockett's body was gathered up with those of Travis and Bowie and the other defenders, thrown onto funeral pyres, and set alight, producing plumes of greasy smoke and mobs of vultures that hovered for days over San Antonio de Béxar. José Juan Sánchez-Navarro said he counted 257 rebel bodies, though there may have been fewer. He reported 110 men killed outright on the Mexican side, and 276 wounded, a figure that is reasonably consistent with other Mexican estimates.

"Long live our country, the Alamo is ours!" an emotional Sánchez-Navarro declared. He proposed to his commanding officer that they commemorate their fallen comrades by burying them in the Alamo and inscribing their names on tablets fashioned from the captured enemy cannon, along with a poem of Sánchez-Navarro's composition honoring "those illustrious, valiant, and untimely victims."

But there were other, more urgent priorities, such as defeating the rest of the insurgent forces, and Sánchez-Navarro's suggestion was not approved. But anyone who visits the Alamo today will find just the sort of thing he had in mind. The church is a deconsecrated place of worship reinvented as

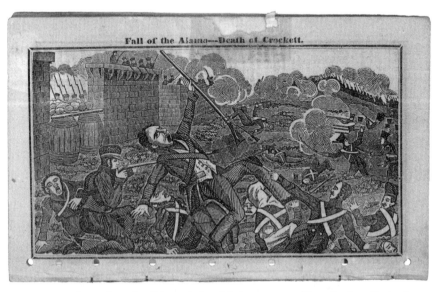

Fall of the Alamo---Death of Crockett.

A very early—and very fanciful—rendering of the last moments of Davy Crockett. Crockett's death would prove to be an inexhaustible subject for painters, poets, and filmmakers.

SUSANNAH DICKINSON, *the wife of Alamo defender Almeron Dickinson, was among the women and children who survived the battle. She last saw her husband when he rushed into her room during the final assault. "My dear wife, they are coming over the wall, we are all lost!"*

a secular shrine, with signs admonishing visitors to be silent and take off their hats, and plaques bearing the names of the fallen heroes of the Alamo. The difference between what exists today and what Sánchez-Navarro proposed is that the names on the plaques are those of the people who lost the battle, not those who won it.

The Alamo is a monument not to a gallant victory but to a holy defeat. The story of the Alamo turned into a myth of deliberate self-sacrifice largely because of something that was believed to have happened inside the fort on the night before the final assault. According to several sources of varying reliability, Travis called the garrison together and told them "our fate is sealed." No help was coming, death was certain for everyone who remained in the fort. With his sword, he drew a line in the sand and asked everyone who was willing to stay and die with him to cross it. Everyone did except for one man named Rose, who escaped over the walls that night.

There is evidence that a man named Louis Rose was a member at some point of the Alamo garrison, that he didn't die in the battle, and that he lived the rest of his life in Nacogdoches, where he was repeatedly called on to corroborate the testimony of heirs who claimed land grants based on the fact that their family members had died in the Alamo. But the story as we know it mostly originated from the pen of William P. Zuber, who said he had heard it directly from his parents when he was fifteen. His parents had heard it from Rose. But Zuber grew up to be a very colorful writer, and he did not commit Travis's supposed speech to paper until decades later, after he experienced what he called "a phenomenal refreshment of my memory." He also admitted that in recalling Travis's stirring address, he "found a deficiency" in it and took remedial measures: "I accordingly threw in one paragraph, which I firmly believe to be characteristic of Travis; & without which, the speech would have been incomplete."

This daguerreotype of the ruined Alamo church was made in 1849. A year later, the U.S. Army would turn the building into a quartermaster depot, in the process altering its shattered roofline into the now-iconic Alamo façade.

It seems extremely likely that the paragraph Zuber supplied, the thing that makes the speech "complete," was the challenge that Travis issued by drawing a line in the dirt. And that line is the linchpin of the Alamo legend. If Travis didn't draw it, if he instead encouraged the men not to give up hope, and perhaps read the letter he had received from Robert Williamson urging him to hold on until help could reach them, then it's a different and more human story. It's about men who did not willingly sacrifice themselves on the altar of Texas freedom but who simply found themselves caught in a deathtrap, counting on reinforcements that never came.

—13—

VENGEANCE

A TEN-YEAR-OLD GIRL NAMED DILUE ROSE LIVED WITH her family on a farm about fifteen miles north of Harrisburg. Harrisburg was a village on the banks of a tributary to Galveston Bay called Buffalo Bayou, up which goods bound for San Felipe could be brought by boat and then carried overland to the Brazos. In December, the Consultation, which had formed the provisional government for a Texas on the verge of separation from Mexico, had named Harrisburg its capital. Now that a declaration of independence had made that separation a reality, Harrisburg was the capital of the "free, sovereign and independent" Republic of Texas. But as self-appointed liberators such as Bernardo Gutiérrez de Lara, James Long, and Haden Edwards had discovered, declaring a republic was not the same thing as creating a viable nation. After the collapse of the provisional government into chaos and the fall of the Alamo, the odds for the survival of Texas could not have been much longer.

Dilue was very much a child of her time and place. She and her parents, brother, and sister had arrived in Texas in 1833 after a troubled two-week voyage from New Orleans that ended with their schooner running aground in a storm on Galveston Bay. Her father, a doctor with aspirations of owning a cotton plantation, moved them from the relative sophistication of Harrisburg, with its two stores periodically supplied from New Orleans, to an isolated farm, where goods and company were scarce. Ropes for plow lines had to be made from the hides of cattle and horses, and hats and bonnets were not store-bought but plaited from straw and palmetto, or woven from a plant called bonnet squash. After a good crop one summer, Dilue's father loaded up a bale of cotton and three or four hundredweight of hides onto a wagon and went to Harrisburg, promising the children he would bring home shoes. "We were so happy over our new shoes we could not sleep," she remembered.

She lived in fear of Indians and escaped slaves, absorbing her parents' and neighbors' attitudes about what they regarded as the subhuman nature of the Africans whom the wealthier planters held in bondage. One day, three white men "and a large gang of negroes" alarmed the Rose family by appearing unannounced at their homestead. One of the white men was a plantation owner who had somehow gotten lost with his slaves out on the prairie. They were all in desperate shape, near starvation. "The negroes acted like dogs," she wrote, "they were so hungry." They were fed under guard, and the next day a neighbor's body servant was assigned the task of taking the traumatized and disoriented slaves to the creek to bathe. "After they were dressed," Dilue reported, "he marched them to the house for mother and us little girls to see. They laughed and chattered like monkeys. They did not understand a word of English. All the men and boys in the neighborhood came to see the wild Africans."

Dilue and her family knew many of the young men who had helped drive the Texas colonies into revolution. William Travis was a frequent visitor to the farm. One day in 1834, Travis came to the Rose property to appear as the attorney for a man accused of stealing one of his neighbor's yearlings. There was no courtroom in the vicinity, so the trial was held in the open air, in a shady square formed by four large trees where the Rose children had built a playhouse for themselves. The accused was found guilty, Travis filed an appeal, and the court adjourned. Afterward, some of the young men who had come to observe the trial wanted to have a dance, but Dilue's mother—who had lost her Bible when their ship ran aground—objected to the idea. She wanted to hear a sermon instead. She dragooned a Mr. Woodruff into giving one, and afterward she and another woman sang "On Jordan's Stormy Banks I Stand and Cast a Wishful Eye."

When Travis left for San Felipe after the trial, he promised to try to look for a new Bible for Mrs. Rose, but he was unable to find one. Determined to repay her hospitality somehow, he sent Dilue and her sister a children's religious instruction book left over from a Sunday school in San Felipe that had been closed down by Father Muldoon, the otherwise easygoing priest who was the face of official Mexican Catholicism in Texas.

After the uprising at Gonzales, Dilue remembered, there was constant talk of war. The teacher who taught classes at her tiny school had run off to join the insurgents. Neighbors were smuggling their slaves back into the United States before they could be liberated by the Mexican troops. When the news came that Santa Anna was marching on San Antonio "everybody was talking of running from the Mexicans."

A few days after Travis wrote his letter of February 24, a courier on his way to Brazoria rode to the Rose homestead with one of the copies that had been urgently printed on Gail Borden's printing press and distributed throughout the colonies. Dilue's mother read the letter to her children. As soon as she was finished, the courier rode off with it to Brazoria. "I remember well the hurry and confusion," Dilue wrote in her memoir. Her uncle James was joining the army to fight Santa Anna, and ten-year-old Dilue spent the next day molding bullets for him while her mother sewed him two new hickory shirts.

On March 12, another courier brought the news that the Alamo had fallen, that Travis was dead. The talk about running from the Mexicans now became a sudden reality. "Then began the horrors of the 'Runaway Scrape,'" Dilue wrote, using the phrase by which the frantic civilian exodus from Santa Anna's armies came to be known.

The Runaway Scrape was another nightmarish centerpiece of the Texas Revolution, an experience that challenged the courage and resilience of Texas women just as acutely as the Battles of Béxar and the Alamo had the men. "If mother shed a tear," one son remembered of the day his family joined the throngs of refugees, leaving everything behind, "I never knew it though there was an unusual huskiness in her voice that day. Mother was brave and resolute, and I heard her say . . . that she was going to teach her boys never to let up on the Mexicans until they got full revenge for all this trouble."

Behind these women were abandoned homes and dead husbands and brothers and sons. "Now what I must say," Mrs. George Sutherland wrote her sister Sally, "(O, God support me). Yes, sister, I must say it to you. I have lost my William. O, yes, he is gone. My poor boy is gone, gone from me . . . slain in the Alamo in San Antonio. Then his poor body committed to the flames." Ahead of them were exhaustion and deprivation. The roads were jammed, and the spring rains so intense that mothers had to carry their children and possessions through waist-deep water. They saw men being seized by alligators as they tried to cross the swollen rivers; they watched in horror as infants were swept away in the current or died of the dysentery and whooping cough that spread in the fetid impromptu camps. They labored to dig out carts and livestock that were bogged down in the mud—"an hourly occurrence east of the Brazos," according to one witness.

They sometimes had to hold marauders and deserters off with pistols or to shame fainthearted husbands into joining the other men who were holding off the Mexican Army at river crossings. Their "courage and fortitude" inspired a Texian soldier named S. F. Sparks to write, "There is no one who can do justice to the women at that time. God bless the women of Texas!"

Dilue Rose and her family became part of the Runaway Scrape the evening that they learned about what happened at the Alamo. Mrs. Rose set out walking with an infant in her arms, Dilue beside her, and Dilue's two sisters in an oxcart driven by their brother. "Sister and I had been weeping all day about Colonel Travis," Dilue remembered. "When we started from home we got the little books he had given us and would have taken them with us, but mother said it was best to leave them."

On March 6, the convention was in session in Washington. The delegates were busy organizing themselves into committees for financing the new republic, organizing its army, and writing its constitution when an express rider delivered the letter that Travis had written three days before. This was the letter that described the ominous situation inside the Alamo, pleaded for reinforcements, and urged the convention to make haste in declaring independence. The delegates were eating breakfast when the letter arrived. They crowded into the convention room, along with the citizens of Washington, to hear it read aloud. None of them knew it, but it was too late to do anything. A hundred and seventy miles to the southwest, in San Antonio de Béxar, Mexican soldiers were already dragging the bodies of Travis and his garrison onto the bonfires.

Robert Potter, a former North Carolina congressman, immediately moved that the convention adjourn and take to the field against Santa Anna. He was, to say the least, a man of action. Back in North Carolina, he had taken a knife and personally castrated two people—a fifty-five-year-old minister and a seventeen-year-old boy—whom he suspected of sleeping with his wife, an act that spawned a vivid new verb: potterize.

The convention voted down Potter's motion. The task of forming a government was critical if the presumptive new nation was to receive any form of recognition or aid from the United States or other countries. (They were, Houston declared, "no better than pirates without one.") But Houston, who had once again been appointed commander in chief, left that same day for Gonzales to try to organize some kind of effective relief for the Alamo and to create a force that would have a chance to defeat Santa Anna's professional army. Houston at last was in charge of something tangible, not just the minuscule regular Texas army, but all the volunteers flooding in from the States to get themselves into the fight. His self-presentation was as ostentatious as ever—he was dressed like an Indian chief, one delegate observed, in buckskins and a poncho-like garment of red flannel. And there were lingering questions about his drinking. When the Texas Declaration of Independence was signed on March 2, his birthday, he later told Mary Austin Holley that he "had a great spree on egg nog that lasted two days!!!" But otherwise he seems to have remained, as he put it, "most miserably cool and sober."

If he was sober when he left Washington, he was chillingly so when he reached Gonzales five days later and learned that the Alamo and the men inside it had been lost. He heard the story from Joe, Travis's slave, and from Susannah Dickinson, whose husband, Almeron, had died in the battle. "All killed, all killed," she said to the families of the Gonzales citizens who crowded around her, desperate to hear news of their loved ones. "For hours after the receipt of the intelligence," an officer in the army wrote, "not a sound was heard, save the wild shrieks of the women, and the heartrending screams of the fatherless children."

Houston had something like four hundred disorganized men under arms in Gonzales, and he knew that thousands of Mexican troops were heading straight for them. There was nothing for him to do but to retreat, to gather up the dispersed components of his army along the way (especially the four hundred men that Fannin had in Goliad) and make a stand someplace where the timing and terrain would be in his favor.

Houston marched his army out of Gonzales, and with it a throng of civilian refugees with all their possessions loaded up onto oxcarts or carried on their backs. Houston ordered ten of his men to stay behind. They were to burn the town in order to deprive Santa Anna's army of any shelter or provisions. The fleeing families of Gonzales found out about this after they had trudged eastward about ten miles and, collapsing in exhaustion, saw the glow of their burning homes on the western horizon.

Before he left Gonzales, Houston ordered Fannin to get out of the presidio in Goliad before another Alamo happened: "We must not depend on Forts; the roads, and ravines suit us best." Fannin was to blow up the presidio and march his men and as much of his artillery as practicable twenty miles east to the town of Victoria, on the Guadalupe River. The rest of the cannon were to be sunk in the river.

Fannin got a late start. He had sent 28 men to nearby Refugio to evacuate Texian families whom he thought were under threat from a loyalist Tejano force led by a prominent ranchero named Carlos de la Garza. The rescue operation turned into a punitive expedition against Garza's men, which backfired catastrophically when General Urrea pinned the Texians down in a nearby mission. Fannin sent out 120 more men to help, but the expedition was splintered and destroyed by Urrea's army, almost all its members eventually captured and executed.

Fannin lost a week by waiting fruitlessly for their return, and when he finally led his men out of the presidio it was too late to evade the Mexican Army. Urrea's cavalry caught up with them in open country only a few miles from Goliad, near the banks of Coleto Creek. Instead of making a dash for the relative safety of the timber along the edges of the creek, as his officers urged him to do, Fannin had his men form into a hollow square. They made a determined stand, repulsing repeated attacks by dragoons and sharpshooters and managing to hold on all day and all night, but by the morning their ranks were filled with wounded men—including Fannin—and they were out of water and out of options. They surrendered and were marched back to Goliad.

General Urrea galloped away to chase down more rebels, leaving a lieutenant colonel named José Nicolás de la Portilla to carry out the explicit and incontrovertible orders of Santa Anna. Fannin and his men were to be executed. "I spent a restless night," Portilla conceded succinctly in his diary. It happened on March 27, Palm Sunday. The Mexicans organized the rebels into four groups, three of which were marched out of the fort and given to understand that nothing terrible was about to happen. They were leaving the fort to gather wood, or to be marched to Matamoros, or perhaps even to be paroled and sent back to the States. Fannin and the rest of the wounded were left behind, supposedly to be sent on later. Herman Ehrenberg, who was among the prisoners, found it odd that the Mexican soldiers guarding them were embarking on a long march without their knapsacks or any sort of baggage. But nobody else seemed to notice, and the men broke into song as they walked along what they thought was the road to liberation. But the soldados, he couldn't help noticing, were "unbearably silent."

The men still couldn't quite process what was happening even as they were ordered to kneel and the Mexican soldiers leveled their muskets at them from barely three feet away. "The idea that they planned to shoot us seemed unthinkable," Ehrenberg wrote.

He miraculously survived the fusillade that erupted. Somehow unhit, he ran through a screen of gunpowder smoke to the banks of the San Antonio River. As he jumped in, he shouted (or so he claims in his memoir), "The Republic of Texas forever!" He was one of twenty-eight men to survive. Three hundred and forty-two did not, including Fannin and the other wounded men, who were shot later inside the fort. Once again the dead insurgents were gathered up into funeral pyres and set ablaze on the prairie.

"I HAVE FOUND THE DARKEST HOURS OF MY PAST LIFE!" SAM
Houston wrote to a friend when he heard the news of Fannin's capture. The
hours would grow even darker when he learned of what became known as the
Goliad Massacre. Houston and his army were camped at a place called Beason's
Crossing, with the rain-swollen Colorado River between him and a Mexican column headed by General Joaquín Ramírez y Sesma. Houston's men were eager
to fight—"He didn't have a man in his army who didn't have a blood grievance
against the Mexicans," remembered a soldier named Creed Taylor. They were
restive and angry and growing contemptuous of their commander's endless and
infuriating deliberation. They had been retreating for over a week, even though a
surge of new recruits had swelled his army to fourteen hundred men.

Nevertheless, he retreated again. He didn't like the odds. Standing and
fighting with his untrained army on the Colorado made no sense to him—
not when Urrea, now unchecked by Fannin or anybody else, was on his side
of the river and could attack his flank or his rear even if he managed to beat
the Mexican forces in front of him.

So Houston ordered a retreat even farther north and east, to the Brazos, to
Jared Groce's plantation, about twenty miles upstream of San Felipe. "I consulted none," Houston admitted. "I held no councils of war." His tight-lipped
internal strategizing enraged his officers and confused his men, but for the
present they were still grudgingly willing to follow him. The march to Groce's
was hard, a rain-soaked slog through fields of mud and the fetid sloughs created by the overflowing Brazos. But once they got there, the weather cleared a
bit. Houston had bought himself two weeks to rest and train his army.

By this time, the convention meeting in Washington had done its work,
or as much work as it could do in the escalating panic of the Runaway
Scrape. In the freezing hall, as crowds of refugees gathered at the ferry
landing to try to make their way to the other side of the Brazos, the delegates drafted and argued over and amended a constitution. "On the approach of death," William Fairfax Gray observed, "they begin to lay aside
their selfish schemes, and to think of futurity."

Texas's Constitution, like its Declaration of Independence, was a somewhat borrowed document, reflecting the values and sometimes the wording
of its American model. There were heat-of-the moment provisions (anyone
unwilling to join the revolution would forfeit his land), and only a single
two-year term of office was allotted to the president, perhaps because the
delegates had already had too much experience with the furious squabbling
of the failed provisional government. The Constitution included a high-

DAVID BURNET *was elected to lead Texas as its interim president in the frantic weeks after independence was declared. He would soon be succeeded and overshadowed by Sam Houston, a man he detested.*

minded Declaration of Rights about power being inherent in the people, and every citizen being at liberty to speak or write, to confront accusers in court, and to be secure in their persons, houses, and so forth. But to modern thinking, these pronouncements were grievously undercut by passages like this one from section 9: "All persons of color who were slaves for life previous to their emigration to Texas, and who are now held in bondage, shall remain in the like state of servitude."

Now that Texas had declared its independence and expressed what it stood for in a constitution, the old provisional government was a relic. The delegates hastily created an interim government to oversee matters until a proper election could be held. The new president was David G. Burnet. His shorthand biography in the supremely useful *Handbook of Texas Online* could serve as a description of most of the men who had brought revolution to Texas—"speculator, lawyer, and politician." Although not elected a delegate to the convention, Burnet had come to Washington anyway and was on hand to offer himself as a candidate. His pedigree, as the fourteenth child of a distinguished New Jersey patriot who had served in the Continental Congress, was impressive. According to the *Handbook*, Burnet's "entire life was a string of disappointments," but most of those failures—political defeat, debt, the enmity of Sam Houston—lay in the future. For now, at least, he had ascended to the presidency of a brand-new country.

The vice president was a man that William Fairfax Gray, despite his belief that Mexicans were "a swarthy, dirty looking people," considered to be "the most interesting man in Texas." The candidates for that designation made up a crowded field, but Gray may have been on target. Lorenzo de Zavala was a cross-pollinated product of revolutionary sophistication and clubby entrepreneurship. He was a long-standing reformer in Mexico who as a young man had been thrown into prison and had passed the time by teaching himself how to be a doctor. He also played the game of Texas land speculation at a high level, acquiring empresario grants and selling them off to New York investors. A prolific author and polemicist, he had written a two-volume history of Mexico and a travel book about the United States that, to add to his cosmopolitan bona fides, was printed in Paris.

The new officers were sworn in at four in the morning amid partisan rancor and growing alarm that the Mexican cavalry was fast approaching. "What shall we do to be saved?" somebody in the assembly moaned the next morning just before the new government decided that in order to preserve itself, it had to get out of town. They became part of the Runaway Scrape, putting the flooded barrier of the Brazos between them and Santa Anna, and heading south to Harrisburg.

---★---

DILUE ROSE AND HER FAMILY WERE ALSO STILL ON THE RUN.
When they arrived at Lynch's Ferry, where Buffalo Bayou and the San
Jacinto River joined a system of sloughs and bays and marshland at the
upper reaches of Galveston Bay, they found five thousand people gathered
there. They had to wait three days before they could cross to the other side.
They made their way to the next river, the Trinity, which had risen beyond
its banks and was clogged with driftwood. Dilue's baby sister was sick. She
went into convulsions as the ferrymen struggled to get the families across
the river. Five days later, after Dilue and her family had crossed a slough
on a homemade raft, the child died. Grieving, exhausted, disoriented, they
buried her in Liberty and stayed there for three weeks.

One April afternoon they heard what they thought at first was thunder. It
echoed from far to the west, beyond the flooded river they had just crossed.
Dilue's father, a veteran of the War of 1812, told them that the sound they
heard was not thunder, but cannon. Somewhere in the sloughs and marshes
and flooded prairies they had just spent five weeks crossing, there was a
battle going on.

They fled east again, not knowing what the battle was or what its outcome might mean. The next day, they saw a man on horseback waving his
hat at them from a distance and yelling that it was safe to turn around: "The
Texas army has whipped the Mexican army and the Mexican army are prisoners. No danger! No danger!"

The man calling out to them was a courier who had been sent by General Houston. He was an Irishman named McDermot who had once been an
actor. He had not slept in a week, and he was pumped so full of adrenaline
that he stayed awake another night, not just telling the refugees the news of
what had taken place at the battle they had heard in the distance but acting
it all out, with such frenetic high spirits that Dilue's mother laughed for the
first time after the death of her little daughter.

This was the Battle of San Jacinto, the improbable, unpredictable victory
that finally tore Texas away from Mexico. It was the dramatic culmination of
Houston's retreat, first across the Colorado and then across the Brazos—a strategic retreat, not a flight. Houston was still looking for his chance, for some
kind of favorable fighting opportunity to present itself. He also had, it seems,
a backup plan. If his wished-for opportunity didn't materialize, he could
always keep retreating, heading north and east toward Nacogdoches and to the
Sabine, where across the river waited the U.S. general Edmund Gaines, with
perhaps as many as twelve thousand men at his disposal. Gaines appeared

more than willing to confront Mexico in a general war if Santa Anna's forces got too close to the conveniently ill-defined border with the United States. It would be just the provocation that Andrew Jackson could use to seize Texas, delivered to him by his former protégé.

As it happened, the backup plan was not needed, though Houston—in his maddening inscrutability—almost lost control of his army. From Harrisburg, President Burnet—who hated Houston—dispatched his secretary of war,

THOMAS RUSK,
the secretary of war of the presumptive Texas Republic, was dispatched by President Burnet to shame Sam Houston into fighting Santa Anna. But Rusk saw something in Houston that Burnet had not, and ended up fighting beside him at San Jacinto and serving with him in the United States Senate.

Thomas Rusk, with a blunt message: "Sir: The enemy are laughing you to scorn. You must fight them. You must retreat no further. The country expects you to fight."

Rusk, in the field, had a higher opinion of Houston and his strategy than Burnet did from Harrisburg. He stayed with the army as it continued to retreat. Meanwhile, Santa Anna, with seven hundred men, broke away from his main force in an attempt to capture the new Texas government at Harrisburg. Burnet and his cabinet barely escaped, scurrying across Galveston Bay in a rowboat. Santa Anna burned Harrisburg to the ground and decided to head toward Lynch's Ferry to intercept Houston on his retreat.

Houston knew from captured intelligence that Santa Anna, separated from his main army, was at the head of a relatively small striking force in the vicinity of Harrisburg. What was still unknown to Houston's men was whether their leader intended to fight. That became clear when the army came to a fork in the road marked by a tree that has entered Texas lore under the name of the Which Way Tree. One road led north, toward Nacogdoches and continued retreat to the Sabine, the other south toward Harrisburg and a certain clash with Santa Anna. Historical opinion differs about whether Houston ordered his men down the Harrisburg fork or simply and silently went along when they marched that way on their own. In any case, they took the branching route of history that led them to the plain of San Jacinto.

They passed the smoldering ruins of Harrisburg and marched on to the banks of Buffalo Bayou, whereupon Houston decided to throw off the cloak of mystery and speak plainly: "We will meet the enemy! Some of us may be killed and must be killed; but soldiers remember the Alamo! The Alamo! The Alamo!"

By the morning of April 20, they were in position, camped in a thick concealing grove of live oaks. To their backs was the bayou, to their left an expanse of marsh leading to Lynch's Ferry where it crossed the San Jacinto River. In the afternoon, the Mexican Army arrived from the opposite direction. Santa Anna ordered his men to set up camp several hundred yards to the south of the Texians, across an open stretch of land owned by an Irish widow and cattle raiser named Peggy McCormick, who had joined the Runaway Scrape with her two sons. Behind the Mexican camp was more marshland and a shallow, boggy body of water known as Peggy's Lake. It was a strikingly vulnerable position. "Any youngster," thought Mexican captain Pedro Delgado, "could have done better."

Santa Anna knew that Houston's army was on the opposite side of the open plain, but neither side could see the other's encampment or divine its intentions. Fighting erupted during the afternoon when Santa Anna sent skirmishers to probe the Texian position. They were repulsed by grapeshot fired from the barrels of a pair of small maneuverable cannon called the Twin Sisters, gifts to the Texas cause from the citizens of Cincinnati. The Twin Sisters were all that Houston had for artillery, but the Mexicans had marched with only a single twelve-pound fieldpiece. The scattered barrages caused a few casualties, as did an attempted cavalry charge launched in open defiance of Houston's wishes by an impulsive Kentucky volunteer named Sidney Sherman.

The grisly main event took place the next afternoon, after the Mexicans received reinforcements and now had about twelve hundred men to face the roughly nine hundred rebels who were camped in the timber on the high bank above Buffalo Bayou. There was no question of retreat for either side, no more patience left among Houston's army for strategic deliberation. It was a question of who was going to attack first. Santa Anna expected an assault in the morning. His men had worked all night creating an impromptu breastwork of brush, timber, piled-up saddles and crates. They were exhausted, as were the reinforcements, led by General Cos, who had marched hard to reach Santa Anna in time. When no assault came or appeared imminent, Santa Anna retired to his tent to take a nap or—according to a legend that has almost but never quite been liberated from history—to pursue the affections of a captured mulatto servant girl named Emily West, forevermore referred to as the "Yellow Rose of Texas."

The city of Houston and its industrial suburbs have almost swallowed

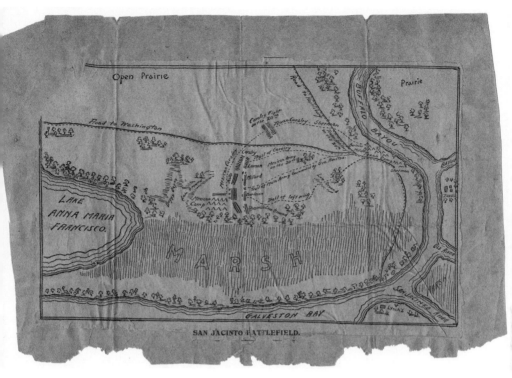

Henderson Yoakum drew this map of the Battle of San Jacinto for his 1856 history of Texas. His friend Sam Houston took him on a tour of the battlefield.

up the battlefield of San Jacinto. The once-transparent Buffalo Bayou is now part of the turbid, much-dredged complex of waterways that make up the Houston Ship Channel complex. The state park that commemorates and protects the site is a clearing within a sprawling overgrowth of refinery towers and oil storage tanks. The battlefield is now dominated and distorted by an 8.5-acre reflection pool and a 570-foot-high white obelisk crowned with a 220-ton Texas star. But you can still see the oak grove where Houston's men camped and from where they set out to attack the Mexican breastworks. And as you walk forward in their footsteps, you can still glimpse the slight ridge of land in the center of the field that kept them hidden from the enemy until they opened fire with the Twin Sisters, abandoned their orderly line of march, and ran forward screaming, "Remember the Alamo!" and "Remember Goliad!"

It was a rout, and then it was a massacre. By the time the surprised Mexicans reached the breastwork, it was too late to mount a coherent defense. Some were cut down by the scything grapeshot of the Twin Sisters; others were killed by Kentucky rifles and shotguns, or stabbed or bludgeoned to death by Bowie knives and tomahawks. General Castrillón, who had futilely argued with Santa Anna for the life of the captured Alamo defenders, was once more a moral hero, standing firm as his men fled in panic until he pitched dead in the grass when a rebel fusillade "riddled him with balls."

Houston had ridden into the battle on a white horse named Saracen. The horse was shot from under him; he mounted another, and was shot through the ankle by a Mexican musket ball. But he stayed on his horse during the fight, doing his best to regain control of his men. It was impossible. Their grudges against Santa Anna were too deep, their blood too high. "You know how to take prisners," one officer told his men in defiance of Houston's order to stop the killing, "take them with the but of your guns, & club guns, right & left, and nocked there brains out." The soldados pleaded for their lives, screaming, "Me no Alamo!" and "Me no Goliad" and "Por Dios, salva mi vida!" When no mercy was forthcoming, many of them fled into the waters of Peggy Lake, where they became vulnerable targets for Texian riflemen on the shore. Eventually, after over six hundred Mexican soldiers lay dead on the field or beneath the water of Peggy's Lake, the killing frenzy slowed down. Only nine Texians were killed.

Most of the rest of Santa Anna's men were taken prisoner, including, on the next day, Santa Anna himself. When he had run out of his tent and grasped the extent of the disaster, he grabbed the reins of a horse and galloped away from the battlefield. It's doubtful that he fled out of cowardice, since during his whole career he had exuberantly exposed himself to danger. More likely he was trying to reach a Mexican division under General Vicente Filisola so that he could launch a counterattack. But his horse gave out, and the only bridge across a deep bayou had been destroyed that morning by a group of rebels—led by the hard-of-hearing Texas hero Esastus "Deaf" Smith—to prevent a Mexican escape or reinforcement.

Santa Anna spent the night in an abandoned house. The next day, a Texian patrol led by a Kentucky volunteer named James Sylvester came upon him hiding in the grass. They didn't know who he was; there was nothing to indicate he was the president general of Mexico instead of just another frightened soldado. Except for maybe the diamond studs under the plain cotton jacket he wore instead of his discarded uniform, and the instinctive hauteur he displayed when he stood up from the grass and presumed to shake Sylvester's hand. When he was led back into Houston's camp, the other captured Mexican officers tried to keep their men quiet as Santa Anna walked past them, but in the end they couldn't prevent the astonished captives from betraying their leader's cover as they called out, "El Presidente!"

Santa Anna was brought before Houston. The victor of San Jacinto was

*A battle flag carried by Texian troops when they attacked the Mexican army at San Jacinto.
It hangs today in the Texas Capitol's House chamber, behind the Speaker's podium.*

lying in the shade of a big post oak tree, dozing despite the pain of his shattered ankle. Colonel John Forbes, the same man who had administered the Texas oath to David Crockett less than four months before, shook him awake. Houston propped himself up on an elbow and looked into the eyes of Santa Anna. In Houston's memory of their conversation, or perhaps in his invention of it, Santa Anna congratulated him on being the conqueror of the Napoleon of the West. That meant, Santa Anna said, Houston was "born to no common destiny, and . . . can afford to be generous to the vanquished."

But Houston, his ankle throbbing, his destiny plain, was not in the mood for rhetorical gallantry. "You should have remembered that, sir," he told Santa Anna, "at the Alamo."

A famous painting by William Henry Huddle of the meeting of the captured Santa Anna and the wounded Sam Houston on the field of San Jacinto.

PART THREE

The

PEOPLE

— *Want* —

EXCITEMENT

— 14 —

AFTERMATH

IN 1955, I WAS SEVEN YEARS OLD AND LIVING IN THE MID-
size West Texas city of Abilene. That spring, I saw a movie
called *Davy Crockett: King of the Wild Frontier* when it came to
the Paramount Theater downtown. The movie had begun
life the year before as a three-part serial on the ABC series
Disneyland. We only had one TV station in Abilene, and it

didn't show ABC programs, so I was unaware of the Davy Crockett madness that had overtaken the country until I walked into the theater one
Saturday afternoon and became one of millions of kids to be jolted alert
by the movie's insanely catchy theme song, bewitched by its buckskin-clad
hero, and haunted by his unfathomable death at the Alamo. The experience
made such a deep impression on me that when I happened to be in Abilene
recently and walked into the still-extant Paramount Theater, I was able to
identify the seat I had sat in sixty years earlier.

I bring this up because after reading over the last several chapters, I see
that like many other writers before me I have been seduced again, now as
an adult, by the high drama of the Texas Revolution. It's almost impossible for someone who grew up white in the Anglo-dominated Texas of the
mid-twentieth century to put aside the idea of the revolution as being not

186

TEXAS!!

Emigrants who are desirious of assisting Texas at this important crisis of her affairs may have a free passage and equipments, by applying at the

NEW-YORK and PHILADELPHIA HOTEL,

On the Old Levee, near the Blue Stores.

Now is the time to ensure a fortune in Land: To all who remain in Texas during the War will be allowed 1280 Acres.
To all who remain Six Months, 640 Acres.
To all who remain Three Months, 320 Acres.
And as Colonists, 4600 Acres for a family and 1470 Acres for a Single Man.
New Orleans, April 23d, 1836.

By the time this broadside appeared in New Orleans, potential recruits to the Texas cause were aware that the Alamo had fallen. But there was still time to fight and, if victorious, acquire "a fortune in land."

just a crucial historical event but also a creation story, even the fulfillment of some sort of unstated prophecy. Viewed through that lens, the victory at San Jacinto reduced everything that preceded it—the years of contentious Mexican rule, the centuries of Indian adaptation to Spanish ambitions, the mysterious millennia of prehistory—to a birth struggle. The Texas that was destined to be had finally emerged. The binary fight between Texians (now known as Texans) and Mexicans was over and won. But the fight was never just between Texans and Mexicans. It was between centralists and federalists, between big-time speculators and small-scale homesteaders, between established colonists with everything to lose and rootless volunteers with sudden fortunes to make, between those Indian nations whose influence was on the rise and those who were on the rocks, between rival Masonic lodges, and between pragmatic philosophers with starkly different opinions about who was a human being and who was not.

And for many of these people, the outcome at San Jacinto was not a concluding triumph or the clear dawning of a new age—it was just something
else to adjust to or exploit. For the members of a Comanche band known
as the Nokonis ("Wanderers"), the chaos of 1836 presented new opportunities to expand their range and improve their fortunes. Sam Houston had
been much concerned about having to fight the Comanches as well as the
Mexican Army during the revolution, but no such alliance ever developed.
For years, though, Anglo settlers had regarded the growing reach of the
Comanches with existential alarm. "Every last one of us," their 1832 petition
for separate statehood within Mexico declared, "is probably threatened with
total extermination by the new Comanche uprising."

But in reality, there was probably as much trading as fighting going on
between the Texians and the Comanches. The new arrivals from the United
States had access to goods—including weapons—from American markets.
The Comanches in turn had horses and mules to barter, many of them taken
in raids against settlements and ranchos on the other side of the Colorado, in
the Old World parts of Mexican Texas, where the conflict between Comanches
and Tejanos had been very bitter for a very long time. But now the Comanches were probing east, toward the isolated homesteads of men and women
who were pushing the boundaries of American expansion into Texas.

———————— ★ ————————

IN MAY 1836, JUST A FEW DAYS SHORT OF A MONTH AFTER THE
Battle of San Jacinto, a Nokoni raiding party approached an imposing, solitary structure rising from the prairie grasslands along the middle stretch of
the Navasota River. The structure was a fort, built by the family labor of its
inhabitants. The Parker clan had arrived from Illinois in 1833—five brothers,
their wives, in-laws, and children. One of them, Daniel Parker, was a fervent
preacher, the founder of the Pilgrim Predestination Regular Baptist Church,
and a man who made it his business to distance himself from anything
that "should bring reproach on the tender cause of God." But he was also
a man of affairs, a former state assemblyman in Illinois, and more recently
a member of the Consultation and of the Texas provisional government
during the revolution. He was rooted enough in society to stay behind when
his younger brothers decided to range far beyond the safety of the town-
ships and build their farms and their fort at the edge of the Cross Timbers,
the immense belt of sandy-soiled gnarly oak forests that stands between the
savannas and piney woods of East Texas and the open plains to the west.

About forty people lived in cabins within the timber stockade of Fort
Parker. It was protected by two-story blockhouses with shooting ports and

a formidable front gate. The Parkers, like many others, had been caught up in the Runaway Scrape. They had been stranded on the west side of the flooded Trinity when word came that Houston's army had defeated Santa Anna and it was safe to come home. They had gratefully returned in time for corn-planting season. Most of the men were outside the walls, working in the fields, when the Comanches came.

There were at least a hundred of them. One of the members of the party, maybe its leader, was a young warrior named Peta Nocona. They came carrying a white flag and pretended that they just wanted a cow. One of the Parker brothers, forty-eight-year-old Benjamin, decided that he had no choice but to walk out of the fort and talk to them. While Rachel Plummer, Benjamin's niece, watched in terror, the Indians killed him with their lances, scalped him, and then stormed into the fort and killed and mutilated the rest of the men there. Rachel's grandmother was lanced through the chest, stripped of her clothes, raped, and left for dead. She somehow survived. Rachel tried to escape through a low door in the back of the fort with her eighteen-month-old son, but as she wrote in a memoir: "A large sulky looking Indian picked up a hoe and knocked me down. I well recollect of their taking my child out of my arms, but whether they hit me any more I do not know, for I swooned away."

The Comanches ransacked the fort and searched the surrounding countryside for the men and women and children who had managed to flee. They killed five people in all and rounded up five captives, including Rachel and her son. The last time she saw the boy was a few days later, during the Indians' escape back to the heart of Comanchería. The Comanches kept him away from her, but she could hear his screams and that of the other captives as they were beaten. She was beaten repeatedly herself, and raped, and forced to watch her relatives' scalps being paraded in front of her eyes. Finally, the Indians brought Rachel's son so that she could nurse him, but when they discovered he had already been weaned they took him away again. "He reached out his hands toward me, which were covered with blood," she wrote, "and cried, 'Mother, Mother, oh, Mother!' I looked after him as he was borne away from me, and I sobbed aloud. This was the last I ever heard of my little Pratt. Where he is, I know not."

She was pregnant at the time with another child, who would be born a few months later and strangled in front of her eyes. But Rachel Plummer would live a while longer. She would be ransomed a year or so later by a group of comancheros, native-born New Mexicans who were in the trading business with the Comanches. She would be reunited with her father, who survived the attack on Fort Parker and led seventeen others to safety

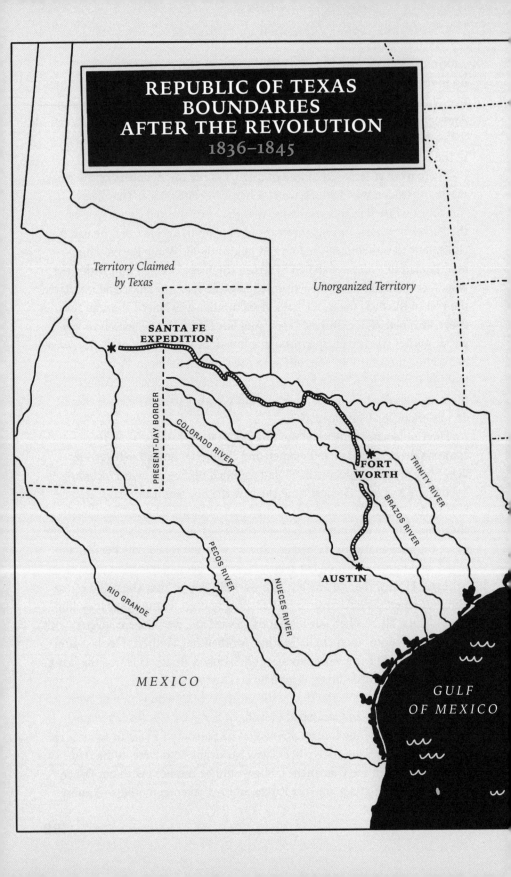

REPUBLIC OF TEXAS BOUNDARIES AFTER THE REVOLUTION
1836–1845

Territory Claimed
by Texas

Unorganized Territory

SANTA FE
EXPEDITION

PRESENT-DAY BORDER

COLORADO RIVER

FORT
WORTH

TRINITY RIVER

BRAZOS RIVER

PECOS RIVER

NUECES RIVER

AUSTIN

RIO GRANDE

MEXICO

GULF
OF MEXICO

through the Navasota bottoms. But she would never be the same, and she predicted, as she wrote the pages of her account, "that before they are published, the hand that penned them will be cold in death." She was right. Rachel Plummer was twenty years old when she died, after giving birth to yet another child who would not live.

Rachel Plummer's ordeal was relatively short-lived, a brutal but not uncommon occurrence in another developing Texas war for dominance. It was a war whose borders would continue to expand, whose savagery would continue to escalate, and whose outcome—decades yet into the future— would have a great deal to do with one of the other traumatized captives who was carried away that day by Peta Nocona. She was one of Rachel's cousins, a ten-year-old girl named Cynthia Ann Parker.

THE REVOLUTION REARRANGED THE GAME BOARD FOR EVERY Indian group in the region. The Cherokees, along with tribes like the Choctaws, Chickasaws, Delawares, Shawnees, and Kickapoos, were recent arrivals in Texas. For a generation, the Cherokees had been pushed west from their ancestral lands in the southern Appalachians to Missouri, Louisiana, and Arkansas, where Sam Houston lived among them during his Big Drunk period. Since the early 1820s, they had been in Texas in significant numbers, living north of Nacogdoches between the Trinity and Sabine Rivers. Their principal chief was a man named Duwali, called "Bowl" or "Bowles" by the Americans. He was old, in his eighties when Sam Houston visited him on February 23, 1836, the day the siege of the Alamo began. There are no portraits of Chief Bowles, but he was half Scottish, with sandy hair and gray eyes, and "his was an English head." Assuming he was dressed in traditional Cherokee fashion, he probably wore a red sash around his waist and a turban on his head.

At some point, Houston presented him with a military hat and a sword. That may have been this occasion, since there was much at stake. Houston had come to make a treaty, to keep Bowles and the Cherokees on the Texian side or at least neutral during the hostilities that had erupted. Bowles was receptive to Houston. The Texian general, after all, had lived with the Cherokees and understood them, and the chief's granddaughter had once made Houston a pair of moccasins. But the Cherokees had recently been visited by emissaries from the Mexican Army as well. Both sides were actively trying to enlist not just the Cherokees, but also the Caddos, Kichais, Wichitas, and other Indian groups of East and Northeast Texas to pitch in against their enemies.

The Cherokees had been trying for years to persuade the Mexican government to give them a grant for the lands they were living on, and Bowles had been loyal to the Mexican Republic, to the point of sitting in judgment during the trial and execution of his fellow Cherokee leader Richard Fields for taking part in the Fredonian Rebellion. He had traveled to Mexico, and had even been made a lieutenant colonel in the Mexican Army. But Mexico never came through with the grant. Houston, on the other hand, was making an offer: if the Cherokees, along with the "associate bands" over which they had influence—the Shawnees, Delawares, Kickapoos, and eight or nine others—promised to remain neutral in the Texas Revolution, they would in return receive a much-reduced but guaranteed swath of the territory they already inhabited. "A firm and lasting peace forever," the treaty read. Bowles and the other chiefs signed, hoping for the best.

Houston then rode off to fight Santa Anna, but the Cherokees were still much on his mind. At about the time when his men were completely losing faith in his leadership and his will to fight, when his army and all of Anglo Texas was in flight and interim president Burnet was writing to say that his enemy was laughing him to scorn, Houston scribbled a hasty, friendly note to Chief Bowles: "I am busy and will only say how da do, to you!"

<hr> ★ <hr>

WHEN THE RAID ON PARKER'S FORT TOOK PLACE, SANTA ANNA was still a prisoner of the Texas government, over two hundred miles to the south. He was being held in the town of Velasco, where the Brazos River enters the Gulf and where Austin's original colonists had first set foot on Texas soil in 1821. The day after his defeat, Santa Anna had sent a letter to General Filisola. "Having yesterday evening had an unfortunate encounter," he cringingly admitted, "I have resolved to remain as prisoner of war in the hands of the enemy."

He ordered Filisola and the divisions under General Gaona and General Urrea to withdraw. He knew that he was a bargaining chip and that he was being kept alive only because he had the power to keep the rest of the Mexican Army at bay. The men he had commanded so ingloriously at San Jacinto were either being held prisoner on Galveston or being eaten by wolves where they had fallen on the battlefield. ("To the devil with your 'glorious history'!" Peggy McCormick is supposed have roared at Houston when she returned to her property and heard him congratulate her on now being the owner of such a sacrosanct spot. "Take off your stinking Mexicans!")

On May 14, Santa Anna signed a document called the Treaty of Velasco. He did so under cordial duress. Even though the agreement stood no chance of being recognized by his government back in Mexico, it had the practical effect of ending the war and helping safeguard his life from the many soldiers and officers in the Texas army who thought he should have been shot on the spot for the ruthless executions he ordered at the Alamo and at Goliad. The treaty had two parts, a public document ending hostilities and requiring all Mexican troops to retreat beyond the Rio Grande, and a secret side agreement, in which Santa Anna was to be repatriated to Mexico, where he pledged to use whatever influence he had left to bring about, among other things, a formal acknowledgment that Texas was now independent.

Sam Houston was not in Texas when the document was signed. The gunshot wound in his ankle had taken a dangerous turn, and he needed the sort of medical treatment that was available only in New Orleans. He left after a staggering display of pettiness on the part of President Burnet, whose jealousy of Houston throbbed as feverishly as the conquering hero's wounded ankle. Houston was, Burnet claimed in an intemperate letter to Mary Austin Holley, a coward who had been forced by his men to fight. He was "universally detested," a "military fop," notable only for "his miserable imbecility."

Burnet did his best to keep Houston from leaving Texas, no doubt worried about the ecstatic hero's welcome he was sure to receive in New Orleans. He first denied him permission to board the *Yellow Stone*, the only steamship then plying the waters of the new republic. When the *Yellow Stone*'s captain refused to leave without the wounded hero of San Jacinto, Burnet intervened once again to prevent Houston from sailing from Galveston in any of the Texas Navy's four ships. Houston booked passage on a schooner instead and disembarked in New Orleans to a frenzy of unambiguous adulation.

Santa Anna also had a rough launch. By the terms of the treaty, he was supposed to be sent home to Mexico. He boarded his ship and bade goodbye to the land pirates who had defeated and captured him, commending them as if they were his dear comrades-in-arms: "I have seen how brave you are in battle, how generous you are in its aftermath. You may count upon my friendship forever . . . please admit this most sincere farewell."

His sincere farewell turned out to be neither sincere nor a farewell. His ship was surrounded by a mob of newly arrived volunteers who had come to Texas determined, now that the actual war was over, to find somebody to fight—or at least shoot. He was not killed, thanks to the intervention of Burnet, who, despite his enmity for Sam Houston, agreed with him that allowing their trophy captive to be executed would not be just bad manners but also catastrophic policy. "A wild and intractable spirit of revenge is abroad among the people," he warned. But Burnet and his cabinet— "perhaps the most imbecile body that ever sat judgment on the fate of a nation," according to one critic—were hard pressed to hold back the tide of vengeance, and for the time being the best that could be done for Santa

Anna was simply to keep him alive. In violation of the secret Treaty of Velasco, he was taken off the boat and held in a room at a nearby plantation, where he spent a long summer being taunted and intimidated and dodging assassination attempts while sometimes chained to a heavy lead ball.

The war was not over—it threatened to erupt again at any moment. New volunteers kept pouring into Texas, led by hotspurs who had their eyes set on the old chimera of taking the war to Mexico by conquering Matamoros. Mexico, meanwhile, had no interest in recognizing the Velasco Treaty— whose terms had been violated in any case when Santa Anna was prevented from sailing to Mexico—and every intention of reconquering Texas at the earliest opportunity. But the Republic of Texas was a reality unless it could be overthrown or unless it collapsed into chaos on its own, and the active hostilities had been reduced for now to simmering possibilities.

Nobody had ever done anything about the dead Mexicans on Mrs. McCormick's property, though for years sightseers picked up the skulls for souvenirs. "A perfect summer scene was presented for contemplation," recalled a Kentucky gentleman attorney named John Hunter Herndon of his visit to the battlefield, just before noting that he "obtained many sculls." He later met a local doctor who had picked up a skull that had washed up in Galveston and watched—in no particular horror—as the man drank whisky out of a vessel "that had yet brains in it." The victors tended to their own dead of the Alamo and of Goliad with much more reverence. Thomas Rusk, who took over command of the army when Houston left for New Orleans, orated over the remains of Fannin and his men, whose bodies had been only haphazardly cremated and whose charred and gnawed-upon bones had been strewn by animals across a wide swath of coastal prairie.

Juan Seguín had been in the Alamo but had been sent out by Travis as a messenger soon after the siege began. He and the twenty members of his Tejano company had fought at San Jacinto. They had been ordered by Houston to affix pieces of white pasteboard to their hats so that the rest of the rebels—particularly the new volunteers, who thought all Mexicans were on the opposite side—could see that they were not part of Santa Anna's army. Seguín was promoted to lieutenant colonel. While in command in San Antonio, he interred the ashes of the Alamo defenders in a solemn military funeral. "The spirit of liberty," he told the soldiers and citizens of San Antonio, "appears to be looking out from its elevated throne with its pleasing mien and pointing to us, saying: 'there are your brothers.'"

And what about Stephen Austin? After six months in the United States with his two fellow commissioners, fund raising and giving speeches from New Orleans to New York, he finally came back to Texas at the end of June.

In a portrait painted of him around this time, probably while he was in New Orleans, he looks older than his forty-two years. It is the picture of someone who has been ill for a long time, his face strangely winnowed, his eyes too big. But those eyes, and the ambition in them, still shone feverishly bright.

Burnet's interim government was scheduled to dissolve after elections were held in September for a permanent government for the Republic of Texas. There were, in the end, three candidates for president: Sam Houston; Henry Smith, who had headed the catastrophically dysfunctional provisional government; and Stephen Austin.

"My labors and exertions to settle this country and promote its welfare are well known," Austin declared when he announced that he was running. "My object has been the general good, and the permanent liberty and prosperity of Texas. In the pursuit of this object I can say with a clear conscience that I have been honest and sincere in my intentions."

It was the sober-sided, almost plaintive statement of a man who embodied a time that history had just surged past. Austin was the opposite of a filibustering adventurer. He was a long-game businessman for whom war had been conceivable only when it became inevitable. He was the wrong man for a Texas brimming with triumphalist bravado, and if he didn't suspect it when he put his name forward for president, he certainly knew it by the time the votes were counted. He lost very badly. Houston beat him ten to one, and even Henry Smith outpolled him by a couple of hundred votes. It wasn't a mindless rejection—among other liabilities, Austin was tainted by association with his good friend Samuel May Williams, a land agent who had been a key player (along with Jim Bowie) in the notorious Monclova land speculations. But it was still a breathtaking defeat, one that an early settler named James Morgan elegantly summarized. "Sam Houston," he wrote, "who had been in Texas about three years, received 5119 votes. Henry Smith, who had made such a tragic and dismal failure of his position as provisional governor, and in a sense, had the blood of both Fannin and Travis on his hands polled a total of 743 votes, while Stephen F. Austin, who was even now dying for the Texas he loved so well and had served so long, and made every sacrifice for, mustered the grand total of only 587 votes."

The Republic of Texas needed a capital where its new president could be sworn in and where its cabinet and congress could meet. Gonzales, San Felipe, and Harrisburg had all been burned to the ground during the Runaway Scrape, and so the seat of government was conferred upon a little clapboard house in the town of Columbia, along the lower reaches of the Brazos River a few miles north of Brazoria.

The house is long gone. The place where Houston stood to take the oath of office is now somewhere in the cold-and-cough aisles of a Walgreens drugstore. But if you want to bring the moment to life, all you have to do is read the words of his inaugural address, through which you can almost experience the president's lingering amazement.

A spot of earth almost unknown to the geography of the age, destitute of all available resources, comparatively few in numbers, we modestly remonstrated against oppression, and, when invaded by a numerous host, we dared to proclaim our independence and to strike for freedom on the breast of the oppressor. . . . We were hunted down as the felon wolf, our little band driven from fastness to fastness, exasperated to the last extreme; while the blood of our kindred and our friends was invoking the vengeance of an offended God, was smoking to high heaven, we met the enemies and vanquished them.

Houston, standing in boots reinforced to support his wounded ankle, finished his address with a characteristic bit of theatre. He gripped his sword, meaning to symbolically surrender it now that he was the president of Texas and no longer its commander in chief. In doing so, he was dramatically overcome with emotion. "His soul," wrote an observer, or somebody who claimed to be one, "seemed to have swerved from the hypostatic union of the body, and to dwell momentarily on the glistening blade."

The new vice president also addressed the assembly. Thirty-eight-year-old Mirabeau Buonaparte Lamar had the most presumptuous name in the new republic and the most propulsive résumé. He had relocated himself to Texas from his home state of Georgia after the Alamo had fallen and Houston's army was retreating from Santa Anna. Lamar had been a newspaper publisher, a state senator, and a failed candidate for the U.S. Congress twice over. In 1830, his twenty-one-year-old wife, Tabitha, died of tuberculosis, and in his grief he exiled himself into the poetic wilderness, writing, among other verses, a poem called "At Evening on the Banks of the Chattahoochee" ("But all the loveliness that played / Around her once, hath fled," lamented the bereaved poet. "She sleepeth in the valley's shade, / A dweller with the dead").

By 1835, Lamar had had enough of dwelling with the dead, and he was ready to head to Texas for all the usual reasons: to make his name, to make his fortune, to recharge his soul. On the afternoon of April 20, the day before the Battle of San Jacinto, he was a private in the Texas army. By the next day, after having saved Thomas Rusk's life in the skirmish that preceded the main battle, he was promoted to colonel and put in charge of the cavalry that advanced along the army's right flank. Soon after, he was named

The poetic sensibilities of Texas president Mirabeau Buonaparte Lamar took a back seat to his ruthlessly pragmatic empire building.

secretary of war and then commander in chief. Now, within the span of six months, he had risen from a common soldier in a demoralized and disorganized army to the vice president of a nation.

Admittedly, it wasn't much of a nation. It had a capital one step up from a log cabin, along with another borrowed building to accommodate the fourteen members of the Texas Senate. "It made my thoughts fly quick and fast when my mind took in the facts," Francis Lubbock marveled when he came to Columbia and found the upstart Congress in session. "This is the capital of a republic." But among the things the capital didn't have was a place for people to sleep. Lubbock had to camp on the ground beneath a live oak tree—"the lodging place of many." The government was greatly in need of basic supplies like stationery and record-keeping books. And the fact that it didn't yet have an official seal or any means of making one meant that the credentials of the ministers whom Houston sent to the United States were not accepted.

The Republic of Texas was also broke. It was over a million dollars in debt. It had wealth in the land it had seized, but no money. The land itself, at least the cultivated parts of it, had been devastated by armies chasing each other across it during the winter and spring of 1836. Juan Seguín's experience was typical. "There was not one of them," he wrote of the families that he escorted back to San Antonio, "who did not lament the loss of a relative and, to crown their misfortunes, they found their houses in ruins, their fields laid waste, and their cattle destroyed or dispersed. I myself found my ranch despoiled; what little was spared by the retreating enemy had been wasted by our own army. Ruin and misery met me on my return."

The new country was also saddled with an unruly army clamoring to invade Mexico, and it would only be a matter of time before Mexico sent troops north to reclaim its territory and destroy a rebel government that in its eyes was no more legitimate than the Green Flag republic of 1813 or the Fredonia republic of 1826. It was pretty clear that in order not to share the fate of those firefly regimes, the Republic of Texas needed help. What it needed, specifically, was to disappear altogether and become part of the United States as soon as possible. There was almost unanimous agreement about this. Annexation was, Austin believed, the "one all absorbing point." He said this in an official capacity, because Houston had recently appointed him Texas's secretary of state.

As the chief diplomat of the republic, Austin lived and worked in Columbia. He didn't have to sleep on the ground, but his combined office and residence was a shed attached to a small house, with neither a stove nor a fireplace to protect his fragile health against the coming winter. One of his first diplomatic initiatives was to get Santa Anna safely and productively out of Texas. He convinced the imprisoned dictator to write a letter to President Jackson and offer his help to bring about an official recognition of Texas by the United States. "Let us establish mutual relations," Santa Anna wrote to Jackson, "so that your nation and the Mexican one may seal a bond of friendship, and together may find an amicable way of giving stability to . . . [the Texan] people."

This was disingenuous blather, and everybody knew it, but it served to help orchestrate a meeting in Washington between Santa Anna and Jackson, with the goal of convincing the United States to formally recognize the Texas Republic. Santa Anna was escorted out of Texas so quietly that it was almost a smuggling operation, but once he and his entourage reached the United States he was welcomed as a puzzling celebrity. He was such a charming and polite villain that nobody quite knew what to think of him. "He is a Spaniard," wrote an army officer who met him, "a slight figure, about 5 ft. 10, of very commanding, dignified appearance, graceful manner and benign countenance. He smiled at his misfortunes, and for my life I could not believe he ever gave the order for the massacre at Goliad." The farther north he traveled, the less ambiguous his reception became. For those who believed that the real goal of the Texas Revolution had always been to add another slave state to the union, Santa Anna was not a rampaging dictator but a champion of freedom. "How can we style him a tyrant," a Rhode Island newspaper asked, since the Mexican leader had "fought and bled to contravene the efforts of those who wished the substantial, the horrible system of slavery?"

—15—

SPARTAN SPIRIT

IN WASHINGTON, DC, SANTA ANNA MET WITH ANDREW
Jackson and with president-elect Martin Van Buren, and was
regaled at state dinners. By the time he was sent home to
Veracruz in the vain hope that he might be able to help bro-
ker some kind of peace between Mexico and Texas, Stephen F.
Austin had been dead for a month. He had developed

pneumonia when a norther blew in, the cold wind infiltrating the unheated
shed of his secretary of state's office. He was moved into the main room
of the house, where he died on a pallet in front of the fireplace. In his last
feverish hour, he announced to the grieving friends tending him, "The independence of Texas is recognized! Don't you see it in the papers?"

His poor delirious mind was several months ahead of reality. The idea of
the United States recognizing Texas was divisive. Acknowledging the legiti-
macy of a breakaway republic that another nation still claimed as its own
would mean trouble—possibly outright war—with Mexico. And recognizing
a slave republic and admitting it into the union was an abolitionist nightmare. Benjamin Lundy, a Quaker activist who had gone to Mexico in the
early 1830s to try to acquire a colonization grant to settle emancipated slaves,
had no illusions about the "real objects" of the Texas Revolution—"to wrest
the large and valuable territory of Texas from the Mexican Republic, in order

to re-establish the system of slavery; to open a vast and profitable slavemarket therein; and, ultimately, to annex it to the United States." His view was fiercely endorsed by former president John Quincy Adams, now in his late sixties and serving in the U.S. House of Representatives, who saw the fight for Texas as only one thing, "a war for the re-establishment of slavery."

But the United States did recognize Texas, thanks to the lobbying of the ministers that Houston sent to Washington, William Wharton and Memucan Hunt; and thanks to Jackson, who had long wished for the United States to possess Texas. It happened the day before the president left office. "I have at length the happiness to inform you," Wharton reported, "that President Jackson has closed his political career by admitting our country into the great family of nations."

But the great family's embrace was rather stiff. Mexico had been independent for only fifteen years, but it was considered a real country, one that other nations would think twice about antagonizing. And outright annexation of Texas by the United States was, for now, a political impossibility.

It took almost ten years for Texas to finally be admitted into that union. In those years, the Republic of Texas proved to be a shaky nation but a proud one. Its unresolved war with Mexico, its growing internal wars with Comanches and other tribes, its bare-bones economy and no-frills governmental appurtenances, its sense of being rejected by what it longed to regard as its mother country: these were ingredients in the identity stew of what it meant to be a Texan. There was the sense of being besieged and underappreciated and isolated, and the need to compensate by being self-reliant, warlike, and inordinately prideful. Texas was a place that thought it wanted to be a state, but at the same time it was developing a fierce national personality that it would never surrender.

Texas had a flag, a single gold star on a blue field. In a few years it would replace that early design with one that echoed the imagery and color scheme of the U.S. flag, with the bold lone star centered on a perpendicular strip of blue, with two broad horizontal stripes of red and white.

Texas had a new capital as well, another temporary one. In December 1836, two brothers named John and Augustus Allen managed to sell the Texas Congress on the idea of relocating from Columbia to a brand-new town they had just laid out a few miles west of the burned-out ruins of Harrisburg on Buffalo Bayou. For symbolic resonance, it was only about fifteen or sixteen miles away from the San Jacinto battlefield; for shameless flattery, it was named Houston; and for the sake of future commerce, it was connected by the supposedly navigable waters of the bayou to Galveston Bay and the Gulf of Mexico. "It is handsome and beautifully elevated, salubrious and well watered," the brothers promised.

The Allen brothers proposed to build a statehouse and other edifices at their own expense and rent them to the government. They would offer comfortable lodgings for the legislators, who were currently forced to sleep on pallets or on the open ground in Columbia. And they did follow through with a relatively imposing two-story capitol, made out of lumber imported from Maine and painted a color that Mary Austin Holley described as peach blossom. But Buffalo Bayou, which was supposed to provide unencumbered access to Galveston for even the largest class of steamboat, was a twisting watercourse filled with snags and overhanging tree branches through which a vessel had to be laboriously cranked forward on improvised windlasses. Sam Houston's executive mansion was a one-room shack with an attached storage shed. On its dirt floor were a single table covered with papers and a scattered array of trunks and camp beds. "We live like hogs," a member of the Texas Congress declared in a letter home to his wife. Others described the new capital city as a "wretched mudhole" and "the most miserable place in the world."

BUT FROM THIS PLACE A VAST NEW COUNTRY WAS TO BE GOV-erned. On the map, Texas had always been a shape-shifting entity. There was never any lasting agreement about where it started and where it ended. One of the first duties of the new Texas Congress was to pass an act to claim its national boundaries. There was a crucial difference between this new geographic vision of Texas and the one that had held sway during the Mexican and Spanish periods. The difference was the river—the Rio Grande—that Texas, heady and greedy with victory, now decided would form its southern and western boundaries.

If you look at a map of Texas today, you can see that it follows the course of the Rio Grande from Brownsville on the Gulf Coast all the way north and west to El Paso, where it veers sharply rightward away from the river into the straight-line geometry that forms the Texas Panhandle. But in 1836, the borders of the Republic of Texas followed the river far past El Paso, all the way into what is now New Mexico. The western border then shot past the origins of the Rio Grande and did not stop until the forty-second parallel, in what is now Wyoming. The Republic of Texas looked roughly like what the state of Texas does now, except that there was much more of it, swelling out to envelop Santa Fe and Albuquerque on the west and, in the north, overtopping the Panhandle with a towering stovepipe.

But look at the map again, this time focusing on a river to the east of the Rio Grande. This is the Nueces, which rises in Central Texas and empties into the Gulf at Corpus Christi. Mexico always regarded the Nueces as the southern boundary of Texas. On the map, the area in South Texas between the two rivers would come to be known as the Nueces Strip. But it was more than a strip, because as the Rio Grande meanders west, away from the Nueces, you can see the extent of Texas widening and opening. Even today, the difference between the Rio Grande boundary and the Nueces boundary is a considerable portion of the state.

According to a U.S. government population estimate made in the summer of 1836, 30,000 Anglo Americans lived in Texas. There were 3,470 Tejanos, 5,000 enslaved people, and a mere handful of free blacks. (Perhaps the most notable of them was Hendrick Arnold, who was born to a white father and black mother. A hunting partner and comrade-in-arms of Deaf Smith, and like Smith married to a Mexican woman, Arnold played a highly visible role in the Siege of Béxar and the Battle of San Jacinto.)

The report also concluded that there were 14,200 Indians in Texas, though certainly this figure is weighted toward the more stationary—and therefore more countable—tribes like the Caddos and Cherokees. Nobody really knew for certain how many Comanches, Kiowas, Apaches, and others lived beyond the line of Texan settlement. Nearly every one of the communities and towns and aspirational cities of the Texas Republic was east of the Nueces. The village of El Paso, far to the west—550 miles from San Antonio—was effectively still a Mexican possession, as was the important trading center of Santa Fe, another 300 miles to its north. In these desert places, the revolution was received as news from a distant land; the nation of Texas existed in an alien world of grassy prairies and verdant forests rapidly being cleared for farms and mills and cotton plantations.

But not rapidly enough. The country with a mudhole for a capital city had an economy with barely a pulse. It was land-rich, though—250 million acres of land that could theoretically be used to lure new tax-paying residents, pay off the debts to its soldiers, and raise revenue from investors. There was so much soil and so little cash that even the carriers employed by Texas's erratic mail service were paid not with currency but with land. But keeping track of legitimate titles in a country built on old Spanish land grants and Mexican colonial claims and rampant speculation was an administrative nightmare. The country's attempts to issue bonds and to borrow money foundered in the wake of the economic depression of 1837. The paper money it printed quickly depreciated, and the private bank it chartered to build canals and railroads was rejected by the public as a "Vampire."

The Texas Army—some 3,600 men—was, in the words of one of its colonels, "bear footed and naked and hongry." Its commanding officer was a hot-tempered Mississippi lawyer named Felix Huston, who had arrived in Texas too late for the fighting and was determined to make up for it by invading Mexico. The similarity of their names must have been a minor source of irritation for President Houston, but in the end, more significant policy clashes led to the president firing the general and replacing him with Albert Sidney Johnston, a graduate of West Point and a veteran of the Black Hawk War. Felix Huston promptly challenged Johnston to a duel and shot him, though Johnston survived his wound and would not die until a quarter century later at the Battle of Shiloh.

The Texas Constitution did not allow the president to succeed himself in office, so when Houston's two-year term was over it was time to step aside. Mirabeau Lamar, Houston's vice president, had become his political enemy and the leader of a faction that was beginning to see Texas not as a fragile country marking time until it could be annexed to the United States, but as a muscular nation willing to push its borders and to aggressively protect itself from Mexicans and Indians. Two prominent officeholders allied with Houston's more pacific philosophy—Peter Grayson and James Collinsworth—were persuaded to run for president, but they couldn't persuade themselves to stay alive. Grayson shot himself in the head after writing an apologetic note to his landlord for "the frightful scene I have made in your house." Collinsworth drank himself into a stupor and drowned when he fell—or probably jumped—from a boat into Galveston Bay.

So Lamar became president. He was short, stocky, slow speaking. But there was something commanding about him. In daguerreotypes taken of him later in life, he poses with his arms crossed, staring into the camera with a self-confidence that could be mistaken—or confirmed—as belligerence. His mouth is straight, his eyes drill into the camera lens. He doesn't look like the wistful author of "At Evening on the Banks of the Chattahoochee." It was Houston—an inferior poet—who had the Byronic soul, who loved to dress in costume and make grand theatrical gestures. He made one at Lamar's inauguration, showing up like George Washington with powdered hair and colonial-era knee breeches. He then took over the platform and gave a farewell address that lasted three hours. Lamar, sensing that Houston would be an annoying act to follow, decided not to speak. Instead, he handed his inaugural address to his secretary and had him read it aloud.

Nevertheless, it was a bold speech. He wanted to "awaken into vigorous activity the wealth, talent and enterprise of the country." On the great question of annexation, Lamar laid it out: "I cannot regard the annexation of Texas to the American Union in any other light than as the grave of all her hopes of happiness and greatness." Grandiose as he was, Houston never saw Texas the way Lamar did, as a great nation in its own right, an imperial power free to make its own policy, to launch its own wars, to ignore all the abolitionist clamor in the United States and unreservedly embrace the institution of slavery, upon which all "hopes of happiness are based."

Lamar wasn't just a saber rattler. He was a poet and classical scholar with a bucolic vision of the empire that his administration aimed to wrest from the hands of its enemies. "Our young Republic," he wrote in his message to Congress a few weeks after his inauguration, "has been formed by a Spartan spirit—let it progress and ripen into Roman firmness, and Athenian gracefulness and wisdom." He was serious about the Athenian part. He introduced legislation that created the foundations of Texas's public schools and universities. But when it came to the Indians who stood in the way of his enlightened slaveholding democracy, he was mercilessly clear: "If the wild cannibals of the woods will not desist from their massacres; if they will continue to war upon us with the ferocity of Tigers and Hyenas, it is time we should retaliate their warfare, not in the murder of their women and children, but in the prosecution of an exterminating war upon their warriors, which will admit of no compromise and have no termination except in their total extinction or total expulsion."

———————— ★ ————————

HE TURNED FIRST TO THE CHEROKEES. THE TEXAS SENATE HAD declined to ratify the treaty that Houston had made with Chief Bowles, calling the Cherokees "the most savage and ruthless of our frontier enemies." It was a galling rebuke to Bowles and his people. They had agreed to stay neutral during the revolution in return for title to their land. Betrayed, Bowles had flirted with the idea of joining a combined force of Mexicans and disaffected Tejanos and rising up against the Texans. In the summer of 1838 there was a tense standoff when the Texas Army under Thomas Rusk, convinced that Bowles was harboring the rebel force, had camped at the edge of a Cherokee village. "I hope to the Great Spirit," Houston wrote pleadingly— or maybe just a little bit menacingly—to Bowles, "that my Red Brother will not make war or join our enemies."

But soon Houston was out of office, and "red brother" was not in his successor's lexicon. When evidence surfaced that another Mexican-Tejano-Indian insurrection was in the works, Lamar lost no time in writing to Chief Bowles with the news that it was time for the Cherokees to leave Texas or to expect a "prompt and sanguinary war." Whether the Cherokees were actually planning to participate in this uprising is unknown, but the suspicion of that possibility was enough of a casus belli for the Texans. Twenty-year-old John H. Reagan was part of the delegation that presented Lamar's letter to Bowles.

Reagan reported that the chief read the letter in silence while sitting on a log. He said he would have to confer with his chiefs and his council before giving an answer. A week or so later the ministers came back. Bowles was candid. He said that he was eighty-three years old and that it did not matter to him whether he lived or died, though he was very much worried for his children and his three wives. He said that he was in a bind. If he fought the whites, they would kill him. If he didn't, his own people would.

He decided to die at the hands of the Texans. The battle took place west of the Neches River, where Chief Bowles made a last stand in a ravine with about 150 warriors. They faced a force of regulars and militias, commanded by Tom Rusk and Edward Burleson, that was three times as large. In the two hours of the climactic conflict, six Texans were killed and thirty-six wounded. The Cherokee losses were much higher, and those who were not killed retreated—leaving Texas behind forever. During the battle, the old chief rode up and down along the rear of his lines on a paint horse, cheering on his men. He waved a sword and wore a silk vest and the military hat that had been given to him by his friend Sam Houston. His horse was shot out from under him. Bowles was hit in the thigh and then in the back. After falling to the ground, he raised himself to a sitting position as his enemies advanced. John Reagan, moved by the chief's "dignity and manliness," called out, "Captain, don't shoot him," to the leader of his company. But the captain shot Bowles through the head anyway, and somebody else scalped him and left his unburied body to rot on the Neches bottomlands that he had tried for so long to secure as a home for his homeless people.

— 16 —

"SAVAGE WARE FARE"

MIRABEAU LAMAR DIDN'T LIKE INDIANS, HE DIDN'T LIKE
Sam Houston, and he really didn't like the capital city
of Houston. Nobody much did. Then as now, it had the
drainage problems of a low-lying coastal city. After a substantial rain, the roads turned into bogs. It was a place of
stagnant water and malarial fevers and perpetually leaky

roofs. Its wildlife was pestering and dangerous. One visitor described being
so beset by giant mosquitoes that he and his party jumped into the waters
of Buffalo Bayou to escape them, only to be chased out of the bayou by alligators, only to encounter a snarling panther on the bank.

In the summer of 1838, when he was running for president, Lamar had
made a sort of campaign trip to one of the westernmost settlements of the
Texas empire, a little cluster of dogtrot houses called Waterloo on the upper
reaches of the Colorado River near where Stephen Austin had once dreamed
of locating a mountain retreat for himself and establishing an academy.
During his visit, Lamar chased down a buffalo and killed it with his pistol.
Afterward he rode up to the top of a hill and gazed out at a landscape that
was far different from the soggy lowlands of Houston. It was in a part of
Texas that rose no more than 2,400 feet above sea level but felt mountainous
all the same, its modest peaks looming above rivers and creeks of clear arte-

sian water, with a sumptuous view of tree-carpeted, undulating ridges, and canyons to the west and thick open prairie to the south and east. Beyond the beauty of the place, what appealed to Lamar was the westward-thrusting feel of it. For someone who thought that Texas should be an unrepentant empire that someday might stretch to the Pacific, this was the place to plant the flag.

After much wrangling in Congress, the site for a new capital was approved. The name "Waterloo" was erased from the map and replaced with "Austin." The city was laid out and built in only nine months under the supervision of Edwin Waller, an old War Party stalwart who had signed the Texas Declaration of Independence and fought the Mexicans at Velasco, where a musket ball struck him in the head but—its force dissipated by the knotted bandana on his forehead—gave him only a black eye.

History does not record the expression on Sam Houston's face or whether he was even present when a train of ox-drawn wagons left the muddy streets of his namesake city, loaded down with the government's archives, along with its officeholders' desks and chairs and spittoons. It wasn't just hurt feelings that made him think Austin was a terrible place to locate the Texas capital. The soon-to-be city was on the far edge of the Texas frontier, vulnerable to Indian attacks and incursions by the Mexican Army. "This is the most unfortunate site upon earth for the Seat of Government," he thundered in a letter when he saw Austin for himself. (He was now serving in the legislature from San Augustine, biding his time before he could run for president again and replace Lamar.) The new capital was "between water, cold region, indifferent and sparse timber. It is removed outside of the settlement, and not a house between here and Santa Fe. . . . I might have been happy in ignorance at home had I known the full extent of Lamar's stupidity."

Austin, like San Antonio, sat at the edge of the Texas highlands, tucked into the craggy limestone buttresses of the Balcones Escarpment. It was eighty miles northeast of San Antonio, but between the two cities there was a tumultuous century of time. Austin was the upstart Americanized capital of Texas, whereas San Antonio still harbored its primal Mexican soul. By now, San Antonio had an Anglo mayor—John Smith, who had been an Alamo messenger—but almost all the other officeholders were of Spanish descent, and only in the past year had city council minutes been rendered in English as well as Spanish. But the Tejanos who lived in San Antonio, as well the Tejanos who lived in the rest of Texas, were starting to feel a growing weight of exclusion. The brilliant Lorenzo de Zavala was dead, having perished from pneumonia after his rowboat overturned on a freezing day in Buffalo Bayou. Juan Seguín was a senator in the new republic, and

José Antonio Navarro was in the Texas House, but besides them there were only two other Tejanos in the government.

Tejanos ran the risk of being distrusted by both Mexico and Texas, constantly forced to choose sides in an endlessly simmering conflict of identity. An attempted reconquest of Texas could come from Mexico at anytime, turning them into refugees again, casting new suspicion on their loyalties. Beneath the wariness with which the Anglos regarded them was something darker, embodied in rhetoric that referred to Mexicans as mongrelized and swarthy and indolent and untrustworthy, as the products of a degraded race. During the war, this sort of vocabulary occasionally slipped from the pens of Anglo leaders like Austin and Houston when they were feeling trapped and vulnerable and uncertain about who was on their side. But by and large the friction between Anglos and the native-born Tejanos had been far more political than racial, the normal squabbling and positioning of allies whose aims might be different but whose enemy was the same. Now it was becoming a dangerous abscess, an assumption of genetic superiority that would poison Texas for many generations. The attitude came easiest to the Americans streaming into the new republic, who had never met Tejanos or written a constitution with them or fought with them on the battlefield. Tejano families who had risked everything for the cause of independence sometimes found themselves being driven into exile into Mexico or Louisiana or, as in the case of Juan Seguín, derided as "unfit for command" by the irascible Felix Huston for not being fluent in English, the new language that had suddenly been imposed upon an ancient Spanish-speaking world.

The Tejano statesman José Antonio Navarro turned his back on his native Mexico to sign the Texas Declaration of Independence. "The pang of severing national allegiance," wrote an observer, "unnerved him."

Relations between whites and Indians were even worse. President Lamar had essentially declared war on any tribe that did not immediately conform to the laws and expectations of the Republic of Texas. To him, the Cherokees and the other immigrant peoples who had been driven west into Texas were "intruders" in a way that his own countrymen certainly were not. "I am far from conceding," he said, "that the Indians, either Native, or Emigrant, have any just cause of complaint." The war of expulsion and extermination that he had unleashed upon the Cherokees was turned upon the Creeks, the Wichitas, the Kickapoos, and the remnants of the once-great Caddos. That was in the forests of the east. Toward the west, directly in the way of the empire that Lamar wanted to push to the sea, were the Comanches.

"MATILDA!" A MAN NAMED ANDREW LOCKHART YELLED ABOVE the chaos of an attack on a Comanche village. "If you are here, run to me!" From inside one of the lodges, fifteen-year-old Matilda Lockhart heard her father's voice. She screamed back as loud as she could to let him know she was in the camp with the Indians who had captured her, but he couldn't hear her above the noise of musket fire and the barking of dogs and the terrified shrieks of women and children.

This happened in the winter of 1839 somewhere along the San Saba River, not far from the mission that had been overrun by Comanches seventy-one years before. The attackers were a force of sixty Texas militiamen. They called themselves, informally, Rangers. The word had come into use during the early days of Austin's colony to describe a mounted force necessary to help defend against Indian attacks. It was a concept that had long been field-tested by Tejanos and their fast-moving spying and pursuit outfits known as *compañías volantes* (flying companies). A "corps of rangers" had been decreed into existence by the Texas provisional government in 1835, but it was not until 1866 that the state legislature would create something officially known as a "Texas Ranger."

With Lockhart and the other Rangers that day were several dozen Lipan Apaches under the leadership of a chief named Castro. The Lipans had discovered a Comanche encampment on the San Gabriel, forty or fifty miles north of Austin, and had enlisted the Texans to join them in a surprise assault on their common enemy. The Texans, especially Andrew Lockhart, were more than eager. Lockhart was a father of nine who had come to Texas in 1829 to settle on the Guadalupe in the DeWitt Colony. The previous fall, his daughter Matilda had been abducted along with four other children while they were gathering pecans along the Guadalupe. The purpose of this raid was to retrieve the captives and bring the wrath of frontier vengeance down upon their abductors.

The Texans and Lipans found, when they reached the San Gabriel, that the Comanches had left, but they followed their trail through a bitter winter storm until they located their camp on the San Saba and attacked in a wild rush, firing indiscriminately into the lodges. The Comanches fled, but the warriors regrouped and drove the Texans back into a cedar brake and then ran off their horses. "We were left afoot more than one hundred miles from home," Noah Smithwick wrote in his memoir of this disastrous campaign.

Matilda Lockhart was lucky she wasn't killed along with the other women and children who must have perished in the attack. "I never felt sorrier for a man than I did for Colonel Lockhart," Smithwick recalled of the forlorn father whose hopes of being reunited with his daughter had just evaporated.

But then, a year later, Matilda Lockhart suddenly appeared in San Antonio.

Twenty-two-year-old Mary Maverick was on hand to witness the terrible things that happened next. She was the wife of Sam Maverick, who had succeeded John Smith as mayor of San Antonio. Sam Maverick was from a South Carolina planter family. He had graduated from Yale, practiced law, and moved to Texas in time to become a key participant in the siege of San Antonio. Now he and Mary lived with their children and slaves in a stone house off the main plaza. They had planted fig and pomegranate trees and built a bathhouse at the edge of the river, beneath a magnificent cypress tree whose buckling roots made serpentine ridges through their yard. Sam kept a "war horse" in the padlocked stable, along with tack and firearms and provisions, so that at a moment's notice he could saddle up and ride off with other members of his Ranger company in pursuit of Indians.

In January 1840, three Comanches of the Penateka band, whose home territory was the southern Texas plains, rode into San Antonio to discuss peace. They were weary of constant border conflicts with the Texans and eager to establish a treaty to open up a more productive trading relationship. They were told that serious peace talks could begin only if they went back to Comanchería and, as a sign of good faith, returned with the thirteen Anglo captives believed to be held by the Comanches.

Two months later they returned. This time there were sixty-five of them, thirty warriors and thirty-five women and children. They came in high spirits, with goods to trade, apparently under the assumption that a formal peace would soon be concluded. But the Texans who received them were far more wary. Albert Sidney Johnston, the republic's secretary of war, had ordered three companies of troops to San Antonio and told the officer in charge that the Penateka chiefs were to be arrested if they didn't produce all thirteen captives.

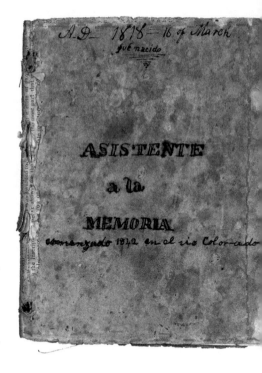

They brought only one. It was Matilda Lockhart. There is debate among historians over exactly what sort of condition she was in. Neither the official reports of what happened that day nor the scant surviving correspondence of the Lockhart family mention anything about Matilda's appearance, but Mary Maverick's memoir couldn't have been more detailed:

> She was in a frightful condition, poor girl. . . . Her head, arms and face were full of bruises, and sores, and her nose actually burnt off to the bone—all the fleshy end gone, and a great scab formed on the end of the bone. Both nostrils were wide open and denuded of flesh. She told a piteous tale of how dreadfully the Indians had beaten her, and how they would wake her from sleep by sticking a chunk of fire to her flesh, especially to her nose. . . . Ah, it was sickening to behold, and made one's blood boil for vengeance.

It may be that the Texans' blood was indeed boiling, or it may be that Mary Maverick's gruesome description—written toward the end of her life—was a latter-day justification for the slaughter that happened next. It took place in a dirt-floored meeting room called the Council House, which was attached to the jail. Twelve of the Comanche leaders were invited for a peace parley. The other eighteen warriors, and the women and children, waited

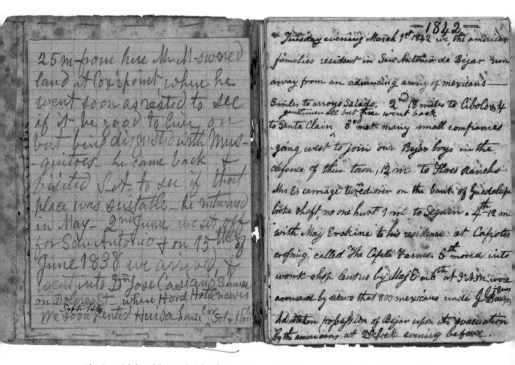

The Spanish hand-lettered title of Mary Maverick's diary reflects the fact that Anglo Texas was a long way from purging itself of its Mexican roots. The vivid diary recounted, among other adventures, the on-the-ground fears of a Mexican invasion.

outside, where the young men entertained themselves and the citizens of San Antonio with bow-and-arrow marksmanship displays while the chiefs and the Texas peace commissioners talked.

Inside the Council House, things quickly went wrong. The Texans demanded that the Indians bring in the rest of the hostages. The Penateka spokesman, a chief named Mukawarrah, said through an interpreter that Matilda Lockhart was the only hostage they had, but they would see what could be done—for a price—to ransom the other captives. A Texas colonel, William S. Fisher, conducted the negotiations. He was also in charge of the troops stationed against the walls of the Council House and guarding the exits. He told Mukawarrah that the other captives had to be returned. Until they were, the chiefs in this room would be held hostage. Betrayed, enraged, realizing they were trapped, the Comanches reached for their weapons and moved for the doors. Within minutes, they were all dead, shot down in a close-range fusillade or stabbed or bludgeoned to death in the savage hand-to-hand fighting that followed. The Indians in the yard outside, who moments before had been peacefully demonstrating their skill with their bows and arrows, turned their weapons on the Texas troops or ran for safety through the streets of San Antonio. The fleeing warriors were hunted from house to house or shot down as they tried to cross the river. They all died. So did five Comanche women and children. The surviving women and children were locked in the jail, next to the Council House, where their chiefs still lay on the blood-saturated dirt floor.

On the Texan side, seven were killed, including a judge and the sheriff and a young man named G. W. Cayce, who had hoped to marry Gertrudis Navarro, a survivor, along with her sister Juana, of the Battle of the Alamo four years earlier. Ten others were wounded.

A Russian doctor and naturalist named Weideman took part in the fight, chasing the fleeing Indians on his horse through the streets of the city. Late that afternoon, while Mary Maverick was visiting a neighbor, Dr. Weideman showed up with two Comanche heads, a male and a female. "I have been long exceedingly anxious to secure such specimens," he told the ladies. He took the heads, as well as the bodies, and put them in a soap boiler so that he could render them down and study their skeletons. The boiler discharged into an *acequia*, which supplied the town's drinking water. When horrified citizens saw what he had done, they had the doctor arrested. "He took it quite calmly," Maverick reported. He assured everyone that the water was safe to drink and that the "Indian poison" had long since run off. He "paid his fine and went off laughing."

There was only lamentation in the Comanche villages when word arrived about what had happened in San Antonio. Their peace ministers had all been massacred, their wives and children—those that managed to survive— held as prisoners in the Alamo. The need for vengeance was unstoppable. Late in that summer of 1840, the Penatekas formed an invasion force with their Kiowa allies and rode down from the Hill Country onto the prairie, into the heart of Anglo Texas. There were about seven hundred of them, and they headed straight for the coast and descended upon a town called Linnville. Linnville was a small community on the shores of Lavaca Bay, only a few miles from where La Salle and his colonists had built their wilderness settlement. It was a perfect target for plunder, since it was a port with a customshouse where goods from the United States were unloaded before being distributed into the interior of Texas.

The several hundred people who lived in Linnville watched as a dust cloud two miles out on the horizon coalesced into a surging nightmarish storm front of screaming men wearing buffalo-horn headdresses and red and black war paint, waving lances and muskets, their horses churning up the prairie as they galloped toward the town. There was no possibility of stopping that sudden oncoming wave, so the citizens of Linnville jumped

EDWARD BURLESON,
*a battle-tested vice president of the Republic of Texas, led Texian forces during the Battle of Béxar
and at San Jacinto, against the Cherokees at Chief Bowles's last stand on the Neches River,
and against the Comanches at the Battle of Plum Creek.*

into boats and rowed themselves out into the bay or just took off swimming, where they were picked up by a ship that was coming into port to unload its cargo. Most of them survived, though the customs agent was killed and his wife captured. From their boats, they watched the marauders ransack and burn their town. The Comanches helped themselves to the goods sitting in the warehouses, trading their buffalo headdresses for top hats, covering their naked painted torsos with frock coats, twirling umbrellas as they rode out of town with the thousands of horses and mules they had liberated from Linnville and nearby Victoria.

It was a victorious caravan but a slow-moving one, far different from the usual lightning strike typical of Comanche warfare. The Indians were burdened with the livestock and warehouse goods they had captured and by the hundreds of women and children who were along on the expedition. Meanwhile, the alarm had spread quickly among the militias and Ranger units, and near the present-day town and barbecue mecca of Lockhart (named after Matilda's uncle Byrd Lockhart, a DeWitt colonist and Alamo courier) two hundred Texans intercepted the Indians' sprawling line of march.

Felix Huston was in command of the Texans, but his tactics proved fruitlessly conventional. He ordered his men to dismount and form up to receive a charge. But the Comanches had no intention of riding straight into a wall of fire. They swarmed around Huston's neat lines, flanking and encircling and harassing the enemy with separate charges while their women and noncombatants kept the huge herd of stolen horses moving behind them.

Within the Texan ranks were men who had more experience fighting Indians than Huston, and far less patience for antiquated military maneuvers. Among them were Edward Burleson and Rangers such as the soon-to-be-legendary Jack Hays, who had had hostile encounters with Comanches while working as a surveyor, and Mathew Caldwell, nicknamed "Old Paint" for the variegated color of his side-whiskers. Caldwell had played a key role in the Battle of Gonzales and had been inside the San Antonio Council House when Mukawarrah and the other Comanche chiefs were killed. Caldwell had been shot in that fight, hit in the leg by a ricocheting ball, but even so he had dispatched two of the chiefs himself, shooting one in the head and beating the other to death with a musket.

A participant in the fight named James Wilson Nichols, whose memoir ranks among the most colorful and idiosyncratic in Texas literature, recorded Huston's remarks to Burleson and Caldwell: "Gentlemen, those are the first wild Indians I ever saw and not being accustom to savage ware fare and both of you are, I think it would be doing you and your men especially great injustace for me to take the command."

That was no problem for Caldwell and Burleson, who led a mounted charge that broke the Comanche momentum, scattered its warriors, and led to a running horseback fight that extended for fifteen miles. Although the conflict did not produce many casualties, it was a grisly enough demonstration of the kind of warfare that could be expected along the Texas frontier in the decades to come. Nichols described encountering an elderly Comanche woman—"this old mother of the forest" —in the midst of the fight. She was apparently guarding three Comanche prisoners—a black slave girl, a woman named Nancy Crosby (who, as it turned out, was the granddaughter of Daniel Boone), and a Mrs. Watts, who was the wife of the customs agent killed in Linnville. When she saw the Texans riding up on her, the old women of the forest turned into a whirlwind of lethality, killing the slave girl with an arrow, Mrs. Crosby with a musket, and firing another arrow into Mrs. Watts, who survived because (according to another witness) the arrow couldn't penetrate her whalebone corset. Nichols killed the old Comanche woman before she could mount her horse and get away. He then joined the pursuit of the Indians on horseback, crossing a creek that was "litterly bridged with packs, dead and bogged down horses and mules." He came across another Comanche woman, lying on the ground and shot through both thighs. A Texan father and son rode up. The father dismounted and handed his reins to his son.

He drew his long hack knife as he strode towards her, taken her by the long hair, pulled her head back and she gave him one imploring look and jabbered something in her own language and raised both hands as though she would consign her soul to the great sperit, and received the knife to her throat which cut from ear to ear, and she fell back and expired. He then plunged the knife to the hilt in her breast and twisted it round and round like he was grinding coffee, then drew it from the reathing boddy and returned the dripping instrement to its scabard without saying a word.

The Texans framed the Battle of Plum Creek as a decisive victory, though most of the Indians got away with most of the horses they had stolen. But the fight blunted the hubris of the Penatekas and only hardened the attitude, preached by people like Mirabeau Lamar and Felix Huston, that when it came to Comanches and the survival of the Texas nation, there could be no such thing as coexistence, only extermination.

Emboldened by having routed the Penateka expedition, the Texans took the fight into Comanchería. It was beyond the government's nonexistent budget to field an army for this purpose, so it was left to the Rangers to head up the Brazos and Colorado and other river valleys in search of Indian villages to destroy. This they did systematically and indiscriminately—one Ranger colonel vaguely alluded to the dead inhabitants of a camp he had just attacked as belonging to "some northern tribe."

The Rangers' salaries, such as they were, were often raised by the communities they protected, but were seriously supplemented by

A stylized depiction of the running horseback fight known as the
Battle of Plum Creek, which took place after the Comanches made a lightning raid
on the Gulf Coast and ransacked the town of Linnville.

plunder—notably by the sale of the horse herds they took away from the smoldering Indian villages. But one has the sense they would have done the job for free. They were young men, by and large, who were drawn to extreme adventure, close comradeship, and dangerous purpose. Over time, they learned to fight like their enemy, traveling without baggage, without tents, without provisions except what they could kill along the way. "Most of them were dressed in skins," recalled a Ranger from San Antonio many years later, "some wearing parts of buffalo robes, deer skins and bear skins, and some entirely naked to the waist, but having leggings and necessary breechclouts."

One thing soon set them apart from the Comanches they hunted: a revolving five-shot pistol invented by Samuel Colt. The Paterson Colt fired

a .36 caliber ball—undersized in comparison with the whopping .44 caliber pistol that would replace it—but the fact that it could discharge five shots in quick succession provided a serious tactical advantage for men who went into war while charging on horseback. The first real test of the weapon—in 1844—occurred along a nameless creek in Central Texas. (It would not be nameless for long, since one of the fight's participants, Sam Walker, would lend his name to the creek and to the next-generation heavy-duty Colt revolver.) Jack Hays, the courteous, mild-seeming former surveyor who was fast becoming the most lethal Ranger leader, was in command of fifteen men who engaged a party of seventy-five Comanches. "Crowd them!" Hays called to his men during the close-order horseback fight. "Powder-burn them!" When the defeated Indians left the field, one Ranger was dead and three were wounded, but forty Comanches had been blasted off their horses by the Paterson Colts. The pistols, Hays wrote in his official report, "did good execution," adding, "I cannot recommend these arms too highly."

—17—

THE BROKEN FLAGPOLE

"I AM INFORMED THAT YOU ARE COLD AND REPULSIVE IN your manners," a political ally of Mirabeau Lamar wrote to the president in 1839. It was intended to be a helpful observation. People would like him more if he could just be a little nicer to them and not so fixated on the "constant occupancy of your mind and important matters of State."

But the condition of the republic was likely to turn any president into a curmudgeon. Lamar's Indian wars had dramatically driven up the national debt, as had his expensive mini-navy of six new ships. Hopeful new residents and their less optimistic slaves were arriving in Texas every day; one visitor recalled passing an incoming convoy of wagons three miles long, carrying over two thousand people. But many of these immigrants had left the United States because of the economic panic of 1837, and that same depression was driving down the market for the cotton they had come to Texas to plant. The state of the country did not inspire confidence in the European powers from which it was seeking recognition, especially when recognizing it could very well create turbulent relations with Mexico, the country that still claimed it. Texas needed money and it needed respect, and it was having trouble finding either. Attempts to arrange a $5 million loan from the United States and from England had gone nowhere, but there was at least one bright spot: France.

In 1838, France launched an improbable little war on Mexico. It was predicated upon claims that a French pastry chef had made against the Mexican government after his shop in Mexico City was destroyed in the street fighting during one of the era's many insurrections. After France had ratcheted the claim up to 600,000 pesos, which Mexico refused to pay, a French fleet arrived and began bombarding Veracruz. The hero of the war, the man who gained credit for repulsing the French, was none other than Santa Anna. He was in the saddle, leading a counterattack against the invaders, when grapeshot from a French cannon killed his horse and shattered his leg. The leg was amputated and eventually buried in a state funeral in Mexico City. The man who had come home in disgrace after losing Texas had managed to once again stir up the adulation of his country and once again become its leader.

With the bitterness between the French and Mexicans still simmering, it was a good time for l'enfant Texas to press its case with imperial France. The French recognized Texas as a sovereign nation, negotiated a trade treaty that spelled out the import duties on Texas cotton in relation to those imposed on French silks and wines, and sent a diplomat named Alphonse Dubois de Saligny as chargé d'affaires. Dubois built an elegant legation on a hill overlooking the new capital—it's still there, one of the oldest surviving buildings in Austin. But thanks to the temperament of their new Texas diplomat, the French, having fought the Chicken War in the previous century and having just recovered from the Pastry War, now found themselves embroiled in the "Pig War." Before Dubois's new official residence was ready, he lived next door to a hotel owned by Richard Bullock. The problem was that Bullock's hogs kept knocking down the fence to Dubois's garden and eating his vegetables, and then breaking into his house to consume his bed linens and state papers. Dubois instructed his servants to kill the hogs. Bullock retaliated by attacking one of the servants on the street with a walking stick, an altercation that Dubois claimed was "one of the most scandalous and outrageous violations of the Law of Nations."

On the surface, the whole affair was something of a joke—"Go it Texas!" chortled one Texas newspaper, "Viva la pigs!"—but it led to the collapse of diplomatic relations and extinguished the possibility of Texas receiving the desperately needed $5 million loan from France.

Lamar's attempt to win Texas a place in the family of nations even extended to its fiercest enemy: Mexico. Through his secretary of state and later through an American special agent with friendly ties to Santa Anna, he pursued a peace treaty that would acknowledge Texas's independence and guarantee its Rio Grande boundary. In return, Texas would pay $5 million. The detail that Texas did not have $5 million ended up being moot, since Mexico—in the pithy words of a Veracruz newspaper called *El Censor*—was "not aware of the existence of a nation called the republic of Texas, but only a horde of adventurers in rebellion against the laws of the government of the republic."

Texas had better luck, after an abortive overture or two, with Great Britain, which, as the world's largest consumer of raw cotton, perceived a national interest in cultivating new markets in a North American country that was neither the United States nor Mexico. It signed treaties with Texas that effectively recognized its independence and offered to help in negotiating peace with Mexico. The treaties were quickly ratified by the Texas Senate. But England, which had a crusading agenda when it came to slavery, insisted on a third treaty that pledged the new republic's aid in the suppression of the slave trade. This too was sent on to the Texas capital for ratification, but strategically delayed until Congress had adjourned and could no longer act on it.

In response, Parliament held up its approval of the other two provisions, leaving Texas still broke, still an unruly, upstart nation in the eyes of much of the world, and still sitting across the Rio Grande from a hostile power that fervently wanted it to disappear from the map. Lamar's answer to this predicament was a disaster known as the Texan Santa Fe Expedition.

Since 1821, there had been a prosperous trade between the United States and Mexico along the Santa Fe Trail, which connected Santa Fe with the Missouri River and St. Louis along a northerly overland route through Missouri, Kansas and Colorado. Why should Texas not siphon off this trade by opening a southerly trail of its own, linking New Mexico with its Gulf Coast ports? Also, since Texas claimed the Rio Grande as its western boundary, the expedition would also serve the diplomatic purpose of convincing the Mexican citizens of Santa Fe—by force if necessary—that their future lay in pledging allegiance to the Republic of Texas. In the words of George Wilkins Kendall, a journalist with the *New Orleans Picayune* who signed on for the adventure, the emissaries from Texas "could not do other than give the people of Eastern New Mexico an opportunity to throw off the galling yoke under which they had long groaned."

But all the groaning ended up being on the Texan side. The 321 members of the Santa Fe party, including soldiers, merchants with wagonloads of goods to sell, and government commissioners such as José Antonio Navarro, mustered north of Austin in June 1841 and took off in high spirits. Someone had even composed a rousing song to see them off:

Forward comrades, firm and steady—
Hearts prepared and rifles ready.

From our mount-encircled valley,
Boldly forward let us sally—
Merrily, Texians march away!
To the hills of Santa Fé.

They intended to march to the Red River and follow it west, but as it turned out the men who claimed to be their guides didn't know the country, and the expedition was soon lost and wandering through, as Kendall described it, "a wide waste of eternal sameness," attacked by Kiowas, eating horses and dogs, almost perishing of thirst. After a hellish crossing of the Llano Estacado, they at last reached New Mexico. But the grateful welcome they expected to receive upon reading their proclamation from their president ("You will see [Texas] become the richest, most powerful nation in America . . . everywhere a Texan sets foot, he transforms barrenness into fertility. Barbarians disappear. . . . Commerce and industry flourish") was painfully distant from reality. They were arrested by the Mexican Army, which still very much regarded this Rio Grande borderland as belonging to Mexico—and the members of the Santa Fe Expedition as criminal intruders—and marched under guard far to the south to prisons in Mexico City.

WHEN NEWS OF THE FULL DEBACLE OF THE TEXAN SANTA FE Expedition reached Austin, Mirabeau Lamar was no longer president. His term ended on December 13, 1841, and the man who was there once again to upstage him on the inaugural platform was none other than his old enemy Sam Houston. It had been a bitter election, with Houston running against yet another old enemy, Lamar's vice president, David Burnet. This was the same David Burnet who, as provisional president in 1836, had taunted Houston for not fighting Santa Anna and then, after Houston's startling victory at San Jacinto, denied him passage to New Orleans to have his ankle wound treated. The campaign to succeed Lamar was predictably bitter, and by the end it had descended into such riotous name-calling and character assassination that Burnet challenged his opponent to a duel. Houston, who didn't rise to the bait, philosophized that "the people are equally disgusted with both of us."

One reason for Houston's equanimity and self-control was the fact that he had recently placed himself in the tempering custody of his third wife. Margaret Lea was from Alabama, but she had happened to be in New Orleans on the day in 1836 when the wounded Houston had arrived at the docks. She was seventeen years old then, part of the crowd welcoming the conquering hero of San Jacinto. They met three years later in Mobile, after

Houston's first term as Texas president. She was twenty-six years younger, but it was an evening of mutual besotment. The evidence is in a poem that Margaret wrote that night, addressed to the flower Houston had presented her ("Doth some tranquilizing power / Breathe in thy rich perfume?"), and in a family story that has them walking together in the garden in the moonlight, with Houston directing her attention to a star in the sky, the Lone Star of their mutual Texas destiny.

Margaret's health was fragile, but her spirit was firm, even a little starchy, which was a good thing for Houston, who was always in danger of throwing himself into the fires of romantic dissolution. She soon had him drinking less, consulting the Bible, and making fewer unnecessary enemies. "Oh gentlemen," the new president and new husband enthused in a speech he gave shortly after his election, "it is woman who blesses her country."

One likes to think it was Margaret who vetoed the inauguration getup he had ordered from Paris—an Elizabethan suit of green velvet, complete with matching cape and floppy hat with a towering tricolored plume. The costume he wore for the event still included a wide-brimmed fur hat and a hunting shirt, but at least it was arguably Texas-themed.

In the wake of Lamar's Texan Santa Fe Expedition, which Houston termed "that silly and vicious project," the Republic of Texas was in renewed danger of reprisals from Mexico. (Lamar had further risked hostilities when he sent half of the six-ship Texas Navy to cruise the Mexican coast in support of Yucatán rebels.) The nation was also more deeply in debt than ever, thanks to the cost of the Indian wars and the construction of a new capital city. The accommodations in Austin were not quite as dire as they had been during Houston's presidential years in his namesake city, when he had resorted to pulling up the floorboards of the "Texian White House" to use for firewood. But the executive mansion turned out to be uninhabitable. In the rush to construct it, the builders used green wood, which shrank as it

MARGARET LEA
first saw Sam Houston when he arrived, badly wounded, to a hero's welcome in New Orleans shortly after defeating Santa Anna.

SAM HOUSTON
in a daguerreotype made at the close of the 1840s. More than a decade had passed since the battle of San Jacinto, but Houston still had the look of a conqueror.

dried, causing the building to fall apart. Instead of taking up residence there, Houston lodged at a boardinghouse owned by a Tennessee widow named Angelina Eberly.

There was no money to pay the government or anybody in it, presumably not even the administration's new secretary of the treasury. "There existed no great use for this office," one observer remembered, "as there was nothing in it that was of special value save promises to pay and some few vouchers."

So Houston's priorities necessarily centered on cost cutting: making treaties with Indians wherever possible instead of raising armies to hound them out of Texas; building trading posts instead of forts; putting the Texas Navy up for sale; and easing up on the saber rattling with Mexico.

On this last point, though, things were already out of his control. "The Mexicans of Mexico," as Mary Maverick put it, "have not forgotten us." Indeed, in March 1842, on Santa Anna's orders, General Ráfael Vásquez led seven hundred troops across the Rio Grande, the river that Texas impudently claimed as its border, and headed toward San Antonio. The invasion came as a surprise. Jack Hays, who was in command of the local Rangers and volunteers, had only a hundred or so men to defend the town, so his forces—along with the town's ladies, who had sewn doubloons into their bustles for safekeeping—withdrew from San Antonio to organize a counterattack. Vásquez, realizing that he would soon be outnumbered, decided that his show of force had been enough. After some light plundering of San Antonio, he retreated back toward the Rio Grande.

The Vásquez invasion was an invitation to an all-out war, a war that Houston very much wanted to avoid. He vetoed a bill from the Texas Congress calling for the invasion of Mexico, and politely evaded clamoring offers of volunteer help from the United States. "Only say you really want men &c &c and all can be had," a Texas official in New Orleans pleaded. "This you may rely on it is so. Many gentlemen have said to me, They will at any time give large sums if Houston wants it."

But Houston didn't want it, not for the purpose of invading Mexico. Once again, he was in the position he had been after the fall of the Alamo, when he had been determined to play for time as everybody around him demanded an immediate engagement. The last thing an insolvent Texas needed was to be swamped with still more rootless volunteer fighters. "If the emigrants come without means," he predicted, "Texas must be destroyed. It will be more fatal than an invasion by fifty thousand men from Mexico."

So Houston maneuvered to keep Texas on a mostly defensive footing. A grinding, confusing war with Mexico would do nothing to advance the goal that still made the most sense for a rapidly disintegrating would-be empire—annexation by the United States.

But then, in September, Mexico invaded again. This time it was a force of 1,200, led by a French-born general named Adrián Woll, who, as a restless young officer, had followed the path of adventure to Mexico, where he offered his services in the fight for independence and later served under Santa Anna in the Texas Revolution. Woll's army sneaked into San Antonio under cover of fog and, after a brief exchange of fire, easily captured the town. More intense fighting came a week later when Jack Hays and a small group of Rangers lured Woll and his army out of San Antonio and across the prairie a few miles to the east, where 225 Texans under Mathew Caldwell—one of the captured members of the Texan Santa Fe Expedition who had just been released from a Mexican prison—had taken up a strong defensive position on the banks of Salado Creek.

One of the men who led daring and repeated cavalry charges against the Texan lines was Juan Seguín. He was now "amongst my enemies" and fighting for the Mexican Army. His plight was emblematic of what had happened to many Tejanos, especially after the suspicion that rained down on anyone of Mexican descent after the twin disasters of the Texan Santa Fe Expedition and the Vásquez invasion. In Seguín's case, he had been accused of treason and—his life under constant threat—forced into hiding at friendly ranchos.

"I had to leave Texas, abandon all," he wrote, "for which I had fought and spent my fortune, to become a wanderer. The ingratitude of those, who had assumed to themselves the right of convicting me; their credulity in declaring me a traitor, on mere rumors, when I had to plead in my favor the loyal patriotism with which I had always served Texas, wounded me deeply."

He was wounded enough to change sides, although as always in the fluctuating borderlands of South Texas the sides were not all that clear. After a six-year exile in Mexico, Seguín was able to come back to Texas and even reenter its public life as a justice of the peace. There were still enough old comrades who trusted him and remembered that he had been a hero of San Jacinto and the man who had buried the ashes of the Alamo dead.

The daylong battle along Salado Creek was a decisive and lopsided victory for the Texans. Woll withdrew from the field after sixty of his men had been killed. Only one of Caldwell's men died. But it was a different story a half mile away, where a force of fifty-three Texas volunteers commanded by Nicholas Dawson were intercepted by Mexican cavalry on their way to join the fight. "Captain," intuited one of his men, "we are in a bad fix." They were indeed. They made a stand in a mesquite thicket, but the spindly branches were no protection against searing grapeshot from the Mexican artillery. Thirty-six of them were either torn apart by cannon fire or killed at close range in the hand-to-hand fighting that followed. Two managed to escape, but the other survivors were taken prisoner and marched with Woll's retreating army back to Mexico.

Up until then, Sam Houston had done his best to appease the Armageddon crowd by posturing and fuming. He had threatened Santa Anna, with transparent theatricality, after the Vásquez invasion: "The Texian standard of the single star, borne by the Anglo-Saxon race, shall display its bright folds in Liberty's triumph on the isthmus of Darien."

But after the outrage of yet another invasion, it was no longer politically possible just to throw up a smoke screen of rhetoric; he had to do something. He ordered General Alexander Somervell to raise a force to cross the Rio Grande into Mexico if he could do so with "a prospect of success." Somervell was a veteran of San Jacinto and, in the dismissive opinion of a private in his army, "a very nice kind Gentleman, but no more fit to Command an Army of men in those times, than a ten year old Boy."

A nice kind gentleman, though, seemed to be what Houston had in mind. His orders to Somervell emphasized caution and "great humanity toward the common people" on the other side of the Rio Grande, rather than righteous vengeance. And the president must have suspected that Somervell would not move with blitzkrieg speed; if he delayed long enough before the onset of winter, it would become impracticable to make the expedition. Houston's heedless and near-fatal charge all those years ago at Horseshoe Bend had perhaps purged him of the impulse to hasten into unpredictable confrontations.

Somervell and his army got off to a slow start, but not slow enough for the operation to be canceled. By the end of November, they were on the march to Laredo, which was theoretically a Texan town on the Texan side of the Rio Grande, though no one had ever tried to enforce that idea. The invading army was an unstable mixture. The legendary Ranger Bigfoot Wallace described its components with elegant concision: "Broken down politicians from the 'old States' that had somehow got on the wrong side of the fence, and had been left out in the cold; renegades and refugees from justice . . . adventurers of all sorts, ready for anything or any enterprise that afforded a reasonable prospect of excitement and plunder."

Somervell lost control of them almost from the start. Even though the citizens of Laredo welcomed the army, it proceeded to ransack the town, making off with so much loot that when it was all piled together, one soldier described it as "a Mountain of no inconsiderable size." Somervell ordered the return of the plunder, and 187 of his men left the army as a result, leaving him with only 550 or so to accomplish the invasion of Mexico. A week later, on December 19, 1842, Somervell called it off and ordered a retreat back to the interior of Texas, but by that time his authority was exhausted. Three hundred of his men refused to join him and decided instead to cross the river to take the town of Mier. But they were overwhelmed and forced to surrender to a brigade led by General Pedro de Ampudia, who treated his prisoners with full military chivalry. Which was lucky for them, since he would soon become notorious for decapitating a rebel leader in Tabasco and then frying his head in oil.

The prisoners were marched to a decrepit hacienda south of Saltillo en route to prison in Mexico City. While there, they engineered a desperate escape. They overwhelmed their Mexican guards, killing five of them, and headed north on stolen horses and mules. After weeks of wandering through a landscape that was nothing but a rumpled immensity of barren mountains, they were recaptured, having long since eaten all their mounts and been driven senseless with thirst.

The order that came from acting president General Nicolás Bravo was comparatively restrained, considering the blanket executions that Santa Anna had ordered after the Alamo and at Goliad seven years before. A hundred and seventy-six beans were put into an earthen jar. Seventeen—a tenth of them—were black. The rest were white. Each man was told to reach into the jar and pull out a bean. If it was a black bean, he would be shot.

One of the men whose life was spared was an assistant surgeon named William F. McMath. He was my wife's ancestor, and I often tell my children that if he had not drawn a white bean, they would never have been born.

One of the men who pulled a black bean out of the jar was Robert Holmes Dunham, who scribbled a letter to his mother that, the last time I checked, is still on poignant display in the Alamo museum.

> Dear Mother,
> I write to you under the most awful feelings that a son ever addressed a mother for in half an hour my doom will be finished on earth for I am doomed to die by the hands of the Mexicans for our late attempt to escape. . . . [It was ordered] by Santa Anna that every tenth man should be shot we drew lots. I was one of the unfortunate. I cannot say anything more I die I hope with firmness may god bless you, and may he in this last hour forgive and pardon all my sins . . . farewell.
> Your affectionate sone,
> R. H. Dunham

ON CONGRESS AVENUE IN DOWNTOWN AUSTIN IS A STATUE OF
Angelina Eberly, the proprietor of the boardinghouse in which President
Houston lived while he was in the capital. No one knows what Angelina
Eberly looked like, but the statue's sculptor, Patrick Oliphant, took the lib-
erty of depicting her as large and furious, no doubt because she needed to
be in scale with the massive cannon she is firing.

If there is a Texas equivalent of St. Lawrence, the third-century martyr
who became the patron saint of archivists and librarians, it is Angelina
Eberly. She accidentally slipped into this role in December 1842, when the
mood of the country was still shaky and incendiary in the wake of the Woll
invasion. Sam Houston had been particularly alarmed about the vulnerable
location of Austin ever since the Lamar administration decreed it into existence as the new capital. A big Comanche raid like the one at Linnville or
another attack from Mexico could leave all those brand-new log buildings in
flames. What worried Houston far more than the buildings, though, were
the government archives, in particular the land office records, which were
the nation's only way of sorting out and enforcing the innumerable claims
and counterclaims about who owned what pieces of Texas land.

After the Vásquez invasion, Houston ordered the government to convene
in Washington, the town on the Brazos where independence had been
declared, but the citizens of Austin wouldn't give up the archives. Doing
so would have meant giving up the last vestiges of their civic economy. But
when General Woll seized San Antonio, and when the breakaway faction of
the Somervell expedition made its disastrous attempt at a revenge raid on
Mexico, moving the archives to a more defensible place became an emergency priority. In October, the president sent two agents to Austin with a
wagon to load up the state department records. Aggrieved Austinites ran
them out of town, but not before perpetrating the ultimate frontier insult of
shaving one of their horses.

After Christmas, Houston tried again. This time he made a grab for all
the archives, sending twenty men and multiple wagon teams. When Angelina Eberly became aware that the intruders were filling the wagons with
the archives, which were kept in the Land Office Building, she took it upon
herself to make use of the town cannon, which was stored in a nearby shed
in anticipation of an Indian attack. The blast didn't kill anybody, but it blew
a hole in the Land Office Building. Houston's men managed to load up the
archives anyway and make a run for it, but the citizens of Austin chased
them down and caught up with them twenty miles away on Brushy Creek.

There were a few tense moments, but in the end the only shot fired during the so-called Archive War came from Angelina Eberly's cannon.

Austin kept the archives, but Houston's Congress still met defiantly in Washington, and as a result Mirabeau Lamar's glorious westward city went, at least for a while, literally to seed. A scientific-minded British adventurer named William Bollaert traveled up the Colorado River to Austin the next August and noted that the once well-defined roads to the capital city were hardly visible beneath the weeds and sunflowers that had overgrown them. Such weedy thoroughfares were known to the angry inhabitants of western Texas as "Sam Houstons." "Alas! Poor Austin," Bollaert wrote, "thy seven hills are nearly deserted, exposed to the marauding of the Comanches." He found the uninhabited president's house to be falling apart, and the empty Capitol "the abode of bats, lizards and stray cattle."

But Austin's abandonment didn't last. The government moved back to the city in the summer of 1845, and it was there, on February 19, 1846, that the ten-year existence of the Republic of Texas was solemnly committed to history. By that time there was a new president, a forty-eight-year-old doctor named Anson Jones. Jones had been part of the medical corps that cared for the wounded Texians after San Jacinto (and ignored the Mexican casualties until Houston promised one of Jones's fellow surgeons $300 to treat them). After the battle, he was appointed the army's apothecary general and later served in the Texas Senate. He was a minister to the United States during Houston's first term and secretary of state in his second.

"Of the four presidents of Texas," lamented an early biographer, "Jones is the least favored by nature. He is of inferior stature, and wanting in beauty of expression. He has not the forcible diction of Burnet, the persuasive grace of Houston, or the noble sincerity of Lamar; but he is courteous, self-possessed, discriminating, and well educated."

Being damned with faint praise was a condition that would hound Anson Jones throughout his political career and through the miserable end of his life, when he descended into depression and chronic jealousy over his more colorful predecessor. (He shot himself in the head in 1858, a few years after telling his son Sam that he had taken the liberty of changing his middle name from Houston to Edward.)

But Jones and Houston had worked well and craftily together as president and secretary of state in guiding Texas toward what they both knew had to be its ultimate destination: union with the United States. After the failure of annexation the first time around, they had dispensed with what Jones called Texas's former "attitude of supplication" and followed instead a strategy of misdirection. The cornerstone of this strategy was to play on American fears of British encirclement of North America. Both countries were claiming possession of Oregon and squabbling over the location of the boundary between the United States and Canada. If the Republic of Texas did not become a part of the United States and became a British client state instead, it would mean the end of the expansionist dream of a continental American empire.

There were plenty of people who didn't share that dream, notably Whig leaders such as Daniel Webster and Henry Clay, who thought that the Union was quite large enough as it was. And to John Quincy Adams and other abolitionists, the annexation of Texas was still nothing but a southern conspiracy to advance the abomination of slavery.

Texas, or at least the idea of Texas annexation, had a friend in John Tyler, who had unexpectedly become the president of the United States after William Henry Harrison died of pneumonia only a month after his inauguration. His ascension threw the Whig Party into turmoil, because Tyler was a Whig in name only, and soon enough not even that. His political philosophy—and his political future—belonged with the Manifest Destiny–minded Democrats.

With Tyler in office, Houston laid the ground carefully. To the British chargé d'affaires in Texas, he dangled the idea that if England could help arrange an armistice with Mexico it would have a very good continental friend in a still-independent Republic of Texas. To Tyler, he expressed his concern that Texas might be forced to fall into the embrace of Great Britain if it could not be annexed to the United States. Texas, Houston wrote to his mentor Andrew Jackson, was being offered to the United States "as a bride adorned for her espousal," but at the same time she was making other plans in case she was spurned once again.

Texans knew, however, that British salvation of the republic would be unlikely, even intolerable. It would come with too big a price: the abolition of slavery. "The institution of slavery," in the words of an outraged Galveston newspaper editorialist, "is engrafted upon our Constitution, and interwoven with the very existence of the Government." Nevertheless, the disingenuous statecraft worked. Texas and the United States signed a treaty of annexation in April 1844, calling for Texas to be admitted into the Union as a territory. But the treaty became a campaign casualty of that year's chaotic U.S. presidential election, and was rejected by the Senate. The Texas bride's long espousal did not finally come to an end until after Houston had left office and Anson Jones became president. By then, the United States had elected an unconflicted expansionist Democrat, James Polk, to succeed John Tyler. Reading the mood of the country, the outgoing president sent Congress a joint resolution calling once again for annexation. This time it was a better deal for Texas, which would come into the Union as a full-fledged state, one

PRESIDENT ANSON JONES
*lowers the flag of the Republic of Texas for the last time. The Texas that had been
an independent nation was now a state.*

that would retain its public lands. And a joint resolution meant a lower bar for success, since it required only a majority vote in each house, not the two-thirds vote in the Senate, which had killed the earlier treaty.

The resolution passed, robustly in the House, squeakily in the Senate. Alarmed at the idea of its runaway province becoming part of a strong and newly aggressive United States, Mexico offered a last-minute deal through British intermediaries. If Texas would reject annexation, Mexico would at last accept its independence. But by then it was too late. Texas wanted, had always wanted, to be part of the United States. When a convention was called to consider the question of annexation there was no debate about the issue, and only one delegate voted against it.

So here was President Anson Jones ascending the speaker's platform in Austin in February 1846 to give his final address—the valedictory not just of a president but also of a country. The wooden dogtrot building on a hill above the Colorado River that had stood vacant except for bats and lizards was now a capital again, with a huge Lone Star flag flying above it.

———————— ★ ————————

IN 1826 OR 1827, A FRENCH INVENTOR NAMED JOSEPH NIÉPCE had managed to fix an image of the view outside his workroom onto a pewter plate—the world's first photograph. But photography remained mostly a laboratory experiment until Louis Daguerre invented a process that made a different type of image fixing—the daguerreotype—available in common life. This happened in 1839, tantalizingly close in time to the battles at the Alamo and San Jacinto and other forever-unseen landmark events of Texas history. Only a few years later, advertisements in Texas newspapers began offering daguerreotype portraits. The first professional photographer to set foot in Texas was a woman known only as "Mrs. Davis," who sailed from New Orleans for Galveston in 1843 and set up a studio there. Neither Mrs. Davis nor, as far as we know, any other photographer was on hand to record the moment when the Republic of Texas ceased to exist, but it's tempting to think about the images from that day that might have been preserved.

Among them would have been the faces on the dignitaries' platform and in the audience. Anson Jones was there, of course, probably sitting next to James Pinckney Henderson, who had done critical diplomatic service as Sam Houston's secretary of state and as minister to France and England, and was about to be inaugurated as Texas's first governor. Houston would have had a place of prominence, and there would have been more eyes straining to get a glimpse of the Raven than anyone else on the platform. There is no record of what he wore that day, but it was unlikely he did not attempt to make some kind of sartorial statement. Juan Seguín's face would not have appeared in the camera lens. He was still in exile in Mexico, still regarded by Anglo Texans as a traitor to the revolution.

But José Antonio Navarro was there, and very glad to be home in Texas. He had spent most of the last four years, ever since setting out as one of the commissioners on the Texan Santa Fe Expedition, in one Mexican prison or another, finally ending up incarcerated in Cuba until being released after a flurry of international diplomacy. He had suffered greatly and was welcomed home as a hero, but he wasn't entirely free from the deepening climate of suspicion toward Tejanos that had arisen in the wake of the Vásquez and Woll invasions. A Galveston newspaper congratulated him on having had a father who was born in Europe, which redeemed him from being "of the abject race of Mexicans." But he didn't speak English, and he had needed a translator for his duties as a delegate to the convention that had written the new state constitution. During the deliberations, he had managed to strike the word "white" from the description of those citizens who would be eligible to vote. The word had been placed in an early draft of the constitution because of fears—as one Anglo delegate put it—of the "hordes of Mexican Indians" who might overrun the ballot box. After all his sacrifices on behalf of Texas, Navarro had enough moral leverage to dismiss that idea as "odious" and to preserve the rights of Tejanos to cast a vote in their new state.

It's possible that the audience packed in front of the capitol on the last day of the Republic of Texas included Navarro's nieces Juana Alsbury and Gertrudis Navarro, or some of the other women or children who had survived the Battle of the Alamo. There were doubtless widows and orphans of the men who had been killed at the Alamo or at Goliad, and many proud veterans of San Jacinto, or the militiamen and Rangers who had fought Comanches at the Battle of Plum Creek or shot them down in the fierce fighting inside the San Antonio Council House. By now, most of them were wearing homespun or even store-bought clothes, not the buckskin hunting outfits that had been common in earlier Texas times. ("Buckskin," remembered Frank Lubbock, "is more romantic and entertaining in romances or pictures than on one's own shanks.")

Perhaps these veterans—young men still—were joined in the crowd of onlookers by the Lipan or Tonkawa scouts who had been their allies against the Comanches or the Mexicans, or by aging men and women of various tribes who had once been "neophytes" during the Spanish mission period—those missions long abandoned, their floors covered in bat guano—and who now were curious to witness the latest revolution of the historical wheel. And there would have been slaves there as well, waiting by their masters' carriages, tending to their horses. Dilue Rose, the girl who had been ten years old during the Runaway Scrape and who wept when she heard of the death of her charming friend William Travis at the Alamo, was now in her twenties. She had married at fourteen a Ranger named Ira Harris. They lived in Columbus, ninety miles away, but perhaps they made the trip to Austin to witness the great transformation and to share memories with others who had fled with them from Santa Anna's army; if so, Dilue might have reconnected with Uncle Ned, the elderly slave of one of those families, who had taken charge of the terrified women and children and gotten them safely out of the flooded bottoms of the Trinity River.

All this is speculation, because there is no photograph of the event, no documentary painting, just scattered reportage and reminiscences. What is known is that Anson Jones tore up his speech, which he thought was "rather a so so affair," wrote a new one at the last minute, and delivered it without looking at his notes. The speech had a resounding conclusion. "The final act in this great drama is now performed," he proclaimed on the occasion that marked for most of his constituents both the end and the beginning of a dream. "The Republic of Texas is no more."

The flagpole broke in two as Anson Jones lowered the emblem of the Lone Star republic for the last time, but Sam Houston managed to step up and catch the flag in his arms before it touched the ground.

—18—

LOS DIABLOS TEJANOS

THE STORY OF A CITY OR A TOWN IS OFTEN TOLD IN ITS street names: names of animals or peoples conquered, names of the rivers and trees and plants that once defined the landscape the city was imposed upon, names of the poets and politicians and generals who left their mark on its identity. But the idea that these names are something more than directional aids, that they are the verbal armature of a town's history, is something that few people who travel those streets ever pay much attention to. For most of us, the names are just names. That was certainly the case with me while growing up in the coastal city of Corpus Christi, a fraying and isolated semi-metropolis in the heart of the South Texas brushlands. I rarely wondered why the downtown streets were called Mesquite or Chaparral or Carancahua or Tancahua, and I never even connected the generic-sounding Taylor Street with the modest granite marker that sat at the edge of a scruffy city park. Chiseled into the granite were the unexciting words "General Zachary Taylor's Army Encamped here in 1845–1846."

In the early 1840s, Corpus Christi was a tiny village centered on a fortified trading post. It sat on a bluff above a bay at the mouth of the Nueces, the river that Mexico still heatedly regarded as the southern boundary of Texas. When Texas voted to enter the Union, everybody knew—or feared,

To his great annoyance, General Zachary Taylor found himself in command of the irregular Texas forces known as los diablos Tejanos *during the Mexican-American War. The Texans were invaluable scouts but, in the opinion of General Taylor, they were also "licentious vandals."*

or hoped—that annexation would mean a war between the United States and Mexico. This was not just because Mexico maintained that the independence of Texas was fraudulent to begin with. It was also because Texas claimed the Rio Grande as its western boundary. It was one thing for Mexico to let Texas go if its loss of territory stopped at the Nueces; perhaps the nation could endure that. But accepting the Rio Grande border was too much. It would mean surrendering an inconceivably huge midcontinent portion of its country and placing its thinly populated California territories at the doorstep of the all-consuming United States.

The language of the joint resolution on annexation was vague on exactly which land made up the new state—only that it would be "the territory properly included within and rightfully belonging to the Republic of Texas." But it was the Rio Grande, the river whose wide westward sweep traced the direction of Manifest Destiny, that President James Polk insisted was the proper and righteous western boundary of Texas.

Less than a month after Anson Jones raised the American flag over the Texas capital, Mexico broke off diplomatic relations with the United States. Juan Almonte, the suave diplomat-soldier who had kept a journal during the siege of the Alamo and had been imprisoned with Santa Anna after San Jacinto, was Mexico's minister in Washington, DC. Before requesting his passports and leaving the country, he declared annexation to be "an act of aggression, the most unjust which can be found recorded in the annals of modern history."

Polk was serenely unmoved by such rhetoric. He was already prepared for war. The previous June, he had ordered General Zachary Taylor, the rumpled sixty-one-year-old hero of the Seminole wars, to lead a force of almost four thousand men to the shores of Corpus Christi Bay. Taylor's army was arguably perched on the peaceable side of the disputed zone between the Nueces and the Rio Grande, but it was still a threatening show of force. It was the largest U.S. military force assembled since the War of 1812, and its whole purpose seemed to be to watch and wait for a suitable provocation.

The eight static months that the army spent in training in Corpus Christi are richly documented, particularly in homesick letters written by young officers such as the future president Ulysses S. Grant. "This morning before I got awake," he wrote in March to his fiancée, Julia Dent, "I dreamed that I was some place away from Corpus Christi walking with you leaning upon my arm, your hand was in mine and I felt very happy. How disappointed when I awoke and found that it was but a dream."

He told Julia about the climate ("delightful and very healthy"), about the prospects for war with Mexico ("we don't believe a word of it"), and about some "terrible visitations of providence." A man drowned in the surf, lightning struck a tent and killed a boy, nine soldiers died when the boilers of a decrepit steamboat exploded in the bay. Grant was perhaps too embarrassed to mention to his beloved that he had been cast as Desdemona in an army production of Othello, but was fired when his fellow officers objected to the unseemly spectacle of a man playing a woman's role.

A twenty-three-year-old lieutenant from Eastport, Maine, with the extravagant name of Napoleon Jackson Tecumseh Dana reported to his wife, Sue, that Corpus Christi was "the dirtiest place, I believe, I was ever in." The constant sea wind drove him crazy, as did the flies and cockroaches and the rattlesnakes that the men sometimes found in the mornings coiled up at their feet. But when he went riding through the prairies, away from the stinking camp and away from the bugs, his mood rose. "You would be so delighted" with the country, he wrote. "All is so wild and romantic. Your buoyant spirit would be unchained, and you would feel so free and happy."

It was not just Sue's buoyant spirit he was frantic to reencounter. "When I come home," he wrote, "I shall want to kiss you all over, and won't you let me do it? I know you will, for you told me on the steamboat you would do everything I want. May I kiss you over and over again on your lips, titties, belly, legs, and between them too? Yes, I must. Tell me, dear one, if I may."

His lustful reveries blossomed in the tedium of endless reviews and inspections, of idle preparations for a war that didn't seem as if it were going to happen after all. "You have no idea, Sue, what a military show we have here and how much of the pomp of war with none of the glory. That is not the worst of it, too. There will be none. I wish I had all my glory and was on my way home again, but let us hold on and see what Mr. Polk is going to do."

Mr. Polk decided to send Napoleon Dana, along with the rest of Zachary Taylor's army, south to the Rio Grande. The order came after the president sent a minister, John Slidell, to Mexico with instructions to try to negotiate a peaceful settlement. The United States would drop its financial claims against Mexico, thereby compensating Mexico for the loss of Texas. It would also offer to buy California outright. But Slidell was pointedly not received, leading him to conclude—as he told Polk—that "a war would probably be the best mode of settling our affairs with Mexico."

Taylor's army marched from Corpus Christi to the north bank of the Rio Grande, a few miles upstream from where it empties into the Gulf. There they built an earthen hexagonal fort just across the river from the thriving Mexican port city of Matamoros, the destination of many a filibuster's dreams. The remains of the fort—Fort Texas—are barely visible these days, just a few weedy hummocks in the middle of a deserted golf course in the city of Brownsville. The banks of that section of the Rio Grande are screened by dense vegetation, but you can still see across the river to Mexico and thereby understand what a taunt it must have been to the people of Matamoros to witness heavy cannon capable of shooting eighteen-pound balls being mounted on those dirt walls and sighted at them across the Rio Grande.

"There was not at that time," Grant remembered of the march toward Matamoros, "a single habitation from Corpus Christi until the Rio Grande

**ANTONIO LÓPEZ
DE SANTA ANNA**
*in a rare mood of repose, almost two decades
after his defeat at San Jacinto. By this time
he had lost a leg fighting the French in the
"Pastry War" and had been exiled from
Mexico after key losses to the Americans in the
battles of Buena Vista and Cerro Gordo.*

was reached." It was a distance of about 170 miles. When you follow the army's route today by car along Highway 77, it is more than possible to understand the bristly emptiness that Taylor's men encountered on their weary march south. "Of this area," decreed an official Texas Land Office map, "nothing is known." Signs still warn drivers—as the highway enters the 825,000-acre domain of the King Ranch—that for the next sixty miles gas will not be available.

This was the Nueces Strip, the subtropical grasslands that made up the heart of the disputed territory between Texas and Mexico. The area was also known as the Wild Horse Desert. "There was no estimating the number of animals in it," Grant wrote in his memoir about one of the mustang herds that swarmed in the distance. "I have no idea that they could all have been corralled in the State of Rhode Island, or Delaware, at one time. If they had been, they would have been so thick that the pasturage would have given out the first day."

U.S. troops disregarding "the ancient limits of Texas" and taking up positions on the banks of the Rio Grande represented, to Mexico, more than a provocation; it was an invasion. The five thousand Mexican soldiers across the river were under the command of forty-two-year-old Major General Mariano Arista, who had seen something of the American character first-hand when he lived, during a brief period of political exile, in Cincinnati. He sent a force of sixteen hundred men across the river. Their mission was to cut off the Americans in Fort Texas from their coastal supply port, a wind-scoured wisp of a village named Point Isabel, twenty-five miles to the east. At a place called Rancho de Carricitos, the Mexicans surprised a detachment of American dragoons under Captain Seth Thornton, killing eleven and capturing Thornton and most of the rest of his men. That was, as much as anything, the official start of the war. Zachary Taylor's summation of the incident to the adjutant general reads as if it were written by someone who had been waiting for something to happen and was now quite satisfied that it had: "Hostilities may now be considered as commenced."

At this point, Santa Anna was no longer president of Mexico, though in the last few years his life had been crammed as usual with personal and political intrigue. His wife had died, and only a month after her state funeral, the one-legged fifty-year-old president married (by proxy) a very wealthy and probably very bewildered fifteen-year-old girl. Then he had been deposed, and then he had been exiled to Cuba. The latest aspirant to leap onto the presidential merry-go-round was Mariano Paredes, who seized power in a coup in late 1845. It fell to Paredes to gather the scattered strands of patriotic fervor and proclaim that Mexico was in the midst of a defensive war. A declaration from the United States followed a few weeks later when Polk learned of the attack on Thornton and his men. Each country claimed it had been invaded by the other.

By the beginning of May, Arista had gotten the rest of his army across the Rio Grande and promptly begun a siege of Fort Texas. Taylor had left five hundred men to hold the fort while he marched the rest of his army to Point Isabel to secure his supply base and bring back provisions. Napoleon Dana was in the fort, and he left a vivid account of the bombardment. The first man killed was a sergeant named Weigart, whose brains were blown out by grapeshot on the ramparts. An hour later, while his body was lying in the hospital tent, a shell burst through and took off what was left of Weigart's head without harming any of the other wounded men or medical personnel. It seemed to Dana that the enemy "had a special spite against that particular man." Several days later, the post's commander, Major Jacob Brown, "a perfect bulldog for the fight," died in agony after a howitzer shell ripped off his leg. Another man was left miraculously unscathed when a shell exploded beneath his legs while he was eating dinner. Fifteen horses were blown up, and so were all the band instruments. A shot from one of the fort's eighteen-pound guns blasted through a house in Matamoros and killed two women. "They ought," Dana wrote to his wife, "to have been out of the way."

The men in Fort Texas were saving their ammunition, preparing for what might be another Alamo, when they heard the sound of heavy cannonading in the distance, eight miles away at a place called Palo Alto. It was the first real battle of the war between the United States and Mexico.

Zachary Taylor had been leading his army back from Point Isabel to relieve Fort Texas when the battle began. He found Arista's army blocking the road, over three thousand men—infantry, cavalry, and artillery—forming a battle line a mile wide. It was the early afternoon of May 8. The full headache-inducing heat of the South Texas sun beat down on a brutal landscape without shade or anything to hide behind but clumps of grass and cactus. Lieutenant Grant was there; it was his first battle. He remembered the intimidating sight of the sun glistening off the massed bayonets of the Mexican infantry and the lance points of the cavalry. The chaparral was an almost impenetrable waist-high forest of thorny, stunted vegetation whose most prominent component was tawny cordgrass as stiff and sharp as razor wire. It would be a hard place for men and horses to maneuver in and an unappealing place for them to die.

The Americans, though considerably outnumbered, had the advantage in artillery—not just in the ordnance but also in its rapid deployment. The gun crews in their red flannel shirts were highly trained and highly mobile. They used horse-drawn limbers to deliver the "flying artillery" to the parts of the battlefield where it was needed most.

There were infantry advances and cavalry charges at Palo Alto, but mostly it was a fearsome artillery battle. Solid shot from the Mexican side fell short at first, the cannonballs rolling and ricocheting in the cordgrass, moving with such bewitching slowness that the men in Taylor's infantry could track them with their eyes and simply step out of the way. Later in the day, when the armies were closer together and the range was shorter, Grant remembered that "some execution was done." In a letter to a friend, he described how a cannonball "struck the ranks a little ways in front of me and nocked one man's

LITH. & PUB. BY SARONY & MAJOR,

head off, nocked the under Jaw of Capt. Page entirely away, and brought several others to the ground . . . the under jaw is gone to the wind pipe and the tongue hangs down upon the throat. He will never be able to speak or to eat."

But the American flying artillery and its exploding shells did far more damage to Arista's men, blowing up the troops as they stood in formation, igniting brush fires that spread through the cordgrass. The wind drove the fires toward the Mexican lines, enveloping wounded men who couldn't move quickly enough to get out of the way. The day ended with the Americans bivouacking on the field, listening in the darkness to the cries of shattered and burned men coming from the Mexican camp. In the morning, they discovered that Arista's army had retreated to a stronger position about five miles away, on the other side of a resaca that was a remnant channel of the Rio Grande, one of the many isolated bodies of standing water in this part of Texas. The fighting at Resaca de la Palma was even fiercer and closer than at Palo Alto on the day before, the chaparral even denser. It was, Grant wrote, "a pel mel affair evry body for himself." The flying artillery could

The battles of Palo Alto and nearby Resaca de la Palma, in the brush country of far South Texas, were the first major conflicts of the Mexican American War.

not maneuver in the tangled brush, and the cavalry found very little open ground in which to make an effective charge. Instead, the men advanced with their muskets and bayonets from one concealing clump of prickly pear or palmetto or mesquite to the next, a brutal few hours of plant-to-plant, hand-to-hand fighting that ended with the Americans breaking the siege of Fort Texas and driving the Mexicans back to the banks of the Rio Grande. Many of them were shot or else drowned under the weight of their equipment before reaching the other side.

The victories at Palo Alto and Resaca de la Palma opened the way for the American invasion of Mexico. The war lasted two years. The national emergency brought Santa Anna once again to power, but after losing battle after battle he fell once more into disgrace and exile. Decisive victories at Monterrey, Buena Vista, and Cerro Gordo led American forces to a conclusive conflict in the heart of Mexico City, and then it was over. Though bitter border hostilities between Texas and Mexico would continue for generations, the 1848 Treaty of Guadalupe Hidalgo settled the matter on paper, settled it in a way that, in the chastened words of Santa Anna, spelled "eternal shame and bitter regret for every good Mexican." Mexico received $15 million for half its territory and an abiding wound to its national soul. The Rio Grande was now the southern boundary of the United States. And the loss of Texas was only part of the humiliation. In all, Mexico was forced to cede 525,000 square miles, land that included all of what is now the American Southwest and all or part of what is now California, Colorado, Utah, Nevada, and Wyoming.

Texans had been crucial and notorious participants in this continent-shattering conflict. Governor James Pinckney Henderson had been in office barely three months when he requested a leave of absence to take command of a Texas volunteer regiment. Well-known Rangers such as Jack Hays, Ben McCulloch, and Samuel Walker joined mounted volunteer companies that were mustered into federal service—no longer officially Texas Rangers, though among this rowdy and independent-minded group the rhetorical distinctions were faint. Most of these men were still relatively young, but many were veterans of a decade or more of savage frontier fighting. They brought experience, and they brought undisguised grudges against Mexicans. McCulloch was born in Tennessee, where he had known both Sam Houston and David Crockett. He had followed Crockett to Texas, arriving too late to die at the Alamo but not too late to settle scores at San Jacinto. Afterward, he joined the Rangers and fought Comanches with Jack Hays and then helped chase the Mexican troops of Generals Vásquez and Woll out of Texas. He had joined the Somervell expedition, too, but had not been part of the breakaway plundering contingent that encountered such misfortune in Mier.

Samuel Walker, younger and more impulsive than McCulloch, had ended up in Mier, where he survived by drawing a white bean and then later making a daring escape from confinement near Mexico City. "War was his element," was the way a friend described Walker, "the bivouac his delight, and the battlefield his playground." He too had fought Indians with Jack Hays, and in the battle where the Colt revolving pistols made their debut, he had been speared by a Comanche lance. He performed important scouting duties for Taylor during the Matamoros campaign and fought at Palo Alto and Resaca de la Palma and Monterrey.

The Rangers were irregular troops with irregular standards. Some of the same men who had fought desperate street battles ten years earlier at the siege of San Antonio found themselves doing the same thing in Monterrey, breaking through the walls of houses to fight the enemy forces with rifle butts and Bowie knives. Some had shot down fleeing Mexican soldados in Peggy Lake during the Battle of San Jacinto. Many had friends or family members who had died at the Alamo or who had been executed at Goliad or Mier. They were primed for an avenging, terrorizing, and highly personal war.

"A rougher looking set we never saw," concluded a volunteer from Louisiana who visited their camp in Matamoros. "Men in groups with long beards and moustaches, dressed in every variety of garment, with one exception, the slouched hat, the unmistakable uniform of a Texas Ranger, and a belt of pistols around their waists."

It was meant to be an admiring verbal portrait, part of the romantic flummery about Texas Rangers that helped captivate the nation. But it did not captivate the Mexican nation. The Rangers were skillful and resourceful warriors but could also be indiscriminate killers. Zachary Taylor had issued a general order before the army left Corpus Christi. Everyone under his command was to

> observe, with the most scrupulous respect, the rights of all the inhabitants who may be found in peaceful prosecution of their respective occupations, as well on the left as on the right side of the Rio Grande. . . .
>
> . . . The general-in-chief has the satisfaction to say that he confides in the patriotism and discipline of the army under his command, and that he feels sure that his orders will be obeyed with the utmost exactness.

These orders were habitually ignored by the men that the Mexicans called *los diablos Tejanos*, men for whom the U.S.-Mexican conflict cloaked a long-simmering partisan war of retribution. Taylor was soon disgusted by his Texas volunteers. He regarded them as "licentious vandals." "The mounted men from Texas," he wrote, "have scarcely made one expedition without unwarrantably killing a Mexican. There is scarcely a form of crime that has not been reported to me as committed by them."

But if not for the intrepid scouting of Texas volunteers like Sam Walker, Taylor and his army might not have been able to win the Battle of Palo Alto and take Matamoros. They would have been taken by surprise by Santa Anna at Buena Vista if McCulloch had not discovered the much larger Mexican force and almost walked up to its campfires while trying get a clear idea of its size.

The war made McCulloch, Hays, Walker, and others into national heroes and cemented the image of Texas Rangers. They were perceived, at their best, as high-minded but bracingly undisciplined warriors; at their worst, as wanton assassins of innocent civilians. "The bushes," observed one chronicler who might have been writing either in admiration or in horror, "skirting the road from Monterrey southward, are strewed with skeletons of Mexicans sacrificed by these desperadoes."

Sam Walker and most of the other Rangers took a sabbatical in the middle of the war, after Monterrey had fallen and a temporary armistice was in place. The Texans' three-month enlistments were up, and their rampaging through the city had become a serious problem. "With their departure," Taylor sighed in relief, "we may look for a restoration of quiet and order in Monterrey."

On a trip to Maryland in December, Walker met with Samuel Colt, who had designed the five-shot revolving pistols the Rangers used against the Comanches. They decided to improve on the old Paterson model and create "the most perfect weapon in the world." This was the Walker Colt, the first six-shooter, a heavy, huge, powerful handgun loaded with enough black powder for its .44 caliber ball to kill a man or a horse at a distance of one hundred yards.

The ferocious new firearm went into production and Walker went back to Mexico, where at the age of thirty he was shot or perhaps lanced in one of the last battles of the war. "I am dying, boys," he was remembered as saying, his last words pure as the lyrics to a classic country song. "I'll never see Texas again."

—19—

THE CRISIS
OF THE CRISIS

Thy task is done. The holy shade
Of Calm retirement waits thee now,
The lamp of hope relit hath shed
Its sweet refulgence o'er thy brow.

SO WROTE MARGARET LEA HOUSTON IN A TEN-STANZA
poem to her husband when his second term as president of
the Republic of Texas ended. Sam Houston no doubt read the
charming verses with loving indulgence, but there was not
much room in his character for "calm retirement." If she knew
her husband at all, which she very much did, Margaret must
have realized that her poem was only a wistful prayer. Two days after the Texas
national flag came down, Houston was elected—along with his old comrade-in-
arms Tom Rusk—to represent the new state of Texas as a U.S. senator.

When he traveled to Washington, DC, to take his seat in the Senate
chamber, Margaret stayed behind at their plantation, a few miles east of the
town of Huntsville. The place was named, in Houston's customary totemic
style, Raven Hill. The new senator reported to Margaret that she was already

something of a legend in the nation's capital for her successful efforts to "tame, and regulate a man who has hereto been deemed untamable."

He was pretty much through with drinking. His last real eruption had occurred shortly after his marriage, when he encountered a bottle of Madeira in the town of Washington while Margaret was away. Delusionally drunk, he ordered a slave to chop down part of his hostess's mahogany four-poster bed with an axe. Margaret was pregnant at the time with their first child, and when she returned to Washington, she brought her formidable mother with her to make sure Houston did not go off the rails again. ("You may have conquered Santa Anna," Mrs. Lea kept reminding her son-in-law, "but you will never conquer me.")

Houston was not yet baptized. He didn't take that step until 1854, after religious counseling by a Baptist minister named George Washington Baines, the great-grandfather of Lyndon Johnson. ("Lord help the fish down below," Houston purportedly said when told that his sins had been washed away in Rocky Creek.) But he enthusiastically grappled with spiritual matters, and a member of the Texas delegation in Washington recalled him praying on his knees every night at bedtime and when he got up in the morning.

But his faith would never be as intense or unyielding as Margaret's. In 1847, she wrote her husband that she was about to be operated on for breast cancer. "With the help of God I hope to sit down to it like a soldier." The surgeon was Houston's trusted friend Ashbel Smith, whose diplomatic services had included being the Texas Republic's chargé d'affaires to England and France. (He was also a proud collector of erotic paintings. "The ladies," remembered a colleague, "afterward said that the doctor should not have exhibited such pictures to them, he being an old bachelor.") Margaret, a fervent Baptist who would not touch alcohol, refused the whiskey that was the only anesthetic Smith was able to offer. She bit down on a silver coin instead while the doctor cut into her breast and removed the tumor. "It is useless to mention," Smith wrote to Houston afterward, "that Mrs. H. bore the pain with great fortitude."

Even though he had mostly conquered himself, Sam Houston was still regarded as a "magnificent barbarian" in Washington, a role that it pleased him to cultivate. He often wore a Cherokee blanket over his shoulders, and on his head a "vast and picturesque sombrero."

Houston approved of the war against Mexico and must have approved of it even more when his old nemesis Santa Anna rose again to power. He was urged into taking a generalship and continuing the fight himself, but he was deep into his fifties by the time the war broke out, creaky from old wounds and apparently satisfied by his conquests that were already written in the

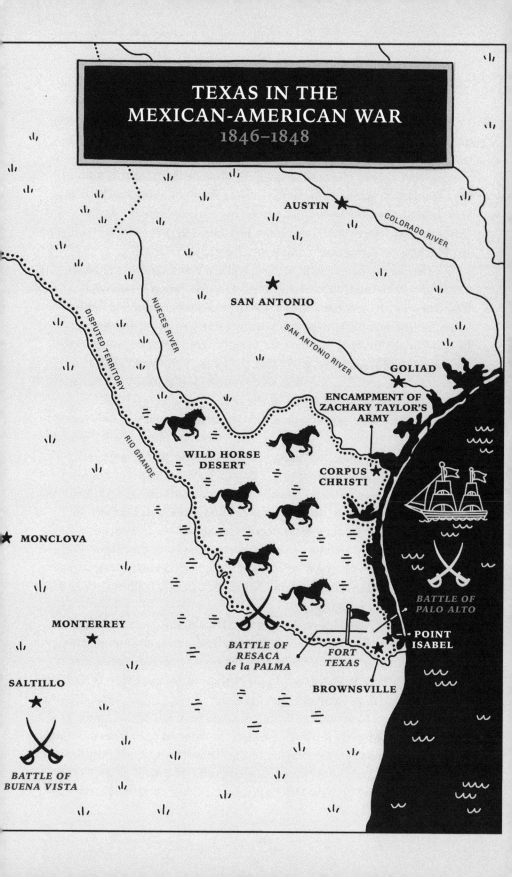

TEXAS IN THE MEXICAN-AMERICAN WAR
1846–1848

AUSTIN

COLORADO RIVER

NUECES RIVER

SAN ANTONIO

SAN ANTONIO RIVER

GOLIAD

DISPUTED TERRITORY

ENCAMPMENT OF
ZACHARY TAYLOR'S
ARMY

RIO GRANDE

WILD HORSE
DESERT

CORPUS
CHRISTI

MONCLOVA

BATTLE OF
PALO ALTO

MONTERREY

BATTLE OF
RESACA
de la PALMA

FORT
TEXAS

POINT
ISABEL

SALTILLO

BROWNSVILLE

BATTLE OF
BUENA VISTA

history books. "I . . . decline all solicitations," he explained to Margaret, "because I love my Dear Wife and little ones [the first two of his eight children had been born by then] more than I favor the honors of this world."

And anyway, things were soon turbulent enough on the political front in the U.S. capital. For almost three decades, the United States had been held together by the dynamic tension resulting from the Missouri Compromise of 1820. That act had managed to quell the growing threat of civil war over the expansion of slavery into the territories of the Louisiana Purchase. Missouri was admitted into the Union as a slave state, balanced by Maine as a free state, and slavery would thereafter be banned in the rest of the Louisiana Purchase lands north of latitude 36 degrees, 30 minutes.

But then came the war with Mexico, and the vast territory that it was forced to cede to the United States. The Missouri Compromise was a tentative-enough agreement to begin with, and neither the slaveholding South nor the Free-Soiler North was willing to allow its cut-the-baby-in-half philosophy to apply to a national map that could now be unfolded all the way to the Pacific. What to do with the lands of the Mexican Cession created a crisis, and Texas became, in the words of the great Whig senator and orator Henry Clay, the "crisis of the crisis."

The problem once again was the Rio Grande, particularly Texas's unyielding claim that the river marked its western boundary. Mexico had disputed that claim strongly enough to fight a war over it, and now that the war had been won and Texas was a part of the United States, the Rio Grande border issue would still not go away. The borders of the new state of Texas had never been properly fixed. In the minds of most Americans, its western margin merely melted away somewhere into the unknown immensity leading to the Pacific and the newly discovered California gold fields. To Texans, that line was clear, and theirs forever by right of conquest. It was the Rio Grande, which meant that Santa Fe was part of Texas, along with half the territory of New Mexico.

The people of New Mexico thought not. Though they were no longer a part of Mexico, they did not consider themselves Texans, any more than they had when Mirabeau Lamar launched his disastrous invitation-intimidation mission to Santa Fe in 1841. Much to the outrage of Texans, that was also the opinion of the U.S. government. Just days after the war ended, Texas decreed that all of eastern New Mexico, including Santa Fe, was a Texas county. The New Mexicans, who had a civilian government that had been formed during the war when Santa Fe was occupied by the army of General Stephen Kearny, emphatically rejected the overture and sent the Texas commissioner home. Toward the end of 1849, New Mexico petitioned Congress for territorial sta-

JOHN SALMON FORD,
better known as Rip Ford, the doctor, scout,
Ranger, soldier, and mayor who was an everyman
of the Texas frontier.

tus. It wanted to be finally free from the groping embrace of Texas, and—even more crucially in light of the sectional wars the Mexican Cession had reignited—it wanted to keep slavery out.

The debate throughout 1850 over whether slavery could be extended into Texas or New Mexico or any of the other territories seized from the Mexicans was, at times, more than just rhetorically intense. At one point, Senator Henry Foote of Mississippi pulled out a horse pistol in the Senate chamber and pointed it at his Missouri colleague Thomas Hart Benton. Civil war was a real possibility, especially after the recently elected Texas governor, a former Ranger and Mexican War veteran named Peter Hansborough Bell, sent another commissioner to New Mexico.

His name was Robert S. Neighbors. Neighbors was thirty-five, tall, dark haired, commanding-looking, and—judging from an 1851 photograph—inclined to fleshiness during those periods of his life when he was not on the verge of starvation. These included a stint in Mexico's infamous Perote Prison after he was captured during the Woll invasion of Texas and a grueling expedition in 1849 to open a wagon road from the interior of Texas to El Paso. On that occasion, he was guided part of the way by the prominent Penateka chief Buffalo Hump, who had led the raid on Linnville and whose Comanche name—Po-cha-na-quar-hip—didn't mean Buffalo Hump at all, but "erection that won't go down." Also in the party was the legendary Indian fighter John Salmon Ford. Ford, a doctor, was better known as Rip, because when he was serving in the Mexican War under Jack Hays, one of his jobs was to write letter after letter to the families of fallen Texans, which he began "Rest in Peace." Ford, who had a rough-hewn literary flair, wrote a sprawling memoir of his years in early Texas. His mule was named "Tantybogus." He referred to the comically quizzical burrowing owls that lived in the prairie dog towns they passed on the way to El Paso as "French Dancing Masters."

Robert Neighbors had served as an Indian agent after annexation and was regarded by the Comanches as an honest broker. He spoke five languages and knew, as very few people did, how to make his way to New Mexico without getting fatally lost—indeed, one reason for his commission was to map out a road there. Otherwise, his instructions were to succeed in New Mexico where the previous commissioner had failed. He was to inform the inhabitants they were now Texans and to form three Texas counties out of the land east of the Rio Grande, from El Paso to Santa Fe. He and his party had a tough time getting there. The two slaves they brought tried to escape, but were tortured and killed by roving scalp hunters. Neighbors and the other survivors were blasted by snowstorms, and their mules started to break down under their burdens, requiring the commissioner to leave behind on the desert floor most of the copies of the Texas Constitution he had brought along.

When Neighbors finally reached El Paso, he won over the roughly five thousand inhabitants in the vicinity to the idea that their destiny lay with Texas. But when he traveled to Santa Fe and tried to organize county elections there, he was met with a wall of hostility. The people of Santa Fe were prepared to resist, and they were backed up by the power of the federal government. The president of the United States was now Zachary Taylor, who favored not just territorial status but also statehood for New Mexico, and who still had fresh memories of the unruliness and belligerence of the Texans who had fought under him during the war. "The whole business is infamous," he declared of what he regarded as Texas's meddling in federal boundary affairs, "and must be put down."

The citizens of Santa Fe were determined to make New Mexico a state, not a Texas county, a state that stood firm against the Texan and southern slave economy. "A curse and a blight," read the resolution about slavery that was adopted at a statehood convention in May, "a moral, social and political evil. . . . We have unanimously agreed to reject it, forever."

Neighbors went back to Texas in defeat, but the crisis of the crisis was not yet over. Governor Bell called a special session of the legislature and asked for two regiments of state troops to be sent to Santa Fe to put down what he and the rest of Texas regarded as an insurrection. "Resolved," declared a legislative committee, "That Texas will maintain the integrity of her Territory at all hazards and to the last extremity."

It was war fever all over again in Austin. Cannons blasted away through the night with symbolic belligerence. A month earlier, Zachary Taylor had fallen ill after assaulting his digestive system with raw vegetables and cherries washed down with glasses of iced milk. A few days later he was dead. The new president was Millard Fillmore, who was no more inclined to support the

Texas claim to New Mexico than Taylor had been. In fact he was ready to deny it by force of arms. "If Texas militia march into any of the other States or into any Territory of the United States," he wrote in a message to Congress, "they become at that moment trespassers; they are no longer under the protection of any lawful authority, and are to be regarded merely as intruders."

The Civil War began in Charleston Harbor in 1861, but in an alternate historical universe it might very well have begun over a decade earlier, in a battle between Texas militia and U.S. government troops somewhere in Comanche country, somewhere out on the arid plains between Austin and Santa Fe. What kept it from happening was the Compromise of 1850, a series of bills that were the culmination of the aging Henry Clay's desperate legislative attempts to hold the country together. As a result of the compromise, California came into the Union as a free state, and the people of Utah and New Mexico were given "popular sovereignty," allowing them to decide for themselves whether slavery would be permitted in their territories. In Washington, DC, the slave trade was abolished, but not slavery itself, and the citizens of free states would be required to return escaped slaves to bondage in the states from which they had escaped.

As part of the compromise, Texas finally gave up New Mexico and the dream of a far-flung Rio Grande border. Its contours would now follow the Rio Grande only as far as El Paso. From there the border would make an abrupt turn back to the east, where it would be finally corralled between the 103rd and 100th meridians, and topped off at latitude 36 degrees, 30 minutes. Gone was New Mexico, gone was the cartographical stovepipe leading all the way to Wyoming. The enormous amorphous thing that had been Texas was still enormous, but now it had a definitive shape, a shape that funneled down to the mouth of the Rio Grande at its southern end, that rose up as a northern panhandle into the Llano Estacado, that jutted far into the Chihuahuan Desert to the west and deep into the Piney Woods on the east. In compensation for surrendering all the land that would not be part of this map, Texas was given a much-needed $10 million in U.S. indemnity bonds.

During the debates over the extension of slavery and the fate of Texas, Sam Houston bared his moderate political soul. He, along with Tom Rusk, had steadfastly represented Texas's interests in the boundary conflict with New Mexico, but his greater passion was for Clay's compromise. Eight years before Abraham Lincoln gave his "house divided" speech, Houston stood in the Senate chamber and asked his colleagues and constituents to pray for the Union, "For a nation divided against itself cannot stand."

Houston represented a slave state that had been a slave country. He himself was a slaveholder, though if gradations of human ownership can be thought to matter, he was on the avuncular end of the scale. (He once impulsively bought a boy from a heartless auctioneer and took him into a nearby store to buy him a sack of candy.) But even though Sam Houston had led a war of rebellion against Mexico, he was no secessionist when it came to the native country of which he was once more a citizen. His support for the Compromise of 1850 and, four years later, his loud opposition to the Kansas-Nebraska Act, marked him as an unyielding unionist and set the table for the political isolation that would end his public career.

The Kansas-Nebraska Act sprang from the presidential ambitions of Illinois senator Stephen A. Douglas. It essentially blasted away the equilibrium between the slave and free states carved out of the Louisiana Purchase, a balance that had been in place for thirty-four years, ever since the Missouri Compromise. Now instead of the northern boundary of the slave section of the country being marked by a line of latitude, popular sovereignty would decide whether the territories of Kansas and Nebraska, which lay above that line, would become slave states or free.

When it came to the path that the United States would follow after the passage of the Kansas-Nebraska act, Houston's foresight was apocalyptically clear. "What fields of blood," he soon predicted, "what scenes of horror, what mighty cities in smoke and ruins—it is brother murdering brother."

Tom Rusk voted in favor of the Kansas-Nebraska Act. Houston was the only Democratic senator from the South to denounce it. He did so not just because of the sectional horrors it would unleash upon the United States, but also because of what it would mean to the Indians living in those territories—for whom a new onslaught of settlement would inevitably bring shattered treaties and displacement. "The Indian," the Raven pleaded helplessly in the Senate, "has a sense of justice, truth, and honor that should find a responsive chord in every heart."

Such convictions set him apart from most hard-bitten Texas thought and drove him into an unlikely political fellowship with abolitionist senators like Charles Sumner. "I have been astonished to find myself so much to his inclining," Sumner wrote as Houston was testing the ground for a run for president in 1852.

Margaret was wary of Houston's very visible presidential ambitions— "Oh, when I think of the allurements that surround you," she wrote him, "I tremble, lest they should steal your heart from God."

But the allurements in the end turned out just to be allurements. Houston was convinced he could win the whole South except for South Carolina if he could just get the Democratic nomination, but he didn't get the nomination—it went to Franklin Pierce. And by the time the next presidential convention rolled around, in 1856, his vote against the Kansas-Nebraska Act had already estranged him from the growing southern virulence of his party.

A lame-duck senator, he was not just hobbled on the national scene but also condemned on the floor of his own state's legislature for his unionist philosophy. Instead of biding his time uselessly in the Senate, he decided to run for governor of Texas against a strict states'-rights aristocrat named Hardin Runnels. Among his reasons: "The people want excitement." The hero of San Jacinto shook every hand in Texas that would shake his back. He traveled over fifteen hundred miles in a red and gold buggy borrowed from a plow salesman, but the tenor of the times was against him, and Runnels beat him by fifteen thousand votes. Houston wasn't all that surprised, or all that bitter. He sensed there was still some destiny left in his sixty-four-year-old life. "The fuss is over, and the sun yet shines as ever," he wrote to Ashbel Smith. "What next?"

—20—

ROBBERS AND LAWYERS

IN MAY 1854, A FEW MONTHS AFTER SAM HOUSTON ROSE in the U.S. Senate chamber to denounce the Kansas-Nebraska Act, a woman named Petra Vela de Vidal walked up the aisle of a small wooden church in Brownsville, Texas. Brownsville had sprung into being with the arrival of Zachary Taylor's army eight years earlier. It was named for Major Jacob Brown, the Fort Texas commander who died when his leg was torn off by an exploding shell during the siege. Brownsville sat on the north bank of the Rio Grande, just across from Matamoros, and was nominally an American town. But this part of Texas, at the bottom of the Nueces Strip, was still very much a Mexican place, far from the Anglo line of settlement on the other side of the Wild Horse Desert.

This was Petra Vela's wedding day. Or if not her wedding day exactly, it was the day when her marriage to a thirty-six-year-old steamboat entrepreneur named Mifflin Kenedy would finally be blessed by the Catholic Church. It's possible that Vela and Kenedy had already been married in a civil ceremony, since they had an infant son together. Petra Vela was thirty-one, a "notably handsome woman of tall and commanding figure," according to a newspaper description written many years later. The description is borne out in photographs taken earlier in her life, in which she faces the camera

PETRA VELA DE VIDAL KENEDY
came from a prominent family on the Rio Grande border. Her marriage to steamboat entrepreneur Mifflin Kenedy bound their fortunes together in an Anglo-Tejano alliance.

straight on, her eyes big and dark, her hair in neat waves, her expression composed and frank.

She and Mifflin Kenedy had needed a dispensation to be married in the Church. He was a Quaker. Though not previously married, Vela had given birth to eight children before she met Kenedy, three of whom were now dead. The father of these children was a Mexican Army officer named Luis Vidal, who had another family with another woman, whom he eventually married instead of Petra. Vidal most likely died of cholera in 1849, leaving Petra as a widow in fact even if not in official designation.

She was born in Mier, the same town in Tamaulipas that was the target of the ill-fated invasion led by renegade members of the Somervell expedition in 1842. Mier had been founded, along with several other towns along the Rio Grande, by a Spanish nobleman named José de Escandón. In the 1750s, the Vela family received some of Escandón's earliest land grants. They became prosperous and landed, with a stone house in Mier and two ranchos on what would become the U.S. side of the Rio Grande.

Petra's father was killed by Apaches in 1846, and she inherited part of his estate. At the time of Luis Vidal's death, she was still a woman of means, though with no husband and with numerous *hijos naturales* (the forgiving Spanish term for children born out of wedlock) to provide for. She was living in Mexico at the time, but soon moved her family across the river to Brownsville.

That was where she met Mifflin Kenedy. He was from Pennsylvania, but had spent a good part of his life on ships and steamboats, roving the oceans and rivers of the world and working his way up from cabin boy to deckhand to captain. He had come to Texas in 1846 to command steamboats carrying troops and supplies up the Rio Grande for Zachary Taylor's army. His pilot on a boat called the *Corvette* was a younger man named Richard King, whom Kenedy had met a few years before when they were working on a steamer in Florida during the Seminole Wars.

After the Mexican-American War, Kenedy and King stayed on in South Texas and became partners with another Anglo businessman, Charles Stillman, in a steamboat company that soon dominated the trade along the Rio Grande, from the river's mouth to the town of Roma, almost two hundred miles upriver. They also bought land, an always-contentious business in that part of Texas, where the owners of Spanish and Mexican land grants had often been driven across the border during the war. When these refugees came back, they were likely to find their property occupied by American or European squatters. Defending their ancestral Spanish titles in what were now American courts was an expensive undertaking, and an uncertain one, especially for working rancheros who weren't members of the new Tejano elite. Many of these people were forced by economic reality to sell out; others were forced at the point of a gun to move on.

"The pore Deveil of a Mexican," wrote an empathetic if not fully literate observer,

> has know chance, he is told by the rober and lawyer he has know
> title to his land and that another person wants the verry land that the

Mexican was borne and rased on and his father before him, and now he is told he has know title. And the very considerat Gentlman that tells the Mexican that his title is not worth any thing makes him an offer of a small amount and advises him to take it and if not there will be know alternative but law and that in . . . Court they know there is know justice for them, they well know the only alternative is to get what the Robber and Lawyer think proper to give him.

The State of Texas set up a commission in 1851 to try to sort out the land title mess along the Rio Grande. But it was a good-faith effort that ended up adding to the confusion, since a substantial portion of the original land titles the commissioners collected went down in a shipwreck off Matagorda Island. Whether people like Mifflin Kenedy or Richard King took full advantage of this chaos in building their land empires is a matter of historical opinion, but they were certainly the sort of men who knew opportunities when they saw them, and they employed a lawyer, Stephen Powers, who was renowned for clearing titles all over the Nueces Strip.

Richard King used his steamboat money to buy a Spanish land grant along Santa Gertrudis Creek about forty-five miles southwest of Corpus Christi. That first 15,500-acre purchase became the nucleus of the 1,300-square-mile feudal entity known as the King Ranch. Not far away, Mifflin Kenedy owned a ranch named Los Laureles. His marriage to Petra Vela brought him more land, including a ranch called Veleño, which his wife had inherited from her grandfather, on the banks of the Nueces.

I think we can assume that Petra Vela and Mifflin Kenedy were in love. They were young when they met, both enterprising and ambitious, both at home in a complex world where the Rio Grande might have marked a border on a map but was in reality a binding force that drew the countries on either bank into an unbreakable dependency. But their marriage was also an alliance, of a kind that was fairly common along the border, a union of family and culture and commerce. Rising Anglo businessmen like Mifflin Kenedy needed credibility and contacts in what was still very much a Mexican world, and Tejana landholders like Petra Vela needed to protect their property from swindlers and speculators, from the sort of men that a French priest in the region decried as "the very scum of society—bankrupts, escaped criminals, old volunteers, who after the Treaty of Guadalupe Hidalgo came into a country protected by nothing that could be called a judicial authority, to seek adventure and illicit gains."

Petra Vela de Vidal Kenedy was now part of the woven, international, interconnected class that had the best chance of thriving in the most lawless part of Texas. All over the state, ever since the revolution, accelerating discrimina-tion and dispossession had been acute facts of Tejano life. Even San Antonio, which had long been the Hispanic center of gravity, was now mostly under Anglo control. The Tejano middle class there of shopkeepers and trades-men had been edged out by American or German immigrants and driven into poorer-paying professions like freight hauling. And even the teamsters were being displaced by Anglo competitors, with such violence that an open war along the San Antonio–Goliad corridor may have left as many as seventy-five Tejano teamsters dead. Thanks to José Antonio Navarro, who had managed to strike the word "white" from the Texas Constitution when it came to voting rights, Tejanos had access to the ballot box in principle, but their votes were routinely compromised or corrupted or outright denied.

And beyond disenfranchisement, there were even starker remedies. "The people of Matagorda County," read a newspaper pronouncement, "have held a meeting and ordered every Mexican to leave the county. To strangers this may seem wrong, but we hold it to be perfectly right and highly necessary. . . . We should rather have anticipated an appeal to Lynch law, than the mild course which has been adopted."

Petra Vela had managed to accommodate herself to this new reality, to find her place in it, in a way that one of her contemporaries never could or would. Juan Cortina was a year younger than Petra Vela. Like her, he was born on the Mexican side of the river, in the town of Camargo, just down-stream from Petra's birthplace of Mier. Like her family, his owned land on the U.S. side. Both he and Petra witnessed the aftermath of the Texans' 1842 Mier invasion. The nineteen-year-old Petra took pity on the wounded and homesick invaders who had been captured in her hometown. "Her self-imposed devotion to the duties of nurse," recalled the Brownsville Herald after her death, "of the suffering and destitute prisoners, won the lasting gratitude of many a bearded and broken-down veteran."

It's likely that the young Juan Cortina—hot tempered, prideful, patriotic, unlettered—would have had a less generous reaction as he stood on the street in Matamoros, watching those ragged Texas captives being paraded through town on their way to Mexico City prisons. He went on to fight another American invasion at Palo Alto and at Resaca de la Palma, and his grievances did not end with the war. "I never signed the Treaty of Guadalupe Hidalgo," he famously declared.

He became a cattle rustler, a crime along the border that was as universal as smuggling and land fraud. When his family's holdings were under threat, when he witnessed his mother being swindled out of a tract of her land, he was pushed to the edge of his fragile endurance. In Brownsville one summer day in 1859, he happened to see Robert Shears, the city marshal, pistol-whipping a man who had once worked at Cortina's rancho. Cortina demanded to know why the marshal was abusing the man, and received an insolent answer. "I punished his insolence," Cortina reported, "and avenged my countrymen by shooting him with a pistol and stretching him at my feet."

Marshal Shears, shot in the shoulder, survived. Cortina rode out of town with the pistol-whipped vaquero on the back of his horse. Though he was an illiterate outlaw with an edgy temper, he had a courtly streak. He wrote to the wounded marshal, offering to pay for his pain and suffering, but the sheriff was not moved, and neither was the grand jury that indicted Cortina for attempted murder. So a few months later, Cortina rode back into town, this time with seventy men and a death list. Shears was on the list, as well as a former cattle-rustling partner named Adolphus Glavecke, with whom Cortina had had a bitter falling-out.

Glavecke escaped being killed, and so once again did Shears, who hid by squeezing himself into a neighbor's oven. But five other men were shot down by Cortina's gang, who rampaged through the streets firing their guns in the air and shouting, "¡Viva México!" and "¡Mueran los gringos!"

"Our object," Cortina declared afterward in the first of several ringingly high-minded pronouncements, "has been to chastise the villainy of our enemies, which heretofore has gone unpunished. . . . These, as we have said, form, with a multitude of lawyers, a secret conclave . . . for the sole purpose of despoiling the Mexicans of the lands and usurp them afterwards." Whatever personal grudges Cortina brought to his uprising, his summary of things sounded extremely accurate to the displaced and disenfranchised Tejanos along the border. "I do not believe that fifty men of Mexican origin," wrote an Anglo postmaster in Brownsville, "can be found on the frontier who do not sympathize with him."

A militia group called the Brownsville Tigers arose to protect Anglo interests from the threat of a growing insurrection. And the fear of what Cortina might unleash—yet another full-scale American-Mexican war—was not confined to the United States side of the river. Mexican national guard troops from Matamoros joined the Tigers in an attack on Cortina's ranch in late October. The Anglos had the benefit of a howitzer taken from one of Mifflin Kenedy's steamers, and Kenedy himself protected his person with a custom-made thirty-pound lead vest that can still be admired today in the Willacy County Historical Museum.

But at the end of the skirmish, the Cortinistas had possession of the cannon, and the Tigers and their allies were in humiliating retreat. After that, the situation grew more and more inflamed, the rumors of Cortina's imperial aims more and more exaggerated. He was falsely reported to have once again overrun Brownsville, killing all its defenders, and to be on the march with an army of six hundred "greaser pelados" to reconquer the Nueces Strip.

A hundred Texas Rangers arrived in Brownsville, but they only made the situation worse when they failed to prevent—or perhaps even participated in—the lynching of a sixty-year-old prisoner who was Cortina's closest and most trusted subordinate. There were more skirmishes, more battles, more pillaging, more murders. Petra and Mifflin Kenedy lost several thousand head of livestock to Cortina's raiders. Dead Rangers were found mutilated in the chaparral, and the Rangers for their part embarked on an indiscriminate killing spree. "The whole country," wrote Major Samuel Heintzelman of the U.S. Army "from Brownsville to Rio Grande City, one hundred and twenty miles, and back to the Arroyo Colorado, has been laid to waste."

Cortina could not read or write, but that didn't prevent him from reaching splendid heights of outraged rhetoric in the *pronunciamientos* he issued. His enemies were "flocks of vampires, in the guise of men." The Mexican race, he declared, "which the Anglo-American . . . tries so much to blacken, depreciate, and load with insults," was in fact "filled with gentleness and inward sweetness . . . adorned with the most lovely disposition toward that which is good and useful."

The climax of what became known as the First Cortina War occurred at Rio Grande City, on the American side of the river across from Cortina's hometown of Camargo. By this time, the original Texas Ranger force had been bolstered by Rip Ford and 53 more men, along with 150 federal troops under Major Heintzelman. They attacked the town, which was held by Cortina's men, in the thick fog of a late December morning. Intense, close-range fighting in the streets spilled over into the chaparral when the insurgents, outgunned and overrun, tried to retreat across the river. There was no accurate tally of how many men Cortina lost in the battle at Rio Grande City—maybe 60, as Heintzelman reported, maybe closer to Rip Ford's estimate of 200. As one Ranger remembered, "We had no use for prisoners."

But Juan Cortina got away, with enough men and enough grievances to ensure that the fight against the "flocks of vampires" that had maliciously alighted in his border country would not subside anytime soon.

21

WARRIORS AND
REFUGEES

I'M LOOKING AT TWO TEXAS MAPS SIDE BY SIDE ON MY
computer screen. I downloaded them from the website of
the Texas General Land Office. One is a beguiling but unpro-
fessional effort, rendered in pastel watercolors by Stephen
Austin. He made the map probably in 1822, shortly after he
began bringing colonists to Texas. He painted the forests
and river valleys in green, the prairies in yellow, Indian villages and domains
in a light wash of pink. Rivers and bays are drawn in ink, their names set
down in Spanish. What is most striking about this map, other than its rustic handmade beauty, is how uncrowded it is. The notations for natural and
man-made features are spaced far apart, and there is nothing but seductive
openness in between. A dozen or more clusters represent centers of Indian
population, but only four places that a Mexican or American or European
might consider a town. These are Laredo, on the Rio Grande, San Antonio
de Béxar, La Bahía, and—far to the east—Nacogdoches.

The other map was published by the New York firm of Johnson and
Browning in 1859. Titled Colton's New Map of the State of Texas, it shows
Texas after all the major border controversies had been laid to rest and

the state had settled on its classic configuration. It is precise and professional; next to it, Austin's earnest hand-painted rendering seems more like a dreamscape. The 1859 map displays the many counties of this new Texas (122 of them) in muted shades of contrasting colors. It shows prominent roads and ferry crossings, though it would be another fifteen or twenty years before such maps were covered with the thick black-and-white lines indicating railroad routes. Most of all, it shows a staggering increase in municipalities. There are four on Austin's map. When I try to count them on Colton's, my eyes cross after about 120, and that's only in the bottom part of the eastern half of the state. In the thirty-nine years between 1820 and 1859, the span of an average lifetime in the middle of the nineteenth century, a whole new galaxy of Texas towns and cities burst into being, with new populations to inhabit them. Not counting Indians, in the years just after Mexico won its freedom from Spain only a few thousand people lived in Texas. By 1859, more than a half million did, 30 percent of them enslaved.

And about that phrase I just used: "not counting Indians." Not only is it blithely dismissive in itself, it assigns a marginal historical status to peoples whose complex alliances and conflicts with one another and with the booming Anglo Texan population were central to the destiny and identity of the state. You can get an idea of this by a glance at the 1859 map. A little bit west of about the ninety-eighth meridian, the counties are there but the towns are not. Westward, beyond the rapidly clearing forests of the east, beyond farm and plantation agriculture, beyond the vast cattle ranches that people like Richard King and Mifflin Kenedy were building in the south, Texas is still empty.

But it was empty only cartographically. West of the line of settlement, the land tended toward the inhospitable, but it was far from uninhabitable. It received considerably less rainfall than the rest of the state, but still had grass for grazing and soil for planting, and plenty of people in Texas were eager to push the frontier west toward the High Plains and the deserts beyond the hundredth meridian. And as always, other people were in their way.

Caddos, Wichitas, Delawares, Shawnees, Kickapoos, Tonkawas, and other Indian groups still clung to existence in Texas. But for a generation, ever since the war against the Cherokees unleashed by President Lamar, they had been pushed west, toward the upper reaches of the Brazos River in north-central Texas. It was the Comanches, particularly the northern bands such as the Yamparikas and Nokonis, who still raided deep into Texas and Mexico from their High Plains strongholds, who continued to hold back the Texan advance into the blank spaces on the map. The "Comanche barrier," as it came to be called by historians, was real, the front line of a war between civilizations.

In the late 1840s and 1850s, the U.S. government built forts up and down the length of Texas, from the Rio Grande almost to the Red River. In the end there were over twenty of them, built at strategic locations that gave the dragoons and, later, the cavalry troopers who garrisoned them a vital advantage in detecting and pursuing Comanche raiding parties. Many of these forts are still visible in one form or another, some reconstructed and repurposed as museums, others—such as Fort Phantom Hill near Abilene—impressing visitors most strongly as moody vestiges, the brick chimney towers of its long-vanished buildings rising against the West Texas skyline with Stonehenge-like mystery.

The purpose of the forts was to secure the line of white settlement, to protect westward-bound immigrants to the California gold fields and stage lines such as the Butterfield Overland Mail. The stages carried passengers and mail along the routes that Robert Neighbors and an army captain named Randolph Marcy had recently pioneered to El Paso, which, at six hundred miles from Austin, was still very much the outer planet of the Texas solar system. But inevitably the forts spurred trade and commerce and in turn pushed the frontier ever farther; and like all frontiers, this one attracted outlaws, speculators, and renegades of every unsavory sort.

Newspaper articles of the time about the Comanche-Texan conflict, and the works of history that followed them, all used the same recurring word: depredation. Comanches "depredated," pillaging ranches and running off livestock, seizing and torturing captives, subjecting enemies that weren't killed outright to blood-freezing barbarities. There was truth in this; the Indian wars on the Texas frontier were gothic and pitiless. But they were also pathetic: scattered conflicts sparked by petty greed, by misunderstandings and mistaken identities, finally escalating into what amounted to an exterminating struggle. And the depredations were by no means all on the Comanche side. "If the world was picked over," wrote Lieutenant William Burnet, who served with the army at Fort Belknap on the upper Brazos and was the son of the republic's interim president, David Burnet, "I do not think there could be found a more vile and worthless set than the people who have squatted along this frontier and who the [news]papers style the 'Brave and injured Frontiersmen.'"

Texas newspapers—particularly those like the *White Man*, whose racist agenda was plainly evident in its title—were often in the business of misinforming and inflaming their readers. They exaggerated the Comanche threat while exalting as Homeric battles the massacres unleashed by white raiders upon defenseless villages.

In fact, after a long run of hegemony on the southern plains, the Comanches were on the defensive. Comanchería had been an empire, but now it was a redoubt, an island battered and eroded by the relentless waves of the Texan advance. The Indian population had been grievously affected by epidemics of cholera and smallpox, and particularly by a sustained drought in the 1840s, which interrupted the normal feeding patterns of the great bison herds, a major Comanche resource. Herds that had once ranged as far as the southern coastal prairies—where they were marveled at by Cabeza de Vaca in the sixteenth century—were scarcer and centered mostly now on the grazing lands north of the Red River.

———— ★ ————

ROBERT NEIGHBORS FAILED IN HIS 1850 ATTEMPT TO CONVINCE the people of Santa Fe to remain part of Texas, but it had been an almost impossible mission in the first place. He was still regarded, in the words of Sam Houston, as "a gentleman of manly and sterling qualities . . . most worthily did he conduct himself." After Neighbors returned, he served in the Texas Legislature, and in 1853 was appointed by the U.S. Commissioner of Indian Affairs to be the supervising agent for Texas. It was a strong choice, and Neighbors backed the idea of establishing reserves where Indians could be protected from aggressive whites, and where they would be expected to sustain themselves as farmers. For the Caddos, Wichitas, and other tribes that came from an agrarian tradition, this cultural shift was at least within reach. Their Brazos River reservation—while it lasted—was something of a success. But the odds were very much against the worn-out, fought-out Penateka Comanches, who agreed to be settled on a reservation farther west along the Clear Fork of the Brazos. Reduced as they were, they were still a nomadic people from a horizonless world whose whole identity was antithetical to the idea of confining borders. "You come into our country," lectured a Penateka chief named Sanaco, "and select a small patch of ground, around which you run a line . . . when everybody knows that the whole of this entire country, from the Red River to the Colorado, is ours and always had been from time immemorial."

But the Penatekas' Clear Fork reservation was surrounded by white people who felt every bit as entitled to this country, and just as willing to seize it from the Comanches as the Comanches had been willing to seize it from the Apaches and the Apaches from the Jumanos. It was probably inevitable that the situation would get worse. Cholera came back, then drought. Raids by northern Comanche bands that had turned their backs on reservation life increased, and the whites who did not know about or care about the differences between bands or tribes settled scores by shooting and scalping the first Indians they came across. "We regard the killing of Indians,"

TEXAS FRONTIER:
U.S. ARMY FORTS BEFORE THE CIVIL WAR
1848–1861

FORT BELKNAP

FORT
PHANTOM HILL

FORT
BLISS

FORT
WORTH

FORT
QUITMAN

FORT
CHADBOURNE

FORT
GRAHAM

FORT
DAVIS

FORT
LANCASTER

FORT
McKAVETT

FORT
CLARK

FORT
McINTOSH

RINGGOLD
BARRACKS

FORT
BROWN

GULF
OF MEXICO

MEXICO

declared a manifesto published by a vigilante group named the Jacksboro Rangers, "of whatever tribe to be morally right and that we will resist to the last extremity the infliction of any legal punishment on the perpetrators."

Neighbors was alarmed. "Every county," he wrote "is raising and arming a band of lawless men who term themselves Rangers." The man who incited the most hate against the Indians, who was one of the founding editors of the *White Man* and led the Jacksboro Rangers, was a former schoolteacher and father of ten named John R. Baylor. He had also been the agent for the Clear Fork Comanches until his obvious hatred of his charges and his clashes with Neighbors, who was his supervisor, led to his dismissal in 1857. Now he and his men were riding boldly onto the reserves, ready to murder any Indian who might be imagined to have committed a crime against the white man.

In the end, the reservations were more a target than a refuge, and in late July 1859 Robert Neighbors closed his office and self-consciously took upon himself the role of Moses, leading the Indians of both the Brazos and the Clear Fork "out of the heathen land of Texas" and onto agency lands in present-day Oklahoma. In all, around 1,500 Indians were escorted by several companies of cavalry to protect them against Baylor's raiders. "The departure," remembered the daughter of one of the Indian agents, "was accompanied by a perfect babel of noise, Indians galloping hither and thither calling to each other; hosts of pappooses shrieking and wailing from fright at seeing so many strange faces and such undue excitement."

The refugees made it safely across the Red River. When it was time for him to return to Texas, Neighbors shook hands with every one of them. He reported to his wife that a Tonkawa chief, Placido, "cried like a child," and that some of the older warriors clung to him and threw themselves onto the ground in grief. "I have labored hard for them," he wrote, "trying to discharge my duty, in the sight of God and man." Neighbors had long known that discharging his duty meant inviting the fury of white men who had no tolerance for the idea that Indians could have any place in the new Texas they were building. On the way back to Fort Belknap, he and his party were attacked one night by marauders who were dressed like Indians. Whether they actually were Indians is dubious, especially since one of the assailants who was killed turned out to be a redheaded white man beneath his war paint.

A few days later, in the little town that had grown up around Fort Belknap, Neighbors finished writing his final reports as an Indian agent, told the district clerk how much he missed his wife and daughter—"I would give all I possess in the world, to see them"—and walked out of the clerk's office, where a stranger shot him in the back with a shotgun and left him to die in the street.

---- ★ ----

LAWRENCE SULLIVAN ROSS RETAINS SOME LINGERING, IF uncertain, name recognition in today's Texas. He became a Confederate general and a two-term governor. Sul Ross State University, a picturesque array of redbrick buildings nestled against the desert mountains of Alpine, is named in his honor. There is also a statue of him on the campus of Texas A&M, where he served as president after leaving the governorship. It is the work of Pompeo Coppini, who lived in San Antonio for much of his life and became the state's most prolific monument maker. The statue depicts an anonymous-looking nineteenth-century man in a frock coat. He has a long tapering goatee and a neatly barbered fringe of hair. There is an Aggie tradition of students leaving pennies at the feet of this bronze muckety-muck during exam time for good luck.

In the winter of 1860, Sul Ross was very much flesh and blood, twenty-two years old, already a captain in the Texas Rangers. His father, Shapley, had served as both an Indian agent and an Indian fighter—no contradiction in those complex times—and two years earlier Sul, on a break from college, had been in charge of a force of Indians from the Brazos River reservation that supported the U.S. Second Cavalry in an attack on a Comanche camp in the Wichita Mountains on the far side of the Red River. The Comanches were a group of Penatekas under the leadership of Buffalo Hump. Although they had renounced the idea of coming onto the Texas reservations, they were in the midst of peace negotiations with federal authorities in Indian Territory when they were attacked.

Ross and his Indian auxiliaries drove off the Comanche horse herd in the surprise attack, forcing the warriors to fight on foot as the troopers thundered through the camp, firing their revolvers and carbines. Buffalo Hump escaped, but about 60 of his people died, and 300 of the Comanches' horses were captured, and 120 of their lodges burned. Among the dozen or so casualties on the attackers' side was Sul Ross, who received both arrow and bullet wounds.

Now he had recovered and was back in the field with his company of twenty Rangers. With them were another twenty troopers from the Second Cavalry and seventy mounted Texas militiamen. They were in pursuit of a party of northern Comanches who the previous month had raided throughout Northwest Texas. The Comanches likely rode under the leadership of Peta Nocona, who as a young warrior had led or at least participated in the raid of Parker's Fort in 1836. This latest round of Comanche reprisals had been vicious. They slaughtered families, burned farms, and stole livestock throughout three counties. Their most brutal attack—certainly the most luridly described—was against a woman named Martha Sherman at a place known as Staggs Prairie. Nine months pregnant, she had been raped, shot through her belly with arrows (killing her unborn child), and scalped alive. They left her for dead, but death only came after four agonizing days.

After the raids, a young settler named Charles Goodnight led a tracking party that located the Comanches' camp along a spring-fed stream called Mule Creek. Mule Creek fed into the shallow gypsum-laced waters of the Pease River, which entered the Red River about fifty miles northwest of today's Wichita Falls. Goodnight joined Sul Ross's force as a scout, leading them in mid-December through the wintry plains north of Fort Belknap. The only protection against the full force of the bitter weather was in shallow valleys filled with stunted hackberries and wiry mesquite forests. On the way, Goodnight found Martha Sherman's Bible, wrapped in a pillowcase.

Goodnight and the militiamen he was riding with soon fell behind, their horses worn out from the forced march. They were not with Ross's Rangers and the cavalry troopers when they spotted the Comanches from a nearby ridgeline. What Ross and his men saw was not the bustling Indian village they had been expecting to find, just a small camp with a few lodges, where about fifteen women and children were busy packing up to move.

Ross decided not to wait for the straggling volunteers. Telling his Rangers he would present a pistol to the first man to take a scalp, he ordered a charge. What happened next went down in Texas history as the Battle of Pease River, though later historians have downgraded it to, at best, a nasty little fight, and at worst a massacre. "I was in the Pease river Fight," a Ranger named Hiram Rogers remembered in 1928, "but I am not very proud of it. That was not a battle at all, but just a killing of squaws."

Ross and his men killed seven Comanches, four of them women. There were various accounts of the fight, a number of them from Ross himself, the most notable in a book published in 1886 as he was running for governor. In that version of events, a dramatic horseback pursuit of Peta Nocona ended with Ross standing over the dying chief as he sang his death song and thrust at the Ranger with his lance. "I could only look upon him with pity and admiration," Ross wrote.

But Peta Nocona was most likely out hunting with his two sons and not on the scene. He would not die for another three or four years. But—and this was why people elevated the sad and tawdry massacre near the Pease River to the upper realms of Texas myth—his wife was there. During the chaos, a Comanche woman wearing a buffalo robe tried to escape on horseback. When she was chased down by one of the Rangers, she turned to him and called out, "Americano!" She had a baby concealed in the robe. Ross rode up and told the man not to fire. "She was very dirty," he recounted in his 1886 version of the events, "both in her scanty garments and her person. But as soon as I looked on her face, I said, 'Why, Tom, this is a white woman. Indians do not have blue eyes.'"

It was Cynthia Ann Parker, who had been abducted from Parker's Fort in 1836, in the same raid in which the Comanches seized Rachel Plummer. Cynthia Ann was nine years old then; she was thirty-three now. She was the mother of three children: the infant girl she had concealed in the buffalo robe, and whose name was Topsannah, or, in English translation, Prairie Flower; and two older sons by Peta Nocona, named Pecos and Quanah.

Charles Goodnight, who had ridden up with the rest of the trailing militia after the fight was over, found her glassy-eyed with horror and disbelief at what had just happened. In fact, what was still happening, since the Rangers and troopers were methodically scalping the dead and ransacking the camp. "We rode right over her dead companions," Goodnight wrote. "I thought then and still think how exceedingly cruel it was."

In the telling of Sul Ross, and in the minds of white Texans, Cynthia Ann Parker had been rescued. But the truth was that she had only been captured once again, savagely torn from her Comanche husband and her two Comanche sons, just as she had once been torn from her Parker family. In both instances, she was forced to undergo a traumatic rebirth. The first rebirth was more far more successful than the second one. Her transition from nine-year-old white girl to Comanche wife and mother had been complete; she couldn't go back.

Cynthia Ann was taken home, though there was really no home to go to. Parker's Fort was abandoned. Her father had been clubbed and scalped before her eyes in 1836. Her mother had died in 1852, still grieving her missing child. Cynthia Ann and Prairie Flower went to live with Cynthia Ann's uncle Isaac on a farm near Fort Worth, but over the next ten years they were passed from one family member to another. Cynthia Ann was treated kindly by her relatives, but with a kind of pitiable bewilderment that she could not find her place again in their world.

She had largely forgotten her native language, and was oppressed by the confinements of houses and rooms. She insisted on sleeping on the floor, on the buffalo robe she had been wearing when Ross's men attacked. She was still very much shaken by what she had experienced, by the massacres at Parker's Fort and on the Pease River, and by who knew what else in the unrecorded years between. She tried to find some degree of solace by kindling a fire on the open ground and staring up at the sky, but in the accounts left behind by family members there was only one moment when she seemed to come alive. That was when her uncle invited to the house a former scout who

This haunting photograph of a shell-shocked Cynthia Ann Parker and her daughter Topsannah (Prairie Flower) was taken shortly after their "rescue" on the Pease River.

had been a Comanche captive and knew the language. When she heard the man speak Comanche, he recalled, "she sprang up with a scream and knocked about half the dishes off the table." She was desperate for news of her two sons, but the man had none. "My heart is crying all the time," she told him.

There was no respite. Prairie Flower, her daughter, died of brain fever when she was nine years old. Cynthia Ann mourned in the Comanche way, taking a knife and slicing her own arms and breasts, bleeding into the earth. She did not live much longer, dying of an unknown cause probably around 1870.

Among the most searing photographs ever taken in Texas is the one that was made of Cynthia Ann and Prairie Flower in a Fort Worth studio in the spring of 1861, only a few months after she was captured by Sul Ross and his men. In it, Cynthia Ann does not so much look into the camera lens as face it down. She is a strong-looking woman, broad, muscled, with big hands. Her face is wide and flat. She wears a bandana and a calico dress. The dress is unbuttoned, folded back on the right side, where Prairie Flower is nursing at her exposed breast. Her dark hair is chopped short, just below her ears. There is no expression on her face, absolutely none, which makes the image that much more incalculably sad. It is the portrait of a shell-shocked woman who has no understanding of where she is or why she is there—only that wherever it is, it is not home.

There was, according to Ross family lore, another captive taken that day at the Pease River besides Cynthia Ann and her daughter. It was a ten-year-old Comanche boy that Sul Ross took home to live with his slaves. He called him Pease Ross. He died sometime in the 1880s, after fathering a daughter with a freed slave named Texana.

Ross inflated the killings at the Pease River into the great concluding act of the frontier, the final battle between savagery and civilization. "The great Comanche Confederacy was forever broken," he wrote when he was governor, "the blow was decisive; their illustrious chief slept with his fathers and with him were most of his doughty warriors."

But the illustrious chief of the Comanches had yet to rise; and he was the son of Cynthia Ann Parker.

— 22 —

I WILL NEVER DO IT

GENERAL ALBERT SIDNEY JOHNSTON HAD BEEN MIRA- beau B. Lamar's secretary of war for the Republic of Texas. He had led Texas volunteers during the Mexican-American War and commanded the U.S. Second Cavalry in its campaigns against the Comanches. In April 1862, a year after the beginning of the Civil War, he was in charge of the entire western theater of the Confederacy. Few people doubted that he was up to the task. Zachary Taylor had been heard to proclaim that he was the finest soldier he had ever commanded. Jefferson Davis, who had been at West Point with Johnston and was now his commander in chief, later called him "the greatest soldier, the ablest man, civil or military, Confederate or Federal, then living."

But on the afternoon of April 6, Albert Sidney Johnston was dead. It happened after the general orchestrated a massive surprise attack against almost fifty thousand Union forces encamped along the Tennessee River near a little log church called Shiloh. After a morning of unparalleled slaughter, Johnston had personally led, from horseback, an infantry charge against a stubborn Union position dug in at a blossoming peach orchard. The attack succeeded, and Johnston rode back in high spirits. Perhaps because a hip wound sustained in his 1837 duel with Felix Huston had left him with nerve damage, he didn't notice that a minié ball had severed the artery behind his right knee.

He was still chatting, full of post-combat adrenaline, when he suddenly turned pale and slumped in his saddle. So much blood had drained from his leg into his boot that he was dead in fifteen minutes.

He was far from being the only Texan to die in the Rebel assault, or in the Union counterattack the next day, when Ulysses Grant's army, reinforced overnight by fresh troops, drove the Confederates back through the bloody fields they had just conquered. Twenty thousand men were killed or wounded at Shiloh, including members of the Eighth Texas Cavalry and the Second and Ninth Texas Infantry.

A private in the Second Texas, shot through the groin on the second day of the fighting, was among the heaps of dead and wounded on the battlefield after

Sam Houston put Albert Sidney Johnston in charge of the Army of the Republic of Texas, a gesture that was not appreciated by his predecessor, who challenged Johnston to a duel and shot him through the hip. Johnston survived, but would later die leading Confederate troops at Shiloh.

the Confederate tide receded. Periodic thunderstorms during the day left the suffering men lying exposed in the churned-up mud. A Union doctor had taken a look at the private, decided he could not be saved, and left him to die, devoting his attention to men who had better prospects for survival. But a chaplain came along later and saw that he was still alive. He searched the wounded man's knapsack for a clue to his identity. He found a Bible that had been struck by a bullet, and in the Bible there was an inscription.

"Are you related to General Houston of Texas?" the chaplain asked after reading the inscription. The private muttered that he was Houston's son. This was Sam Houston Jr., Sam and Margaret's oldest child, who a year before had pridefully marched in ranks as his father, waving the same sword and wearing the same outfit he had worn at San Jacinto, had performed the honorary duty of drilling the new recruits.

Sam Jr. survived his groin wound, just as his father had survived his at the Battle of Horseshoe Bend almost half a century earlier. He would become a doctor and the author of "a rare find" among Texana collectors, an obscure volume of short stories and articles called *Sam Houston's Rambling Rustlings*.

Margaret Houston, as she often did at moments of flooding emotion, composed a poem when she learned that her son was alive:

> But for the guardian care that kept
> My patriot boy on Shiloh's plain,
> His youthful form would now have slept,
> With thousands of the noble slain.

Margaret characteristically attributed her son's survival to the "guardian care" of God. But if it had not been for that Union chaplain, who, along with the rest of the country, was very much aware that Sam Houston of Texas had stood firm against secession, Sam Jr. might have been given only a cursory blessing and left to bleed to death in the Shiloh mud.

IN 1859, HOUSTON ONCE AGAIN REANIMATED HIS POLITICAL corpse. Hardin Runnels, who had decisively beaten him for governor two years earlier, had become vulnerable for all sorts of reasons. During his administration, the simmering violence along the Rio Grande began to boil over and clashes between Texans and Indians in Northwest Texas took on a renewed fury.

"You whipped me like a cur dog," Houston said to the voters when he decided to take on Runnels again, acknowledging that they were still bitter over his stand on the Kansas-Nebraska Act. "If I was wrong, I own it and take it all back, and if you were wrong I forgive you. So we will start even again."

Secession was very much in the air, and slavery still very much regarded as the bedrock right of every white Texan. Houston offered no objection to slavery, but he outfoxed his opponent when it came to Runnels's plan to reopen the African slave trade, which had been outlawed since before the days of the republic. Houston framed Runnels's proposal not as a moral outrage but as a simple supply-and-demand problem. "Reopen the African Slave Trade," he argued, "and . . . Your present stock of negroes would fall in value."

Despite his Unionist sins, Houston won the election, was inaugurated in December, and moved into the new Governor's Mansion in Austin, just southwest of the boxy, inelegant limestone Capitol erected in 1853 to replace the log cabin Capitol of the republic.

As governor, Houston revisited an idea that he had flirted with as a U.S. senator—a big, crazy, dangerous idea that had more in common with the imperial dreams of his besotted youth than with the calm statesmanship of his later years. Shortly after his inauguration, the trouble on the Rio Grande heated

Sam Houston shortly before his death in 1863, still plagued by his old war wounds and rapidly winding down. "A man of three score years and ten, as I am," he wrote, not entirely persuasively, "ought, at least, be exempt from the charge of ambition."

up again. Juan Cortina had been defeated in the battle at Rio Grande City but had certainly not capitulated. After one of Mifflin Kenedy and Richard King's steamboats found itself in the middle of a crossfire between Cortina's men and Rip Ford's Rangers, Ford led several incursions across the river. The inevitable result was that the tensions along the border escalated even more.

Houston's think-big solution to the lingering problems between Texas and Mexico was nothing less than the formation of an American protectorate, which would have required nothing less than another American invasion. Houston had a paternalistic fondness for the Mexican people, who were "mild, pastoral and gentle" but who were being constantly misled by "demagogues and lawless chieftains." But even though there was plenty of agitated feeling along the border—"The 'Greaser' and Gringo can never live harmoniously together," declared a citizen of Rio Grande City, "unless the latter largely predominate"—the United States had already fought an all-out war with Mexico and wasn't in the mood for another one.

The country, instead, seemed determined to go to war with itself over the intractable issue of slavery and its expansion. In 1860, the Republicans nominated Abraham Lincoln for president. The Democrats split in half; the southern wing of the party withdrew from the convention where Stephen Douglas was being nominated and chose their own candidate, John Breckinridge of Kentucky. But it turned out to be a four-way race for president because another party emerged, the Constitutional Union Party. It was made up mostly of former Whigs who were moderates without a home after the breakup of their own party, and of orphans of the fraying nativist Know-Nothing Party. Its purpose was to avoid war and preserve the Union. Houston was still a national hero in some quarters for his opposition to the Kansas-Nebraska act, and for a while—until his support began to slide on the second ballot—it looked as if he instead of Tennessee's John Bell would end up carrying the banner of the Constitutional Union Party.

Houston lost, but that didn't prevent an ecstatic demonstration in support of the Texas Governor in New York or brushfire enthusiasm in the dwindling pockets of moderate thought in Texas, where he was still popular. He did his best to save his state from "the yawning gulf of ruin" by embarking on a speaking tour, pleading with his fellow Texans to remain in the Union. But the election of Lincoln in November 1860 pulled history inexorably in the opposite direction. South Carolina seceded in December, followed in the next month by Mississippi, Florida, Alabama, Georgia, and Louisiana.

It was now Texas's turn to decide. In modern times, Texas is not generally thought of as a southern state. Its western half—its cowboy half, its plains-and-desert half—acts as a kind of psychic counterweight to the cotton-kingdom identity that links it with the Old South. But in 1860, it was powered by the same economy and saturated with the same ethos as the slaveholding states that had rushed to secede from the Union. Only about 27 percent of its white population owned slaves, compared with almost 50 percent in states such as South Carolina and Mississippi, but the slaveholders were the elite, and most of the wealth and influence in Texas was in their hands. Voices here and there decried the institution of slavery, but for the most part, Unionists like Sam Houston were a long intellectual reach from being abolitionists.

"Negroes For Sale." If you were a newspaper reader in Texas in the years leading up to the Civil War, you would have found nothing discordant in such an advertising headline or in the text that followed: "We have just arrived and permanently located in Galveston with a large lot of young and likely Virginia and North Carolina Negroes, which we will sell on reasonable terms. We have made arrangements for fresh supplies during the season and will always have on hand a good assortment of field hands, house servants and mechanics. Persons wishing to buy Negroes would do well to give us a call before purchasing elsewhere."

This was from the Galveston slaving firm of McMurry & Winstead, whose main competitor was a slave market—the largest west of New Orleans—run by a former mayor of the city, John S. Sydnor. Hometown slave dealers operated in Houston, Austin, and San Antonio, and out-of-state firms advertised their wares in newspapers throughout Texas. There was nothing peculiar (in the modern sense of the word) about what was antiseptically known as the peculiar institution. "Peculiar" referred instead to something specific or particular, like a regional custom or accent. White Texans embraced the southern conception of slavery as something that was not just normal but ordained in heaven and enshrined in human logic.

"Slavery came to the Southern man," wrote Rip Ford in a philosophical time-out from chasing Mexican bandits and Comanches, "authorized by the Supreme Law of the Land. It came to him authorized by time, and custom, and law. The assumption in the Declaration of Independence that 'all men are created equal' was not intended to include the African race, or was a falsehood on its face. It was an institution sanctioned by the Bible, and it had all the authority of time to uphold it."

To John Henry Brown, a newspaper editor and veteran of the Plum Creek fight and the Somervell expedition, a person from Africa was self-evidently "an inferior grade of being," with "wool instead of hair on his head." But by virtue of bracing work under the salubrious Texas climate, he "attains his highest civilization in slavery."

A slave manifest for a ship bound for Galveston from New Orleans in 1838—proof that the phrase "human cargo" was not a figure of speech.

Such platitudes had no coherence in the parallel universe inhabited by the bondsmen. "Who I am, how old I am, and where I was born I don't know," confided one elderly Texas man in the 1930s named William Hamilton to a researcher for the Works Progress Administration. That note of cloudy fatalism is evident throughout the slave narratives that the WPA collected. The accounts feature kind masters and cruel masters, paternalistic Christmas celebrations mixed with hideous tortures, heartbreaking separations, ceaseless work that was crushing to body and mind: "The [cotton] rows were a mile long, and no matter how much grass was in them, if you left one sprig on your row, they beat you nearly to death." The conditions of bondage were not uniform. There were slaves who were cowboys as well as slaves who labored all day in the fields. There were slaves who strolled in the cities in their best clothes as well as slaves who lived and worked on the edge of starvation and were housed in filthy shacks. There were slaves who had authority over others, who were trusted with money and errands, and

THE PEOPLE WANT EXCITEMENT

Cotton was the dominant crop in Texas, and picking it was the dominant labor of African Americans, most of whom didn't own their land but worked for shares as tenant farmers.

those who lay on their pallets at night, enduring the agony of the salt that had been rubbed into their lacerated backs and desperately plotting how to outwit the master's hounds. One enslaved man named John Barker remembered his grandfather's inventive method of throwing dogs off the scent. He would catch horned toads, put them in the fireplace until they were dried, and then crush them with a bottle until he had a powder that he could use to coat the bottom of his shoes and scatter along his escape route.

Jeff Hamilton was the name of the thirteen-year-old boy that Sam Houston once impulsively bought off a slave block in Huntsville. Hamilton's almost lifelong association with Houston was extraordinary enough for him to write an autobiography. But in other ways he was representative of the many thousands of Texas slaves who lived out lives that would never be chronicled. Born in Kentucky, he was transported to Texas when he was three years old, along with his mother and the rest of the slaves belonging to a family of "quality aristocrats" who decided to make a new beginning in the Republic of Texas.

But the new beginning was a disaster. The softhearted master was killed by Indians, and his widow married a dissolute gambler who sold Jeff to pay an overdue bill for two barrels of whiskey. "I turned my head for one last look at my mother," he remembered. "She was standing in the cabin door, holding her apron to her face and sobbing in a kind of hopeless way."

"Here's a little nigger for sale—cheap!" Hamilton remembered his master calling out to the crowd in Huntsville after he was ordered to stand on an auction block for hours in front of a general store. He stood hatless under the full force of the East Texas sun, weeping in terror, on display in front of a crowd of scrutinizing strangers, thirsty and hungry, tormented by a display of gingerbread in the store's window.

He was rescued by Sam Houston, although of course that isn't the right word. He was bought. But his relief at escaping into the custody of a man like Houston was complete and—at least as rendered in his as-told-to-a-white-author autobiography—almost unqualified: "The very sound of my master's voice swept away my fears. From that time on, he was my hero and I was his loyal slave."

Part of Hamilton's duties was to dress—almost every day—Houston's forever-unhealing wounds from the Creek War as well as the ankle that had been shattered by a Mexican musket ball at San Jacinto. "He told me once when I was dressing it that the doctors in New Orleans took from his ankle twenty-three pieces of bone," Hamilton recalled. "He also said that no one on earth would ever know what agony he suffered from his wounded ankle for two or three months after the battle."

———————— ★ ————————

SAM HOUSTON DID HIS BEST TO QUELL THE SECESSIONIST ardor that gripped his state, setting off on another speaking tour and resisting demands to call a special session that would give the legislature the legal cover to convene a secession convention. "I am making my last effort," he confided to a friend, "to save Texas from the yawning gulf of ruin."

But in the end, he had no choice but to call the session and stand by as the Secession Convention, on February 1, 1861, passed an ordinance of secession by a vote of 166 to 8. Jeff Hamilton wrote that Houston appeared before the convention on the day before the vote was taken. Hamilton said that he accompanied the governor to the floor of the House of Representatives, but a door was slammed in his face before he could enter, so he watched from the balcony as Houston pleaded with his colleagues one last time, bared his right arm and shoulder to display his old wounds, and declared, "I know what war is."

The legislative vote for secession had to be confirmed by a popular referendum, scheduled for February 23. The convention ordered ballots to be printed with the choices "For Secession" and "Against Secession," along with a voters' guide entitled "Declaration of Causes Which Impel the State of Texas to Secede from the Federal Union." Among the grievances listed was the North's "debasing doctrine of the equality of all men, irrespective of race or color—a doctrine at war with nature, in opposition to the experience of mankind, and in violation of the plainest revelations of the Divine Law."

Even before the referendum was voted on, the Committee of Public Safety, created by the convention, sent emissaries to San Antonio to see to the surrender of arms and supplies in possession of the federal government. The man in charge of the Department of Texas was General David Twiggs, who was seventy-one years old and had been in the service of the U.S. Army all his adult life. He hesitated just a little too much, and was taken into custody by a Texan force of several hundred men led by Ben McCulloch. They were supplemented by a hundred members of the Knights of the Golden Circle, a secret society that dreamt of a future slave empire radiating from a base in Havana throughout Mexico, the Caribbean basin, and the American South and Southwest. The insurgents quickly occupied all the buildings in San Antonio where federal supplies were kept, including the Alamo, or what was left of it. Most of the old mission walls had been torn down, and only the church and convent were still standing. The army had built a roof over the church, which during the time of the siege was an open ruin, and had augmented its ragged, crumbling facade with the curved parapet by which the world has recognized the building ever since.

"You have treated me shamefully," Twiggs complained to McCulloch as he and his army marched out of town. He wept like a child, according to one writer. "You, sir, without papers, without any notice, have assembled a mob and forced me to terms."

The popular referendum on secession was more decorously done. And it was decisive. There were 122 organized counties in Texas, and 104 of them voted for secession. The popular vote was three-to-one in favor. But there were interesting pockets of Unionist or at least worried thought, particularly in Central Texas counties populated with freethinking German immigrants and abutting the Indian frontier, which, with the withdrawal of federal troops, would be left—at least for the moment—unprotected.

Texas seceded from the Union on March 2, 1861, Sam Houston's sixty-eighth birthday and the twenty-fifth anniversary of Texas's Declaration of Independence from Mexico. The Secession Convention voted on March 5 to officially become part of the Confederate States of America. On March 14, it decreed that all state officers—including especially the governor—sign an oath of allegiance to the Confederacy. That was a step too far for Sam Houston. "Margaret," he told his wife after a sleepless night spent pacing around in his socks on the upper floor of the Governor's Mansion, "I will never do it."

Houston was a famous whittler, and a pretty good one, judging by the letter opener he carved in the shape of an alligator, which is on display today at the Sam Houston Memorial Museum in Huntsville. His great friend Ashbel Smith recognized his whittling habit as an outward manifestation of intense, coiling thought. "Whenever I saw him turn over in his hands the trifling piece of wood I knew he was making a forward move in his cogitation."

On March 16, 1861, his whittling was furious. He sat in his first-floor office in the Capitol while in the chamber upstairs his name was called to present himself and take the oath. It was called three times. He never stirred, never appeared—just kept whittling. The next day, he pointedly showed up for work as governor, but the office was no longer his. Edward Clark, a veteran of the Mexican-American War who had been his lieutenant governor, was sitting at his desk. They exchanged strained pleasantries, and Houston gathered up his things and left.

Before he and his family were evicted from the Governor's Mansion, Houston—according to Jeff Hamilton—burned a letter in the fireplace, an act of incineration guaranteed to break the hearts of archivists everywhere. It was a letter from Abraham Lincoln, offering to make Sam Houston a major general in the Army of the United States and to provide him with fifty thousand troops to keep Texas in the Union. According to Hamilton, Houston was tempted. He brought in four friends and asked their advice. One of them thought Houston should take Lincoln's offer. The other three felt strongly otherwise. The people of Texas had made their decision, they argued. Nothing would change their opinion, and if Houston led an army against them it would only mean needless slaughter.

"Gentlemen," Houston replied as he threw the letter into the fireplace, "I have asked your advice, and I will take it, but if I were ten years younger I wouldn't."

★

IN JUNE, A FEW MONTHS AFTER TEXAS SECEDED AND SAM Houston was turned out of office, a young woman from Ohio named Lucy Stevens attended the commencement ceremonies at Baylor College in the town of Independence, a few miles west of Washington-on-the-Brazos, where the Texas Declaration of Independence was signed. Lucy had come to Texas to visit her aunt's family, who had settled along the Brazos Valley in

1835. During the festivities, she met Edward Clark, the new governor, whom she found to have a "remarkably pleasant countenance."

The grand finale of the graduation programs was a "Secession Play," a stirring pageant that began in mourning, with a young woman representing the United States dressed in crepe, wearing a crown of black. But then came the figures of the seceded Southern states, adorned in radiant white and accompanied by Abraham Lincoln's "long and heart piercing wail." The play ended in triumph as the girls representing the South rose up together, defying Lincoln's threats, declaring they would never be slaves, and breaking the chains that bound them to the oppressive Union.

The sad but thrilling parable of rebirth and affirmation took place before the blockading and invasion of Texas ports, before twenty-four thousand Texans died from disease or from fighting at places like Shiloh and Elkhorn Tavern and Chickamauga and Vicksburg, and before a vicious war of partisan retribution took root within the borders of Texas.

A much darker vision of secession crept into the dreams of an Englishwoman named Amelia Barr. She and her Scottish husband, Robert, sailed to Texas in 1856, trying to escape personal and financial calamities. Yellow fever raging in Galveston prevented them from landing, but a steamer took them up Buffalo Bayou to Harrisburg. On the way, they passed the plain of San Jacinto, and Barr was charmed to see that the captain of the boat removed his hat. "We are going to live among heroes," she told her accountant husband.

Barr, who would later become a feverishly prolific novelist, recorded her Texas adventures in a robust autobiography called *All The Days of my Life: The Red Leaves of a Human Heart*. She wrote about the eerie nighttime bayou, its surface stippled with alligators; the great flocks of cranes that populated the prairies, with "their tocsin shout of Kewrrook! Kewrrook! Kewrrook!"; about frontier delicacies such as bear paws preserved in Madeira wine ("The paws then look like walnuts, but are said to excel any tidbit known to epicures"); and about the redoubtable Texas women she encountered, who were "nearly without exception fine riders and crack shots, and quite able, when the men of the household were away, to manage their ranches or plantations, and keep . . . faithful guard over their families and household."

The Barrs settled in Austin, where Robert had a job with the state comptroller until he was advised to resign before his antislavery views became known. But Amelia was briskly in line with prevailing Texas thought. "An unreasonable detestation of slavery," she wrote, "was one of Robert's prejudices or principles. . . . The majority of our small matrimonial frets were on this subject."

Nevertheless, Amelia was impressed with the grand old figure of Sam Houston, and was present in the gallery on the day he refused to sign the oath. It was during this anxious time that she had her horrifying secession nightmare:

> I was on a vast plain, dark and lonely, with the black clouds low over it, and the rain falling in a heavy, sullen downpour; and, as I stood with clasped hands, but without the power to pray, a great white arch grew out of the darkness. It seemed high as heaven, and wide as the horizon, and I wondered at its beauty and majesty. But, as I looked, I saw a black line down the center of it grow to a visible break, and this break grow wider and wider, until one-half of the arch fell to the ground, amid groans and cries, far off, but terrible.

The calamity that she envisioned as far off was much closer to home than she realized. Indeed, even before Lincoln's election and the secession referendum, parts of North Texas had erupted into paranoia and chaos. What became known as the "Texas Troubles" began in July 1860, and their unlikely cause was the introduction of a new consumer product called the prairie match. Prairie matches had phosphorous tips that could be ignited not just by friction but also by the indirect heat of a record 110-degree summer. The matches seem to have combusted in several dry-goods stores on the same day, burning down buildings in Denton and Pilot Point and a small town of 168 people on the Trinity River called Dallas. Most of the businesses on Dallas's main square burned down that day, including the offices of its weekly newspaper, the *Dallas Herald*. The cause of the conflagration wasn't yet known, but that didn't prevent the editor of the *Herald* from eagerly jumping to the conclusion that it was arson, the opening act of a slave rebellion orchestrated by fanatic white abolitionists. In a world where the 1831 Nat Turner rebellion was still a living memory and the John Brown raid on Harpers Ferry still a fresh one, panic was an easy register to reach. A Tarrant County man reported to his brother:

> they ar Whipping about thirty Negros pr Day the Negros ar Confessing all about the plot they say that the Abolitionists have promised them there freedom if they would burne all the towns Down in the State allso they was to breake out on the Sixty Day of August when the men was all gon to the Election than kill all the Wimmin and Children that they could all the likly young ladies they Was to save for Wives for themselves

Somewhere between thirty and a hundred black people and suspected white collaborators were lynched during the course of the reprisals that summer. The number of slaves who were whipped or beaten until they acknowledged the existence of the bogus abolitionist plot must have been much higher. One of the men who suffered a particularly unpleasant and undignified demise was a Methodist minister named Anthony Bewley. The Methodists had broken apart over the issue of slavery. Bewley, a member of the antislavery, northern faction of the church, had left Texas when the troubles broke out. But after he was accused of being a member of an abolitionist secret society called Mystic Red, he was apprehended in Missouri by bounty hunters, brought back to Texas, and hanged, according to an article in the *White Man*, for being one of "Sam Houston's 'viceregents of God.'" His body was so indifferently buried that the knees poked up out of the ground. Three weeks later, somebody dug it up, hacked the remaining flesh from the bones, and threw the skeleton up on the roof of a storehouse. Local boys got into the spirit of things and climbed up on the roof, where they "set up the bones in a variety of attitudes by bending the joins of the arms and legs, and . . . mocked [the remains] by crying, 'old Bewley,' 'old abolitionist', etc."

No doubt some of those boys who played with the preacher's bones were among the 25,000 volunteers who signed up to fight for the Confederacy when the war broke out—or among the 90,000 who enlisted or were conscripted during the course of the conflict. Their units had cohesive-sounding names like the Third Texas Cavalry or the Sixth Texas Infantry, but their appearance was as irregular as that of Sam Houston's army during the revolution. The men arrived with every kind of weapon, from hand-me-down squirrel guns to the latest styles of revolvers and Bowie knives. One Texas cavalry unit even carried lances—as a kind of homage, one suspects, to their ancestral Mexican and Comanche enemies. Uniforms, when they existed, varied from regiment to regiment. There were enough shades of Confederate gray to merge into federal blue. The flashier uniforms—sometimes including leopard-skin pants—tended to belong to the cavalry, and that was where most volunteers wanted to be. "It was found very difficult to raise infantry in Texas," wrote a British military observer, "as no Texan walks a yard if he can help it."

Gettysburg, Sharpsburg, Manassas, Shiloh, Vicksburg, Chickamauga, the Wilderness: the great battles of the Civil War took place far from Texas, but Texans fought in all of them. They fought in units like Terry's Texas Rangers and Hood's Texas Brigade, names that still have a hallowed Lost Cause resonance among some Texas citizens, even as others are leading the fight to rename schools and streets bearing the names of Confederate leaders and remove their statues from public parks and universities.

Members of Company C of Terry's Texas Rangers, always ready for a fight and full of attitude.

Terry's Texas Rangers was officially known as the Eighth Texas Cavalry. It was organized early in the war by Benjamin Franklin Terry, a wealthy planter who, along with a business partner, built the first stretch of railroad in Texas. (Well, he didn't actually build it—slaves did.) Terry's Rangers were mounted troops, armed with Colt revolvers and Bowie knives. Judging from a famous photograph of five members of Company C taken in 1861, Terry's men were as cocky and lethal as their notorious forebears who were known to the Mexicans as *los diablos Tejanos*. In the photo, four of the five men are wearing hats with a Lone Star badge on the crown, but otherwise their uniforms are a mishmash of frontier and military styles. Their beards and mustaches are scant and scruffy, their hair is long, their posture relaxed, but their attitude confrontational. It is easy to imagine these men as part of the drunken group that J. K. P. Blackburn wrote about in his reminiscence of serving with the Rangers. One night, encamped in Nashville, some of the men had gone to see a play, a reenactment of the Pocahontas and John Smith story. As the actress playing Pocahontas was flinging her body under a war club to save Smith, one of the Rangers in the gallery "whipped out a six-shooter and fired upon the supposed executioner with the remark that 'his mother had taught him to always protect a lady when in danger.'" The shot went wild, and the offending actor lived, but two policemen died in the melee that followed.

Terry himself was killed in his regiment's first battle near Woodsonville, Kentucky, shot through the head during a Union ambush, but the name "Terry's Texas Rangers" stayed with the regiment and proved indelible. John Bell Hood's tenure at the head of his namesake brigade was relatively brief as well. He led the Texas Brigade for only six months until he was promoted to division commander, and during the war the outfit was augmented with troops from Georgia, South Carolina, and Arkansas. Nevertheless, it retained the name Hood's Texas Brigade, and the eroded letters on the granite monument erected to the brigade's memory on the state Capitol grounds spell out an observation from Jefferson Davis that ranks high on the list of Texas accolades: "The troops of other states have their reputation to gain. The sons of the Alamo have theirs to maintain."

"The gallant Hood of Texas," as he was referred to in a song with music borrowed from "The Yellow Rose of Texas," was a Kentuckian and West Point graduate. Before the Civil War, he had served along the Texas frontier in the Second U.S. Cavalry. In a fight against the Comanches on the Devil's River, he had been wounded in the left hand by an arrow. He later lost the use of his entire left arm after being hit by a shell fragment at Gettysburg, and another wound at Chickamauga led to the amputation of his right leg.

JOHN BELL HOOD,

the commander of Hood's Texas Brigade, had to be strapped by aides into his saddle after he lost an arm and a leg in Civil War battles.

(After that, it took three aides to lift the general into the saddle and strap him there so that he wouldn't fall off.)

Hood's Brigade fought in twenty-four battles in 1862 alone, including Second Manassas and Gaines's Mill. And on the single bloodiest day in American history, it attacked Union forces through a cornfield outside the Maryland town of Sharpsburg, just to the west of Antietam Creek. "The hottest place I ever saw on this earth or want to see hereafter," one survivor remembered. "There were shot, shells and Minie balls sweeping the face of the earth, legs, arms and other parts of human bodies were flying in the air like straw in a whirlwind." One regiment of the brigade, the 1st Texas, which had 226 men going into the fight, lost 186 of them, the highest percentage of casualties in either army during the entire war. By the time of Lee's surrender at Appomattox, the cumulative number of killed and wounded in the brigade reached 61 percent.

Although the Texas version of the rebel yell—with its sampling of Comanche war whoops—was heard on every major Civil War battlefield, the majority of the approximately ninety thousand Texans who enlisted or were conscripted during the course of the conflict served in what was called the Trans-Mississippi, the theater of war that lay to the west of the strategically vital river. That meant not just Texas but most of Louisiana and Arkansas, as well as Kansas, Missouri, and the Indian Territories north of the Red River. The Trans-Mississippi also included New Mexico, the territory of the upper Rio Grande that Texans had long coveted as part of the prize won for defeating Santa Anna's army.

In the summer of 1861, in the early months of the war, Texas tried to seize it again, this time for the Confederacy. John Baylor, the former editor of the *White Man*, turned his attention from murdering peaceable Indians in Northwest Texas to leading an invasion force into southern New Mexico. He had fewer than three hundred volunteers, but the Second Texas Mounted Rifles routed the federal troops there and set the stage for a much larger, brigade-strength campaign led by General Henry Hopkins Sibley, a much-decorated veteran of the Mexican-American War who had once gone snow-blind while trying to climb Mount Popocatépetl outside Mexico City. Sibley intended to finish conquering the Southwest for the Confederacy, but that dream fell apart when Union forces destroyed his supply train after an intense battle at Glorieta Pass, east of Santa Fe.

— 23 —

WITH THROBBING HEARTS

WHEN YOU THINK ABOUT IT, IT'S REMARKABLE HOW much conflict some of the Texans who fought in the Civil War managed to compact into one lifetime. Ben McCulloch is only one example. He fought at San Jacinto. He joined the Texas Rangers and fought Indians with Jack Hays. He was shot in the arm in a duel. After the Comanches launched their invasion of the Texas coast, he was in the middle of the Battle of Plum Creek. He was part of the force that drove Vásquez and Woll back to Mexico. He was a member of the Somervell expedition. During the Mexican-American War, he fought at Monterrey and infiltrated enemy lines at Buena Vista. At the start of the Civil War, he drove General Twiggs and his federal army out of San Antonio. That same year, he became a brigadier general in the Confederate army and led a force from Texas into southwestern Missouri, where he joined with General Sterling Price to defeat Union troops under General Nathaniel Lyon at a crucial battle the South called Oak Hills and the North Wilson's Creek. His warrior's life finally came to an end the next year at the Battle of Elkhorn Tavern when he was shot in the heart while scouting an attack against a federal position on the other side of a snake rail fence.

Colorado

Kansas

Missouri

Oklahoma

Arkansas

**BATTLE OF
GLORIETA PASS**
MARCH 26–28,
1862

New
Mexico

Texas

**BATTLE OF
MANSFIELD**
APRIL 8, 1864

**BATTLE OF
SABINE PASS**
SEPTEMBER 8, 1863

Louisiana

**TREUE der UNION
MONUMENT**

**BATTLE OF
NUECES**
AUGUST 10, 1862

**BATTLE OF
GALVESTON**
JANUARY 1, 1863

**BATTLE OF
PALMITO RANCH**
MAY 12–13, 1865

*GULF
OF MEXICO*

TEXAS IN THE CIVIL WAR
1862–1865

Another battle-forged old Texan, Rip Ford, found himself back in action after secession. He was ordered to the Rio Grande to secure the border between Brownsville and Laredo for the Confederacy. It was a crucial errand. As Union troops began blockading Texas ports, the only safe way for Texas to get its cotton out of the state, sell it, and raise funds for vital war needs was to send it across the Rio Grande to Matamoros, from where it could be taken to the Mexican port of Bagdad and loaded onto ships.

In South Texas, the war reawakened and to some degree reconfigured the old Anglo-Tejano conflicts that had been stewing there since the filibustering days of James Long. It was a complex, almost out-of-sight pocket of the Civil War. Besides the struggle between North and South on the American side of the border, there was a distorted-mirror conflict on the Mexican side, where the French invaded in December 1861 with the intention of installing a Habsburg archduke, Ferdinand Maximilian, as the emperor of Mexico. The Rio Grande theater of the war was a confusing tangle of big-picture geopolitics, shape-shifting alliances, and long-standing blood feuds.

Speaking of blood feuds, Juan Cortina returned to the scene. During what came to be called the Second Cortina War, he was, Ford believed, colluding with Unionists in Texas and elsewhere and "organizing a foreign force to invade Texas. . . . I can not tell where the storm may burst."

It burst in Zapata County, near the little town of Carrizo. Ford was not present for the battle. The fighting fell to another Tejano, a prosperous merchant and former Laredo mayor named Santos Benavides. Benavides was no abolitionist, and no Unionist, though in the 1830s he had fought with the Mexican federalists against the centralist government. He was more than comfortable with secession, and as someone who had crossed into Mexico to track down runaway slaves, he was certainly comfortable with slavery. He joined the Confederate army as a captain, commanding a cavalry regiment made up mostly of fellow Tejanos from the Laredo area. It was Benavides and his men who overran Cortina's partisans at Carrizo. The fight lasted only a few minutes. There were no casualties on the Confederate side, but Cortina's men were hit hard. The survivors (including Cortina) were driven across the Rio Grande. Eleven Cortinistas were captured, but this being the border, they were not detained in a living state for long. "Before attacking Cortina," Benavides wrote Ford, "I particularly ordered my men not to arrest any of the bandits, but to kill all that fell into their hands. Consequently I have no prisoners."

Benavides was among roughly 2,500 Tejanos who fought for the Confederacy during the Civil War. Some joined willingly, others were conscripted. Some fought in ranks with Hood's Brigade at places like Gettysburg and Chickamauga, some with the Second Texas Mounted Rifles at Glorieta Pass.

Others—like those in Benavides's company—fought closer to home along the Rio Grande border, protecting their homes and property from avenging partisans like Juan Cortina and from Union troops organized in Mexico or arriving by sea from New Orleans. Tejanos fought for the Union as well, almost a thousand of them. They fought in U.S. cavalry regiments like the one commanded by Edmund Jackson Davis, a Texas lawyer and district judge who refused to sign the oath to the Confederacy and left the state to throw himself into the struggle against it.

Another Union force operating along the lower Rio Grande was called Vidal's Independent Partisan Rangers. At its head was Adrián Vidal, the combustible and disappointing son of Petra Vela, and the stepson of Mifflin Kenedy. Vidal started out fighting on the Confederate side, like Benavides. He appears to have inherited the martial spirit and leadership skills of his natural father, but he was short on self-control and long on grievances and soon grew disenchanted with the Confederacy. In the fall of 1863, he joined up with the Union forces that had just invested Brownsville. But his identification with the opposing side was not long-lived either. He eventually ended up deserting the Union as well, crossing the river, and falling in with the Mexican insurgency against the French invaders. He was captured by the imperialists in 1865 and shot for treason. His body was sent home to his mother. Mifflin Kenedy was distraught about the fate of his wayward stepson, whom he had personally mentored in the steamboat business. "I write with a heavy hand," he confided to a friend, "as my boy has been shot at Camargo. As bad as he is, I would have saved him if [I] could."

———— ★ ————

PEOPLE LIKE ADRIÁN VIDAL, INHERITORS OF COMPLICATED legacies, operated in the confusing eddies and back channels of the Civil War. And the embrace of secession and of the Confederacy was far from monolithic in Texas. About a third of the state's residents, after all, were enslaved. And in parts of Texas, in those counties that had voted against secession, Unionist sentiment could be strong.

In the little Hill Country town of Comfort, which is about fifty miles northwest of San Antonio, a lonely little granite obelisk sits in a patch of parkland on a bluff above Cypress Creek. Three German words are carved onto the southern face of the shaft: *Treue Der Union*—True to the Union. Elsewhere on the monument are listed the names of some of the sixty-eight men who were killed—*Gefallen*—on the banks of the Nueces and Rio Grande during the summer and fall of 1862. It is one of the few monuments to the Union ever erected on Confederate soil, and the names incised upon it—

names like Bauer, Luckenbach, Weyershausen—testify to the depth of German influence in this part of Texas, and to the cultural and political dilemmas that entrapped many German Texans during the Civil War.

"Nowhere does the German race prosper better than here," declared a German tract promoting immigration to Texas in the 1840s. The words were advertising hyperbole, but if they had been entirely untrue there wouldn't have been such a steady surge of German settlers arriving in the years just before and after independence. By 1850, they were more than 5 percent of the population. They came as Mexican colonists originally, as had the Europeans of Scots-Irish descent seeking land grants in the days of the empresarios.

The first wave of German immigration came at the urging of a man named Christian Friedrich Dirks, who had been in the loyal service of the Duke of Oldenburg until the duke discovered that Dirks was no longer loyal and decided that his services were no longer wanted. Escaping an embezzlement charge required a change of name and a change of scene, and that was how the newly christened Johann Friedrich Ernst arrived in Texas in 1831. He secured a league in Austin's colony and began writing letters to friends back in northwestern Germany—letters that were published in the newspapers—extolling the Texas paradise he had discovered. Soon people began leaving their fragmented, played-out farmsteads in places like Oldenburg, the Münsterland, and Holstein and coming to join Ernst to try their luck in the bountiful black soil between the Brazos and the Colorado.

In the next decade, after Texas had become an independent republic and was offering colonization grants of its own, more Germans arrived. The new immigrants disembarked in Texas under the auspices of the Adelsverein, also known as the Verein zum Schutze deutscher Einwanderer in Texas (Society for the Protection of German Immigrants in Texas.) The altruistic-sounding name was somewhat misleading, since the society was formed by a group of titled aristocrats interested as much in the profits they would gain from a surging German presence in Texas as in the offer of a new start to struggling families. These new families ended up farther west than the first group of Germans, staking out farms in the picturesque but thin-soiled Hill Country. They established towns like New Braunfels and Fredericksburg, where fachwerk houses and fortress-like buildings of hand-cut limestone still line the streets today.

The first commissioner-general in charge of the Adelsverein settlers bore the distinctly un-Texan title of Friedrich Wilhelm Carl Ludwig Georg Alfred Alexander, Prince of Solms, Lord of Braunfels, Grafenstein, Münzenberg, Wildenfels, and Sonnenwalde. Prince Solms was a dashing and romantic-minded character who had become infatuated with Texas in part because

of an alluring German novel he had read on the subject, and who believed that the Teutonic adventure in this new land would bring "new crowns to old glory." In addition to lending part of his titled name to the town of New Braunfels, he helped create a short-lived Texas utopian community of free-thinkers called The Forty. One of the members of The Forty was a young man named Friedrich Schenck, who, in a letter home to his mother, revealed a wide-eyed, searching soul whose mood swung in a short arc from sighing contentment to outright rapture: "A strange melancholy came over me when, from a hilltop, my eye looked out over the immeasurable plains and the evening sun spread its magic shadows over the valleys and poured its purple over the peaks of the highlands. The heavenly silence of nature, in eternal harmony here with itself for thousands of years, grips the soul of man more powerfully than organ tones or church hymns."

Schenck was deeply impressed by almost everything he experienced in Texas, but there is one passage in his letter, about a visit from a Comanche delegation, that is particularly striking when considered against the merciless wars that festered between that nation and the Anglo Texans. "I could tell you all so much," he wrote, "about those slender, half-naked children of the wilderness, of the agility of the young warriors and of the luminous eyes of the beautiful amazons. . . . One would have to know the language of these people to comprehend their spiritual development."

THE PEOPLE WANT EXCITEMENT

"Nowhere does the German race prosper better than here." That was the pitch made to German immigrants, who made a new home in Texas and built old-world towns such as New Braunfels.

Schenck's idealism about Indians was one thing, but it was the pragmatic negotiating skill of Prince Solms's successor, John Meusebach, that forged an important and lasting treaty in 1847 between the Comanches and the Germans who aspired to settle on their hunting grounds in the land between the Llano and Colorado Rivers.

Conflict between the Germans and the Indians was mitigated by the Meusebach-Comanche treaty, but the "beardmen," as old-time Texans referred to the German settlers, sometimes found themselves in hostile territory anyway. The enlightened views of idealists like Friedrich Schenck were bound to collide with prevailing Texas thinking. "Unfortunately," Schenck reported to his mother after describing the joys of cultivating the Texas soil, "this happy picture of Texas farm life is also disturbed below by the curse of slavery . . . the feelings of the Germans bristle against such practice, as it is contrary to the holiest right of man—freedom!"

Not all Germans in Texas were hostile to slavery, but there was a discernible overall resistance to secession, most strikingly in areas like Gillespie County, home to Fredericksburg, where the vote for remaining in the union reached 96 percent. Ferdinand Lindheimer, the great Texas botanist and editor of a New Braunfels newspaper called the *Neu-Braunfelser Zeitung*, urged his readers to keep their heads down in the coming conflict. "When in Texas," he wrote, "do as the Texans do. Anything else is suicide and brings tragedy to all our Texas-Germans."

But his voice went unheeded by a core of militant German Unionists in the Hill Country, some of them refugees from the failure of the liberal European revolutions of 1848. They banded together to form the Union Loyal League, which, among other things, discouraged enlistment in the Confederate army and stood ready as partisans to assist in a federal invasion of Texas. In August 1862, fearing that they were about to be imprisoned or worse, sixty to seventy German Unionists decided to flee to Mexico. They took their time, not knowing that they were being pursued by a force of Confederate cavalry and state militia. A week or so after setting out, they were camped along a bend in the Nueces River, in a grassy prairie meadow fringed by cedar trees. They were only about forty miles from the Mexican border. "At 4 o'clock in the morning," remembered one of the survivors, August Hoffmann, "our enemies came."

During the ugly fight that followed, about half of the Unionists bolted through the trees. Some of them—like August Hoffmann—managed to make it home or to Mexico, but most of the other escapees were captured and hanged one by one, or died in a later battle with Confederate troops at the Rio Grande. The rest of the Germans who were surprised on the Nueces that morning stood their ground, putting up an intense fight despite being caught entirely unprepared. But not long after daylight, all these men were either dead on the field or wounded. The wounded were dragged off into the trees and shot in the head. The Confederates buried their own dead but left the bodies of the Unionists to rot on the ground. Their bones lay there until the end of the war, when they were gathered up and buried, and their names memorialized on the unlikely monument in the middle of Comfort.

There is a semantic historical squabble over whether this incident should be referred to as the Battle of the Nueces or the Massacre of the Nueces. No such parsing is required for what happened a few months later in one of the North Texas counties that voted against secession. This part of the state, as demonstrated by the prairie match conflagration that led to the Texas Troubles in 1860, was a region of dangerous instability. This was due in part to its nervous frontier proximity to Comanche, Kiowa, and Wichita raiders, who had been emboldened by the withdrawal of federal troops. It also lay along the newly established Butterfield Overland Mail route, which originated in St. Louis, crossed Texas, and terminated in San Francisco. Many of the people in this area had come from or had ancestral ties to places like Kansas and the border states of the Upper South. Only 10 percent of the population of Cooke County, whose northern border ended at the Red River, owned slaves and felt a strong economic kinship with the plantation South. But they were alert and alarmed. As a minority population, they feared an insurrection from Unionists who might collaborate with Indians, with Kansas abolitionists, or with rebellious slaves.

On October 1, they struck. A colonel of the Texas state troops named James Bourland arrested 150 men suspected of being Union fifth columnists. Colonel William Young, who the year before had led the Eleventh Texas Cavalry across the Red River to capture three federal forts in Indian Territory, handpicked a jury, stacking it with slaveholders—like himself and Bourland. During the trial, in Gainesville, the jury condemned seven of the men and hanged them one by one from an elm tree outside town. But that wasn't enough for the mob that had begun forming during the proceedings. They stormed the courtroom, seized fourteen more, and lynched them all. The next week, Young was bushwhacked. Then nineteen more of the men who had been arrested were retried and condemned to death, with Young's avenging son Jim supervising the proceedings. The condemned men were taken to the hanging tree and dispatched at the steady rate of two per hour. The county buried some of them in shallow graves by the banks of a nearby creek, graves easily disturbed by rooting animals. Not long after, a girl saw a hog carrying something in its jaws down a Gainesville street. It was her stepfather's arm.

"Reason had left its throne," decided a local minister about what came to be known as the Great Hanging. It was a clear enough judgment about the situation not just in the northern tier of Texas counties during the Civil War but also in the Hill Country, across the Indian frontier, and along the Rio Grande border. Far from the great battlefields in the East and the South, much of Texas remained on the ragged edge of the Civil War, where the titanic struggle trickled down to local clashes among vigilantes, night riders, infiltrators, committees of safety, spies, and saboteurs. To Kate Stone, a twenty-two-year-old woman who fled across the Sabine after the fall of Vicksburg, Texas was "the dark corner of the Confederacy." She used the phrase "dark corner" over and over in her diary. She didn't like anything about the place, its "whiteheaded children and buttermilk," its "desolate wind-swept" prairies. "And, oh, the swarms of ugly, rough people, different only in degrees of ugliness. There must be something in the air of Texas fatal to beauty." A stalwart secessionist, she felt she had landed in a throbbing hive of confusion "where Union feeling is rife, and where the principal amusement of loyal citizens is hanging suspected Jayhawkers."

But not all the fighting was insular and indirect. A coastal invasion of Texas was very much on the to-do list of Abraham Lincoln and his war planners in Washington. In October 1862, while the citizens court in Gainesville was trying and hanging its prisoners, a Union gunboat, the *Harriet Lane*, named for former president James Buchanan's niece, steamed into Galveston harbor with a demand that the city surrender. Backing up the *Harriet Lane* were seven ships in a flotilla commanded by William Renshaw. It was an auspicious time to attack Galveston: the island was lightly defended, thanks to Brigadier General Paul Octave Hébert, the Confederate commander of the District of Texas. Hébert, a swaggering autocrat who had been first in his class at West Point, was unimpressed by his troops. Francis Lubbock, whom we last saw as a young man camping out beneath a tree after wandering into the new capital of the Republic of Texas, was now the state's governor. His opinion of Hébert was that he was "somewhat bewildered by the magnitude of the task assigned him."

Whether out of bewilderment or tactical prudence, Hébert had decided that the Texas coast was indefensible. Before the Union fleet arrived, he had moved most of his artillery out of Galveston and onto the mainland. As a result, Renshaw took the city almost without resistance. A month later, Hébert was replaced by John Bankhead Magruder. Magruder, supposedly the "handsomest soldier in the Confederacy," was nicknamed "Prince John" for his luxe personal tastes. But he was also confident where Hébert had been cautious, and on New Year's Day 1863 he took Galveston back, commanding a Confederate strike force in the middle of the night over a railroad bridge that led across the bay to the island. The land attack stalled under fire from the Union ships, but just in time two river steamers that the Confederates had converted into gunboats sailed into the harbor. The steamers were of the "cotton-clad" class, that is, the men on deck were protected by bales of cotton. One of the vessels, the *Neptune*, was sunk by a shell from the *Harriet Lane*, but the surviving ship, the *Bayou City*, kept steaming ahead, its sharpshooters firing from behind cotton bales at the crews on the copper-plated hulls of the Union gunboats. Then it rammed the *Harriet Lane* and boarded her. Both of the *Harriet Lane*'s senior officers were mortally wounded in the hand-to-hand fighting. The ship's second in command, Edward Lea, had a father who was in Galveston with the Confederate forces. The senior Lea boarded the captured ship, found his son, and held him as he died. The boy's last words were "My father is here."

After another of Renshaw's ships ran aground in the battle, he ordered the withdrawal of the Union fleet and decided to blow up his own flagship before it could fall into Confederate hands. In the process, he accidentally blew himself up as well. The recapture of Galveston heartened Texans, with what one writer described as "an electric thrill." Union strategists, on the other hand, were profoundly irritated at the loss of a port that they considered almost as crucial as Mobile and New Orleans.

The electric thrill of Magruder's victory was quickly transmitted up the Brazos River to the little town of Travis, where Lucy Stevens, the young woman who had attended the secession pageant at Baylor a year and a half before, heard the news from her Uncle Pier. She and a group of girls had spent New Year's afternoon fortune-telling, consulting the drops of coffee in a teaspoon for cosmic clues about when they would be married. All of them, the teaspoon said, would be married within a year—except for Lucy's friend Sallie. "She poor child," Lucy mourned to her diary, "was to wait eleven."

Lucy spent the next few days knitting socks for Confederate soldiers and fretting about a rumored uprising of "Dutch & Negroes." The rumor was false, and so far the war had not brought great hardship to her family or circumscribed its bounteous New Year's Day menu—"Baked ribs, sausage, liver hash, sweet potatoes, fried & egg bread & sure enough coffee." But even though Galveston was back in Confederate hands, the Union blockade was tightening. The next Christmas, Lucy's cousin Sarah wrote in her diary: "No stocking hung up tonight for the first time, Santa Claus cannot run the blockade."

In the summer of 1863, Vicksburg fell to Ulysses Grant's armies, giving them control of the Mississippi and effectively cleaving Texas and the rest of the Trans-Mississippi from the main body of the Confederacy. But the Union had not given up on invading Texas, especially with the French up to destabilizing mischief in Mexico. That September, a Union fleet from New Orleans that included four gunboats and twenty-two transport ships carrying an expeditionary force of five thousand troops tried to establish a beachhead at Sabine Pass, the narrow channel at the border of Texas and Louisiana where the Sabine River threads its way into the Gulf. From there the Federals planned to follow the railroad west to capture Houston.

The upper part of the channel was guarded by a fort built of earth and logs by slave labor, and manned by forty-seven Irish dockworkers known as the Davis Guards. In the fort were six pieces of artillery under the command of Lieutenant Richard Dowling, a Houston saloon magnate who was the "President and Cashier" of the Bank of Bacchus, a sort of theme bar that cheekily masqueraded as a financial institution, offering "exchanges," "drafts," and "deposits" in the form of drinkable currency.

Dowling and his few dozen men and his six guns were all that stood in the way of a massive Union invasion force. The artillery crews in the fort had been drilling for weeks, sighting their smoothbore cannon and howitzers at stakes driven into the channel for target practice. On the morning of September 8, they hunkered down and held their fire while a heavily armed Union side-wheel steamer, the *Clifton*, entered the channel and began blasting away at the fort. After a while the *Clifton* withdrew, returning that afternoon with the three other gunboats. The four vessels advanced up the channel to attack the fort and to cover the landing of Union troops farther downstream.

Dowling's men were waiting for the ships to reach the target stakes that had been driven into the channel. Two of their cannon faced north and couldn't yet be trained on an enemy coming from the south. That left them with four artillery pieces against the combined twenty-six heavy guns on board the attacking ships. And against the 1,200 men that would be landed during the bombardment to attack the fort from the landward side. When Dowling's men finally opened fire, they made up for what they lacked in ordnance numbers with precision, steady nerves, and a dangerously rapid firing rate that left them with powder burns and seared hands from over-heated barrels they had no time to let cool. In less than an hour, two of the Union gunships were knocked out of the fight and left in the channel for the rebels to seize as prizes. The other two, along with the transport ships full of the Union soldiers who never had a chance to step onto the mucky marshland to invade Texas, steamed back out into the Gulf. In their startled necessity to get back to New Orleans as soon as possible, the surviving ships had to lighten their loads, throwing ammunition, rations, and wagons overboard. The mules that had been brought along to haul supplies for the invasion were jettisoned as well. So that they wouldn't have a chance of swimming to shore and falling into enemy use, their legs were hobbled before they were pushed overboard. The armada steamed away as the terrified mules struggled in vain to keep their noses above the green Gulf waters.

The unlikely victory at the Battle of Sabine Pass was a jolt of inspiration for Confederate Texans. The powder-burned members of the garrison received a special medal and the praise of Jefferson Davis, who described the battle as "one of the most brilliant and heroic achievements in the history of the war." Dick Dowling's hero status rose to Alamo-defender levels. "With throbbing hearts," went the patriotic verse composed by Mrs. M. J. Young, "and lifted hands / We name him—'DOWLING! OF THE PASS'!" In 1905, he was commemorated with a monument in the center of Houston, an honor that Sam Houston himself did not receive until twenty years later.

But the Union was not through with the idea of invading Texas, and several months later seven thousand troops came ashore without resistance at Brazos Island, just north of the mouth of the Rio Grande. They were commanded by Napoleon Jackson Tecumseh Dana, the homesick young lieutenant who had written letters of such explicit longing to his wife, Sue, in

1846 from Zachary Taylor's camp in Corpus Christi. The war had brought him back to the Texas coast as a major general in the Union army, bearing wounds suffered at Cerro Gordo during the Mexican-American War and more recently at Sharpsburg. His men quickly invested Brownsville and made their presence known as far north as Matagorda Island. They were supported by the Texas Union Cavalry under Edmund Davis and John Haynes, who seized key positions along the lower Rio Grande.

It looked like a massive Union thrust into Texas from the coast was imminent, and the Confederates steeled themselves to meet it. "Shall the Lincolnites tread on our forefathers' dust?" asked another poem, urgently and prosaically titled "The Expected Texas Invasion": "The answer reverberates—nay!"

But the great battle for the Texas homeland never occurred. Most of the Union troops along the coast were withdrawn, leaving only a small force of 1,200 men at Brazos Island. A Texas cavalry force under Rip Ford reoccupied Brownsville and retook control of the Rio Grande.

Meanwhile, the Union troops that had been withdrawn from Texas were redeployed for an invasion of the state from the northeast via the Red River. If it succeeded, the expedition, under General Nathaniel Banks, would bring all of Louisiana under Union control, isolate Texas from the rest of the Confederacy, and capture 150,000 bales of cotton stored in Shreveport. It didn't succeed. A Confederate attack under General Richard Taylor smashed Banks's army at the Battle of Mansfield in northern Louisiana on April 8, 1864, and pursued them to a village called Pleasant Hill, where another furious battle was fought the next day. After Pleasant Hill, the Union forces were in retreat, the grand prospects of seizing Shreveport and penetrating Texas via the Red River in ruins.

The invasion of Texas had been checked, but in a war that would not be won. Members of Hood's Texas Brigade—"shot to pieces," in the words of one veteran—were among the Texans present when Robert E. Lee surrendered the Army of Northern Virginia to General Grant at Appomattox Court House on April 9, 1865. Out of the 5,300 men who had served in the brigade, only 617 were left.

There was defiance at first. Even as the paroled Confederate troops were making their way back to Texas, the governor, Pendleton Murrah, was urging Texans to fight on. So were General Magruder and Lieutenant General Edmund Kirby Smith, who headed the Trans-Mississippi Department of the Confederacy and had yet to surrender the fraying army under his command. That did not happen until June. After that, Smith, Magruder, and Murrah, along with other prominent officers and officials of Confederate Texas, fled to Mexico.

A little over a month after Appomattox, a few weeks before Kirby Smith's surrender, there was an anticlimactic final Civil War battle. It was fought at a place called Palmito Ranch, not far from the old Palo Alto battlefield amid the chaparral and barren sand flats east of Brownsville. The federal force on Brazos Island, among them the black troops of the Sixty-Second Regiment of the U.S. Colored Troops, had crossed over from the island to attack Confederate positions on the mainland.

"This may be the last fight of the war," Rip Ford mused to himself, just before leading a cavalry charge that broke the Union lines. It *was* the last fight of the war, and Confederate Texans had won it. "Boys," Ford told his men when it was over, "we have done finely."

Ford reported that he had only five men wounded, though it may have been more. The casualties were higher for the federal forces, several dozen killed and wounded. Among the dead men lying in the sand beneath the South Texas sun that day was a twenty-two-year-old Union soldier from Indiana named John Jefferson Williams, the very last man to die in the Civil War.

——————— ★ ———————

"THE DREAM IS OVER," AMELIA BARR WROTE IN HER DIARY ON May 25. "No southern independence now." She wept as the soldiers from the Rio Grande, victorious at Palmito Ranch but defeated in the larger war, paraded through the streets of Austin. "Through every deprivation and suffering, through hunger and thirst, though heat and cold, weary, ragged, weather-beaten and battle-scarred, they had carried aloft their flag with the single star." She was less moved when the men paraded into the Capitol and demanded to be paid in gold or real estate, or when they began looting the government stables the next day.

About a month later, a Union general named Gordon Granger arrived in Galveston. He issued a series of general orders. General Order Number 3 read, in its most crucial part, "The people of Texas are informed that, in accordance with a proclamation from the Executive of the United States, all slaves are free."

It was June 19—a day that would be commemorated and celebrated by the word "Juneteenth." "When Marse Bob came home," a slave named Andrew Goodman recalled when the news of emancipation reached Smith County, "he sent for all the slaves. He was sitting in a yard chair, all tuckered out, and shook hands all around, and said he was glad to see us. Then he said, 'I've got something to tell you. You are just as free as I am. You don't belong to nobody but yourselves. We went to war and fought, and the Yankees done whipped us, and they say the niggers are free. You can go where you want to go, or you can stay here, just as you like. He couldn't help but cry."

Jeff Hamilton, Sam Houston's slave, was already free, or at least that was his impression. It might not have been strictly true, since at the time of Houston's death his twelve slaves were still listed as personal assets. But according to Hamilton, Houston had called all his slaves together after Lincoln issued his preliminary Emancipation Proclamation in September 1862. "You, and each of you, are now free," he told them.

Whether it was a legal act or just a magnanimous rhetorical gesture, Hamilton remembered it fondly. Houston was almost seventy by then, in failing health, living in a commodious rented house in Huntsville that was shaped like a steamboat. Officially retired from public life, he was far from retiring when it came to his opinions or his legacy. When General Hébert placed the state under martial law in May 1862, Houston was once stopped by a sentry who asked to see his pass from the provost marshal. "Go to San Jacinto," he told the soldier, "and learn my right to travel in Texas."

One day, toward the end of his life, Houston ordered Jeff Hamilton to drive him from his namesake city to that storied old battlefield on Buffalo Bayou. On the way, Houston sat in silence, remembering. When they got to San Jacinto, he climbed painfully down from the buggy, feeling the old war wounds that had never healed. He sat down beneath the very tree where he had received Santa Anna as a prisoner. He sat there "for a long time," Hamilton wrote, "never speaking to me or looking at me. He had a far-off look in his eyes, which I couldn't help but notice were wet."

He died in the Steamboat House of pneumonia, in the presence of Margaret and all his children but one, on July 26, 1863. His last words were "Texas! Texas! Margaret."

— 24 —

RECONSTRUCTED

ONE OF THE PEOPLE PROCLAIMED FREE ON JUNETEENTH
was a woman named Lucy Grimes. She lived in the East
Texas secessionist stronghold of Harrison County and
worked in the household of a white woman, also named
Grimes, to whom Lucy had presumably been enslaved until
emancipation. Lucy had a child, ten or twelve years old, who
found some money lying around in the house one day and went outside to
play with it. Mrs. Grimes, outraged, ordered Lucy to whip her child as punishment for theft. When Lucy wouldn't do it, Mrs. Grimes called on two
men named Anderson and Simpson.

Anderson and Simpson were both former Confederate soldiers.
Anderson came from a respectable family, but Simpson was a "desperado."
Mrs. Grimes told them that she wanted Lucy punished for disobeying her.
The men then abducted Lucy and took her into a pine forest two miles from
the house. They tore off her clothes, whipped her viciously with either a
whip or a strap, and then took a club and beat her head in. Her grown son
went looking for her when she didn't come home and discovered her lying
in the woods. She either was dead when he found her or died soon after.

The son went to see Lieutenant Colonel H. S. Hall to report the murder of his mother. Hall was the subassistant commissioner for freedmen in

the northeastern district of Texas. He had commanded U.S. Colored Troops during the war, had lost an arm at Petersburg, and was now one of the military officers charged with maintaining order in Texas until a government could be established that would be loyal enough to the Union for the former Confederate state to be readmitted to the United States.

Hall wanted to see justice done for this brutal murder, but the chief justice of the county court refused to issue a warrant. There was no one to testify in the case except Lucy Grimes's son, he said, and "negro testimony" was not allowed in Texas courts. Her killers therefore went free.

Lucy Grimes was killed in December 1865, more than half a year after Kirby Smith's surrender ended the Civil War in Texas. She was no longer a slave, but not yet a citizen, and in the eyes of Anderson and Simpson probably not even a full human being. She lived in a time and place in which she could be savagely murdered with impunity over a trivial matter. Peace may have come to Texas, but it was a grudging peace, an imposed peace. During his months in Texas, Colonel Hall had become acquainted with many of the area's most prominent citizens, the wealthy planters and professional men who now lived under the military jurisdiction of the government that had defeated the South. They acknowledged their situation but chafed at their powerlessness and waited for the world to be turned right again.

"There seems to be a very general desire—an earnest wish," Hall testified to a congressional committee, "to be immediately admitted into the Union, which takes the shape of a demand of an absolute right. But there is no real love expressed for the government; on the contrary, there is an expression of hatred for the people of the north, and of Yankees generally, while the idea seems to be that they should at once obtain possession of the political privileges and powers which they once had."

The decade following the end of the Civil War was the era of Reconstruction, a time when the balance of power in Texas surged dramatically between victors and vanquished, when a bold new promise of social justice rose and then collapsed and then lingered unfulfilled far into the next century and the next.

———————— ★ ————————

THE TEXAS CAPITOL, WHERE SAM HOUSTON HAD SAT WHITTLING while refusing to answer the call to take the Confederate oath of office, burned down in November 1881. It was replaced seven years later by a commanding structure of red granite whose dome, crowned by a statue of a grimacing Goddess of Liberty, reaches 566 feet above the ground. The building is dominated by a great central rotunda, which rests beneath the echoing

The Goddess of Liberty statue, sixteen feet high, was the crowning touch when the new Texas State Capitol building was completed in 1888. She helped boost the building's height, making it fifteen feet higher than the national capitol. One-upping Washington, DC, has always been a Texas priority.

218-foot-high vault of the interior dome. The curved wall on all four floors of the rotunda features official portraits of Texas governors, going back (and up) to Henry Smith. Every time a new governor is inaugurated, the portrait of the outgoing one is moved a space to the left. When there is no more room on the ground floor, the procession of older governors spirals up into the higher floors of the dome.

Recently, I climbed the stairs to the third floor, where Sam Houston and most of the circa-1860s governors were currently displayed. I was curious to see whether there was a portrait of Andrew Jackson Hamilton. There was. It shows a man with a neat haircut and a mild-looking middle-manager face. His upper lip is clean shaven, but he has an explosive chin beard that reaches down to his chest buttons and is distinguished by two perfectly parallel columns of gray.

I was unsure whether Hamilton would be honored with an official state portrait because he was not an elected governor, but an appointed one. He was placed in that role by Andrew Johnson, who became president upon the assassination of Lincoln. Hamilton presided over Texas as it wrote a new constitution and formed a new government that would renounce secession, renounce slavery, and prove its loyalty to the United States.

Hamilton was well known in Texas and in Washington. He had represented the state in Congress, where he had worked unsuccessfully to try to turn back the tide of secession. He was back in Texas during the first year or so of the war, but it was an uncomfortable place to be a Unionist Democrat, so he slipped away to Mexico and eventually to Washington, ending up as a brigadier general in the Union army. (His wife, Mary Jane, stayed behind in Austin, where reprisals swiftly fell upon her and the six Hamilton children. While she was visiting friends one day, arsonists burned down their home.)

The postwar Texas that President Johnson turned over to provisional governor Hamilton was a wide canvas of grief (tens of thousands of Texans dead or wounded) and of violence and social chaos. The war had taken a deep toll in all sorts of ways, but thanks to people like Dick Dowling and his Irish cannoneers at Sabine Pass, Texas had managed to escape the destruction that would have followed an outright invasion. The state's economic basis had more or less survived. Throughout the war, ranchers were at the mercy of raids from Indians emboldened by the pullout of U.S. forces and from bandits and deserters from the Confederate army. But they were still able to get their livestock to market through and into Mexico. Members of the planter class (those with twenty or more slaves) were still able to get in their crops during the war. Cotton could not be shipped from blockaded ports like Galveston, and so, like cattle, had to take advantage of a Mexican workaround. Had one of the land or sea invasions succeeded, the slaves on those plantations and farms might have fled to Union lines, but as it turned out most of them had little choice but to remain where they were, keeping their heads down and waiting to see what happened next.

Now the war was over and the slaves were free, but nothing about that radical change was simple. Planters still needed workers, and former slaves needed a way to support themselves. In many cases, the solution was an uneasy accommodation: free blacks worked for former masters either for wages or for shares as tenant farmers. Sometimes the difference between outright slavery and voluntary employment dissolved into a rhetorical distinction. A contract might bind blacks to long hours, restrict their movements, keep them living in the same quarters they had inhabited as slaves, and throw them on the mercy of the landowner for food and clothing, whose cost was deducted from their wages.

The Bureau of Refugees, Freedmen, and Abandoned Lands, better known as the Freedmen's Bureau, was a scattershot agency established by Congress to intervene in such conditions, to keep an eye out for unjust treatment both in the courts and in the cotton fields, to help establish black schools, and to prevent former slaves from being casually lynched or shot down in the streets. In trying to safeguard the passage of African Americans from bondage to something like viable citizenship, the Freedmen's Bureau had a big job to do, and a big hostile state to do it in. It was a quasi-military institution, an agency of the U.S. Army that was headed in Texas by a rapidly rotating cast of high-ranking Union officers. Many of the fifty or so men who served as its district agents were army officers as well. The army was theoretically the enforcing arm of the bureau, but the federal troops that entered the state in great numbers just after the war (mostly as a show of force against the French on the Mexican border) were quickly demobilized, leaving a scant force of just three thousand to contend with the infinite violations of comity likely to rise among a seething Texas populace coming to terms with the reality of conquest and occupation.

The Freedmen's Bureau had civilian agents as well. Some of them were northern postwar arrivistes regarded as opportunists and labeled across the defeated South as carpetbaggers. Some were from the antisecessionist, pro-Reconstruction ranks of Texas residents labeled derogatorily as scalawags. And a few, like George T. Ruby, were black.

Ruby was born in New York in 1841, was educated in Portland, Maine, and traveled to Haiti as a correspondent for the *Pine and Palm*, a Boston newspaper "devoted to the interests of freedom, and of the colored races of America." He was urbane and ambitious, with friendly but piercing eyes, a precise part in his hair, and facial hair in the style of a garland that draped over his thin cheeks. He worked as a teacher in Louisiana, but after being beaten by a white mob there, came to Texas in 1866. In Galveston, he took another teaching job, joined the Union League (a secret political organization designed to bolster Republican candidates and organize black votes), and began work as a traveling agent for the Freedmen's Bureau. He formed Union League chapters along the way, honing the listening skills and forming the political contacts that would later make him a player in Texas state government.

But he would have to wait to take his place in the political arena. History wasn't quite ready to seat him yet. There were no African Americans among the elected delegates to the 1866 convention charged with writing a new state constitution for Texas. No African Americans in Texas were yet allowed to vote. In calling the convention, Governor Hamilton was serious about bringing Texas into line with the Reconstruction conditions expected by the federal government. When it came to the political rights of freedmen, though, those expectations were light. President Johnson, who had already twice vetoed civil rights bills passed by his warring Republican Congress, had no great interest in extending suffrage or much else to former slaves except the raw freedom that had been granted to them by the Thirteenth Amendment. His instructions to Hamilton, in the proclamation that appointed him provisional governor, were palpably fuzzy. They merely invested the delegates to the convention "with authority to exercise within the limits of said State all the powers necessary and proper to enable such loyal people of the State of Texas to restore said State to its constitutional relations to the Federal Government."

Reading between the lines, and aware of Johnson's increasingly testy relationship with his radical Congress, Hamilton thought it would be a good idea for the convention to at least ratify the Thirteenth Amendment. To bring Texas back into the embrace of the Union, the convention would also need to renounce secession and repudiate the state's Confederate war debt. He went as far as to argue that to guarantee readmission to the Union, the convention should grant the rights of citizenship—even, possibly, the vote—to freed slaves. The delegates to the convention and the men who voted for them (women's suffrage was still a long way into the next century) were required by Johnson's Amnesty Proclamation to take an oath. "I do solemnly swear or affirm," it went, "in the presence of Almighty God, that I will henceforth faithfully support and defend the Constitution of the United States and the Union of the States thereunder. And that I will, in like manner, abide by and faithfully support all laws and proclamations which have been made during the existing rebellion with reference to the emancipation of slaves, so help me God."

One can imagine the feelings boiling inside the former Confederates as they raised their hands to take that oath—men who had fought, been wounded, lost sons in a bitter war against that same Union of the States. But enough of them sincerely spoke or merely spat out the words to qualify as delegates. The convention, which assembled in Austin in February, was dominated by men who had served as officers or enlisted men in the Confederate army. Not all of them convened in a spirit of defiance. Some of them had been Unionists and had voted against secession, but when the war came, they loyally and gravely took up arms to fight for Texas. Others were pragmatists and moderates whose main priority was just to put the pieces of their former world back together.

Radical Unionists were also part of the political fabric of the convention, but when it came time to elect officers and write the constitution, they were outgunned by a conservative coalition formed from the reanimated remains of the Democratic power elite that had existed before the war. One big item on their agenda, in the words of former Texas Supreme Court justice and secession leader Oran M. Roberts: "keep Sambo from the polls."

The delegates were willing to renounce secession, but not in the way the Union radicals wanted them to—to declare it had been null and void from the beginning. That would have meant that every Texas law or act passed during the war was null and void as well. They argued over this ab initio question like philosophers for a month. It encompassed crucial issues of practicality—were marriages invalidated? were debts?—but at its core was a lingering something about honor and pride. Calling secession fundamentally null and void meant subtly admitting that there had never been any constitutional basis for secession, that the states had not just liberated themselves from the U.S. government but had committed treason against it.

In the end, the delegates did vote to renounce the right of secession, but not in the retroactive way that the ab initio stance implied. They did not, as Hamilton urged them to do, ratify the Thirteenth Amendment, but they at least bowed to the reality that it existed and that slavery was abolished. And any generosity of spirit that the new constitution extended to the people who had once been slaves was limited. Blacks would be allowed to own and sell property and to testify in court if the case in question pertained to them. "A system of public schools for Africans and their children" was written into the new constitution, to be paid for by taxes imposed specifically on black people. But contrary to the hopes of radical Unionists, and of course of freedmen themselves, blacks would not be allowed to vote, hold office, or serve on juries.

The voters of Texas ratified the constitution in June 1866, an election in which they also chose a new governor, whose face can be found next to Hamilton's on the portrait carousel in the Capitol rotunda. James Throckmorton was a doctor turned lawyer turned politician, and a Whig turned Democrat. He had been a Sam Houston man before the war, had voted against secession, and had even been in the room when Houston burned the letter from Abraham Lincoln offering him federal troops to help Texas stay in the Union. Despite his antisecessionist stance, and despite his chronic debilitating kidney problems, Throckmorton fought on the Confederate side in the war and emerged from it as a thoroughgoing conservative, primed to lead the fight against African American rights and the radical Republican Congress in Washington. To the most hardened minds in Throckmorton's Conservative Union Party, the word "Reconstruction" was understood to mean something more like "Restoration," a putting back into place the undisturbed Texas that once had been.

Running against Throckmorton was Elisha Pease. Pease was from the Texas revolutionary generation. He had been with the "Come and Take It" men at Gonzales, had helped write the republic's constitution, and had already held the office of governor, from 1853 to 1857. As governor, he had been farseeing, establishing hospitals, erecting state buildings, helping create the financial architecture that would fund public schools and universities. But 1866 was a nearsighted time, dominated by the same great overriding theme that promises to endure in Texas unto eternity: get the federal government off our backs.

Throckmorton outballoted Pease by an overwhelming four-to-one margin. The new constitution was approved as well. The legislature that convened after the election promptly refused to ratify the Fourteenth Amendment, which would have granted the full benefits of citizenship to African Americans, a population that many white Texans still thought should, by divine ordinance, be slaves. They believed the sentiments contained in the "Declaration of Causes" stating why Texas had seceded from the Union, a document that warned of "the debasing doctrine of the equality of all men, irrespective of race or color—a doctrine at war with nature."

Instead of ratifying the Fourteenth Amendment, the legislature codified the limitations to be imposed on freedmen's lives. Texas's "black codes" were not as harsh as those enacted by some other southern states, but the line they drew was clear enough: no voting, no jury service, no court testimony in any case that happened to involve a white person, no vagrancy, no impudence, no riding in the same railway cars as whites. Black people could not work for more than a month without signing a contract—filed with the county clerk—that essentially turned their lives over to the needs of their employers. Limits on their personal conduct were backed by force of law. Legislators spelled out financial punishments against black workers who pretended to be sick "for purposes of idleness." The state made it its business to ensure that household contractees "shall, at all hours of the day or night, and on all days of the week, promptly answer all calls . . . to be especially civil and polite to their employer, his family and guests."

Remember David Burnet, the interim president of the Republic of Texas, who had once chastised Sam Houston for being slow to fight Santa Anna? He was now seventy-eight. His wife was dead. His four children were dead as well, the last of them killed while fighting for the Confederacy in Alabama. He and Mirabeau Lamar had once planned to write a book that would cast what they regarded as some much-needed shade on the reputation of Sam Houston, but Lamar—who died in 1859—had devoted his final literary energies to a limp little book of poetry.

Burnet had one last role to play in Texas history, though it too would prove to be abortive. The legislature chose him and Oran Roberts as U.S. senators. But when they traveled to Washington in November 1866, along with a recently elected congressional delegation, they were blocked from taking their seats in the Senate and House chambers.

That August, President Johnson had proclaimed the insurrection in Texas officially over, adding even more hopefully that "peace, order, tranquillity, and civil authority now exist in and throughout the whole of the United States of America." But his political adversaries in Congress, who were steadily gaining the upper hand against Johnson, believed no such thing. They knew that Burnet and the others could not take the "Ironclad Oath," promulgated in 1862 but now required of governmental officers, affirming that they had never fought for or encouraged "any pretended government." The new Texas Constitution and the black codes its legislature had passed were clear evidence that Texas assumed it could just ease back into the Union without correcting its unredeemed attitudes about racial justice.

When the Radical Republicans decisively seized control of Congress in the 1866 midterm elections, they took away Johnson's velvet hammer of Reconstruction and hefted a sledgehammer. The first of their four Reconstruction Acts was passed one day in the spring of 1867. The date of March 2 may have been accidental, but an old-guard white Texan could not have seen it as anything but the ultimate historical insult. March 2 was Texas's sacred day of independence from Mexico, it was Sam Houston's birthday, it was the day when Texas voted to secede from the Union. Now it was the day that an uncommonly prideful region would once again find itself dominated by the rule makers in a distant federal capital.

Texas was placed under direct military control. General Philip Sheridan commanded the district that oversaw Texas. In charge of Texas itself

was General Charles Griffin, who had fought in Mexico and in the bloodiest campaigns of the Civil War. Impatient and quick-tempered, he did by
fiat what Texans had refused to bring about by law. He began the process of
registering voters—white and black. Taking the Ironclad Oath was required
of anybody wanting to cast a ballot or serve on a jury or run for office. Governor Throckmorton protested. Governor Throckmorton was removed from
office. He was replaced by Elisha Pease.

General Griffin himself was not long on the Texas scene. He was engaged in the business of removing district and state supreme court judges
suspected of disloyalty when he died that September of yellow fever at the
age of forty-one. He was replaced by another general, Joseph Reynolds, who
continued the work of undermining the old secessionist power base and
replacing it with loyal Unionists and newly enfranchised blacks.

For Texas to be readmitted into the Union, it needed yet another new
constitution, one that seriously confronted the new promise of racial equality. So another constitutional convention was convened and more delegates
were elected. This time the convention was dominated not by the former
Confederates who had produced the rejected 1866 constitution but by a
resurgent wave of scalawags, that is, homegrown Texas Unionists. And
there was another big difference in the cast of characters who reported for
duty in the state Capitol in June 1868. There were ten delegates, ten people,
whose presence in this gathering as voting members would have been—only
a few years earlier—utterly unimaginable to most Texans.

The ten delegates were black men. The polished, freeborn, highly educated, well-traveled New Englander George Ruby was one of them. The
others had been born slaves. Most of them had, by one means or another,
learned to read and write. Each had emerged from slavery and carved out
a profession—wheelwright, cobbler, blacksmith, Methodist preacher. They
were politically ambitious, or they wouldn't have been there. They had been
aided in their rise by the Freedmen's Bureau and had met crucial constituents in the secret conclaves of the Union League.

The Union League wasn't the only secret society in Texas during that
summer of 1868. There were also the Knights of the White Camelia, the
Knights of the Rising Sun, and—seeping into the state earlier in the year—
something called the Ku Klux Klan. The Klan started out in Tennessee as
a self-consciously cryptic social club, with ghostlike robes and hoods and
absurd leadership titles like Grand Cyclops or Grand Magi. But when it
came to the men who were drawn to the Klan there was only a fine line between the spoofy and the sinister.

The constitutional convention, a chaotic and contentious affair, lasted through the summer, ran out of funds and out of gas, reconvened in December, and finally stumbled to a discordant end in February of the next year. While the delegates debated the tired old ab initio question regarding secession, the Klan was busy with an agenda of intimidation and murder, raiding black political rallies and Freedmen's Bureau schools throughout northeastern Texas. In Jefferson, a deep-woods town of ten thousand that was an important port on the Red River, the head of the Freedmen's Bureau was an idealistic young white man named George Washington Smith. A New Yorker who had been wounded at Gettysburg, he had come to Jefferson after the war to go into business with his uncle. He had political ambitions and had been elected as a delegate to the constitutional convention, but he was home in October while the convention was in recess. "He was correct," one of his colleagues remembered, "almost austere. He never drank, smoked, chewed, nor used profane language."

For too many of the white citizens of Marion County, Smith's presence in their midst was a chronic outrage. His fervent work on behalf of African Americans could only be explained as some sort of unnatural interracial impulse, an "unbridled licentiousness." In the end, he was a carpetbagger who died because of his carpetbag. On the way home from a political rally, he had given his valise into the keeping of several local freedmen, who were then robbed by local white vigilantes. Smith's demand that the bag be returned to him led to an argument, which led to a gunfight. Smith escaped unhurt and gave himself up to an army major in charge of the local Freedmen's Bureau, who unfortunately turned him over to the local authorities. "If you surrender me to these men," he told the major, "they will kill me."

He was right. A mob made up of members of the Knights of the Rising Sun overwhelmed the soldiers guarding the calaboose, executed two of the freedmen who had been arrested with Smith, and then forced their way into Smith's cell. The cornered prisoner fought off with his fists the first man who came inside and desperately tried to bar the others by throwing his weight against the door, but it was soon over. After Smith was shot in the head, each of the eighteen or so assailants took turns firing a symbolic bullet into his body—"that each one might participate in the triumph."

A local newspaper, the *Jefferson Times*, concluded in a satisfactory tone that Smith's murder was more than justified: "The sanctity of home, the peace and safety of society, the prosperity of the country, and the security of life itself demanded the removal of so base a villain."

In July, in the town of Millican, a railroad community in Brazos County, there was a bloody event that contemporary newspapers and subsequent histories referred to as a "riot," but that Governor Pease, writing to his wife,

Lucadia, was probably much closer to the mark in calling a "massacre." The particulars are hazy, but the violence apparently started when the Ku Klux Klan descended upon Millican during a Methodist church service led by an activist black preacher named George Brooks. The freedmen in Brooks's congregation were accustomed to going about armed to protect themselves against just such a visit. They fired back, the Klan retreated, and both sides prepared for outright war. Brooks organized a militia to protect the freedmen's community where most of the African Americans lived. But soon train cars heading toward Millican were filled with armed and aggrieved white men: local peace officers, rowdies recruited from saloons and whorehouses, and vengeance-minded Klansmen. The black "riot" that followed when this force assaulted the freedmen's community left only blacks dead—as many as fifty or sixty of them. There were no white casualties. Brooks appears to have been killed in the fight or tracked down and murdered later.

For the alarmed white citizens of East Texas, the Millican battle was just another example of how the natural order that they and their ancestors had fought for and believed in was coming apart in front of their eyes. In the opinion of a Kentucky newspaper called the *Hickman Courier*, the constitutional convention then meeting in Austin was determined "to disarm all the whites, arm all the negroes . . . and establish negro supremacy upon the basis of both law and brute force. It is a terrible state of things, truly."

Perhaps no one could have lamented the old world that was passing away with more authority than Henry McCulloch, the younger brother of Ben McCulloch and almost his equal in Texas Ranger lore. Reacting to the Millican troubles, the Plum Creek veteran and former Confederate general wrote a letter to the editor of an Austin newspaper from a locality called "Ranger's Home." He wrote with a plaintive, how-could-this-be-happening tone. He had never countenanced violence, he said, but enough was enough. The time had come for people to defend themselves against Radical Republican rule, against the carpetbaggers who were stirring up "the poor, ignorant, misguided negroes." Everything would be fine if the officers of the Freedman's Bureau and the Union League would just leave Texans to sort things out for themselves and run their own affairs. Instead, the offices of the state were "filled by men who have no sympathies with or regard for the welfare of the people among whom they simply live, as masters, whose political prejudices will not enable them to look upon a late rebel as anything less than a demon, sent from the region of darkness, and who can look upon a carpet-bagger, radical, scalawag or negro as not inferior to an angel sent from the regions of the blessed, and negroes not only equals, but superiors, socially and politically, to any true Southern gentlemen."

THE DELEGATES TO THE 1868–1869 CONSTITUTIONAL CONVEN-
tion never quite succeeded in writing a constitution. Even though the secessionist Democrats had been mostly sidelined in the gathering, there was no
particular harmony among the Republicans, who were split between moderate and radical factions. The radicals, led by the convention president, E. J. Davis, wanted to deny
the vote to former Confederates.
They also wanted to divide the state
in half, to simply jettison the "dark
corner of the Confederacy" and
create a new state out of western
Texas that would be an enlightened,
Union-minded utopia. In the end,
it all dissolved into procedural warfare and almost into outright violence, to the point that pistols were
drawn. When the delegates finally
left the hall, an army officer called in
to protect Davis ordered the doors
nailed shut.

E. J. DAVIS,
a fervent anti-secessionist, fled to Mexico and
fought for the Union. When the Civil War was
over, he returned to Texas and served as governor
during Reconstruction, only to discover that there
was still "a slow civil war going on here."

A constitution finally emerged
from the fracas, though it was
signed by only forty-five of the
ninety delegates and had to be
cobbled together from the official records, which had to be pried from the hands of an assistant secretary who was arrested while running away with them. The new document,
though, succeeded where the 1866 Constitution had failed, at least when it
came to meeting the demands of the Republican Congress in Washington
for readmitting Texas to the Union. Its most crucial provision was found in
Article VI, which granted the right to vote to every male citizen "without
distinction of race, color or former condition."

In the statewide elections of November 1869, the voters of Texas—which
now included 56,905 duly registered African American men—approved the
new constitution and, with exquisite narrowness (a margin of 809 votes
out of almost 80,000 cast), chose E. J. Davis over A. J. Hamilton for governor. For the first time, black Texans were elected to public office—twelve to

MATTHEW GAINES
was one of the first black Texans elected to public office after a raucous
constitutional convention gave African Americans the right to vote.

the House and two to the Senate. Among them were the polished George Ruby and a former slave preacher named Matthew Gaines. At five feet and 125 pounds, Gaines was a bantamweight political fighter, but fearless and uncompromising. "He has neither [the] culture nor shrewdness of Ruby," a newspaper writer observed with what was probably admiration, "but has more hard stupid sense."

After the Texas Legislature ratified the Thirteenth, Fourteenth, and Fifteenth Amendments to the U.S. Constitution in February 1870, President Ulysses Grant signed a bill restoring Texas to the Union. Reconstruction was formally over, but the Civil War showed every sign of smoldering into eternity.

Governor Edmund Jackson Davis: "Certainly the name of no Texan," wrote the historian Charles William Ramsdell, "has gone down to posterity so hated as his." Ramsdell made this judgment in 1910, long before posterity had rolled out to its present extent. It was probably true enough at the time, at least among a plurality of white Texans, for whom Reconstruction and the Republican state government that arrived in its wake remained a live and bitter memory. Most of us might think differently today, just as we might find the pages of Ramsdell's seminal Reconstruction history to be filled with musty attitudes and misty Confederate memories. Here, for example, is Ramsdell describing, in what seems like approving terms, the terror inflicted on black communities by night-riding Klansmen: "Sometimes giant horsemen, shrouded in ghostly white, some of them headless, passed at midnight through the negro settlements, disarming and frightening the superstitious freedmen out of their senses, but otherwise doing no harm. A community thus visited was usually quiet for some time thereafter."

The governor that so many white Texans at the time thought of as a tyrant was, according to a much friendlier assessment, "a magnificent specimen of manhood, standing over six feet, broad shouldered, deep-chested, strong and clean-limbed, with a face whose every feature denoted inflexible will and a courage that would not quail before any danger."

Davis had been a strong antisecessionist in the days leading up to the Civil War and a vigorous fighter for the Union cause after it broke out. He was in San Antonio, serving as a district judge, when General Twiggs was forced to surrender the city to the insurgent Texans under Ben McCulloch. One of the federal officers in San Antonio who was briefly imprisoned by the rebels was the commander of the Second U.S. Cavalry, Lieutenant Colonel Robert E. Lee. Davis and Lee spent some time together afterward, and Davis did his best to convince his new friend to set his ancestral loyalty to Virginia aside and fight for the Union. But both Davis and Lee knew that that wasn't going to happen. When they finally said good-bye, they shook hands in tears.

Davis refused to take the Confederate oath, and as a result had to flee to Mexico, and then to New Orleans and Washington, where he offered his services to Lincoln to help take Texas back for the Union. When his strong-willed wife, Lizzie, tried to follow her husband out of Texas, with their two young children, she was informed by a former groomsman at her wedding, now a Confederate colonel, that if she attempted to cross the Rio Grande "you will be shot, and your body will float down the river." When she was later told that if her husband came back to Texas at the head of Union troops she should be prepared to have her throat cut, she said, echoing the brave words on the Gonzales battle flag, "Come and cut it!"

Lizzie Davis managed to smuggle herself and her children into Mexico without being murdered. Her husband, meanwhile, kept trying to smuggle himself in, along with the 1st Texas Cavalry regiment that he commanded. He was captured in Mexico and barely escaped being hanged. After some diplomatic back-and-forth he was released, and then he and his troops tried to get back into Texas again as part of the Union armada that was turned away by Dowling's men at Sabine Pass. He eventually made it onto Texas soil—or at least mud—when he landed with General Dana's forces at Brazos Santiago in November 1863. From there he pursued Santos Benavides's Confederate partisans up the Rio Grande, and even made efforts to recruit the mercurial Juan Cortina into a cross-border alliance with Union forces.

Now E. J. Davis was the leader of the state that he had been driven out of and that he had spent the war trying to recapture for the United States—an entity that many of his fellow citizens still regarded as an enemy country.

"There is a slow civil war going on here," he said in a speech shortly after his inauguration, "and has been ever since the surrender of the Confederate armies."

He was referring to the unflagging outlawry and vigilantism and partisan warfare that still gripped Texas, particularly in its eastern quadrant. The violence often manifested itself in grudge matches between families that quickly combusted into regional wars. Several of these entered Texas lore as famous feuds. There was, for instance, the Sutton-Taylor feud, a dark and long-running pageant of shootings, lynchings, and bushwhackings. There was the Lee-Peacock feud, which was centered on a cluster of northeastern Texas counties known as the Four Corners. The densest, gloomiest, most heavily forested corner was the Wildcat Thicket, where a not-so-former rebel guerrilla named Bob "Man Eater" Lee ensnarled himself in a bitter conflict with a Union League leader named Lewis Peacock. Two hundred people were dead before it was over, including both Lee and Peacock. Lee died first, by bullets or strychnine or maybe both. In reprisal, Peacock was ambushed by shotgun-wielding Man Eater partisans and blasted into bloody shreds on his way to the outhouse. A neighbor, at breakfast with his family, heard the shots and said, unsurprised, "There, they've got Peacock, I figure."

And then there was the Confederate deserter Cullen Montgomery Baker. He went by the gallant sobriquet of "Swamp Fox of the Sulphur" and inspired a novel by Louis L'Amour, but he seems to have been an unhappy alcoholic sociopath who never rose above drab and dreary criminality. He rampaged along the Texas-Louisiana border, targeting blacks and Freedmen's Bureau agents. "If I could sink this whole country into hell by stamping upon the ground," he once raged, "I would stamp with all my power, and send it and every living creature, with myself, into the infernal regions."

Everyone knew that Texas was riven with this sort of lawlessness, and that something needed to be done about it. But to out-of-power Democrats, to disenfranchised aristocrats of the former Confederacy, to a put-upon yeomanry that was far from ready to accept former slaves as fellow citizens, Governor Davis's new Republican government might as well have been Santa Anna all over again. The legislation bundles rolled out by the administration were quickly christened the Obnoxious Acts by their opponents, mostly because they strengthened the hand of the governor and centralized Republican power. The number of judicial districts was increased, allowing Davis to pack the courts with his own appointments. He controlled the registration of voters. His patronage powers extended to the vacant elective offices that needed to be filled at every level of state government. Elections were moved forward to give Davis and his fellow Republicans more time to consolidate their grip on the state. The governor had the power to designate which newspapers could print public notices, putting advertising revenue directly into the pockets of loyal Republican publications that would "radiate civilization into the darkest corners of the state."

Davis's law enforcement agenda rattled his Democratic opponents, who were already primed to think he was capable of dictatorial overreach. It was bad enough that he created a state militia, with the governor as its commander in chief, and empowered himself to declare martial law. But there was also his state police force, with a sizable number of armed African Americans in its ranks, perhaps as many as 30 percent. The State Police became known, among defiant white Texans, who had about as much desire to be policed from the power center in Austin as they did to be reconstructed by the federal government, as the "Governor's Hounds." A tombstone in Guadalupe County of a presumed offender has the governor's name wrong but the prevailing attitude right: "Thomas J. Smith 1869: Killed by W. W. Davis and his nigger police."

One place where the law had a particularly loose sway was Hill County, about sixty miles south of Dallas. Hill County was the home base of the notorious Kinch West gang and was already on Governor Davis's cleanup list when a black man and woman were murdered after they stopped at a grocery store. One of the killers was the son of James J. Gathings, the wealthiest man and biggest former slaveholder in the county, who was not happy about being made considerably less rich by emancipation. When the State Police pursued the killers to his house, Gathings told them, "You cannot search my house with your damned negro police." They entered the house anyway, with pistols drawn, but Gathings had stalled them long enough for his son and his associate to get away. Gathings then recruited a mob, "arrested" the policemen, and had a compliant local judge try them for forcible entry. The scene in the courtroom was tense, the black police officers on trial confronting a hostile crowd armed with shotguns and six-shooters. The defendants somehow managed to get bail and get out of town with their lives.

In response, Davis declared martial law in Hill County and levied a $3,000 fine on Gathings for assaulting the police. But his son got away with killing a man and a woman, and Gathings—"robbed," declared a newspaper writer, "by a negro State Policeman of $3,000 in gold"—was later reimbursed by the Democratic legislature that turned Davis out of office.

Davis also declared martial law in Walker County, where a sixty-eight-year-old freedman named Sam Jenkins had the audacity to press charges against a gang of white men who had beaten him almost to death. The men, after being no-billed by the grand jury, brazenly followed Jenkins out of the courtroom and shot him to death on the road home. A courageous district judge named J. P. Burnett issued an arrest warrant for the murder and put the men on trial. One night as he was leaving the courtroom, the judge narrowly missed being assassinated when the defendants' friends opened fire on him. While he was being shot at, another battle raged inside the courtroom, where the defendants themselves pulled concealed six-shooters provided by "benefactors" and opened fire on the State Police that were guarding them. Nobody was killed, but pretty much everybody was wounded. Two of the defendants escaped. The one who didn't—and was later finally convicted—was named Outlaw.

In Walker County, and in Limestone and Freestone Counties, where Davis also declared martial law, attempts at law enforcement had a way of resulting in insurrection, and sometimes almost into open race war. The town of Groesbeck was—or would soon become—the seat of Limestone County. It was located between the Brazos and the Trinity only a few miles from where Cynthia Ann Parker had been captured in 1836. In 1871, Groesbeck erupted into confused violence when four black members of the Special Police (a kind of State Police auxiliary force) attempted to arrest two white men in a bar. There was a shoot-out, one of the white men ran out, and the policemen shot him dead in the street. "Kill the damned nigger state police," the dead man's partner was heard shouting to the populace. Meanwhile, one of the policemen was quoted as proclaiming that he had "just killed a white son of a bitch."

The policemen dodged into the mayor's office to escape an escalating mob of outraged white citizens, who were soon pouring into the streets of Groesbeck armed with shotguns liberated from an auction house. The men were finally rescued from lynching by a posse of State Police led by a man named Merritt Trammell, who would later turn outlaw and become known as the "notorious negro."

The State Police had been created by Davis for a pragmatic and worthy reason—to protect the lives of freedmen and ordinary white citizens from terrorizing outlaw gangs—but that didn't mean the police didn't occasionally stoop to some extrajudicial killing of their own. The most egregious offender was Jack Helm, who had spiraled up like a bat from the dark caverns of the Sutton-Taylor feud. He already had a reputation as a notorious bushwhacker (on the Sutton side of the conflict) when he was somehow appointed a State Police captain. Probably under his orders, two brothers named Henry and William Kelly, who had recently been arrested, fined, and released for shooting up a circus in Lavaca County, were taken from their homes one August morning in 1870 by three men who were members of Helm's State Police company. "I think from the looks and actions of the men," Henry's wife, Amanda, warned the Kelly brothers' mother, "that they are after doing something wrong." Her instincts were precise. Watching from the trees, she saw the police shoot William Kelly in the act of lighting his pipe. Then they shot Amanda's husband, Henry, off his horse. "A general firing of guns by the party at the bodies on the ground by the parties then ensued," she wrote in her coolheaded report of the cold-blooded murder of her husband and brother-in-law.

Such outrages didn't do much to strengthen Governor Davis's hand when it came to his Republican government's brief reign and its attempt to impose civility and equality on a Texas not configured for either. The administration faced growing hostility from planters, who considered themselves overtaxed, and from railroad magnates, who demanded more and more state subsidies and debt relief. And its purity of purpose was undercut by corruption—the governor's adjutant general ran off to Belgium with $35,000 in stolen state funds. There was also plenty of history behind the adversarial reaction to Davis's reforms. Texas was still a hard frontier world. It had been seized from Mexico and from the Indians by force of arms and by an unpitying righteousness of thought. Its people—those who had not come there in bondage, those who had not been driven onto reservations or been culturally and politically overswamped, those who had not died in battle or of disease in the Civil War—were on high alert, suspecting that any change decreed from Austin would turn out to be a threat. They considered their financial well-being to be under assault, as well as their pride, as well as some standard of liberty they could never quite define but always stood ready to defend. Here was how their plight was described for them by Richard Coke in 1873 when he accepted the Democratic nomination for governor: "You have been living under a government given over to tyranny, usurpation, and violence to vested rights—to the rights of person and of property . . . have lived under a government that does not pretend to represent the people of Texas, to help the people of Texas, or to take any note of the wants of the people of Texas, but who derive all their inspiration from Washington City, their central depot."

Coke—a big man with a big booming voice—buried E. J. Davis in the election that followed, 85,549 votes to 42,663. The white voters he represented, wrote Charles Ramsdell, "were determined that E. J. Davis should never again rule over Texas, that radical-carpetbag-negro domination was to be ended."

But the election ended in chaos, and that was because of a semicolon. A man named Rodríguez had been arrested for voting more than once. His attorneys argued that he was innocent because the election itself was illegal. Why was that? Because a semicolon that had been placed in a bland clause of the Texas Constitution could, with exquisite parsing, be interpreted to indicate that the election was supposed to take place over four days, not the single day on which the polls were actually open.

The Texas Supreme Court, which heard the case, was full of judges appointed by Davis. In Texas's most notorious grammatical ruling, they came down on the defendant's side and voided the election as unconstitutional.

Davis had no illusions about what the will of the people had been. He knew he had lost the election, and lost it badly. But he couldn't ignore his own supreme court, even though Coke and the Democrats were demanding to take over the reins of state government at once. The more Davis stalled, the more heated things got. Worried that the Democrats were going to seize the executive offices, the governor called in the militia. He also deployed a unit called the Travis Rifles, one of whose organizers was Sam Houston's youngest son, Andrew Jackson Houston. But the Travis Rifles, once they arrived at the Capitol, refused to protect Davis and threw their allegiance instead to Coke. They mustered on the upper floor of the Capitol while Davis's militia, many of them African Americans, patrolled the basement. Meanwhile, the building was ringed by partisans from both sides, including hundreds of freedmen. They had raced out of their homes and businesses to the Capitol grounds in support of the Republican governor, who was all that stood between them and the certain hollowing-out of their civil rights that would come under the Democrats.

It would not have taken much of a spark to set off a shooting war inside the Capitol between the black militia and the Travis Rifles, along with a bloody race riot throughout Austin and the rest of Texas. Davis telegraphed President Grant, asking him to send federal troops to keep the peace. Grant declined, leaving Davis no choice but to yield and allow Coke to be inaugurated. The governor ordered his forces to stand down. He left the Capitol to the cheers of the black men in his militia.

Lizzie Davis, the governor's wife, was not pleased with Grant's refusal to send troops. As she and her husband were packing their furniture in the Governor's Mansion, she took down a painting of the president. The woman who had once invited her Confederate enemies to cut her throat wouldn't hold back her Texan defiance now. She stomped her foot through the canvas.

Hide hunters at work during the great buffalo slaughter that began on the Texas plains in the 1870s. "It was sheer murder," one of them remembered.

25

THE END OF COMANCHERÍA

IF YOU WERE A BUFFALO HUNTER ON THE SOUTH PLAINS in the 1870s, you worked in a mobile processing plant. Your job might be shooter, skinner, teamster, cook, camp tender, or some sort of apprentice-level jack-of-all-trades. You followed your prey across the llano, through a landscape that was narcotic in its vast sameness but also capable of thrillingly

subtle changes—a lone tree in the distance, a modest swell or dip of land, a sudden shift of color or texture as the grass responded to a barreling storm sky overhead or even a single passing cloud.

Hunters generally worked in teams of four or five men, but if you were with a big outfit, you might travel in, or alongside, as many as thirteen or fourteen wagons, pulled by oxen or steers or mules. Some of the wagons were for carrying supplies; others were sturdy, big-framed vehicles for hauling buffalo hides back to the railhead of Dodge City, Kansas, or—as the business began to boom in Texas—to the teeming, lawless "hide town" of Fort Griffin on the Clear Fork of the Brazos.

If you were a skinner, you stripped the carcasses and hauled them back to camp from the kill sites. It was a hard, stinking, never-ending job. A good winter's hunt for a large outfit might result in 4,500 buffalo to be skinned and butchered. Sixty-two thousand pounds of meat—tongues, hams, humps, backstraps—had to be cured in the field in makeshift smokehouses made out of hackberry logs and covered with hides.

If you were a hunter, the essential tool of your trade was the Sharps "Big Fifty" rifle. It weighed as much as sixteen pounds and shot fifty-caliber cartridges that cost twenty-five cents apiece, ten times the going market value of a pound of buffalo meat. The cartridges held around a hundred grains of powder, but the hunters often boosted their velocity by packing in a little more. The result was a weapon that could kill a buffalo from a distance of five hundred to six hundred yards. "Shoots today," went an Indian assessment of the reach of the Sharps rifle, "and kills tomorrow."

A hunter typically approached a herd from downwind, set his Sharps up on a pair of crossed sticks, and searched for the herd leader, the creature in the grazing multitude stretched across the plains that was the most alert and would be the soonest to react to any sense of danger. The idea was to shoot the animal through the lungs, a killing shot that would throw it back and sideways on its haunches, so that the buffalo landed more or less on the same footprint of grassland it had just been occupying. This was much preferable to a shot through the heart, which might allow the wounded animal to run two hundred yards until it died. If that happened, the rest of the herd would panic and stampede. The first buffalo had to be dropped immediately. Then, with the rest of his targets milling about in stalled confusion, the hunter could kill methodically, concerned only about the octagonal barrel of his rifle overheating if he fired too rapidly. "All you had to do," a hunter named Frank Mayer reminisced, "'was pick them off one by one, making sure you made a dropping kill at every shot, until you wiped out the entire herd. Then you went to another and repeated the process. . . . It was sheer murder."

In addition to the big cartridges the hunters used for killing buffalo, they often carried one that they might need to use on themselves. It was no mere rumor that buffalo hunters caught on the plains by enraged Indians could be subjected to hideous and prolonged deaths. One day a man named McRae recalled to Mayer that he "came upon the body of a teamster, who had been stripped, scalped while alive, his privates cut off and stuck into his mouth and fastened there with a sinew cord. Fat pine splinters had been stuck into his flesh from ankles to chin until he resembled a hedgehog. These were ignited at his feet, causing an upward slow flame which literally roasted him alive. His body had been fastened to a dead tree trunk with his own chains."

To solve the problem of meeting such a horrible end, McRae invented a "poison vial," a thin glass tube filled with hydrocyanic acid. "If Indians seem fit to capture you," McRae advised his young protégé, "bite hard on the tube. It's sure medicine against scalping and torture."

The vials were needed because in hunting the buffalo with such efficiency, the hunters were spiking the threat against the Plains Indians to a frightening new order of magnitude. "The Indians realized very keenly," wrote J. Wright Mooar, the man who introduced industrial-scale bison slaughter to Texas, "that the work of the buffalo hunters was the real menace to the wild, free life they wished to lead, and never lost an opportunity to wreak vengeance." The Kiowa chief Kicking Bird was less romantic. "The buffalo," he said, "is our money. . . . We love them just as the white man does his money."

Wright Mooar, from Pownal, Vermont, was a nineteen-year-old former streetcar conductor when he showed up in Hays City, Kansas, and saw his first buffalo. He was cutting wood for the soldiers at Fort Hays when he was hired to procure 500 buffalo hides for a local fur trader who was in touch with an English firm interested in developing a market for buffalo leather. Mooar promptly shot 557 buffalo. He sent the extra 57 hides to his brother, a jewelry store clerk in New York City. Once trend-crazy New Yorkers caught sight of this exotic product from the Wild West, piled high in a wagon rumbling along to an import company on Pine Street, the great buffalo herds of the American West were doomed. They would be mostly exterminated in only six years.

In the summer of 1873, Mooar led a scouting trip south, following the Canadian River into the Texas Panhandle. He had heard rumors of plentiful buffalo there, ready to be exploited for the new hide market he had helped create. The rumors were confirmed beyond his expectations. "In this lonely land," he wrote, "we found the great herd, millions upon millions, fattening on the grass of those mighty uplands. . . . For five days we had ridden through and camped in a mobile sea of living buffalo."

THAT THOSE BUFFALO WOULD NOT BE LIVING FOR LONG WAS more than apparent to the increasingly beleaguered Indians who remained on the Texas plains or who persisted in hunting or raiding there from their reservations in Indian Territory north of the Red River.

The Civil War had not failed to send its destabilizing shock waves deep into the Texas frontier and beyond. Indians, just like whites, had to make decisions about whose side to fight on or avoid fighting on, about what new threats would be closing in and what new opportunities would be opening up. The reservations of Indian Territory north of the Red River in present-day Oklahoma seethed with every sort of partisan dissension. Raids and wholesale massacres took place among tribes that had once commanded sprawling lands but were now reduced to living on government parcels, and that might be at the mercy of blood enemies suddenly liberated onto the warpath by the confusion of the white man's conflict. The Choctaws and Chickasaws—who had been moved out of Texas into Indian Territory—allied themselves with the Confederacy, in large part because many of the wealthier members of the tribe were slave owners. The Tonkawas were pro-Confederate, or were thought to be. In any case, a hundred of them, including Placido, the chief who "wept like a child" when Robert Neighbors had said good-bye to him on the reservation, were killed in an attack on the Wichita agency launched by an alliance of tribes that might have been Union sympathizers or might have just been settling old grievances.

The Kickapoos, an Algonquian-speaking people from the Great Lakes region, had been splintered apart and driven steadily southward for two hundred years. A contingent ended up in Mexico, where they fought Comanche and Kiowa raiders on behalf of the Mexican government. Kickapoos who had been living in Indian Territory decided to escape the growing Civil War spillover there and make their way through West Texas to join their brethren in Mexico. They came in two waves. Each one was discovered and attacked along the way by Confederate soldiers and Texas militiamen who either assumed they belonged to a hostile tribe or didn't care. But the Kickapoos were well armed and well organized. Near present-day San Angelo, they fought off a mixed force of regular troops and militia in a pitched battle at a place called Dove Creek. They killed twenty-six Texans and wounded sixty before finally escaping into Mexico. With that kind of welcome in Texas, it was not long before they got into the reprisal business, crossing the Rio Grande and raiding ranches throughout the brush country of South Texas.

Of the Comanche bands, the Penatekas were the most settled at the start of the Civil War, or the most broken. They had agreed to take up residence on the Clear Fork reservation, but were so harassed and preyed upon there by Texan settlers that they were relocated by Robert Neighbors to agency land on the other side of the Red River. For the other bands, especially the indomitably minded Quahadis, who claimed the llano as their home territory, the war sparked a new surge of aggression against the white intruders they called *taibos*. For one thing, the abandonment of forts by federal troops and the imperfect Confederate and militia attempts to fill the gap had made the western frontier wide open again for raiding. Raiding was more important to the Indians than ever, since the war and blockades had cut off their supplies of firearms and other manufactured goods. There was now much more livestock to carry off as well, since the ranches that had been carved out of the frontier were home to a growing multitude of unfenced and often, with their owners off to war, unprotected cattle. And an epic drought was finally ending, renewing the grass, luring the buffalo back to the southern plains. The great herds that J. Wright Mooar discovered along the Canadian River in 1873 had not gone unnoticed by the Indians. Their renewed raiding, along with the revivification of their most important resource, kept drawing them back down onto the Texas plains and into an apocalyptic collision course with their *taibo* enemies.

For generations, the Comanches had maintained a strong alliance with the Kiowas, another nomadic tribe that had migrated south from as far away as Canada, evolving into a horse culture along the way. Comanches and Kiowas had a history of raiding together deep into Mexico on well-trampled war trails under the light of the full moon, the span on the lunar calendar that settlers from Big Spring to Querétaro learned to fear as the "Comanche Moon."

Maybe the reason the two tribes meshed so well was that they were alike but not too alike. They were both mobile, horse-and-buffalo societies in which male honor and prestige was dependent on feats of war. But their cultures were different. As a people, the Comanches tended to be looser, more individualistic, more improvisational. Kiowa life was stratified, with warriors channeled into one of six soldier societies, and the people as a whole born into a caste system whose ranks, while not necessarily rigid, were clearly delineated. Kiowas had firmer notions about cosmology, a stronger cultural taste for religious ritual. From their creator, they had received ten medicine bundles, actual sacred objects that were guarded and revered and contained within themselves the *dwdw*, or sacred power, that flowed through the universe. The Kiowas held yearly sun dances and recorded their history in pictographs painted on buffalo hides. These "hide calendars" are spookily compelling, particularly one image commemorating an 1833 meteor shower, which depicts a hairless, fetus-like human form hovering in space between what looks like the barrel of a cannon and a cluster of swirling black stars.

A Kiowa war chief named Satanta (or White Bear) was one of the marquee names at a council called by the recently established congressional Indian Peace Commission at Medicine Lodge Creek, in Kansas, in 1867. He was a renowned warrior in his late fifties who owned a shield decorated with a white woman's scalp. His face had a proud, probing look, and he deployed a long-winded speaking style that led the white peace commissioners, either in exasperation or admiration, to label him the "Orator of the Plains." One of the other senior Kiowa representatives was a man with a confusingly similar name to Anglo ears, Satank (or Sitting Bear). Satank was nearly seventy, still lithe and wiry, and cultivated an un-Indian-like droopy mustache. He had a well-earned incorrigible grudge against the whites and was not shy about expressing it. "The white man once came to trade; now he comes as a soldier. . . . He builds forts and plants big guns on their walls. . . . He now covers his face with the cloud of Jealousy and anger and tells us to be gone, as an offended master speaks to his dog."

The commissioners also got an earful from Ten Bears, a Comanche chief from the Yamparika band. He was older even than Satanta and Satank. In photographs, he wears a pair of spectacles that give him an air of scholarly benevolence. Who knows whether what was rendered into English was a strict translation of his words, or whether his speech was given a romantic twilight glow by sympathetic reporters in attendance at the council. In any case, the plaintive statement that emerged takes its place alongside Travis's Alamo letter as a classic of Texas documentary literature:

> I was born under the prairie, where the wind blew free and there was nothing to break the light of the sun. I was born where there were no enclosures and everything drew a free breath. . . . I know every stream and wood between the Rio Grande and the Arkansas. I have hunted and lived over that country. I live like my fathers before me and like them I lived happily. . . . If the Texans had kept out of my country, there might have been peace. . . . But it is too late. The whites have the country which we loved, and we wish only to wander on the prairie til we die.

"If the Texans had kept out of my country." Ten Bears must have known how impossible his reverie was. The Texans could not have kept out of this country any more than the Comanche or Kiowa could have. And so the settlers had bloodily pressed the line of white settlement westward in the years before the Civil War, only to be bloodily pushed back as army protection evaporated and the frontier forts were all but abandoned. With few troops to protect them, the people who had staked out homesteads in the most fought-over stretch of prairie in Texas, the rolling grasslands north of the Clear Fork of the Brazos River, organized themselves into militias, conducted their own patrols and raids, and even built their own civilian forts.

It isn't hard to imagine the vulnerability these settlers must have felt, especially if you happen to be driving alone at night along some lonely two-lane road through the prairie expanses of Young County or Eastland County. The lush native grasses are mostly gone, lost to agriculture and overgrazing and replaced by latter-day invaders such as broomweed or buffelgrass. The woodlands along the creeks and riverbanks are gnarlier and more chaotic

Satanta Kiowa chief

The Kiowa chief Satanta. An army officer once described him as
"a picture of fallen savage greatness."

than they were back in the days when stately belts of trees rose from undisturbed soil. But it still feels primeval and isolated. And if there's a full moon rising above the landscape with all its menacing wattage, it's easy enough to think of it as a Comanche moon, and to imagine a dog's suddenly silenced warning bark, gunshots coming from the next homestead along the Brazos, the echoing screams of women and children being carried away into the night, the disbelieving shrieks from some unfortunate ranger or teamster or farmer being exactingly tortured to death.

The moon had begun to wax on October 13, 1864, and the terror was bright. This was the date of the Elm Creek raid, which was perhaps the largest assault on Texas settlements since the summer of 1840, when outraged Comanches attacked the Texas coast in force to avenge the slaughter of their chiefs in the Council House fight. This time a party of several hundred Kiowas and Comanches swept down along the Brazos and its Elm Creek tributary, attacking ranches, running off livestock, killing and capturing whomever they encountered. Among the people in their path was a thirty-nine-year-old widow and grandmother named Elizabeth Ann Carter Fitzpatrick.

Texans have long had a warm feeling in their quasi-national consciousness for women who are strong, independent minded, entrepreneurial, and hard to kill. In those categories, I'm not sure anybody beats Elizabeth Fitzpatrick. She was born in Alabama. She was epileptic. When she was sixteen years old, she was daring or defiant enough to marry a free black man. With their two mixed-race children, they moved to Texas and lived on the sharp edge of the frontier, settling near Fort Belknap. She operated a kind of boardinghouse and community center called the Carter Trading House. Her husband was murdered. Her second husband disappeared. Her father-in-law was murdered. She married for a third time, and her new husband was also murdered. On the day the Comanches and Kiowas began their raid along Elm Creek, she was at her trading house with her teenage son, her married daughter, and three grandchildren. There was another family there as well, a slave woman named Mary Johnson and her three children.

Elizabeth Fitzpatrick had already lost three family members to murder. Now she would lose almost all the others. The Indians killed her daughter and youngest grandchild right away. They did not kill her thirteen-year-old son until the next day, after he and Elizabeth and the other survivors of the initial attack had been carried into captivity. Her two surviving granddaughters—Lottie and Millie—were then taken from her and given or traded away to other tribes or bands.

Elizabeth was held by the Kiowas until she was rescued, a little over a year later, by U.S. troops that had moved back into Texas after the war had ended.

Lottie, the older of her two surviving granddaughters, was also set free, though marked physically as well as mentally with tattoos on her arms and forehead. We don't know what Elizabeth endured during her captivity with the Kiowas, but we know that she endured it. Despite her grievous losses, she appears to have stepped briskly back into life. On her release, she was sent to Council Grove, Kansas, where, in a former school for Kaw Indians she went to work cooking and sewing and providing emotional support of the I've-been-there-myself variety to a group of fellow Indian captives.

Until her death in 1882, she never stopped searching for Millie, her two-year-old granddaughter. The Indians, when later questioned about Millie's fate, said that she died of exposure or starvation during the first winter of her captivity. But Elizabeth didn't believe it, and perhaps she was right. The Indians may have been covering for a Kiowa warrior named Au-Soant-Sai-Mah, who was said to have taken the girl into his family and lovingly raised her. If that story is true, Millie Durgan became Sain-To-Hoodle, a name that means "She Killed A Cow." She grew up, married a Kiowa husband, and had nine children. Her true identity was not revealed until 1931, three years before she died.

Elizabeth Fitzgerald wasn't the only victim of the Elm Creek raid who never gave up hope that her family could be recovered. A man named Britt Johnson was the husband of Mary Johnson, the enslaved woman who had been at the trading house with her three children when the Comanches and Kiowas attacked. The Johnsons were the property of a local rancher named Moses Johnson. Out of progressive inclinations, practical considerations, or both, Britt's owner had given him considerable latitude, making him foreman of his ranch and trusting him to come and go as his duties dictated. Britt Johnson was off somewhere on ranch business when the raid happened, but he got to Elizabeth Fitzgerald's place soon after—soon enough to find the body of his young son James lying in the dirt outside the burned-out trading house. He buried James and then went after his captured wife and two daughters, risking his scalp by traveling deep into Comanche territory again and again, following whatever leads he could find, never giving up until they were finally ransomed in the summer of 1865.

Britt Johnson was reunited with his shattered family, but whatever happy ending might have resulted was short-lived. In 1871, when he was no longer a slave but the respected proprietor of a local freighting business, he and two other black teamsters were hauling goods along a wagon road leading to Fort Griffin when they were attacked by Kiowas. The place where it happened is on private ranch property, but on a summer day when the brush isn't too high you can stand on the ranch gate and see, a hundred yards or so in the distance, the rough-hewn gravestone that bears his name and those of his two companions, along with a chiseled description of their fate that is so prosaic it is almost poetic: "Killed by Indians 1871."

The mutilated bodies were found by other teamsters and later buried on the spot where they died by a cavalry patrol. Johnson was discovered behind a dead horse that he had used as a barricade. Scattered around his body was further evidence of this legendarily determined man's last stand: 173 expended rifle and pistol shells.

Britt Johnson was killed a little more than three years after the Medicine Lodge Treaty, which established a 2.9 million-acre Comanche and Kiowa reservation in what is now a swath of southwestern Oklahoma between the Red and Washita Rivers. The idea that the Comanches and Kiowas would placidly take up residence as farmers, surrendering the hunting and raiding culture that defined them as a people, turned out to be a fantasy. This was in no small part due to the practical demands of feeding and supplying the Indians on the reservation, which were undercut by bureaucratic incompetence and corruption. Upon discovering they could not thrive, or even survive, on the diet of salt pork and cornmeal grudgingly supplied by the U.S. government, many of the Comanches and Kiowas who had signed the treaty and gone onto the reservation soon threw down their hoes and tossed away their third-rate government-issued white man's clothing. President Ulysses Grant, who took office in 1869, was determined to sweep away the cynicism and cronyism that had defiled the reservation system. He placed the reservations under new management. Gone were the partisan appointees from the Office of Indian Affairs. Taking their place were Quakers. "If you can make Quakers out of the Indians," the president dreamily reflected, "it will take the fight out of them."

The new agent on the Kiowa and Comanche reservation was a committed and energetic Iowa Quaker named Lawrie Tatum. He arrived in Indian Territory and discovered the obvious: the reservation had become not a homeland for the Indians but a refuge, a base from which to launch raids across the Red River into Texas and then return to for sanctuary and government supplies. "If Washington don't want my young men to raid in Texas," one of the Comanche chiefs told Tatum, "then Washington must move Texas clear away, where my young men can't find it."

Satanta and Satank, the two Kiowa chiefs who had signed their names to the Medicine Lodge Treaty, helped orchestrate an attack on a civilian wagon train in May 1871. This happened four months after the death of Britt Johnson and in the same vicinity, the stretch of rolling grassland in Young County that became known as the "most dangerous prairie in Texas." Among the other Kiowa leaders that day was a chief named Big Tree—

BIG TREE
*was captured along with his fellow Kiowa leader Satanta and prosecuted in the
first murder trial ever conducted against Native Americans.*

"a remarkably handsome Indian," in one white man's recollection. And
there was also a medicine man of powerful influence whose Kiowa name of
Maman-Ti translates roughly to "Sky Walker."

As the Kiowas watched the Butterfield Stage road from hiding, what
looked like a rich target rolled by: a military wagon, obviously carrying
someone of importance, guarded by an escort of the black troopers that the
Indians called Buffalo Soldiers. Sky Walker, in consultation with an oracular
owl skin, insisted on not attacking the wagon. The medicine wasn't right, he
argued. Something better would come along later.

It did, and very soon afterward a civilian wagon train passed by on the way to Fort Griffin. Sky Walker gave his assent this time, and the Indians attacked and killed seven of the teamsters, captured their mules and cargo, and carried them off to their reservation beyond the Red River. A cavalry sergeant named Henry D. Gregg described one of the horrors he encountered when his patrol rode up afterward to the scene of the fight: "Stripped stark naked and fastened by a chain in the fire was the body of the wagon master of the train. One side was burned to a crisp and the limbs were twisted out of all shape by the action of the flames. He had been scalped alive and hot ashes poured upon his bleeding skull, and, notwithstanding all this, life was not yet extinct, as was evidenced by his wildly rolling eyeballs. He died immediately after, however."

This was the sort of fate that might have happened to William Tecumseh Sherman, the commanding general of the U.S. Army, if Sky Walker had gotten a different reading from his owl medicine. Sherman, along with General Randolph Marcy, was one of the occupants of the wagon that the Kiowas had let pass. He was on an inspection tour of the troubled Texas frontier, traveling between Fort Belknap and Fort Richardson. The news of what had happened to the wagon train traveling behind him shocked and infuriated Sherman. He headed north to the Kiowa and Comanche reservation. There was no trouble in identifying the perpetrators of the Salt Creek Prairie attack. "If any other Indian comes here," Satanta frankly admitted to Lawrie Tatum when he went to the reservation headquarters at Fort Sill to draw his rations, "and claims the honor of leading the party he will be lying to you, for I did it myself."

There was a tense moment when Sherman ordered the arrest of Satanta, Big Tree, and Satank. A Kiowa chief named Lone Wolf threatened the general by cocking his carbine, causing the soldiers to level their weapons. Satanta threw up his hands and pleaded for peace, even though it meant he would be put in irons and sent back to Texas to be tried for murder in the town of Jacksboro. He and Big Tree were loaded into one wagon, Satank into another. Satank by now was seventy-one or thereabouts, but age had only hardened him. As the wagon labored along, he sang the death song of his Koitsenko warrior society:

> O sun, you remain forever, but we Koitsenko must die.
> O earth, you remain forever, but we Koitsenko must die.

Singing, he scraped the skin off his wrists as he worked his way out of his manacles. He had somehow hidden a knife, and when his hands were free he stabbed the soldier who was guarding him. He grabbed a rifle from another soldier and might have gotten away if it had not jammed. As it was, he was shot dead in the road. The Tonkawa scouts who were with the army were allowed to take his scalp.

Satanta—whom a lieutenant described as "a picture of fallen savage greatness" —was sent on with Big Tree to Jacksboro. During his trial, Satanta, the Orator of the Plains, had the opportunity to hear what it sounded like when an ambitious young white prosecutor orated against him to a jury. In this proceeding, the first murder trial ever conducted against Indians, the prosecutor, Samuel W. T. Lanham, called out Satanta as "the arch fiend of treachery and blood—the cunning Cataline."

The two Kiowa chiefs were found guilty and sentenced to hang. But their trial was a national event that troubled the consciences of Americans who were aware of the immemorial chain of injustices suffered by Native Americans, and who lived far enough away from places like the Salt Creek prairie for mercy to seem like a simple enough gesture. E. J. Davis was still governor at that point. A progressive man by nature, he bowed to progressive pressure and commuted Satanta's and Big Tree's sentences to life imprisonment. A few years later, they were set free on parole, though with the stern condition they would be imprisoned again at the first sign of more Kiowa raiding. That wasn't nearly enough for General Sherman, who wrote a blistering letter to Davis: "I believe Satanta and Big Tree will have their revenge . . . and if they are to take scalps, I hope that yours is the first that will be taken."

BLUNT THINKING WAS A TRAIT THAT SHERMAN SHARED WITH his combative subordinate General Philip Sheridan, who commanded from Chicago the Military District of the Missouri, which incorporated the Department of Texas and all the Indian insurgencies therein. When, in 1875, even the hard-hearted Democratic Texas legislature pondered doing something to save the buffalo from extinction, it was Sheridan who set them straight. So what if the buffalo hunters kill all the buffalo, he told the legislature: "They are destroying the Indians' commissary . . . For the sake of lasting peace, let them kill, skin, and sell until the buffaloes are exterminated. Then your prairies can be covered with speckled cattle and the festive cowboy."

At the top of the Texas Panhandle, in a lush grassy meadow two miles north of the Canadian River, was a place called Adobe Walls. It came by that name because a group of buffalo hunters who arrived in March 1874 to set up a trading post found the ruins of what some of them speculated was an old Spanish mission. In reality, it was the site of an earlier trading post that had been built in the 1840s and soon abandoned. The crumbling walls became the site of a battle in 1864 when Kit Carson led a force of volunteers and Indian auxiliaries out of New Mexico to pursue a group of Comanches and Kiowas whose raids along the Santa Fe Trail had threatened to sever traffic and communications between the Union forces holding New Mexico and the rest of the United States. Carson and his men attacked a Kiowa village, an assault that stirred up a massive and unexpected Indian reprisal that threatened to annihilate them. Thanks to Carson's cool strategic thinking and the skillful deployment of the two mountain howitzers that his men had brought with them, they managed to fight the Indians to a draw and make their way back to Fort Union in New Mexico. (Carson wasn't the only strategist on the battlefield. Satanta, who was very much an active participant on the Kiowa side, had once stolen a bugle from a military post and had learned to play it. He sowed confusion among the cavalry's ranks by playing "Retreat" every time Carson's bugler sounded "Advance.")

Now there was to be a second battle of Adobe Walls, a conflict that would help trigger the defeat of the once-unconquerable Plains Indians and finally drive them out of Texas.

The hide hunters who came to the vicinity of Adobe Walls in 1874 erected a complex of log buildings chinked with sod and surrounded by an eight-foot-high corral fence made out of cottonwood trunks cut from the banks of nearby creeks. It was as lonely an enterprise as could be imagined—two stores, a blacksmith shop, a saloon set down on a sweeping immensity of grass. Its purpose was to provide the buffalo hunters—who called themselves "runners"—a place to sell their hides and get supplies without having to make the long trip north to Dodge City.

The presence of a white man's trading post in the heart of the rapidly diminishing buffalo range—in violation of the terms of the Medicine Lodge Treaty—was the ultimate provocation for the Indians of the southern plains. The Comanches and Kiowas on their reservation were already close to starving. Despite the pleading of the agents, the supply of government rations was often scant and late. "We come in from our camps on issue day, to get our rations," fumed the Kiowa chief Big Bow, "only we find little here. We carry that home, divide around among the people. It is soon gone, and our women and children begin to cry with hunger, and that makes our hearts feel bad. A white man's heart would soon get bad to see his wife and children crying for something to eat, when he had nothing to give them."

Life on the reservation was miserable, demeaning, and dangerous. Beyond the reservation, where the buffalo runners were slaughtering the Indians' food supply at a rate that the human mind could barely process, life was growing insupportable. A few months after the hunters had built their outpost at Adobe Walls, a young Comanche from the Quahadi band named Isa-tai summoned a gathering—a sun dance—in provocative proximity to the southern border of the Comanche-Kiowa reservation. Isa-tai translates in English to something like "Wolf Shit," a name that might cause modern readers to chortle but did nothing to undermine the regard in which he was held, at least briefly, by his fellow Comanches. He was a prophet who had correctly predicted the onset of a blizzard and the course of a comet across the heavens, and who claimed that his medicine was strong enough to protect him and his fellow warriors from *taibo* bullets.

Isa-tai's preaching ignited the pride and aroused the vengeful feelings of the Indians attending the sun dance. The war party he assembled was substantial, perhaps 250–300 warriors, made up mostly of Comanches, Kiowas, and Southern Cheyennes. But Isa-tai wasn't the only leader. He may have been the messianic instigator, but the party's war chief was another young Comanche. Born a member of the Nokoni band, he had taken up residence with the Quahadis as a teenager. He was battle tested, aggressive, and as aggrieved as any Indian on the Texas plains. His name was Quanah. Rendered into English, the word sounds intriguingly unwarlike: Fragrance. Quanah was the son of Cynthia Ann Parker, who had been taken as an eight-year-old girl from Parker's Fort in 1836 and rechristened Naduah by the Comanches. His father was Peta Nocona, the warrior who had captured her. Now his father was dead. There is a long-running debate about whether he was killed on that horrific day on the Pease River when Sul Ross and his Rangers attacked the Comanche camp, or whether he was elsewhere at the time and died of illness a few years later. That is what Quanah later insisted happened. Either way, Quanah was now without family. One of the epidemics brought to his country by the *taibo* had carried away his younger brother. Most wrenchingly, his mother and sister had been seized in the Pease River fight when he was still a boy, as suddenly as if they had been carried off by one of the mythic monsters of Comanche lore—the Great Cannibal Owl. Quanah did not know where they were. He did not know that his sister Prairie Flower had died of brain fever in some white man's settlement. He did not know that his mother, who had told her white family, "My heart is crying all the time," was dead as well. Like Elizabeth Fitzgerald, like Britt Johnson, all he could do was to hope that his family was alive and that someday he would be reunited with them.

The attack on Adobe Walls, led by Quanah and Isa-tai, took place just before dawn on a day in late June 1874. There was one woman in the compound, a cook named Hannah Olds, and twenty-eight men. Among them was Bat Masterson, a young buffalo runner who would later gain a lasting Wild West reputation as a lawman in Dodge City before becoming a sportswriter in New York and serving as the model for Sky Masterson in Damon Runyon's *Guys and Dolls*. And there was Billy Dixon, thought by some to be "the meanest man" among the hide hunters but thought by himself to be a considerate spirit who always remembered his mother's admonition to be kind to animals. (Except, of course, buffalo.) "In all my after life," he wrote in his autobiography, "I never forgot her words. Often on the Plains and in the wilderness did I turn my horse or wagon aside rather than injure a road lizard or a terrapin that was unable to get out of the way."

The battle plan that Isa-tai and Quanah had devised was simple: a surprise assault on the sleeping occupants of Adobe Walls. But the merchants and hidemen weren't sleeping, at least not all of them. They had been aroused in the middle of the night by the noise of what James Hanrahan, the saloon owner, said was a cracked ridgepole holding up the sod roof. That may or may not have been true. Wright Mooar, who was out on the buffalo plains at the time, claimed that Hanrahan had found out an attack was coming but did not tell the hunters, worried that they would abandon the outpost and leave his inventory undefended. Wanting everyone awake and vigilant, he had shot off his rifle in the middle of the night and pretended the sound was the ridgepole breaking.

Whichever version of the story is to be credited, the result was the same. There were enough men awake to hear the war cries of the Indians and swiftly react. Billy Dixon, like many of the hunters and teamsters at Adobe Walls, had been sleeping out in the open next to his Sharps rifle when he was awakened by the commotion inside the saloon. Having decided to get an early start on that morning's hunt, he was in the process of packing when he saw "a large body of objects advancing vaguely in the dusky dawn."

The nature of those oncoming shapes became clear all too suddenly: "Then I was thunderstruck. The black body of moving objects suddenly spread out like a fan, and from it went up one single, solid yell—a war whoop that seemed to shake the very air of the early morning. Then came the thudding roar of running horses, and the hideous cries of the individual warriors each embarked in the onslaught. I could see that hundreds of Indians were coming."

Dixon made a dash for one of the stores, where, from behind the sod walls, he and the other trapped hidemen put up a desperate close-quarters fight, the rooms filling with gun smoke as both defenders and Indians shoved their rifles through the chinking to shoot point-blank at one another. A pair of brothers who were teamsters were sleeping outside in their wagon when the attack began. They hid in the bed of the wagon in the midst of the

ISA-TAI

was a visionary Comanche leader, held in high regard until his medicine failed him at the 1874 Battle of Adobe Walls.

fight until they were discovered. They were killed along with the Newfoundland dog that was trying to protect them. The Indians scalped the teamsters, and then they scalped the dog.

Isa-tai's confident prediction that the war party was immune to white men's bullets proved disastrously wrong. The Indians—faced with extremely accurate fire from men with far-shooting Sharps rifles whose daily work had served to perfect their marksmanship—lost as many as thirty men before it was all over. The hide hunters lost only three. Quanah was wounded. Isa-tai, who observed the battle from a distance, his body clothed in nothing but yellow medicine paint, suffered the career-ending humiliation of having his horse killed by a long-range bullet from one of the sharpshooters. In rage and frustration, one of the Cheyennes even turned on him and started beating him with his quirt. "You got polecat medicine!" he sneered.

This incident was followed by an even more spectacular shot, one that has been credited by tradition, if not quite vetted by history, to Billy Dixon. After the Indians called off the attack, leaving the unrecoverable bodies of dead warriors lying around the corrals and buildings of Adobe Walls, they hung around the vicinity, maintaining a loose siege. Two days after the initial assault, one of them was sitting on his horse on a low butte far away from the sheltered buffalo hunters. Shot off his horse, the warrior hit the ground before the report of the rifle that killed him was audible. It was the most famous "shoots today, kills tomorrow" shot of all, at a distance of three-quarters of a mile, or perhaps even more.

The great war party, shocked and demoralized following the failure of Isa-tai's magic, finally withdrew and fragmented. The buffalo hunters who dared to remain at Adobe Walls after the attack shored up the fortifications and decorated them with a gloating medieval display. "Twelve Indian heads," crowed a scout who rode in with an army column that August, "minus hair, feathers and other thum mim, now adorn the gateposts of the corral."

The Indians had struck hard but failed. Now General Sherman directed the U.S. Army to strike back, to put an end once and for all to the "renegade" Indians who would not settle on reservations or who continued to exploit them for strategic advantage. What happened next was called the Red River War. It was a campaign of encirclement that took place over the remaining summer and fall of 1874 through the spring of 1875, and that involved five army expeditions tightening the noose from every direction, from as far away as Kansas and New Mexico, around the heart of the remaining Kiowa and Comanche resistance on the eastern edge of the Llano Estacado. It was a war relatively light on casualties but devastating and stark in its results.

The battles of the Red River War were mostly skirmishes and ambushes and running fights involving Indians who found fewer places to hide as they were pursued by Texas Rangers or by the converging field forces of the U.S. Army. It was conducted during a summer drought so intense that thirst-crazed troopers reportedly sliced open veins to drink their own blood. When the drought broke there were blinding rainstorms and howling northers.

Billy Dixon, scouting for the column commanded by Colonel Nelson Miles, which had marched down from Kansas, found himself in yet another desperate situation, on a much smaller scale than at Adobe Walls but representative of the kind of perilous isolated fighting that characterized the Red River campaign. He and five other men accidentally encountered a hundred or so Kiowas and Comanches out on the plains along a tributary of the Washita River. Two of the men were badly wounded at once. Dixon and the others found the only cover available, a shallow depression created by wallowing buffalo. Through a long thirsty afternoon and a long frigid night, Dixon kept the Indians at a distance with accurate fire from his Sharps, and ran out to the exposed ground twice to drag each of the stranded men back to the shelter of the buffalo wallow. All the others except Dixon were wounded as well, and one of the men he had dragged to safety begged the others "in piteous tones to shoot him and put an end to his terrible sufferings." They didn't, but he died during the night. In the morning, Dixon crawled out again, somehow evaded the encircling Indians, and brought back help. He and the four surviving scouts were awarded the Medal of Honor for "cool courage, heroism, and self-sacrifice," though Dixon's medal was later rescinded when it was discovered he was a scout and not officially a member of the army. The loss of the medal pained him less than the loss of his "dearest treasure," his mother's picture, the only one of her he had, which had been in a pocket of the coat tied behind his saddle when his horse ran off.

Afterward, he wrote, it was always his intention to go back out onto the llano someday, find the spot where the fight had taken place, and mark the grave of his comrade who had died in the buffalo wallow. But he never did, and he regretted it. "Every night the same stars are shining way out there in the Panhandle, the winds sigh as mournfully as they did then, and I often wonder if a single settler who passes the lonely spot knows how desperately six men once battled for their lives where now may be plowed fields and safety and the comforts of civilization."

While Dixon and his fellow scouts were besieged in their buffalo wallow, one of the five cavalry columns was making preparations to ride north from Fort Concho, which had been established after the Civil War in west-central Texas (near present-day San Angelo). It was a force that included some six hundred men from the Fourth Cavalry and the Tenth and Eleventh Infantry. Serving as scouts were a dozen Tonkawas and thirteen recruits from the people known as Black Seminoles, descendants of the escaped slaves who in the eighteenth century had allied with the Seminoles in Florida, and over time and under pressure had drifted west and south to Mexico.

The unit was commanded by Colonel Ranald Slidell Mackenzie, a well-born New Yorker whose great-grandfather had been Alexander Hamilton's assistant secretary of the treasury and whose father, a naval officer with a literary bent, had written a two-volume history of John Paul Jones. Mackenzie tended to be private and taciturn; a West Point classmate described him as "inexpressive" and "immobile." Nevertheless, he graduated at the head of his class and performed with such grim, dogged proficiency in the Civil War that he had been brevetted to major general by the age of twenty-four. "I regarded Mackenzie," Ulysses Grant wrote in his memoirs, "as the most promising young officer in the army."

Mackenzie had been wounded six times, including by a shell fragment that carried off the first two fingers of his right hand. The Indians he fought in Texas after the war knew him as Bad Hand. In 1873, under orders from Sheridan, he had violated the international border and led troops across the Rio Grande to suppress Kickapoo raiders. The year before, he had had somewhat less success in leading an expedition against the Comanches. In a place called Blanco Canyon, at the base of the llano, his encampment had been attacked in a brazen middle-of-the-night charge. The Indians targeted the troopers' horses, frightening them so thoroughly that they pulled up their picket pins and stampeded down the canyon. One of Mackenzie's officers described the leader of the raid: "A large and powerfully built chief . . . on a coal black racing pony. Leaning forward upon his mane, his heels nervously working in the animal's side, with six-shooter poised in the air, he seemed the incarnation of savage, brutal joy." He was describing Quanah, the half-*taibo*, half-Comanche son of Cynthia Ann Parker and Peta Nocona. And it was Quanah who ended up that night with Mackenzie's favorite horse, an iron-gray pacer.

Now Bad Hand was headed back to what was left of Comanchería at the head of the most punishing component of the five-pronged offensive designed to destroy Indian resistance forever on the South Plains. Within a week of leaving Fort Concho, his scouts were once again probing along the edge of the Caprock, the stark massif, undercut with creeks and canyons, that rears up out of the West Texas landscape, sometimes a thousand feet high, and marks the unmistakable beginning of the Llano Estacado. Mackenzie's army was camped in Tule Canyon one night in late September when the Comanches made another brazen nighttime attack, under a Comanche Moon

It was the "inexpressive" Colonel Ranald Slidell Mackenzie, missing two fingers and known to the Indians as Bad Hand, who pursued the Comanches and Kiowas to their last redoubt in Palo Duro Canyon.

bright enough for one of the officers to read the *New York Herald* by. This time Mackenzie was better prepared. He had already lost part of his horse herd, along with own mount, to Quanah's raiders, and so he made sure to surround the herd with skirmishers, and not just to picket the horses but also to hobble their legs with inch-thick rope so that they could barely move.

The attack failed, but the Indians sniped at the soldiers all night, and at daybreak Mackenzie ordered one of his companies to counterattack. A lieutenant who was among the men chasing the Indians across the plains later recalled, as an older man, what he saw that day: "The sun, rising in our rear, seemed to light up the entire line of hostiles, in their full dress of gaudy paint and feathers as they turned in their saddles to fire at us, scurrying across the prairie in rapid flight. I recollect well saying to myself; now look and take it all in, for with the rapid advance of civilization and settlement on the frontier, the like of this I will never see again."

The Indians vanished, in the words of another of Mackenzie's officers, "as completely as if the ground had swallowed them." In a sense, it had. They had retreated to the floor of Palo Duro Canyon, the most startling geographic feature of the High Plains. Palo Duro, the second-largest canyon in the United States, is an abrupt rupture in the flat tableland of the Texas Panhandle. Though carved by the Prairie Dog Town Fork of the Red River over many millions of years, it attacks the eye with its suddenness, as if the unmarked surface of the llano had just been savagely ripped apart. It is a sprawling, spidery declivity, 120 miles long and 800 feet deep, in which strata of geologic time are almost shockingly exposed in bright multicolored bands of rock.

Looking down from the rim of the canyon at daybreak on the next morning, September 28, Mackenzie and his men could see Comanche and Kiowa villages—hundreds of tepees in all—strung out in the hazy distance along the riverbed. Mackenzie ordered an attack, which meant his men had to lead their horses single file along a narrow, precipitous trail before they could reach the canyon bottom and form up for a charge. They were spotted on their way down, and the Indians began a frantic retreat, gathering their families and driving their horse herds up the canyon. "As we galloped along," wrote Captain R. G. Carter, "we passed village after village of Indian lodges both on the right and left, all empty and totally abandoned. The ground was strewn with buffalo robes, blankets, and every imaginable thing, in fact, that the Indians had in the way of property."

The fleeing warriors sniped at Mackenzie and his men from the canyon rim, but there was only one serious casualty—a bugler shot through the stomach—and by the afternoon the outcome was clear. Though the Indians lost only three men killed, the Battle of Palo Duro Canyon was a shattering blow from which they could not realistically hope to recover. Facing winter, they had lost everything: food, forage, weapons, clothing, precious possessions, and a hitherto undiscovered canyon sanctuary.

And horses. The spoils of war included almost 1,500 of them. Mackenzie selected 350 of the best horses to distribute among his scouts as payment and inducement for their dangerous work. But he knew that it would be impossible to guard the rest of the herd against Indian attempts to recapture them. So he had them shot. "It seemed a pity to be compelled to kill them," Carter wrote, "but there was no other alternative. It was the surest method of crippling the Indians and compelling them to go into and stay upon their reservations." For the men burdened with the task, it took an entire day to kill over a thousand horses.

The Red River War dragged on until the following June, but it would be hard to find a more definitive close to the centuries-long reign of the Comanches than the methodical execution of the creatures that had defined them as a people and propelled them to their destiny on the Texas plains.

Satanta, the chief who had been convicted of murder and paroled on condition that the Kiowas never again take to the warpath, surrendered a week or so after the Palo Duro battle to the commander in charge of the troops at the Cheyenne agency. With him were his fellow parolee Big Tree and 143 men, women, and children. An indication of how hounded and dispossessed they had become can be seen in the inventory of arms taken from them. All that the thirty-seven warriors in the group had available to fight off the pursuing columns of the U.S. Army were thirteen rifles, three pistols, eighteen bows, and four lances. Satanta claimed he had not been part of the hostilities, but the army wasn't in the mood to believe him—and anyway, the fact that the Kiowas had gone to war meant that his parole was revoked. He was thought to be more dangerous than Big Tree, who was released. Satanta was sent to prison in Huntsville, where he was put to work building roads in a forest country that must have seemed menacing and claustrophobic to a plains-dwelling Kiowa. "When I roam the prairies I feel free and happy," he once said, "but when I sit down I grow pale and die." On the day after a deputy marshal told him he had no chance of ever being free again, he killed himself by jumping out of a second-story balcony onto the prison courtyard. (He is now buried at Fort Sill, but until 1963 his body was interred in a plain pine box in the Huntsville convict cemetery that was known as Peckerwood Hill.)

Quanah's band of four hundred or so Quahadis had escaped the rout at Palo Duro and were still at large, along with several hundred good horses. Throughout a wet, stormy winter, they managed to evade the soldiers who had converged on the Panhandle and were relentlessly mopping up whatever opposition remained. Mackenzie chased Quanah all over West Texas, without success. That March, after taking command of Fort Sill at the Comanche and Kiowa reservation, he sent out a peace ambassador, a doctor named Jacob Sturm, who was married to a Caddo woman, to find Quanah and talk him into surrendering.

Guiding Sturm were a man named Wild Horse and two other reservation Comanches. They located the Quahadi camp along a small stream not far from the spot in Scurry County where, the next year, J. Wright Mooar would perform the symbolic medicine-robbing feat of shooting a white buffalo. ("A freak of nature," declared Mooar's biographer, Charles G. Anderson, "and a god to the Indians.")

Sturm found Quanah to be surprisingly receptive to his overtures. There is anecdotal speculation that Quanah came to the conclusion that it was time to go to the reservation during a vision quest in which he watched a wolf trot and an eagle soar toward the northeast, in the general direction of Fort Sill. In any case, reported Strum back to Mackenzie, "We are again in counsel, and Quanah, a young man of much influence with his people, made a speech in favor of coming in . . . As his authority seems to be absolute, they all agreed to start tomorrow."

And so they did, though they took their time. The journey to reach Fort Sill became a monthlong valedictory trek through a way of life that was gone, through country that was no longer theirs. Quanah surrendered to Mackenzie in person. Their encounter was described as "undramatic," though perhaps there was so much emotion coursing below the surface of two unrevealing men that any drama would have been offensive.

Quanah had a question for Mackenzie: where were his mother and sister? The colonel didn't know. He wrote to a quartermaster stationed in the town of Denison and asked him to find out. There is no record of how Quanah reacted when the reply came back that they were dead.

— 26 —

FENCED IN

The red man was pressed from this part of the west
He's likely no more to return
To the banks of Red River where seldom if ever
His flickering camp fires burn.

THESE WORDS ARE BURIED IN THE VERSES OF "HOME ON the Range," a song most people know only by its enveloping, closed-loop refrain. "Home on the Range" is almost more a hymn than a song, a testament to a world that is both gorgeously present but achingly ungraspable—"like a maid in a heavenly dream," as another verse puts it. And whatever regret its lyrics might express for the plight of real people driven from Texas is mostly a sentimental trope, part of an overall nostalgia for times that are gone and old ways that have vanished.

Still, it's a great song, even a candidate for the greatest American song. Its origins and authorship are hazy. A Kansas doctor claimed to have written it in 1873 with the help of a lyricist from a neighboring dugout. The song was then called "The Western Home," and its awkward lyrics included a paean to a local riverbank "where seldom if ever / Any poisonous herbage doth grow."

But the Texas folklorist and ballad collector John A. Lomax was convinced that the song predated the Kansas songwriting team. He didn't believe that such songs even had authors. They just seemed "to have sprung up as quietly and mysteriously as does the grass on the plains." In 1908, Lomax walked into the Buckhorn Saloon in San Antonio, which then as now featured one of the world's largest and most eccentric collections of animal horns. For several years, Lomax had been on the hunt in Texas for cowboy songs. He had discovered "The Old Chisholm Trail" in a saloon, had learned "The Buffalo Skinners" from an actual aging buffalo skinner in Abilene, and a Gypsy woman in Fort Worth had been the unlikely source of "Git Along, Little Dogies."

When he told the proprietor of the Buckhorn that he was looking for cowboy songs, he was referred to an African American man who used to be a camp cook for a cattle outfit and who now operated an outdoor beer saloon. Lomax hauled his Edison recording machine with its five-foot horn to the man's establishment in a mesquite grove behind the Southern Pacific depot. There, for the first time, he heard somebody sing America's signature cowboy anthem.

His informant told Lomax that he had made a half-dozen trips up the Chisholm Trail in his youth, and that "Home on the Range" was one of the songs that the trail hands sang during the long slow trek from the brushlands of South Texas to the railhead at Abilene, Kansas. The Chisholm was one of several Texas trails that brought longhorns to market and achieved legendary status during the period of the great cattle drives, which spanned the years after the Civil War to 1890.

The cattle drives had something—well, let's say a lot—to do with the transformation of the cowboy from a dust-eating laborer to the embodiment of rootless romantic self-sufficiency. John Lomax, after maybe collecting one too many cowboy songs, fell pretty hard himself: "He sits his horse easily as he rides through a wide valley, enclosed by mountains, clad in the hazy purple of coming night. . . . Dauntless, reckless, without the unearthly purity of Sir Galahad though as gentle to a pure woman as King Arthur, he is truly a knight."

The men—and a few women, and at least one woman who pretended to be a man—who drove the herds north were as likely to call themselves waddies as cowboys. They were usually prohibited from carrying guns because a stray shot could stampede the cattle, as could the striking of a match or the rumble of thunder. Many of them were teenagers. About a quarter of them—like Bose Ikard, who was born into slavery but became a crucial associate and trusted friend of Charles Goodnight—were black. Some were Tejanos or Mexicans whose ancestral cattle-herding skills reached deep into a time before there were any Anglos in Texas.

Whatever knightly glamour a newly hired waddie imagined would be involved in trailing cattle for up to 1,500 miles was soon forgotten in an unspooling daily routine of fatigue and drudgery and chronic thirst. If you were a drag driver, one of the two lowliest positions on a ten- or eleven-man crew, you rode behind the herd and finished the day by spitting and coughing and hacking the dust out of your lungs. "I have seen them come off herd," a trail hand named Teddy Blue Abbott reminisced, "with the dust half an inch deep on their hats and thick as fur in their eyebrows and mustaches, and if they shook their head or you tapped their cheek, it would fall off them in showers." The work could also be grimly distasteful. For instance, something had to be done with the calves that were born along the trail in the spring and could not keep up with the herd. "I had a pistol," wrote a cowboy named Branch Isbell, "and it was my duty to murder the innocents each morning while their pitiful mothers were ruthlessly driven on. . . . Being the executioner so disgusted me with six-shooters that I have never owned—much less used one from that time to this."

But despite all that, the trail drives were remembered by their participants—those who weren't killed by lightning or by Indians, or flattened in a stampede ("horse and man . . . mashed into the ground as flat as a pancake")—as a life's interlude of freedom and wonder. In memory, they represented a time when each day brought to these farm-raised kids new country to see and new sensations to absorb. There was the pastoral peace of serenading the bedded-down cattle at night, two riders making opposing circles around the herd, trading off verses to "Home on the Range" or one of the many other cowboy songs that John Lomax eventually recorded. There was the punishment of a "dry drive," forty or fifty miles without water, when the men's lips cracked and bled as they rode through the alkali dust, the cattle so dehydrated they staggered forward almost blind. And there was the eeriness of an approaching storm: the way the charged atmosphere would cause the

A Texas "cow boy" at large on the soon-to-vanish open range.

ears of the horses and the horns of thousands of apprehensive cattle to glow green with phosphorescence, and the hail that followed, powerful enough to knock out jackrabbits. Or the terror of hearing a panther scream in the middle of the night. "My thick hair," recalled a waddie about that particular unearthly sound, "went straight up and has never thoroughly settled down."

Charles Goodnight, who had been a young scout for Sul Ross when Cynthia Ann Parker was recaptured on the Pease River, and would become over the course of his life the inarguable personification of the Texas cowman, summed up the appeal of going up the trail better than anybody: "We were solitary adventurers in a great land as fresh and new as a spring morning, and we were free and full of the zest of darers."

★

THE GREAT CATTLE DRIVES THAT TOOK PLACE FROM 1866 TO

the end of the 1880s were a kind of industrial spasm, a response to a sudden hunger for a commodity—longhorn cattle—that had become so bountiful and free-ranging in Texas that to some observers they were effectively no different from wild game. There was no real market for Texas cattle until after the Civil War, when a new, nationwide demand for beef coincided with the development of railroad lines in Missouri and Kansas, from which the cattle could be loaded onto cars and shipped to St. Louis and other cities farther east.

Longhorns were the descendants of the Spanish cattle that had entered the New World with Cortés, that accompanied entradas into Texas from Coronado onward, and that formed the basis of Spanish and then Mexican ranching culture. Over the generations, they ended up being bred—deliberately or haphazardly—with English-derived varieties of cattle brought by Anglo colonists in the 1820s. The result was something of an apparition. In Texas today, a number of "game ranches" stock all sorts of outlander creatures for recreational hunters to dispatch, but no oryx, aoudad, bongo, or water buffalo is quite as exotic as the homegrown longhorn steers you see every so often grazing along the side of the highway. Their horns are not just long, but freakishly so, spreading as much as eight feet from tip to tip, and sometimes taking a dip or a twist along the way, so they end up looking less like a natural animal horn than a contorted piece of driftwood.

Spanish cattle provided the stock that gave rise to the creation of ranching in South Texas during the colonial era, just as the vaqueros who had perfected the techniques of working with cattle from horseback provided a base of expertise and experience that helped turn Anglo American farmers into cowboys. The first vaqueros were soldiers who joined Spanish expeditions into Texas from their homes in northern provinces such as Nuevo León or

Nuevo Vizcaya and ended up working on the large ranchos along the San Antonio River valley that supplied beef to the padres and neophytes at the missions, or for private rancheros like Gil Ibarvo, Martín De Léon, and Erasmo Seguín. Vaqueros rounded up and marked or branded cattle, but the great majority of longhorns in Texas were still half-wild *orejanos*, the Spanish term for cattle that bore no sign of ownership, or fully wild *cimarrones*. (The English word "maverick" comes courtesy of Samuel Maverick, the Battle of Béxar veteran, former mayor of San Antonio, and Texas land baron who was uninterested in branding his cattle and had enough sway to assume that people would know that they were his.)

Cattle were slaughtered for hides and tallow, but for a long time the market for rangy beef was thin outside Texas. During the last few decades of the eighteenth century, vaqueros made small-scale drives to Mexico and to Louisiana along the Camino Real, which led through the old mission fields of East Texas. After the revolution, Anglo Texans tried Louisiana again, but weeks of trudging through swamps and forests, where the cattle were driven mad by heel flies, made the cost-benefit ratio tricky. Far better was the Shawnee Trail, an old Indian hunting trace along which herds could be driven north from the brush country of San Antonio, across the Red River, and through eastern Indian Territory to population centers in Missouri and as far north as Illinois. That worked for a few years, until Missouri farmers noticed that their domestic cattle were refusing to eat, becoming glassy-eyed and nearly paralyzed, and dropping dead in a high-temperature delirium. It was a tick-borne illness to which the longhorns were immune. Nobody knew the exact cause, however, which only increased the sense of menace from these wild, spiny, almost prehistoric-looking creatures who seemed to be sowing death among the defenseless Herefords and Holsteins they passed along the Shawnee Trail. The Missourians tried ineffective legislative defenses against "Texas fever," but when that didn't work they formed committees of vigilance and turned back the herds by force of arms.

Texas drovers faced the same lack of welcome in eastern Kansas when they shifted the trail westward to bypass the Missouri state line. Then the Civil War all but dried up the market, especially after the fall of Vicksburg, which gave the Union control of the Mississippi and blocked Texas from supplying beef to the Confederacy via New Orleans. Something like five million cattle were in Texas before the start of the war, and with so many of their owners off fighting the Union or serving in the Frontier Regiment guarding the settlements from the Indians, the longhorns ran wild. As they propagated, their unbranded offspring grew even more longhorn-like, their horns getting longer and twistier, their colors variegating into a profusion

Waddies on the trail, taking a break from their dust-eating chores.

of browns, blacks, brindles, and grays—every shade of the natural palette of the Texas landscape. They also bred an attitude of defiance—"fifty times more dangerous to footmen," in the opinion of Colonel Richard Irving Dodge, "than the fiercest buffalo."

Fortunately, it wasn't queasy footmen but highly motivated equestrian entrepreneurs like Charles Goodnight who began to round up these beasts when the Civil War ended and the northern states—flush with victory but short on beef after supplying the Union armies—opened a powerful new marketing opportunity. Cattle on the ground in Texas were worth three or four dollars a head. If you could get them to a northern city, they would be worth ten times that. The math was inspiring, and it created the cattle drives that in turn created a big piece of the evolving Texas identity. In the never-shy words of the writer and Lone Star myth keeper J. Frank Dobie, the drives were "the greatest, the most extraordinary, the most stupendous, the most fantastic and fabulous migration of animals controlled by man that the world has ever known or can ever know."

There were three main cattle corridors: the Goodnight-Loving Trail, the Chisholm Trail, and the Western Trail. Their names still carry a charge in a state where very little moseying takes place anymore and traffic moves on interstate highways designated by cold numbers. The first of these routes was named for Charles Goodnight and his partner, Oliver Loving, but pioneered by an Ohio native named James Patterson. Goodnight was thirty in 1866 when he and Loving combined their herds and made their first drive to Fort Sumner, New Mexico, where 8,500 Navajos and Mescalero Apaches were desperately in need of food on their reservations. Oliver Loving was fifty-four, a former freight hauler and store owner in Palo Pinto County, a father of nine who had driven a herd all the way to Colorado before the war and sold it for enough gold to present his five daughters with matching golden rings.

Goodnight, Loving, and sixteen men embarked on a June day with two thousand cattle from Young County. The trail swerved west, straight across much of Texas to the Pecos River, before turning north into eastern New Mexico. It was a wide detour that largely avoided the turbulent Comanche and Kiowa country but led the herd across hellish, waterless wastes and then to riverbeds full of quicksand and alkaline ponds that might as well have been straight poison for the thirsty longhorns. Goodnight and Loving lost 20 percent of their stock along the way to drowning or dehydration, their bones sunk in the mud or strewn along the salt lakes beyond the Horsehead Crossing of the Pecos. But they made a profit when they arrived in Fort Sumner, enough to warrant another drive that same year. The next year they did it again, but this time the losses were human as well. Loving, scouting alone,

The novelist Larry McMurtry teaching a creative writing class at Rice University in 1972. Though a confirmed chronicler of contemporary Texas, his imagination was still tethered to the bygone world of the trail drives, which would lead to the publication in 1985 of Lonesome Dove, *the all-time world champion Texas novel.*

was mortally wounded in an Indian attack. He somehow survived for three days before being found by Mexican teamsters and then dying of gangrene.

The song "Oh, Bury Me Not on the Lone Prairie," was composed in 1879 by a pair of trail drivers who had heard a dying companion beg them not to inter him in the middle of nowhere on the far side of the Red River. It also echoed the homesick sentiments of Oliver Loving, whose last request to Charles Goodnight was to have his body transported back to Texas. It isn't clear whether Goodnight drove his partner back himself or contracted the mournful job out to somebody else, but if all this is starting to sound familiar, it's probably because you either read Larry McMurtry's novel *Lonesome Dove* or watched the miniseries that was made from it.

Delivering cattle to scattershot markets in the West via the Goodnight-Loving Trail was a profitable though perilous enterprise. The big play was in the cities of the East and the North, if they could be reached. To do that, a cattle trail needed to connect with a railroad, which is what the Chisholm Trail did. The trail was named for a trader and Indian interpreter—he spoke twelve dialects—named Jesse Chisholm, who had laid out a wagon road connecting his trading posts in Indian Territory with central Kansas. Using that road as the northern part of a cattle trail originating in Texas was the idea of a young sparkplug named Joseph McCoy. McCoy went looking for a place far enough from the Texas fever quarantine zone that cattle could be loaded onto the Kansas Pacific Railroad. A nothing-happening town named Abilene in northeastern Kansas turned out to be just what he wanted. It was "a very small, dead place" of log huts with dirt roofs, where the keeper of the town's one saloon sold souvenir prairie dogs to tourists passing through on the train. The economy was about to improve. McCoy built stockyards and pens and loading chutes and then sent word to Texas that he was open for business.

In that year, 1867, 35,000 cattle were assembled from as far south as Brownsville and from along feeder trails in South or Central Texas and driven north through San Antonio, Austin, Waco, and Fort Worth. They crossed out of Texas at a treacherous ford called Red River Station and pressed on through Indian Territory and most of Kansas before arriving at McCoy's railroad siding in Abilene. There was a problem in getting beasts with eight-foot-wide horns through the five-foot-wide doors of railroad cars, but there were men on hand to twist their heads through the openings or, when that didn't work, to saw off their horns. The next year, more than 75,000 cattle made their way up the trail, and by 1871 the numbers had increased almost tenfold to 700,000. Abilene did so much to solve the supply-and-demand problem of Texas cattlemen that my boyhood hometown of Abilene, Texas, was named in its honor when it was established in 1881.

The Chisholm Trail faded away during the mid-1870s when new quarantine laws in Kansas forced the drovers to develop another route farther to the west. This trail, the Western Trail, led straight up through the heart of the last contested ground of the Comanches and Kiowas, but by the time it was in use Miles and Mackenzie and their armies had driven the Indians across the Red River onto their reservations. The southern buffalo herd was almost gone, too. The trail drivers were usually assessed a fee—payable in cattle, tobacco, or other goods—to pass through Indian Territory. From there the trail led to the railroad at Dodge City, the Kansas town that had once been the headquarters of the buffalo slaughter but, with its newfound cattle prosperity, was blossoming into what one headline writer in 1878 called "The Beautiful, Bibulous Babylon of the Frontier."

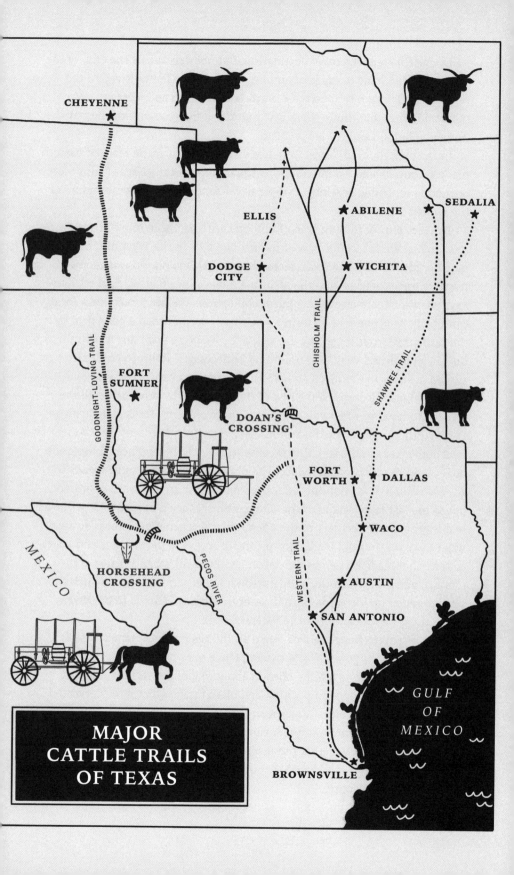

CHEYENNE

ELLIS

ABILENE ★

SEDALIA ★

DODGE
CITY ★

WICHITA ★

GOODNIGHT-LOVING TRAIL

CHISHOLM TRAIL

SHAWNEE TRAIL

FORT
SUMNER ★

DOAN'S
CROSSING

FORT
WORTH ★   ★ DALLAS

★ WACO

MEXICO

HORSEHEAD
CROSSING

PECOS RIVER

WESTERN TRAIL

★ AUSTIN

★ SAN ANTONIO

GULF
OF
MEXICO

MAJOR
CATTLE TRAILS
OF TEXAS

BROWNSVILLE

Dodge City was the main destination, but not necessarily the end, of the Western Trail. Some herds kept ambling north to the Platte River, to the railhead at Ogallala, Nebraska, or much farther north and west into Wyoming and Montana, where there was a world of free grass untouched by the vanishing buffalo and ready for cattle.

In the end, the trail drives were not just how Texas cattle reached eastern markets, but also how a million or so square miles of the Great Plains were opened to ranching, sparking a whole new economy for the western half of the United States.

By 1880, almost four and a half million cattle had been moved from Texas to slaughterhouses in the East or to grazing lands in the West. But in the next decade the trail drives staggered to an end. One reason was renewed hostility to Texas fever, and the resulting quarantines that blocked off Kansas and other destinations. ("A burnt child shuns the fire," declared a local cattleman, "and some of us from Kansas have been burned a good deal by the cattle trail from Texas. We are sick of it; we don't want any more of it.") But the epic drives were also becoming unnecessary. Railroad construction surged in Texas in the 1870s and 1880s, connecting every major city, and finally connecting Texas to the rest of the nation. Why drive cattle all the way to Dodge City when you could load them onto the Texas and Pacific in Fort Worth, or deliver them to a local slaughterhouse?

Another reason the trail drives came to an end: the unfenced grasslands of Texas were unfenced no longer. The phrase "open range" still speaks to an American itch for unimpeded movement across an unbroken continent, but in the last few decades of the nineteenth century it ceased to describe a real way of life. In the days of the open range, a rancher's business strategy wasn't to own the land itself, but to control access to the streams and watercourses that made cattle raising viable. Land was all around, a vast commons of grass on which the animals wandered and grazed, from which they were rounded up for branding and for organizing into herds to be driven north along the Chisholm or the Western Trail.

That began to change in 1874 when an Illinois inventor named Joseph Glidden received a patent for "a twisted fence-wire having the transverse spur wire D bent at its middle portion about one of the strands A of said fence-wire, and clamped in position and place by the other wire Z, twisted upon its fellow, substantially as specified." It was a deliriously complex description for a supremely simple invention—a length of wire with impaling barbs woven into it. Whether the inspiration for barbed wire was to keep livestock contained or to keep dogs out of Mrs. Glidden's flowerbeds is apparently open to dispute.

But would barbed wire work to keep unruly longhorns from breaking out? The answer came two years later when a salesman for the Washburn & Moen Company, the firm marketing the product, staged a demonstration in San Antonio. John Warne Gates would later become famous as an oilman and flamboyant gambler known as "Bet a Million" Gates, but in 1876 he was just a portly young wire hustler in a bowler hat and ostentatious checked pants that were a little too tight. He had met resistance from ranchers who refused to consider ordering "bob wire" because they didn't believe it would contain their cattle and instead would just create inviting wounds to host screwworm flies. To prove them wrong, Gates organized an extravaganza in Military Plaza that took its inspiration from a medicine show that had just come to town, in which a master salesman named Doc Lighthall entered the plaza in a gilded chariot and proceeded to promote a blood purifier named Radway's Sarsaparillion Resolvent.

Military Plaza was the old Plaza de Armas of Spanish days, the scene of much house-to-house fighting in the Battle of Béxar and still very much the throbbing center of San Antonio, full of shopping stalls and the outdoor Mexican food vendors known as chili queens. Gates fenced the plaza in with barbed wire as a crowd gathered, eager to see him fail and taking bets to that effect. Before the main event, there was a rodeo with bulldoggers and trick riders, and then Gates began to extol his product, calling barbed wire "light as air, stronger than whiskey, cheaper than dirt!"

Forty confused and frightened longhorn steers were led into the enclosure and harried toward the perimeters by a Mexican vaquero holding two flaming torches. The demonstration worked spectacularly well. The cattle strained and pushed one another against the eight strands of barbed wire strung up between mesquite fence posts. The wire held, and the longhorns, after their initial terror, settled into place.

And so barbed wire happened. Thanks to Bet a Million Gates's showmanship, and to more down-to-earth field tests carried out by farmers and ranchers, Texas got fenced. The demand for barbed wire was overwhelming, and even took its inventor, Joseph Glidden, by surprise. When a client telegraphed an order, Glidden telegraphed back, thinking there had to have been a misprint. Surely the man was only asking for a hundred pounds of barbed wire. No, the reply came, the order was right the first time: a hundred tons.

Barbed wire, along with the windmill, which was introduced onto the Great Plains at about the same time, radically changed Texas. Cattle kingdoms, the great unmarked expanses where livestock ranged freely until rounded up, became ranches with fenced pastures—big pastures, to be sure, but no longer limitless. Barbed wire changed cattle too. It spelled the end of the time when longhorns propagated indiscriminately on the open range, and made possible the careful cultivation of specific strains of blooded cattle. And it moved farmers west, out from the coastal prairies and up onto the plains, where they could plant crops and raise livestock that would be protected from the rampages of half-wild cattle.

It was far from a smooth transition. Cowmen accustomed to feeding their cattle on the free grass of Texas public lands found themselves fenced out by big landowners, who now more than ever controlled access to streams and water holes. And worse, those landowners were sometimes absentee capitalists. A Chicago syndicate sold bonds to wealthy British investors such as the Earl of Aberdeen for the purpose of buying three million acres in the Panhandle from the State of Texas to create the vast XIT Ranch. The Matador Land and Cattle Company, headquartered in Dundee, Scotland, owned a big piece of the plains below the Caprock. "Away with your foreign capitalists!" declared an omnibus rant in the Fort Worth newspaper that pretty much summed up the prevailing grievances of white Texans: "The range and soil of Texas belong to the heroes of the South. No monopolies, and don't tax us to school the nigger. Give us homes as God intended and not gates to churches and towns and schools. Above all, give us water for our stock."

Saboteurs organized themselves into secret fence-cutting societies with names like the Owls, Blue Devils, or Javelinas, and snipped away at the "devil's hat band." Things got bad enough that the state legislature finally made fence cutting a felony enforced by the Texas Rangers.

At about the time Bet a Million Gates was demonstrating his barbed wire, Charles Goodnight was busy establishing a ranch at the bottom of Palo Duro Canyon. This was in the heart of the Llano Estacado, which a recent handbook for immigrants called "the only uninhabitable portion of Texas." Goodnight thought otherwise, as had the Comanches and Kiowas who had been driven from the canyon by Mackenzie's soldiers only a few years before. Goodnight and his men gathered up the Indians' abandoned lodge poles to use as rafters for the dugout that served as their first ranch headquarters. They built smudge fires out of dried buffalo dung to drive away the blowflies that emerged in a pestilential mass from the thousands of rotting buffalo carcasses left scattered across the llano by the hide hunters. Goodnight's ranch ended up being called the JA, after John Adair, the man who bankrolled its expansion. Adair was an arrogant Northern Irish aristocrat—"an overbearing old son-of-a-gun," in Goodnight's probably cleaned-up-for-print words—but the partnership was productive. The ranch in the Palo Duro grew to 1.3 million acres, thanks to Goodnight's canny and sweeping acquisitiveness. "I wanted that cañon," he told his biographer, J. Evetts Haley. "I took all the good land and all the water I could get. . . . Every good ranch in the country, every place a man was liable to come, I took." And though he was as much an avatar of the open range as anyone alive, he fenced it in with barbed wire.

Charles Goodnight was fierce looking in his youth, in his middle age, and deep into his dotage. His hair and beard turned white, but in photographs his penetrating, disapproving countenance is undiminished. But he didn't seem to scare off women, neither his beloved wife, Molly, nor the twenty-seven-year-old nurse-secretary he married when he was a widower of ninety-one. Molly was born Mary Ann Dyer. She was a schoolteacher whose family had come to Texas from Tennessee in the 1850s. In photographs, she appears almost as stern looking as her husband, but she was a nurturing soul who became known as the "Darling of the Plains" and the "Mother of the Panhandle" for her kindness to cowboys and to orphaned baby buffalo. When she first came to the Panhandle, Molly was in the company of John Adair's wife, Cornelia. Lady Adair, a product of Philadelphia and New York, was a dauntless society adventurer who loved nothing better than hunting buffalo and riding sidesaddle across hundreds of miles of open country. After helping establish the ranch, she departed the llano for her husband's Irish estate, leaving Molly Goodnight alone in a part of the country where the nearest female company was forty-five miles away.

At some point, she may have crossed paths with Lizzie Johnson Williams, though Williams lived even farther away, in Hays County. They had cattle and ranching in common, though whether a Panhandle earth mother like Molly Goodnight would have gotten along with a business-minded cattle queen like Lizzie Johnson Williams is a matter of speculation. Williams was the daughter of a strict Central Texas schoolmaster nicknamed "Old Bristle Top." Like the young Molly Goodnight, she became a teacher, a "rather austere and firm" one in the opinion of her students. The impression is reinforced, fairly or not, by a studio photograph taken when she was in her thirties, in which she is wearing a dress of brush-popping practicality and a look of almost ruthless determination. She was thirty-nine in 1879 when she married a widower named Hezekiah Williams and promptly signed him to the equivalent of a prenuptial agreement. He was a jovial drinker, and she was a hard-nosed businesswoman with assets she did not care to put at risk. She already had multiple income streams: from teaching; from a successful career as a writer of short stories, such as "Lady Inez; or the Passion Flower, an American Romance," that appeared in main-

LIZZIE JOHNSON WILLIAMS
was a no-nonsense cattle queen who drove herds up the Chisholm Trail and supplemented her ranching income by publishing floridly romantic short stories.

stream national publications like Frank Leslie's *Illustrated Weekly*; from bookkeeping for ranchers; and finally from her own cattle enterprise. She rounded up mavericks, branded them with her registered brand, and contracted to send them up the Chisholm Trail. She even went up the trail herself, eating dust along with the waddies, accompanied by her husband but not in business with him, since they were herding their separate brands to market. She kept a steely control over her cattle and her finances, and over the years she had to repeatedly bail her dissolute husband out, once even ransoming him from bandits in Cuba. But when he died, she seems to have fallen apart, living out her life as a magnificently strange and disagreeable old lady who, though she owned ranches and property all over Texas, as well as a big piece of the city of Austin, dressed so raggedly that people stopped her on the street to offer her money. It would never have occurred to diners in 1920 or so at the Maverick Cafe in Austin, as they watched this solitary, crotchety old woman argue with the proprietor about the price of her vegetable soup, that they were in the presence of an actual maverick, one of the remnant personalities of the fading Texas frontier.

★

FADING, BUT NOT GONE. BY 1879, THE COMANCHES AND KIOWAS were no longer in the way of white dominance in Texas—they were in fact no longer in Texas at all except for sporadic hunting expeditions or unsanctioned outbreaks from their reservations beyond the Red River. Only a few Native American groups maintained any kind of ancestral foothold in the state. The Alabamas and Coushattas, two historically allied tribes sharing a mutually understandable Muskogean language, had migrated into East

Texas toward the end of the eighteenth century and carved out settlements and pathways in the unbroken, disorienting forest gloom of the Big Thicket. They had been diplomatically adroit enough to win the goodwill of even Mirabeau Lamar, and had managed to hang on to some vestige of Texas soil in Polk County after almost every other tribe had been driven from the state. And eight hundred miles to the west, in the village of Ysleta del Sur, downriver from El Paso, there were still a few hundred members of the Tiguas, descendants of the Tiguex people whom Coronado had warred against in the 1540s. After the Pueblo Revolt in 1680, some of the Tiguas had accompanied the fleeing Spaniards downriver to El Paso, and there they remained, on land that had been swindled away from under their feet by various promoters and state legislators.

The Lipan Apaches, who had once controlled much of Texas and fought so bitterly against the Spanish, had mostly retreated to Mexico, where they had joined with another Apache band, the Mescaleros, in cross-border raiding until they were routed by Ranald Mackenzie in 1873. The surviving Lipans ended up at the Mescalero reservation in southeastern New Mexico, near present-day Ruidoso.

It was an Apache chief of the Chiricahua band, from beyond the Black Range in western New Mexico, who sparked the last of the Indian wars in Texas. Beduiat, better known as Victorio, was around fifty-five years old in 1880, a veteran partisan who had fought with Apache war leaders such as Nana and Geronimo but had done his best to accommodate himself and his people to the undeniable reality of defeat. But he was pushed too far when the government decreed that they had to move from their traditional homelands to the overcrowded and inhospitable confines of the San Carlos Reservation in southeastern Arizona. He led several followers off the reservation and began raiding throughout New Mexico and Texas and into Mexico.

The war that was fought against Victorio took place mostly in the driest and least populated part of the state, the region west of the Pecos River. The Trans-Pecos is a hard place to fight a war, a sun-hammered expanse of endless creosote flats interrupted by looming desert mountains. But it was familiar territory for the buffalo soldiers of the Tenth Cavalry, who had chased Comanches and Kiowas all throughout it, and who had lost four men to thirst in 1877 during a disastrous expedition that went eighty-six hours without water.

The Tenth was stationed at Fort Concho and farther west at Fort Davis, which had been built at the base of a picturesque box canyon guarding the San Antonio—El Paso road. Today it is one of the best preserved Texas forts, located only a few miles up Texas Highway 17 from the fashionably remote hipster paradise of Marfa. Strolling along its parade ground, beneath the cracked columns of volcanic rock rearing overhead, it's easy to comprehend how truly remote a posting it was back in 1880, and how every patrol that wandered outward from it into the waterless immensity the Spanish called the *despoblado* had to reckon with the real possibility of never returning.

Buffalo soldiers got their name, it is thought, because Indians regarded the hair on top of black troopers' heads to have a textural kinship with buffalo fur. The Tenth was commanded by fifty-four-year-old Colonel Benjamin Grierson, who, despite being afraid of horses as a child, had become a lionized cavalry officer in the Civil War. All the other officers in this African American regiment were white as well, except for one: Lieutenant Henry O. Flipper, the first black man to graduate from West Point. Flipper had distinguished himself in the Red River War and would do so as well in the campaign against Victorio.

Grierson and his buffalo soldiers pursued Victorio for 1,500 miles throughout the Trans-Pecos and into New Mexico, but the Apaches eluded them and slipped across the Rio Grande into Mexico. Victorio was a gifted strategist, both when fighting and in flight, but he was being pursued across a landscape where his choices, particularly when it came to water, were limited. Aware of this, Grierson shifted his own strategy. When he received word that Victorio had once again crossed into Texas, he had his men stake out the few springs and waterholes where he knew the Apaches would have no choice but to stop. This led to a fight on July 30 at a place called Tinaja de las Palmas, near the present-day town of Sierra Blanca, and to another, more climactic one a week later, after Grierson ordered a forced march of sixty-five miles to the next waterhole. His men outpaced Victorio in time to set up an ambush in the Sierra Diablo Mountains, in a canyon leading to Rattle-snake Springs. Victorio sniffed out the ambush, but he was desperate for water, and in his repeated assaults against the buffalo soldiers in the canyon, and in a failed attack against Grierson's supply train, he may have lost as many as 30 of his 150 warriors. Three buffalo soldiers died, three were wounded, and another disappeared during the skirmish, presumably carried off by the Apaches to a merciless and vengeful death somewhere along their retreat back to Mexico.

That October, a Mexican Army force led by Colonel Joaquín Terrazas trapped Victorio and his followers in a cluster of desert peaks known as Tres Castillos. Victorio was wounded early in the battle that followed, and during the night he predicted to a young Mescalero warrior that "the end will be at sunrise." It was. Terrazas assaulted their position at dawn, and the last of Victorio's renegade Apaches died in hand-to-hand fighting or were picked off by Mexican *cazadores*. The Tarahumara scout who had shot and wounded Victorio the day before was awarded two thousands pesos for his scalp.

Kennedy, Wilberforce, O.

LIEUTENANT HENRY FLIPPER
was the first black man to graduate from West Point, but his promising military career ended in ruins on the Texas frontier. "The trap," he wrote, "was cunningly laid."

Rattlesnake Springs turned out to be the last Indian battle on Texas soil, fought against a once-mighty native power that had been steadily eroded over the centuries by the Comanches, the Spaniards, the Mexicans, the Texas Rangers, and finally by a U.S. Army regiment made up mostly of men—like Henry Flipper—who had been born into slavery.

LIEUTENANT FLIPPER'S CONTRIBUTIONS IN THE CAMPAIGN

against Victorio and in the Red River War did not go unrecognized. In the opinion of Benjamin Grierson, he had "steadily won his way by sterling worth and ability, by manly and soldierly bearing, to the confidence, respect and esteem of all with whom he has served or come in contact." In recognition of his service, he was named acting quartermaster and post commissary at Fort Davis. But what seemed like a next step up the career ladder turned out to be the preamble to a court-martial.

"Never did a man walk the path of uprightness straighter than I did," Flipper bitterly wrote in his memoir, "but the trap was cunningly laid and I was sacrificed."

It's doubtful there really was an elaborate conspiracy to end Flipper's military career. It's easier to take him at his word when he writes that most of the white officers at Fort Davis treated him with patronizing tolerance. As the lone black officer, he was not just emotionally isolated but also burdened with a racial pioneer's responsibility of never making a false step. At the same time, he smoldered with resentment at his treatment. He saw the officers who thwarted and tormented him as "hyenas." He noted that he routinely went on horseback excursions with a young white woman, the sister-in-law of his troop commander. A fellow officer who later thought that Flipper had been unduly punished qualified his concern by noting, "Our wives and daughters must be considered."

The problem had to do with missing funds for which Flipper, as commissary officer, was responsible. The amount was almost four thousand dollars. Flipper had no training or experience in bookkeeping, was careless about his personal finances, and naively thought he could write a personal check to cover part of the loss until he could locate the missing money. Unfortunately, there wasn't any money in his San Antonio bank account to cover the hot check. But he had recently sold an autobiography, and with the unfounded optimism of freelance writers throughout the centuries, he hoped his royalties would arrive in time.

They didn't. He was arrested by the post commander, Colonel William R. Shafter, charged with embezzlement, and thrown into the guardhouse.

Interestingly, the white civilians who lived around Fort Davis sprang to Flipper's defense and took it upon themselves to raise the money to cover the missing commissary funds. But the lieutenant was court-martialed anyway. "Tried and punished by the commanding officer of this post with a severity which is unexampled in the history of the service," pleaded his attorney during the trial, "tried and punished by the trumpet voice of the press which has heralded every idle dream of suspicion as the burden of my client's sin, he now comes before you to be tried again and he asks you . . . if he has not been punished enough for the errors into which he was led by circumstances."

Not quite enough. Although he was found innocent of embezzlement, Flipper was convicted of "conduct unbecoming an officer and gentleman" and dismissed from the army in December 1881. He never gave up trying to overturn his conviction, but he didn't allow himself to grow stagnant in resentment. Tough-minded, ambitious, fluent in Spanish, he carved out a career as a surveyor and mining engineer in the Southwest, Mexico, Venezuela, and Alaska. He published memoirs, English translations of books on Spanish mining law and combustible materials, and even an article about Estebanico, the black slave who had been shipwrecked with Cabeza de Vaca and walked across some of the same country where Flipper, as an officer in the Tenth Cavalry, had pursued Victorio almost three and a half centuries later.

After Flipper's conviction, the judge advocate general appealed for leniency, stating his belief that the officer was guilty of no more than carelessness and that "there is no case on record in which an officer was treated with such personal harshness and indignity." The appeal went unanswered by President Chester A. Arthur. Flipper died in his eighties in 1940, with the verdict of conduct unbecoming an officer and a gentleman still hanging over his reputation. But in 1976, after lobbying from his descendants, he was granted a retroactive honorable discharge, and in 1999 he was given a full pardon by President Bill Clinton in a White House ceremony. There is a bust of him today on the grounds of West Point.

──────── ★ ────────

A YEAR AFTER HENRY FLIPPER'S COURT-MARTIAL, ANOTHER man who would be tried—and convicted—for embezzling stepped off a train at a town halfway between San Antonio and Laredo. William Sydney Porter was nineteen years old, a pharmacist from North Carolina whose mother had died of tuberculosis when he was three. Afraid that he might be developing the disease himself, he had come to Texas on the advice of a family friend, a doctor who thought the searing climate would be beneficial.

The La Salle County town of Cotulla, where Porter relocated, had a reputation. "Cotulla!" conductors supposedly announced as the train neared the station. "Everybody get your guns ready." It sat on the edge of the Nueces Strip, the forever-contested land between that river and the Rio Grande. Trouble in the Nueces Strip had never died down, and never really would, but the years after the Civil War had been a particularly incendiary time, with Anglo and Mexican bandits crossing the river from both sides to steal cattle and settle long-simmering grudges over stolen land and stolen honor. In 1875, a slight, dapper-looking Texas Ranger captain named Leander McNelly was authorized to raise a forty-man company and bestow law and order on the Nueces Strip. McNelly had seen a lot of fighting in the Civil War—at the New Mexico Battle of Val Verde, at Galveston, at the Battle of Mansfield, and in numerous bloody guerrilla skirmishes when he was a twenty-year-old captain leading a company of mounted irregulars whose job was to create havoc with the Union's attempt to invade Texas via the Red River.

The fact that McNelly, who was barely in his thirties, was already dying of tuberculosis when ordered to the Nueces Strip did not prevent him from carrying out his duties with a grim completeness that has been both celebrated and reviled, depending on your position regarding illegal border crossings, summary executions, and torture. He retained a sadistic associate named Jesús Sandoval—a "perfect Chesterfield in politeness"—whose specialty was extracting information from captured bandits or those suspected of being bandits by dangling them by the neck from a hangman's noose. When it came to the actual hanging, he was the soul of courtliness. "He is so kind and considerate," wrote one of McNelly's men, "that it . . . would almost be a pleasure to be hanged by such a nice gentleman."

A telegram that McNelly sent to the Texas adjutant general demonstrates the taciturn satisfaction that he took in fulfilling his duty: "Had a fight with raiders, killed twelve and captured two hundred and sixty beeves. Wish you were here."

At one point, in November 1875, McNelly led his men across the Rio Grande in pursuit of Mexican bandits and 400–500 head of cattle stolen from Texas ranches. The Rangers were on a tight budget, but their outfit had been generously supplemented during a stop at the King Ranch, where Richard King had presented McNelly with a prize bay to replace the mount he had driven to exhaustion while crossing the Wild Horse Desert. A storekeeper in Corpus Christi, Sol Lichtenstein, had also been generous, providing them with the Sharps rifles that would soon become the weapon of choice for buffalo hunters. "They were boogers," one of McNelly's men remembered. "That fifty caliber bore looked big enough for a gopher to crawl through."

McNelly's men attacked a place called Rancho Las Cuevas on the other side of the border, but had to retreat when they stirred up a counterattack by three hundred or so heavily armed men, a combined force of rustlers and the Ranger-like Mexican lawmen known as rurales. Besieged on the Mexican side of the border, McNelly managed to get off a telegram to the Texas adjutant general: "The Mexicans are in my front . . . [number] about four hundred. What should I do?"

Among the opinions received, from U.S. Secretary of War William Belknap and from the colonel commanding the regular army on the other side of the border, was: surrender to the Mexican authorities. "Give my compliments to the Secretary of War," McNelly replied, "and tell him and his United States soldiers to go to hell."

The standoff ended in a hastily arranged armistice, with the Rangers and the recovered cattle withdrawing across the river, preventing an international war but leaving twenty-seven rurales and bandits dead on the field.

They weren't the only casualties of McNelly's raid. "Is it the truth you want?" an old vaquero once asked the historian Walter Prescott Webb while he was researching his 1935 history of the Texas Rangers. He then told Webb about being a boy and watching in horror as McNelly and his men launched their attack on the people of Las Cuevas, shooting down his relatives and friends with their rifles and Colt revolvers.

Though the book that Webb produced is often thought of today as an antiquated paean to the Rangers, the author must have taken at least some of what the old vaquero told him to heart, because in other writings he frankly wished that McNelly had been killed at the Alamo or Goliad: "Had he performed the remarkable feats there on behalf of freedom that he performed in the Nueces Strip, mainly on behalf of a few stolen King cattle, he would have been a heroic figure in Texas history."

But he was heroic enough for the men who served under him. They revered him, and at least one of them, George Durham, dreamed of reuniting with McNelly in the Texas Ranger afterlife. "When I get Over Yonder," he wrote, "I want to go back to work for Captain if he's still running an outfit."

A year before he died in 1877, McNelly was succeeded by Lee Hall, the son of the doctor in North Carolina who had advised William Sydney Porter to move to Texas. Hall had served as captain of McNelly's earthly outfit for three years before retiring from the Rangers in 1880 to manage a big ranch south of the Nueces. Porter lived on this ranch for two years, dabbling in sheepherding and ranch chores but devoting his mental energy to the sort of saturation-level reading, watching, and listening common to young aspiring writers. One of the people he paid the most attention to was Lee Hall, an imposing, hard-drinking Ranger specimen who was also a loquacious retailer of anecdotes about cattle rustling, fence cutting, epic feuds, and the pistol-wielding psychopaths he had encountered in the thorny *brasada* of the Nueces Strip.

Porter left the ranch in 1884 and moved to Austin, where he worked as a draftsman at the General Land Office and then as a bank teller. He started a weekly humor newspaper called the *Rolling Stone*, which lasted for a year before going under. Porter went under as well, arrested for embezzling bank funds and sent to an Ohio penitentiary. He was thirty-five then; he would be dead by forty-seven. He spent his three years in prison working as a pharmacist and writing short stories under the pseudonym O. Henry. Upon release, he moved to New York and developed into one of the most famous writers in the world. In 1907, a few years before he died, he published a collection of short stories called *The Heart of the West*. A number of the stories featured Texas Rangers and outlaws and the South Texas brush country he had gotten to know in his time on the ranch. The protagonist in one of the stories, "The Caballero's Way," is a Ranger named Sandridge— "Six feet two, blond as a Viking, quiet as a deacon, dangerous as a machine gun"—who is on the trail of a charismatic young killer named the Cisco Kid. The story has a nice descriptive paragraph or two about prickly pear flats, but it mostly reminds you why the author has never quite been welcomed into the hallowed academic precincts patrolled by literature professors. "The Caballero's Way" is sentimental, self-satisfied, and preposterous, with a typical O. Henry surprise ending—in this case, the Ranger hero is double- or even triple-crossed by the remorseless Cisco Kid.

WILLIAM SYDNEY PORTER
was a sickly pharmacist who headed to Texas for his health. The stories he found there helped turn him into O. Henry—one of the most popular writers in the world.

What makes the story interesting is that the Cisco Kid seems to have been inspired to some degree by John Wesley Hardin, whose name recognition as a Texas outlaw is probably even greater than O. Henry's as a short-story writer. Porter would have heard about him from Lee Hall, who as a Ranger captain had overseen the tentacular operation that captured Hardin in Pensacola, Florida, in 1877.

The arrest was sensational national news. Hardin, still in his early twenties, was the "Grand Mogul of Texas desperadoes." He had come of age bearing a grudge in the miserable, vengeful climate of Reconstruction. ("In those times," he wrote, "if there was anything that could rouse my passion it was seeing impudent negroes, lately freed, insult or abuse old, wounded Confederates."). Hardin's father, a Methodist minister, had named him for John Wesley, but if he was hoping for a tolerant and liberal-minded son he was disappointed. John Wesley Hardin, a charming character of conniving intelligence, was briefly a molder of young minds in Navarro County when at fifteen he was hired as a schoolteacher. His students were impressed that he prayed every morning before class. They would have been even more impressed to learn that he had already killed four men. The next year he would kill two more, including one who cried out, "Oh, Lordy, don't shoot me any more," as Hardin drunkenly pumped him full of bullets.

In 1871 he did what so many rootless young men in Texas did: he joined a cattle outfit and headed up the Chisholm Trail to Abilene. By the time he returned, he had killed another ten people. Back in Texas, he threw himself into the Sutton-Taylor feud. He was on the Taylor side, and one of the people he killed was Jack Helm, the rogue State Police officer who had murdered the Kelly brothers.

When Hardin was arrested in Florida, it was for the murder of a deputy sheriff, but by then he may have killed as many as thirty men, including one that, according to legend, he dispatched for snoring. The "knight of the six-shooter," as one newspaper referred to him, enchanted the crowds who came to see him as he was escorted back to Texas for his trial. The Texas Rangers who guarded him were particularly impressed. They handed him unloaded six-shooters so he could demonstrate his famous "border roll," a gun-twirling maneuver he had bragged about using in Abilene when Wild Bill Hickok once tried to arrest him.

He was locked up for almost sixteen years in the forbidding-looking state penitentiary that the Texas Legislature had ordered built in 1848 in Sam Houston's hometown of Huntsville. The penitentiary was known (and is still known) as the "Walls" for the twenty-foot-high walls of red brick that surrounded it. Hardin's first order of business on arriving at the Walls was to escape. He recruited dozens of fellow convicts in an audacious attempt to tunnel beneath the prison grounds and surface inside the armory, where the plan was to seize the guns, capture the guards, and "liberate all who wished to go except the rape fiends." But the plan was discovered, as were subsequent attempts, for which Hardin was mercilessly flogged with a leather strap. After a while, he stopped trying to escape and settled into prison life, plotting a longer and slower release through guile and charm. He studied theology and became the president of the prison's debating club, once arguing in the affirmative on women's rights. He read law, conned a judge into supporting his release ("You ought to read Victor Hugo's masterpiece, Les Miserables," the judge wrote him), got a governor's pardon, passed the bar, and became a licensed attorney. At forty-one, he married a rebellious and impressionable fifteen-year-old girl, who ran back home to her parents after a week. He moved to El Paso, where he opened a law practice. The *El Paso Times* was maybe a little too hopeful in observing that "forty-one years has steadied the impetuous cowboy down to a quiet, peaceable man of business." The line between law enforcement and criminality was blurry in El Paso, where being a sheriff or a constable did not necessarily mean that you might not be available for a hired killing.

In El Paso, Hardin made the awkward transition from knight of the six-shooter to scary drunk. "I would feel my very bones chill," recalled his landlady, "when he looked at me with his darting little serpentine eyes."

He had been working on an autobiography but had only gotten up to his law studies in prison when he was ambushed one August day while shooting dice. His assailant was John Selman, formerly the leader of a notorious outlaw gang but now the local constable. It remained undetermined whether Selman shot him because of a personal argument or because Hardin had neglected to pay Selman his fee for helping murder the husband of one of his clients. In any case, he was dead on the floor of the Acme Saloon. As his body lay there for hours with his blood pooling and his brains leaking out of his head, the citizens of El Paso streamed in and took a last look at the man who had been a cowboy, a killer, and a chronicler of his own notorious life.

—27—

TURN TEXAS
LOOSE

IT ISN'T TRUE, AS TEXAS SCHOOLCHILDREN HAVE LONG believed, that Governor James Hogg saddled his two daughters with the names Ima Hogg and Ura Hogg. Not quite true, anyway. There was never a Ura Hogg, but there was an Ima. The governor named his only daughter after the heroine of an epic Civil War poem—*The Fate of Marvin*—written by his older brother. Hogg later claimed that he and his wife, Sallie, "never noticed the play of her name until it was called to our attention." Ima's grandfather, however, saw the problem as soon as he got word of what the baby was going to be called, and hurried to the Hogg home in the northeastern Texas town of Mineola to put a stop to it. But he got there too late; she had already been christened.

Ima Hogg lived until 1975, a renowned philanthropist, art collector, and preservationist. She never married and suffered from time to time with depression, but there is no evidence that she was ever scarred by her name or harbored any resentment toward the man who had given it to her. On the contrary, she worshipped him.

When Ima Hogg was born, her father was a thirty-one-year-old district attorney and rising politician in the Democratic Party, which, after the ouster of E. J. Davis and his Republican regime, was effectively the only political party in Texas. James Hogg's father had served as a brigadier general in the Confederate army and died from dysentery during the siege of Corinth when James was eleven. As a young man, James worked as a typesetter on East Texas newspapers and then as a sharecropping farmer and an employee at a cotton gin. In 1869, he joined in to help subdue a gang of assassins who had ridden into the town of Quitman to kill the sheriff. A few months later, when he was eighteen, the same men lured him to an isolated house across the Sabine and shot him in the back. He lay there bleeding on a bed all night and half the next day. The doctor who finally arrived had no surgical instruments and used a stick to probe the wound, which was perilously near the spine. The doctor finally gave up trying to remove the bullet and went home.

Hogg somehow survived, though it took a long time for the wound to heal and for his spirits to rebound. He was in a state of deep despondency until one day, while walking alone in the woods, he heard the song of a mockingbird. He was probably not the first Texan to feel restored to life by the piercing, ricocheting musicality of *Mimus polyglottos*, no doubt part of the reason it became the Texas state bird. (Although that did not happen until 1927, when the legislature declared with unbothered anthropomorphism that the mockingbird "is a singer of distinctive type, a fighter for the protection of his home, falling, if need be, in its defense, like any True Texan.")

Hogg sprang back—and spread out. ("I have never," he wrote near the end of his life, "been willing to stand by and see the spare-ribs, back-bones, sausages, chitlings and sauce, spoil.") At over three hundred pounds, he was corpulent, but also tall and imposing. His big face, made bigger by his receding hairline, was usually clean shaven, but at periods in the 1890s it was obscured beneath an impressive, broom-like beard. He was friendly and unpretentious, a natural campaigner and powerful public speaker. The first Texas governor to be born in Texas, he emerged at a critical time, when the state sat on the hinge of modernity.

The Reconstruction government of E. J. Davis was definitively swept away in the election in 1873. The new regime, led by Governor Richard Coke, called itself a "redeemer" government. It saw its mission as the redemption of the state from the humiliation and subjugation that followed its defeat in the Civil War. Under the Redeemers, Texas would once again be self-reliant, self-determining, and wary, almost phobic, of rules and regulations. All this was reflected in a new state constitution, ratified in 1876, which began with a lofty-sounding Bill of Rights but got down to business in the articles that followed, which systematically scaled back the reach of government. The governor's term was reduced to two years, the appointment power of the office diluted, its annual salary cut from $5,000 to $4,000. Senatorial terms were trimmed from six years to four years. Judges were to be elected, not appointed. The legislature would no longer meet every year, but every other year. It was a document drafted by people who preferred to be left alone, to keep their affairs close at hand and their government at arm's length. It's an attitude still in force in Texas today. So is the 1876 Constitution, though by now it has been amended 491 times.

Redemption essentially reinstalled the same wealthy planter class that had been in charge of Texas before the Civil War. In Texas, as elsewhere in the South, they were called Bourbon Democrats. The name probably referred to the monarchial family that had resisted the French Revolution, but it more aptly evoked whiskey-drinking men of affairs leisurely plotting the course of things from the shade of their verandahs.

They had a hands-off attitude about business, particularly the railroad business. Railroads had begun to operate in Texas as early as 1853, but it was not until after the war, during the 1870s, that the transportation revolution came storming in. Major railroads such as the Texas and Pacific and the International and Great Northern soon spanned the length and breadth of Texas and linked it to the rest of the continent. In 1870 there were 583 miles of railroad track in the state. Thirty years later there were almost 10,000, and Texas was on its way to having more miles of track than any state in the country. The building of the railroads inevitably sparked profound changes, bringing farmers and settlers into the empty counties that lay beyond the rapidly eroding frontier line. One after another the forts that had guarded Texans against the Indians were deactivated. The Indian resistance had been broken, and the forts were no longer needed. A newspaper called the *Frontier Echo*, which was printed in Jacksboro, northwest of Fort Worth, had to keep relocating farther and farther west to justify its name. All along the track being laid, new towns came into being, and older towns began to develop into cities. Railroads helped spur a major lumber industry in the Piney Woods of East Texas, in part because of a demand for crossties (500,000 of them in 1880 alone). Logs that once had to be transported by boat down the Neches and Sabine Rivers could now be shipped by rail all over Texas and the United States.

The proliferation of the railroads fostered a new business: railroad robbery. Its most famous practitioner was an outlaw named Sam Bass. Bass, like John Wesley Hardin, had driven cattle up the trails to Kansas. Unlike Hardin, he was not a natural-born man-killer. According to the Texas Ranger James B. Gillett, who wrote about him in his memoir, *Six Years with the Texas Rangers*, he was just "an honest, sincere and clean young man" who had fallen in with

"An honest, sincere and clean young man" was the way one Texas Ranger described Sam Bass (seated). Except for the honest part, it may have been an accurate description of the notorious bank robber.

the wrong crowd after driving cattle to Dodge City. He was with a gang that robbed a passenger train in Nebraska, carrying away $60,000 in newly minted $20 gold pieces. The money was divided among the five bandits. Three of them were soon killed by army patrols and sheriff's posses, but Bass and an associate named Jack Davis traveled back to Texas with their gold coins hidden in the bottom of a wagon. On the way home, they camped near a cavalry detachment that had been sent in pursuit of the train robbers. Brazenly, or perhaps just to be friendly, they sauntered over to the unsuspecting troopers' campfire and chatted amiably with them until bedtime.

Back in Texas, Bass put together a new gang. During the spring of 1878, they robbed four trains, but their haul was minuscule compared with the take from the Nebraska robbery, and they quickly sparked a pursuing swarm of Rangers and other law enforcement personnel. The gang ended up in splinters, with one dead and several others captured. One of the captured men, Jim Murphy, agreed to deliver Sam Bass in exchange for his own freedom. Somewhat to his credit, he did so with a heavy heart, since "his former chief had been kind to his family, had given them money and provisions, and . . . it would be ungrateful to betray his friend."

Murphy was allowed to skip bond and rejoin the gang as an informer. By then, Sam Bass was out of money. He spent his last $20 coin from the Nebraska train robbery at a saloon in Waco. While Bass was selling a horse, Murphy sent a note to John B. Jones, the leader of the Texas Rangers' Frontier Battalion: "We are on our way to Round Rock to rob the bank. For God's sake be there to prevent it."

Round Rock—currently a booming suburb of Austin whose amenities include the Lone Star Bakery, the home of the world's greatest doughnuts—was at that time a small community along the Chisholm Trail. It was named for a distinctive circular boulder that still can be seen rising from the bottom of Brushy Creek.

When Bass, Murphy, and the two other men with them arrived in town, General Jones and three other Rangers were waiting for them, along with two deputy sheriffs. Eight more men from the nearest Ranger company, 115 miles away in San Saba, had ridden all night and were almost to Round Rock when Bass and his two remaining associates walked into a store to buy tobacco. The wanted men promptly shot the deputy sheriffs who had followed them inside. Then they ran outside and into a street battle with the Rangers. One of the bandits was killed. Bass was shot through the hand and in the back, but with the help of his surviving friend managed to mount his horse and ride off.

The next morning, the Rangers found him sitting beneath an oak tree. He had told his friend to leave him there, that he was done for. The man had reluctantly ridden away, and the mortally wounded Bass had walked to a nearby house and asked a frightened woman there for a drink of water. She gave it to him, and he staggered back to the shade of the tree. Though desperately thirsty, he was too weak to hold the cup to his lips. The bullet that had entered his back had shredded his kidney. He died the next day, on his twenty-seventh birthday, after remarking deliriously, "The world is bobbing around."

Sam Bass's tombstone in the Round Rock cemetery bears an existential inscription written by his sister: "A brave man reposes in death here. Why was he not true?"

---- ★ ----

THE LIVES OF MOST TEXANS DURING THE LAST DECADES OF
the nineteenth century had little to do with trail drives or bank robberies or
shootouts in dusty streets. Most of them were not cowboys or ranchers but
farmers. Between the end of the Civil War and the dawn of the new century,
the population of the state surged dramatically, from roughly eight hundred
thousand people in 1870 to over three million in 1900. Even though cities
grew dramatically as well, 83 percent of Texans still lived rural lives. The
population of the major cities—San Antonio, Houston, Dallas, Galveston,
Austin—typically tripled in that period, but the number of farms quintupled.

Cotton was still the dominant crop, and it would become even more so as
farmers began to follow the market, shifting from growing a range of crops
to feed their families to planting more and more cotton to sell for cash. Subsistence agriculture was giving way to the monetized, commodified production of a single staple, to a modern world in which necessities more and
more were bought and sold from the proceeds of cotton rather than grown or
hunted for personal use. Participants in this new market faced new obstacles.
For one thing, almost half of all farmers didn't own the land they worked.
They were tenant farmers, laboring on somebody else's acreage for a share
of the crops produced. Many of them were former slaves or the children of
slaves. In some East Texas counties, as much as 80 percent of the black population worked as tenant farmers. The few that were fortunate enough to be
able to supply their own plows and seeds and mules fared much better as tenants than the sharecroppers who owned nothing but their backs and hands,
and who had to mortgage their share of the speculative proceeds to landowners in order to provide food and clothing for their families. It was easy enough
for such a sharecropper to find himself on a lifelong treadmill of debt, since
the price of cotton was unpredictable and interest rates were correspondingly,
sometimes stratospherically, high—as much as 150 percent.

As more and more immigrants moved to Texas, the more the price of
land increased, and as more and more cotton hit the market, the more its
price fell. And farmers were at the mercy of the unregulated railroads when
it came to the cost of shipping that cotton. The Redeemer government was
chummy and accommodating to railroads, giving them sixteen sections of
land (a section is 640 acres, or 1 square mile) for every mile of track laid.
The law was repealed in 1882, but before that happened the railroad companies came into possession of thirty-two million acres of Texas public land.
Five million of those acres belonged to the Texas and Pacific, which belonged to the New York robber baron Jay Gould. Gould and C. P. Hunting-

ton, of the Southern Pacific, were both building railroads across Texas. Their routes converged east of El Paso, and they found their interests converging as well. By allying their two companies, which controlled half the railroad mileage in Texas, they created a monopoly that engaged in a bit of track sharing and a lot of rate fixing.

Hurt by falling prices, beset by droughts, gouged by collusion among Gilded Age railroad magnates, farmers in Texas began to organize themselves into agrarian movements. One of these was a national association called the National Grange of the Order of Patrons of Husbandry. The Grange was a social organization that welcomed isolated farm families into a communal identity ablaze with secret trappings. Its officers had titles such as "worthy master" and "worthy assistant steward," its meetings featured rituals involving symbolic farm implements, and it even had a version of the Ten Commandments, with injunctions such as "Thou shalt not leave thy straw but shalt surely stack it for thy cattle in the winter" and "Thou shalt have no Jewish middlemen between thy farm and Liverpool to fatten on thy honest toil."

The Grange's focus had more to do with progressive husbandry than progressive politics. Its suggestion to farmers who were trapped in tenancy or hammered by railroad pricing was not to take the bait of the modern world. Instead of literally betting the farm on a money crop like cotton, they should plant diverse crops and become self-sufficient, like their yeoman forebears. "Make no war upon railroads," the Texas worthy master, W. W. Lang, admonished. An old-school Democratic ruralist, he also believed that cities were places where "depravity finds friendship."

But these were the wrong sentiments for an industrializing, urbanizing, fierily political time. Farmers needed a sharper edge than the Grange, with its educational fairs and secret pageantry, could provide. And making war upon the railroads was not out of the conversation. When the Grange faded, a new and more activist organization, the Farmers' Alliance, coalesced around distressed farmers who were still looking for some sort of leverage against the tycoons and big landowners and foreign syndicates that were cornering the prosperity market in Texas.

The Farmers' Alliance held a convention in Cleburne in 1886 and, with its fifty-thousand-member voice, demanded "freedom from the onerous and shameful abuses that the industrial classes are now suffering at the hands of arrogant capitalists and powerful corporations." What this meant in practice was, among other things, that Texas public land should be sold not just to railroad companies and speculators but also to individual settlers in parcels small enough for them to afford. It meant coining silver as well as gold and expanding the circulation of money to help raise the prices of farm commodities, and it meant creating some sort of authority to regulate railroads in order "to secure to the people the benefits of railroad transportation at reasonable cost."

The grievances expressed by the Farmers' Alliance were echoed by the Knights of Labor, a powerful national labor union that opened a Texas front at about the same time that farmers began to sharpen their political agenda. The farmers and the Knights had a common adversary in Jay Gould and his Texas and Pacific Railway. In 1885, the Knights had won an important round with Gould when they organized a strike against one of his other holdings, the Wabash, St. Louis & Pacific Railway, after the Wabash slashed workers' wages and expanded their working hours. That strike ended in victory for the union and a spectacular surge in its membership. In the spring of the next year, 1886, there was another strike, this one kindled by an incident in the East Texas town of Marshall in which a railroad foreman was fired for attending a union meeting on company time. It soon blossomed into a conflagration known as the Great Southwest Strike, which paralyzed freight traffic throughout Texas, Arkansas, Illinois, Kansas, and Missouri and created something close to open warfare between the Knights of Labor and the strike breakers, militiamen, Rangers, special deputies, and Pinkerton detectives that Gould and the state governments mobilized to defeat them.

The feverish stakes were outlined clearly enough in a union circular: "Gould the giant fiend, Gould the money monarch, is dancing . . . over the grave of our order, over the ruin of our homes and the blight of our lives. Before him the world has smiled in beauty, but his wake is a graveyard of hopes, the cyclone's path of devastation and death."

The Great Southwest Strike put people in literal graveyards as well. In April 1886, a train leaving Fort Worth came to an unexpected stop at a place called Buttermilk Switch, where a group of four strikers had just thrown open a switch and others were waiting nearby with rifles. On the train were a dozen or so men with ties to law enforcement. They were led by an acting city marshal named Jim Courtright, who was, as described by an Atlanta newspaper, "a typical border ruffian . . . a red-handed tough."

It was certainly true that Courtright had had a porous relationship with the law, since he had recently been tried (and acquitted) for murdering two men in New Mexico who he claimed were squatters. Courtright stepped off the train and arrested the four men who had pulled the switch. The other strikers raised their rifles. Courtright supposedly called out, "For God's sake don't shoot!," a plea that went unheeded, either by him or by the strikers. Witnesses testified that the marshal opened fire first—a credible enough scenario, since his instinctive reaction to a fight was to storm into it. "They said that his hands," wrote Eugene Cunningham, the author of a book about gunfighters with the genius title of *Triggernometry*, "snapping to the butts of the .45s in their cut-down holsters, were like racing snakes streaking into holes."

It wasn't a "massacre," as a newspaper article referred to it, but for the next few minutes a lot of bullets went flying. Three peace officers were shot, one mortally. Several of the strikers were probably wounded or killed as well, but there was no accounting of the casualties on their side, because all the union men fled into the woods. Courtright was unscathed, though he would die the next year when, as the owner of a Fort Worth detective agency, he tried to extort protection money from Luke Short, who occupied something of Courtright's same commodious space between criminality and law enforcement. The two men met outside the White Elephant saloon. Courtright went for his gun, but Short was faster and shot off the thumb of his assailant's right hand. That wouldn't have been a problem, since Courtright was ambidextrous, but in the time it took to shift his gun to his left hand, Short managed to shoot him three more times.

The violence at Buttermilk Switch, combined with the bloodier Haymarket Riot in Chicago the next month, and the inconvenience of having rail traffic brought to a standstill throughout much of Texas, swayed public opinion away from the striking railroad workers. The Great Southwest Strike ended up being a disaster that staggered the Knights of Labor. But several decades of hard-core Redeemer government in Texas had generated a tide of reform that wasn't going to subside.

"There is one peril," Jay Gould believed. It was "injudicious interference by Congresses and State Legislatures with business. . . . The peril is legislation. That is the danger always." Gould had a business-at-all-costs philosophy that has rarely been out of rhythm with the engine of Texas politics, but the last part of the nineteenth century was a time inflamed by populist resentment. A Farmers' Alliance spokeswoman named Mary Elizabeth Lease summed up the opinion of the have-not farmers and laborers in a memorable address: "The great common people of this country are slaves, and monopoly is the master. The West and South are bound and prostrate before the manufacturing East. . . . Our laws are the output of a system which clothes rascals in robes and honesty in rags." In her opinion, farmers should "raise less corn and more Hell."

★

ALL OF WHICH BRINGS US BACK TO JAMES HOGG, WHO BECAME

Texas's attorney general in 1886, the same year when Sul Ross—the Texas Ranger who was renowned for recapturing Cynthia Anna Parker and who had then gone on to become a Confederate general—was elected governor.

Ross was a popular, nontoxic, mild-tempered Democrat. During the first of his two administrations, the new Capitol, the one that looms today at the foot of Congress Avenue in Austin, was completed and dedicated. (It was paid for, as most big things in Texas were paid for at the time, by the sale of a chunk of the public's land—in this case, the Panhandle acreage that became the XIT Ranch. Convicts, many of them poor blacks, quarried the granite, and fabricated the new Capitol's ornamental ironwork in prison shops.)

As attorney general, Hogg was politically attuned to the swelling chorus of populist thought. Texas had been founded on a gospel of self-reliance and small-to-the-point-of-vanishing government, but its new chief law enforcement officer represented an emerging coalition that put him in conflict with the monopolists, tycoons, and land barons for whom Texas had once been a rugged paradise of noninterference. One of these was none other than Charles Goodnight, who, along with other big landowners, had been cannily using a law that allowed them to acquire grazing leases on public lands set aside for school funding. Goodnight and other Panhandle ranchers made sure to gobble up the leases for the "children's grass" at the minimum auction price set by the State Land Board by agreeing not to bid against one another. When the legislature in response raised the minimum price from four cents an acre to eight cents an acre, Goodnight—a grand master of cantankerousness— staged a scene that harked back in spirit to the old "Come and Take It" days. He and several other ranchers went to an Austin bank, withdrew over a hundred thousand dollars in cash—the amount that they claimed they owed based on the four-cent rate—piled it into a wheelbarrow, strapped on their gun belts, and paraded up Congress Avenue to the General Land Office. Their payment was refused, but their defiant theatrics were duly registered.

"You cannot legislate for me," Goodnight later lectured the State Land Board. "I was on the frontier carrying a gun when I should have been in school. I served the State as a ranger for four years. I put in my life to make this a free country and haven't been paid a cent for it."

Goodnight embodied what was by then the old Texas, the Texas that had been forged into being by Indian fighters and trail drivers, by men who had seized or homesteaded land, who had fenced it and fought for it against nesters and fence cutters and cattle rustlers and Austin bureaucrats. It was inevitable that he would be in the way of people like Jim Hogg, who possessed no memories of the Texas Revolution, had been too young to fight in the Civil War, and had come of age at a time when the Comanche empire that had held back the invasion of Texas since the days of the Spanish was finally crumbling.

The railroads were crucial to the modernization of Texas but they were also in Hogg's way, inasmuch as they tended to combine forces just as

JAMES HOGG

in a clean-shaven phase after his consequential governership had ended and his post-Spindletop oil fortune was just beginning to grow.

Goodnight and his Panhandle ranchers had done in attempting to consolidate and control their markets. As attorney general, Hogg pursued a trust-busting agenda, notably against rate-fixing railroad consortiums and insurance companies. He would have preferred not to engage in the thorny but unavoidable issue of Prohibition, which had achieved gale force in Texas when the Woman's Christian Temperance Union set up a state branch in 1883. Prohibition was something considerably more than a thou-shalt-have-no-fun stricture imposed onto a sinful society by the hard-shell churches that found fertile soil in Texas. It was intimately linked with a real problem—families shattered and terrorized by alcoholism—and by women's growing determination to have a say in how the world was structured.

Hogg was an overenthusiastic eater but a moderate beer-and-wine man who adhered to his father's admonition never to drink in saloons. "If you were to ask me if I am opposed to temperance and sobriety," he cagily expressed in a public letter, "then I should cheerfully tell you no." But though he didn't mind using the power of government to rein in corpora-tions, he balked at Prohibition, both because of its "utter impracticability" and because of a philosophical conviction that "men cannot be made moral, forced into temperance or whipped into religion."

On the other hand, they could be maneuvered into compliance, which is what Hogg did when he took on the syndicate that had built the new Capitol and forced it to fix the leaky roof, which had manifested itself on the very day that the building was dedicated. And he was elected gover-nor in 1890 in large part on his promise to create a commission that would oversee the railroads and the shipping prices they could charge. If your eyes are starting to glaze over at the prospect of reading multiple pages about freight-hauling regulations, don't worry—I'll keep it short. We can agree that the words "Texas Railroad Commission" sound pretty boring, but in truth the agency had a profound human impact far into the next century as it went from merely regulating railroads to regulating oil and gas pipelines, along with production and pricing, thereby essentially ordering the world's energy economy until the rise of OPEC in the 1970s.

Governor Hogg appointed John H. Reagan to head the three-man board of the Texas Railroad Commission. Reagan, known as the "Old Roman," was one of the great Texas political sages. As a young man, he had fought in the Battle of the Neches against the Cherokees, and it was he who had implored (in vain) his militia captain not to shoot the dying Chief Bowles. In the early days of Texas statehood, he had been elected to Congress, but resigned at the beginning of the Civil War and became the postmaster general of the Confed-eracy. He was captured along with Jefferson Davis at the end of the war and imprisoned in Boston at Fort Warren. While there he wrote a famous letter to the people of Texas, admonishing them to accept the reality of defeat, "recog-nize the supreme authority of the Government of the United States," and "recognize the abolition of slavery, and the rights of those who have been slaves to the privileges and protection of the laws of the land."

The Fort Warren letter sent Reagan into the political wilderness, but only for a time. Over the years, what had sounded to some Confederate Texan ears like treacherous appeasement began to be appreciated for its statesmanlike pragmatism. Reagan had made a comeback and was a U.S. senator when he was offered the chairmanship of Hogg's railroad commission. By then he was in his seventies, every bit as rotund as the governor who appointed him, but still with the penetrating, narrow-gauge eyes of the frontiersman he had once been.

Even with the Texas Railroad Commission to bolster his populist bona fides, Hogg faced a lively buzz of opposition when he ran for reelection in 1892. The Farmers' Alliance was irritated that one of its own had not been appointed to the commission board, and that the board was appointed in the first place, instead of being elected directly by the people. Like many other farmers throughout the South, members of the Farmers' Alliance were heavily invested in the concept of the U.S. government building warehouses where they could store their crops as collateral against short-term loans. But Texas Democrats, even reform-friendly ones like Hogg, didn't want the federal government to build warehouses or do much of anything else in their former sovereign republic. The idea, in the words of Richard Coke, was "absurd and preposterous."

As a result, many of the farmers who might have supported Hogg were seduced away by the newly formed People's Party. It was led in Texas by a former district judge named Thomas L. Nugent, a deep-thinking Swedenborgian who believed in the perfectibility of human beings, even Texans, but who had pretty much given up on the Democratic Party, which he regarded as a plutocrat's clubhouse that could not be trusted "to bear the hopes of toiling and struggling humanity." Nugent was not the only candidate the governor had to worry about. When George Clark, a Confederate veteran of Gettysburg and a prominent railroad attorney, failed to beat Hogg for the Democratic nomination, he formed his own conservative insurgency, which featured the alarming-sounding campaign slogan "Turn Texas Loose."

In all, seven parties or fragments of parties competed to steer Texas into the twentieth century in this crucial election. Among them was the still-breathing Republican Party, which had split along a stark racial divide. "Do you feel the strong current of your Gothic blood stir in your veins to-day?" a member of a breakaway Republican convention stirringly quizzed his fellow delegates. "Are you ready to assert the spirit of white men in this country and govern it?"

They were. They called themselves the Lily-White Republicans. Their candidate for Texas governor was Andrew Jackson Houston, the son of Sam Houston. But Houston and the Lily Whites were a minority faction of a minority party. The Republicans proper were in the firm control of a deft politician named Norris Wright Cuney. Cuney was the Texas-born son of a slave mother and a planter father. He grew up to be a Union League protégé of George Ruby and such an ascendant figure in Republican ranks that President Benjamin Harrison awarded him the prize patronage post of Galveston customs collector in 1889. The *New York Evening Telegram* described him approvingly as "a finely built copper-hued man," but closer to home the *Houston Post*—which backed Hogg—saw Cuney as a transparent opportunist, a "dark-skinned white man."

Snort the *Post* might, but as the leader of the mostly African American Republican Party of Texas, Cuney commanded a significant voting bloc and was a power player on both the local and national scene. He was deeply fond of Shakespeare and Byron, of Italian opera and traditional Irish music, but not to the extent that his European tastes confused or subverted his racial identity. He considered himself—as his daughter Maud put it in the subtitle of her loving biography—"A Tribune of the Black People." Earlier in his career, he had helped organize a black longshoremen's union and had taken advantage of a strike by white workers to integrate the Galveston docks. When the Texas Senate passed a Jim Crow bill requiring blacks to ride in separate railroad cars, an inflamed Cuney wrote, "All such legislation is futile and iniquitous and cannot possibly withstand our advancing humanity and civilization." His rhetoric was even more scorching after he sent Maud to study at Boston's New England Conservatory of Music. He was informed by the executive committee of the school that his daughter, because of "a large number of pupils who are affected by race prejudices," would, regrettably, have to find a place to live off campus. "I notice with extreme reluctance," Cuney snapped back, "the bewildering fact that glorious Massachusetts . . . can furnish an institution of learning, capable of surrendering her world-wide fame, won in the fields of humanity and christian endeavor, at the demand of a dying prejudice which your great State has done so much towards rendering nauseous in the eyes of enlightened humanity."

But being a tribune of the black people did not mean that Cuney was predictable in his politics. The Republican Party, he preached, "is not a cast iron institution, it is reasonable, flexible, liberal and patriotic." What that meant in practice was that Wright Cuney was as probusiness as pretty much any fusty old white Democrat. To him, the People's Party—which went so far as to advocate government ownership of railroads—was hardly distinguishable from outright socialism. For that matter, so was the mainstream reform agenda of Governor Hogg. Instead of supporting either party, or running a Republican candidate who would be doomed to defeat, Cuney steered his majority-black party into a strange-bedfellows alliance with George Clark, the "Turn Texas Loose" leader of the breakaway Democrats. Hogg's campaign found itself facing—in an expression that the governor was too refined to use himself— "Three C's—Clark, Cuney and the Coons."

But James Hogg won the election anyway, beating both Clark and Nugent. A key engineer of his victory was Edward Mandell House, the wealthy son of a Houston banker. House was trim and dapper, with a meek, unobtrusive face that made him look—as the historian H. W. Brands once quipped to me—like Stuart Little, the mouse protagonist of E. B. White's famous children's book. He was almost as furtive as a mouse, too, studiously keeping behind the scenes as he organized rallies, flooded the state with leaflets, and brokered crucial deals. "It pleased his imagination," a slightly less-than-admiring acquaintance later wrote, "to look upon himself as a sort of kingmaker, to exert power without incurring responsibility, to put other men on the high road to office . . . For him politics was a game, it delighted him to move the pieces on the board."

The gamesmanship skills that House honed during the Hogg campaign came in handy as he orchestrated the elections of three subsequent Texas governors. He later helped Woodrow Wilson win the presidency, and he became such an indispensable adviser and operative in Wilson's administration that the president called him "my second personality." House also delved into fiction, writing *Philip Dru: Administrator; A Story of Tomorrow, 1920–1935*, the second-worst utopian political novel ever written by a rich, powerful Texan. (First place goes to H. L. Hunt for *Alpaca*.) A brief passage from *Philip Dru* is enough to demonstrate why House was more at home writing policy papers than fiction: "[Dru] further directed that the tax on realty both in the country and the city should be upon the following basis:—Improvements on city property were to be taxed at one-fifth of their value, and the naked property either in town or country at two-thirds of its value. The fact that country property used for agricultural purpose was improved, should not be reckoned."

Jim Hogg's success and the relatively moderate views of the governors who succeeded him gave rise to a wave of Progressivism that helped Texas coast over the bar from the old century to the new. It was not just politics, though; it was something deeper—the cultural ripening of a state in which the blood wars and titanic frontier clashes of the last several hundred years were starting to recede into legend and legacy.

ASHBEL SMITH, THE FORMER SURGEON GENERAL OF THE ARMY

of the Republic of Texas, collector of erotic paintings, and great friend of Sam Houston, was nearing eighty when he gave an address in 1882 to dedicate the laying of the cornerstone of the main building of the University of

The University of Texas rises upon an Austin hill in 1883.

Texas. He and three thousand onlookers gathered in Austin less than a mile north of the site where ground had been broken for the soaring new Capitol a month earlier. He observed that the university was the culmination of something that the "founders of Texas" had envisioned from the beginning, an institution that "cements the victory of San Jacinto and consecrates that battle as one of the few decisive battles of the world . . . to free institutions, to virtue and to power."

Indeed, a university for Texas at roughly this spot near the banks of the Colorado had been a wistful dream of Stephen Austin, and the actual site had been chosen by the Texas Congress in the early days of the republic. "Let me . . . urge it upon you, gentlemen," President Mirabeau Lamar told his legislators in 1838, "not to postpone this matter too long." But there were Indian wars, border wars, range wars, secession, Union invasions, and the furor of Reconstruction to otherwise occupy the minds of Texans, and it was not until over forty years later that ground was finally broken for the University of Texas, along with another public institution of higher learning, Texas Agricultural and Mechanical College, in College Station.

"Smite the rocks with the rod of knowledge," Ashbel Smith predicted confidently in his address, "and fountains of unstinted wealth will gush forth." But it was small-scale smiting at first. When the university opened for business in September 1883, it had only eight professors, all men, the majority recruited from outside the state. Among them was Oran Roberts, the president of the secession convention, who after the war was elected senator and sent to Washington along with David Burnet, where the new Radical Republican Congress refused to seat them. He later became governor; his term ended just as the University of Texas was opening for business, and he signed on as its law professor. He was, according to one presumably sympathetic fellow Democrat, "a man that everybody laughed at and everybody loved and venerated." He wrote books on law and history and earned the nickname "Old Alcalde," which is why the University of Texas alumni magazine still retains the curious title *Alcalde*.

Only 100 students attended classes on that first day, though enrollment swelled over the academic year to 221, including 58 women. An aspiring young poet and German scholar named Jessie Andrews was the first woman to enroll in the new university, the first to graduate, and the first to teach a class there. It might also have been a thriving environment for a young woman like Maud Cuney if the university had accepted African American students.

"It is well to consider what trouble the colored people may give," warned one of UT's regents. Besides, Texas in its imagined magnanimity had already decreed that black students should have a college of their own, Prairie View A&M, where they could acquire "scientific instruction in agricultural and industrial arts" without disturbing the Lone Star universe by studying literature or philosophy. Speaking of philosophy, a black legislator named Robert Lloyd Smith was elegantly succinct in explaining why he voted for an appropriation bill for the segregated university: "I know that I cannot enter the University of Texas as a student, but I would rather place the fate of my race in the hands of the educated, rather than to put it in the hands of the ignorant."

In the beginning there were not many more books in the library than students in the university. That changed because of a long-faced Swedish immigrant with the enchanting name of Swante Palm. At various times in his life, Palm had been a postmaster, bookkeeper, meteorologist, and diplomat, but he is remembered for being Texas's earliest and most passionate book collector. The twelve thousand volumes of his personal library in Austin included pretty much every book ever written about Texas and the Southwest, along with a definitive collection of Swedish Bibles and up-to-date volumes on archeology, literature, and evolution. In 1897, when he was eighty-two, he donated almost all of these books to the University of Texas, carefully loading them wagonload by wagonload from his house in Austin, accompanying them to the campus, and spending the remaining two years of his life as an assistant librarian of his own library, making sure the books he had spent a lifetime accumulating and keeping safe were properly shelved and catalogued.

———— ★ ————

THE IMAGES OF SWANTE PALM AND ORAN ROBERTS WERE PRE- served in marble busts created by another notable example of Texas's emerging cosmopolitanism. She was a German sculptor named Elisabet Ney. Ney arrived in the state in 1872, gusting along on the winds of her self-dramatizing personality. "Here is where I shall live and die!" she proclaimed when she arrived at her new Texas home, in Waller County near the town of Hempstead. Ney was married to a Scottish doctor, who seems to have grimly acquiesced in her insistence that their marriage be their little secret. ("She anxiously treated me as an outsider," he remembered, "in order to appear before the world as independent.") They bought Liendo, a plantation carved out of an old Spanish land grant. It was only a few miles from where Sam Houston had rested his army on the far side of the Brazos while being chased by Santa Anna during the Runaway Scrape.

Elisabet Ney was almost forty when she came to Texas. She was already famous in Europe for her marble renderings of German monarchs and philosophers. A photograph of her taken around this time depicts a resolute, very handsome woman with a high pale forehead and shoulder-length ringlets of dark hair. Garibaldi, for one, had been bewitched by her as he sat for a portrait bust. "Votre physiognomie," the great Italian revolutionary ventured to her in French, "est très bonne." But she appears to have been interested in Garibaldi's physiognomy mostly to the degree that she could sculpt it, and she was even less swoony when it came time to create a statue of King Ludwig II of Bavaria. "Begin your work!" the king supposedly commanded when she arrived in his presence for the initial sketching, to which the equally imperious Ney supposedly replied, "I will begin, Your Majesty, when I am ready."

She was tempestuous, angry, generous, and smothering. "From quite early," she once wrote, "my life has been a protest against the subjection to which women were doomed from their birth." When she went riding, not sidesaddle in a long skirt, but wearing men's pants, with her legs visibly astride, she sent shock waves through Waller County. At public appearances in Austin, where she built a studio that is now a museum devoted to her work and life, she ignored any fashions but her own, dressing in an all-encompassing dark cloak and a floppy medieval-looking cap.

Her two-year-old son died soon after she and her husband moved to Texas, and her response was searingly artistic. She locked herself in her

When she left Europe to make a new life in Texas, Elisabet Ney was already a famous sculptor. Among her subjects was Guiseppe Garibaldi, who was smitten with her "physiognomie."

bedroom all night with the boy's body, emerging in the morning with a death mask of his face. Because the child had died of highly contagious diphtheria, she was told by a doctor that he should be cremated. There is no real reason to give credence to the local legend that she performed the ritual herself in the fireplace, but if she had, it wouldn't have been completely out of character. She was such an overbearing mother to her surviving son, so fierce in her determination to shape and manage every aspect of his emerging self, that he fled from her in defiance as soon as he was old enough to do so.

She had better luck leaving her mark on Texas. "After so many of the great men of the civilized world sat for me," she remarked before leaving Europe, "I would like to model the greatest of the wild men." Two of her full-scale marble statues of Texas wild men can be seen today at the state capitol; in fact, they can hardly be missed, since they flank the main entrance to the rotunda. They stand there in poses of bloodless, regal stillness: Sam Houston wearing buckskins, an Indian blanket thrown over his shoulder, a sword at his side; Stephen Austin with the barrel of a Kentucky rifle leaning against his shoulder and an unscrolling map in his hands. A few years before she died, in 1907, Ney completed a monument to Albert Sidney Johnston, whom she depicted as a recumbent Confederate knight lying within his gothic tomb in the Texas State Cemetery in Austin. Her own grave, in Hempstead, near Liendo, is uncharacteristically modest—just her name and her dates and one reverberant word: "Sculptress."

Elisabet Ney was far from the only visual artist at the end of the nineteenth century who glanced backward, back to the misty dawning of Texas. Another German immigrant, Hermann Lungkwitz, was by that time at the close of a long career spent painting romantic, almost rapturous San Antonio street scenes and Hill Country landscapes. The canvases of his Paris-born contemporary Théodore Gentilz were sparer, less color saturated. Gentilz painted moody contemplations of the San Antonio missions, and there is a bewitching stillness that seeps into his work even when it depicts dynamic events like fandangos and horseback corridas. Like so many other Texas-based artists and writers (including me), Gentilz couldn't avoid the Alamo. He produced narrative paintings of the 1836 battle and haunted renderings of the Alamo church during its long afterlife as a historical ruin in the center of San Antonio. Both Robert Onderdonk, a New Yorker who came to Texas in 1879, and Henry McArdle, an Irishman who settled in Texas after the Civil War, produced lusty, congested, chaotic paintings of the last moments of the Alamo defenders. You can hardly miss the contemporary Anglo attitude toward Mexicans in both paintings.

Ney at work in her Austin studio in 1892. In the background is her statue of Sam Houston, marble versions of which stand in both the foyer of the Texas Capitol and the National Statuary Hall in the United States Capitol.

In McArdle's *Dawn at the Alamo*, which hangs in the Senate Chamber of the Capitol, Santa Anna's *soldados* are snarling and sneaky. In Onderdonk's *The Fall of the Alamo*, they are a vicious, onrushing horde bent on annihilating Davy Crockett and a group of stalwart last-standers who are calmly and judiciously preparing for their heroic deaths.

Onderdonk was a vivid action painter, but he was also at home in pastoral modes—though not to the extent of his more famous son Julian, whose lush, impressionistic depictions of wildflower-covered Hill Country swales accidentally unleashed upon the world the much-loved but also much sneered-at genre known as the bluebonnet painting. In the work of another young painter, Frank Reaugh, the Texas landscape is all about distances and horizons, a dusty pastel world occupied mostly by longhorn cattle, which seem less like herded beasts than like independent creatures embarked on some mysterious errand of their own.

IT WAS NATURAL FOR THE TEXAS ART-
ists at century's end to produce images of lore
and longing. There was a powerful history to
record and a raging myth to nurture. History
meanwhile was moving on, and as usual the
living present was not necessarily as heroic
or bucolic as the remembered past. That was
especially the case for Texans whose identity
had not been forged by nostalgia for the Lost
Cause of the Confederacy or the triumphant
birth struggles of the old republic.

"The foremost man of all the world,"
declared a Texas legislator named A. W. Terrell
in 1889, "is the Anglo-Saxon American white
man." A dubious proposition, but not when
it came to brute political leverage. Despite
occasional minority power brokers like Norris
Wright Cuney, white men were still in charge
in Texas. This was especially true in the
Nueces Strip, where the pattern for Anglo
encroachment into Tejano territory had long
been established. The means for acquiring
control and ownership of old Spanish-Mexican
land grants ranged from legal to legalistic to outright seizure and terrorism.
Defending title, especially for Tejano landowners who had fled across the
border after the Mexican-American War or were later driven out by Texas
Rangers acting as the de facto enforcement arm of Anglo landowners,
meant mounting an expensive legal case in what was essentially a foreign
court. One Tejano claimant was told that in order to testify on his own
behalf, his "character for truth and veracity had to be established by the
testimony of two white men."

Even Captain Leander McNelly of the Rangers, no stranger to off-the-
books law enforcement remedies, was appalled by some of the blatant violence he witnessed along the border. "The acts committed by Americans are
horrible to relate," he reported back to Austin in 1875. "Many ranches have
been plundered and burned, and the people murdered or driven away."

Through decades of displacement, the Anglo ranching culture and power
structure pushed landowning Tejanos to the margins of a country they had

Henry McArdle's Dawn at the Alamo—*eight feet tall and thirteen feet wide—is a sort of grisly bookend to his equally massive canvas depicting the Battle of San Jacinto. Both paintings hang in the Senate chamber of the Texas Capitol.*

once dominated. Tejano ranches were swallowed up by white empire build-ers, aided by the bankers, lawyers, politicians, and Rangers (*los rinches*) they either employed or deployed. They were aided as well by the lingering cus-toms of the old feudal world that had existed along the border before their arrival, a world in which powerful *patrones* commanded the allegiance and ruled the lives of the lower-class workers—the *peons*—who depended upon them for food and shelter and protection.

The peonage system was still alive, but now the *patrones* were likely to be newly arrived white men, not the Old World hacendados whose ancestors had fought their way into Texas after the conquest of Mexico. In Cameron County, which included Brownsville, the man to see was James B. Wells. Wells's place of birth, in 1850, was St. Joseph Island, a spectacularly wild and isolated bar-

This 1903 painting by Robert Onderdonk, which hangs in the entry hall of the Texas Governor's Mansion, typifies the Alamo mythology that remained unchallenged in Texas for many years: courageous and upright Anglos facing a skulking Mexican horde.

rier island across the bay from Corpus Christi. His father was a New England sea captain who had come to Texas during the revolution and served the cause as a privateer, guarding the coast against Mexican ships. Young Jim Wells left his desolate sandbar to study at the University of Virginia and then came back to Texas to finish studying law. He became the protégé and law partner of Stephen Powers. He also married Powers's niece. By the time he was in his thirties, Wells had built and set himself at the controls of a Democratic political machine whose gears spun throughout not just Cameron County

but also neighboring Starr, Hidalgo, and Duval Counties. It was similar to the boss rule that had taken root in the eastern metropolises after the Civil War, powered by the same sort of favor granting, graft, and reliable voter roundups. But boss rule in South Texas managed to impose itself onto a long-established culture of patronage and peonage. For people like Jim Wells and the other Anglo bosses who followed him, the accumulation of power was partly a matter of assuming the identity of protector and provider.

"I have lived among them," Wells reflected back with paternalistic nostalgia a few years before his death. "I have tried to so conduct myself as to show them that I was their friend and they could trust me. . . . I buried many a one of them with my money and married many a one of them. It wasn't two or three days before the election, but through the years around, and they have always been true to me."

There's no reason to think he was being disingenuous. The relationship between Wells and the Mexican American vaqueros and laborers and sharecroppers who made up his constituency was a complex welter of emotional ties and power dynamics. But it was also true that a border boss like Wells could hardly regard election days as an afterthought. Elections, after all, were what the whole system was about. There were plenty of compliant voters in Wells's brushland fiefdom who could be efficiently rounded up for a visit to the polls and a thank-you fiesta. There were also Mexicans living on the other side of the border who could be counted on to cross the river and help boost the turnout in a foreign election.

—28—

BIPEDAL BRUTES

"I AM IN SEARCH OF MY CHILDREN," WROTE A GALVESTON resident named Kitty Hanley in 1880 to the editor of the *Southwestern Christian Advocate.* "I belonged to a gentleman by the name of Patten, was separated from my children in Harrison county, Texas, several years before the late war. The oldest a girl named Esther, the other a boy named Sam. In a division of Mr. Pattern's estate myself and children fell to Mr. Hanley, who married Mr. Patten's daughter. I was afterward carried to Montgomery county by Mr. Jim McCown. I have not heard from my children since. If there is any way in which I can find them I would be glad of your assistance."

The letter, like most of the other notices the *Advocate* published in its "Lost Friends" column from 1877 until the early decades of the twentieth century, is businesslike, respectful, scrubbed clean of heartbreak or rage. The *Advocate*, a Methodist newspaper published in New Orleans, was sent to preachers and post offices all over the former Confederacy in an effort to bring together families that had been thoughtlessly pulled apart by the demands of slave commerce. "I desire to find my parents," stated another letter, written by a man in the town of Midway, Texas, who signed himself "Si Johnson." Mr. Johnson must have been approaching his fifties when the letter was published in 1881, since he remembered being five years old in

1834 when his mother, Edna Thompson, was sold in a property division after the death of her owner. "My mother said, the morning she was going to leave, 'My son you must be a good child.'"

The history of Texas continued to accrue, to be written, sung, painted, and celebrated, but there was a shadow history beneath it, a story that had not yet been composed but was waiting to be discovered in forlorn newspaper inquiries like these about scattered slave families, or in county courthouses full of unconfirmed Tejano land titles, or at river fords and mountain passes and forest clearings where Indian camps and villages had once been, and that were now places to hunt for souvenir arrowheads. But this darker story was not entirely hidden. It had a tendency to erupt every now and then into plain sight.

In 1893, about 8,000 people lived in the town of Paris, in northeastern Texas between the Red and Sulphur Rivers. Paris was the seat of Lamar County, situated in rolling prairie country watered by creeks and streams and dotted with isolated mottes of trees rising out of the waxy black soil. It was a farming community and a railroad center on the route of the Texas and Pacific and three other lines. When the town was incorporated, in 1844, it was named after the French capital. It was probably not as ironic-sounding a name to the earnest, hardworking sodbusters of the Republic of Texas as it is to modern ears. The 1984 Wim Wenders movie *Paris, Texas* coasted a long way on its droll title alone. A few years later, after the movie had achieved cult-classic status, the citizens of Paris, deciding they might as well be in on the joke, erected a sixty-five-foot-tall replica of the Eiffel Tower close to the center of town, and later topped it with a giant red cowboy hat.

A few miles west of the Eiffel Tower is Paris's Evergreen Cemetery. One of the graves there is of three-year-old Myrtle Vance, who died violently in 1893 and whose resting place is marked by an eroding statue of a little girl sitting on a rock and sadly contemplating her folded hands resting in her lap. There is no grave for Henry Smith, the young black man who was accused of murdering her. "Body lost or destroyed" is the sole citation on the online grave-marker database I consulted. That's because there was nothing much left of him after he had been burned alive and his charred bones taken away from the site as souvenirs.

Myrtle's body was discovered in some brush on a day in late January. She had been murdered, probably strangled to death, though the rhetorical description of the crime soon took flight, prompting a local bishop to declare that she had been "first outraged with demoniacal cruelty and then taken by her heels and torn asunder in the mad wantonness of gorilla ferocity."

Smith may have been guilty of killing Myrtle Vance. There was no trial to

The gruesome lynching of Henry Smith, accused murderer of three-year-old Myrtle Vance, was the subject of a celebratory postcard. "Never in the history of civilization," wrote Ida B. Wells of the citizens of Paris, Texas, "has any Christian people stooped to such shocking brutality and indescribable barbarism."

convict him, but there was a possible motive, since Smith had had several violent run-ins with Myrtle's father, a Paris policeman named Henry Vance. There was also circumstantial evidence. The day before Myrtle's body was found, several witnesses noticed Smith walking through town with a young white girl—later assumed to be Myrtle Vance—in his arms.

After the crime was discovered, the suspect fled east to Arkansas, but he was apprehended and brought back to Texarkana, which straddles the Texas-Arkansas border. Five thousand furious people were waiting at the train station there, eager to watch the "negro ravisher" pay for his crime, but several prominent citizens from Paris intervened and pleaded with the Arkansas crowd to let the train pass. They were not asking for mercy for Smith or demanding that he have his day in court. They wanted to get him alive to Paris so they could have him for themselves.

"Never in the history of civilization," wrote the journalist and activist Ida B. Wells about what happened next, "has any Christian people stooped to such shocking brutality and indescribable barbarism."

A postcard circulated after the terrible events of February 1, 1893, is titled "Little Myrtle Vance Avenged." The photograph on the front shows a portion of the ten thousand or so onlookers crowding against a specially built ten-foot-high scaffold erected on vacant land near the Texas and Pacific depot. Many of the people are on horseback, and others stand under umbrellas in the drizzly cold. The open prairie beyond the scaffold is wrapped in a sodden haze. The figures climbing the stairs to the wooden platform or already standing on it are indistinct as well. It is unclear from the photograph what has happened or is about to happen, but the lurid newspaper articles leave no doubt.

Bars were closed and school classes were dismissed so that all the citizens of Paris and those who had ridden in on trains and on horseback throughout East Texas could watch Henry Smith as he was paraded through town "upon a carnival float in mockery of a king upon his throne." When the procession reached its destination, he was led up the scaffold and tied to a stake. His shirt and coat were ripped off and torn into scraps that were thrown to the crowd.

For generations, Texas frontier families had lived in fear of the inhuman suffering they might face if they were to fall into the hands of hostile Comanches. What happened in the prosperous farming community of Paris that day should have shattered any illusion that sanctioned, ritualistic torture was something practiced only by their Indian enemies.

"For God's sake," a local minister—a black man, like some of the others in the crowd—called out when he saw what was about to happen. "Send

The body of seventeen-year-old Jesse Washington after his lynching in what would become known as the "Waco Horror."

the children home." But he was met with a chorus of angry parental voices shouting, "Let them learn a lesson."

"I love children," the minister later told a newspaper, "but as I looked about the little faces distorted with passion and the bloodshot eyes of the cruel parents who held them high in their arms, I thanked God that I have none of my own."

As the father of the murdered child, Henry Vance inaugurated the proceedings. He and his fifteen-year-old son and two of Myrtle's uncles slowly rolled red-hot irons up Smith's body, starting with the soles of his feet. It went on for two hours. Smith writhed and screamed in agony as the avenging Vance family patiently applied the irons. When his entire body had been seared, the Vance men burned out his eyes and then shoved another glowing iron down his throat.

He was still alive when they poured coal oil over him and over the wooden scaffold. They set him on fire, but the flames also burned through the ropes that bound him to the stake. Blind, maddened by pain, he somehow managed to leap down off the scaffold. But there was nowhere to run—the dense crowd that had come to see him die extended outward for a hundred yards. Somebody put a rope around his neck, and they hoisted him back into the fire, back onto the burning scaffold. Beneath it, cut into one of the wooden crosspieces collapsing into ash along with Henry Smith's bones, was the single word "Justice."

Governor Hogg was sickened. He called what happened in Paris a "terrible holocaust," a prime example of "Mobocracy" at work. But the word "mob" conjured up something different from what had happened in Paris and kept happening throughout Texas and the South until the 1940s. The killing of Henry Smith was not a spontaneous eruption of vengeful wrath; it was a meticulously planned, civically sanctioned pageant of slow death. No one was punished for the crime, and the legislature did not act on Hogg's impassioned proposal for an antilynching law. Such a law was finally passed four years later, in 1897, but it didn't prevent scenarios such as the 1916 lynching known as the "Waco Horror," in which seventeen-year-old Jesse Washington was seized from the courthouse moments after being convicted of the murder of a white woman. His death was more haphazardly orchestrated than Smith's, but every bit as gruesome and savage. Fifteen thousand people packed the streets in front of city hall to watch, and afterward his mutilated, castrated, charred body was thrown in a sack and publicly displayed in front of a blacksmith shop.

One of the people who heard about the ghoulish lynching of Henry Smith was a nine-year-old girl named Jessie Daniel. She lived 150 miles south of Paris in Palestine, another Texas town named for another place. One of its earliest residents and city fathers was Daniel Parker, the fiery preacher uncle of Cynthia Ann Parker and a leading proponent of "Two Seedism," an eccentric doctrine maintaining that Eve, when she sinned against God in the Garden of Eden, "had received the Serpentine nature . . . the seed of Satan," which sparked an eternal war between the divine and the diabolical.

Parker's theology may have been abstruse, but it was hard to argue, especially after the evil of Henry Smith's lynching, that the devil's seed did not lay ready to germinate in the human soul. As a child, Jessie Daniel witnessed the ravages of the epidemics that swept through Palestine; one neighbor family lost a baby a year for nine years. "Mob rule," she would later write, "is the typhoid fever . . . of the South."

She was a lonely child, ignored by her progressive-minded but indifferent father. She grew even lonelier after she married an army surgeon named Roger Ames, who seems to have more or less shunned her, as did his upper-crust Mississippi family. When Jessie Daniel Ames was thirty-one, her husband died of blackwater fever in Guatemala. Being a widow hardened her a little. "Since the day of my husband's death," she wrote, "I have put on a bold front to prevent anyone's feeling sorry for me." It may have also have liberated her from the fate of being a subservient and resented wife and propelled her into the urgent work of women's suffrage and civil rights. In 1930, she founded an organization whose name hits the modern ear with contrasting notes of bygone horror and gentility: the Association of Southern Women for the Prevention of Lynching.

———— ★ ————

AS FAR AS I KNOW, JESSIE DANIEL AMES NEVER MET WILLIAM Cowper Brann. He was dead by the time she was barely in her teens. They might have admired each other's outspokenness and shared some unorthodox ideas, but Brann was not someone to recruit for an antilynching campaign. "I like the negro in his place and his place is in the cotton patch" is about the kindest thing he ever said about African Americans. "The baleful shadow of the black man," he wrote with his trademark feverishness, "hangs over every Southern home like the sword of Damocles, like the blight of death—an avatar of infamy, a decree of damnation."

And yet he was a reformer, or at least a rhetorical one, the editor of an incendiary newspaper, the *Iconoclast*, that had its headquarters in Waco but enjoyed a nationwide circulation of 100,000. Born in Illinois, Brann came to Waco in 1894 by way of newspaper jobs and other enterprises in St. Louis, Galveston, Austin, San Antonio, and Houston. While he and his wife, Carrie, were living in Austin, their thirteen-year-old daughter killed herself with a morphine overdose, leaving behind a suicide note that read in part, "I don't want to live. I could never be as good as you want me to. I was born for a rowdy and you would be ashamed of me."

Her death was a tragic misreading of her father's character. If there was ever an editorialist who was "born for a rowdy," it was William Cowper Brann. And Waco turned out to be the perfect place for him to practice his full-blown sarcastic mischief. The town was named for the Indian tribe that

BIPEDAL BRUTES

had lived long ago near the junction of the Bosque and Brazos Rivers, about a hundred miles north of present-day Austin. A trading post established there in 1844 grew into a modest town along the edge of the Chisholm Trail, which grew still further into a city of 20,000 after it became a railroad hub. By then, the ferry that used to haul people and goods across the Brazos had been replaced by a world-class suspension bridge and the city's preferred nickname was no longer "Six Shooter Junction" but the "Athens of Texas."

To Brann, though, Waco was "the religious storm-centre of the Universe," a description that would become eerily apt a century later during the siege of the Branch Davidian compound. What Brann meant was that Waco was the home of his favorite target, the Baptist bluenoses in charge of Baylor University, the proud institution that put the Athens in the "Athens of Texas."

WILLIAM COWPER BRANN
in the editorial office of the magazine he launched to instruct and inflame Waco and the world.

Brann himself never went to any college. His education was scrappier. Before he became a newspaperman, he had been a salesman, a railroad brakeman, a semiprofessional baseball pitcher, and the manager of an opera company. But he was ferociously well read, and the many volumes of his verbiage are loaded with references to Carlyle, Macaulay, Shakespeare, Malthus, and Byron, as well as displaying an encyclopedic summoning power for classical literature and world history. All this knowledge was dragooned into the service of bluster and provocation. "It Strikes to Kill," read an advertisement for the *Iconoclast*, and you can see the attitude in a studio portrait taken of him around 1896. He has the lean face and frame of a man who doesn't have time for lunch. His eyes are narrow and piercing, his mouth is set in what reads as a permanent half smirk.

The photo was taken about two years before he died at the age of forty-three, after having relentlessly summoned up the outrage of the staunch Baptists of Baylor University. He was kidnapped, beaten, threatened with lynching and tarring and feathering, and ordered to get out of Waco. He stayed right where he was, and he gleefully raised the stakes, calling out his enemies in the *Iconoclast* as "bipedal brutes," "scorbutic brats," and "intellectual eunuchs," as well as "splenetic-hearted hypocrites and pietistical dead-beats—who should have been hanged with their own umbilicular cords at birth."

Four people were dead before it was all over. The first shoot-out came after a judge named G. B. Gerald, a hot-tempered supporter of Brann's, had gotten into a spectacular stair-tumbling, thumb-biting fistfight with J. W. Harris, the editor of the *Waco Times-Herald*. A few weeks later, the fight reignited when Judge Gerald exchanged fire with Harris and his brother in front of a Waco drugstore. The judge shot Harris through the neck and then was shot twice from across the street by the editor's brother. But a metal button deflected one of the bullets, and the other struck an arm that had already been rendered useless by a wound received many years before in the Civil War at Manassas. The old judge walked across the street, dodging bullets from the gun of his remaining assailant, and shot him at such close range that his shirt collar caught on fire.

"There are not Baptists enough in Texas to drive [the *Iconoclast*] out of this town," Brann wrote a few months later. "If they kill the editor, another and a better man will step into his shoes and continue the old fight against hypocrites and humbugs, against all that loveth and maketh a lie."

They did kill the editor. It happened on April 1, 1898, when a man named Tom Davis stepped into the street behind Brann and shot him through the middle of the back. But there was one last salvo from the *Iconoclast*. Gravely wounded, Brann turned around, propped himself on an elbow, and emptied his pistol at Davis. Both men died lingering deaths. Brann's funeral procession was the largest that Waco had ever seen, the streets lined with mourners or perhaps gloating onlookers. He is buried in Waco's Oakwood Cemetery, beneath a tombstone depicting his face in profile and a sculptural rendering of the "lamp of truth." But the face has a bullet hole in it, and vandals made off with the lamp.

—29—

SCORPIONS AND HORNY TOADS

IT'S EARLY IN THE AFTERNOON ON A BLINDINGLY BRIGHT April day in El Paso. I've just had lunch (an estimable plate of mole enchiladas) at the L&J Cafe, which has occupied the same location on Missouri Avenue since 1927. Across the street is the fifty-two-acre Concordia Cemetery, a parched expanse of sacred desert ground backgrounded by the treeless slopes of the Franklin Mountains. Ground squirrels and lizards skitter across the tombstones. John Wesley Hardin is buried here, in a weird house-shaped cage erected to deter souvenir hunters. Above the padlocked doorway is a metal plate adorned with two six-shooters. The inscriptions on many of the graves are written in Chinese characters, memorializing the immigrants who came to Texas to finish building the Southern Pacific Railroad and who stayed and put down roots in El Paso even after the Exclusion Act of 1882, which suspended Chinese immigration. There are also buffalo soldiers of the Ninth and Tenth Cavalry interred here, in a new, walled-off section of the cemetery where each tombstone is inscribed with a pair of crossed swords and the dual mottos "We can; We will!" and "Ready and Forward!"

I'm driving home to Austin today. If I take the more scenic, southern route, parting with I-10 at Van Horn to follow Highway 90 through Marfa and Alpine, I'm looking at a little over 600 miles. And if for some reason I wanted to press on to the Louisiana border it would be another 275 miles until I got out of Texas. Texans are used to such distances—we're used to driving for ten or twelve hours and never leaving our state. The speed limit on the stretches of interstate highway that lead through the unpopulated expanses of West Texas is 85 miles an hour. There is little incentive to slow down and read every historical marker, to learn about the story behind every river ford or every county seat or every stop on the Butterfield stage route. There is no time to tour every dusty museum in every town center bypassed by the freeway. But every single mile thrums with history.

A little west and north of downtown El Paso, for instance, in a scruffy industrial neighborhood about a hundred yards from a much-diminished Rio Grande, is the spot where, in 1598, the expedition led by Juan de Oñate forded the river on its way to establish a Spanish colony in the Pueblo country of New Mexico that Coronado had entered almost sixty years earlier. This place was called El Paso del Río del Norte, the Pass across the River of the North. Ahead was a wide gap between two mountains, through which the Spanish trace known as El Camino Real de Tierra Adentro led all the way up the Rio Grande to Santa Fe.

The pass marked the divide not only between two mountain ranges but also between what would become two very different countries. A year after Oñate moved on to secure the Spanish claim to New Mexico, another expedition arrived in El Paso del Norte to establish a mission on the west bank of the Rio Grande, the seed that became today's sprawling Mexican metropolis of Ciudad Juárez. Juárez and El Paso inch up to their respective banks of the Rio Grande, so close together geographically that they could almost be one city. But they are also nations and worlds apart, the narrow seam of the river connecting them like the contrasting patchwork on a quilt.

As I drive out of town on my way to Austin, I follow Socorro Road south along the river. This road—El Paso's Mission Trail—leads past two missions and a presidio chapel that were erected after the Pueblo Revolt in 1680 in northern New Mexico made refugees of the Spanish colonists and their Tigua and Piro allies, driving them south again to El Paso. The missions look different from the Alamo and the other San Antonio missions, which were built from limestone quarried in the craggy and verdant Hill Country. The facades of the El Paso missions are painted white, as white as bones that have bleached beneath the desert sun.

The last stop along the Mission Trail is the little community of San Elizario, where another imposing white chapel faces a leafy square and a grid of old adobe buildings. It is no news to anyone that Texans always stand ready to proclaim something in our state to be the best or biggest or first. We have lately been encouraged to insist that the first Thanksgiving took place not in Massachusetts but in Texas. Twenty-three years before the Pilgrims sat down for dinner with the Wampanoags, Oñate, on his way up the Rio Grande, held a feast with the local inhabitants who lived on the site of San Elizario, a people called the Manso, who were later absorbed into one or another of the Apache bands of the Southwest.

Heading back to Austin, I can't shake the presence of an ancient, invisible history, a story that reaches deeper than anything I'll be able to recount in this book. A large part of that feeling comes from the land itself. This part of Texas is certainly not untouched—like the rest of the state, it has been overgrazed, mined, pumped dry, scraped clean, used up, insulted in a thousand different ways—but its vastness and emptiness overrides every other impression. It's a raw stretch of creation that goes on forever, despoiled but somehow untouched.

The highway leads east past the conical peaks of long-dormant volcanoes, through dry alluvial plains, through the art-world destination of Marfa, a town that began as a railway water stop in 1883 and improbably evolved into a wry end-of-the-earth hangout for fashionistas and celebrities. The high-art vibe might have been set by a woman named Hanna Strobridge. She was the wife of the Southern Pacific superintendent in charge of building the railroad, and it is supposed that he left the creative work of naming the stops to his spouse. Mrs. Strobridge was either reading *The Brothers Karamazov* or had it in mind when she passed through, and she named the town-to-be after one of the novel's characters, Marfa Ignatieva. Texas was never the impermeable barrier to culture that some people want to think it was. A literary honorific was also bestowed in the same decade on another West Texas start-up town, three hundred miles to the northeast. Today the locals pronounce it "Bront," with a hard t at the end, but it was named for Charlotte Brontë, the author of *Jane Eyre*.

On past shallow mountains forged from volcanic eruptions thirty-five million years ago, along a broad pass leading through collapsed calderas and then tightening into road cuts and corridors of fine-grained lava rock. In the late afternoon I arrive at Langtry, a barely there desert community in Val Verde County. It is perched on the site of an old railroad grading camp overlooking a massive limestone chasm carved by the Rio Grande and known as Eagle Nest Canyon. There isn't much that is human-scaled to take in except the Judge Roy Bean Visitor Center, a little museum devoted

to the life and strange career of
the man who called himself, not
entirely inaccurately, the "Law
West of the Pecos." Bean had
come to Texas by way of several
shadowy adventures with the law
south of the river, in California,
and in New Mexico. His real first
name was not Roy but Fauntel-
roy. He pared it down to Phantly
and then apparently dispensed
with it altogether, no doubt reasoning that it would not serve
him well among trigger-happy
associates in the freight-hauling
and saloon-keeping businesses.
He made his way west from San
Antonio in 1882, when he was in
his fifties. He had been described
as "handsome as an Adonis"
during his California days, but
he was probably on his way to
hard-drinking grizzletude by the
time he opened a tent saloon for

*Judge Roy Bean claimed to have named the town of
Langtry in honor of the English actress Lillie Langtry.
Unfortunately, they never met. By the time she made
it to the middle-of-nowhere outpost on the Pecos River
where she was held in such high regard, her number-
one fan was in his desert grave.*

the workers on the Galveston, Harrisburg and San Antonio Railway who
were laying track in the Pecos country to link up with the Southern Pacific,
heading from California.

He opened his first establishment at a place called Vinegarroon, named
after a particularly impressive species of scorpion. At that time Vinegarroon
was in Pecos County, over a hundred miles from the county seat, Fort Stockton. "There is the worst lot of roughs, gamblers, robbers, and pick-pockets,
collected here I ever saw," wrote a Texas Ranger captain charged with maintaining order among the workers and hangers-on in the railroad camps.
What the place needed was a justice of the peace, and the honor somehow
fell to Roy Bean. "He might have been a murderer and a robber and a thief,"
recalled a woman who had known him when she was a girl, "but he was
good in his way."

His qualifications, other than owning a copy of the Revised
Statutes of Texas, were vague at best, but he embarked on the twin
tasks of dispensing justice and whiskey with great enthusiasm. When

Vinegarroon folded, he moved his law shop and his saloon a few miles west to Eagle Nest and the new town of Langtry. It was named for a railroad engineer named George Langtry, but Bean claimed he christened the place in honor of the ravishing British actress Lillie Langtry, who, in addition to starring in plays such as *She Stoops to Conquer* and *As You Like It*, had a prominent real-life role as the mistress of the Prince of Wales. Bean may not have named the town after her, but the actress—born on the Isle of Jersey—had a bewitching sobriquet that he borrowed for his combination saloon and courthouse.

In the Jersey Lily, according to one biographer, Bean sold "grizzly-bear jism" as an aphrodisiac. I don't know whether this is true (how exactly was it procured?), but he did have a captive black bear, named Bruno, that he taught to drink beer for the amusement of railroad passengers on the Sunset Route who stepped off the train in Langtry. As a judge, he was just as capricious and high-spirited as he was a host. He once appropriated $40 from a dead man, fining the corpse for carrying a concealed weapon. He had a fondness for the Irish rail workers, who were liberal patrons of his saloon, but a distaste for the Chinese, who tended to hold tight to their money. The most persistent folklore riff about Roy Bean is that he once let an Irishman who murdered a Chinese laborer go free because, after consulting the Revised Statutes, he said he could find no mention of "any law against killing a Chinaman."

His growing infatuation led him to construct an opera house near the Jersey Lily. He hoped to entice Lillie Langtry to perform there. She knew of his interest. He wrote her fan letters and she wrote back. She regretted not being able to visit the town that she was misled into thinking had been named after her. But she did offer to bestow upon it an ornamental drinking fountain. "Roy Bean's quick reply," she noted in a memoir, "was that it would be quite useless, as the only thing the citizens of Langtry did not drink was water."

By the time of his death, in 1903, his frontier eccentricities had made such reliably good copy that he was nationally, even world, famous. He and Lillie never met, but less than a year after he died she passed through Langtry in a private railway coach on her way to performances in San Francisco. She paid a visit to the famous saloon. Some of the besotted cowboys in attendance tried to present her with the gift of another of Roy Bean's pet bears, but the animal broke its chain before the train pulled out and ran away across the desert, with the cowboys in pursuit and shooting at it. She was, however, later sent the judge's revolver, inscribed by Langtry's town fathers. "This pistol," they wrote, "kept order in the Jersey Lilly Saloon."

A FEW MILES EAST OF LANGTRY, PAST THE VANISHED SITE OF Vinegarroon, Highway 90 crosses the Pecos River over a towering bridge just a few miles upstream from where the Pecos meets the Rio Grande. I pull off the highway at a scenic overlook, get out of the car, and stand there for a moment, thinking: what a state! There are few other places where Texas seems quite so endless, so remote, so geologically emphatic and eternal. The river enters my field of vision from the north, a wide grayish-greenish ribbon sluicing around the bend through a deep canyon of slick limestone pockmarked with shallow, amphitheater-sized rock shelters.

In one of those shelters, high up on the canyon wall, is Texas's most ancient, most gloriously perplexing work of art. I can see the shallow cave from where I stand at the overlook, but the painting itself—the White Shaman mural—is hidden in deep shadow. Twenty-six feet long, it is a series of faded pictographs made thousands of years ago whose most prominent feature is a row of five vertical, vaguely humanlike figures, each with a red crest like the tip of an unstruck match, each of their handless arms holding what appear to be torches. In the view of Carolyn Boyd, an artist who has studied the mural for many years and has written a book about it, these five central figures are pilgrims journeying into the heart of a mystic world. "It is a creation story," she believes, "detailing the birth of the sun and the dawn of time."

Past the rock shelter and its depiction of a world before time, out of sight beyond the bend of the river, is the old Pecos High Bridge, which Roy Bean's tent saloon customers constructed to connect Texas to the rest of the Southwest via the Sunset Route of the Southern Pacific. Toward the southwest, in the opposite direction, the Pecos slides into its confluence with the Rio Grande. The stark canyon the river has incised here is three hundred feet deep. It flows sluggishly between unscalable cliffs of Devils River limestone, past more overhangs still haunted by the pictographs of ancient peoples.

It is almost too much to take in. The land is too big, and its history too various and unrevealing. I get back into the car and head home, the landscape's desert palette shifting to sage green and then to full-blown springtime grassiness and leafiness the farther east I travel. There are always vultures somewhere along the way, but the roadrunners that kept slipping across the highway a few hours back are no longer present. Adobe houses give way to Alsatian architecture around Castroville, where the lush fading-light foliage of oaks and pecans erases the memory of desolate creosote flats.

I'm still traveling on something of a rural highway, at least until it enters the gravitational pull of San Antonio, its outer loops lined with shopping malls and theme restaurants and gargantuan convenience stores featuring a hundred gas pumps. Before I get to this unbroken urban thicket, I notice abandoned houses and motels moldering on the side of the road, and pass through picturesque town squares that once supported thriving everyday businesses—clothing stores, movie theaters, bakeries—but that are now home only to struggling specialties like tea shops and Pilates studios.

Every such place is its own unwritten historical marker, a mute record of some success or failure, some expression of human hope or enterprise that once existed but is now no more. Thinking about these places, and the generations of people who lived in them and whose names might have appeared in a census report or a phone book but never in a newspaper article or a volume of history, reminds me that the story of Texas has always played out beneath and beyond the canopy of Big History. So let's scale down for a moment. Who, for instance, might be considered the unlikeliest Texas hero of all time?

HIS NAME WAS OLD RIP. THOUGH HE WASN'T A PERSON, HE was certainly a personage. Old Rip was a horny toad, which is an animal also known throughout Texas as a horned toad or horned frog. It is a reptile, though, and not, as the name implies, an amphibian. Horny toads are properly known as Texas horned lizards. They're small creatures, only a few inches in length. Their bodies are flat and armored with spiky protrusions, most strikingly the backward thrusting horns on their heads, but also the pointy rows on their backs and along their flanks. Horny toads are harmless, though when they feel under threat they can inflate themselves like a puffer fish and spray blood from their eyes for up to four feet.

"The horned lizard," concludes one author, "is surprisingly charismatic." One of the people who fell under the species' spell was Joe Chadwick, who passed through Texas in 1834 as an assistant to the artist George Catlin and died two years later, along with the rest of Santa Anna's prisoners, at Goliad. "Joe's fancy for horned frogs has grown into a sort of frog-mania," Catlin wrote about Chadwick as they crossed the plains, "and his eyes are strained all day, and gazing amongst the grass and pebbles as he rides along, for his precious little prizes, which he occasionally picks up and consigns to his pockets." Four decades later, a pair of literary travelers named H. F. McDanield and N. A. Taylor were equally entranced. "Now imagine this creature," they wrote, "with all his horns and monstrous assemblage, increased in size to an elephant or buffalo, and conceive yourself coming upon him unawares on the wide prairie or in the deep forests!"

Horny toads made as striking an impression on people in West Texas in the 1950s as they did in the century before. They were everywhere in Abilene when I was a kid. Before pesticides and habitat loss turned them into a threatened species, you couldn't walk across a vacant lot without encountering a dozen of them. They were easy to catch and strangely in demand. At the 1964 Boy Scout Jamboree in Valley Forge, one Texas troop brought three thousand live horny toads to trade with scouts from other parts of the country for less dazzling goods like neckerchief slides and Order of the Arrow patches. Some gas stations would give you a horny toad as a premium for filling up your tank.

At the close of the nineteenth century, the creatures were abundant, as they were almost everywhere in Texas, in Eastland County, named after Captain William Mosby Eastland, one of the men who had the misfortune to draw a black bean in Mier. The county seat, about a hundred miles west of Fort Worth, was also named Eastland. The courthouse burned down in 1896, and construction began the next year on a replacement. A boy named Will Wood was playing with a horny toad he had captured when his father, the county clerk, came home one day for lunch and, on a whim, borrowed it and decided to drop into a hollow space in the cornerstone of the new courthouse. He wanted to test a local theory that horny toads could live indefinitely without food or water.

Thirty-one years later, in 1928, the courthouse was already inadequate, mostly because of the economic and population changes brought about by the oil boom in Eastland County. It was demolished to make room for a newer and larger building. On a February day, a crowd gathered to watch as the cornerstone was opened. The people of Eastland had heard the rumor that a horny toad had been placed in it three decades before, along with a Bible, and the local newspaper had drummed up a feverish curiosity about its fate.

It was a Methodist minister who first peered into the opened cornerstone and announced, "There's the frog!"

The thing that was lifted out of the cornerstone was "flat as a dollar," dusty, unmoving. Then one of its hind legs started to twitch. "The durn thing's alive," someone called out.

"When first taken from its score-and-a-half year tomb," the *Dallas Morning News* reported of the Lazarus-like spectacle, "where no light, air nor water had a chance to penetrate, the frog's eyes were closed and it seemed

"The durn thing's alive!" Old Rip, the world's most celebrated horny toad, supposedly survived thirty-one years of entombment in the cornerstone of the Eastland County courthouse.

dead. Soon, however, its pale eyelids blinked and then opened. . . . It wriggled a bit, then settled back into lethargy, seemingly ready to go to sleep for another third of a century."

They called it, of course, Rip Van Winkle—soon shortened to Old Rip. The horny toad was instantly world famous, and a legal battle erupted over who owned him—Eastland County or Will Wood, the now-grown man whose father had slipped Old Rip into the cornerstone thirty-one years earlier. The court intrigue, however, did not prevent Wood from taking the horny toad on tour, including a stop at the White House to meet President Coolidge.

"The president's remarks to Rip were not announced to the public," Wood telegraphed home to Eastland, "but are assumed to have been friendly rather than scientific."

Old Rip survived for a little less than year. Will Wood's daughter left him out on the porch in a gold-fish bowl during a norther, and he died, we are told, of pneumonia. His body was embalmed by a local funeral home and laid in a tiny, specially con-structed silk-lined casket.

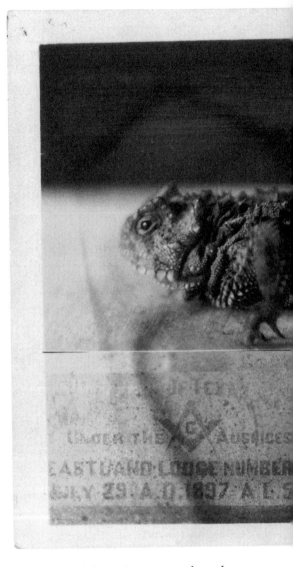

You can pay your respects to Old Rip today. He reposes in his casket in a little glass-walled mausoleum built into the courthouse that replaced the one in which he had been entombed while alive. It may not be the original Old Rip—probably isn't, really—since there is a rich legacy of grave robbing when it comes to the world's most celebrated horny toad. And then there is the question, of course, whether the story of his long survival in the cornerstone could pos-sibly be true. Skeptics argued that someone had used sleight of hand to slip a live horny toad into the cornerstone just as it was opened, but witnesses such as the Methodist minister passionately maintained that no such hoax had occurred. Learned professors examined Old Rip and speculated upon the survival potential of the Texas horned lizard. The closest any of them came to a con-clusive scientific statement was "nothing is impossible with God."

The last time I visited Old Rip's tomb, I found myself pondering not so much the mystery of his longevity as the three decades of history that had occurred beyond his supposed cornerstone imprisonment in the East-land County Courthouse. Time may have stood still for Old Rip, but not for Texas. Here's what happened while he slept.

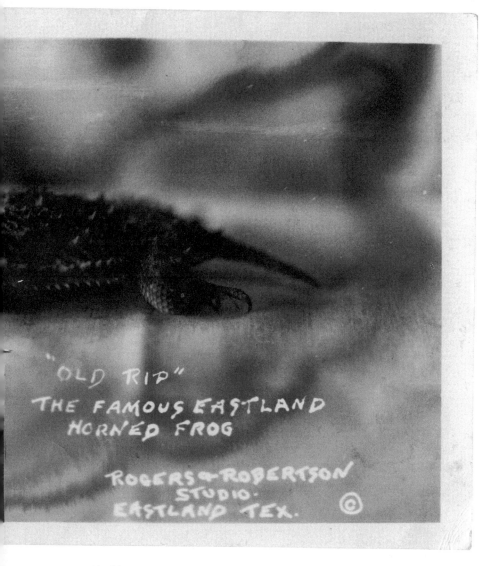

After his resurrection, Old Rip was famous enough to be on a postcard and to travel to Washington, DC, to meet Calvin Coolidge.

★

PART FOUR

— While —

OLD RIP SLEPT

★

—30—

A THOUSAND
LITTLE DEVILS

IN THE TENTH MONTH OF OLD RIP'S CONFINEMENT, THIRTY-
nine-year-old Theodore Roosevelt arrived in San Antonio
and sat down for breakfast in the Menger Hotel. It was
May 15, 1898. Only a few weeks earlier, the United States had
declared war against Spain, a development that Roosevelt
thoroughly approved of. "I had preached," he wrote in his
book *The Rough Riders*, "with all the fervor and zeal I possessed, our duty to
intervene in Cuba, and to take this opportunity of driving the Spaniard from
the Western World."

In Roosevelt's mind, a war with Spain over Cuba would be a net gain for
America. It would free the Cuban people from the weight of Spanish oppression; reinforce the 1823 Monroe Doctrine, which warned European powers
not to meddle in the Western Hemisphere; give the American people something lofty to think about; and provide a containable little shooting war in
which the U.S. Army and Navy could dust off their skills. The February 1898
explosion that sank the American battleship *Maine* in Havana Harbor and
killed 260 men provided a righteous casus belli, though whether the ship

THEODORE ROOSEVELT
in San Antonio while recruiting the Rough Riders. TR's time in Texas was brief, but he and the Lone Star State were made for each other.

was destroyed through hostile action or an internal coal fire that blew up the magazine has never been conclusively determined.

Whatever it was that caused the *Maine* to explode, war had come, and Roosevelt had immediately resigned from his post as assistant secretary of the navy and, along with Colonel Leonard Wood, a veteran of the Apache Wars in Arizona, formed the First U.S. Volunteer Cavalry, one of three cavalry regiments called for by the secretary of war "to be composed entirely of frontiersmen possessing special qualifications as horsemen and marksmen." It was a regiment that Roosevelt and his men, and soon the whole world, called the Rough Riders.

The Rough Riders were recruited from Arizona, New Mexico, and the Indian and Oklahoma Territories. They also came from another unlikely sphere: Roosevelt's circle of acquaintances on the East Coast, polo players and steeplechase riders and yachtsmen from the Ivy League, and denizens of exclusive clubs like the Knickerbocker and the Somerset. This "Fifth Avenue Crowd" had, along with the rest of the Rough Riders, come to San Antonio for an intensive few weeks of drill and training.

Roosevelt's company arrived five days before he did. It visited the Alamo and the other San Antonio sights before going into camp with the hunters, cowboys, and prospectors who made up the other companies in the regiment. The Rough Riders from the territories were, in Roosevelt's rhapsodic recollection, "a splendid set of men . . . tall and sinewy, with resolute, weather-beaten faces, and eyes that looked a man straight in the face without flinching." He also found plenty of recruits in Texas, former Rangers many of them: "[They] needed no teaching. . . . They were splendid shots, horsemen, and trailers. They were accustomed to living in the open, to enduring great fatigue and hardship, and to encountering all kinds of danger."

This described just the sort of man that Roosevelt himself longed to be, and to a remarkable degree he had already succeeded. Fourteen years earlier, Roosevelt had moved to Dakota Territory from New York to become a rancher. The cattle boom that he and his aristocratic friends were investing in promised big financial rewards and bracing tests of manhood. Afflicted with asthma and plagued by grief (his wife and his mother had died on the same day), Roosevelt put his career in state and national politics on hold to reinvent himself as a rugged and self-reliant cattle baron. The Porcellian Club dandy who called out instructions such as "Hasten forward there!" to his ranch hands was soon, via a determined effort of self-transformation, regarded by the locals as "a fearless bugger."

He was a source of curiosity and entertainment for the citizens of San Antonio, galloping a "rough and hardy" bay horse up and down St. Mary's Street while crowds gathered on the sidewalks to watch. "The animal had plenty of mettle," the *San Antonio Daily Express* reported, "but Col. Roosevelt mastered him."

Roosevelt spent his time in the city drilling the men on foot and on the "plunging steeds" that he imagined they would ride into battle, though his famous assault on San Juan Hill (actually, a neighboring promontory called Kettle Hill) turned out to be a foot charge. He was in San Antonio for only a few weeks. By the end of May, he was on his way with the Rough Riders to Cuba, lustily reading a book called *À Quoi Tient la Supériorité des Anglo-Saxons* on the long train journey to their embarkation point in Tampa.

But the memory of his presence lingers in San Antonio, most notably in the famous bar of the Menger Hotel, where a plaque makes the outsized claim that it was the place where Roosevelt actually "recruited" the Rough Riders.

Roosevelt might have encountered an ex-Ranger or two in the bar and talked them into signing up for his regiment, but I like to think of him not at the Menger bar but at the hotel's restaurant, where he had breakfast on the morning of his arrival in San Antonio. The Menger is across the street from the Alamo, built on ground where a desperate group of Texian defenders had, in the final minutes of the battle, left the walls of the overrun mission and tried to make a stand out in the open before being run down by

Mexican lancers. Roosevelt would have known he was breakfasting on sacred Texas ground, and it's inconceivable he would not have found time to stroll across the street that morning and enter the dark, hushed shrine that the Alamo church had become in the half century since the battle. "We . . . were glad," he wrote in *The Rough Riders*, "that our regiment had been organized in the city where the Alamo commemorates the death fight of Crockett, Bowie, and their famous band of frontier heroes."

He had already paid homage, in his own Fifth Avenue way, to the spirit of Crockett and Bowie. Before moving to Dakota, he had stopped in at Tiffany & Co. to order a custom-made Bowie knife whose sterling silver repoussé handle featured an engraving of a buckskin-clad Davy Crockett–like frontiersman. In the Badlands, he made a point of acquiring his own fringed buckskin shirt, made to order by a local seamstress.

It is not hard to imagine Theodore Roosevelt as the ultimate honorary Texan. As an enthusiastic destabilizer of empires, he would have been right at home in the Alamo, among men who had risen up in revolt against Mexico, and perhaps even more at home with the generation of filibusters who preceded them, who had confidently set out to seize Texas from Spain.

★

SAN ANTONIO WAS STILL THE BIGGEST CITY IN TEXAS WHEN Roosevelt passed through with the Rough Riders. The 1900 census listed 53,321 people living there. It was ahead of Houston by nearly 10,000 residents, and its population was double that of Austin's. Dallas, in third place with 42,638, was still, even by Texas standards, a young city. It had erupted from a trading post and ferry planted on a rocky ford of the upper Trinity River—some four hundred miles inland from where the river discharges into the Gulf of Mexico. The trading post had been built in 1841 by a restless Tennessee lawyer named John Neely Bryan. Bryan served as postmaster for the Republic of Texas, but his political career never quite caught fire, and his life was full of flight and turmoil. He made a brief foray into the California gold fields in 1849 and later sent himself into exile for five years after shooting a man who he claimed had insulted his wife. His complicated life ended in Austin in 1877 at what was then called the State Lunatic Asylum. If his legacy had been a little stronger, the great city he helped spark into being might have borne his name. As it happened, nobody quite remembered whom the place was named after. There are a handful of possibilities. Among them are George Mifflin Dallas, the vice president of the United States under James K. Polk; or his brother, a naval commodore in the War of 1812; or a friend of Bryan's named Joseph Dallas.

Dallas had something of an identity problem from the beginning. Besides that question mark hanging over its name, over the course of time it became fashionable, particularly among the worldly wags of other Texas cities, to argue that Dallas had no reason to exist in the first place. It didn't spring from a river port or a military installation or a commanding chunk of geography. But it was near the meeting place of several significant Indian trails, as well as the confluence of the West Fork and Elm Fork of the Trinity. It was also at the intersection of two of the primitive roads later decreed into being by the Republic of Texas, one of them aspirationally named the Central National Highway. In the 1870s, it became a railroad crossroads as well, and a location that had once been only marginally convenient became strategic. Texas needed a transportation hub for shipping its raw products, particularly cotton, to manufacturing centers in the East and the North, and with the arrival of the railroads Dallas quickly assumed that role. Its status as a cotton market soon made it a merchandising center as well, with German Jewish businessmen like Philip, Isaac, and Alexander Sanger opening dry-goods shops that would morph into flagship department stores. A salesman at Sanger Brothers, Herbert Marcus, had a sister, Carrie, who worked as a blouse buyer at another department store, A. Harris and Company. The two of them joined forces with Carrie's husband, Abraham Lincoln Neiman, to start an enduring little retail enterprise named Neiman-Marcus.

─────────── ★ ───────────

IN 1900, GALVESTON WAS TEXAS'S FOURTH-LARGEST CITY. ITS population, soon to be brutally subtracted by more than 15 percent, was 37,789. There was no mystery about the origins of Galveston's name. It was named for Bernardo de Gálvez, the viceroy of New Spain who, when he was governor of Spanish Louisiana, had secured the Mississippi for the American colonies in their fight against Great Britain. Gálvez never set sail on the great bay, Bahía de Gálvezton, that bore his name, nor set foot in the settlement established on the vulnerable sandbar at the bay's mouth, where Jean Lafitte had once entertained Jane Long.

Galveston had become a venerable, elegant, and thriving tropical port. Lafitte's Maison Rouge was long gone, as were the shanties and gambling parlors that made up his pirate settlement of Campeche, but in their place had risen a city with a wide central esplanade, electric lighting, an imposing opera house, churches, and magnificent residential palaces designed with Victorian abandon by an Irish-born architect named Nicholas Clayton. The wealthy families that ran Galveston—the Moodys, the Sealys, and the Kempners, among others—had formed an organization called the Deep

Water Committee that, by 1896, had succeeded in building jetties and dredging a channel that turned the shallow waters of Galveston harbor into a deepwater port, ending for a moment the threat from the rival port city of Houston, at the upper end of Galveston Bay. "Though fifty miles inland," H. F. McDanield and N. A. Taylor noticed about Houston during their trip to Texas in the 1870s, "the sea knocks at her doors, and she has only to heed the summons." Galveston made sure to heed the sea's summons before Houston could, and its colossal investment paid off. Galveston outpaced New Orleans to become America's largest cotton port, exporting goods worth $86 million dollars in the last year of the century.

But Galveston was not a relatively sheltered inland port like New Orleans. It was an island, rising only 8.9 feet above sea level at its highest point, fully exposed on its windward side to the open Gulf of Mexico. Its vulnerability had something to do with its turn-of-the-century, edge-of-the-world enchantment.

Not everyone shared in the island's magic. If you were one of the women and children employed at Galveston's new cotton mill, for instance, you worked thirteen-hour days on a sweltering factory floor under the scrutiny of sadistic foremen, barely able to see your loom because the lightbulbs overhead were spaced so far apart.

For the wealthy or middle-class residents of the island, for tourists from the mainland with time and money enough to take the train across the bay for a seaside vacation, Galveston in early September 1900 was a beguiling place to be. Mule-drawn streetcars took bathers down to the beach and delivered guests to another of Nicholas Clayton's confections, the multi-tiered, multigalleried Beach Hotel, from whose turret a massive pennant fluttered in the mild Gulf breeze.

Pavilions with restaurants and dance floors extended out over the water on pilings, and commodious bathhouses were available for those who didn't see the point of spending money on the portable bathhouses that were moved up and down the beach and in and out of the water by horses.

Most people didn't wear their wool bathing suits to the beach. They kept them in the bathhouses and bathing pavilions and changed into them once they got there. A man named Lloyd Fayling, a former deputy U.S. marshal who was now a district manager for a publishing company, had been patronizing a bathhouse called the Pagoda all during the summer of 1900, swimming for hours every day. He was proud of his bathing suit, "which was of a particularly vivid color and attracted some attention."

At one o'clock in the afternoon of Saturday, September 8, he went to the Pagoda once again, not to swim but to get a view of the tropical storm that

had just struck the island. "People were already somewhat alarmed at the situation," he wrote later, "but no one thought that the storm was going to be anything more than one of our usual damp spells."

The storm had been predicted, but without any particular sense of alarm or specificity. In that morning's edition of the *Galveston News*, an update was squeezed onto page 10, speculating that "the tropical disturbance has changed its course or spent its force before reaching Texas." Isaac Cline, the meteorologist who headed the Galveston bureau of the U.S. Weather Service, had an ominous feeling but couldn't back it up with instrument readings. "The usual signs which herald the approach of hurricanes," he recalled, "were not present in this case."

But they were presenting themselves on Saturday afternoon to Lloyd Fayling and the others gathered at the beach, where the waves were already flooding the streets and crashing over the piers and pilings. Fayling saw half the Pagoda crumble into the sea, but he raced along the boardwalk to the surviving half and managed to rescue his bathing suit. As he stood there, bewitched by the phosphorescent glow of the rising ocean, he noticed that a gale was blowing from the north, across the mainland and the long fetch of Galveston Bay. The onrushing sea was powerful, driven by the approaching Gulf storm, but the waves pounding onto the beach were facing a strong headwind that convinced Fayling this was no tropical storm but a full-blown hurricane. "I then realized that something was going to drop," he remem-

*The hurricane and flood that destroyed Galveston in 1900 was
the worst natural disaster in American history.*

bered, "and started for town, bathing suit in hand, and informed all the
people I met that they had better get into the higher parts of the town."

But no part of town was high enough to withstand the savage two-front
assault of wind and water that hit Galveston that day. "Things beginning to
look serious," wrote a young woman who worked at a local hospital. The
letter she composed during the storm and never had a chance to send was
unsigned, though it somehow survived, even if its author may not have.
"Should feel more comfortable in the embrace of your arms," she confided
to her unknown addressee. "Darkness is overwhelming us, to add to the
horror. Dearest—I—reach out my hand to you. my heart—my soul."

The winds of the hurricane reached 120 miles an hour. They whipped
down at first from the north, driving the waters of Galveston Bay over the
wharves and dockside businesses along the leeward side of the island and
on its eastern point. The north wind suppressed the water that was building
on the Gulf side, but when the cyclonic winds shifted at about two in the
afternoon, that dammed-up ocean surge was released as well, inundating
the city's streets as the screaming wind tore apart houses and churches and
proud municipal edifices.

While trying to ride out the storm in their stoutly built houses, many
Galveston residents quickly realized they needed to chop or drill holes

in their floors so that the rising water would provide some sort of ballast against a wind strong enough to lift houses off their foundations and send them sailing on the floodwaters to join a growing pile of debris that in turn shoved down more buildings and crushed the occupants that had sought shelter in them.

"It sounded as if the rooms were filled with a thousand little devils," one survivor wrote of the shrieking wind that broke her house apart. Cast onto the stinking, slimy, debris-filled waters, the people of Galveston struggled to keep from drowning or from being bludgeoned or decapitated by a shrapnel slurry of window glass, bricks, wooden beams, and roofing slate. The wind and water stripped off their clothes. The occupants of still-standing houses long remembered looking out their windows at the pale naked bodies of terrified men and women screaming for help as the tide swept them helplessly along under the moonlight. In a forlorn attempt not to be separated, families tied themselves together with clotheslines, but that only ensured that each drowning person pulled down the next. A family of eight in the western part of the city died that way.

It was far worse at St. Mary's Orphanage, an imposing brick edifice facing the beach, which the sea tore down like a sandcastle. Each of the nuns there—members of the Sisters of Charity of the Incarnate Word—tied herself to a group of children. They led the orphans in a hymn, "Queen of the Waves," which called upon the intercession of the Blessed Virgin Mary to calm the seas.

> Help, then sweet Queen, in our exceeding danger,
> By thy seven griefs, in pity Lady save;
> Think of the Babe that slept within the manger
> And help us now, dear Lady of the Wave.

But the orphanage collapsed under the wind and waves even as the children sang. Three older boys, who had not been roped together, survived. The rest—ninety children and ten nuns—were among the dead in the worst natural disaster in American history.

There was never a precise count of the people who perished. At least 6,000 died, probably many more. Lloyd Fayling, the former U.S. marshal who had saved his colorful bathing suit but barely escaped drowning in an underwater tangle of telegraph wires, helped lead the effort to put the city under martial law and do something about the dead bodies that were everywhere, either lying in plain grotesque sight or hopelessly impacted in ramparts of debris that were thirty feet high.

A ground-level view of one of Galveston's main streets.
Though much of the city was ground into rubble by the storm, a few architectural
showpieces—like the Bishop's Palace, in the background—still stand today.

Men and boys were conscripted into gathering up the decomposing dead. The stench of death was as thick as the foot-deep carpet of slime and mud that covered every surface. There was no way to identify most of the bodies by sight, no way to give them a proper burial. At first they were loaded onto barges, sash weights tied to their feet, and dumped into the Gulf. But the tide brought them back, in even more horrible condition than before, and there was nothing to do but burn them. There were fires all over the island, on once-thriving city streets that had been scraped back to bare sand by the hurricane.

"What a terrible fire!" a correspondent from the *New York Journal* named Winifred Black said to a nearby stranger on the boat as she was crossing from the mainland and saw the flames all over Galveston. She speculated that some of the larger surviving buildings in town had caught fire.

"Buildings?" the man said. "Don't you know what is burning over there? It is my wife and children."

The Lucas gusher
that erupted on the
coastal mound known
as Spindletop and
changed the history
of the world. The well
spewed crude oil for
nine days. "Now that
we've got her, boys,"
Anthony Lucas asked
his drilling crew,
"what are we going
to do with her?"

—31—

GUSHERS

"IT IS NECESSARY TO HAVE A CITY HERE," W. L. MOODY
Sr. told a reporter a few days after the storm had all but
erased Galveston from the earth. Moody, a decorated
Confederate veteran, had become a Galveston cotton and
banking magnate. After the hurricane, the city's ruling elite
promptly took direct control of the recovery of the city, and
not incidentally of the city itself. "Businessmen and methods are what we
need now in Galveston," they declared, "men who know their duty to the
city and are not afraid to perform it."

That meant getting rid of the old, cumbersome, ineffective—but
democratic—city government and replacing it with what amounted to a
kind of municipal martial law. The twelve aldermen who had represented
Galveston wards were eliminated; in their place would be four commissioners
and a "mayor-president" chosen by the governor. Though the commissioners
were soon changed from appointed to elected, in order to provide some
semblance of representative government, the emergency structure that
Galveston put in place worked with such blunt efficiency that it soon
spread to five hundred other American cities. Within a few years, the city
commissioners of Galveston had overseen the construction of a seventeen-
foot-high seawall to repel any future killer waves from the Gulf. Temporary

canals were dug so that 16.3 trillion cubic yards of sand could be dredged from the ship channel and distributed over the residential part of the island, raising the city fifteen feet above the flood zone. It was an engineering project of such outrageous magnitude that the chairman of the New York Bondholders' Committee thundered, when presented with the proposal, "Galveston is not in her right mind yet."

With its seawall built, its ground raised, and much of its island mystique restored, Galveston came back, but could not hold on to the promise that had distinguished it before the great 1900 storm. By 1930, it was still a thriving port, but the initiative had been stolen by Houston, which had dredged its own fifty-two-mile deepwater channel across the bay to the open sea. Houston, not Galveston or even New Orleans, was now the largest cotton port in the nation.

But it was another cargo moving through the Port of Houston that would change Texas forever and shock the world into a new age.

On a summer day in 2017, I joined a group of a hundred or so retirees in purple T-shirts that read "Swingin' Seniors." We were boarding a boat—the *Sam Houston*—docked at the turning basin of the Port of Houston. The port has offered free tours of its facilities on this vessel since 1958, tours that are so inscrutably popular that they are often booked up for almost a year. I sat with the captain in the wheelhouse of the *Sam Houston* as he guided the boat toward Galveston Bay along the dredged and widened mouth of Buffalo Bayou, a few miles downstream from where the Allen brothers had founded the town of Houston just after the Battle of San Jacinto. The water was scummy and laden with trash washed into the port from Houston streets and sewer drains and overflowing creeks. Cargo ships were unloading, barges were plying the bay, and dredges were pumping out silt to make sure the channel remained deep and wide enough to accommodate oceangoing traffic. In his off hours, the *Sam Houston*'s captain told me, he was a surfer, not on the Gulf beaches but in the channel itself. If you didn't mind the less-than-enchanting seascape, you could catch a ride on the wake of one of those big ships that might last for five miles.

History was deeply layered here, or maybe it would be more accurate to say deeply submerged. Somewhere among the warehouses and railroad sidings and grain elevators that lined the ship channel was the spot where Sam Houston had once crossed Buffalo Bayou with his army to advance upon the Mexicans at San Jacinto. At the halfway point of the tour was a stretch of green lawn on the right bank in front of the Pasadena Refining plant. Beneath the trees there, barely visible from the wheelhouse of the *Sam Houston*, an old-style historical marker made of granite commemorated the place where Santa Anna had been captured. And if the boat had continued a little farther down the drowned bayou, it would have come across the San Jacinto battlefield itself, marked by its 567-foot-high tower of victory.

But all around us, on either side of the ship channel, were other, less deliberate monuments to Texas history: the sprawling refineries with their distillation towers and cracking units and tank farms and thick nests of pipelines that turned crude oil into gasoline and transported it across the world.

Oil was never "discovered" in Texas; it was just always there. It was the "scum" that surviving members of the De Soto and Moscoso expeditions had found seeping up out of the Texas surf in 1543 and then used to seal the gaps in their leaky handmade rafts while they were tortured by clouds of mosquitoes. A three- or four-acre pond in the forests between the Brazos and Sabine Rivers was apparently regarded by local Indians—the Bidais and Deadose—as a useful resource, since blobs of lubricant in the form of petroleum percolated up from its sulfurous shallows. When the Anglos came, they called the place Sour Lake. In the little community of Sour Lake today, on the side of an out-of-business Mexican restaurant that faces Highway 105, a fading mural depicts a group of Indians wading through the water and staring down at floating, fetid-looking brown lumps. "All over the lake's surface," an early visitor noted, "there is an escaping gas that ignites as quickly as gunpowder the moment that a match is applied to it."

Yet the place was, improbably, a mecca. On the mural, next to the scene of the Indians staring down at the petroleum seeping up out of Sour Lake, is a full-length portrait of Sam Houston standing in front of a long-vanished resort hotel with an explanatory text below: "Houston seeks mudbath."

Houston was indeed one of the guests who traveled to Sour Lake to take therapeutic baths and drink the supposedly medicinal waters. In fact, he sought relief there in the summer of 1863, just before he died. A few years earlier, Frederick Law Olmsted, in his narrative about his travels through Texas, left a vivid description of a sulfurous, gaseous resort. "The approach to the rude bathing-houses," he remembered, "is over a boggy margin, sending up a strong bituminous odor, upon pools in which rises a dense brown, transparent liquid, described as having the properties of the Persian and Italian naphthas."

At the time, there was no compelling use for petroleum that extended much beyond its restorative powers. It was handy, however, for jobs that required some sort of lubricant or sealant, and the dried-up, oil-saturated mud on the banks of Sour Lake could even be sliced up and burned like candles. And there were enterprising do-it-yourself types like the farmer in Liberty County who sank a pipe three feet into his backyard and, with the aid of a funnel, diverted the natural gas that emanated from the ground into his house, where he used it for cooking and lighting.

Oil production during the first part of the nineteenth century meant mostly capturing and diverting the gas that rose naturally from the ground or gathering the petroleum deposits that seeped up out of foul-smelling bogs like Sour Lake. That changed after 1859, when Edwin Drake, a former railroad conductor, drilled a well in Titusville, Pennsylvania, and struck oil sixty-nine feet below the ground. All at once there was an oil industry, though at that point petroleum was used mainly for illumination, not power. Whale oil in lamps was on the way out, replaced by the cleaner-burning kerosene that could be refined from crude oil.

A pig, not a geologist, determined the site of the first oil well in Texas. Two farmers in the Big Thicket, only a few miles from Sour Lake, saw tarry splotches on their pigs and followed them to the viscous pit in the middle of the forest where they had been wallowing. In 1865 one of the farmers contracted with a Galveston man named Edward Von Hartin, who built a wooden derrick over the tar wallow. Over and over a mule laboriously pulled a weight to the top of the derrick, whereupon it would be released to slam into the earth. Von Hartin was able to penetrate a hundred feet by using this process, but it wasn't deep enough. Texas had its first dry hole.

But oil was struck the next year at a place a few miles east of Nacogdoches fittingly known as Oil Springs. Lyne Taliaferro Barret was a clerk who had risen to become a partner in an East Texas mercantile firm. He leased some land on which to prospect for oil, but the Civil War interrupted his plans, and it wasn't until 1866 that he was able to drill, using an eight-foot steam-powered auger. He and his four partners in the Melrose Petroleum Oil Company struck oil at 106 feet—ten barrels a day—the first Texans to bring in a well. But like many wildcatters who would follow him, Barret had to face the fact that fortune wasn't going to be on his side. Oil prices were low in 1866, Reconstruction tensions were high, and eastern investors were more interested in proven Pennsylvania oil fields than Texas tar pits. Barret capped his well, had eleven children, served as master of his local Masonic Lodge, became a justice of the peace, and died. Twenty years after he was forced to abandon the site he called Oil Springs, forty producing wells were crowded together there, along with Texas's first pipeline and its first refinery.

Even then, oil was only a sidelight industry. The oil that was coaxed out of the ground using old-fashioned cable tool rigs and fishtail drill bits, and hauled to railheads by wagon along Big Thicket logging roads, had too much sulfur in it and too little paraffin to make it practicable for refining into kerosene. It was better suited to low-grade applications like lubricating machinery, firing boilers, or spraying onto dusty Texas streets. One Central Texas rancher who accidentally struck oil while drilling for water made $7.08 after selling forty-eight barrels.

A higher-quality grade of oil was discovered in the town of Corsicana. Corsicana, about sixty miles southeast of Dallas, was in Navarro County, named for the Tejano patriot José Antonio Navarro. The county seat in turn was named in honor of his parents, who had been born in Corsica. In 1894, The Corsicana Water Development Company underwent a name change to the Corsicana Oil Development Company after three water wells drilled in the middle of town struck oil instead. It was an unwelcome development at first, but the report from a Pennsylvania chemist determined that the product might be as marketable as water. In 1900, the Corsicana oil field produced 839,554 barrels, nothing compared to what would soon take place in Texas, but enough for a greasy forest of derricks to sprout from the front yards of the town's residents, and for oil to flow off the roofs of their houses into the streets.

And Corsicana turned out to be a crucial testing ground for an infant industry. Cable tool rigs, which up to then had been the standard workhorses of the oil field, chipping away into the ground with percussive force, were soon superseded by rotary drills, which could reach oil sands lying at a thousand feet in days rather than weeks. The process of refining was also refined as new techniques were deployed for removing the sulfur content from crude oil, resulting in kerosene that Corsicana boosters declared had "Quality as Good as Pennsylvania's."

The quality may have been there, but quantity had yet to erupt from the East Texas soil. That didn't happen until the first month of 1901, just south of the town of Beaumont, atop a vast spreading mound that was no more than fifteen feet higher than the surrounding coastal prairie. This low-slung landmark went by the name Sour Spring Mound or Big Hill or—most indelibly—Spindletop. It got that name because of a pine tree that rose from the mound in stark isolation, giving it the look of a spindle.

It could be argued that Spindletop is one of the most important locations in the history of the world, but you don't get that impression today as you drive along a spur road off the main highway from Beaumont to Port Arthur, past a dreary industrial neighborhood in which rusting oilfield equipment is scattered in the vacant acreage between RV parks and correctional facilities. If there's a sign directing tourists to Spindletop, I missed it. But finally, after turning onto a side road that led across the railroad tracks and past a random collection of unmoving pumpjacks, I came to an observation platform with a view of—almost nothing. There was only flat, scraggly, boggy coastal plain, with a whiff of sulfur in the air.

The landscape would have been more enticing before oil was discovered at Spindletop, but even then it was a malodorous sort of place, with a series of sumps and springs discharging water that smelled like gunpowder and the ground offering up hissing columns of gas.

When Dick Dowling and his Irish cannoneers repelled the U.S. Navy at the Battle of Sabine Pass in September 1863, one of the men who took part in the fight was a gunsmith named Robert Higgins. Higgins had moved his family from Georgia and settled in Sabine Pass just before Texas seceded from the Union. After the battle, Dowling gave Higgins the task of traveling to nearby Beaumont to warn its citizens to watch out for Union soldiers who might have managed to get ashore. While he was there, he was also to suggest a suitable place where any prisoners of war could be housed. Higgins found just the spot—the big mound with its network of sour-smelling springs. He raised a flag to mark it.

Thirty-eight years later, this was the place where the first great Spindletop gusher came in. And that happened because of Robert Higgins's son.

———— ★ ————

PATTILLO HIGGINS WAS BORN THREE MONTHS AFTER THE Battle of Sabine Pass and came of age in Beaumont during Reconstruction. He had a probing, tinkering intelligence and a rowdy spirit that had festered into real menace by the time he was seventeen. In 1881 he was part of a gang that attacked worshippers in an African American church with slingshots and what the newspaper described as homemade torpedoes. Higgins exchanged fire with one of the deputies dispatched to restore order, mortally wounding him in the groin and stomach. One of the deputy's shots hit Higgins in the left arm.

Pattillo Higgins lost his arm but was acquitted of murder after convincing a jury that he had fired in self-defense. A free man but still a troubled one, he went to work for a lumber company, given the perilous chore of driving logs down the Neches River, even though he had only one arm and couldn't swim. A few years later he had a religious awakening after listening to a preacher at the Galveston Opera Hall. "I used to put my trust in pistols," he wrote to his brother afterward. "Now my trust is in God and I feel much safer."

He became a respectable businessman, the owner of a brickyard, and a church deacon who taught a girls' Sunday school class, sometimes amusing his young students by taking them on excursions to the Spindletop mound, poking a hole in the ground with a stick, and striking a match to ignite the escaping gas.

Higgins was an autodidact, developing self-generated theories about geology and religious salvation at about the same steady rate. After taking a tour of Indiana and Ohio brickyards—looking for ways to improve the efficiency of his own manufacturing business—and after getting a close-up look at the petroleum industry in Pennsylvania, he came home convinced that there was no reason that the oil he needed to fire his kilns couldn't be found in his own East Texas neighborhood, particularly in the fume-rich acreage that made up the Spindletop mound. But his vision was far grander than that. He planned not just to discover oil but also to build an entire oil-based metropolis, "an inland manufacturing and commercial city" complete with a seaport, pipelines, and refineries.

He called it Gladys City, after Gladys Bingham, one of the young girls in his Sunday school class, with whom he was inappropriately smitten. "Don't let the boys kiss you," he once sternly warned his students. "Don't let them put their hands on you or lean up against you. The boys are ignorant and full of animal nature." His nervous paternalism further manifested itself in his habit of legally adopting young girls, one of whom he ended up marrying.

Gladys City never happened, at least not on the scale and with the coherence that Higgins had originally envisioned. By the time the first earth-shaking well came in at Spindletop, Higgins had been largely sidelined. He had had to sell off most of the acreage he controlled on the mound, and his vision of a great oil-bearing anticline beneath the surface was increasingly regarded by investors not as prophecy but as lunacy. The town of Beaumont, wrote a state geologist who arrived to appraise Higgins's theory, should look for industries that would not involve "frittering her money away upon the idle dreams or insane notions of irresponsible parties in the vain outlook for either oil or useful gas."

A series of wells drilled on the mound in the mid-1890s seemed to bear out this harsh opinion. But then, in 1899, Higgins made the acquaintance of someone who believed, as he did, that there was oil somewhere beneath the coastal prairies of Texas, and that Sour Spring Mound was the place to find it. "I can say right now," Anthony Lucas wrote to Pattillo Higgins that year, "that you will have good cause to be pleased of having met me."

Anthony Lucas was known as Captain Lucas for his service in the Austrian Navy. Born on the Dalmatian coast, he immigrated to the United States at age twenty-four. He became an engineer and, like Higgins, a self-taught geologist. Lucas was convinced, from his drilling explorations in Louisiana, that the salt domes of the Gulf Coast held more than salt; and with his imposing six-two frame, his neatly bald head, and his faintly mysterious accent, he gained the confidence of hard-to-impress Pittsburgh oil pioneers

After oil was discovered on Spindletop, derricks sprouted like mushrooms, creating the first of Texas's muddy, malodorous boom towns.

John H. Galey and James M. Guffey, who tapped into the Mellon banking fortune to finance the well that they planned to drill on Spindletop.

The well was begun—spudded, in the drilling jargon that would soon became familiar throughout Texas—on October 27, 1900, only a few weeks after the beachside funeral pyres of Galveston had stopped smoldering. Three superbly pragmatic brothers from Corsicana—Al, Curt, and Jim Hamill—had been contracted to do the drilling. They built a sixty-four-foot derrick from green logs that had been floated down the Neches River, and made good progress with their rotary rig until they hit quicksand at 160 feet. At that point, Curt Hamill remembered, it was like "trying to drill a hole in a pile of wheat." They inched down, improvising as they went. The water they pumped into the well wasn't heavy enough to keep the hole open in those porous sands, so they enlisted some nearby cattle to churn up the clay in a slush pit, thus inventing one of the indispensable tools of the oil business: drilling mud.

Spindletop came in on January 10, 1901. The sky over the mound had been scoured clear early that morning by a fast-moving norther. What first erupted from the center of the earth was a violent spume of mud and rock and drilling pipe that shook and sorely tested the structural integrity of the derrick that

A drilling crew on Spindletop, several years after the Lucas gusher came in.

the Hamill brothers had designed and hammered together. It tore away the heavy crown block and other equipment and cast them out onto the prairie. The crew desperately put out a fire that had started in the firebox and then watched from a distance as the roaring mud geyser finally subsided.

When things were quiet again, Al Hamill dared to look down into the drill hole. He saw something that looked alive—black, viscous, and heaving. He got out of the way just in time to avoid being blasted into the air by a column of crude oil that shot out of the hole with such force that it soared far above the top of the derrick, high into the winter sky, before raining back down onto the earth.

"Now that we've got her, boys," Lucas reportedly said to the Hamill brothers a few days later, when the geyser had still not abated and the countryside and farmers' crops for miles around were covered with a blanket of oil, "what are we going to do with her?"

It took nine days to tame what became known as the Lucas gusher. The ever-resourceful Hamill brothers came up with another invention, a method of capping the well that involved a team of horses dragging a carriage with a gate valve over the open pipe and shutting down the monstrous flow of oil.

When Lucas had asked Al Hamill the month before for a prediction about how much oil they might find, Hamill had guessed 50 barrels a day. He was off by approximately 950,000 barrels.

The oil that came out of the gusher was heavy greenish crude, and it was thought that it would not be particularly valuable for refining into kerosene. But another use awaited it, one that would arrive soon enough and power the engines of the new century. "There will be a good market for fuel oil," John Galey thought, "when the country has had time to adjust itself to using liquid fuel."

THE LUCAS GUSHER AT SPINDLETOP UNLEASHED A NEW economy, along with new Texan archetypes in the form of wildcatters and roughnecks and newly minted fat-cat oil barons. The fattest of the fat cats was former governor James Hogg, who got in on the frenzy early, forming a syndicate with four other partners to gobble up leases and drill new wells all over Spindletop. Their syndicate was later absorbed into the Texas Company, which in 1959 changed its name to Texaco. (Among the other major oil companies that could trace their ancestry to the Spindletop discovery were Exxon, Mobil, Gulf, and Sun.) Hogg was a frequent visitor to Beaumont, and on one occasion he turned himself into an eye-popping apparition. When a thunderstorm left the streets of the city flooded, he commuted from his hotel to the Texas Company office in a skiff pulled through the water by a hard-trudging African American bearer. Hogg's three-hundred-pound body mass rested in a chair borrowed from the hotel, his pants legs rolled up to reveal his pale calves, an umbrella hovering over his head. He looked, in the words of the oil historian Walter Rundell Jr., "like Cleopatra on her barge."

Pattillo Higgins did not sail into wealth quite so elegantly. After some legal squabbles with his former partners in his Spindletop holdings, he entered into a long and prickly career as an uncredentialed, practical-minded geologist, self-schooled in the surface-reading arts of "moundology" and "creekology." He formed companies and lost control of them in takeover bids, he bought up leases and drilled wells and made a fortune, but had his wildcatter's share of bad luck—pulling out of a play too early, getting into it too late, finding himself pushed aside by the major oil companies that had mushroomed into existence after Spindletop. The religious precepts with which he shielded himself against his own reckless nature were rigid and tiresome—he once lectured his aged, widowed mother about her harmless pastime of reading lighthearted romance novels. All his life, he never stopped looking for oil, chipping away at the ground with his pick on vacations while his family fished and picnicked. All the oil fields he claimed to have located were shown on a "measles" map, so called for the red pinpoints marking the discovery sites. On the day he died—at the age of ninety-one—he signed up ten thousand acres of leases. In a photograph from a few years earlier, when Higgins was eighty-eight and a guest of honor at Beaumont's celebration of the fiftieth anniversary of the discovery of oil at Spindletop, he stands stiffly in front of a fake boomtown storefront, holding a Stetson hat in his right hand. His hairless, maybe toothless head pokes up from his shirt collar like a turtle's, and his frail body looks swallowed up in the billowy tailoring of his 1950s suit. His left sleeve hangs empty past his shot-off arm. "They did not believe me then," Higgins was quoted as saying around this time, "and they will not believe me now."

In the photograph, a sign above Higgins's head reads "Gladys City Oil, Gas & Mfg. Co.," the name of the company he started as the basis for a model industrial community at Sour Spring Mound. The real Gladys City, which sprang into being after Spindletop, was short-lived, a crowded, chaotic boomtown that would be replicated throughout Texas during the following decades. Oil was soon discovered at Sour Lake, and then at other East Texas sites such as Saratoga and Baston, and then near the Red River in Electra and Burkburnett, and then a little farther south in the hitherto sleepy communities of Ranger and Desdemona, and then throughout the great dried-up, down-warped ancient seabed that sprawls beneath much of West Texas and is known as the Permian Basin.

The entrepreneurs and oil-field workers who swarmed to these boomtowns immediately overpowered whatever accommodations were at hand. Roughnecks threw up palmetto huts, tarpaper shacks, and tents to live in. Hotels and boardinghouses rented out not just beds but chairs. "Oil companies," reported a Wichita Falls newspaperman about the scene in Burkburnett, "are being formed on the sidewalk or in the middle of the street." Local proprietors and city officials did whatever they could to participate in the frenetic moneymaking atmosphere, including a justice of the peace in East Texas who acted as a sort of pimp for the town's prostitutes, gathering them together on the balcony of a hotel so that prospective lawbreakers could ogle them before deciding whether they wanted to pay the "fine" the judge read out for each woman.

In some of these towns, like Sour Lake, land was sold off into parcels as small as one-thirty-second of an acre, with the derricks erected on them close enough together to fret out the sunlight. The men who worked them waded through the muck of overflowing slush pits—"The struggle between men and mud was close-locked," recalled a participant named Charlie Jeffries—while breathing varieties of escaping sulfurous gas that ranged from the highly toxic to the—once you got used to it—strangely agreeable. The densest part of the Sour Lake field was a narrow drilling strip called the Shoestring. "Here the wells were thickest," wrote Jeffries, "here the mud was deepest; here the gas was strongest; here the boilers roared the loudest; here the efforts of men had the fullest play. . . . This was the place with which men with pride of action liked to identify themselves."

Texas—parts of it anyway—was now a big beautiful hellhole. And the scattered, seeping tar that Indians had once used to soothe their aching limbs or caulk their canoes had just given the formerly neglected Mexican province a big nudge toward the center of the world.

—32—

LIGHT COMING
ON THE PLAINS

THE MOVIE IS CALLED *THE BANK ROBBERY*. IT IS A SILENT film released in 1908, produced by the Oklahoma Natural Mutoscene Company and starring Bill Tilghman, the real-life U.S. deputy marshal who had apprehended Bill Doolin, the leader of the Wild Bunch gang, in Eureka Springs, Arkansas. Tilghman not only starred in the film but also directed it—poorly but fascinatingly. It's a creaky two-reeler about a group of bank robbers who are pursued by a posse and dispatched, all but one of them, in a brisk shoot-out.

The gang leader is played by Al Jennings, who by the time the film was made had become a reformed celebrity train robber. He had been pardoned by President Theodore Roosevelt and had inspired a short story ("Holding Up a Train") that appears to have been a collaboration between Jennings and O. Henry, published under O. Henry's name. Jennings had also been an attorney, with two of his brothers, in a law practice in Woodward, Oklahoma. In 1895, one brother was killed and another wounded in a saloon gunfight with a local lawyer named Temple Lea Houston, the youngest of Sam and Margaret Houston's eight children.

The Bank Robbery is primitive filmmaking. Tilghman's occasional attempts to move the camera are jerky and distracting, and though the close-up had yet to be invented, he rarely manages to maneuver his actors close enough to the lens for their features to even register. Almost all the scenes are shot in one long take, and there is no storytelling beyond a raw procession of events. But the movie is also grippingly authentic. The actors ride their horses with a supple, untaught expertise, and they and the extras who play (and are) the townspeople of Cache, Oklahoma, appear to be wearing their own clothes, not the stylized Western outfits later invented by Hollywood costumers.

Toward the end of the film, we catch a glimpse of one of the members of the posse as he rides past the camera after the climactic gunfight. His horsemanship, like that of the others, is casually expert. He wears a black vest over a white shirt, a stubby bowtie at his collar, a commodious black cowboy hat on his head. He would be unremarkable in this company except for one thing: the two tight braids beneath his hat brim that identify him as an Indian.

It is Quanah, the last warrior chief of the Comanches, a featured player, along with other distinguished or notorious western celebrities, in one of the first narrative movies ever made. He is in his sixties and only a few years from his death, in 1911, but he is lithe and energetic and probably having fun by pretending to round up outlaws with Bill Tilghman.

By the time the movie was made, it had been thirty-two years since Quanah had led his Quahadi Comanches onto the reservation in Indian Territory and surrendered to Ranald Mackenzie. Mackenzie was long dead. After serving as commander at Fort Sill, he was ordered north to subdue the Northern Cheyenne in Wyoming and the Utes in Colorado. Not long after he completed those assignments, his sanity began to mysteriously unravel. He died, paranoid and incoherent, at the age of forty-eight.

Quanah on the other hand had undergone an unlikely resurgence, displaying a canny adaptiveness to the white man's world and the grim realities of reservation life. He was about thirty when his life as a Comanche warrior came to an end, young enough to address the possibility of reinventing himself, old enough to be patient and pragmatic about how to do so. We don't know what if anything his mother ever said to him about her life as a *taibo* before she was seized from the Parker homestead as a girl, but the fact that Quanah was half white, and knew it, must have aided in his confident transformation from war leader to reservation potentate.

He did this by consolidating his power among the demoralized bands of the Comanche-Kiowa reservation, and by convincing the agents and ranchers and politicians he got to know that he was someone they could do business with. A federal inspector who met Quanah at the height of his influence concluded that he "would have been a leader and a governor in any circle where fate may have cast him—it is in his blood." Two years after the end of the Red River War, he won the respect of Mackenzie by leading a Comanche expedition to track down a group of Indians who had fled the reservation. After weeks of tracking the renegades across the high plains, he caught up with them and convinced them to give up a hopeless dream of escape in a world now controlled and circumscribed by the *taibo*.

And the buffalo were gone. That fact was driven home the next spring when Quanah led a hunt south of the Red River into Texas and found nothing but cattle eating the grass that had once supported the vast buffalo herds. At Palo Duro, the site of the Comanches' and Kiowas' last defeat, Quanah met Charles Goodnight, who as a young man had been a scout for the Ranger company under Sul Ross that had kidnapped his mother, and who now owned the canyon heartland of Comanchería. They had a testy initial meeting but became friends, to the point that Goodnight gave him a Durham bull for his own burgeoning cattle herd and later complimented him on his table manners.

In middle age, Quanah was, as his personal letterhead testified, "Principal Chief of the Comanches." He had accumulated eight wives, much to the annoyance of white Indian commissioners, and fathered twenty-four children. He had reportedly invested $40,000 in a short-haul railroad, the Quanah, Acme and Pacific, and there was also now a Texas town named in his honor. "It is well," he was quoted as telling the citizens who had gathered to see their town's namesake. "You have done a good thing in honor of a man who has tried to do right both to the people of his tribe and to his pale faced friends. May the God of the white man bless the town of Quanah." He had an eight-bedroom, two-story house with stars painted on the roof. (As of this writing, it's a collapsing ruin behind a failed amusement park in Cache, Oklahoma.) Among his white friends was the president of the United States, Theodore Roosevelt, whom he entertained in the Star House and hosted on a wolf hunt. "In his youth a bitter foe of the whites," Roosevelt said of Quanah, "now painfully teaching his people to travel the white man's stony road."

His life, toward the end, was full, but there was still the part of him that had been ripped away when his mother—Naduah, Cynthia Ann—was abducted on the Pease River. Cynthia Ann Parker was dead, but Quanah— now going by both his Comanche and *taibo* names, Quanah Parker—arranged the only reunion he could. He found out where his mother was buried by placing ads in Texas newspapers. He lobbied for a bill that would allow him to bring her home to Oklahoma. ("Me have family graveyard," he told a crowd at the Texas State Fair in 1910, "and me want bury my mother there.")

The law was passed, and Cynthia Ann's bones were disinterred in Texas and reburied in Oklahoma. Quanah spoke at her funeral. "Forty years ago my mother died. She captured by Comanches, nine years old. Love Indian and wild life so well no want to go back to white folks. All same people anyway, God say. I love my mother. . . . Comanche may die today, tomorrow, ten years. When end comes then they all be together again. I want see my mother again then."

That spiritual opportunity came for Quanah less than three months later when he became ill on a train and staggered into the Star House, dying of heart failure. A white physician attended him, but afterward was asked to leave the room. He was replaced by a Comanche medicine man, who called out to the Great Father, "Our brother is coming," and imitated the piercing call of an eagle. He was dead twenty minutes after entering his house. He was buried beside his long-lost mother, under a headstone that read:

Resting Here Until Day Breaks
And Shadows Fall and Darkness Disappears is
Quanah Parker
Last Chief of the Comanches

Five years after Quanah's death, another silent movie was made, this one titled *Old Texas*. It was a nostalgic vanity project about the passing of the frontier, produced by Charles Goodnight when he was eighty years old. Goodnight appears in it briefly at the beginning and sort of narrates the silent film through a series of title cards. "Listen!" the first one reads, "he tells the story." A brief image shows the white-bearded Goodnight sitting beneath a tree and acting out the role of patriarchal storyteller to a cluster of fascinated listeners, and then the story flashes back to scenes of his Texas adventures.

The most interesting part of the film is an old-time buffalo hunt, or at least a vestige of one, by Kiowa warriors. For years, Goodnight had been building up a small buffalo herd, primarily at the urging of his wife, Molly, a heartsick witness to the slaughter of the buffalo who had urged her husband to do something to prevent their total extinction. In October 1916, and then again in December, he invited a group of Kiowa men to come down to his ranch in the Palo Duro and kill a buffalo the old-fashioned way, with bows and arrows. The *Amarillo Daily News* deemed it the "Plain's Last Buffalo Hunt." For the Indians, it was the "Last Kill of Their Race."

As captured in the flickering footage of *Old Texas*, the hunt is not as dynamic or as dramatic as that headline makes it seem. Its climax is the slow death of a single exhausted, frightened buffalo encircled by a group of aging

Kiowa horsemen. But it created enough local excitement for the *Amarillo Daily News* to call it the "Greatest Gathering Ever Witnessed in the Panhandle." According to the paper, "a large portion of the eleven thousand people who were there went home declaring it was the greatest day of their lives."

I wonder whether one of those people might have been a new faculty member at the West Texas State Normal College in the town of Canyon, a few miles beyond the western rim of Palo Duro. Georgia O'Keeffe was twenty-eight when she arrived in Canyon in September to become the sole teacher in the college's art department, responsible for classes in design, costuming, and interior decoration. She was sick off and on during that academic quarter, and she wasn't the sort to blindly follow a crowd, but it's hard to imagine her not being interested in witnessing Charles Goodnight orchestrate the concluding act of the great Texas frontier drama.

We know that she was deeply drawn to the landscape in which the hunt took place. On Saturday mornings, alone or with students or fellow faculty members, she would climb down the same steep, snaking trails that the Comanches and Kiowas and Mackenzie's troopers had used to reach the floor of Palo Duro Canyon. She would stare in artistic agitation at the sun-bathed red and rose and white bands of eroded sediment all around her—a chromatic wonderland of geology. "I can't help it," she once exclaimed, "it's all so beautiful!"

O'Keeffe had lived in the Panhandle before. In 1912, when she was twenty-four and no longer able to afford to live in New York or continue her studies at the Art Students League, she had boarded a train for far-distant Amarillo to become the drawing supervisor for the town's public schools. She was something of an apparition in Amarillo—a lean young woman, her hair pulled straight back to showcase her stark and striking features. Later, when she returned to live in Canyon, she dressed somewhat like the nuns who taught her at a convent boarding school in Wisconsin, in spooky robe-like garments and black dresses accented only by a severe white collar. "There was something insatiable about her," a friend remembered of O'Keeffe after her first Texas stint, "as direct as an arrow and hugely independent."

She took artistic possession of the landscape. The room she rented in Canyon, a spare room in a professor's house, was strikingly austere—no curtains, no furniture except an iron bed and a wooden crate. But what mattered was the window that faced east, into the Texas sunrise. "That was my country," she later wrote. "Terrible winds and a wonderful emptiness."

She had been working mostly in black and white on the advice of the New York photographer and gallery owner Alfred Stieglitz, her formidable mentor, champion, and eventual husband. But what she saw from

During her two stints as an art teacher in Texas, Georgia O'Keeffe saw something in the "wonderful emptiness" of the Panhandle that stirred her imagination and helped shape her vision as a painter.

her window and from her excursions into Palo Duro expanded her palette and helped her find her way as an artist. Her letters are full of descriptions of color and light and of wild visual yearning. "Tonight I walked into the sunset," she wrote to her friend Anita Pollitzer, "to mail some letters—the whole sky—and there is so much of it out here—was just blazing—and grey blue clouds were riding all through the holiness of it."

She left Texas in 1918, but the color and scale and isolation of the Panhandle seems never to have left her consciousness, and the abstract watercolors she made there—a painting called *Sunrise*, and a series known as *Light Coming on the Plains*, are as much about the awakening of a soul as they are about the dawning of a new day.

★

AS CHARLES GOODNIGHT WAS WRAPPING UP HIS LEGACY

through the new art of film and Georgia O'Keeffe was finding novel ways to paint the sunrise, the winds of Progressivism were still intermittently blowing through Texas. James Hogg died in 1906. "Time for you to get up, Papa," his daughter, Ima, called out just before finding him dead in his bed on March 3, the day after Texas Independence Day. The night before, knowing how ill he was, he had told a friend that he would like for a pecan tree to be planted at the head of his grave and a walnut tree at his feet. "And when these trees shall bear, let the pecans and walnuts be given out among the plain people."

The man who sat at the governor's desk at the time of Hogg's death was Samuel W. T. Lanham. Lanham, the last Confederate veteran elected to that office, was famous as the district attorney who had prosecuted Satanta and Big Tree at their sensational trial and conviction in Jacksboro in 1871. The gentlemanly, moss-bearded Lanham had also been a long-serving member of Congress. Like several governors before him, he had been picked for the office by Edward House, the deep-background political operative who had managed Hogg's campaign and those of the three victorious gubernatorial candidates who followed him. House was not exactly dazzled by Lanham, who was old and tired and who later complained that he "was very happy for years and years" before becoming governor. But House thought his candidate was genial and pliable—"we could commit him to any line of policy that we thought best."

Lanham would not have objected to the plain people having a few pecans and walnuts, but he wasn't going to shake any trees to make it happen. ("The people," House presumed to assume, "wanted no disturbance.") The new governor was a business-friendly chief executive, naturally gravitating toward the conservative end of the Democratic spectrum. And since the Republicans were then a spent force and the Texas Populists had split into irreconcilable factions during the 1896 presidential election, the Democrats were still the only game in town. "We have only one political party in Texas," a future governor, Oscar Colquitt, would declare, "but there are enough political fights in that one for half a dozen."

Among the fights were those over Prohibition, women's suffrage, taxes, corruption, education, prison reform, and the growing problems of farmers trapped in tenancy as well as the regulation of railroads, insurance companies, and the lumber companies that were cutting down the old-growth forests of East Texas at a frightening rate. During the sleepy Lanham years, a Progressive coalition reconstituted itself around this cluster of issues and in 1906 voted a real reformer into the Governor's Mansion. His name was Thomas Campbell, a fifty-one-year-old lawyer who had once been the court-appointed receiver for Jay Gould's International & Great Northern Railroad when it was flailing financially. Campbell saved the railroad from bankruptcy and went on to serve briefly as its general manager, long enough to consider himself schooled in the evils of Gould's monopolistic business practices. In his official governor's portrait, he could be mistaken for a backward-looking scold, with a brushy downturned mustache and fierce black eyebrows looming over glaring, disapproving eyeballs. But he was close to being the antithesis of the old Bourbon Democrats, for whom, in the words of the *Dallas News*, state government was a constant threat, "a huge octopus of special bureaus, special commissionerships and special inspectorships, with arms and tentacles stretching in every direction and applying its inquisitorial and suctorial powers to every form of business and industry, to every recess of private life."

According to one of Campbell's political opponents, the new half-man, half-octopus governor had "a knife up his sleeve for railroads . . . and . . . corporations of any magnitude." With the backing of a reform-minded legislature, he beefed up the tax base (though no personal income tax, then or ever, has been allowed to trouble the sleep of Texans). He promoted antitrust legislation and the regulation of insurance companies and banks. His administration reined in lobbyists and speculators, encouraged conservation, and addressed some of the worst abuses in the Texas prison system, notably the practice of leasing out the labor of prisoners to private contractors.

———————— ★ ————————

IF YOU WERE WHITE AND CONSIDERED YOURSELF A PROGRES-
sive Texan during the first couple of decades of the twentieth century, you were also likely to be in favor of Prohibition. The idea that the government had the right and the duty to outlaw the production and sale of alcoholic beverages had become bound up with the political philosophy of reform-

ers who believed that government had a role to play not just in breaking up trusts or regulating corporations but in perfecting human nature. Alcohol, stated Texas Prohibition activists at a meeting in 1910, "is the greatest menace of the twentieth century to civic righteousness, clean politics, pure elections and the sanctity of the ballot box. . . . It is the lion in the pathway of the onward march of the Christian religion in its supreme struggle to uplift humanity, save men and women from sin, and evangelize the world."

Statewide Prohibition did not become a reality until 1918, when the legislature ratified the Eighteenth Amendment. But Prohibition already existed in much of the state through local-option elections that banned alcohol in a growing number of towns and counties. The Prohibitionists—the drys—had more sway among middle-class whites than among blacks and Mexican Americans, not to mention German Texans, whose idea of progressive enlightenment had never had anything to do with shuttering biergartens.

For old-line Texas types like Senator Joseph Bailey—the "greatest living American" according to one of his cronies, the lumber magnate John Kirby—Prohibition was not just impractical but also sinister, one more example of the government octopus slithering into places where it didn't belong. He darkly prophesied Prohibition's future: "There will not be a square foot of territory in the United States where it will be unlawful for negroes and white people to intermarry."

Bailey had been in favor of Prohibition as a young political comer several decades earlier, and as a senator he went along with the Progressive agenda when it came to railroad regulation and corporate taxes. But he was theatrical, quick-tempered, and seducible. Once, in the U.S. Senate Chamber, he attacked a colleague who had accused him of libel and might have choked him to death if he had not been pried off his victim by two other senators. He was accused of influence peddling in his murky relations with a subsidiary of Standard Oil. Though the charges dogged him for the rest of his political life, he was exonerated, and he trumpeted his official innocence in an address to the Texas Legislature, congratulating himself on his deliverance from the evils of legal scrutiny: "I have walked through the fire and, thank God, like the Hebrew children, a spirit walked with me, preserving my garments from even the smell of the flame."

Where women were concerned—and women were concerned very much in these years leading up to the passage of the Nineteenth Amendment, which finally secured for them the right to vote—Bailey was a gentlemanly troglodyte. For instance, he was worried about what might happen if a wife or mother found herself in a jury room "locked up overnight with strange men deliberating upon a case, the testimony in which it might happen

U.S. officials posing in front of the Brownsville customs house after a successful hunt for illegal liquor during Prohibition.

MINNIE FISHER CUNNINGHAM
saw the potential of literary societies and women's clubs as a political power base. She ran for the Senate in 1927 against the handpicked candidate of the Klan, coming in fifth in the Democratic primary.

would be such that a woman of refinement would not be willing to discuss with her neighbors of her own sex."

Sometimes, though, he dropped the mask of courtly concern and just let his plain old exasperation show. "If a woman wants something done," he pointed out, "she wants it done and she will not hear about the right way and wrong way of doing it. She believes that any way is the right way of doing what ought to be done. This mental infirmity has been thoroughly demonstrated in the discussion of this question of woman suffrage itself, as well as in the question of prohibition."

Minnie Fisher Cunningham might have been the sort of woman he had in mind when he made these remarks. In 1912, she was living in Galveston and had just been elected to membership in a local social organization exclusive enough to be limited to twenty-five women. It was called the Wednesday Club, and like many other similar groups around the state, it was part of the Texas Federation of Women's Clubs.

Cunningham at that time was thirty years old. She had grown up in Walker County near the town of New Waverly, another Texas place name with a literary inspiration, in this case the novels of Walter Scott. Her father, Horatio Fisher, had been a Confederate officer. Her mother, Sallie, was raised in plantation gentility in the years before the Civil War, in conditions that—as Minnie later wrote—"contrasted blackly against the lives of their slaves." By the time Minnie was born, that world was long gone and the family was cash poor, living among farm tenants who had once been their slaves, and struggling to make some kind of profit with a market garden despite the high freight rates charged by the railroad to take their produce to Houston.

Horatio Fisher, a Hogg Democrat, served in the state legislature and was a justice of the peace. His daughter gravitated toward populism but was every bit as politically minded as he was—though in a world in which a woman couldn't vote or run for office, politics was a frustrating passion. She wanted to be a doctor, but the idea of a female developing too close an acquaintanceship with the human body made her parents squeamish, so they sent her to pharmacy school instead. She went to work in a Huntsville drugstore. Though an accredited pharmacist, she made only half of what the male clerks did. "Equal pay for equal work," she said in an interview in the 1950s, "made a suffragette out of me."

In Huntsville she met "the best-looking man I ever saw." Like Minnie's father, B. J. Cunningham was politically active, serving as a county attorney before getting into the insurance business. Nevertheless, they seem to have had a drab marriage at best. They had no children, and by the time Cunningham had drunk himself to death, in 1927, they had been separated for ten years. Minnie's reaction to his death was tantalizingly ambivalent. "I miss him so," she told a friend. "Isn't that awful? And unexpected too."

The Wednesday Club she joined in Galveston in 1912 was in theory a literary study club, but in practice it and other such organizations acted as grassroots staging grounds for women who had political ambitions but were shut out of the electoral process. Minnie Cunningham quickly rose to become secretary of the Wednesday Club, nudging it away from anodyne literary analysis to an urgent grappling with new feminist ideas. She also joined the Women's Health Protective Association, which, among other initiatives, pressured Galveston for pure milk ordinances; helped found the Galveston Equal Suffrage Association; and then took over statewide leadership of the Texas Equal Suffrage Association. By the end of her career, she had helped form the National League of Women Voters, been an influential national advocate and lobbyist for the passage of the Nineteenth Amendment, made a run for the U.S. Senate and another for governor, and helped create the eternally embattled liberal touchstone the *Texas Observer*. When she was an old lady, she lived alone in Walker County, where she sold pecans by the side of the road and blasted armadillos with a shotgun when they tried to invade her garden. One of her last political acts was to manage the local Democratic headquarters and help deliver her county for John F. Kennedy in the presidential campaign of 1960. I read a whole book about her, and the only instance of second-guessing I could find was when she acquiesced in a request from the president of the Texas Federation of Women's Clubs not to press the issue of women's suffrage at a 1914 convention. "I can't help regretting," she wrote, "that I didn't make a scene."

IN LATER LIFE, MINNIE FISHER CUNNINGHAM WORKED OPENLY for civil rights issues like desegregation, but for the first few decades of the twentieth century the Progressive movement had little concern for blacks or Mexican Americans nor any tactical energy to spend on their behalf. Cunningham politely evaded the request of an African American women's club to join the Texas Equal Suffrage Association. Black women were also excluded from membership in the umbrella organization, the Texas Federation of Women's Clubs, and as a result they formed their own version, the Texas Association of Colored Women's Clubs.

Since Reconstruction, white Texans had been employing various means to keep black voters out of polling places. The least formal was brute intimidation. "Few white men went unarmed on election day," a resident of Robertson County remembered. "The courthouse at Franklin was lined with about forty Winchester rifles, and no Negro votes were cast there." There was also legislative sleight of hand. In 1879, a legislator named Alexander Terrell, who had opposed secession but fought for the Confederacy, proposed a poll tax. On the surface, a poll tax was a way to inject integrity into the electoral process by weeding out destitute citizens whose votes could theoretically be bought. But it was transparently not just that. "Unless," Terrell wrote to Oran "Old Alcalde" Roberts, "some flank movement can be made on the mass of ignorant negro voters, we will soon be at Sea in Texas."

The poll tax faced a headwind when it was first introduced—notably from cash-strapped members of the fading Populist Party and from border bosses like Jim Wells, who had already invested quite enough money to buy the votes of Mexican American voters and didn't like the idea of having to pay twice. Terrell kept trying, though, and by 1903 he had his flank movement in the form of an alliance between white populists and Hogg Democrats, neither of which had any particular passion for black enfranchisement. A poll tax of $1.50 went into effect, and the passage of other election reforms a year later consolidated the Democrats' one-party power and kept blacks from voting in its primaries. To participate in the process meant first affirming, "I am a white person and a Democrat."

It was much the same in Texas as it was throughout the South, except that Texas wasn't the South, not quite. Though it was a place of seething racial tensions, of Jim Crow laws, of voter intimidation, of rising white supremacy, Texas was not foundering in an old identity but bursting into a new one. The Indians were mostly gone, but a phantom frontier reflex remained, a righteous sense of westward conquest that had been in play ever since Mirabeau Lamar envisioned a Texas nation stretching to the Pacific. The filibusters and colonists who had originally come to Texas from the South had for generations made their homes among, and made war with, Mexicans who still regarded Texas as a torn-away part of their own sovereign country. The Texas consciousness had been stretched enough, broken enough, tested enough, annealed enough to become its own thing. And now it was developing into a matrix of competing but somehow complementary mythologies—cowboys, oilmen, visionaries, murderers, iconoclasts. The Texas spirit, noted a writer named M. G. Cunniff, who breezed through the state in 1906 on assignment for a magazine called the *World's Work*, "is a coolly arrogant self-sufficiency. Tasks which other, older, more compact, and more populous commonwealths cannot accomplish, Texas can—and does. It is alive and awhir with a buoyant business progressiveness. . . . The consistency and lusty promise of Texas cannot now be matched in the Union."

Partly this was a conscious sense of self-inquiry on the part of Texans. Texas history was already being taught in schools, and as Cunniff noted, "You gather from Texas conversation that the massacre of the Alamo happened last month." Indeed, the Alamo was one of the cultural symbols that prompted Texas to put some distance between itself and the rest of the South. Texans didn't need to embrace the Lost Cause of the Confederacy; they already believed that they were a people born out of the ashes of a sacred defeat.

The physical Alamo, though, was almost allowed to disappear. After the battle in 1836, the Mexican Army had torn down almost all the mission walls and buildings, leaving only the roofless church and the two-story convent building, where some of the most gruesome fighting had taken place. The church was later used as a quartermaster's depot by the U.S. Army, which built a new roof and crowned its shattered facade with the curving, bell-shaped architectural feature that eventually became a worldwide visual icon. But when the army moved out in the 1870s, the church reverted to an empty, useless building full of trash and bat guano. And the old convent was sold to private owners, who turned it into a grocery warehouse. "Amazement and disgust" was the reaction of a Texas tourist expecting to encounter a reverent, meditative space, but instead found "sacks of salt, stinking potatoes, odorous kerosene and dirty groceries."

Adina De Zavala, a former schoolteacher with a passionate interest in Texas history, which might have sprung from the fact that she was the granddaughter of the Tejano hero Lorenzo de Zavala, had the same reaction. So did Clara Driscoll, a worldly young ranch heiress from South Texas who was descended from two grandfathers who had fought in the Texas Revolution. The two of them joined forces to save the Alamo from destruction, though they later fell out—quite bitterly—over exactly what should be saved. From her travels in Europe, Driscoll had visions of the church standing in alluring, mysterious isolation in the middle of a plaza, like the Pantheon in Rome. To her, the convent building was an aesthetic distraction. But to De Zavala, the convent was just as historic and sanctified, just as anointed with the blood of Texian and Tejano dead, as the church itself. In 1908, fearing that demolition of the convent was nigh, she made national news by barricading herself in it for three

ADINA DE ZAVALA
was so horrified at the potential destruction of the Alamo convent that she barricaded herself inside it, touching off a bloodless second siege of the Alamo.

CLARA DRISCOLL
was determined to save the Alamo from ruin, but her romantic European vision for the site set her on a collision course with Adina de Zavala.

days. Unfortunately, the grocery warehouse was empty by then, and she had not planned well for a siege. She had no food or water, and the sanctified building was overrun with rats. With the doors padlocked, only a tiny porthole offered access to the outside—and it was not even big enough for a kindly deputy sheriff to pass a glass of water through. She had to stoop down while he poured the contents into her open mouth.

By the time the fracas—dubbed with less whimsy than you might think as the Second Battle of the Alamo—was finally over, at least part of the convent had been saved, and it and the Alamo church were placed in the keeping of the Daughters of the Republic of Texas, an organization that had splintered into Driscoll and De Zavala factions. But the preservation war between these two strong-minded clubwomen obscured an evolving consensus that the story of Texas added up to something more than history. It was a legacy. But the questions of whose legacy it was and what it meant were still unsettled. Texas history, like Texas soil, was something to be seized.

—33—

SEDICIOSOS

THE GRAVES OF JESUS BAZÁN AND HIS SON-IN-LAW
Antonio Longoria are located in a small family cemetery in
northwestern Hidalgo County, deep in South Texas, close to
the Mexican border. There is a modern county road nearby,
but the graves were dug many years ago at the edge of an
older, unpaved road no longer in use. Jesus Bazán was sixty-
seven when he died on a September day in 1915. His son-in-law was forty-
eight. He died the same day. Their tombstones give no account about what
happened to them, only the word *"Murió"*—"Died." But no doubt there were
friends and family members who would have preferred to see another word
carved there: *"Asesinado"*—"Murdered."

The manner of their deaths was nothing special, if you take into account
the way things were during the terror years of 1915 and 1916 in the lower Rio
Grande valley. Bazán and Longoria were traveling down the road when a
group of Texas Rangers under Captain H. L. Ransom came along and shot
them off their horses. The Rangers had a list, and one of the names on it
was Longoria. The fact that Antonio was the wrong Longoria, or that Bazán
had been vouched for as a law-abiding citizen by a nearby Anglo rancher,
meant little to Ransom. He and his men rode away, leaving Bazán and Longoria dead on the ground, under the piercing South Texas sun. The bodies

472

stayed there, unburied. The families of the murdered men fled their homes, convinced they would be killed as well if they tried to retrieve their loved ones. Tejanos driving their wagons down the road skirted around the bodies, fearful that a show of human sympathy would mean, to the Rangers, proof of conspiracy. After five days, nearby ranchers, disturbed by the stench of decomposition, finally ventured out to bury them.

Bazán's and Longoria's names are recorded, their bodies buried, but there has never been anything close to a full accounting of the hundreds, and more likely thousands, of people who were killed along the border and left in the chaparral or dumped into resacas during the violence that was sparked by the Mexican Revolution of 1910–1920.

In Texas, this was a war of raids and reprisals concentrated mostly throughout the Rio Grande valley, the same trouble spot previously best known as the Nueces Strip. "Valley" is an unconvincing word for a thorny

Bolton & Mitchell,   LAREDO, TEXAS.

GREGORIO CORTEZ,
to the sheriff who tried to arrest him, was nothing more than a "medium-sized Mexican." But a tragic gunfight and an epic manhunt turned him into a Tejano folk hero.

tropical expanse of country without any hills or mountains in sight, but nevertheless that's what it's called.

The trouble began—well, it can't really be said to have begun at any particular moment. It had been seething for at least a century, since the arrival of the first Anglo colonists. It had flared into open conflict during Juan Cortina's raid on Brownsville, during the confusing turmoil of the Civil War, and in 1891 after a Texas newspaper publisher named Catarino Garza, a veteran of gunfights and court battles with Texas Rangers, raised an army and initiated a brief cross-border war whose goal was to unseat Mexican president Porfirio Díaz. And then, in 1901, there was the case of Gregorio Cortez, a vaquero working on a ranch in Karnes County. The local sheriff, who was looking for a "medium-size Mexican" wanted for horse theft, approached Cortez and his brother. There was a tense, garbled interrogation in Spanish that ended when the sheriff shot the brother. Cortez in turn killed the sheriff, took flight, and evaded hundreds of law officers throughout Central and South Texas for ten days before he was finally captured. His artful elusiveness, combined with the conviction that he was innocent, turned him into an instant folk hero for Tejanos trying to survive in an Anglo universe of tightening injustice and casual suspicion.

Things got worse for Tejanos when the railroads reached the Rio Grande valley in 1904, opening the region up to commercial agriculture and delivering by special excursion trains an epic population surge of Anglo farmers and businessmen. A *Houston Chronicle* writer exulted in the new world that the railroads were creating "through the range of the longhorn, across the ranches, over the dominion of the rattler and horned frog." The population of the "Magic Valley," as the promoters called this part of South Texas, doubled in ten years. Land prices soared; ranches were subdivided into farms. "We are witnessing," declared the confidently hyperbolic *Collier's* magazine, "the largest migration of human beings that has ever taken place since history began to be recorded."

But it was not just the dominion of the rattler and horned frog that was coming to an end, but also the deep-rooted ranching culture that Tejanos had invented. The promotional literature of one of the new development companies put it succinctly: "The golden glow of the brush fires against the night sky, where land is being cleared for cultivation, truly typifies the passing of the old civilization and the coming of the new."

This new civilization meant higher taxes to go with the higher land prices, forcing small ranchers to sell out to developers and turning vaqueros into field workers. And many cash-poor Tejanos found out that owning land was different from keeping it, since it required money they didn't have to uphold a claim in court against a rich and well-connected claimant. "I told him to pack up his doll rags and piss on the fire" is the way one encroacher described ordering away the Tejano he considered to be squatting on his land.

Following on the heels of this huge cultural shift came destabilizing shock waves from a climactic power struggle across the border. Porfirio Díaz had been the iron-fisted Mexican president of Mexico since 1876. When he was challenged in 1909 by a reformist candidate, Francisco Madero, he had him arrested for sedition. Madero managed to escape to San Antonio. There, in a house on Santa Rosa Avenue, he wrote and published a manifesto—*Plan de San Luis Potosí*—that ignited the Mexican Revolution. The *Plan* declared that all Mexico should arise at the same hour of the same day "to eject from power the audacious usurpers whose only title of legality involves a scandalous and immoral fraud."

This call to action sparked a complex, fragmented uprising throughout Mexico as rebel armies led by leaders such as Francisco "Pancho" Villa and Emiliano Zapata helped bring Madero to power in 1911. "Madero has unleashed a tiger!" Porfirio Díaz grumbled on his way to exile in Paris. "Now let us see if he control it!"

He couldn't, and was dead at the age of thirty-nine a little more than a year later, assassinated after being deposed in a coup by General Victoriano Huerta, the counterrevolutionary dictator whose oppressive rule was known as "La Mano dura" (the Hard Hand). But by 1914 Huerta too was gone, replaced by Venustiano Carranza, the head of one of the many revolutionary armies fighting for power in the ever-splintering Mexican Revolution.

The revolution certainly didn't bump to a stop at the Rio Grande. The U.S. side of the river was populated now not just with Tejanos whose lands and occupations were disappearing under the flood of Anglo immigration, but also with a steady flow of Mexican refugees desperate to escape the violence in their country. The sense of an impending reckoning was kept alive by influential publications like *Regeneración*, an anarchist newspaper that had once been headquartered in San Antonio and was spearheaded by two brothers named Ricardo and Enrique Flores Magón. By the time the civil war in Mexico had reached its full chaotic force, the Flores Magón brothers were in exile in Los Angeles, but the activist call to arms of their newspaper and the political organization they had founded, the Partido Liberal Mexicano, still echoed along the borderlands of Texas and Mexico.

One particularly fervent reader of *Regeneración*, and a close friend and correspondent of Ricardo Flores Magón, was an activist and woman of letters named Sara Estela Ramírez. Born in Mexico, she had lived in Laredo since she was seventeen, where she became a teacher and then a widely read contributor to newspapers such as *El Demócrata Fronterizo* and *La Crónica*.

"Revolution approaches!" Ricardo Flores Magón notified the Mexican and Mexican American women who read his newspaper, in an editorial titled "A La Mujer." Flores Magón sported a modern-trending Salvador Dali mustache, but his instructions to women had a past-century patriarchal ring. While acknowledging that they were sisters in the struggle ("If men are slaves, you are too"), he told them that their duty was "to help man; to be there to encourage him when he vacillates; stand by his side when he suffers; to lighten his sorrow; to laugh and to sing with him when victory smiles."

Sara Estela Ramírez never got to read Flores Magón's lecture about how revolutionary women should behave. By the time it was published, in September 1910, she had been dead a month. Some unknown illness claimed her at the age of twenty-nine. But she had already issued a feminist directive, her own version in poetry of "A La Mujer." Its title ("¡Surge!") translates in English as "Rise Up!"

> Rise up! Rise up to life, to activity, to
> the beauty of truly living; but rise up radiant
> and powerful, beautiful with qualities, splendid
> with virtues, strong with energies.

When she died, Ramírez was eulogized in *La Crónica*, one of the newspapers she had contributed to, as "La Musa Texana." *La Crónica* was published in Laredo and was a family enterprise, operated by Nicosio Idar—a former vaquero on the King Ranch—and his children Clemente, Eduardo, and Jovita. Jovita wrote Sara Estela Ramírez's obituary. She had begun her career as a teacher, but the conditions she encountered in Laredo's segregated Mexican American schools sparked her outrage and animated her investigative instincts. She joined her family's newspaper, whose motto was "We work for the progress and the industrial, moral, and intellectual development of the Mexican inhabitants of Texas," and reported from all over the Rio Grande valley, covering the lynchings and land thefts and other crimes against Tejanos that were likely to go unremarked in Anglo publications.

In 1911, Nicosio Idar organized a conference in Laredo called the Primer Congreso Mexicanista, a major civil rights gathering that brought Tejanos from all over Texas and Mexico. Among the items on the agenda were women's rights, and after the congress Jovita Idar became the first president of La Liga Feminil Mexicanista (League of Mexican Women).

Ricardo Flores Magón, whose idea of a woman's role in the struggle was to shore up the vacillating will of her man, might not have known quite what to make of the take-charge attitude of someone like Jovita Idar, who wrote articles for *La Crónica* with titles such as "Debemos Trabajar" ("We Should Work"). When the Mexican Revolution broke out, she crossed the border to Nuevo Laredo to volunteer as a combat nurse for Carranza's forces. In 1913, back on the Texas side of the border, she made enemies when she published an editorial in the newspaper *El Progreso* denouncing President Wilson's intervention in Mexico. The Texas Rangers were sent to close down the paper, but when they got there and encountered Jovita Idar standing in the doorway with her arms crossed, refusing to budge and refusing to let them in, they decided they'd better come back another day.

"THINGS DID NOT LOOK RIGHT," ONE TEJANO RESIDENT RE-
membered of those tremulous years in Texas. "Something queerly fantastic, unnatural, seemed to be hovering over the Valley and along the river front."

In January 1915, Basilio Ramos, a twenty-four-year-old Mexican citizen, educated in Norman, Oklahoma, and a former employee at a beer company in the South Texas town of San Diego, was apprehended in McAllen, deep in the Valley. In his pockets were several letters of introduction from prominent insurrectionists in Mexico, including one that said, "I am convinced his testicles are in the right place."

But the document that mattered, whose discovery ignited the revolutionary tinder along the Rio Grande, was a manifesto that would be known as the "Plan of San Diego." It was the blueprint for an apocalyptic uprising against "the Yankee tyranny which has held us in iniquitous slavery since remote times." The plan called for the independence of all five U.S. states bordering Mexico, states that would then be formed into a new independent republic that might at some future date—"if it be thought expedient"—annexed to Mexico. The land taken from the Indians would be returned. This new republic would offer African Americans freedom and equality and help them seize neighboring American states so that they could create their own independent nation. It would even "grant them a banner, which they themselves shall be permitted to select."

JOVITA IDAR
began her career as a teacher but, inflamed by the injustices she saw around her in South Texas, soon joined the family newspaper business, becoming a wide-ranging reporter and an activist who was not afraid to face down the Texas Rangers.

The Plan of San Diego might have been dismissed as fancifully far-reaching if it had not been for, among other incendiary passages, Article 7, which stated as clearly as anything could be stated: "Every North American over sixteen years of age shall be put to death; and only the aged men, the women, and the children shall be respected; and

The publication of the Plan of San Diego—a manifesto calling for an uprising against the "Yankee tyranny"—caused universal alarm along the Rio Grande and led to a spate of reprisals that darkened the reputation of the Texas Rangers.

on no account shall the traitors to our race be spared or respected." Another such document surfaced the next month, decrying the gringos' "hatred of races which closes the doors to schools, hotels, theaters and all public establishments to the Mexican, black and yellow, and divides the railroads and all public meeting places into areas where the savage 'white skins' meet and constitute a superior class." This document promised not just to end segregation but to create "Universal Love," in part by seizing lands from capitalist overlords and delivering them, and the railroads that crossed them, into the collective keeping of the proletarians.

It's hard to know how direct an influence these manifestos had on the events that followed, since the storm of violence didn't really break until that summer, when groups of *sediciosos*—as the insurgents came to be called—began a series of sporadic raids on farms and ranches, and burned a railroad trestle near McAllen. At first it seemed more like freelance banditry, but the sense of there being at least an attempt at command and control came with the publication of a third manifesto in late August, grandly claiming that the *sediciosos* maintained a "General Headquarters" in San Antonio. It was signed by a fifty-year-old former deputy sheriff named Luis de la Rosa ("First Chief of Operations") and by Aniceto Pizaña ("Chief of the General Staff"), a rancher, a poet of outraged political verses, and a fervent follower of the Flores Magón brothers. The authors declared that the territory to be seized from the United States would be called, with blazing irony, the Republic of Texas.

"The moment has arrived," the document promised. By then, there had already been a number of targeted attacks, including the assassinations of a rancher named A. L. Austin and his grown son, Charles. Austin was the head of the Sebastian Law and Order League and an abusive overseer of the Tejanos who worked on his ranch. "Every time he kicked a Mexican," a local deputy sheriff recalled, "he made an unrelenting enemy." He and Charles were taken from their house and shot dead in a nearby field. Austin's wife, Nellie, related with chilling precision what she saw after the marauders left the house: "I first went to my husband and found two bullet holes in his back one on each side near his spinal column. . . . My husband was not quite dead but died in a few minutes thereafter. I then proceeded to my son Charles who was lying a few feet from his father; I found his face in a large pool of blood and saw that he was shot in the mouth, neck and in the back of the head and dead when I reached him."

A few days later there was a full-scale attack on the King Ranch. It happened at Norias, one of the five divisions of the ranch, which by then commanded a great swath of the South Texas map and was the size of an inconspicuous country. (Ten years later, under the stewardship of Richard King's widow, Henrietta, and her son-in-law Robert Kleberg, it would vault in size to well over a million acres.) The manager of Norias was Caesar Kleberg, Robert's cousin. He was in Brownsville when he got word that an attack might be brewing, and he sent out a call for help. Army troops, deputies, and Rangers rushed by train to the Norias ranch house. The Rangers were out scouting when a group of *sediciosos* charged the house with Mauser rifles. Inside were only sixteen defenders—soldiers, ranch employees, and a few civilians from Brownsville who had come along hoping to pitch into a fight.

One of the civilians was an immigration inspector named D. P. Gay Jr., who later set down a florid account of the desperate two-and-a-half-hour battle, during which the defenders lost four men wounded but finally drove off the *sediciosos* after killing at least five. "Knowing there were 75 or 80 bandits," Gay wrote, "I could not help from thinking of those immortals, Travis, Bowie, and Crockett and their memoriable [*sic*] fight at the Alamo, when a hundred and eighty red-blooded Americans fought about five thousand greasers."

But nothing as conclusive or inspiring as the Alamo ever took place in the grubby race war that had erupted in South Texas. There were only raids, bushwhackings, casual executions, and showcase atrocities like the one that befell a U.S. Army private named Richard Johnson. He was captured by rebels during an attack on the town of Progreso on the north bank of the Rio Grande and taken across the river. The next time his fellow soldiers saw him, his head, stuck on a pole, was staring back at the United States of America.

In late September 1915, a party of *sediciosos* attacked the ranch of a man named James Ballí McAllen, an Irish immigrant who had married into a Tejano family with roots in Texas going back to a Spanish land grant they had received in 1799. When the assault came, only McAllen and his cook were home. Her name was Doña María de Agras, a former *soldadera* who had fought with Madero against Porfirio Díaz. With McAllen firing and Agras loading his handcrafted Greener shotgun and Winchester rifles, they killed two of the attackers and fatally wounded at least one other, and somehow managed to avoid being hit themselves by any of the five hundred bullets that aerated the house. A Ranger captain who arrived at the scene after the battle was particularly impressed by Doña María's coolness under fire: "Fresh from the revolutions in her native land, she was inured to the sight of bloodshed. During the attack on the ranch, she had no intention of remaining a passive spectator."

It was the search for the perpetrators of the McAllen ranch raid that led to the Rangers' mistaken—and indifferent—killing of Jesus Bazán and Antonio Longoria. Their deaths were part of a rampage of retribution, chronicled in gloating photographs that have considerably darkened the already complicated reputation of the Texas Rangers. In the most famous of these photos, taken after the Norias raid, three Rangers pose on horseback, having roped the dead bodies of four *sediciosos* that they seem to be planning to drag through a brushy pasture. In another, a Ranger has plopped a sombrero onto a skull and is holding it out with one hand as if contemplating the fate of Yorick while he points a pistol at its eye socket.

The atrocities were certainly not all on the Anglo side, but the legacy of the uprising was tighter oppression against Mexican Americans and a renewed and codified attitude of superiority on the part of whites. In the triumphant hindsight of a Hidalgo County deputy sheriff, the white race "had fought for all it had ever gained, and it had gained much since its trek from the shores of Albion to the chaparral fringes of the Rio Grande, therefore fighting was not new to it as attested by the gruesome skeletons found even at this late day, twenty years after, in the wilderness, lying in neatly arranged rows, side by side, each with a trim, round hole in the forehead squarely between the empty eye-sockets—'Brands' of the Texas [R]angers' 'irons,' the never-failing 45-Colts."

J. T. Canales, a Brownsville lawyer, sometime political beneficiary of Jim Wells's Valley machine, and the only Tejano member of the state legislature, introduced a bill in 1919 whose intention was to starve the Rangers of state resources. The bill ended up being sandbagged, but it led to a joint House and Senate investigation into Ranger conduct, for which Canales served as the prosecuting attorney. He did his job fervently but skittishly, perhaps because he was convinced that at any moment he would be assassinated by Frank Hamer, a particularly intimidating six-foot-three-inch slab of Texas Ranger who would later lead the manhunt and ambush that killed Bonnie and Clyde.

Canales had reason to be worried. "You are . . . complaining," he claimed Hamer told him, "to the Governor and the Adjutant General about the Rangers, and I am going to tell you if you don't stop that you are going to get hurt."

As it turned out, Canales lived to be ninety-nine years old, not dying until 1976. The investigation he launched brought modest reforms. The Texas Rangers were not exactly punished for their exterminating missions along the border, but the hearings brought at least some of that behavior into public view, where it could be decried by any Texans who were willing to be alarmed. "These young men, hot blooded young fellows without much education," one witness told the committee, recalling Zachary Taylor's assessment from almost three-quarters of a century earlier about *los diablos tejanos*, who had been such unruly allies during the Mexican-American War, "men who are willing to go out and risk their lives for forty, fifty, or sixty dollars a month and lead the kind of lives they do, are not the type of men you want to entrust the lives and properties of the citizens to without throwing around them some safeguard."

THE VIOLENCE THAT ERUPTED ALONG THE BORDER AFTER THE discovery of the Plan of San Diego was a prismatic piece of a revolution that had already torn Mexico from north to south and that in turn was part of a global revolutionary upheaval. It provoked a series of responses from the Woodrow Wilson administration: blockading Vera Cruz, recognizing the Carranza government, and, in the end, sending a "punitive expedition" to capture Pancho Villa after he attacked the United States by raiding the town of Columbus, New Mexico, and killing eight soldiers and ten civilians. The massive retaliatory response—with over six thousand infantry and cavalry troops and air support in the form of eight aircraft from the 1st Aero Squadron—was led by General John J. Pershing. Pershing was stationed at Fort Bliss in El Paso and had, the year before, lost his wife and three daughters in a house fire in San Francisco. ("Can it be true? Can it be true?" he had howled to the universe.) The expedition not only failed to capture Villa, but also inflamed the Mexican people and ended up stumbling into a fight with Mexican regular troops at the Battle of Carrizal, where it suffered a chastening defeat. After that, and after some complex diplomacy between the Wilson and Carranza administrations, Pershing and his men headed home.

The punitive expedition mostly skirted Texas, and other signature events of the vast Mexican Revolution occurred outside the state's borders. But as always when there was conflict on or below the Rio Grande, Texas—subject to the laws of geography and history—was inevitably pulled in. For instance, after Pancho Villa and Pascual Orozco conquered Ciudad Juárez for Madero in 1911, they crossed the international bridge to celebrate with ice cream at the Elite Confectionary in El Paso. In August 1914, shortly after Villa and fellow rebel general Álvaro Obregón captured Mexico City and sent President Huerta into exile, they were met by Pershing for a congratulatory handshake on the international bridge leading to El Paso and then escorted to Fort Bliss for a banquet. Obregón was back in El Paso in 1916, though the handshake this time was awkward because he had lost his right arm in fighting Villa, now a bitter enemy of both Obregón and the Carranza government he represented, and of the United States. While Pershing was five hundred miles deep into Mexico still chasing Villa, Obregón and Hugh Scott, the U.S. Army's chief of staff, held a secret meeting at the city's finest hotel, the Paso del Norte, where they tried but failed to secure an agreement that would allow Pershing's expedition to remain on Mexican soil without igniting a full-scale war with Mexico itself. (Even though the country was torn apart at the moment, it had not forgotten the unifying sensation of being invaded by the United States.)

A few days after the Obregón-Scott meeting, Mexican raiders once again struck on Texas soil, this time far from the lower Rio Grande valley in the Big Bend hamlet of Glenn Springs. They killed three soldiers and the young son of a storekeeper. Another raiding party in nearby Boquillas made off with two more civilian prisoners. This led to a minor punitive expedition spearheaded by a chauffeur-driven Cadillac packed with twelve army sharpshooters. They never caught the marauders but managed to recover the prisoners alive.

Victoriano Huerta, who had deposed President Madero and ordered his assassination, ended up dying in Texas. He was arrested in El Paso in 1915 on charges of violating American neutrality for conspiring with agents of the German government. Sweltering in the county jail in his undershirt, he told reporters on the Fourth of July, "I am enjoying the novel experience of being in jail in liberty-loving America on the very day you celebrate liberty and justice and independence." The ice water served in jail, he added, "is a little thin." He was transferred to Fort Bliss, where the accommodations were better but where his mood and his health steadily sank. He drank heavily, turned yellow with jaundice, and died. An autopsy revealed cirrhosis of the liver, though rumors persisted that he had been assassinated by a mysterious doctor who appeared one night to perform a purposefully incompetent operation.

Throughout this uncertain period, Texas cities such as El Paso and San Antonio were crowded with figures of whom such shadowy scenarios could be believed, with exiles or plotters from one warring Mexican faction or another, along with reporters, spies, motion picture crews, and every imaginable species of opportunist or idealist. One of them was a flamboyant and notorious doctor named Aureliano Urrutia, who lived in San Antonio until his death in 1975 at the age of 103. Urrutia was distinguished by the black opera cape he habitually wore, and by his spectacular sculpture garden, whose centerpiece was a replica of the Winged Victory of Samothrace—which can still be glimpsed out of the corner of your eye as you drive along Hildebrand Avenue in San Antonio.

Urrutia was famous for being one of the first surgeons to successfully separate conjoined twins, but he was better known for the dark speculations that followed him wherever he appeared. As a cabinet officer in the Huerta administration, he had been one of the men accused of murdering Belisario Domínguez, a liberal senator who had memorably raised his voice in defiance of the president. Urrutia was believed to have not only participated in his murder but also used his surgical skills to remove his tongue, and then

Mexican Revolution leaders Pancho Villa (center) and Álvaro Obregón (right) with General John J. Pershing in a short-lived display of comity at the international bridge at El Paso.

to proclaim, "This tongue that called for the assassination of General Huerta will never say another word!"

Another bitter enemy of Urrutia was General Frederick Funston, who had won the Medal of Honor for service in the Philippines and commanded the U.S. Army's Southern Department during the worst of the border troubles along the Rio Grande and the hunt for Pancho Villa. Urrutia had a serous grudge against Funston because the general had arrested him in 1914 when he tried to flee Mexico as Huerta was losing his grip on power. It's a fact that Funston dropped dead of a heart attack in the lobby of the St. Anthony Hotel at the age of fifty-one while listening to an orchestra play the "Blue Danube" waltz. It's merely a legend, but a pretty good one, that just before Funston collapsed, Urrutia strolled through the hotel in his opera cape and looked in his direction. The last thing the general experienced was *mal de ojo*, the penetrating, murderous stare of the doctor's evil eye.

—34—

PA

DURING THIS TIME OF INSURRECTION AND REPRISAL
along the Rio Grande, the governor of Texas was a man
named James Ferguson, also known as "Farmer Jim" and—
somewhat later—"Pa" Ferguson. He was in his midforties,
bland-looking, a little portly. If you were to judge only by
photographs, he would appear to be the visual embodiment
of an earnest, anonymous public servant.

He was anything but. He was a magnetic, grandiose, bullying, and
crooked personality whose hands had to be repeatedly pried away from the
levers of power for the next quarter century.

You can get a sense of his blunt appeal to the electorate by visiting the
Dolph Briscoe Center for American History at the University of Texas and
asking to see box 3P46 of the James E. Ferguson Papers. In there you will
find two old-fashioned school tablets, one with a blue jay on the cover and
one with the brand name Conqueror of the Chiefs, whose cover features a
buckskin clad frontiersman gazing off toward the horizon. Ferguson used
the tablets to draft speeches and platforms for his out-of-nowhere run for
the office of Texas governor in 1914. He apparently commandeered them
from one of his two school-age daughters, since on the back of the blue

JAMES FERGUSON
during the early years of his notorious political career.

tablet there is a child's colored-pencil drawing of three golden-haired ladies in fancy sheath dresses.

Ferguson's penmanship on these brittle pages is aggressive, and the thoughts he sets down with his thick pencil strokes are fluid and urgent. An occasional word or phrase is crossed out, but by and large there are no second thoughts. "Who is this man," he writes,

who has never held office, who has never been even a justice of the peace, who has never been a county attorney, a county judge, or if you please, a member of the Texas legislature, who [has] never even run for state senator, who is this man from Temple who contrary to all the precedents of political slate making in Texas, quietly passes by all other state offices and seeks at one great bound to land himself in the great office of governor. Who is he?

Listen while I tell you. My friends I am a plain private citizen of Texas.

But plain and private were not traits that even Jim Ferguson's loving daughter Ouida would have thought to apply to him. As she wrote quite accurately in her dual biography of her parents, "Daddy was the stormy petrel of Texas politics." There was nothing in his past to suggest that he had ever considered being plain and private anything but rhetorical ammunition. He was born on a farm near the little town of Salado in Central Texas in 1871. At sixteen, his intransigence about doing chores got him kicked out of a prestigious local school, after which he wandered out west for two years before returning to Bell County. He more or less faked his way into becoming a lawyer, skipping law school, reading up a little bit on the profession, and heading straight to his bar exams, where the three lawyers who examined him—chums of his late father, a circuit-riding minister—asked him zero questions and then saluted his success with a round of whiskey.

He married a young woman named Miriam Wallace, the daughter of a prosperous rancher and farmer who lived six miles away. Miriam was as introverted as her new husband was brash. She was a strikingly apolitical homebody in a time when there was an unstoppable surge of interest in the expanding potential of women in American society. Miriam Ferguson was a devoted churchgoer, but the socially conscious denizens of the women's clubs were not her crowd. In 1914, only a decade before she would become the first female governor of Texas, she told an interviewer, "I have really given little thought to the subject of women's suffrage. My husband has always attended to every business care. I have never had to feel the responsibility of any of that sort of thing, and even if I had the right to vote, I do not think that I would care to use the right."

With Miriam's inheritance to back him, Jim Ferguson became one of the owners of a bank in the nearby town of Temple. He also bought a big house and a farm and made himself known in Democratic political circles, especially on the anti-Prohibition side. Prohibition was the dominant issue when he ran for governor in 1914. Ferguson positioned himself—with the help of a slush fund from brewers—as the candidate of the wets. "If I am elected Governor," he declared, "and the Legislature puts any liquor legislation up to me, pro or anti, I will strike it where the chicken got the axe."

A phrase like "where the chicken got the axe" was not accidental. Ferguson, a rich bank president with a chauffeur, posed as "Farmer Jim," a plain-spoken rural populist who promised to bring common business sense to state government and "banish from Texas the agitator and political grafter."

It was not yet obvious that Farmer Jim was himself a high-functioning political grafter. He preferred not to lean too heavily on the contentious issue of Prohibition, but instead focused his concern on the plight of tenant farmers, whose numbers had grown substantially in the last few decades and whose votes, therefore, had too. The fact that Ferguson wasn't particularly generous as a banker when it came to making farm loans didn't dissuade him from being a champion of the landless masses. "One man says that he has a right to do with his land as he pleases," he wrote in his—or his daughter's—Conqueror of the Chiefs tablet. "Now then let us see where this leads to. If one man has the right to do as he pleases with his land then he has the right to make every tenant, his wife, children cats dogs and chickens get out in the lane or public road."

Ferguson adroitly won the Democratic nomination for governor over his opponent, Thomas Ball, and then the essentially pro forma general election that followed. Ball, the dry candidate, had let slip that he belonged to the Houston Country Club, but assured the voters that even though drinks were sold there, he never indulged. Neither did he play golf, even though it was a golfing club. During the campaign, Ferguson visited the Houston Country Club and painted it as a den of sin, pretending to be aghast that it was filled with men playing billiards and card games and knocking back fifteen-cent drinks. "It had probably not occurred to some of you good prohibitionists," he said, "that you were really running a high-toned saloon man for governor." And when Ball received the endorsement of President Woodrow Wilson, Ferguson turned it into an unforgivable federal intrusion into Texas's business and an insult to "those sacred principles for which the gallant Confederate soldiers fought and bled on so many Southern battlefields."

As governor, Ferguson moved to patch things up with Wilson. He sent the president a condolence letter upon the death of his wife and traveled to Washington to discuss the escalating problems with Mexico. Wilson's Texas confidant, that great political seer Edward House, sized Ferguson up shortly after his election and prophesied that he would "be one of our most successful governors" because he had "common sense and courage" and "the faculty of making friends instead of enemies."

It did not seem like a spectacularly wrong call at first. Governor Ferguson had an instinct for stuntsmanship. He offered fifty dollars to the first Texas woman to produce triplets. He saw no shades of gray in the troubles along the Rio Grande, ordering Captain Ransom of the Rangers—the notorious assassin of Jesus Bazán and Antonio Longoria—to make the border problems go away if he had to "kill every damned man down there."

Farmer Jim appeared to have a heartfelt interest in improving the state's low ranking in education, particularly when it came to underfunded rural schools and the 15 percent of the Texas population that remained illiterate. But as a high school dropout who had been (unfairly) mocked during the campaign for his overall ignorance of history and grammar, he was primed for a grudge match with the pooh-bahs of higher education, most especially those who had supported his opponent. He promptly engineered the ouster of Edward Blackshear, the principal of Prairie View Normal and Industrial College. Prairie View was a state-supported college established in 1876 "for the benefit of Colored Youth." Blackshear, a highly regarded educator, was, naturally enough as the head of a segregated college, black. In Ferguson's mind, the principal was doubly disqualified to serve, both because he had been a supporter of Thomas Ball and Prohibition and because "a negro has no business whatever taking a part in the political affairs of the Democratic party, the white man's party."

When the Fergusons took up residence in the Governor's Mansion in Austin, they found themselves in enemy territory. The blustery small-town banker who had talked himself into the state's highest office was not prepared for the suspicion and condescension awaiting him in the hotbox of Texas Progressivism. That applied to his wife as well. The Fergusons' daughter Ouida Ferguson Nalle remembered Austin as a "social and political whirlpool" dominated by three warring social groups: the intolerably smug "old Austin set," the "University group, who bask in their intellectual superiority," and "the politicos," most of whom "are endowed with colossal ego, convinced that they have been sent by the people to save the State government from the other two groups, whom they call high-hat snobs."

Miriam Ferguson was completely at sea in this environment. "My mother," Ouida observed, "had never possessed, nor had she attempted to cultivate, the slightest tendency toward diplomacy." She hired a social secretary to help her manage, but this read like an act of farm-girl desperation to the alert, gossiping classes of Austin.

Governor Ferguson eventually managed to alienate all three factions that Ouida described. To begin with, he launched a frontal assault on the University of Texas, an always-reliable target for populist politicians. The new governor tromped right over the cherished conviction expressed by one professor that "politics have no more to do with the appointments at the University of Texas than they do with the canals on Mars." For Ferguson, politics had everything to do with the university, and everything to do with everything else. He intended to liberate the institution from the snooty elitist clique running it, including a classics professor named William J. Battle, who, upon the resignation of his predecessor, had been appointed acting president of the university. Ferguson demanded the resignations of Battle and a handful of other faculty members, one of whom was John A. Lomax, the inventive collector of cowboy songs. For several of the people Ferguson wanted fired, such as a journalism professor who was a vocal opponent of the governor, the motive was pure political payback. For others the reasons were obscure. When asked why he was determined to have the men on his list removed from the university, Ferguson's answer was concise: "I don't have to give any reasons. I am Governor of the State of Texas."

Battle's successor as president was a theology professor named Robert E. Vinson, to whom Ferguson made the same demands to purge the university of professors he found objectionable. When Vinson refused, the governor invited him to "the biggest bear fight that had ever taken place in the history of the State of Texas."

It didn't go well for the governor. He dismissed his opponents as "trickster lawyers, plodding pedagogues and whispering politicians," but failed to take into account that many of them had a sentimental fealty to the state's flagship university. Among them was James Hogg's son Will, a former member of the University of Texas Board of Regents and a power player in the influential Ex-Students' Association. Ferguson's attempt to pack the board of regents with appointees who would do his bidding led to an investigation by the legislature, which began to uncover the shell game that Ferguson had for years been playing with his own imperiled finances. His bank in Temple was a particularly busy clearinghouse in which he deposited an alarming amount of state funds, reaping interest payments that should have gone to the state treasury. Ferguson escaped impeachment, and though the committee found that he deserved "the severest criticism and condemnation," he was merely censured. He escaped, but he couldn't contain his fury at the professoriate. When the new appropriation bill for the University of Texas reached his desk, he theatrically vetoed it and the bear fight started up again. That resulted in his impeachment in the House of Representatives, and to a trial in the Senate, which began in August 1917. Among the charges was one of contempt, because the governor would not reveal the source of an "unusual and questionable" loan of $156,500. Ferguson, the lawyer who had never gone to law school and had been admitted to the bar without being asked a single question, decided to represent himself at trial. The most memorable thing he said in his defense was "Is it any crime for a man to borrow $156,500?"

Ferguson was found guilty by the Senate of political meddling in the University of Texas, misuse of state funds, and official misconduct. He resigned the day before the Senate could remove him from office. Ferguson called this episode his "attempted impeachment," though it was very much an accomplished fact. The Senate had declared him "disqualified to hold any office of honor, trust or profit under the State of Texas." Ferguson denied the reality of that as well, declaring his intention to run for governor again the next year, in 1918.

For now, the ex-governor and his family vacated the mansion so that Lieutenant Governor William Hobby could move in. They left the Austin snobs behind and returned to Temple. "It is really a relief for me to get back into private life for a time," was the way Ferguson spun his forced retrenchment. He and his family did not receive a rousing welcome in Temple. Childhood friends of the Ferguson children taunted them. The ex-governor showed up at a parade in downtown Temple, expecting to be greeted with hearty handshakes, but found nobody willing to talk to him. Standing alone on an empty sidewalk, watching the parade go by, Farmer Jim was already plotting his comeback.

—35—

WAR AT HOME
AND ABROAD

BUT FIRST THERE WAS WORLD WAR I. "TO THE AVERAGE
American," the Dallas-based newspaper *Farm and Ranch*
observed in August 1914, a few days after Germany invaded
Belgium, causing Britain to declare war, "the war in Europe
is unintelligible. Who knows what they are fighting about
and what ends are hoped of achievement." But the faraway
conflict kept creeping closer to the United States. A hundred twenty-eight
American lives were lost when a German U-boat sank the *Lusitania*, a British passenger liner that was also transporting munitions to England, in
1915. The next year, the German government declared unrestricted submarine warfare, a high-stakes calculation meant to prevent American shipments from reaching British forces before they could be defeated. That
led to the United States breaking off diplomatic relations with Germany.
Edward House was with his friend Woodrow Wilson in Washington a few
days before the decision was made. "The President was sad and depressed,"
according to House, "and I did not succeed at any time during the day in
lifting him into a better frame of mind."

Pershing's troops had just returned from Mexico, and relations between the

United States and the Carranza government were still sore, when American diplomats got wind of a coded message from the German Foreign Office to the Mexican government that had been intercepted and decoded by British intelligence. The so-called Zimmerman Telegram was almost as explicit and alarming to Texans as the Plan of San Diego had been. In the event of the United States not remaining neutral in the war, the Germans stated, "We make Mexico a proposal or alliance on the following basis: make war together, make peace together, general financial support and an understanding on our part that Mexico is to reconquer the lost territory in Texas, New Mexico, and Arizona."

Carranza didn't act on the offer. The dream of a deeply riven Mexico reconquering Texas, fighting the United States in another all-out war, was impractical. But there were still Texans alive whose grandfathers had been killed at the Alamo and at Goliad, or who had charged the Mexican Army with Sam Houston at San Jacinto, or who had fought off the forces of Vásquez and Woll when they tried to retake Texas in 1842. Americans in general were outraged at Germany aiming their bellows at the smoldering fire of U.S.-Mexico relations, but for Texans the stakes were personal.

One descendant of the Texas revolutionary aristocracy, however, was cautious about the prospect of war with Germany. Thanks to the endorsement of House, Albert Sidney Burleson was Wilson's postmaster general, one of three Texans in the president's cabinet. His grandfather was Edward Burleson, who had replaced Stephen Austin as the Texian commander during the siege of San Antonio. Edward Burleson had fought at San Jacinto, had led Mirabeau Lamar's army against Chief Bowles and against the Comanches at Plum Creek, had served as vice president of the Republic of Texas and as a spy in the Mexican-American War. His son Edward Jr. also fought in that war, and fought Indians as well, and was a conscription officer in the Confederacy. I'm guessing that his son was named in honor of the Confederate general Albert Sidney Johnston, but Albert Sidney Burleson was a politician, not a soldier. On the streets of the nation's capital, he always carried an umbrella and dressed with such black-clad severity that his colleagues called him the "Cardinal." He was a faintly progressive free-silver advocate who introduced airmail delivery to the United States but who also stood squarely for segregation and criticized Wilson when the president came aboard on issues like women's suffrage and thereby trod upon the "sound old principles" of the country.

Burleson, unlike his other Texas colleagues in Wilson's cabinet—Attorney General Thomas Watt Gregory and Secretary of Agriculture David F. Houston—was hesitant to declare war on Germany. "I regret this step," he said, in striking historical contrast to the warring spirit that drove his grandfather, "but there is no other way. It must be carried through to the bitter end."

BY THE TIME THE WAR IN EUROPE STARTED, MORE THAN FOUR million people were living in Texas, making it the fifth-largest state in the country. Its biggest cities—San Antonio, Dallas, Houston, and Fort Worth— had three times as many residents as they did in 1900. From this expanding population base, almost two hundred thousand Texans served in uniform in World War I. Some were in regular army units like the Ninetieth Division, made up mostly of Texas and Oklahoma draftees and known as the "Alamo" Division. Others were men who were already serving in the National Guard or who had enlisted following the exhortations of the mightily distracted Governor Ferguson. A few months before his impeachment trial, Ferguson posed the questions "[What] greater life can a man live than that of sacrifice? What greater death can he die than that for principles?" National Guard units from Texas and Oklahoma, including an Oklahoma regiment with guardsmen from Indian tribes, like the Choctaws and Cherokees, that had been pushed out of Texas, formed the Thirty-Sixth Division. The Thirty-Sixth later called itself the Arrowhead Division, but when it began training at Camp Bowie, near Fort Worth, its members were the Panthers, with an insignia depicting a mountain lion in full attack mode.

A few Texans got to France shortly after the Americans entered the war in April 1917, including the incomparably named Brigadier General Beaumont Bonaparte Buck, and Warren R. Jackson, a marine who had been a student at Sam Houston Normal College and who would go on to write a lively account of his experiences in combat called *His Time in Hell*. Most of the troops didn't arrive until the summer of 1918, in time to help break the German spring offensive at places like Belleau Wood, Soissons, Chateau-Thierry, and the Saint-Mihiel salient.

As the war began, the fighting was not just overseas. Soldiers of the Third Battalion of the Twenty-Fourth Infantry, one of the regiments set aside for black troops, arrived in Houston at the end of July 1917, almost a full year before most Texans disembarked in France. Their job was to stand guard during the construction of a new training site called Camp Logan. It was a demeaning assignment for men who had fought in the Southwest, in Cuba, and in the Philippines, and who had only recently returned from chasing Pancho Villa with General Pershing. But it was part of a new reality for black troops, who were increasingly sidelined from significant combat roles and were being treated instead as a kind of auxiliary force whose presence in the army was merely endured. "We must not eat with them," the French military reported to its officers after receiving a directive from Pershing about how they were expected to behave around black U.S. soldiers, "must not shake hands or seek to talk or meet with them outside the requirements of military service. We must not commend too highly the black American troops, particularly in the presence of Americans."

Nevertheless the Third Battalion was initially pleased to be in Houston and not at its regimental encampment in New Mexico or out in the middle of the Chihuahuan Desert, where for two years it had had nothing to look at "save sand, rocks, and sage brush." There were trees and parks in Houston, along with the beckoning soldierly amenities of a major city.

The men of the Third Battalion were accustomed to sitting with whites in streetcars in the Philippines and in San Francisco, to playing baseball with them in New Mexico. But now they were in the enforcement zone of the Jim Crow South. "When I took my battalion to Houston," the battalion's white commander, Colonel William Newman, wrote after the violence that took place that August, "I knew that the Texans' idea of how a colored man should be treated was just the opposite of what these 24th Infantrymen had been used to."

Newman was speaking from experience, since one of his soldiers had been murdered by a Texas Ranger in Del Rio the year before, "for no other reason than that he was a colored man." He likely also was thinking of what had happened in Brownsville in 1906, only weeks after black soldiers from another regiment, the Twenty-Fifth Infantry, arrived at their posting at Fort Brown. The year 1906 was a noticeably bad one to be an African American in Texas, just after the poll tax and white primaries had gone into effect, and in the middle of a decade that would see at least a hundred lynchings. It was also the year when segregation, already in force on railroads, was extended to streetcars, and when volunteer black militia units in Texas—centers of pride and tradition—were informed by the legislature that they were no longer allowed to exist.

The black soldiers who reported for duty that year at Fort Brown were met by a white citizenry that was, at best, unreceptive. "Whenever you nigger soldiers," a customs inspector advised one private after threatening to blow his brains out for failing to show due Jim Crow deference, "see a white man on the sidewalk talking to ladies, get off the sidewalk and into the street." The affronts piled up, tensions rose, and after a local white woman accused a black soldier of raping her, all passes at Fort Brown were canceled. That night, a local bartender was killed and a police lieutenant was wounded in downtown Brownsville in what the mayor claimed was an organized rampage by as many as twenty uniformed men from the Twenty-Fifth. Twelve enlisted men were arrested, but a Cameron County grand jury didn't see enough evidence to charge them. That didn't matter to the inspector general of the army, who assumed that blame for the shooting resided with the men at Fort Brown, and who managed to convince President Theodore Roosevelt—already feeling political heat for having invited Booker T. Washington to dinner at the White House—to dishonorably discharge all 167 of them. In 1972, more than sixty years later, the Nixon administration agreed to make the discharges honorable. But by then, only one of the 167 men was still alive. He received a $25,000 pension.

HOUSTON IN 1917 HAD ALL THE ELEMENTS OF THE SAME racial storm that had been brewed up in Brownsville eleven years earlier. The soldiers of the Twenty-Fourth arrived on a Saturday, and most of them went out that night to investigate the entertainment possibilities of Houston. They had little tolerance for the streetcar segregation laws and even confiscated the signs dictating where "colored" passengers were supposed to sit. The next night, a near riot occurred when a conductor ordered two platoons of soldiers off his streetcar because they were overflowing into the "white" section.

That was only the first weekend. Things declined steadily from there. The provost guards from the camp were treated with contempt by the local police. Colonel Newman humiliated his own military police by taking the advice of the local police chief and relieving them of their sidearms. The soldiers guarding Camp Logan while it was under construction showed little tolerance for the taunts they received from the white workers. At one tense point, a black guard trained his rifle on a white construction worker who had almost knocked him down with a load of lumber. Then a black employee at the camp was knifed to death during a payroll scuffle. The guards arrested the white assailant, whose friends claimed that they had heard the man's dying words, and that he had goaded the soldiers to "wipe out the whites."

In August, two Houston policemen were pursuing a pair of teenagers for gambling when they barged into the house of a black housewife. "You all God damn nigger bitches," one of the officers, Lee Sparks, lectured her, "since these God damn sons of bitches of nigger soldiers come here, you are trying to take the town." When a private on a pass into Houston from the infantry camp saw the woman being harassed and tried to intervene, Sparks pounded him on the head with his six-shooter and hauled him off to jail. A black provost guard named Charles Baltimore went to investigate the fate of his fellow trooper. "I don't report to no niggers," Sparks told Baltimore before beating him over the head as well and then shooting at him as he tried to escape. Baltimore was captured, thrown into jail, released, and was back in camp that night. But a rumor persisted among the black soldiers of the Third Battalion of the Twenty-Fourth Infantry that Corporal Baltimore had been murdered. Before that could be cleared up, another rumor erupted that a white mob was on its way to attack the camp.

"There will be hell popping tonight," one of the soldiers was heard to prophesy. The man who led the mutiny and the rampage that followed was a thirty-five-year-old sergeant from I Company named Vida Henry. He was, one of his white officers testified, a leader "that the men of the company seemed to respect and obey without question." It's impossible to say whether Henry suddenly snapped and merely took charge of what happened next, or whether it was something he had taken an active part in planning all along. But he was the one who told the hundred or so men who took part to "get plenty of ammunition and save one for yourself," and who called out "right face" as he marched them out of camp and into the streets of Houston with bayonets fixed to their Springfield rifles.

Their objective, more or less, was the police station, but they opened fire along the way at random cars driving down the road, at people sitting on their porches, at lawmen rushing to confront them. By the time it was all over—two hours later—fifteen white people, including four police officers, were dead. Twelve others were wounded, one mortally.

Four of the black mutineers also died, including Henry. During one of the exchanges of gunfire, he was shot in the shoulder. He wanted to continue on to attack the police station, but by that time most of the men knew it was pointless to keep marching when they had stirred up the whole white population of Houston into a state of merciless reprisal. Their only hope of surviving was to give up the raid and sneak back into camp. "You all can go in," Henry told them. "I ain't going in. I ain't going to camp no more."

He asked several of the men to shoot him, but they wouldn't do it. They shook hands with him instead as they filed away a few hours past midnight, leaving him alone beneath a chinaberry tree along the railroad tracks. They had not gone far when they heard a rifle shot. His body was found the next morning. There are conflicting accounts of how he died. He might have shot himself in the head with his Springfield rifle, or he might have been clubbed and bayonetted by assailants unknown.

Three courts-martial followed. The first of them, in which 64 members of the Twenty-Fourth Infantry were judged in a courtroom at Fort Sam Houston in San Antonio, was the largest murder trial in the history of the United States. By the time all the proceedings were over, 110 men were found guilty. Most of them were given life sentences, but 19 were hanged. Thirteen of the condemned men went to the gallows together in a mesquite clearing along

Salado Creek outside San Antonio. The group included Charles Baltimore, the provost guard whose rumored death had helped spark the mutiny. It was a cold December dawn, with a bonfire burning. The condemned men all refused blindfolds, and when the commanding officer called out, "Attention!" they stepped onto the trapdoors with military polish.

"Unwept, Unhonored, and Unsung," read the headline in the *Houston Press* a few days after the riot; "Two Negro Soldiers Are Buried." The story was

The black soldiers of the Twenty-Fourth Infantry who rioted in Houston in 1917 were tried in three separate courts-martial. This was the scene at the first proceeding, the largest murder trial in American history, which included sixty-four defendants.

about the under-cover-of-darkness disposal of the bodies of Sergeant Henry and Private Bryant Watson, another mutineer killed the night of the riot.

Their families were not contacted, and no markers were put on their graves. But on the hundredth anniversary of their deaths, I drove to Houston to witness a ceremony in College Park Cemetery, where they had been buried, only a few blocks from where they had died. If Henry and Watson had committed an infamous crime a century ago, no mention of it was made

der Trial in the History of the United States.
Court Martial of 64 members of 24th. Infantry U.S.A.
iny and murder of 17 people at Houston Tex. Aug 23, 1917.
l Held in Gift Chapel. Ft Sam Houston.
---Nov 1, 1917 - Brig Genl. George K. Hunter. Presiding.
- Judge Advocate.   [Counsel for Defense.
phin, Asst.   "   [Maj. Harry S. Grier.
s guarded by 19th. Infantry. Co. "C" Capt. Carl J Adler
hted by. W. C. Lloyd. San Antonio Tex. Reproduction not allowed

that morning. They had died before the court-martial and so had never been convicted of anything. Among the hundred or so people gathered at their grave sites that morning there was a conviction that if history could not absolve their crimes, it could at least explain them.

A group of buffalo soldier reenactors, in black campaign hats, dark blue blouses, and yellow-striped cavalry pants, marched toward two black-draped tombstones to present the colors. After prayers and speeches, two uniformed marines solemnly lifted the drapes to reveal the tombstones and the names and dates incised there—no mention of mutiny or murder, just birth dates and death dates and the incontrovertible acknowledgment that the men buried there had served their country in World War I.

★

NOT ALL AFRICAN AMERICAN TROOPS WERE HELD STATESIDE during the war. Twelve thousand Texans from segregated regiments made the voyage to France. Only a few hundred of them ended up being engaged in combat; for the most part, they were assigned to the same behind-the-scenes support roles as their counterparts back home. But in France they got a glimpse of a different and, for them, much less vicious world. Despite Pershing's directive, they were treated by the French Army and the French people without any particular condescension or hostility. "I have but one desire," wrote a black Texas soldier after discovering that the prejudice he had experienced all his life back home was not globally applied, "and that is to be able to go all over our land and tell of my experiences in the democratic France, and the manly qualities displayed by our soldiers under conditions so very foreign to those at home."

One extremely unpleasant thing that Europe and the United States had in common in 1918, the year that most of the American troops landed, was influenza. The epidemic known as the Spanish flu came in waves, first hitting the United States during the summer and then coming back, with much more ferocity, in the fall. More than 650,000 Americans died from the disease—up to 50 million died worldwide—and it struck with particular virulence in crowded military posts like Fort Bliss in El Paso or in newly opened training facilities like San Antonio's Camp Travis or Fort Worth's Camp Bowie, or in ships carrying troops across the Atlantic. (In a two-month period, 4,000 men died of disease on those ships.)

One of the people who came down with the flu was a twenty-eight-year-old newspaper reporter from Indian Creek, Texas, named Katherine Anne Porter. She was born in a log cabin in 1890 and would live long enough to cover the launch of Apollo 17, the last manned mission to the moon, for

Playboy magazine. Her ties to Texas were deep. Her parents had been married by an old Baptist minister named Noah Byars, who in 1836 was one of the owners of the drafty building in Washington-on-the-Brazos that hosted the signers of the Texas Declaration of Independence. "I was fed from birth," Porter later wrote of her Texas upbringing, "on myth and legend."

But grim reality overtook myth and legend early on. When Katherine—or Callie, as she known then—was two years old, her mother died while giving birth to her younger sister, and her father fell into a haunted lassitude from which he never recovered. The family was rescued by her stern and indefatigable sixty-five-year-old grandmother, Catharine Ann Skaggs Porter. Despite being a widow who had raised nine children and lost her own daughter in childbirth the day before her daughter-in-law died, "Cat" Porter brought her bereaved son and his children to live with her in her house in the little town of Kyle, about twenty miles south of Austin.

"I do not believe that childhood is a happy time," her granddaughter would later write. "It is a time of desperate cureless bitter griefs and pains, of shattering disillusionments, when everything good and evil alike is happening for the first time, and there is no answer to any question."

Katherine Anne Porter escaped childhood by marrying at sixteen, the first of four troubled or unsatisfying marriages and many love affairs. ("I have no hidden marriages," she told an interviewer late in life, "they just sort of slip my mind.") She escaped Texas by moving to Chicago to try to become a movie actress. She had the looks for it—a precisely symmetrical face, wide-set dark eyes, and a pensive mouth. She claimed she found the "ideal of prettiness" to be "nauseating," but the dramatic glamour shots that track her long literary career suggest an abiding fascination with her own appearance. She found work as an extra in a few silent movies, but the experience was unfulfilling and demeaning, and she moved on.

There was more authenticity

KATHERINE ANNE PORTER,
born in a log cabin in Indian Creek, made a point of putting distance between herself and Texas.

in writing, even if it was only advertising copy disguised as poetry, as in this early contribution to the *Gulf Coast Citrus Fruit Grower and Southern Nurseryman*:

> Ye shivering ones of the frozen North, list to my happy song
> Of the seventh heaven nestled here below,
> In our rich, fertile valleys, midst sunkissed fruits and flowers
> In Texas, by the Gulf of Mexico

In October 1918, just as the influenza epidemic was cresting, she moved to Denver to work as a court reporter on the *Rocky Mountain News*. That was when she was stricken. Her fever spiked to 105 and remained there for nine days. Her hair fell out. Her colleagues at the paper prepared an obituary, and her family back in Texas, hearing that she was near the end, began to make funeral arrangements. "It just simply divided my life," she remembered of this hovering moment, "cut across it like that. So that everything before that was just getting ready, and after that I was in some strange way altered, ready."

A shot of strychnine brought her back from the verge of death. The hair that had been black grew back white, and though she would go on to write theater and movie reviews and unembarrassed fluff such as a column called "Let's Shop with Suzanne," Texas's first great literary artist emerged from that Denver sickbed. (She was not shy in pointing this out: "I am the first and only serious writer," she declared in 1958, "that Texas has produced.") She always had a distant and difficult relationship with Texas, particularly after her acclaimed 1939 book *Pale Horse, Pale Rider* lost the prize for best book from the Texas Institute of Letters to a collection of old-timey buried-treasure tales by J. Frank Dobie. But in the title story, her main character, in a raging flu fever, remembers her home state with incandescent clarity: "And her memory turned and roved after another place she had known first and loved best, that now she could see only in drifting fragments of palm and cedar, dark shadows and a sky that warmed without dazzling. . . . There was the long slow wavering of gray moss in the drowsy oak shade, the spacious hovering of buzzards overhead, the smell of crushed water herbs along a bank, and without warning a broad tranquil river into which flowed all the rivers she had known."

TEXAS DOUGHBOYS SERVING FAR AWAY IN FRANCE MUST HAVE had similarly vivid dreams of home. Some made it back; some did not. The war took, through combat or disease, the lives of over five thousand Texans. When the University of Texas built its football stadium in 1924 and called it

Memorial Stadium, the names of the Texan dead were inscribed on a huge bronze entablature. Eighty-five of the dead were professors or students or alumni of the university. When I went to a football game not long ago at the much-renovated stadium, I noticed the plaques that had been put up in their memory along the stairway concourses. On many of the plaques, beneath the name of a dead member of the UT family, was the notation "Killed at St. Étienne, France."

I knew about Saint-Étienne. I had written a novel called *Remember Ben Clayton*, in which the title character fought and died there. During the course of researching the book, I went to France to walk across the battlefield. Saint-Étienne-à-Arnes is a tiny village in the Champagne region of northeastern France, no more than a few hundred people. In 1918, the village and the chalk-and-limestone ridge known as Blanc Mont, about a half mile to the south, were knotty enemy strong points during the great offensive that finally broke through the Germans' Hindenburg Line and brought about the end of the war. By the time the six-week Meuse-Argonne battle was over, more than 26,000 members of the American Expeditionary Force had been killed.

Blanc Mont and Saint-Étienne made up a small pocket in that sprawling battle, but it was a bloody pocket. The French had been trying for three days to dislodge the Germans from the summit of Blanc Mont when the American Second Division was thrown into the effort. It carried the ridge, but only after being sliced apart at the top by deadly counterattacks. Texas Marine Warren Jackson, who took part in the fight, remembered simply, "The men on the front paid the bill."

When the ridge was taken, the Germans retreated to Saint-Étienne, which like Blanc Mont was heavily fortified. It fell to the untested Texans and Oklahomans of the Thirty-Sixth Division's 141st and 142nd Infantry to take over from the exhausted marines and assault the village.

"Picture if you can that scene," Chaplain C. H. Barnes, who was on the ground with the 142nd, instructs readers about the American attack on the heavily fortified village. "Call on all the power of your imagination and see those men as they move slowly, steadily forward into barbwire entanglements, while gigantic cannon are booming, huge shells screaming through the air, high explosives bursting, shrapnel whizzing on all sides, snipers firing from hidden positions, machine guns click, click, click, click, doing their deadly work while the air is filled with gas."

It's easier to picture the scene when reading Barnes's regimental history than it is while standing on the battlefield. A monument now rests on the bitterly fought-over summit of Blanc Mont, though an authoritative World War I website maintains that it "might be the least visited monument on the

Western front." Old trench works trace across it like healed-over surgical scars, but the grass is green and the birds are singing and the view across the sugar beet fields toward nearby Saint-Étienne is clear, with no fog of noxious gas.

In the village, where the Germans forces prepared for a last stand in the cemetery, digging trenches through the grave sites, you can see tombstones and vaults defaced by bullets and shell fragments from the Thirty-Sixth's ferocious final assault. ("There was not a square foot of air space," one participant remembered, "through which bullets were not flying.") There is still barbed wire tangled in the grass in places, and just back of the cemetery I came across an unexploded French grenade bleached white by a century of sun.

"Texans Heroic in First Battle," the *New York Times* reported of the fight at Saint-Étienne. One of the most heroic was Corporal Samuel M. Sampler of Decatur, who was awarded the Medal of Honor for single-handedly taking out an enemy machine-gun position and then also single-handedly forcing the surrender of twenty-eight German soldiers. The casualties that resulted from the taking of Blanc Mont and Saint-Étienne added up to 1,300 men killed and wounded. Among the dead were Panthers such as John H. Green, a sergeant in the 142nd. Chaplain Barnes, who compiled eyewitness battle reports, reported that Green was shot "by machine gun bullets which penetrated left chest and right abdomen and right leg between hip and knee." "He lived but a few minutes," Barnes went on to write. "The last words heard that he said, 'Get those kraut-eating devils.'"

France's Marshal Pétain reportedly proclaimed the Blanc Mont–Saint-Étienne engagement "the greatest single achievement of the 1918 campaign." It is almost forgotten today, though not by the 142nd Infantry, whose regimental patch features the shattered church steeple of Saint-Étienne.

---------- ★ ----------

PRIVATE DAVID BARKLEY, A NINETEEN-YEAR-OLD FROM SAN
Antonio, was serving in the 356th Infantry during the final days of the campaign. On November 9, just two days before the armistice, he and another man volunteered to swim across the Meuse River to locate the position of the German forces on the opposite side. It was a perilous mission, not just because they would be slipping behind enemy territory but also because the water was searingly cold. They managed to get the critical intelligence they needed, but on the way back across the river Barkley's body seized up with cramps and he drowned. For his heroism, he was awarded the Medal of Honor. After his body was shipped home, it received the ultimate Texas tribute of lying in state in the Alamo. A school and an army camp were named for him, and in 2003 a statue was erected in his birthplace of Laredo.

Barkley's father, a career soldier, had abandoned his family after moving them to San Antonio, leaving thirteen-year-old David to support his mother and sister. His mother was a Tejana named Antonia Cantu, but Barkley went to some effort to keep that fact a secret when he enlisted. Even though Mexican Americans were not forced into segregated units as black soldiers were, he suspected that if his ancestry were discovered he wouldn't be trusted with frontline duty. In his letters home, he begged his mother never to use her Spanish surname when she was writing him. "Just tell them it's Barkley," he instructed her. The army never found out. He is still listed as David Bennes Barkley in most service records and historical citations, but these days Tejanos tend to sideline the official name and refer to him as David Barkley Cantu.

Barkley was one of thousands of Texans of Mexican American heritage who enlisted or were drafted into military service during World War I. Among the most fervent was a schoolteacher just about to turn thirty named José de la Luz Sáenz. He had recently married his brother's widow, a descendant of Gregorio Esparza, one of the Tejanos who had died defending the Alamo. Sáenz was a dedicated teacher, but a visibly opinionated one, chafing against the practice of segregated Mexican schools and serving as a local president of the mutual aid society known as the Mexican Protective Association. He was teaching at an all-Mexican school in the Central Texas town of Dittlinger when the war broke out. He didn't wait to be drafted but enthusiastically joined up, in part for the chance it offered to impress upon Anglo Texans that Tejanos were fellow patriots who were willing to fight but expected the full rights of citizenship in return.

"Until now," he wrote to his students when he took his wartime leave of the school, "I have used pencil and pen to wage trying battles for the educational advancement of our people. You will soon hear that I am holding a rifle in the very same trenches of France and upholding our people's pride for the glory and honor of our flag. . . . Long live Washington! Long live the star spangled banner! Long live our raza!"

Sáenz wrote a book about his experiences in the war, and its grand Spanish title—*Los Mexico-Americanos en La Gran Guerra y Su Contingente en Pro de la Democracia, la Humanidad y La Justicia*—highlights his aspirations that Mexican American participation in the great world struggle would lead to overdue social changes back home in benighted Texas.

But the book isn't a manifesto; it's a *diario particular*, a journal of his personal experiences in the war. Sáenz, who was fluent in English and Spanish and could read French, and whose memoir is studded with references to Victor Hugo, Dante, and Cincinnatus, applied for officer training school, but did so fully aware that "the general understanding is that this is not for Mexican soldiers. That may be the case, but I want to give it a try."

His application was not acted upon. Even though he remained an enlisted man, his language skills turned out to be in crucial demand, and as he marched with the Ninetieth Division through France he was kept busy at headquarters translating French army documents. But that work did not keep him out of harm's way during the concluding months of the war, when the Ninetieth was pushing hard against the German lines at Saint-Mihiel, through the Meuse-Argonne, and into Germany. Before he entered combat, knowing his chances of being killed were high, he wrote a beyond-the-grave missive to his wife: "This is my last letter to you. This moment had to arrive sooner or later. It is here." He told her he was honor bound to fight "as long as the horrible and long-standing prejudice continues in Texas against our raza. . . . Our purpose is to demonstrate our dignity as a people before the whole world. It is necessary to fall where the best have died, and you can be sure that I will have fallen as a man of worth."

He did not fall, though there were many near misses, as when German shells landed nearby and vaporized comrades or blew their shredded bodies into the treetops. "Some of these sights cannot be imagined," he wrote at one point, just after describing the sight of a dead German soldier whose "very handsome" head, along with its trailing windpipe and lungs and heart, was all that was left of him. "They are on the battlefield," he wrote of his dead friends, "in the trenches, behind tree trunks, and in foxholes. . . . When I see all this I cannot help but think of the ungrateful nature of man. The dead are destined to be forgotten. . . . Who will care about the soldiers of my raza after the sacrifice? There they are, Simón González, José González, José Garcia, Moisés Carrejo, and so many others."

Sáenz and his fellow soldiers were often witnesses to dogfights in the sky above their trenches as American pilots pursued German planes attempting to shoot down observation balloons. Of one aerial engagement, he wrote, "The [German] plane nosedived with a winding motion like a wounded bird. One of the pilots—we do not know if he was dead or alive—fell from the sky like a lifeless leaf from a dried-up tree, spinning and spinning until he smashed into Mother Earth."

Sáenz may very well have been watching the exploits of the Ninety-Fourth Aero Squadron, better known as the "Hat in the Ring" squadron for the unit marking on the side of its planes, a red, white, and blue top hat encircled by a red ring.

The squadron had trained at Kelly Field in San Antonio, then the largest flying school in the world, and one of a dozen fields in Texas where pilots

JOSÉ DE LA LUZ SÁENZ
*was a schoolteacher from Central Texas. He told his
students that he had enlisted to fight in World War I
to help advance Mexican American rights, "upholding
our people's pride for the glory and honor of our flag."*

were trained in the new arts of aviation surveillance and combat. Kelly Field was named for Lieutenant George E. Kelly, who had been a student of Lieutenant Benjamin Foulois, whose thesis for the Signal Corps School at Fort Leavenworth—"The Tactical and Strategic Value of Dirigible Balloons and Aerodynamical Flying Machines"—and his fifty-four minutes aloft in an early Wright Flyer had landed him the assignment of being the army's sole aviator in 1910. Foulois and another pilot, Philip Orin Parmalee, flew between Laredo and Eagle Pass in March 1911 in the first demonstration of aerial reconnaissance. Foulois then flew his plane across the border to help Pershing's punitive expedition search out Pancho Villa from the air. A month later, he was back in San Antonio at Fort Sam Houston, where Kelly—one of his three pilot trainees—died in a crash landing of one of the army's three airplanes.

It's no coincidence that Kelly, Brooks, Ellington, and most of the other airfields in Texas were named for flyers killed in crashes during the early, experimental days of aviation. But the high death rate didn't keep young Texans out of the sky. Clyde Balsley escaped a career working in his mother's bakery in San Antonio by sailing to France and working as a volunteer ambulance driver in the early days of the war. He ended up becoming a member of the Lafayette Escadrille, one of the thirty-eight American pilots who flew for France before the United States entered the war. Balsley and the other members of the French Air Service learned their perilous craft at training academies with names such as the "School of Perfection and Combat" and the "School of Acrobacy."

"For a long period the Lafayette Escadrille had enjoyed enviable luck," Balsley remembered, before describing how he became the first American pilot in history to be shot down: "Around and around us the Huns flew, their machine guns spitting streams of lead. . . . Suddenly I was lifted almost out of my seat, my head swam dizzily, my legs became limp and heavy, releasing the controls. The machine spun over on its back, and bounded wildly downward."

He somehow managed to land his Nieuport between the trench lines and haul himself out. Eight surgeries later, he was still alive, and the next year was the hero-groom in a celebrity wedding to the silent film star Miriam MacDonald.

Had either the French or the American army allowed women to fly, 101-pound Katharine Stinson of San Antonio might have been a participant in one of the dogfights over the trenches of the western front. "Well, other people have done it!" she explained in a magazine article, titled "Why I Am Not Afraid to Fly," after she had become famous. "And if they can do it, I don't see why I can't. No one taught me to loop the loop. I figured out how it was done, and went ahead and did it."

Stinson claimed that she became an aviator for an oddly practical reason. As a teenager, she badly wanted to go to Europe and study music—"If I could only become a music teacher. . . . I should be perfectly happy." But she had no money to go abroad, and no way to raise it, until she read in the newspaper about pilots and how much they earned by doing stunts for spectators over open fields. So that was what she did, though in the process she forgot about teaching music and became the world's most famous female pilot instead. She had been flying for five years when she tried to volunteer as a pilot in the war. She was twenty-six then, a lithe, beaming young woman in a tam-o'-shanter who wore her hair in long dark tresses like a Victorian heroine. She had already flown farther and longer than any pilot ever had without stopping, setting a distance record of 606 miles between San Diego and San Francisco. Her celebrity status was formidable—"She was America's sweetheart of the airways," one author remembered, "as surely as Mary Pickford was America's sweetheart of the silent screen"—but it was of no use in convincing the army to accept her services. Instead, she went to England and France and volunteered for terrestrial duty as an ambulance driver. It was grueling work in the damp European cold, and it undermined her robust health. She developed tuberculosis and never flew again, though she had a long second act as an architect in Santa Fe and lived to be eighty-six.

At about the same time that Katharine Stinson was driving ambulances in France, Bessie Coleman—another Texas woman with visions of flight—was working as a manicurist in Chicago. She was nominally married to a man fourteen years older, but there's no indication that the woman who was soon to become known as the "wonderful colored aviatrix" had more than a fleeting enthusiasm for conventional married life. The first black woman in history to fly an airplane was born in 1892 in a one-room cabin in Northeast Texas but grew up mostly in Waxahachie, a farming town and county seat thirty miles south of Dallas. Her mother, Susan Coleman, who was born in 1865, the year of emancipation, gave birth to thirteen children, nine of whom survived past childhood. Her father, George Coleman, a day laborer, had enough Native American blood to claim tribal rights in Indian Territory, and in 1901, when Bessie was nine, he left his family behind and moved to Oklahoma.

Susan Coleman, left alone to provide for her children, went to work as a housekeeper for a local white couple. In her own home, she enforced rigorous and prideful standards, making sure that the table was set, that manners were upheld, and that aspirations were alive—especially aspirations of breaking through racial barriers. "We learned Harriet Tubman at Mother's knees," one of Bessie's sisters remembered.

"You can't make a race horse out of a mule," Susan Coleman once admonished Bessie. "If you stay a mule, you'll never win the race."

There was no way Bessie Coleman was ever going to be a mule. She was a driven, restless, beautiful, and instinctively self-promoting racehorse. After moving to Chicago, she was giving a manicure one day when her brother John, who had served overseas in the war, wandered in drunk and began unspooling anecdotes about the French women he had encountered overseas. Some of them, he said, had even flown airplanes.

That was enough motivation for Bessie to begin looking for a flying teacher. No one in that infant field in America would take on a young black woman as a student, so she decided to go to France. She gave up her manicurist job to manage a chili parlor, where the pay was better, signed up for French lessons, and talked several prominent black men in Chicago into more or less sponsoring her dream to sail across the Atlantic and enroll in a seven-month course at the École d'Aviation des Frères Caudron. From her room in a nearby town, she had to walk nine miles every day to the airfield. She learned to fly and to do acrobatics in a Curtis JN-4, better known as a Jenny, a biplane with a forty-foot wingspan whose engine had to be primed with castor oil by a mechanic while she waited in the cockpit.

She returned to the United States as a celebrity—"a full-fledged aviatrix," as one newspaper described her, "the first of her race."

She was twenty-nine when she got her French flying license, but throughout her brief career she would routinely subtract four or five or six years from her age. In the air circuses in which she demonstrated her flying skills, she wore a fetching military-looking uniform that included a Sam Browne belt, puttees, and a sleek leather coat.

She was badly injured in a crash when her plane stalled and crashed during an air show in Santa Monica in 1923. "My faith in aviation," she telegraphed to her fans from her hospital bed, "and the useful [sic] of it will serve in fulfilling the destiny of my people isn't shaken at all."

She was airborne again as soon as she healed and could find the financing for another plane. She made a triumphal tour of Texas in 1925. During an aerial circus in San Antonio, another daring black woman named Liza Dilworth agreed to parachute off the wing of Coleman's plane.

But she wasn't daring enough to do it twice, and Bessie began taking over the parachute jumps herself. On a spring day in 1926, after she had visited and given an inspiring speech to every black school in Jacksonville, Florida, she went up in her new Jenny to scout locations for the jump she would make the next day at the air show. She was sitting in the rear seat, with her seat belt unbuckled so that she could get a good view over the edge of the cockpit while another pilot flew the plane. At one thousand feet, the plane went into a tailspin after a loose wrench slid into the control gears. The aircraft nose-dived and then flipped, and at five hundred feet Bessie Coleman fell out, her body turning over and over in the air until she landed with what one witness reported as a "sickening thud."

The coffin was closed at her funeral in Chicago, but that didn't discourage ten thousand people from filing past it. And every April 30, the day of Bessie Coleman's death, African American pilots still fly over Lincoln Cemetery to drop flowers on her grave.

---------- ★ ----------

WOODROW WILSON'S "SECOND PERSONALITY," THE INDISPENSable and ubiquitous Colonel House, played an important but ultimately wrenching role in the conclusion of World War I. He was dispatched by the president to France in October 1918 to negotiate the details of the ceasefire and to ensure that the conditions Wilson had outlined in his Fourteen Points speech were taken seriously by the Allies. But the Wilson-House twinship suffered a fatal severing during the peace talks in Paris the next spring. The president grew ill and asked House to take his place in the meetings, during which the colonel made the grievous mistake of not demanding that Wilson's great dream of a league of nations be part of the treaty. When he found out, Wilson felt irretrievably betrayed.

"When you take a man like House," Wilson's personal physician claimed that the president told him, "and put him in a place the like of which no other man ever occupied in the world, take him into your innermost confidence, unbosom your very soul to him, and then this man is seduced by the flattery of others and goes back on you in a crisis—what a blow it is! It is harder than death."

The last time the two men spoke was at the train station in Brest as the president was returning home to the United States after the signing of the Treaty of Versailles. His parting words to the Texas kingmaker who had once been his shadow self were icy and concise: "Goodbye, House." They never saw each other again, and when Wilson died, five years later, House was not invited to his funeral.

Most of the Texas troops were home by the time Wilson was sailing back to the United States. "There here had been talk among the bunch," Warren Jackson remembered of the day he learned of the armistice, "that the war might end anytime. However, when I was waked on that morning of 11 November 1918, to be told that the war would cease that day, the thought was inconceivable. To be told that someone would be flying to the moon would have been easier to believe."

People in Texas greeted the news of the end of the war with a clangy chorus of fire station bells and sirens and patriotic songs. Civil War veterans, those who were still spry enough in their seventies or eighties, marched in the welcome-home parades. "Let's not have a grouch in the whole town," a Fort Worth newspaper decreed, "not a single one—while the boys are coming home."

When he got back to Texas, Private Sáenz was grateful to be home but wary of the future. He attended a welcome-back dance for returning heroes at the Rice Hotel in Houston, and couldn't help but notice that he and his fellow Tejano doughboys were mostly ignored by the hosts. On the way to San Antonio the next day, he found the vegetation that he saw outside the train window to be saturated with cultural complexities: "Corn, the historic plant of our indigenous raza, shines in all its splendor and beauty. When I set my eyes on the first cactus, the legendary symbol of our Aztec past, I saw a beauty in the humble plant that I had never imagined. Like other plants, it is condemned to extinction. The Europeans have declared an all-out war against it like the one they leveled against the indigenous people who lived here."

Sáenz was hopeful that patriotic service in the war might ease some of the generations-deep prejudice and distrust that Tejanos faced, but he wasn't naive about it. He would have been aware, for instance, of one of the signal atrocities that took place along the border during the aftershocks of the Mexican Revolution. It happened in a little village called Porvenir on the U.S.

side of the Rio Grande in remote Presidio County in January 1918, a month before Sáenz wrote his farewell letter to his students and joined the army. That Christmas, Mexican raiders had attacked the 125,000-acre Brite Ranch, which was known for the white-faced Hereford cattle it bred and sold all across the country. The ranch was so large and so far from any population center that it had its own store and post office, which the raiders looted after a tense siege during which three bystanders were killed, including a mailman whose throat was cut after he was hung from the rafters in the store.

The inevitable reprisal came from a dozen or so Texas Rangers and local ranchers, accompanied by forty army troopers from a Presidio County cavalry outpost. They descended on Porvenir just after midnight, awakened the 140 people who lived there, and ordered them out of their houses. While the villagers shivered with fear and cold in the freezing January night, the soldiers searched for stolen goods from the Brite Ranch raid. They found none, but that didn't stop the Rangers from marching fifteen male residents of Porvenir, ages sixteen to seventy-two, to a nearby bluff and methodically executing them. A schoolteacher, one of two Anglos who lived in the village, testified later that "one of the soldiers rode back and seeing what the Rangers had done (the moon was shining nearly as bright as day), cursed them, and told them 'what a nice piece of work you have done tonight.' . . . The Rangers and four cow-men made 42 orphans that night." The surviving villagers transported their dead across the river and didn't come back. In their absence, the soldiers burned down the jacales that had once made up the town.

Sitting in a booth in the Rice Hotel a year and a half later, present for but not quite participating in the homecoming festivities for him and his fellow doughboys, José de la Luz Sáenz became pensive: "I mulled my past in light of what was before me. I thought anxiously of my many dark moments and my wishful thinking, of the numerous memories and encouraging hopes for the future. All of this may soon fade away like smoke. We may have to face harsh realities and bitter truths tomorrow."

He knew enough, from his studies of history and his own participation in it, not to expect too much. The world had been remade by the war, but Texas was still Texas, and it was folly to think that all those "bitter truths" were now consigned to the past—not when a Spanish word for future was *porvenir*.

— 36 —

THE BLACKSNAKE WHIP

DR. HIRAM WESLEY EVANS WAS ONCE DERIDED FOR BEING a "small-time dentist," but what was wrong with that? A modest, manageable dental practice across the street from the Neiman-Marcus department store in Dallas was exactly the sort of business that someone who called himself "the most average man in America" might conduct. It was said that he lacked eloquence, but he had a kindly looking face and he struck people as direct and affable.

Evans was from Alabama originally, but at the beginning of the 1920s he was living in Dallas and swiftly working his way up the ranks of an organization that was enjoying a startling new revival among small-business owners like himself, and among white men and women from every class and profession who felt unsettled or threatened or enraged by the changes that had been set upon the world after the end of the war. "I will show you girls smoking cigarettes in public places," wrote Billie Mayfield, the owner of a Houston newspaper called *Colonel Mayfield's Weekly* and the outraged spirit guide to this new Gomorrah. "I will show you girls drinking whisky like the old time bar room bum. I will show you Main street shop windows filled

The Imperial Wizard of the Ku Klux Klan —"the most average man in America"—was a Dallas dentist named Hiram Wesley Evans.

with silver whisky flasks. . . . I will show you around Houston after 11:00 at night, not less than 300 automobiles parked by the road side with the lights out. . . . I will take you to the Majestic theater and let you hear a few of the modern jokes and see the modern audience scream every time the comedian pulls a dirty one." And he wasn't even mentioning the real menace: the blacks and Jews and Catholics who were forever corrupting Anglo-Saxon Protestant Americanism.

The organization whose goal was to put a stop to this pollution, and of which Hiram Evans was such an ascendant member, was the Ku Klux Klan. But it was a different Klan from the one that had terrorized blacks during Reconstruction. It was more open, more mainstream, more politically canny. It thought of itself, in the words of a *Houston Chronicle* article, as "an organization of true Americans whose motive was to teach and inspire Americanism as we came to know it during the war . . . a bulwark of loyalty to the flag and nation."

It was also something of a pyramid scheme. Field organizers called kleagles were responsible for recruiting new members, and they savvily began at the top, securing the imprimatur of a community's business or political elite and then working their way down the white class ranks to the confused and aggrieved masses. It cost $10 to join the Klan—a fee that was known as a klectoken. Of that $10, $4 went into the pocket of the kleagle. Another $1 went to his supervisor, 50¢ to the realm (i.e., state) leader, known as the Grand Goblin, and $2.50 to the national organizer, the Imperial Kleagle. If you were a new Klansman and wanted a robe—which you did—you had to rent one from the organization for $6.50. Membership was so robust—up to 700,000 in 1922—that a Georgia "nightshirt factory" was lit up twenty-four hours a day while turning out robes and the floppy hoods that Klan members referred to as helmets.

The first Texas "klavern" of the reanimated KKK was begun in Houston by the Klan's Imperial Wizard, William Joseph Simmons, an alcoholic hustler and disgraced Methodist minister whose opening protocol for meetings was to set two guns on a table and call out, "Bring on your niggers!" His "Invisible Empire" was publicly introduced at a parade that was the culmination of a Confederate veterans reunion in 1920. In front of a hundred thousand people, Klan members in full night-rider outfits marched down Houston's Main Street. They accompanied a float depicting a hooded judge passing down sentences on various malefactors, and a series of banners reading, "We were here yesterday, 1866," "We are here today, 1920," and "We will be here forever."

I don't know whether the friendly dentist Hiram Evans was present at this seminal occasion, but it was an event he certainly would not have

One Hundred

Americans

wanted to miss. In short order, he had become the Exalted Cyclops of the Dallas klavern, the state's largest. He was also part of a group of masked men who in the spring of 1921 abducted a black man named Alex Johnson who worked as a bellman at Dallas's Adolphus Hotel, the Beaux Arts namesake of brewing titan Adolphus Busch. Johnson had been accused of some sort of improper intimacy with a white woman, and for this he was driven six miles out of town, where he was lashed with a whip and threatened with lynching. Evans and the rest of his tormentors decided to let him live, but not before burning the letters KKK into his forehead with acid.

Only a few months later, Evans skyrocketed to the position of Imperial Kligrapp (national secretary) of the Klan, and a few months after that he had maneuvered Simmons straight out of office. At its national klonvokation in 1922, the Klan named Evans the new Imperial Wizard. A delegate explained that one of the reasons the Texan won the election was that "Texas was the star Klan state."

Hiram Evans had a smoother, less dissolute, more focused approach than his predecessor, doing his best to position the Klan in the public eye as a fraternal movement instead of a terrorist group. When he wasn't actively torturing black people, he could sound notes of plummy paternalism, as in this 1924 speech to the "Second Imperial Klonvokation" in Kansas City:

> We are accused of hostility to the Negro, and that is not true. The Klan is the Negro's best friend, because it proposes to help solve the problem which his presence in America brings.
>
> The problem is one which the white men of America are in honor bound to see solved with all fairness to the Negro. The Negro is not here by his own wish; we brought him. We cannot assimilate him. We cannot permit a race so different to mix with ours. The Negro is not a menace to Americanism in the same sense that the Jew or Roman Catholic is a menace. He is not actually hostile to it. He is simply racially incapable of understanding, sharing in or contributing to Americanism.

Evans's narrow-gauge understanding of Americanism was under particular strain in the early 1920s. It was one of those times in our history when the lid was coming off the box. The war and its dizzying social ramifications had given new momentum to long-stewing issues like women's suffrage and Prohibition. Activists like Minnie Fisher Cunningham adroitly linked the idea of a woman's right to vote with the contributions they had made to the war effort by selling Liberty bonds, planting war gardens, serving as army or navy nurses, working for the Red Cross, or—like

Katherine Stinson—risking their lives on the front by driving wounded soldiers in ambulances. Cunningham was a political pragmatist and wasn't above exploiting the xenophobia and suspicion that were natural consequences of the war. If German-speaking Texas men—"our alien enemy"—could vote, why not presumably patriotic Texas women?

The Nineteenth Amendment, giving women the right to vote, was passed by Congress in 1919 and ratified in 1920, but Texas women got something of a jump on the voting process during a special session of the legislature in the spring of 1918, a few months before American troops arrived in force in France. This happened just as Jim Ferguson was plotting an attempted comeback. William Hobby had become governor when Ferguson was impeached, but Farmer Jim had been unable to tolerate his political exile for more than a few months and was now determined to reclaim the Governor's Mansion. To Ferguson's audacious thinking, the fact that the legislature had forbidden him from running for office again was a baseless technicality, since he had resigned one day before the Senate officially removed him from office. So here he was again, declaring that the mild-looking, hair-parted-in-the-middle Governor Hobby was a "sissy," dismissing the legislature that had dismissed him as a den of crooks, and renewing his satisfying feud with the University of Texas. To Ferguson, the university was an autocracy on par with that of the evil kaiser, and among its many sins was the propagation of useless research, like that of the professor who the impeached governor claimed had gotten a research grant to prove "you cannot grow any wool on the back of the armadillo."

The threat of the return of Ferguson helped give women the ballot in Texas. It would require a national constitutional amendment for women to be able to vote in general elections, but a change in state law would allow them to vote in primary elections. And primary elections in a one-party state like Texas were everything. Minnie Cunningham was quick to let it be known that if the special session produced such an outcome, women would be pleased to support Hobby at the ballot box. "Vote in hand," she reasoned, "we will quite naturally concentrate on the man who enfranchised us."

In the election that November, the boost that women gave Hobby helped bury Ferguson in the primary—not that he would ever stay dead. And the election made history of another sort. Cunningham and the Texas suffragists enlisted a female candidate—Annie Webb Blanton—to run for state superintendent of public instruction. Blanton was a college English professor and the author of unexciting books like *Review Outline and Exercises in English Grammar*, but she proved to be a political knife fighter in her campaign against the incumbent, whom she painted as a tool of the brewery interests. In 1918, when many brewers were German Americans and the war had brought on widespread anti-German hysteria, this was close to a charge of being an enemy agent. With her opponent thrown off his guard and the newly unleashed women's vote behind her, she cruised to victory in the Democratic primary, carrying every county but one. Women couldn't yet vote for her in the general election, but that didn't matter, since she was unopposed. She was the first woman to win statewide office in Texas.

The special session in 1918 that gave women the half-vote had been called because of another issue that wouldn't relinquish its historic grip. The growing ranks of the temperance movement had harried Governor Hobby out of his safe middle-ground position on Prohibition. He was pressed into introducing legislation to outlaw the sale of alcohol within ten miles of military bases. This would, predicted a Baptist newspaper, "protect our soldier boys against evils more deadly than all the horrors and carnage of the battlefields." The law was passed and the soldiers were protected—at least until they were shipped off to the real battlefields in France.

During the same session, Texas became one of the first states to ratify the Eighteenth Amendment to the U.S. Constitution, and the next year it amended its own constitution to make Prohibition a reality before it went into effect for the whole nation, in 1920. The Eighteenth Amendment, outlawing "the manufacture, sale, or transportation of intoxicating liquors," had a Texan pedigree. Its primary sponsor was Morris Sheppard, who occupied the U.S. Senate seat that Joe Bailey had resigned in 1913. Sheppard was as progressive as Bailey had been Paleozoic. He was genial, sharply focused, short—five feet, four inches tall—and, surprisingly enough, not a hypocrite when it came to the horrors of alcohol. It was observed by a colleague that he was only one of three members of the Senate who voted for Prohibition who didn't drink. Indeed, he was "the driest of the drys." He had come under the thrall of temperance after joining the Methodist Church, and reportedly after seeing a picture in a biology textbook of the wreckage of an alcoholic's stomach. By the time he attended Yale Law School, he had given up liquor for good, determined to pursue his studies and subsequent political career with knightly purity.

"We are coming to understand," he had declared in a Senate speech in 1917, "that the engine of the body must have the same care as the engine of the aeroplane, the battleship, the railway train, the steamship, or the automobile; that the trade in alcohol is a form of sabotage which the human machine can not endure."

The virtues of abstemiousness were in vogue, but so was wild abandon. Less than a year after Sheppard introduced his Prohibition amendment, federal officials busted a hardworking still and destroyed four hundred gallons of moonshine on property that the senator owned. It wasn't Sheppard's operation—it was his lawless cousin's—but it was a lively and embarrassing demonstration of the practical limits of a virtuous public stance.

★

IN THE ABSTINENCE DEPARTMENT, EVEN SHEPPARD COULDN'T compete with Pat Neff. Neff was the son of a Texas Ranger and a devoted frontier mother named Isabella, who lived into her nineties, in time to see her son inaugurated in 1921 as governor. (When she died, he deeded their family property to Texas, creating one of its first state parks and naming it Mother Neff State Park in her honor.)

"It cannot be said that he was like other boys," remembered Neff's roommate at Baylor. "Strange to say, though a Texan born and a rustic, to this day he has never shot a gun, baited a fish hook, used tobacco in any form, nor drunk anything stronger than Brazos water."

Neff may have been a bewilderingly prim specimen for Texans to absorb—"Even Christ," someone observed, "made wine and went fishing"—but he was more in sync with the times than his main opponent for the Democratic governor's nomination, who was none other than Joe Bailey. Bailey mocked his nondrinking, nonsmoking, nonfishing opponent as "the wild man from Waco" and ran a rearguard campaign against blacks ("It's partly a matter of smell"), tax collectors, women anywhere outside the kitchen, Prohibition, and federal agents who threatened to bring down the wrath of the law onto "your good wife" for "squeezing the juice out of her own grapes for use on her own table."

Bailey, doing his best to turn back a half century or so of time, observed at one point in the campaign—apparently with some weird sort of approval—that Christ had never ridden in an automobile. That was one example the God-fearing Pat Neff didn't follow. He drove all through Texas by himself, six thousand miles in his own Model T, patching his own tires, shaking hands at blacksmith shops and small-town drugstores, and finally beating Bailey in a runoff by almost eighty thousand votes. The Wild Man From Waco went on to his inauguration, but not to an inaugural ball, since one of the things Pat Neff didn't think people should do was dance.

What Neff stood for was, as he put it in a written address to the citizens of Texas, "that righteousness that exalteth a nation." But righteousness was even scarcer in the state than usual, not least because of the new horizons of illegal enterprise that had been made possible by Prohibition and by the Volstead Act, its enforcement arm. "The good name of Texas is at stake,"

Neff fretted. "Vice in its most baleful and pernicious form is flaunting itself in the face of the people. The robber, the holdup man, the thief, the burglar, the gambler, the bootlegger and the murderer are all busy today with their respective professions. . . . Lawlessness seems atmospheric."

That was true nowhere more than in Galveston, which as an old pirate port had long ago set its table to take advantage of the glorious business opportunities that illegal alcohol represented. "Prohibition," Gary Cartwright wrote in his history of the island, "was a jackpot waiting to pay up."

Like other crime-friendly localities along the U.S. coasts, Galveston had its Rum Row. Vessels loaded with booze from Caribbean ports would anchor out at sea and unload their cargo onto shallow-draft boats that would stealthily slip into one of the numberless coves or unpatrolled piers along Galveston Bay. The smuggling was handled by two rival syndicates—the Beach Gang and the Downtown Gang—that were already running bars and vending-machine rackets and gambling joints. The leaders of the gangs presented themselves as pillars of the community, passing out toys at Christmas and contributing to charity and civic initiatives. When Prohibition came, a Sicilian-born barber named Rosario Maceo saw his chance to step up to something more lucrative when one of the smuggling gangs asked to use his beach cottage to stash a load of liquor. Soon Rose Maceo and his brother Sam (né Salvatore) had invested in the scene themselves, opening a "soda shop" that was a none-too-subtle front for bootleg liquor, and then in 1926 partnering with a couple of mobsters named Ollie Quinn and Dutch Voight on a glitzy air-conditioned nightspot and gambling den called The Hollywood Dinner Club, a venue that eventually hosted stars such as Frank Sinatra, Peggy Lee, and Guy Lombardo, and where Fred Astaire once picked up a paycheck as a dance instructor.

A decade and a half after The Hollywood opened, the Maceo brothers outdid themselves when they opened the Balinese Room, the much-loved, much-raided Polynesian-themed supper club that sat at the end of a pier reaching out into the Gulf. Prohibition had been repealed by then, but gambling was still illegal. The Maceo brothers dealt with that problem by stationing a hostess at the entrance to the club. When the Texas Rangers arrived to bust the place, she greeted them politely and pressed a buzzer at her feet, prompting the band in the Balinese Room to break into a warning rendition of "The Eyes of Texas." By the time the lawmen had made it through "Rangers' Run" to the business end of the pier, the gambling tables had flipped over and were hosting only harmless games of bridge and checkers, and the band was announcing, "And now, ladies and gentlemen, we give you, in person, the Texas Rangers!" (When Hurricane Ike destroyed the place in 2008, heartbroken Galvestonians combed through the crashing surf, hoping to retrieve some battered souvenir fragment of its glory days.)

THE LAWLESS ATMOSPHERE THAT GOVERNOR NEFF PREACHED

against also inevitably settled on boomtowns like Ranger. Nowadays, Ranger is a lonely little hamlet of a couple thousand people, with a museum in its old train depot, a surprisingly sprightly junior college, and some dreary downtown buildings with broken windows and a long-faded mural depicting an oil well with the words "Welcome to Roarin' Ranger" beneath it. Oil was discovered at Ranger in 1917, and by the early 1920s, around the time my father-in-law—the son of an oilfield roustabout—was born there, the town's population of 750 or so had been slammed by a population wave that might have reached thirty thousand—though nobody had time to take a proper count. There was nothing resembling infrastructure to accommodate such a startling influx of people. The trains coming to Roarin' Ranger were so packed that prospective oil-field workers had to ride on top of the cars and stand on the cowcatchers. When it rained, which it did for about two years, the streets turned into deep soggy channels. Since everybody in town was an entrepreneur, the problem was soon solved by pop-up ferry operators who hauled people from the one side of the street to the other on mud sleds or just hoisted them on their backs. Food was scarce, but money could be insanely bountiful. One visitor to Ranger, frustrated at not being able to buy a milkshake, went out and leased two hundred acres, bought thirty-eight cows, and started his own dairy.

Ranger may have been a tough town to find a milkshake in, but gambling and bootlegging and prostitution were throbbing enterprises—just the sort of place for the Texas Rangers to clean up. After the abuses that came to light during the Canales hearings, the Ranger force had been reduced (to only seventy-five officers and men). The organization was making an effort to shift its legacy away from the taint of casual assassination and back to law enforcement.

The Rangers tried their luck in Ranger, busting the Commercial Hotel, the town's central vice venue, and arresting ninety patrons. But there was too much money being made, and too many local law officials in on the action, for any charges to stick. The fines of the arrested men were kindly paid by the hotel's proprietors, and when the proprietors themselves went on trial, the boomtown jury promptly found them not guilty.

The Rangers had more effect in another boomtown called Mexia, a farming town in Limestone County not far from where the Parker family had built their fort on the edge of the Anglo frontier, and from which in 1836 the Comanches had carried away Rachel Plummer and Cynthia Ann Parker. It was a frontier place once again, though now a chaotic and industrial one, with a row of derricks—the Golden Lane—running along an oil-bearing formation called the Mexia Fault, and an unruly population that had spiked from 4,000 to 40,000. The lawlessness there was intense enough for Governor Neff to dispatch twenty Rangers—by then, almost half of the shrunken Ranger force—to raid a couple of thriving vice palaces called the Winter Garden and the Chicken Farm.

In charge of the Winter Garden raid was thirty-four-year-old Frank Hamer, the man who a few years back had threatened J. T. Canales with unspecified unpleasantness for "complaining" about the conduct of the Texas Rangers in South Texas.

Walter Prescott Webb included a semi-hagiographic sketch of Hamer in his book about the Texas Rangers. (Only semi-hagiographic because, in a bid for objectivity, Webb tallied up the Ranger's "faults," which were pretty much limited to stubbornness, poker, and impolitic integrity.) "If all criminals in Texas," Webb asserted, "were asked to name the man that they would most dread to have on their trail, they would probably name Captain Frank Hamer without hesitation."

It was true enough, even though Webb lamented that the passing of the old frontier had left such towering and lethal figures as Hamer marooned in a world where they were as likely to traverse the Texas landscape behind a steering wheel as upon a saddle, busting up moonshiners' stills instead of attacking Comanche camps. Whether Hamer himself felt out of time is another question. A natural horseman and a dead shot, he had an exquisite woodsy expertise when it came to tracking animals, calling birds out of the trees, or impaling harmless armadillos through their heads with a thrown knife. (As a boy, he said, "I made up my mind to be as much like an Indian as I could.")

But there was no nostalgic hesitation when Hamer and his fellow Rangers burst into the Winter Garden with shotguns and machine guns, or studied aerial photographs to locate moonshiners' camps. The twentieth century was here, and the Texas Rangers had crossed over to it. They "cleaned up" Mexia and the surrounding area, only to see it quickly revert to anarchy, since so many of the local judges, district attorneys and sheriffs were part of the criminal architecture. In the end, Governor Neff had to declare martial law, backing up the Ranger force with the National Guard.

———————— ★ ————————

THE MEMBERS OF THE NEW KU KLUX KLAN WERE ALSO, IN their minds, backing up Neff in the battle to suppress vice. The Klan flat-

*The very lethal, much-wounded Texas Ranger Frank Hamer,
shown here as a young enforcer of the law.*

tered itself that it had arisen to address the moral confusion and licentious-ness unleashed by World War I and the response to Prohibition. Its masked and robed members interrupted church services to win over congregations with donations of money or clothes or Christmas gift bags. But its true work was on the vigilante side, enforcing its ideas of righteous conduct and racial purity. "Again the blacksnake whip cracked and fell," wrote a *Dallas Times-Herald* reporter with unseemly enthusiasm. He had been invited along by the Klan to witness the whipping of a railroad dispatcher who was sus-pected of molesting a twelve-year-old girl. "The prisoner tugged against his bonds and sagged limply. The flitting of a myriad of fireflies in the damp weeds of the humid bottomlands made the scene a weird one. The hoot of owls and croaking of frogs on the river bank drowned the victim's groans."

Moral malefactors across the state—real or accused, or merely supposed—were beaten, tarred and feathered, castrated, and murdered. Many of the victims—like the black Houston dentist abducted and surgically sterilized for having some sort of relationship with a white woman—were punished for racial trespassing. But patrolling the color line was only part of the Klan's self-appointed mission. Its adherents were also vigilantes for virtue, as in the case of Beulah Johnson, a white woman who was employed at a hotel in the little town of Tenaha. The Klan, on hearing that she had remarried without legally divorcing a previous husband, convicted her of bigamy, kidnapped her, cut off her hair, stripped her, slathered her body with coal tar, then dumped her back in town.

In Williamson County, north of Austin, a white man named R. W. Bur-leson, a door-to-door salesman for the Real Silk Hosiery Company, was handed a warning in the form of an otherwise blank piece of paper with the letterhead of Klan Klavern 178. He was under scrutiny because of his rumored immoral relationship with a white woman, a family friend ten years his senior. A month and a half later, he was waylaid on a stretch of road near the San Gabriel River, threatened with castration, and then chained naked to a tree. The men who had abducted him took turns whip-ping him with a leather strap until, covered with blood, "as raw as a steak" from his knees to his waist, he finally broke down and confessed (falsely) to an immoral association.

The whipping stopped then. The Klan drove Burleson to the town of Tay-lor, tossed him out of a truck, poured creosote over his lacerated body, and then left him chained to another tree. He managed to extricate himself and make his way to the door of a nearby boardinghouse. "If Satin [sic] himself had walked into the Harbor House," wrote the local paper, "it would not have caused greater consternation than did R. W. Burleson last night, sock salesman out of Waco, when he appeared on the porch . . . before the boarders shortly after dusk with a chain locked around his neck and his head and face covered with black creosote."

It was the sort of outrage likely to be condemned by newspapers like the *Dallas Morning News* and the *Houston Chronicle*, by leading citizens like Houston mayor Oscar Holcombe, by state legislators like Wright Patman and Sam Ealy Johnson Jr. (the father of Lyndon Johnson), and by former Texas attorney general Martin McNulty Crane. Crane once discovered a group of Klan members burning a cross on his lawn and walked out of the house in his bathrobe. His questions to them—"Why do you come to my house in the middle of the night? . . . What can I do for you?"—were so disarmingly reasonable that the men could think of no better way to react than to disperse and go home.

"When a government ceases to enforce her laws," Governor Neff had declared in a message to the legislature, "it ceases to be a government and becomes a mob." But when it came to the Ku Klux Klan, his words were disturbingly hollow. "Why So Silent, Governor?" asked a frustrated *Houston Chronicle* editorial writer about Neff's chronic reticence to call out the Klan by name. Maybe he had a secret appreciation for the way the Klan went about its law enforcement agenda, maybe he was just a wily "business progressive" who knew his state and couldn't afford to alienate all the chamber of commerce types and law enforcement officials who were either members of the Klan themselves or applauding its work.

The man who had never baited a hook probably had no intention of targeting the Klan when he appointed a twenty-eight-year-old lawyer named Dan Moody to fill out the term of the just-resigned district attorney for Travis and Williamson Counties. "I have not the shadow of a doubt," Neff told Moody, "that you have the ability to make your administration as prosecuting attorney one that will strike terror to the hearts of the criminally inclined."

What Neff might not have anticipated was that Moody would be very interested in the criminal hearts of the members of the Ku Klux Klan, specifically the men who had chained R. W. Burleson to a tree, whipped him, and covered him with creosote for the crime of some sort of imagined indelicacy with a woman. Moody was determined, as he later said, to place "the Klan in the dock" and to show the people of Texas "how strong it had become, how arrogant were its pretensions, what a menace it was to the peace and order of the State."

Dan Moody's mother was a math teacher. His father was old enough—almost sixty when Dan was born—to have trailed cattle to Missouri before becoming mayor and justice of the peace in the Central Texas town of Taylor. Their ambitious, industrious son taught himself how to be an electrician and then wired houses to put himself through college. He was tall, with slightly wavy red hair and an expression in his eyes that, in old photographs at least, is combatively direct.

In September 1923, six months after R. W. Burleson's ordeal, Moody began prosecuting the men who had abducted and beaten him. The trials were held in the Williamson County courthouse in Georgetown. A statue outside the

DAN MOODY
became a rising star in Texas politics when, as a young district attorney, he dared to take on the Ku Klux Klan in a criminal trial.

building honors the young district attorney. Moody is depicted as coatless, ready for action in a form-fitting vest and rolled-up sleeves, his hat in one hand and a law book in the other. It's maybe a little too idealized, a little too pugnacious, but Jessie Daniel Ames, the suffragist and antilynching advocate who sat through the trials, noted that Moody—a crusading prohibitionist who was said to have never tasted alcohol—"seemed drunk on fight."

The proceedings, which involved the sequential prosecution of five of the men accused of assaulting Burleson, turned out to be a sensation. "The great auditorium of the county's temple of justice," wrote the local newspaper, "was crowded from the opening hour each day until the close at night." Among those watching the results closely were the Klan members who sent threatening notes to Moody and to James R. Hamilton, the presiding judge. "A close friend informed me," one of them wrote in an anonymous letter to Hamilton, "he understood the plan was to take you out, shave your head, tar you, [and] ride you on a rail. . . . This was held in abeyance hoping you would let up on your persecution of the Klan and its membership and turn your efforts toward the real menace to our city, viz., bootlegging."

Unintimidated, the judge pressed on, and so did Moody, who by the time the trials ended in February 1924 had secured the convictions of all five defendants and become a shooting star in progressive Texas politics. "And ladies," a local county judge thought it relevant to point out, "he's totally unmarried."

<hr />

★

THE SAME YEAR HE BEAT THE KLAN IN COURT, MOODY BEAT IT
at the ballot box. He defeated the Klan-backed candidate to become the state's youngest attorney general. The 1924 election year in Texas was a significant one, certainly so in the reckoning of Jim Ferguson, who on January 3 had predicted in the pages of his self-promoting newspaper, the *Ferguson Forum*, "The most momentous political year in the history of Texas is now upon us."

And where there was momentousness, there was Farmer Jim, who as usual was tirelessly trying to spring himself from political exile. In 1920, he had announced his candidacy for president of the United States, declaring in a campaign broadside that he had "more real friends and more mean enemies than any man that ever lived in the Lone Star State." His presidential run did not make much of an impression—only eighty-five people showed up for his opening campaign speech—but that didn't dissuade him from running for the U.S. Senate in 1922. (As an impeached governor, he was barred from holding state offices, but not federal ones.)

The near-comatose incumbent in that race was Charles Culberson, a former governor who had represented Texas in the Senate since 1899 but had not set foot in the state for the last ten years. Culberson was old and frail and a problem drinker, known around Washington as the "sick man of the Senate." Ferguson owed the old man a few political favors, but that didn't stop him from joining the scrum of challengers determined to unseat him. After a runoff, Ferguson's main competition for the Senate seat turned out to be Earle Mayfield, a member of the State Railroad Commission and the handpicked candidate of Hiram Evans and the Ku Klux Klan. For this race, Ferguson, who was already on record as being against Prohibition and against women voting, decided he could create productive political mischief by being against the Klan as well. He thus presented Texans with the interesting problem of whether to vote for a demonstrated crook or for an obvious tool of the Invisible Empire.

To give you an idea of what a perverse choice it was, Jessie Daniel Ames, who was the president of the League of Women Voters and who in a few years would found the Association of Southern Women for the Prevention of Lynching, felt forced to back Mayfield, the Ku Klux Klan candidate, against Ferguson. At least Mayfield didn't want to take the ballot out of women's hands. And then there was Prohibition, that still dearly held pillar of progressive belief. A journal called *Home and State* put the issue clearly to its readers: "Of recent weeks the metropolitan press of Texas has overflowed with denunciation of the Ku Klux Klan and yet has been as silent as an oyster on the question of bootleggers and moonshiners. . . . Candidily [*sic*], of the two evils we would take the Ku Klux Klan."

Ferguson campaigned with his usual thrilling invective, calling his opponent, among other things, "a lowdown, stinking, contemptible, pusillanimous, gambling little upstart hypocrite." But with his strange-bedfellows coalition of the Klan and disheartened progressives, Mayfield won the runoff by 44,000 votes and then the general election. Although Moody had won his convictions and also won his race for attorney general in that election, Mayfield's victory had helped remind voters that the Klan was perilously close to the center of Texas cultural and political life. One case in point: even as Dan Moody was putting the organization on trial in Williamson County, Imperial Wizard Hiram Evans was welcoming seventy-five thousand Klansmen, along with their wives and children, to the officially designated "Ku Klux Klan Day" at the State Fair of Texas.

Jim Ferguson had lost a round in his defeat for the U.S. Senate in 1922, but in 1924 he was back in action, ready to be the Texas governor again. He tried at first to promote the illusion that his impeachment had been invalid, but when that didn't fly, he just put his wife Miriam's name on the ballot and sent her out on the campaign trail. The unassertive woman who was on record as saying things like "Personally, I prefer that men shall attend to all public matters" was an obvious placeholder for her husband. Nobody was naive enough to believe that Farmer Jim, if Miriam won, wouldn't be the real governor.

The 1924 election was not just a race for political office. It was a referendum on the Ku Klux Klan. A Klan publication in Houston predicted as much: "It is going to be the greatest and fiercest political battle ever waged in Texas. The fight is between the K.K.K.'s and the J.J.J.—Jew, Jug, and Jesuits."

Ferguson once again positioned himself—or his wife—as the anti-Klan candidate, but since he was such an all-embracing bigot, he did so with dizzying hypocrisy. He wasn't about to allow the Klan to get the upper hand when it came to anti-Semitism, so he went after them in the pages of the *Ferguson Forum*, claiming "an unholy alliance between the Big Jews and the Big Ku Klux, where the Ku Klux are to get the big offices and the Big Jews are to get the big business." He even attacked Hiram Evans, the Klan's Imperial Wizard, for the outrage of allowing his black servant to ride with him in a whites-only Pullman car. "All along you have said," he lectured the Klan in the pages of the *Forum*, "that you were in favor of white supremacy. . . . Now your present grand gizzard is a 'nigger lover.' "

The official candidate was nowhere nearly as incendiary as her husband. "I know I can't talk about the Constitution and the making of laws and the science of government," she frankly admitted, and about the highest campaign pitch she could reach was when she affirmed, "I have a trusting and abiding faith 'that my Redeemer liveth.'" It pained her that this faith was not shared by her husband. "Men of his type," she sighed in a statement soon after the announcement of her candidacy, "need Christ in their hearts at all times more than men of milder natures."

But it was one of those familiar times in Texas history in which milder natures were in short supply. Two of the men running against Miriam for the Democratic nomination attacked each other relentlessly—a questionable strategy, since they had the same last name and created enough confusion to cancel each other out. For her part, Mrs. Ferguson left the thunderbolt hurling to her husband. She allowed herself to be posed for photographs at the family farm in a borrowed sunbonnet while peeling peaches and hoeing the garden. It was a bogus tableau—Miriam never wore bonnets, had no interest in farmwork, and had an active dislike of cows—but it was campaign catnip to the press. Her new campaign identity was further sealed by the fact that the candidate's name—Miriam Amanda Ferguson—got shorthanded to M. A. Ferguson in the newspapers, and from there it was no stretch to get to Ma Ferguson and for Farmer Jim to have another enduring nickname—Pa.

Ma and Pa triumphant: the Fergusons soon after Miriam—subbing for her impeached husband—was named the Democratic nominee for Texas governor.

It was Ma's bonnet against the Ku Klux Klan's hood when the Democratic primary was held in August. Mrs. Ferguson won decisively against Hiram Evans's handpicked "klandidate," a judge and World War I veteran named Felix Robertson, whose own father and grandfather had been Confederate generals. In the general election, the Republican she faced was a University of Texas Law School dean that Pa dismissed as a "little mutton headed professor with a Dutch diploma." He put up a spirited fight and polled decently, but Texas was still a Democratic state with a bent for novelty, and so it elected Miriam Ferguson. She was very nearly the first female governor in the history of the United States. On the same day that Ma was elected in Texas, Wyoming's Nellie Tayloe Ross was chosen in a

special election to fill the governor's seat vacated by her husband, who had died in October. But she got the first-ever record because her inauguration took place less than two weeks before Ferguson's.

"I am now going home," Ma's professor opponent said in defeat, "and, like our genial friend, Mr. Pickwick, I am going to 'reflect on the mutability of human affairs.'"

Whether or not he came to any conclusions, there was a lot of mutability to reflect over. The victory of the Fergusons more or less sealed the fate of the Klan's dominance in Texas, even though, as one critic, a Methodist minister, observed, "so far as the Klan was involved, Ferguson and his cohorts triumphed simply because they out-kukluxed Ku Kluxism."

The departing governor, Pat Neff, left a white rose for Mrs. Ferguson in his office as a hopeful symbol of executive purity. He also left a Bible, open to the verse in Psalm 119 reading, "Thy word is a lamp unto my feet, and a light unto my path." It was a nice try, but as soon as Jim Ferguson saw the Bible, he closed it, set it and the white rose aside on a nearby windowsill, and informed his newly elected wife, "Sunday school is dismissed. The Governor's office is now open for business."

———— ★ ————

BOY, WAS IT. FOR THE NEXT TWO YEARS, WHILE
Mrs. Ferguson occupied the governor's chair, her husband threw himself into the work of rebuilding the shaky family fortune, trying to reclaim his even shakier reputation, and settling scores with his enemies. When it came to income, he appears to have quickly identified several potential streams of influence-peddling revenue. Pa's newspaper, the *Ferguson Forum*, proved especially handy in this regard. Before the election, it was a shoestring affair that didn't make enough in advertising to pay its mailing costs. That changed overnight. Ferguson printed special editions of the *Forum* that were swollen with ads from just the sort of firms—brewers, asphalt manufacturers, banks, oil companies, utilities—that were likely to appreciate an influential friend high up in state government. It was also suggested—that is, required—that all state employees buy a one-dollar subscription to the *Forum*.

Jim Ferguson was not a member of the three-person Texas Highway

MIRIAM AMANDA FERGUSON *in the governor's chair. She was almost—but not quite—the first woman governor in American history, though not because of any progressive inclinations of her own. "I prefer," she stated, "that men shall attend to all public matters."*

Commission, but that didn't prevent him from dropping in on its closed-door meetings and sharing his wisdom about which oddly high bidders should be awarded road-building contracts. The road business in Texas at that time was booming. There were 16,445 miles of state highways. There were almost a million cars in the state, and the Texas Highway Commission had $20 million to spend. And Jim Ferguson, as the unofficial but unmistakable head of this commission, was more than happy to award contracts to the firms that were the most generous advertisers in his newspaper.

"The highway department revelations were only the big show under the big tent." That was the conclusion of Don H. Biggers, a West Texas newspaper editor, former state legislator, and author of an exasperated satirical summary of the career of Farmer Jim, whose rococo title deserves to be printed in full: *Our Sacred Monkeys: Or, 20 Years of Jim and Other Jams (Mostly Jim), the Outstanding Goat Gland Specialist of Texas Politics: A Thousand Chuckles and a Thousand Facts, Showing the Amusing Humbuggery of the Whole Business, Particularly since Jim Broke Into the Game in 1914.*

Biggers went on to point out that Ferguson's "little sideshow" scandals were "scattered all over the premises." Among them: charging cash to newspapers and magazines for interviews with the governor, taking kickbacks (allegedly) from publishers to have their textbooks selected by Texas schools, and granting a suspicious number of pardons—3,595 of them during Ma's two-year term. Nobody ever quite proved that the pardons were for sale, but the anecdotal evidence just kept rolling in, with $5,000 often attached as a price tag. Among the most abiding stories of the Ferguson years is the one in which a man riding in an elevator with the governor accidentally stepped on her foot. He said, "Pardon me," to which Ma answered (drolly, one hopes), "You'll have to see Jim."

There was some serious friction between Jim Ferguson and Attorney General Dan Moody—as Don Biggers noted with sarcastic understatement in *Our Sacred Monkeys*, "Jim and Dan were not mated for political harmony." There was no chance for friendly relations when Moody was actively investigating the highway commission's odd habit of awarding contracts to the highest bidders, or blocking Pa's attempt to get the Texas Senate to pass an amnesty bill restoring his right to run for state office. "The war is on," the governor's agitated husband declared when Moody got in his way, "and I do not know where it will end."

Well, it ended with Dan Moody beating Miriam Ferguson in the 1926 governor's race. By that time, most of the state's largest newspapers had come out against Ma and Pa, and the governor herself, after a brush with impeachment, had vainly tried to calm the roiling political waters churned up by her husband, by declaring January to be "Laugh Month."

Texans had had enough (for now) of Jim Ferguson. They delivered a stinging rebuke in the form of an almost two-to-one victory for Moody in the Democratic primary runoff. But Governor Ferguson kept writing pardons up until the day she and her husband grudgingly left office, including one for Murray Jackson, one of the men that Moody had spectacularly convicted when he put the Klan on trial a few years before.

"If I am condemned and criticized," Mrs. Ferguson speechified on her way out of the governor's office, in words that might very well have been penned by her grandiose, grievance-minded husband. "I shall not murmur because I remember that Sam Houston, the Father of Texas, paid the same penalty."

Everyone must have winced at that unsolicited reminder of the contrast between the state's glorious past and its grasping present, but Texas moved on. The national press, looking for a suitable Lone Star hero, predicted that the newly elected thirty-three-year-old Dan Moody, the "implacable foe of the Ku Klux Klan," would be the next Abraham Lincoln. The *Philadelphia Inquirer* even reported that he had "the most brilliant blue eyes this writer has ever seen in a human head." In the end, he turned out to be a perfectly okay governor: a little stiff, not exactly a political maestro, and not even an antiracist. (In later life, he led a group of anti–New Deal Democrats called the Texas Regulars, who espoused, among other things, "the purity of the white race.") But he was earnest and incorruptible, and when he announced his candidacy for a second term in January 1928 there was no doubt that he would be reelected.

But it was too soon to write off Jim Ferguson. Like Old Rip, who emerged desiccated but breathing from the cornerstone of the Eastland County courthouse that same year, he was still somehow strangely viable.

★

PART FIVE

The
EMPIRE
— of —
TEXAS

—37—

MUSIC AND MAYHEM

BY THE END OF THE 1920S, TEXAS HAD A STATE BIRD (THE
mockingbird), a state flower (the bluebonnet), a state tree
(the pecan), and a state song. "Texas, Our Texas," according
to Christian Wallace, who tore the song to shreds in a 2016
Texas Monthly article, is "a brassy alma mater . . . a sugary
concoction of obtuse patriotic sentiment and rubber-wristed
backslapping, a mouthful of cotton candy."

But there are those of us who like it, or at least can't quite help being
suckered in by it, by its determination to present Texas as a magisterial
realm where its citizens are privileged by God to live.

The idea of a state song was Pat Neff's, who initiated a contest to provide one while he was governor. Out of 286 entries, the eventual winner
of the $1,000 prize came from a songwriting team from Fort Worth, Wil-
liam J. Marsh and Gladys Yoakum Wright. Marsh, born in England, was a
music professor at Texas Christian University whose later works included an
opera called *The Flower Fair at Peking*. He was also a devout Catholic with an
interest in sacred music, which may explain why "Texas, Our Texas" gnaws
on at a liturgical pace and has been found persistently unsingable by generations of Texas elementary school students. The lyrics were written by Gladys

Yoakum Wright, whose great-uncle, Henderson Yoakum, was a close friend of Sam Houston's and the author of a seminal history of Texas. Wright's unabashed words—"Texas, Our Texas! All hail the mighty State! / Texas, Our Texas! So wonderful so great!"—have the brute force necessary to slap awake her collaborator's sleepy melody, and—if you're in a chauvinistic frame of mind—it can be a stirring anthem.

But even those of us who have a secret fondness for "Texas, Our Texas" recognize that it's official music, state-approved music, real in its own way but nothing like the polyphonous Texas soundtrack that had been emerging for decades all on its own, unbidden by gubernatorial decree.

Scott Joplin had been dead and long removed from Texas soil by the time "Texas, Our Texas" was performed for the first time in the state Capitol. He died in 1917 of syphilis at the age of forty-nine in a New York hospital. But he was Texas born and, to an important degree, Texas educated. The son of a former slave, he had musical instincts and the good fortune as a boy in Texarkana to make the acquaintance of a German-born music professor named Julius Weiss, who gave him a proper, though informal, education in music practice and theory. It was enough to equip him with a career as a piano player in whorehouses and saloons in the wide world beyond the Red River, where his specialty was the intricate haywire style of playing that was known at first as "ragged time." Joplin composed music himself, and—thanks to the lessons of Professor Weiss—he could write it down, which led to a lucrative publishing career. "Maple Leaf Rag," whose sheet music he published in 1899, sold 100,000 copies in a year. He was proud and opinionated when it came to his syncopated compositions. "That real ragtime of the higher class is rather difficult to play," he informed aspirants in the introduction to a book of piano exercises he published in 1908, "is a painful truth which most pianists have discovered. Syncopations are no indication of light or trashy music, and to shy bricks at 'hateful ragtime' no longer passes for musical culture."

Music snobs inclined to shy bricks at ragtime would probably not have ventured too close to a Dallas area off Elm Street known as Deep Ellum. The old freedmen's town had grown into a heady entertainment district alive with domino parlors, brothels, and music clubs. It was here, probably around 1912, that two sharecroppers' sons started playing music together. Blind Lemon Jefferson would have been nineteen or twenty then. He had been sightless, or mostly so, from birth. Huddie Ledbetter was a few years older. Born in Louisiana, he had been scraping around Texas for a few years, playing in saloons and dives.

Jefferson's journey to international blues fame was smoother than Ledbetter's, but substantially briefer. The composer of the plaintive song "See

That My Grave Is Kept Clean" and of "Black Snake Moan" (whose unforgettably chilling lyrics include the lines "I ain't got no mama now" and "Mmm, black snake crawlin' in my room") was discovered by a scout for Paramount Records and whisked off to Chicago to launch a robust recording career. His flexible, high-pitched voice—"He hollered like someone was hitting him all the time," remembered another blind bluesman, the Reverend Gary Davis—was rustically appealing to consumers of what was then called "race music." But he lived only a few years after leaving Texas, dropping dead of a heart attack in the middle of a Chicago snowstorm. His body was sent home to be buried in Freestone County, in a forlorn black graveyard that is now proudly known as the Blind Lemon Memorial Cemetery. The inscription on his tombstone reads: "Lord, It's One Kind Favor I'll Ask of You. See that my Grave is Kept Clean."

Blind Lemon Jefferson was thirty-six when he died. Huddie Ledbetter made it to sixty-one. His career was slower to take off than Jefferson's, possibly because for much of his early life he was incarcerated. He went to prison in 1918 for murder, acquired the nickname Lead Belly somewhere along the way, and was pardoned after seven years by Pat Neff, who was impressed with Ledbetter's twelve-string virtuosity and confident vocals. Neff had heard him sing during several inspection visits to Texas prison farms. One of Lead Belly's compositions that favorably struck the governor was a song titled "Governor Pat Neff," which featured the lyrics "If I had you Governor Neff like you got me, / I'd wake up in the morning, I would set you free."

Neff did set him free, but Lead Belly was back in prison five years later on a charge of assault, this time in Angola, Louisiana. His visitors there included John Lomax, then in his mid-sixties and still tenaciously on the hunt for folk songs and work songs to record. With him was his eighteen-year-old son Alan. "I'll never forget," Alan told PBS's *American Roots Music* about Lead Belly. "He approached us all the way from the building where he worked, with his big twelve-string guitar in his hand. He sat down in front of us and proceeded to sing everything that we could think of in this beautiful, clear, trumpet-like voice that he had, with his hand simply flying on the strings. His hands were like a whirlwind and his voice was like a great clear trumpet."

Aaron Thibeaux "T-Bone" Walker eventually pushed the blues ("that ol' feelin'," in the words of Lead Belly) toward the electric horizon. He grew up in the Oak Cliff section of Dallas but made his way over to Deep Ellum in time to be of service to Blind Lemon Jefferson, who needed somebody to help lead him down the crowded streets from one gig to the next, and to pass around a tin donation cup while he was singing. T-Bone Walker went on to cut his first record in Dallas—"Wichita Falls Blues"—in the same year

Huddie Ledbetter, better known as Lead Belly, was convicted of murder as a young man but was paroled after he met Pat Neff and impressed the governor with a song—flatteringly titled "Governor Pat Neff"—that pleaded for his release.

that his Deep Ellum mentor collapsed and died in Chicago. Jefferson was on the obese side, but Walker was lithe and irrepressibly physical, a musical acrobat who danced and did the splits and, when he electrified the blues in the 1930s, created a style legacy that led down through the generations to Chuck Berry and Jimi Hendrix.

Jim Rob Wills, a fiddle player whose day job was cutting hair at Hamm's Barber Shop in the Panhandle town of Turkey, moved to Fort Worth in 1929, where he found work as a blackface performer in a medicine show and started a two-man dance hall band. By then he had shortened his name to Bob Wills. Western swing, the exuberant, yipping, yodeling, fiddle and steel-guitar musical expression he was helping invent, had some blues shooting through it, but at heart it was white man's music—not untroubled by history, but not committed like the blues to the exploration of personal and ancestral pain. But it was still people's music, and the people needed it. Nineteen twenty-nine, the year that both Wills and T-Bone Walker made their first records, the year that "Texas, Our Texas" was adopted as the state song, the year that Blind Lemon Jefferson died in the snow, was also the year when, on October 29, sixteen million shares were traded in one panic-stricken day on the New York Stock Exchange, leading to the collapse of the stock market and the beginning of the Great Depression.

"WHY DON'T SOMETHING HAPPEN?" A DEEPLY FRUSTRATED young woman named Bonnie Parker had written in her diary the year before. She was seventeen, living in an industrial community across the Trinity River from Dallas whose name, Cement City, could not have been more evocative of the stuck-in-place life she considered herself to be enduring. She was a high school dropout, married at fifteen to a man whose name she had tattooed on her inner thigh but who had soon gotten bored and essentially run out on her. "Let all men go to hell!" she confided to her diary after a lonely New Year's Eve with a girlfriend. "But we are not going to sit back and let the world sweep by us."

This was not just angsty teenage rhetoric. Bonnie Parker had a real fear of the world sweeping by her. She was pretty, flirtatious, verbal, troublesome, and recklessly ambitious. There had to be a way out of Cement City, and if she could only find it she believed she had the makings of a poet or a movie star. But right now she was a waitress, and soon enough not even that.

At first, the stock market collapse and all that it portended seemed like a distant issue to most Texans, a problem for Wall Street and the investor class of a faraway East Coast culture. Texas did not have an imaginary, spec-

*An outlaw portrait taken around the time of Bonnie Parker's
poetic prophesy—"it's death for Bonnie and Clyde."*

ulative economy; it had cotton and lumber and livestock and oil. "More and
more it appears," the editor of the *Houston Post-Dispatch* wrote in an attempt
to enforce calm less than a month after Black Tuesday, "the changes in stock
prices are purely an affair of and for stock speculators."

But as he wrote this, the Dallas restaurant where Bonnie Parker worked
was already closing due to a sudden shortage of customers. She became one

of the eight million people in the United States who were out of a job. She was living with her mother, doing her best to help pay the rent by babysitting and housecleaning when she met Clyde Barrow at a friend's house in 1930. He was twenty, short and slight but sharply dressed, and in suspicious possession of a nice car. Barrow had grown up on farms in East Texas, where his father worked on shares, but when cotton prices fell after the end of the war the family moved to West Dallas, a shantytown suburb from which the office buildings of thriving downtown Dallas gleamed like an unreachable Oz. The Barrows lived in a campground, and Clyde's father worked as a junkman, picking up scrap metal in a horse-drawn cart. Like Bonnie, Clyde was determined to enter the sealed-off world of prosperity and glamour that was tauntingly visible in movies and magazines. He was upwardly mobile in a criminal sort of way, having graduated from stealing chickens and turkeys to stealing cars.

They fell hard for each other, although soon after they met Clyde was hauled off to jail for car theft. "They only think you are mean," Bonnie wrote to him. "I know you are not, and I'm going to be the very one to show you that this outside world is a swell place, and we are young and should be happy like other boys and girls."

To help him get back into the outside world, she smuggled a gun into the McLennan County jail in Waco so that he and two other prisoners could escape. But he was back in custody soon enough, this time sent to Huntsville and the notorious Eastham Prison Farm. Eastham was known as the "Bloody 'Ham," because so many prisoners routinely chopped off their own toes to escape the hellish ten-hour days of field work. Eastham also had a reputation for appalling food, sadistic prison guards, and wanton predation by fellow inmates. Clyde Barrow had gone into the Texas prison system as a dapper, high-spirited thief; he left it with a darkened soul. He was repeatedly raped by another, more powerful prisoner, and one day he killed his assailant by crushing his skull with a lead pipe. Nobody was charged with the killing, which was written off as self-defense, and in February 1932, Clyde was free on parole, though he was on crutches when he was released and would never walk right again. Two months before, despairing that there was no way out of an eternity of field work but the traditional Eastham remedy, he (or a helpful friend) had chopped off his left big toe and part of the next one.

Bonnie had no hesitation about joining the gang that Clyde formed after his release. She was caught after the botched robbery of an East Texas hardware store and confined to jail for a few months before being released when the grand jury believed—or at least chivalrously chose to believe—her story that Clyde and the gang had kidnapped her and forced her to participate in the robbery. She passed the time in jail by composing poems, emerging with a collection called *Poetry from Life's Other Side,* written on old bank forms.

She was still in jail when Clyde Barrow's gang killed its first victim, during a robbery at a general store in Hillsboro. The fact that an innocent man had died at their hands didn't seem to trouble Bonnie, who was mad for excitement and shared Clyde's rationalized grudge of having been forced into criminality. "They made him what he is today," she told her family. "Folks like us haven't got a chance."

The robberies escalated, and so did the killings, and so did the range of Bonnie and Clyde's increasingly desperate life on the run. For two years they evaded pursuit in stolen cars through eight states, killing civilians who got in their way and police officers, marshals, and prison guards who tried to stop them. They escaped two chaotic shootouts, including one in Missouri that resulted in the death of Clyde's older brother, Buck. Another misadventure occurred when Clyde was driving seventy miles an hour along a dark road in 1933. The car he had stolen soared off the road and rolled over. Acid from the smashed battery flowed down the length of Bonnie's right leg, burning it in places down to the bone. She survived, but from then on she had a painful, hopping gait, and sometimes had to be held upright by Clyde, who himself had only eight and a half toes to stand on.

By that time, their intoxicating highwayman romance had degenerated into a drawn-out, cold-blooded killing spree. And the outcome for the notorious and glamorous outlaw couple—who were rumored to have once danced to the Western swing music of Bob Wills's fiddle band at the Crystal Springs Dance Pavilion in Fort Worth—was increasingly obvious. A few weeks before she died, Bonnie presented her mother with another original poem, and not a terribly bad one either, called "The End of the Line." The last of its sixteen stanzas reads:

> Some day they'll go down together;
> And they'll bury them side by side,
> To a few it'll be grief—
> To the law a relief—
> But it's death for Bonnie and Clyde.

That death was orchestrated by Frank Hamer. No longer a Texas Ranger, he was a temporary state investigator earning $180 a month whose sole job was to track down and apprehend Clyde Barrow and Bonnie Parker. Hamer had had a rough few years. In May 1930, in the Northeast Texas town of Sherman, he and three Rangers and a handful of other law officers had been all that stood between a black farmhand named George Hughes who was accused of rape and an unhinged mob of thousands determined to break into the courthouse to lynch him.

Hamer and his Rangers held back the mob by beating its leaders over the head with their .45s. That worked for only a while. "If you put your foot on the step," Hamer told one of the men as he guarded a stairway leading up to the courtroom where the trial was getting underway, "I will shoot it off."

He did, and Hamer did. That held the attackers back long enough for the Rangers to take the prisoner from the courtroom and lock him in the court clerk's steel vault on the second floor. But the enraged citizens of Sherman set fire to their own courthouse and slashed the hoses of the firemen who arrived to put out the blaze. By that evening, Hamer and his men had been forced to retreat to the county jail, a block from the courthouse, where they had to dodge lighted sticks of dynamite thrown from the crowd. The furor of the lynch mob reached such an insane pitch that one woman held up her baby and called out to the National Guard soldiers who had arrived to help Hamer and his men. "Shoot it," she screamed at them, "you yellow, nigger lovin' soldiers! Shoot it!"

It ended with George Hughes dying of smoke inhalation in the vault as the courthouse burned down around him. His body was dragged behind a car, hanged, and burned for further desecration, and a thousand African American citizens of Sherman fled in terror as the white mob began to burn down their homes and businesses. It took the arrival of three hundred more National Guard troops and the imposition of martial law to restore order.

Hamer emerged with his hero status not totally intact. "One Riot, One Ranger" had been the unofficial motto of the Texas Rangers since the turn of the century, when, supposedly, a captain named Bill McDonald had stepped off a train alone to quiet a brewing Dallas mob. "Where's the rest of the outfit?" the mayor had asked. "Rest, hell!" McDonald replied. "You ain't got but one riot, have you?"

But this time, the riot had overwhelmed the Rangers. Hamer, one of the most authoritative, intimidating figures in Texas Ranger history, a veteran of many gunfights and unkillable receiver of many gunshots, had lost his prisoner to a lynch mob. But that wasn't the reason he was no longer a Texas Ranger. In January 1933, he was fired, along with the entire Ranger force of forty-four men, by Miriam Ferguson.

Yes, she was the governor again. Dan Moody had been succeeded by Ross Sterling, one of the founders of Humble Oil, a man who was so wealthy and who had such farsighted career goals that he had built a replica of the White House for himself on the shores of Galveston Bay. But he assumed office just as the Depression was tightening its grip, when Texas banks were closing, the price of both cotton and oil were falling, and state revenues were dwindling while state expenses were rising. The stage was set for a populist candidate, and who could be more populist than Ma and Pa Ferguson? With the help of some energetic ballot packing, they edged out Sterling in the Democratic primary. But Sterling was still governor, and he sent Hamer and the Rangers to look into the voter fraud. They discovered barrels full of fake ballots and observed that "great numbers of tramps were taken off freight trains . . . and were herded to the polls by election officials." The investigation was a gesture that Jim Ferguson did not appreciate, and as soon as his wife took the governor's oath for the second time, he had her dismiss the entire Ranger force and replace them with friendlier and more compliant faces.

Hamer had taken a leave of absence before the axe fell, but he was still out of a job until he was hired to track down Bonnie and Clyde in February 1934. The manhunt lasted until May and ended in western Louisiana, where Hamer and five other lawmen, acting on information from a gang informant, hid themselves in the brush on the side of a country road, waiting for the outlaws' car to appear.

"As daylight came," Hamer remembered, "a few cars passed, and occasionally a logger's truck. . . . It was probably about 9:10 when we heard a humming through the pines that was different from that made by the other motors. A car was coming from the north at a terrific speed, singing like a sewing machine."

Hamer knew that Bonnie and Clyde were extremely dangerous and not likely to give themselves up—they had already killed nine peace officers— but he hated the thought of shooting a woman. His plan to give them a chance to surrender evaporated when one of his deputies opened fire. After that, it was a full-on barrage, all the lawmen firing at once with shotguns, rifles, and pistols. Bonnie was wearing a red dress and a white tam hat. In the recollection of one of the officers, she "screamed like a panther" as she was hit more than forty times. Some accounts say she was holding a pistol in her hand, others a sandwich. Her body was bent forward, her head between her knees. Next to her, in the driver's seat, Clyde slumped with dead weight against the steering wheel. "When all was said and done," one of the officers recalled about seeing the results of the ambush when he peered into the death car, "they weren't nothing but a bunch of wet rags."

—38—

THE BOY FROM
THE HILL COUNTRY

TEXANS HAD TAKEN A TIME-OUT FROM THEIR LONG HIS-
tory of being a one-party state to vote for Herbert Hoover,
a Republican, for president in 1928 over Al Smith, who—as
a Catholic, a New Yorker, and an opponent of Prohibition—
struck the traditional Texas voter as an alien Democratic
species. But the Depression had taken hold by the time of
the next presidential election, in 1932, when Texans were hungry enough
and snarky enough to call the armadillos that they were reduced to hunting for food "Hoover hogs." So the vote swung decisively back to the Democrats, to Franklin Roosevelt and his running mate, John Nance Garner.

Garner held the home-state advantage. He was a white-haired, bristly-
eyebrowed, cigar-gumming Texan in his mid-sixties. In 1902 he was first
elected to the House of Representatives, where for years he kept his head
down, saying little, making no speeches, steadily gaining expertise and
seniority until he became Speaker in 1931. He was born in a log cabin a few
years after the Civil War in the Northeast Texas town of Blossom Prairie.
The country was so thinly populated back then that the baseball team he
played on had to pull from so many local communities that it went by the

JOHN NANCE GARNER,
*from Uvalde by way of Blossom Prairie, was Franklin Roosevelt's vice president
and part of his Texas power trust.*

wonderfully aggregate name of Blossom–Coon Soup Hollow. Garner became
a lawyer and moved west beyond San Antonio to a town on the southern
edge of the Hill Country called Uvalde. He was already a crusty character,
serious about poker and serious about drinking, when he was elected to
the state legislature in 1898. Among the bills he introduced was one that
would have made the cactus the state flower. The bluebonnet lobby was too
powerful for the bill to pass, but Garner got the most lasting of his many
nicknames out of it: Cactus Jack.

At the apex of his long career in the House, when he was elected Speaker,
Garner gave an acceptance speech memorable for its crotchety clarity: "I
made no promises as a candidate for this office," he said, "and I make none
now." But that didn't mean his ambitions stopped there. The next year, he
actively campaigned for the Democratic nomination for president, but released his delegates at the convention when he saw he would lose, and
expressed the hope that they would vote for Roosevelt.

As vice president, Garner used his formidable legislative skills to help
steer the president's recovery bills and New Deal programs through Congress. But he was far from the only Texan in FDR's power sphere. There was
also the magnificently bald, sad-eyed congressman Sam Rayburn, who had

been Cactus Jack's campaign manager during his brief presidential run. Rayburn was a graduate of East Texas Normal College, but his political education had begun when he was a young boy on a forty-acre farm in the Northeast Texas town named for the Goliad commander James Fannin. Working in the cotton fields from the age of five, he had watched as the profits from his family's crop disappeared into the pockets of mortgage holders and middlemen and the railroads, which charged unfair rates to get the cotton to market. All that, along with having a father, a Confederate veteran, who

The very powerful and very lonely Sam Rayburn, the longest-serving Speaker of the House in United States history. He was one of the Texans who became a force in Washington politics during the FDR administration.

"never stopped hating the Yankees" for the Republican Reconstruction regime imposed on the South after the Civil War, turned young Rayburn into a lifelong Democrat. When he was twelve, he had a boyhood epiphany when he heard Joseph Weldon Bailey—then a congressman—speak at a church tent meeting in Bonham. "He went on for two solid hours," he remembered of that starstruck moment "and I scarcely drew a breath the whole time. I can still feel the water dripping down my neck."

Transfixed, the barely teenage Rayburn vowed to someday run for the Texas Legislature, become its Speaker, and then get elected to Congress by the age of thirty. All of which he did. He was a hot-tempered and incorruptible presence there, a man who could not be bought and who regarded lobbyists, a friend of his wrote, "with a venomous hatred."

Though he was bashful and uncertain around women, he managed to get married in 1927, fifteen years after he was elected to Congress. It took him nine years to propose, by which time he was in his mid-forties. His bride was almost twenty years younger. They were married for three months. Something went mysteriously wrong, and the divorce was so crushing that Rayburn never attempted marriage again. He plighted his troth instead to the House of Representatives, though he maintained a wistful reverie of "having a little towheaded boy to teach how to fish."

Decades later in his career, when he became the longest-serving Speaker in U.S. history, the *New York Times* dubbed him "Mr. Everything," an honorific that was a grade above his usual affectionate nickname Mr. Sam. He first became an indispensable force during the early years of the Roosevelt administration, serving as chairman of the powerful Interstate and Foreign Commerce Committee, playing a major role in reining in the unregulated Wall Street dealing that had unleashed the Depression, and helping create the Rural Electrification Administration, which brought electricity at long last to places like the Texas Hill Country, where the paleolithic darkness was relieved only by lanterns and hearth fires.

Another Texas member of Roosevelt's team was Tom Connally—"the only man in the United States Senate," in the judgment of an observer of that institution, "who could wear a Roman Toga and not look like a fat man in a nightgown." I guess that means that with his six-foot bearing and big face and tight wavy hair, he carried himself with immutable gravitas. He didn't wear a toga, but deep into the 1930s he hadn't purged his closet of his Edwardian wardrobe, since he was still seen around town in a frock coat and detachable collar, with a pince-nez hanging from a black ribbon. Connally was a reliable New Deal Democrat, though he and FDR had a break in their political alliance in 1937 when he refused to go along with the president's attempt to boost the fortunes of his legislation by his "court-packing" plan to expand the number of justices on the Supreme Court.

And then there was Jesse Jones, the courtly and shrewd Houston mandarin whose empire had originated in a prosperous family farming business and grown to include banks, oil, lumber, real estate development, and newspapers—he owned the *Houston Chronicle*. He had never cared to run for elective office, and had never needed to. His great wealth and his business efficiency naturally found him a cozy chair in the power suites of Texas and Washington. He had helped finance the Houston Ship Channel and had brought the 1928 Democratic National Convention to Houston by hand delivering a $200,000 check to the bidding committee in Washington and then throwing himself into the effort to build—in only sixty-four days—the convention hall that Houston didn't happen to have handy. Now that Roosevelt was president, Jones was the chair of the mighty government agency known as the Reconstruction Finance Corporation, which functioned as a bank to fund marquee New Deal programs like the Works Progress Administration and the Tennessee Valley Authority.

———— ★ ————

LYNDON BAINES JOHNSON WILL SOON BE WEAVING IN AND OUT of these pages, so now—during the New Deal years, when he first started to make a national impression—is probably as good a time as any to introduce him. Or maybe to leave the introduction to his mother, Rebekah Baines Johnson, who was of course very much present at his birth. "Now the light came in from the east," she wrote about the fateful Texas Hill Country morning of August 27, 1908, "bringing a deep stillness, a stillness so profound and so pervasive that it seemed as if the earth itself were listening. And then there came a sharp, compelling cry—the most awesome, happiest sound known to human ears—the cry of a newborn baby; the first child of Sam Ealy and Rebekah Johnson was 'discovering America.'"

Rebekah Johnson—who as a girl had once set her sights on writing a historical novel—did not blush at recollecting her first child's birth as a dramatic, world-changing event. She was twenty-seven when Lyndon was born, in a lonely dog-run cabin on the banks of the Pedernales River. Lyndon's younger brother, Sam Houston Johnson, had the opinion that their mother "was probably the best-educated woman in the whole county." Rebekah's grandfather was the Baptist preacher who had ministered to Sam Houston. Her father was a lawyer, newspaper editor, and former Texas secretary of state. She had experienced a refined childhood, growing up in a two-story stone house near the town of Blanco. "I love to think of the gracious hospitality of that home," she later wrote, "of the love and trust, the fear of God, and the beautiful ideals that made it a true home." But Blanco turned out to be a temporary paradise. While she was away at college in Waco (she studied literature at Baylor), her father went broke, moved the family to Fredericksburg, and died two years later.

In Fredericksburg after college, Rebekah worked as an elocution teacher and a stringer for the Austin newspaper. Among the people she interviewed was Sam Ealy Johnson, the rising politician who held the same seat in the Texas Legislature that her father had once occupied. In photographs taken when he was a young man, Sam Johnson looks a lot like his more famous son: tall and rangy, with a pinched mouth and giant ears. He was a lot like Lyndon in other ways as well: gregarious, aggressively persuasive, brimming with appetite, propelled by a natural-born arrogance. "Hell," a neighbor recalled of this particular family characteristic, "the Johnsons could strut sitting down."

As a legislator, Sam Johnson was notable from the start, introducing one successful bill after another, including the one that authorized the state to buy the deteriorating Alamo. ("Santa Anna took the Alamo," wrote a newspaper reporter, "that was 1836. Sam Johnson saved the Alamo—that was 1905.") He was a people's Democrat who had a reputation for honesty and who had refused to bow to pressure when the oil and railroad interests tried to keep the legislature from investigating Senator Joe Bailey for doing their bidding.

Rebekah Baines's interview with Sam Johnson in 1907 led to a fast-paced courtship and marriage that same year. It was also the year that her husband decided not to run again for the legislature. He had started out his political career in debt and ended up broke, having lost all his money by speculating in cotton futures. So he decided to become a farmer and moved himself and his new wife away from the relative cosmopolitanism of Fredericksburg to a sagging shack in the isolated heart of the thin-soiled Hill Country. Rebekah Johnson brought along her volumes of Tennyson and Browning, her exquisitely thin china teacups, but like generations of Texas pioneer women before her she was thrust into a world of loneliness and grueling physical labor. "At last," she wrote, "I realized that life is real and earnest and not the charming fairy tale of which I had so long dreamed."

Her new baby, though, was right at home. At picnics, Lyndon Johnson wriggled out of his parents' grasp to jump into the arms of strangers. "Sam, you've got a politician there," one of them told his father. "I've never before seen such a friendly baby."

But as Johnson grew up, his eager openness turned out to be only one thread in a blindingly complex character tapestry. His father drank too much. His mother's enveloping love could sometimes mysteriously disappear. He

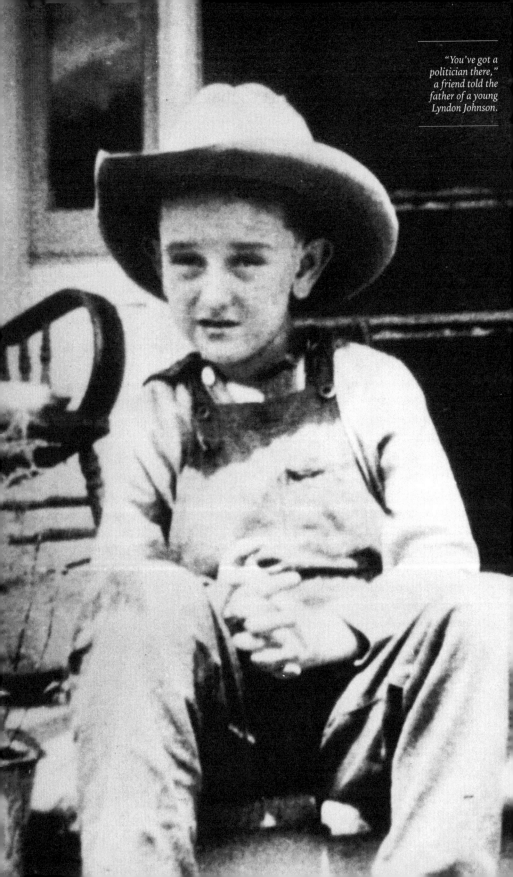

had terrible dreams. In one of them, sparked by the cattle-driving tales he had heard from his grandfather, and by the reality of witnessing his grandmother paralyzed by a stroke, he saw himself sitting in a chair all alone, immobile and helpless on the Texas plains, screaming for his mother as a herd of stampeding cattle thundered toward him.

Look up Lyndon Johnson in the indexes of his biographers and you'll find phrases such as these: "grandiosity of," "deceit and skullduggery of," "need for love and attention," "obsequiousness," "bragging and exaggeration," "confidence/assurance and insecurity," "courage and cowardice," "viciousness," "compassion for poor," "sense of inherited superiority," "fear of losing," "conducts business in bathroom."

All these contradictory traits were streams channeling their way into a great river of personality. In 1927, Lyndon Johnson came flooding out of Johnson City—a town founded by a distant cousin, where the family had moved when Lyndon was five—to enroll at Southwest Texas State Teachers College in San Marcos. At that time, Johnson City was a tiny rural-crossroads community with no running water or electricity. San Marcos, at the eastern edge of the Balcones Escarpment, between Austin and San Antonio, population 5,000, was by comparison a surging cosmopolis. Earlier Johnson City students who had found their way to the college there had been flummoxed by the electric lights in their rooms. When they wanted to go to sleep and were unable to figure out how to turn off the glowing globes that hung from the ceiling, they just hid the still-glowing lights in a drawer.

Johnson was somewhat worldlier than that. After his father had been reelected to the legislature, Lyndon had spent time in the Capitol, staring down from the House gallery and soaking in all the deal making taking place on the floor. And when he was sixteen he and several boyhood friends had set off on an escapade to California that ended up lasting more than a year. By the time he had hitchhiked the thirty miles from Johnson City to San Marcos to go to college, he had a rampaging sense of ambition and a genius-level homing instinct for the places where power existed and the hidden sources where it could be kindled. Almost immediately upon arriving at college, he began shamelessly ingratiating himself with its president, Cecil Evans, fetching his newspaper in the morning, carrying his wife's groceries. In a little over a month, the new freshman had created a job for himself as the president's de facto assistant, and when he began writing editorials for the student newspaper, he made sure his flattery was smotheringly thick: "Great as an educator and as an executive, Dr. Evans is greatest as a man."

Student offices were dominated by an organization called the Black Stars. With Lyndon Johnson on campus, the Black Stars were soon dominant no longer. He took command of a rival group called the White Stars and turned it from a wan student-activity alternative to a governing powerhouse. His energy was inspiring and bewildering. He brought campaigning, caucusing, and horse-trading to student offices that few people cared about and that previously had been sleepily doled out. When Lyndon Johnson showed up among the seven hundred students clustered in this isolated college in Central Texas, he brought politics with him.

When he was a sophomore, Johnson interrupted his class work to take a job teaching at a school in Cotulla, the same South Texas town where William Sydney Porter had gotten off the train many years before to recover from tuberculosis and listen to stories about John Wesley Hardin. When Johnson arrived in 1928, Cotulla had three thousand residents, most of whom were Tejanos who spoke only Spanish and worked for Anglo ranchers and farmers. He taught at the town's "Mexican school," and for the nine months he was there, he was also, at nineteen years old, its principal. Looked at through a contemporary lens, his time in Cotulla might seem like the idealistic field work of a naive young savior—one who made $125 a month, filled his charges briefly with hope and inspiration, and then headed off again to finish his degree. But this was also Lyndon Johnson at his best. He had big cultural blind spots—he forbade the use of Spanish in his school, and his Texas history lessons were tales of Anglo triumphalism—but he was serious about helping his students envision breaking out of their closed-in horizons. He organized sports teams, paid for equipment out of his own salary, and furiously goaded the students into believing that their horizons were limitless, that in this country any one of them, if they wanted it bad enough and worked hard enough, could be anything they dreamed of being. He felt for the kids in his school, he identified with them in their isolation, and he projected on them the same fevers that were burning in him. "He told us," one of the students remembered many years later, "we were looking at the future president of the United States."

When he got a job a few years later as secretary to Richard Kleberg, the King Ranch heir who was a newly elected U.S. congressman, Johnson quickly saw the benefit of having a distracted boss. He seized control of the congressman's Washington office, driving the staff sometimes to work eighteen hours a day, demanding that every letter or request from every constituent be answered the same day, not with a form letter but with an emphatic personal response. When he joined the Little Congress, an organization of congressional secretaries, he did the same thing he had done with the White Stars at Southwest Texas State Teachers College—discovered a hitherto neglected power source and boosted its amperage, turning it from an incon-

Lyndon Johnson proposed marriage to Claudia Taylor on the day they met. She said yes, and from then on the sense of excitement in Lady Bird's life "certainly didn't decline."

sequential parliamentarian society into something glamorous and important enough to command the attention of big-time political figures such as Huey Long and Fiorello La Guardia.

Johnson was in Austin on a business trip for Kleberg when he met Claudia Taylor. She had just graduated from the University of Texas and had taken a year off before having to decide whether to become a secretary or a teacher or a journalist, waiting to "see where fate led." She had grown up in a big slave-built white-columned house in the town of Karnack, deep in the pine forests of East Texas. Her father was a hard-driving businessman who owned stores and cotton gins and 65,000 acres of land—the richest man in the county. Her mother—cultured, ethereal, and fragile—had died when Claudia was five, and was remembered by her almost as a ghost. "I have a vague memory of her having some sort of illness and losing some of her hair, and from then on she did wear turbans a good deal, and she would walk through the house very swiftly."

Claudia had long been known in the family as Lady Bird, a nickname given to her either by her black nurse, Alice Tittle (who thought her "as purdy as a lady bird") or—as she related in an oral history a few years before she died—by two black childhood friends. She was shy, lonely, self-possessed, bookish (she read *Ben-Hur* when she was eight years old), but also—as she grew older—confident and determined.

"There was something electric going," she recalled of her first meeting with Lyndon Johnson. "He came on strong, and he was very direct and dynamic. I didn't know quite what to make of him."

On the day they met, they rode around Austin in his car and he proposed marriage—or rather insisted on it. She thought he was joking at first, but he took her to meet his parents the next day, and then to the King Ranch to meet the Klebergs, and a few months later he hustled her through the doors of a church in San Antonio, still arguing her into marriage as they walked up the aisle to the altar, where the minister he had summoned at the spur of the moment was waiting.

"My sense of excitement mounted," she remembered of their honeymoon in Mexico and their first few weeks together, "and certainly didn't decline. I just found it more interesting as we went along."

They went along with blurry speed. Lady Bird's new husband vowed that when he went back to Washington it would be as a congressman, and a few years later—after amassing more power and expertise running the Texas division of FDR's National Youth Administration, after strategic assaults of flattery upon influential Texas elders like Sam Rayburn, after a grueling, gutter-level campaign in which two days before the election he had surgery that saved him from a ruptured appendix—Lyndon Johnson was the congressman for the Tenth Congressional District of Texas. He was twenty-eight years old when he arrived in Washington in 1937, and he was there to stay.

LYNDON JOHNSON
FOR
UNITED STATES SENATOR

ND UNITY
B DONE"

A Panhandle homestead during the Dust Bowl of the 1930s. The family who lived in the house in this photo managed to hold on, but most of their neighbors were forced to leave and look for a new life someplace where the soil hadn't been blown away.

— 39 —

CENTENNIAL

BEFORE THE GREAT DEPRESSION VISITED TEXAS, AN OLD Testament–style catastrophe had been brewing for years in the High Plains of the Panhandle. The wheat farmers there, in response to a surplus market, had done what farmers all throughout the southern plains had done: plowed up more land and planted more wheat in an effort to stay even as the market price for their crop dropped by two-thirds. The waving grass-lands that had bewitched Coronado and his men, that had fed the great herds of buffalo and the cattle that replaced them, had been torn up by plows and lately by exponentially more efficient gasoline-powered tractors. Great swaths of famous ranches like the XIT had been targeted as agricul-tural land and aggressively peddled to farmers—"Get a farm in Texas while land is cheap," the ads read, "where every man is a landlord!"

But it was the deep, tightly laced roots of the native buffalo and grama grasses that had held the soil in place throughout the ages as the ever-scouring wind, unblocked by trees or geography, swept across the plains. Now millions of acres of that grassy sod were gone, with nothing left to stop the wind from carrying the remaining dirt away. Beginning in the early 1930s, dark towering columns reaching from the ground up to 10,000 or more feet into the atmosphere began to coast ominously toward Panhandle

A duster strikes:
"the blackest dark
you ever saw."

towns such as Dalhart and cities such as Amarillo. There was no word yet
for what they were. They weren't sandstorms, or at least the kind of sandstorms that anybody had experienced before. They became known as black
dusters or black blizzards. Even though the winds that drove them might be
blowing at sixty miles an hour, they approached seemingly without fury, at a
stately, indomitable pace across the landscape. Ahead of the dusters, the sky
turned black with birds flying frantically to escape.

"It was just like a high wave rolling over and over toward you," an employee of Charles Goodnight's old JA Ranch recalled. "When it got to you,
it looked like it had hit the ground about a hundred yards on the other side
of you. From then on it was so dark that you couldn't strike a match and see
the light. . . . It was the blackest dark you ever saw."

There was enough dust in those storms to create a greasy atmospheric
texture—"not just black," one woman remembered, "not just thick—it was
black thick." And the storms had a granular invasiveness. The dust slipped
through the minute crevices of even the best-built homes. There were
people who swore it could penetrate glass. The black dusters were alive
with atmospheric electricity that caused barbed wire to glow green with
St. Elmo's fire and lifted the tails of horses and shorted out cars. Jackrabbits were electrocuted by static electricity, and men learned not to shake
hands during a storm because the charge it would generate could knock
them over.

A storm would last for days, and then another one might come along
a few weeks later. The masks issued by the Red Cross would be so coated
with black blizzard residue that they were unusable. People died from silico-
sis and bronchitis, and from something called dust pneumonia, an infection
that took hold after the lungs filled up with dust.

As for the places where those people lived and died or fled from in the
great Dust Bowl exodus, photographs from that time are bleakly iconic:
abandoned farms and homesteads, weathered boards with the paint stripped
away, lonely windmills rising out of choking drifts of dust, tumbleweeds
nestled against barbed-wire fences, providing a substrate for the accumulation of unnatural dunes. These are vistas filled with drifts and banks that
the black-and-white photography fools you into thinking might have something to do with Christmas, until you realize you're looking not at a snowy,
wintry panorama but at a landscape that is dead and buried. When the
dusters finally stopped blowing through, around 1937, almost a third of the
farmers in the Texas Panhandle had given up and left.

★

EVEN AS THE DEPRESSION GOT UNDER WAY, HOPE WAS SURG-
ing in one place in Texas, at least for a while. This was in and around the
East Texas town of Kilgore, which was destined to become not only the boyhood home of the pianist Van Cliburn but also the birthplace of the Kilgore
Rangerettes, the world's first women's precision drill team, whose motto
was "Beauty Knows No Pain." But by the time of the stock market crash,
Kilgore was just another town of only a thousand or so people in the center
of a region whose farming population had already been hit hard by drought
and plummeting cotton prices. During the 1920s, geologists from some
of the major oil companies scouted out the area, knowing that beneath it,
at fairly shallow depths, ran the oil-rich formation known as the Woodbine Sand. But the Woodbine was vast, and the odds of any particular well
ending up in the right spot were so long that the majors and most wildcatters were lured by better prospects elsewhere.

That was not the case with Columbus Marion Joiner, who would soon
become known as "Daddy of the Rusk County Oilfield," and then just "Dad."
He was sixty-six when he arrived in East Texas in 1926, way past his physical
prime and permanently bent over at the waist, but his fast-talking acuity
was still sharp. He had served in the Tennessee Legislature for a single term
before heading to Oklahoma to try his skill in the oil business. His specialty
was to charm widows into selling him their mineral rights. He had prospered
briefly, but was seriously down on his luck by the time he came to Texas.
He was following a wildcatter's hunch that there was oil to be found in the
Woodbine under Rusk County. Soon with him was his old partner, a man
named Joseph Idelbert Durham, who called himself Doc Lloyd and passed
himself off as a geologist—in fact, not just a geologist, but also "one of the
greatest living scientists."

In a past life, Doc Lloyd had studied enough pharmacy to become a
snake-oil entrepreneur and promote his products at his own medicine show.
He had six ex-wives, was six feet in height, and weighed three hundred
pounds (or probably more). He was even older than Dad Joiner and was still
a hustler at seventy when he came to East Texas. The two of them were a
formidable pair—the earnest, seasoned wildcatter with a nose for oil and the
seemingly unassailable scientist armed with a report on Rusk County's oil
potential, a "Geological, Topographical, and Petroliferous Survey" that he
had written himself and that was pure fiction.

The funny thing was, they struck oil. Not only that, they discovered the
East Texas oil field, the biggest yet known in the world, a pool of oil forty-

three miles long and twelve and a half miles wild, sprawling over five Texas counties. It happened in 1930 after they had already drilled two failed wells on the farm of a widow named Daisy Bradford. But the Daisy Bradford No. 3 was different. Because it had already shown signs of life, in the form of a geyser of oil-laced mud, eight thousand spectators were present on the October day in 1930 when Joiner's crew began to bore through the cement plug blocking the hole. It was a shoestring operation, a "poor boy" well. They were out of firewood to power the boilers and had to throw in old tractor tires, whose smoke blackened the air as night fell. Around nine o'clock, a column of oil spewed through the burning tire smoke when the well finally came in, showering down upon the farmers and their families who had been standing there for a day and a half, waiting for something momentous to happen.

A famous photograph taken a month earlier, after the Daisy Bradford No. 3 had passed the drill-stem test, which confirmed it was likely to be a productive well, shows Dad Joiner in a necktie and straw boater shaking hands with Doc Lloyd, who wears a cowboy hat and whose stomach is ballooning out over the belt holding up his khaki jodhpurs. Standing with them around the wooden derrick is the Daisy Bradford No. 3 drilling crew, and among them, also wearing a straw boater, with a cigar in his mouth, is a man that Dad Joiner had just met: an oilman named Haroldson Lafayette Hunt.

H. L. Hunt at that time was forty-one, not yet extravagantly wealthy. But he was doing all right in the oil business, even if his financial life was still on the skittery side. He was operating more than a hundred wells, and his company, Hunt Oil, had offices in Shreveport and El Dorado, Arkansas. He lived in Shreveport, or maybe in Dallas. It was hard to say, because he had a family in each place, and neither knew the other family existed. He was a bigamist with two wives who had six children from one marriage and four from the other. He had been a child prodigy who could read the newspaper aloud at the age of three and was breast-fed by his mother until he was seven. He was magnetic, arrogant, and restless; and he had a tendency toward paranoia that came into full anticommunist flower in the 1950s.

"I believe we have the biggest thing found in Texas," the Daisy Bradford's driller told a newspaper reporter just after the well came in. It was an opinion that H. L. Hunt shared, even though a few days later the well's flow started easing off and the magnitude of Joiner's find was in doubt. But it was not in doubt to Hunt, who had hired a spy to feed him information about a well that another company was drilling northwest of the Daisy Bradford, and whose success would confirm that the Daisy Bradford No. 3 was not an isolated windfall but a signal that there was a seemingly inexhaustible reservoir of oil in this part of the Woodbine.

DAD JOINER
*(in necktie) and his self-styled geologist, Doc Lloyd (in oversized jodhpurs),
congratulating themselves on bringing in the Daisy Bradford No. 3, the well that opened up
the world's greatest oil field. The man in the straw boater with the cigar in his mouth
is H. L. Hunt, who is about to get away with most of the profits.*

But Dad Joiner was in trouble. He held the leases to over five thousand acres, but to raise money to drill his wells he had sold far more investment certificates than he could redeem. When he struck oil and his investors wanted their money, his pyramid scheme came to light, and he was forced to hide out in the Baker Hotel in Dallas. That was where H. L. Hunt found him, and that was where he made a deal with Joiner to pay him $30,000 up front, along with $1.305 million in future oil payments, for a field that would eventually return over five billion barrels of oil. It was one of the greatest business deals in Texas history, though maybe more than a little bit skeezy, since, because of his spy network, Hunt knew more than Joiner did about the potential value of his property. They closed their deal at midnight and celebrated with cheese and crackers. Hunt went on to become the richest man in the country. Dad Joiner, though, was never as rich as he thought he deserved to be, and when he died in 1947—following a series of lawsuits launched by his embittered wife and children after he ran away to Mexico to marry his young secretary—all that he had left in the way of assets was his house and his car.

There was no doubt, though, that Dad Joiner with his oversold certificates, and Doc Lloyd with his baseless geological know-how, had stumbled onto something really big. Two years after the Daisy Bradford No. 3 came in, the East Texas oil field—now known as the Black Giant—was hosting 5,652 producing wells. A young roughneck named Gerald Lynch was typical of the men who smelled opportunity in the new discovery during the Depression. "I was broke as a convict," he remembered, "needed a job, and East Texas was booming. I headed for Kilgore."

He found a familiar sight: a small town swamped with brand-new dance halls and hamburger stands, with derricks wedged in between buildings and looming over graveyards, with boomtown entrepreneurs throwing up privies so that they could charge new arrivals ten cents for each bathroom visit. Traffic was so bad that driving through the scant few blocks of downtown Kilgore suddenly took over two and a half hours. The East Texas oil field was the most intense boom so far in Texas history, and for people like Gerald Lynch it was a lifeline in the midst of a grim economic time. Life in the oil fields was dangerous. Men died from explosions and falls from derricks. They died when cables broke and came whipsawing across the drilling platform or when they lost their footing and got sucked down into sludge pits. And the pay wasn't great, but it was pay. It was better than having to stand in line at a soup kitchen or hauling your family to California to work in the fields.

And the discovery of the East Texas oil field represented a new chance not just for roughnecks and tool pushers, but also for down-on-their-luck wildcatters and independent operators, since the Woodbine was shallow and could be drilled the way Dad Joiner had, using somebody else's cast-off equipment, rusty drill pipes, boilers salvaged from old cotton gins, and creaky wooden derricks.

But the ease of production, and the gargantuan size of the field, set Texas up for a big fall. Suddenly there was too much oil. Crude that was selling for $1.10 a barrel when the Daisy Bradford No. 3 came in was down to 5 cents a barrel a year or so later. The obvious solution to the problem was to impose drilling limits, a temporary expedient that the big companies could weather but that could drive the small operators—who were still making a shaky profit even when the price of oil was bottoming out—quickly out of business.

The Texas Railroad Commission, the state agency set up during the Hogg administration to regulate freight and passenger fees, had expanded its jurisdiction so that it was now also in charge of pipelines and oil production. It proclaimed a drilling limit: the East Texas oil field could produce only 160,000 barrels a day—less than a third of what was already coming in. Everything else was "hot oil," a product not much different from moonshine liquor in the eyes of the regulators.

H. L. Hunt and other big operators had pressed for exactly the sort of limits—known as proration—that the Railroad Commission imposed, but so many people ignored the new rules that Governor Ross Sterling declared martial law and sent in the National Guard to close down the field. That worked for a little while, but the purveyors of hot oil got wily quick. They deployed left-handed valves that looked closed when they were open; they built hidden pipelines and dummy oil wells. One man ran pipes to his bathroom and installed a harmless looking plumbing valve so that he could operate his well out of sight of regulators as he soaked in his tub.

Real moonshiners, though, were on their way out of the picture. Prohibition hadn't quite worked out when it came to improving the character of the American people. Senator Morris Sheppard, the Texan who wrote the text of the Eighteenth Amendment, and who believed with all his heart that alcohol was a toxic affront to the well-regulated functioning of the "human machine," had argued in 1930 that "there is as much chance of repealing the Eighteenth Amendment as there is for a hummingbird to fly to the planet Mars with the Washington Monument tied to its tail."

But by then the hummingbird was already beating its way to the troposphere. People were weary of Prohibition, the Depression had dried up the funds that made enforcing the Volstead Act even remotely possible, and a tax on legal alcohol was beginning to seem like a handy way to provide revenue for the government. The ratification of the Twenty-First Amendment in 1933, which repealed Prohibition, gave Texans who were tired of buying their liquor through bootleggers or at speakeasies something to celebrate during an otherwise dark time.

———————— ★ ————————

THERE WAS SOMETHING ELSE TO CELEBRATE: TEXAS ITSELF. IN 1936, a hundred years had passed since Sam Houston had defeated Santa Anna on Peggy McCormick's San Jacinto pastureland, and now the nation-state created by that eighteen-minute battle paused to congratulate itself and gaze back at its history in amazement and approval. I've already described the Texas Centennial Exposition, the monumental Art Nouveau buildings hurriedly erected on the grounds of Fair Park in Dallas, the robotic dinosaurs, the seven-hundred-foot-long reflecting pool, and the historical pageant performed daily on the world's largest stage. What the exposition meant to Texans, in linking their present Depression reality with their imagined glorious past, is harder to sketch. Over six million people visited the fair. A representative pilgrim, maybe, was my grandmother Ruby King McLaughlin, born in Ennis, Texas, in 1885, the daughter of a Confederate cavalry trooper who served in Bradford's Regiment during the Civil War, helping guard Galveston against federal invasions. In 1936 she was a widow with an eighteen-year-old son (my father) and a thirteen-year-old daughter. My father died before I was born, so I never heard from him about the automobile excursion they took from Tennessee to Texas. My grandmother never mentioned it, and my Aunt Dorothy, when she was old, brought up the journey she had taken as a teenager only in passing, as a way to comment on how much easier highway travel had grown during her long life. It was only after her death that I connected that adventurous and tedious road trip with its Centennial destination. Now it's left to me to speculate about the motivation for the journey—a need on my grandmother's part to see Texas again, to show it off to her Tennessee-born children?—and about the reactions the three of them might have had to the wonders on display.

Who might have been circulating among them in the crowds as they strolled down the great Esplanade toward the Texas Hall of State, past the water fountains that leapt in time to "The Yellow Rose of Texas"? Maybe Andrew Jackson Houston? The only surviving child of Sam and Margaret Houston was eighty-two. He had made failed runs for governor in 1910 and 1912, honoring his mother's natural temperance and his father's late-in-life sobriety by positioning himself as a candidate of the Prohibition Party. After his defeat, he turned to writing about Texas history, producing newspaper and magazine articles and a book about his father's San Jacinto campaign. At the time of the Texas Centennial, he was in charge of the very ground where that battle took place, serving as superintendent of the San Jacinto battlefield. Keenly interested in the astonishing milestone that Texas had reached, he had been following the Centennial rivalry that had developed between Dallas and Fort Worth.

Fort Worth, which was thirty miles west of Dallas and had begun in 1849 as a frontier garrison near the confluence of the Clear and West Forks of the Trinity River, was now—thanks to its history as a cattle trail and railroad hub, as well as an oil, banking, and meatpacking center—a prairie metropolis of 170,000 people. Its undisputed first citizen, the newspaper publisher and philanthropist Amon Carter, supposedly had such disdain for the neighboring city to the east that he brought a sack lunch whenever he had to visit there, committed to not spending a dime in Dallas.

Now, in the state's centennial year, Carter engaged the over-the-top New York impresario Billy Rose to create a spectacle in Fort Worth—where, he affirmed, "the West begins"—to draw the spotlight away from the grand exposition in Dallas ("where the East peters out"). Rose showed up in Fort Worth wearing a ten-gallon hat and a deputy's badge, walking around with a two-headed snake, and promising to stock an attraction called the "Frontier

Follies" with one thousand beautiful girls. "The exposition in Dallas will show the progress of art, education and culture during the last 100 years," he noted, "but my exposition will show just the opposite."

"Is Texas celebrating its independence," wondered the son of the hero of San Jacinto when this news reached him, "or the birth of musical comedy?"

Alex Ferguson, Pa Ferguson's younger brother, was a visitor to the exposition. Alex had no doubt that Jim was a crook—"He is my brother and I know him" is the reason he gave for supporting his opponent in the 1929 governor's race—and he had bitter personal feelings toward him after Jim had spent six years trying to break their late sister's will, which gave pretty much everything to Alex and another brother and only a hundred dollars to their problem sibling, Farmer Jim. As they were touring the fairgrounds, Alex's son Sam asked him why he was carrying a six-shooter. He told the boy that it was in case they ran into his uncle.

Jeff Hamilton, Sam Houston's former slave, was ninety-six years old and much appreciated by white statesmen and historians for his generous comments about Houston and his seemingly untroubled recollections of a benevolent master-slave relationship. I don't know whether he made it to Dallas for the exhibition, but he was present at one of the statewide centennial events, the dedication of a historical marker at the site of Sam Houston's old summer getaway on the shores of Galveston Bay, and he was called upon to speak. "That old Negro made the finest address of the day," in the judgment of the president of the Centennial Association. "He recounted, with all the ease and poise of a veteran after-dinner speaker, humorous episodes, campaign yarns, and some of the deadly thunderbolts 'Old Sam' hurled at political enemies."

Hamilton had what he called "rheumatics," but he was sharp of mind and wit and didn't look, a visitor noted, a day over eighty. He had never been to school, but he could read. He lived in the Central Texas town of Belton and had for almost fifteen years had been the janitor at Mary Hardin-Baylor, the women's college there. The professors lent him books, and he read so much that the school's president once joked to a visitor that his janitor had read enough Texas history and English literature to qualify for a postgraduate degree.

The governor during the Centennial year was the personable, New Deal–friendly James V. Allred, better known to his friends and Texas voters as Jimmie. Sometime during 1936, Jeff Hamilton came to Austin, and Allred accompanied him to the Treaty Oak, a massive live oak that grew on what used to be the western boundary of the city. The last time Hamilton had seen the Treaty Oak, he was in the company of Sam Houston. "Jeff," Ham-

The Centennial of 1936 presented an opportunity for Texas to position itself as a rising state, no longer a vestige of the defeated South.

The Grand Esplanade at the Texas Centennial Exposition. The fountains in the reflecting pool leapt in rhythm to "The Yellow Rose of Texas."

ilton remembered Houston telling him, "I want you to remember what I am going to tell you about this tree. The Indians have been coming here for hundreds of years. They would hold their war councils and have their war dances and other ceremonies under its shade. . . . It got to be looked on by them as a holy tree."

In Hamilton's recollection, Houston told him that the tree was "holy" to the Indians and almost as holy to the Texians because it was under its branches that Stephen Austin had made one of the first treaties with the Comanches. Houston also told Hamilton about the time the great naturalist John James Audubon came to visit him when he was president of the Republic of Texas, and how on Houston's recommendation he had traveled to Austin to see "this king of all Texas trees." When Audubon returned, he told Houston that "he was sure the tree must be at least five hundred years old and that it should live hundreds of years more."

He was right, probably. The Treaty Oak that Jeff Hamilton stood under with Sam Houston, and then seventy-five years later with Governor Allred, is still alive at the time of this writing, though it suffered a near-death experience in 1989 when it was poisoned with a deadly herbicide by a feed-store employee who was said to have been trying to entrap its psychic energy to win the love of a woman. The "holy tree" underwent drastic emergency pruning, and its spreading canopy is significantly diminished, but it's still alive, still revered, and still producing acorns.

—40—

PASSIONATE ONES

SCHOOLCHILDREN, OF COURSE, WERE AMONG THE VISITORS
to the great fair. Governor Allred suspended classes statewide for two days "in recognition of the unprecedented
educational advantages offered at the Texas Centennial
Exposition." There were special railroad rates for school
groups, and one town, Nacogdoches, commandeered the
city's taxis to send students to Dallas.

No doubt some of the children who saw the exhibits at the exposition
and came home filled with the requisite fervor for their state were from a
school in the little town of New London, in the center of the Black Giant oil
field and only a few miles from where Dad Joiner had drilled the Daisy Bradford No. 3. The town had originally been called London, in that East Texas
way of naming hopeful little villages in honor of great world capitals. But
"New" was added when the residents discovered they weren't the first Texas
town to claim a post office with that name.

Many of the students at the New London junior and senior high school
(from fifth to eleventh grade) were children of oil-field workers who had
swarmed in during the boom. These families were far from well off, but
the school district was flush with new tax money. It was one of the richest
districts in the United States, and the school was almost brand-new, a

sprawling two-story brick building with a roof of red Spanish tile. But the money wasn't likely to be endless—that was the nature of booms—and so the school cut costs wherever it could, despite an occasional extravagance like the electric floodlights that illuminated the football field. One way to save money, the school board had covertly decided, was to tap into the waste gas released by a nearby refinery. Waste gas had no value as a salable commodity, but it was common practice in the area to divert it for use in gas-fired heaters. It was essentially free. By using waste gas, the school could be heated for only about $250 a month.

On a Thursday in March 1937, the New London school was busy preparing for a number of out-of-town interscholastic contests that would begin the next day. Classes were canceled for Friday, but the PTA would be meeting on Thursday afternoon. On days when the PTA met, the students were usually let out early, at three, but because the next day was a holiday they were kept until the usual dismissal time of three thirty.

Students had been complaining about headaches and sore eyes for a week or so, but nobody had been able to find the source of the problem. In fact, natural gas, which is odorless, was steadily being channeled via a pipe coupling buried in the ground outside the school and was invisibly pooling on the bottom floor of the building. At 3:17 on Thursday, March 18, just thirteen minutes before the end of the school day, a shop teacher turned on the power switch of an electric sander and set off a spark.

A student named Helen Beard was walking down the hallway with her younger sister Marie when the explosion happened. It launched her into the sky, where, before losing consciousness, she gazed down in shock-filled wonder at the unfathomable commotion below.

Her mother was sitting in her car outside the school, waiting to pick up her daughters, when she saw the building in front of her blow up. The blast lifted her car and turned it around, and then showered it with dislodged bricks.

"Good God, all our children are dead!" another mother was screaming a few moments later. If there was anything to be thankful for that day, it was the fact that she was wrong. Only about half of the 600 or so children in the school were dead, or would die from their injuries. The survivors included the two Beard sisters. Helen was blown into the parking lot, where her mother, staggering out of her ruined car, managed to find her. Her little sister Marie was dug out of the rubble and, presumed dead, taken to a funeral home, where her whimpering alerted a Methodist minister that she was still alive.

The Beard family was almost miraculously fortunate. "You couldn't look anywhere," a witness remembered, "without seeing a pile of dead boys and girls." The shredded bodies of children rained down on passing cars. They

"Good God, all our children are dead!" The aftermath of the New London school explosion in 1937.

hung from telephone wires. "I gathered two tubs full of hands, arms, legs, and feet for which I could find no bodies," an ambulance driver recalled. "I helped to gather nearly a bushel basket full of shoes—tiny shoes that kiddies wear—in which we found no feet. They were just shoes, laced and tied and which had been blown completely from the victims' bodies."

One of the first reporters to witness the horrors of the New London explosion was Walter Cronkite, a twenty-year-old dropout from the University of Texas who was working out of the United Press bureau in Dallas. "I did nothing in my studies," he wrote many years later, after a long career of reporting on wars and catastrophes, "nor in my life to prepare me for a story of the magnitude of that New London tragedy, nor has any story since that awful day equaled it."

Among the collapsed classroom debris that frantic rescuers and parents searched through to find children who might still be alive was a blackboard with a chalk-written message from some chemistry or civics class whose teacher and students were now dead or grievously hurt or waking into a new life of searing memory: "Oil and natural gas are East Texas' greatest mineral blessings. Without them this school would not be here."

One of the children who survived the explosion was nine-year-old Carolyn Jones. In the middle of spelling class, her teacher had heard "the first awful rumble," quickly threw open the windows, and yelled to her pupils, "Get out of here." Before any of them could act, the room collapsed. Carolyn escaped being seriously injured, but her older sister did not. Like so many other mangled children, she could be identified only by the clothes she had worn to school that morning—a pink print dress that her mother had sewn for her.

Only a week after the disaster, Carolyn Jones was in Austin, standing on a chair so she could peer over the Speaker's podium to address the House Chamber at the Capitol. "Out of this explosion," she told them, "we have learned of a new hazard that hovers about some of our school buildings. If this hazard can be forever blotted out of existence, then we will not have completely lost our loved ones in vain."

The House members tearfully applauded her speech, and the legislation they subsequently voted on—to add a putrid-smelling chemical called mercaptan to natural gas so that a leak could be detected—remains the legacy of the worst school disaster in American history.

———————— ★ ————————

"SAN ANTONIO IS—AS IT HAS ALWAYS BEEN—A PLACE OF
romance, a city where mañana (tomorrow) and quien sabe (who knows) ever have been and still are words of significance."

This observation is from a guidebook to San Antonio published in 1938 as part of the New Deal's Federal Writers' Project. This Depression-era publication, like almost all the other guidebooks written since, presents readers with a salute to the city's Old World charm, its markets and fiestas and tortilla vendors and picturesquely crumbling missions. It wasn't a fantasy—the Spanish colonial landmarks and Mexican rhythms were real—but there was another San Antonio, one of far grittier authenticity, that remained out of the line of the typical tourist's sight, particularly in that celebratory centennial year.

San Antonio's West Side was where most of the city's one hundred thousand Spanish-speaking residents lived. Many were native-born Tejanos, others were immigrants from Mexico who had fled to Texas during the revolutionary years. It was a zone of real poverty, one of the worst slums in the country, where almost nobody had indoor plumbing and three-fourths of the population in an age of electricity still lit their houses with kerosene lamps.

As many as twenty thousand of the people who lived on the West Side—men, women, and children—found seasonal work as pecan shellers, either in the plants operated by a big local firm called the Southern Pecan Shelling Company, or just by operating out of their own homes as contractors. At the plants, they sat at long tables and cracked the nuts or dug out the meat with picking knives. The conditions were grim. There were no bathrooms, no windows. On hot days the doors at the end of the room might be open, but otherwise the pecan dust that hung in the air had nowhere to go except to settle into the lungs of the shellers. "At the end of the day there was a brown haze in the sheds," one of the workers remembered, "and I think that is why several family members contracted tuberculosis."

The business of pecan shelling had been mechanized a few decades before, but the Depression brought cheap labor, and it was more cost-efficient for the pecan companies just to hire people to do the work by hand than to buy and maintain the machines. The workers' pay came in envelopes from a local bank that cheerily advised them, "Let a Bank Account shelter you on that Rainy Day! The Acorn from which wealth grows is—Saving!"

But to a pecan sheller, a savings account was as distant a prospect as a Park Avenue penthouse. Pay was tied to the amount of pecan meat produced, seven cents for a pound of intact halves and six cents for pieces. The typical weekly income for a sheller in 1938 was $2.73. The median yearly income for a family of five was less than $300. To the company's owners, the low wages were easily justified by what they imagined to be the workers' inborn low expectations. "The Mexicans don't want much money," one of the owners concluded. "Compared to those shanties they live in, the pecan shelleries are fine. They are glad to have a warm place to sit in the winter.

Like these San Antonio pecan shellers, generations of Mexican Americans in Texas were trapped in unhealthy labor that paid poverty wages.

They can be warm while they're shelling pecans, they can talk to their friends while they're working. . . . If they get hungry they can eat pecans."

But after the pay for a rendered pound of pecans was reduced by a penny at the beginning of 1938, somewhere between six thousand and eight thousand shellers went on strike. It was an impromptu strike at first, but it soon acquired an experienced, disciplined leader named Emma Tenayuca. She was only twenty years old, weighed 108 pounds, and was five feet, one and a half inches tall. "It was right she would be called La Pasionara," another Texas labor leader of that time, Latane Lambert, remembered many years later, "because in her shrill little voice she would make your spine tingle."

La Pasionara roughly translates as "the Passionate One," a fitting name for a girl who went to her first political rally at the age of six, learning the words to "The Internationale" ("Arise ye workers from your slumbers / Arise ye prisoners of want"), and quickly moved on to the writings of Karl Marx and of the Flores Magón brothers. In an oral-history interview given to the *Texas Observer* in 1983, when she was in her sixties, Tenayuca floated the suggestion that her unusual last name tied her father's lineage far back in time to the Aztec empire. Her mother's family traced itself back to the

EMMA TENAYUCA
behind bars—not for the first time. She was first arrested when she was sixteen, but by the time she led the pecan shellers strike she had become a real threat to business as usual in San Antonio.

mission Indians who had been part of the Spanish retrenchment at San Antonio after the East Texas missions were abandoned near the end of the eighteenth century. "I am satisfied," she said, "that we have been here quite a long time."

In her first years of high school, she joined the women's auxiliary of the League of United Latin American Citizens. LULAC, organized in Corpus Christi in 1929, included among its aspirational members José de la Luz Sáenz, who brought the perspective of World War I veterans to the fight for Mexican American civil rights. But LULAC proper was a men's outfit, and though the middle-class businessmen and lawyers who founded it were sincere and energetic when it came to tackling racial discrimination, they must have seemed stuffy to the impatient young radical in their auxiliary ranks.

She was sixteen the first time she went to jail, after joining the picket line of a group of women who were striking against a San Antonio cigar factory. After high school, she got a job as a hotel elevator operator and washed jars at a pickle factory, but her real work was organizing. "She would go house to house," a fellow activist remembered of her efforts to enlist members into an organization called the Workers Alliance, "up one street and down another, listening to them, asking them to join the union. . . . She organized pickets and told people they had rights."

As the leader of the pecan strike, Emma Tenayuca was promptly arrested. She had already been pegged as a communist agent by San Antonio's police chief. "The Tenayuca woman," he said after one of her previous arrests, "is a paid agitator sent here to stir up trouble among the ignorant Mexican workers."

If she was an agitator, she was an unpaid one, and the Mexican workers she was stirring up were far from ignorant about the conditions of their own lives. But there was also the fact that she was a communist. She had joined the party the year before and married Homer Brooks, the secretary of the Texas Communist Party. It was an incendiary affiliation that led to what should have been natural allies in the struggle, like LULAC, keeping their distance from La Pasionara. And the threat of godless communism guaranteed the hostility of the Catholic Church. "In the midst of this community," a Catholic newspaper warned, "exists a woman by the name of Emma Tenayuca who wants to spread disorder and hatred. . . . Don't give your names to her when she comes around to solicit them. Warn people when she comes around. Mrs. Tenayuca de Brooks is not a Mexican, she is a Rusofile, sold out to Russia."

Tenayuca was forced to resign from the leadership of the strike by the Catholic Church and by the union that represented the pecan shellers— both were wary of her Communist connections— but she paid no heed to her expulsion. She was out on the street the next day organizing workers.

The taint of communism also caused problems with the Congress of Industrial Organizations, the federation of industrial worker unions that moved in to take over management of the strike. Tenayuca signed the papers they presented her, removing herself as the pecan shellers' strike leader, but she acted as if she had never capitulated. She went right back to giving speeches out on the streets, writing circulars, and assigning strikers to their

positions on the picket lines. She instructed them not to provoke the police by making eye contact with them, but there was plenty of havoc anyway. The police beat the strikers with axe handles, repeatedly teargassed them, hauled them into jail on flimsy charges. None of that stopped Tenayuca from holding rallies in the streets, speaking to five thousand pecan workers at a time.

The strike ended a few months after it started, in the wake of an arbitrated agreement guaranteeing workers the minimum wage of twenty-five cents an hour set forth by the newly passed Fair Labor Standards Act. But it was only a faint victory, because the owners of the pecan-shelling companies simply went back to using shelling machines rather than pay workers the increased rate.

Emma Tenayuca ran quixotically for Congress the next year on the Texas Communist Party ticket, and even persuaded San Antonio's just-elected mayor, Maury Maverick, to allow the use of the city auditorium for the party's state convention. Maury Maverick was as close as you could get to Anglo royalty in San Antonio. His grandfather was Sam Maverick, who had guided Texian forces when they attacked the town in 1836 and who later became the Gulf Coast cattle baron who gave his name to wild, unbranded calves.

His grandson Maury was well aware of how the family name had entered the language as an against-the-grain accolade by the time he wrote his autobiography, *A Maverick American*. "The stork brought me into the world," he declared with hearty Texas chauvinism in its opening chapters. "I remember it exactly. I can recall the first thing I saw in my flight was the Alamo when I sat bolt upright in the diaper which was in the stork's bill. Even though the stork had to hold his mouth tightly shut, he was telling me about the heroes of the Alamo."

But even with his illustrious pedigree, Maverick wasn't bulletproof, not in the poisonous political climate of Texas in the 1930s. The convention he allowed to be held in the auditorium was overrun by a mob of five thousand that forced its way past the police cordons and did its best to dismantle the building and terrorize the convention's communist delegates. Emma Tenayuca barely escaped, hustled out through a back door under a nervous police guard. Maury Maverick was hanged in effigy but stood firm, announcing, "The civil liberties of everybody in San Antonio, even Emma Tenayuca, will be upheld."

Maverick was defeated in the next election. Tenayuca divorced her husband and fell out of love with communism as well after learning of Stalin's terror regime. She moved to San Francisco, got a college degree, and came back to San Antonio fifteen years later to teach elementary school. For the rest of her life, she was more or less a private citizen—no longer the public firebrand immortalized in a photograph taken at a Workers Alliance demonstration in front of San Antonio's city hall the year before the pecan shellers' strike, with her arm raised and her hand clenched into a fist, the embodiment of defiance and youthful confidence.

You can get a sense of what she must have been like by watching a video interview that was made about ten years before her death, in 1999. She is wearing a gray sweater almost the exact shade of her short wavy hair, and she is testy and exasperated with the interviewer. She quizzes him about whether he is a Christian or whether he has read Voltaire. She gives him the names of books he needs to check out of the library at once, and condescendingly tells him that they are "very very simple." When asked what her goal was in helping the workers during the pecan shellers' strike, she almost jumps out of her chair in exasperation: "Food!"

The interviewer keeps angling for a moment of self-reflection, but it isn't forthcoming. When he tells her that the people of San Antonio now regard her as a heroine, her patience is once again severely tested. "Look," she demands, "do you know how busy I was kept? You think I had time to pick up a paper and cut it out because my picture was in it?"

★

FAR ACROSS THE POLITICAL AND PERSONALITY DIVIDE FROM Emma Tenayuca was another Passionate One. His name was Wilbert Lee O'Daniel, but everybody called him Pappy. In 1938 he was close to fifty, a pleasant, slightly pudgy man with dimples and slicked-back hair. Originally from Kansas, he had been in Texas since 1925, working as the general manager of a Fort Worth firm called the Burrus Mill and Elevator Company. It manufactured Light Crust Flour, which was used for baking by housewives all over the state.

At the time, Bob Wills was playing in a musical trio that had a show on a local low-power radio station. Their show was sponsored by the Aladdin Lamp Company—hence the group's name, the Aladdin Laddies. But the lamp company pulled its support, and the trio was in need of a new sponsor. O'Daniel knew nothing about radio advertising, but he agreed to sponsor the group for a threadbare seven a.m. broadcast. The Aladdin Laddies became the Light Crust Doughboys. They were a bust at first, and O'Daniel fired them. After Bob Wills pleaded with O'Daniel to take them back, he agreed to sponsor the show again if the Doughboys would work a forty-hour week for the flour mill to justify the expense.

O'Daniel regarded the western swing that Wills and his band were playing as "hillbilly music," but the label didn't matter—the Light Crust Doughboys started to catch on. And so, accidentally, did O'Daniel. When the regular announcer for the show failed to appear one day, O'Daniel took his place and strode into a new career. It turned out that hidden inside the flour salesman was a born showman. He could sing—he had a pleasant baritone that was a cozy fit with the primitive radios of his listeners—and he delivered a smooth and shameless cornball homily to his growing audience, instructing them to follow the scriptures and be kind to their mothers. He was especially bullish on motherhood. "Hello there, mother, you little sweetheart," he might say at the beginning of his program. "How in the world are you anyway, you little bunch of sweetness?"

He also erupted as a poet and songwriter, dashing off songs like "Beautiful Texas," "Sons of the Alamo," a song about the flu called "Kachoo! Kachoo! Kachoo!" and—motherhood again—"The Boy Who Never Grew Too Old to Comb His Mother's Hair."

By 1935, he had his own company, Hillbilly Flour. Bob Wills and the Doughboys had quit two years earlier amid a flurry of lawsuits, and now O'Daniel had a new band called the Hillbilly Boys. He sold so much flour he now had a net worth of a half million dollars. His radio show, which aired at 12:30 every day, began with a woman's voice calling out "Please pass the biscuits, Pappy," and all over Texas listeners tuned in to hear Pappy talk and listen to his gluten-rich theme song:

> I like bread and biscuits,
> Big white fluffy biscuits—
> Hillbilly Flour makes 'em grand.
> So while we sing and play
> And try to make folks happy,
> We hope you'll say,
> "Please pass the biscuits, Pappy."

A thought occurred to Pappy in the spring of 1938: why not run for governor? Never mind that he knew nothing about politics or government and had never even paid his poll tax so that he could vote in Texas. He believed in the Golden Rule and the power of name-brand marketing to sell flour, and he even had a platform in mind: the Ten Commandments. He claimed that a blind man who was frustrated with cynical politicians had sent him a letter pleading with him to run. What do you think? he asked his radio audience during a Palm Sunday broadcast. Letters came flooding in, he reported, 54,499 listeners begging him to run and only 4 people thinking that maybe he had better not.

"From the Texas plains and hills and valleys," he declared in a Mother's Day speech, "came a little breeze wafting on its crest more than 54,000 voices of one accord—we want W. Lee O'Daniel for governor of Texas."

His campaign was a sensation. More people turned out to hear him speak—forty thousand people at one rally—than had ever assembled before in Texas political history. He started his rallies with a concert by the Hillbilly Boys, featuring vocal solos by Leon Huff and Kitty Williamson, aka the "Texas Rose." "Beautiful Texas," his signature song, was always featured. Its proudly insipid lyrics ("Beautiful beautiful Texas / Where the beautiful bluebonnets grow") were a perfect match for his vacuous campaign. As the crowds poured in to see him, his flour sales doubled. "Boy, is business good," he marveled. He promised everyone in Texas over sixty-five a pension of $30 a month, blithely indifferent to the fact that if those payouts were to happen they would quadruple the budget for a state already

"Pass the Biscuits Pappy" with the Hillbilly Boys, the second iteration of his band.

so strapped for money that it couldn't repair the leaky roof in its Capitol. (Members of the legislature had to hold umbrellas over their heads when they conferred in the House Chamber.) If somebody asked Pappy whether he was planning to raise taxes to pay for his pension idea, he would turn to his band and say, "All right, boys, give 'em a tune."

He wasn't the only candidate for the Democratic nomination. Pa Ferguson tried to get Ma to run again, but she wouldn't. Even so, there were twelve contenders, including one of Ferguson's cousins. At least two of them, the state's attorney general and the chairman of the Railroad Commission, were deadly serious establishment candidates. O'Daniel beat them all without even a runoff and then of course as a Democrat sailed on to victory in the general election.

"Texas, it appears, has once more turned wild and woolly," reported the *Washington Post* in a typically agog national reaction. "Latest reports from the Lone Star state indicate that it has chosen a radio crooning flour broker, until recently quite unknown to the public, to be its next governor."

Sixty thousand fans of Pappy O'Daniel, Hillbilly Flour, and "Beautiful Texas" mobbed the inauguration in Austin. It was a bright beginning, but

The flour salesman, warbler, song-writer, and unlikeliest of Texas governors, W. Lee "Pappy" O'Daniel. He loved his mother, he loved Texas, and he loved the Ten Commandments.

the results were predictable. O'Daniel had no idea how to govern, and his attempt to pay for his pension plan with the then-unthinkable notion of a sales tax led to one state representative calling him out as a "crooning corporal of the panoplied forces of financial marauders."

The man who presented himself to the voters as a humble man of the people, as a man who was never too proud to comb his mother's hair, had no problem with vetoing bills that would have provided beds for orphans or with cozying up to big business or undercutting the influence of unions.

He got reelected anyway; he was just too much fun. In that 1940 election, Jim Ferguson finally prevailed upon his wife to run again. It was Ma and Pa against Pappy. But the old carnival populism of Jim Ferguson belonged to a different, pre-radio age. Even with Jim working the levers once again, Miriam Ferguson couldn't do better than fourth place for the Democratic nomination.

In the first year of his second term, O'Daniel was busy railing against "labor union racketeers" like Emma Tenayuca when a new opportunity presented itself. The able and conscientious U.S. senator from Texas, Morris Sheppard, sixty-five years old, died in the spring of 1941. His personal physician thought he died from the stress of serving as the chairman of the Senate's Military Affairs Committee at a time when the United States was being steadily drawn into the convulsion of World War II.

As governor, O'Daniel was obliged to select a "suitable and qualified" person to keep the Texas seat warm for a few months until a special election could be held in June, when the voters would select a replacement for Sheppard. There were plenty of suitable and qualified people to choose from, but most of them came with the disadvantage of being known to the voters, and therefore would be in a strong incumbent position—and therefore a threat—if Pappy decided to run for the vacant Senate seat himself.

What Governor O'Daniel needed was somebody really old, somebody unlikely to have ambitions beyond the few months of an interim appointment. He announced his decision on April 21, 1941, when he came to speak at the San Jacinto Monument on the 105th anniversary of the battle that had won Texas its independence from Mexico.

"At this very hour—3 p.m.," he said, "the destiny of Texas hung precariously in the balance five years more than a century ago." After rhapsodizing about that astounding victory and the immortal hero who had commanded the Texian forces that day, Pappy O'Daniel announced his choice for the man who would occupy Sam Houston's old seat in the U.S. Senate: his still-living-but-barely son, eighty-six-year old Andrew Jackson Houston.

A photograph taken that day shows the plump, beaming governor standing next to his new appointee, a cadaverous remnant of old Texas glory. Andrew Jackson Houston lived in a modest frame house with his two daughters, neither of whom thought he had any business at his age and in his condition traveling all the way to Washington to serve in the Senate. When reporters called to interview him, they were told by his daughters that he was too fatigued to even answer the telephone.

But he traveled to Washington anyway, the oldest man ever to enter the U.S. Senate. He attended one committee meeting, appeared on the floor a few times, and then died. In his twenty-four days in the Senate Chamber, he had time to introduce one bill. It was for the creation of a historical museum at San Jacinto, the last act of a man who had spent much of his lifetime nurturing his father's legacy, tending his old battlefield, and serving as the last direct link to the man who was in command at the moment of Texas's bloody nativity.

"above and beyond the call of duty"

DORIE MILLER
Received the Navy Cross
at Pearl Harbor, May 27, 1942

The nation needed inspiration after Pearl Harbor, and Doris Miller—as depicted on this recruiting poster—was one of the people who provided it.

—41—

TEXANS AT WAR AGAIN

THE HEAVYWEIGHT BOXING CHAMPION OF THE USS *WEST* *Virginia*, which was moored along Battleship Row in Pearl Harbor, Hawaii, had the unlikely first name of Doris. According to family lore, this was because his mother, Henrietta Miller, who worked as a sharecropper with her husband, Connery, on a farm outside Waco, had longed for a daughter after having given birth to two sons. In the navy, to take the edge off his girl's name, Doris was known as Dorie. He was six feet three and a thick-bodied 225 pounds. Quiet and easygoing, he held his formidable temper in check for the boxing ring.

Because he had enlisted in 1939, Miller was not able to take advantage of the reforms of the Selective Training and Service Act, which was passed the next year; it at least in theory opened all branches of the services to African Americans. His duties were limited to that of mess attendant—shining officers' shoes, doing their laundry, making their beds, and serving their food. As a member of the Messmen Branch, he had never been trained on his ship's weapons or allowed to handle them. "Just think of it!" the *Waco Messenger*, the black newspaper in Miller's hometown, railed a few months before the Japanese attack on Pearl Harbor. "The only way Negroes can die in Uncle Sam's democratic Navy is—slinging hash."

595

Miller was picking up laundry in the junior officers' room when the first of a series of aerial torpedoes and bombs struck the *West Virginia* during the Japanese surprise attack on December 7, 1941. The forward part of the ship was ripped apart, much of the crew disappearing in the towering flames or brought down by jagged metal fragments, exploding ammunition, and poisonous fumes. Miller threw himself into the work of hauling burned and bleeding survivors onto the quarterdeck as Japanese pilots continued to strafe the ship.

He helped carry the ship's mortally wounded captain from the bridge to a less exposed place behind the conning tower. Mounted forward of the tower were two fifty-caliber machine guns, operable but unmanned. Doris Miller had never fired such a weapon before, and was technically forbidden from doing so, but none of that mattered on a burning, sinking ship filled with dead and wounded crewmen.

"It wasn't hard," he later testified. "I just pulled the trigger and she worked fine."

The Japanese pilots, recalled another Texas survivor, "were so low you could see them grinning." Miller kept shooting until the ammunition was gone and he was ordered, along with the rest of the surviving crew, to abandon ship. "I actually downed four Japanese bombers," a newspaper article published the next month quoted him as saying. "I might have brought down more—but I am positive of four."

He was wildly overstating his beginner's luck. He might have shot down one plane, but his more likely contribution to the defense of Pearl Harbor that day was simply the valuable harassing fire from his machine gun. Nevertheless, he received the Navy Cross for "distinguished devotion to duty, extraordinary courage and disregard for his own personal safety."

World War II had begun for the United States, and Doris Miller, a black mess attendant from Central Texas, was one of its first heroes. In time, his face would appear on a recruitment poster and a commemorative postage stamp; a U.S. Navy frigate would be named for him, along with schools and auditoriums and parks; and his wild turn at one of the *West Virginia*'s machine guns would be caustically celebrated in "Negro Hero," a poem by Gwendolyn Brooks:

> Still—am I good enough to die for them, is my blood bright enough to be spilled,
> Was my constant back-question—are they clear
> On this? Or do I intrude even now?
> Am I clean enough to kill for them, do they wish me to kill
> For them or is my place while death licks his lips and strides to them
> In the galley still?

It was another Texan—the venerable and consequential Tom Connally, now the chairman of the Senate Foreign Relations Committee—who introduced a resolution on December 8 declaring war against Japan. Connally, in his telling, was not just shocked at what had happened but also furious about America's lack of preparedness. At a meeting in the White House on the night of the attack, he exploded at Roosevelt after the president briefed the cabinet on what had happened at Pearl Harbor, told them about the ships that were lost and the men killed, and then looked down at the floor and said, "I guess that's all." "That's all?" Connally protested loudly. "Hell's fire, didn't we do anything?"

He next directed his outrage toward Secretary of the Navy Frank Knox.

"Didn't you say last month that we could lick the Japs in two weeks? Didn't you say that our navy was so well prepared and located that the Japanese couldn't hope to hurt us at all? . . . Why did you have all the ships at Pearl Harbor crowded in the way you did? . . . And why did you have a log chain across the mouth of the entrance to Pearl Harbor, so that our ships could not get out?"

But Connally understood his blast of hindsight was irrelevant: "A long, hard war lay ahead for the United States. And when we said good-by to the President, we left the past behind us with an understanding that we would concentrate on the future."

Part of that future was thrust into the hands of Admiral Chester Nimitz, the chief of the navy's Bureau of Navigation. He and his wife, Catherine, heard the news about Pearl Harbor over the radio as they were listening to a broadcast of the New York Philharmonic Orchestra. After an announcer broke in, Nimitz kissed his wife good-bye and told her, "I won't be back until God knows when."

His instincts were prescient. A little more than a week later, he was jumped over twenty-eight other, more senior admirals to become the new commander in chief of the Pacific Fleet. "Tell Nimitz," Roosevelt said to Knox, "to get the hell out to Pearl Harbor and stay there till the war is won."

It may seem odd that the National Museum of the Pacific War is located in Fredericksburg, Texas, a town far from the Pacific, smack in the middle of a landlocked expanse of limestone and granite hills about eighty miles west of Austin. But Fredericksburg was the boyhood home of Chester Nimitz, and the museum building is the repurposed hotel built by his grandfather, Charles Nimitz, in the 1850s. The Nimitzes were from a played-out aristocratic family that had come to Texas with Baron von Meusebach in one of the early waves of German migration. By the time he arrived in Fredericksburg in 1846, Chester's grandfather was a veteran of the German merchant marine who was given to nostalgic reveries of his old seafaring life. These were passed on to his grandson, whose father had died before his birth and who lived in the Nimitz Hotel with his widowed mother. The building, then as now, was a Main Street landmark in Fredericksburg: a sprawling structure of fifty rooms, half Victorian mansion, half dry-docked steamboat, with a crow's nest from which to survey the stony sea of the Texas Hill Country.

Inspired by his grandfather's tales, and by his own wanderlust, Chester Nimitz traveled far from Texas to attend the U.S. Naval Academy in Annapolis, Maryland. As a twenty-two-year-old ensign, he was given command of a decrepit destroyer in the Philippines. He once ran it aground, but wrote such an honest, unvarnished report of his own negligence that he escaped a career-ending court-martial. He served on a submarine during World War I, and twenty years before the Japanese attack on Pearl Harbor he directed the construction of a submarine base there.

When he was ordered to take command of the Pacific Fleet, he was fifty-six years old, five feet nine inches tall, with white hair, sharp blue eyes, a resolute expression, and a left hand that was missing part of its ring finger—the result of an accident with the cogs of a diesel engine. When he was a midshipman, someone had called him "that man of cheerful yesterdays and confident tomorrows."

The naval war he would be fighting spanned sixty-eight million square miles of ocean. "If there's one place bigger than Texas," Nimitz quipped in a Honolulu speech to far-from-home Texas servicemen, "it's the Pacific Ocean." It was impossible to predict any confident tomorrow when the conflict that began at Pearl Harbor might finally be over. "The war will end," Nimitz told a reporter in his direct, taciturn way, "when the Japanese have been hunted down in all those regions and their striking power destroyed."

It was on his flagship, the USS *Missouri*, that the Japanese would surrender on September 2, 1945, but that event was a transformed world away from Christmas Day 1941, when Nimitz arrived at the devastation of Pearl Harbor. His first order of business was to salvage both ships and morale. He did so steadily and patiently, building up the fleet's strength until he was able to deploy it throughout the Pacific in a chain of battles—in the Coral Sea, at Midway, in Leyte Gulf—that were among the greatest naval engagements in history.

It was Chester Nimitz who pinned the Navy Cross on the chest of his fellow Texan Doris Miller on a spring day in 1942. "This marks the first time

ADMIRAL CHESTER NIMITZ,
*a landlocked son of the Texas Hill Country, signs the peace treaty with Japan
on board the* USS Missouri.

in this conflict," the admiral said, "that such high tribute has been made in the Pacific Fleet to a member of his race."

Early the next year, Miller was back in the States, being honored at a ceremony in Waco and touring the country to promote sales of war bonds. By the time he returned to the Pacific, he had been promoted to ship's cook third class and was reassigned to the escort carrier *Liscome Bay*. The ship was supporting the invasion of the Gilbert Islands in 1943 on the day before Thanksgiving when a torpedo from a Japanese submarine struck its starboard side, next to the bomb magazine. Over six hundred of its nine hundred crew members died, Miller among them. His body was never found, but one of the survivors remembered a haunting sight: a plucked, frozen Thanksgiving turkey that ship's cook Doris Miller was scheduled to prepare the next day improbably floating upon the oil-covered surface of the open Pacific.

MORE THAN 725,000 TEXANS, MEN AND WOMEN, SERVED IN
uniform during World War II. While writing this chapter, I listened to old
recordings of Perry Como and Bing Crosby crooning "Deep in the Heart
of Texas" and Bob Wills and his Texas Playboys (the band he formed after
leaving the Light Crust Doughboys) playing "New San Antonio Rose." Both
songs were big hits during the early days of the war. What would it have been
like, I wonder, to be besieged on Wake Island, or to be about to go ashore
at Tarawa or Saipan, and to hear those musical tributes to a home five or
six thousand impossible miles away across the Pacific? "New San Antonio
Rose," in particular, still vibrates with an epic plaintiveness. The song had
been called just "San Antonio Rose" when Wills first recorded a tossed-off
instrumental version in 1938. Irving Berlin's music publishing company liked
what it heard but wanted lyrics, so Wills and the band came up with those as
well and added "New" to the title of the revised version. There was a genius
quality to the lyrics. Lines such as "Deep within my heart lies a melody" and
"A moonlit path that only she would know" bump up against real poetry.
Although the song is a jaunty fiddle tune, with Wills's high-pitched yowling
intruding playfully in the background, the rich lazy tenor of the lead vocalist,
Tommy Duncan, grounds it as an aching homesick anthem.

Whether Dwight David Eisenhower had any nostalgia for Texas is uncertain. The man who would become the supreme commander of the Allied
forces and the thirty-fourth president of the United States was born a Texan
in the town of Denison on October 14, 1890. Denison, north of Dallas, hugs
the banks of the Red River at the Oklahoma border. At the end of 1941, it
had become known, at least to itself, as the "Egg Breaking Capital of the
World." That was because it had a couple of egg-drying businesses that were
transformed into a supercharged industry when the war opened up a massive market for powdered eggs.

But this was long after Eisenhower had left. The future president's early
life as a Texan was flickeringly brief. His father, the bankrupt owner of a general store in Hope, Kansas, had moved his family to Denison in 1889, planning
to find work on the railroad known as the KATY (Missouri-Kansas-Texas),
which had sparked the town's fortunes when it arrived in 1872. But he was
only able to get a menial job wiping down and lubricating locomotives, and
to afford the rent on a rundown sooty house that was only yards away from
the train tracks. That was where Eisenhower was born. He was less than a
year old when the family moved back to Kansas. They made such a fleeting
impression on the town that it wasn't until the middle of the war, when Gen-

eral Ike Eisenhower was one of the most famous people in the world and on the cover of every magazine, that someone in Denison made the connection. A retired schoolteacher wrote to him and asked whether he had once lived there. When he wrote back that he had, the town bought the house, fixed it up, and welcomed him home after the war with a parade and a celebratory breakfast in the tiny parlor where he had once been an infant.

Eisenhower was also in Texas when the war broke out. He was stationed at Fort Sam Houston in San Antonio, recovering from shingles, basking in his recent success in leading the Third Army in a victorious war games exercise in Louisiana, and in the middle of a deep nap when the phone rang with the news about Pearl Harbor. A week later he was in Washington, where, after being urgently questioned by Army Chief of Staff General George C. Marshall about how to win this new war, he sat down at a typewriter and, hunting and pecking with one finger, wrote a memo headed "Steps to Be Taken."

Pappy O'Daniel was also in Washington. After the predictable death of the aged Andrew Jackson Houston, he had predictably put himself forward as a candidate for the special election he called for the late Morris Sheppard's Senate seat. The election had been abundantly wacky and subversive, "the biggest carnival in American politics," according to *Time* magazine. There were almost thirty candidates, including formidable contenders such as the communist-hunting congressman Martin Dies; the state attorney general, Gerald Mann, known as the "Little Red Arrow" from his football days at Southern Methodist University; and that ever-revving human ambition machine Lyndon Johnson. But also in the running was a cousin of Judge Roy Bean; a man styling himself as a commodore whose platform was the creation of a five-ocean navy; and a laxative magnate who awarded a free mattress at his rallies to the couple with the most children. There was also a doctor named John Brinkley, who had obtained his license (valid in only eight states) from the Eclectic Medical University in Kansas City, who believed that "all energy is sex energy," and who had invented the surgical process of inserting goat gonads into the testicles of men who were cursed with "no pep."

Lyndon Johnson had the backing of FDR and, even more crucially, the dollars of George and Herman Brown, the brothers who controlled Brown & Root, the Texas-based construction firm that Congressman Johnson had helped turn into a national powerhouse when he saw to it that it received the authorization for a major dam-building project northwest of Austin. The Browns were lavish in their gratitude. "I hope you know, Lyndon," George Brown had written in 1939, "I am going to try to show my appreciation through the years to come with actions rather than words."

What that meant in practice was a steady snowfall of money, enough for

Johnson to employ enough advance men and sound trucks, print enough posters, and buy enough ads to blanket the state—and to mount an "All-Out Patriotic Revue" to rival Pappy O'Daniel's crowd-pleasing campaign extravaganzas. Brown & Root's money also took a more direct route, straight into the pockets of the machine politicians and border bosses who acted as brokers for Tejano and Mexican votes in places like the West Side of San Antonio and the Rio Grande valley. "The Mexican voter," as one observer of this process described it, "was marched to the polls, generally by a half-breed deputy sheriff with two six-shooters, a Winchester rifle, and a bandoleer of ammunition, to perform the sovereign act of voting. He entered the polls, one at a time, was handed a folded ballot which he dropped in the box, was given a drink of Tequila, and then was marched out."

Duval County, between Corpus Christi and Laredo, was the South Texas fiefdom presided over by the Parr family. The dynasty had been founded by a ruthlessly inventive *patrón* named Archie Parr, who gained control of the Duval Democratic Party machine following the mysterious 1907 assassination of the powerful county tax assessor. After decades of corruption, more killings, and a timely courthouse fire that destroyed potentially incriminating financial records, the Parrs were still firmly in control of Duval, though by the time of the 1941 senatorial election Archie was in his eighties. The iron fist had been bequeathed to his son George—aka the Duke of Duval—fresh out of prison for tax evasion and running the family business of countywide vote selling.

But the Johnson team made a miscalculation when it reported the votes it had bought from South Texas bosses like George Parr too early after the election, giving O'Daniel the opportunity to scramble to make up the difference in yet-unreported East Texas counties, where "an amazing change of votes" suddenly took place. Pappy was also helped by people like Pa Ferguson, back in the action now as the general counsel of the Texas Brewers Association. Why would the brewers be in favor of electing O'Daniel, a man who believed that liquor was as evil as motherhood was good, to the U.S. Senate? Simple: they wanted him out of the state.

So O'Daniel won the election with a flurry of last-minute bought-and-paid-for returns that put him ahead of Johnson by a bit more than a thousand votes. Sworn into office in August, he startled his new colleagues by making a speech on only his second day as a senator, a breach of know-your-place protocol that broke even Huey Long's record for brazen grandstanding. (Long had had the patience to wait until his third day.)

In the speech, Pappy patted himself on the back for winning the election ("I have always enjoyed a good scrap") and acknowledged the "fear that

Texas would send to the United States Senate a hillbilly musician, a radio crooner, or a flour salesman who might perchance lower the dignity of this great deliberative body."

"I do like hillbilly music," he confirmed to his bewildered senatorial audience, adding, "I want to say frankly that I intend to continue to like hillbilly music and to use the radio to talk to the people of this nation."

It was not just the brewers who were happy to have O'Daniel out of the state, bestowing the gift of his personality on the stuffed-shirt solons of Washington, DC, and leaving Texas alone. Another beneficiary of his absence was Lieutenant Governor Coke Stevenson, who ascended to the governorship upon Pappy's election to the Senate. Stevenson was an exceedingly popular Texas politician—when he ran for lieutenant governor, he carried every one of the state's 254 counties. He was self-made, born in a log cabin, a former freight hauler who famously taught himself history Abe Lincoln–style, fervently reading by the light of hearths and campfires. He was in his early fifties when he became governor, square of jaw, receding of hairline, honest and upright, seldom glimpsed when not ruminatively puffing on his pipe. When it came to his politics—well, as one of his critics noted, he was "as liberal as the people." Which meant, in Texas in the early 1940s, he was a hard-line small-government, white-supremacist conservative.

Stevenson was chummy with the anti-Roosevelt faction of the Texas Democratic Party, which called itself the Texas Regulars and whose members included now-senator Pappy O'Daniel and a throng of oilmen, lobbyists, attorneys, movie chain moguls, and others who had a natural aversion to taxes, unions, and governmental regulations. The Texas Regulars ran advertisements in the newspapers reminding Texans to "keep the White in Old Glory," and their official platform had planks such as "Return of state rights which have been destroyed by the Communist-controlled New Deal" and "Restoration of the supremacy of the white race, which has been destroyed by the Communist-controlled New Deal."

Stevenson kept a lookout for the interests of his friends in the oil business. He opposed wellhead taxes, for instance, and wartime gasoline rationing. He considered gasoline to be kin to those other sacred tools of the frontier—"the saddle, the rifle, the ax, and the Bible"—that had made Texas what it was.

When asked by a lobbyist about the great issues of the day facing the Texas government, which he headed, "those questions," he replied, "usually take care of themselves." He did virtually nothing when a race riot was ignited in Beaumont in 1943 after a black man was falsely accused of raping a white woman. And even though there was a world war raging, he would

GOVERNOR COKE STEVENSON,
also known as "Calculatin' Coke." Great issues like those that faced Texas, he calculated, "usually take care of themselves."

not raise taxes or agree to spend the money to call a special session of the legislature to allow the Texans who were fighting in Europe or in the South Pacific to have their poll taxes waived so that they could vote.

One of the issues that refused to take care of itself during Stevenson's two terms in office was the latest round of turmoil at the University of Texas campus. O'Daniel and Stevenson had stacked the board of regents with men disposed to regard the professors in Austin as agents of a "far reaching evil." The regents told the university's president, Homer Rainey, a former pitcher on one of the baseball teams of the Texas League, to fire four economics professors with New Deal leanings. Rainey refused. He also stood in their way when they tried to root out the professor who put John Dos Passos's admired but "obscene" novel *The Big Money* on an undergraduate reading list, and when they claimed that the university harbored a "nest of homosexuals."

In 1944, the regents fired Rainey, which led to an outburst of student protests, including a mock funeral in which pallbearers carried a coffin labeled "Academic Freedom" while the university's Longhorn Band played Chopin's "Funeral March."

BUT BY THAT TIME THERE HAD ALREADY BEEN PLENTY OF REAL funerals. World War II would claim the lives of almost twenty-two thousand Texans—in the Philippines, North Africa, New Guinea, on the open sea, in the open air, on Pacific atolls and islands, in Sicily, in Italy, and throughout the beaches, towns, hedgerows, and forests of France and Belgium and Germany.

A global war can't be condensed easily into a chapter-length survey, so I'll just enter some coordinates of time and place and personality and drop us down, say, with the Thirty-Sixth Infantry Division on the banks of the Rapido River in southern Italy in January 1944. The Thirty-Sixth was the Texas National Guard unit that had been activated into federal service during World War I, that had fought at Saint-Étienne and on many other battlefields, and that now was in the midst of the invasion of Italy. The men of the Thirty-Sixth had already come a long hard way. They had landed in Salerno nineteen weeks earlier and had been fighting their way inland ever since, taking enough casualties (over 60 percent in one rifle company) that the division's Texas identity had been seriously diluted by emergency replacements from the rest of the country.

One of the most wrenching losses was that of Captain Henry Waskow, who commanded a company in the 143rd Infantry. Waskow was twenty-five, studious and serious, "a sweet little oddball," as one of his classmates at Belton High School remembered him. "In this war," the correspondent Ernie Pyle famously recalled, "I have known a lot of officers who were loved and respected by the soldiers under them. But never have I crossed the trail of any man as beloved as Captain Henry T. Waskow, of Belton, Texas."

He was killed on December 14 in the fighting around San Pietro, after eating breakfast and trying to toast a piece of bread on a coat hanger over a can of Sterno. "When we get back to the States," he told one of his men, "I'm going to get me one of those smart-aleck toasters where you put the bread in and it pops up." He was struck in the chest by shrapnel on Hill 1205 shortly thereafter. His body was taken down on a pack mule and laid on the ground by a stone wall. The men of his company stared down at him in silent grief. "Gradually," Pyle wrote, "one by one I could sense them moving closer to Captain Waskow's body. . . . One soldier came and looked down, and said aloud, 'Goddamn it.' That's all he said, and then he walked away."

A little more than a month later, the Thirty-Sixth was near the east bank of the Rapido, a relatively narrow but cold and swift-flowing river. The division's assignment was to cross the river into the Liri Valley and break through the Gustav Line, the German defensive network whose left flank led to a 1,700-foot pinnacle capped by the sixteenth-century monastery known as Monte Cassino. The heights above the river, and the mountain gullies and caves hidden from Allied sight, were dense with interconnected artillery emplacements and machine gun nests, and both sides of the Rapido were heavily mined and strewn with barbed wire.

The division's staff engineer concluded, after a pre-attack reconnaissance, "First that it would be impossible for us to get to the river. Secondly, that we couldn't cross it, and third, if we got across the river there was no place to go."

General Fred Walker, the commander of the Thirty-Sixth, had reached the same conclusion. "We have to cross the Rapido in the San Angelo area," he wrote in his diary. "But how? The equipment available for crossing is unsuitable. The improvised foot bridges—planks lashed to rubber boats—will be heavy and clumsy to carry by hand to the river. The larger rubber boats are heavy and cumbersome. They will easily be punctured by shell fire and will be difficult to launch and use as ferries because of the high banks and swift current. . . . We are undertaking the impossible, but I shall keep it to myself."

A lot of people up and down the chain of command knew, or at least suspected, that crossing an unfordable river into an open field of fire like the Liri Valley was the embodiment of tactical folly. "We had the feeling we were being sacrificed," one survivor of the Rapido remembered. Nevertheless, it was decreed to be a strategic necessity, a way to distract the German forces in Italy from the main event, Operation Shingle, the Allied landing scheduled to take place at Anzio.

The river was a formidable obstacle in itself. It was deep enough to drown in, it had a powerful current, and the water was close to freezing. But there were also the dense minefields that the Germans had sown on the American side of the river, and that had to be cleared by men probing through the wet mud with bayonets. Securing this corridor came at a great cost—"we are getting an epidemic of horrible mine wounds," a field surgeon reported. The engineers marked the cleared path with white tape, but by the time the attack finally began, on the night of January 20, many of those markers had been obliterated by German shell fire, and men stumbled helplessly into the minefields.

Everything that General Walker had predicted came true, and worse. Already burdened with fifty pounds of equipment, the men had to carry their quarter-ton boats in the darkness through the open boggy plain that led to the river. Along the way they were strafed by machine-gun fire or blown apart by the screaming *Nebelwerfer* mortars known to the Germans as "she-wolves."

When the boats were finally launched into the river, many of them were so cut up by shrapnel that they quickly sank. Others caught the current wrong and capsized. In one sinking boat, eight of the twelve occupants drowned before they were halfway across the river. Those who managed to make it to the other side found themselves trapped and cut off, with no radio contact, no supplies, and often no weapons or ammunition to fight with.

The attack failed, but the need for a diversion persisted, and so the Thirty-Sixth was ordered to attack again the next day, in broad daylight. Perhaps fortunately, there was no way to get enough new boats or replacements for the men who had been killed or wounded into position before nightfall, so the attack took place once again in darkness. But it was even worse than the day before. More men managed to get across, only to be targeted by artillery, overrun by German infantry, or drowned or shot while trying to make their way back to the American side. The experience of Company E of the 141st Regiment, which was made up of mostly Mexican American troops, was representative. They were pinned down by machine-gun fire against a row of barbed wire and encircled by German troops, their captain calling out either—people remembered it differently—"Fire wholeheartedly, men!" or "Fire foolheartedly, men!" before he was cut down and the survivors were forced to surrender. It was one of those E Company men, Sergeant Manuel Rivera from El Paso, who best summed up the folly of the Rapido assault. "If you didn't get wounded, if you didn't get killed, if you weren't captured, [then] you weren't at the river."

There was a grievous casualty rate: 1,330 men killed or wounded, another 770 captured. "I had 184 men," one company commander in the 143rd Infantry reported. "Forty-eight hours later I had 17. If that's not mass murder, I don't know what is."

The Germans lost only a little over 200 men, and gloated over their victory after the battle by means of a captured American carrier pigeon. It flew back to the east bank of the Rapido River with the message "We look forward to your next visit."

—42—

THE SHOW OF SHOWS

A FEW MONTHS LATER, ON D-DAY AT OMAHA BEACH, THE casualties were just as terrible, but this time there was no mockery, no defeat. Among the Texans who took part in the Normandy landings and who afterward assumed legendary status was Earl Rudder, who in civilian life had been a rancher, a teacher, and a football coach at Tarleton Agricultural

College. By the time of D-Day, he was a lieutenant colonel and the commander of the Second Ranger Battalion—Rudder's Rangers—when they were given the unnerving task of assaulting Pointe du Hoc, the 100-foot cliff that reared upward between the invasion beaches of Omaha and Utah and that threatened both with a battery of 155 mm guns. "It can't be done," one skeptic declared after hearing about the plans for storming straight up this natural citadel. "Three old women with brooms could keep the Rangers from climbing that cliff."

But Rudder attacked the problem like the football coach he had been, practicing and drilling his men for weeks ahead of time, making mock assaults under live fire, getting the feel of the scaling ladders and rocket-propelled grappling hooks they would use to climb the promontory. The training paid off spectacularly well. The Rangers arrived at the base of Pointe du Hoc on the early morning of June 6 and, dodging rifle fire and hand grenades from the enemy above, managed to reach the summit, find and disable the guns, and

EARL RUDDER
after leading his Rangers to the summit of Pointe du Hoc.

gain control of their position within two hours of scrambling out of their British assault boats. They were aided in the initial proceedings by the fourteen-inch guns of the battleship *Texas*, now serving in its second world war.

Rudder's Rangers accomplished their mission only to find themselves cut off and having to fight off counterattack after counterattack by German forces filtering back in through the extensive trench networks they had dug into the top of the point. "I gave up hope of getting off Pointe du Hoc alive," a *Stars and Stripes* writer remembered. "No reinforcements in sight, plenty of Germans in front of us, nothing behind us but sheer cliffs and [the] Channel."

By the time relief finally arrived, on the third brutal day, only about 75 of the 225 men who had come ashore with Rudder were alive or unwounded. Rudder had been hit twice within the space of thirty minutes, first by a German bullet in the leg and once by shell fragments in the chest and upper arm. He nonetheless stayed in command, refusing to be evacuated. In the opinion of a corporal who lived through Pointe du Hoc, "If Colonel Rudder had not led us in this battle, there would not have been any survivors."

Rudder managed to live through the rest of the war, leading men through other hellscapes such as Hürtgen Forest and the Battle of the Bulge, and then entering Texas politics and being elected land commissioner in 1956. He became the president of Texas A&M a few years later. He died fairly young, at

59—troubled all his life by the bits of shrapnel working their way through his shoulder—but he lived long enough to be confounded by the political and cultural sea changes of the 1960s. He once canceled a sanctioned A&M performance by Johnny Cash after the singer was arrested on drug charges in El Paso. When Cash performed off campus at a local dance hall, he dedicated his song "Dirty Old Egg Sucking Dog" to Earl Rudder, probably not knowing that the middle-aged, overweight, grayer-than-gray college administrator he was mocking was the man who had stormed the impregnable heights of Pointe du Hoc and helped turn the course of World War II. A few years later, during the cultural upheavals of 1968, Rudder put potential student agitators on notice. "The dissidents will have a hell of a fight," he warned in a speech, "and this pot-bellied president will be up in the front ranks leading it."

★

WHILE RUDDER'S RANGERS WERE FIGHTING THEIR WAY UP Pointe du Hoc on the morning of June 6, 1944, the men who had landed on Omaha Beach to their east were being slaughtered by the fire coming from German machine-gun nests at the top of the bluffs.

When I was in high school, our family's yard in Corpus Christi backed up to that of a friendly geologist and his wife, Joe and Melba Dawson. Mr. Dawson was slender, with a prominent nose and slicked-back hair. He would have been in his fifties then. I barely knew him, too caught up in the tortured self-consciousness of an acne-cursed teenager to have any curiosity about a neighbor who seemed unremarkable in every way. As far as I know, he never talked about his World War II experiences to anyone in our family, so it was a surprise to see him appear at the televised fiftieth anniversary of the D-Day landings in Normandy in 1994 and to hear him introduced by the chairman of the Joint Chiefs of Staff. "When history books are written," General John Shalikashvili told the people gathered at the American cemetery above Omaha Beach, "about the great invasion of France, you may not necessarily read of Joe Dawson, but . . . no history will be complete without him."

Stephen Ambrose, in his account of D-Day, published that same year, made a point of singling out Joe Dawson, whose "dash, boldness, initiative, teamwork, and tactical skills were outstanding beyond praise." On D-Day, Dawson was a thirty-year-old captain, the commander of the Sixteenth Infantry Regiment's G Company, part of the storied First Infantry Division known as the Big Red One. The war had already taken him through Algeria, Tunisia, and Sicily, and the horrors he had seen had branded his soul with a crusading urgency that was half fatalism. "The visions of the future must be based on the precepts of common understanding," he wrote to "My Dearest Family" from Sicily in July 1943, "but the world will see a blood bath that will make this war now existent seem puny in contrast. . . . Dear ones, this letter may have a solemn portent, but realize that I am seeing life in a measure far greater than one can envision from a distance."

The week before the invasion of France, he wrote from England, "When the big day comes, you will undoubtedly be wondering about me, and where I am, and how I fit into the show of shows. All I can say, dearest ones, is that I shall be giving everything within my power, and the enemy will know that there is one outfit led by a long, lanky Texan who means business."

When his landing craft touched down under furious fire on Omaha Beach, Dawson jumped out first. Two others were able to get off before an artillery shell blew up the other thirty-three men in the boat behind him. As mortars exploded and machine-gun fire raked the beach, the surviving members of G Company from the other boats instinctively crouched behind a mounded shingle of sand, but Dawson, quickly realizing it was a suicidal position, rallied them forward to the base of the high bluffs overlooking the beach.

With bangalore torpedoes, they blew holes through the concertina wire. But the slope leading up the bluff beyond the wire was a minefield. Two men who had tried to climb it earlier lay dead, and the slope was exposed to machine-gun fire from an emplacement on the crest of the bluff. But Dawson led his men upward anyway, stepping on the bodies that marked where the mines had already exploded, making their way through a scything storm of bullets. During the last part of the climb, Dawson crawled up a steep defile that temporarily hid him from the machine gun nest, only a few yards away. He pulled the pins on two grenades, stood up, and—in a kind of quick-draw contest—threw the grenades and killed the German gunners just as their barrels were turning toward him.

In doing so, he created a way out for the men trapped in the inferno of Omaha Beach. A path leading to those seaside bluffs—and to the liberation of France and the conquest of Germany—had been wedged open by his heroism. "Words can never describe," Dawson wrote home that next week, "the hell that was created on the beach that I stormed. God was with me, and I survived to get the job done, but it was terrible."

THERE WAS ANOTHER TEXAS HERO OF WORLD WAR II WHOSE acquaintance I had sort-of made. Though I never saw Audie Murphy in real life, he was a lingering boyhood presence, the star of 1950s westerns such as *The Kid From Texas*, *Tumbleweed*, *The Guns of Fort Petticoat*, and *Ride a Crooked Trail*. Even as a seven- or eight-year-old kid, I could tell that there was something not quite right about him as a movie star. He was short, but unlike other undersized screen presences—Alan Ladd, for instance—he *seemed* short. His Texas accent was too specific, too real. And in a movie genre dominated by grizzled presences like John Wayne or Randolph Scott, Audie Murphy looked barely old enough to play the lead in a high school play.

He was, as it turned out, something of an accidental cowboy hero, the beneficiary of his crossover fame as the most decorated soldier in World War II. Audie Murphy was a young man who had won every decoration for valor the United States had to give, including the Medal of Honor. It was James Cagney who wired Murphy during the closing months of the war and invited him to come to Hollywood, took him under his producer's wing, and signed him up for acting lessons. "I saw Audie's picture on the cover of *Life* magazine," Cagney remembered, "and said to myself, 'There is the typical American soldier.' . . . I saw that Audie could be photographed well from any angle, and I figured that a guy with drive enough to take him that far in the war had drive enough to become a star."

But Cagney also noticed something else. The first time he met Murphy, at the Los Angeles airport, he was struck by how thin he was, what a pallor he had. His new movie-star prospect was in "such a nervous condition that I was afraid he might jump out of a window."

Audie Murphy had been through a lot in his twenty years—had been, in the title of his memoir and the movie that would be made from it—*To Hell and Back*. He was born into poverty in 1924 to a tenant farming family in Hunt County in north-central Texas. When the war broke out, he was sixteen, with a fifth-grade education, working in a radio repair shop in the county seat of Greenville, which promoted itself as having the "blackest land" and the "whitest people." He stood five feet, five and a half inches and weighed 112 pounds. Two years later, serving with the Third Division in North Africa, he had grown a little taller but still "didn't look sixteen years old."

A woman in Greenville remembered him as being sensitive and easily hurt, "a sad type person." But in combat, which he soon experienced an unbelievable amount of in Sicily, the Italian peninsula, and France, he developed into a focused, remorseless, intelligent, and highly skilled killer—he would have been very much at home on the Texas frontier, rangering with Jack Hays or Rip Ford. By the time he won the Medal of Honor, he was already a legend in the Third. "I don't suppose there was a real veteran in the whole division who was not aware of him," one man remembered. "If Murphy was in the front lines, we in the rear area went to sleep. But if we got word that he was falling back, we prepared to get the hell out of there. When Murphy started retreating, it was time to clear out fast."

A day when Audie Murphy famously did not retreat was January 26, 1945. This was during the intense fighting when the German Army was making a defiant stand west of the Rhine in an area called the Colmar Pocket. Murphy by that time was a second lieutenant, in command of a company that had started out with 235 men but had lost so many to death and wounds and trench foot that there were only 18 left. They had been ordered to hold a position at the edge of a forest. The winter air was raw, and the ground so frozen that it was impossible to chip a foxhole out of it.

When two hundred Germans, with six tanks, began to attack, Murphy ordered his men back into the trees. He stayed out in the opening, shooting at the advancing enemy with his carbine and directing artillery strikes over the radio. German shells had already hit an American tank destroyer, which stood burning a few yards away. When Murphy had emptied his rifle, he leapt up on top of the tank vehicle. He knew that the gasoline and ammunition below could explode at any moment, but he stayed there anyway, mowing down the advancing Germans with its fifty-caliber machine gun and continuing to call out artillery coordinates. When someone on the other end of the line asked him how close he was to the enemy, he said, "Just hold the phone and I'll let you talk to one of the bastards."

Though he was standing alone out in the open, facing down an enemy only yards away as he fired from the deck of the burning tank destroyer, at one point killing 12 Germans in a single burst from the machine gun, he almost magically survived. The tank destroyer blew up only minutes after he finally got down from it. He had killed or wounded 50 German soldiers, part of a personal wartime tally of 240. He wrote in *To Hell and Back* that he felt "no exhilaration at being alive. . . . Existence has taken on the quality of a dream in which I am detached from all that is present."

To some degree, that was true of the rest of his brief life. Though Murphy became a movie star and a reasonably respected actor, a best-selling author, and even a successful song lyricist (his best known country lament was "Shutters and Boards"), the war-strung nerves that James Cagney had noticed that day at the Los Angeles airport never quite settled. When he died in a plane crash in 1971 at the age of forty-five, Audie Murphy was a compulsive gambler, an insomniac with a pill problem, an actor with a fast-fading career, and a half-forgotten hero from another age.

★

SAM DEALEY, ANOTHER MEDAL OF HONOR WINNER, HAD A smoother start in life than Audie Murphy. He was the nephew of George Bannerman Dealey, the owner and editor of the anti-Klan *Dallas Morning*

News, one of the founders of Southern Methodist University, and a president of the Philosophical Society of Texas. (The Philosophical Society was an organization whose origins went all the way back to 1837, whose charter members included the immortal mortal enemies Mirabeau Lamar and Sam Houston, and whose areas of cogitation included "animals . . . Aboriginal tribes . . . Natural curiosities . . . Mines . . . And the thousand other topics of interest which our new and rising republic unfolds to the philosopher, the scholar, and the man of the world.")

The name Dealey acquired a hard-to-shake shadow in 1963 when Dealey Plaza—named in honor of George despite his protestations, and originally conceived as a pleasing, parklike entrance to downtown Dallas—became the site of John F. Kennedy's assassination. But during World War II, Sam Dealey's record as a submarine commander helped keep the civic luster of the family name bright. The beginning of his career, though, was unpromising. His grades were so low and his demerits so high at the U.S. Naval Academy that he "bilged out" in his first year. Alarmed and abashed, he paid a visit to his congressman in Washington and talked him into giving him another chance and restarting his appointment.

In his thirties when the war came, he was given command of the USS *Harder*, one of a new class of faster, heavily armed submarines, with six torpedo tubes in its bow and four in its stern. In those days, submarines were named for fish. Most of the glamorous fish names had already been taken by then, and Dealey and his men had to make do with a fighting ship named for an unremarkable species of South African mullet. But they compensated with the sub's pennant, which featured a pugnacious fish smoking a cigar, a torpedo tucked under one fin, with the slogan "Hit 'em Harder" above.

"I think I'm going to enjoy this war," Dealey wrote his family the day he took command of the *Harder* in 1942. That seems to have been true. "The *Harder*," reported a headquarters officer after visiting the ship, "was the most high-spirited boat I ever saw. . . . Dealey, as you know, was a most modest, self-effacing man with but one goal in mind—to sink Jap ships and get the war ended as soon as possible. Officers and men of his ship absolutely worshipped him. . . . They tasted a lot of glory with him, and this in itself put their morale at the very highest level."

Dealey liked officers who could sing and thereby join in the nightly underwater songfests featuring old favorites such as "In the Gloaming" and "Don't Fence Me In." One of the officers had gone to school with the singer Dinah Shore. She became the *Harder*'s "Guardian Angel," framed photos of her securely attached to wardroom and mess room walls to give hope to the crew as they were being bombarded from above by depth charges.

As a submarine commander, Dealey's instinct was for exuberant aggression. You can see it on display in his patrol logs: "The *Harder* was in the middle of an enemy convoy and I felt like a possum in a hen house."

And of course it was on display where it counted, in the dangerous waters of the southwestern Philippines, between the Sulu Archipelago and Borneo. During four spectacularly lethal days in June 1944, the *Harder* sank four (possibly five, and even possibly six) Japanese destroyers.

On his next patrol, his sixth, Dealey led a wolf pack of submarines that destroyed four Japanese merchant ships and three frigates—bringing *Harder*'s wartime toll to somewhere between sixteen and twenty enemy vessels. But Dinah Shore's protective magic wore off on an August morning on the west coast of Luzon. The commander of one of the submarines in Dealey's wolf pack caught a last distant glimpse of the *Harder*'s periscope as it disappeared beneath the surface, pursuing a Japanese minesweeper trying to break for the open sea out of Dasol Bay. An hour later, he heard the sonic echo of fifteen depth charges. One of them, at least, must have struck the *Harder*, because neither the sub nor its high-spirited Texas skipper was ever seen again.

---- ★ ----

FOR PEOPLE LIVING ALONG THE TEXAS COAST, SUBMARINE warfare was not something taking place on the other side of the world. It was unnervingly immediate. "They were expecting the biggest invasion you ever saw to come into Galveston," remembered one of the men who worked on the city's coastal defenses. It was far from an unrealistic fear after the attack on Pearl Harbor. A few people still alive in Galveston likely had vivid childhood memories of the Union invasion during the Civil War, and since the city was a significant port for oil tankers and guarded the approach to the Houston Ship Channel and its spidery tangle of petrochemical plants, its strategic importance in a modern war was glaringly plain. In Galveston today is an obscure but prominent landmark at the base of a luxury hotel just across Seawall Boulevard from the Gulf beach. It's a huge disc of concrete that erupts out of a grassy swale bordered by palm trees. The horizontal slit in the casement that faces the sea once harbored coastal guns that fired thousand-pound shells. During World War II, this gun emplacement was the bristly seaward facade of a post known as Fort Crockett. It was one of three coastal batteries built to protect Galveston from the German U-Boats that began to enter the Gulf in 1942 and that routinely attacked and sank tankers sailing from Texas ports.

Most beaches on Galveston were closed to the public. Blackouts were ordered, throwing the island back in time to the primeval darkness of the

Karankawa days. In the Hotel Galvez, each formerly luxurious room housed fourteen coastguardsmen sleeping on steel bunk beds, the ocean views blocked by permanent blackout curtains. Blimps 250 feet long, armed with bombs and fifty-caliber guns, coasted forth from their stations along the Texas shoreline for improbable slow-moving air-sea battles with German submarines in the Gulf.

The submarine threat had faded by the summer of 1943, but by then German commanders had sunk fifty-six ships in the Gulf of Mexico and damaged another fourteen. No submarines ever appeared within eyeball distance of Galveston, but if you were driving along Seawall Boulevard, you couldn't have missed another reminder of a continent-spanning war. At Fort Crockett, behind a ten-foot-high fence topped with barbed wire and guarded by searchlights and watchtowers, men in denim jackets with a white *P* on the back were mowing and raking the grounds. They were German soldiers, among the almost fifty thousand prisoners of war being held in Texas in dozens of camps.

It wasn't just POWs captured in battle who found themselves behind barbed wire in Texas. There was another category of detainee: "enemy aliens" already living in the United States. These were people whose German, Japanese, or Italian ties put them under a noxiously indiscriminate cloud of suspicion. Many of them had been arrested and deported to Peru and other Latin American countries. The Immigration and Naturalization Service operated three internment camps in Texas. The largest of them— with five hundred buildings spread across almost three hundred acres— was on the outskirts of Crystal City, a town whose name referred to once-sparkling artesian springs that were now mostly dry, depleted in the service of turning this desert-like location thirty miles from the Mexican border into "the spinach capital of the world." Spinach had been so good to Crystal City that in 1937 it erected a fiberglass statue of Popeye in front of city hall. The whimsical gesture was lost on many of the Mexican migrant workers who picked the spinach. "We hated that statue," José Ángel Gutiérrez, an activist who grew up in Crystal City, recalled. "The statue symbolized our servitude to the spinach and the Anglo owners of the company."

The new Crystal City internment facility was built on the site of a migrant-labor camp, a primitive place with outdoor privies and no running water where Mexican field workers had been housed while they picked produce. The new camp was a big leap forward; its amenities included a swimming pool, schools, stores, libraries, and a beer hall for the German detainees. But it was still a prison, and its end-of-the-earth location was disorienting, especially if you were a newly designated enemy alien from San Francisco or New York.

*"Enemy aliens"
with ties to the Axis
powers were detained
during the war in
Texas camps like this
one in Crystal City.
The camps provided
schools, libraries, and
movie theaters for the
detainees, but there
was no mistaking
they were prisons.*

Of the internment camps in Texas, Crystal City was the only one built for families. Spouses and children of enemy aliens swept up after Pearl Harbor were put on trains and shipped off to the Texas desert to join them. This helped relieve, to some degree, the trauma of family members whose loved ones had suddenly disappeared for inexplicable reasons. (One German father in Cleveland, Mathias Eiserloh, was incarcerated and sent away partly because a feuding neighbor told the FBI that he kept quicklime in his basement to dispose of murdered bodies and had built a flat roof on the top of his house for use as a landing pad for Axis gyro-copters.)

The families arrived under guard at the train station in San Antonio and were sent on by army buses to Crystal City, where they were driven past the statue of Popeye, through a gate guarded by machine-gun-wielding soldiers in towers, and into briefing sessions, where they were instructed in the unanticipated skills they would need in their new South Texas home—among them, how to suck the poison out of a rattlesnake bite.

"There was no place like Crystal City," Mathias Eiserloh's daughter remembered decades later with lingering bitterness. "So many families living behind the barbed wire, many of us born in America, humiliated and betrayed by our government."

—————— ★ ——————

AMONG THE TEXANS WHO FOUND THEMSELVES PROPELLED TO unexpected prominence by the war was Oveta Culp Hobby, a thirty-six-year-old former parliamentarian of the state legislature. She had gotten that job when she was only twenty. "Oveta," her mother was once heard to remark, "was never young." The daughter of a state legislator, she was a no-nonsense workhorse from the beginning, even though she had been named after the heroine of a romance novel. She was an avid childhood reader of the *Congressional Record*. In Sunday school, when she was five, she was handed a temperance pledge by her teacher. She refused to sign—on the grounds, as she later recalled her reasoning, that while she was "pretty sure it [drinking] was something I wouldn't do now, I wasn't sure I might not want to do it in the future."

When she was twenty-five, she ran for the state legislature, and lost partly because her opponent called her out as a "parliamentarian," trusting that the word would have a fifth-columnist, saboteur-like ring to his district's voters. After her defeat, she went to work for the *Houston Post-Dispatch*, soon to be consolidated into the *Houston Post*. The newspaper's president was the former governor William Pettus Hobby, the man who had defeated Pa Ferguson in 1918. Hobby was a fifty-three-year-old widower

"If there are no rules," wrote former state parliamentarian Oveta Culp Hobby, "confusion results." When she was named head of the Women's Army Auxiliary Corps, she deployed her skills to bring order and purpose to a mass enlistment of women eager to defend their country.

when Oveta Culp met him; she was twenty-six.

"I never thought about a romance," she said many years later. "I was quite busy and I really didn't have marriage on my mind."

But she married Hobby anyway—"I always felt so at ease with him." She called him "Governor." After they were married, she threw herself into civic and philanthropic causes, displaying a keen executive ability. She was also cool under fire. She and her husband were flying to the Centennial Exposition in Dallas in a private plane when flames erupted in the cockpit and the pilot crash-landed in a cotton field. Oveta, two months pregnant, managed to drag her unconscious husband out of the plane just before the fuel tank erupted. Then she borrowed a car from a local field hand and drove Governor and the badly burned pilot and copilot to a nearby hospital. After that, she collected her nerves and produced a book about parliamentary law. "In every field of life," she wrote, "it is necessary to have rules which one observes. In meetings, if the rules are not followed, or if there are no rules, confusion results."

She became executive director of the *Houston Post,* and a few years later she and her husband bought the paper from Jesse Jones. It made sense that such a disciplined, connected, and collected personality would be summoned to Washington in a time of national emergency. In May 1942, Oveta Culp Hobby was sworn in as head of the newly created Women's Army Auxiliary Corps, which received a status upgrade a year later when "auxiliary" was dropped and women for the first time were allowed to be part of the regular army.

Women rushed to enlist—thirteen thousand of them on the first day that applications were accepted, almost a hundred thousand by the end of the war. Hobby was given the rank of major, and later colonel. Since there were not yet army uniforms for women, she was sworn in while wearing a dress and a wide-brimmed picture hat. She finally got a uniform, but for a while it was the only one in existence. She wrangled with the Army Quartermaster Corps over the final design of the WAAC uniform—the quartermasters disapproved of pleats because they were a waste of cloth. The ensemble ended up being topped with a severe-looking billed cap like something out of a Foreign Legion movie. The female recruits were not fond of it, but it looked good enough on Colonel Hobby's earnest, small-featured face to become known as a "Hobby Hat."

Uniforms were only one small element in the complex bureaucratic undertaking of creating a women's army where none had existed before. Thousands of women had to be trained and deployed, many of them overseas. Jobs for them had to be expanded beyond default secretarial duties to front-and-center work as pilots, radio operators, flight dispatchers, motor pool mechanics, and gas-balloon chemists. Logistical objections and blatant misogyny from the regular men's army had to be confronted, along with the disapproval of civilian traditionalists (the WAACs, in the opinion of one Catholic Church publication, existed "to break down the traditional American and Christian opposition to removing women from the home and to degrade her by bringing back the pagan female goddess of de-sexed, lustful sterility").

In addition, Colonel Hobby had to contend with the initial deep skepticism of African Americans, who assumed that her background as a southerner guaranteed that any black women who managed to become a WAAC would be serving under Jim Crow rules. The director of the National Negro Council predicted that Hobby would be "imbued with the mores and undemocratic practices of a state like Texas."

But Hobby worked quickly to overcome that expectation. She announced that at least forty black women would be in the first group of officer candidates. She made a recruiting speech to a black sorority at Howard University, intervened when an army recruiting officer in North Carolina refused to accept black applicants, and made a point to be at the docks to bestow an official farewell when an African American battalion of WAACs sailed off to duty in England.

She wore herself out. She ended up being hospitalized for six weeks with exhaustion and resigned just before the end of the Pacific war. But she returned to the national stage in the Eisenhower administration as the second female cabinet member in American history, serving as the head of the new Department of Health, Education, and Welfare. And for most of the rest of her life, she remained a force in Texas politics as the president and editor of the *Post*, as the vastly wealthy owner of television and radio stations, and as the sole female member of the "8-F Crowd," Houston's informal power-player cabal that met in Herman Brown's suite in the Lamar Hotel—eight floors below Jesse Jones's penthouse—to decide such things as who should

Hobby made a seamless transition from military commander to civilian mover and shaker.

own oil pipelines or where airports should be built or who should be president. Her much-older husband died in 1964, but Oveta Culp Hobby held onto the *Post* and onto power for decades longer, finally passing away in 1995. In firm command till the last, she helped write her own eulogy. Her son, former lieutenant governor Bill Hobby, was asked to describe his late mother in one word. He chose "intimidating." But another family member, Hobby's daughter-in-law Janet, added a little more amplification: "All she wanted was for someone to designate an objective standard for achievement, and she would dominate by sheer, dogged and undeniable merit."

★

IN JUNE 1947, OVETA CULP HOBBY WAS A PASSENGER ON THE
Pan American clipper *America* when it made the first regularly scheduled
round-the-world passenger flight in the history of commercial aviation. The
trip, which lasted thirteen days, took the passengers—among whom were
newspaper publishers like herself, mayors, businessmen, and State Department officials—on a dizzying itinerary that included the recently defeated Empire of Japan. At a luncheon in Tokyo, Hobby sat next to General
Douglas MacArthur and peppered him with questions about food shortages
and the pace of democratization and disarmament. She saw firsthand the
horrible effects of the Allied bombing of Tokyo, and en route to the city on
the *America*, she had looked out of the airplane windows at what was left of
Hiroshima and Nagasaki—"mute reminders of the atomic bomb."

She may have known that it was a fellow Texan—and a fellow
Houstonian—who had dropped the bomb on Nagasaki, which killed at
least seventy-five thousand people. His name was Captain Kermit Beahan, a
graduate of Rice University and a veteran bombardier of precise skill. "Kevin
was a true artist with a bombsight," wrote Charles Sweeney, his pilot on
the Nagasaki mission. "If it was possible to deliver a bomb to its intended
target, he was the man to do it." He was such an auteur with his Norden
bombsight and so effortlessly proficient at picking up women that his
fellow crewmen named their B-29 after him—*The Great Artiste*. The aircraft
accompanied the *Enola Gay* on its August 6, 1945, mission to drop the atomic
bomb on Hiroshima. Three days later, Beahan and the rest of the *Great
Artiste* crew, though now flying in a different airplane, attacked Nagasaki
with an even more powerful bomb, one known as Fat Man.

The day he called out, "Bombs away!" and unleashed the bomb that
destroyed Nagasaki and ended World War II was Kermit Beahan's twenty-
seventh birthday. In an official armed forces film clip of him taken about a
week later, he stands on an airfield in front of a B-29. His uniform sleeves are
rolled up to his biceps, he has a Clark Gable mustache, and he speaks with a
broad southern accent. He appears to have been rather clumsily coached in
how to present himself to the camera in an aw-shucks, everyman way.

"Captain Beahan," the interviewer asks in a staccato newsreel voice,
"what was your most outstanding experience on this historic flight?"

"I suppose," Beahan answers, "it was when the clouds opened up over
the target of Nagasaki. The target was there, pretty as a picture. I made the
run, let the bomb go"—at this point he looks into the camera with a grin
that might be forced or might be natural—"that was my greatest thrill!"

CAPTAIN KERMIT BEAHAN,
"a true artist with a bombsight" and the man who dropped the atomic bomb on Nagasaki.

On the fortieth anniversary of the bombing, when Kermit Beahan was a soon-to-be-retired technical writer for Brown & Root, he was interviewed again, this time by the *Houston Chronicle*. He said he would never apologize for his participation in the bombing of Nagasaki, but perhaps four decades of reflection had changed the way he remembered what he saw that day. "It looked," he said, "like a picture of hell."

—43—

A NEW TEXAS

A DUST STORM WAS KICKING UP ONE FREEZING AFTER-
noon as I stood outside President George W. Bush's childhood home in Midland. This was in January 2018, and Midland
—situated in the heart of the Permian Basin—was in the
throes of reanimation. Thanks to the recent lifting of a forty-
year-old ban on crude oil exports, the price of West Texas
Intermediate was $65 a barrel, more than double what it had been two years
before. And breakthroughs in fracking technology, which had brought about
a revolution in domestic oil production, meant that Interstate 20 between
Midland and nearby Odessa was a slow-moving procession of eighteen-wheelers
hauling oilfield equipment. The highways were lined with the prefabricated
buildings of companies offering fire-resistant clothing, pumpjack components,
storage tanks, and well-logging and perforating services. Cheap motel rooms—
with views of leafless mesquite branches festooned with windblown trash—
were going for rates you might expect to pay in Manhattan or London.

But there were no views today as the dust came in and browned out the
horizon and the nearby downtown buildings. Tumbleweeds—not indigenous
to Texas, but a European invader whose seeds arrived in the United States
with nineteenth-century agricultural shipments—bounded across thoroughfares and residential streets, snagging in the undercarriages of cars.

The Bush home, on West Ohio Avenue, was a modest one-story house with gray siding, a bay window, and a fenced yard with a long-uninhabited doghouse. It was open to the public. Compared with tours of other presidents' homes I had visited, this one didn't last long. There was not all that much to see in a 1,500-square-foot house: a living room, a den, a kitchen, a hallway with a shelf for a rotary telephone, and three bedrooms. One of the rooms, with knotty-pine walls and bookshelves filled with representative toys and books from the 1950s, had been the bedroom of the young George W. Bush, who was five years old when he and his parents and his sister Robin moved into this house in 1951.

My visit to this humble historical attraction left me saturated with nostalgia. I never lived in Midland; but when I was five, in 1953, my widowed mother remarried, and she and my brother and I moved with our new oilman father from Oklahoma City to Abilene. Abilene was 150 miles east of Midland, but the two cities shared a fundamental West Texas vibe: a cluster of utilitarian downtown office buildings rising from a scraggly landscape, flat and dusty residential streets lined with cinderblock fences and unimpressive houses like the ones the Bush family or ours lived in, a sense of overpowering, unimpeded, unlovely space in every direction. When we came to Abilene, it felt to me that we had landed at the edge of a great emptiness where the frontier was still a living memory. Indeed, when twenty-four-year-old George Herbert Walker Bush brought his own young family to West Texas in 1948 from Connecticut, only seventy-four years had passed since the last stand of the Comanches at the Battle of Palo Duro Canyon.

"Poppy" Bush was the patrician son of a U.S. senator. He was a product of Andover and of Yale, where he was the captain of the baseball team. But between prep school and college there was the war. Bush enlisted in June 1942 on the day he turned eighteen. He went into pilot training and became one of the youngest flying officers in the navy. He got a cursory glimpse of a different part of Texas during training at the Corpus Christi Naval Air Station, and his torpedo-bomber squadron sailed to the war in the Pacific on board a newly commissioned light aircraft carrier named—after the eternally fabled Texas battle—the USS *San Jacinto*.

It was from the deck of the *San Jacinto* that Bush flew his Avenger torpedo bomber in September 1944 on a mission to destroy a Japanese radio tower on the Pacific island of Chichi-Jima. Just before he dropped his bombs on the target, his plane was struck by antiaircraft fire. Bush managed to scramble from the cockpit and bail out. He thought his two fellow crewmen had bailed out as well, but they were never seen again, and he drifted down into the ocean alone, bleeding and gasping from the smoke that had filled the cockpit. Paddling a tiny inflated life raft with his hands, he desperately tried to pull away from the tide carrying him back to the Japanese-held island. Before he was helplessly delivered up to the enemy, or killed by machine-gun fire from a Japanese gunboat, he was pulled out of the water by an American submarine. A month later he found his way back to the *San Jacinto*. He went on leave, got married to Barbara Pierce, a girl he had met three years before at a Greenwich Country Club dance, and then reported back to duty and waited for the order to vanish into the inferno of the invasion of mainland Japan. But then Kermit Beahan released Fat Man over Nagasaki, and suddenly George H. W. Bush had the opportunity to figure out what to do with a life that had just been unexpectedly extended.

"What you need to do is head out to Texas and those oil fields," advised an influential family friend who offered Bush a ground-level job in Odessa with a firm called IDECO, the International Derrick and Equipment Company. Odessa was Midland's scruffier neighbor. It was twenty miles to the west, and many miles from anywhere else. El Paso was 280 miles away to the west, Fort Worth 320 miles to the east. Odessa was a cowtown that had developed into a stop on the Texas and Pacific Railway and boomed after oil was discovered in 1926. Among the accounts of how it got its name, the most dismissible is that there was once a beautiful Indian maiden in the vicinity with the unlikely name of Odessa. The most credible is that it was named for some obscure reason or another after the Russian port city on the Black Sea. When the Bushes arrived, it was still a relatively small town with fewer than thirty thousand people. Though Odessa would one day feature a full-scale replica of Shakespeare's Globe Theater and an eight-foot-tall statue of the "World's Largest Jackrabbit," in 1948 its allurements were scant. The closest things to scenery were the oil derricks on the horizon and a nearby hole in the ground that was the site of a long-ago meteorite impact.

George and Barbara Bush and two-year-old Georgie lived at first in a rented duplex where they shared a bathroom with the mother and daughter prostitutes who entertained their clients next door. They rented another house a few months later. In Odessa, George Bush learned about the virtues of chicken-fried steak and the inadvisability of wearing his Bermuda shorts among oil-field workers. Barbara learned that the smell of gas was a persistent atmospheric condition and did not mean that an apocalyptic explosion was imminent.

It was not long before Bush, in the words of a friend, "caught the fever" of the oil patch and made the jump from selling oilfield equipment to setting up, with the help of family connections, his own exploration company. By this time, the Bushes were living in the little house on West Ohio Avenue in

GEORGE AND BARBARA BUSH
doing their best to fit in as Texans at the Midland Rodeo grounds in 1950. With them are their first two children: George W. (Georgie) on horseback, and Robin on her father's shoulders.

Midland, and there were two other children, three-year-old Robin and new-born John Ellis, known as Jeb. One day Robin woke up and told her mother, "I don't know what I'm going to do today. I'm either going to lie on the bed and look at books or rest outside and watch cars go by." Barbara thought it was odd that her energetic three-year-old girl was suddenly filled with such lassitude. She took her to their doctor in Midland. A blood test revealed that she had leukemia. "What do we do?" her parents asked, and the doctor's blood-freezing advice was not to do anything. "You should take her home, make life as easy as possible for her, and in three weeks' time, she'll be gone."

It was impossibly practical advice to follow, and there were months of visits back and forth to Sloan-Kettering Institute in New York for treatment, but in the end her life was not saved and her death only deferred. "I have a vivid memory of the day my parents told me that Robin had died," George W. Bush wrote many years later. He was at Sam Houston Elementary School when he saw his parents pull up in their pea-green Oldsmobile in the middle of the school day. "As I sprinted over to the car, I thought that I saw Robin's blond curls in the backseat. I was so excited that she had come home. But when I got to the car, she wasn't there. Mother hugged me tight and told me she was gone. On the drive home, I saw my parents cry for the first time."

Two future presidents in front of the modest Bush family house on West Ohio Avenue in Midland.

The day after their daughter died, George and Barbara Bush played golf. It must have been the saddest eighteen holes ever played. "We just got up and went out," Barbara recalled in a 1988 *Texas Monthly* interview, sounding still in a grief-induced daze. "Played golf. Didn't tell anyone. I later thought that if people had seen us, they would have said, 'Why are those people doing that?'"

THE TEXAS THAT THE BUSH FAMILY EXPERIENCED AS EMBRAC-ing, disorienting, and heartbreaking was in important ways a different place from the Texas that had existed before the war. More people now lived in its cities than on its farms or ranches, a change that had been stealing over the state for generations but that finally arrived when a wartime manufacturing surge brought workers to the shipyards and aircraft factories and petrochemical plants that had sprung into being in small and large Texas cities. And with so many men overseas, thousands of those new jobs were open to women.

The new urban growth could be dizzying. Corpus Christi, where George H. W. Bush received his aviator wings at the naval air station and where Reynolds Aluminum had built a new plant, doubled its population during the 1940s. Houston, San Antonio, Dallas, Fort Worth, and other Texas cities pulsed with new residents and new industries, producing steel and paper and airplanes and chemicals. And of course there was still oil, along with its ever-expanding subsidiary businesses. Lord Curzon's famous bromide about World War I, that "the Allied cause had floated to victory on a wave of oil," applied to World War II as well, and a lot of that oil came from Texas, from the fields of stupendously rich oil barons such as H. L. Hunt, Clint Murchison, Hugh Roy Cullen, and Sid Richardson. Texas alone produced almost twice as many barrels—five hundred million—during the war as the Axis powers combined. But the problem had been to find a way to get that oil to the refineries on the East Coast.

It was wildly impractical to transport it all by rail. Ninety percent of Texas oil reached eastern refineries via tankers that carried it through the Gulf of Mexico, around the Florida Straits, and up the Atlantic coast. But once World War II was underway, those sea-lanes became a shooting gallery for German U-boats. What was needed, and needed fast, were pipelines that would deliver East Texas oil across half the continent to the refineries in Philadelphia and elsewhere in the East. The two pipelines that were constructed for that purpose were called the Big Inch—twenty-four inches in diameter, to transport crude oil—and the slightly smaller Little Big Inch, which would carry kerosene and other refined products. The pipelines were built under the supervision of the Texas oilman Jubal Richard Parten. J. R.

Parten was not nearly as conniving as J. R. Ewing, the fictional centerpiece of the TV show *Dallas*, who would one day make his initials famous. Parten was a big player—a former president of the Independent Petroleum Association of Texas and a member of the University of Texas Board of Regents, among other things—but unlike Texas wildcatters and pot stirrers of the time, he was a non-crusty political moderate, even sort of a liberal when it came to things like academic freedom and free speech.

Fifteen thousand roustabouts began work on the Big Inch and the Little Big Inch in 1942. The Big Inch was started first. It ran for 1,254 miles—dug into the earth, buried beneath rivers and bored through mountain ranges, from Longview, Texas, to the Sun Oil refineries in Marcus Hook, Pennsylvania. The world's longest pipeline, a construction project of almost inconceivable scale spanning the complicated geography of seven states, took only a little over a year to build and for the oil that won the war to begin flowing from Texas.

When it came to the superheated industrial economy that followed in the wake of World War II, there was hardly a better example than the thriving, malodorous town of twenty thousand called Texas City. It was on the western shore of Galveston Bay, between the island city of Galveston and the ship channel leading to the mighty port of Houston. By 1947, Texas City was the fourth-largest port on the Gulf Coast. It had tripled in size in seven years. Surprisingly, no other town had seized on the definitive name Texas City until three developer brothers from Duluth, Minnesota, did so in the 1890s when they bought up 10,000 acres of marshy Galveston Bay shoreline to create what they believed would be a major shipping center. Texas City survived the 1900 hurricane and was in place when Spindletop came in a year later. Then came refineries, tank farms, pipelines, chemical plants—a chaotic no-nonsense cityscape of squatty storage tanks, cracking towers, and flaring gas that one tugboat captain described as "an ominous Oz."

"I feel like I'm sitting on a keg of dynamite," the thirty-nine-year-old pastor of St. Mary's Catholic Church told a friend in March 1947. Father Bill Roach was probably not talking about a literal explosion. More likely he was making an oblique reference to his own interior volatility. He had the tortured demeanor of a saint, a man who had taken it upon himself not just to save souls but also to heal injustice. He had found plenty of souls in peril in the dives and whorehouses of Texas City, but when he called the city "a wicked place, a very wicked place" in a Sunday sermon, he was referring to glaring social inequity and environmental devastation as well as personal sins.

"It is needless," he wrote in a provocative ad he bought in the local newspaper, "to point out to the citizens the primitive and sordid conditions under which we are living. For a sewage disposal plant we are using our front yard, that is, the bay. For a garbage incinerator, we dig large trenches on the prairie, leaving the community open to the potential danger of epidemics. . . . Our Mexican and Negro sections are a disgrace. . . . Both of these areas are over-populated. . . . Two and three families are living in one or two rooms. . . . Outdoor toilets, open sewage."

On the morning of April 16, 1947, though, the residents of Texas City noticed something that was disconcertingly lovely. A fire was coming from the docks, from a French ship named the *Grandcamp*, one of the several thousand freighters known as Liberty ships that had been built during the war to deliver troops and supplies to Allied forces. In its holds, among other cargo, were five million pounds of ammonium nitrate, shaped into pellets and packed into over fifty thousand moisture-proof plastic bags. Ammonium nitrate was a key ingredient in the bombs and other high explosives that had leveled cities in World War II. It was also a fertilizer that promised to help feed a devastated postwar world.

Just before eight in the morning, one of the stevedores loading the rest of the cargo smelled burning paper and soon saw small eruptions of flame. They were quenched by fire retardant and fire hoses, but more kept leaping out until the whole cargo was smoldering and a strange pastel palette of multicolored smoke began streaming from the *Grandcamp*'s hold. "If that wasn't a fire," a high school girl who was watching the colorful blaze from a second-floor classroom window said to her friends, "that would be one of the prettiest things I've ever seen."

Twenty-seven of the twenty-eight men of the Texas City volunteer fire department rushed to the scene to help the French crew put out the flames, and the novel spectacle of a burning ship fatally drew hundreds of townspeople to the docks.

The decks of the *Grandcamp* began to heave from the heat, and the water in which the ship floated began to boil. The explosion happened a little after nine. The *Grandcamp* blew apart in a screeching, fiery cascade of molten metal fragments that vaulted into the sky and fell upon the buildings and people of Texas City, killing those that had not already been incinerated or blasted away in the explosion's massive shock wave. A dark mushroom cloud appeared over the city. Two planes flying over the port were broken apart and knocked out of the sky. A bus traveling down the highway four miles away was lifted into the air, and the concussive force of the blast knocked out windows in Houston, forty miles away.

Father Roach was not killed at once. He was hauled out of the inferno, his eyes wild and open as if they were staring at a vision of the hell he had predicted. They were still open when he died later that day. All the members

Texas City, on Galveston Bay, was an exemplar of the surging Texas industrial economy after World War II. But that was before something went terribly wrong.

of the Texas City fire department and of the French crew that had tried to save the ship were killed. At the nearby Monsanto plant, 145 workers were dead, and the forty-acre plant itself was a jagged, poisonous ruin. Pieces of bodies were everywhere, and those who managed to survive the blast staggered through smoke and flames, clothes blown off, limbs blown off or broken, bodies covered in a thick sheen of oil and chemical residue and the molasses that had also been part of the ship's cargo. Many of the white survivors, covered in this black goop, could no longer be identified by their race, and they were thrown into trucks and driven to Galveston, where they were treated in the segregated black ward of the hospital.

Another Liberty ship in the port, the *High Flyer*, was also carrying ammonium nitrate, and when the blast occurred it was blown into the hull of a neighboring vessel. The captain ordered the crew to abandon ship; its own combustible cargo was on fire. That night, after heroic volunteer tugboat crews managed to cut its anchor chain and try without success to tow the *High Flyer* out of its slip, it too exploded, in an eruption even more powerful than the one that destroyed the *Grandcamp*. This time, though, there were no curious onlookers, and only two people died when the *High Flyer* went up. But the new explosion blasted through tank farms and chemical plants, creating an unholy slurry of crude oil, styrene, sulfur, toluene, and every other flammable or gaseous product released from the destroyed petrochemical complex. It also finished the job that the *Grandcamp* had started, further leveling the neglected black and Hispanic neighborhoods that to Father Roach had been an exhibit of Texas City's toxic racism.

The official death toll was 581. That included the bodies of those that could be identified and those, known to be dead, whose bodies had been vaporized or incinerated or could never be found. But many other people in Texas City that day were never accounted for, so the true total may have been much higher.

Of the 468 bodies deposited at the local funeral home and at a makeshift morgue in the garage of a gas station, 63 could not be identified. It was decided that they would be buried in the same location, with best guesses made about which body parts should go into which coffins. Preliminary arrangements were made for a parcel of land a few miles away in the town of Hitchcock to be used for the burial, but the citizens there wanted to know beforehand whether there were any black people among the dead. When they were told there were, they canceled the deal. The Episcopalian pastor in charge of the burials was so disillusioned that he didn't speak about it for many years. "I expected, somehow," he said, "that people would come together in such a way that things like that would never happen. It hit me right in the stomach."

— 44 —

YE SHALL KNOW
THE TRUTH

THE UNKNOWN AFRICAN AMERICANS REFUSED BURIAL IN
Hitchcock were not the only minority citizens having trouble
finding a place for themselves in postwar Texas, either in
death or in life. For instance, there was a trim, scholarly,
balding Houston mail carrier from Houston. His name was
Heman Sweatt. In 1946, the year he put himself forward

as a plaintiff in a court case designed to challenge the University of Texas's segregated law school, Sweatt was thirty-three. His father, an activist member of the Houston branch of the National Association for the
Advancement of Colored People, had fought to make white insurance companies sell their policies to black railway clerks. He had a powerful influence on his son, as did Melvin B. Tolson, who taught Sweatt English at
Wiley College in Marshall, Texas. (He also taught the civil rights leader
James Farmer). Tolson was not just a professor but also an electrifying debate coach—Denzel Washington would later play him in a movie—and
a rising man of letters who in 1947 was named poet laureate of Liberia.
His best-known poem, published in the *Atlantic Monthly*, was called "Dark
Symphony," a howling burst of outrage and racial pride. "They tell us to

Heman Sweatt finally won his fight to register at the University of Texas law school in 1950, but by then his long and bitter fight against segregation had begun to erode his health.

forget," begins one representative stanza, "Democracy is spurned. / They tell us to forget / The Bill of Rights is burned."

Listening today to a recording of Tolson reading this poem—in the bugling, theatrical intonations of a performer-professor—it's easy to see how Heman Sweatt could have been stirred up to a pitch of righteous struggle. After graduation, he wrote newspaper columns, became—like his father—an active voice in the NAACP, and helped raise money to launch lawsuits against Texas's infamous whites-only Democratic primary, which was finally squelched by the U.S. Supreme Court in 1944. (The law had been challenged twenty years earlier when another graduate of Wiley College, the El Paso physician Lawrence Nixon, presented his poll-tax receipt at a Democratic primary polling place and was turned away.)

In February 1946, Heman Sweatt, accompanied by a delegation of prominent black Texas activists, including the firebrand NAACP officer Lulu White, presented himself at the main building of the University of Texas, a recently completed edifice dominated by a twenty-seven-story tower, and the biblical promise "Ye Shall Know the Truth and the Truth Shall Make You Free" chiseled above a main entrance that led to intimidating interior spaces with names such as the Hall of Noble Words.

But noble words and liberating truth were empty promises to the black citizens of Texas, for whom an education in this building was forbidden. Sweatt nevertheless was politely received by a phalanx of administration officials led by Theophilus Painter, the zoology professor (and noted expert on the chromosomal structure of the salivary glands of fruit flies) who had assumed the troubling mantle of UT president after the firing of Homer Rainey. Sweatt presented his college transcript to Painter and asked to be admitted into the law school. After the university registrar assured Sweatt and the NAACP leaders that he "did not have any more than the normal amount of prejudice against Negroes," the meeting ended in an inconclusive muddle. President Painter asked for an opinion from Grover Sellers, the Texas attorney general and a man who was, according to a colleague, "not real smart, but lovable." Painter was direct about his predicament: "This applicant is a citizen of Texas and duly qualified for admission to the Law School at the University of Texas, save and except for that the fact that he is a negro."

The response from the attorney general, a response that filled Sweatt with what he described as "vomitous contempt," was that segregation was still enshrined in Texas. If Heman Sweatt wanted to study the law or any other professional calling, he could do so at Prairie View A&M, the school that the state had created for the higher education of blacks. Never mind that Prairie View didn't have a law school. Texas would create one for

Sweatt so that he would never, as Sellers promised elsewhere, "darken the door of the University of Texas."

Theophilus Painter sent Heman Sweatt an official letter of rejection. Sweatt responded by suing for admission to the law school. In hearings at the Travis County Courthouse in Austin, Sweatt's writ was denied, on the blatantly fictional basis that a "substantially equivalent" law school for black students existed at Prairie View. Sweatt was then caught up in another round of court proceedings, which resulted in the frantic creation of a new law school that would function to keep Heman Sweatt and other black applicants out of the all-white, Hall of Noble Words sanctum of the University of Texas. The state leased three rooms on the bottom floor of a downtown office building, hired a few moonlighting law professors, and sent Sweatt a letter declaring that it was pleased to inform him that he was entitled to attend the brand-new School of Law of the Texas State University for Negroes. But Sweatt never showed up to register at the law school built expressly to keep him out of the all-white university that had denied him admission. Nor did anybody else. The School of Law of the Texas State University for Negroes—forever after enshrined in civil rights lore as the "basement school"—put a sign on its window that it was "closed until further developments."

Further developments included the fact that Sweatt's case eventually reached the U.S. Supreme Court, where it was transformed into a direct assault on the whole concept of separate-but-equal facilities. Sweatt neatly summarized his feelings in an article published in the *Texas Ranger*, a University of Texas student magazine: "Please remember that I asked for Education—not Negro education."

One of the lawyers who argued Sweatt's case before the Supreme Court was Thurgood Marshall. Sweatt was not in Washington when the opinion came down. He had just finished delivering mail in Houston on June 5, 1950, when Marshall called him on the phone and told him, "We won the big one!" The unanimous decision of the Court was that Heman Sweatt had been denied his legal rights under the Fourteenth Amendment. *Sweatt v. Painter* became one of the crucial cases that set the stage for *Brown v. Board of Education* four years later, the case that would declare the concept of requiring separate schools for blacks and whites unconstitutional.

So Heman Sweatt enrolled at the University of Texas Law School—the hitherto white one—after all. Four years had gone by since he first presented his transcript to Theophilus Painter. He was now thirty-seven and, as he wrote to Lulu White, "a complete emotional wreck." After four years of tense litigation, of being heralded and reviled, of having his life threatened, his nerves and his health had taken a beating. When he attended his first classes, he was welcomed by some white students, but terrorized by others. Shortly after he arrived, a cross was burned on campus. His tires were slashed. He developed stomach ulcers and appendicitis and broke up with his wife.

He flunked out of the law school he had worked tirelessly to enter. He moved to Atlanta, earned a master's degree, went to work for the National Urban League, and—after a lifetime of dicey health—died of a heart attack in 1982. In 2005, the Travis County Courthouse in Austin, only a few blocks from the basement law school he had refused to attend, and where he had been ruled against in his original suit against the University of Texas, was named in his honor.

WHEN SHE PRESENTED HERSELF AT A FUNERAL HOME IN THE South Texas town of Three Rivers in 1948, Beatrice Longoria experienced the same sort of polite turnaway that Heman Sweatt had faced when he presented his transcript to the University of Texas. She was twenty-nine, the same age that her husband, Felix, would have been if he were still alive. They had met at sixteen, married at eighteen, had a daughter at twenty-one. Three years after her birth, in 1944, Felix enlisted. He and Beatrice spent their last night together in a rented room in Belton, near Fort Hood, where he went for basic training. They danced a polka and said good-bye, and she never saw him again. In June 1945, on the Philippine island of Luzon, during one of his first combat encounters, he was killed by a Japanese sniper.

His body was buried overseas and then, after three and a half years, finally shipped home across the Pacific. Beatrice wanted him buried in Three Rivers, where he had grown up and where their daughter—Adela, whom they called Adelita—was born. She planned to use the chapel at the funeral home there for Felix's wake. But when she mentioned the idea, the two funeral directors seemed oddly taken aback. They left her alone to talk in private, and then one of them, a man named Tom Kennedy, walked over to her and suggested that she make other arrangements. He told her she could not use the chapel for her husband's wake because "the whites would not like it."

She left the funeral home and began, as Kennedy had suggested, to make other arrangements. But the more she thought about what she had been told—that her husband, who had sacrificed his life for his country, who had won a Bronze Star, a Purple Heart, and a Combat Infantryman Badge, could not be honored in the funeral chapel of his own hometown—the more it kept gnawing away at her sense of injustice. After a while, she couldn't let it alone, and so she went to Corpus Christi to meet with a man whom she had been told could help her.

Doctor Hector García was another neighbor of ours in Corpus when I lived there in the early 1960s. His son, also named Hector, was one of my closest boyhood friends. The doctor would say a cordial hello to us when we charged into the García house on Peerman Place, and then he would retreat into his impressive study. I knew almost as little about him as I knew about Joe Dawson—he was just a neighbor, the father of a friend. My parents spoke of him with a kind of generalized respect, but I didn't really know why, and I would have been surprised to hear that there would one day be a statue of him and a highway named for him, and that he would be awarded the Presidential Medal of Freedom by Ronald Reagan.

When Beatrice Longoria contacted him in 1949, García was thirty-five. Although born in the Mexican state of Tamaulipas, he was raised in the South Texas town of Mercedes after his family fled across the border to escape the chaotic violence of the Mexican Revolution. There were seven children in the enterprising García family. At a time when schools and hospitals actively discriminated against Mexican Americans, six of them became doctors. With his medical degree, García served in North Africa and Europe during World War II with the Medical Corps. He ended up as a major, his innate personal authority bolstered by his official rank, so he grew confident that when he issued orders to the Anglo soldiers under his command they would be followed. He married an Italian woman with a PhD in philosophy, returned with her to Texas after the war, and began a medical practice in Corpus Christi. One early morning when he was working in the hospital, he came across a Tejano patient, a fellow veteran, lying in the hall. The Mexican ward was full. García called the hospital administrator at two in the morning and demanded that his patient be given a room in the Anglo ward. Just like that, he desegregated the hospital. Soon after, he founded the American G.I. Forum, a veterans aid society that evolved into a powerfully influential organization focused on the civil rights of Mexican Americans.

García was primed to confront the outrage of the funeral home's refusal to host Felix Longoria's wake. Only months before, he had led an investigation into the grievous inequities that had long prevailed in South Texas. "I have never seen," he concluded, "such general disregard for the welfare and health of any people anywhere in Europe or Africa, even in wartime." He and his committee photographed and documented the unheated, unventilated one-room jacales, with no running water and rampant disease, where Tejano workers and their families lived. They found chickens in their coops living in better conditions than the human beings that tended them. They saw the signs barring Mexicans from entering restaurants or hotels or movie theaters, and the unmissable contrast between the tidy brickwork of the expansive Anglo schools and the shoddy gap-planked wooden shacks with open privies outside where Tejano children were housed for their education.

After García met with Beatrice Longoria, he launched a public relations assault, firing off seventeen telegrams to state and national officials. The most consequential of these was to Lyndon Johnson, who was the junior senator from Texas.

A WHOLE LOT OF LORE AND A WHOLE LOT OF WRITING—NOTABLY,

the second volume of Robert A. Caro's commanding biography of LBJ—has collected around the 1948 Senate race in Texas, in which Johnson narrowly defeated and/or narrowly stole the election from Coke Stevenson. That contest began with Senator Pappy O'Daniel's decision not to run again. After seven years in the Senate, O'Daniel had a 7 percent approval rating. As the founder of the Light Crust Doughboys, he would one day be inducted into the Texas Radio Hall of Fame, but no such honors awaited him as a statesman. His decision to stop representing Texas in Washington was, in one newspaper's judgment, "the one most constructive act" of his improbable political career.

The scramble to succeed him winnowed down to a two-man Democratic race between Lyndon Johnson and Coke Stevenson. As governor, Stevenson had been known for his frustratingly unhurried habits of mind and had earned the sort-of-admiring nickname Calculatin' Coke. But he was not quite as calculating as his opponent. For instance, Johnson made a point of courting the out-of-power but still influential governor team of Jim and Miriam Ferguson, and when Pa died after a stroke in 1944 Johnson showed up at the funeral, something that Stevenson did not do. Ma noticed the gesture, and called upon the aging legions of Ferguson loyalists in East Texas to turn out for Election Day.

But Johnson's Senate race got off to a rocky start—or more precisely, to a stony one. "It never entered his mind," one of his aides remembered, "that he wasn't going to pass this stone. . . . It was a personal trial of his; he just had to tough it out." He was referring to a kidney stone that signaled its existence almost as soon as the candidate entered the contest. It began as a nagging dull pain and then intensified into ever-tightening agony. But Lyndon Johnson wanted to be a senator almost as much as anyone had ever wanted anything, and though he needed surgery the thought of missing even a day of campaigning was almost more torture than the condition that left him sweating and gasping in pain. He finally decided to fly to the Mayo Clinic for what he hoped would be a nonsurgical procedure, but when that didn't work he kept putting the operation off, jumping up and down or ordering his aides to drive him over bumpy roads in the faint hope that it would jostle the stone through his ureter.

In the end, he had the operation and, with nearly two weeks lost, threw himself back into the campaign with the same furious will with which he had tried to make his body heal on its own. He had plenty of money to spend. It came from George and Herman Brown, grateful for the shipbuilding contracts he had steered to Brown & Root during the war, and for the contracts for military bases he had secured for them afterward. It came from Sid Richardson, the Fort Worth oilman who counted among his possessions an entire Texas island called St. Joseph, a barren twenty-two-mile-long strip of sand and surf across a narrow ocean pass from the fishing village of Port Aransas. (In 1937, Richardson had hosted President Roosevelt on a tarpon-fishing trip in the Gulf waters off St. Joseph. While they were fishing, the president received news about the tragedy of the German zeppelin *Hindenburg* and wired his condolences to Adolf Hitler.)

Johnson's money came from people like Howard Hughes Jr., the Houston-born only son of the man who in the years after Spindletop had invented an indispensable drill bit for grinding through obdurate rock. When his father died, Howard Jr. took control of the tool company and the fortune that came with it and became a daring and dashing round-the-world pilot, highly successful movie producer, aircraft tycoon, and decades later a mad hermit living alone in the penthouse of his Las Vegas hotel.

Johnson had money and a gift for appearing to be on every side of every issue—he was somehow backed, the *Dallas Morning News* marveled, by "a variety of business tycoons, left-wing laborites, corporation lawyers, New Dealers, anti–New Dealers, etc." He also had a helicopter. He was the first politician to use one. The vastness of Texas was perfect for such an innovative outreach tool. While stolid old Calculatin' Coke was riding around the state, puffing his pipe in the passenger seat of a Plymouth driven by his nephew, Johnson was hopping in the air from one city or lonely hamlet to the next, greeting the people that came to see him and his helicopter by tossing his Stetson into the crowd with godlike beneficence as he descended. (His aides then scurried out to grab the hat back, or buy it if they had to, from the lucky mortal who had caught it.)

"We were getting a thousand people in a town of a thousand," one of those aides remembered. But the result, after a July primary election eliminated a third candidate and sent Johnson and Stevenson into a runoff, was about as narrow as it could be. The return from the Texas Election Bureau five days after the second primary vote showed Johnson behind Stevenson by 349 votes. But that was an unofficial return. The chess game then began, with the candidates making calls to the vote brokers who could bring in enough ballots to shift the tally one way or the other.

The place to get those precious new votes was from the feudal kingdoms of South Texas, particularly from bosses like George Parr, who controlled not only Duval County but had some sway next door in Jim Wells and other border counties where voters could be called in if necessary from across the Rio Grande. "The moon is high," some unnamed official is said to have casually reported to the Johnson forces. "The river is low. How many votes do you need?"

In Precinct 13 in Jim Wells County, there fortuitously appeared a previously uncounted 203 votes. The tally in that now-legendary tin ballot box—box 13—was spectacularly suspicious: 202 for Johnson, only 1 for Stevenson. Even more suspicious was the fact that the names of the voters were in alphabetical order and all were written in a different color of ink from that used for the rest of the precinct's voter list.

Stevenson dispatched a team of lawyers to Alice, the county seat of Jim Wells County, to inspect the suspicious voting list of box 13. They were warned ahead of time, as one of the lawyers remembered, "that they were known to kill people down there." When they got to Alice, they found themselves being tracked as they walked down the street by a group of sullen, heavily armed enforcers. And it turned out that the voting list they wanted to see was locked away in a bank that just happened to be owned by George Parr. They were not allowed to see it and were advised to get out of town.

That didn't sit right with Coke Stevenson, who went down to Alice himself, this time accompanied by Frank Hamer, now sixty-four years old, no longer a Texas Ranger but working for the Texas Company. But he was still in possession of Old Lucky, his single-action Colt .45 revolver, which he had a special Ranger commission to carry. "He appeared to be an old man," one of Stevenson's lawyers thought. But he revised that impression as Hamer walked with Stevenson down the dusty main street of Alice on the way to Parr's bank, past ranks of menacing, heavily armed border henchmen—"when Frank Hamer walked down the street," the lawyer remembered, "those clusters of people parted." People on the sidewalks were whispering Hamer's name in awe. When the group reached the bank, more pistoleros barred the way. Hamer scattered them, at least according to lore, with one word: "Git!"

But the battle over who won the 1948 Democratic nomination for Texas senator wasn't settled that day in Alice. Nor was it settled a week later at a meeting of the Democratic Party's State Executive Committee in a Fort Worth hotel, where one member had a heart attack amid the heart-pounding tension as the committee rejected, by a vote of 28 to 29, Stevenson's claim that the election had been a fraud. It would take a furious legal scramble and a last-

Election officials in South Texas proudly—gloatingly?— displaying the notorious box 13, whose suspicious contents helped Lyndon Johnson win the 1948 Texas Senate race.

minute decision from Supreme Court justice Hugo Black—effectively shutting down Stevenson's investigation of ballot-box tampering—to clear the way for Johnson's victory. But nothing could clear the air. The 1948 senatorial primary election would remain the closest (out of almost 1,000,000 votes cast, Johnson led by only 87) and cloudiest in Texas history.

———————— ★ ————————

WHEN HECTOR GARCÍA SENT HIS TELEGRAM ABOUT FELIX

Longoria to the new senator from Texas, the response came with lightning alacrity. Lyndon Johnson, who had been affected by the rank prejudice he had seen as a nineteen-year-old principal at the "Mexican school" in Cotulla, was genuinely outraged.

"I deeply regret," he wired García, "that the prejudice of some individuals extends even beyond this life. I have no authority over civilian funeral homes. Nor does the federal government. I have today made arrangements to have Felix Longoria buried with full military honors in Arlington National Cemetery here in Washington, where the honored dead of our nation's wars rest."

So Felix Longoria was not buried in his hometown of Three Rivers, but in faraway Arlington Cemetery on a cold drizzly February day in 1949. His widow wore a borrowed fur coat. The financial offerings from Tejanos that had flooded into García's office or to the G.I. Forum—donations as small as a nickel—had paid for the expenses of the Longoria family's trip to Washington. The secretary of the Mexican Embassy was there, with a military escort and a bouquet of flowers. So was General Harry H. Vaughan, President Harry Truman's military aide. Lyndon and Lady Bird Johnson made sure to come as well. In gratitude, Beatrice Longoria had reserved two seats beside her for the senator and his wife. But if Johnson saw an opportunity for political theater in Felix Longoria's posthumous wanderings, he was canny enough not to exploit it too openly. He made a point of standing in the rain—and making sure that the general did too.

THE OWNER OF THE FUNERAL HOME THAT HAD REFUSED ITS services to the Longoria family claimed that it had all been a "misunderstanding," but if it was simply a misunderstanding, it was a resonant one that amplified an ages-old narrative of Anglo dominance and hardened the reputation of Texas as the pitiless, blighted, cactus-and-rattlesnakes undergrowth of an otherwise flowering republic. The state was also guilty of, well, poor taste. This was personified by the greed, rowdiness, eccentricity, and right-wing snarliness of its preposterously wealthy oilmen. If Texas, as Carl Sandburg once observed while reviewing a book of poems by the Texas author Boyce House, is a "peculiar blend of swagger and valor," by the middle of the twentieth century the mix was a little off. The valor was sputtery, but the swagger was fully engaged.

For example, there was "Silver Dollar" Jim West, the son of Big Jim West, a lumber and cattle magnate who became vastly richer when he partnered with Hugh Roy Cullen on a series of wells around Houston in the 1920s. When he died, in 1941, Big Jim left behind an estate worth seventy million dollars and an oddball son named James Marion West, who earned his nickname because of his basement full of silver dollars, stored in racks and kept shiny by the daily ministrations of an employee. In a truly remarkable photo of him, he stares at the camera with unearthly intensity, a wide-brimmed Stetson on his head, a Daddy Warbucks cigar sticking out of his mouth, and a shiny revolver in his hand. His portly body is adorned with some sort of stubby novelty tie, a shirt pocket full of six or eight pens, and a Texas Ranger badge. The badge was an honorary one, bestowed upon a law enforcement groupie who was happiest when riding around in patrol cars or screeching up to crime scenes in one of his eleven Cadillacs equipped with police radios and submachine guns. He was very generous to the police and the sheriff's department and the Rangers, and they were tolerantly grateful to him in turn.

It's hard to tell from the photograph whether the badge is the one he accessorized with nine diamonds. It's also unclear whether the pants he is wearing—held up both by suspenders and a wide leather belt with an eight-inch-wide belt buckle—are one of the pairs he had customized with extra-commodious saddle pockets. Those pockets were where he stuffed his silver dollars every time he ventured out of his mansion in Houston's River Oaks neighborhood. Making a jingle-jangle sound as he walked, he would pass out silver dollars with chuckling paternalism to waiters and doormen and down-on-their-luck vagrants. He threw silver dollars into the deep ends of swimming pools so that he could watch kids dive for them. But his benevolence had strictly enforced limits. On one Halloween, when teenage trick-or-treaters targeted his home, he drove them off with tear gas.

The peculiarity potential of the wealthy Texas oilman was also realized—though in a much more benign form—in a man named Edgar B. Davis. Davis was on his last legs and almost eighty as Texas rolled into the 1950s. He was also broke and being hounded by the authorities in his native state of Massachusetts for unpaid income taxes. Though he had once weighed 350 pounds—described as "a prodigious eater of terrapin and Welsh rabbit"—he had wasted away to under 200 and lived alone in a little white house in Luling, the town in Caldwell County whose main street had been gratefully renamed in his honor and where some of the residents drove around with custom license plates reading "Luling—The Home of Edgar B. Davis."

The reason that Davis was such a hero to the people of Luling was not just that he had discovered oil there in 1922, but also that he had shared his wealth—more than twelve million dollars when he sold out to Magnolia—with a generosity that bordered on financial suicide. "I have no right to any of this money," he once said. "I'm called a success, but there's as shadowy a line between success and failure as between sanity and insanity."

Davis comfortably straddled both lines. He was, to be sure, no Texas version of Scrooge McDuck, luxuriating among his millions in a secure vault. Soon after he made the Magnolia deal in 1926, he celebrated by hosting the inhabitants of three counties—2,317 square miles—to a barbecue. He may have fed as many as forty thousand guests. He bestowed two swimming pools upon Luling, and two youth clubhouses—one for blacks and one for whites. He was fond of the Central Texas landscape and sponsored an art competition—with the highest cash prize ever awarded—for wildflower paintings.

And then there was *The Ladder*, the awful play upon which he squandered much of the rest of his incalculable fortune. This came about because Davis, an ardent spiritual pilgrim, met a newspaperman in San Antonio and convinced him to write a play about reincarnation, with a cast of characters who start out in an English castle in 1300 and end up in New York City in 1926. "Here's the theatre, and here's the play," he told the producer he hired, "and here's a million dollars. How can it fail?"

Well, of course it did fail. The kindest thing that any critic wrote about it was that it was "quite a long play." But Davis continued to throw money at it for two years, giving away free tickets, sending his crestfallen producer on a glitzy European vacation so that he could regain his morale, and at one point trying to hire Eugene O'Neill to rewrite the play into a semblance of coherence. Davis was a tireless tinkerer of his quixotic project. Here is a cable he sent while he was abroad in Russia and couldn't stop thinking about the play: "URGENT ACT TWO SCENE ONE CHANGE MARGARET'S LINE FROM QUOTE OH HOW BEAUTIFUL UNQUOTE TO QUOTE AH HOW BEAUTIFUL UNQUOTE DAVIS."

Whether his money was generously bestowed or wantonly thrown away, Davis was Zen about it. "I am perfectly happy," he told Stanley Walker, a Texas-born journalist, in 1949, two years before he died.

Davis could not have been more different from the turbulent, archetypal wildcatter Glenn McCarthy, though both men seemed to be in pursuit of an ungraspable goal that transcended mere oil money. In the recollection of the future Watergate prosecutor Leon Jaworski, who encountered him in the 1930s, the young McCarthy "looked a little like Barrymore's Hamlet." This was before he hit it big with a series of wells near Beaumont, where he was born in 1907, only a few years after Anthony Lucas brought in Spindletop in the same vicinity. McCarthy had a flamboyant, tempestuous personality. He had curly dark hair and a rakish mustache, with a potato nose and a brooding, challenging expression in his eyes. A photo taken of him in the 1940s on a Hill Country bird hunt says it all. His tough-guy pose is as authentic (even if carefully curated) as the rotund Diamond Jim West's is bogus. He is in three-quarter profile, standing on a promontory with the rocky landscape spread below him. He holds a shotgun with casual expertise, his shirt is halfway unbuttoned, and he is gazing indifferently in the direction of the camera lens. He looks like a Heathcliff of the Texas moors.

McCarthy had been expelled from Rice, gotten into innumerable brawls, and heroically saved men's lives on collapsing oil derricks. On his first discovery well, he encountered so many delays in getting a rig working that drilling still hadn't begun on the last day of his lease—which would expire at

The Texas wildcatter Glenn McCarthy, straight out of central casting and in full swashbuckling mode.

midnight. To make the deadline, he grabbed a chain tong (a big oil-field pipe wrench) and began pounding it into the ground, hand drilling his own well.

By the late 1940s, after the obligatory wildcatter's experience of winning and losing several fortunes, he owned 400 producing oil and gas wells, a ranch, a twenty-two-story office building, and a gnawing hunger for something much more, something along the lines of the bedazzled appreciation of the world at large.

His solution: a project that would be, in the opinion of the *Houston Chronicle*, "perhaps the greatest ever undertaken by an individual in Texas." This project was the Shamrock Hotel, a magnificent edifice that McCarthy imagined as the largest building between New York and Los Angeles, a must-see, must-stay place that would place Houston and Glenn McCarthy where they rightfully belonged: at the center of the universe.

The Shamrock Hotel cost twenty-one million dollars. It had eighteen stories, 1,100 rooms, and the largest hotel swimming pool in the world—large enough to water-ski in. By the time it was completed, in 1949, McCarthy was fatally in hock to the New York insurance company that had advanced him the money based on its valuation of his oil reserves. Compared to the opening of the Shamrock, Edgar B. Davis's three-county barbecue blowout was a snack tray. McCarthy thought the opening of his hotel should coincide with the Houston premiere of a major motion picture, so he became a movie producer and bankrolled a film called *The Green Promise*, starring Walter Brennan and Natalie Wood. To christen his hotel, he invited almost every big star in Hollywood and chartered a special train to bring them from Los Angeles to Houston. The Shamrock's lobby was dominated by a life-size portrait of McCarthy, and though its decor and pastel color scheme—eighty-two shades of green!—were beautiful to its impresario, critics such as Frank Lloyd Wright thought it looked like the inside of a jukebox.

The carefully crafted grand opening of the hotel ended up a scene of wondrous chaos. The ceremony started three hours late and was mobbed by a thousand or so uninvited guests, who broke through the police barricades, stormed into the Emerald Room, consumed all the food, and interrupted what was supposed to be a national radio broadcast featuring Dorothy Lamour. It was a disaster—Miss Lamour fled to her room in tears—but in the eyes of some observers it was the most exciting thing to happen in Texas since the Alamo. The event was immortalized, sort of, in the closing scenes of the 1956 movie *Giant*, based on Edna Ferber's novel. James Dean plays a character loosely modeled on the Shamrock's owner, but the actor's mumbling magnetism was of a different order from Glenn McCarthy's clear-cut pugnacity.

McCarthy had control of the Shamrock for only a few years. His fortunes turned again, and the insurance company that had fronted him the money for the hotel began to sell off his assets. The Shamrock was bought by the Hilton Hotels Corporation, which took down the portrait of McCarthy in the lobby and replaced it with one of Conrad Hilton.

But nobody could ever think of the Shamrock without thinking of Glenn McCarthy. In 1982, when he was seventy-five, I interviewed him for a magazine story in the hotel he had built. He drove himself to the Shamrock in a dust-covered Delta 88 whose floorboards were littered with Styrofoam coffee cups. When he got out of the car, he put on a black riverboat gambler's hat, cocking it to one side. He had a growling voice and an impassive expression. He looked like someone you should choose your words carefully around, or you might end up in an unanticipated fistfight of the sort that he once was famous for. He showed me his pocket watch, which he was dropping off at the hotel jeweler to have cleaned. "It's a Patek," he said, "and it's real good. . . . And those diamonds are not little chippy diamonds either."

We sat in the dining room for lunch, at a table overlooking the inland sea that was the Shamrock's swimming pool.

"The Shamrock let the world know that there was a Houston," said the jeweler, who had joined us.

"He's telling you the truth," McCarthy said. "I used to get mail that just said Glenn McCarthy, Shamrock Hotel. It didn't even say Houston on it. There wasn't anybody in the United States who didn't know where the Shamrock Hotel was, and there wasn't anybody in Europe . . . Anybody that was alive then had heard of the Shamrock."

He reminisced about the famous people who had stayed here, talked a little about Howard Hughes ("He wasn't crazy. He was a genius.") and about his own brief career as a movie producer. "I'm not much interested in movies anymore," he said. "I haven't seen one in two years. I don't like bebop and rock n' roll and all that horseshit."

When I asked him if it ever made him depressed that he didn't own the hotel anymore, he snapped at me. "I don't get depressed, " he said. "I built it, I paid cash for it, I sold it for cash, and the hotel's still here."

Except that now it isn't. It was torn down in 1987 to become a parking lot for Houston's expanding Texas Medical Center. Before it was demolished, nine hundred people paraded from downtown Houston to form a protective ring around the hotel to try to save it. There were T-shirts that read: "Tearing down the Shamrock would be like tearing down the Alamo."

One of the people in the crowd of protestors was Glenn McCarthy, eighty ravaged years old and a year and a half away from his own demise.

— 45 —

THE LORD TAKES A SLEEPING PILL

IN 1952, JANIS JOPLIN WAS A NINE-YEAR-OLD GIRL LIVING in Port Arthur, the coastal town just north of Sabine Pass where Dick Dowling and his Irish dockworkers had blocked the Union invasion of Texas in 1863. Willie Nelson was nineteen, recently discharged from the air force and attending Baylor University in Waco. Buddy Holly, a high school student in Lubbock, was busy making a home recording, with his friend Bob Montgomery, of songs called "Take These Shackles From My Heart" and "I'll Just Pretend." Mance Lipscomb, a tenant farmer in Grimes County and the son of a slave, was fifty-seven years old. He had changed his first name from Bowdie to Mance in honor of an old man named Emancipation. Sam Hopkins, who had altered his own first name to Lightnin' in 1946, was a forty-year-old blues musician from the little town of Centerville, by then recording in Houston. Narciso Martínez, raised in Brownsville, was also forty and a master of the conjunto style that fused northern Mexican music with German and Czech polkas. He played the accordion so nimbly and so fast that he was known as "El Huracán del Valle" ("The Hurricane of the Valley"). Dale Evans—born Lucille Wood Smith in Uvalde—was starring and singing in a television series

TOM LEA
in his studio, hunkered down in front of a study of one of his beloved Texas murals.

called *The Roy Rogers Show*, which bore the name of her fourth husband. Roy Orbison was a high school student in the tiny West Texas oil town of Wink. The Wink Wildcats had just won the state championship. Roy was not a football hero, though, just an unsung member of the school's marching band who shoveled road tar during the summer for the county and played in local honky-tonks with a group called the Wink Westerners. "There are so many ways," he confided to a friend, "to be lonesome in West Texas."

Then there was Tom Lea, an El Paso writer and painter, who was forty-five. As an illustrator for *Life* magazine during the war, he had painted horrifying images of combat—including a defining GI portrait titled *Marines Call It That 2,000 Yard Stare*—and had just published his second novel, *The Wonderful Country*, which he illustrated. Another painter, John Biggers, was twenty-seven. He had been born in North Carolina but was now the head of the art department at Texas Southern University in Houston, whose name had recently been changed from the Texas State University for Negroes. In 1950, he had won a drawing contest at Houston's Museum of Fine Arts but had not been invited to the awards reception because black people were allowed into the museum only on Thursdays. Américo Paredes, born in Brownsville and named by his parents for the sixteenth-century Italian explorer Amerigo Vespucci, had just completed his undergraduate

AMÉRICO PAREDES,
folklorist turned novelist, at work transcribing an audiotape.

degree at the University of Texas. He had served in the war as a writer and editor for *Stars and Stripes* and was a few years away from beginning his dissertation on the border tragedy of Gregorio Cortez, which would become the book *With His Pistol in His Hand.* John Graves, who lost the vision in one eye to a Japanese grenade on Saipan, was thirty-two, a "desperately aspirant writer" preparing for a Hemingwayesque sojourn in Spain, not yet secure enough in his Texas heritage to begin writing his classic book *Goodbye to a River.* Mary Elizabeth Spacek, whom her parents called Sissy, was a three-year-old child in Quitman, Texas. In Corpus Christi, Farrah Fawcett was two years older. Her name was originally spelled "Ferrah," and it may have been bestowed upon her by her father, an oil-field contractor, who believed it to be the Arabic word for "joy." The Rhode Island–born Charles McCarthy was nineteen, a student at the University of Tennessee who would soon rename himself Cormac and, a couple of decades later, move to El Paso and weave the West Texas landscape into novels of incomparable bleakness and incantatory prose rhythms.

This is just a core sample of some of the manifestations of Texas identity that were pushing their way to the surface at the halfway point of the twentieth century. Meanwhile, Texas was its familiar visible self. The state's Democratic Party, secure in its hegemony since the end of Reconstruction,

JOHN GRAVES,
who took a canoe trip down the Brazos and turned the experience into one of the classics of Texas literature.

was showing signs of coming apart. There were the Texas Regulars, who in 1948 had thrown in with the die-hard Deep South segregationist "Dixiecrats" led by South Carolina governor Strom Thurmond. There were the moderate-ish establishment Democrats who nevertheless crossed party lines in 1952 to vote for the Republican (and sort of Texan) Dwight Eisenhower for president against the liberal Illinois governor Adlai Stevenson. Then there was the progressive Democratic faction, which enthusiastically voted for its party's presidential candidate, despite the snarky prediction of the current Texas first lady about Stevenson: "No one who wears white shoes will ever be elected president of the United States."

One Texan who did not live to see 1952 was Beauford Jester. He was elected governor in 1946 after defeating Homer Rainey, the University of Texas president who had been ousted by Coke Stevenson's board of regents. Jester died in office in the summer of 1949, at the age of fifty-six, after he left Austin on a midnight train for Galveston one night in July. The special legislative session he had called had just adjourned, and he was headed to the island for a vacation and what he called a "secret mission." He was probably referring to a planned medical checkup and not—as still-circulating rumors would have it—an onboard assignation with an unknown woman in whose company the married governor was speeding south. In any case, he was officially alone and unresponsive when a porter tried to wake him up in his Pullman car early the next morning.

In life, Jester had had a moderate political soul, campaigning on the promise to follow the "people's path." But once settled in the Governor's Mansion, he was pushed rightward by the strong prevailing winds of conservative business interests. Wariness of unions pressed him to sign the 1947 Texas right-to-work law, resentment of minorities and the enshrinement of the code of states' rights led him to oppose anti-poll-tax and antilynching laws proposed by President Harry Truman's administration. He characterized the Fair Employment Practices Committee, whose aim was to end racial discrimination in government workplaces, as an assault on "racial purity laws." But he was only a pragmatic hardliner, not a temperamental one. He softened some of those views later in his tenure, after the contentious 1948 presidential election, in which he helped keep establishment Texas Democrats from bolting the party along with the Dixiecrats. And during the remaining year of his governorship the legislature passed a sweeping education law that doubled the state's spending for schools and consolidated its education bureaucracy. But enough lawmakers were skeptical of the bill, or hostile to the taxes that would be needed to pay for it, or suspicious of the whole idea of public education, that a third of the House members bolted from the Capitol so that they wouldn't have to vote. It was one of the first such quorum breaks, which would become familiar entertainment to students of the eccentric workings of the Texas Legislature. The sergeant at arms managed to round them all back up, cornering them in the bars where they were hiding or, in one case, chasing a fleeing solon as he ran through a startled woman's house and out her backyard. He was apprehended, covered with mud, in the middle of a creek bed.

When Jester died, the lieutenant governor in line to succeed him was Allan Shivers.

"You're kidding," Shivers replied when a reporter called to tell him the governor was dead. "It's too early in the morning for pranks."

Shivers was forty-one. He had grown up in deep East Texas, the son of a county judge and a sternly religious mother—she wouldn't allow a deck of cards in the house—whose first name was Easter. As a young state senator, first elected when he was twenty-seven, he was pro-labor and pro old-age pensions, but he sometimes dressed as a plutocrat, with spats and a walking cane. He was tall, slender, dark haired and married to an equally tall, slender, dark-haired woman named Marialice, who had grown up in a twenty-four-room house in the Rio Grande valley built by her father, one of the wealthy land developers who had brought about the Anglo agricultural boom in South Texas. When Shivers was new to the legislature, Ma Ferguson was still the governor, and he was counseled by her aging husband on, of all un-Fergusonian things, how not to be bitter. "I want to give you one bit of advice," Pa told him. "Don't let yourself get to hating so many people that you don't have time to like anyone."

Beauford Jester was the first Texas governor to die in office, and Shivers was inaugurated in an impromptu ceremony at his farm near Woodville. Twenty-five hundred people came, including a delegation of Alabama-Coushatta Indians. Local Boy Scouts were deployed to help direct the flow of traffic overwhelming the rural roads.

Shivers turned out to be a skillful and confident governor, with early whispers of a progressive agenda. "Texas, the proud Lone Star State," he said in a speech whose chastening observations would still ring true today, "first in oil—48th in mental hospitals. First in cotton—worst in tuberculosis. First in raising goats—last in caring for its state wards. These things are unthinkable. Texas can do this job."

But like Jester, Shivers ended up tacking rightward, and—perhaps because of the wealth he had married into—seemed to feel comfortable there. His aide Jake Pickle—later a liberal congressman—paid him a compliment that could serve as the ultimate midcentury Texas accolade: "He wasn't mean, he was just tough."

One of the issues that Shivers inherited was a legalistic sea battle between Texas and the federal government over which of them owned title to the submerged lands in the Gulf of Mexico beyond the state's shoreline. There was oil there—by 1949, the state had taken in a tidy seven million dollars in lease bonuses earmarked for the Permanent School Fund. Similar potential bonanzas awaited in the territorial waters of other coastal states, but Texas was unique, since it had come into the Union as an independent country. In December 1836, six months after the Battle of San Jacinto, when Mexican corpses were still rotting on Peggy McCormick's pasture and the shattered bones of Sam Houston's ankle were still knitting themselves together, the Republic of Texas had stipulated its seaward boundaries: "beginning at the mouth of the Sabine River, and running west along the Gulf of Mexico three leagues from land, to the mouth of the Rio Grande."

It was the "three leagues from land" part that suddenly meant everything. The old Spanish measurement of three leagues meant that Texas owned the seabed 10.5 miles offshore from low tide (hence the term "tidelands"). But the U.S. government, spurred by the prospect of oil revenues and by the security concerns made manifest during World War II, ruled that the states' claims extended to only three miles. Beyond that was federal ter-

ritory. The difference mattered especially to Texas oilmen. If the federal government got control of the tidelands, they would have to pay 37.5 percent royalties on their profits, compared with the far more forgiving 12.5 percent that the state imposed. But there was also a spasmodic identity reaction, going back to Texas's robust nationalistic past and its declaration during the 1850 border crisis that it would "maintain the integrity of her Territory at all hazards and to the last extremity."

Two recent U.S. Supreme Court decisions had ruled against Texas's claim to the tidelands. Sam Rayburn, the Texan who was in the middle of his long run as Speaker of the House, had tried to work out a compromise. But the tidelands controversy was a natural hard-line issue. It became even more so after the oil interests decided to have fun with billboard and television advertising that frightened children and parents into thinking that their schools would disappear if the state lost offshore royalties. "My kids came running in from the TV set like Paul Revere," a bewildered father reported, "tears streaming from their eyes, saying 'Pa, they're trying to take our tidelands away!'"

Rayburn saw the way this was going. With his protégé Lyndon Johnson's help, he managed to pass a bill giving the state its 10.5-mile claim, but President Truman vetoed it. In the eyes of the executive branch, the pesky state of Texas was up to its old grabby tricks again, and Truman declared he could not tolerate "robbery in broad daylight."

That meant the war was on between the conservative Texas Democrats and the national standard bearers of their party. At the Democratic National Convention in 1952, there was a bitter fight over which delegation from Texas would be seated: the loyalist Democrats, led by Maury Maverick, or the vacillating faction of the party, which Governor Shivers controlled. Sam Rayburn was the convention chairman, and he seated the Shivers group, claiming that the governor had made a pledge to him to support the Democratic candidate to emerge from the convention. But that candidate was Adlai Stevenson, who was pointedly opposed to Texas's expansive tidelands claim. As for Shivers, he didn't remember an ironclad pledge to Sam Rayburn, only a fuzzy statement of intent. (Rayburn remembered it, though—"I'll have to take that boy's pants down before I'm through.") In any case, thus was born the Shivercrats, who strayed from the Democratic Party corral and did a previously unthinkable thing in Texas politics. They voted for a Republican, Dwight D. Eisenhower, for president, and Texas kept its tidelands.

"Sometimes a man just gets to wondering if the Lord is taking sleeping pills or something," Maury Maverick sighed the next year. "He sure isn't keeping check on politics down here in Texas."

BUT IN TEXAS IN THE 1950S, WHEN EVERYBODY WAS CONVINCED
that the Lord was—or ought to be—on their side, politics came to pivot on
who feared godless communism the most. Not that everything was about
politics. The rise of Communist China, the Korean War, the Soviet development of nuclear weapons, and the threat of enemy spies within fostered a
doomsday edginess that could be exploited into hysteria but was also a credible part of the daily atmosphere. I can remember as a nine- or ten-year-old
kid walking down Benbrook Street in Abilene, on my way to the Elmwood
shopping center to buy a comic book at the drugstore, and seeing one of the
bombers from the newly opened Dyess Air Force Base flying overhead. Not
knowing then whether it was an American or a Soviet plane, I would freeze
on the sidewalk, waiting to see if in the next few moments I would live or die.

Texas oilmen also feared nuclear annihilation, almost as much as they
feared the end of the oil depletion allowance, the customary tax break for oil-
well earnings that they had come to consider a sacred birthright. Their suspicion of an overreaching federal bureaucracy thirsty for the tidelands and full
of Soviet spies and East Coast lawmakers greedy for more tax money brought
them into a natural kinship with people like the Wisconsin senator Joe
McCarthy, who had whipped up a merciless search for communist infiltrators.

Hugh Roy Cullen's approval was emblematic. "Senator McCarthy," he
said, "has done more than anyone to throw the pinks and Reds out of the
country. I hope Senator McCarthy keeps all the Communist spies running
until they get to Moscow." In Houston, a wealthy cattle rancher launched
a fund drive to present Joe McCarthy with a brand-new Cadillac as a wedding present. It was outfitted with every accessory except, as one wit com-
mented, a left-turn indicator. The keys were handed to the senator in a
Washington, DC, ceremony, along with a proclamation from Governor Shivers that read: "Joe McCarthy—a real American—is now officially a Texan."

H. L. Hunt was very much among the smitten when it came to McCarthy.
Hunt was by then in his sixties, white haired, pink faced, balding, and
bow-tied. He was arguably the richest man in America (though he "never
got around to tallying it up") and now had a third "secret family" that he
had begun with a young Hunt Oil secretary. (All told, he had fifteen children.) He was maybe a few years away from the full flower of his eccentricity—when he looked, as one journalist wrote, "like the kindly judge in an
early Shirley Temple movie." He carried his lunch in a paper bag, hand sold
something called Gastro-Magic digestive tablets in the drugstore on the
ground floor of his thirty-two-story office building, crept around his house

on all fours ("I'm a crank about creeping!"), and wrote and self-published a strange novel called *Alpaca*, about a fictional republic whose citizens were allotted multiple votes based on the taxes they paid, and which included both the entire constitution of Alpaca and a sizzling love story with dialogue such as: "'Yes,' he said, kissing her upturned face, 'the same old moon which now rises above the saw-toothed line of cedars on yonder mountain crest. And we haven't forgot, have we?—the sound of splashing waves against the Riviera beach, that night when the world stood still, and did not move at all?'"

H. L. Hunt, a eulogist remarked at his funeral in 1974, "moved in and about the timberlines of life where the timid fear to venture." But he worried very much that the forest was full of communists and subversive agents of every sort, and so when he met Joe McCarthy in Dallas in 1952, the two men bonded over a game of gin rummy and a shared sense of paranoia. Hunt had started a right-wing radio show called *Facts Forum*, whose reach was relatively anemic until he met McCarthy. He hired three of the senator's associates, pumped more money into it, and boosted it into a nationwide radio, television, and publishing enterprise. It languished after a few years, but Hunt liked the idea of having a national bully pulpit so much that he created an iteration in 1958 called *Life Line*, which was broadcast in fortyseven states and stalwartly stood up for Christianity and free enterprise against communism and big-government gremlins.

Martin Dies, a veteran hand when it came to hunting communists, was back on the scene in the 1950s after a decade or so in the political wilderness. Dies was from the West Texas town of Colorado City, which had been a major center of the "bone business" after the buffalo were all but wiped out in the 1870s and their bones, still littering the Texas plains, became marketable for use in everything from phosphate ash to buttons. (Piles of buffalo bones at places like Colorado City could stretch for a half mile, thirty feet high, on either side of the train tracks.)

Dies was first elected to Congress in 1931, starting out as a supporter of the New Deal but soon veering into anti-union, anti-agitator territory and becoming, in 1938, the first chairman of the investigative committee later known as the House Un-American Activities Committee. The people he targeted as communist sympathizers included the ten-year-old child star Shirley Temple (in whose movies—as we have seen—H. L. Hunt would have been castworthy as a kindly uncle) and the sociologist Maurice Parmelee, who was suspected not just of being red but of being tan all over, since he was the author of a book titled *Nudism in Modern Life: The New Gymnosophy*.

Dies was reelected to Congress in 1953, in time to lend his voice once again to the anticommunist harmonies being sung by groups like the

*Congressman Martin Dies's list of Communist sympathizers
to keep an eye on included Shirley Temple.*

Minute Women, a national organization whose members wore a red, white, and blue lapel pin with the slogan "Guarding the Land We Love."

Texas was a stronghold of the Minute Women. The Houston branch was particularly active, its members coming from the middle and upper classes. The organization was strongly represented in Houston's wealthiest enclave, River Oaks, where the wives of doctors and oilmen were vigilantly on the lookout for anything that might seem like socialized medicine or could threaten the oil depletion allowance. One of these Houston Minute Women, ruefully looking back on her old self in those fevered days, admitted that "members were interested in keeping a purity of the white race." She also remembered, "I was concerned about socialism, concerned about big government, things were happening too fast. I could see a Brave New World coming."

The Minute Women were on the lookout for people like George Ebey, who had been hired in 1952 as a deputy superintendent for Houston's schools. Ebey, from Oregon by way of California, was suspect from the beginning. As a leader of the American Veterans Committee, he had promoted communist-sounding initiatives like "racial and religious cooperation week" and was on the record as being against "the red mist of hysteria."

We've Got Your Number, Dr. Ebey was the title of a mimeographed booklet, written by a Mrs. W. J. Edwards, that welcomed the new deputy superintendent to Houston. Among the outrages that Ebey had committed: he had called for "the training of children in non-discriminatory behavior," an insult to proud Americans like Mrs. Edwards, who, as she put it, "cherish their prejudices."

The next year, after helping foment pressure to investigate Ebey for his supposedly pinkish past, the Minute Women came out in force at a school board meeting that decided whether he could keep his job. The investigation took the form of a hazy 348-page report into his character and career. Ebey was allowed to see it only a few hours before the meeting—"thumb through it pretty fast," his outraged lawyer was told. Not that it would have mattered how much of it he had been able to read. The fact that Ebey had once expressed his approval of racially integrated schools in Portland was probably enough to guarantee the 4–3 vote that cost him his job.

Ebey and his family bitterly packed up and went back to California, where he got a job—with a government security clearance—working on defense contracts. "I find it a bit ironic," he said, "that probably my most significant contribution to education came from being lynched professionally by savages in a community where I was relatively a stranger."

But the "savages" he was referring to, among them the Minute Women from River Oaks, were still on the watch. They monitored classes at the University of Houston to spy on potentially subversive professors, they targeted ministers for the sin of "pre-marital counseling," they joined in the hounding of two high school teachers who had read aloud to their students portions of D. H. Lawrence's *Studies in Classic American Literature*—an act "tantamount to practicing communism."

The most notorious—and most unhinged—of the Houston Minute Women was Bertie Maughmer, the wife of a police lieutenant who was a former president of the Houston Police Officers Association. The upper-crust matrons of the Minute Women grew increasingly wary of the blue-collar Mrs. Maughmer, who had a screaming need for attention and a colorfully abrasive personality. Nevertheless she managed to get herself elected parliamentarian of the school board, a platform from which she sniffed out communist, United Nations, and New Deal influences in geography and economics textbooks. To her vigilant mind, the National Education Association, free-lunch programs for students, and of course integration were all toxic manifestations of communist infiltration. "I'd rather go to jail," she declared, "than see my kids go to school with niggers."

666   THE EMPIRE OF TEXAS

She did go to jail, at least briefly, but not for the crime of keeping her children out of school. It was because she shot her husband. Her marriage had been "sheer hell," she said, and one night she decided she had had enough. "I've been trying to warn you," she said, as she took her husband's .357 Magnum and pointed it at him as he stood before her in his underwear, "and trying to tell you that it was going to turn out like this."

She shot him in the stomach, but in a frantic fit of thoughtfulness called an ambulance. He lived, and returned his wife's favor by helping influence a grand jury not to indict her. She reluctantly agreed that it was best for her to resign from the school board—a homicidal parliamentarian was bad for the image of the Minute Women.

— 46 —

GIANT

ALLAN SHIVERS WAS REELECTED IN 1952 AND AGAIN IN
1954, breaking with a Texas tradition that governors served
only two terms. Opposing him for the Democratic primary
in both elections was Ralph Yarborough, a lawyer, former
district judge, combat veteran, and lieutenant colonel with
General Douglas MacArthur's occupation forces in Japan.

Yarborough was almost fifty when he took on Shivers for the first time. He
was a grinning, happy-to-be-here liberal, unafraid of corny bromides like the
one that became his political slogan: "Put the jam on the lower shelf so the
little man can reach it." He was also a serious intellectual with an incomparable home library and, as one of his aides recalled, "the most incredible
cross-referenced mind."

Shivers easily squelched Yarborough's challenge in 1952, but two years later
"Smilin' Ralph" was a big enough threat that Shivers partisans hired a black
man to drive a brand-new Cadillac through the overheated racist precincts of
East Texas. The car had Yarborough bumper stickers plastered all over it, and
the driver's instructions were to behave rudely and haughtily when he stopped
for gas and to announce loudly that he was working for Mr. Yarborough.

The Supreme Court's *Brown v. Board of Education* decision, which ordered
the integration of public schools and overturned the doctrine of separate but

equal, dropped like a bag of rattlesnakes into the middle of the 1954 campaign. "All of my instincts," Shivers responded, "my political philosophy, my experiences and my common sense revolt against this Supreme Court decision. . . . As far as the state of Texas is concerned, there are no changes to be made in the way we are conducting our schools."

The specter of the end of segregation gave Shivers a boost, but he wasn't yet in the clear. When Yarborough forced him into a runoff, the governor's campaign rolled out a frightening TV spot that looked as if it might have inspired *The Twilight Zone* or *Invasion of the Body Snatchers*. When you watch that twelve-minute film, *The Port Arthur Story*, today, you have a clear window into the ominous world of Red Scare Texas. Port Arthur had been the scene of a strike by retail workers against several stores in the city, a strike that the Texas attorney general claimed was the work of "proven Communist leadership."

The film begins with images of empty streets, empty sidewalks, empty businesses, and the voice of a mournful, how-could-this-have-happened narrator: "This is a city in Texas: Port Arthur. A year ago it was a thriving city. Children played. Women shopped. Businessmen drank coffee in the restaurants. That was one year ago. Today, it is deserted."

Well, it might have been deserted because these scenes were filmed at five in the morning. Nevertheless, it was "a city strangled, almost plunged into economic ruin by the plot of a red-tinged union who invaded Texas." And Ralph Yarborough, we learn, is "right in bed with them."

And finally the canny, the cynical, the irresistible call to arms to a populace steeped in defiant history: "True Texans in Port Arthur are fighting back, building the defenses for Texas against the foreign invasion of grasping control. Will Texans hold Texas? Fannin did, Bowie and Crockett, Sam Houston and Travis did. Will you? Will you?"

It's unclear whether Shivers put his personal imprimatur on all this agit-prop. ("Allan really doesn't like to demagogue," one of his aides said, "but he was about to lose the race.") But his campaign's appeal to the fear of communism, the fear of integration, and an atmospheric suspicion of pretty much everything (Yarborough was in favor of chiropractors!) did the trick and delivered Shivers back to the Governor's Mansion.

But his third term was a disaster, collapsing in a black hole of scandal involving the revelation of a suspicious personal real estate deal that returned a 1,700 percent profit in six months; corrupt state commissioners who received kickbacks from unbridled insurance companies; and Shivers's seeming involvement in a land-sale scheme meant to help veterans but that instead lined the pockets of a crooked state land commissioner and his cronies.

And then, in the last months of his tenure, there was an ugly showdown

in the town of Mansfield, about fifteen miles southeast of Fort Worth. Following the *Brown* decision, Texas schools—at least those away from the East Texas and Central Texas epicenters of segregationist doctrine—began allowing black students into their schools with relatively little turmoil. That wasn't the case in Mansfield, where the Fifth Circuit Court of Appeals had come down hard and ordered the desegregation of the school system. The situation there was blatant. White elementary school students went to school in a spacious brick building; black students had a four-room schoolhouse without indoor toilets or running water. Until a year before, when a well was dug, they and their teachers had to bring water from home. There was no high school for the black kids. They had to ride a bus to a segregated school in Fort Worth. The bus let them out twenty blocks away and didn't pick them up until two hours after the school day ended.

As the day approached for black students to enroll, the white citizens of Mansfield let their thoughts be known. Crosses were burned in the black section of town, a black effigy was strung up in Main Street with a sign reading: "This Negro tried to go to a white school." On the first day of registration, two hundred people, carrying signs with slogans such as "Coons ears $1.00 a dozen," surrounded the school. The next day the mob was twice as large, and it beat up an assistant district attorney who had been sent to report back on conditions. Alarmed at the violence, Shivers sent in the Texas Rangers, but not for the reason you might think. They were there not to protect students as they entered the school, but to make sure they did not. The governor regarded the mob intimidation as an "orderly protest against a situation instigated and agitated by the National Organization [*sic*] for the Advancement of Colored People."

Shivers had accumulated enough baggage by 1956 to know that there was no chance of a fourth term. But it was a presidential election year, and he wanted to go out in a leadership role by heading the state delegation at the Democratic National Convention. But Sam Rayburn had been waiting to pull his pants down, and now he did. He let it be known that he wanted Lyndon Johnson to head the delegation and to be the state's favorite-son candidate for president. The announcement surprised Johnson and threw him into a fight with Shivers he didn't want or think he needed, but the two men gamely assassinated each other's characters—with Shivers reminding the world of George Parr and box 13, and Johnson calling Shivers a demagogue—before LBJ carried away the necessary precinct votes to head the delegation.

Defeated by Johnson and Rayburn (whom he compared to Santa Anna, still enshrined as Texas's eternal villain) and their alliance with the party's labor and liberal factions, Shivers headed off to practice law in the political afterlife. That left the field for the governor's race open to a cast of characters that included Yarborough, the curmudgeonly West Texas historian J. Evetts Haley, and—back again!—Pappy O'Daniel. Haley regarded integration as such a mortal menace that he proposed a showdown at the Red River: he and the Texas Rangers against the enrobed eastern eggheads of the Supreme Court. For his part, Pappy was concerned that putting black and white kids in school together would lead to "little parties" at which "nature will take its course, they intermarry and the mongrel race takes over."

But the voters sloughed off Haley and O'Daniel on Election Day and threw Yarborough into a race with the candidate of the conservative establishment, Price Daniel. Daniel was a three-time Texas attorney general (he had represented the University of Texas in the Heman Sweatt case), a champion of the holy tidelands crusade, and a current U.S. senator from Texas. But he wanted to be governor more than he wanted to be senator, and he had the backing of oil and business interests and—not insignificantly—Fess Parker, the easygoing Fort Worth–born actor whose performance as the title character in Walt Disney's new popular-culture juggernaut, *Davy Crockett: King of the Wild Frontier*, represented at that moment the embodiment of undiluted Texanness.

Price Daniel won, and Ralph Yarborough lost the governor's race for the third time. But the election had a happy effect on Yarborough's political career, since Price Daniel's Senate seat became vacant. The special election that followed featured twenty-two candidates, including the formidable Martin Dies, but Yarborough's liberal support in Texas, after so much paranoia and poison had leaked into the atmosphere, was running at flood tide.

So Yarborough went to Washington as the junior senator from Texas. He joined Lyndon Johnson, whose rise to power in the Senate had been stunningly swift—from the suspect victor of a clouded election ("Landslide Lyndon") in 1948 to Senate majority leader in 1955. His engine of ambition was still madly pumping as he set about to master the rules and procedures of the Senate and to master the people in it. "No senator," remembered the Senate page Bobby Baker, "had ever approached me with such a display of determination to learn, to achieve, to attain, to belong, to get ahead. He was coming into the Senate with his neck bowed, running full tilt, impatient to reach some distant goal I then could not even imagine." His instinctive strategy had two poles: a sometimes cringeworthy, submissive deference to influential older men like Rayburn and Georgia senator Richard Russell, and a raw physical dominance that manifested itself in what observers came to call the "treatment." The *Washington Post*'s Ben Bradlee described it this way: "You really felt as if a St. Bernard had licked your face for an hour, had pawed you all over. . . . He never just shook hands with you. One hand was

The author Edna Ferber did not endear herself to Texans, and was once even kicked off the King Ranch. But she was happy to share her opinions about Texas with the readers of her novel Giant.

shaking your hand; the other hand was always someplace else, exploring you, examining you. And of course he was a great actor, bar fucking none the greatest. . . . It was just a miraculous performance."

I HAVEN'T FOUND A RECORD OF EDNA FERBER EVER MEETING

Lyndon Johnson, but if she had been subjected to the treatment I can only imagine her recoil at this oozy Texas power display. Ferber was in her sixties and one of the best-selling novelists in the country—the author of *Show Boat* and the Pulitzer Prize winner *So Big*, and a regular at the Algonquin Round Table—when she visited the King Ranch in 1947 as a guest of Robert Kleberg, the grandson of Richard and Henrietta King, and his wife Helen. The Klebergs' daughter remembered that Ferber informed her father that she was going to write a novel about him and his immense ranch. He replied that he would rather she didn't. She said that she was going to anyway. As she grew more and more imperiously insistent, Robert Kleberg turned to his daughter and told her to call Ferber's driver and tell him, "She wants to leave now and won't be coming back."

She left, but her mind was set. She began to conduct research, or at least absorb impressions, as she traveled from one big ranch to another. Her hauteur was dazzling. When one woman offered to introduce her to some other local ranchers, she replied, "Oh, no, I don't want to know any more people like you."

She plowed her distaste of Texans into her 1952 novel *Giant*. The book was close to being a cartoon, or at best a satire, of the gaudiness and chauvinism of the big ranching and oil elites who had entertained her at their ranches and petroleum clubs. The story tracks twenty-five years in the life of a Virginia bride who marries Bick Benedict—one of Texas's "great mahogany-faced men bred on beef"—and moves to a geographically impossible two-and-a-half-million-acre ranch that spreads from the shores of the Gulf of Mexico to the "cloud-wreathed mountains far far to the north." To survive, the bride must turn herself into a kind of anthropologist of the exotic and imperfect Texans she encounters. "Here in Texas," she explains at one point to a fellow outlander, "we are very modern in matters of machinery and agriculture and certain ways of living. Very high buildings on very broad prairies. But very little thinking or broad viewpoint."

Ferber was appalled at the treatment of Mexican Americans that she witnessed in Texas, and that too went straight into her book, along with her horror of Texas man-food. ("Leslie found that the steak once cut could not be chewed. She felt her face flushing scarlet, she tried to swallow the leathery mass, it would not go down.")

The novel was a major best seller, but it got a bristly reaction in Texas. Partly this was because Ferber saw things she didn't like and wasn't shy about puncturing wealthy, beef-fed Anglo Texans' illusions about their noble possession of the Lone Star State. Ferber got the Texas vernacular subtly wrong but the historical reality exactly right when she had Jett Rink say, "Who gets hold of millions of acres without they took it off somebody!"

But the fact that Ferber dared to tell uncomfortable truths did not necessarily mean she had written a good novel. "For sheer embroidery of fact," Lon Tinkle, the book editor of the *Dallas Morning News*, wrote with justifiable harrumphment, "an art at which Texans are rarely surpassed—Miss Ferber takes the cottonseed cake. She has us all riding around in our own DC-6's. . . . Imagination goes overboard and what you have is a sort of mongrel biography, neither flesh nor fish but indisputably foul."

The 1956 movie, which starred Rock Hudson, Elizabeth Taylor, and James Dean and premiered fourteen months after Dean was killed at the age of twenty-four when he wrecked his new Porsche Spyder on a California highway, confronted the racial themes that were central to Ferber's novel but went easy on her snooty indictments of Texas. It was mostly a critical success—"James Dean's talent," wrote George Christian, then a movie critic, later LBJ's press secretary, "glows like an oilfield flare."

Not all of Ferber's snark was omitted, though. In one scene, the oil-rich Bick Benedict sits by his new swimming pool with business buddies and politicians singing the praises of the oil depletion allowance. "That oil tax exemption," one of them says, "is the best thing to hit Texas since we whupped Geronimo." This ahistorical remark (Geronimo was not whupped in Texas) is not contradicted by any of the other characters, but exception is taken by Bick's wife, Leslie, who steps into the frame to lecture these conniving Texas cronies about proper eastern values. "How about an exemption for the depletion of first-class brains?" she asks, referring to her doctor father, who "spent his life saving other people's lives. How about some tax exemption there?"

Texas oilmen turned movie critics and bombarded the producer and director with demands that the scene be cut, that it would do "irreparable harm," and that the elimination of the allowance that Elizabeth Taylor seemed to be arguing for would "be a death blow to our industry." But the scene stayed in, and the oil business somehow survived.

———— ★ ————

GIANT WAS FILMED OUTSIDE MARFA, IN PRESIDIO COUNTY, AND its principal set was the headquarters building of Bick Benedict's vast ranching spread, an improbable Victorian mansion rising all alone, with no fences or outbuildings or roads or shade trees, out of the board-flat Chihuahuan Desert. (Its false front stood there for decades, a corroding tourist attraction, before the telephone poles that held it up were all that remained.)

The parched grasslands surrounding the great house remind us that much of the 1950s unfolded during a period best summed up by the title of Elmer Kelton's novel of that period, *The Time It Never Rained*. Nancy Hagood Nunns, a rancher in the Hill Country community of Junction, remembered that one of the Christmas presents she received in 1951 was a raincoat. "It was the color of a green Coke bottle and trimmed in white, buttoned up the front, and had a full circular skirt. It was quite a raincoat, but it was never worn. We referred to it in the family as 'the virgin raincoat.' . . . [I] just outgrew it before it started to rain."

It stopped raining around 1950—or perhaps as early as 1947—and didn't start again until 1957. "Just another dry spell, men said at first," Kelton wrote in his novel. "Ranchers watched waterholes recede to brown puddles of mud that their livestock would not touch. They watched the rank weeds shrivel as the west wind relentlessly sought them out and smothered them with its hot breath. They watched the grass slowly lose its green, then curl and fire up like dying cornstalks."

The drought finally swept over so much of Texas that by the end of it, 236 out of the state's 254 counties had been declared disaster areas. Farmers and ranchers stared hopefully at the sky day after day, but year after year no rains came, no new grass grew in the pastures, only the mesquite and cedar that came in to claim overgrazed land. "The cattle would weaken down," Kelton remembered, "and then the wild hogs would just start eating 'em while they were alive. They'd be laying there bawling, and those wild hogs'd be eating on 'em."

Cattle died, and penguins in the Dallas zoo died, victims of the unbroken heat wave. The drought sparked epochal changes in the way Texans lived their lives. Almost 100,000 of the state's 345,000 farms disappeared, their owners giving up and moving to the cities, accelerating even further the rural-to-urban shift in the state. Not just livelihoods, but the landscape itself was forever changed, since the drought brought about the construction of many of Texas's present-day dams and reservoirs, which in turn recalibrated the salinity ratios of bays and estuaries. (Gone for a generation, for instance, were the tarpon—the "silver kings"—which had brought Franklin Roosevelt for a fishing trip to the Texas coast in 1937 and that had been part of the economic lifeblood of coastal villages like Port Aransas.)

But it wasn't just the forces of nature that were altering Texas. In 1956, work had just begun outside Corsicana on the state's first piece of the Interstate Highway System. President Eisenhower's dream of a seamless highway network connecting every state and every major city in the United States would become, until China brought its own system into being in 2011, the largest public-works project in the history of the world. A Texan named Frank Turner, who would become known as the "Father of the Interstate," was Eisenhower's choice as chief engineer of the project. His description of what he had been charged to accomplish must have sounded almost dream-like to motorists of the 1950s, accustomed to patchwork roads that could change radically from state to state: "A system of highway pieces all joined together so that you could get from anywhere to everywhere."

The Texas portion of the Interstate Highway System took thirty-six years to complete, but to the citizens of a state that stretched sideways for eight hundred miles the interstates came to be regarded as indispensable and natural as air. And let us pause to salute another Texan, Richard Oliver, who worked in the maintenance division of the Texas Highway Department and whose winning design of a red, white, and blue shield clearly displaying the interstate highway number achieved a ubiquity bordering on immortality.

Then there was air-conditioning, which was beginning to make Texas bearable. In the previous century, a dogtrot cabin with its central breeze-way could be surprisingly cool, even in the brain-melting heat of a Texas summer. But this sort of natural cross-ventilation had its limits, especially in growing cities with office buildings rising above streets of superheated asphalt. The cafeteria of Houston's Rice Hotel laid claim to being the first building in Texas to be cooled by refrigerated air, and by 1928 the twenty-one-story Milam Building, in San Antonio, became the first high-rise struc-ture in the United States to feature air-conditioning, a system that took its inspiration from the compressors used to cool German mine shafts.

But if you were alive in Texas in the 1950s and it was summer, you most likely lived in a world of fans and evaporative coolers and were on the look-out for signs like the ones outside movie theaters, which featured penguins standing next to igloos or arctic blocks of ice urging passersby, "Come on in. It's cool inside."

In May 1958, a lanky, balding, thirty-four-year-old electrical engineer moved to Dallas from Milwaukee just in time to experience a Texas summer. His name was Jack Kilby, and he was a new hire at Texas Instruments, an electronic-equipment company that had grown out of an earlier firm, Geo-physical Service, Inc., which specialized in seismological exploration for oil and, during the war, submarine detection.

A peculiarity of working for TI was that all its employees took vacation at the same time, in July. Well, all but one. Since Kilby was new at the company

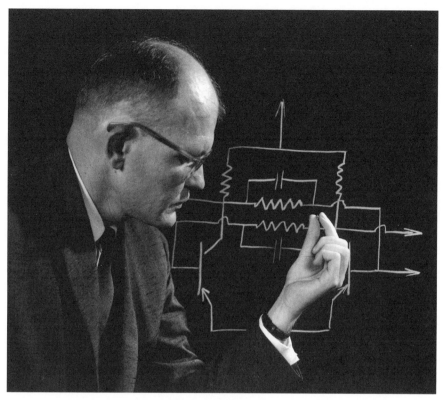

JACK KILBY
and his integrated circuit helped prove that not everything in Texas has to be big.

and not yet eligible for a vacation, he was left alone in the semiconductor lab. TI at that time was trying to solve a problem that bedeviled everyone in the relatively new field of transistors, the miniaturized circuits that had replaced old-fashioned vacuum tubes as a way to transmit and control electrical charges. The problem was that transistors were not miniature enough. Each circuit contained dedicated components such as resistors, capacitors, and diodes, all of which had to be connected by wires. The potential for what these semiconducting devices could do appeared limitless, but the hardware got in the way. There were too many wires, too many components, too many circuits—a conceptual ceiling known to scientists as the "tyranny of numbers."

With everyone at Texas Instruments on vacation, Kilby noodled around on the problem, free of distractions. A pragmatic engineer who had spent World War II repairing radio transmitters in India, he was on the trail of a practical, workable solution. "You could design a nuclear-powered baby bottle warmer," he once mused, "and it might work, but that's not an engineering solution."

On July 24, 1958, Kilby set down some ideas in a notebook. If you didn't know better and came across his drawings, you might think he was trying to invent a mousetrap. In fact, he was sketching the future. The device he invented that day was the integrated circuit. It had no wires, no separate components made out of metal or carbon or ceramics. It was all one elegant thing, a chip of silicon with all the critical components embedded into it.

It won Kilby the Nobel Prize in Physics in 2000, and it changed the world. Robert Noyce, an engineer at California's Fairchild Semiconductor, independently came up with a similar invention six months later, and is generally regarded as a kind of coinventor, but it was Jack Kilby, working in a Dallas lab in the summer of 1958, just after the great Texas drought of the 1950s finally broke, who first conceived the idea of the integrated circuit, the device that led the world into the information age.

Unlike Bick Benedict of *Giant*, Kilby was a newcomer to Texas, but no more a newcomer than Sam Houston or Davy Crockett or H. L. Hunt had once been. And he quickly made the case that Texas was no longer necessarily a place where worth and wealth were measured in oil leases or pastureland. Texas was now a place where a two-and-a-half-million-acre ranch like the Benedicts' Reata had to make room for a silicon chip that was a tiny fraction of the size of a human fingernail.

— 47 —

A GAMBLIN' MAN

IN 1960, I WAS IN THE SEVENTH GRADE AT ST. PATRICK'S
Catholic elementary school in Corpus Christi. Farrah Fawcett was a grade ahead of me, though not yet a part of Texas
history. It was sixteen years before she would set the world
ablaze—and presumably unsettle her teachers, the Sisters of
the Incarnate Word and Blessed Sacrament—by posing in
a red bathing suit and a blinding smile for what became the best-selling
poster ever. At the moment, as mandated by the Texas Legislature, we
seventh-graders were learning about our state's history. We had been taken
down a notch by Alaska, which became the forty-ninth state in 1959, making
Texas no longer the biggest state in the Union and necessitating an amendment in the state song—what had been "largest and grandest" was now
"boldest and grandest."

Our primary Texas history text, if you could call it that, was a paperback
book distributed free of charge to Texas students by the Mobil Oil Company.
It was called *Texas History Movies* and had run as a cartoon strip in the *Dallas Morning News* in the 1920s before being repackaged as a textbook for the
students of Texas. It was a black-and-white comic book, full of attitude, its
characters expressing themselves in sassy speech-bubble asides. It was also
more than a little racist, with irascible Anglo Texans calling Mexicans things

681

like "greasers" and "tamale eaters," and Indians expressing themselves with words like "ugh" and "heap big feller."

It didn't occur to me to ask my Mexican American friends in the class what they thought of *Texas History Movies*, or to think about how they might have felt when school was let out on a November day in 1960 so that everyone could be bused downtown to see John Wayne's new movie, *The Alamo*, in which Santa Anna was depicted more or less as a proto-Soviet tyrant bent on suppressing American freedoms.

At least there weren't any signs saying "No Mexicans" to keep my fellow students from being able to watch the gallant deaths of the Alamo defenders. Had there been any black students in our class of Anglos and Mexican Ameri-

Black students from Wiley College making their presence felt at a lunch counter sit-in in Marshall, Texas.

cans, they probably would have been allowed in as well, although it had been only a few years since I had last noticed the "white" and "colored" water fountains in Texas department stores. The process of integrating restaurants and theaters and golf courses and state parks—not to mention schools—was still unfolding. For instance, the previous spring, a group of students from Wiley and Bishop, the two influential black colleges in Marshall, in Harrison County, had risked their lives to integrate lunch counters at a Woolworth's department store and at the local bus station. On the way, one of their cars was pelted with rocks, and when they entered Woolworth's—dressed neatly in suits and sports clothes—they found, according to the store manager, "every peace officer in the county." The manager turned off the lights and

closed the store, and when another group of students came back half an hour later they found a full house—all the seats at the lunch counter were filled by police officers. They tried again a few days later and were arrested. Most of the students got only "a heart-to-heart talk" about how agitating for their rights would worsen racial relations, but for one of them the lecture was accompanied by a policeman slapping him around and poking his eye with a finger and threatening him with death if he returned to town.

The embattled but resolute black students drove back to their colleges, most likely in the same car that had been dented by white men's rocks. And if they were listening to the car radio along the way they were probably—given the slim pickings of 1960s AM radio—listening to white men's music. Roy Orbison had a big hit that year. The kid from Wink who had found so many ways to be lonesome in West Texas—who, with his soft, pale, beady-eyed face, was the opposite of what a rock 'n' roll star was supposed to look like—had written and recorded a song, "Only the Lonely," that blasted forth from his haunted teenage insecurity. A few years before, he had married a gorgeous sixteen-year-old Odessa girl, Claudette Frady, who had had to reas-

ROY ORBISON
may have been born without rock-star looks, but that didn't matter when he opened his mouth to sing.

sure her mother, perplexed about why her daughter would have chosen someone so homely, that "it's not outside but what's inside people that counts."

Roy had written the song while sitting alone in a car outside his house in Wink, feeling all alone at night but also sensing that his loneliness was not a solitary burden but something he shared with the world—"the club is very big." The recorded version of the song begins with a smooth introductory vocal, a series of nonsense syllables that doesn't prepare the listener for Orbison's shivering, soul-piercing falsetto, which rips right out of the bland sonic background.

The international success of the song was proof of Orbison's observation that loneliness is a big club. The song may be universal, but it still conveys a particularly Texan kind of loneliness. Orbison's voice, once he found it, had the tonal sweep of Texas itself. It was like a mournful wind drifting over the empty plains.

When he died of a heart attack at the age of fifty-two, his wife, Claudette, had been dead for over twenty years. She was killed in a motorcycle wreck in 1966. Roy, riding ahead of her, turned around when he heard the ambulance siren. He got there in time to see her body lying on the highway. "He sat there paralyzed," a witness said, "and laid his head down." Two years later, two of his sons died in a house fire. The timelessly relevant lyrics of "Only the Lonely" were also painfully prophetic.

———————— ★ ————————

ON JANUARY 20, 1961, OUR FAMILY WAS INVITED TO WATCH
John F. Kennedy's presidential inauguration at a neighbor's house. The neighbor had a color television, the first one any of us had seen. "Color" was a generous term. The image on-screen differed from what we would have seen in black-and-white only because it had a blurry pastel wash. The new technology made this unfolding Texas moment—when Lyndon Johnson took the oath of office as vice president of the United States—seem curiously antique, like something depicted in an old hand-tinted photograph.

THE EMPIRE OF TEXAS

Watching that same video today, I'm struck by how strong and confident Johnson looks, though with his weary, deeply lined face and his gray hair slicked back, he appears older than his age, which at that time was fifty-two. It was remarkable that he was still alive. In 1955, riding in a limousine from Washington, DC, to a Virginia estate owned by Brown & Root, he had felt closed in and overheated, with a growing pain in his chest. "If only," he said to the chauffeur, "I hadn't eaten that cantaloupe at lunch."

Cantaloupes were the least of Lyndon Johnson's problems. He was facing the consequences of a frenetic lifetime regimen of compulsive smoking and drinking and overwork and overeating—he had gained forty pounds in 1955 alone. When Johnson was finally persuaded that he was experiencing a heart attack and not indigestion, he was taken to Bethesda Naval Hospital in an ambulance. He was in great pain on the way. "Doctor," he said to the physician who was riding with him, "let me ask you something. Will I be able to smoke again if this is a heart attack?" When the doctor told him no, Johnson said, "I'd rather have my pecker cut off."

After surviving the heart attack, he did stop smoking, at least until he left the presidency in 1969, and he started to lose weight as well. "He became," one of his aides remembered, "the god-damnedest diet fanatic that ever lived." But he couldn't quite abide the doctors' prescription of extreme rest and no excitement whatever—"It would kill him if he relaxed," Sam Rayburn said.

Lyndon Johnson made a disingenuous observation in 1956, after his favorite-son candidacy for president came to nothing, that "no Texan wants to be vice president." His appetite for power was not diminished by his heart attack. If anything, he was in an even bigger hurry than before, since he now had convincing evidence to support the fatalistic family lore he had heard since childhood—that all Johnson men died young from heart problems.

Johnson was still a dominant force after his heart attack, still the Senate majority leader and, along with Sam Rayburn, one of the towering figures of the national Democratic Party. He wanted very much to be president, and to achieve that end he strove to become—as Herbert Hoover once said about Franklin Roosevelt—a "chameleon on plaid."

"I never had any bigotry in me," Lyndon Johnson testified about his own character. That would have been a surprise to some of the proudly bigoted Texas tycoons who poured money into his campaigns, or to a mentor like Georgia's senator Richard Russell, who had been gratified by Johnson's maiden speech in the Senate, which was an argument against a federal civil rights bill. Robert Parker, a black postal worker who owed his job to Johnson and in return was expected to moonlight without pay as his pri-

vate bartender and chauffeur, suffered through his job without Johnson ever
using his name, addressing him only as "boy" or "nigger" or "chief." "I can't
be too easy with you," Johnson confided to Parker one day when they were
alone. "I don't want to be called a nigger-lover."

Johnson's bids for the presidency in 1956 and 1960 depended on his old trick
of seeming to be all things to all people. Though he had opposed Truman-
sponsored anti-poll-tax and antilynching legislation in 1948, eight years
later he was one of only three southern senators not to sign the so-called
Southern Manifesto, whose retrograde aim was to dismantle *Brown v. Board
of Education* and make the country safe once again for segregation. And in
1957 he shepherded the passage of a civil rights bill, though he made sure it
was watered down enough—with very little federal enforcement power to
back up its provisions—to be approved by the Senate. The 1957 Civil Rights
Act turned out to be a somewhat symbolic gesture, but not an empty one,
and Johnson knew it. It was historic—the first civil rights legislation to be
passed in eighty-two years—and it pointed directly at the future. "We've
started something now," Johnson said, "Don't worry, it's only the first."

The reviews of Johnson's motives and methods in passing this legislation were mixed, but nobody doubted his mastery. "He is the first Southern
Democratic leader since the Civil War," wrote one columnist, "to be a
serious candidate for Presidential nomination and, if nominated, to have a
fair chance of winning."

"If nominated"—that turned out to be the problem. Lyndon Johnson
was not conflicted about becoming president, but something about an open
public admission of that fact, declaring that he was indeed a candidate,
held him back. His political instincts and experience led him to plot behind
the scenes, to equivocate, to throw up smoke screens, to wait to seize his
chance at a brokered convention. He was too late when it came to recognizing the élan and youthful appeal of his main rival, Senator John Kennedy.
When Kennedy sent his brother, Robert Kennedy, down to Johnson's ranch
on the Pedernales to try to determine whether the Texas senator was running, Johnson assured him that he wasn't. But LBJ also seized an opportunity to humiliate Bobby Kennedy, goading him into a deer-hunting excursion on the ranch. When Kennedy, far out of his urban-elite comfort zone,
fired the shotgun his host had selected for him, he ended up flat on his back
from the recoil. "Son," Johnson told him, sowing the seeds of a lifelong
enmity, "you've got to learn to handle a gun like a man."

But Lyndon Johnson waited too long, and outsmarted himself. On July 13,
1960, Kennedy won the nomination on the first ballot. But there was a surprise in store the next morning for Johnson. Kennedy wanted him on the

ticket as vice president. Johnson was well aware of what a former vice president from Texas, John Nance Garner, had thought of his office—"It's not worth a bucket of warm piss." On the other hand, the vice presidency might not be a blind alley, but a route forward. Former congresswoman Clare Boothe Luce asked Johnson on the night of the inaugural ball why he had chosen to accept Kennedy's offer. "Clare," he said, "I looked it up: one out of every four Presidents has died in office. I'm a gamblin' man, darlin', and this is the only chance I got."

Kennedy's inauguration took place on a cold but brightly sunny January day. Among the dignitaries who spoke was eighty-six-year-old Robert Frost, who had written a poem for the occasion called "Dedication." But when the old white-haired New England bard came to the podium and held the page in front of him and began to read, he managed only a few seemingly random words and phrases, as if he were translating from a language he barely knew. Was he having a stroke? The president-elect and the other dignitaries in their seats behind the podium reacted by staring stonily ahead, pretending that nothing was amiss, hoping the situation would somehow resolve itself.

But Lyndon Johnson saw what was wrong: the glare from the sun was too bright for the aged poet to see the words on the page. The new vice president stood up, and with an old-fashioned inaugural top hat shielded Frost's eyes. Frost grabbed the hat out of Johnson's hand and said, "Let me have that," an irascible response that caused the dignitaries and the vast audience to laugh and applaud. The tension was broken, the nation was saved from an embarrassing spectacle, and it was Lyndon Johnson who had displayed the initiative and leadership that the moment required. But it would be almost three frustrating years before his cynical gamble would pay off and he could take the lead again.

—48—

WELCOME
MR. KENNEDY

THERE WAS A VORTEX DRAWING JOHN F. KENNEDY TO
Dallas. It was a vortex of dissension, confusion, hate, pride,
and fear. Kennedy had chosen Lyndon Johnson as his running
mate because he needed to carry Texas, but there was no place
in Texas that had a darker view of Kennedy and Johnson than
Dallas did. It was the state's feverish headquarters of anti-
communism, anti-Catholicism, anti-Semitism, anti-fluoride, anti–federal
overreach, anti-school-milk programs, prosegregation activism, and pro-
American militancy. It wasn't monolithically so. Plenty of Dallas citizens
had copies of Kennedy's book *Profiles in Courage* on their bedside tables,
and before JFK clinched the nomination, the city had a "Ladies for
Lyndon" club, complete with uniforms of blue scarves and candy-striped
jackets designed by Neiman-Marcus on the instructions of its owner, the
cosmopolite Stanley Marcus. But Marcus got a reading on the brewing
right-wing atmosphere as soon as he endorsed Kennedy. "Nothing I had
done publicly up to that time," he wrote, "caused so much reaction among
our customers. The fact that Kennedy was a Catholic was not discussed,
but worse than being a papist, he was suspected of being against the

oil depletion allowance, which was a cardinal sin in the petroleum and country clubs of the state."

Dallas was the home of Bruce Alger, the U.S. congressman who was the first Republican to represent his district since Reconstruction. Alger was dashing looking, Princeton educated, and a decorated bomber pilot who had written a well-observed book about his experiences in the war. He was elected in 1954 as a moderate conservative who believed in "gradualism" and not outright denial when it came to integration. "It would be foolhardy," he said, "of any of us to think we can turn the clock back and deny rights to any of our citizens because of race." But he held that position only as long as it was politically workable, and after an election challenge in 1956 he had a conversion experience. No longer was he the voice of go-slow stateliness. He was the lone vote in the House of Representatives—348 to 1!—who dared to stand up for the principle that the federal government should not give free milk—"socialized milk"—to schoolchildren. He asserted that mixing "filthy with clean children" in the same school was not part of God's plan. "Who can ever repeal the law of nature," he wanted to know, "that birds of a feather flock together?"

His views may have changed, but he was still pretty good-looking, and his swoony Gary Cooper vibe might have been one reason why he rallied so many affluent young housewives to his cause. His own wife, though, considered herself a "political widow"—or something more unfortunate than that. She claimed in her divorce petition that after Alger won his congressional election in 1954, he had made her watch while he had sex with a prostitute.

The world's largest Methodist church was in Dallas. So was the world's largest Presbyterian church. So was the world's largest Baptist church. The fifty-year-old pastor of the First Baptist Church, shepherding a flock of 18,500 Dallas souls, was an avuncular, craggy-faced premillennialist named W. A. Criswell, who preached hard against integration and racial equality. ("They are not our folks. They are not our kind. They don't belong to the same world in which we live.") He was famous for the chuckles he elicited when in a speech to the South Carolina state legislature he mentioned the bugs that infested Texas lawns, claiming that the NAACP had outlawed the term "chigger": "It has to be Cheegro! Idiocy! Foolishness!" And of course he was against Kennedy. Among his reasons: "The election of a Catholic as president would mean the end of religious freedom in America."

One of the First Baptist parishioners who eagerly hearkened to the word of the Reverend Criswell was one of the country's richest men, H. L. Hunt, now in his early seventies, living in a mansion modeled after Mount Vernon. In his front yard were a cannon and a twelve-foot-high sign announcing the

Rising from the plains: Dallas in the early 1960s.

THE REVEREND W. A. CRISWELL
of the First Baptist Church proudly ministered to the conservative elite of Dallas. H. L. Hunt was
a member of his congregation.

daily schedule for his *Life Line* radio broadcasts. This was around the time
that Hunt was promoting his novel, *Alpaca*. It was a paperback, printed on
cheap paper, and much smaller than a regular book. No doubt Hunt intended
for it to be carried around in people's pockets or purses for quick and constant reference. And why not? After all, Hunt admitted, "I am the best writer
I know." At a big book signing for *Alpaca* in February 1960, the young daughters from his latest marriage stood behind him and sang "How much is
that book in the window?" to the tune of "How Much Is That Doggie in the
Window?" and then cried out at the end, as their beaming, wispy-haired, billionaire cheapskate father signed his books, "*ALPACA!* Fifty cents!"

Ted Dealey might have been one of the people in line to buy a copy of
Alpaca that day, though more likely the author had one sent to his office, a
courtesy for the publisher of the *Dallas Morning News*. Dealey was a few years
younger than Hunt. His father was George Dealey, the newspaper's founder,
whose statue overlooked the downtown plaza named in his honor. His
cousin was Sam Dealey, the heralded but doomed submarine commander
of the USS *Harder*. Ted had spent much of the war as a correspondent for
his newspaper and had been present on the deck of the USS *Missouri* when
the Japanese signed the surrender agreement. As a young reporter in the
1920s, he had helped lead the *News*' attack against the resurgent Klan. He

held a master's degree in philosophy from Harvard. He had the casual, vivid writing style of a veteran newspaperman, and as he approached his seventies he was developing a nostalgia for the old Dallas of his youth, which he looked back upon with blinkered fondness. ("Nor were there any racial problems that I can remember," he wrote in his awkwardly titled memoir, *Diaper Days of Dallas,* a few chapters after mentioning the lynching of an innocent black man in 1910. "The colored people of the community and the citizens with white skins got along peaceably and amicably.")

But Ted Dealey was no longer quite so content. His temperature, and his newspaper's, had spiked in response to the feverish climate of latter-day Dallas. The New Deal he had embraced as a younger man he now saw as a pernicious example of big-government meddling, and Kennedy as president would bring more of the same, only with the Catholic Church calling the shots. "The President of the United States," declared a *News* editorial in October 1960, "should be a man who can be trusted to fear God and honor his oath of office, no matter what all the bishops in the hierarchy may presume to order."

On November 4, 1960, four days before the presidential election, Lyndon and Lady Bird Johnson flew to Dallas on one of their last campaign stops. When their motorcade arrived at the downtown Baker Hotel, they were met by Bruce Alger and a sizable crowd of upper-middle-class women, many of them in mink coats—hence their immortal designation as the Mink Coat Mob. The Republican housewives of Dallas—"The prettiest bunch of women I ever saw in my life," according to Alger—were running up and down the street, pinning Nixon buttons on businessmen walking by on their way to work. Some of them were waving campaign signs for John Tower, the nattily dressed political science professor from Midwestern University in Wichita Falls, who was running against Lyndon Johnson for senator. (LBJ was on the ballot as both a senatorial and a vice presidential candidate. Running for two offices at the same time had been prohibited by Texas law until Johnson, with a simple phone call, arranged things otherwise.)

But they carried other signs as well, with slogans such as "Texas Traitor" and "Judas Johnson." Alger held up a placard that read, "LBJ Sold Out to Yankee Socialists," and shouted, "We're gonna show Johnson he's not wanted in Dallas." When the Johnsons tried to enter the hotel, the women pressed in on them, booing and yelling insults. One of them grabbed the white gloves that Lady Bird was holding in one hand and threw them in the gutter. It got worse when the Johnsons tried to walk across the street so that he could give a speech in the Adolphus Hotel. The crowd by then was bigger and uglier, jostling and jeering at them as they tried to make their way across Commerce Street. When they finally got to the lobby of the Adolphus, it was the scene of a riot. A fight had broken out between the Mink Coat Mob and their male auxiliaries, on one side, and, on the other, the Johnson supporters who had gathered there to welcome the candidate.

Lady Bird was frightened and appalled, but Johnson quickly saw that this mob of spitting, hate-filled demonstrators was exactly the boost he needed to help carry Texas for Kennedy. Instead of hurrying through the lobby, he took a dramatic slow walk as he shielded his wife from the spittle and jabbing signs. "No man is afraid to facing up to such people," he said later. "But it is outrageous that in a large civilized city a man's wife can be subjected to such treatment. Republicans are attacking the women, and the children will probably be next."

In the election that took place four days later, Kennedy squeaked past Richard Nixon in Texas by forty-six thousand votes. It might have been the madness in the Adolphus lobby, documented by photographers and news crews, that made the difference. Nixon thought so, and he blamed Bruce Alger. "We lost Texas," he said, "because of that asshole congressman."

———————— ★ ————————

BUT THE DALLAS FURIES STILL RAGED AFTER THE ELECTION, as became clear when Adlai Stevenson, the U.S. ambassador to the United Nations, accepted an invitation from Stanley Marcus to give a speech in Dallas in October 1963 on United Nations Day. His appearance was a melee almost from the start. "Surely, my dear friend," Stevenson called out from the podium to a man who tried to shout him down just after Marcus made his introduction, "I don't have to come here from Illinois to teach Texas manners, do I?"

Much of the crowd applauded, but "Surely, my dear friend" was exactly the sort of stuffy Eastern liberal pinko locution that was bound to ratchet up the resentment of the UN-hating members of the audience. They continued to interrupt his speech, waving upside-down American flags, calling out, "Kennedy will get his reward in hell. Stevenson is going to die."

He managed to finish the speech, and supporters in the room responded with lengthy applause and heartfelt apologies. But there was still the matter of getting out of Dallas alive. Stevenson was escorted out a stage door, but the protestors in front of the auditorium spotted him and were on him before he could reach his limousine, spitting in his face and calling him a communist and a traitor. One woman, the wife of a Dallas insurance executive, took her sign—which read, "Adlai, Who Elected You?" and was attached to a stout piece of wood—and whapped him over the head with it. She later claimed that she hadn't meant to actually hit the U.S. ambassador to the United Nations, but that she had been "pushed from behind by a Negro."

"Adlai got what was coming to him." That was the opinion of Dallas's most incendiary personality, General Edwin Walker. Walker was about to turn fifty-four. He had short dark hair, emphatic dark eyebrows, and a military mien that was somewhat undercut by an awkward public-speaking style and a tendency to break into tears when reminiscing about the men he led in Germany in the Twenty-Fourth Infantry Division. He was a war hero in both World War II and Korea, and was briefly something of a civil rights hero as well, since he had commanded the troops that protected the black students trying to enroll in Central High School in Little Rock, Arkansas.

But that was in 1957, and now Walker was out of uniform and no longer taking orders from anybody. "I was on the wrong side," he told people about his role in integrating Central High. In 1961, he was relieved of his command in Europe for trying to indoctrinate his troops with literature from the right-wing John Birch Society. He defended himself before a Senate committee by declaring, "I am a Christian martyr, personally victimized by the international Communist conspiracy," and afterward punching a reporter in the eye. That same year, 1962, he ran unsuccessfully for the Democratic nomination for Texas governor against Lyndon Johnson's protégé John Connally, but he was still waging war against the "conspiracy from within" that was trying to topple American values and integrate its schools.

In September 1962, he was again in command at a school segregation fight, but this time he was leading a Molotov cocktail–throwing mob that tried to prevent James Meredith from registering at the University of Mississippi. Two people died, and twenty-eight U.S. Marshals were wounded by gunfire. Attorney General Robert Kennedy ordered Walker arrested. He was taken into custody at bayonet point and, on the suspicion that he was insane, sent to a federal psychiatric prison for evaluation. While incarcerated, he behaved like a prisoner of war, refusing to divulge anything but his name, rank, and serial number. He was finally sent home to Dallas, on the condition that he take a psychological examination. At the Dallas airport, he got a hero's welcome, with people holding up signs reading, "Walker for President in 1964." The next month, November 1962, he aced his exam at Parkland Hospital. He was officially sane.

John Kennedy would have disagreed. "We're heading into nut country today," he told his wife on the morning of November 22, 1963, in their suite at the Hotel Texas in Forth Worth, a little less than an hour before leaving for Dallas.

But Kennedy was eager to be in Texas. He needed to raise money, and he needed to carry the state in the 1964 election, a prospect that—as seen by the toxicity in Dallas—was becoming worrisome. Political lore has it that he also came to quell, or at least keep an eye on, an intraparty dispute between Senator Ralph Yarborough and John Connally, who had been elected the year before as governor. Connally later testified that this "was pure hogwash." He said the split had nothing to do with him but was between Yarborough and Vice President Johnson over patronage issues. Maybe so, but there was no great affection between Connally and Yarborough. Jack Valenti, a Johnson consultant, remembered that the Texas senator and the Texas governor had a "venomous" relationship. "The antipathy that raged between these two men," he said, "bordered on pathological hatred."

Valenti regarded John Connally as "the most charismatic man in American public life." The new Texas governor certainly looked more like what a Texas governor ought to look like than almost any of his predecessors—although Jacqueline Kennedy thought he was "too pretty to be handsome." He was in his midforties when he was elected, his wavy dark hair just going gray. He was tall and straight with a patrician nose and a chin that his biographer, James Reston Jr., referred to as the "Great Jawbone."

Connally was born thirty miles southeast of San Antonio near Floresville. His father (who was six-five and so rugged-looking that people called him "Old Man Texas") was a tenant farmer, his mother a schoolteacher. John was the fourth of their eight children. He never knew his older brother, who had burned to death as an infant when he accidentally rolled into the hearth. As a boy, Connally picked cotton on the family farm, dragging a sack between the rows as he shuffled along on kneepads cut from old tires. Walking "many a mile" behind a team of mules, he broke the turf with a turning plow—"I used to take off my shoes because the soil behind the plow felt so good to walk in."

He made his way to the University of Texas, where he studied law, be-

The morning of November 22, 1963, Love Field in Dallas. Governor John Connally stands to welcome President and Mrs. Kennedy into the fatal limousine.

came student body president, orated for the Athenaeum Literary Society on topics such as "Is There Such a Thing as a Virtuous Woman?," joined the Curtain Club, and acted in plays with the future movie stars Eli Wallach and Zachary Scott. "The line between dramatics and politics, I found, was a thin one," he noted. Also at UT, he met his future wife, a girl named Idanell Brill, who was known as Nellie and had been certified by the student body as both a Bluebonnet Belle and one of the Ten Most Beautiful on campus.

He met Lyndon Johnson after he got a grant through the National Youth Administration, whose regional office Johnson headed, to shelve books at the Texas Supreme Court for seventeen cents an hour. When he was twenty-two, Connally became Johnson's congressional secretary and the beneficiary of his mentor's pragmatic political wisdom. "There is nothing in the world more useless," Johnson once told him, "than a dead liberal."

Connally joined the navy and served on the aircraft carrier USS *Essex* as a flight direction officer, a kind of air traffic controller for the ship's fighter planes during the frenzied kamikaze battles late in the war. He was LBJ's campaign manager for the notorious 1948 Senate election, and later worked as legal counselor and adviser to the billionaire Fort Worth oilman Sid Richardson. In 1959, he and Nellie lost their teenage daughter, Kathleen. She had become sullen and uncommunicative, and her parents strongly suspected she was secretly pregnant by her high school boyfriend. "I accused Kathleen and Bobby of lying to us," Connally recalled in an exquisitely painful chapter of his memoir. "She repeated once again that nothing was wrong. And then I slapped her. Even as I did it, I wished that I hadn't. A thousand times since—maybe more—I have wanted to call back my hand."

The next day, she and her boyfriend drove to Oklahoma and got married by a justice of the peace. Then they went to Florida. A month later, Connally got a call from the Tallahassee sheriff, who told him his daughter had been shot in the head. Startled, Connally asked how bad it was. The sheriff was brutally blunt: "Couldn't be worse. Half her head was blown away."

The Connallys never knew whether she had deliberately killed herself with her boyfriend's shotgun, or whether he had tried to seize it from her as she was pointing it at her head and it accidentally went off. In either case, their daughter's death was—until November 22, 1963—the defining tragedy of their lives.

"WELCOME MR. KENNEDY TO DALLAS." THAT WAS THE HEADING of a black-bordered full-page ad that ran in the *Dallas Morning News* on the morning of November 22. Paid for by something called the American Fact-Finding Committee, it featured a laundry list of grievances against the president, including the sale of wheat and corn to communist countries, the White House's hosting of the Yugoslav president—and "Moscow's Trojan Horse"—Marshal Tito, and the administration's tendency to "go soft on Communists, fellow-travelers, and ultra-leftists in America."

The ad was not an official expression of the views of the newspaper, or of Ted Dealey, its publisher. Those were conveyed in an anodyne pleasantry on the editorial page, in which the paper expressed its interest in "extending the hand of fellowship to the President of the United States and his attractive wife." But Dealey had approved the ad, and John Kennedy knew

The full-page ad that ran in the Dallas Morning News *the day of the president's visit. Once you read past the headline, it wasn't much of a welcome.*

Lee Harvey Oswald in custody after Kennedy's murder.

exactly what Dealey thought of him. Two years before, the president had invited a group of Texas publishers to an off-the-record get-acquainted session at the White House. To the great embarrassment of his colleagues in the room, Dealey interrupted Kennedy in the middle of his welcoming talk and informed him, "You and your administration are weak sisters. . . . We need a man on horseback to lead this nation—and many people in Texas and the Southwest think that you are riding Caroline's tricycle."

The resounding irony is that the person who killed Kennedy was not a murderous ideologue who emerged from the right-wing hatred of Dallas, not someone who considered the president an unhorsed weakling who was going too easy on Khrushchev and Castro, but a twenty-four-year-old Marxist whose target of choice, the previous April, had been none other than General Edwin Walker, whom he regarded as "the most dangerous man in America."

Walker was not hard to find. He lived in a five-thousand-square-foot house on Turtle Creek Boulevard, one of Dallas's premium neighborhoods. The distress signal of three upside-down American flags flew in the yard, along with Confederate and Texas flags and a giant sign that read, "Get the U.S. Out of the U.N." The house was filled during the day with volunteers, with the attractive young men whom the general called his "adjutants." (In 1976, he was arrested for propositioning an undercover policeman in a Dallas park.)

On the night of April 10, 1963, Walker was alone. His aides had left, and he was sitting in his study, filling out his income tax forms. Lee Harvey Oswald was watching him. He had positioned himself in an alley behind a wooden fence with the Mannlicher-Carcano rifle he had ordered through the mail, along with a cheap Japanese telescopic sight, for $19.95. Oswald had a clear shot. It was only 120 feet from where he stood to where Walker sat at his desk, pencil in hand, staring down at his tax forms in concentration. But the bullet Oswald fired nicked the edge of the window frame on its way to the general's head, changing its course enough that it just riffled his hair before slamming into the wall.

"I missed," Oswald told his wife Marina the next morning.

———— ★ ————

WE ALL KNOW THAT HE DIDN'T MISS HIS NEXT TARGET—AT
least those of us do who accept the conclusion that Lee Harvey Oswald was the sole assassin of John F. Kennedy. There are not enough pages in this book, or room in my head, to engage with the ever-spiraling conspiracy theories, or even to recount all the events of that day and the days that followed: Nellie Connally's remark to Kennedy—the last words he heard in his life—"Well, Mr. President, you can't say that Dallas doesn't love you," just before the shot

that hit the president in the back and exited the throat and almost fatally wounded her husband; the next shot, which blew off the right front half of Kennedy's head; the race to Parkland Hospital (where Edwin Walker had been judged sane the year before); Oswald's escape attempt and murder of the Dallas police officer J. D. Tippit; his capture in the Texas Theatre, where a movie called *War Is Hell*, which featured a filmed introduction by Audie Murphy, was playing; his live-on-television killing by the nightclub owner Jack Ruby.

Then there is the eerie still point in this unreal swirl of events: the most famous photograph in Texas history, taken on Air Force One by the official White House photographer, Cecil Stoughton, two hours and eight minutes after Kennedy was shot in Dealey Plaza. The masterful composition of the image is due of course to the photographer's skill, but also to the cramped conditions in the airplane's stateroom and the dictates of the man at the picture's center. Johnson invited everyone on the plane to witness him taking the oath of office, and he told them where he wanted them to be. Standing in front of him in the photograph, holding a Catholic missal, is sixty-seven-year-old Sarah T. Hughes, the first woman appointed a state district judge in Texas and the first to serve as a federal district judge. ("Sonny," Sam Rayburn had told Bobby Kennedy when he tried to block her nomination for the federal post because she was too old, "everybody seems old to you.")

Judge Hughes is wearing a print dress with fuzzy polka dots. We see her only from the back, and the tilt of her head as she gazes up at the face of the tallest person in the room creates a commanding visual vector. LBJ's expression is solemn and steady. His left hand is on the missal, his right raised to the level of his creased ear lobes. Lady Bird Johnson, standing to his right, looks dazed but composed. Jack Valenti, squeezed into the picture on the left side of the frame, is looking at the judge, but because his face is above her head, his eyes seem to be drilling into the viewer, challenging us to witness what is happening. Then, to the left of Johnson, in her blood-and-brain-spattered pink Chanel suit, is Jacqueline Kennedy, her face subtly contorted in shock and anguish—the most haunted facial expression in Texas history since Cynthia Ann Parker stared into the camera at a Fort Worth photographer's studio in 1861.

Every American, every Texan, who was alive then has a memory of hearing the news of Kennedy's murder. The assassination would become all the more

The photograph taken on the Texas tarmac that seared itself into the memory of the world.

vivid to us because our state would no longer be regarded by the rest of the nation as merely an overblown, self-important province, but a place to be reviled and condemned and avoided. Dallas was labeled the "city of hate."

I have my own memories of that day, but I'll defer to my friend Lawrence Wright, who gave us the best account in his memoir, *In the New World*, of what it was like to be a young Texan in 1963 and to hear the news that Kennedy had been killed. Larry was in a high-school algebra class when the principal came over the public-address system to tell the students that the president had been shot. "In that instant," he wrote, "the world we knew shattered and collapsed. It happened—the something we had been waiting for. It happened! We were dazed and excited. We turned in our chairs and looked into each other's faces, finding grins of astonishment. Later, when reports appeared about Dallas schoolchildren laughing at the news, I wondered if I hadn't laughed myself. . . . All I knew was that life could change, it had changed at last. Hadn't we known! Hadn't we been scared of exactly this?"

—49—

EL DEGÜELLO
REPRISE

THE NIGHT BEFORE HE DIED, KENNEDY MADE AN APPEAR-
ance at the Rice Hotel in Houston at a gala put on by LULAC,
the League of United Latin American Citizens. Just before
going down to the Grand Ballroom where the gala was taking
place, he had had a tense conversation with Lyndon Johnson
about the very public split between Ralph Yarborough and the

Johnson-Connally axis of the Texas Democratic Party. Yarborough was in
full sputter. He had just become aware of how thoroughly John Connally
was trying to cast him into the shade during the president's trip: no seat for
the Yarboroughs at the head table for an Austin fund-raiser scheduled for
the next night after the trip to Dallas, and not even an invitation to a reception afterward at the Governor's Mansion. Earlier that day in San Antonio,
Yarborough had taken revenge by refusing to ride in the vice president's car
in the motorcade.

Jackie Kennedy, after seeing Johnson angrily exit the president's suite,
asked her husband what the argument had been about. "That's just Lyndon," he told her. She confided to him that she didn't like John Connally at
all—"I just can't bear him sitting there saying all these great things about

himself." "For heaven's sakes," Kennedy told her. "Don't get a thing on him, because that's what I came down here to heal. I'm trying to start by getting two people in the same car."

There is surviving footage of the Kennedys and the Johnsons as they dropped into the LULAC gathering a few minutes later. It's remarkable, given the tense scene that had just taken place, how relaxed they all appear. Jackie Kennedy had been nervously memorizing and practicing some remarks in Spanish in her stateroom on Air Force One on the flight from Washington, a few bromides about *el gran estado de Texas* and *La noble tradición española*. When she delivered the talk, it went over thunderously well, the LULAC audience applauding and yelling out, "¡Viva!"

The visits to San Antonio and Houston were brief but important stops for the president. San Antonio and Bexar County were, as its congressman, Henry B. González, told Kennedy on Air Force One, "Viva country." Kennedy had won Texas in 1960 by only 46,257 votes, and the support of Mexican American leaders such as González and Hector García, who had organized "Viva Kennedy" clubs across the state, had made a difference.

But the fact that the relatively middle-class members of LULAC could gather for a gala in a fancy hotel ballroom to salute the president they had helped elect did not mean that the ancient tensions between Anglos and Tejanos were no longer alive. The West Side of San Antonio, for example, was home to some of the poorest neighborhoods in America, where the unemployment rate was almost four times as large as that of the city taken as a whole, and where people still lived in dirt-floored shacks with no running water and walls and roofs made out of scavenged pieces of metal. And then there was the part of South Texas bucolically known as the Winter Garden because of its year-round agricultural yield, where the Bracero Program, established by the United States during World War II to compensate for a projected shortage of manpower, was coming to an end. Braceros were guest workers from Mexico who in theory would work on short-term contracts and receive adequate pay and housing before returning to their homes in Mexico. But the program also opened the door to a flood of undocumented immigrants that South Texas farmers were happy to hire in an off-the-books way, perpetuating the exploitation that had been going on for decades—"legalized slavery," in the words of a Department of Labor official. All this culminated in 1954 in a xenophobic backlash, a government program derisively called Operation Wetback, that rounded up undocumented workers and sent them back across the border in one of the biggest mass deportations in American history.

Before and after the Bracero Program, in places like Starr County in the Valley, conditions among farmworkers were likely to be as eternally bad as ever: forty cents an hour to pick cantaloupes under the South Texas sun, no bathrooms or medical services provided, and sometimes no water. "I remember we would drink from puddles left by the irrigation system," one worker recalled a half century later, "full of frogs and crickets. We would push the critters out of the way and drink."

In the early sixties, the most visible champion of Mexican American rights in Texas—"Super Mex," he was called on the West Side of San Antonio—was Congressman Henry B. González. He was in his late forties, part of the rising postwar generation of Texas minority activists. He came from a family that had arrived in the New World from Spain in 1561. For many generations they had been governmental officials in Mapimí, the silver-mining region of northern Mexico. González's great-great-grandfather had celebrated

The Bracero Program promised better conditions for Texas farm workers, but when it came to migrant labor, the reality almost always fell short.

THE EMPIRE OF TEXAS

his daughter's wedding by ordering a path made of silver constructed from the family's house to the door of the church. But during the Mexican Revolution the family fled north, settling among San Antonio's refugee population. Henry González's father was the general manager of a Spanish-language newspaper called *La Prensa*, and when Henry was growing up the house was a meeting place for Mexican intellectuals in flight from the turmoil on the other side of the Rio Grande. The boy had an intellectual side of his own, copying out the essays of Matthew Arnold, reading Thomas Carlyle aloud while honing his oratorical skills, a la Demosthenes, with rocks in his mouth. But his erudition was lost on the racial enforcers who threw him and his friends out of public parks and swimming pools, and on the Anglo schoolchildren who taunted him with labels like "Meskin greaser."

He served as a military translator during World War II, alerting his superiors to Nazi plans to send submarines into the Gulf. After the war, he wanted to join the FBI, but he was turned down, and he suspected it was because he was a Mexican American. ("Oh, they were very racist.") Instead he became a juvenile probation officer, then a San Antonio city councilman, and then, in 1956, the first Tejano to serve in the Texas Senate since José Antonio Navarro in the 1840s. He was still a freshman senator when he launched into a famous twenty-two-hour filibuster against a school bill meant to ease the way for local school districts to enforce prohibitions against integrating black students. "The Irish have a saying," he proclaimed in full Demosthenes mode, "'It's easy to sleep on another man's wounds.' Well, what's the difference? Mexican, Negro, what have you. The assault on the inner dignity of man, which our society protects, has been made. . . . We all know in our hearts and minds that it is wrong."

He ran for governor in 1958 against Price Daniel, but—as the journalist Ronnie Dugger observed of his hopeless race against

a popular prosegregationist governor—"Gandhi might as well have run for governor of South Africa before he returned to India."

In 1961, though, he was elected to Congress from his San Antonio district. Combative and passionate by nature, he surrendered nothing of his personality once he took his seat in Washington. He felt free to tell President Kennedy that he was "full of bullshit," and when he heard that another congressman had called him a communist, he accosted him in the hallway outside the House Chamber and told him to take off his glasses. The man refused, but González hit him anyway.

González may have had a scrappy political personality, but he was also an establishment player during a time when the traditional political architecture was crumbling. This was happening in places like Crystal City, the former site of the World War II internment camp, where Mexican Americans accounted for 80 percent of the population. To them, Crystal City was known as Cristal, and they perceived themselves as living in a different town from the one they shared with the Anglos who ruled city hall and the school system and owned the major employer, the Del Monte processing plant. But that power imbalance was about to change. "The rumor in the barrio," remembered the Chicano activist José Ángel Gutiérrez, who had recently graduated from high school in Crystal City, "was that five Mexican Americans were going to run for all five seats on the city council."

They were called Los Cinco Candidatos, and their success depended on the registration of Mexican American voters, which depended upon payment of the still-extant poll tax. "In retrospect," Gutiérrez wrote, "it seems crazy that we were forced to buy the right to vote by collecting $1.75 from poor, migrant, seasonal farmworker families who felt they had better uses for the money, such as buying one hundred pounds of potatoes or a case of Southern Select or Jax beer." To raise money for the poll taxes, volunteers put on cakewalks and dances and sold tamales. They were aided by the Teamsters and by a new political organization that had grown out of the Viva Kennedy clubs and was known by the acronym PASSO (Political Association of Spanish-Speaking Organizations).

The mild-looking, bespectacled Gutiérrez was just a teenager, but he was already developing a reputation as a scorching speaker. "They say there is no discrimination," he told the audience at a Cinco Candidatos rally, "but we have only to look around us to know the truth. . . . We look at the schools. . . . The houses we live in. . . . The few opportunities. . . . The dirt in the streets. . . . And we know."

He also attracted the attention of a *pinche rinche* (i.e., a "fucking Ranger") by the name of A. Y. Allee, who—Gutiérrez says—cornered him one night

Chicano activists began to suspect Henry "Super Mex" González of being too cozy with the Washington establishment.

after a rally and told him to stop making speeches and "making the Meskins act crazy." Allee was in the act of slapping him around when Gutiérrez's mother appeared from her house a half block away, pointing a shotgun at the Ranger captain and at the police who were with him. "I could believe neither my eyes or ears; my mother was 'packing,' and she was facing down the *pinches rinches!*"

Gutiérrez's mother somehow got away with it, and Los Cinco Candidatos got away with it, too, winning the election and installing a Mexican American mayor and four other city officials in city hall in 1963. After the election, the new mayor, Juan Cornejo, claimed that Allee had roughed him up by banging his head six times into a sheetrock wall. The responses of Governor Connally and Senator Yarborough after Cornejo pressed charges illustrated the Texas reality-perception divide. "I urge your complete cooperation with the Rangers and Captain Allee," Governor Connally told the mayor, whereas Yarborough declared that men such as Allee "are a relic of a primitive age in Texas which should have passed away with the frontier."

A few years after the election in Crystal City, there was another demonstration of the emerging Chicano movement in the Rio Grande valley. A group of union officers from the National Farm Workers Association dispatched by Cesar Chávez arrived in Starr County to organize local farmworkers—who were demanding, among other things, a minimum wage of $1.25 an hour. The Texas Rangers were once again deployed. It depended on where you stood whether they were there to preserve law and order or to intimidate the striking workers and ensure that they did not succeed. After a month, the farmworkers and their families set out on a three-hundred-mile march north from the Rio Grande to the Capitol in Austin to set their grievances in front of the governor.

John Connally by then was in his second term and, one suspects, still coming to terms with the fact that he was alive. "Oh, my God, it hurts! It hurts!" he had screamed when he arrived at Parkland Memorial Hospital after being shot in the front seat of the president's car. The bullet that had torn downward from his shoulder through his chest—and then into his wrist and thigh—had collapsed his lung. "The governor is not expected to live," a nurse told one of Lyndon Johnson's aides. Henry González was at the hospital, and he was handed two paper bags filled with the governor's effects and told to sign for them.

Connally survived, though he lost mobility in his shattered wrist, and the bullet that had clipped his lung interfered with his breathing for the rest of his life. And for two months after the assassination, he dreamed every night of being shot at—"under a never-ending series of scenarios."

Connally was a bit gun-shy when it came to the marchers from the Rio Grande valley. He didn't want to meet them in Austin and seemed to be under the impression that their presence there might provoke a riot like those taking place elsewhere in the country. But he traveled to New Braunfels, fifty miles south of Austin, and conferred with the farmworkers on the highway in the blazing August heat. He was genial and respectful— "My door has been open . . . And it's gonna continue to be open"—but later a Catholic priest with the marchers neatly summarized the gulf between establishment politicians like John Connally and the upstart Chicano movement. "Governor Connally," he said, "is the symbol of gringo paternalism. I could see that out on the road that day. He was the tall Texan looking down and patting the Mexican on the head."

As the 1960s passed turbulently on, even a longtime champion of Mexican American rights like Henry B. González could not escape the suspicion of paternalism by younger, more militant advocates like Gutiérrez or by González's onetime protégé Willie Velásquez.

González had spoken to the Rio Grande marchers when, after meeting and being cordially dismissed by Connally, they had continued on to a rally in Austin. But he had refused to join a protest against the Texas Rangers earlier that summer in Rio Grande City, on the pretext that it would mean meddling in the politics of another congressional district. In reality, he was alarmed at what he perceived to be the "race hate" that had crept into the Chicano movement, and he didn't like its style either—their "brown berets, combat boots, serapes, rolled blankets slung over shoulder and chest in campaign style, mustaches and-or beards."

González belonged to the old guard, to the anticline of the seismic upheavals that were warping the structure of the country during the Vietnam War era. He had little in common with groups like the Mexican American Youth Organization, founded by—among others—Gutiérrez and Velásquez. MAYO evolved into the Raza Unida Party and made some respectable political showings in South Texas. But the title of MAYO's newspaper, *El Degüello*, told you everything you needed to know about its initial attitude: "El Degüello" was the take-no-prisoners bugle call Santa Anna had ordered played for the besieged defenders of the Alamo. José Ángel Gutiérrez went so far as to characterize Henry B. González as a kind of honorary gringo and to declare, in words that might have sounded alarming to those who remembered the incendiary Plan of San Diego, "It's too late for the gringo to make amends. Violence has to come."

When people called him a communist, as that congressman had done, or a *cabrón vendido* (bastard sellout), as some MAYO militants did during a rhetorical ambush at one of his talks, González always politely asked them to remove their glasses before he punched them out.

Once, González was waylaid before a lecture he was supposed to give at the University of Colorado at Boulder and then spirited away to a classroom, where he was detained by a group of activists who had decided to put him on trial. "We find you guilty," the "judge" concluded, "and you are a traitor."

"Well," Henry B. González replied, "you're a little dumb shit."

— 50 —

THE VOICE OF GOD

BARBARA JORDAN WAS TWENTY YEARS YOUNGER THAN
Henry B. González, not yet a member of the hated establishment, but like González she had pragmatic political instincts that tended to set her apart, as a minority leader, from the raging temper of the times. And like him, she had a personal inkling of uncommon destiny. "Whoever heard of an outstanding pharmacist?" she once asked by way of talking herself out of a pharmacy career. She got some of that attitude from her maternal grandfather, John Ed Patten, who had owned a candy shop in Houston's Fourth Ward. Late one night as he was closing up, someone ran in, grabbed some money off his counter, and disappeared into the night. Patten got a gun and gave chase, a near fatal mistake. It was only a year after the Camp Logan Riot, and an armed black man running through the Houston streets at night was a natural target for the police, who opened fire. Patten claimed at his trial that he didn't know it was the police who were shooting at him—he just heard a voice calling out in the darkness: "Catch that nigger, he's got a gun." He shot back, wounded one of the officers, and was shot through the hand when he tried to surrender. He went to the state penitentiary for six years.

When he came out, he had lost the candy store, so he started a junk business, hauling metal scraps and rags in a mule-drawn wagon through downtown Houston. He was outraged when his daughter Arlyne, Barbara's mother, settled into a conventional marriage with a young man who sang in the choir of her Baptist church. He wouldn't come to his daughter's wedding, punishing her for her rejection of some undefined future grandeur. When his granddaughter Barbara was born, he projected his aspirations onto her instead. "He felt himself quite different," she remembered of her grandfather, "just a little cut above the ordinary man, black or white." He singled Barbara out from his other grandchildren, gave her extravagant gifts, read to her from a book titled *Songs for the Blood Washed* about "the resolute few who dare go through," and warned her never to marry.

His own claim to being one of the resolute few went unfulfilled. He died after he fell down drunk on the railroad tracks and a passing train severed his legs. But he passed on to his granddaughter an internal sense of brewing magnificence. "I decided that I was not going to be like the rest," she wrote. "I believed I was going to be a lawyer, or rather something called a lawyer, but I had no fixed notion of what that was."

Certainly, it had something to do with her voice, a voice that she studiously cultivated through church recitations and debate competitions but that was also an innate gift. "She had it in the cradle," her debate coach at Texas Southern University, Tom Freeman, said of her voice. Its spectacular orotundity—every syllable building and rolling like an ocean wave—was so rich, so perfect that it was almost a parody of what an orator was supposed to sound like. "I thought I was listening to God," reported a woman who heard Barbara Jordan speak in public for the first time. The voice was godlike not just in its all-commanding tone but also in the sense that it seemed to have no beginning. The girl and then woman who deployed it was a black Texan from segregated Houston's Fourth Ward, but there was no accent, nowhere in particular to place it. It was the voice of someone determined to create herself and announce herself to the world.

At first the voice trumpeted more than it delivered. Freeman, Barbara's TSU debate coach, used it as a shock weapon. "She could not argue, she could not think on her feet, all she could do was speak. So I would take her down to mesmerize the audience and then the fellas [she was the only woman on the team] would come along and clean up afterward."

But the content would not be long in arriving. Barbara Jordan was accumulating plenty of stark experience to draw upon. When she and her teammates traveled in Freeman's car to college debates in Chicago or New York or Cambridge, they had to pack their own food as they drove through the southern states, since most restaurants and cafes wouldn't serve blacks. When they stopped for gas, they couldn't use the restrooms, just the out-

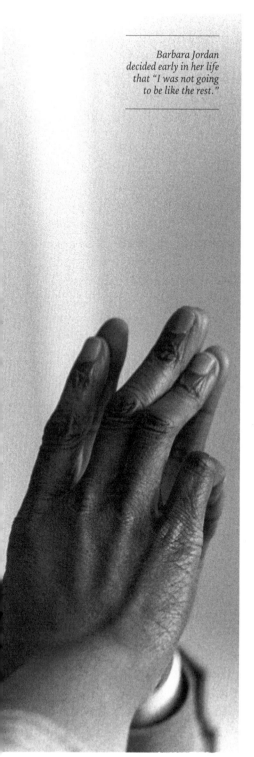

houses marked "Colored" in the fields behind the stations. It was only when they arrived at the eastern colleges for their debates that they "could go in the front door."

In law school at Boston University, she quickly realized that she "could no longer orate and let that pass for reasoning." And she came face-to-face with the limitations of her separate-but-equal education in Texas: "Separate was not equal; it just wasn't. . . . I was doing sixteen years of remedial work in thinking."

She got a law degree, passed the bar, returned to Houston, and practiced law for a while out of her parents' house. She made two unsuccessful runs for the state legislature. She did well enough with African American voters, but since candidates had to run countywide and blacks made up only 20 percent of the population of Harris County, she was facing what seemed like an immovable barrier.

"Is politics worth staying in for me?" she asked herself. She thought about moving to another state, but she didn't want to: she was a Texan. Her family and friends pressured her to get married. She didn't want to do that either. A wife, she thought, "was the ward of her man; she was always to be available at her husband's side no matter where he had to go or what he had to do. She must always be prepared to turn and kiss his puckered lips."

Jordan was staunchly quiet about her private life and never made any announcements about her sexuality,

but there's enough alarm in her description of traditional man-woman marriage to suggest there were other reasons for her lack of interest in it. In any
case: "I made the decision, and it was a fairly conscious one, that I couldn't
have it both ways. And that politics was the most important thing to me."

Fortunately for her political future, Lyndon Johnson was now president.
"He lay on his huge bed in his pajamas watching television," Jack Valenti
wrote of Johnson on the night of Kennedy's assassination, "as the world,
holding its breath in anxiety and fear, considered that this alien cowboy
[had] suddenly become the leader of the United States."

But if there was one thing the alien cowboy knew how to do, it was how to
run Washington and make legislation happen. Five days after becoming president, he appeared before a joint session of Congress and let it be known that
his sacred priority was to pass his dead predecessor's long-stalled civil rights
legislation. "We have talked long enough in this country about equal rights,"
he declared. "We have talked for a hundred years or more. It is time now to
write the next chapter and to write it in the books of law."

The Civil Rights Act of 1964, which Johnson steered through Congress,
and the Voting Rights Act, which passed the next year, altered the political
landscape for Barbara Jordan and other minority candidates. She was no
longer relegated to a hopeless run in a majority-white district. A new single-
member district in Houston included the Fifth Ward, which was 38 percent
black. She ran in 1966 and won. She was the first African American to serve
in the Texas Senate since 1882, and the first African American woman to ever
become a senator. And she wasn't alone in the history department. That
same year, two black men, Curtis Graves and Joseph E. Lockridge, were
elected to the Texas House.

As a legislator, she turned out to be a convivial workhorse, popular
across the political spectrum. Her thunderous voice might have given the
impression she was all about judgment and righteousness, but she had a
sense of fun and made a point of learning how to get along, to the degree
that her liberal critics—and there certainly were some—started to wonder
whether she was trying to become "a black LBJ."

The president, recognizing and appreciating the raging ambition that
drove her, took her under his wing. She looked up to Johnson but not to his
presumed heir, Governor John Connally. She had worked against him in 1962
and didn't like his retrograde stand on civil rights or the fact that he tended
to ignore her presence. But she was popular with her fellow legislators. The
summer before she defeated Curtis Graves for a U.S. House of Representatives seat in 1972, she was given the honor of being named Governor for a
Day. "Governor Jordan," Leon Jaworski told the audience at the ceremony in

the Senate Chamber, "stands before us as the central figure in a new page in Texas history."

For a while, it seemed as if his prediction was certain to come true. Jaworski was not the only one who saw her star rising in the firmament. Journalists and politicians heralded her as "the best politician of this century" and "the salvation of American politics." When she arrived in Washington, she quickly won—with the support of President Johnson—a seat on the thirty-eight-member House Judiciary Committee, which become the legislative body that voted on the articles of impeachment against Richard Nixon during the Watergate crisis. During the hearings, she thanked the chairman for giving the junior members of the committee "the glorious opportunity of sharing the pain of this inquiry." A stout woman in a matronly pink knit suit, she delivered her remarks as she sat at the dais, leaning forward into the microphone, now and then adjusting her glasses, speaking with real anger and mellifluous, precise phrasing. "Today I am an in-quis-i-tor. And hyperbole would not be fictional and would not overstate the solemnness that I feel right now. My faith in the Constitution is whole, it is complete, it is total! And I am not going to sit here and be an idle spectator to the diminution, the subversion, the destruction of the Constitution!"

When the committee adjourned and she walked out of the Rayburn Building that night, she was met by a crowd waving their fists in the air and screaming, "Right on!" She rode this wave of national adulation to the 1976 Democratic National Convention, where—sixty pounds lighter—she gave a keynote address. There were over two minutes of standing ovations and gavel pounding for silence before she was able to speak. She began by offering herself—the first African American woman to give a keynote presentation at a national convention—as "one additional bit of evidence that the American Dream need not forever be deferred."

In the excitement that followed the speech, some talked of the American Dream being extended to her becoming Jimmy Carter's running mate, but she was pragmatic enough to see through it. "It is not my turn," she said. "When it's my turn, you'll know it."

It seems likely that it was her health, and not some newly developed aversion to fame or power, that got in her way and robbed her of her turn. She retired from Congress at the end of her third term, in 1979, and went back to Texas to teach at the University of Texas. She was hobbled by multiple sclerosis and then diagnosed with leukemia. In 1988, her companion, Nancy Earl, came home from shopping one day and found her floating unconscious in their Austin swimming pool. She survived, but she had gone into cardiac arrest and afterward her health problems escalated. "I believe I have a spirit that is not going to disappear," she told a friend, but her body was clearly on a mortal track. She was in a wheelchair for the next eight years, and died at fifty-nine in 1996.

An emotional Ann Richards gave her eulogy, and made a point of confronting a century or so of tired old cowboy and wildcatter stereotypes: "She forever redefined what it meant to be a Texan in the eyes of this nation."

—51—

THE TOWER

IN THE SUMMER OF 1980, A FORMER HIGH SCHOOL
teacher burst through the doors of a Baptist Church in the
East Texas town of Daingerfield. He was wearing a bulletproof vest and was armed with two pistols and two semiautomatic rifles. He yelled, "This is war!" before he opened
fire, killing five people and wounding another ten. In 1991,
a man drove his pickup truck through the front window of a Luby's cafeteria in Killeen and declared, "This is payback day!" He killed twenty-
three people and wounded twenty-seven more before killing himself. At
Fort Hood, in 2009, an army psychiatrist opened fire with a semiautomatic
pistol. The toll that time was thirteen dead and more than thirty wounded.
Five years later there was another shooting at Fort Hood, with four people—
including the gunman—dead, and twelve others shot but surviving. In 2016,
in Dallas, five police officers were killed and nine others—plus two civilians—were wounded when an assailant opened fire during a downtown
protest against police violence. In November 2017 there was a church massacre in Sutherland Springs, east of San Antonio, when a man who had been
court-martialed by the air force and convicted of assaulting his wife and
son killed twenty-six worshippers and wounded another twenty. Then, on
May 18, 2018, in the small community of Santa Fe, between Houston and

Galveston, a seventeen-year-old student killed eight fellow students and two teachers and wounded thirteen others with a shotgun and a .38 revolver. He surrendered to police instead of killing himself, as he'd planned, and said later that he had spared students he liked "so he could have his story told."

At the time of this writing, the Santa Fe school shooting is the most recent out-of-nowhere massacre in Texas, but it follows many others across the nation, including the attack on the Marjory Stoneman Douglas High School in Parkland, Florida, on February 14, 2018, which left seventeen students and teachers dead and another seventeen with various degrees of lifelong suffering from gunshot wounds.

It would be useless to argue that there was a clear beginning point, some sort of understandable origin, to all these assaults, but what happened on August 1, 1966, in Austin at the University of Texas, was very much an unprecedented horror. That was when twenty-five-year-old Charles Whitman, who had been an Eagle Scout and a marine before enrolling at UT to study architectural engineering, began shooting from the observation deck of the university's 307-foot-high Tower, a landmark that was at that time the tallest building in Austin other than the Capitol. "You know," Whitman had said to a friend five years earlier while staring up at the Tower, "that would be a great place to go up with a rifle and shoot people."

There is a photo of Whitman and his wife, Kathy, taken in the summer of 1966 when they visited the Alamo—a grinning young couple in the shadow of a stone arch, paying their respects to the shrine of Texas liberty. Whitman has a severe flattop haircut, and his engineer-style short-sleeved dress shirt is blindingly white. Nothing to indicate that in two weeks he would kill his mother in her apartment—probably by strangling her and bashing in the back of her head. He covered her body with a floral bedspread and left a note—"I have just taken my mother's life. I am very upset over having done it. . . . Let there be no doubt in your mind that I loved the woman with all my heart." Then he went to his house and, in the early hours of the morning, stabbed his sleeping wife five times in the chest with a hunting knife.

At about eleven o'clock that morning, he left his house with his marine footlocker. It was packed with siege supplies, including water jugs, an alarm clock, food enough for several days, an extension cord, and earplugs. He went shopping that morning and bought a rifle and a shotgun, though he already had two rifles and three pistols in the arsenal that he packed in or around the footlocker, loaded onto a dolly, and rode with up the elevator to the Tower's observation deck. Before he opened fire on the campus below, he killed a receptionist. He also killed two sightseers and wounded two more who had come to the top of the Tower to take in its unobstructed view of Austin.

Eighteen-year-old Claire Wilson and her boyfriend, Tom Eckman, were the first people Whitman targeted on the ground, a few minutes before noon. Claire was eight months pregnant. She was wearing a maternity dress that Tom had picked out for her. Like Claire, Tom was a member of the Students for a Democratic Society. The two of them had once driven to the Rio Grande valley to show their support for striking farmworkers. It was a searing Texas August day, and Tom was dressed in a short-sleeved plaid shirt that gave no hint of his political leanings. But he had a mustache, an early stylistic indicator of the social upheavals that were about to descend on the country as Lyndon Johnson's war in Vietnam escalated.

"All of a sudden I felt like I'd stepped on a live wire," Claire Wilson remembered, "like I'd been electrocuted. . . . Tom said, 'Baby—' and reached out for me. Then he was hit. . . . Tom never said another word. I was lying next to him on the pavement, and I called out to him, but I knew he was dead."

Claire Wilson was alive, immobile and bleeding on the open plaza where she had fallen in the nearly hundred-degree heat. The sniper's bullet had killed her baby. "It was something giant," she said of her suffering there. "It went beyond pain."

As she lay on the plaza, Whitman methodically continued firing through his four-power scope. Counting Claire Wilson's unborn baby boy, he killed fourteen people. He wounded thirty-one others. In those days before the concept of SWAT teams had taken root, the police response was improvisational. The shooting had been going on for almost an hour and a half when two police officers, Houston McCoy and Ramiro Martinez, made their way to the observation deck and blasted the sniper to death with pistol and shotgun fire.

Claire Wilson was among those who survived. She would have bled to death had it not been for two students who risked their lives by running out onto the open plaza while Whitman was shooting and carried her to safety.

There was no easily accessible precedent in 1966 for what Whitman had done, no template for how to react, only a bewildered search for a reason why. Kinky Friedman, a future gubernatorial candidate who in the 1970s was something of an outrage artist with a band called Kinky Friedman and the Texas Jewboys, wrote a jauntily toxic song called "The Ballad of Charles Whitman," which featured the lyrics "There was a rumor / About a tumor / Nestled at the base of his brain."

The doctor who performed the autopsy on Whitman's body did find a pecan-sized tumor in the sniper's brain, but it likely had nothing to do with his shooting spree, which was patiently and studiously planned and showed no evidence—in its skillful sharpshooting—of motor impairment. No one has had a pinpoint explanation of why he did it, but in the decades to come,

In 1966, Charles Whitman began shooting from the University of Texas tower and, in an instant, shattered the illusion of safety in public places.

as mass shootings became increasingly commonplace, Charles Whitman's motivation gradually lost its aura of mystery.

There was no established ritual for how individuals or institutions should respond to this kind of indiscriminate slaughter. The University of Texas more or less never mentioned it. In 2007 a small memorial plaque was installed at an ornamental turtle pond in the shadow of the Tower, but it wasn't until 2016, fifty years after the shootings, that an imposing granite monument—listing the names of the dead—finally appeared on campus.

I arrived as a student at the university a year after the massacre, and it was the strangest thing: nobody said a word about it. Nobody mentioned that the Tower, rising above the campus, had been the sniper's perch, or that the open spaces we crossed between classes had been a killing zone and could very well be one again. Once I drove from Austin to the East Coast with a group of friends, one of whom was John Fox. He later changed his name to Artly Snuff, played with an Austin band called the Uranium Savages, and lived in a corn-themed group house called the Corn Palace. Just another keeper of the Austin weirdness flame. Neither during our nonstop cross-country conversation nor in several decades afterward did he ever mention that he had been on the campus that day when Whitman opened fire, and that he had been one of the two students who ran out onto the open plaza, lifted Claire Wilson off the searing, blood-soaked concrete, and saved her life.

★

MAYBE PART OF THE REASON WHY THE UT TOWER WAS NEVER exclusively identified with mass murder was because of football. I know: I've come to football, part of the foundational identity of modern Texas, shockingly late in this book. This is mostly because of willful ignorance. Two-a-day high school football practices in the August heat of South Texas, combined with an overall athletic ineptitude and a peculiar inborn indifference to the game itself, purged me of the normal football mania expected of a sane and healthy young midcentury Texan.

Nobody ever missed anything by not watching me warm the bench on my school's team, but high school football was never a backwater attraction in Texas. In cities like Wichita Falls or Abilene or Odessa or Waco or Brownwood, it was a feverish form of entertainment and a sacred rite of tribal bonding. It was the same in hamlets that were not big enough to field full-strength teams but developed a high-velocity parallel universe version of the sport known as six-man football. *Friday Night Lights*, H. G. Bissinger's classic book, captures in its title alone a sense of the bonding, the yearning, and the magic of Texas high school football. But there were Thursday nights, too, just as intense, just as crucial for a sense of shared victory or defeat, when the African American teams of the Prairie View Interscholastic League faced off in the years before integration.

Then of course there was college football. I was at the University of Texas during the Darrell Royal years, when the exalted coach led the Texas Longhorns to national championships in 1969 and 1970. On those occasions, the deadly Tower glowed orange at night, floodlit with the dominant school color, banks of windows on its successive floors strategically lit to form a gleaming white "1."

Darrell Royal was born in the Dust Bowl town of Hollis, Oklahoma, just across the Red River, in 1924. His mother died when he was four months

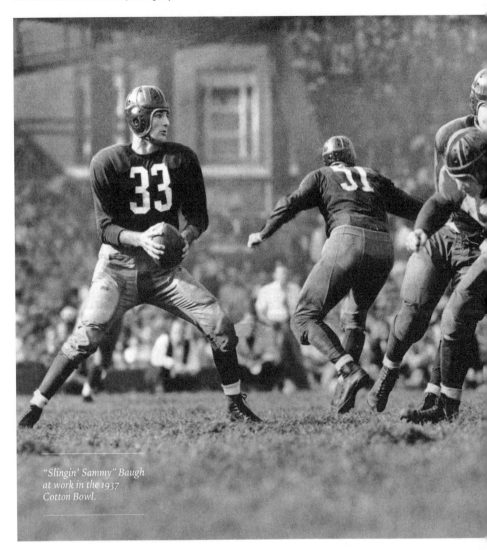

"Slingin' Sammy" Baugh at work in the 1937 Cotton Bowl.

old. The cause was cancer, but he was told she died while giving birth to him. He absorbed that lie, and the inchoate guilt that came from it, into his personality. "It was awfully hard, just a real hard childhood": that was the opinion of his wife, Edith, who grew up not far from Darrell on a cotton farm on the Salt Fork of the Red River. "He was a poor boy," she added, "and he was so lonely." But he was also, according to one of his high school coaches, "the workingest kid you ever saw."

He joined the U.S. Army Air Forces during the war and got noticed while playing football for the Gremlins, the Third Air Force team. After the war, he was a star for the University of Oklahoma. He was a punter and defensive back in 1947 when OU went up against the University of Texas Long-

horns in a famously rowdy game in the Cotton Bowl that ended with enraged Oklahoma fans indiscriminately bombarding the field with soda bottles and seat cushions. Royal and the Sooners lost against a UT team that featured the great quarterback Bobby Layne as well as Tom Landry, a young defensive safety who, as a copilot on a B-17, had survived thirty bombing missions over Europe during the war.

Royal was an all-American player, but his destiny was in coaching. One sportswriter's opinion in those early days was that he "owns one of the most brilliant masses of football cerebellum we've seen caged in one skull."

It was not Darrell Royal's cerebellum alone that created the wishbone offense. "Like many great works of art," Jim Atkinson wrote in *Texas Monthly*, "the wishbone was equal parts genius, plagiarism, and luck." Royal and a UT assistant coach named Emory Bellard developed it out of new thinking about old ideas of how to improve upon the stodgy T formation, in which the running backs line up neatly behind the quarterback in the shape of a *T*. With the new offense, that formation was skewed: the fullback scooted up behind the quarterback, and the two running backs were splayed out behind them like the prongs of a wishbone. The setup, once it was mastered, gave the quarterback a hard-to-track set of options—he could hand off to the fullback, pitch to a halfback, run the ball himself, or pass to a receiver downfield.

There were some false starts, but the new offense was deployed in its full mesmeric power in a 1968 game against OU in which the UT quarterback, James Street, led a late charge from the Longhorns' own 15-yard line that won the game by leaving the Sooner defense as hypnotized as the victims of a shell game.

College football glory was by no means in sole possession of the University of Texas. In the 1930s, the Horned Frogs of Texas Christian University, in Fort Worth, fielded teams that showcased the exalted passing of the quarterbacks Sammy Baugh and Davey O'Brien. O'Brien, who was a nimble 150 pounds and hence called "Little Davey," set a Southwest

In the opinion of sportswriter Dan Jenkins, SMU's Doak Walker was "quite simply the greatest all-round college football player who ever lived."

Conference passing record—1,457 yards—that stood for ten years. He won the Heisman Trophy and played for two seasons with the Philadelphia Eagles before dropping out of pro football to join the FBI. Samuel Adrian Baugh got his nickname, Slingin' Sammy, while playing third base for TCU's baseball team. But his powerful throwing arm made an even bigger impression when he played quarterback, both at TCU and later in his record-setting career with the Washington Redskins, where he supernally deployed the forward pass during a time when the football itself—stubbier and rounder—was harder to drill through the air toward a target. The Redskins' owner, George Preston Marshall, tried to exploit Baugh's rugged Texas looks by instructing him to wear a cowboy hat and boots in the nation's capital. Baugh didn't like cowboy boots—they hurt his feet—but he went along with the typecasting when he starred—woodenly—in a cowboys-versus-Nazis western serial called *King of the Texas Rangers*. Despite his dislike of cowboy boots, Baugh eased into ranching after his football career ended, and had enough credibility in that role that Robert Duvall— preparing to play Gus McCrae in *Lonesome Dove*—picked up a few of his gestures after visiting him at his ranch. "Something told me to go out there and hang around with him," Duvall told me. "He was straight as a ramrod. He was like a Texas Ranger himself."

Texas A&M was also a hive of mojo before the Aggies' coach, Bear Bryant, was lured home to Alabama in 1957. The Mustangs of Southern Methodist University, in Dallas, had won six Southwest Conference titles by 1947, and they had an extraordinary talent in Doak Walker, whose iconic handsomeness was to Texas football what John Connally's was to Texas politics. Walker won the Heisman Trophy in 1948. A plaque at the main entrance to the Cotton Bowl reads: "The House That Doak Built." That's because so many people wanted to see Walker play that SMU outgrew its campus stadium and had to move its home games to the larger venue in Dallas's Fair Park. And even the Cotton Bowl turned out to be too small for Doak's fans—they had to expand it and double its capacity. He was, the sportswriter Dan Jenkins insisted, "quite simply the greatest all-round college football player who ever lived. Did you hear me? Ever lived."

Walker and Bobby Layne played together in high school, and they were reunited after they turned pro and played together for the Detroit Lions. But by the early 1960s, they were both retired—Walker said he wanted to "get out while I still have all my teeth and both my knees." His knees were still good when, later in life, he moved to Colorado and married a former Olympic downhill skier who had told him, the first time he heedlessly attacked the slopes, "You're going to have to learn to steer!" It was skiing that killed

him. He had a terrible fall at the age of seventy-one on a January day in 1998. Paralyzed, he died nine months later.

Tom Landry had played at UT with Bobby Layne and against Doak Walker when he was at SMU, went to the pros as well, playing and then coaching for the New York Giants. That was where he started wearing his famous fedora. He was trimly bald and had grown up in Mission, in the subtropical heart of the Rio Grande valley, so there was a priority in keeping his head warm in the blizzardy north. He retained the hat after becoming the first coach of the Dallas Cowboys and wore it throughout his career, paying no attention to the fact that—when it came to cowboy headgear—a fedora was contraindicated. (An image of the hat is etched into his cenotaph at the Texas State Cemetery.)

Landry coached the Cowboys throughout the 1960s, but the team didn't really break through until the early 1970s, when they won their first Super Bowl. They were supremely raw in their debut, in 1960, finishing the season with a sad tally of 0–11–1. The fact that they started out with a hometown star, an SMU prodigy named Don Meredith, whose nicknames ranged from Southern Meredith University to Dandy Don, failed in those early years to translate into magic—though in 1966 and again in 1967 Meredith came within a hair of leading the team to championships against the Green Bay Packers. He retired after the next season to become a color commentator, actor, and TV pitchman for Lipton Tea. He missed the glory days of the Cowboys but helped build the foundation. As the sportswriter Joe Eisenberg concluded, "Someone had to serve as the laboratory rat as the city developed the harder edge that came with the pros. It was [Meredith's] destiny to become the sacrificial figure on whom Dallas lost its innocence as a sports town."

Texans in general had yet to become accustomed to professional football. The real focus was still on the college game. For a long time, the mostly Texas schools of the Southwest Conference maintained a whites-only roster. That began to change in 1965 when SMU coach Hayden Fry recruited a black wide receiver from Beaumont named Jerry LeVias. LeVias was small— five-seven and 150 pounds, and he had had polio as a child—but his physical limitations were easier to deal with than the racial isolation and intimidation he experienced as a Mustang. His grandmother insisted that he wear number 23, for Psalm 23. He needed some "fear no evil" encouragement, because his life as the only black player at SMU was, he said, a "living hell." He endured hate mail and racial slurs, and not all of it from opposing teams. Teammates avoided him. Nobody would be his roommate. Once somebody spit in his face. All this while he was receiving all-conference honors and leading SMU to its first Cotton Bowl appearance since the Doak Walker days.

But Darrell Royal's Texas Longhorns were still a white team. There were no black players on the field at UT's 1969 matchup with the Arkansas Razorbacks, which has been dubbed the "Big Shootout," the "Game of the Century," and—puzzlingly—"the biggest thing to happen in the Southwest Conference since the Alamo."

The Longhorns' victory in Fayetteville that day hinged on a play that Royal called when Texas was down six points in the fourth quarter, facing a fourth down on its own 43-yard line with less than five minutes to play. The pressure was insane: 45,000 Razorback fans were screaming

JERRY LEVIAS
found his life as a black player at SMU to be a "living hell."

from the stands, the game was being broadcast nationwide, and both President Nixon and Billy Graham were in attendance. It would have been, for most coaches, an excellent time to punt and regroup, but Royal had a different attitude—"I just thought it was time to swing from the floor."

He called 53 Veer Pass, a risky play that had never worked before. Royal's offensive coordinator thought the coach had gone nuts and, calling down from his position in the press box, pleaded with him to change his mind. Royal got tired of listening and took off his headphones. "Y'all aren't going to believe this call," the quarterback, James Street, told his players in the huddle. "But it will work."

And it did. Street threw a beautiful downfield pass that was thrillingly caught by Randy Peschel. After a few more plays the game was tied, and then the UT place kicker—whose immortal name was Happy Feller—scored the extra point and clinched the game for the Longhorns, 15–14.

I've written all this to give the impression I know what I'm talking about, as if I might have been there myself in Fayetteville for the Game of the Century. In fact, I was so self-righteously tuned out of football at the time that

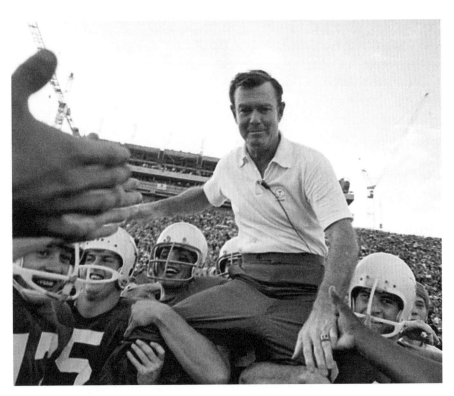

DARRELL ROYAL

after putting his "football cerebellum" to use in defeating Arkansas in 1970.

I barely knew the game was happening. But after the final whistle blew it was impossible to be ignorant of the fact that the earth had joyfully slipped off its axis. The streets of Austin turned into an instant bumper-to-bumper parade of honking cars and raving, drunken fans. Those were the tear-gas years at Texas's signature university, when almost every week some kind of march or demonstration against the Vietnam War could be counted on to disintegrate into chaos, with the police dispersing the crowd and smashing the heads of fleeing protestors with nightsticks. But when it came to something to get worked up about in Texas, football was and would remain the ruling passion.

— 52 —

VIGIL ON THE
PEDERNALES

IT WAS JULY 20, 1969, A LITTLE AFTER TEN A.M. TEXAS
time, when Buzz Aldrin descended a ladder leading from the
Eagle, the Apollo 11 lunar module, onto the Sea of Tranquil-
ity. He was the second human being to set foot on the moon.
A few hours earlier, after the LM landed but before Neil
Armstrong preceded him out of the tiny hatch, Aldrin had

gotten out his "personal preference kit," which contained a small chalice, a
wafer, and some wine, and given himself communion. He had wanted to do
this publicly, reading a passage from the Gospel of John back to the people
on earth, but NASA had asked him not to. This was because of an Austin-
based atheist named Madalyn Murray O'Hair, who was regarded—not only
because of her unpopular cause but because she was personally belligerent
and obnoxious—as the "Most Hated Woman in America." Just six months
before, O'Hair had sued the U.S. government for violating the separation
of church and state by allowing the crew of Apollo 8 to read from the book
of Genesis as they orbited the moon. (It was an easy call for the Supreme
Court: since the offense had taken place almost a quarter million miles away
from Earth, the case was dismissed for "want of jurisdiction.")

There were Texas finger-prints all over the mission that put human footprints on the lunar soil.

Armstrong was waiting for Aldrin when he climbed down the ladder and watched the lunar dust scatter with eerie precision as he set his foot onto it for the first time. There was an awkward pause when Aldrin felt a sudden imperative to urinate—"Neil might have been the first man to step on the moon," he wrote, "but I was the first to pee in his pants on the moon." When he had a chance to look around, the words he chose to describe what he saw were "Beautiful. Beautiful. Magnificent desolation."

Sam Houston's name was not, as most people believe, the first word spoken on the moon. When the craft had touched down on the lunar surface several hours earlier, a few seconds of technical chatter passed between the crew and the Manned Spacecraft Center before Armstrong said, "Houston, Tranquility Base here. The Eagle has landed."

But when I think of Aldrin's phrase "Magnificent desolation," I can't help thinking of Texas first, particularly the part of Texas that greeted Cabeza de Vaca and Estebanico and the rest of the survivors of the Narváez expedition who washed ashore onto a landscape of wild wretched nothingness in November 1528. Most scholars believe they landed on either Galveston Island or on Follett's Island, just across a narrow channel from Galveston's western end. That put them roughly fifty miles from the spot on the western shore of Galveston Bay where, 441 years later, technicians at their computer screens in Mission Control guided a new generation of voyagers to the moon.

The launch site for the Mercury, Gemini, and Apollo manned space-flight programs was at Cape Canaveral, Florida, half a continent away from the fringes of Houston, where the Manned Spacecraft Center was located. Houston was where the astronauts trained and from where the flights were directed. Lyndon Johnson was vice president when the site for the center was chosen, and he certainly played a part in steering it to Texas. Almost two dozen possibilities were considered before an undeveloped expanse of bay shoreline twenty-five miles southeast of downtown Houston was selected. The congressman whose district abutted the place where the center was built was Albert Thomas, the chairman of the powerful House Appropriations Committee and the former Rice University roommate of Johnson's faithful financial benefactor George R. Brown. And it was Brown & Root that secured most of the contracts to construct the vast utilitarian buildings of the MSC.

While Armstrong and Aldrin were bounding along the surface of the moon, the president of the United States made a call from the Oval Office. "Because of what you have done," he told the astronauts, "the heavens have become a part of man's world."

But the president on the phone was not Lyndon Johnson; it was Richard Nixon. On March 31, 1968, at the end of a television address to the nation on Vietnam, LBJ had announced, "I shall not seek, and I will not accept, the nomination of my party for another term as your president." Even allowing for the yellowish tint of most of the ancient videos of that speech available today, LBJ looks terrible, sallow and worn-out, his voice defeated, his eyes barely discernible behind the fishbowl glare of his glasses.

Lyndon Johnson in wistful retirement after leaving the presidency. "I asked so little in return. Just a little thanks."

What had happened? Most of all, Vietnam, the disastrous, unwinnable war that he had ratcheted up America's involvement in, had conducted with chronic duplicity, and could not bring to a palatable, much less honorable, end. In January, a few months before his speech, the Vietcong and the North Vietnamese Army had launched a massive coordinated assault throughout South Vietnam. The offensive, named for the Vietnamese lunar New Year, Tet, shattered the illusion that the United States was anywhere close to any sort of victory. Walter Cronkite, the Texan who had covered the New London explosion as a young reporter and was now, in his perch as the anchor of *CBS News*, the "nation's most trusted person," concluded one broadcast with the observation that the United States was "mired in stalemate."

Johnson was savvy enough to know that Cronkite's verdict represented a tipping point for his own credibility. The president had lost the trust of his citizens. His overall approval rating was at 41 percent. The Great Society he had envisioned at the beginning of his presidency—a country finally cured of racism, poverty, and unequal education, where every citizen would experience the "full equality which God enjoins and the law requires"—was fraying into class and racial warfare. Senator Bobby Kennedy, whom Johnson had humiliated at his Pedernales Ranch and called "Sonny," was preparing to challenge him for the 1968 Democratic nomination. Senator Eugene McCarthy already had, and had done worrisomely well in the New Hampshire primary, coming within seven points of the president. And Johnson wasn't sure whether he could survive another term. He had had

THE EMPIRE OF TEXAS

surgery while in office to remove his gallbladder and another kidney stone. The grueling recovery had led to a fresh round of national derision aimed at the Texas rube who had accidentally become president. Never a paragon of bodily discretion, he had lifted his shirt at Bethesda Naval Hospital to proudly display to reporters the surgical scar on his pallid belly. The editorial cartoonist David Levine took the deadliest aim, depicting a morose LBJ pointing to a scar in the shape of Vietnam.

Lyndon Johnson, who had towered over Texas like no one since Sam Houston, was beset by a sense of futility and self-pity. "I spilled my guts out," he told Doris Kearns Goodwin, in getting the Civil Rights Act of 1964 through Congress. . . . I tried to make it possible for every child of every color to grow up in a nice house, to eat a solid breakfast, to attend a decent school, and to get a good and lasting job. I asked so little in return. Just a little thanks. Just a little appreciation. That's all. But look at what I got instead. . . . Riots in 175 cities. . . . Young people by the thousands leaving their universities, marching in the streets, chanting that horrible song about how many kids I had killed that day.

He was also having that old dream again, the one about being paralyzed while runaway cattle thundered toward him. "After thirty-seven years of public service," he said, "I deserved something more than being left alone in the middle of the plain, chased by stampedes on every side."

After leaving office, he returned home to his Hill Country ranch, grew his hair long, and unburdened himself of the responsibility of keeping his appetites in check for the sake of the country. When his presidential library was dedicated, on May 22, 1971, it was, according to a friend, "the greatest day in the world," and the former president "was in hog-heaven." The occasion was barely marred by the two thousand antiwar demonstrators behind the police barricades keeping them away from the new building, which resembled an ancient monolithic tomb. I was among the protestors that day, but I wasn't the vocal type and don't remember joining in the "Hey, hey, LBJ" chant that the former president believed was so unfair. Besides, my heart wasn't really in it—maybe because Lyndon Johnson was already beginning to seem more tragic than evil, a tormented personality powered by a furious two-cycle engine of nobility and venality.

He lived for two more years. One January afternoon in 1973, alone in his ranch bedroom, he died of the heart attack that he had always known was coming. He was sixty-four. On the morning of January 25 there was an elaborate state funeral in Washington, DC. Afterward, Lyndon Johnson's body was flown home to Texas on Air Force One, the plane in which he had once traveled with John Kennedy's body in the opposite direction after the assassination, and in which he had taken the oath of office as president.

He was buried that same afternoon, in a family cemetery set within a low stone wall on the banks of the Pedernales. It was a steely cold day, and thousands of people had been crowding the roads and waiting in the open air since early that morning. The Fifth Army Band played the "Star-Spangled Banner." The Thirty-Sixth Infantry fired a salute from six 105 mm howitzers, a concussive blast that echoed across the landscape and startled the squirrels scrambling in the live oak branches above the open grave. Billy Graham and John Connally gave eulogies. "Along this stream," Connally said, drawing on the oratory and stage skills he had learned as a young collegiate actor, "and under these trees he loved, he will now rest. He first saw light here. He last felt life here. May he now find peace here."

Had he been a witness to his own funeral, and been able to take note of the people gathered that day on the Pedernales, Johnson might not have been in an especially peaceful frame of mind. In a sense, the business-minded, guardedly progressive Texas Democratic legacy whose custodian and guiding spirit he had been for so long was going to the grave with him. You could glimpse the future in Connally himself, who had once been Johnson's heir apparent but was now Richard Nixon's. ("I believed," Nixon wrote, "that John Connally was the only man in either party who clearly had the potential to be a great president. He had the necessary 'fire in the belly,' the energy to win, and the vision to lead.") Connally had briefly been Nixon's secretary of the treasury before heading a political organization called Democrats for Nixon. Three months after Lyndon Johnson's burial, he dropped the Democratic facade entirely and did the hitherto unthinkable: turned Republican.

Of course, plenty of mourners at the ranch that day would stay Democrats. It's hard to imagine Ralph Yarborough ever allowing his heart to bleed for any other party. He had come to say good-bye to Johnson, even though his relationship with the former president had been testy at best. Yarborough was now out of office, having lost the 1970 Democratic senatorial primary to Lloyd Bentsen.

Like Tom Landry, Bentsen was from the Rio Grande valley town of Mission—whose motto was "Home of the Grapefruit"—and had also served on bombers in World War II (and was shot down twice). But Landry's father had run a paint and body shop in Mission, whereas Bentsen's father—Big Lloyd—had made a fortune in pretty much everything there was to make a fortune in in Texas, including real estate, ranching, oil, and banking. In manner, his son did not exude Texanness, as Johnson and Yarborough did. "I've never seen him sweat," a friend once remarked, a telling trait for someone who grew up in the miasmal climate of South Texas. He was chilly and debonair, or maybe just courtly and debonair, with monogrammed shirt cuffs and a thin-lipped sphinxlike smile. But after beating Yarborough in the Democratic primary, Bentsen defeated the Republican candidate, George H. W. Bush, whose Lone Star mojo was still a work in progress, in the general election. "I guess there were just too many Democrats," Bush concluded after his loss.

Yes, there were a lot of Democrats in Texas, but not for long. The political crowd at Lyndon Johnson's interment represented the gathering of a clan that was slipping from power and slipping from definition. Bentsen's centrist political profile was close enough to LBJ's that it made sense for him to be among the group of family and friends positioned inside the three-foot-high fence of Hill Country limestone that ringed the grave site. Dolph Briscoe, who had been inaugurated as the new governor of Texas nine days earlier, was unlikely to carry on the Johnson political tradition—or any political tradition. The legislature had no idea what Governor Briscoe meant when he announced, "Politics is not a game, and I will not play it." But he would prove true to his word, flying home to his vast ranch on weekends and disconnecting the phone. He was in his fifties, with a generic slicked-back-hair-and-glasses look that could have belonged as easily to a small-town hardware clerk as to the chief executive of one of the world's rowdiest nation-states. His most remarkable physical attribute was the "UT" that had been burned onto his chest at the University of Texas by a branding iron wielded by another student, the King Ranch heir Dick Kleberg. Dolph Briscoe, like Kleberg, was one of the largest landowners in Texas. His ancestral ranch, called Catarina, sprawled near the south-central Texas town of Uvalde. He was so inscrutable in his political leanings that the summer before, when he led the Texas delegation at the Democratic National Convention, he managed, in successive votes, to pledge his state to both George Wallace and George McGovern.

How exactly had this gentleman rancher who wouldn't play politics become governor? Pan around to some of the other people gathered on the banks of the Pedernales that day to lay Lyndon Johnson to rest and you can begin to understand how it might have happened. Here is Briscoe's immediate predecessor as governor, Preston Smith, wearing glasses with bold black frames, the only point of visual emphasis on a mild face beneath a bald head. Smith had launched his political career—at least in his imagination—at the age of nine on his family farm in Williamson County. "I was walking down a cotton row behind a span of mules," he recalled, "and reading an old newspaper about Governor Jim Ferguson. That was the first time I'd read about a governor and I decided right then and there I wanted to be governor."

He set his course, and after making money in the movie theater business and serving as a state senator and lieutenant governor for six years under John Connally, he was elected in 1968. On January 19, 1971, he was sworn in for his second term. In his inaugural address, he predicted a happy future for Texas, but let slip that "we must live in the midst of yesterday's mistakes."

As it turned out, yesterday's mistakes were perilously fresh. The day before Smith took office, the Securities and Exchange Commission had filed a lawsuit against Frank Sharp, a Houston real estate heavyweight who had created a four-thousand-acre development in the southwestern part of the city that he called Sharpstown. Among his other assets was a bank, also named Sharpstown, and a life insurance company. Very soon it was revealed that Sharp had made loans from his bank to a host of state officials, among them the new governor and Gus Mutscher, the Speaker of the House. (He's also in attendance at Johnson's funeral, listening to Anita Bryant sing "The Battle Hymn of the Republic.") The legislators used the money from the loans to buy stock in Sharp's insurance company, which they then sold after Sharp worked his magic and inflated their value. The quid pro quo in the deal was a set of cozy banking laws that Sharp needed the legislature to pass, and that Mutscher obligingly brought to the floor in a special session.

The citizens of Texas, when all this became clear, were in a scorching mood. "Imagine for a moment," wrote the *Houston Post* columnist Lynn Ashby when Mutscher and two other defendants went on trial in Abilene for bribery, "facing the jury box where the men in coonskin hats and leather jackets sit—holding their rifles and powder horns—explaining for them that they died for the glory of unsecured loans and bank stock."

Mutscher was found guilty and sentenced to five years' probation. Preston Smith wasn't charged, but there was enough for investigators to chew on in his relations with Frank Sharp for the governor to be declared an unindicted coconspirator. And for his political career to be over. He tried to run for a third term, but he was swimming against a riptide of voter fury. He and half the members of the legislature were swept out of office in the greatest political purge in Texas history.

Preston Smith was sixty when Sharpstown brought him down, but Ben Barnes was twenty-six years younger. (He is the six-foot-three-inch, ruddy-faced young man with wavy red hair standing among the Johnson intimates inside the fence.) Barnes's future, until Sharpstown happened, was a strato-spheric Texas saga waiting to be written. He grew up on a forty-acre pea-nut farm in Comanche County, put himself through UT, and sharpened his good-old-boy skills while selling Electrolux vacuum cleaners door-to-door. ("You couldn't invent a better training program for a political career," he testified in his memoir.) He was elected to the Texas House of Representatives at twenty-two in a startling shoe-leather campaign in which he beat a well-known, well-loved war hero. Four years later he was Speaker of the House. Four years after that, after carrying all 254 Texas counties, he was lieutenant governor, which is by no means as subordinate an office as it might sound. In Texas, the lieutenant governor has a lot of muscle to flex. He (or she, though no woman has held the position at the time of this writing) is in charge of all Senate committee appointments and assignments and in teeing up legislation. For Barnes, the position was the perfect launching pad for the next steps—governor, senator, vice president, and, everybody almost assumed, president.

"He is always hurrying somewhere, and he is always selling something," Paul Burka once observed in *Texas Monthly*, "and that something is himself. Not directly; he doesn't boast. Rather, he believes. . . . You go into a conversation with him . . . vowing to be on guard, but it doesn't matter. You come out thinking, 'Wow!'"

Barnes had an instinctive Texas way of relating. Once, when he was trying to get votes for a sales tax bill, he drew an imaginary line in the carpet in the lieutenant governor's office and, a la Travis at the Alamo, called out, "Every one of you that's going to vote for this bill, I want you to step across this line."

Lyndon Johnson set the bar for Ben Barnes about as high as it could be set. "He's a redhead, like Thomas Jefferson," the former president said at a fund-raiser in 1970, "and, like Thomas Jefferson, Ben Barnes will be president! Show us the way, Ben! Where you lead us, we will follow! . . . Ben Barnes will someday be the next president of the United States from Texas!"

But that was before Sharpstown. Barnes wasn't indicted, but his highly interesting financial life—the investments in radio stations and motels and shopping centers that were out of scale with his modest Speaker's salary, and the fact that he once took out a sixty-thousand-dollar loan from another bank owned by Frank Sharp—ended up in the hamper with all the dirty laundry. He too ran for governor in 1972, on a platform of constitutional reform, open government, tax code revision, and "I never met Frank Sharp." But like Preston Smith, he didn't even make the Democratic primary runoff.

"I'd just turned 34 years old," the presumed successor to Lyndon Johnson wistfully recalled many years later, "and my career in elective politics was over."

SHARPSTOWN CREATED AN ONSLAUGHT OF REFORM, THOUGH not enough to break the male Anglo lock on state government. Still, the 1972 gubernatorial election, in which Preston Smith and Ben Barnes got plowed under, helped aerate the political soil of Texas. There was an unexpectedly vital Democratic challenger, for instance, in Frances Farenthold, universally known as Sissy. Elected to the Texas House in 1968, she was its sole female member. There were 149 men and her. (Across the rotunda, in the Senate Chamber, Barbara Jordan was the only woman.) Sissy Farenthold came from an ancestral matrix of influential Texas families, from entrepreneurs and empresarios and Indian scouts and a chief justice of the state

Lyndon Johnson with Ben Barnes, the political up-and-comer that LBJ predicted—wrongly—would be "the next president of the United States from Texas."

supreme court. She had gone to Vassar and to the University of Texas Law School, and had married a Belgian aristocrat whose family had a genetic vulnerability to Von Willebrand disease, a condition like hemophilia in which the blood is missing an important clotting protein. In 1960, the Farentholds' three-year-old son, Vincent, had gotten up in the night all alone and bled to death after hitting his head against the bathroom sink.

That tragedy no doubt had something to do with the *Texas Observer*'s impression that Sissy Farenthold was a "melancholy rebel." But she also had an inborn tendency toward depression and was so shy that she found her first campaign to be an "unbelievable torment." She was also dyslexic. But perhaps her experience with anxiety, disability, and deep personal loss helped sharpen her sense of empathy. As a director of the Legal Aid office for Nueces County, she witnessed such poverty and inequity that she later recalled it as "a soul-searing experience."

Her shyness may have made it difficult for her to pass out leaflets and ask people for their vote, but it didn't keep her from expressing her opinion. As the Sharpstown scandal was coming to light, she refused to allow her name to be used on a resolution congratulating Governor Preston Smith on his birthday, and called instead for a full-dress House-Senate investigation of the blatant influence peddling that was happening during his administration. She was one of the ringleaders of the "Dirty Thirty," the thirty House members who banded together to keep Gus Mutscher from using his Speaker's power to make the scandal go away. "The unsavory smell of corruption," she said, "hangs like a rabid blanket over Texas."

She did better than Preston Smith or Ben Barnes in the Democratic primary. When the race narrowed, she was the only candidate left standing for a runoff with Dolph Briscoe. But even though 1972 was arguably the busiest reform year ever in Texas, the state wasn't ready for a woman who was willing to make heretical pronouncements such as "the Texas Rangers are a festering sore."

In the end, Democratic primary voters were more ready to embrace a million-acre rancher than a woman who kept talking about rancid blankets and festering sores, and Dolph Briscoe won the runoff by ten points. But the days when a Democrat could motor on to victory in the general election with just a friendly wave to his Republican challenger were coming to an end. The Republican, a schoolteacher and state senator from Corpus Christi named Hank Grover, troubled Briscoe's election-night sleep by coming within five percentage points of the Democrat's lead. And there was another near spoiler this time. La Raza Unida, which had grown out of José Ángel Gutiérrez's

Crystal City victories, was running a third-party candidate. Ramsey Muñiz was an attorney, a former Baylor football star, and a button-pushing public speaker with a strapping pair of 1970s sideburns. He could not have been a more jolting contrast to Dolph Briscoe's colorless complacency. "We're poor, man, I mean we're poor!" he railed to his Mexican American voters. "And nobody wants to do nothin' about it! You still kissin' the Democratic party, thinkin' they gonna save you, and they ain't gonna do it!"

La Raza Unida's slogan, borrowed from the black civil rights movement, was "Venceremos," meaning "We will overcome." Muñiz did well enough—6 percent of the vote—for him to try again in 1974, but infighting between La Raza Unida's factions and increasingly overheated rhetoric ("the only good gringo is a dead gringo") broke the party apart. And Muñiz's life came apart not long afterward. He was arrested in 1976 and spent five years in prison for smuggling marijuana. He was convicted of drug charges again in 1982, was incarcerated for another two years, and then—a decade later—apprehended again (framed, he and his advocates claimed) for possession of ninety pounds of cocaine. He was sent to Leavenworth Federal Penitentiary, sentenced to life without parole, far beyond the average prison time in Texas of 3.74 years for nonviolent offenders. (As of this writing, he is seventy-five years old and has been in Leavenworth for twenty-four years.) "From the beginning," he wrote from prison in 2002, "I knew that suffering, sorrow, grief, loneliness and eventually confinement would be my companions for principles."

———————— ★ ————————

A shy campaigner and a "melancholy rebel," Sissy Farenthold nevertheless threw herself into a vigorous reform campaign for governor in the wake of the Sharpstown scandal.

LIFE HAD NEVER BEEN EASY FOR THE

inmates—principled or not—of Texas prisons either. In 1972, an inmate named David Ruiz brought what would turn out to be an extremely consequential class-action lawsuit against William Estelle, the director of the Texas Department of Corrections. *Ruiz v. Estelle* charged that overcrowding, harsh and capricious discipline, and other conditions in Texas prisons met the definition of "cruel and unusual punishment" prohibited by the Eighth Amendment of the U.S. Constitution. After eight years and a 129-day trial, a federal district judge with the ringing name of William Wayne Justice ruled for Ruiz and his seven fellow plaintiffs in 1980, setting the stage for wholesale reforms and thirty years of federal oversight over the Texas prison system.

But Fred Gómez Carrasco, the inmate who orchestrated the 1974 takeover of the education center of the Walls Unit in Huntsville and set off an eleven-day standoff, the longest prison siege in American history, had no particular interest in *Ruiz v. Estelle* or solidarity with inmates who were agitating for better conditions. "I know there's a lot of people who want prison reform," he said, "and I don't want to have anything to do with them."

All he wanted was to get out of prison and back to his life as the head of the biggest drug-running operation in South Texas, an enterprise whose heroin-smuggling receipts were measured in tens of millions of dollars. He was said to have been responsible for at least fifty killings. A shootout with police in San Antonio the year before had left him with multiple bullet wounds. At the Walls, he had to walk with a cane, and he was humiliated by his prison job as a janitor—it "galled his soul," in the words of a prison chaplain who was one of his hostages.

Carrasco and two fellow conspirators who were in his thrall took over the library and the prison school during a typing class for inmates on a July afternoon. They were armed—Carrasco loyalists had smuggled pistols into the prison by hiding them in cans of peaches and packaged hams. The siege went on for eleven terror-filled and bewildering days. It was unclear for a while exactly what Carrasco wanted and how he was planning to achieve it. But he had a big bargaining chip: fifteen civilian and inmate hostages, including the chaplain and six women who worked as teachers or librarians.

One of Carrasco's two confederates was an obvious sadist; the other had a rudderless personality and was happy to follow his leader's orders. Carrasco, though, had what he imagined to be an outlaw gallantry. He was generally cool-headed, and so considerate to his hostages that the chaplain sorrowfully concluded he "could have been a fine gentleman, but instead, he was a cold-blooded killer." His courtliness showed when one of the hostages faked a heart attack: he not only let her go but also ordered the prison director to send her two dozen roses, and then directed the other hostages to send her a get-well note. He signed it, along with his two henchmen, just under the line "With all our love."

He also wanted to look sharp when he left the penitentiary. He demanded new clothes to replace the abductors' prison whites, and specifically said that his suit should come from the brand Hart Schaffner & Marx and cost twice as much as those of his associates. "If the clothes are not good," he warned, "I will kill the hostages." He was equally particular about the

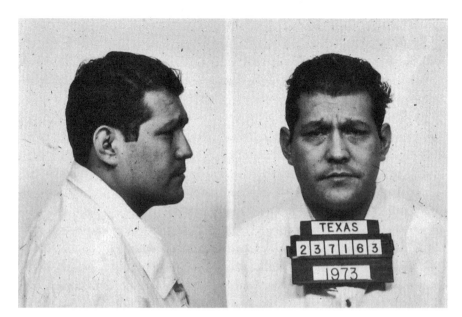

FRED CARRASCO
had no interest in prison reform, only in prison escape.

food that was delivered to him and the hostages. At one point, when ordering the exasperated prison authorities to provide Kentucky Fried Chicken, he instructed them to "make it, how do you say it, crunchy."

William Estelle, the director of the TDC and the defendant in the *Ruiz v. Estelle* lawsuit, did his best to keep Carrasco from killing anybody while he desperately stalled for time. He even went so far as to allow three thirty-pound bulletproof steel helmets to be fabricated in the prison machine shop according to Carrasco's specifications. And he agreed to Carrasco's demand for an armored escape truck.

But Carrasco knew he wouldn't be allowed to walk out of the education building into an awaiting armored truck without resistance, so he set to work building what came to be known as the Trojan Taco, a seven-hundred-pound six-foot-high protective box made out of chalkboards and bookshelves and lined with thick, bullet-stopping law books from the prison library. The hostages, sensing release after eleven deeply fretful days, eagerly threw themselves into the construction of this contraption, even decorating it with pictures of historical bad boys Santa Anna and Emiliano Zapata that they had torn out of encyclopedias.

Carrasco and his two lieutenants, wearing their bulletproof steel helmets with a narrow slit for the eyes, shuffled inside the Trojan Taco down a ramp toward the armored truck. Each of them was handcuffed to one of the female hostages. There wasn't room for everyone inside, so the other hostages were handcuffed to the outside of the box to serve, along with the law books, as another layer of bulletproofing.

Police officers, FBI agents, Texas Rangers, and TDC officers watched this strange procession as the Trojan Taco rolled forth across the prison yard on its squeaky plastic casters. There was no way they were going to allow Carrasco to make it to the armored truck. The plan was to topple the box with high-pressure hoses and disarm the would-be fugitives. But it didn't work, and as soon as the water blasted the Taco, Fred Carrasco, handcuffed to a forty-seven-year-old prison teacher named Elizabeth Yvonne Beseda, dropped his mask of chivalry and shot her through the heart. Rudy Dominguez, one of the other hostage takers, had the same lethal reaction, killing the librarian, Judy Standley, who was handcuffed to him.

In the crazy shootout that followed, as the officers fired at the Taco, and Carrasco and the others shot back through its gun ports, Dominguez was killed, the prison chaplain was seriously wounded, and Carrasco shot himself through the head. Only one of the hostage takers, Ignacio Cuevas, survived. He was convicted of capital murder and, seventeen years later, executed in the prison he had never escaped.

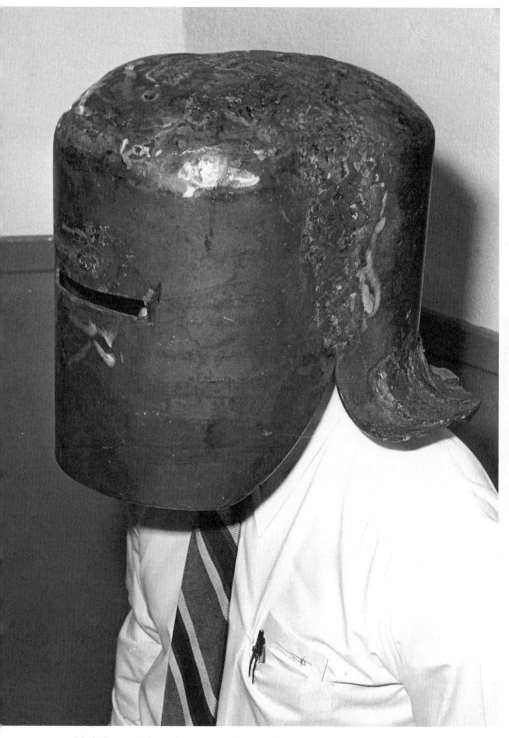

One of the bulletproof helmets that Carrasco demanded that the prison machine shop manufacture for the shootout he knew was coming.

— 53 —

A SIDE TO BELONG TO

NORMA MCCORVEY, WHO AS "JANE ROE" STUMBLED INTO the national discourse on the same day that Lyndon Johnson died, was, according to her own description, "a rough woman, born into pain and anger and raised mostly by myself." Her mother called her "a die-hard whore" and admitted, "I beat the fuck out of her. You can only take so much of nerviness. She was wild. Wild."

Norma was born in Louisiana. Her ancestry was Cajun and Cherokee. Her grandmother was a prostitute and fortune-teller who had leveraged herself up to the ownership of a prosperous whorehouse. She drove around steamy Baton Rouge in a Lincoln Continental with a mink stole around her neck.

Norma's father, a TV repairman, moved the family to Houston when she was in grade school. Then he disappeared. A year later he came back and moved them to Dallas. When she was ten years old, Norma robbed a gas station and used the money to flee to Oklahoma City with her best friend. The two girls talked a hotel manager into giving them a room, but after a maid discovered them kissing, he pounded on the door and called out, "What are you two girls doing in there?" Norma fled via a fire escape, but was caught by the police and sent by a judge to a Catholic boarding school. But after telling a nun who criticized the way she ironed a shirt in the

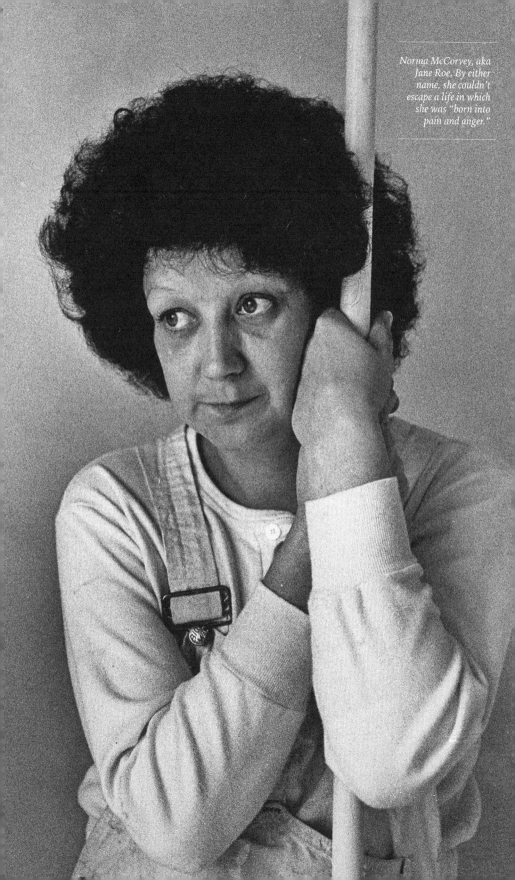

Norma McCorvey, aka Jane Roe. By either name, she couldn't escape a life in which she was "born into pain and anger."

laundry to "shove her fucking shirt up her fucking ass," she was kicked out and sent to the Gainesville State School for Girls. When she was released at fifteen, she got a job as a roller-skating carhop in Dallas and met Woody McCorvey when he drove up and luridly ordered "a furburger and a cherry coke." They got married and moved to California. When she told him she was pregnant, he went into a rage and beat her up.

She returned to Dallas and gave birth to a daughter. According to McCorvey's memoir *I Am Roe*, her mother—angry that her daughter was drinking and taking drugs and hanging out in a lesbian bar—essentially seized the baby girl, removing her from Norma's custody and replacing her in the crib with a plastic doll.

Two years later, at nineteen, McCorvey got pregnant again by another man and gave the baby up for adoption. She went to work for a carnival, in charge of the creatures in an animal freak show—a five-legged calf, a two-headed snake, a "poor old dog with no hair," which was billed as having elephant skin. While working there, she got pregnant once more. "I didn't want to give birth to another unwanted child," she wrote. "I didn't want to have to give up another child. I didn't want a child to be born with me as its mother."

This was in 1970. Abortion was illegal in Texas. It was legal in only six states—Alaska, California, Hawaii, New York, Oregon, and Washington. Norma McCorvey couldn't afford to travel to any of them, but she had a glimmer of possibility when she was put in touch with two women, both lawyers, whom she met one February day in an Italian restaurant in Dallas. The women, Linda Coffee and Sarah Weddington, had been among the few female students in their classes at the University of Texas Law School. They were in their twenties. Coffee was from Houston and, after trying and failing to get a job at one of Texas's male-dominated law firms, she had been hired as a clerk by Sarah Hughes, the federal judge who had sworn in Lyndon Johnson on the day of Kennedy's assassination.

She and Sarah Weddington were on a mission: to find a plaintiff through whom they could challenge Texas's antiabortion statute, first passed originally in 1854, in federal court. "We both felt strongly," Weddington remembered, "that it was not the government's business to prohibit abortion, and we were deeply sympathetic to the personal tragedies that resulted from anti-abortion laws."

It was a particularly personal issue for Weddington. Born in Abilene, the daughter of a Methodist minister, she was the leader of her high school chapter of Future Homemakers of America. In Texas at that time, future home-making was serious business. Weddington played on the girl's basketball team in high school, and was puzzled about why girls could use only half the court and were required to pass the ball after dribbling twice. Her physical education instructor explained that dribbling too much and running back and forth on the full court was too taxing for females. "Young women," she explained, "must preserve their reproductive capacity; after all, it is their meal ticket."

Weddington got pregnant in her third year of law school. Her boyfriend and future husband didn't want children. She wrote in her memoir that she "had no strong feelings either way." But in the end her feelings were strong enough to take her to Eagle Pass, Texas, and then across the Rio Grande. Abortion was illegal in Mexico too, but a doctor in the town of Piedras Negras was competent and willing to perform the procedure for $400 in cash.

The operation went smoothly but made Weddington think of the women who had not been so fortunate, who had bled to death or died from the infections that could result from illegal abortions.

In the Italian restaurant, Weddington and Coffee asked McCorvey whether she would be willing to help them. Hoping that this would be the answer to her getting a safe abortion, she said she would.

"In her excitement," McCorvey wrote, "Sarah began describing the road the lawsuit would take—through district courts and appeals courts, state courts and federal courts. Early on, I lost the thread of what she was saying. But I kept nodding anyway."

That was how Norma McCorvey became Jane Roe, the pseudonym that Weddington and Coffee used in the original *Roe v. Wade* lawsuit, filed in the Dallas federal district court in 1970. The "Wade" in the suit was Henry Wade, the cigar-chomping Dallas County district attorney who six years earlier had prosecuted Jack Ruby for the murder of Lee Harvey Oswald. The hearing, which McCorvey didn't attend, was in front of a three-judge panel that included Sarah Hughes, and their finding was unanimous: the Texas abortion laws were "unconstitutionally vague . . . in violation of the Due Process Clause of the Fourteenth Amendment."

But on the ground, nothing changed. Wade appealed, and in the meantime the court refused to issue an injunction that would have prevented doctors from being prosecuted for performing abortions. The case went to the Supreme Court, where Sarah Weddington—twenty-seven years old, and in the midst of a successful campaign for the Texas House of Representatives—made her case to nine robed male eminences. On January 22, 1973, in a 7–2 decision, the court bought her argument and held that a woman's right to privacy, protected under the Fourteenth Amendment, extended to abortion. Three Texas women—Weddington, Coffee, and McCorvey—had created a lawsuit that not only brought down a state law but also jackhammered the foundation that supported antiabortion legislation in the rest of the United States. It was a

When Sarah Weddington argued Roe v. Wade *before the Supreme Court, it was personal. Years before, she had had to cross the border into Mexico for an abortion.*

victory, McCorvey had hoped early on, "that would allow me, and millions of other women, to be in control of our own destinies."

But Jane Roe's destiny was still rocky. Abortion was legal, but Norma McCorvey never got one. The gestation of the baby she was carrying outpaced the start-and-stop timing of her legal proceeding. The case was still on appeal when she gave birth. She signed the adoption papers, was given a shot to dry up her unneeded breast milk, and then went home and out on the street to buy every sort of illegal pill she could find. She washed them all down with a bottle of Wild Turkey and lay on the couch in a novelty T-shirt with psychedelic lettering that read: "Fuck you."

But she survived her suicide attempt. She fell in love with a woman named Connie Gonzalez and started a housecleaning business. She learned about the Supreme Court's Jane Roe decision one day when she came home from work, opened a beer, and picked up the newspaper. There it was, just below the fold and the news about Lyndon Johnson's death.

She remained anonymous until 1984—"a scared and angry cleaning woman, a person just trying to get through the day without crying or shouting or drinking herself unconscious." But then she decided it was time to stop hiding behind the name Jane Roe. She did interviews, she was played by Holly Hunter in a TV movie, and she became an activist in the increasingly furious abortion wars—a hardscrabble heroine to one side, an opportunistic baby murderer to the other. She even claimed to have been fired upon in her home in the night, though Gonzalez, who lived with her, later denied it.

McCorvey wrote that she felt used and condescended to by the stylish, well-educated, unconflicted feminist warriors of the pro-choice movement. She sensed that she was being held up as a useful figurehead when the camera lights were on, but made fun of as soon as the crowds went away: "Though the pro-lifers saw me as their nemesis, the one responsible for killing all the babies, those on 'my side' looked at me as nothing but an inconvenient nuisance, a woman who had to be tolerated."

And after she went to work at an abortion clinic, she felt even more distance from the ideal she was supposed to represent. She began to see herself as "involved in a bloody, dehumanizing business," increasingly horrified at the way the word "tissue" was used to describe what were plainly tiny body parts in the clinic freezer. After a group called Operation Rescue set up its headquarters next door to the abortion clinic, she became friendly with her presumed enemy neighbor, an evangelical minister named Flip Benham. He baptized her in a swimming pool. She later alienated him by being baptized again, this time as a Catholic. She spent the rest of her tormented life by speaking out against abortion, scrounging for income, both demanding and regretting her place in history. She wrote two memoirs—the first, *I Am Roe*, was dedicated to "all the Jane Does who died for Choice"; the second, *Won by Love,* chronicling her pivot to religion and the pro-life movement, was dedicated to "all the children who have been torn apart by abortion."

She died at sixty-nine of heart failure in an assisted-living center in the Houston suburb of Katy. Six or seven years before her death, she made her acting debut in a Christian-themed movie called *Doonby*. She played an elderly sad-eyed widow who tries to talk a young woman out of an abortion. It was an amateur performance but a credible one, backed up by a life of rootlessness, self-destruction, and colliding epiphanies. Erin Way, the actress playing the young woman, got to know McCorvey on the set and offered perhaps the best summary of the tormented person who was Jane Roe: "She feels at the end of the day a little bit like she doesn't have a side that she can belong to."

———————— ★ ————————

ROE V. WADE WAS NOT THE ONLY THING THAT MADE TEXAS IN the 1970s a pulse point of the woman's movement. In November 1972, eight months after Texas became one of the first states to ratify the national Equal Rights Amendment, it passed its own amendment to its mossy old 1876 Constitution, which, among other things, had historically not allowed married women to control their own separate property without the oversight of their husbands. The amendment was the result of a dogged, fifteen-year-effort led by the Texas Federation of Business and Professional Women and in particular by its president and legal counsel, Hermine Tobolowsky. Tobolowsky was from San Antonio. Her father was a Lithuanian immigrant who caught on early to her opinionated nature and debating skills and steered her to law school at the University of Texas. She and the 10 other women in their class of 350 were likely to be regarded as irritants. One of her professors came up with a list of prospective husbands for her, just to get her married and out of his classroom so that a man could take his rightful place there instead of her. She didn't listen, married whom she wanted (the credit manager of a Dallas department store), and years later deployed her legal training to sweep away the patronizing cobwebs of the Texas Constitution. To those (men, for the most part) who held that an amendment was not a priority and that discrimination against women could be corrected when necessary by legislation, she replied with a brisk not-so: "Legal equality for every citizen—man or woman—is a basic democratic right which is too precious to be left to the whim of government."

Even though Sissy Farenthold lost the gubernatorial race to Dolph Briscoe, 1972 turned out to be a threshold year for female representation in the

Texas Legislature. True, there were only six women elected, five to the House and one to the Senate, but that was more than had ever gained entry to those chambers at any one time. Among the new House members was Sarah Weddington; she beat a runoff opponent who dismissed her as "that sweet little girl." There was also Eddie Bernice Johnson, the first African American elected to the Texas House from Dallas, who as of this writing is serving her thirteenth term in Congress; and a young Republican from Houston named Kay Bailey, who had been the press secretary to Anne Armstrong, the powerhouse diplomat, presidential counselor, and cochair of the Republican National Committee. (Even though Barbara Jordan and Ann Richards generated more sizzle when they gave their keynote speeches at the Democratic National Conventions in 1976 and 1988, it was Anne Armstrong who was the first woman to fill that crucial speaking spot when she took the podium at the 1972 Republican convention.) Kay Bailey—she would become known as Kay Bailey Hutchison after she married in 1978—approached the idea of feminism with a smidge of internal dissonance: "I believe in equal rights for women," she said, "but I like being protected." But she worked with Weddington and other Democratic colleagues to pass landmark women's-rights legislation. And later, when she was a U.S. senator, she wrote a book of profiles about Texas women with the we-don't-need-to-be-protected-after-all title *Unflinching Courage*.

In 1977, Texas was the site of the National Women's Conference, a government-sponsored convocation—"Four Days That Changed the World," in the opinion of *Ms.* magazine—held on a November weekend in Houston. Thousands of women were there, as delegates, demonstrators, or onlookers, the largest gathering of American women ever. Not all of them were in agreement, especially when it came to contentious issues like abortion and gay rights, but there weren't many dissenters from the harmonious words of speakers such as Coretta Scott King. "Let this message go forth from Houston," she declaimed, "and spread all over this land. There is a new force, a new understanding, a new sisterhood against all injustice that has been born here. We will not be divided and defeated again."

The event took place in the Albert Thomas Convention Center, where a stage—dominated by the word "WOMAN" in twelve-foot-high letters—had been erected by an all-female crew. Two thousand runners had taken turns carrying a festival torch all the way from Seneca Falls, New York, the site of the convention in 1848 that launched the women's suffrage movement. There was some impressive logistical trouble involving overbooked hotel rooms, but Barbara Jordan, in her keynote speech, warned the delegates not "to be brainwashed by people who predict chaos and failure for us. Tell them they lie and move on."

A Houston convention center was the site of the 1977 National Women's Conference.

Other Texas women who were or would become famous took their places at the podium or on the platform. Lady Bird Johnson was there. Sarah Weddington spoke, as did Liz Carpenter, the opinionated and quick-witted former aide to Lyndon Johnson and press secretary to Lady Bird. (It was she who wrote LBJ's eloquently brief message to the nation after the assassination. "This is a sad time for all people. I ask for your help—and God's.") Now she was leading the national fight for ratification of the ERA and asking her audience, "Are we to be forever shackled by the unending audacity of elected men?"

Ann Richards, the future governor of Texas, also spoke. She was a forty-four-year-old Travis County Commissioner who, the writer Prudence Mackintosh noted, "reminds me of Barbara Stanwyck in *The Big Valley*, ordering rustlers off the place."

"I rise," Richards told the convention hall, "on behalf of my two daughters who cannot find women in the history texts of this country."

Carpenter and Richards and others, such as the *Texas Observer* journalist Molly Ivins, were already an identifiable subcategory of progressive Texas women—strong willed, caustically funny, perpetually exasperated by all the grinning, patronizing good ol' boys clogging the avenues of power. They were part of the reason that Texas not only ratified the ill-fated ERA but also stood by the amendment when every other southern state rejected it.

If Lottie Beth Hobbs had had her way, Texas would have turned its back on women's liberation along with the rest of the South. She lived in Fort Worth but, like Sarah Weddington, was a native of Abilene. She grew up in the Church of Christ there, attended Abilene Christian College, and worked in defense plants during World War II. The Church of Christ's teachings about wives being submissive to husbands did not seem to squelch her natural entrepreneurial spirit, since after the war she became an in-demand speaker for women's Bible classes (though she wasn't allowed to lecture to men) and the prolific author of books with pastel cover images of birds and children and with titles like *You Can Be Beautiful* (about "God's plan for inner beauty") and *Your Best Friend* (i.e., Jesus Christ.)

Hobbs was the founder of Women Who Want to Be Women, an organization determined to derail the ERA. Most of its members came from a Church of Christ background. Its key talking points were covered in a famous pamphlet that Hobbs wrote called *Ladies Have You Heard?* It was also known as the "Pink Sheet" because it was printed on pink paper to bolster its message of complacent femininity. "God created you," the Pink Sheet instructed, "and gave you a beautiful and exalted place to fill. . . . Yet, a tiny minority of dissatisfied, highly vocal, militant women insist that you are being exploited as a 'domestic drudge' and a 'pretty toy.' And they are determined to 'liberate' you—whether you want it or not!"

When it came to the National Woman's Conference in Houston, Lottie Beth Hobbs—as another of the traditionalist leaders phrased it—"put on the full armor of God . . . and met the challenge of Women's Lib head-on."

She did this by organizing a competing event, which brought fifteen thousand people to the National Pro-Family Rally. It took place across town, in the Astro Arena. The arena was part of the Astrodome complex. As soon as it had opened, in 1965, the Astrodome had become a symbol of Texas bluster: the home of the Houston Astros, the "Eighth Wonder of the World," the first-ever air-conditioned domed stadium, its playing field carpeted with the latest in Texas gaucherie, an artificial grass know as Astroturf.

"We salute a great lady," Phyllis Schlafly, the national conservative-values guardian, wrote of Lottie Beth Hobbs and her counterprogramming triumph, "who saw her 'impossible dream' crowned with the glory of success." She compared the dueling rallies in Houston to the crucial Battle of Midway. "Likewise, the Battle of Houston dealt a crippling blow to the anti-family forces of Women's Lib. The war isn't over. . . . But there is now no question which side will win."

Mary Kay Ash, the founder of Mary Kay Cosmetics, already considered herself to be on the victorious side. Born in Hot Wells, south of San Antonio, in 1918, she now lived in Dallas—though not yet in her famous pink mansion. But she was already all about pink, including her clothes and her product packaging and the pink Cadillac Coupe de Villes she presented to her top salespeople. (The Cadillacs had custom paint jobs designed to match a shade of blush that Ash had found pleasing.) It makes sense in a chromatic way that she would also have been impressed enough with Lottie Beth Hobbs's "Pink Sheet" to have it distributed to the ladies who sold her cosmetics door-to-door and through home parties. But although she apparently shared Women Who Want To Be Women's attitudes, she had never been hesitant about liberating herself. She started her own company after working at two other direct-sales companies and witnessing how the men she had trained were swiftly promoted above her and paid more. "One of my strongest reasons for starting Mary Kay Cosmetics," she said, "was my determination to give other women the opportunity I felt I had always been denied."

It would have been interesting to see what would have happened if Mary Kay Ash had driven up to the National Women's Conference in her pink Cadillac to listen to all the debates over abortion and lesbian rights and the seizing of political power. But it was not to be. She already knew what a woman needed. "From 14 to 40," she said, "she needs good looks, from 40 to 60, she needs personality, and I'm here to tell that after 60, she needs cash."

— 54 —

DON'T BE SO
SELF-RIGHTEOUS

IT'S TIME TO TALK, BRIEFLY, ABOUT CHILI. REMEMBER way back in this book when we encountered J. C. Clopper, the high-spirited and verbose young wanderer from Cincinnati who traveled through Texas in 1828? One of the things he noticed during his visit to San Antonio was that when the inhabitants "have to pay for their meat in market a very

little is made to suffice a family. It is generally cut into a kind of hash with nearly as many peppers as there are pieces of meat—this is all stewed together."

He was describing what would become the official state food of Texas, a thick, often fiery slurry of meat, dried peppers, onions, oregano, cumin— pretty much everything except beans, which are included only if the cook is willing to risk the derision of chili purists.

It is one of those ancient grab-all dishes whose origins are impossible to pinpoint. The same is true of Texas barbecue, which is an evolutionary mash-up of the meat-smoking techniques of Caddo Indians, of the Spanish shepherds and vaqueros of New Spain, and of the slaves and slaveholders from the American South, all their traditions fused and arguably perfected by the German and Czech immigrants who came to Texas in the nineteenth century and opened meat markets that sold slow-smoked leftovers on the side.

At the moment, there is far more artisanal-food hysteria about barbecue in Texas than there is about chili, so I wouldn't be surprised if in the future it—or some other regional specialty like breakfast tacos—toppled chili as the official state food. But it's doubtful whether the dish's mystique will ever dissipate. In the unlikely event I ever open a chili parlor, I'm going to name it The Lady in Blue. That would be in honor of Sor María Jesús de Ágreda, the Spanish nun with the blue cloak who claimed to have visited the Indians of Texas in her mystical bilocation wanderings during the 1620s. Among the ever-fruitful legends about her is one in which she not only preached to the Jumanos and other tribes about the Catholic faith, but also handed them a chili recipe.

There is no direct link between Texas chili and Middle Eastern oil, but the two viscous fluids were of great interest to Everette Lee DeGolyer. He was born in a sod hut in Kansas in 1886 and grew up in Oklahoma. By the time he moved to Texas, in the centennial year of 1936, he was already one of the world's most renowned geologists as well as a very wealthy man. Among other things, he had discovered the Potrero del Llano No. 4 well in 1910, which brought in 110,000 barrels a day and opened up the immensely productive Golden Lane fields of Mexico. He didn't look like a wildcatter, at least not a wildcatter in the Glenn McCarthy mold. He was short and pudgy, and his scholarly curiosity roamed everywhere. He described the California-Spanish mansion he built in Dallas as "a Los Angeles architect's idea of what a Mexican rancher should have if he struck oil." The centerpiece of the house was a library stacked to the ceiling with rare books on Texas, the Southwest, and Mexico. He seemed to have read them all, and was authoritatively dismissive of Texas bookstores ("the ones in Mexico are far superior") and Texas writers, all of whom, "contemporary and bygone, have . . . failed to capture, the true flavor, the vastness, the unique character of Texas and Texans." (No offense taken.)

DeGolyer helped found Texas Instruments, the eventual incubator of Jack Kilby's integrated circuit. He started the world's leading petroleum-consulting firm. He wrote the *Encyclopaedia Britannica* entry on Santa Anna. He also became one of the earliest and most enterprising of chili scholars. He theorized that the dish in its true form originated as "the pemmican of the Southwest," a dehydrated mixture of beef, fat, and chile peppers that Texas cooks packed away for traveling to the California gold fields or up the cattle trails to Kansas. He was probably wrong about this—no doubt something like it was being eaten among the Tejanos of San Antonio long before

EVERETTE DEGOLYER
*(seated) as a young geologist. He would become, among other things, a noted chili scholar and a
prophet who foresaw the rise of Middle Eastern oil.*

the gold rush or the cattle drives—but even if his scholarship was debatable, he did win first prize in the chili contest at the 1948 State Fair of Texas.

Among his other not-so-small accomplishments was the role he played during World War II, when, as a deputy in the Petroleum Administration for War, he was sent overseas to Saudi Arabia and other Middle Eastern countries to size up their oil-producing potential. "We haven't seen anything but a pretty barren land on this whole trip," he wrote home to his wife at one weary point. "In fact Texas is a garden in comparison with some places we have been."

But he grew more and more aware of the staggering resources waiting to be discovered in this seemingly empty land. In a speech in 1940, he suggested that a "galaxy of fields of the first magnitude" existed in the Middle East, but the reality he found on his trip throughout Iraq, Iran, Kuwait, Bahrain, Qatar, and Saudi Arabia far outstripped his expectations. He came back convinced that there were twenty-five billion barrels of proven and probable reserves in those countries—in fact, the amount would turn out to be much larger. "The center of gravity of world oil production," he wrote, "is shifting from the Gulf-Caribbean area to the Middle East—to the Persian Gulf Area."

THE EMPIRE OF TEXAS

THE IMPACT ON TEXAS OF ALL THAT OIL WOULD BE PROFOUND,
but maybe not as profound as the impact Texas had on the countries under
whose sands it lay. It all began with the Texas Railroad Commission, which
was created in the Governor Hogg years to regulate intrastate railroad charges
but whose mandate vastly expanded after the discovery of the East Texas oil
field, when the sudden overabundance of oil made it crucial for somebody to
set production rates in order to stabilize prices. The eventual success of the
Texas Railroad Commission in determining how much a barrel of oil would
cost all over the world did not go unnoticed. One of the people who found
the organization particularly fascinating was Juan Pablo Pérez Alfonzo, who
was the minister of development in Venezuela before being exiled after a 1948
coup. During his years in Washington, DC, he spent time at the Library of
Congress studying the history of the oil industry. That was where he learned
about the Texas Railroad Commission and started to wonder how its success in regulating prices might be applied to his own oil-rich but exploited
country. When the Venezuelan dictatorship that had exiled him was toppled,
he returned to Caracas and became minister of mines and hydrocarbons. In
his new role, he began to explore the idea of a global consortium that would
allow the oil-producing countries of the world to do what the Texas Railroad
Commission had been doing for them—control the price of oil.

Another student of the Texas Railroad Commission was Abdullah Tariki,
also known as the "Red Sheikh." Tariki, the son of a Saudi Arabian camel magnate and caravan operator, studied in Austin at the University of Texas. His
experience there in the 1940s was mixed. People assumed he was a Mexican
and treated him as such, not allowing him into bars or movie theaters. On the
other hand, like Pérez Alfonzo, the more he studied geology, the more interested he found himself becoming in the Texas Railroad Commission. In 1959,
when Tariki was the Saudi oil minister, the two men were introduced over a
Coca-Cola at the Arab Oil Congress in Cairo. "You're the one I've been hearing
so many things about," the Venezuelan student of the Texas Railroad Commission said to the Saudi student of the Texas Railroad Commission.

Thus was born, if I may grossly simplify, the Organization of Petroleum
Exporting Countries. And it was OPEC that, in 1973, decided to cut oil im-
ports to the United States in a hostile response to its support of Israel in the
Yom Kippur War. The American economy, crippled by inflation, was already
in poor shape when the embargo began. Thanks to OPEC, the price of a
barrel of oil (around $3) quadrupled and would keep on climbing throughout
the decade. And there was not nearly enough of it. Half-mile-long lines at

stations led to gas rationing, and a system of even-odd days for filling up. To save fuel, the speed limit was lowered and daylight-saving time was brought out of mothballs for the first time since World War II.

Texans suffered these inconveniences along with the rest of the country, but at the same time those ever-rising prices juiced the state's oil-producing, oil-exporting economy into another boom. By the early '80s, oil was at almost $40 a barrel, ten times what it had been a decade earlier. Job creation surged along with the price of oil, personal income tripled, construction cranes loomed over the downtowns of Houston and Dallas and Austin. Bright new banks and savings and loans sprang up on sleepy street corners, entrepreneurs surged into the state, along with the oil-field workers and lawyers and accountants and construction workers and restaurant and hotel staffs needed to service a mushrooming economy. I remember the billboards all over Houston in those years that read "Business Cards in Eight Hours." In those pre-digital days, when printing something as simple as a card required weeks of waiting time, it was a thrilling promise, a measure of the state's accelerated pulse rate.

Turn Your Eyes toward Texas is the title of a dual biography of Sam and Mary Maverick written by Paula Mitchell Marks, and that sentiment—expressed in one of Sam Maverick's letters from 1838, when Texas was a paradise of possibility—could have served as the state's motto nearly a century and a half later. It was only natural that a nation with an inflated economy and a deflated morale would find hope in a state whose engine had gone into overdrive with petrochemical and human energy. Texans found themselves alive in a cultural moment where they were not just tolerated by the rest of the country but also sometimes emulated. It was the era of Texas chic, of mechanical bulls and hip Texas-themed New York hangouts such as The Lone Star Café, and of the movies *Urban Cowboy* and *Semi-Tough* and *North Dallas Forty*. The TV series *Dallas* first aired in 1978, and though its dominant character, J. R. Ewing, was the same old ruthless oilman that the entertainment industry had been cycling through movie and TV screens and magazine features for decades—the embodiment of Texas greed and showiness—audiences were invited to reconsider that stereotype with a sly appreciation that bordered on approval.

It didn't hurt Texas's shiny new image that the Dallas Cowboys were in the middle of a record-breaking NFL winning streak. They were now known as "America's Team," a once-unimaginable description for a team from a state that had for so long been regarded as a loud-mouthed intruder stagger-ing into the prim garden party of the national consciousness. In those years, the Cowboys' quarterback was Roger Staubach, who led the team to Super Bowl victories in 1972 and 1978. Like Sam Houston, Staubach was a come-

Herbert and Bunker Hunt testifying in 1980 before the House subcommittee investigating the collapse of the silver market—and how the Hunt brothers may have brought it about.

from-behind specialist. In 1975, when he completed a fifty-yard Hail Mary pass to Drew Pearson in the last thirty-two seconds to win a championship game against the Minnesota Vikings, it was the football equivalent of Houston's pursued and cornered Texian army winning the Battle of San Jacinto.

In those boom times, Texas cachet reached around the world. Once, working on a magazine story, I was walking through a remote, wretched, hurricane-racked village on the west coast of Madagascar. When a barefoot Malagasy kid asked me in broken French where I was from and I answered in broken French that I was from Texas, his face lit up in wonder and delight and he said, "J. R.!"

J. R. Ewing and his fictional world had obvious roots in the real-life saga of H. L. Hunt. In the origin story of the series, the father of J. R. and the founder of Ewing Oil is Jock Ewing, who in 1930—the same year that Hunt hoodwinked Dad Joiner into selling him the great East Texas oil field—swindled his partner, Digger Barnes, out of massive royalties.

Four years before *Dallas* debuted, the body of eighty-five-year-old H. L. Hunt was on display in the real Dallas, lying in an open casket at W. A. Criswell's First Baptist Church. He was dressed in a dark pinstriped suit, and even in death his bulbous face still had its peculiar baby-pink skin tone. The thirteen surviving children of his three families were there, including his daughter June, who sang one of her father's favorite hymns, with the refrain "I shall know Him, by the print of the nails of His hand."

MUCH FEUDING AND INTRIGUE AND LITIGATION AMONG THOSE
thirteen children followed in the years to come. And during the Texas boom
years, Hunt's high-rolling legacy was perpetuated by the exploits of two of his
sons from his first marriage, Nelson Bunker Hunt and William Herbert Hunt.
Bunker and Herbert—they both went by their middle names—were proud
custodians of their father's eccentricity. Bunker was in his forties when
H. L. Hunt died. He had a froggish-looking face with glasses and slicked-
back hair and weighed 275 pounds. His younger brother Herbert was lighter
and had the conventional, near-handsome appearance of a neighborly banker.
With their siblings in H. L. Hunt's first family, they controlled Placid Oil and
its vast oil reserves, which toward the end of the 1970s was generating a million dollars a day. Even so, Bunker and Herbert made pronounced gestures
toward normality. They were listed in the Dallas phone book. During the gas
crisis, Herbert—whose family's oil reserves were valued at $2 billion—slipped
into the back of a long line at a service station and sat there for two hours
with his wife and the family dog. Bunker had his extravagances—five hundred
race horses, a $50 million collection of ancient coins—but as one writer put it,
he "is the kind of guy who orders chicken-fried steak and Jell-O, spills some
on his tie, and then goes out and buys all the silver in the world."

That was not an exaggeration, about the chicken-fried steak and Jell-O, or
about the silver. Buying all the silver in the world was pretty much what the
Hunt brothers embarked on in the 1970s. It was a perilous time: inflation was
undermining the value of the dollar, and to ever-alarmed conservative minds
like Bunker Hunt's, the world was still very much under threat from communist gremlins. "Bunker," said one of his rare-coin dealers, "was just obsessed
with the idea that the Russians were coming over the Rockies."

Fiscal security no longer resided in paper money or in commodities contracts—"Any damn fool can run a printing press," Bunker said—but in solid
objects that inflation could not touch. Like silver. When the Hunts started
buying the metal in mega quantities in 1973, they weren't buying paper contracts, but real silver ingots, so many of them that by the time they were
through, the storage costs were three million dollars a year. The Hunt
brothers denied the colorful story testified to by one of their employees
about forty million ounces of silver being loaded into armored cars and
then chartered 707s from the exchanges in Chicago and New York, flown to
Zurich, and then deposited in several Swiss banks, all the while under guard
by armed cowboys from Bunker's Circle T Ranch.

Soon the Hunt brothers owned 9 percent of all the silver in the world.

They also owned less tangible silver assets in the form of stock market positions: they controlled 69 percent of all the silver futures contracts listed on COMEX, the New York exchange specializing in metals trading. The Hunts always maintained that they never had any intention of cornering the market, but the regulators at the Commodity Futures Trading Commission were not convinced. "Do you think there's any possibility these guys are just having fun, just horsing around?" one of the commissioners asked his colleagues at a CFTC meeting in 1979. "Is this a little game they're going through?"

If it was just a game, it was a fantastically lucrative one, at least at first. Silver was selling at about $3 an ounce in 1973, when the Hunts started to load it into their armored cars. By January 1980, they and their Saudi coconspirators had managed to drive it up past $50 an ounce. It was only a matter of time, one of the regulators warned, before "they'll have all the silver in the world."

COMEX clamped down and imposed new restrictions on silver trading. The Chicago Board of Trade went further, imposing rules that kept the Hunts and other speculators from buying any more silver at all. Silver prices started to drop, and so did Bunker and Herbert Hunt's hitherto limitless wealth. The Hunts hadn't used their own money to buy up all that silver—they had borrowed it from investment banks—and as the price of silver fell, those banks started issuing margin calls, demanding real money as collateral for the falling price of all those glistening silver ingots and futures contracts. The brothers didn't have it, and the banks that had lent them the money were facing their own margin calls and had no option but to unload silver, dropping the price further until, on March 27, 1980—"Silver Thursday"—the per-ounce price fell to $10.80.

It was the scariest trading day on Wall Street since the stock market crash of 1929. Bunker and Herbert Hunt were almost wiped out, though they didn't actually go bankrupt until after the big oil bust of the 1980s delivered the fatal blow. Still, it was really bad. They ended up being mortgaged, quite literally, down to their lawn mowers. It's very doubtful, as that regulator speculated, that they were just horsing around and not really trying to buy up all the silver in the world, but even if that were the case the fun was over. "A billion dollars," Bunker famously lamented during the worst of it, "isn't what it used to be."

———————— ★ ————————

TEN MONTHS AFTER SILVER THURSDAY, RONALD REAGAN WAS sworn in as the fortieth president of the United States. Reagan had been harried during his pursuit of the 1980 Republican nomination by a Republican primary opponent who was now his vice president, George Bush. By this time, Bush was fifty-six and had accumulated an extensive résumé in

BILL CLEMENTS
—the *"fire by friction man" who became Texas's first Republican governor since Reconstruction.*

government: Harris County chairman of the Republican Party, U.S. congressman, ambassador to the United Nations and to China, and director of the CIA. Public service had waylaid him for years in Washington, New York, and China, but he was still a resident of Texas. When it came to being perceived as a Texan, though, he never seemed to get credit for time served. Ralph Yarborough, who beat him in the raw 1964 Texas senatorial election, had called him out as a carpetbagger, "the Connecticut candidate." It was an unfair shot, because by that time Bush had lived in the state for sixteen years, was fond of pork rinds and barbecue, and had never repeated his rookie mistake of wearing Bermuda shorts in public in Midland. He was also a successful oilman, though nowhere near the stratospheric level of the Hunt or Murchison or Richardson families. In 1959, the year he and Barbara moved from Midland to Houston, his company, Zapata Off-Shore, had a respectable 195 employees and four rigs operating in the Gulf.

"Something was stirring at the political grass roots in Texas," Bush had suspected as far back as 1960, when a Democratic presidential ticket that featured native son Lyndon Johnson had barely eked out a victory in Texas; and the winner of the special election for Johnson's vacated Senate seat was John Tower. Tower was the first Republican since Reconstruction to win statewide office in Texas, and his victory helped inspire conservative Texas Democrats to look into the mirror and realize that all along there had been a Republican face staring back at them.

Now the nation's vice president was a Republican from Texas. The state's governor was a Republican, too, the first since E. J. Davis was forced out of office in 1874. Texas's new chief executive, elected in 1978, was Bill Clements. Clements was very wealthy and very gruff. He had helped found an offshore drilling company called SEDCO (Southeast Drilling Company) and had served in the Nixon and Ford administrations as deputy secretary of defense. He believed himself to be "Texan to his toenails" and deployed an ornery demeanor to prove it. "I'm a nuts and bolts guy," he told me once while I was interviewing him for a magazine profile. "I'm a fire by friction man. I'm not long on self-indulgence. I'm a why and a wherefore guy."

Clements was proud of being an Eagle Scout, an all-state high school football player, and an oil-field roughneck in South Texas. "Back then," he told me of his roustabout youth, "you could make more money working on a rig than you could as a lawyer or a graduate engineer. . . . I went where the rigs went. I lived at the bakery for a dollar a day, room and board. I ate 'em out of house and home." True to his Texas toenails, he had amassed an impressive collection of the sort of literature that Texans unblushingly call Texana. In his SEDCO office were ten-foot-high shelves filled with volumes such as *Bigfoot Wallace, A Dynasty of Western Outlaws,* and *Cow by the Tail*—all of them arranged by author and catalogued on file cards. Like all Texas governors, he was publicly worshipful of Sam Houston, and maybe privately of the opinion that in holding Houston's former office he was sharing in his outsized legacy. "He never recovered from Texas' seceding from the Union," Clements said. "It broke his heart. . . . For twenty-five years here's a man who had only one thing on his mind, and that was Texas."

During Clements's first term, one of the offshore rigs owned by SEDCO, Ixtoc 1, had a blowout while drilling in the Bay of Campeche. The explosion led to a monstrous environmental insult; 10,000–30,000 barrels of oil a day leaked into the Gulf of Mexico until the well was finally capped almost ten months later. Clements's unvarnished manner was generally appreciated, but less so when a tide of oil was heading toward the Texas beaches and he was arguing that it was "much ado about nothing." His suggestion for the coastal residents who were worried about a little crude washing ashore: "Pray for a hurricane."

That wasn't his only infelicitous outburst. "Just another Mexican with an opinion" is the way he once dismissed Dr. Jorge Bustamante, Mexico's leading demographer. And only a few years after Houston hosted the National Women's Conference, maybe he should have thought twice before proclaiming that "no housewife was qualified to sit on the Public Utility Commission."

By the end of his first term, he was being perceived as a bit too much of a throwback, and he was defeated for reelection by the state's Democratic attorney general. The new governor, Mark White, was in his early forties. With his sandy hair and oversized 1980s glasses, White had a nonthreatening, Rotary Club appearance that contrasted sharply with the growly take-charge visage of Bill Clements. He was talented, and his agenda was admirable—he was a champion of public education who wanted skills tests for students and competency exams and salary raises for teachers. But as a politician he probably could have benefited from cultivating a sharper edge. "There's no profit in being White's friend," one of the premier scrutinizers of Texas politics, Paul Burka, once observed, "and no loss in being his enemy."

On the other hand, there was something daring about him, as when he crept up to the third rail of Texas politics with a law known as the "no pass, no play" rule, which barred public school students from participating in sports and other extracurricular activities if they hadn't passed all their courses. Putting education ahead of football in Texas was a shocking, unholy act. Whole teams were sidelined, along with bands and cheering squads. The rule struck at the heart of the small towns where football was everything. The DeKalb Bears of Northeast Texas, for example, were undefeated and gearing up for their greatest season when all of a sudden they were defeated by algebra.

White was unapologetic. "We are in a world race," he explained to the *New York Times*, "and we have not even heard the starting gun. The rest of the world is sweeping past us. The oil and gas of the Texas future is the well-educated mind. But we are still worried about whether Midland can beat Odessa at football."

Yes, very worried: White's embrace of "no-pass, no-play" was one of the reasons he ended up a one-term governor. But he also had the great misfortune to be presiding over Texas when the economy came crashing down, when the boom was finally over and oil dropped to the unthinkable low of $10 a barrel. This was in 1986, the sesquicentennial year, the 150th anniversary of Texas's independence from Mexico. There was a birthday cake—the largest cake in the history of the world. It weighed 90,000 pounds and filled the floor of an Austin sports arena. Great Britain, one of the three countries that had recognized Texas after it declared its independence, sent Prince Charles as a guest of honor. He cut into the cake with a lusty blow from a curved sword.

But the sesquicentennial celebration had as much to do with keeping up Texas's spirits in its suddenly dismal present-day economy as with glorifying its past. The state was entering its "see-through years," so named because all those high-rise buildings constructed in Texas downtowns during the boom years were now empty of inhabitants and office furniture, their tiers of windows framing unobstructed views of the opposite horizon. Mark White was turned out, and the voters, thinking that maybe His Orneriness Bill Clements could shock Texas back to life, elected him governor again with 53 percent of the vote. But even Clements, a zealous no-tax, no-spend Republican, had to raise taxes to try to make up a deficit of $6.5 billion dollars, which had gobbled up a $1 billion surplus generated by previously soaring oil prices.

And Clements found himself the focus of a scandal during his second term. Since it was a scandal about football, it was even worse—politically speaking—than the Ixtoc 1 oil spill. It came to light that Clements had been the chairman of the board of governors of SMU when the Mustangs, the school's sizzling Southwest Conference championship team, was given the "death penalty" by the National College Athletics Association for doling out $61,000 to players from a secret boosters' slush fund. Among other penalties, the Mustangs' 1987 season was canceled, and the team was barred from bowl games and live television broadcasts until 1989. Clements hadn't made or approved any payments, but when he was made aware of what was going on, he didn't put a stop to it. In fact, when challenged by a fretful SMU official about the ongoing infractions, he advised him, in a trademark outburst of Clementsian crankiness, "to calm down and not be so self-righteous."

★

THEN THERE WAS THE 1980S SAVINGS AND LOAN CRISIS, THE

result of a nationwide paroxysm of greed on the part of bankers, brokers, accountants, developers, lawyers, lobbyists, politicians, and every conceivable species of quick-money artist, all of which Texas had in abundance. Once upon a time, before the crusade for deregulation found its full expression in Ronald Reagan's presidency, savings and loan institutions were known as

MARK WHITE
being sworn in for his first and only term as governor. He made the mistake of messing with high school football.

thrifts, a word whose very meaning was obliterated in the fast-trading frenzy of the 1980s. They were grassroots institutions, owned by their depositors, and their primary business was to fund humble home mortgages.

When they were deregulated, S&Ls became switching stations for high-velocity real estate deals that used depositors' investments as crazy money. The land-flipping schemes became so egregious that one participant recalled a row of tables lined up all the way down the hall in an office building: "The loan officers would close one sale and pass the papers to the next guy. It looked like kids registering for college."

"The S&L model," remembered the novelist Ben Fountain, who found himself in the bizarre center of it all as a new hire at a high-rolling Dallas law firm, "wasn't about producing things or providing a service to meet a naturally occurring demand. It was all about spinning wealth out of thin air through the creative manipulation of capital, cash flow, and hard assets. The deal itself became the product."

Obscene extravagance was a big part of the adrenaline rush. "You think it's easy eating in three-star restaurants twice a day six days a week?" Don Dixon, the president of Dallas's Vernon Savings and Loan, once complained after taking a "gastronomique fantastique" spin through Europe, courtesy of his depositors' money. He was later convicted of twenty-three counts of fraud—"the highest of the high fliers among the savings and loans crooks," according to U.S. Attorney General Dick Thornburgh. But other crooks aspired to even higher flying, the most ambitious of whom was Stanley Adams, the owner of Lamar Savings Association in Austin. He was indicted for misapplying $121 million of the thrift's funds, but the real reason he is remembered today, when so many S&L grifters' names have been forgotten, is that he once applied to the attorney general with apparent seriousness to build a branch of his institution on the moon. His proposal was rejected as "speculative."

As the S&L schemes began to come to light and come apart, the floundering perpetrators turned their suspicious eyes toward the FSLIC, the Federal Savings and Loan Insurance Corporation, which Congress had established in 1934 to insure consumers in case a thrift failed. The high rollers worried that any money appropriated to the FSLIC would be used to seize the insolvent institutions and save the taxpayers from having to bail them out further. In the words of one advocate for troubled Texas S&Ls, "There were just too many of us that are true Americans to put up with that kind of stuff."

They had a friend in Jim Wright, the powerful Democratic congressman who in January 1987 became Speaker of the House. Wright was from Fort Worth. He had won a Distinguished Flying Cross as a B-24 bombardier in World War II, and there was no indication that he had ever trimmed his eyebrows since. As a public servant, his moments of glory were intermittent, but those soaring Mephistophelean tangents of reddish hair remained magnificent. Wright had taken right-side-of-history stands as far back as the 1950s, when he had refused to sign the Southern Manifesto and supported the 1957 Civil Rights Act, but now he was on the side of that weary  gastronome Don Dixon and other S&L owners who were convinced they were being persecuted by government regulators. As Speaker, he moved energetically to undermine the FSLIC's budget so that it could no longer put so tight a squeeze on his donors and business partners back in Texas.

Wright was an aggressive, manipulative Speaker—"a heavy-handed son of a bitch," in the opinion of the not-so-light-a-touch-himself Republican congressman Dick Cheney. But in his longevity in the Speaker's office, he was no Sam Rayburn. His efforts on behalf of skeezy S&L operators ended up being folded into a Republican-driven ethics investigation that included scrutiny of a memoir he wrote called *Reflections of a Public Man*, whose bulk sales to interested parties, and the subsequent royalties paid to its author, were a convenient work-around to abiding by House rules that prohibited members from charging speaking fees. He was forced to resign after only two and a half years on the job—brought down, he said, by "mindless cannibalism."

JIM WRIGHT
was a powerful Washington insider from Fort Worth, who lost his job as Speaker of the House during the 1980s S&L scandals.

"Every Texan is in a box today," Lyndon Johnson's old press secretary, George Christian, told the *New York Times* during the deadly deceleration of the Texas economy. By "every Texan," he was really talking about the world-striding, empire-building sort that was still embodied, though a bit shakily, by John Connally.

Connally's defection to the Republican party in 1973 had caused a furor among Democrats, leading to the ultimate Texas insult, delivered courtesy of Liz Carpenter: "It's a good thing John Connally wasn't at the Alamo. He'd be organizing Texans for Santa Anna now."

In switching parties, Connally was only a step or two ahead of other conservative Texans, since the state was destined to be as monolithically Republican as it had once been unassailably Democratic. Even so, his political future ended up on the side of the road. Lyndon Johnson might have predicted as much for his former protégé. "I should have spent more time with that boy," he said after Connally joined the Nixon cabinet as secretary of the treasury. "His problem is he likes those oak-paneled rooms too much."

Nixon had passed over Connally for Gerald Ford as his vice president after Spiro Agnew resigned over bribery charges. Had he not, Connally, instead of Ford, would have assumed the presidency when Nixon resigned. Then, in 1975, it was Connally's turn to be on trial for bribery, accused of taking illegal kickbacks from the Associated Milk Producers, Inc. The last thing John Connally needed was a "milk scandal," and he imperiously scoffed at the charge that he had taken a $10,000 bribe. ("They haven't printed enough money to buy me.") Barbara Jordan testified as a character witness at his trial in federal court. So did, somewhat equivocally, Lady Bird Johnson. She said that no one doubted his integrity, even though "some folks don't like him."

He was acquitted, but Mrs. Johnson's observation was unfortunately borne out, at least in a political sense. When he ran for the 1980 Republican presidential nomination, a tall silver-haired silver-tongued Texan with a hefty-for-the-times war chest of $11 million, the only person who seemed to like John Connally was Mrs. Ada Mills of Clarksville, Arkansas. After a fourteen-month primary campaign, she turned out to be his only delegate.

After that, Connally was through with politics, but not with making money. Those were still the boom years, when oil prices were still climbing ever higher. "We were all bulletproof," remembered J. Edward Pennington, the president of the superstar investment partnership Connally formed with Ben Barnes, who, like Connally, had once been thought a sure bet to be a Texas successor to the LBJ presidential legacy. The Sharpstown scandal and the milk scandal had, among other things, shattered that particular dream, but there was still real estate, and plenty of deregulated S&Ls were dying to lend money to big players like a former Texas governor and a former Speaker of the Texas House. "We're beginning an era of prosperity like America hasn't dreamed of," Connally predicted in 1983, two years after forming his partnership with Barnes, "and Texas will be at the forefront of it."

They made deals, and in this supercharged economy, the challenge, the high, was to make them as fast as possible. Barnes and Connally soon had fifteen big-scale developments in play—office buildings, country clubs, hotels, luxury homes, racetrack condos in New Mexico, and beachside condos on South Padre Island. They were paid for with money borrowed at 18 percent interest and backed by the partners' personal guarantees. So when the savings and loan business went down, and the real estate business went down with it, Barnes and Connally found themselves exposed in a blast zone of financial ruin. "The man who once signed the nation's money," the former treasury secretary plaintively observed of his plight, "had lost his own."

The bankruptcy auction of John and Nellie Connally's personal possessions at a Houston showroom in 1988 was, depending on your level of sympathy for two men who embodied the frenetic deal making of the times, either the ultimate Texas gloat fest or a wrenching display of shattered fate. "He seemed to be the fulfillment of the mythology of Texas," an observer noted of John Connally, who sat there with his wife in folding chairs, listening to the auctioneer and the fall of the gavel as furniture, Picasso lithographs, elephant tusks, saddles, shotguns, china, the very chair that John Connally had sat in as governor were sold. Some of the items found their way back to them, courtesy of friends who were moved to buy prized possessions and return them to their former owners. A stranger from Georgia bid on the silverware the Connallys had bought when they were married, and handed it back to Nellie after the auction with the comment, "No woman should lose her wedding silver."

The hardest thing for John Connally to let go of was a life-size stone statue of St. Andrew that had once stood outside Westminster Abbey. He and Nellie had bought it on a trip to London and brought it home to Texas. Connally admitted to being inordinately fond of it: "[When] the movers came with their truck to the ranch to ship our belongings, I asked them to pack that piece last. When there was nothing else left, I gave it a hug and walked into the house."

Somebody must have returned the St. Andrew statue to them, because it now stands in front of the Connallys' black granite grave marker in the Texas State Cemetery.

★

EVEN AS JOHN CONNALLY'S GOODS WERE BEING SOLD OFF, Texas was beginning to make itself whole again. The semiconductor revolution that Jack Kilby had helped create with his integrated circuit was pointing the state to a more diversified economy, one in which a drop in the price of oil was not necessarily a bullet to the state's brain. And in its political personalities, it was diversifying as well.

"Our work is not done, our force is not spent!" George H. W. Bush told the Republican National Convention in New Orleans when he accepted his party's nomination for president in August 1988. It was an emphatic speech, most famous for a promise—"Read my lips: no new taxes"—that was rousing in the moment but politically fatal in the long run. "I know what it all comes down to," Bush declared, emphasizing his eight years' experience as vice president, "after all the shouting and the cheers—is the man at the desk. . . . My friends, I am that man."

The words were commanding, but the voice that delivered them was stuck at a mild, polite register that was reminiscent of the soothing tones used by Fred Rogers, the host of the children's television show *Mister Rogers' Neighborhood*. By contrast, there had been plenty of Texas slyness and swagger at the Democratic National Convention the month before, when the party's dreary candidate, Michael Dukakis, had been overshadowed by an electrifying keynote speech by Ann Richards.

"I'm delighted to be here with you this evening," she began, "because after listening to George Bush all these years, I figured you needed to know what a real Texas accent sounds like."

Richards later admitted being so nervous that when she reached for a glass of water at the podium her hand was shaking too much to pick it up. But to the television audience she was all slow-burning self-confidence. She was fifty-four at the time, the state treasurer of Texas, a recovering alcoholic with a silver bouffant that looked like an iceberg. In a not-so-distant previous life, she had been on the board of directors of Mad Dog, Inc., a hard-partying absurdist collective of Texas writers and artists and drug-fueled hangabouts whose motto was "Doing Indefinable Services to Mankind" and whose credo, as set forth in its articles of incorporation, was "Everything that is not a mystery is guesswork."

Richards had grown up outside Waco. Her parents hailed from Texas farm communities named Bug Tussle and Hogjaw. She had once dressed up at an Austin Mad Dog party as a giant tampon to greet the visiting editor of the *New York Times*. Now, improbably, her rowdy Texanness had brought her to a national stage and to the beguiled attention of the country. "Poor George," she said in her sarcastic drawl about the Midland oilman who was still dogged by his preppy upbringing, "he can't help it. He was born with a silver foot in his mouth."

Never mind that she had stolen the line; a *New York Times* reporter had used it two decades earlier in an obituary about an upper-crust parks commissioner. Everything else about Ann Richards that evening was original, further evidence that Texas could still not quite be mistaken for the rest of the United States.

Ann Richards introduces her deeply Texan self to the world at the 1988 Democratic National Convention.

— 55 —

BAPTISM OF FIRE

"THE LORD WILL ROAR FROM ZION," PREDICTS THE prophet in the book of Amos, "and utter his voice from Jerusalem; and the habitations of the shepherds shall mourn, and the top of Carmel shall wither."

This is a reference to Israel's Mount Carmel, the place where Elijah triumphed over the 450 false priests and prophets of Baal. In 1935, a man named Victor Houteff, a Bulgarian-born former washing-machine salesman who led a heretical offshoot of the Seventh-day Adventist Church, chose the name Mt. Carmel for a religious community he established a few miles northwest of Waco.

His group was called the Davidian Seventh-day Adventist Association in acknowledgment of King David, whose throne they believed Jesus would one day come to earth to reclaim. Houteff billed himself as a new Elijah, sent to earth to announce the Second Coming of Christ. But his very mortal death in 1955 threw his congregation into confusion and dissension. Out of the doctrinal power struggle arose yet another splinter group, which would come to be known as the Branch Davidians, led by a former oil-field worker named Ben Roden.

By that time, the Branch Davidians had relocated Mt. Carmel to a spot on the prairie twelve miles east of Waco. When Roden died, in 1978, his strong-willed widow, Lois, seized the Branch Davidian leadership from another claimant, her son George. Lois Roden seems to have been a passionate soul who meant business and was on fire with revelation. Once, in the darkness of an early morning, she woke up and saw a "vision" pass by her window: "It was of a silver angel, shimmering in the night." Roden interpreted the angel to be the Holy Spirit, a female manifestation of God. She also believed that when the prophesied end of the world was approaching, it would be necessary for the righteous—the Branch Davidians—to pass through a baptism of fire before they could be resurrected.

Lois Roden was in her early sixties, a severe-looking prophet with oversized old-people eyeglasses, when a young man named Vernon Wayne Howell arrived at Mt. Carmel in 1981. Born in Houston to an unmarried fourteen-year-old mother, he was a high school dropout who had found school a torment. He had a learning disability and was mocked by his classmates, who called him "Mr. Retardo." But he was also a visionary who believed he was in direct communication with God, a claim not endorsed by the pastor of his Seventh-day Adventist church, whose daughter Howell had gotten pregnant. "Disfellowshipped" from the church, he found his way to the Branch Davidians of Mt. Carmel, where he fell into a sexual and spiritual union with the much-older Lois Roden. ("I don't know how in the world [he] was able to persuade her," one church member speculated. "It had to be something in scripture—you know, similar to what Eve experienced with the serpent.")

Lois Roden died in 1986. Howell succeeded her as the sect's leader, but only after a surreal showdown with her son George, who dug up a decades-buried Branch Davidian corpse and demanded that Howell prove his powers by resurrecting it. Howell declined, which led to a gunfight. No one was killed, but afterward Howell's claim to leadership was secure and George Roden was cast out.

Howell had visited Israel in 1985, and it was there he had one of the more emphatic of his many epiphanies. On Mount Zion, he was visited by angelic entities who explained to him the secret of the mysterious seven seals in the book of Revelation. Indeed, he believed himself to be the seventh angel mentioned in the book, the one whose revelations would be the most crucial. He was also, he revealed, an end-time iteration of King David, and he later came to believe he was the manifestation of Christ.

"Revelation 1," he told a radio interviewer, "says that I am the root and offspring of David, the bright morning star. Peter says that prophecy is a light that shines in the dark places until the day-spring, day-star arises in your heart. So you see Christ is this great light. I am the light of the world."

He rechristened himself after this vision, changing his name legally in 1990. The new name referred to King David and to the Hebrew form of

Cyrus, the name of the Persian king who freed the Jews from the Babylonian captivity. Vernon Wayne Howell was now David Koresh.

EVERY YEAR IN SAN ANTONIO DURING THE FIRST WEEK OF

March—a time that Texas history obsessives refer to as the High Holy Days—a series of public events marks the anniversary of the siege and fall of the Alamo. There are reenactments, wreath layings, a reading of Travis's famous "Victory or Death" letter, musketry volleys, artillery displays, and a solemn dawn ceremony on March 6, the day of the climactic battle.

No such pageantry commemorates the second most famous siege in Texas history, the one that began on February 28, 1993, at the Branch Davidian compound near Waco and ended two months later in a grotesque, wind-driven inferno. Indeed, when I visited the site on April 19, 2018, the twenty-fifth anniversary of the FBI assault, almost no one was there. I drove through an open gate off Double EE Ranch Road, where, in a stretch of verdant pastureland, stands a memorial to those who died, listing their names and ages and declaring, "For 51 days, the Davidians and their leader, David Koresh, stood proudly."

A few hundred yards past the memorial was the site where that standoff took place. The Mt. Carmel compound, a sprawling, cheaply built conglomeration of meeting rooms and dormitories that Koresh's followers referred to as the Anthill, had been gone for a quarter of a century, burned down in the final assault. But a simple church had been rebuilt there for the few surviving Texas members of the Branch Davidian faith, and remnants of the original structure were scattered about the pastoral landscape. The community's concrete-lined swimming pool, next to the gymnasium at the back of the Anthill, was still there, half filled with stagnating green water. And a few dozen yards away, amid tangled undergrowth and a "Keep Out" sign, was a scorched, flattened, twisted eruption of orange-tinted metal—all that was left of the buried school bus that was part of an underground tunnel system through which some of the Branch Davidians tried to escape on the day of the conflagration.

Koresh and his followers began building the Mt. Carmel complex in 1988. Within a few years, 150 or so people were living there, all of them under the sway of Koresh's messianic magnetism. He was a marginally talented musician, playing guitar and fronting a Mt. Carmel band that played in bars around Waco. His sermons were wearisome, hours-long, brain-crunching exegeses about the book of Revelation and the unrevealed secrets of the seven seals and the coming apocalypse of the American Babylon. "Despite his easy ways," remembered David Thibodeau, the drummer in his band and

Vernon Wayne Howell rechristened himself David Koresh after a biblical epiphany in which he discovered that he was meant to be "the light of the world."

one of the survivors of the Waco tragedy, "I couldn't avoid the slow realization that there appeared to be a very dark side to David's 'truth.' It seemed that he expected to be destroyed, along with anyone who followed him. The possibility that the forces loose in the world would reject and kill him was always on David's mind; and if the world rejected his message, his death was inevitable and terrible."

Koresh had also taken on a busy sexual burden. An epiphany he claimed to have experienced in 1989 led him to believe it was his responsibility to father the twenty-four children who would grow up to be the elders described in Revelation as seated around the throne of God, all clothed in white and wearing crowns of gold. As he interpreted things, this meant that the other men at Mt. Carmel were to remain celibate and, if necessary, to give up their wives to marry their leader.

"It's a toughie," Koresh acknowledged to his shocked male followers.

He didn't live long enough to provide all twenty-four elders, but he did father seventeen children, many of them to underage mothers. Once, when the voice of God commanded him to "Take Michele as a wife," he had sex with a twelve-year-old girl who, two years later, gave birth to a daughter.

Koresh was wide open to charges of, at least, statutory rape. And after a dissenter left the compound and alerted the authorities, he was investigated by the Texas Department of Human Services for child abuse as well, though no charges were ever filed.

What was of immediate concern to the Bureau of Alcohol, Tobacco and Firearms were reports of the Branch Davidians stockpiling firearms, buying powdered aluminum and dummy hand grenades, and converting legal semiautomatic AR-15 rifles into illegal automatic weapons. The ATF, despite the fact that Koresh was often in Waco and could be apprehended away from Mt. Carmel, came up with a plan of "dynamic entry": approach the compound in force and by surprise, arrest its leader, and search the property for a forbidden arsenal.

But the raid—Operation Trojan Horse—quickly unfolded into disaster. The Davidians were tipped off by a member who was away from Mt. Carmel and had spotted some of the eighty or so ATF agents in full combat gear that had been convoyed that morning from nearby from Fort Hood, with three National Guard helicopters in the air above them.

The ATF learned that it had lost the element of surprise, but decided to go ahead with the raid anyway—a spectacularly ill-fated decision that led to a raging gun battle between government agents and a civilian religious group that had been primed by David Koresh to anticipate the apocalypse. The agents shot five of the Davidians' dogs as they raced toward the front doors of the compound. Koresh met them, holding open one of the double doors. He was unarmed, but slow to comply when the agents started calling out, "Police! Search warrant! Get down!" That was when somebody—either the ATF or the Branch Davidians (there is plenty of forensic speculation on that front)—opened fire.

As bullet rounds tore through the flimsy plywood of the buildings and the assailants tossed flash-bang grenades through the windows, one of Koresh's followers picked up the phone and called 911. "Call it off!" he yelled. "There are women and children in here! We want a cease-fire! If they don't back off we're going to fight to the last man."

There was a cease-fire, but only after almost two hours, and after four ATF agents were dead and another sixteen wounded. Five Davidian defenders had been killed as well, and four more wounded, including Koresh, who had been shot in the wrist and the hip.

His disciples thought Koresh was going to die, but he lived through the next fifty-one days as the FBI took over from the ATF and surrounded the compound. The siege was in part an ongoing negotiation to talk the Davidians into coming out and in part a blunt application of crude psychological warfare on the part of the government. Power was cut to the compound, searchlights swept across the buildings at night, and loudspeakers played a variety of unendurable sounds: rabbits being slaughtered, clocks ticking, babies crying, Nancy Sinatra singing "These Boots Are Made for Walking."

Twenty-one children were sent out, and fourteen adults as well left during the siege, but the majority of the Davidians stayed with Koresh. He was in pain from his seeping hip wound and urinating blood, but he was still the dominant presence, preparing the Mt. Carmel residents for some sort of end-time rendezvous. Early in the siege, he promised the negotiators he would lead his people out, but then he changed his mind. He would not surrender. "My Commander-in-Chief told me to wait," he said.

And the more he waited, the more the forces arrayed against him demanded a climax. There were over 700 law enforcement officials—FBI and ATF agents, along with state and local police—and a rough daily average of a thousand members of the media watching, weighing in, waiting for something to happen.

A plan was devised, the Jericho Plan. The compound would be assaulted in slow stages, over a period of two days, with tear gas. Janet Reno, the U.S. attorney general, was assured that the tear gas would not harm the children or the pregnant mothers still inside. Nor would it cause a fire. But it would force the people out.

"It was not law enforcement's intent," stated a report compiled later by the Justice Department, "that this was to be D-Day."

But to the people inside Mt. Carmel, D-Day was exactly what it looked like. "This is not an assault," the FBI's chief negotiator's voice claimed—pleaded—over a loudspeaker as two tanks modified with thirty-foot booms began punching through the walls and depositing tear gas cylinders inside. They were followed by Bradley Fighting Vehicles shooting more gas from almost four hundred canisters.

The FBI waited for the tear gas to drive the Davidians out, but it didn't. Neither did the fires that began hours later, about noon, and quickly ravaged the buildings, propelled by the wind blowing across the Central Texas prairie. Of the eighty-five people who were in residence at Mt. Carmel at the time of the attack, only nine survived. Eighteen children under the age of ten perished. So did two unborn children. The arguments about how the fire started rages on to this day. Did Koresh and his followers deliberately burn down Mt. Carmel to bring on a prophesied purification by fire? Or did the bulldozing tanks kill some of the Davidians by burying them in falling concrete and dooming the rest when the tear gas canisters delivered by the Bradleys—made up of a chemical powder called CS in a solution of methylene chloride—accidentally ignited lanterns and cans of diesel fuel, as well as the Molotov cocktails the defenders had assembled and the hay bales they had propped against the walls to help absorb bullets?

In either case, the FBI's assault was a nightmarish blunder. Some of the Branch Davidians died from blunt trauma wounds from falling concrete,

The apocalyptic end of the Branch Davidian compound known as Mt. Carmel—the tragic end of a bungled siege and the fulfillment of a fiery prophecy.

others from smoke inhalation, others from close-range execution-style gunshot wounds, others from burning alive. "Most of the burned bodies," a report concluded, "were unrecognizable as humans."

David Koresh died of a gunshot wound to the head, either self-inflicted or administered by a follower. He was buried, with one of his wives and six of his children—those whom he prophesied would one day be among the twenty-four to surround the throne of God—in a Tyler cemetery. His grave marker reads, "In His Father's Hands," but a more resonant summing up might be the words he left on his mother's answering machine during the siege—"I'll see y'all in the skies."

★

GOVERNOR ANN RICHARDS HAD BEEN IN OFFICE A LITTLE OVER two years when the Waco tragedy happened. In the opinion of her friend and biographer Jan Reid, "Ann was snookered and used by federal agents who wanted to go in like a platoon of military commandos." Responding to an ATF claim that the Branch Davidians were manufacturing methamphetamines, she had approved the use of three Texas Air National Guard helicopters. The government denied that any agents fired down on the compound from the helicopters, though survivors of the siege argued very much the opposite.

The thought of all those bullets flying into and out of Mt. Carmel in a

THE EMPIRE OF TEXAS

battle pitting heavily armed federal agents against apocalypse-minded citizens equipped with their own paramilitary gear and weapons had an effect on Ann Richards. It was probably one of the reasons she vetoed a Republican bill calling for a referendum on allowing Texans to carry concealed firearms, something that had been illegal since 1871, when a law established a minimum $25 fine for anyone who dared to carry a pistol "on or about his person, saddle, or in his saddle bags."

The law exempted people who lived in a "frontier county," where there could be "incursions by hostile Indians." It's doubtful that it was ever consistently enforced, and even though Texas was the first state to pass such a law, it should not be assumed that it was the result of peaceable-kingdom progressive thought. (A good rule of thumb: never assume anything of the sort when it comes to Texas.) The law was passed by a Reconstruction Republican government nervous about gun-toting ex-Confederates. It was kept on the books when the Democrats came back to power and were nervous about gun-toting ex-slaves.

But Ann Richards was determined to keep the law in force—she wanted to save Texas from "the amateur gunslingers who think they will be braver and smarter with gun in hand." She vetoed the bill, but that only inspired the Republicans to put a concealed-carry referendum on their primary ballot the next spring, which passed with 79 percent of the vote. She had just invented what Texas politicos now refer to as the "Ann Richards Rule"—that is, keep away from people's guns or lose your political future.

She hadn't had an easy time in becoming governor in the first place. "Richards Wins in Mudslide" was the headline of the *Dallas Times Herald* after she won an unseemly Democratic primary during which she took direct aim at the integrity of one of her opponents, former governor Mark White, claiming that he had "lined his pockets" while in office; and during which she had to continually dodge the question whether she—a founding member of Mad Dog, Inc.—had ever used drugs.

In the general election, she was pitted against Clayton Williams, a fifty-eight-year-old West Texas rancher, oilman, and banker. He had a wide, face-splitting grin and a pleased-with-himself presence that harked back a little to the Pappy O'Daniel days, all the more so because like O'Daniel, Claytie—as he was known—was a political novice. But he had a white cowboy hat, he could ride a horse, and he had an appealingly simpleminded agenda. He wanted to build more prisons, give drug dealers the death penalty, and introduce young criminals to "the joys of bustin' rocks."

Among his campaign slogans was one that would work for Donald Trump decades later: "Make Texas Great Again." "I want to give back to

CLAYTON "CLAYTIE" WILLIAMS
promised to return Texas to the good old days of his youth. But that didn't work out.

our kids," Williams promised, "the Texas my father gave to me." But there was one thing he wasn't willing or able to give back. Back in the 1950s, his father, Clayton Williams Sr., had taken energetic advantage of Texas's "rule of capture" law, which gave landowners more or less unfettered access to any water flowing beneath the surface of their property. In drilling fifty-two wells to irrigate his own land, he dried up Comanche Springs, a lush desert watering hole in Fort Stockton that had been the pride of the town and a stopping place for desert nomads since before the time of Cabeza de Vaca.

Decades later, Claytie was continuing his father's work, extracting groundwater to irrigate his twelve thousand acres. When he was asked on

the campaign trail whether the springs might come back if he stopped pumping thirty million gallons of water a day from the aquifer, he was direct: "They might, but I'm not going to do it."

When it came to entertainment value, the contest between Clayton Williams and Ann Richards was the most fun the state had had in a long time. Both candidates embodied in an undiluted way what a Texan was, or at least what people wanted to believe a Texan was. There was the sarcastic, wisecracking, bighearted, formerly hard-drinking Ann Richards, with her white crest of what was fondly known in Texas as big hair. ("I rat the tar out of it," her hairdresser confessed. "Then spray the hell out of it. We defy gravity.") And there was Clayton Williams, the Texas A&M graduate who sobbed when he heard the "Aggie War Hymn"; who implied that with him in the governor's chair, Texas could "ride horseback into the 21st century"; who promised that he would not just defeat his opponent but would "head and hoof her and drag her through the dirt"; and who notoriously joked to the press—when they were huddled in misery during a wet and freezing night at his ranch—that they should aspire to the easygoing attitude of a rape victim: "If it's inevitable, just relax and enjoy it."

Williams later admitted he had a habit of shooting himself in the foot, and then he would "load 'er up and blast away again."

The self-inflicted coup de grace came at a joint appearance late in the campaign, after Claytie called Ann Richards a liar. She said she was sorry he felt that way, and held out her hand. He refused to shake it. It was one thing to characterize women as rodeo animals that needed to be headed and hoofed and dragged through the dirt, or to make a grotesque joke about rape, but it turned out to be quite another not to shake a woman's hand. There was just enough chivalry left in Texas for people to be horrified, and Ann Richards squeaked past Clayton Williams to become the state's second female governor.

—56—

TEXANS VERSUS TEXANS

TEXAS, BY NOW ALMOST A SOLIDLY REPUBLICAN STATE, was ready to accept a Democratic woman as its leader, given the uncouth alternative. But two years after Richards won the election, the nation decided that another Texan, George H. W. Bush, would leave office as a one-term president. Bush—the Man at the Desk—had led the country with often superlative managerial skill, though maybe without enough of what he once unfortunately referred to as "the vision thing." A native sense of discretion and a career spent in foreign policy helped him understand that the last thing the suddenly shifting world order needed was for the United States to gloat about the Berlin Wall coming down. "I'm not going to go dance on the wall," he said. He assembled a world team to go to war with Saddam Hussein after the Iraqi dictator invaded Kuwait. He orchestrated a subtle and nimble response to the collapse of the Soviet Union.

But Bush was in a corner from the day he took office, and he knew it. A mounting deficit was going to mean a government shutdown unless some sort of meaningful bipartisan budget deal could be reached. "We don't need to do that this year": that was the opinion expressed shortly after the 1988 election by James Baker, the powerhouse Houston-born lawyer who was Bush's longtime close friend, his tennis partner, and now his secretary of state. But the reckoning couldn't be put off forever, and in the summer of 1990 Bush agreed to raise taxes—or, in the see-through euphemism the White House put out, to "tax revenue increases."

"Firestorm on 'Right,'" Bush explained to Baker in a note he scrawled around this time. "[And] in Press re Read Lips break of word."

Not much decoding was necessary. The man who had declared "Read my lips: no new taxes," was saying yes to new taxes. Ronald Reagan might have explained it away, or gotten away with it somehow, but he had had the vision thing, and the courtly George Bush did not. Bush, who had made so much of his life in Texas, who had created a business there and raised his children there and listened (for real!) to country music there, could have used a bit more of something—certitude? ruthlessness? bluster? luck?—that was commonly regarded as an essential component of the Texas personality.

It wasn't fair that a war hero president who had declared in his inaugural address that one of America's goals was "to make kinder the face of the nation and gentler the face of the world" should be pictured on the cover of *Newsweek* in proximity to the word "wimp." It wasn't fair that a man who had once bought pork rinds at Midland grocery stores was ridiculed for being out of touch with the daily lives of ordinary Americans when he expressed polite enthusiasm while being shown a next-generation supermarket scanner. And it wasn't fair, or at least it was unfortunate, when another Texan, an inarguably authentic one, came along just in time to help torpedo his reelection.

Ross Perot was born Henry Ray Perot in 1930, in Texarkana, the Northeast Texas city that is so flush against the Arkansas border that it is essentially two cities in one, divided by its main street, State Line Avenue, into Texarkana, Texas, and Texarkana, Arkansas. Perot's middle name was legally changed to Ross when he was twelve, a gesture on the part of himself and his parents to honor an older brother—Gabriel Ross Perot—who had died before he was born. The designation "H. Ross Perot" had been accidentally bestowed upon him by a *Fortune* magazine writer working on a profile titled "The Fastest Richest Texan Ever." Perot thought the unshakable *H* was ostentatious and much preferred to be known just as Ross.

He was five-six with a blunted, downward-thrusting nose and a scorched-earth haircut that made his big ears look like birds that had been flushed out of hiding. His high-register voice had a nagging, peppery, I-can't-believe-you-don't-know-this-already quality to it. The note of impatience was integral to his personality. It had taken him only sixteen months to become an Eagle Scout, a process that usually takes four or five years. When he was a seventeen-year-old freshman at Texarkana Junior College, he persuaded the board of regents to relocate the institution. As a prudish, teetotaling lieutenant (j.g.) on a destroyer, he complained directly to the secretary of the navy about his degenerate shipmates: "I have found the Navy to be a fairly Godless organization. . . . I do not enjoy the prospect of continuing to be subjected to drunken tales of moral emptiness, passing out penicillin pills, and seeing promiscuity on the part of married men."

Perot owned a company called EDS—Electronic Data Systems—that he founded after working as a salesman for IBM and noticing that the companies he was selling computers and computer systems to did not really know what to do with them or how to integrate them into their business cultures. EDS, which Perot began in 1962 with a thousand-dollar investment, filled that void and made its owner a billionaire.

Perot laid down a moralistic corporate culture of the sort he had pined for as a naval officer. His employees had to take lie detector tests to ensure they weren't drug users. Adulterers were subject to dismissal. And the people (mostly men) who worked for EDS hewed to a strict dress code—suits, white shirts, no facial hair—even when fashions were uncaged in the late 1960s. He was also the architect of the "no pass, no play" education initiative, the high-minded but gruesomely unpopular 1984 policy that had helped cause Governor Mark White to lose a second term.

The leader of EDS was a take-charge, can-do, red-tape-cutting action hero intolerant of slow-moving governmental bureaucracy. His concern about American POWs had led him to charter an airliner in 1969 in a bold but unsuccessful attempt to deliver three hundred tons of food and medicine and mail to North Vietnamese prisons. He had better luck on the heroism front in 1979. Two EDS employees had been jailed in Tehran on the eve of the Iranian Revolution as a result of a business dispute between Perot's company and the government. To break them out of prison, Perot assembled a team headed by a retired army colonel and made up of EDS employees with combat experience, stipulating that "these guys had to have been in live combat where they saw the man hit that they shot."

As it turned out, the commandos didn't need to kill anybody. The EDS hostages were released when Iranian revolutionaries stormed the country's prisons and freed its occupants. In the chaos that followed, the two men made it to the Hyatt Hotel in Tehran, where some of Perot's employees met them and got them across the border to Turkey. The colonel in charge of the operation later depicted the daring rescue as a "spring outing." Still, when Perot entered the 1992 presidential race, challenging both Bush and Bill Clinton as an independent candidate, he came loaded with the aura of a man who could get things done and wasn't going to wait around to do them.

At that time, Bush's son George W. was living in Dallas, where he had determinedly assembled an investment group to buy a Major League baseball team, the Texas Rangers. As comanaging general partner of the team, he worked out of the ninth floor of a Dallas office building, from which he had a clear view of Ross Perot's downtown campaign headquarters. He saw that something ominous was stirring, and he picked up the phone to call his father in the Oval Office. "I want to tell you what's going on outside my window," he told the president. "We've got a problem here. There are like ten cars deep with people stopping to get bumper stickers. You can't write this guy off."

The elder Bush had known Perot a long time and thought his candidacy was "a big massive ego trip" and that Perot was "a highly wired up, strange little egomaniac." The problem, though, was that his poll numbers in the spring of 1992 were better than Bush's and better than Bill Clinton's. He blew onto the national weather map like a Texas norther. A fed-up, quick-fix, anti-Washington billionaire seemed for a while like the perfect anti-dote to a president who was out of touch, who was tired, who—by his own admission—had "never been too hot with words." He had proved it by reading aloud, in front of a New Hampshire audience, the reminder note on a cue card ("Message: I care") and then in another speech, apropos of nothing, blurted out, "Don't cry for me, Argentina."

Perot's campaign, though, was erratic and profoundly weird. In July, he decided to withdraw from the race. But a few months later, in October, a month before the election, he announced that he was back, claiming that he had dropped out in the first place because Republican mischief makers had somehow attempted to sabotage his daughter's wedding. Bush, who had had an 89 percent approval rating after the Gulf War, had sunk below 30 percent by the summer of 1992, and Ross Perot reentering the race and showing up on the debate stage didn't help. Caught between the wacky, jabbering Perot and the youthful and suavely empathetic Bill Clinton, Bush looked like a man that history had already chosen to pass by.

"How's it going, son?" George H. W. Bush asked George W. Bush on Election Day.

"Not so good," his son replied. "The exit polls are in, and it looks like you're going to lose."

He might very well would have lost anyway, even without Perot. Clinton easily took the electoral college, but the popular vote—43 percent for Clinton, 38 percent for Bush, and 19 percent for Perot—reflected how deeply disruptive an ill-tempered Texas billionaire could be.

"I DID ACTUALLY MEET SELENA IN THE GALLERIA MALL IN Houston. But I didn't say much to Selena because I wasn't a celebrity. I just saw her and said hello and kept it moving."

That was Beyoncé Knowles's recollection of meeting Selena Quintanilla. This happened sometime in the early 1990s, probably around the time when Ross Perot was busy making George Bush's life miserable and when Selena's

President George H. W. Bush. He never quite got credit for being a Texan.

third album, *Entre a mi Mundo*, with signature songs such as "Como La Flor" and "Que Creías," was beginning to boost the popular young Tejana singer into real stardom. Beyoncé was maybe ten or eleven. She was right in pointing out that she was not a celebrity, but she was already attracting attention as part of a dancing and singing group of preteen performers called Girls Tyme. They played venues like rodeos and malls and theme parks. ("It don't get much bigger than AstroWorld!" an excited Beyoncé once announced.)

Beyoncé Knowles lived only a few miles from AstroWorld near Houston's Third Ward, a historically African American neighborhood in the heart of the sprawling city. In 1872, the Reverend Jack Yates, a former slave and Baptist minister, had led a fundraising drive among other residents who had recently escaped from slavery to buy a ten-acre parcel of land in the Third Ward and create a green space known as Emancipation Park. A century later, prosperous black neighborhoods had emerged along Brays Bayou to the east of Rice University and the Texas Medical Center. That was where Beyoncé grew up, on a street called Parkwood Drive. Her father was Matthew Knowles, a highly successful salesman of medical systems for Xerox who drove a Jaguar XJ6. Her mother Tina, born in Galveston, was the daughter of French-speaking Louisiana Creoles whose family name, Beyincé, was also spelled "Buyincé" and "Boyance." In junior high, Tina was a singer, performing with a trio called the Veltones.

To a young Texan like Beyoncé Knowles, who aspired to a certain kind of flashy, costume-and-dance-driven pop stardom, Selena must have seemed like a heaven-sent inspiration. Selena was young herself, probably only a year or so past twenty when Beyoncé encountered her at the Galleria, but she had signed with Capitol Records at eighteen and secured a lucrative sponsorship agreement with Coca-Cola the year before. Beyoncé didn't speak Spanish—neither did Selena at her age—but there was no communication barrier when it came to performance style. Selena had a powerhouse, spectrum-wide singing voice and nonstop dance moves that were delivered with a sultriness that felt good-natured and authentic.

Selena Quintanilla was born in Freeport, a city at the mouth of the Brazos River, where her father, Abraham, worked for Dow Chemical. Less than 10 percent of the residents in that part of Texas were Hispanic, but Abraham had grown up in Corpus Christi, where the Mexican American population was heavily in the majority. As a teenager in Corpus, he was part of a group called the Dinos, which specialized in doo-wop numbers like "In the Still of the Night" and wore matching collarless jackets. They were shunned by Anglo club owners who didn't want Mexican Americans singing in their establishments, and were heckled in other clubs by the Tejano clientele. "Play Spanish music!" they demanded. "Who do you think you are, gringos or something?"

Chastened and confused, the Dinos became Los Dinos and began surfing what a Dallas promoter called *la onda chicana*, the Chicano wave, cutting an album called *Los Dinos a Go Go* and having some success with original songs and with Spanish covers of English pop hits. But they didn't have enough success to make a living, and Quintanilla moved to Lake Jackson and took a job with Dow. Although his musical career had been foreclosed on by reality, his ambition was reawakened through his children. "When I realized that Selena could sing," he said, "I saw the continuation of my dreams."

"It gave you chill bumps how powerful her voice was," one of Selena's childhood friends remembered. Abraham Quintanilla gave up his job at Dow to run a Mexican restaurant in Lake Jackson, where he made sure the diners were introduced to "the sensational nine-year-old singer."

The restaurant went bust after a year, and Quintanilla moved the family to Corpus Christi, where he worked at his brother's truck-leasing business and threw himself into managing a new, reconstituted version of his old band. Now it was Selena y Los Dinos, featuring not just Selena but also her brother A. B. and sister Suzette. Over the years, Tejano music had continued to evolve. It now drew not only from conjunto, which was a fusion of Mexican border influences and the polka rhythms of Czech and German and other European Texas transplants, but also from the percussive Latin American *cumbia* sound and the smooth big-band stylings known as *orquesta*. It was a Spanish-language omnibus expression of Texas-Mexican identity that could be dialed up or down, from honky-tonk two-stepping to dancing and singing showmanship designed to fill stadiums.

Quintanilla, "the ultimate stage father," according to one observer, sensed the opportunity and drove his children hard, grilling Selena on Spanish pronunciation, conveying the family band from gig to gig in a bus called Big Bertha. Sometimes they made only enough money to buy dinner at Whataburger, the Corpus Christi–based hamburger chain that, along with Blue Bell Ice Cream and HEB grocery stores, ranked high on the list of most-beloved Texas businesses.

The band's fortunes eventually prospered, and its audience grew, but at a cost. Selena's father pulled her out of school in the eighth grade so that she could be on the road, leaving her to finish high school by correspondence. She sang to increasingly populous and adulatory audiences, but offstage her social life was narrowly centered on her family as they logged miles in Big Bertha throughout Texas and the Southwest. She never had a date and was chaperoned everywhere, though after Abraham Quintanilla hired a talented

SELENA QUINTANILLA
—*"it gave you chill bumps how powerful her voice was."*

lead guitarist, Chris Perez, to perform with the band, she covertly fell in love. "You're dead," Perez thought to himself after he first kissed Selena. "Abraham is going to kill you." There was no bloodshed, but when he found out what was going on Quintanilla fired Perez, which led to Selena skipping out on an El Paso concert to marry Perez at the Nueces County Courthouse in Corpus Christi. Quintanilla had no choice but to welcome his new son-in-law into the family and hire him back to play lead guitar.

After her startling act of defiance, Selena settled back into her identity as a dutiful, hardworking, unfailingly gracious music professional. To her new husband, "Selena was, in a word, *good.*"

"God, if only I was like Selena." It was a wish that could have been whispered by many thousands of young girls or women, by a starstruck aspirant like Beyoncé Knowles. But in this case the person dreaming of that remote possibility was Yolanda Saldívar, the thirty-three-year-old president of the Selena fan club and manager of the singer's fashion boutiques. Saldívar was a former nurse with an assertive, possessive personality and a checkered employment history. Her devotion to Selena was obvious and intense—there was a shrine-like room in her house dedicated to the singer. She seemed to believe that they were more than friends, more than business associates, that they shared a powerful emotional connection, a mother-daughter bond. "In my opinion," Abraham Quintanilla later said, "she was living her life through Selena." Chris Perez never thought of her as a threat—she was just, as he would later bitterly describe her, "a small, sad, ugly little woman."

Yolanda Saldívar's belief that she was the irreplaceable center of Selena's world was a delusion that could not survive Quintanilla's growing suspicion that she was embezzling money from his daughter's boutique business. It all ended horribly in Corpus Christi on a March day in 1995 when Selena went alone to meet Saldívar in her room at a Days Inn motel. Saldívar had bought a gun a few weeks before. When Selena confronted her about missing financial records, she took it out of her purse and fired. Selena was hit in the shoulder. She managed to stagger to the motel lobby, where she cried out, "Help me! Help me! I've been shot," and collapsed onto the floor, bleeding to death from a severed artery.

Saldívar ran to her truck, locked herself in, and began a hysterical stand-off with the police that lasted almost ten hours. She held the gun to her head, threatening suicide, but finally surrendered. Seven months later, she was convicted of first-degree murder and sentenced to at least thirty years in prison.

Outside a downtown auditorium overlooking Corpus Christi Bay, people began lining up at four a.m. two days after Selena's death to pass by her closed coffin. The mourners—almost sixty thousand by the end of the day—

were solemn and orderly, but some of them grew agitated after a rumor began to circulate that the coffin was empty. The lid was finally opened to reveal the twenty-three-year-old Selena lying shockingly still with a single rose in her hand.

Between Corpus Christi and San Antonio, in the brushlands of South Texas, still mostly populated by Tejanos, thousands of drivers turned on their lights in memory of Selena as they cruised down Interstate 37. The motel where she was shot instantly became a pilgrimage site, some people just needing to stand there and stare, others coldly scavenging the grass and flowerbeds for some trace of Selena's spilled blood.

The paroxysm of grief that followed her death passed most Anglo Texans by—most of them, including me, had barely heard of her. But to the many, many Texans who, like Selena, were products of the centuries-deep hybrid heritage of the Texas and Mexican borderlands, her murder was as unexpected and unreal a crime as the assassination of President Kennedy had been a generation before.

The shock of Selena's death is likewise a historical event, a thing of the past, but she is still the focus of steady veneration. The last time I was in Corpus, I drove by her memorial, which is called Mirador de la Flor and whose centerpiece is a statue of the singer in three-quarter profile, looking out over the water of Corpus Christi Bay. Surrounding the statue, staring at it, taking pictures of it, setting flowers on it, were twenty or more teenage girls, born after the 1995 death of the Tejano singer the memorial commemorated. I thought it was close to a sure bet that one or two of them were named Selena.

"LADIES AND GENTLEMEN," SAID THE MODERATOR, A FRIENDLY- looking man in his early forties, wearing a dark blue suit and balancing a clipboard on his knee, "on behalf of the underwriters, the sponsors, and the producers, I welcome you to the 1990 Texas governor's debates."

You might not have guessed that this polished TV host was the same person who, as a child in Midland, had poisoned his sister's goldfish by pouring vodka into its bowl. Or who as a young—and then not-so-young—man was a snarky, aimless problem drinker who had once turned to one of his parents' friends at the dinner table and asked her, "So, what is sex like after fifty?"

But George W. Bush had quit drinking in 1986—more or less cold turkey, though with an assist from a slow-burning religious awakening. Now, in the second year of his father's presidency, he was the public face of a big-business baseball team and an obvious aspirant for political office. He had made a premature run for Congress in 1978, in the West Texas district where he had grown up. "Son," the aging former governor Allan Shivers warned him, "you can't win." Shivers was right. Bush's Democratic opponent, a state senator named Kent Hance, had triumphed in part by managing to slander Bush for the crime of having had an elite education on the East Coast. "While Kent Hance," the narrator of one of Hance's radio ads announced, "graduated from the University of Texas Law School, his opponent . . . get this, folks . . . was attending Harvard."

After serving in Congress, Hance began swimming with the Texas political tide and turned into a Republican. He was one of four Republican primary candidates in the debate that Bush was moderating that night. Among them was the eventual winner, Clayton Williams, who would be the eventual loser to Ann Richards. What is striking, watching that debate today, is the fact that none of those men arguing about abortion, education, and campaign finance reform would become governor of Texas. Only the moderator would.

Bush had thought about running for governor that year, but decided to bide his time. He didn't feel ready, especially when it came to facing a crowded field of primary opponents. As the president's son, he had celebrity to draw on but not much else. In his portfolio were a DUI, a failed congressional bid, and an oil company—named Arbusto (Spanish for "bush," but also, unfortunately, for "shrub")—that had cratered in the 1986 oil bust. But his position with the Rangers was providing him with executive experience and a means of road-testing himself as a public figure, since as an owner of the Rangers he was called upon to give speeches and talk to the media and knock around with the fans. It provided him with lots of money, too. To buy into the team, he had cobbled together an investment of just over $600,000. But after the citizens of Arlington—a city halfway between Dallas and Fort Worth—built the Rangers and their owners a gleaming new stadium at taxpayer expense, and after the team was sold to a new owner, Bush's initial buy-in multiplied twenty-five times to almost $15 million.

When he decided to run against Ann Richards, in 1994, his mother—from whom he had inherited his needling and direct sense of humor—played the role of Allan Shivers, who had died in 1985 and was no longer around to discourage the younger generation. "George," she told her son, "you can't win."

She was just acknowledging the apparently obvious. Ann Richards had turned out to be a popular governor; her approval ratings were at 60 percent. But one of the people who didn't believe she was indomitable was Karl Rove. The Denver-born, Austin-based Rove had been a proud Republican warrior nerd in his youth, and in his forties he still had a youthful, smooth-faced, crafty look that led Bush to nickname him Boy Genius. Also, he really

ANN RICHARDS
in 1992, during her memorable one term as Texas governor.

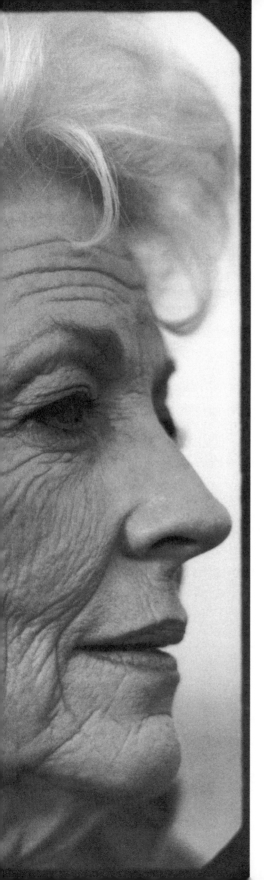

was a genius, a dazzling political strategist whose memory vaults were loaded with obscure political data—county-by-county vote tallies of ancient campaigns, names of long-forgotten candidates and ward bosses—reaching back to the days of William McKinley.

Rove had known the Bushes since 1973, when he had worked for George H. W. Bush when he was the chairman of the Republican National Committee. When he was twenty-nine, Rove had orchestrated the defeat of a venerable and long-serving Democratic incumbent, Babe Schwartz, an event so unexpected the *Galveston Daily News* ran a headline reading simply, "Island in Shock." Then he had helped Bill Clements regain the governorship from Mark White. ("We woke up every morning and got hammered," Mark McKinnon, who worked for White, recalled of Rove's blitzkrieg direct-mail campaign. "We would wake up with Karl's fist in our face.") He managed to help get a Republican, Tom Philips, elected chief justice of the formerly all-Democratic Texas Supreme Court—creating a breach that would turn the whole court Republican a decade later. And he was on hand to service the careers of Rick Perry, who would become the longest-serving governor in Texas history, and of Kay Bailey Hutchison, who became Texas's state treasurer in 1990 and then won a U.S. Senate seat in a blowout special election in 1993.

All these victories pointed to the idea that Texas was still a conservative state and was becoming even more so, and that a liberal governor like Ann Richards, who was running against the idea that Texans should be able to carry concealed weapons, was a historical anomaly, a mere detour on the state's inevitable march to total Republican domination. "Richards' facade looked big and imposing," Karl Rove remembered, "but the foundation was weak. . . . My analysis showed that there was enough swing in the electorate to pull off an upset."

Richards was vulnerable in other ways too, distracted by her sudden upgrade to national progressive icon—the straight-talking, bighearted, mordantly witty, white-haired grandmother whose mission was to end white males' domination of Texas and "let the people in." "There was a real strange sense," remembered Joe Holley, one of the governor's speechwriters, "that she almost didn't want to win."

You wouldn't have necessarily gotten that impression while watching her one debate with George W. Bush. She came across as articulate, experienced, compassionate, and complex. But she also looked tired, with a not-quite-below-the-radar disdain for the son of the man who had been born with a silver foot in his mouth, with whom she had to share this stage. Bush in turn was disciplined and polite, slipping out of questions about his business failures and his favored-son status in the National Guard during the Vietnam War to pound down on his carefully curated core issues: welfare reform, tort reform, education, and juvenile justice. "I had seen enough politics," he wrote later, "to know you can't really win a debate. You can only lose by saying something stupid or looking tired or nervous."

———— ★ ————

"I'VE SERVED WITH FOUR GOVERNORS," TEXAS'S POWERFUL and legendarily incendiary lieutenant governor, Bob Bullock, proclaimed two years after Bush won the 1994 election, "and this one here has the stuff to be president of the United States!"

Like George W. Bush, like Ann Richards, like Sam Houston, Bullock was a recovering alcoholic. But he was also bipolar, subject to surges of creative mania that had helped transform the comptroller's office, when he held that position, into a strikingly efficient operation that overhauled the state's musty financial life. He had a team of enforcers called "Bullock's Raiders" to collect delinquent taxes, and he had not one but two state airplanes at his disposal, useful when he wanted to fly to other states to study their tax-collecting policies or, less officially, to audit their debauched nightlife. He was the sort of "amateur gunslinger" that Ann Richards might have had in mind when she vetoed the concealed-carry law. Earlier in his career his pistol tended to fall out of his pocket when he was drunk, and fellow picnickers were advised to duck their heads if he decided to enjoy some impromptu al fresco target shooting. One night at the Quorum Club, a political hangout in Austin, he pulled a gun on a waiter and held the barrel against his head as he complained about the service.

He didn't care for lithium, his bipolar medicine, because "it took the edge off" his personality. He may have had a point, because his personality was all edge. But he did finally manage to go into rehab, sober up, enter into a stabilizing marriage, and distill his own once-raging political ambitions into a humble credo: "Do what's good for Texas." This included sprucing up the state cemetery (he didn't like the rundown look of his future resting place) and decreeing into being a state history museum bearing his name and statue. But the edge was still there. For example, once when he was hustling along bills in the Senate Chamber in his role as lieutenant governor, and had grown annoyed with a senator who kept agitating to speak, he finally put down his gavel and said, "The chair recognizes the crybaby from Waco."

Paul Hobby, the grandson of Oveta Culp Hobby and the son of former lieutenant governor Bill Hobby, had worked for Bullock, and he counseled George W. Bush about how to deal with him. "Turn the other cheek," he advised about the inevitable moment when Bullock would blow his lid over something or other. "It's just a temporary eruption. It's a sugar imbalance. It's whatever you want it to be. But don't take it personally."

And lo, it wasn't long before Bullock informed the new governor that he was "a cocky little motherfucker." Bush smiled in reply, the beginning of a beautiful friendship. The volatile old-guard Democrat and the new Republican governor had a mutual interest in not falling on their respective faces, and Bush's campaign themes of welfare reform, education, and so forth weren't that far off from an already agreed-upon Democratic agenda. Bush and Bullock and Speaker Peter Laney had breakfast every week and harmonized so well together that the governor's whole campaign program sluiced smoothly through the legislative pipeline, making Bullock's prediction that Bush had "the stuff to be president" more than just polite speculation.

As an Austin writer and parent in the back half of the 1990s, I often found myself at parties or panel discussions or school assemblies with George and Laura Bush. Our daughters and the Bush twins, Barbara and Jenna, met during their junior high years, hit it off, and became close friends. I first met their mother at an annual meeting of the Texas Institute of Letters, the writers' organization that had originally convened in 1936 at the Centennial Exposition's Hall of State, and that three years later passed over Katherine Anne Porter for its first fiction prize.

It seemed odd at first that the new Republican First Lady would show up—apparently out of innocent curiosity—at the annual gathering of the schlumpy and grumpy Texas literati. We didn't yet realize that in certain key ways she was one of us, a child of the Texas plains for whom reading had been both an adventure and a retreat, an activity that could simultaneously seize the imagination and stave off loneliness. She was a decade and a half away from publishing her memoir, *Spoken from the Heart*, but when I eventually read its early sections about growing up in Midland, it stirred up a Proustian storm of my own Texas memories: the summer car rides during which "in the heat my skin stuck to the upholstery until I would have to peel it off like a thick roll of sticky tape"; the sound of croaking frogs from nearby rain-filled depressions in the landscape that had once been buffalo wallows; the exotic thrill of a trip to San Antonio to see the Alamo and the live alligators that used to be part of the lobby decor of the Menger Hotel.

The statewide Texas Book Festival that Laura Bush founded was in its fifth year during the unreal presidential race of 2000, when the exceedingly close voter margins in Florida created such chaos on election night that the race ultimately had to be determined by a controversial 5–4 Supreme Court vote a month later. Three nights after the inconclusive election, a party for the book festival was held in the Governor's Mansion. Outside the mansion, news vans and reporters who had come to Austin from across the world to report the results of the election were marooned until it could be decided.

But nobody was as marooned as George W. Bush, who had thought it was all over when Al Gore called to concede on election night, only to have Gore call again and retract his concession. Normally, Bush operated on a wide range of modes. He could do gravitas, along with heckling insouciance and startling candor, and his jokes could be so deliciously bad that you had to believe they were part of his overall strategy of wanting to seem, in his own famous malapropism, "misunderestimated." ("I was a history major," I once heard him say as president while chatting with a recent college graduate. "Now I'm a history maker!")

That night, though, the usual looseness felt a bit forced, and the bandaged boil that had appeared on his right cheek hinted at the volcanic tensions under the surface of a man who still did not know whether he was going to be president of the United States. Things were much better at a Governor's Mansion Christmas party a month later. He was now the president-elect, and aides were handing him notes from prospective cabinet members as a band called Rotel and the Hot Tomatoes played in the reception room. The boil was gone, and his face was sweaty from dancing with my high-school-age daughter, Dorothy, who had just taught him a dance of her own invention called "Circumnavigate That Ass."

He stood there talking to a group of us, in front of the big Robert Onderdonk painting of the fall of the Alamo, about his recent excruciatingly polite sixteen-minute conversation with Al Gore, during which Bush had said, "Mr. Vice President, I just want you to know you're a tough competitor," and Gore had frostily replied, "Thank you very much."

The history of the moment we were taking in was amplified by the history everywhere around us, in this building that had been the residence of James Hogg and Ma and Pa Ferguson and Ann Richards, that John Connally had come home to, still a bit short of breath after being shot in the lung by Lee Harvey Oswald. The place where Lizzie Davis, furious about what she believed was the betrayal of her husband by Ulysses Grant's Reconstruction government, had taken down the president's portrait and kicked her foot through it. The place where Sam Houston, after receiving Lincoln's offer of troops to lead an army against his fellow Texans to save the Union, had hesitated, wrestling with his conscience and his abilities, before tossing the letter into the fireplace.

★

THE NEXT TIME I SAW GEORGE W. BUSH WAS EIGHT AND HALF months later. Laura had just opened the inaugural National Book Festival gala and was hosting a reception at the White House the next day for the Texans who were participating in it. It was a Sunday, and what I remember most from that morning is standing off to the side in the West Sitting Room, listening to the president make small talk with a cluster of old friends. In a few minutes he would be called to the Rose Garden, where he was scheduled to flip a coin to determine which NFL team would receive the kickoff in the season's opening game. But at the moment there wasn't all that much to do, and as he sat there in his shirt sleeves talking about a Red River boundary dispute between Texas and Oklahoma while he was governor, he grinned at Barney, his Scottish terrier, who was sitting at his feet, gnawing away at a chew toy. Being president of the United States, it seemed to me at that moment—on September 9, 2001—was a pretty easy job.

Three days later Bush was standing in the smoldering, twisted ruins of the World Trade Center, his arm draped around the shoulders of a New York firefighter named Bob Beckwith, speaking through a bullhorn to the first responders around him and to the world. "I can hear you!" he said, when some of the firefighters called out that they were having trouble making out what he was saying. "The rest of the world hears you! And the people who knocked these buildings down will hear all of us soon!"

George W. Bush at the ruins of the World Trade Center, channeling his not-so-inner Texan at the most critical moment of his presidency.

Was it a Texas moment, an example of what Carl Sandburg meant when he wrote that the state features a blend of valor and swagger? Bush was a sometimes affected but mostly real Texan. I don't know whether he was consciously channeling that particular identity that day, but if you were looking for it, you could hear it in his accent, see it in his posture, sense it in some heady aura of destiny that would help drive the nation into endless wars in Afghanistan and Iraq.

And it wasn't as if Bush hadn't drawn on his Texas bona fides before. In 1999, when he was governor, the Texas golf legend Ben Crenshaw had asked him for a favor. Crenshaw was the captain of America's Ryder Cup team, and he wanted Bush to give them a pep talk after the European team had opened up a wide lead and victory seemed like a distant prospect. On the last, desperate day of the match, Bush appeared and read them Travis's letter from the Alamo, the immortal "Victory or Death" letter, the "I shall never surrender or retreat" letter that every Texan learns by heart in seventh grade.

A British reporter for the *Telegraph* was shocked by the behavior the governor inspired in the American golfers. He found their confidence appalling. The players, he wrote, "their heads full of the Alamo, were high on the worst kind of patriotism, the chest-beating sort."

It was nothing short of "ugly jingoism," the reporter fumed. Maybe, but Travis's words—written 163 years earlier from the headquarters room of a crumbling Spanish mission on the cusp of an epic defeat—still had the power to deliver an unlikely victory.

DAVY CROCKETT'S
FAIRY PALACE

YOU DON'T THINK ABOUT WHALES WHEN YOU THINK about Texas, but they're here, cruising through the waters of the sacred tidelands—humpback whales, fin whales, sperm whales, and even occasionally sleek, two-toned, high-finned orcas. Every once in a while a pod of these cold-water predators better known as killer whales surfaces in the Texas Gulf, astonishing the tarpon fishermen and offshore oil-rig roustabouts who think such creatures are found only in the waters of the Pacific Northwest or of Antarctica.

Imagine a humpback whale erupting out of the warm blue Texas waters on a spring day, twisting and rolling in the air and landing full on its back, its white-tipped pectoral fins adding a final percussive slap as it sinks again beneath the surface. And in the air above this fifty-foot-long, forty-ton animal, flying through the dissipating molecules of its exhaled breath, is a three-inch-long ruby-throated hummingbird that weighs less than a nickel. On its annual migration from Central America along the great Central Flyway, which leads right over Texas, it has been thrumming its little wings nonstop across the entire Gulf of Mexico, its heart beating 1,260 times a minute as it travels twenty miles a day.

It will arrive in Texas about the same time that the whooping cranes at the Aransas National Wildlife Refuge, near Corpus Christi, start to leave on their annual migration to their nesting grounds in Canada. They are the tallest birds in North America, five feet high, with a span of seven feet between the black-tipped edges of their white wings. Texas is the winter home of the last wild flock of a species that once numbered in the tens of thousands but—as I write this—has only a little over four hundred closely monitored and carefully protected individuals.

The naturalist and artist John James Audubon, who painted and described the whooping crane, visited Texas in 1837, the year after the Texian army's defeat of Santa Anna. He collected as scientific souvenirs a few of the Mexican skulls that were still lying unburied on the San Jacinto battlefield, and he visited Sam Houston in the new national capital on Buffalo Bayou that bore his name. The "President's mansion" was a log house, crammed with trunks and paper and camp beds resting on a muddy dirt floor. When Audubon met Houston, he detected "a scowl in the expression of his eyes that was forbidding and disagreeable." Nevertheless, the president was cordial, inviting the naturalist and his party "to drink grog with him, which we did, wishing success to the new republic."

Audubon was unimpressed by the filth and disorder of that new republic's capital—"shanties, cargoes of hogsheads, barrels, etc. were spread about the landing; and Indians drunk and hallooing were stumbling about in the mud in every direction." But even though he had lost twelve pounds on this expedition, and even though he was plagued by mosquito bites and his legs were swollen, he was not immune to the beauty of the country surrounding Galveston Bay.

"Ah, my dear friend," he wrote home, "would that you were here just now to see the Snipes innumerable, the Blackbirds, the Gallinules, and the Curlews that surround us;—that you could listen as I now do, to the delightful notes of the Mocking-bird, pouring forth his soul in melody as the glorious orb of day is fast descending toward the western horizon;—that you could gaze on the Great Herons which, after spreading their broad wings, croak aloud as if doubtful regarding the purpose of our visit to these shores!"

Audubon's observations are just one reminder of the obvious fact that the human history of Texas is part of an infinitely broader chronicle, that while Spanish friars were building missions in the East Texas forests and buffalo soldiers were fighting Comanches and Apaches during the last years of the Indian wars, there were also ruby-throated hummingbirds beating doggedly across the ocean and snow-white whooping cranes filling the skies and, of course, great buffalo herds—on the eve of their near extermination—spreading across the plains and the prairies.

THESE WERE THE SORTS OF THOUGHTS THAT OCCUPIED MY mind recently in Lubbock when I was in Mackenzie Park watching the inhabitants of the city's local prairie dog town. A number of communities in West Texas feature a living prairie dog exhibit like this one, a tourist attraction that pays homage in a low-grade sort of way to the once-boundless creature fecundity of old Texas. Over the decades I've spent a lot of hours standing at the cinderblock borders of these urban prairie dog towns. I'm fascinated by the animals' eternal vigilance and by their complex vocabulary of barks and chirps and yips, a warning system that researchers believe is precise enough to distinguish not just specific predators—hawks, coyotes, snakes—but also subtle visual differences within species. When, for instance, Coronado passed through the high plains in 1541, the prairie dogs were already familiar with human beings, but when they were standing sentinel they would have had to come up with a new prairie dog word to describe the danger presented by a man atop a horse, an animal they had never seen before.

Lubbock was on the itinerary of a sort of wrapping-up tour I had devised for myself. Finished with the chronological tyranny of this book, I was at large in Texas in the best way a Texan can be: driving aimlessly, indulging in random thoughts while listening to a self-selected Lone Star playlist. In this part of the country, the playlist was heavy on Bob Wills and Buddy Holly and, of course, Roy Orbison. Also the Flatlanders, the Lubbock supergroup comprising Joe Ely, Butch Hancock, and Jimmie Dale Gilmore. It was Gilmore's rendition on a solo album of "I'm So Lonesome I Could Cry" that I kept playing again and again. His voice was so beautifully creaky, so vulnerable and wary—"Did you ever see a night so long / When time goes crawlin' by?"—that it seemed no accident that he had grown up in one of the cities of these endless, uncaring plains.

Earlier, I had been up in the Panhandle, delighted to receive an invitation to visit the JA, the immense ranch that Charles and Molly Goodnight and John and Cornelia Adair had built in the Palo Duro country after the Comanches were driven out. From the front gallery of the elegant, sprawling ranch house, I could see the plains across which Mackenzie had pursued Quanah and his people into the canyon for that last, heartbreaking fight. If you looked at satellite images of the floor of the canyon, I was told, you could still make out the circular indentations where the Comanche and Kiowa tipis once stood. But to encounter ancient traces of things closer at hand, I just needed to walk around to the back of the house, where the juniper-log cabin that Charlie Goodnight built with his own hands in the 1880s still stood just yards away from the commodious modern kitchen.

When I drove through Canyon, a few miles to the west, I pulled over in a quiet residential neighborhood and turned off the ignition in front of a home on 20th Street. It was a gray prairie-style house from early in the last century, with a deep front porch and a dormer room projecting from the roofline. The dormer had a set of white-framed windows facing east. This was the room that Georgia O'Keeffe had rented in the house of a fellow faculty member at West Texas State Normal College when she was a young art instructor, and those were the windows she looked out through, staring at the horizon, watching the light coming on the plains. "It is absurd the way I love this country," she wrote.

I thought of Georgia O'Keeffe's untried love for Texas as I stood at the Horsehead Crossing of the Pecos River in Crane County, southwest of Odessa, a few days later. Her initial enthrallment with the state might have faded fast had she been with Rip Ford and Robert Neighbors when they were blazing a wagon route to El Paso in 1849, or if she had been a jostled passenger on the Butterfield Stage a decade later, or been a waddie with Charles Goodnight and Oliver Loving as they were opening a cattle trail to New Mexico in 1866. The river at the Horsehead Crossing was narrow, greenish, and shallow, a vivid strip of color against the mute desert palette. Here, near where Goodnight and Loving had lost hundreds of cattle as they stampeded for water after a dry three-day drive, I listened to "Little Joe the Wrangler," the cowboy song about a vagrant kid from an abusive home—"a little Texas stray and all alone"—who begs to join a cattle outfit and ends up getting "smashed to a pulp" in a stampede. It's a tender song, but as harsh and inexorable as a Cormac McCarthy novel.

———————— ★ ————————

NORTH TO ODESSA, EAST ON I-20, AND PAST THE TOWN OF Sweetwater. It was the wrong time of year for the annual Sweetwater Rattlesnake Roundup. Just as well. I had attended this strange and disturbing event many years earlier, and my dreams were still troubled by the memory of watching the local Jaycees stretch out the snakes they had captured during the year on a chopping block and strike off their heads with a machete blow. In Texas, rattlesnakes were still somehow immune from any animal-rights considerations granted to other species, still the only creatures I could think of that were regarded as so irredeemably evil that they were subject to public execution.

At Sweetwater, I left the interstate and headed northeast to Archer

City, where fewer than two thousand people lived. But thanks to the novel *The Last Picture Show*, and the movie made from it, the town is unshakably emblematic of the dreary and isolated rural West Texas of the mid-twentieth century. *The Last Picture Show*, one of Larry McMurtry's early novels, is set in a lightly fictionalized version of Archer City called Thalia in the book and Anarene in the movie. This was where McMurtry grew up, starved for any sort of distraction or any hint of transcendence. ("People have no idea," he once said, "how empty the world is out here. They don't understand its bleakness.")

The Archer City of McMurtry's youth was, the writer remembered, "a bookless town, in a bookless part of the state—when I stepped into a university library, at age eighteen, the whole of the world's literature lay before me unread, a country as vast, as promising, and, so far as I knew, as trackless as the West must have seemed to the first white men who looked upon it."

McMurtry—as much a Texas bibliophile as the previous century's Swante Palm—cured his hometown of its booklessness in spectacular fashion. After the success of *Lonesome Dove*, he all but took over the one-street downtown of Archer City, turning vacated storefronts that had once housed businesses like automobile dealerships into colossal bookstores. At its peak, Booked Up—as the enterprise was known—expanded to four bookstores—not a bad showing in a one–Dairy Queen town.

It was no longer such a thriving business. McMurtry's dreams of establishing a "book town" that would become a worldwide destination foundered on the shores of Texas reality, and in 2012 he held an auction, sold off 300,000 of his 450,000 volumes, and closed down all but one of the bookstores.

But it was a noble and eccentric experiment, and as I finished browsing at the remaining store—Booked Up #1—and drove out of town on Main Street, I thought about the last time I was here, back in about 2010, when McMurtry's book town was in full flower. It was in August, a West Texas afternoon at its worst—probably 110 degrees in the full glare of the sun. Nobody was out in the heat except for one person. Larry McMurtry, Texas's greatest living author, dressed in a T-shirt and shorts, seventy-something years old, was pushing a wheelbarrow full of books from one of his stores to the next, filling in, volume by volume, the cultural emptiness that had once oppressed him as a child.

————————— ★ —————————

SOUTH OF DALLAS, I MERGED ONTO I-35, LISTENING TO WILLIE

Nelson sing "Uncloudy Day" and "Blue Eyes Crying in the Rain" and "Angel

Flying Too Close to the Ground." It struck me that one of the keys to Willie's (nobody calls him anything but Willie) enduring tenor voice is the fact that it also flies too close to the ground. It never soars—it just skims along at contour level. The way it saunters unconcernedly behind the beat leaves listeners in mild suspense and can short-circuit unprepared musicians. ("Don't get too caught up in what he's doing," one sideman cautions, "because he'll take you up the creek and dump you.")

I was still listening to his songs seventy miles later when I drove past the little town of Abbott, population 300, give or take, where Willie Nelson was born one momentous day in 1933. He was five years old when he made his performing debut, standing on a flatbed truck at a family picnic a few miles outside town and reciting a poem that he had written himself.

> What are you looking at me for?
> I ain't got nothin' to say.
> If you don't like the looks of me,
> You can look some other way.

———————— ★ ————————

I SPENT ONE NIGHT AT HOME IN AUSTIN BEFORE SETTING OFF on the road again. Pulling out of my driveway, looking west, I noticed the residential street rising and falling toward the jumbled hills on the other side of Lake Austin (the dammed-up Colorado River) several blocks away. One of the streets that ran parallel to the river was Balcones Drive, named for the word that Spanish explorers used to describe those cracked upthrust pediments of limestone, the "balconies" that marked the edge of the great Edwards Plateau. There are dividing lines and transition zones like this all over Texas, places that provide a vivid snapshot of how geology determines history. My Austin neighborhood was one, the border between fertile blackland prairie and the hard, thin-soiled country that once beckoned pilgrims to the High Plains and the mountains beyond: the place where the West begins.

A few houses away from ours, at the end of a cul-de-sac, was the official residence of the chancellor of the University of Texas System. The current occupant was Admiral William McRaven, who before coming to UT had been the head of the U.S. Special Operations Command and was the architect of Operation Neptune Spear, the 2011 raid on the Al-Qaeda compound in Abbottabad, Pakistan. Next door to him lived Mike Judge, the writer and director of the movies *Office Space* and *Idiocracy* and the television series *Silicon Valley*. Judge was also the creator of *King of the Hill*, the animated television series whose protagonist, Hank Hill, was the purest distillation of a

Texas everyman ever to appear on any screen. It might be a worthy historical observation about the big tent of Texas identity, or it might just be a meaningless factoid, but either way I thought I'd point out that the man who oversaw the death of Osama Bin Laden once lived next door in Texas to the man who created Beavis and Butthead.

In Austin, I drove past the Capitol but didn't stop. The great granite building would be mostly empty except for tourists and seventh-grade Texas history students on field trips. Most of them would be gazing up at the dizzying interior dome or checking out the history artworks in the South Foyer: the full-length portrait of Davy Crockett on one side and the painting of Sam Houston accepting Santa Anna's surrender at San Jacinto on the other; and the statues of Houston and Stephen Austin by Elisabet Ney guarding the entrance to the rotunda. There would be nobody in the Senate and House Chambers except for the visitors whose curiosity took them that far down the corridors, where they could study Henry McArdle's gigantic history paintings of the Alamo and San Jacinto.

The legislature was not in session. It had already fulfilled its constitutional responsibility of meeting every two years, and unless a new special session was called it would be another year before it resumed its biennial lawmaking. The current governor, Greg Abbott, was a former attorney general who had spent much of his life in a wheelchair. When he was twenty-six, he was paralyzed below the waist when a tree fell on him while he was jogging. Abbott's predecessor was Rick Perry, who stepped up from his post as lieutenant governor when George W. Bush became president. He served as governor for a historically long time—more than fourteen years. Perry had presidential aspirations, and as a conservative Republican governor with leading-man looks from the second most populous state, it seemed for a while as if the planets might align for him. But his campaigns in 2012 and 2016 were both misfires. Then, curiously, what might have been a rock-bottom moment for another out-of-work politician turned out to be something of a reboot. In 2016, after he had dropped out of the race, he appeared as a contestant on *Dancing with the Stars*. There have been a lot of strange moments in Texas history—the Pig War, Lillie Langtry being presented with Judge Roy Bean's pet bear—but I'm not sure anything quite compares with former governor Rick Perry stepping out onto the dance floor in a black western-cut suit with white oak-leaf-cluster appliqués, handing a corn dog to his dance partner, and doing his best to perform a cha-cha to a song called "God Bless Texas." It was winningly godawful, and a few months later Donald Trump nominated Perry to be his secretary of energy.

By now, the Republican dominance of Texas was a completed thing. No Democrat had held statewide office since Bob Bullock was reelected lieutenant governor in 1994. And the state's current political agenda was to steer Texas straight to the far-right horizon. One of the reigning issues in the 2017 legislative session was captured in Senate Bill 6, which would have brought the force of law to the effort to make transgender people use public bathrooms that corresponded to the sex on their birth certificates. It passed in the Senate, but Speaker Joe Straus, a beleaguered but adroit Texas moderate, calmly saw to its suffocation in a special session.

There was also the sanctuary cities bill, Senate Bill 4, which, unlike the "bathroom bill," was passed into law. Its specific purpose was to require often-reluctant local law enforcement agencies to cooperate with federal authorities in deporting undocumented immigrants. But it was also part of a broader resurgence of anti-immigrant thought that animated the conservative Republican base of white rural and suburban Texans.

Texas had come into existence because in the 1820s, Mexico had an immigration problem and was searching for a way to stop the unregulated flood of Anglo settlers fleeing misfortune and looking for new opportunities in a new country. Now the reverse was happening, had been happening for many decades. Even though illegal border crossings were in decline, because of a constellation of factors related to the American and Mexican economies, a renewed sense of alarm had been steadily kindled on the Texas side of the Rio Grande, a mind-set of imminent threat that could be followed back to the Vásquez and Woll invasions of 1842, to the cross-border raids of Juan Cortina, and to the violence of the Mexican Revolution of 1910.

An element of the new threat climate was an old suspicion: that Mexican and Central American immigrants were here for the purpose of stealing American jobs and freeloading on American social services. But there were also fears of a more recent vintage, brewed out of post-9/11 anxiety: cartel violence, drug smuggling, human trafficking, terrorism. All this was why the sanctuary cities bill passed; why so many Texas politicians were enthusiastically on board with the priorities of the Trump administration, which included the extremity of first separating children from parents who had brought them to the border to escape Central American violence and then housing them in repurposed Walmarts and tent cities; why immigration control was relentlessly evolving into a militarized enterprise, a web of federal and state agencies building walls and fences, manning surveillance towers, operating gunboats, drones, and surveillance blimps. And why Texas showed a new willingness to turn its ever-complicated but living border with Mexico into a stone-cold barrier.

ON THE PLAYLIST AS I LEFT AUSTIN: ASLEEP AT THE WHEEL,
Townes Van Zandt, Lyle Lovett, Beyoncé, Selena, Narciso Martínez, Marcia
Ball, and the two unrelated Joplins, Scott and Janis. I saw Janis Joplin only
once in person, at an impromptu concert in an open meadow south of
Austin. I was close enough to the stage to make out the feathers she was
wearing in her hair, to see the Southern Comfort bottle she held in one
hand as she sang. "Now I want y'all to listen to a new song from somebody
you're going to be hearing a lot about," she told us that summer night. The
songwriter she was talking about was a Texas native named Kris Kristof-
ferson, and the song—the first time any of us had heard it—was "Me and
Bobby McGee."

She sang with uninhibited performance joy, but also with a detectable
vibe of hurt and defiance. She had grown up in Port Arthur, an unhappy,
tormented high school beatnik with severe acne but with a raw, confident
singing voice that amazed her and her friends. She developed something
of a reputation as a singer at the University of Texas, but she dropped out
and left Austin after only a year. One of the reasons might have been a
fraternity-sponsored "Ugliest Man on Campus" contest. Somebody had
cruelly drummed up write-in votes on her behalf.

Just before hitchhiking to San Francisco, she wrote and recorded a song
called "So Sad to Be Alone." Anyone who has ever been the least bit impatient with Janis Joplin's cosmic indiscipline and raucousness should listen
to it. It isn't much of a song, but it may be one of the most heartbreaking
pleas for human connection ever recorded. Janis accompanies herself on
autoharp and sings in a voice that uncharacteristically never breaks into a
caterwauling chorus or ventures beyond a beaten-down and pitiable register: "The dusty road calls you," it goes, "You walk to the end. / It's sad,
so sad to be alone."

She came back to Texas after a year and a half in California. She was
by then an eighty-eight-pound heroin addict whose concerned friends
had pooled their money for bus fare to send her home to her parents in
Port Arthur. She stayed in Texas long enough to enroll at Lamar Tech, to
straighten up her life a bit, to get dumped by a fiancé, to increase the power
of her singing. Then it was back to San Francisco and drugs and alcohol and
stardom, which is roughly the point at which I caught up with her on that
night outside Austin. It would have been July 1970, three months before she
overdosed in Hollywood in a room at the Landmark Motor Hotel, her nose
broken from falling facedown on the floor, her clenched hand holding $4.50.

I MEANDERED NORTHEAST FROM AUSTIN, 150 MILES TO

Huntsville, the home place of Sam Houston, the town where the Texas news icon Dan Rather got his start in journalism, and the end-of-life location for the 361 death row inmates who "rode the thunderbolt" back in the days of the electric chair—and of the over 500 more who have been executed by lethal injection after the chair, "Old Sparky," was retired in 1964. Texas has rarely been troubled by second thoughts about the death penalty. It executes nearly five times as many people as Oklahoma, the next most lethal state. Partly this is because state appellate judges in Texas are elected and consequently aware that their political fortunes are subject to the approval of a historically reliable law-and-order electorate. Even Ann Richards, the most liberal Texas governor since Thomas Campbell, knew where not to tread. ("I recommend," a campaign adviser wrote in an internal memo during her first gubernatorial race, "that your response to any questions regarding this issue should be that as governor you would uphold the death of juveniles and mentally retarded killers.")

Death row is located in the Texas Department of Correction's Polunsky Unit, about forty miles east of Huntsville, but when it comes time for execution the condemned men (and sometimes women) are transported to the Walls Unit of the Texas State Penitentiary, which occupies a massive footprint only a few blocks from Huntsville's quaint downtown.

The redbrick fortress of the Walls has been much modified and expanded since the days when John Wesley Hardin debated the rights of women and studied law there, and when a demoralized Satanta made his suicidal leap from the second floor of the prison hospital, but it's still a jarring apparition.

At the Texas Prison Museum, on the side of the freeway, I stopped to take a look at Old Sparky. The chair was disturbingly attractive, high backed, made of solid oak. The convicts who built it in the 1920s took obvious pride in its craftsmanship, putting it together not with nails but with wooden pegs, staining it in a way that brought forth the warmth of the wood. Even the leather cuffs that bound the condemned man's hands and feet in place during his electrocution seemed like fashion flourishes. ("Have a seat, please," these men were told by the warden when it was time for those cuffs to be strapped on.)

Also in the museum was one of the three crude bullet-proof helmets that Fred Carrasco had demanded that the prison machine shop manufacture for his escape during the 1974 siege that took place at the Walls. It looked like something from a steampunk nightmare, a cube of dented steel with an eye slit that gave it an expression of inhuman scrutiny. Compared to Fred Carrasco's helmet, Old Sparky was a lovingly wrought object of beauty.

Before I left Huntsville, I stopped at Sam Houston's grave. His monument was designed by the Italian-born sculptor Pompeo Coppini, who lived and worked in San Antonio for most of the first half of the twentieth century, and whose statues and memorials—including the Cenotaph in front of the Alamo—are liberally scattered across Texas. I'm generally an admirer of Coppini's work, but this elaborate grave marker, which features a bas-relief of the great conqueror triumphantly waving his hat astride an ill-proportioned horse, is not his best. The most memorable thing about it is the carved marble inscription at its base, a quotation from Houston's mentor, Andrew Jackson: "The World Will Take Care of Houston's Fame."

Hard to argue with that prophecy, especially when you drive south from Huntsville on Interstate 45, past the sixty-seven-foot-high statue of Sam Houston on the side of the highway and toward the city that bears his name—the fourth most populous city in the United States, whose Consolidated Metropolitan Statistical Area covers 9,444 square miles, an expanse larger than New Jersey, and is inhabited by 2.3 million people speaking 145 languages.

The San Jacinto battlefield is part of the immense Greater Houston area. So is Allen's Landing, the place on the banks of Buffalo Bayou that John and Augustus Allen had proposed in 1837 as the port for the city they planned to develop, which would bear Sam Houston's name and be the new capital of the Republic of Texas. The Allen brothers laid out the town and got busy selling lots and lobbying the new government to move the capital from Columbia. "No place in Texas more healthy," they claimed, which was false. They also claimed that Buffalo Bayou was a perfectly navigable path to the sea, also false. Some people saw through the hype. "A splendid map of the city," one skeptic wrote, "was carried on the wings of the wind to distant places to catch in time the greedy speculator and allure the uninitiated."

Had the Allen brothers lived roughly a century and a half later, they might have had corner suites in downtown Houston at 1400 Smith Street, the fifty-floor office tower that once was the headquarters of the Enron Corporation. Enron began life as a company that transmitted natural gas and ended up as a company that sold air. It charged into an era of competitive greed by inventing dubious new horizons of business creativity, shifting from relatively tangible energy contracts to an array of inscrutable "derivatives" with which it could buy and sell and speculate in coal and electricity, broadband communications, and even the very weather of the planet. Profits were imaginatively inflated, and losses were dumped into splintering companies that were created for the purpose of keeping any bad news off Enron's books. Of course it couldn't go on like that forever, and by 2001, when its stock price had fallen from $90 a share to less than $1, Enron collapsed in an earth-shattering bankruptcy that sent many of its executives to prison and also took down its once-venerable accounting company, Arthur Andersen.

I stopped for lunch at a banh mi place on the other side of downtown, in a strip mall within sight of the former Enron building. Houston has almost 150,000 Vietnamese American residents, part of a surging international population that makes it one of the most ethnically diverse cities in the United States. The noontime rush made it seem as if almost half that population was in the restaurant with me—young Asian men and women in business suits and surgical scrubs on their lunch breaks from nearby office buildings and hospitals. It did not seem that long ago, and indeed wasn't that long ago, that I was interviewing Vietnamese refugees at a government resettlement site in the Houston suburb of Missouri City. These were the "boat people," who had fled their country after the fall of Saigon and had endured storms, hunger, and pirate atrocities before—if they were lucky—being rescued by a freighter and delivered to the bewildering safety of Texas. I remember how dazed and thin those people looked, how a grown son carried his aged mother on his back, speaking softly and reassuringly to her in Vietnamese. A young boy who had been given a can of pink Play-Doh was modeling a water buffalo on the facility's concrete steps. Now, I reckoned, he might be a prosperous paterfamilias, the owner of a restaurant or a fleet of shrimp boats or a busy fish market along the shore of Galveston Bay in Seabrook. He would have arrived in Houston just in time to learn English, to make a new start, to take advantage of that old billboard promising business cards in eight hours.

In other words, he would be a Texan, just like all the immigrants before him to this outsized state that sits at the center of the nation but stands consciously apart from it. People viewing Texas from the outside have always recognized that there is something different about it, not just in its expanse but in its attitude also, in its annoying, ineradicable mythic presumption. But it's hard to live here and not feel, just a little, that presumption stirring inside you. So many kinds of people have fought over the geography of Texas for so long, and competed for their places in its ever-changing culture, that there is a kind of harmony of conflict, a hard-earned conviction that the word "Texan" belongs to you as righteously as it does to anyone else.

WHEN I BROKE OUT OF THE HOUSTON TRAFFIC, I DROVE WEST
on Highway 90 toward Fayette County and the painted churches built by
Czech immigrants after they began coming to Texas in the 1840s. I stopped
at the site of the mostly vanished town of Praha—the Czech spelling of
Prague—to visit St. Mary's Church of the Assumption, completed in 1895.

It was a clear late-spring afternoon on the Texas prairie, and the white
steeple of the church was exquisitely backlit by the cloudless blue sky. In
front of the church, to the left, was a much smaller structure, a stone shrine
honoring the Boys of Praha, the young men, representing an entire generation of a town that had less than a hundred residents, who were killed
during a twelve-month span in World War II.

The church was an austere gothic structure from the outside, but when
I walked through its doors I was met with a blast of color. St. Mary's was
crowded with brightly rendered religious statuary and Stations of the Cross
figures, but what really drew my eye was the warm blue of the painted
sky overhead on the vaulted tongue-and-groove ceiling. There were panels
depicting vines and flowering plants and, above the altar, a midair convocation of three angels surrounding a radiant hovering cross. This was the work
of a Swiss-born artist named Godfrey Flury, who was married in this church
shortly after he finished painting it.

Homesick Texas Czechs established places like this to remind them of
the ornate churches in their distant homeland. Once, during a visit to the
Czech Republic, I stood in the church in the little village of Brusperk, near
the larger municipality of Frýdek-Místek, where my own Czech ancestors—
many generations deep—had been married and buried. The church was
every bit as vibrant as St. Mary's, and I realized today how consoling it must
have been for those immigrants—fleeing oppression or chasing dreams in
the United States—to kneel in one of these pews and remember home in a
brilliant suffusion of sacred color.

The painted churches reminded me that there were other paintings I
wanted to see again, specifically, the 4,000-year-old art of the Pecos Canyonlands, the fading rock-shelter murals of shamanic creatures and secret rituals
that had been no more perplexing to those unknown people than the depictions of Jesus and Mary were to the immigrant Czechs. But those canyons
were far away to the west, three hundred miles, and there were many other
Texas things closer at hand to see for the first time or to revisit.

I wouldn't have minded reprising the bike ride along the Mission Trail in
San Antonio that I had taken several years before with Larry Wright, when

he was working on his book *God Save Texas* and I was working on this one. We had started at the southernmost of the five missions, San Francisco de la Espada, and pedaled our way up the chain—to San Juan Capistrano, to Concepción, to San José—until we were in the heart of San Antonio and in front of Mission San Antonio de Valero, the Alamo. Standing in Alamo Plaza that summer day, eating the Mexican snow cones known as *raspas,* I had the same sense of wonder I had always had in front of this ancient blood-soaked edifice. Tourists were clopping by in horse-drawn carriages and wending in and out of the Ripley's Believe or Not! Museum and other carnival attractions that had taken over the block of latter-day buildings where the west wall of the mission once stood, where Travis had written his "Victory or Death" letter in his command headquarters. Big plans were under way to try to bring some semblance of historical coherence and respect to this venerable site, but the plans were inevitably contentious because the Alamo had by now been the bewildering urban centerpiece of San Antonio longer than it had been a Spanish mission or a Texian fort. (The level of confusion about the Alamo can be summed up by the reaction of my three-year-old granddaughter when she saw it for the first time: "Is that Davy Crockett's fairy palace?")

ALSO ON MY TO-DO LIST: I WANTED TO RIDE THE LOS EBANOS ferry, still hand operated, which crossed the Rio Grande near McAllen. I wanted to backtrack to the east to see the bucolic old inland port of Jefferson on the Red River. It had been many years since I had crossed the border at Eagle Pass and driven downriver on the Mexican side to see the old mission of San Juan Bautista and the presidio of Guerrero, which was the genesis of the Texas missions and the staging area for Santa Anna's thrust across the Rio Grande to put down the rebellion in Texas. I wanted to see that crucial place again. And though I wasn't as young as I was when I climbed to the highest point in Texas, the 8,749-foot summit of Guadalupe Peak, I thought I could make it again if I took it slow and brought plenty of water.

And as long as I was in a climbing mood, why not drive to Big Bend National Park and hike once again in the Chisos Mountains, which rise like a massive broken castle almost eight thousand feet from the floor of the Chihuahuan Desert. When you trek to the summit of the Chisos and stare out beyond the South Rim, you are facing the most magnificent view in Texas— an undulating series of desert mountains like frozen ocean waves that reach past the Rio Grande and endlessly deep into Mexico.

Then there were the petroglyphs at Hueco Tanks in the desert east of El Paso, and the site of the Taovaya village on the Red River, where the

Comanches and Norteños had forted up and driven away the Spanish forces trying to avenge the massacre of the priests at San Saba. And I had forgotten to write about Babe Didrikson Zaharias, the Olympic gold medalist in multiple categories and the greatest female golfer in the world, who, in addition to mastering every possible sport, had won a prize for her sewing at the 1931 Texas State Fair. There was a museum in Beaumont showcasing her accomplishments that I should see. I should also visit the Sam Rayburn Museum in Bonham, as well as a hundred other museums and battlefields and archives and barbecue places and Mexican restaurants and dance halls and swimming holes and acequias and river crossings where old wagon ruts were embedded in the limestone.

It was too much. Texas was too large, too old. It was impossible to see one thing, to bring into focus one period or person in its history, without having the anxious feeling that you were missing a galaxy of other moments and personalities.

So I gave up and settled on just one thing I wanted to see before I drove home to Austin. I had been there before, but wasn't sure I could find it again. It was a solitary live oak tree by the side of a county road south of San Antonio, just off Interstate 35 beyond the city's outer loop. After a few false turns and a phone call to a historian friend, I located it again and parked the car on the shoulder of the empty two-lane road on whose edge it sat.

Years ago, somebody had told me what it was. I would never have been able to discern it by myself. It was just a kind of scar, much healed over, in the trunk of an old tree. No different, really, from any accidental gouge that might have been inflicted on this live oak in the hundreds of years it had been growing here.

The tree stood next to a modern road, but it was an ancient road, the Camino Real, that it had once marked. I could make out the overgrown, contoured traces of that old byway a few yards away. The scar in the tree was no accident of nature. It was a cross carved centuries ago by a Spanish friar on one of the many entradas across the unmapped lands of Tejas.

It was remarkable to me that it was still here, still pointing the way, still registering a moment of long-ago prayer or idle carving. But it could not last long. It was fading away, as our contemporary marks on the landscape will, as the words of this book will. Like everything that now seems present and visible but is steadily being lost to the engulfing past, it was one more vestige of the Texas that used to be.

ACKNOWLEDGMENTS

WHEN DAVID HAMRICK, THE DIRECTOR OF THE UNIVER-
sity of Texas Press, asked me if I might be interested in
writing a history of Texas, my first thought was that maybe
he should ask a historian instead. It was a project that
seemed too large, too crucial, to entrust to a novelist and
magazine writer whose limited formal education in history
included a D in a college course on the Roman Empire.

So I said no to Dave, but then I said yes. Turning away from this opportunity made me feel like a painter who had just been handed a giant blank
canvas and who—for abstruse reasons of credentialing and acute reasons
of fear—was forbidding himself from touching it. Gradually I realized that
being intimidated by a task was not the same thing as being unready for it.
A lot of my life, and a lot of my career, had been channeling me in the direction of this book. Except for my first five years, spent abroad in Oklahoma,
I have lived in Texas all my life. For over forty years I've been writing about
the state for *Texas Monthly*, in articles and essays that have almost all, in one
way or another, tended to be as much about the past as the present. As a
journalist, I was never quite as interested in the top layer of time, which I
was supposed to be covering, as I was in the history rumbling beneath it.
For that fortuitous grounding, I'll always be grateful to Mike Levy, *Texas
Monthly*'s founder, and to its editors and staff.

I've written two historical novels set in Texas—*The Gates of the Alamo* and
Remember Ben Clayton—and the years of research that went into trying to
make them historically as well as fictionally credible had a deep impact on
me and gave me an enhanced respect for the work of every sort of historian,

from academic to unaffiliated, from those who write sweeping narratives (such as this one is intended to be) to those who spend their lives examining some unexciting-to-relate but crucial-to-understand fragment of the past. Ann Close was my editor at Alfred A. Knopf for both of those books, as she has been for several others, and I've always greatly appreciated her editorial guidance and the support of the entire Knopf team.

When I first began thinking about how I was going to attack this book, I had enlightening conversations with Don Carleton, the director of the Briscoe Center for American History, and Jesús F. de la Teja, the former Texas State Historian and now the chief executive officer of the Texas State Historical Association. Light Townsend Cummins, like Frank de la Teja, is a former Texas State Historian and was generous in sharing an early draft of the authoritative Texas bibliography—*Discovering Texas History*—that he had edited with Bruce A. Glasrud and Gary D. Wintz.

For major help or just welcome little courtesies along the way, I'm grateful to an expansive list of people and institutions: Mark Smith and Jelain Chubb of the Texas State Library; Brian Roberts, Jonathan Jarvis, Marybeth Tomka, and Susan W. Dial of the University of Texas's Texas Archeological Research Laboratory; Mark Lambert and James Harkins of the Texas General Land Office; Bruce Winders, the curator of the Alamo; Jim Bruseth of the Texas Historical Commission and his wife and co-author Toni S. Turner, who allowed me to accompany them to the fascinating and forlorn site of La Salle's Fort St. Louis; Bill Hensel of the Port of Houston, and Doug Mims, captain of the M/V *Sam Houston*; Angela Holder of the National Buffalo Soldiers Museum; Mark Updegrove, Jennifer Cuddeback, and Brian McNerney of the LBJ Presidential Library; Victoria Ramirez of the Bullock Texas State History Museum; Zach Roberts of the George H. W. Bush Presidential Library; Rebecca Russell of the Woodson Research Center at Rice University; Alex Hunt, Timothy Bowman, Maureen Hubbart, A. J. McCormick, and Kaycie Timm of the Center for the American West at West Texas A&M University; Amy Von Lintel, also of West Texas A&M; Warren Stricker of the Panhandle Plains Museum; Sue Prudhomme and Eric Ray of the Museum of the Coastal Bend; and J. P. Bryan, the founder of Galveston's wondrous J. P. Bryan Museum, along with the museum's director, Joan Marshall, and Mary Lou Hollender, its director of development.

I'm thankful also for various insight boosts or hospitality provided by Walter Buenger, Carol Dawson, Tom Harrigan, Evan Smith, Jim Harrigan, Robert Sharp, Zach Ernst, S. C. Gwynne, Luci Johnson, Philipp Meyer, Ben Barnes, Regan Gammon, Ricardo Ainslie, Karl Rove, Alvin Lynn, Cina Forgeson, Victor Emanuel, Phil Collins, Jay O'Brien, Brian Sweany, Ninia

Ritchie, Paul Hutton, James Donovan, Robert Duvall, Dick Reavis, Lou Berney, Jeff Salamon, David Grogan, Bruce Winders, Joe Bill Sherrod, Bret Anthony Johnston, Andres Tijerina, Ty Cashion, Georgia and Chuck Kitsman, Chris and Kade Matthews, Tim Taliaferro, Alan Huffines, Jan Reid, and Jack and Dee Turner.

Some eminent Texas historians agreed to review the manuscript in whole or in part and to alert me to any mistakes or missteps or foolish conclusions they found therein. They of course made some excellent discoveries, and I made corrections accordingly, but readers should be assured that whatever errors still exist are my responsibility and not the fault of this distinguished panel. Warm thanks in this regard to Stephen L. Hardin, Light Cummins, Paula Mitchell Marks, Bill Minutaglio, and George Diaz.

In addition, it was a great relief, and a real pleasure, to work with Christian Wallace and Emily McCullar of *Texas Monthly* as they carefully fact-checked the manuscript, diplomatically calling my attention to errors both forgivably small (somebody's age being a year off) to howlingly huge (oops, wrong century!).

My friends William Broyles, James Magnuson, Bill Wittliff, and Lawrence Wright helped to convince me that writing a history of Texas was within my authorial range, and they provided encouragement whenever I began to fret that it wasn't. Bill Broyles read the manuscript and made valuable comments, as did Larry Wright. Larry and I have had many memorable adventures together during our long friendship, but among the best of them was the bicycling excursion we took along San Antonio's mission trail, as well as a trip to Abilene where we discovered that, unbeknownst to our younger selves, we had gone to school across the street from each other. (For more on that, including a schoolyard lightning strike that almost ended Larry's career before it began, see his book *God Save Texas*.)

For decades, Larry and Gregory Curtis and H. W. Brands and I have had breakfast together on Monday mornings. The long-running discussions that take place have often involved each other's works in progress, so it was natural that this book would be field-tested to some extent in their company. Greg is a particularly insightful editor (he edited *Texas Monthly* for over twenty years) and Bill Brands is an esteemed and uncannily prolific biographer and historian with total recall of American history. This book—and my life in general—has benefitted greatly from those Monday breakfasts.

There was no possibility of having breakfast with my great friend Elizabeth Crook—she's a restless night owl and needs her morning sleep—but in countless lunches and probably thousands of phone conversations her wisdom and sometimes her wisecracks have helped immeasurably to shape and steady the course of my career.

I wish I could take credit for the profuse and arresting illustrations in this book, but that was the result of Dave Hamrick's original vision and of Chuck Bailey's expert and tireless research in tracking down the images. (And special thanks in this regard to the Briscoe Center, which was particularly generous when Chuck came calling.) We were all delighted by the lighthearted maps produced by Margaret Kimball, and I'm grateful to Gary Zaboly for allowing me to repurpose the authoritative Alamo sketch that he originally drew for the endpapers of *The Gates of the Alamo*. Kip Keller, who copy edited this book, matched his exactitude to my persnicketyness (Kip, did I spell that right? Is it even a word?) with graceful efficiency, and made the process of reviewing his comments a pleasure. And it was my good fortune that UT Press entrusted the design of this book to Erin Mayes, whose artistry is visible on every page. For the heavy lifting required for indexing, I'm grateful to Kay Banning, and for proofreading to Rebekah Fowler and Luke Torn.

In-house at the Press itself, my editor Casey Kittrell was always an unflappable presence, undemanding but quietly directing. I have no idea how Lynne Chapman, the senior manuscript editor, managed to keep her sanity while bringing order to all the scattered components and citations of my many drafts, but she somehow did, and even managed to convince me that the disarray was never as great as I imagined. Dustin Kilgore likewise kept things moving ahead with seeming effortlessness on the design and production side of things. Gianna LaMorte has been a champion of this book from the beginning, and the architect of ever-inventive ways to bring it to the attention of readers, even including the publication of a preview volume called *They Came from the Sky*. Cameron Ludwick has also been a pleasure to work with as she helps this book make its way into the world. Thanks also to the other members of the UT Press team—Demi Marshall, Robert Devens, Robert Kimzey, Bailey Morrison, Angelica Lopez-Torres, Andrew Hnatow, Cassandra Cisneros, Joel Pinckney, Brenda Jo Hoggatt, Dawn Bishop, and Kate Shannon—who have been aiders and abettors of this outsized publishing project. And it's important to note that the project would not have been viable in the first place without the support of Bill Powers, the former president of the University of Texas at Austin, Victoria Corcoran, and the remarkable members of the UT Press advisory board.

Any acknowledgments I make in any book I write would be incomplete to the point of meaninglessness if I didn't mention, with deep gratitude, my steadfast agent and friend Esther Newberg.

It would be nice to make a clean break here and not get my family all mixed up in a list of what should probably be professional thank-yous, but I don't know where to draw that line, especially since my wife, Sue Ellen, our daughters, Marjorie, Dorothy, and Charlotte, and our sons-in-law, Rodney, Mike, and Zach, have all weighed in with welcome opinions and suggestions during the years it took to write this book. (Sue Ellen's advice, as always, was inspiringly direct: "Just hurry up and get it over with.") And during those years our family has happily expanded to include six grandchildren— Mason, Travis, Maisie, Romy, Sonny, and Gladys. It has been the joy of my life to use my book advance to treat them all to LuAnn Platters almost every week at Luby's cafeteria.

Finally, even though I've already mentioned Dave Hamrick several times, it's time to bring him back for a curtain call. Without his vision, determination, goading (sometimes), and generosity (always), I would never have embarked upon the long journey that has ended, with so many debts to so many people, upon this final page.

NOTES

THESE CHAPTER NOTES WILL, I HOPE, BE HELPFUL TO readers who want to explore with more precision a certain period or aspect of Texas history. For myself, I think of them as tent stakes anchoring what often threatened to become a wild and billowing canvas. I also took comfort in realizing that writing a sweeping narrative history of Texas was not necessarily an impossible task. Plenty of other writers have done it before me, and whether their specific books are cited in these chapter notes or not, I wanted to make sure I mentioned at least those that were the most useful to me when it came to information or inspiration.

Henderson Yoakum's *History of Texas* was published long ago, in 1855, but by then there had already been enough Texas history to fill two volumes, and Yoakum was an observer of much of it, having fought in Mexico with Jack Hays and served as Sam Houston's lawyer. (He even consulted with Houston while writing his book.) Much closer to our own time is T. R. Fehrenbach's *Lone Star: A History of Texas and the Texans*. *Lone Star* was published in 1968 and is, of course, a product of its time, a bit assailed these days for being what seems to some like a pulse-pounding chronicle of Anglo conquest and racial determinism. I stayed away from Fehrenbach while writing this book—his mythic cadences are too contagious and his aura of authority is too intimidating—but I can remember enough of *Lone Star* to understand that one of the main reasons it is a target is that it is still, after half a century, the monumental Texas history book.

Randolph B. Campbell's *Gone to Texas: A History of the Lone Star State*, is less imposing in a literary sense. Its tone is a bit more professorial—no surprise, since it was written by an esteemed professor of his subject—but it is

836

also more current and encompassing. Campbell powers deep into the twentieth century, whereas Fehrenbach only briefly ventures beyond all the rousing blood-letting of the nineteenth.

Campbell's book, published in 2003, was followed three years later by James L. Haley's *Passionate Nation: The Epic History of Texas*. Haley is not a professor and not affiliated with a university; he's a prolific Texas historian and biographer, and he has a lively freelance prose style that makes *Passionate Nation* a great pleasure to read.

Campbell's and Haley's histories served as road maps for me while I was trying to chart the narrative span of my own book. The same can be said of textbooks like *Texas: Crossroads of North America*, by Jesús F. de la Teja, Ron Tyler, and Nancy Beck Young (now in its 2015 second edition); *The History of Texas*, by Robert A. Calvert, Arnoldo De León, and Gregg Cantrell (fifth edition); and the current fourth edition of *Beyond Myths and Legends: A Narrative History of Texas*, by Kenneth W. Howell, Keith J. Volanto, James M. Smallwood, Charles D. Grear, and Jennifer S. Lawrence.

Henderson Yoakum might have had the advantage of checking in with Sam Houston himself when he wrote his history of Texas in the 1850s, but, on the other hand, he didn't have access to an encyclopedic website like the Texas State Historical Association's Handbook of Texas Online, which grew from a two-volume desk reference in 1952 into an ever-expanding online resource that is a crucial first stop for anyone curious about anything having to do with Texas. Another dazzling digital resource is Texas Beyond History (https://www.texasbeyondhistory.net), produced by the Archeological Research Laboratory at the University of Texas at Austin, in partnership with Texas State University and more than two dozen other historical and archeological departments, commissions, archives, and organizations. It bills itself, quite accurately, as "The Virtual Museum of Texas' Cultural History." Then there is the Portal to Texas History, created by the University of North Texas Libraries, which is just what its title says it is: a front door that opens seamlessly to a digital universe of primary sources.

Some of the books that were always on my desk while I was writing *Big Wonderful Thing*, serving as context-builders and morale-builders if not always sources for particular citations, were *Texas: A Historical Atlas*, by A. Ray Stephens, with cartography by Carol Zuber-Mallison; *Texas Through Time: Lone Star Geology, Landscapes, and Resources*, by Thomas E. Ewing, with contributions by Heather Christensen; *Roadside Geology of Texas*, by Darwin Spearing; *Lens on the Texas Frontier*, by Lawrence T. Jones III; the always-crucial *Texas Almanac*; and a recent volume of bibliographic essays that I've already mentioned in my acknowledgments, *Discovering Texas History*, edited by Bruce

A. Glasrud, Light Townsend Cummins, and Gary D. Wintz, which was the compass I came to rely upon when orienteering through the wilderness of Texas historiography.

PROLOGUE. BIG TEX

SOURCES
Cavalcade of Texas souvenir program; Kuh, *The Artist's Voice*; Ragsdale, *The Year America Discovered Texas*

NOTES
Texanize Texans: Ragsdale, 9.
mirror the accomplishments of Texas: Ragsdale, 8.
patient, loyal, patriotic attitude: Ragsdale, 232.
The Cavalcade of Texas will march on forever:
  Cavalcade of Texas souvenir program, 29.
the Westminster Abbey of the Western World:
  Ragsdale, 255.
I salute the Empire of Texas: Ragsdale, 247.
I couldn't believe Texas was real: Kuh, 189.

1. CASTAWAYS

SOURCES
Boyd, *White Shaman Mural*; Cabeza de Vaca, *Narrative*; Chipman, *Spanish Texas*; Goodwin, *Crossing the Continent*; Hanke, *All Mankind Is One*; Hickerson, *The Jumanos*; Hodge and Lewis, *Spanish Explorers in the Southern United States*; Krieger, *We Came Naked and Barefoot*; Reséndez, *A Land So Strange*; Ricklis, *The Karankawa Indians of Texas*; Schneider, *Brutal Journey*; Shafer, *Painters in Prehistory*; Texas Department of Public Safety, "Padre Island"; Weber, *The Spanish Frontier in North America*; Weddle, *Spanish Sea*

NOTES
explore, conquer, populate and discover: Schneider, 19.
used to waylay shipwrecked sailors: Texas Department of Public Safety.
This occupation served me very well: Cabeza de Vaca, 97.
very difficult for some to believe: Cabeza de Vaca, 25.
vipers that kill men when they strike: Cabeza de Vaca, 106.
the first dwellings we saw: Cabeza de Vaca, 147.
going the route of the setting sun: Cabeza de Vaca, 150.

things would go very well for them: Cabeza de Vaca, 153–154.
they had walked across the continent: Cabeza de Vaca, 122. (According to Adorno and Pautz, the editors of Cabeza de Vaca's account, they didn't really set out until midsummer 1535, when they left the Avavares.)
they should not kill them or take them as slaves: Cabeza de Vaca, 156.
[They] experienced great shock: Cabeza de Vaca, 159.
Are these Indians not men?: Hanke, 4.
Indians and all other people who may later be discovered: quoted in Hanke, 21.
But such distant moral declarations: Weddle, 157.

2. GOLDEN CITIES

SOURCES
Bolton, *Coronado*; "Coronado's Report to the King of Spain"; Flint and Flint, *Coronado Expedition*; Hallenbeck, *Journey of Fray Marcos*; Hodge and Lewis, *Spanish Explorers*

NOTES
greatest thing in the world: Hallenbeck, 18.
satiated with fear: Hallenbeck, 34.
bigger than the city of Mexico: Hallenbeck, 34.
You can inspect the documents: Flint and Flint, 617–618.
no more landmarks than as if we had been swallowed up: "Coronado's Report to the King of Spain."
The country is like a bowl: Hodge and Lewis, 362.
vast prairie dog towns: Hodge and Lewis, 363.
The country they traveled over: Hodge and Lewis, 383.
lived like Arabs: Hodge and Lewis, 330.
straw and skins: "Coronado's Report to the King of Spain."
the real Coronado was no more: Bolton, 331.
This expectation of death: quoted in Hodge and Lewis, 369.

3. WOE TO US

SOURCES
Arnold and Weddle, *Nautical Archeology of*

Padre Island; Hodge and Lewis, *Spanish Explorers*

NOTES

sank into a deep despondency: Hodge and Lewis, 229.
The Governor longed to be again: Hodge and Lewis, 246.
they could but laugh: Hodge and Lewis, 263.
A dark viscous scum: Hodge and Lewis, 263.
Woe to us who are going to Spain: Arnold and Weddle, 33.
helpless to protect the decency: Arnold and Weddle, 41.

4. THE LADY IN BLUE

SOURCES

Colahan, *Visions of Sor María*; Fedewa, *María de Ágreda*; Hickerson, *The Jumanos*; Kendrick, *Mary of Ágreda*

NOTES

in the kingdoms of Quivira and the Jumanas: Colahan, 111.
I say that she is a catholic and faithful Christian: Fedewa, 192, 193.

5. VOYAGEURS

SOURCES

Bruseth, *From a Watery Grave*; Bullock Texas State History Museum, *La Belle: The Ship That Changed History*; Chapa, *Texas and Northeastern Mexico*; Foster, *La Salle Expedition to Texas*; Parkman, *La Salle and Discovery*; Weddle, *La Salle, the Mississippi, and the Gulf*; Weddle, *Wilderness Manhunt*; Weddle, *The Wreck of the Belle, the Ruin of La Salle*

NOTES

this thorn which has been thrust: Weddle, *Wilderness Manhunt*, 89.
much pity among us: Chapa, 135.
Oh, beautiful French women: quoted in Weddle, *Wilderness Manhunt*, 187. This is my translation (with the help of Ricardo Ainslie) of the Spanish version found in de León, Chapa, and Sánchez de Zamora, *Historia de Nuevo León*, 218–219 (Oh, francesas hermosas / que pisabais de estos prados frescas rosas; / y con manos de nieve / tocabais blanco lirio en campo breve).
possession of this country of Louisiana: Parkman, 191.
a Noah's Ark: quoted in Foster, 85.
a tremendous inflammation of the throat: Foster, 124.

It is better not to mope: quoted in Foster, 139.
This is a man who has lost his mind: Weddle, *La Salle, the Mississippi, and the Gulf*, 103, 113.
was interested only in his own opinion: quoted in Foster, 103.
discretion of wolves: Foster, 199.
had little trouble slaughtering them all: Weddle, *La Salle, the Mississippi, and the Gulf*, 237.

6. GOD'S WORK

SOURCES

J. Barr, *Peace Came*; Bolton, *Athanase de Mézières*; Bolton, *Spanish Exploration in the Southwest*; Campbell, *Gone to Texas*; de la Teja, *San Antonio de Béxar*; W. Dunn, "Apache Relations in Texas"; Chipman and Joseph, *Spanish Texas*; Gwynne, *Empire of the Summer Moon*; Hackett, "Marquis of San Miguel de Aguayo"; "Itineraries of the De León Expeditions"; J. Jackson, *Imaginary Kingdom*; "Letter of Fray Damian Massanet"; Nathan, *San Sabá Papers*; Wallace and Hoebel, *Comanches*; Weddle, *San Sabá Mission*

NOTES

very pretty alcove: Bolton, 377–378.
I delivered to the governor a staff: "Itineraries of the De León Expeditions," 416.
it is easily to be seen: "Letter of Fray Damian Massanet," 387.
witchcraft, superstitions, and deceits of the devil: J. Barr, 59.
despicable meat of crows: Chipman and Joseph, 116.
did not spare . . . the lives of the chickens: quoted in Hackett, 197.
far flung heathen land: quoted in Hackett, 201.
eternal dwellers in the infernal caverns: W. Dunn, 235.
Each year at a certain time: Gwynne, 60.
the model of the fabled Thessalian Centaur: quoted in Wallace and Hoebel, 49.
persuading and catechizing: Nathan, 1.
All Hell is joined to impede this enterprise: Weddle, 67.
[I was] filled with amazement and fear: Nathan, 85.
his face was hideous and extremely grave: Nathan, 86.
personal defects and a complete ignorance: Weddle, 122.
as a ship anchored in mid-Atlantic: Weddle, 170.
such a knowledge of these provinces: Bolton, *Athanase de Mézières*, 86.
They venerate it: Bolton, *Athanase de Mézières*, 296.

imaginary frontier: quoted in J. Jackson, 197.
distinguished only in their color: Campbell, 83.

7. FILIBUSTERS

SOURCES

Bradley, *"We Never Retreat"*; Garrett, *Green Flag over Texas*; Hatcher, "Arredondo's Report"; "Memoir of Colonel Ellis P. Bean"; Wilson and Jackson, *Philip Nolan and Texas*

NOTES

less pleasing in practice than in speculation: Wilson and Jackson, 72.
I found that he was sincerely my friend: "Memoir of Colonel Ellis P. Bean."
God keep us from their hands: Bradley, 16.
assuming a proper direction: Garrett, 86.
Behold the empire of Mexico: quoted in Garrett, 144.
The volunteer expedition from the most insignificant beginning: quoted in Garrett, 162.
the dark myst of ignorance, slavery and corruption: quoted in Bradley, 42.
rank among the most extraordinary expeditions: Bradley, 73.
employed in lolling on his sofa: quoted in Bradley, 81.
great bravery: Hatcher, 229.

8. GOD SPEED YE

SOURCES

Bradley, *"We Never Retreat"*; Brindley, "Jane Long," Chipman and Joseph, *Notable Men and Women*; "French Exiles in Texas 1818"

NOTES

advanced at an amazing rate: Chipman and Joseph, 247.
We enjoyed the greatest tranquility: "French Exiles in Texas 1818."
Our intention is to take the country: quoted in Bradley, 167.
God speed ye: quoted in Bradley, 142.
beyond description, beautiful, fertile: quoted in Bradley, 171.
nothing . . . [but] tame submission: quoted in Bradley, 145.
trifling expedition: quoted in Bradley, 161.
an uncouth giant: Brindley, 221.
unexampled in the annals of war: Bradley, 190.
gave me the unfortunate idea: quoted in Bradley, 204.
the energies of masculine vigor: quoted in Brindley, 235.
Oh, brighter than that planet, love: Bradley, 212.

9. THE TEXAS DREAM

SOURCES

Annual Report of the American Historical Association for the Year 1919, vol. 2, *The Austin Papers*, pt. 1 [hereafter cited as *Austin Papers*, pt. 1]; Austin, "Journal"; Austin Papers, Briscoe Center; Barker, *Life of Stephen F. Austin*; Cantrell, *Stephen F. Austin*; Clopper, "Journal"; Fowler, *Santa Anna*; Jackson, *Indian Agent*; Jackson, *Texas by Terán*; Lee, *Mary Austin Holley*; Stephen F. Austin to Mary Austin Holley (November 17, 1831; December 25, 1831; December 29, 1831; and January 14, 1832); Stephen F. Austin to Samuel May Williams, July 1, 1832; July; Torget, *Seeds of Empire*

NOTES

but a shadow of his former self: Austin Papers, pt. 1, 408.
here is hundreds Travelling hundreds of Miles: Barker, 9.
lay the foundation: Cantrell, 42.
swore he would force his way into my house: Austin Papers, pt. 1, 352
I am . . . with out a Dollar: Austin Papers, pt. 1, 288.
His fever has returned this day: Austin Papers, pt. 1, 394–395.
a small, quite handsome gentleman: quoted in Cantrell, 92.
raise your Spirits: Austin Papers, pt. 1, 393.
I started on with a heavy heart: Austin, 287.
The general face of the country: Austin, 289.
It was a wild, howling, interminable solitude: Austin to Holley, November 17, 1831.
the glorious news of the Independence of Mexico: Austin, 296.
the land along the Colorado River: Austin, 303.
a most beautifull situation: Austin, 306.
it appears to be the General rage: quoted in Cantrell, 109.
cuts me off from all protection: quoted in Cantrell, 114.
having assumed those natural and imprescriptable rights: Austin Papers, Briscoe Center; also Austin Papers, pt. 1, 601.
go about with their constitution in their pocket: Jackson, *Texas by Terán*, 100.
Strangers to each other: quoted in Cantrell, 181.
absolute Lord and Master: Jackson, *Indian Agent*, 61.
corrupt and despotick Mexican government: quoted in Cantrell, 184.
The flag of liberty: quoted in Jackson, *Indian Agent*, 65.

A small party of infatuated madmen: quoted in
Cantrell, 184.
*Labyrinth of trouble and Vexation and responsi-
bility*: quoted in Cantrell, 154.
something like disgust towards the world: quoted
in Cantrell, 228.
difficult and dark question: Cantrell, 190.
we will have nothing but poverty: Torget, 95.
*The state prohibits absolutely and for all time
slavery*: Torget, 100.
curse of curses: quoted in Cantrell, 189.
he descried an Indian: Austin, 305.
An American population will be the signal:
Austin, 305.
My lot is cast in the wilderness: quoted in
Cantrell, 167.
amuse myself and do good to others: Cantrell, 232.
their lofty gambols and wild manoeuvres: Clopper, 57.
the snowy brightness of her well turned forehead:
Clopper, 72.
Farewell! Edward: Clopper, 63.
small spare little old batchelor: Clopper, 60.
the soul of this emporium of chaos: quoted in
Fowler, 91.
friend of liberty: Fowler, 81.
Suffice it to say: Clopper, 61.
There is no power like that to the north: Jackson,
Texas by Terán, 178–179.
In the act of ceding Texas: Jackson, *Texas by
Terán*, 179.
an execrable traitor who ought to be punished:
Jackson, *Texas by Terán*, 179.
They pull their teeth: Jackson, *Texas by Terán*,
101.
If the colonization contracts in Texas: quoted in
Cantrell, 219.
One's feelings in Texas are unique and original:
quoted in Lee, 233.
farewell once more: Austin to Holley,
December 25, 1831.
My ambition was to redeem this fine country:
Austin to Holley, December 29, 1831.
One word from me now: Austin to Holley,
December 29, 1831.
Gardens, and rosy bowers, and ever verdant groves:
Austin to Holley, December 29, 1831.
On our ponies we will scamper: Austin to Holley,
January 14, 1832.
We shall go for Independence: Austin to Holley,
December 29, 1831.
We were all enchanted with Texas (photo cap-
tion): Holley.
How horrid is civil war: Austin to Williams.
Texas is lost: quoted in Cantrell, 255.

10. THE CONSEQUENCE OF FAILURE

SOURCES
Barker, *Life of Stephen F. Austin*; Cantrell,
Stephen F. Austin; Davis, *Three Roads to the
Alamo*; R. Gray, *Visit to Texas*; Hansen,
Alamo Reader

NOTES
The time has come to strike a decisive blow: Han-
sen, 337.
impede the rapidity of their motions: Hansen,
338.
the country was placed: quoted in Barker, 438.
The common soldiers at this post: R. Gray, 95–96.
Among these strangers: R. Gray, 214.
He hungered and thirsted for fame: quoted in
Davis, 205.
blaze away upon the fort: Davis, 270.
Mexicans have learned a lesson: quoted in Davis,
273.
a sort of Mad Cap: Cantrell, 259.
The consequence of a failure: Cantrell, 265.
Others have died in less than one hour: Cantrell,
270.
Good God what a blow: Cantrell, 271.
state criminal of the greatest seriousness: Cantrell,
279.
a very sprightly young lady: Cantrell, 298.

11. COME AND TAKE IT

SOURCES
Campbell, *Gone to Texas*; Cantrell, *Stephen
F. Austin*; Clarkson, *Food History Almanac*;
Clopper, *Journal*; Crook, "Sam Houston
and Eliza Allen"; Davis, *Three Roads to the
Alamo*; de la Teja, *Revolution Remembered*;
Ehrenberg, *With Milam and Fannin*; J. L.
Haley, *Sam Houston*; S. Hardin, *Texian Iliad*;
James, *Raven*; Jenkins, *Papers of the Texas
Revolution*; Jenkins and Kesselus, *Edward
Burleson*; Lester, *Life of Sam Houston*; Lukes,
"DeWitt, Green"; Siegel, *Political History*;
Smithwick, *Evolution of a State*

NOTES
all are for energetic resistance: quoted in Davis,
448.
submission men: Davis, 457.
Listen not to men who have no home: Davis, 454.
A gentle breeze shakes off a ripe peach: Cantrell,
307.
let those ungrateful strangers know: Campbell,
129.
as enthusiastic in praise of the country: Lukes.
dissipation [and] neglectful indolence: Clopper,
67.

much embarrassed in his affairs: Lukes.
took a header from his horse: Smithwick, 71.
I can not remember that there was any distinct
understanding: Smithwick, 71.
We are all captains: S. Hardin, 8.
War is our only recourse: quoted in Cantrell,
312.
It certainly bore little resemblance to the army:
Smithwick, 75.
well satisfied that the beginning of the revolution:
de la Teja, 77.
This conduct, all the more scandalous: de la Teja,
133.
democracy in its most extreme form: Davis, 38.
almost industrial scale: Davis, 99.
When fired by anger: Davis, 94.
cut his heart strings: Davis, 215.
very successful in securing a fair portion: Davis,
152.
I know that she had a deep hold on Bowie's affections: Smithwick, 127.
little better than pounded charcoal: quoted in
S. Hardin, 34.
The Army must follow them right into the town:
quoted in S. Hardin, 33.
In the name of almighty God: Jenkins, 2:322.
The taking of Bexar is very difficult: Jenkins,
2:321.
the organization of a regular army: Jenkins,
2:321.
terraqueous machine and the repulsive-sounding
meat biscuit: Clarkson, 129.
the best speech . . . I have ever heard: Jenkins,
2:323.
tall, large, well formed, fascinating man: quoted
in J. L. Haley, 90.
a most remarkable foot: quoted in Siegel, 51.
If we should live, our wealth must be boundless:
quoted in Siegel, 88.
a herdsman, and spend the rest of his life: Lester, 54.
My God, is the man mad?: quoted in J. L. Haley,
66.
There is a thousand different tails a float: quoted
in Crook, 16.
his suspicion that she might not be virtuous:
Crook, 14.
she was repulsed by his running sore: J. L. Haley,
57.
I wish they would kill him: quoted in Crook, 6.
like some magnificent ruin: quoted in J. L.
Haley, 59.
a broken-down sot and debauchee: quoted in
S. Hardin, 57.
be careful in executing the great trust reposed in
you: Jenkins, 2:415.
The little Gentleman shewed the disposition of a
viper: quoted in James, 2.

greatly astonished & mortified: Lukes.
A pretty Texas girl: Ehrenberg, 6.
the hero of thirty battles who was never known to
retreat: Jenkins and Kesselus, 3.
don't care a looking company of men as could be
found: Jenkins and Kesselus, 30.
On the left, denuded shore of the river: Ehrenberg, 41.

12. THE ALAMO IS OURS!

SOURCES

Davis, *Three Roads to the Alamo*; de la Teja,
Revolution Remembered; Ehrenberg, *With
Milam and Fannin*; W. Gray, *Diary*; Hansen,
Alamo Reader; Huson, *Dimmitt's Comman-
dancy*; Jenkins, *Papers of the Texas Revolution*;
Looscan, "Micajah Autry"; Potter, "Texas
Revolution"; Shackford, *David Crockett*;
Zaboly, *Altar for Their Sons*

NOTES

It is all important: Jenkins, 2:321.
Save the dignity of our Government: quoted in
Huson, 193.
We were surrounded with crude bumpkins: quoted
in Huson, 194.
We considered ourselves almost invincible: Ehren-
berg, 95.
I do solemnly swear that I will bear true allegiance:
Shackford, 217.
He has rather an indolent appearance: quoted in
Davis, 391.
any future republican government: Shackford,
217.
He could not live without being before the public:
quoted in Davis, 407.
I am rejoiced at my fate: Davis, 417.
We stand guard of nights: Looscan, 320.
We know not what day, or hour: Hansen, 649.
I shall identify myself with your interests: Han-
sen, 140
The salvation of Texas depends in great measure:
Hansen, 19–20.
Col. Neill & Myself: Hansen, 20.
Travis strained every nerve: Hansen, 17.
They are worn down & exhausted with the war:
Hansen, 17.
We are determined to sustain it: Hansen, 21.
The great problem I had to solve: Hansen, 345.
Poor fellows: de la Teja, 194.
The Mexican army cannot come to terms: Han-
sen, 331.
I am a better judge of my military abilities: Jen-
kins, 4:398.
We reminded him constantly of the probable fate:
Ehrenberg, 153.

Col. Fannin is said to be on the march: Hansen, 36.
We have had a shower of bombs and cannon balls: Hansen, 37.
Let the Convention go on and make: Hansen, 37.
thought Washington a disgusting place: W. Gray, 108.
It is laid out in the woods: W. Gray, 108.
The pang of severing national allegiance: Potter, 9.
You cannot know my anxiety, sir: Hansen, 601.
He wanted to cause a sensation: Hansen, 421.
Night came and with it the most sober reflections: Hansen, 421.
he related the affair with much modesty: Hansen, 77.
example of Arredondo: Hansen, 420.
voiced principles regarding the rights of men: Hansen, 420.
It seemed as if the furies had descended upon us: Hansen, 425.
even been expected to die: Hansen, 48.
The bodies with their blackened and bloody faces: Hansen, 426.
Where be thy sarcasms now: Zaboly, 245.
My dear wife, they are coming over the wall (photo caption): Hansen, 50.
Long live our country, the Alamo is ours: Hansen, 404.
our fate is sealed: Hansen, 245.
a phenomenal refreshment of my memory: Hansen, 267.
I accordingly threw in one paragraph: Hansen, 254.

13. VENGEANCE

SOURCES

Castañeda, *Mexican Side*; Constitution of the Republic of Texas (1836); Ehrenberg, *With Milam and Fannin*; W. Gray, *Diary*; J. L. Haley, *Sam Houston*; S. Hardin, "Hard Lot"; S. Hardin, *Texian Iliad*; D. Harris, "Reminiscences I"; D. Harris, "Reminiscences II"; Hansen, *Alamo Reader*; Henson, "Burnet, David Gouverneur"; R. Hunter, *Narrative*; Jenkins, *Papers of the Texas Revolution*; Moore, *Eighteen Minutes*

NOTES

We were so happy over our new shoes: D. Harris, "Reminiscences I," 113.
and a large gang of negroes: D. Harris, "Reminiscences I," 97.
The negroes acted like dogs: D. Harris, "Reminiscences I," 98.
On Jordan's Stormy Banks I Stand and Cast a

Wishful Eye: D. Harris, "Reminiscences I," 102.
everybody was talking of running from the Mexicans: D. Harris, "Reminiscences II," 160.
I remember well the hurry and confusion: D. Harris, "Reminiscences II," 160.
Then began the horrors of the Runaway Scrape: D. Harris, "Reminiscences II," 162.
I never knew it though there was an unusual huskiness in her voice: S. Hardin, "Hard Lot," 37.
Now what I must say: S. Hardin, "Hard Lot," 42.
an hourly occurrence east of the Brazos: S. Hardin, "Hard Lot," 38.
There is no one who can do justice to the women at that time: S. Hardin, "Hard Lot," 39.
When we started from home we got the little books: D. Harris, "Reminiscences II," 162.
no better than pirates without one: Hansen, 622.
had a great spree on egg nog: Hansen, 622.
most miserably cool and sober: J. L. Haley, 120.
not a sound was heard, save the wild shrieks: quoted in S. Hardin, *Texian Iliad*, 163.
We must not depend on Forts: Jenkins, 5:58.
I spent a restless night: Castañeda, 244.
unbearably silent: Ehrenberg, 200.
The idea that they planned to shoot us seemed unthinkable: Ehrenberg, 202.
I have found the darkest hours of my past life: quoted in S. Hardin, *Texian Iliad*, 183.
He didn't have a man in his army: quoted in S. Hardin, *Texian Iliad*, 180.
I consulted none: quoted in S. Hardin, *Texian Iliad*, 184.
On the approach of death: W. Gray, 133.
All persons of color who were slaves: Constitution of the Republic of Texas.
speculator, lawyer, and politician: Henson.
a swarthy, dirty looking people and *the most interesting man in Texas*: W. Gray, 89, 120.
What shall we do to be saved: W. Gray, 133.
The Texas army has whipped the Mexican army: D. Harris, "Reminiscences II," 168.
Sir: The enemy are laughing you to scorn: S. Hardin, *Texian Iliad*, 189.
We will meet the enemy: S. Hardin, *Texian Iliad*, 199.
Any youngster could have done better: quoted in S. Hardin, *Texian Iliad*, 202.
riddled him with balls: S. Hardin, *Texian Iliad*, 213.
take them with the but of your guns: R. Hunter, 16.
Me no Alamo: S. Hardin, *Texian Iliad*, 215, 213.
born to no common destiny: quoted in J. L. Haley, 154.

14. AFTERMATH

SOURCES

Cantrell, *Stephen F. Austin*; "Chronicles of Oklahoma"; *Columbus (GA) Ledger-Inquirer*; de la Teja, *Revolution Remembered*; Everett, *Texas Cherokees*; Fowler, *Santa Anna*; Frankel, *Searchers*; J. L. Haley, *Sam Houston*; Hämäläinen, *Comanche Empire*; S. Hardin, *Texian Macabre*; Houston, *Writings*; Jenkins, *Papers of the Texas Revolution*; Lack, *Texas Revolutionary Experience*; La Vere, *Texas Indians*; Lubbock, *Six Decades in Texas*; Parker and Plummer, *Rachel Plummer Narrative*; Siegel, *Political History*; P. Williams, *Jackson, Crockett and Houston*; Williams and Barker, *Writings of Sam Houston*

NOTES

Every last one of us is probably threatened: quoted in Hämäläinen, 200.
should bring reproach on the tender cause of God: Frankel, 14.
A large sulky looking Indian: Parker and Plummer, 93.
He reached out his hands toward me: Parker and Plummer, 96.
that before they are published, the hand that penned them: quoted in Frankel, 51.
his was an English head: "Chronicles of Oklahoma."
A firm and lasting peace forever: La Vere, 169.
I am busy and will only say how da do, to you: Everett, 77.
Having yesterday evening had an unfortunate encounter: Jenkins, 6:15.
To the devil with your glorious history: quoted in J. L. Haley, 154.
He was universally detested: quoted in Siegel, 38.
I have seen how brave you are in battle: quoted in Fowler, 179.
A wild and intractable spirit of revenge: Jenkins, 7:207.
perhaps the most imbecile body that ever sat judgment: Lack, 106.
A perfect summer scene was presented for contemplation: S. Hardin, 173.
that had yet brains in it: S. Hardin, 175.
The spirit of liberty: de la Teja, 156.
My labors and exertions to settle this country: quoted in Cantrell, 350
Sam Houston, who had been in Texas about three years: quoted in Siegel, 55.
A spot of earth: Houston, 448
His soul seemed to have swerved: Williams and Barker, 451–452.

But all the loveliness that played: Reprinted in the *Columbus (GA) Ledger-Inquirer*, May 7, 1978. Available at the Muscogee County (GA) Archives, http://files.usgwarchives.net/ga/muscogee/newspapers/poemexto2260gnw.txt.
the lodging place of many: Lubbock, 36.
There was not one of them who did not lament the loss: de la Teja, 89.
one all absorbing point: quoted in Cantrell, 361.
Let us establish mutual relations: Fowler, 181.
He is a Spaniard: P. Williams, 236.
How can we style him a tyrant: Fowler, 181.

15. SPARTAN SPIRIT

SOURCES

Adams, *Speech*; Cantrell, *Stephen F. Austin*; de la Teja, Marks, and Tyler, *Texas*; Everett, *Texas Cherokees*; Gambrell, *Mirabeau Buonaparte Lamar*; J. L. Haley, *Sam Houston*; S. Hardin, *Texian Macabre*; Hogan, *Texas Republic*; Kerr, *Seat of Empire*; Lamar, *Papers*; [Lundy], *War in Texas*; Siegel, *Political History*

NOTES

The independence of Texas is recognized: quoted in Cantrell, 364.
to wrest the large and valuable territory of Texas: [Lundy], 3.
a war for the re-establishment of slavery: Adams, 8.
I have at length the happiness to inform you: quoted in Siegel, 77.
It is handsome and beautifully elevated: quoted in S. Hardin, 78.
We live like hogs: quoted in S. Hardin, 98.
wretched mudhole: quoted in S. Hardin, 95–96.
rejected by the public as a Vampire: Hogan, 98.
bear footed and naked and hongry: quoted in J. L. Haley, 182.
the frightful scene I have made in your house: Kerr, 7.
awaken into vigorous activity: quoted in Gambrell, 201.
I cannot regard the annexation of Texas to the American Union: Lamar, 321.
hopes of happiness are based: Lamar, 320.
has been formed by a Spartan spirit: Lamar, 349.
If the wild cannibals of the woods: Lamar, 352.
the most savage and ruthless of our frontier enemies: de la Teja, Marks, and Tyler, 237.
I hope to the Great Spirit: quoted in Everett, 94.
prompt and sanguinary war: quoted in Everett, 104.

16. "SAVAGE WARE FARE"

SOURCES

G. Anderson, *Conquest of Texas*; Cox, *Texas Rangers*; Gwynne, *Empire of the Summer Moon*; Houston, *Writings*; Lamar, *Papers*; Mary Maverick, *Memoirs*; McDowell, *Now You Hear My Horn*; Smithwick, *Evolution of a State*; Sowell, *Early Settlers and Indian Fighters*

NOTES

This is the most unfortunate site upon earth: Houston, 2:322.
between water, cold region, indifferent and sparse timber: Houston, 2:322.
I am far from conceding: Lamar, 353.
If you are here, run to me: quoted in Gwynne, 81.
corps of rangers: Cox, 46.
something officially known as a Texas Ranger: Cox, 187.
We were left afoot: Smithwick, 157.
I never felt sorrier for a man: Smithwick, 157.
She was in a frightful condition: Maverick, 44.
I have been long exceedingly anxious: Maverick, 38.
paid his fine and went off laughing: Maverick, 39.
Gentlemen, those are the first wild Indians I ever saw: McDowell, 60.
this old mother of the forest: McDowell, 63.
litterly bridged with packs: McDowell, 64.
He drew his long hack knife: McDowell, 66.
some northern tribe: Anderson, 192.
Most of them were dressed in skins: quoted in Cox, 79.
Powder-burn them: Sowell, 320.
I cannot recommend these arms too highly: quoted in Cox, 92.

17. THE BROKEN FLAGPOLE

SOURCES

de la Teja, *Revolution Remembered*; Gambrell, *Anson Jones*; J. L. Haley, *Passionate Nation*; J. L. Haley, *Sam Houston*; S. Haynes, *Soldiers of Misfortune*; Hogan, *Texas Republic*; Hollon, *William Bollaert's Texas*; Houston, *Writings*; Kendall, *Texan Santa Fé Expedition*; Kerr, *Seat of Empire*; McDonald, *José Antonio Navarro*; McDonald and Matovina, *Defending Mexican Valor*; Mary Maverick, *Memoirs*; Nance, *Attack and Counterattack*; Roberts, *Star of Destiny*; Siegel, *Political History*; Torget, *Seeds of Empire*; Wallis, *Sixty Years on the Brazos*

NOTES

constant occupancy of your mind: quoted in Siegel, 138.

one of the most scandalous and outrageous violations: quoted in Kerr, 156.
Viva la pigs: quoted in Siegel, 163.
not aware of the existence of a nation: Siegel, 124–125.
could not do other than give the people of Eastern New Mexico: Kendall, 2.
Forward comrades, firm and steady: quoted in McDonald, 168.
a wide waste of eternal sameness: Kendall, 110.
You will see [Texas] become the richest, most powerful nation: quoted in McDonald, 167.
the people are equally disgusted with both of us: quoted in J. L. Haley, 226.
Doth some tranquilizing power: Roberts, 19.
it is woman who blesses her country: quoted in J. L. Haley, 228.
that silly and vicious project: quoted in J. L. Haley, 239.
There existed no great use for this office: Wallis, 158.
The Mexicans of Mexico have not forgotten us: Maverick, 27.
Only say you really want men: J. L. Haley, 247.
If the emigrants come without means: J. L. Haley, 247.
He was now amongst my enemies: de la Teja, 119.
I had to leave Texas, abandon all: de la Teja, 118.
Captain, we are in a bad fix: quoted in Nance, 366.
The Texian standard of the single star: quoted in S. Haynes, 16.
a prospect of success: Houston, 3:170.
a very nice kind Gentleman: quoted in S. Haynes, 31.
Broken down politicians: quoted in S. Haynes, 45.
a Mountain of no inconsiderable size: quoted in S. Haynes, 55.
Alas! Poor Austin: Hollon, 198.
Of the four presidents of Texas: Gambrell, 485.
attitude of supplication: Torget, 276.
as a bride adorned for her espousal: quoted in J. L. Haley, 246.
The institution of slavery is engrafted upon our Constitution: quoted in Torget, 243.
of the abject race of Mexicans: quoted in McDonald, 203.
to dismiss that idea as odious: McDonald and Matovina, 20.
Buckskin is more romantic: quoted in Hogan, 46.
The Republic of Texas is no more: quoted in Gambrell, 418.

18. *LOS DIABLOS TEJANOS*

SOURCES

K. Bauer, *Mexican War*; Broyles, "King Ranch"; Cox, *Texas Rangers*; Ferrell, *Monterrey Is Ours!*; Fowler, *Santa Anna*; Grant, *Personal Memoirs*; A. Greenberg, *Wicked War*; S. Haynes, *Soldiers of Misfortune*; "Joint Resolution for Annexing Texas"; Robinson, *Texas and the Mexican War*

NOTES

the territory properly included within and rightfully belonging: "Joint Resolution for Annexing Texas."
an act of aggression, the most unjust: quoted in K. Bauer, 16.
I dreamed that I was some place away from Corpus Christi: Grant, 905–906.
delightful and very healthy: Grant, 898.
the dirtiest place, I believe, I was ever in: Ferrell, 7.
All is so wild and romantic: Ferrell, 18.
When I come home: Ferrell, 22.
You have no idea, Sue, what a military show we have here: Ferrell, 26.
a war would probably be the best mode: quoted in A. Greenberg, 79.
There was not at that time: Grant, 63.
Of this area nothing is known: Broyles, 167.
There was no estimating the number of animals in it: Grant, 62.
the ancient limits of Texas: Robinson, 26.
Hostilities may now be considered as commenced: Robinson, 25.
had a special spite against that particular man: Ferrell, 60
a perfect bulldog for the fight: Ferrell, 61.
They ought to have been out of the way: Ferrell, 62.
some execution was done: Grant, 67.
struck the ranks a little ways in front of me: Grant, 914.
pel mel affair evry body for himself: Grant, 915.
eternal shame and bitter regret for every good Mexican: Fowler, 281.
War was his element: S. Haynes, 20.
A rougher looking set we never saw: Cox, 108.
observe, with the most scrupulous respect, the rights of all: Robinson, 16.
licentious vandals: Cox, 110.
The mounted men from Texas: Cox, 118.
The bushes . . . are strewed with skeletons: Cox, 118.
With their departure: Robinson, 72.
the most perfect weapon in the world: Cox, 112.
I'll never see Texas again: Cox, 117.

19. THE CRISIS OF THE CRISIS

SOURCES

Bordewich, *America's Great Debate*; Ford, *Rip Ford's Texas*; Gwynne, *Empire of the Summer Moon*; J. L. Haley, *Sam Houston*; Neighbours, *Robert Simpson Neighbors*; Roberts, *Star of Destiny*; Wallis, *Sixty Years on the Brazos*

NOTES

Thy task is done: quoted in Roberts, 108.
tame, and regulate a man: Roberts, 128.
You may have conquered Santa Anna: Roberts, 100.
Lord help the fish down below: J. L. Haley, 333.
With the help of God I hope to sit down to it like a soldier: quoted in Roberts, 150.
The ladies afterward said that the doctor should not have exhibited: Wallis, 160.
It is useless to mention: quoted in Roberts, 151.
magnificent barbarian: Bordewich, 159.
vast and picturesque sombrero: Bordewich, 159.
I . . . decline all solicitations: Roberts, 143.
erection that won't go down: Gwynne, 92.
French Dancing Masters: Ford, 121.
The whole business is infamous: Bordewich, 255.
A curse and a blight: Bordewich, 254.
That Texas will maintain the integrity of her Territory: quoted in Neighbours, 98.
If Texas militia march into any of the other States: quoted in Bordewich, 308.
For a nation divided against itself cannot stand: quoted in J. L. Haley, 305.
What fields of blood: quoted in J. L. Haley, 328.
The Indian has a sense of justice: quoted in J. L. Haley, 322.
I have been astonished: quoted in J. L. Haley, 312.
Oh, when I think of the allurements that surround you: quoted in J. L. Haley, 301.
The people want excitement: quoted in J. L. Haley, 344.
The fuss is over, and the sun yet shines as ever: quoted in J. L. Haley, 352.

20. ROBBERS AND LAWYERS

SOURCES

"Documents on the Brownsville Uprising"; Monday and Vick, *Petra's Legacy*; Montejano, *Anglos and Mexicans*; Thompson, *Cortina*

NOTES

notably handsome woman of tall and commanding figure: Monday and Vick, 39.

has know chance, he is told by the rober and *lawyer*: Thompson, 32.
the very scum of society: quoted in Montejano, 32.
The people of Matagorda County: quoted in Montejano, 28.
Her self-imposed devotion to the duties of nurse: Monday and Vick, 21.
I punished his insolence: Thompson, 37.
Our object has been to chastise the villainy: "Documents on the Brownsville Uprising."
I do not believe that fifty men of Mexican origin: quoted in Thompson, 51.
greaser pelados: quoted in Thompson, 61.
The whole country from Brownsville to Rio Grande City: quoted in Thompson, 77.
flocks of vampires, in the guise of men: "Documents on the Brownsville Uprising."
We had no use for prisoners: quoted in Thompson, 80.

21. WARRIORS AND REFUGEES

SOURCES
G. Anderson, *Conquest of Texas*; Carlson and Crum, *Myth, Memory, and Massacre*; Frankel, *The Searchers*; Gwynne, *Empire of the Summer Moon*; Holden, *Lambshead before Interwoven*; Neighbours, *Robert Simpson Neighbors*

NOTES
If the world was picked over: G. Anderson, 324.
a gentleman of manly and sterling qualities: quoted in Neighbours, 99.
You come into our country: quoted in Gwynne, 164.
We regard the killing of Indians: quoted in G. Anderson, 319.
Every county is raising and arming a band of lawless men: quoted in G. Anderson, 319.
out of the heathen land of Texas: quoted in G. Anderson, 322.
The departure was accompanied by a perfect babel: Neighbours, 274.
cried like a child: quoted in Neighbours, 280.
I would give all I possess in the world, to see them: quoted in Neighbours, 282.
I was in the Pease river Fight: quoted in Carlson and Crum, 5.
I could only look upon him with pity and admiration: quoted in Carlson and Crum, 34.
Americano: Frankel, 69.
She was very dirty: quoted in Carlson and Crum, 34.
We rode right over her dead companions: quoted in Frankel, 70.

she sprang up with a scream: quoted in Frankel, 84.
The great Comanche Confederacy was forever broken: Gwynne, 180.

22. I WILL NEVER DO IT

SOURCES
Amelia Barr, *All the Days of My Life*; Blackburn, "Reminiscences"; Campbell, *Empire for Slavery*; "Declaration of Causes"; Flanagan, *Sam Houston's Texas*; Foote, *Civil War*; *Galveston Weekly News*; Hamilton, *My Master*; J. L. Haley, *Sam Houston*; Houston, *Writings of Sam Houston*; Reynolds, "Reluctant Martyr"; Roberts, *Star of Destiny*; Thompson, *Cortina*; Tongate, *Another Year*; Tyler and Murphy, *Slave Narratives*; A. Williams, "Houston, Sam, Jr."; E. Williams, *Hood's Texas Brigade*; Wooster, *Texans in the Civil War*

NOTES
the greatest soldier, the ablest man: quoted in Foote, 169.
Are you related to General Houston of Texas?: Houston, 404.
a rare find: A. Williams.
But for the guardian care that kept: quoted in Roberts, 315.
You whipped me like a cur dog: quoted in J. L. Haley, 362.
Reopen the African Slave Trade: quoted in J. L. Haley, 363.
mild, pastoral and gentle: quoted in J. L. Haley, 366.
The Greaser and Gringo can never live harmoniously together: quoted in Thompson, 81.
A man of three score years and ten (photo caption): J. L. Haley, 413.
the yawning gulf of ruin: quoted in J. L. Haley, 382.
Negroes For Sale: *Galveston Weekly News*, September 27, 1859.
Slavery came to the Southern man: Tyler and Murphy, xxviii.
an inferior grade of being: Tyler and Murphy, xxviii, xxvix.
Who I am, how old I am, and where I was born: Tyler and Murphy, 10.
The [cotton] rows were a mile long: Tyler and Murphy, 50.
quality aristocrats: Hamilton, 1.
I turned my head for one last look at my mother: Hamilton, 4.
Here's a little nigger for sale—cheap: Hamilton, 5.
The very sound of my master's voice: Hamilton, 9.

He told me once when I was dressing it: Hamilton, 31.
I am making my last effort: quoted in J. L. Haley, 382.
I know what war is: Hamilton, 73.
debasing doctrine of the equality of all men: "Declaration of Causes."
You have treated me shamefully: quoted in Wooster, 18.
Margaret, I will never do it: quoted in J. L. Haley, 390.
Whenever I saw him turn over in his hands: Flanagan, 183.
Gentlemen, I have asked your advice: Hamilton, 76.
remarkably pleasant countenance: Tongate, 25.
long and heart piercing wail: Tongate, 25.
We are going to live among heroes: Amelia Barr, 181.
their tocsin shout of Kewrrook! Kewrrook! Kewrrook!: Amelia Barr, 184.
The paws then look like walnuts: Amelia Barr, 193.
nearly without exception fine riders and crack shots: Amelia Barr, 211.
An unreasonable detestation of slavery: Amelia Barr, 227.
I was on a vast plain, dark and lonely: Amelia Barr, 220.
they ar Whipping about thirty Negros: quoted in Campbell, 226.
Sam Houston's viceregents of God: quoted in Campbell, 228.
set up the bones in a variety of attitudes: Reynolds, 350.
as no Texan walks a yard if he can help it: quoted in Wooster, 31.
whipped out a six-shooter and fired: Blackburn, 48.
There were shot, shells and Minie balls: quoted in E. Williams, 106.

23. WITH THROBBING HEARTS

SOURCES

Allan, *Allan's Lone Star Ballads*; Amelia Barr, *All the Days of My Life*; Campbell, *Empire for Slavery*; T. Cutrer, "Hébert, Paul Octave"; T. Cutrer, "Magruder, John Bankhead"; DeBruhl, *Sword of San Jacinto*; de la Teja, *Lone Star Unionism*; Ford, *Rip Ford's Texas*; Gallaway, *Texas*; J. L. Haley, *Sam Houston*; Hertzberg and Schenck, "Letter"; Hoffman, "German-American Pioneer"; T. Jordan, *German Seed in Texas Soil*; Lich and Moltmann, "Solms-Braunfels, Prince Carl of"; McCaslin, *Tainted Breeze*; "Newspaper advertisement for the Bank of Bac-

chus"; Pickering and Falls, *Brush Men*; Stone, *Brokenburn*; Thompson, *Vaqueros in Blue and Gray*; Tongate, *Another Year*; Tyler and Murphy, *Slave Narratives*; Wooster, *Texans in the Civil War*

NOTES

organizing a foreign force to invade Texas: quoted in Thompson, 17.
Before attacking Cortina: quoted in Thompson, 22.
I write with a heavy hand: quoted in Thompson, xv.
Nowhere does the German race prosper better than here: quoted in T. Jordan, 40.
new crowns to old glory: Lich and Moltmann.
A strange melancholy came over me: Hertzberg and Schenck, 159.
I could tell you all so much: Hertzberg and Schenck, 162.
beardmen: Hertzberg and Schenck, 161.
Unfortunately, this happy picture of Texas farm life: Hertzberg and Schenck, 157.
When in Texas, do as the Texans do: de la Teja, 107.
At 4 o'clock in the morning: Hoffman, 496.
Reason had left its throne: quoted in McCaslin, 67.
the dark corner of the Confederacy: Gallaway, 155.
whiteheaded children and buttermilk: Stone, 223–224.
And, oh, the swarms of ugly, rough people: Stone, 223–224.
where Union feeling is rife: Stone, 223–224.
somewhat bewildered by the magnitude of the task: T. Cutrer, "Hébert, Paul Octave."
handsomest soldier in the Confederacy: T. Cutrer, "Magruder, John Bankhead."
My father is here: quoted in Wooster, 67.
an electric thrill: Wooster, 68.
She poor child was to wait eleven: Tongate, 83.
Dutch & Negroes: Tongate, 84.
Baked ribs, sausage, liver hash: Tongate, 83.
No stocking hung up tonight: Tongate, 22.
President and Cashier of the Bank of Bacchus: "Newspaper advertisement for the Bank of Bacchus."
one of the most brilliant and heroic achievements: quoted in Wooster, 92.
With throbbing hearts: Allan, 113.
The answer reverberates—nay: Allan, 123.
shot to pieces: quoted in Wooster, 169.
Boys, we have done finely: Ford, 390, 391.
No southern independence now: Amelia Barr, 249–250.
The people of Texas are informed that: Campbell, 249.

I've got something to tell you: Tyler and Murphy, 115.
You, and each of you, are now free: quoted in J. L. Haley, 407.
Go to San Jacinto: quoted in DeBruhl, 399.
He sat there for a long time: quoted in J. L. Haley, 408.
Texas! Texas! Margaret: quoted in J. L. Haley, 415.

24. RECONSTRUCTED

SOURCES

Bean, "Death of a Carpetbagger"; Campbell, *Gone to Texas*; Constitution of the State of Texas (1866); Constitution of the State of Texas (1869); Crouch and Brice, *Cullen Montgomery Baker*; Crouch and Brice, *Governor's Hounds*; "(1866) Texas Black Codes"; *Galveston Daily News*, September 6, 1873; *Hickman (KY) Courier* ("A Regular War"), August 15, 1868; A. Johnson, "Amnesty Proclamation"; A. Johnson, "Proclamation 139"; A. Johnson, "Proclamation 157"; McCulloch, "Letter from Gen. H. E. McCulloch"; Moneyhon, *Edmund J. Davis*; E. M. Pease to Lucadia Pease, July 24, 1868; *The Pine and Palm* [electronic resource]; Pitre, *Through Many Dangers*; Ramsdell, *Reconstruction in Texas*; Smallwood, Crouch, and Peacock, *Murder and Mayhem*; *Statutes at Large*, 37th Cong., 2nd sess.; U.S. Congress, *Joint Committee on Reconstruction*, pt. 4: "Florida, Louisiana, Texas"

NOTES

desperado: U.S. Congress, *Joint Committee on Reconstruction*, 47.
negro testimony: U.S. Congress, *Joint Committee on Reconstruction*, 47.
There seems to be a very general desire: U.S. Congress, *Joint Committee on Reconstruction*, 46.
devoted to the interests of freedom: *The Pine and Palm*.
with authority to exercise within the limits: A. Johnson, "Proclamation 139."
I do solemnly swear or affirm: A. Johnson, "Amnesty Proclamation."
keep Sambo from the polls: quoted in Campbell, 272.
A system of public schools for Africans and their children: Constitution of the State of Texas (1866), Article X.
for purposes of idleness: "(1866) Texas Black Codes."
peace, order, tranquillity, and civil authority: A. Johnson, "Proclamation 157."

any pretended government: *Statutes at Large*, 37th Cong., 502.
He was correct, almost austere: Bean, 267.
unbridled licentiousness: Bean, 268.
If you surrender me to these men: quoted in Bean, 270.
that each one might participate: Bean, 277.
The sanctity of home, the peace and safety of society: quoted in Ramsdell, 231.
in calling it a massacre: E. M. Pease to Lucadia Pease.
to disarm all the whites, arm all the negroes: *Hickman (KY) Courier*.
the poor, ignorant, misguided negroes: McCulloch, August 15, 1868.
without distinction of race, color or former condition: Constitution of the State of Texas (1869), Article VI.
He has neither [the] culture nor shrewdness of Ruby: quoted in Pitre, 171.
Certainly the name of no Texan: Ramsdell, 49.
Sometimes giant horsemen, shrouded in ghostly white: Ramsdell, 233.
a magnificent specimen of manhood: Moneyhon, 6.
you will be shot, and your body will float: quoted in Moneyhon, 50.
Come and cut it: quoted in Moneyhon, 50.
There is a slow civil war going on here: Moneyhon, 170.
There, they've got Peacock: quoted in Smallwood, Crouch, and Peacock, 8.
If I could sink this whole country into hell: quoted in Crouch and Brice, 67.
radiate civilization into the darkest corners: Ramsdell, 299.
Thomas J. Smith 1869: Crouch and Brice, 49.
You cannot search my house: quoted in Crouch and Brice, 64.
robbed by a negro State Policeman of $3,000 in gold: quoted in Crouch and Brice, 71.
six-shooters provided by benefactors: Crouch and Brice, 81.
Kill the damned nigger state police: quoted in Crouch and Brice, 100.
just killed a white son of a bitch: quoted in Crouch and Brice, 99.
notorious negro: Crouch and Brice, 103.
that they are after doing something wrong: quoted in Smallwood, Crouch, and Peacock, 47.
A general firing of guns by the party: quoted in Smallwood, Crouch, and Peacock, 44.
You have been living under a government: *Galveston Daily News*, 2.
were determined that E. J. Davis: Ramsdell, 315.

25. THE END OF COMANCHERÍA

SOURCES
C. Anderson, *In Search of the Buffalo*; Baker and Harrison, *Adobe Walls*; Carter, *On the Border with Mackenzie*; Cozzens, *Eyewitnesses to the Indian Wars*; Dixon, *Life of "Billy" Dixon*; Frankel, *Searchers*; Grant, *Personal Memoirs*; Gwynne, *Empire of the Summer Moon*; J. L. Haley, *Buffalo War*; J. L. Haley, *Passionate Nation*; King, "Salt Creek Prairie"; Leckie, *Military Conquest*; Lynn, *Kit Carson*; F. Mayer, "Buffalo Harvest"; Mooar, *Buffalo Days*; "Native American Relations in Texas"; Neeley, *Last Comanche Chief*; Nye, *Carbine and Lance*; Robinson, *Bad Hand*; *San Francisco Chronicle* ("An Indian Massacre: Some Thrilling Experiences in Texas"), December 4, 1892

NOTES
Shoots today and kills tomorrow: Mooar, *Buffalo Days*, 20.
All you had to do was pick them off: F. Mayer.
came upon the body of a teamster: F. Mayer.
If Indians seem fit to capture you: F. Mayer.
The Indians realized very keenly: Mooar, 79.
The buffalo is our money: quoted in Haley, *Passionate Nation*, 354.
In this lonely land: Mooar, 36.
The white man once came to trade: quoted in Haley, *Buffalo War*, 7.
I was born under the prairie: quoted in Gwynne, 227.
If you can make Quakers out of the Indians: quoted in Frankel, 103.
If Washington don't want my young men to raid: quoted in Frankel, 103.
most dangerous prairie in Texas: King.
a remarkably handsome Indian: *San Francisco Chronicle*, December 4, 1892, 10.
Stripped stark naked and fastened by a chain: *San Francisco Chronicle*, December 4, 1892, 10.
If any other Indian comes here: quoted in Leckie, 149.
O sun, you remain forever: quoted in Leckie, 153.
a picture of fallen savage greatness: "Native American Relations in Texas."
the arch fiend of treachery and blood: Leckie, 154.
I believe Satanta and Big Tree: quoted in Leckie, 154.
They are destroying the Indians' commissary: quoted in Haley, *Buffalo War*, 25.
We come in from our camps on issue day: quoted in Haley, *Buffalo War*, 42.
the meanest man: Baker and Harrison, 7.
In all my after life: Dixon, 17.
a large body of objects advancing vaguely: Dixon, 157.
Then I was thunderstruck: Dixon, 157.
You got polecat medicine: Haley, *Buffalo War*, 75.
Twelve Indian heads: Haley, *Buffalo War*, 131.
in piteous tones to shoot him: Dixon, 209.
dearest treasure: Dixon, 205.
Every night the same stars are shining: Dixon, 210.
inexpressive and immobile: Grant, 772.
I regarded Mackenzie: Grant, 40.
A large and powerfully built chief: Gwynne, 11.
The sun, rising in our rear: Robinson, 169.
as completely as if the ground had swallowed them: quoted in Haley, *Buffalo War*, 175.
As we galloped along: Carter, 489.
It seemed a pity to be compelled to kill them: Carter, 495.
When I roam the prairies I feel free: quoted in Nye, 255.
A freak of nature: C. Anderson, 66.
We are again in counsel: quoted in Neeley, 143.
Their encounter was described as undramatic: Neeley, 146.

26. FENCED IN

SOURCES
Abbott and Smith, *We Pointed Them North*; Browning, "From Outlaw to Attorney"; Collins, *Crooked River*; Cox, *Texas Rangers*; Dobie, *Longhorns*; Durham and Wantland, *Taming the Nueces Strip*; Flanagan, *Trailing the Longhorns*; Gard, "Fence-Cutters"; Glasrud and Searles, *Buffalo Soldiers*; J. L. Haley, *Charles Goodnight*; J. Hardin, *Life of John Wesley Hardin*; T. Harris, *Black Frontiersman*; Henry, "The Caballero's Way"; J. Hunter, *Trail Drivers of Texas*; Hutton, *Apache Wars*; Leffler, "Cotulla, TX"; Leonard, *Men of Color*; Lomax, *Cowboy Songs and Other Frontier Ballads*; Lomax, "Half-Million Dollar Song"; Metz, *John Wesley Hardin*; Robinson, *The Fall of a Black Army Officer*; Shelton, "Lizzie E. Johnson"; Webb, *Great Plains*; Wendt and Kogan, *Bet a Million!*; R. Wright, "Beginnings of Dodge City"

NOTES
The red man was pressed: Lomax, "Half-Million Dollar Song."
where seldom if ever / Any poisonous herbage doth grow: Lomax, "Half-Million Dollar Song."
to have sprung up as quietly and mysteriously: Lomax, *Cowboy Songs and Other Frontier Ballads*, xxiv.
He sits his horse easily: Lomax, *Cowboy Songs and Other Frontier Ballads*, xxiii.

with the dust half an inch deep: Abbott and Smith, 62.

I had a pistol: J. Hunter, 573.

horse and man . . . mashed into the ground: Abbott and Smith, 37.

My thick hair: J. Hunter, 233.

We were solitary adventurers: quoted in Flanagan, 169.

fifty times more dangerous to footmen: quoted in Webb, 213.

the greatest, the most extraordinary: Dobie, x.

a very small, dead place: Webb, 220.

The Beautiful, Bibulous Babylon: R. Wright.

A burnt child shuns the fire: quoted in Flanagan, 154.

a twisted fence-wire: quoted in Webb, 300.

light as air, stronger than whiskey: quoted in Wendt and Kogan, 48.

The range and soil of Texas: quoted in Gard, 4.

devil's hat band: quoted in Gard, 1.

the only uninhabitable portion of Texas: quoted in Haley, 276.

an overbearing old son-of-a-gun: quoted in Haley, 301.

I wanted that cañon: quoted in Haley, 303.

Old Bristle Top: Shelton, 350.

rather austere and firm: Shelton, 350.

the end will be at sunrise: quoted in Hutton, 257.

steadily won his way by sterling worth: quoted in Leonard, 189.

Never did a man walk the path of uprightness: T. Harris, 37.

tormented him as hyenas: T. Harris, 37.

Our wives and daughters must be considered: Glasrud and Searles, 138.

some damned nigger at the bottom of it: Glasrud and Searles, 134.

tried and punished by the trumpet voice: Glasrud and Searles, 139.

there is no case on record: Glasrud and Searles, 140.

Everybody get your guns ready: Leffler.

He is so kind and considerate: quoted in Collins, 193.

Had a fight with raiders: quoted in Cox, 250.

They were boogers: quoted in Collins, 187.

The Mexicans are in my front: quoted in Collins, 227.

Give my compliments to the Secretary of War: quoted in Collins, 227.

Is it the truth you want?: quoted in Collins, 11.

Had he performed the remarkable feats: Durham and Wantland, x.

When I get Over Yonder: Durham and Wantland, 178.

Six feet two, blond as a Viking: Henry.

Grand Mogul of Texas desperadoes: Metz, 172.

In those times: J. Hardin, 15.

Oh, Lordy, don't shoot me any more: quoted in Metz, 20.

knight of the six-shooter: Metz, 177.

liberate all who wished to go: J Hardin, 126.

You ought to read Victor Hugo's masterpiece: quoted in Metz, 211.

forty-one years has steadied the impetuous cowboy: quoted in Browning.

I would feel my very bones chill: quoted in Metz, 253.

27. TURN TEXAS LOOSE

SOURCES

Allen, *Great Southwest Strike*; Alvord, "T. L. Nugent"; Anders, *Boss Rule in South Texas*; Alwyn Barr, *Reconstruction to Reform*; Bell, "Bad Day at Round Rock"; Berry, *UT History 101*; Cotner, *James Stephen Hogg*; E. Cunningham, *Triggernometry*; E. Cutrer, *Art of the Woman*; DeArment, *Jim Courtright*; Gillett, *Six Years with the Rangers*; Grayson, "Colonel's Folly"; J. L. Haley, *Charles Goodnight*; Hare, *Norris Wright Cuney*; Hodgson, *Woodrow Wilson's Right Hand*; Hometown, "Buttermilk and Blood"; House, *Philip Dru*; Lane, *University of Texas*; Perman, *Road to Redemption*; Pitre, *Through Many Dangers*; Spratt, *Road to Spindletop*; State Symbols USA, "Mockingbird"; Tijerina, *Tejano Empire*; Wallace, Vigness, and Ward, *Documents of Texas History*; Whisenhunt, *Texas*; "Written in Stone"

NOTES

never noticed the play of her name: Bernhard, xi.

is a singer of distinctive type: quoted in State Symbols USA, "Mockingbird."

I have never been willing to stand by: Bernhard, 276.

an honest, sincere and clean young man: Gillett, 164.

his former chief had been kind to his family: Gillett, 167.

We are on our way to Round Rock: Gillett, 170.

The world is bobbing around: Bell.

Thou shalt not leave thy straw: "Written in Stone."

Make no war upon railroads: quoted in Perman, 234.

depravity finds friendship: quoted in Whisenhunt, 161.

freedom from the onerous and shameful abuses: Wallace, Vigness, and Ward, 238.

to secure to the people the benefits: Wallace, Vigness, and Ward, 239.

Gould the giant fiend: quoted in Allen, 88.

a typical border ruffian: quoted in DeArment, 201.
For God's sake don't shoot: Hometown.
snapping to the butts of the .45s: E. Cunningham, 285.
There is one peril: quoted in Spratt, 158.
The great common people of this country: quoted in Spratt, 207.
raise less corn and more Hell: Spratt, 207.
children's grass: Spratt, 126.
You cannot legislate for me: quoted in Haley, 393–394.
If you were to ask me if I am opposed: quoted in Cotner, 131.
men cannot be made moral: Cotner.
recognize the supreme authority of the Government: Wallace, Vigness, and Ward, 202.
absurd and preposterous: quoted in Alwyn Barr, 126.
to bear the hopes of toiling and struggling humanity: Alvord, 67.
Are you ready to assert the spirit: quoted in Alwyn Barr, 185.
a finely built copper-hued man: quoted in Hare, 109.
dark-skinned white man: quoted in Hare, 123.
All such legislation is futile: quoted in Hare, 129.
a large number of pupils: quoted in Hare, 132.
I notice with extreme reluctance: Hare, 132–133.
is not a cast iron institution: quoted in Cotner, 306.
Three C's—Clark, Cuney and the Coons: Cotner, 307.
It pleased his imagination: quoted in Grayson.
my second personality: quoted in Hodgson, 9.
[Dru] further directed that the tax: House, 177.
cements the victory of San Jacinto: quoted in Lane, 26.
Let me . . . urge it upon you, gentlemen: quoted in Berry, 3.
Smite the rocks with the rod of knowledge: quoted in Berry, 8.
a man that everybody laughed at: Alwyn Barr, 42.
It is well to consider what trouble: Lane, 57.
I know that I cannot enter the University of Texas: quoted in Pitre, 200.
Here is where I shall live: quoted in E. Cutrer, 92.
She anxiously treated me as an outsider: quoted in E. Cutrer, 37.
Votre physiognomie: quoted in E. Cutrer, 43.
I will begin, Your Majesty: quoted in E. Cutrer, 59.
my life has been a protest: quoted in E. Cutrer, 176.

I would like to model the greatest: quoted in E. Cutrer, 132.
The foremost man of all the world: quoted in Alwyn Barr, 205.
character for truth and veracity: quoted in Tijerina, 123.
Many ranches have been plundered and burned: quoted in Tijerina, 126.
I have lived among them: quoted in Anders, 13.

28. BIPEDAL BRUTES

SOURCES
Carr, "Remembering the 'Wizard of Words'"; Carver, *Brann and the Iconoclast*; Hall, *Revolt Against against Chivalry*; Hogg, "Message of the Governor"; *Lost Friends*; Mertins, *Little Myrtle Vance Avenged*; *New York Sun*, February 2, 1893; Parker, *Views on the Two Seeds*; Wells, *Red Record*

NOTES
I belonged to a gentleman: *Lost Friends*.
My mother said, the morning she was going to leave: *Lost Friends*.
first outraged with demoniacal cruelty: quoted in Wells.
negro ravisher: *New York Sun*, February 2, 1893.
Never in the history of civilization: Wells.
Little Myrtle Vance Avenged: Mertins.
upon a carnival float in mockery of a king: Wells.
For God's sake: Wells.
I love children: Wells.
a prime example of Mobocracy: Hogg.
had received the Serpentine nature: Parker.
Mob rule is the typhoid fever: quoted in Hall, 4.
Since the day of my husband's death: quoted in Hall, 16.
I like the negro in his place: quoted in Carr.
The baleful shadow of the black man: quoted in Carver, 43.
I don't want to live: Carver, 24.
the religious storm-centre of the Universe: quoted in Carver, 123.
It Strikes to Kill: Carver, 71.
bipedal brutes: Carver, 156, 173.
There are not Baptists enough in Texas: Carver, 173.

29. SCORPIONS AND HORNY TOADS

SOURCES
Boyd, *White Shaman Mural*; *Dallas Morning News*, February 19, 1928; Estleman, *Roy and Lillie*; Manaster, *Horned Lizards*; McDaniel and Taylor, *Coming Empire*; Skiles, *Judge Roy Bean Country*; Sonnichsen, *Judge Roy Bean*; Welch, *Legendary Texas Horned Frog*

NOTES

handsome as an Adonis: Skiles, 3.

There is the worst lot of roughs: quoted in Skiles, 7.

He might have been a murderer: quoted in Skiles, 18.

grizzly-bear jism: Estleman, 11.

any law against killing a Chinaman: Sonnichsen, 137.

Roy Bean's quick reply: quoted in Skiles, 171.

This pistol kept order: Skiles, 175.

It is a creation story: Boyd, 1.

The horned lizard: Manaster, 1.

Joe's fancy for horned frogs: quoted in Welch, 95.

Now imagine this creature: McDanield and Taylor, 245.

There's the frog: Welch, 35.

flat as a dollar: McDanield and Taylor, 67.

The durn thing's alive: quoted in Welch, 35.

When first taken from its score-and-a-half year tomb: Dallas Morning News, February 19, 1928.

The president's remarks to Rip: quoted in Welch, 52.

nothing is impossible with God: quoted in Welch, 75.

30. A THOUSAND LITTLE DEVILS

SOURCES

Greene and Kelly, *Night of Horrors*; Knowlton, *Cattle Kingdom*; Larson, *Isaac's Storm*; McDanield and Taylor, *Coming Empire*; Rayburn, "Rough Riders"; Roosevelt, *Rough Riders*; *San Antonio Daily Express*, May 18, 1898

NOTES

I had preached with all the fervor and zeal I possessed: Roosevelt, 11.

to be composed entirely of frontiersmen: Rayburn, 113.

a splendid set of men: Roosevelt, 21.

[They] needed no teaching: Roosevelt, 28.

Hasten forward there: quoted in Knowlton, 170.

a fearless bugger: Knowlton, 169.

rough and hardy bay horse: Roosevelt, 34.

The animal had plenty of mettle: *San Antonio Daily Express*, May 18, 1898.

We . . . were glad: Roosevelt, 43.

Though fifty miles inland: McDanield and Taylor, 10.

which was of a particularly vivid color: Greene and Kelly, 77.

People were already somewhat alarmed: quoted in Greene and Kelly, 76.

the tropical disturbance: quoted in Larson, 143.

The usual signs which herald: Larson, 15.

I then realized that something was going to drop: quoted in Greene and Kelly, 77.

Should feel more comfortable in the embrace: Greene and Kelly, 13.

It sounded as if the rooms were filled: Greene and Kelly, 109.

Buildings?: quoted in Greene and Kelly, 37.

31. GUSHERS

SOURCES

Bixel and Turner, *Galveston and the 1900 Storm*; Block, *Sour Lake*; Cartwright, *Galveston*; Linsley, Rienstra, and Stiles, *Giant under the Hill*; McDaniel, *Pattillo Higgins*; Olmsted, *Journey through Texas*; Rundell, *Early Texas Oil*; Wallace, Vigness, and Ward, *Documents of Texas History*

NOTES

It is necessary to have a city here: quoted in Bixel and Turner.

Businessmen and methods are what we need: quoted in Bixel and Turner, 92.

Galveston is not in her right mind yet: quoted in Cartwright, 187.

All over the lake's surface: quoted in Block, 17.

The approach to the rude bathing-houses: Olmsted, 376.

Quality as Good as Pennsylvania's: Rundell, 26.

I used to put my trust in pistols: quoted in McDaniel, 24.

an inland manufacturing and commercial city: McDaniel, 38.

Don't let the boys kiss you: quoted in McDaniel, 96.

frittering her money away: quoted in McDaniel, 47.

I can say right now: Linsley, Rienstra, and Stiles, 60.

trying to drill a hole in a pile of wheat: quoted in Linsley, Rienstra, and Stiles, 93.

Now that we've got her, boys: quoted in Linsley, Rienstra, and Stiles, 123.

There will be a good market for fuel oil: quoted in Linsley, Rienstra, and Stiles, 128.

like Cleopatra on her barge: Rundell, 39.

They did not believe me then: quoted in McDaniel, 147.

Oil companies are being formed: quoted in Rundell, 96.

The struggle between men and mud: quoted in Wallace, Vigness, and Ward, 255.

Here the wells were thickest: Wallace, Vigness, and Ward, 255.

32. LIGHT COMING ON THE PLAINS

SOURCES
Acheson, *Joe Bailey*; *Amarillo Daily News*, October 7, 1916; Anders, *Boss Rule in South Texas*; Alwyn Barr, *Reconstruction to Reform*; Cotner, *James Stephen Hogg*; Cunniff, "Texas and the Texans"; de la Teja, Marks, and Tyler, *Texas*; Giboire, *Lovingly, Georgia*; Gould, *Progressives and Prohibitionists*; Guttery, *Representing Texas*; Gwynne, *Empire of the Summer Moon*; Lisle, *Portrait of an Artist*; McArthur and Smith, *Minnie Fisher Cunningham*; Neeley, *Last Comanche Chief*; Roberts and Olson, *Line in the Sand*; Roosevelt, *Outdoor Pastimes*; Wallace, Vigness, and Ward, *Documents of Texas History*

NOTES
would have been a leader and a governor: quoted in Neeley, 224.
Principal Chief of the Comanches: Gwynne, 304.
It is well: quoted in Neeley, 228.
In his youth a bitter foe of the whites: Roosevelt, 113.
Me have family graveyard: quoted in Neeley, 231.
Forty years ago my mother died: quoted in Neeley, 233.
Our brother is coming: quoted in Neeley, 235.
Plain's Last Buffalo Hunt: *Amarillo Daily News*, October 7, 1916.
Last Kill of Their Race: *Amarillo Daily News*, October 7, 1916.
Greatest Gathering Ever Witnessed in the Panhandle: *Amarillo Daily News*, October 7, 1916.
I can't help it, it's all so beautiful: quoted in Lisle, 100.
There was something insatiable about her: quoted in Lisle, 68.
Terrible winds and a wonderful emptiness: quoted in Lisle, 63.
Tonight I walked into the sunset: Giboire, 183.
Time for you to get up, Papa: quoted in Cotner, 577.
And when these trees shall bear: quoted in Cotner, 576.
was very happy for years and years: quoted in Guttery, 99.
we could commit him to any line of policy: quoted in Alwyn Barr, 221.
The people wanted no disturbance: quoted in de la Teja, Marks, and Tyler, 333.
We have only one political party in Texas: quoted in de la Teja, Marks, and Tyler, 335.
a huge octopus of special bureaus: quoted in Acheson, 33.
a knife up his sleeve: quoted in Anders, 87.
is the greatest menace of the twentieth century: Wallace, Vigness, and Ward, 267.
greatest living American: quoted in Gould, 16.
There will not be a square foot of territory: quoted in Gould, 24.
I have walked through the fire: Wallace, Vigness, and Ward, 265.
locked up overnight with strange men: quoted in Acheson, 354.
If a woman wants something done: quoted in Acheson, 357.
contrasted blackly against the lives of their slaves: quoted in McArthur and Smith, 8.
Equal pay for equal work: quoted in McArthur and Smith, 30.
the best-looking man I ever saw: quoted in McArthur and Smith, 23.
I miss him so: McArthur and Smith, 138.
I can't help regretting: quoted in McArthur and Smith, 138.
Few white men went unarmed on election day: quoted in Alwyn Barr, 199.
Unless some flank movement can be made: quoted in Alwyn Barr, 204.
I am a white person and a Democrat: quoted in Alwyn Barr, 201.
is a coolly arrogant self-sufficiency: Cunniff, 7269.
You gather from Texas conversation: Cunniff, 7270.
Amazement and disgust: quoted in Roberts and Olson, 202.

33. SEDICIOSOS

SOURCES
Amberson, McAllen, and McAllen, *I Would Rather Sleep*; Flores Magón, "A La Mujer"; Gavito, "La Leyenda sobre la Mutilación"; Harris and Sadler, *Plan de San Diego*; Harris and Sadler, *Texas Rangers and Mexican Revolution*; Hart, *Revolutionary Mexico*; Hurst, *Pancho Villa and Pershing*; B. Johnson, *Revolution in Texas*; Madero, "Plan of San Luis Potosí"; Montejano, *Anglos and Mexicans*; Orozco, "Cortez Lira, Gregorio"; S. Ramírez, "¡Surge!"; Rausch, "Death of Victoriano Huerta"

NOTES
medium-size Mexican: Orozco, "Cortez Lira, Gregorio."
through the range of the longhorn: quoted in Montejano, 107.
We are witnessing the largest migration: quoted in Montejano, 108.
The golden glow of the brush fires: quoted in B. Johnson, 29.

I told him to pack up his doll rags: quoted in B. Johnson, 34.
to eject from power the audacious usurpers: Madero.
Madero has unleashed a tiger: quoted in Hart, 247.
If men are slaves, you are too: Flores Magón.
Rise up! Rise up to life: S. Ramírez, 227.
Something queerly fantastic: quoted in B. Johnson, 38.
I am convinced his testicles: quoted in Harris and Sadler, 9.
the Yankee tyranny: quoted in B. Johnson, 2.
hatred of races which closes the doors: quoted in B. Johnson, 80, 81.
General Headquarters in San Antonio: Harris and Sadler, 39.
The moment has arrived: quoted in Harris and Sadler, 39.
Every time he kicked a Mexican: quoted in B. Johnson, 77.
I first went to my husband: quoted in B. Johnson, 78.
Knowing there were 75 or 80 bandits: quoted in B. Johnson, 200.
Fresh from the revolutions in her native land: quoted in Amberson, McAllen, and McAllen, 482.
had fought for all it had ever gained: quoted in B. Johnson, 200.
You are . . . complaining: quoted in B. Johnson, 174.
men who are willing to go out: quoted in Harris and Sadler, 458.
Can it be true?: quoted in Hurst, 44.
I am enjoying the novel experience: quoted in Rausch, 144.
This tongue that called for the assassination: Gavito. ("Esta lengua que llamó asesino al General Huerta, no volverá a pronunciar palabra alguna.")

34. PA

SOURCES
James E. Ferguson Papers, box 3P46; Gould, *Progressives and Prohibitionists*; Nalle, *Fergusons of Texas*; Wallace, Vigness, and Ward, *Documents of Texas History*; Wilson, *In the Governor's Shadow*

NOTES
who has never held office: James E. Ferguson Papers, box 3P46.
Daddy was the stormy petrel of Texas politics: Nalle, 83.
I have really given little thought to the subject of women's suffrage: quoted in Wilson, xv.

If I am elected Governor: quoted in Gould, 126.
banish from Texas the agitator: Ferguson Papers, box 3P46.
One man says that he has a right: Ferguson Papers, box 3P46.
It had probably not occurred to some of you: quoted in Gould, 135.
those sacred principles for which the gallant Confederate soldiers: quoted in Gould, 141.
be one of our most successful governors: quoted in Gould, 158.
kill every damned man down there: quoted in Wilson, 61.
a negro has no business whatever: quoted in Gould, 56.
social and political whirlpool: Nalle, 83.
My mother had never possessed: Nalle, 83.
politics have no more to do with the appointments: quoted in Gould, 188.
I don't have to give any reasons: quoted in Nalle, 192.
the biggest bear fight: quoted in Nalle, 194.
trickster lawyers, plodding pedagogues: Nalle, 196.
the severest criticism and condemnation: quoted in Wilson, 113.
unusual and questionable loan: Wallace, Vigness, and Ward, 270.
Is it any crime for a man to borrow $156,500?: quoted in Gould, 218.
attempted impeachment: quoted in Gould, 218.
disqualified to hold any office of honor: Gould, 218.
It is really a relief for me: quoted in Gould, 218.

35. WAR AT HOME AND ABROAD

SOURCES
A. Anderson, "President Wilson's Politician"; Ball, *They Called Them Soldier Boys*; Balsley, "Lafayette Escadrille"; C. Barnes, *142nd Infantry*; Buckley, *American Patriots*; Christian, *Black Soldiers in Texas*; Culver, *Day the Airmail Began*; "Forgotten Victory"; Givner, *Katherine Anne Porter*; Gould, *Progressives and Prohibitionists*; Grayson, "Colonel's Folly"; R. Haynes, *Night of Violence*; Jackson and Clark, *His Time in Hell*; Porter, *Collected Stories*; J. Ramírez, *To the Line of Fire*; Reich, "Soldiers of Democracy"; Rich, *Queen Bess*; Sáenz, Zamora, and Maya, *World War I Diary*; C. Smith, "Houston Riot of 1917"; Stinson, "Not Afraid to Fly"; Stout, *South by Southwest*; Unrue, *Katherine Anne Porter*; Warren, "Porvenir Massacre"; White, *From Panthers to Arrowheads*; Wooster, *Texans in the Great War*; Zimmermann Telegram

NOTES

To the average American: quoted in Gould, 150.

The President was sad and depressed: quoted in Wooster, 29.

We make Mexico a proposal or alliance: Zimmermann Telegram.

his colleagues called him the Cardinal: A. Anderson, 347.

sound old principles: A. Anderson, 345.

but there is no other way: quoted in Wooster, 32.

[What] greater life can a man live: quoted in White, 9.

We must not eat with them: quoted in Buckley, 163.

save sand, rocks, and sage brush: quoted in R. Haynes, 60.

When I took my battalion to Houston: quoted in R. Haynes, 64.

for no other reason than that he was a colored man: C. Smith, 88.

see a white man on the sidewalk: quoted in R. Haynes, 54.

wipe out the whites: R. Haynes, 78, 79

since these God damn sons of bitches: quoted in R. Haynes, 94.

I don't report to no niggers: quoted in R. Haynes, 97.

There will be hell popping tonight: quoted in R. Haynes, 103.

that the men of the company seemed to respect: quoted in R. Haynes, 116.

get plenty of ammunition and save one for yourself: quoted in R. Haynes, 127.

You all can go in: quoted in R. Haynes, 165.

Two Negro Soldiers Are Buried: Christian, 207.

I have but one desire: quoted in Reich, 1484.

I was fed from birth: quoted in Unrue, 16.

I do not believe that childhood is a happy time: quoted in Unrue, 27.

I have no hidden marriages: quoted in Givner, 86.

ideal of prettiness: quoted in Stout, 99.

Ye shivering ones of the frozen North: Stout, 29.

It just simply divided my life: quoted in Givner, 126.

I am the first and only serious writer: quoted in Stout, 165.

And her memory turned and roved: Porter, 298.

The men on the front paid the bill: Jackson and Clark, 184.

Picture if you can that scene: C. Barnes, 30.

might be the least visited monument: "Forgotten Victory."

There was not a square foot of air space: quoted in Ball, 109.

Texans Heroic in First Battle: White, 157.

by machine gun bullets which penetrated left chest: C. Barnes, 109.

Just tell them it's Barkley: quoted in J. Ramírez, xiv.

Until now I have used pencil and pen: Sáenz, Zamora, and Maya, 35.

the general understanding is that this is not for Mexican soldiers: Sáenz, Zamora, and Maya, 87.

This is my last letter to you: Sáenz, Zamora, and Maya, 179.

They are on the battlefield: Sáenz, Zamora, and Maya, 165.

The [German] plane nosedived: Sáenz, Zamora, and Maya, 102.

School of Perfection and Combat: Balsley, 68, 69.

For a long period the Lafayette Escadrille: Balsley, 70.

Well, other people have done it: Stinson, 37.

If I could only become a music teacher: Stinson, 60.

She was America's sweetheart of the airways: Culver, *Day the Airmail Began*, quoted on The Early Birds of Aviation, "Katharine Stinson Otero, 1891–1977," www.earlyaviators.com/estinka1.htm.

wonderful colored aviatrix: Rich, 59.

We learned Harriet Tubman at Mother's knees: quoted in Rich, 9.

You can't make a race horse out of a mule: quoted in Rich, 14.

a full-fledged aviatrix: Rich, 35.

My faith in aviation: Rich, 70.

sickening thud: quoted in Rich, 110.

When you take a man like House: quoted in Grayson.

Goodbye, House: Grayson.

There here had been talk among the bunch: Jackson and Clark, 211.

Let's not have a grouch in the whole town: quoted in Ball, 162.

Corn, the historic plant of our indigenous raza: Sáenz, Zamora, and Maya, 459.

one of the soldiers rode back: Warren.

I mulled my past: Sáenz, Zamora, and Maya, 458.

36. THE BLACKSNAKE WHIP

SOURCES

K. Anderson, *Dan Moody*; Bernstein, *Ten Dollars to Hate*; Biggers, *Our Sacred Monkeys*; Boatman, Belshaw, and McCaslin, *Galveston's Maceo Family*; Brown, *Hood, Bonnet, and Jug*; Campbell, *Gone to Texas*; Cartwright, *Galveston*; Evans, *Klan of Tomorrow*; Gould, *Progressives and Prohibitionists*; Hendrickson, Collins, and Cox, *Profiles* in *Power*; E. Jackson, "Speeches of Morris Sheppard"; McArthur and Smith, *Minnie Fisher Cunningham*; Stanley, "Booze, Boomtowns, and Burning Crosses"; Wagner, "Culberson, Charles Allen"; Webb, *Texas Rangers*; Wilson, *In the Governor's Shadow*

NOTES

small-time dentist: Bernstein, 124.

the most average man in America: quoted in Brown, 75.

I will show you girls smoking cigarettes: quoted in Bernstein, 74.

an organization of true Americans: quoted in Brown, 51.

nightshirt factory: Brown, 50.

Bring on your niggers: quoted in Bernstein, 20.

Texas was the star Klan state: quoted in Brown, 75.

We are accused of hostility to the Negro: quoted in Evans, 14.

our alien enemy: quoted in McArthur and Smith, 61.

Governor Hobby was a sissy: Wilson, 136.

you cannot grow any wool on the back of the armadillo: quoted in Gould, 236.

Vote in hand: McArthur and Smith, 61.

protect our soldier boys against evils: quoted in Gould, 232.

the driest of the drys: Hendrickson, Collins, and Cox, 31.

We are coming to understand: E. Jackson, 61.

It cannot be said that he was like other boys: quoted in Brown, 13.

Even Christ made wine and went fishing: quoted in Gould, 272.

the wild man from Waco: quoted in Brown, 16.

It's partly a matter of smell: quoted in Brown, 266.

your good wife: quoted in Gould, 262.

The good name of Texas is at stake: quoted in Brown, 24.

Prohibition was a jackpot waiting to pay up: Cartwright, 208.

And now, ladies and gentlemen: Boatman, Belshaw, and McCaslin, 91.

If all criminals in Texas: Webb, 519.

I made up my mind to be as much like an Indian: quoted in Webb, 521.

Again the blacksnake whip cracked and fell: quoted in Bernstein, 114.

The prisoner tugged against his bonds: Bernstein, 114.

as raw as a steak: Bernstein, 8.

If Satin [sic] himself: quoted in Bernstein, 9.

Why do you come to my house in the middle of the night?: quoted in Bernstein, 150.

When a government ceases to enforce her laws: quoted in Stanley, 32.

Why So Silent, Governor?: Bernstein, 306n.

I have not the shadow of a doubt: quoted in Anderson, 28.

the Klan in the dock: quoted in Bernstein, 211.

seemed drunk on fight: quoted in Bernstein, 208.

The great auditorium of the county's temple of justice: quoted in Bernstein, 199.

A close friend informed me: quoted in Bernstein, 201.

And ladies, he's totally unmarried: quoted in Bernstein, 221.

The most momentous political year: quoted in Wilson, 150.

more real friends and more mean enemies: quoted in Wilson, 143.

sick man of the Senate: Wagner.

Of recent weeks the metropolitan press: quoted in Bernstein, 161.

a lowdown, stinking, contemptible: quoted in Bernstein, 160.

Personally, I prefer that men shall attend: quoted in Brown, 219.

It is going to be the greatest and fiercest political battle: quoted in Brown, 211.

an unholy alliance: quoted in Brown, 215.

All along you have said: quoted in Brown, 234.

I know I can't talk about the Constitution: quoted in Brown, 219.

Men of his type: Campbell, 372.

little mutton headed professor: quoted in Campbell, 373.

I am now going home: quoted in Brown, 251.

so far as the Klan was involved: quoted in Brown, 240.

Sunday school is dismissed: quoted in Brown, 254.

The highway department revelations: Biggers, 70.

little sideshow: Biggers, 70.

You'll have to see Jim: quoted in Brown, 273.

Jim and Dan were not mated for political harmony: Biggers, 71.

The war is on: Brown, 266.

Laugh Month: Brown, 296.

I shall not murmur: quoted in Brown, 340.

implacable foe of the Ku Klux Klan: Bernstein, 235.

the most brilliant blue eyes: Bernstein, 235.

the purity of the white race: Bernstein, 250.

37. MUSIC AND MAYHEM

SOURCES

Boessenecker, *Texas Ranger*; Find a Grave, "Lemon Jefferson"; Guinn, *Go Down Together*; Jenkins and Frost, *I'm Frank*

Hamer; Joplin, *School of Ragtime*; Lomax, oral history; "Leadbelly Talking about the Blues"; Procter, "Great Depression"; Wallace, "Texas, My Texas"

NOTES
a brassy alma mater: Wallace.
is a painful truth which most pianists have discovered: Joplin, 3.
He hollered like someone was hitting him: Find a Grave.
I'll never forget: Lomax.
that ol' feelin': "Leadbelly Talking about the Blues."
Why don't something happen?: quoted in Guinn, 51.
Let all men go to hell: quoted in Guinn, 50.
More and more it appears the changes in stock prices: quoted in Procter.
They only think you are mean: quoted in Guinn, 57.
They made him what he is today: quoted in Guinn, 123.
If you put your foot on the step: quoted in Boessenecker, 362.
Shoot it, you yellow, nigger lovin' soldiers: quoted in Boessenecker, 168.
Rest, hell: quoted in Boessenecker, 26.
great numbers of tramps: quoted in Boessenecker, 384.
As daylight came: quoted in Jenkins and Frost, 231.
screamed like a panther: quoted in Jenkins and Frost, 232.
When all was said and done: quoted in Guinn, 341.

38. THE BOY FROM THE HILL COUNTRY

SOURCES
Caro, *Path to Power*; Dallek, *Lone Star Rising*; Gillette, *Lady Bird Johnson*; D. Goodwin, *Lyndon Johnson*; Green, "Connally, Thomas Terry"; Hendrickson, Collins, and Cox, *Profiles in Power*; Roberts and Olson, *Line in the Sand*

NOTES
I made no promises as a candidate for this office: quoted in Hendrickson, Collins, and Cox, 50.
never stopped hating the Yankees: Caro, 306.
He went on for two solid hours: quoted in Caro, 308.
with a venomous hatred: quoted in Caro, 326.
having a little towheaded boy to teach: quoted in Hendrickson, Collins, and Cox, 109.
the only man in the United States Senate: quoted in Green.
bringing a deep stillness: quoted in Goodwin, 21.
was probably the best-educated woman: quoted in Caro, 57.
I love to think of the gracious hospitality: quoted in Caro, 51.
Hell, the Johnsons could strut sitting down: quoted in Caro, 42.
Santa Anna took the Alamo: quoted in Roberts and Olson, 277.
At last, I realized that life is real and earnest: quoted in Caro, 53.
Sam, you've got a politician there: quoted in Dallek, 32.
Great as an educator and as an executive: quoted in Caro, 149.
He told us we were looking at the future president: quoted in Caro, 171.
see where fate led: Gillette, 44.
I have a vague memory of her having some sort of illness: quoted in Gillette, 12.
as purdy as a lady bird: Dallek, 113.
There was something electric going: quoted in Gillette, 50–51.
My sense of excitement mounted: quoted in Gillette, 63.

39. CENTENNIAL

SOURCES
C. Dawson, *Miles and Miles of Texas*; J. Dawson, *High Plains Yesterdays*; Egan, *Worst Hard Time*; Hamilton, *My Master*; Hinton and Olien, *Oil in Texas*; Hurt, *Texas Rich*; J. Jones, *Billy Rose Presents*; *Lebanon (PA) Daily News*, April 5, 1949; Lynch, *Roughnecks, Drillers, and Tool Pushers*; *March of Time* radio series advertisement, *Time*; Okrent, *Last Call*; *Time*, June 22, 1936; Wilson, *In the Governor's Shadow*

NOTES
Get a farm in Texas while land is cheap: quoted in Egan, 24.
It was just like a high wave: J. Dawson, 184–185.
not just black, not just thick: quoted in J. Dawson, 205.
one of the greatest living scientists: Hinton and Olien, 169.
Geological, Topographical, and Petroliferous: Hinton and Oilen, 265.
I believe we have the biggest thing found in Texas: quoted in Hurt, 83.
I was broke as a convict: Lynch, 54.
there is as much chance of repealing the Eighteenth Amendment: quoted in Okrent, 330.

the West begins: Inez Robb, "Fort Worth–Dallas Feud Is His Invention," *Lebanon (PA) Daily News*, April 5, 1949, 14. Available at https://www.newspapers.com/clip/3980193/fort_worthdallas_feud_is_his_invention.

The exposition in Dallas will show the progress: quoted in Jones, 29.

Is Texas celebrating its independence: quoted in *March of Time* radio series advertisement, 83.

He is my brother and I know him: quoted in Wilson, 175.

He told the boy that it was in case: C. Dawson, 48.

That old Negro made the finest address: quoted in Hamilton, vii.

Jeff, I want you to remember: Hamilton, 79.

this king of all Texas trees: Hamilton, 80.

40. PASSIONATE ONES

SOURCES

Abigail and Leon, "Tenayuca, Emma Beatrice"; Brown and Wereschagin, *Gone at 3:17*; Caro, *Path to Power*; Crawford, *Please Pass the Biscuits*; *Dallas Morning News*, April 22, 1941; Dingus, "New London School Explosion"; Federal Writers' Project, *San Antonio*; Green, *Establishment in Texas Politics*; Maury Maverick, *Maverick American*; McKay, *W. Lee O'Daniel*; Menefee and Cassmore, *Pecan Shellers of San Antonio*; Ragsdale, *Year America Discovered Texas*; Rips and Tenayuca, "Living History"; Shapiro, "Pecan Shellers of San Antonio"; Tenayuca, oral history interview; Vargas, "Tejana Radical"; "Walter Cronkite Remembers"

NOTES

in recognition of the unprecedented educational advantages: quoted in Ragsdale, 290.

Good God, all our children are dead: quoted in Brown and Wereschagin, 73.

You couldn't look anywhere: quoted in Brown and Wereschagin, 73.

I helped to gather nearly a bushel basket: quoted in Brown and Wereschagin, 73.

Oil and natural gas: Dingus.

the first awful rumble: quoted in Brown and Wereschagin, 228.

Out of this explosion we have learned of a new hazard: quoted in Brown and Wereschagin, 229.

San Antonio is—as it has always been: Federal Writers' Project, 5.

At the end of the day there was a brown haze: quoted in Abigail and Leon.

Let a Bank Account shelter you: Shapiro, 232.

Compared to those shanties they live in: quoted in Menefee and Cassmore, 50.

It was right she would be called La Pasionara: Rips and Tenayuca, 7.

I am satisfied that we have been here: Rips and Tenayuca, 7.

She would go house to house: Abigail and Leon.

The Tenayuca woman: quoted in Vargas, 564.

In the midst of this community: quoted in Vargas, 569.

I remember it exactly: Maverick, 20.

The civil liberties of everybody in San Antonio: quoted in Rips and Tenayuca, 13.

very very simple: Tenayuca, oral history interview.

How in the world are you anyway: quoted in Caro, 696.

I like bread and biscuits: Crawford, 28.

From the Texas plains and hills and valleys: quoted in Caro, 700.

Boy, is business good: quoted in Crawford, 36.

All right, boys, give 'em a tune: quoted in Crawford, 32.

Texas, it appears, has once more turned wild and woolly: quoted in McKay, 47.

crooning corporal of the panoplied forces: quoted in Green, 26.

suitable and qualified person: McKay, 390.

At this very hour—3 p.m.: *Dallas Morning News*, April 22, 1941, 16.

41. TEXANS AT WAR AGAIN

SOURCES

R. Atkinson, *Day of Battle*; Braudaway, "John R. Brinkley"; Brooks, *Street in Bronzeville*; Caro, *Path to Power*; Caro, "Search for Coke Stevenson"; Chamberlain, "Doris Miller"; T. Connally, *My Name Is Tom Connally*; Crawford, *Please Pass the Biscuits*; Dallek, *Lone Star Rising*; Driskill and Casad, *Chester W. Nimitz*; Green, *Establishment in Texas Politics*; McKay, *W. Lee O'Daniel*; *Pittsburgh Courier*, January 2, 1943; Sapper, "Aboard the Wrong Ship"; Schultz, *Crossing the Rapido*; L. Smith, *River Swift and Deadly*; F. Walker, *From Texas to Rome*; Wooster, *Texans in World War II*

NOTES

The only way Negroes can die in Uncle Sam's democratic Navy: quoted in Sapper, 3.

It wasn't hard: quoted in Sapper, 4.

were so low you could see them grinning: quoted in Wooster, 19.

I actually downed four Japanese bombers: Pittsburgh Courier, January 2, 1943, 4.
distinguished devotion to duty: Chamberlain.
Still—am I good enough to die for them: Brooks, 44–45.
then looked down toward the floor: Connally, 249.
A long, hard war lay ahead: Connally, 250.
I won't be back until God knows when: quoted in Driskill and Casad, 106.
Tell Nimitz to get the hell out: quoted in Driskill and Casad, 109.
that man of cheerful yesterdays and confident tomorrows: quoted in Driskill and Casad, 128.
If there's one place bigger than Texas: quoted in Driskill and Casad, 198.
The war will end: quoted in Driskill and Casad, 141.
This marks the first time: Chamberlain.
Egg Breaking Capital of the World: Wooster, 39.
the biggest carnival in American politics: quoted in Crawford, 45.
all energy is sex energy: Braudaway.
I hope you know, Lyndon: quoted in Dallek, 176,
All-Out Patriotic Revue: Caro, Path to Power, 715.
The Mexican voter: quoted in Caro, 721.
an amazing change of votes: Dallek, 223.
I have always enjoyed a good scrap: quoted in McKay, 503–504.
as liberal as the people: Caro, "Search for Coke Stevenson."
keep the White in Old Glory: Green, 50.
the saddle, the rifle, the ax, and the Bible: Green, 79.
those questions usually take care of themselves: quoted in Green, 82.
far reaching evil: Green, 83.
nest of homosexuals: Green, 87, 88.
a sweet little oddball: quoted in Schultz, 93.
In this war, I have known a lot of officers: quoted in Schultz, 93.
I'm going to get me one of those smart-aleck toasters: quoted in Schultz, 94.
Gradually, one by one I could sense them moving closer: quoted in Schultz, 95.
First that it would be impossible: quoted in Smith, 17.
We have to cross the Rapido: Walker, 300, 302.
We had the feeling we were being sacrificed: quoted in Schultz, 130.
we are getting an epidemic of horrible mine wounds: quoted in Schultz, 147.
Fire wholeheartedly, men: quoted in Schultz, 188.
If you didn't get wounded: quoted in Schultz, 187.

I had 184 men: quoted in Atkinson, 348.
We look forward to your next visit: Atkinson, 348.

42. THE SHOW OF SHOWS

SOURCES

Critical Past, "Captain Kermit Beahan"; Gambrell, "Philosophical Society of Texas"; Graham, No Name on the Bullet; Hatfield, Rudder; Hobby, Around the World; Hobby, Mr. Chairman; Hurt, "Last of the Great Ladies"; Kingseed, From Omaha Beach; Lockwood and Adamson, Through Hell and Deep Water; New York Times, "Kermit Beahan"; Pando, "Oveta Culp Hobby"; "President Clinton at D-Day 50th Anniversary"; Russell, Train to Crystal City; Sweeney, War's End; Wiggins, Torpedoes in the Gulf; Winegarten, Oveta Culp Hobby

NOTES

It can't be done: quoted in Hatfield, 94.
I gave up hope of getting off Pointe du Hoc alive: quoted in Hatfield, 150.
If Colonel Rudder had not led us in this battle: quoted in Hatfield, 156.
The dissidents will have a hell of a fight: quoted in Hatfield, 385.
When history books are written: "President Clinton at D-Day 50th Anniversary."
dash, boldness, initiative, teamwork: Ambrose, 352.
The visions of the future: Kingseed, 99.
When the big day comes: Kingseed, 143.
Words can never describe: Kingseed, 154.
I saw Audie's picture on the cover: quoted in Graham, 130.
such a nervous condition: quoted in Graham, 129.
didn't look sixteen years old: Graham, 37.
a sad type person: quoted in Graham, 20.
If Murphy was in the front lines: quoted in Graham, 72.
Just hold the phone: quoted in Graham, 89.
no exhilaration at being alive: quoted in Graham, 92.
animals . . . Aboriginal tribes . . . Natural curiosities: Gambrell.
I think I'm going to enjoy this war: quoted in Lockwood and Adamson, chap. 8.
The Harder was the most high-spirited boat: quoted in Lockwood and Adamson, chap. 15.
The Harder was in the middle of an enemy convoy: quoted in Lockwood and Adamson, chap. 13.

They were expecting the biggest invasion: quoted in Wiggins, 120.
We hated that statue: quoted in Russell, 42.
There was no place like Crystal City: quoted in Russell, xix.
Oveta was never young: quoted in Winegarten, 3.
pretty sure it [drinking] was something: quoted in Winegarten, 4.
I never thought about a romance: quoted in Hurt, 148.
I always felt so at ease with him: Hurt, 148.
In every field of life: Hobby, 26.
to break down the traditional American and Christian opposition: quoted in Pando, 113.
imbued with the mores: quoted in Pando, 92.
He chose intimidating: quoted in Pando, 2.
All she wanted was for someone: quoted in Pando, 2.
mute reminders of the atomic bomb: Hobby, 7.
If it was possible to deliver a bomb: Sweeney, 111.
Captain Beahan: Critical Past.
It looked like a picture of hell: quoted in New York Times, "Kermit Beahan."

43. A NEW TEXAS

SOURCES
G. W. Bush, 41; A. Cunningham, "Good-Bye to Robin"; Meacham, Destiny and Power; Minutaglio, City on Fire

NOTES
What you need to do is head out to Texas: Meacham, 77.
caught the fever: quoted in Meacham, 92.
I don't know what I'm going to do today: quoted in A. Cunningham, 80.
You should take her home: Cunningham, 80.
As I sprinted over to the car: Bush, 56.
We just got up and went out: Cunningham, 82.
an ominous Oz: quoted in Minutaglio, 4.
I feel like I'm sitting on a keg of dynamite: quoted in Minutaglio, 11.
a wicked place, a very wicked place: quoted in Minutaglio, 19.
It is needless to point out to the citizens: quoted in Minutaglio, 13.
If that wasn't a fire: quoted in Minutaglio, 118.
I expected, somehow: quoted in Minutaglio, 214.

44. YE SHALL KNOW THE TRUTH

SOURCES
Abilene (TX) Reporter-News, March 20, 1950; Boessenecker, Texas Ranger; Burrough, Big Rich; Caro, Means of Ascent; Carroll, Felix

Longoria's Wake; Dallek, Lone Star Rising; Gillette, "Heman Marion Sweatt"; Green, Establishment in Texas Politics; Harrigan, "Main Street"; Lavergne, Before "Brown"; Tolson, "Dark Symphony"; S. Walker, "Where Are They Now?"

NOTES
They tell us to forget democracy is spurned: Tolson, 315.
did not have any more than the normal amount of prejudice: quoted in Lavergne, 102.
not real smart, but lovable: quoted in Lavergne, 105.
This applicant is a citizen of Texas: quoted in Lavergne, 104.
vomitous contempt: quoted in Lavergne, 109.
darken the door of the University of Texas: quoted in Lavergne, 110.
substantially equivalent: Lavergne, 136.
basement school: Lavergne, 151.
Please remember that I asked for Education: quoted in Lavergne, 223.
We won the big one: quoted in Lavergne, 253.
a complete emotional wreck: Gillette, 181.
the whites would not like it: quoted in Carroll, 56.
I have never seen such general disregard: quoted in Carroll, 35.
the one most constructive act: quoted in Dallek, 298.
It never entered his mind: quoted in Caro, 198.
a variety of business tycoons: quoted in Dallek, 325.
We were getting a thousand people: quoted in Dallek, 306.
The river is low: quoted in Green, 114.
that they were known to kill people: quoted in Caro, 323.
He appeared to be an old man: quoted in Boessenecker, 454.
when Frank Hamer walked down the street: quoted in Caro, 327.
Git: Caro, 327.
I deeply regret that the prejudice: Carroll, 66.
peculiar blend of swagger and valor: Abilene (TX) Reporter-News, March 20, 1950, 7; available at Barry Popik, The Big Apple (blog), November 25, 2007, https://www.barrypopik.com/index.php/new_york_city/entry/texas_is_a_blend_of_valor_and_swagger_carl_sandburg.
Luling—The Home of Edgar B. Davis: Walker, 35.
I have no right to any of this money: Walker, 45.
Here's the theatre, and here's the play: Walker, 42.
quite a long play: Walker, 40.
URGENT ACT TWO SCENE ONE: Walker, 44.

I am perfectly happy: Walker, 35.
looked a little like Barrymore's Hamlet: Burrough, 170.
perhaps the greatest ever undertaken: quoted in Burrough, 176.
It's a Patek: Harrigan, "Main Street," 158–159. All quotations from the interview are from this source.
I don't get depressed: Harrigan.

45. THE LORD TAKES A SLEEPING PILL

SOURCES
Amburn, Dark Star; Bartley, Tidelands Oil Controversy; Carleton, Red Scare!; Galveston Daily News, July 11, 1949; Graves, Myself and Strangers; Green, Establishment in Texas Politics; J. L. Haley, Passionate Nation; Hunt, Alpaca; Kinch and Long, Allan Shivers; Porterfield, "Hunt's Long Goodbye"; San Antonio Express and News, September 15, 1968; Time, "Education: Bertie & the Board"; L. Wright, "The Tide Turns"

NOTES
There are so many ways to be lonesome: quoted in Amburn, 19.
desperately aspirant writer: Graves, 27.
No one who wears white shoes: quoted in Wright, 332.
secret mission: Galveston Daily News, July 11, 1949, 1.
racial purity laws: Green, 108.
You're kidding: quoted in Kinch and Long, 59.
I want to give you one bit of advice: quoted in Kinch and Long, 15.
Texas, the proud Lone Star State: quoted in Kinch and Long, 74.
He wasn't mean, he was just tough: Wright, 330.
beginning at the mouth of the Sabine River: quoted in Bartley, 82.
maintain the integrity of her Territory: quoted in Haley, 267.
My kids came running in from the TV set: quoted in Green, 147.
robbery in broad daylight: quoted in Green, 143.
I'll have to take that boy's pants down before I'm through: quoted in Wright, 338.
Sometimes a man just gets to wondering: Green, 151.
Senator McCarthy has done more than anyone: quoted in Carleton, 137.
Joe McCarthy—a real American: quoted in Carleton, 228.
secret family: San Antonio Express and News, September 15, 1968, 1-K.

like the kindly judge: San Antonio Express and News, September 15, 1968, 1-K.
I'm a crank about creeping: quoted in Porterfield, 67.
Yes, he said, kissing her upturned face: Hunt, 129.
moved in and about the timberlines: Porterfield, 68.
members were interested in keeping: quoted in Carleton, 125.
racial and religious cooperation week: quoted in Carleton, 184.
the training of children: quoted in Carleton, 186.
thumb through it pretty fast: quoted in Carleton, 212.
I find it a bit ironic: quoted in Carleton, 223.
pre-marital counseling and tantamount to practicing communism: Carleton, 231, 250.
I'd rather go to jail: Time, "Education: Bertie & the Board."
sheer hell: quoted in Time, "Education: Bertie & the Board."
I've been trying to warn you: Carleton, 294.

46. GIANT

SOURCES
A. Bauer, "Ralph Yarborough's Ghost"; Burnett, "When the Sky Ran Dry"; Campbell, Gone to Texas; Dallek, Lone Star Rising; C. Dawson, Miles and Miles of Texas; Ferber, Giant; Fuermann, Reluctant Empire; Giant script; Gilbert, Ferber; Graham, Giant; Green, Establishment in Texas Politics; Hendrickson, Collins, and Cox, Profiles in Power; Kelton, Time It Never Rained; "Port Arthur Story"; T. Reid, "Texas Edison"; Thompson and O'Connor, Marfa and Presidio County

NOTES
Put the jam on the lower shelf: Hendrickson, Collins, and Cox, 163.
the most incredible cross-referenced mind: Bauer.
All of my instincts: quoted in Green, 156.
proven Communist leadership: quoted in Hendrickson, Collins, and Cox, 157.
This is a city in Texas: "Port Arthur Story."
Allan really doesn't like to demagogue: quoted in Green, 165.
This Negro tried to go to a white school: Fuermann, 204.
orderly protest against a situation: quoted in Campbell, 427.
nature will take its course: quoted in Green, 175.
No senator had ever approached me: quoted in Dallek, 378.

You really felt as if a St. Bernard: quoted in
Dallek, 474.
She wants to leave now: quoted in Thompson
and O'Connor, 198.
Oh, no, I don't want to know any more people:
Thompson and O'Connor, 198.
great mahogany-faced men bred on beef: Ferber,
45.
cloud-wreathed mountains: Ferber, 3.
Here in Texas we are very modern: Ferber, 46.
Leslie found that the steak once cut: Ferber, 117.
Who gets hold of millions of acres: quoted in
Graham, 11.
For sheer embroidery of fact: Gilbert, 188.
James Dean's talent: quoted in Graham, 241.
That oil tax exemption: *Giant* script.
be a death blow to our industry: Graham, 237.
It was the color of a green Coke bottle: quoted in
Burnett.
Just another dry spell: Kelton, 1.
The cattle would weaken down: quoted in
Burnett.
A system of highway pieces: quoted in Dawson,
222.
You could design a nuclear-powered: quoted in
Reid, 106.

47. A GAMBLIN' MAN

SOURCES
Amburn, *Dark Star*; Caro, *Master of the Senate*; Caro, *Passage of Power*; Dallek, *Lone Star Rising*; *Texas Observer*; "Bold Sit-Ins in Marshall"; Leuchtenburg, *FDR Years*; Zambrano, *"Texas History Movies"*

NOTES
greasers and tamale eaters: Zambrano.
every peace officer in the county: *Texas Observer*, 1.
a heart-to-heart talk: *Texas Observer*, 2.
it's not outside but what's inside: quoted in
Amburn, 74.
the club is very big: quoted in Amburn, 90.
He sat there paralyzed: quoted in Amburn, 147.
If only I hadn't eaten that cantaloupe: quoted in
Caro, *Master of the Senate*, 621.
Doctor, let me ask you something: quoted in
Caro, *Master of the Senate*, 624.
He became the god-damnedest diet fanatic: quoted
in Caro, *Master of the Senate*, 631.
It would kill him if he relaxed: quoted in Caro,
Master of the Senate, 628.
no Texan wants to be vice president: quoted in
Dallek, 504.
chameleon on plaid: Leuchtenburg.
I never had any bigotry in me: quoted in Caro,
Master of the Senate, 712.

I can't be too easy with you: quoted in Caro,
Master of the Senate, 717.
We've started something now: quoted in Caro,
Master of the Senate, 1003.
He is the first Southern Democratic leader: quoted
in Dallek, 527.
Son, you've got to learn to handle a gun: quoted
in Caro, *Passage of Power*, 71.
It's not worth a bucket of warm piss: quoted in
Caro, *Passage of Power*, 110.
Clare, I looked it up: quoted in Caro, *Passage of
Power*, 115.

48. WELCOME MR. KENNEDY

SOURCES
Caro, *Passage of Power*; J. Connally, *In History's Shadow*; Dealey, *Diaper Days of Dallas*; Marcus, *Minding the Store*; Miller, *Nut Country*; Minutaglio and Davis, *Dallas 1963*; Reston, *Lone Star*; "Testimony of Mr. and Mrs. Connally"; Valenti, *This Time, This Place*; L. Wright, *In the New World*; L. Wright, "They Hate Us So Much"

NOTES
Nothing I had done publicly up to that time: Marcus, 252.
It would be foolhardy: quoted in Miller, 79.
socialized milk: Miller, 84.
filthy with clean children: quoted in Miller, 82.
Who can ever repeal the law of nature: quoted in
Miller, 82.
political widow: quoted in Minutaglio and
Davis, 58.
They are not our folks: quoted in Minutaglio
and Davis, 13.
The election of a Catholic as president: Wright,
"They Hate Us So Much," 150.
I am the best writer I know: Minutaglio and
Davis, 27.
ALPACA! Fifty cents: Minutaglio and Davis,
28.
The colored people of the community: Dealey, 150.
The President of the United States: quoted in
Minutaglio and Davis, 55.
The prettiest bunch of women I ever saw in my life:
quoted in Minutaglio and Davis, 58.
We're gonna show Johnson: quoted in Minutaglio and Davis, 62.
No man is afraid to facing up to such people:
quoted in Minutaglio and Davis, 65.
We lost Texas: quoted in Minutaglio and
Davis, 66.
I don't have to come here from Illinois: quoted in
Minutaglio and Davis, 245.
Kennedy will get his reward in hell: quoted in
Minutaglio and Davis, 246.

pushed from behind by a Negro: quoted in Minutaglio and Davis, 249.
Adlai got what was coming to him: quoted in Minutaglio and Davis, 256.
I was on the wrong side: quoted in Minutaglio and Davis, 167.
I am a Christian martyr: quoted in Minutaglio and Davis, 153.
conspiracy from within: Minutaglio and Davis, 168.
We're heading into nut country today: quoted in Minutaglio and Davis, 302.
was pure hogwash: "Testimony of Mr. and Mrs. Connally."
The antipathy that raged: Valenti, 6.
the most charismatic man in American public life: Valenti, 6.
too pretty to be handsome: quoted in Reston, 246.
Great Jawbone: Reston, 415.
I used to take off my shoes: Connally, 27.
The line between dramatics and politics: Connally, 4.
There is nothing in the world more useless: quoted in Connally, 53.
She repeated once again: Connally, 155.
Couldn't be worse: Connally, 158.
Moscow's Trojan Horse: quoted in Minutaglio and Davis, 293.
extending the hand of fellowship: quoted in Minutaglio and Davis, 292.
You and your administration are weak sisters: quoted in Minutaglio and Davis, 108.
the most dangerous man in America: Miller, 101.
I missed: quoted in Minutaglio and Davis, 216.
Sonny, everybody seems old to you: quoted in Caro, 334.
In that instant, the world we knew shattered: L. Wright, *In the New World*, 63.

49. *EL DEGÜELLO* REPRISE

SOURCES

Behnken, *Fighting Their Own Battles*; J. Connally, *In History's Shadow*; Diaz, "Texas Farmworker"; Dugger, "Gonzales of San Antonio"; Gutiérrez, *Making of a Chicano Militant*; Manchester, *Death of a President*; Montejano, *Quixote's Soldiers*; Reston, *Lone Star*; *Texas Observer*, "Confrontation"; *Texas Observer*, "Shock Waves from Popeye Land"

NOTES

That's just Lyndon: quoted in Manchester, 82.
¡Viva!: Manchester, 67.
Viva country: quoted in Manchester, 70.
legalized slavery: quoted in Behnken, 105.
I remember we would drink: quoted in Diaz.
Super Mex: Dugger, part 5, 7.
Meskin greaser: Dugger, part 2, 20.
Oh, they were very racist: Dugger, part 3, 15.
The Irish have a saying: quoted in Behnken, 59.
Gandhi might as well have run for governor: Dugger, part 3, 24.
full of bullshit: Dugger, part 4, 15.
The rumor in the barrio: Gutiérrez, 36.
In retrospect, it seems crazy: Gutiérrez, 37.
They say there is no discrimination: quoted in Behnken, 88.
making the Meskins act crazy: Gutiérrez, 44.
I could believe neither my eyes or ears: Gutiérrez, 44.
I urge your complete cooperation: *Texas Observer*, "Shock Waves from Popeye Land," 6.
Oh, my God, it hurts! It hurts!: quoted in Reston, 277.
The governor is not expected to live: quoted in Reston, 281.
under a never-ending series of scenarios: Connally, 177.
My door has been open: *Texas Observer*, "Confrontation," 10.
Governor Connally is the symbol: quoted in Behnken, 109.
brown berets, combat boots, serapes: Montejano, 287n94.
It's too late for the gringo: quoted in Montejano, 112.
cabrón vendido: Montejano, 109.
Well, you're a little dumb shit: Dugger, part 5, 11.

50. THE VOICE OF GOD

SOURCES

Broyles, "Making of Barbara Jordan"; Freeman, "Dr. Freeman Reflects"; Gittinger and Fisher, "LBJ Champions Civil Rights Act"; L. Johnson, "Address before a Joint Session"; B. Jordan, Democratic National Convention Keynote Speech; B. Jordan, Statement on the Articles of Impeachment; Jordan and Hearon, *Barbara Jordan*; Richards, Eulogy for Barbara Jordan; Rogers, *Barbara Jordan*

NOTES

Whoever heard of an outstanding pharmacist?: Broyles, 130.
Catch that nigger, he's got a gun: quoted in Rogers, 17.
He felt himself quite different: Jordan and Hearon, 8.

the resolute few who dare go through: Jordan and Hearon, 23.

I decided that I was not going to be like the rest: Jordan and Hearon, 64.

She had it in the cradle: Broyles, 130.

I thought I was listening to God: quoted in Broyles.

She could not argue: Freeman.

could go in the front door: Jordan and Hearon, 79.

could no longer orate: Jordan and Hearon, 93.

Separate was not equal: Jordan and Hearon, 93.

Is politics worth staying in for me?: Jordan and Hearon, 117.

was the ward of her man: Jordan and Hearon, 118.

I made the decision: Jordan and Hearon, 119.

He lay on his huge bed in his pajamas: quoted in Gittinger and Fisher.

We have talked long enough: Johnson.

a black LBJ: Broyles, 200.

stands before us as the central figure: quoted in Rogers, 166.

the best politician of this century: Broyles, 127.

Today I am an in-quis-i-tor: B. Jordan, Statement on the Articles of Impeachment.

Right on: Jordan and Hearon, 199.

one additional bit of evidence: B. Jordan, Democratic National Convention Keynote Speech.

It is not my turn: Jordan and Hearon, 234.

I believe I have a spirit: quoted in Rogers, 333.

She forever redefined what it meant: Richards.

51. THE TOWER

SOURCES

J. Atkinson, "Texas Primer"; Cartwright, *Turn Out the Lights*; Colloff, "96 Minutes"; Robert Duvall; Friedman, "Ballad of Charles Whitman"; Harvey, "Integrating SWC Took Heavy Toll"; Lavergne, *Sniper in the Tower*; Maher and Bohls, *Long Live the Longhorns!*; McEachern, *DKR*; Politi, "Texas School Shooter"; J. Reid, "Blood of the Lamb"; Ross, "53 Veer Pass"; Thetford, "Walker, Ewell Doak, Jr."; Woodbury, "Ten Minutes in Hell"

NOTES

This is war: Reid, 144.

This is payback day: Woodbury.

so he could have his story told: Politi.

You know, that would be a great place: Colloff.

I have just taken my mother's life: Lavergne, 103.

All of a sudden I felt like: quoted in Colloff.

It was something giant: quoted in Lavergne, 103.

There was a rumor: Friedman.

It was awfully hard, just a real hard childhood: quoted in McEachern, 9.

the workingest kid: quoted in McEachern, 8.

owns one of the most brilliant masses: quoted in McEachern, 29.

the wishbone was equal parts: Atkinson.

Something told me to go out there: Robert Duvall, telephone interview with the author, June 2018.

quite simply the greatest: quoted in Reid.

get out while I still have all my teeth: quoted in Thetford.

You're going to have to learn to steer: quoted in Reid.

Someone had to serve as the laboratory rat: quoted in Cartwright.

living hell: Harvey.

the biggest thing to happen in the Southwest Conference: Maher and Bohls, 173.

I just thought it was time to swing: Ross.

Y'all aren't going to believe this call: quoted in Maher and Bohls, 171.

52. VIGIL ON THE PEDERNALES

SOURCES

Aldrin, *Return to Earth*; "Apollo 11 Astronauts"; Aterryazios, "Ramsey Muñiz"; B. Barnes, *Barn Burning*; Behnken, *Fighting Their Own Battles*; Burka, "Ben Barnes"; J. Connally, *In History's Shadow*; Deaton, *They Threw the Rascals Out*; Dallek, *Flawed Giant*; Draper, "Blood of the Farentholds"; D. Goodwin, *Johnson and the American Dream*; Harper, *Eleven Days in Hell*; L. Johnson, "Decision to Not Seek Reelection"; Meacham, *Destiny and Power*; "Ramsey Muñiz Video"; Nelson, "Lloyd Bentsen"; *O'Hair v. Paine*, 397 U.S. 531 (1970); Reston, *Lone Star*; G. Smith, "Why Does Dolph Briscoe"

NOTES

want of jurisdiction: *O'Hair v. Paine*, 397 U.S. 531 (1970).

Neil might have been the first man: Aldrin, chap. 8.

Beautiful. Beautiful: Aldrin, chap. 8.

Houston, Tranquility Base here: Aldrin, chap. 8.

Because of what you have done: "Apollo 11 Astronauts."

I shall not seek: Johnson.

nation's most trusted person: Dallek, 506.

mired in stalemate: quoted in Dallek, 506.

full equality which God enjoins: quoted in Dallek, 82.

in getting the Civil Rights Act of 1964: Goodwin, 340.

After thirty-seven years of public service: Goodwin, 343.

the greatest day in the world: quoted in Dallek, 609.

Along this stream and under these trees: Connally, 215.

I believed that John Connally: quoted in Reston, 443.

I've never seen him sweat: Nelson.

I guess there were just too many Democrats: quoted in Meacham, 150.

Politics is not a game: Smith.

I was walking down a cotton row: quoted in Deaton, 60.

we must live in the midst of yesterday's mistakes: quoted in Deaton, 11.

facing the jury box: quoted in Deaton, 34.

You couldn't invent a better training program: B. Barnes, 27.

He is always hurrying somewhere: Burka.

Every one of you that's going to vote: B. Barnes, 173.

He's a redhead: B. Barnes, 186.

I'd just turned 34 years old: B. Barnes, 215.

melancholy rebel: quoted in Draper.

unbelievable torment: Draper.

a soul-searing experience: quoted in Deaton, 66.

The unsavory smell of corruption: quoted in Deaton, 36.

the Texas Rangers are a festering sore: Deaton, 92.

We're poor, man: Muñiz.

the only good gringo is a dead gringo: Behnken, 184.

From the beginning: Aterryazios.

I know there's a lot of people who want: quoted in Harper, 22.

galled his soul: quoted in Harper, 28.

could have been a fine gentleman: quoted in Harper, 156.

With all our love: Harper, 228.

If the clothes are not good: quoted in Harper, 53.

make it, how do you say it, crunchy: quoted in Harper, 53.

53. A SIDE TO BELONG TO

SOURCES

Jones and Winegarten, *Capitol Women*; Mackintosh, "Good Old Girls"; McArthur and Smith, *Texas through Women's Eyes*; McCorvey, *I Am Roe*; McCorvey, *Won by Love*; Nemy, "Liz Carpenter"; Nemy, "Mary Kay Ash"; "What Really Happened in Houston," *Phyllis Schlafly Report*; Prager, "Accidental Activist"; *Roe v. Wade*, 314 F. Supp.

1217 (N.D. Tex. 1970); Spruill, *Divided We Stand*; Stokes, "Mary Kay Cosmetics"; Tobolowsky, "For Equal Rights Amendment"; Weddington, *Question of Choice*

NOTES

a rough woman, born into pain and anger: McCorvey, *I Am Roe*, 2.

a die-hard whore: Prager.

What are you two girls doing in there?: McCorvey, *I Am Roe*, 26.

shove her fucking shirt: McCorvey, *I Am Roe*, 29.

a furburger and a cherry coke: McCorvey, *I Am Roe*, 42.

poor old dog with no hair: McCorvey, *I Am Roe*, 100.

I didn't want to have to give up another child: *I Am Roe*, 104.

We both felt strongly: Weddington, 51.

Young women must preserve: Weddington, 22.

had no strong feelings either way: Weddington, 15.

In her excitement: McCorvey, *I Am Roe*, 120.

unconstitutionally vague: *Roe v. Wade*, 314 F. Supp. 1217 (N.D. Tex. 1970).

that would allow me, and millions of other women: McCorvey, *I Am Roe*, 124.

Fuck you: McCorvey, *I Am Roe*, 133.

a scared and angry cleaning woman: *I Am Roe*, 171.

Though the pro-lifers saw me as their nemesis: McCorvey, *Won by Love*, chap. 4.

involved in a bloody, dehumanizing business: McCorvey, *Won by Love*, chap. 9.

all the Jane Does who died for Choice: McCorvey, *I Am Roe*, dedication.

all the children who have been torn apart: McCorvey, *Won by Love*, dedication.

She feels at the end of the day: Prager.

Legal equality for every citizen: Tobolowsky, 1074.

that sweet little girl: quoted in Jones and Winegarten, 163.

I believe in equal rights for women: quoted in Jones and Winegarten, 159.

Four Days That Changed the World: Spruill, 2.

Let this message go forth from Houston: quoted in Spruill, 7.

to be brainwashed by people who predict chaos: quoted in Spruill, 220.

This is a sad time for all people: Nemy, "Liz Carpenter."

Are we to be forever shackled: Spruill, 219.

reminds me of Barbara Stanwyck: Mackintosh, 153.

I rise on behalf of my two daughters: quoted in Mackintosh, 153.

God's plan for inner beauty: From a de-

scription of the book on its Amazon page, https://www.amazon.com/You-Can-Be-Beautiful-Beauty/dp/0913838012.
God created you: quoted in McArthur and Smith, 247.
put on the full armor of God: quoted in Spruill, 237.
We salute a great lady: Phyllis Schlafly Report.
One of my strongest reasons: Stokes.
From 14 to 40: Nemy, "Mary Kay Ash."

54. DON'T BE SO SELF-RIGHTEOUS

SOURCES

Adler, *Mollie's Job*; Barron, "Remembering Bill Clements"; Burka, "Remembering Bill Clements"; Burka, "Strange Case of Mark White"; Burrough, *Big Rich*; G. H. W. Bush, "Acceptance Speech"; Clopper, "Journal"; Clymer, "Jim Wright Dies"; J. Connally, *In History's Shadow*; Elkind, "Going for Broke"; Fountain, "Jackpot of the Plains"; Gregory, *Stupid History*; Harrigan, "Governor's New Clothes"; Klein, "Little Bit of a Snake"; Kleinfield, "He Had Money"; M. Mayer, *Greatest-Ever Bank Robbery*; Meacham, *Destiny and Power*; Pittsburg *Post-Gazette*, March 28, 1980; Porterfield, "Hunt's Long Goodbye"; J. Reid, *Let the People In*; Reinert, "Not Guilty"; Reinhold, "Connally's Texas-Sized Troubles"; Reinhold, "Impact of Texas School Law"; Reston, *Lone Star*; Richards, speech, Democratic National Convention; Stutz, "Bill Clements"; *Texas Week Magazine*, "'Failing,' Texas Writers"; Waldman, *Who Robbed America?*; Yergin, *The Prize*

NOTES

have to pay for their meat: Clopper.
a Los Angeles architect's idea: Texas Week Magazine, "'Failing,' Texas Writers," 30.
the ones in Mexico are far superior: Texas Week Magazine, "'Failing,' Texas Writers," 30.
We haven't seen anything but a pretty barren land: Yergin, 374.
galaxy of fields of the first magnitude: Yergin, 374.
The center of gravity of world oil production: quoted in Yergin, 375.
You're the one I've been hearing so many things about: quoted in Yergin, 499.
I shall know Him: Porterfield, 66.
the kind of guy who orders chicken-fried steak: Pittsburg Post-Gazette, "Texas' Silver-Plated Billionaire Hunt Has Midas Touch with Money," March 28, 1980.

Bunker was just obsessed: quoted in Burrough, 388.
Any damn fool can run a printing press: quoted in Burrough, 390.
Do you think there's any possibility: quoted in Burrough, 396.
they'll have all the silver in the world: quoted in Burrough, 398.
A billion dollars: quoted in Burrough, 404.
Something was stirring: Meacham, 114.
Texan to his toenails: quoted in Burka, "Remembering Bill Clements."
I'm a nuts and bolts guy: Harrigan.
you could make more money: Harrigan.
He never recovered from Texas' seceding: Harrigan.
much ado about nothing: quoted in Burka, "Remembering Bill Clements."
Pray for a hurricane: Stutz.
Just another Mexican with an opinion: quoted in Adler, 274n.
no housewife was qualified: quoted in Burka, "Remembering Bill Clements."
There's no profit in being White's friend: Burka, "Strange Case of Mark White," 136.
We are in a world race: Reinhold, "Impact of Texas School Law."
to calm down and not be so self-righteous: quoted in Barron.
The loan officers would close one sale: quoted in Waldman, 35.
wasn't about producing things: Fountain.
gastronomique fantastique: quoted in Waldman, 2.
the highest of the high fliers: Kleinfield.
rejected as speculative: Gregory, 146.
There were just too many of us: quoted in Mayer, 11.
a heavy-handed son of a bitch: Clymer.
mindless cannibalism: Clymer.
Every Texan is in a box today: Reinhold, "Connally's Texas-Sized Troubles."
It's a good thing John Connally: quoted in Reston, 453.
I should have spent more time with that boy: quoted in Reston, 434.
They haven't printed enough money to buy me: quoted in Klein, 40.
some folks don't like him: quoted in Reinert.
We were all bulletproof: Elkind, 218.
We're beginning an era of prosperity: quoted in Elkind, 124.
The man who once signed the nation's money: Connally, 307.
He seemed to be the fulfillment: quoted in Reston, 307.
No woman should lose her wedding silver: Connally, 314.

[When] the movers came: Connally, 310.
Our work is not done, our force is not spent: Bush.
I'm delighted to be here with you this evening:
   Richards.
Everything that is not a mystery is guesswork:
   Reid, 50.

55. BAPTISM OF FIRE

SOURCES
Jarboe, "Meet the Governor"; McGaughy,
   "First to Ban Open Carry"; Newport,
   Branch Davidians of Waco; Reavis, *Ashes of
   Waco*; J. Reid, *Let the People In*; Thibodeau,
   Waco; *Waco: Madman or Messiah*, interview
   with Charles Pace

NOTES
It was of a silver angel: quoted in Newport, 158.
I don't know how in the world: *Waco: Madman or
   Messiah*, part 1.
Revelation 1 says that I am the root: Newport,
   183.
Despite his easy ways: Thibodeau, 52.
It's a toughie: Thibodeau, 50.
Take Michele as a wife: Thibodeau, 103.
dynamic entry: Newport, 246.
Police! Search warrant! Get down: Reavis, 140.
Call it off: Thibodeau, 162.
My Commander-in-Chief told me to wait: *Waco:
   Madman or Messiah*, part 2.
It was not law enforcement's intent: quoted in
   Reavis, 266.
This is not an assault: quoted in Reavis, 276.
Most of the burned bodies: Thibodeau, 257.
I'll see y'all in the skies: Thibodeau, 172.
Ann was snookered: Reid, 373.
on or about his person: McGaughy.
incursions by hostile Indians: McGaughy.
the amateur gunslingers: Reid, 374.
Richards Wins in Mudslide and *lined his pockets*:
   Reid, 229, 227.
I want to give back to our kids: Jarboe, 122.
They might, but I'm not going to do it: Jarboe,
   154.

I rat the tar out of it: quoted in Reid, 265.
ride horseback, head and hoof her, and *if it's inevitable*: quoted in Reid, 240, 251.
load 'er up and blast away again: quoted in
   Reid, 260.

56. TEXANS VS. TEXANS

SOURCES
G. H. W. Bush, *Decision Points*; G. H. W.
   Bush, Inaugural Address; G. W. Bush, *41*;
   L. Bush, *Spoken from the Heart*; "Bush's
   Unforgettable 9/11 Bullhorn Speech";
   Draper, *Dead Certain*; Gaines and Dorning,
   "Myth of Perot's Iran Rescue"; Gwynne,
   "Genius"; Hodgkinson, "Bush's Patriot
   Games"; "Mariah, Beyonce, Katy, Jlo";
   Meacham, *Destiny and Power*; McNeely and
   Henderson, *Bob Bullock*; Patoski, *Selena*;
   Perez, *To Selena*; J. Reid, *Let the People In*;
   Rove, *Courage and Consequence*; Shenk-
   man, "Iran Rescue"; Taraborrelli, *Becoming
   Beyoncé*; Texas Republican Gubernatorial
   Primary Debate; "20/20—Selena's Killer,
   Part 1"; Updegrove, *Last Republicans*; L.
   Wright, "Man from Texarkana"

NOTES
the vision thing: Meacham, xxii.
I'm not going to go dance on the wall: G. W.
   Bush, 195.
We don't need to do that this year: quoted in
   Meacham, 409.
tax revenue increases: Meacham, 414.
Firestorm on Right: Meacham, 416.
to make kinder the face of the nation: G. H. W.
   Bush, Inaugural Address.
The Fastest Richest Texan Ever: Wright, 34.
I have found the Navy: quoted in Wright, 31.
these guys had to have been in live combat:
   Shenkman.
spring outing: Gaines and Dorning.
I want to tell you what's going on: quoted in
   Updegrove, 239.
a big massive ego trip and *a highly wired up*:
   Meacham, 503, 514.

never been too hot with words: quoted in
  Meacham, 250.
Message: I care: G. W. Bush, 229.
Don't cry for me, Argentina: Meacham, 499.
How's it going, son?: G. W. Bush, 243.
I did actually meet Selena: "Mariah, Beyonce,
  Katy, Jlo."
It don't get much bigger than Astroworld:
  Taraborrelli, loc. 651.
Play Spanish music: quoted in Patoski, 21.
When I realized that Selena could sing: quoted in
  Patoski, 36.
It gave you chill bumps: quoted in Patoski, 37.
the sensational nine-year-old singer: Patoski, 41.
the ultimate stage father: Patoski, 54.
You're dead: Perez, 39.
Selena was, in a word, good: Perez, 32.
God, if only I was like Selena: Patoski, 121.
*In my opinion, she was living her life through
  Selena*: "20/20—Selena's Killer, Part 1."
a small, sad, ugly little woman: Perez, 569.
Ladies and gentlemen: Texas Republican Guber-
  natorial Primary Debate.
So, what is sex like after fifty?: G. H. W. Bush,
  Decision Points, 33.
Son, you can't win: G. H. W. Bush, *Decision
  Points*, 39.
While Kent Hance graduated: quoted in G. H. W.
  Bush, *Decision Points*, 40.
George, you can't win: G. H. W. Bush, *Decision
  Points*, 53.
Island in Shock: Gwynne, 86.
We woke up every morning and got hammered:
  Gwynne, 87.
Richards' facade looked big and imposing: Rove,
  82, 84.
There was a real strange sense: Reid, 390.
I had seen enough politics: G. H. W. Bush, *Deci-
  sion Points*, 54.
I've served with four governors: quoted in
  Draper, 390.
it took the edge off: McNeely and Henderson,
  129.
Do what's good for Texas: McNeely and Hen-
  derson, 176.

The chair recognizes the crybaby from Waco:
  quoted in McNeely and Henderson, 211.
It's just a temporary eruption: quoted in
  McNeely and Henderson, 256.
a cocky little motherfucker: McNeely and Henderson, 259.
in the heat my skin stuck: L. Bush, 29.
the sounds of his parents' choked sobs: L. Bush,
  61.
I can hear you: "Bush's Unforgettable 9/11
  Bullhorn Speech."
their heads full of the Alamo: Hodgkinson.

EPILOGUE

SOURCES
Draper, "O Janis"; S. Hardin, *Texian Maca-
bre*; Harrigan, *Comanche Midnight*; Hol-
landsworth, "Minor Regional Novelist";
K. Jones, "Georgia O'Keeffe"; McMurtry,
In a Narrow Grave; Nelson, *The Facts of Life:
And Other Dirty Jokes*; Patoski, *Willie Nelson*;
D. Reid, *Have a Seat, Please*; J. Reid, *Let the
People In*; Rhodes, *John James Audubon*

NOTES
a scowl in the expression of his eyes: quoted in
  Rhodes, 399.
shanties, cargoes of hogsheads, barrels: Rhodes,
  399.
Ah, my dear friend: quoted in Harrigan, 82.
It is absurd the way I love this country: Jones.
People have no idea: Hollandsworth.
a bookless town: McMurtry, 63.
Don't get too caught up: Patoski, 476.
What are you looking at me for?: Nelson, 10.
The dusty road calls you: quoted in Draper, 183.
I recommend that your response: quoted in
  J. Reid, 222.
Have a seat, please: D. Reid, 15.
No place in Texas more healthy: quoted in Har-
  din, 81.
A splendid map of the city: quoted in Hardin,
  82.

BIBLIOGRAPHY

Abbott, E. C., and Helena Huntington Smith. *We Pointed Them North: Recollections of a Cowpuncher*. Norman: University of Oklahoma Press, 1939. Reprint, 1955.

Abigail, R. Matt, and Jazmin Leon. "Tenayuca, Emma Beatrice." Handbook of Texas Online, February 10, 2016; modified January 26, 2017. https://tshaonline. org/handbook/online/articles/fte41.

Acheson, Sam Hanna. *Joe Bailey: The Last Democrat*. New York: Macmillan, 1932.

Adams, John Quincy. *Speech of the Hon. John Quincy Adams in the House of Representatives on the State of the Nation: Delivered May 25, 1836*. New York: Piercy, 1836.

Adler, William M. *Mollie's Job: A Story of Life and Work on the Global Assembly Line*. New York: Simon and Schuster, 2001.

Ajemian, Robert. "Where Is the Real George Bush?" *Time*, January 26, 1987. http://content.time.com/time/subscriber/article/0,33009,963342-3,00.html.

Aldrin, Buzz. *Return to Earth*. New York: Random House, 1973. Kindle.

Allan, Francis D. *Allan's Lone Star Ballads: A Collection of Southern Patriotic Songs, Made During Confederate Times*. Galveston: Sawyer, 1874.

Allen, Ruth A. *The Great Southwest Strike*. University of Texas Publication 4214. Bureau of Research in the Social Sciences. Austin: University of Texas, 1942.

Alvarez, Elizabeth Cruce, ed. *Texas Almanac, 2014–2015*. Denton: Texas State Historical Association, 2014.

Alvord, Wayne. "T. L. Nugent, Texas Populist." *Southwestern Historical Quarterly* 57, no. 1 (July 1953): 65–81.

Amberson, Mary Margaret McAllen, James A. McAllen, and Margaret H. McAllen. *I Would Rather Sleep in Texas: A History of the Lower Rio Grande Valley and the People of the Santa Anita Land Grant*. Denton: Texas State Historical Association, 2003.

Ambrose, Stephen E. *D-Day*. New York: Simon and Schuster, 1994.

———. *Eisenhower*. Vol. 1: *Soldier, General of the Army, President-Elect, 1890–1952*. New York: Simon and Schuster, 1983.

Amburn, Ellis. *Dark Star: The Roy Orbison Story*. New York: Carol, 1990.

American Oil and Gas Historical Society. "First Lone Star Discovery." https://aoghs.org/petroleum-pioneers/first-texas-oil-well.

Anders, Evan. *Boss Rule in South Texas: The Progressive Era*. Austin: University of Texas Press, 1982.

Anderson, Adrian. "President Wilson's Politician: Albert Sidney Burleson of Texas." *Southwestern Historical Quarterly* 77, no. 3 (January 1974): 339–354.

Anderson, Charles G. *In Search of the Buffalo: The Story of J. Wright Mooar*. Seagraves, TX: Pioneer, 1974.

Anderson, Gary Clayton. *The Conquest of Texas: Ethnic Cleansing in the Promised Land, 1820–1875*. Norman: University of Oklahoma Press, 2005.

Anderson, Ken. *Dan Moody: Crusader for Justice*. Georgetown, TX: Georgetown Press, 2008.

Annual Report of the American Historical Association for the Year 1919. Vol. 2, *The Austin Papers*, part 1. Edited by Eugene C. Barker. Washington: Government Printing Office, 1924.

Annual Report of the American Historical Association for the Year 1919. Vol. 2, *The Austin Papers*, part 2. Edited by Eugene C. Barker. Washington: Government Printing Office, 1924.

"Apollo 11 Astronauts Talk with Richard Nixon from the Surface of the Moon." Posted on YouTube by the AT&T Tech Channel, July 20, 2012, https://www.youtube.com/watch?v=ieGKIh3k0AI.

Arnold, J. Barto, III, and Robert S. Weddle. *The Nautical Archeology of Padre Island: The Spanish Shipwrecks of 1554*. New York: Academic Press, 1978.

Aterryazios, Diana. "Ramsey Muñiz." *Texas Monthly*, November 2002. https://www.texasmonthly.com/articles/ramsey-muniz.

Atkinson, Jim. "Texas Primer: The Wishbone Offense." *Texas Monthly*, October 1985. https://www.texasmonthly.com/the-culture/texas-primer-the-wishbone-offense.

Atkinson, Rick. *The Day of Battle: The War in Sicily and Italy, 1943–1944*. New York: Holt, 2007.

Austin, Stephen F. "Journal of Stephen F. Austin on His First Trip to Texas, 1821." *Quarterly of the Texas State Historical Association* 7, no. 4 (April 1904): 287–307.

Austin Papers. Dolph Briscoe Center for American History, University of Texas at Austin.

Baker, T. Lindsay, and Billy R. Harrison. *Adobe Walls: The History and Archaeology of the 1874 Trading Post*. College Station: Texas A&M University Press, 1986.

Ball, Gregory W. *They Called Them Soldier Boys: A Texas Infantry Regiment in World War I*. Denton: University of North Texas Press, 2013.

Balsley, Clyde. "The Story of the Lafayette Escadrille." As told to Paul Adams. *Bellman*, July 20, 1918, 68–72.

Barker, Eugene C. *The Life of Stephen F. Austin, Founder of Texas, 1793–1836*. Austin: University of Texas Press, 1969.

Barnes, Ben. *Barn Burning, Barn Building: Tales of a Political Life, from LBJ to George W. Bush and Beyond*. With Lisa Dickey. Albany, TX: Bright Sky, 2006.

Barnes, C. H. *History of the 142nd Infantry of the Thirty-Sixth Division: October 15, 1917, to June 17, 1919; Including a Sketch of First Oklahoma Infantry and Seventh Texas Infantry*. [Blackwell, OK]: Blackwell Job Printing, 1922.

Barr, Alwyn. *Reconstruction to Reform: Texas Politics, 1876–1906*. Dallas: Southern Methodist University Press, 2000.

Barr, Amelia E. *All the Days of My Life: An Autobiography—The Red Leaves of a Human Heart*. New York: Appleton, 1913.

Barr, Juliana. *Peace Came in the Form of a Woman: Indians and Spaniards in the Texas Borderlands*. Chapel Hill: University of North Carolina Press, 2007.

Barron, David. "Remembering Bill Clements and the SMU Death Penalty." *Houston Chronicle*, May 30, 2011. https://blog.chron.com/sportsupdate/2011/05/remembering-bill-clements-and-the-smu-death-penalty.

Bartley, Ernest R. *The Tidelands Oil Controversy: A Legal and Historical Analysis*. Austin: University of Texas Press, 1953.

Bauer, A. J. "Ralph Yarborough's Ghost." *Texas Observer*, September 21, 2007. https://www.texasobserver.org/2590-ralph-yarboroughs-ghost-fifty-years-after-his-election-to-the-senate-many-overlook-his-legacy-but-the-patron-saint-of-texas-liberals-still-has-something-to-teach-a-new-generation.

Bauer, K. Jack. *The Mexican War, 1846–1848*. New York: Macmillan, 1974. Reprint, Lincoln: University of Nebraska Press, 1992.

Bean, Christopher. "Death of a Carpetbagger: The George Washington Smith Murder and Stockade Trial in Jefferson, Texas, 1868–1869." *Southwestern Historical Quarterly* 112, no. 3 (2009): 262–292.

Behnken, Brian D. *Fighting Their Own Battles: Mexican Americans, African Americans, and the Struggle for Civil Rights in Texas*. Chapel Hill: University of North Carolina Press, 2011.

Bell, Bob Boze. "Bad Day at Round Rock: Sam Bass Gang vs. Texas Rangers." *True West*, June 1, 2010, www.truewestmagazine.com/bad-day-at-round-rock.

Bernhard, Virginia, ed. *The Hoggs of Texas: Letters and Memoirs of an Extraordinary Family, 1887–1906*. Austin: Texas State Historical Association, 2014.

Bernstein, Patricia. *Ten Dollars to Hate: The Texas Man Who Fought the Klan*. College Station: Texas A&M University Press, 2017.

Berry, Margaret C. *UT History 101: Highlights in the History of the University of Texas*. Austin: Eakin, 1997.

Biggers, Don Hampton. *Our Sacred Monkeys, or 20 Years of Jim and Other Jams (Mostly Jim), the Outstanding Goat Gland Specialist of Texas Politics*. Brownwood, TX: Jones Printing, 1933.

Bixel, Patricia Bellis, and Elizabeth Hayes Turner. *Galveston and the 1900 Storm*. Austin: University of Texas Press, 2000.

Blackburn, J. K. P. "Reminiscences of the

Terry Rangers, I." *Southwestern Historical Quarterly* 22, no. 1 (July 1918): 38–77. Available at JSTOR, https://www.jstor.org/stable/30234772?seq=1#page_scan_tab_contents.

Block, W. T. *Sour Lake, Texas: From Mud Baths to Millionaires, 1835–1909.* Liberty, TX: Atascocita Historical Society, 1995.

Boatman, T. Nicole, Scott H. Belshaw, and Richard B. McCaslin. *Galveston's Maceo Family Empire: Bootlegging and the Balinese Room.* Charleston, SC: History Press, 2014.

Boessenecker, John. *Texas Ranger: The Epic Life of Frank Hamer.* New York: Dunne, 2016.

Bolton, Herbert Eugene, ed. *Athanase de Mézières and the Louisiana-Texas Frontier, 1768–1780.* Vol. 1. Cleveland: Clark, 1914.

———. *Coronado: Knight of Pueblos and Plains.* New York: Whittlesey House, 1949.

———. *Spanish Exploration in the Southwest, 1542–1706.* New York: Charles Scribner's Sons, 1916. Reprint, Andesite Press, 2017.

———. *Texas in the Middle Eighteenth Century.* Vol. 3: *Studies in Spanish Colonial History and Administration.* Berkeley: University of California Press, 1915. Reprint, London: Forgotten Books, 2018.

Bordewich, Fergus M. *America's Great Debate: Henry Clay, Stephen A. Douglas, and the Compromise that Preserved the Union.* New York: Simon & Schuster, 2012.

Boyd, Carolyn E. *The White Shaman Mural: An Enduring Creation Narrative in the Rock Art of the Lower Pecos.* With contributions by Kim Cox. Austin: University of Texas Press, 2016.

Bradley, Edward A. *"We Never Retreat": Filibustering Expeditions into Spanish Texas, 1812–1822.* College Station: Texas A&M University Press, 2015.

Brands, H. W. *Lone Star Nation: The Epic Story of the Battle for Texas Independence.* New York: Doubleday, 2004.

Braudaway, Doug. "Dr. John R. Brinkley: The Goat-Gland Man." Val Verde County Historical Commission, http://vvchc.net/marker/dr-brinkley.html.

Brindley, Anna A. "Jane Long." *Southwestern Historical Quarterly* 56, no. 2 (October 1952): 211–238.

Brooks, Gwendolyn. *A Street in Bronzeville.* New York: Harper and Brothers, 1945.

Brown, David M., and Michael Wereschagin. *Gone at 3:17.* Lincoln, NE: Potomac, 2012.

Brown, Norman D. *Hood, Bonnet, and Little Brown Jug: Texas Politics, 1921–1928.* Col-

lege Station: Texas A&M University Press, 1984.

Browning, John G. "From Outlaw to Attorney at Law: The Brief Legal Career of John Wesley Hardin," *Journal of the Texas Supreme Court Historical Society* 7, no. 2 (Winter 2018), www.texascourthistory.org/Content/Newsletters//Journal%20Winter%202018%20Vol%207%20No%202.pdf.

Broyles, William, Jr. "The King Ranch." *Texas Monthly,* October 1980.

———. "The Making of Barbara Jordan." *Texas Monthly,* October 1976.

Bruseth, James E., and Toni S. Turner. *From a Watery Grave: The Discovery and Excavation of La Salle's Shipwreck, "La Belle."* College Station: Texas A&M University Press, 2005.

Buckley, Gail. *American Patriots: The Story of Blacks in the Military from the Revolution to Desert Storm.* New York: Random House, 2002.

Bullock State History Museum. *La Belle: The Ship That Changed History.* Edited by James E. Bruseth. Published for the Bullock State History Museum by Texas A&M Press, 2014.

Burka, Paul. "Ben Barnes." *Texas Monthly,* September 2001. https://www.texasmonthly.com/articles/ben-barnes-2.

———. "Remembering Bill Clements." *Texas Monthly,* May 30, 2011. https://www.texasmonthly.com/burka-blog/remembering-bill-clements/.

———. "The Strange Case of Mark White." *Texas Monthly,* October 1986.

Burke, Robert. "The Day Texas City Lost Its Fire Department." Firehouse, May 1, 2007. https://www.firehouse.com/rescue/article/10505314/the-day-texas-city-lost-its-fire-department.

Burnett, John. "When the Sky Ran Dry." *Texas Monthly,* July 2012. https://www.texasmonthly.com/articles/when-the-sky-ran-dry.

Burrough, Bryan. *The Big Rich: The Rise and Fall of the Greatest Texas Oil Fortunes.* New York: Penguin, 2009.

Bush, George H. W. Acceptance Speech, 1988 Republican National Convention. YouTube, https://www.youtube.com/watch?v=gZCwsEozANM.

———. Inaugural Address, January 20, 1989. Available at the American Presidency Project, www.presidency.ucsb.edu/ws/index.php?pid=16610.

————. *Decision Points.* New York: Crown, 2010.

Bush, George W. *41: A Portrait of My Father.* New York: Crown, 2014.

Bush, Laura. *Spoken from the Heart.* New York: Scribner, 2010.

Cabeza de Vaca, Álvar Núñez. *The Narrative of Cabeza de Vaca.* Edited, translated, and with an introduction by Rolena Adorno and Patrick Charles Pautz. Lincoln: University of Nebraska Press, 2003.

Calvert, Robert A., Arnoldo De León, and Gregg Cantrell. *The History of Texas.* 5th ed. Chichester, UK: Wiley-Blackwell, 2014.

Campbell, Randolph B. *An Empire for Slavery: The Peculiar Institution in Texas, 1821–1865.* Baton Rouge: Louisiana State University Press, 1991.

————. *Gone to Texas: A History of the Lone Star State.* 3rd ed. New York: Oxford University Press, 2017.

Cantrell, Gregg. *Stephen F. Austin: Empresario of Texas.* New Haven, CT: Yale University Press, 1999.

Carleton, Don E. *Red Scare! Right-Wing Hysteria, Fifties Fanaticism, and Their Legacy in Texas.* Austin: Texas Monthly Press, 1985.

Carlson, Paul H., and Tom Crum. *Myth, Memory, and Massacre: The Pease River Capture of Cynthia Ann Parker.* Lubbock: Texas Tech University Press, 2010.

Caro, Robert A. "My Search for Coke Stevenson." *New York Times,* February 3, 1991. https://www.nytimes.com/1991/02/03/books/my-search-for-coke-stevenson.html.

————. *The Years of Lyndon Johnson: Master of the Senate.* New York: Knopf, 2002.

————. *The Years of Lyndon Johnson: Means of Ascent.* New York: Knopf, 1990.

————. *The Years of Lyndon Johnson: The Passage of Power.* New York: Knopf, 2012.

————. *The Years of Lyndon Johnson: The Path to Power.* New York: Knopf, 1982.

Carr, William R. "Remembering the 'Wizard of Words.'" January 19, 1998. Brann the Iconoclast, www.heritech.com/pridger/brann/brann.htm#pin.

Carter, Robert G. *On the Border with Mackenzie; or, Winning West Texas from the Comanches.* Washington, DC: Eynon, 1935.

Cartwright, Gary. *Galveston: A History of the Island.* Fort Worth: Texas Christian University Press, 1998.

————. *Turn Out the Lights: Chronicles of Texas During the 80s and 90s.* Austin: University of Texas Press, 2000.

Carver, Charles. *Brann and the Iconoclast.* Austin: University of Texas Press, 1957.

Castañeda, Carlos E. *Our Catholic Heritage in Texas, 1519–1936.* Vol. 2: *The Mission Era: The Winning of Texas, 1693–1731.* Austin: Von Boeckmann-Jones, 1936.

————, trans. *The Mexican Side of the Texas Revolution (1836) by the Chief Mexican Participants.* Dallas: Turner, 1928. Reprint, 1956.

Cavalcade of Texas. Souvenir program. Dallas, 1936.

Chamberlain, Gaius. "Doris Miller" Great Black Heroes, January 25, 2012. www.greatblackheroes.com/government/doris-miller.

Chapa, Juan Bautista. *Texas and Northeastern Mexico, 1630–1690.* Edited by William C. Foster. Austin: University of Texas Press, 1997.

Chipman, Donald E., and Harriett Denise Joseph. *Notable Men and Women of Spanish Texas.* Austin: University of Texas Press, 2010.

————. *Spanish Texas, 1519–1821.* Austin: University of Texas Press, 2000.

Christian, Garna L. *Black Soldiers in Jim Crow Texas, 1899–1917.* College Station: Texas A&M University Press, 1995.

"Chronicles of Oklahoma." Oklahoma State University website, http://digital.library.okstate.edu/Chronicles/v032/v032p029.pdf.

Clarkson, Janet. *Food History Almanac: Over 1,300 Years of World Culinary History.* Lanham, MD: Rowman and Littlefield, 2003.

Clopper, Joseph Chambers. "J. C. Clopper's Journal and Book of Memoranda for 1828: Province of Texas." *Quarterly of the Texas State Historical Association* 13, no. 1 (July 1909): 44–80.

Clymer, Adam. "Jim Wright Dies at 92; House Speaker Resigned amid Ethics Charges." *New York Times,* May 6, 2015.

Colahan, Clark A. *The Visions of Sor María de Agreda: Writing, Knowledge, and Power.* Tucson: University of Arizona Press, 1994.

Collins, Michael L. *A Crooked River: Rustlers, Rangers, and Regulars on the Lower Rio Grande, 1861–1877.* Norman: University of Oklahoma Press, 2018.

Colloff, Pamela. "96 Minutes." *Texas Monthly,* August 2006. https://www.texasmonthly.com/articles/96-minutes.

Connally, John. *In History's Shadow: An American Odyssey.* With Mickey Herskowitz. New York: Hyperion, 1993.

Connally, Tom. *My Name Is Tom Connally.*

As told to Alfred Steinberg. New York: Crowell, 1954.

Constitution of the Republic of Texas (1836). Texas Constitutions 1824–1876. Tarlton Law Library website, https://tarltonapps.law.utexas.edu/constitutions/texas1836/general_provisions.

Constitution of the State of Texas (1866). Texas Constitutions 1824–1876. Tarlton Law Library website, https://tarltonapps.law.utexas.edu/constitutions/texas1866/a10.

Constitution of the State of Texas (1869). Texas Constitutions 1824–1876. Tarlton Law Library website, https://tarltonapps.law.utexas.edu/constitutions/texas1869/a6.

"Coronado's Report to the King of Spain Sent from Tiguex on October 20, 1541." New Perspectives on the West, PBS (KLRU). www.pbs.org/weta/thewest/resources/archives/one/corona9.htm.

Corridos y Tragedias de la Frontera. "Gregorio Cortez: A Texas Mystery." Updated May 7, 2001. Liberal Arts Instructional Technology Services, University of Texas at Austin. http://www.laits.utexas.edu/jaime/jnicolopulos/cwp3/icg/cortez/index.html.

Cotner, Robert C. *James Stephen Hogg: A Biography*. Austin: University of Texas Press, 2014.

Cox, Mike. *The Texas Rangers: Wearing the Cinco Peso, 1821–1900*. New York: Doherty, 2008.

Cozzens, Peter. *Eyewitnesses to the Indian Wars, 1865–1890. Volume Three: Conquering the Southern Plains*. Mechanicsburg, PA: Stackpole Books, 2003.

Crawford, Bill. *Please Pass the Biscuits, Pappy*. Austin: University of Texas Press, 2004.

Critical Past. "Captain Kermit Beahan, Bombardier of B-29 That Dropped Atomic Bomb on Nagasaki." YouTube, July 15, 2014. https://www.youtube.com/watch?v=kxGBtFNI2lc.

Crook, Elizabeth. "Sam Houston and Eliza Allen: The Marriage and the Mystery." *Southwestern Historical Quarterly* 94, no. 1 (July 1990): 1–36.

Crouch, Barry A., and Donaly E. Brice. *Cullen Montgomery Baker: Reconstruction Desperado*. Baton Rouge: Louisiana State University Press, 1997.

Crouch, Barry A., and Donaly E. Brice. *The Governor's Hounds: The Texas State Police, 1870–1873*. Austin: University of Texas Press, 2011.

Culver, Edith Dodd. *The Day the Airmail Began*. Kansas City: Cub Flyers Enterprises, 1971.

Cunniff, M. G. "Texas and the Texans." *World's Work*, March 1906, 7267–7288. Available at the Internet Archive, https://archive.org/stream/worldswork11gard#page/7266/mode/2up.

Cunningham, Amy. "Good-Bye to Robin." *Texas Monthly*, February 1988.

Cunningham, Eugene. *Triggernometry: A Gallery of Gunfighters*. New York: Press of the Pioneers, 1934. Reprint, digital ed., Pickle Partners, 2016. https://play.google.com/books/reader?id=24zjDAAAQBAJ&printsec=frontcover&pg=GBS.PT3.

Cutrer, Emily Fourmy. *The Art of the Woman: The Life and Work of Elisabet Ney*. College Station: Texas A&M University Press, 1988.

Cutrer, Thomas W. "Hébert, Paul Octave." Handbook of Texas Online, June 15, 2010. https://tshaonline.org/handbook/online/articles/fheo9.

———. "Magruder, John Bankhead." Handbook of Texas Online, June 15, 2010; modified January 18, 2013. https://tshaonline.org/handbook/online/articles/fma15.

Dallek, Robert. *Flawed Giant: Lyndon Johnson and His Times, 1961–1973*. New York: Oxford University Press, 1998.

———. *Lone Star Rising: Lyndon Johnson and His Times, 1908–1960*. New York: Oxford University Press, 1991.

Davis, William C. *The Pirates Laffite: The Treacherous World of the Corsairs of the Gulf*. New York: Houghton Mifflin, 2005.

———. *Three Roads to the Alamo: The Lives and Fortunes of David Crockett, James Bowie, and William Barret Travis*. New York: Harper Perennial, 1999.

Dawson, Carol. *Miles and Miles of Texas: 100 Years of the Texas Highway Department*. With Roger Allen Polson. College Station: Texas A&M University Press, 2016.

Dawson, John C. *High Plains Yesterdays: From XIT Days through Drouth and Depression*. Austin: Eakin, 1985.

Dealey, Ted. *Diaper Days of Dallas*. Nashville: Abingdon, 1966.

DeArment, Robert K. *Jim Courtright of Fort Worth: His Life and Legend*. Fort Worth: Texas Christian University Press, 2004.

Deaton, Charles. *The Year They Threw the Rascals Out*. Austin: Shoal Creek, 1973.

DeBruhl, Marshall. *Sword of San Jacinto*. New York: Random House, 1993.

"Declaration of Causes: February 2, 1861—A declaration of the causes which impel the State of Texas to secede from the Federal Union." Texas State Library and Archives Commission website, https://www.tsl.texas.gov/ref/abouttx/secession/2feb1861.html.

de la Teja, Jesús, ed. *Lone Star Unionism, Dissent, and Resistance: Other Sides of Civil War Texas*. Norman: University of Oklahoma Press, 2016.

———, ed. *A Revolution Remembered: The Memoirs and Selected Correspondence of Juan N. Seguín*. Austin: Texas State Historical Association, 2002.

———. *San Antonio de Béxar: A Community on New Spain's Northern Frontier*. Albuquerque: University of New Mexico Press, 1995.

———. *Tejano Leadership in Mexican and Revolutionary Texas*. College Station: Texas A&M University Press, 2010.

de la Teja, Jesús F., Paula Marks, and Ron Tyler. *Texas: Crossroads of North American*. Boston: Houghton Mifflin, 2004.

de León, Alonso, Juan Bautista Chapa, and Fernando Sánchez de Zamora. *Historia de Nuevo León, con noticias sobre Coahuila, Tamaulipas, Texas y Nuevo México*. Edited by Israel Cavazos Garza. Monterrey: Fondo Editorial Nuevo León, 1985.

Devereaux, Linda. "Barret, Lyne Taliaferro." Handbook of Texas Online, June 12, 2010. https://tshaonline.org/handbook/online/articles/fba80.

Diaz, Joy. "Texas Farmworker: 1966 Strike 'Was like Heading into War.'" NPR, August 12, 2016, https://www.npr.org/2016/08/12/489491157/texas-farmworker-1966-strike-was-like-heading-into-war.

Digital Austin Papers. http://digitalaustinpapers.org.

Dingus, Anne. "The New London School Explosion." *Texas Monthly*, March 2001. https://www.texasmonthly.com/articles/the-new-london-school-explosion.

Dixon, Olive K. *Life of "Billy" Dixon: Plainsman, Scout and Pioneer*. Revised ed. Dallas: Southwest Press, 1914.

Dobie, J. Frank. *The Longhorns*. Boston: Little, Brown, 1941. Reprint, Austin: University of Texas Press, 1980.

"Documents on the Brownsville Uprising of Juan Cortina." Archives of the West, 1856–1868. KLRU/PBS, www.pbs.org/weta/thewest/resources/archives/four/cortinas.htm.

Donovan, James. *The Blood of Heroes: The Thirteen-Day Struggle for the Alamo—and the Sacrifice That Forged a Nation*. New York: Back Bay, 2013.

Draper, Robert. "The Blood of the Farentholds." *Texas Monthly*, April 1992. https://www.texasmonthly.com/articles/the-blood-of-the-farentholds.

———. *Dead Certain*. New York: Free Press, 2007.

———. "O Janis." *Texas Monthly*, October 1992.

Driskill, Frank A., and Dede W. Casad. *Chester W. Nimitz: Admiral of the Hills*. Austin: Eakin, 1983.

Dugger, Ronnie. "Gonzalez of San Antonio." Part 2: "From Revolution to the Capital." *Texas Observer*, April 11, 1980, 8–10, 20–22.

———. "Gonzalez of San Antonio." Part 3: "The South Texas Cauldron: Guns, Disease, Politics, Victory." *Texas Observer*, May 9, 1980, 15–24.

———. "Gonzalez of San Antonio." Part 4: "The Establishment." *Texas Observer*, October 17, 1980, 4–6, 14–22.

———. "Gonzalez of San Antonio." Part 5: "The Politics of Fratricide." *Texas Observer*, December 12, 1980, 1, 6–11, 15–19.

Dunn, Jeff. "The Mexican Soldier Skulls of San Jacinto Battleground." The Friends of the San Jacinto Battleground, www.friendsofsanjacinto.com/sites/default/files/uploads/MexicanSkulls4-1-10.pdf.

Dunn, William Edward. "Apache Relations in Texas, 1718–1750." *Quarterly of the Texas State Historical Association* 14, no. 3 (January 1911): 198–275.

Durham, George, and Clyde Wantland. *Taming the Nueces Strip*. Austin: University of Texas Press, 1962.

Egan, Timothy. *The Worst Hard Time*. Boston: Houghton Mifflin, 2006.

Ehrenberg, Herman. *With Milam and Fannin: Adventures of a German Boy in Texas' Revolution*. Translated by Charlotte Churchill. Dallas: Tardy, 1935. Reprint, Austin: Pemberton, 1968.

"(1866) Texas Black Codes." BlackPast website, www.blackpast.org/primarywest/1866-texas-black-codes.

Elkind, Peter. "Going for Broke." *Texas Monthly*, October 1986, 122–127, 216–230, 238.

Elliott, Debbie. "Galveston: Destruction and Reconstruction." NPR, September 10, 2005. https://www.npr.org/templates/story/story.php?storyId=4840557&t=1534502932050.

Estleman, Loren D. *Roy and Lillie: A Love Story*. New York: Forge, 2010.

Evans, H. W. *The Klan of Tomorrow and the Klan Spiritual: Addresses by H. W. Evans, Imperial Wizard, Delivered at the Second Imperial Klonvokation Held in Kansas City, Missouri, September 23, 24, 25, and 26, 1924*. Published by Knights of the Ku Klux Klan, 1924.

Everett, Dianna. *The Texas Cherokees: A People between Two Fires, 1819–1840*. Norman: University of Oklahoma Press, 1990.

Ewing, Thomas E. *Texas through Time: Lone Star Geology, Landscapes, and Resources*. Austin: Bureau of Economic Geology, University of Texas, 2016.

Federal Writers' Project of the Works Progress Administration in the State of Texas. *San Antonio: An Authoritative Guide to the City and Its Environs*. San Antonio: Clegg, 1938.

Fedewa, Marilyn H. *María of Ágreda: Mystical Lady in Blue*. Albuquerque: University of New Mexico Press, 2009.

Fehrenbach, T. R. *Lone Star: A History of Texas and the Texans*. New York: Macmillan, 1968.

Ferber, Edna. *Giant*. Garden City, NY: Doubleday, 1952. Reprint, New York: Harper Perennial, 2000.

Ferguson, James E. Papers. Dolph Briscoe Center for American History, University of Texas at Austin.

Ferrell, Robert H., ed. *Monterrey Is Ours! The Mexican War Letters of Lieutenant Dana, 1845-1847*. Lexington: University Press of Kentucky, 1990.

Flanagan, Sue. *Sam Houston's Texas*. Austin: University of Texas Press, 1964.

———. *Trailing the Longhorns*. Austin: Madrona, 1974.

Flint, Richard. *No Settlement, No Conquest: A History of the Coronado Entrada*. Albuquerque: University of New Mexico Press, 2008.

Flint, Richard, and Shirley Cushing Flint, trans. and eds. *Documents of the Coronado Expedition, 1539–1542: They Were Not Familiar with His Majesty, nor Did They Wish to Be His Subjects*. Dallas: Southern Methodist University Press, 2005.

Flores, Dan. *Journal of an Indian Trader: Anthony Glass and the Texas Trading Frontier, 1790–1810*. College Station: Texas A&M University Press, 1985.

Flores Magón, Ricardo. "A La Mujer." *Regeneración*, September 24, 1910. Available at the Anarchy Archives, "Ricardo Flores Magón: Collected Works," http://dwardmac.pitzer.edu/Anarchist_Archives/bright/magon/works/regen/mujer.html.

Foote, Shelby. *The Civil War: A Narrative; Fort Sumter to Perryville*. New York: Random House, 1958.

Ford, John Salmon. *Rip Ford's Texas*. Edited by Stephen B. Oates. Austin: University of Texas Press, 1963.

"Forgotten Victory—Part I: Capturing Blanc Mont Ridge." Doughboy Center, www.worldwar1.com/dbc/bm1.htm.

Foster, William C. *The La Salle Expedition to Texas: The Journal of Henri Joutel, 1684–1687*. Austin: Texas State Historical Association, 1998.

———. *Spanish Expeditions into Texas, 1689–1768*. Austin: University of Texas Press, 1995.

Fountain, Ben. "Jackpot of the Plains." *Texas Monthly*, February 2013. https://www.texasmonthly.com/articles/jackpot-of-the-plains.

Fowler, Will. *Santa Anna of Mexico*. Lincoln: University of Nebraska Press, 2009.

Frankel, Glenn. *The Searchers: The Making of an American Legend*. New York: Bloomsbury USA, 2014.

Freeman, Thomas F. "Dr. Freeman Reflects on His Relationship with Barbara Jordan," 1975. Texas Archive of the Moving Image, http://texasarchive.org/library/index.php/2013_00005.

"French Exiles in Texas 1818." Sons of DeWitt Colony Texas website, www.sonsofdewittcolony.org/frenchexiles.htm.

Friedman, Kinky. "The Ballad of Charles Whitman." Genius, https://genius.com/Kinky-friedman-the-ballad-of-charles-whitman-lyrics.

Fuermann, George. *Reluctant Empire: The Mind of Texas*. New York: Doubleday, 1957.

Gaines, William, and Mike Dorning. "The Myth of Perot's Iran Rescue." *Chicago Tribune*, July 9, 1992.

Gallaway, B. P., ed. *Texas: The Dark Corner of the Confederacy*. 3rd ed. Lincoln: University of Nebraska Press, 1994.

Gambrell, Herbert. *Anson Jones: The Last President of Texas*. Garden City, NY: Doubleday, 1948. Reprint, Austin: University of Texas Press, 1988.

———. *Mirabeau Buonaparte Lamar: Troubadour and Crusader*. Dallas: Southwest Press, 1934.

———. "Philosophical Society of Texas." Handbook of Texas Online, June 15, 2010; modified November 2, 2017. https://tsh-

aonline.org/handbook/online/articles/
vtp04.

Gard, Wayne. "The Fence-Cutters." *South-western Historical Quarterly* 51, no. 1 (1947): 1–15.

Garrett, Julia Kathryn. *Green Flag over Texas: A Story of the Last Years of Spain in Texas.* Austin: Pemberton Press, 1969.

Gavito, Sofia Mireles. "La Leyenda sobre la Mutilación de la Lengua de Belisario Domínguez." *La Voz del Norte*, May 12, 2013. www.lavozdelnorte.com.mx/semanario/2013/05/12/la-leyenda-sobre-la-mutilacion-de-la-lengua-de-belisario-dominguez.

Genoways, Ted. "The Shape of Droughts to Come." *Texas Monthly*, July 2018. https://www.texasmonthly.com/the-culture/drought-to-come-agriculture-water-crisis.

"George W. Bush's Unforgettable 9/11 Bullhorn Speech." Posted to YouTube by Rare Media, September 7, 2016. https://www.youtube.com/watch?v=lOkQ-at_olw.

Giant. Script, adapted by Fred Guiol and Ivan Moffat from Edna Ferber's 1952 novel. Drew's Script-o-Rama, http://www.script-o-rama.com/movie_scripts/g/giant-script-transcript-james-dean.html.

Giboire, Clive, ed. *Lovingly, Georgia: The Complete Correspondence of Georgia O'Keefe and Anita Pollitzer.* New York: Simon & Schuster, 1990.

Gilbert, Julie Goldsmith. *Ferber: Edna Ferber and Her Circle.* New York: Applause, 1978, 1998.

Gillett, James B. *Six Years with the Texas Rangers: 1875 to 1881.* Austin: Von Boeckmann-Jones, 1921.

Gillette, Michael L. "Heman Marion Sweatt: Civil Rights Plaintiff." In *Black Leaders: Texans for Their Times,* edited by Alwyn Barr and Robert A. Calvert, 156–188. Austin: Texas State Historical Association, 1981.

———. *Lady Bird Johnson: An Oral History.* Oxford: Oxford University Press, 2012.

Gittinger, Ted, and Allen Fisher. "LBJ Champions the Civil Rights Act of 1964." *Prologue* 36, no. 2 (Summer 2004). https://www.archives.gov/publications/prologue/2004/summer/civil-rights-act-1.html.

Givner, Joan. *Katherine Anne Porter: A Life.* Rev. ed. Athens: University of Georgia Press, 1991.

Glasrud, Bruce A., Light Townsend Cummins, Gary D. Wintz. *Discovering Texas History.* Norman: University of Oklahoma Press, 2014.

Glasrud, Bruce A., and Michael N. Searles, eds. *Buffalo Soldiers in the West: A Black Soldiers Anthology.* College Station: Texas A&M University Press, 2007.

Goodwin, Doris Kearns. *Lyndon Johnson and the American Dream.* New York: St. Martin's Griffin, 1976.

Goodwin, Robert. *Crossing the Continent, 1527–1540: The Story of the First African-American Explorer of the American South.* New York: HarperCollins, 2008.

Gould, Lewis L. *Progressives and Prohibitionists: Texas Democrats in the Wilson Era.* Austin: University of Texas Press, 1973.

Graham, Don. *Giant: Elizabeth Taylor, Rock Hudson, James Dean, Edna Ferber, and the Making of a Legendary American Film.* New York: St. Martin's, 2018.

———. *No Name on the Bullet: A Biography of Audie Murphy.* New York: Viking Penguin, 1989.

Grant, Ulysses S. *Personal Memoirs of U. S. Grant; Selected Letters, 1839–1865.* New York: Library of America, 1990.

Graves, John. *Myself and Strangers: A Memoir of Apprenticeship.* New York: Knopf, 2004.

Gray, Robert S. *A Visit to Texas in 1831.* 3rd ed. Houston: Cordovan Press, 1975.

Gray, William Fairfax. *Diary of Col. William Fairfax Gray: From Virginia to Texas, 1835.* Houston: Gray, Dillaye, 1909. Reprinted as *Diary of Col. William Fairfax Gray: From Virginia to Texas, 1835–1836.* Houston: Young, 1965.

Grayson, Cary T. "The Colonel's Folly and the President's Distress." *American Heritage* 15, no. 6 (October 1964). www.americanheritage.com/content/colonel%E2%80%99s-folly-and-president%E2%80%99s-distress.

Green, George N. "Connally, Thomas Terry." Handbook of Texas Online, June 12, 2010. https://tshaonline.org/handbook/online/articles/fco36.

———. *The Establishment in Texas Politics: The Primitive Years, 1938–1957.* Norman: University of Oklahoma Press, 1979.

Greenberg, Amy S. *A Wicked War: Polk, Clay, Lincoln, and the 1846 U.S. Invasion of Mexico.* New York: Knopf, 2012.

Greenberg, Sanford N. "White Primary." Handbook of Texas Online, June 15, 2010; modified November 3, 2015. https://tshaonline.org/handbook/online/articles/wdwo1.

"Green DeWitt, 1787–1835: Empresario

from Missouri, Founder of the DeWitt Colony." Sons of DeWitt Colony Texas website, www.sonsofdewittcolony.org//dewitt&kerr2.htm.

Greene, Casey Edward, and Shelly Henley Kelly, eds. *Through a Night of Horrors: Voices from the 1900 Galveston Storm.* College Station: Texas A&M University Press, 2000.

Gregory, Leland. *Stupid History: Tales of Stupidity, Strangeness, and Mythconceptions throughout the Ages.* Kansas City: Andrews McMeel, 2009.

Groneman, Bill. *Eyewitness to the Alamo.* Guilford, CT: Lone Star Books, 2017.

Gutiérrez, José Angel. *The Making of a Chicano Militant: Lessons from Cristal.* Madison: University of Wisconsin Press, 1998.

Guttery, Ben R. *Representing Texas: A Comprehensive History of U.S. and Confederate Senators and Representatives from Texas.* BookSurge, 2008.

Gwynne, S. C. *Empire of the Summer Moon: Quanah Parker and the Rise and Fall of the Comanches, the Most Powerful Indian Tribe in American History.* New York: Scribner, 2010.

———. "Genius." *Texas Monthly*, March 2003.

Habig, Marion A. *The Alamo Chain of Missions: A History of San Antonio's Five Old Missions.* Chicago: Franciscan Herald Press, 1968.

Hackett, Charles W. "The Marquis of San Miguel de Aguayo and His Recovery of Texas from the French, 1719–1723." *Southwestern Historical Quarterly* 49 (October 1945): 193–214.

Hagan, William T. *Quanah Parker, Comanche Chief.* Norman: University of Oklahoma Press, 1993.

Haley, James L. *The Buffalo War: The History of the Red River Indian Uprising of 1874.* Garden City, NY: Doubleday, 1976.

———. *Passionate Nation: The Epic History of Texas.* New York: Free Press, 2006.

———. *Sam Houston.* Norman: University of Oklahoma Press, 2004.

Haley, J. Evetts. *Charles Goodnight: Cowman and Plainsman.* Boston: Houghton Mifflin, 1936. Reprint, Norman: University of Oklahoma Press, 1949.

Hall, Jacquelyn Dowd. *Revolt against Chivalry: Jessie Daniel Ames and the Women's Campaign against Lynching.* New York: Columbia University Press, 1979.

Hallenbeck, Cleve. *The Journey of Fray Marcos de Niza.* Dallas: Southern Methodist University Press, 1949. Reprint, 1987.

Hämäläinen, Pekka. *The Comanche Empire.*

New Haven, CT: Yale University Press, 2008.

Hamilton, Jeff. *My Master: The Inside Story of Sam Houston and His Times.* Dallas: Manfred, Van Nort, 1940. Reprint, Austin: State House Press, 2007.

Hanke, Lewis. *All Mankind Is One: A Study of the Disputation Between Bartolomé de Las Casas and Juan Ginés de Sepúlveda in 1550 on the Religious and Intellectual Capacity of the American Indians.* 1974. Reprint, DeKalb: Northern Illinois University Press, 1994.

Hansen, Todd, ed. *The Alamo Reader: A Study in History.* Mechanicsburg, PA: Stackpole, 2003.

Hardin, John Wesley. *The Life of John Wesley Hardin, as Written by Himself.* Seguin, TX: Smith & Moore, 1896.

Hardin, Stephen L. "A Hard Lot: Texas Women in the Runaway Scrape." *East Texas Historical Journal* 29, no. 1 (1991): 35–45.

———. *Texian Iliad: A Military History of the Texas Revolution.* Austin: University of Texas Press, 1996.

———. *Texian Macabre: A Melancholy Tale of a Hanging in Early Houston.* Abilene, TX: State House Press, 2007.

Hare, Maud Cuney. *Norris Wright Cuney: A Tribune of the Black People.* New York: Wood, 1913.

Harper, William T. *Eleven Days in Hell: The 1974 Carrasco Prison Siege at Huntsville, Texas.* Denton: University of North Texas Press, 2004.

Harrigan, Stephen. *Comanche Midnight.* Austin: University of Texas Press, 1995.

———. "The Governor's New Clothes." *Texas Monthly.* May 1981. https://www.texasmonthly.com/articles/the-governors-new-clothes.

———. "Main Street." *Texas Monthly*, February 1983, 158–159.

Harris, Charles H., III, and Louis R. Sadler. *The Plan de San Diego: Tejano Rebellion, Mexican Intrigue.* Lincoln: University of Nebraska Press, 2013.

———. *The Texas Rangers and the Mexican Revolution: The Bloodiest Decade, 1910–1920.* Albuquerque: University of New Mexico Press, 2004.

Harris, Dilue. "The Reminiscences of Mrs. Dilue Harris, I." *Quarterly of the Texas State Historical Association* 4, no. 2 (October 1900): 85–127.

———. "The Reminiscences of Mrs. Dilue Harris, II." *Quarterly of the Texas State His-*

torical Association 4, no. 3 (January 1901): 155–189.

Harris, Theodore D., ed. *Black Frontiersman: The Memoirs of Henry O. Flipper*. Fort Worth: Texas Christian University Press, 1997.

Hart, John Mason. *Revolutionary Mexico: The Coming and Process of the Mexican Revolution*. Berkeley: University of California Press, 1987.

Harvey, Randy. "Integrating SWC Took Heavy Toll on LeVias." *Houston Chronicle*, August 21, 2013. https://www.houstonchronicle.com/sports/columnists/harvey/article/Integrating-SWC-took-heavy-toll-on-LeVias-4750988.php.

Hatcher, Mattie Austin. "Joaquin de Arredondo's Report of the Battle of the Medina, August 18, 1813." *Quarterly of the Texas State Historical Association* 11, no. 3 (January 1908): 220–236.

Hatfield, Thomas W. *Rudder: From Leader to Legend*. College Station: Texas A&M University Press, 2011.

Haynes, Robert V. *A Night of Violence: The Houston Riot of 1917*. Baton Rouge: Louisiana State University Press, 1976.

Haynes, Sam W. *Soldiers of Misfortune: The Somervell and Mier Expeditions*. Austin: University of Texas Press, 1990.

Hendrickson, Kenneth E., Jr., Michael L. Collins, and Patrick Cox, eds. *Profiles in Power: Twentieth-Century Texans in Washington*. Austin: University of Texas Press, 2004.

Henry, O. "The Caballero's Way." 1907. Available at the Literature Network, www.online-literature.com/o_henry/1002.

Henson, Margaret Swett. "Burnet, David Gouverneur." Handbook of Texas Online, June 12, 2010; modified May 10, 2016. https://tshaonline.org/handbook/online/articles/fbu46.

Hertzberg, H. T., and Friedrich Schenck. "A Letter from Friedrich Schenck in Texas to His Mother in Germany, 1847." *Southwestern Historical Quarterly* 92, no. 1 (July 1998): 144–165. Available at the Portal to Texas History, https://texashistory.unt.edu/ark:/67531/metapth101212/m1/172/?q=schenck.

Hickerson, Nancy Parrott. *The Jumanos: Hunters and Traders of the South Plains*. Austin: University of Texas Press, 1994.

Hickman (KY) Courier. "A Regular War." August 15, 1868. Available at *Millican "Riot,"*

1868. http://millican.omeka.net/items/show/184.

Hinton, Diana Davids, and Roger M. Olien. *Oil in Texas: The Gusher Age, 1895–1945*. Austin: University of Texas Press, 2002.

Hobby, Oveta Culp. *Around the World in 13 Days with Oveta Culp Hobby*. Privately printed, 1947.

———. *Mr. Chairman*. Oklahoma City: Economy, 1936.

Hodge, Frederick W., and Theodore H. Lewis. *Spanish Explorers in the Southern United States, 1528–1543*. New York: Barnes and Noble, 1959.

Hodgkinson, Mark. "Bush's Patriot Games beyond the Pale." *Telegraph*, September 16, 2004. https://www.telegraph.co.uk/sport/golf/rydercup/2386848/Bushs-patriot-games-beyond-the-pale.html.

Hodgson, Godfrey. *Woodrow Wilson's Right Hand: The Life of Colonel Edward M. House*. New Haven, CT: Yale University Press, 2006.

Hoffman, David R., ed. "A German-American Pioneer Remembers: August Hoffmann's Memoir." *Southwestern Historical Quarterly* 102, no. 4 (April 1999): 486–509. Available at the Portal to Texas History, https://texashistory.unt.edu/ark:/67531/metapth101219/m1/558/?q=hoffman.

Hogan, William Ransom. *The Texas Republic: A Social and Economic History*. Austin: Texas State Historical Association, 2006.

Hogg, James Stephen. "Message of the Governor to the Twenty-Third Legislature on the Subject of Lynch Law." 1893. In *Speeches and State Papers of James Stephen Hogg, Ex-Governor of Texas, with a Sketch of His Life*. Edited by C. W. Raines. Austin: State Printing Co., 1905. Available at the Portal to Texas History, https://texashistory.unt.edu/ark:/67531/metapth29400/m1/246/?q=lynch%20law.

Holden, Frances Mayhugh. *Lambshead before Interwoven: A Texas Range Chronicle, 1848–1878*. College Station: Texas A&M University Press, 1982.

Hollandsworth, Skip. "The Minor Regional Novelist." *Texas Monthly*, July 2016. https://www.texasmonthly.com/the-culture/larry-mcmurtry-minor-regional-novelist.

Holley, Mary Austin. *Texas. Observations, Historical, Geographical, and Descriptive, In a Series of Letters, written during a Visit to Austin's Colony, with a view to a permanent settlement in that country, in Autumn of 1831*. Baltimore: Armstrong & Plaskitt,

1833, https://archive.org/details/texasobservationooholl/page/n9.

Hollon, W. Eugene, and Ruth Lapham Butler, eds. *William Bollaert's Texas*. Norman: University of Oklahoma Press, 1956.

Hometown. "Buttermilk and Blood (Part 2): 'For God's Sake, Don't Shoot.'" *Hometown by Handlebar* (blog), May 24, 2013. http://hometownbyhandlebar.com/?p=6900.

House, Edward Mandell. *Philip Dru, Administrator: A Story of Tomorrow, 1920–1935*. New York: Huebsch, 1912.

Houston, Sam. *The Writings of Sam Houston, 1813–1863*. Edited by Amelia W. Williams and Eugene C. Barker. 8 vols. Austin: University of Texas Press, 1938–1943.

Howell, Kenneth W., Keith J. Volanto, James M. Smallwood, Charles D. Grear, and Jennifer S. Lawrence. *Beyond Myths and Legends: A Narrative History of Texas*. 4th ed. Wheaton, IL: Abigail, 2013.

Hudson, Charles. *Knights of Spain, Warriors of the Sun: Hernando de Soto and the South's Ancient Chiefdoms*. Athens: University of Georgia Press, 1997.

Hunt, H. L. *Alpaca*. Dallas: H. L. Hunt Press, 1960.

Hunter, J. Marvin, ed. *Trail Drivers of Texas: Interesting Sketches of Early Cowboys and Their Experiences on the Range and on the Trail during the Days That Tried Men's Souls*. San Antonio: Jackson, 1920, 1923. Reprint, Austin: University of Texas Press, 1992.

Hunter, Robert Hancock. *The Narrative of Robert Hancock Hunter*. Introduction by William D. Wittliff. Austin: Encino, 1966.

Hurst, James W. *Pancho Villa and Black Jack Pershing: The Punitive Expedition in Mexico*. Westport, CT: Praeger, 2008.

Hurt, Harry, III. "The Last of the Great Ladies." *Texas Monthly*, October 1978.

———. *Texas Rich*. New York: Norton, 1981.

Huson, Hobart. *Captain Philip Dimmitt's Commandancy of Goliad, 1835–1836*. Austin: Von Boeckman-Jones, 1974.

Hutton, Paul Andrew. *The Apache Wars: The Hunt for Geronimo, the Apache Kid, and the Captive Boy Who Started the Longest War in American History*. New York: Crown, 2016.

"Itineraries of the De León Expeditions of 1689 and 1690." American Journeys Collection: Document No. AJ-019. Wisconsin Historical Society Digital Library and Archives.

Jackson, Edgar M. "An Analysis of Selected Speeches of Morris Sheppard." Master's thesis, Texas Technological College, August 1968. https://ttu-ir.tdl.org/ttu-ir/bitstream/handle/2346/59409/31295004270889.pdf?sequence=1.

Jackson, Jack, ed. *Imaginary Kingdom: Texas as Seen by the Rivera and Rubí Military Expeditions, 1727 and 1767*. With annotations by William C. Foster. Austin: Texas State Historical Association, 1995.

———. *Indian Agent: Peter Ellis Bean in Mexican Texas*. College Station: Texas A&M University Press, 2005.

———, ed. *Texas by Terán: The Diary Kept by General Manuel de Mier y Terán on His 1828 Inspection of Texas*. Translated by John Wheat. Austin: University of Texas Press, 2000.

Jackson, Ron J. Jr. and Lee Spencer White. *Joe: The Slave Who Became an Alamo Legend*. Norman: University of Oklahoma Press, 2015.

Jackson, Warren R., and George B. Clark. *His Time in Hell: A Texas Marine in France: The World War I Memoir of Warren R. Jackson*. Novato, CA: Presidio, 2001.

James, Marquis. *The Raven: A Biography of Sam Houston*. Indianapolis: Bobbs-Merrill, 1929. Reprint, Austin: University of Texas Press, 1988.

Jarboe, Jan. "Meet the Governor: Clayton Williams." *Texas Monthly*, October 1990, 119, 122, 125, 148–156.

Jenkins, John H. *Papers of the Texas Revolution, 1835–1836*. Ten volumes. Austin: Presidial Press, 1973.

Jenkins, John H., and H. Gordon Frost. *I'm Frank Hamer: The Life of a Texas Peace Officer*. Austin: State House Press, 1993.

Jenkins, John H., and Kenneth Kesselus. *Edward Burleson: Texas Frontier Leader*. Austin: Jenkins, 1990.

Johnson, Andrew. "President Johnson's Amnesty Proclamation." *New York Times*, May 30, 1865. https://www.nytimes.com/1865/05/30/archives/president-johnsons-amnesty-proclamation-restoration-to-rights-of.html.

———. "Proclamation 139—Reorganizing a Constitutional Government in Texas." June 17, 1865. Available at the American Presidency Project, www.presidency.ucsb.edu/ws/?pid=71947.

———. "Proclamation 157—Declaring That Peace, Order, Tranquillity, and Civil Authority Now Exists in and Throughout the Whole of the United States of America." August 20, 1866. Available at the American Presidency Project, www. presidency.ucsb.edu/ws/?pid=71992.

Johnson, Benjamin Heber. *Revolution in Texas: How a Forgotten Rebellion and Its Bloody Suppression Turned Mexicans into Americans.* New Haven, CT: Yale University Press, 2003.

Johnson, Lyndon B. "Address before a Joint Session of the Congress," November 27, 1963. Video available on You-Tube, https://www.youtube.com/watch?v=LF0TxpxIMA0.

———. "Remarks on Decision to Not Seek Reelection," March 31, 1968. Video available on YouTube, https://www.youtube.com/watch?v=2-FibDxpkbo.

"Joint Resolution for Annexing Texas to the United States." Texas State Library and Archives Commission website, https://www.tsl.texas.gov/ref/abouttx/annexation/march1845.html.

Jones, Jan. *Billy Rose Presents Casa Mañana.* Fort Worth: Texas Christian University Press, 1999.

Jones, Kathryn. "Georgia O'Keeffe: Canyon and Sky." *Texas Highways*, November 2013. www.texashighways.com/culture-lifestyle/item/460-georgia-o-keeffe-canyon-and-sky.

Jones, Lawrence T., III. *Lens on the Texas Frontier.* College Station: Texas A&M University Press, 2014.

Jones, Nancy Baker, and Ruthe Winegarten. *Capitol Women: Texas Female Legislators, 1923–1999.* Austin: University of Texas Press, 2000.

Jordan, Barbara. Democratic National Convention Keynote Speech, July 12, 1976. Part 1. Posted to YouTube by TSUJordanArchives, September 5 2012, https://www.youtube.com/watch?v=Bg7gLIx__-k.

———. Statement on the Articles of Impeachment, July 25, 1974. You-Tube, https://www.youtube.com/watch?v=UG6xMglSMdk.

Jordan, Barbara, and Shelby Hearon. *Barbara Jordan: A Self-Portrait.* New York: Doubleday, 1979.

Jordan, Terry. G. *German Seed in Texas Soil: Immigrant Farmers in Nineteenth-Century Texas.* Austin: University of Texas Press, 1966.

Keener, Charles Virgil. "Racial Turmoil in Texas, 1865–1874." Master's thesis, North Texas State University, 1971. Available at https://digital.library.unt.edu/

ark:/67531/metadc663776/m2/1/high_res_d/1002774009-Keener.pdf.

Kelton, Elmer. *The Time It Never Rained.* New York: Forge, 1999.

Kendall, George Wilkins. *Narrative of the Texan Santa Fé Expedition: Comprising a Description of a Tour through Texas.* 2 vols. New York: Harper, 1844. Reprint, London: Sherwood, Gilbert, and Piper, n.d. [1845?].

Kendrick, T. D. *Mary of Ágreda: The Life and Legend of a Spanish Nun.* London: Routledge & Kegan Paul, 1967.

Kerr, Jeffrey Stuart. *Seat of Empire: The Embattled Birth of Austin, Texas.* Lubbock: Texas Tech University Press, 2016.

Kinch, Sam, and Stuart Long. *Allan Shivers: The Pied Piper of Texas Politics.* Austin: Shoal Creek, 1973.

King, Steve M. "Salt Creek Prairie." Handbook of Texas Online, June 15, 2010. https://tshaonline.org/handbook/online/articles/ryseu.

Kingseed, Cole C., ed. *From Omaha Beach to Dawson's Ridge: The Combat Journal of Captain Joe Dawson.* Annapolis, MD: Naval Institute Press, 2005.

Klein, Joe. "A Little Bit of a Snake." *New York Magazine*, December 3, 1979, 39–44.

Kleinfield, N. R. "He Had Money, Women, an S&L; Now Don Dixon Has Jail." *New York Times*, March 17, 1991.

Knowlton, Christopher. *Cattle Kingdom: The Hidden History of the Cowboy West.* New York: Houghton Mifflin Harcourt, 2017.

Koontz, Giacinta Bradley. "Little Katie Stinson." Aviation Pros, April 24, 2008. https://www.aviationpros.com/article/10378266/little-katie-stinson.

Krieger, Alex D. *We Came Naked and Barefoot: The Journey of Cabeza de Vaca Across North America.* Austin: University of Texas Press, 2002.

Kuh, Katharine. *The Artist's Voice: Talks with Seventeen Artists.* New York: Harper and Row, 1962.

Lack, Paul D. *Texas Revolutionary Experience: A Political and Social History, 1835–1836.* College Station: Texas A&M University Press, 1995.

Lamar, Mirabeau Buonaparte. *The Papers of Mirabeau Buonaparte Lamar.* Vol. 2. Edited by Charles Adams Gulick Jr., with the assistance of Katherine Elliott, archivist, Texas State Library. Austin: Baldwin and Sons, 1922.

Lane, J. J. *History of the University of Texas:*

Based on Facts and Records. Austin: Henry Hutchings, State Printer, 1891.

Larson, Erik. *Isaac's Storm: A Man, a Time, and the Deadliest Hurricane in History.* New York: Vintage, 2000.

La Vere, David. *The Texas Indians.* 2004. Reprint, College Station: Texas A&M University Press, 2013.

Lavergne, Gary M. *Before "Brown": Heman Marion Sweatt, Thurgood Marshall, and the Long Road to Justice.* Austin: University of Texas Press, 2010.

———. *A Sniper in the Tower.* Denton: University of North Texas Press, 1997.

Leckie, William H. *The Military Conquest of the Southern Plains.* Norman: University of Oklahoma Press, 1963.

Lee, Rebecca Smith. *Mary Austin Holley: A Biography.* Austin: University of Texas Press, 1962.

Leffler, John. "Cotulla, TX." Handbook of Texas Online, June 12, 2010. https://tshaonline.org/handbook/online/articles/hgc16.

Leonard, Elizabeth D. *Men of Color to Arms! Black Soldiers, Indian Wars, and the Quest for Equality.* New York: Norton, 2010.

Lester, C. Edwards. *The Life and Achievements of Sam Houston: Hero and Statesman.* New York: Hurst, 1883.

"Letter of Fray Damian Massanet to Don Carlos de Siguenza." American Journeys Collection: Document No. AJ-018. Wisconsin Historical Society Digital Library and Archives.

Leuchtenburg, William E. *The FDR Years: On Roosevelt and His Legacy.* Chapter 1 excerpted in the *Washington Post*, November 19, 1995. www.washingtonpost.com/wp-srv/style/longterm/books/chap1/fdryears.htm?noredirect=on.

Lich, Glen E., and Günter Moltmann. "Solms-Braunfels, Prince Carl of." Handbook of Texas Online, June 15, 2010; modified May 6, 2016. https://tshaonline.org/handbook/online/articles/fso03.

Linsley, Judith Walker, Ellen Walker Rienstra, and Jo Ann Stiles. *Giant under the Hill: A History of the Spindletop Oil Discovery.* Austin: Texas State Historical Association, 2002.

Lisle, Laurie. *Portrait of an Artist: A Biography of Georgia O'Keeffe.* New York: Washington Square, 1980.

Lockwood, Charles A., and Hans Christian Adamson. *Through Hell and Deep Water.* New York: Greenberg, 1956. Reprint, Pickle Partners Publishing, 2015. Kindle.

Lomax, John A., ed. *Cowboy Songs, and Other Frontier Ballads.* New York: Sturgis and Walton, 1910. Reprint, Charleston, SC: Bibliobazaar, 2008.

———. "Half-Million Dollar Song: Origin of 'Home on the Range.'" *Southwest Review* 31, no. 1 (Fall 1945): 1–8.

Long, Jeff. *Duel of Eagles: The Mexican and U.S. Fight for the Alamo.* New York: William Morrow & Co., 1990.

Looscan, Adéle B. "Micajah Autry, a Soldier of the Alamo." *Quarterly of the Texas State Historical Association* 14, no. 4 (April 1911): 315–324.

Lord, Walter. *A Time to Stand: The Epic of the Alamo.* New York: Harper and Brothers, 1961. Reprint, New York: Open Road Media, 2012.

Lost Friends: Advertisements from the "Southwestern Christian Advocate." Historic New Orleans Collection, 2016. See https://www.hnoc.org/database/lost-friends/ads-images/18800325_LostFriends_7th%20ad.jpg (Hanley); https://www.hnoc.org/database/lost-friends/ads-images/18810317_LostFriends_7th%20ad.jpg (Johnson).

Lubbock, Francis Richards. *Six Decades in Texas; or, Memoirs of Francis Richard Lubbock, Governor of Texas in Wartime, 1861–63.* Austin: Jones, 1900.

Lukes, Edward A. "DeWitt, Green." Handbook of Texas Online, June 12, 2010; modified on July 11, 2016. https://tshaonline.org/handbook/online/articles/fde55.

[Lundy, Benjamin]. *The War in Texas: A Review of Facts and Circumstances, Showing That This Contest Is the Result of a Long Premeditated Crusade against the Government, Set on Foot by Slaveholders, Land Speculators &c., with the View of Establishing, Extending and Perpetuating the System of Slavery and the Slave Trade in the Republic of Mexico; By a Citizen of the United States.* Philadelphia: Merrihew and Gunn, 1836.

Lynch, Gerald. *Roughnecks, Drillers, and Tool Pushers: Thirty-Three Years in the Oil Fields.* Austin: University of Texas Press, 1987.

Lynn, Alvin R. *Kit Carson and the First Battle of Adobe Walls: A Tale of Two Journeys.* Lubbock: Texas Tech University Press, 2014.

Mackintosh, Prudence. "The Good Old Girls." *Texas Monthly*, January 1978.

Madero, Francisco Madero. "The Plan of San Luis Potosí." October 5, 1910. Available at History of the Americas 1, http://staff.4j.lane.edu/~hamill/americas/ayala.htm.

Maher, John, and Kirk Bohls. *Long Live the*

Longhorns! 100 Years of Texas Football. New York: St. Martins, 1993.

Manaster, Jane. *Horned Lizards.* Austin: University of Texas Press, 1997.

Manchester, William. *The Death of a President.* New York: Harper and Row, 1967.

March of Time radio series advertisement, *Time,* June 22, 1936, 83.

Marcus, Stanley. *Minding the Store.* Boston: Little, Brown, 1974. Reprint, Denton: University of North Texas Press, 1997.

"Mariah, Beyonce, Katy, Jlo, Gaga Remember Selena Quintanilla." Posted to YouTube by Cristhian Ramos, February 9, 2014. https://www.youtube.com/watch?v=Uowo6L1IuMI.

Marks, Paula Mitchell. *Turn Your Eyes toward Texas: Pioneers Sam and Mary Maverick.* College Station: Texas A&M University Press, 1989.

Maverick, Mary A., George Madison Maverick, and Rena Maverick Green. *Memoirs of Mary A. Maverick.* San Antonio: Alamo Printing, 1921.

Maverick, Maury. *A Maverick American.* New York: Covici and Friede, 1937.

Mayer, Frank H. With Charles B. Roth. "The Buffalo Harvest." New Perspectives on the West. PBS, www.pbs.org/weta/thewest/resources/archives/five/buffalo.htm.

Mayer, Martin. *The Greatest-Ever Bank Robbery: The Collapse of the Savings and Loan Industry.* New York: Scribner's Sons, 1990.

McArthur, Judith N., and Harold L. Smith. *Minnie Fisher Cunningham: A Suffragist's Life in Politics.* New York: Oxford University Press, 2003.

———. *Texas through Women's Eyes: The Twentieth-Century Experience.* Austin: University of Texas Press, 2010.

McCaslin, Richard B. *Tainted Breeze: The Great Hanging in Gainesville, Texas, 1862.* Baton Rouge: Louisiana State University Press, 1994.

McCorvey, Norma. *I Am Roe: My Life, "Roe v. Wade," and Freedom of Choice.* With Andy Meisler. New York: HarperCollins, 1994.

———. *Won by Love.* With Gary Thomas. Nashville: Thomas Nelson, 1997.

McCulloch, H. E. "Letter from Gen. H. E. McCulloch." Austin *Weekly State Gazette,* August 15, 1868, 2.

McDaniel, Robert W. *Pattillo Higgins and the Search for Texas Oil.* With Henry C. Dethloff. College Station: Texas A&M University Press, 2000.

McDanield, H. F., and N. A. Taylor. *The Coming Empire, or Two Thousand Miles in Texas on Horseback.* New York: Barnes, 1877.

McDonald, David R. *José Antonio Navarro: In Search of the American Dream in Nineteenth-Century Texas.* Denton: Texas State Historical Association, 2010.

McDonald, David R., and Timothy M. Matovina. *Defending Mexican Valor in Texas: José Antonio Navarro's Historical Writings, 1852–1857.* Abilene, TX: State House Press, 1995.

McDowell, Catherine W., ed. *Now You Hear My Horn: The Journal of James Wilson Nichols, 1820–1887.* Austin: University of Texas Press, 1967. Reprint, Austin: University of Texas Press, 2010.

McEachern, Jenna Hays. *DKR: The Royal Scrapbook.* With Edith Royal. Austin: University of Texas Press, 2012.

McGaughy, Lauren. "First to Ban Open Carry, Texas Could Be One of Last to OK It." *Houston Chronicle,* December 22, 2014.

McGowen, Stanley S. "Battle or Massacre? The Incident on the Nueces, August 10, 1862." *Southwestern Historical Quarterly* 104, no. 1 (2000): 64–86.

McKay, Seth Shepard. *W. Lee O'Daniel and Texas Politics, 1938–1942.* Lubbock: Texas Technological College Research Funds, 1944.

McMurtry, Larry. *In a Narrow Grave: Essays on Texas.* Austin: Encino, 1968. Reprint, with a new preface, New York: Liveright, 2018.

McNeely, Dave, and Jim Henderson. *Bob Bullock: God Bless Texas.* Austin: University of Texas Press, 2008.

Meacham, Jon. *Destiny and Power: The American Odyssey of George Herbert Walker Bush.* New York: Random House, 2015.

"Memoir of Colonel Ellis P. Bean." Sons of DeWitt Colony Texas website, www.sonsofdewittcolony.org/beanmemoirs.htm.

Menefee, Selden C., and Orin C. Cassmore. *The Pecan Shellers of San Antonio: The Problem of Underpaid and Unemployed Mexican Labor.* Washington: Government Printing Office, 1940.

Mertins, J. L. *Little Myrtle Vance Avenged.* Paris, Texas, February 1, 1893. Photograph, Library of Congress, www.loc.gov/pictures/item/2016648613/resource/.

Metz, Leon. *John Wesley Hardin: Dark Angel of Texas.* Norman: University of Oklahoma Press, 1996.

Miller, Edward H. *Nut Country: Right-Wing Dallas and the Birth of the Southern Strategy.* Chicago: University of Chicago Press, 2016.

Minutaglio, Bill. *City on Fire: The Forgotten Disaster That Devastated a Town and Ignited a Landmark Legal Battle*. New York: HarperCollins, 2003.

———. *First Son: George W. Bush and the Bush Family Dynasty*. New York: Times Books, 1999.

Minutaglio, Bill, and Steven L. Davis. *Dallas 1963*. New York: Twelve, 2014.

Monday, Jane Clements, and Frances Brannen Vick. *Petra's Legacy: The South Texas Ranching Empire of Petra Vela and Mifflin Kenedy*. College Station: Texas A&M University Press, 2007.

Moneyhon, Carl. *Edmund J. Davis of Texas: Civil War General, Republican Leader, Reconstruction Governor*. Texas Biography Series 2. Fort Worth: Center for Texas Studies at TCU and TCU Press, 2010.

Montejano, David. *Anglos and Mexicans in the Making of Texas, 1836–1986*. Austin: University of Texas Press, 1987.

———. *Quixote's Soldiers: A Local History of the Chicano Movement, 1966–1981*. Austin: University of Texas Press, 2010.

Mooar, J. Wright. *Buffalo Days: Stories from J. Wright Mooar as Told to James Winford Hunt*. Edited by Robert F. Pace. Abilene: State House Press, 2005. Originally published in *Holland's Magazine*, 1933.

Moore, Stephen L. *Eighteen Minutes*. Dallas, Taylor, 2004.

Muñiz, Ramsey. "Ramsey Muniz Video." Posted to YouTube by David Contreras, April 14, 2017, https://www.youtube.com/watch?v=K6lwolKIyMA.

Nalle, Ouida Ferguson. *The Fergusons of Texas, or "Two Governors for the Price of One"; A Biography of James Edward Ferguson and His Wife, Miriam Amanda Ferguson, Ex-Governors of the State of Texas*. San Antonio: Naylor, 1946.

Nance, Joseph Milton. *Attack and Counterattack: The Texas-Mexican Frontier, 1842*. Austin: University of Texas Press, 1964.

Nathan, Paul D., trans. *The San Sabá Papers: A Documentary Account of the Founding and Destruction of San Sabá Mission*. Edited by Lesley Byrd Simpson. San Francisco: John Howell, 1959.

"Native American Relations in Texas." Texas State Library and Archives Commission, https://www.tsl.texas.gov/exhibits/indian/index.html.

Neeley, Bill. *The Last Comanche Chief: The Life and Times of Quanah Parker*. New York: Wiley, 1995.

Neighbours, Kenneth Franklin. *Robert Simpson Neighbors and the Texas Frontier, 1836–1859*. Waco: Texian, 1975.

Nelson, Mark. "Lloyd Bentsen: The Last of the Old-Line Texas Democrats?" *D Magazine*, August 1982. https://www.dmagazine.com/publications/d-magazine/1982/august/lloyd-bentsen.

Nelson, Willie. *The Facts of Life: And Other Dirty Jokes*. New York: Random House, 2002.

Nemy, Enid. "Liz Carpenter, Journalist, Feminist, and Johnson Aide, Dies at 89." *New York Times*, March 20, 2010. https://www.nytimes.com/2010/03/21/us/politics/21carpenter.html.

———. "Mary Kay Ash, Who Built a Cosmetics Empire and Adored Pink, Is Dead at 83." *New York Times*, November 21, 2001. https://www.nytimes.com/2001/11/23/business/mary-kay-ash-who-built-a-cosmetics-empire-and-adored-pink-is-dead-at-83.html.

Newcomb, W. W., Jr. *The Indians of Texas: From Prehistoric to Modern Times*. Austin: University of Texas Press, 1961.

Newport, Kenneth G. C. *The Branch Davidians of Waco: The History and Beliefs of an Apocalyptic Sect*. New York: Oxford University Press, 2006.

"Newspaper Advertisement for the Bank of Bacchus." *Houston Tri-Weekly Telegraph*, September 20, 1860. Available on the website of the Woodson Research Center, Fondren Library, Rice University, accessed November 23, 2016, http://exhibits.library.rice.edu/items/show/514.

New York Sun. "Burned at the Stake: A Black Man Pays for a Town's Outrage." February 2, 1893. Available at History Matters, http://historymatters.gmu.edu/d/5487.

New York Times. "Kermit Beahan, 70, Bombardier on Plane That Dropped A-Bomb." March 11, 1989. https://www.nytimes.com/1989/03/11/obituaries/kermit-beahan-70-bombardier-on-plane-that-dropped-a-bomb.html.

Nye, W. S. *Carbine and Lance: The Story of Old Fort Sill*. Norman: University of Oklahoma Press, 1937. Reprint, 1969.

O'Hair v. Paine, 397 U.S. 531 (1970). Opinion available at Justia, https://supreme.justia.com/cases/federal/us/397/531.

Okrent, Daniel. *Last Call: The Rise and Fall of Prohibition*. New York: Scribner, 2010.

Olmsted, Frederick Law. *A Journey through Texas, or A Saddle-Trip on the Southwestern Frontier*. New York: Dix, Edwards, 1857.

Reprint, Lincoln: University of Nebraska Press. 2004.

Orozco, Cynthia E. "Cortez Lira, Gregorio." Handbook of Texas Online, June 12, 2010; modified April 13, 2017. https://tshaonline.org/handbook/online/articles/fco94.

Palmer, Jerrell Dean, and John G. Johnson. "Big Inch and Little Big Inch." Handbook of Texas Online, June 12, 2010; modified November 16, 2016. https://tshaonline.org/handbook/online/articles/dob08.

Pando, Robert T. "Oveta Culp Hobby: A Study of Power and Control." Dissertation, Florida State University, 2008.

Parker, Daniel. Views on the Two Seeds. 1826. Reprinted as "Daniel Parker's Treatise on the Two Seeds," 2004, by the Old School Particular Baptist Library, www.particularbaptistlibrary.org/LIBRARY/Theology/Treaties%20on%20the%20Two%20Seeds%20-%20Parker.pdf.

Parker, James W., and Rachel Plummer. The Rachel Plummer Narrative: A Stirring Narrative of Adventure, Hardship and Privation, in the Early days of Texas, Depicting Struggles with the Indians and Other Adventures. Palestine, TX, 1926.

Parkman, Francis. La Salle and the Discovery of the Great West. 1869. Reprint, New York: Modern Library, 1999.

Patoski, Joe Nick. Selena: Como la Flor. New York: Little, Brown, 1996.

———. Willie Nelson: An Epic Life. New York: Little, Brown, 2008.

Pease, E. M., to Lucadia Pease, July 24, 1868. Available at the Portal to Texas History, https://texashistory.unt.edu/ark:/67531/metapth712791.

Perez, Chris. To Selena, with Love. New York: Celebra, 2013.

Perman, Michael. The Road to Redemption: Southern Politics, 1869–1879. Chapel Hill: University of North Carolina Press, 1984.

"What Really Happened in Houston." Phyllis Schlafly Report 11, no. 5 (December 1977).

Pickering, David, and Judy Falls. Brush Men and Vigilantes: Civil War Dissent in Texas. College Station: Texas A&M University Press, 2000.

The Pine and Palm (electronic resource). Stanford University Libraries, https://searchworks.stanford.edu/view/9679491.

Pitre, Merline. "The Evolution of Black Political Participation in Reconstruction Texas." East Texas Historical Journal, 26, no. 1 (1988): 36–45. Available from ScholarWorks, https://scholarworks.sfasu.edu/cgi/viewcontent.cgi?referer=https://www.google.com/&httpsredir=1&article=1970&context=ethj.

———. Through Many Dangers, Toils and Snares: Black Leadership in Texas, 1868–1898. College Station: Texas A&M University Press, 2016.

Politi, Daniel. "Texas School Shooter Spared People He Liked 'So He Could Have His Story Told.'" Slate, May 19, 2018. https://slate.com/news-and-politics/2018/05/texas-school-shooter-spared-people-he-liked-so-he-could-have-his-story-told.html.

"Port Arthur Story (1954), The." Texas Archive of the Moving Image, www.texasarchive.org/library/index.php/The_Port_Arthur_Story_(1954).

Porter, Katherine Anne. The Collected Stories of Katherine Anne Porter. New York: Harcourt, Brace and World, 1965.

Porterfield, Billy. "H. L. Hunt's Long Goodbye." Texas Monthly, March 1975, 63–69, 92–94.

Potter, R. M. "The Texas Revolution: Distinguished Mexicans Who Took Part in the Revolution of Texas, with Glances at Its Early Events." Magazine of American History, October 1878, 577–603. Available at the Internet Archive, https://archive.org/stream/texasrevolutiondoopott#page/no/mode/2up.

Poyo, Gerald E. Tejano Journey, 1770–1850. Austin: University of Texas Press, 2010.

Prager, Joshua. "The Accidental Activist." Vanity Fair, January 18, 2013. https://www.vanityfair.com/news/politics/2013/02/norma-mccorvey-roe-v-wade-abortion.

"President Clinton at D-Day 50th Anniversary." June 6, 1994. Video available at C-SPAN, https://www.c-span.org/video/?57592-1/president-clinton-day-50th-anniversary.

Ragsdale, Kenneth B. The Year America Discovered Texas: Centennial '36. College Station: Texas A&M University Press, 1987.

Ramírez, José A. To the Line of Fire: Mexican Texans and World War I. College Station: Texas A&M University Press, 2009.

Ramírez, Sara Estela. "¡Surge!" La Crónica, April 9, 1910. Reprinted in Jesse Alemán, "Narratives of Displacement in Places That Once Were Mexican," in The Cambridge History of Latina/o American Literature, edited by John Morán González and

Laura Lomas, 216–231 (Cambridge: Cambridge University Press, 2018).

Ramsdell, Charles. *Reconstruction in Texas.* New York: Columbia University Press, 1910. Reprint, Austin: University of Texas Press, 1970.

Rausch, George J., Jr. "The Exile and Death of Victoriano Huerta." *Hispanic American Historical Review* 42, no. 2 (May 1962): 133–151.

Rayburn, John C. "The Rough Riders in San Antonio, 1898." *Arizona and the West: A Quarterly Journal of History* 3, no. 2 (Summer 1961): 113–128.

Reavis, Dick J. *Ashes of Waco: An Investigation.* New York: Simon and Schuster, 1995.

Redpath, James. "The Pine and Palm." *Pine and Palm,* May 18, 1861. Available from the American Historical Association, https://www.historians. org/teaching-and-learning/teaching-resources-for-historians/sixteen-months-to-sumter/newspaper-index/boston-and-new-york-pine-and-palm/the-pine-and-palm.

Reich, Steven A. "Soldiers of Democracy: Black Texans and the Fight for Citizenship, 1917–1921." *Journal of American History* 82, no. 4 (March 1996): 1478–1504.

Reid, Don. *Have A Seat, Please.* With John Gurwell. Huntsville, TX: Texas Review Press, 2001.

Reid, Jan. "Blood of the Lamb." *Texas Monthly,* March 1983, 140–147, 191–206.

———. "The Immortals." *Alcalde,* December 2013. https://alcalde.texasexes. org/2013/12/the-immortals.

———. *Let the People In: The Life and Times of Ann Richards.* Austin: University of Texas Press, 2013.

Reid, T. R. "The Texas Edison." *Texas Monthly,* July 1982.

Reinert, Al. "Not Guilty." *Texas Monthly,* June 1975. https://www.texasmonthly.com/articles/not-guilty.

Reinhold, Robert. "Impact of Texas School Law Hits Home with Football Season." *New York Times,* November 25, 1985.

———. "John Connally's Texas-Sized Troubles." *New York Times,* September 14, 1986.

Resendez, Andres. *A Land So Strange: The Epic Journey of Cabeza de Vaca.* New York: Basic Books, 2009.

Reston, James, Jr. *The Lone Star: The Life of John Connally.* New York: Harper and Row, 1989.

Reynolds, Donald E. "Reluctant Martyr: Anthony Bewley and the Texas Slave Insurrection Panic of 1860." *Southwestern Historical Quarterly* 96, no. 3 (1993): 345–361.

Rhodes, Richard. *John James Audubon: The Making of an American.* New York: Doubleday, 2004.

Rich, Doris L. *Queen Bess: Daredevil Aviator.* Washington, DC: Smithsonian Books, 1993.

Richards, Ann. Eulogy for Barbara Jordan, Austin, Texas, January 20, 1996. Text available at Speech Vault, www.speeches-usa.com/Transcripts/ann_richards-eulogy.html. Video available on YouTube, https://www.youtube.com/watch?v=cUhtya1CuM4.

———. Speech, Democratic National Convention, 1988. YouTube, https://www.youtube.com/watch?v=wtIFhiqS_TY.

Ricklis, Robert A. *The Karankawa Indians of Texas: An Ecological Study of Cultural Tradition and Change.* Austin: University of Texas Press, 1996.

Rips, Geoffrey, and Emma Tenayuca. "Living History: Emma Tenayuca Tells Her Story." *Texas Observer,* October 28, 1983, 7–15.

Roberts, Madge Thornall. *Star of Destiny: The Private Life of Sam and Margaret Houston.* Denton: University of North Texas Press, 1984.

Roberts, Randy, and James S. Olson. *A Line in the Sand: The Alamo in Blood and Memory.* New York: Free Press, 2001.

Robinson, Charles M., III. *Bad Hand: A Biography of General Ranald S. Mackenzie.* Abilene: State House Press, 1993.

———. *The Fall of a Black Army Officer: Racism and the Myth of Henry O. Flipper.* Norman: University of Oklahoma Press, 2008.

———. *Texas and the Mexican War: A History and a Guide.* Austin: Texas State Historical Association, 2004.

Roe v. Wade, 314 F. Supp. 1217 (N.D. Tex. 1970). Text of the opinion available at Justia, https://law.justia.com/cases/federal/district-courts/FSupp/314/1217/1472349.

Rogers, Mary Beth. *Barbara Jordan: American Hero.* New York: Bantam, 1998.

Roosevelt, Theodore. *Outdoor Pastimes of an American Hunter.* New York: Scribner's, 1906.

———. *The Rough Riders.* New York: Scribner's, 1899. Reprint, New York: Library of America, 2004.

Ross, Stephen. "53 Veer Pass." *Barking Carnival,* December 6, 2010.

https://www.barkingcarnival.
com/2010/12/06/53-veer-pass.
Rove, Karl. *Courage and Consequence: My Life
as a Conservative in the Fight*. New York:
Simon and Schuster, 2010.
Rundell, Walter, Jr. *Early Texas Oil: A Photo-
graphic History, 1866–1936*. College Sta-
tion: Texas A&M Univeristy Press. 1977.
Russell, Jan Jarboe. *The Train to Crystal
City: FDR's Secret Prisoner Exchange and
America's Only Family Internment Camp
during World War II*. New York: Scribner,
2015.
Sáenz, José de la Luz, Emilio Zamora, and
Ben Maya. *The World War I Diary of José de
la Luz Sáenz*. College Station: Texas A&M
University Press, 2014.
Sapper, Neil. "Aboard the Wrong Ship in the
Right Books: Doris Miller and Historical
Accuracy." *East Texas Historical Journal* 18,
no. 1 (1980): 3–11. Available from Schol-
arWorks, http://scholarworks.sfasu.edu/
ethj/vol18/iss1/5.
Scheer, Mary L., ed. *Women and the Texas Revo-
lution*. Denton: University of North Texas
Press, 2012.
Schneider, Paul. *Brutal Journey: Cabeza de Vaca
and the Epic First Crossing of North America*.
New York: Holt, 2007.
Schultz, Duane. *Crossing the Rapido*. Yardley,
PA: Westholme, 2010.
Sealy, Edward Coyle. "Galveston Wharves."
Handbook of Texas Online, June 15, 2010;
modified July 7, 2017. https://tshaonline.
org/handbook/online/articles/etg01.
Shackford, James Atkins. *David Crockett: The
Man and the Legend*. Chapel Hill: Univer-
sity of North Carolina Press, 1986.
Shafer, Harry J. *Painters in Prehistory: Archeol-
ogy and Art of the Lower Pecos Canyonlands*.
San Antonio: Trinity University Press,
2013.
Shapiro, Harold A. "The Pecan Shellers of
San Antonio." *Southwestern Social Science
Quarterly* 32, no. 4 (March 1952): 229–244.
Shelton, Emily Jones. "Lizzie E. Johnson: A
Cattle Queen of Texas." *Southwestern His-
torical Quarterly* 50, no. 3 (1947): 349–366.
Shenkman, Richard. "An Iran Rescue That
Worked." *Washington Post*, June 1, 1980.
https://www.washingtonpost.com/
archive/opinions/1980/06/01/an-iran-
rescue-that-worked/493d046d-72e1-
4f2f-961c-c18af804ec50/?utm_term=.
b1c26aa13c7e.
Siegel, Stanley. *A Political History of the Texas
Republic, 1836-1845*. Austin: University of
Texas Press, 1956.

Skiles, Jack. *Judge Roy Bean Country*. Lubbock:
Texas Tech University Press, 1996.
Smallwood, James, Barry A. Crouch, and
Larry Peacock. *Murder and Mayhem: The
War of Reconstruction in Texas*. College Sta-
tion: Texas A&M University Press, 2003.
Smith, C. Calvin. "The Houston Riot of
1917, Revisited." *Houston Review* 13 (1991):
85–95. Available at www.studythepast.
com/4333_spring12/materials/houston-
riot1917_houstonreview.pdf.
Smith, Griffin, Jr. "Why Does Dolph Briscoe
Want to be Governor?" *Texas Monthly*,
February 1976. https://www.texas-
monthly.com/politics/why-does-dolph-
briscoe-want-to-be-governor.
Smith, Julia Cauble. "Corsicana Oilfield."
Handbook of Texas Online, June 12,
2010; modified July 22, 2016. https://tsh-
aonline.org/handbook/online/articles/
doc03.
Smith, Lee Carraway. *A River Swift and
Deadly: The 36th "Texas" Infantry Division at
the Rapido River*. Austin: Eakin, 1997.
Smithwick, Noah. *The Evolution of a State, or,
Recollections of Old Texas Days*. Compiled
by Nanna Smithwick Donaldson. Austin:
Gammel Book Company, 1900. Reprint,
independently published, 2016.
Sonnichsen, C. L. *Judge Roy Bean: Law West
of the Pecos*. Old Greenwich, CT: Devin-
Adair, 1943. Reprint, Boerne, TX: Mock-
ingbird, 2016.
Sowell, A. J. *Early Settlers and Indian Fighters of
Southwest Texas*. Austin: Jones, 1900.
Spearing, Darwin. *Roadside Geology of Texas*.
Revised ed. Missoula, MT: Mountain
Press, 1991.
Spratt, John Stricklin. *The Road to Spindle-
top: Economic Change in Texas, 1875–1901*.
Austin: University of Texas Press, 2014.
Spruill, Marjorie J. *Divided We Stand: The
Battle over Women's Rights and Family Values
That Polarized American Politics*. New York:
Bloomsbury, 2017.
Stanley, Mark. "Booze, Boomtowns, and
Burning Crosses: The Turbulent Gov-
ernorship of Pat M. Neff of Texas,
1921–1935." Master's thesis, University
of North Texas, August 2005. https://
digital.library.unt.edu/ark%3A/67531/
metadc4834/m2/1/high_res_d/thesis.pdf.
State Symbols USA. "Mockingbird."
www.statesymbolsusa.org/sym-
bol-official-item/texas/state-bird/
mockingbird.
*Statutes at Large, Treaties, and Proclamations of
the United States of America, from December*

5, *1859, to March 3, 1863*. Edited by George P. Sanger. Vol. 12. 37th Congress, 2nd session, 1862. Boston: Little, Brown, 1863. Available at *A Century of Lawmaking for a New Nation: U.S. Congressional Documents and Debates, 1774–1875*, Library of Congress, http://memory.loc.gov/cgi-bin/ampage?collId=llsl&fileName=012/llsl012.db&recNum=533.

Stephens, A. Ray. *Texas: A Historical Atlas*. Norman: University of Oklahoma Press, 2010.

Stinson, Katharine. "Why I Am Not Afraid to Fly." *American Magazine*, January 1919, 36–37, 60–66.

Stokes, Don. "Mary Kay Cosmetics: Capture the Vision." 1981. Texas Archive of the Moving Image, www.texasarchive.org/library/index.php/Mary_Kay_Cosmetics_-_Capture_the_Vision.

Stone, Kate. *Brokenburn: The Journal of Kate Stone, 1861–1868*. Edited by John Q. Anderson. Baton Rouge: Louisiana State University Press, 1955. Available at the Internet Archive, https://archive.org/stream/brokenburnthejou00876mbp#page/n9.

Stout, Janis P. *South by Southwest: Katherine Anne Porter and the Burden of Texas History*. Tuscaloosa: University of Alabama Press, 2013.

Stutz, Terrence. "Bill Clements, Texas' First GOP Governor in More than A Century, Dies." *Dallas Morning News*, May 29, 2011. https://www.dallasnews.com/obituaries/obituaries/2011/05/29/bill-clements-texas-first-gop-governor-in-more-than-a-century-dies.

Sweeney, Charles W. *War's End: An Eyewitness Account of America's Last Atomic Mission*. With James A. Antonucci and Marion K. Antonucci. New York: Avon, 1997.

Taraborrelli, J. Randy. *Becoming Beyoncé: The Untold Story*. New York: Grand Central, 2015. Kindle.

Tenayuca, Emma. Oral history interview by Luis R. Torres, c. 1987. José Angel Gutiérrez Papers, MS 24, box 31, University of Texas at San Antonio Libraries. https://medialibrary.utsa.edu/Play/9046.

"Testimony of Mr. and Mrs. John B. Connally, Dallas, Tex." House Select Committee on Assassinations, 95th Congress, 2nd session, September 6, 1978. Available via the Kennedy Assassination Home Page, http://mcadams.posc.mu.edu/russ/m_j_russ/hscacon.htm.

Texas Department of Public Safety. His-

torical Museum and Research Center. "Padre Island." 1960. Available at the Texas Archive of the Moving Image, http://www.texasarchive.org/library/index.php?title=Padre_Island.

Texas Observer. "Bold Sit-Ins in Marshall." April 1, 1960, 1–2.

———. "The Confrontation." September 16, 1966, 9–11.

———. "Shock Waves from Popeye Land." May 16, 1963, 6–7. http://archives.texasobserver.org/issue/1963/05/16#page=6.

Texas Republican Gubernatorial Primary Debate. February 8, 1990. Available at C-SPAN, https://www.c-span.org/video/?11170-1/texas-republican-gubernatorial-primary-debate.

Texas Week Magazine. "'Failing,' Texas Writers Keep Trying." August 24, 1946, 30–31.

Thetford, Michael Wayne, Jr. "Walker, Ewell Doak, Jr." Handbook of Texas Online, June 15, 2010. https://tshaonline.org/handbook/online/articles/fwamr.

Thibodeau, David. *Waco: A Survivor's Story*. With Leon Whiteson and Aviva Layton. Originally published as David Thibodeau and Leon Whiteson, *A Place Called Waco* (New York: PublicAffairs, 1999). Reprint, New York: Hachette, 2018.

Thompson, Cecilia, and Louise S. O'Connor. *Marfa and Presidio County, Texas: A Social, Economic, and Cultural Study, 1937 to 2008*. Vol. 1: *1937–1989*. Xlibris, 2014.

Thompson, Jerry D. *Cortina: Defending the Mexican Name in Texas*. College Station: Texas A&M University Press, 2007.

———. *Vaqueros in Blue and Gray*. Austin: Presidial, 1976. Reprint, Austin: State House, 2000.

Tijerina, Andrés. *Tejano Empire: Life on the South Texas Ranchos*. College Station: Texas A&M University Press, 1998.

———. *Tejanos and Texas Under the Mexican Flag, 1821–1836*. College Station: Texas A&M University Press, 1994.

Time. "Education: Bertie and the Board." August 15, 1960. http://content.time.com/time/subscriber/printout/0,8816,939782,00.html.

Tobolowsky, Hermine D. "For Equal Rights Amendment." *Texas Bar Journal*, December 1963, 1004, 1074–1076.

Tolson, Melvin G. "Dark Symphony." *Atlantic Monthly*, September 1941, 314–317.

Tongate, Vicki Adams. *Another Year Finds Me in Texas: The Civil War Diary of Lucy Pier Stevens*. Austin: University of Texas Press, 2016.

Torget, Andrew J. *Seeds of Empire: Cotton, Slavery, and the Transformation of the Texas Borderlands, 1800–1850.* Chapel Hill: University of North Carolina Press, 2015.

"Traces of Texas." Facebook post, December 18, 2013. https://www.facebook.com/TracesofTexas/posts/676572302374902.

"20/20—Selena's Killer, Part 1." Excerpt from a 1995 episode of the news program *20/20.* Posted to YouTube, April 9, 2010, https://www.youtube.com/watch?v=ElTfi3AZyHI.

Tyler, Ron, and Lawrence R. Murphy, eds. *The Slave Narratives of Texas.* Austin: Encino, 1974. Reprint, Austin: State House, 1997.

Unrue, Darlene Harbour. *Katherine Anne Porter: The Life of an Artist.* Jackson: University Press of Mississippi, 2005.

Updegrove, Mark K. *The Last Republicans: Inside the Extraordinary Relationship between George H. W. Bush and George W. Bush.* New York: HarperCollins, 2017.

U.S. Congress. *Report of the Joint Committee on Reconstruction.* Part 4: "Florida, Louisiana, Texas." *Reports of the Committees of the House of Representatives Made During the First Session of the Thirty-Ninth Congress, 1865–66.* Vol. 2. Washington: Government Printing Office, 1866. Available at the Internet Archive, https://archive.org/stream/jointreconstr00congrich#page/n643.

U.S. House. *The Reports of the Committees of the House of Representatives Made during the First Session, Thirty-Ninth Congress, 1865–66.* 3 vols. Washington, DC: Government Printing Office, 1866. Available from Google Books, https://books.google.com/books?id=rDs4AQAAMAAJ&printsec=frontcover#v=onepage&q&f=false.

Valenti, Jack. *This Time, This Place: My Life in War, the White House, and Hollywood.* New York: Crown, 2007.

Vargas, Aragosa. "Tejana Radical: Emma Tenayuca and the San Antonio Labor Movement during the Great Depression." *Pacific Historical Review* 66, no. 4 (November 1997): 553–580.

Wagner, Robert L. "Culberson, Charles Allen." Handbook of Texas Online, June 12, 2010; modified February 24, 2016. https://tshaonline.org/handbook/online/articles/fcu02.

Waldman, Michael. *Who Robbed America? A Citizen's Guide to the Savings & Loan Scandal.* With the Staff of Public Citizen's Congress Watch. New York: Random House, 1990.

Walker, Fred L. *From Texas to Rome: A General's Journey.* Dallas: Taylor, 1969.

Walker, Stanley. "Where Are They Now? Mr. Davis and His Millions." *New Yorker,* November 26, 1949, 35–47.

Wallace, Ernest, and E. Adamson Hoebel. *The Comanches: Lords of the South Plains.* Norman: University of Oklahoma Press, 1986.

Wallace, Ernest, David M. Vigness, and George B. Ward, eds. *Documents of Texas History.* 2nd ed. Austin: Texas State Historical Association, 2002.

Wallis, Mrs. Jonnie Lockhart. *Sixty Years on the Brazos: The Life and Letters of Dr. John Washington Lockhart, 1824–1900.* Los Angeles: Privately published, 1930.

"Walter Cronkite Remembers." The New London School Explosion, http://nlsd.net/Recollections05.htm.

Warren, Henry. "The Porvenir Massacre in Presidio County, Texas, on January 28, 1918." Henry Warren Collection, box 4, folder 88, Archives of the Big Bend, Sul Ross State University, Alpine, Texas.

Webb, Walter Prescott. *The Great Plains.* New York: Grosset and Dunlap, 1931.

———. *The Texas Rangers: A Century of Frontier Defense.* Boston: Houghton Mifflin, 1935.

Weber, David J. *The Mexican Frontier, 1821–1846: The American Southwest under Mexico.* Albuquerque: University of New Mexico Press, 1982.

———. *The Spanish Frontier in North America.* New Haven, CT: Yale University Press, 1994.

Weddington, Sarah. *A Question of Choice.* New York: Putnam's Sons, 1992. Reprint, 40th anniversary ed., New York: Feminist Press, 2013.

Weddle, Robert S. *The French Thorn: Rival Explorers in the Spanish Sea, 1682–1762.* College Station: Texas A&M University Press, 1991.

———. *La Salle, the Mississippi, and the Gulf: Three Primary Documents.* College Station: Texas A&M University Press, 1987.

———. *The San Sabá Mission: Spanish Pivot in Texas.* College Station: Texas A&M University Press, 1999.

———. *Spanish Sea: The Gulf of Mexico in North American Discovery, 1500–1685.* College Station: Texas A&M University Press, 2000.

———. *Wilderness Manhunt: The Spanish Search*

for La Salle. College Station: Texas A&M University Press, 1999.

———. *The Wreck of the Belle, the Ruin of La Salle*. College Station: Texas A&M University Press, 2001.

Weems, John Edward. *Men Without Countries: Three Adventurers of the Early Southwest*. Boston: Houghton Mifflin, 1969.

Welch, June Rayfield. *O Ye Legendary Texas Horned Frog!* Irving, TX: Yellow Rose, 1993.

Wells, Ida B. *A Red Record: Tabulated Statistics and Alleged Causes of Lynching in the United States, 1892–1893–1894.*" Chicago: Dono-hue and Henneberry, 1895. Unpaginated text available at the Internet Archive, https://archive.org/stream/theredre-cord14977gut/14977.txt.

Wendt, Lloyd, and Herman Kogan. *Bet a Million! The Story of John W. Gates*. New York: Bobbs-Merrill, 1948.

Whisenhunt, Donald W., ed. *Texas: A Sesqui-centennial Celebration*. Austin: Eakin, 1984.

White, Lonnie J. *From Panthers to Arrowheads: The 36th (Texas-Oklahoma) Division in World War I*. Austin: Presidial Press, 1984.

Wiggins, Melanie. *Torpedoes in the Gulf: Galves-ton and the U-Boats, 1942–1943*. College Sta-tion: Texas A&M University Press, 1995.

Williams, Amelia W. "Houston, Sam, Jr." Handbook of Texas Online, June 15, 2010. https://tshaonline.org/handbook/online/articles/fho74.

Williams, Edward B. *Hood's Texas Brigade in the Civil War*. Jefferson, NC: McFarland, 2012.

Williams, Paul. *Jackson, Crockett and Houston on the American Frontier: From Fort Mims to the Alamo, 1813–1836*. Jefferson, NC: McFarland, 2016.

Wilson, Carol O'Keefe. *In the Governor's Shadow: The True Story of Ma and Pa Fergu-son*. Denton: University of North Texas Press, 2014.

Wilson, Maurine T., and Jack Jackson. *Philip Nolan and Texas: Expeditions into the Unknown Land, 1791–1801*. Waco: Texian, 1987.

Winders, Richard Bruce. *Crisis in the South-west: The United States, Mexico, and the Struggle over Texas*. Lanham, MD: Row-man & Littlefield, 2002.

———. *Mr. Polk's Army: The American Military Experience in the Mexican War*. College Sta-tion: Texas A&M University Press, 2000.

Winegarten, Debra L. *Oveta Culp Hobby: Colo-nel, Cabinet Member, Philanthropist*. Austin: University of Texas Press, 2014.

Winegarten, Ruthe. *Black Texas Women: 150 Years of Trial and Triumph*. Austin: Univer-sity of Texas Press, 1995.

Woldert, Albert. "The Expedition of Luís de Moscoso in 1542." *Southwestern Historical Quarterly* 46 (October 1942).

Wood, Peter H. "La Salle: Discovery of a Lost Explorer." *American Historical Review* 89, no. 2 (April 1984): 294–323.

Woodbury, Richard. "Ten Minutes in Hell." *Time*, October 28, 1991. http://content.time.com/time/subscriber/article/0,33009,974133,00.html

Wooster, Ralph A. *Texas and Texans in the Civil War*. Austin: Eakin, 1995.

———. *Texas and Texans in the Great War*. Buf-falo Gap, TX: State House, 2009.

———. *Texas and Texans in World War II*. Forth Worth: Eakin, 2005.

Wright, Lawrence. *In the New World: Growing Up in America, 1964–1984*. New York: Knopf, 1987.

———. "The Man from Texarkana." *New York Times Magazine*, June 28, 1992.

———. "The Tide Turns." *Texas Monthly*, January 1986.

———. "Why Do They Hate Us So Much?" *Texas Monthly*, November 1983.

Wright, Robert M. "The Beginnings of Dodge City." Chapter 7 of *Dodge City: The Cowboy Capital and the Great Southwest in the Days of the Wild Indian, the Buffalo, the Cowboy, Dance Halls, Gambling Halls, and Badmen*, 1913. Available at Legends of America, www.legendsofamerica.com/ks-dodgecitybeginnings.html.

"Written in Stone: The Ten Commandments of the Grange." 1874. Available at His-tory Matters, http://historymatters.gmu.edu/d/5027.

Yergin, Daniel. *The Prize: The Epic Quest for Oil, Money and Power*. New York: Simon and Schuster, 1990. Reprint, New York: Free Press, 2009.

Yoakum, Henderson. *History of Texas from Its First Settlement in 1685 to Its Annexation to the United States in 1846*. New York: Red-field, 1856.

Zaboly, Gary S. *An Altar for Their Sons: The Alamo and the Texas Revolution in Contempo-rary Newspaper Accounts*. Buffalo Gap, TX: State House Press, 2011.

Zambrano, Mike, Jr. "Texas History Movies." Handbook of Texas Online, January 23, 2018. https://tshaonline.org/handbook/online/articles/edtyk.

Zimmermann Telegram. 1917. Available at Our Documents, https://www.ourdocu-ments.gov/doc.php?flash=false&doc=60&page=transcript.

ILLUSTRATION CREDITS

Maps by Margaret Kimball

pp. 358–359 Courtesy of the Library of Congress

pp. 362–363 Courtesy of the Library of Congress

p. 365 Courtesy Woodson Research Center, Fondren Library, Rice University

p. 372 DeGolyer Library, Southern Methodist University, Lawrence T. Jones III Texas Photographs

p. 375 Wikimedia Commons/Public Domain

p. 380 Austin History Center, Austin Public Library

p. 386 Courtesy of Getty Images

p. 393 Ima Hogg Photographs, di_07641, The Dolph Briscoe Center for American History, The University of Texas at Austin

p. 398 Prints and Photographs Collection, di_11388, The Dolph Briscoe Center for American History, The University of Texas at Austin

p. 401 Austin History Center, Austin Public Library

p. 403 Austin History Center, Austin Public Library

pp. 404–405 The State Preservation Board, Austin, Texas

pp. 406–407 Friends of the Governor's Mansion, Austin

pp. 410–411 Courtesy of Getty Images

p. 413 Courtesy of Library of Congress

p. 414 Austin History Center, Austin Public Library

p. 416 Courtesy of The Texas Collection, Baylor University, Waco, Texas

p. 421 DeGolyer Library, Southern Methodist University, Lawrence T. Jones III Texas Photographs

p. 422 William Downey/Wikimedia Commons/Public Domain

pp. 426–427 Courtesy of Eastland County Museum

pp. 428–429 DeGolyer Library, Southern Methodist University, Lawrence T. Jones III Texas Photographs

p. 433 Courtesy of UTSA

pp. 438–439 Courtesy of Texas State Library and Archives Commission

p. 441 Courtesy of Sisters of Charity of the Incarnate Word via the Associated Press

p. 442 By Trost Studio, Prints and Photographs Collection, di_02302, The Dolph Briscoe Center for American History, The University of Texas at Austin

p. 450 Courtesy of Texas Energy Museum, Beaumont, Texas

p. 451 Courtesy of Texas Energy Museum, Beaumont, Texas

p. 460 © Georgia O'Keeffe Museum; image courtesy of the Georgia O'Keeffe Museum

pp. 464–465 Robert Runyon Photograph Collection, RUN08690, The Dolph Briscoe Center for American History, The University of Texas at Austin

p. 466 Austin History Center, Austin Public Library

p. 467 Austin History Center, Austin Public Library

p. 470 Courtesy of Texas State Historical Association and Texas Tejano

p. 471 Adina Emilia De Zavala (Adina Emilia De) Papers, di_00930_02, The Dolph Briscoe Center for American History, The University of Texas at Austin

p. 473 Courtesy of Texas State Library and Archives Commission

p. 477 Courtesy of UTSA

pp. 478–479 Robert Runyon Photograph Collection, RUN00096, The Dolph Briscoe Center for American History, The University of Texas at Austin

p. 485 Robert Runyon Photograph Collection, RUN00196, The Dolph Briscoe Center for American History, The University of Texas at Austin

p. 487 Courtesy of the Library of Congress

pp. 498–499 U.S. National Archives and Records Administration

p. 501 Courtesy of the George Platt Lynes Estate

p. 507 Nettie Lee Benson Latin American Collection, University of Texas Libraries, The University of Texas at Austin

p. 514 Courtesy of the Library of Congress

History, The University of Texas at Austin

p. 692   Courtesy of Southern Baptist Historical Library and Archives, Nashville, Tennessee

pp. 696–697   Courtesy, Fort Worth Star-Telegram Collection, Special Collections, The University of Texas at Arlington Library, Arlington, Texas

p. 699   DeGolyer Library, Southern Methodist University

p. 700   Shel Hershorn Photograph Collection, e_sh_0198, The Dolph Briscoe Center for American History, The University of Texas at Austin

pp. 702–703   LBJ Library photo by Cecil Stoughton

pp. 706–707   Courtesy of Getty Images

pp. 708–709   By Russell Lee, Henry B. Gonzalez Collection, e_hbg_0015, The Dolph Briscoe Center for American History, The University of Texas at Austin

pp. 711   Henry B. Gonzalez Collection, e_hbg_0003, The Dolph Briscoe Center for American History, The University of Texas at Austin

pp. 716–717   LBJ Library photo by Frank Wolfe

p. 724   Shel Hershorn Photograph Collection, e_sh_0199, The Dolph Briscoe Center for American History, The University of Texas at Austin

pp. 726–727   Courtesy of the Associated Press

p. 728   DeGolyer Library, Southern Methodist University, Southern Methodist University Campus Memories

pp. 730–731   Courtesy of Getty Images

p. 733   Courtesy, Fort Worth Star-Telegram Collection, Special Collections, The University of Texas at Arlington Library, Arlington, Texas.

p. 734   Courtesy of the Associated Press

p. 736   NASA

pp. 738–739   LBJ Library photo by Frank Wolfe

p. 745   Courtesy of Texas State Library and Archives Commission

pp. 746–747   By Malvern D. Lusky, Frances Tarleton Farenthold Papers, e_sf_0047, The Dolph Briscoe Center for American History, The University of Texas at Austin

p. 749   Texas Prison Museum

p. 751   Texas Prison Museum

p. 753   Courtesy of the Associated Press/Bill Janscha

p. 756   PICB 11116, Austin History Center, Austin Public Library

pp. 760–761   Courtesy of the *Houston Chronicle*

p. 766   DeGolyer Library, Southern Methodist University, Everette Lee DeGolyer, Sr. Papers

p. 769   Courtesy of Getty Images

p. 772   Courtesy of the Associated Press

pp. 776–777   By Ted Powers, William P. Hobby Sr. Family Papers, di_05739, The Dolph Briscoe Center for American History, The University of Texas at Austin

pp. 778–779   Courtesy of the Fort Wort Star-Telegram Collection, Special Collections, The University of Texas at Arlington Library

p. 783   Courtesy of Getty Images

p. 787   YouTube screen grab

p. 790   Courtesy of the Associated Press/Ron Heflin

pp. 792–793   Ave Bonar Photographs, di_11569, The Dolph Briscoe Center for American History, The University of Texas at Austin

pp. 796–797   Shel Hershorn Photograph Collection, di_01324, The Dolph Briscoe Center for American History, The University of Texas at Austin

p. 799   Courtesy of Getty Images

p. 802   Courtesy of John Dyer

pp. 806–807   The Museum of Fine Arts, Houston. Museum purchase funded by Joan and Stanford Alexander in honor of Peter R. Coneway, on the occasion of his birthday, 94.119 © Annie Leibovitz/Trunk Archive

pp. 812–813   Courtesy George W. Bush Presidential Library and Museum.

INDEX

—C—

Cabeza de Vaca, Álvar Núñez: on bison, 24, 266; and Charrucos, 23; and Estebanico, 377; food sustaining, 51; Indian followers of, 26–27, 28; and Karankawa Indians, 22, 40; *La relación*, 23–25, 25, 26; route of, 26, 27, 29, 32, 33, 38, 92, 792

Caddoan-speaking people, 14

Caddo Indians: agrarian tradition of, 266; and Apaches, 61, 65; and barbecue, 764; and James Bowie, 134–135; centralized governmental system of, 59, 61; and Christianity, 61–62; in East Texas, 37–38, 45, 52–54, 59, 61; and French explorers, 59, 63, 66; population of, 203, 264; and Texas Revolution, 191; trading routes of, 112; and war of extermination, 210

Cagney, James, 612, 614

Caldwell, Mathew, 216, 227

California, 238, 239, 244, 253

Calvert, Robert A., 837

Camargo, Mexico, 260, 262, 296

Cameron County, Texas, 405–407

Camino Real, 97, 101, 361, 829

Campbell, Randolph B., 836–837

Campbell, Thomas, 462, 824

Camp Bowie, Fort Worth, 494, 500

Camp Logan, Houston, 494, 495, 496–500, 714

Camp Travis, San Antonio, 500

Canada, 232, 335

Canadian River, 10–11, 333, 335

Canales, J. T., 482, 523, 524

Canary Islands, 65

Cantrell, Gregg, 837

Cantu, Antonia, 505

Cantu, David Barkley, 504–505

Canyon, Texas, 459, 818

Cape Canaveral, Florida, 737

Caprock, 351, 370

Carlyle, Thomas, 707

Caro, Robert A., 644

Carpenter, Liz, 762, 779

carpetbaggers, 313, 319, 320

Carranza, Venustiano, 475–476, 483, 493

Carrasco, Fred Gómez, 748–750, 749, 824–825

Carrejo, Moisés, 506

Carrizo, Texas, 295

Carson, Kit, 344

Carter, Amon, 572

Carter, Jimmy, 719

Carter, R. G., 353

Carter Trading House, 338

Cartwright, Gary, 522

Casas, Juan Bautista de las, 84

Cash, Johnny, 610

Castañeda, Francisco, 128

Castañeda, Pedro de, 33, 35

Castillo, Alonso del, 24

Castrillón, Manuel, 163, 179–180

Castro, Fidel, 701

Castro (Lipan Apache chief), 210

Castroville, Texas, 424

Catarina ranch, 742

Catholic Church: and Stephen F. Austin, 105; and John F. Kennedy, 688, 689, 693; Ku Klux Klan's targeting of, 515, 518, 531; and Michael Muldoon, 107; and Emma Tenayuca, 584; on Women's Army Auxiliary Corps, 622

Catlin, George, 76, 425

cattle drives: and Sam Bass, 385–386; and Chisholm Trail, 356, 364, 366, 368, 372, 381, 387; and Civil War, 361; daily routine of, 357, 360; and Goodnight-Loving Trail, 364, 365–366; map of major cattle trails, 367; and market for Texas cattle, 360, 361, 364; and waddies, 356, 357, 360, 362–363, 372, 818; and Western Trail, 364, 366, 368

cattle raids, 378–379, 392, 512

Cavalcade of Texas (outdoor pageant), 4–5

Cayce, G. W., 214

CBS News, 738

Central National Highway, 436

Central Texas, 366, 447

Chadwick, Joe, 425

Champ d'Asile (Field of Asylum) colony, 90

Chapa, Juan Bautista, 49, 56

Chapman, John Gadsby, and portrait of David Crockett, 146, 147

Charles, Prince of Wales, 775

Charles III (king of Spain), 75

Charles V (king of Spain), 20, 23, 39, 41

Charrucos, 23

Chávez, Cesar, 711

Cheney, Dick, 778

Cherokee Indians: battle of, with Texas Army, 205, 206, 394; and Haden Edwards, 108; and Fredonian Rebellion, 109; and Sam Houston, 138, 139–140, 191, 192, 205, 206; and Mirabeau Lamar, 205–206, 210, 264, 493; and Mexican government, 191–192; population of, 203; and Texas Revolution, 191, 192, 205, 206; Texas Senate on, 205; and World War I, 494

Chicago Board of Trade, 771

Chicano movement, 711–713

Chicano wave music, 801

Chichimeca peoples, 41

Chickasaw Indians, 191, 334

Chicken Farm, 524

Chicken War, 63–64, 221

Chihuahua, Mexico, 81, 83

Chihuahuan Desert, 27, 57, 253, 677, 828

Childress, George, 156

chili, 764, 765–766

China, 678

Chinese immigrants, 418, 423

Chiricahua band, 373

Chisholm, Jesse, 366

Chisholm Trail, 356, 364, 366, 368, 372, 381, 387

Chisos Mountains, 828

Choctaw Indians, 191, 334, 494

cholera, 124, 127, 135, 145, 152, 258, 266

Christensen, Heather, 837

Christian, George, 676, 779

Church of Christ, 762

Cíbola, Seven Cities of, 29–31, 41, 43, 45–46, 69

Cicúique (pueblo), 31, 34

cimarrones (cattle), 361

Cincinnatus, 505

Circle T Ranch, 770

Ciudad Juárez, Mexico, 419, 483

civil rights: and African Americans, 718, 747; and Minnie Fisher Cunningham, 468; and Lyndon Johnson, 685, 686, 718, 740; and Mexican Americans, 583, 643, 706, 711–712; and Tejanos, 476; and Edwin Walker, 695

Civil Rights Act of 1957, 686, 778

Civil Rights Act of 1964, 718

Civil War: Confederate veterans of, 511, 515; and Indians, 312, 333–335; and Albert Sidney Johnston, 204, 274–275; postwar conditions in Texas, 312, 551–553; and Rio Grande, 295, 296, 300, 301, 305, 306; and slavery, 253, 278, 394; Texans fighting in, 287, 290, 292, 293, 295; Texas battles in, 294; Texas surrender in, 305–306, 309; Union blockades of Texas ports in, 285, 295; and Unionist sentiment in Texas, 254, 255, 276, 278, 279, 283, 295, 296–297, 299–301, 312, 315, 318, 321. *See also* Reconstruction; secession

Clark, Edward, 284, 285

Clark, George, 395–397

Clay, Henry, 232, 250, 253

Clayton, Nicholas, 436–437

Clear Fork Comanche reservation, 266, 268, 334

Clear Fork of the Brazos, 266, 331, 336, 338

Murphy compared to, 612; and Robert Neighbors, 251, 818; portrait of, *251*; and Second Cortina War, 295; on slavery, 279

Fort Belknap, 265, 268, 270, 338, 342

Fort Bliss, El Paso, 483, 484, 500

Fort Brown, Texas, 495–496

Fort Concho, San Angelo, 350–351, 373

Fort Crockett, Galveston, 616–617

Fort Davis, Texas, 373–374, 376–377

Fort Defiance, Goliad, 142

Fort Griffin, Texas, 331, 339, 342

Fort Hood, Texas, 642, 721, 788

Fort Parker, Texas, 188–189, 191, 192, 269, 271, 345, 523–524

Fort Phantom Hill, 265

Fort Richardson, Jacksboro, 342

Fort St. Louis, 49, 51–52, 54–56, 59

Fort Sam Houston, San Antonio, 497–498, 507, 601

Fort Sill, Oklahoma, 342, 354, 456

Fort Stockton, Texas, 729

Fort Sumner, New Mexico, 364

Fort Texas, 239, 240, 241, 243, 256

Fortune, Jan Isbelle, 5

Fortune magazine, 795

Fort Union, 344

Fort Warren, Boston, 394–395

Fort Worth, Texas: and cattle drives, 366, 368, 572; population of, 494, 572, 631; as railroad hub, 572; and ranching, 370; and Texas Centennial, 572–573

The Forty, 298

Foulois, Benjamin, 507

Fountain, Ben, 777

Fourteenth Amendment, 316, 323, 641, 755

Fox, John "Artly Snuff," 725

France: recognition of Republic of Texas by, 90, 220–221; war of, with Mexico, 221; in World War I, 503–504, 509; in World War II, 605. *See also* French explorers

Franciscans: and Jumanos, 43–44; and Lipan Apaches, 65; missions of, 43, 58–59, 62, 63–64, 69, 72

Fredericksburg, Texas, 297

Fredonian Rebellion, 109, 111, 113, 192, 198

free blacks, 203, 313

freedmen, 308–309, 314, 320, 327, 329

Freedmen's Bureau, 313–314, 318, 319, 320, 325

Freeman, Tom, 715

Freestone County, Texas, 326

French Air Service, 507

French and Indian War, 75

French Army, 500

French explorers: and Caddo Indians, 59, 63, 66; and Comanches, 74; and Karankawa Indians, 49, 51, 52, 53, 54; and Seven Years' War, 75; in Spanish territory, 48–55, 62–63, 64

French Revolution, 82, 385

Friedman, Kinky, 723

Friedrich Wilhelm Carl Ludwig Georg Alfred Alexander (prince of Solms), 297–299

Friends of Mexican Emancipation, 90

Frontier Echo (newspaper), 385

Frontier Regiment, 361

Frost, Robert, and "Dedication," 687

Fry, Hayden, 732

FSLIC (Federal Savings and Loan Insurance Corporation), 777–778

Funston, Frederick, 485

—G—

Gable, Clark, 624

Gaines, Edmund, 176–177

Gaines, Matthew, 322, 323

Gainesville, Texas, 301, 302

Gainesville State School for Girls, 754

Galey, John H., 450, 452

Galveston, Harrisburg and San Antonio Railway, 422

Galveston, Texas: Confederate recapture of, 302, 303; cotton trade in, 312, 437, 443; Deep Water Committee of, 436–437; docks of, 396; and gun emplacement of Fort Crockett, 616–617; hurricane of 1900, 437–441, *438–439, 441,* 443–444, 450; and Jean Lafitte, 92–93, 112; and James Long, 92, 93; population of, 388, 436; as port city, 437, 444; and Prohibition, 522; seawall of, 443–444; slave trade in, 279; tourism of, 437–438; Union attack on, 302, 572, 616; yellow fever in, 285

Galveston Bay: and Anahuac, 116, 121; and John James Audubon, 816; and Buffalo Bayou, 201; and Houston, 437, 444; and Sam Houston, 573; and hurricane of 1900, 438–439, 444; and Jane Long, 93, 94, 436; and Prohibition, 522; and Texas City, 632

Galveston Bay and Texas Land Company, 138

Galveston Equal Suffrage Association, 468

Galveston Island, 93, 737

Galveston News, 438

Gálvez, Bernardo de, 436

gambling, 522, 523

game ranches, 360

Gaona, Antonio, 192

García, Hector, 643–644, 647–648, 705

Garcia, José, 506

Garcitas Creek, 47, 48, 51–52, 53, 54–55, 59

Garibaldi, Guiseppe, 400

Garner, John Nance, 550–551, *551,* 687

Garza, Carlos de la, 171

Garza, Catarino, 473

Gates, John Warne, 369–370

Gathings, James J., 326

Gault Site, 11–12

Gay, D. P., Jr., 481

gay rights, 759

Gemini manned spaceflight program, 737

General Order Number 3, emancipation of slaves, 306

Gentilz, Théodore, 402

Geophysical Service, Inc., 678

Georgia, 278

Gerald, G. B., 417

German immigrants, 283, 296–297, 299–300, 463, 764–765

Germany: and World War I, 492–493, 494, 503–506, 508; and World War II, 605–607, 609, 610, 611, 614, 616–617

Geronimo (Apache chief), 373, 676

Giant (Ferber), 652, 675–676, 680

Giant (film), 652, 676–677

Gilbert Islands, 599

Gillett, James B., and *Six Years with the Texas Rangers,* 385–386

Gilmore, Jimmie Dale, 817

"Git Along, Little Dogies," 356

Glasrud, Bruce A., 838

Glavecke, Adolphus, 261

Glenn Springs, Texas, 484

Glidden, Joseph, 368–369

Goliad, Texas: James Bowie's defense of, 142; and James Fannin, 152, 154, 155, 171; Goliad Massacre, 172–173, 193–194, 199, 230, 235, 245, 425, 493; naming of, 128; Texians' capture of, 128–129; William Travis's plea for help from, 154

Gómez Farías, Valentín, 123–125

Gómez Pedraza, Manuel, 113–114

"Gone to Texas," 134

Gonzales, Texas: Battle of Gonzales, 127–128, 141, 169; and Sam Houston, 171; and reinforcements for the Battle of the Alamo, 152, 158, 170, 171; and Runaway Scrape, 195; and siege of San Antonio de Béxar, 129, 130

Gonzalez, Connie, 757

922   INDEX

World Trade Center, 811
World War I: and anti-German hysteria, 519, 520; armistice that ended, 511; and aviation, 507–508; and Blanc Mont and Saint-Étienne, France, 503–504, 605; effects of, 526; Mexican Americans serving in, 505–507, 511–512, 583; and Chester Nimitz, 598; and race relations, 494–500; Texans serving in, 494–495, 502–503; and Treaty of Versailles, 511; and Woodrow Wilson, 492–493, 510–511; women's contributions to, 518–519
World War II: African Americans serving in, 595, 599–600; and bombing of Hiroshima and Nagasaki, 624–625, 628; and Bracero Program, 705; and George Herbert Walker Bush, 627–628; casualties of, 605, 607, 608, 609, 827; and D-Day, 608–609, 610, 611; and Sam Dealey, 614–616; and Everette Lee DeGolyer, 766–767; and Dwight D. Eisenhower, 600–601; and Fort Crockett, 616–617; and Hector García, 643; and German U-boats, 616, 631; and Henry B. González, 707; high explosives used in, 633; internment camps of, 617, 618–619, 620, 710; and Felix Longoria, 642; Mexican Americans serving in, 607; and Audie Murphy, 612, 613; and Chester Nimitz, 597–599, 599; Texans serving in, 600, 605–607; U.S. involvement in, 592, 597; and Women's Army Auxiliary Corps, 621–622; and Ralph Yarborough, 668
Wright, Frank Lloyd, 652
Wright, Gladys Yoakum, 540–541
Wright, Jim, 778, 778–779
Wright, Lawrence, 703, 827–828
Wright, Norris, 133
Wyoming, 202, 368, 456

—X—

Xalapa, Mexico, 123
XIT Ranch, 370, 392, 563

—Y—

Yamparikas, 264, 336
Yarborough, Ralph: and George H. W. Bush, 773; and John Connally, 696, 704; and governor's race of 1954, 668–669; and governor's race of 1956, 696; and Lyndon Johnson's funeral, 741; as political campaigner, 670–671;

and Allan Shivers, 668; as U.S. senator, 673, 696, 711
Yates, Jack, 800
yellow fever, 285, 318
"The Yellow Rose of Texas," 3, 178, 290, 572
Yellow Stone (steamship), 193
Yoakum, Henderson: on history of Texas, 541, 836, 837; and map of Battle of San Jacinto, 179
Yom Kippur War, 767
Young, Jim, 301
Young, Mrs. M. J., 304
Young, Nancy Beck, 837
Young, William, 301
Young County, Texas, 336, 340, 364
Ysleta del Sur, Texas, and Tiguas, 373

—Z—

Zaboly, Gary, and Alamo compound, 160–161
Zacatecas, Mexico, 41, 126
Zaharias, Babe Didrikson, 829
Zapata, Emiliano, 475, 749
Zapata Off-Shore, 773
Zavala, Lorenzo de, 108, 175, 208, 470
Zimmerman Telegram, 493
Zuber, William P., 165–166
Zuber-Mallison, Carol, 837
Zuni River, 30
Zunis, 31

COLOPHON

The text of this book is set in Iowan Old Style, a typeface designed by John Downer, which draws inspiration from both ancient Roman inscriptions and American twentieth-century hand lettering. The display face is set in Knockout, designed by Jonathan Hoefler, which draws inspiration from nineteenth-century American wood type.

DESIGN AND COMPOSITION
EmDash, Austin, Texas

JACKET PRINTING
Phoenix Color,
Hagerstown, Maryland

PRINTING AND BINDING
Sheridan, Chelsea, Michigan

ACQUIRING EDITOR AND PHOTO EDITOR
David Hamrick

EDITOR
E. Casey Kittrell

MANUSCRIPT EDITOR
Lynne Chapman

COPYEDITOR
Kip Keller

FACT CHECKERS
Christian Wallace
Emily McCullar

INDEXER
Kay Banning

PROOFREADER
Rebekah Fowler

PHOTO PERMISSIONS
Chuck Bailey
Angelica Lopez-Torres
Andrew Hnatow
Sarah McGavick

PRODUCTION MANAGER
Dustin Kilgore

PRODUCTION COORDINATOR
Sarah Mueller

PRODUCTION ASSISTANT
Cassandra Cisneros